CASES AND MATERIALS

COPYRIGHT

SIXTH EDITION

by

ROBERT A. GORMAN
Kenneth W. Gemmill Professor of Law Emeritus
University of Pennsylvania

JANE C. GINSBURG
Morton L. Janklow Professor of
Literary and Artistic Property Law
Columbia University School of Law

NEW YORK, NEW YORK
FOUNDATION PRESS

2002

COPYRIGHT © 2002 By FOUNDATION PRESS

       395 Hudson Street
       New York, NY 10014
       Phone Toll Free 1–877–888–1330
       Fax (212) 367–6799
       fdpress.com

All Rights Reserved
Printed in the United States of America

ISBN 1–58778–375–4

 TEXT IS PRINTED ON 10% POST
CONSUMER RECYCLED PAPER

To
BENJAMIN KAPLAN

An inspiring teacher and scholar, who has shaped the study of Copyright and has instilled in generations of students a deep appreciation of the links between law and culture

*

PREFACE TO THE SIXTH EDITION

The past decade has witnessed an extraordinary ferment in the field of Intellectual Property in general and Copyright in particular. New technologies enable all individuals in the United States, and indeed the world, to create new works of literature, music, art, film and software -- and to disseminate those works instantanously and around the globe. In a world in which we are all "content providers" and content users, little wonder that old social, economic and legal paradigms are being challenged. Little wonder, too, that there has been a burst of activity on the part of Congress to accommodate the diverse industry and public interests, on the part of the courts to resolve litigative conflict, and on the part of the Copyright Office to study, elucidate and implement the rapidly evolving congressional commands. As never before, the public has become energized and engaged by Copyright disputes – the Napster case being only one obvious example – and major litigations often move quickly from the courtroom to the negotiation table at which new business models are devised.

This casebook is designed to capture these developments in a way that is comprehensive, informative, stimulating and teachable. We have aimed to preserve the same general approach as in earlier editions, and the same general mix of materials, including primary and secondary sources, textual notes and problems for class discussion. Our updating has taken account of both the internet environment (including not only Napster but also encrypted motion picture disks, disseminators' secondary liability and fair use, the interpretation of pre-digital contract language, and international legal issues) -- and the more "traditional" issues as they evolve as well (including constitutional challenges to the lengthening term of copyright, the protectability of governmental materials, and parodies of classic literary and film works).

We wish to express our appreciation to the many teachers of Copyright, too numerous to mention, who have made helpful suggestions for improvements in the book and have more generally stimulated our thinking about coverage and pedagogy. We also wish to thank William J. Roberts of the Copyright Office and Eric J. Schwartz, Esq. for reviewing certain of the materials. And we are especially grateful to Samuel A. Lambert of the Columbia Law School Class of 2002, who contributed extensively and painstakingly in both substantive and technical ways in the preparation of this new edition.

November 1, 2001

*

SUMMARY OF CONTENTS

TABLE OF CONTENTS

TABLE OF CASES

Principal cases are in bold type. Non-principal cases are in roman type. References are to Pages.

CASES AND MATERIALS

COPYRIGHT

*

CHAPTER 1

THE CONCEPT OF COPYRIGHT

A. HISTORICAL PERSPECTIVE

1. ENGLAND AND THE STATUTE OF ANNE

Our whole law relating to literary and artistic property is essentially an inheritance from England. It seems that from the time "whereof the memory of man runneth not to the contrary," the author's right to his or her manuscript was recognized on principles of natural justice, being the product of intellectual labor and as much the author's own property as the substance on which it was written. Blackstone, 2 Commentaries 405, associates it with the Law of Occupancy, which involves personal labor and results in "property," something peculiarly one's own (as implied by the Latin root "proprius"). But ages before Blackstone, an Irish king had enunciated the same principle in settling the question of property rights in a manuscript: "To every cow her calf."

When printing from type was invented and works could be reproduced in quantities for circulation, however, it seems that the author was without protection as soon as the work got into print.

In 1556, the Stationers' Company, made up of the leading publishers of London, was established by royal decree for the primary purpose of checking the spread of the Protestant Reformation by concentrating the whole printing business in the hands of the members of that company. Printing was subject to the orders of the Star Chamber so that the Government and the Church could exercise effective censorship and prevent seditious or heretical works from getting into print. Hallam, 1 Constitutional History 238. This was essentially a means of controlling the press and in no sense afforded protection to authors.

Under this decree all published works had to be entered in the register of the Stationers' Company and in the name of some member of that company. By virtue of this entry, and supported by the Star Chamber, the stationer successfully claimed the sole right to print and publish the work for himself, his heirs, and assigns forever. In the course of time, and especially after the last of the old Licensing Acts expired in 1694, the ban against unlicensed printing was lifted and independent printers began to spring up and invade the sacred domain of the Stationers' Company. As a result, the company applied to Parliament for a law to protect its alleged rights in perpetuity against these pirates. As the event turned out, the stationers got much less than they had reckoned on, for Parliament, instead of recognizing their perpetual rights, proceeded to pass a law

1

limiting the exclusive right of publication to a paltry term of years. Drone, Law of Property in Intellectual Productions 69 (1879).

This law was the celebrated Statute of Anne (8 Anne c. 19, 1710), the first statute of all time specifically to recognize the rights of authors and the foundation of all subsequent legislation on the subject of copyright both here and abroad. *See* Ransom, The First Copyright Statute (1956). Because of its historical importance in relation to the study of our own copyright laws, it is well to note some of its provisions.

Title.

"An Act for the Encouragement of Learning, by Vesting the Copies of Printed Books in the Authors or Purchasers of such Copies, during the Times therein mentioned."

Preamble.

"Whereas Printers, Booksellers and other Persons have of late frequently taken the Liberty of Printing, Reprinting, and Publishing ... Books and other Writings without the Consent of the Authors or Proprietors ... to their very great Detriment, and too often to the Ruin of them and their Families:

For Preventing therefore such Practices for the future, and for the Encouragement of Learned Men to Compose and write useful Books; May it please your Majesty that it may be Enacted...."

Key Provisions.

1. Exclusive right of author of new work to print book for fourteen years;

2. Renewal period of fourteen years if author living;

3. Registration requirement
   a. register title at Stationers' Hall
   b. deposit nine copies at official libraries;

4. "... if any other Bookseller, Printer, or other Person whatsoever, ... shall Print, Reprint or Import ... any such Book or Books without the Consent of the Proprietor ... then such Offender or Offenders shall forfeit such Book or Books to the Proprietor or Proprietors of the Copy thereof, who shall forthwith Damask and make Waste Paper of them; and further, that every such Offender or Offenders shall forfeit one Penny for every Sheet which shall be found in his, her, or their Custody."

While the statute seemed plain enough, the stationers nevertheless still contended that their perpetual rights were not taken away but that the purpose of the Act was merely to enable them to obtain speedier relief against piracy, this being the only thing they had sought from Parliament in the first place. For more than half a century the lower courts sustained them in this view by granting many injunctions, even after the expiration of the term fixed by the statute. But in the famous case of *Donaldson v. Becket,* 4 Burr. (4th ed.) 2408, 2417, 98 Eng. Rep. 257, 262 (H.L. 1774), the House of Lords overruled a case decided only five years earlier by the King's Bench, *Millar v. Taylor,* 4 Burr. (4th ed.) 2303, 98 Eng. Rep. 201 (K.B. 1769), and determined that copyright (i.e., the exclusive right to publish and sell copies) had never existed as a right at common law. The full House of Lords thus rejected the divided decision of the judicial branch of the House of Lords, which had ruled that copyright had existed at common law; that prior to adoption of the Statute of Anne, common-law copyright existed in perpetuity even after publication of the work; but that (according to some reports of the decision) the Statute of Anne substituted a limited term of statutory protection with regard to published works. (Other reports of the decision indicate that a bare majority of the judges determined that the Statute of Anne did not in any way limit common-law copyright.) The various opinions of the judges of the House of Lords and the decision of the full House in *Donaldson v. Becket* are meticulously examined in Abrams, *The Historic Foundation of American Copyright Law: Exploding the Myth of Common Law Copyright,* 29 Wayne L. Rev. 1119, 1156–71, 1188–91 (1983).

The Statute of Anne expressly sanctioned the importation of books in foreign languages without the recognition of any rights on the part of the foreign authors; but it said nothing about importation of books in English printed or reprinted abroad. Such a contingency seemed out of the question, as the printing business had not as yet become a flourishing institution in the Colonies. But later on, had Benjamin Franklin chosen to enlarge his printing plant, it is conceivable that books rather than tea might well have become the bone of contention leading to the Revolution.

The Statute of Anne has long been treated as a startling result of the parliamentary process. Perhaps the most significant shift in English law was its recognition of the rights of authors, and not merely those of printers and booksellers.

2. THE COLONIES AND THE CONSTITUTION

After the close of the Revolution, all of the Colonies except Delaware passed laws to afford a measure of protection to authors, pursuant to a recommendation of the Continental Congress, 24 Journals, Continental Congress 326 (1783), and the entreaties of Noah Webster. While many states patterned their statutes after the Statute of Anne, many others mingled natural rights rhetoric with the more utilitarian inspiration of the English model. See Massachusetts, Act of March 17, 1783, the preamble to which states:

> Whereas the improvement of knowledge, the progress of civilization, the public weal of the community, and the advancement of human happiness, greatly depend on the efforts of learned and ingenious persons in the various arts and sciences: As the principal encouragement such persons can have to make great and beneficial exertions of

this nature, must exist in the legal security of the fruits of their study and industry to themselves; and as such security is one of the natural rights of all men, there being no property more peculiarly a man's own than that which is procured by the labor of his mind.

Reprinted in Solberg ed., Copyright Enactments of the United States 14 (1906). Connecticut, New Hampshire, Rhode Island, North Carolina, Georgia, and New York also enacted copyright laws combining natural rights and public-benefit rationales. *See* Solberg at 11, 18, 19, 25, 27, and 29; *see also* Crawford, *Pre–Constitutional Copyright Statutes,* 23 Bull. Copyright Soc'y 11 (1975).

But whatever the state copyright statute's philosophy, these laws were limited in their operation to the boundaries of each state. Hence, if an author in one state wished to secure protection for his work throughout the other states, he was obliged to comply with a multitude of laws. *See Hudson & Goodwin v. Patten,* 1 Root 133 (Conn.1789), for a clash of interests between the assignees of copyright in different states. The same situation prevailed at that time in Europe, but on this side of the Atlantic, where all spoke the same language and read the same books, a uniform national law soon became imperative.

The framers of the Constitution, therefore, embodied in that immortal instrument a simple and direct clause empowering Congress "to promote the progress of science and useful arts, by securing for limited times to authors and inventors the exclusive right to their respective writings and discoveries." U.S. Const., art. I, sec. 8, cl. 8. *See* Fenning, *The Origin of the Patent and Copyright Clause of the Constitution,* 17 Geo. L.J. 109 (1929). It should be noted that this clause does not use the terms "copyrights" and "patents," but nevertheless covers both forms of property. The selection of the "writings" of "authors" terminology for copyrights was made by the committee on detail or style and the clause was adopted by the Constitutional Convention without debate.

Some contemporaneous light on the clause is often sought from the succinct, if not enigmatic, comment of Madison in The Federalist, No. 43 at 279 (Mod. Lib. ed. 1941):

> The utility of this power will scarcely be questioned. The copyright of authors has been solemnly adjudged, in Great Britain, to be a right of common law. The right to useful inventions seems with equal reason to belong to the inventors. The public good fully coincides in both cases with the claims of individuals. The States cannot separately make effectual provision for either of the cases, and most of them have anticipated the decision of this point, by laws passed at the instance of Congress.

3. THE FIRST UNITED STATES COPYRIGHT STATUTE

There is no committee report on the first federal Copyright Act of May 31, 1790, 1 Stat. 124, and the Act itself must be looked to for enlightenment as to its purpose and policy. Congress adopted the system of formalities and restrictions inaugurated by the old Statute of Anne, which, as we saw earlier, had been enacted purely as a municipal measure to replace the Licensing Acts and, incidentally, curb the pretentious claims to perpetual copyright on the part of the members of the Stationers' Company.

The Act of 1790 assured protection to the author or his assigns of any "map, chart or book" for fourteen years upon:

(1) recording the title, prior to publication, in the register book of the clerk's office of the district court where the author or proprietor resided;

(2) publishing a copy of the record so made in one or more newspapers for four weeks; and

(3) depositing a copy of the work itself in the office of the Secretary of State within six months after publication.

The privilege of renewal of the copyright for fourteen more years was granted to the author or his assigns on condition of again entering the title and publishing the record. The renewal term, as in the Statute of Anne, was dependent on the survival of the author throughout the first term. By subsequent Act, 2 Stat. 171 (1802), the notice of entry, including the date thereof, was required to be inserted in every copy of the published work. Suitable penalties were provided in the case of infringement.

There was also a provision against the unauthorized use of an author's manuscript, thus recognizing the old common-law right before publication, without requiring the proprietor to observe any formality. With respect to published works, however, Congress seemed extremely solicitous to safeguard the public in general from offending against the Act and incurring the penalties through ignorance of the copyright claim. It is not clear why it was deemed necessary to shift the burden from those who might want to use the work to those who created it, but presumably it was because copyright is in the nature of a monopoly and, therefore, "odious in the eye of the law." Likewise, the courts at the beginning construed the Act very strictly and hence the author was obliged to proceed with the utmost caution along the tortuous copyright route lest any slip prove his undoing.

Wheaton v. Peters, 33 U.S. (8 Pet.) 591 (1834), like *Donaldson v. Becket* in England, posed the questions whether common-law copyright existed in the United States, and, if it did, whether and to what extent the enactment of the federal Copyright Act abrogated common-law copyright. Plaintiff Wheaton was a former Reporter for the United States Supreme Court. Defendant Peters, Wheaton's successor as Reporter, sought to publish "Consolidated Reports" of Supreme Court decisions. Peters' work included decisions previously reported in published volumes by Wheaton. Wheaton alleged infringement of his federal statutory and common-law copyrights in the reports.

The Supreme Court observed that while an author had the right at common law to prevent another from depriving him of his manuscript, and to prevent the unlawful publication of an unpublished work, the case raised the different question whether, once the work was published, the common law recognized a copyright in the form of "a perpetual and exclusive property in the future publication of the work."

The Court held that there was no federal common-law copyright. Rather, the question would be resolved under the law of the state where Wheaton's work was published, Pennsylvania. In determining whether Pennsylvania recognized common-law copyright, the Court held that two matters must be addressed: First, did England recognize common-law copyright? Second, even if it did, did Pennsylvania adopt that aspect of the English common law or, alternatively, develop its own common-law copyright? Reviewing *Donaldson v. Becket,* the Supreme Court determined that the existence and scope of common-law copyright in England was "a question by no means free from doubt." The Court then ruled that, regardless of the state of common-law copyright in England, the concept had not been adopted in any form in England until after Pennsylvania had developed its own common law. The Court concluded that English common-law copyright was not part of the common law of Pennsylvania, and that Pennsylvania had not developed a common-law copyright of its own.

The Court went on to state its view that common-law copyright in published works had not existed in any state. Rather, the right to copy and sell published works was entirely a creation of Congress. Wheaton's sole recourse, then, was to federal statutory copyright. But Wheaton's federal statutory claim also failed because, upon publication of his work, Wheaton had not complied strictly with all the requirements of the Copyright Act. (The Court also observed, in passing, that no one was entitled to a copyright in the text of the Court's decisions.)

4.   STATUTORY REVISION

Step by step after the 1790 statute, new subjects were added, and the scope and term of protection enlarged. In 1802, prints were added (2 Stat. 171); in 1831, musical compositions (4 Stat. 436), but not the right of public performance (this right came for the first time in 1897, Rev. Stat. § 4966). At the same time (1831), the first term was extended to twenty-eight years with the privilege of renewal for fourteen years solely to the author or his widow and children. In 1856, dramatic compositions, with the right of public performance thereof, were added (11 Stat. 138); in 1865, photographs (13 Stat. 540); in 1870, paintings, drawings, sculpture, and models or designs for works of the fine arts. This Act of 1870 (16 Stat. 212, Rev. Stat. § 4948–71) facilitated the whole process by centralizing the copyright business in the Library of Congress, then located in the Capitol Building.

5.   THE 1909 ACT

The Copyright Act of 1909—which, with minor amendments, was the law in force for nearly 70 years—was the outcome of several years of painstaking labor and extensive discussion. Because the Act was ultimately a composite of several tentative bills and proposals embodying different points of view and often clashing interests, there was a good deal of incoherence, inconsistency and opaqueness in certain sections; this caused no little perplexity on the part of both the public and the courts in interpreting the statute.

Nonetheless, the 1909 Act made some notable improvements over the preexisting law. For example: (1) for published works, copyright was declared to begin with the publication of the work with copyright notice (rather than from the date of filing the title); (2) statutory copyright was made available for unpublished works designed for exhibition, performance or oral delivery; (3) the renewal term of protection was extended by 14 years, thus increasing the maximum possible copyright term to 56 years; and (4) the certificate of registration was declared to be prima facie evidence of the facts recorded therein in relation to any work.

After the passing of half a century, pressure mounted for the comprehensive revision and modernization of the Copyright Act. For one thing, the development of the motion picture, the phonograph, radio, television, and other techniques of aural and visual recording, together with changes in business methods and practices, created new factors to be considered. For another, the marketing of copyrighted materials across international boundaries, and the desirability of affording greater protection to U.S. authors abroad, focused increased attention upon the wisdom of conforming U.S. copyright law in greater measure to the norms of international copyright laws and treaties.

6. THE 1976 ACT

A comprehensive project along these lines was authorized by Congress in 1955. Under this authorization, the Copyright Office prepared a number of legal and factual studies of the major substantive problems inherent in any revision of the law. Distribution of these studies gave rise to the healthy interchange of ideas, comments, and suggestions necessary for the development of an improved law. (In addition, they serve as valuable research tools irrespective of their original purpose and have accordingly been published in an Arthur Fisher Memorial Edition, in honor of the Register of Copyrights who launched the project.) In July 1961, Register Kaminstein submitted to Congress a detailed report of his tentative recommendations for revision with a view to the introduction, after further public comment, of a new proposed law. *Report of the Register of Copyrights on the General Revision of the U.S. Copyright Law, Report to House Committee on the Judiciary,* 87th Cong., 1st Sess. (1961). (A 1965 *Supplementary Report* and 1975 *Draft Second Supplementary Report* were later issued by the Register.)

Legislative activity on the revision continued, with new bills submitted virtually every year from 1964 on. An important piece of legislative history is embodied in S. Rep. No. 94–473, 94th Cong., 1st Sess. (1975), which preceded the 1976 vote. A comprehensive House Judiciary Committee report, H.R. Rep. No. 94–1476, 94th Cong., 2d Sess. (1976), recapitulated significant segments of the tortuous legislative history. The exhaustive section-by-section discussion of the bill in that House Judiciary Committee report is widely regarded as the definitive expression of "legislative intent" on the provisions of the 1976 Copyright Act. (Passages from the House Report are set forth where pertinent and helpful throughout this casebook.) The differences between the chambers were resolved in a conference report, H.R. Rep. No. 94–1733, 94th Cong., 2d Sess. (1976), which was accepted by both houses, and the President approved Public Law 94–553, 90 Stat. 2541, on October 19, 1976.

The 1976 Act marked a significant philosophical departure from the centuries-old traditions reflected in the Statute of Anne, the first U.S. statute in 1790, and the 1909 statute. At the same time, much of the substance of the 1909 Act will remain with us, either directly or indirectly, well into the twenty-first century, if not indefinitely.

The key provisions of the 1976 law included the following:

(1) A single federal system of protection for all "original works of authorship," published or unpublished, from the moment they are fixed in a tangible medium of expression. (Pertinent state law is expressly preempted.)

(2) A single term of protection generally measured by the life of the author(s) plus 50 years after his or her death, with a term based on publication (or creation, in the case of unpublished works) reserved only for special situations, such as works made for hire.

(3) A provision for an inalienable option in individual authors generally permitting termination of any transfer after thirty-five years, but with the transferee still permitted to exploit derivative works produced under the transfer before it was terminated.

(4) A provision for notice on visually perceptible copies distributed to the public, with some flexibility as to the form and position of the notice, curative provisions for notice deficiencies, and incentives for use of a proper notice, as well as for prompt registration.

(5) Recognition of a fair use limitation on exclusive rights (with an indication of the criteria for its applicability) as well as other limitations in favor of nonprofit, library, educational, and public broadcasting uses.

(6) Imposition of copyright liability on cable television systems and jukeboxes that use copyrighted material, but subject to compulsory license provisions and other limitations.

(7) Establishment of a Copyright Royalty Tribunal to review or establish rates under compulsory licenses and to provide for certain distributions to claimants under such licenses.

(8) Provisions implementing divisibility of copyright ownership.

During the long progress of the revision effort, three significant matters were resolved by separate legislative action. First, beginning on September 19, 1962, terms of renewal copyrights that would otherwise have expired were extended so as to bring these copyrights under the protection of the new Act. Second, in 1971 and 1974, limited federal copyright protection was extended to recorded performances insofar as duplication of recordings was concerned, but not as to independently recorded imitation of sound or as to the performance of the recordings. Third, a National Commission on New Technological Uses of Copyrighted Works (CONTU) was established to study new technology, such as computers and reprography, for recommendation to Congress of detailed provisions to replace the stopgap provisions in the 1976 Act governing these fast-moving areas. Several amendments were recommended by CONTU in its Final Report of July 31, 1978 and were adopted by Congress on December 12, 1980. Pub. L. 96–517.

7.   INTERNATIONAL COPYRIGHT PROTECTION AND ITS IMPACT ON U.S. COPYRIGHT LEGISLATION

During the republic's first hundred years, the U.S. was a "pirate nation," with respect to foreign works of authorship. By the end of the nineteenth century, however, the general movement for international copyright began to gather momentum and there was much agitation for it in this country as well as abroad. The United States therefore ultimately enacted the so-called International Copyright Act of 1891 (26 Stat. 1106), whose terms made copyright available for the first time to foreigners—but only on the hard condition of their complying with the age-old requirements of entry of title, notice, and deposit, as well as that of American manufacture of "any book, photograph, chromo or lithograph." Thus it was essentially a national rather than an international measure, maintaining a good part of the century-old pattern of "encouraging learning" by granting incentives to *American* authors, while permitting pirating of most foreign works. There may have been some cultural, if not ethical, justification for allowing freebooters to offer inexpensive foreign reprints at a time when it could be said that no one "in the four quarters of the globe . . . reads an American book." (Statement of Sidney Smith in 1820, quoted in *United Dictionary Co. v. Merriam Co.,* 208 U.S. 260, 264 (1908).) But toward the end of the nineteenth century it seemed to many, especially those abroad, that more than a token international protection was needed.

The result was the Berne Convention, which established an International Copyright Union in 1886. Under this Convention, as subsequently amended, protection was made automatic throughout all the countries acceding to it on behalf of the authors and artists of every country in the world, whether inside or outside of the Union, and without the need to comply with any formalities whatever, the sole condition being publication of the work in any Union country not later than the date of publication elsewhere. The protection of unpublished works under the Convention was and still is limited to citizens or residents of a Union country. Beginning with a membership of only ten countries, the Berne Union, by January 1, 1999, counted 133 countries as adherents, among them almost all of the leading countries of the world, including the United States and the People's Republic of China. Periodic revisions of the Convention have taken place at

Paris (1896), Berlin (1908), Rome (1928), Brussels (1948), Stockholm (1967), and Paris (1971). In 1996, the WIPO Copyright Treaty and the WIPO Performers and Phonograms Treaty resulted from a diplomatic conference to draft a new international instrument that would address a variety of problems spawned by new technology, as well as the neighboring rights of producers and performers.

The U.S. did not initially adhere to the Berne Convention. Until the 1976 Act, our law conflicted with that treaty's norms in several respects, including formalities and duration. The need for U.S. participation in the international copyright system nonetheless became increasingly clear, as exports of U.S. copyrighted works grew following World War II. If, at that time, comprehensive revision of the United States law to conform with the Berne Convention seemed unlikely, the formation of the United Nations and the establishment of UNESCO offered a new international organ through which some compromise might be reached.

In 1952 success was achieved with the signing of the Universal Copyright Convention. This multilateral treaty, which did not alter the obligations of the Berne Convention as among its adherents, offered a new route for international protection. Works by a national of a member nation, as well as works first published within its borders, were protected in every other member nation. Domestic formalities were excused if all published copies of the work bore a prescribed notice, or if the work remained unpublished.

The United States, in 1954, was one of the first nations to ratify the Universal Copyright Convention, amending its domestic law slightly more than necessary to comply with its treaty obligations. Public Law 743, 83d Cong., 68 Stat. 1030 (1954). The Convention became effective in 1955. As of June 1998, 94 nations had ratified the Universal Copyright Convention.

In October 1988, the United States at last ratified the Berne Convention. Changes in our internal copyright law accompanied the ratification. Congress determined that the Berne Convention's substantive provisions were not self-executing; i.e., that the Convention's mandates were not directly incorporated into domestic law, but must be implemented by domestic legislation. As a result, Congress amended the copyright law to remove those inconsistencies with Berne standards which still persisted under the 1976 Act.

The most significant of these amendments included modification of the provision on notice of copyright to make notice optional rather than mandatory; elimination of the need, as a prerequisite to suit, to record transfers of rights; and initial substitution of negotiated licenses for the previous "compulsory license" publicly to perform musical compositions on jukeboxes (the compulsory license remained as a residual measure in the event private negotiations fail). The legislation also modified the registration provisions of the Act but only with respect to Berne works of foreign origin. Claimants in these works need no longer register as a prerequisite to suit (fulfillment of these formalities remains necessary, however, to obtain certain enhanced remedies). Pre-suit registration remains required for works of U.S. origin.

8.   Subsequent Amendments to the 1976 Copyright Act

In almost every year beginning in 1990, Congress made further substantial changes in the copyright law. In 1990, Congress enacted the Visual Artists Rights Act, the Architectural Works Copyright Protection Act, and the Computer Software Rental Amendment. The Visual Artists Rights Act affords authors of certain pictorial, sculptural and photographic works limited rights of attribution and integrity in the original physical copies of their works. The Architectural Works Copyright Protection Act grants protection to completed architectural structures as well as plans and models. The Computer Software Rental Amendment, which closely follows the 1984 Record Rental Amendment, grants to copyright owners of computer programs the exclusive right to authorize (or to refuse to authorize) rentals of copies, even after their first sale.

In 1992, Congress provided for automatic renewal of the copyright terms of pre–1978 Act works then in their first term of copyright. Congress also modified the fair use exception to make clear that a work's unpublished status does not preclude successful invocation of the fair use defense. Moreover, for the first time, Congress directly, albeit only partially, addressed the problem of private copying in the Audio Home Recording Act of 1992. This law imposed a surcharge on digital audio tape (DAT) recorders and recording media, to be distributed among song writers and publishers, and performers and producers of sound recordings. The law also obliges manufacturers of DAT machines to include a "serial copy management system," to prevent recording subsequent-generation tapes from the initial tape copy. The law does not, however, impose levies or other restrictions concerning analogue audio recording devices or media; indeed, it explicitly exempts private analogue audio copying from liability for copyright infringement.

Legislation adopted in 1993 abolished the Copyright Royalty Tribunal and replaced it with ad hoc royalty arbitration panels, which have the powers both to adjust statutory compulsory-license royalty rates and to distribute collected royalties among claimants.

In 1994, Congress restored copyright protection to non-U.S. works from Berne Convention and World Trade Organization countries whose U.S. copyrights had lapsed due to failure to comply with the notice requirement, or due to failure to renew the registration of copyright at the conclusion of the first 28–year term under the 1909 Act. So long as these works remain under copyright in their countries of origin, they retrieved their U.S. copyright protection as of January 1, 1996. The copyright restoration legislation also contains detailed provisions reconciling the interests of restored rights-holders with the rights of "reliance parties" who had exploited the works before the copyrights were reinstated.

In 1995, and again in 1998, Congress extended the public performance right to digital transmissions of sound recordings, instituting a full right with respect to interactive digital transmissions, and a compulsory license regime for most other digital transmissions.

In 1998 Congress also adopted the "Digital Millennium Copyright Act," and the "Sonny Bono Copyright Term Extension Act." The former act incorporates provisions preventing the circumvention of technological protections of works, and preventing the removal or alteration of "copyright management information." The latter act, which includes "fairness in music licensing" provisions, extends the term of copyright from 75 years from publication, or the life of the author plus 50 years, to 95 years from publication, or life plus 70. The "fairness in music licensing" section expands the exemption enjoyed by certain small businesses from liability for performing music through receipt of radio and television transmissions.

B.   GENERAL PRINCIPLES

United States Constitution

Article I, Section 8, Clause 8.

The Congress shall have power . . . To promote the Progress of Science and useful Arts, by securing for limited Times to Authors and Inventors the exclusive Right to their respective Writings and Discoveries.

Report of the Register of Copyrights on the General Revision of the U.S. Copyright Law 3–6 (1961)

B.   *The Nature of Copyright*

1.   *In General*

In essence, copyright is the right of an author to control the reproduction of his intellectual creation. As long as he keeps his work in his sole possession, the author's absolute control is a physical fact. When he discloses the work to others, however, he makes it possible for them to reproduce it. Copyright is a legal device to give him the right to control its reproduction after it has been disclosed.

Copyright does not preclude others from using the ideas or information revealed by the author's work. It pertains to the literary, musical, graphic, or artistic form in which the author expresses intellectual concepts. It enables him to prevent others from reproducing his individual expression without his consent. But anyone is free to create his own expression of the same concepts, or to make practical use of them, as long as he does not copy the author's form of expression.

2.   *Copyright as Property*

Copyright is generally regarded as a form of property, but it is property of a unique kind. It is intangible and incorporeal. The thing to which the property right attaches—the author's intellectual work—is incapable of possession except as it is embodied in a tangible article such as a manuscript, book, record, or film. The tangible articles containing the work may be in the possession of many persons other than the copyright owner, and they may use the work for their own enjoyment, but copyright restrains them from reproducing the work without the owner's consent.

Justice Holmes, in his famous concurring opinion in *White–Smith Music Publishing Co. v. Apollo Co.* (209 U.S. 1 (1908)), gave a classic definition of the special characteristics of copyright as property:

> The notion of property starts, I suppose, from confirmed possession of a tangible object and consists in the right to exclude other[s] from interference with the more or less free doing with it as one wills. But in copyright property has reached a more abstract expression. The right to exclude is not directed to an object in possession or owned, but is now in vacuo, so to speak. It restrains the spontaneity of men where, but for it, there would be nothing of any kind to hinder their doing as they saw fit. It is a prohibition of conduct remote from the persons or tangibles of the party having the right. It may be infringed a thousand miles from the owner and without his ever becoming aware of the wrong.

3.   *Copyright as a Personal Right*

a.   Generally

Some commentators, particularly in European countries, have characterized copyright as a personal right of the author, or as a combination of personal and property rights. It is true that an author's intellectual creation has the stamp of his personality and is identified with him. But insofar as his rights can be assigned to other persons and survive after his death, they are a unique kind of personal rights.

.   .   .

4.   *Copyright as a Monopoly*

Copyright has sometimes been said to be a monopoly. This is true in the sense that the copyright owner is given exclusive control over the market for his work. And if his control were unlimited, it could become an undue restraint on the dissemination of the work.

On the other hand, any one work will ordinarily be competing in the market with many others. And copyright, by preventing mere duplication, tends to encourage the independent creation of competitive works. The real danger of monopoly might arise when many works of the same kind are pooled and controlled together.

C.   The Purposes of Copyright

1.   Constitutional Basis of the Copyright Law

. . . As reflected in the Constitution, the ultimate purpose of copyright legislation is to foster the growth of learning and culture for the public welfare, and the grant of exclusive rights to authors for a limited time is a means to that end. A fuller statement of these principles was contained in the legislative report (H. Rep. No. 2222, 60th Cong., 2d Sess.) on the Copyright Act of 1909:

The enactment of copyright legislation by Congress under the terms of the Constitution is not based upon any natural right that the author has in his writings, for the Supreme Court has held that such rights as he has are purely statutory rights, but upon the ground that the welfare of the public will be served and progress of science and useful arts will be promoted by securing to authors for limited periods the exclusive rights to their writings. The Constitution does not establish copyrights, but provides that Congress shall have the power to grant such rights if it thinks best. Not primarily for the benefit of the author, but primarily for the benefit of the public, such rights are given. Not that any particular class of citizens, however worthy, may benefit, but because the policy is believed to be for the benefit of the great body of people, in that it will stimulate writing and invention to give some bonus to authors and inventors.

In enacting a copyright law Congress must consider . . . two questions: First, how much will the legislation stimulate the producer and so benefit the public, and, second, how much will the monopoly granted be detrimental to the public? The granting of such exclusive rights, under the proper terms and conditions, confers a benefit upon the public that outweighs the evils of the temporary monopoly.

2.   The Rights of Authors and the Public Interest

a.   In General

Although the primary purpose of the copyright law is to foster the creation and dissemination of intellectual works for the public welfare, it also has an important secondary purpose: To give authors the reward due them for their contribution to society.

These two purposes are closely related. Many authors could not devote themselves to creative work without the prospect of remuneration. By giving authors a means of securing the economic reward afforded by the market, copyright stimulates their creation and dissemination of intellectual works. Similarly, copyright protection enables publishers and other distributors to invest their resources in bringing those works to the public.

b.   Limitations on Author's Rights

Within reasonable limits, the interests of authors coincide with those of the public. Both will usually benefit from the widest possible dissemination of the author's works. But it is often cumbersome for would-be users to seek out the copyright owner and get his permission. There are many situations in which copyright restrictions would inhibit dissemination, with little or no benefit to the author. And the interests of authors must yield to the public welfare where they conflict.

Chafee, Reflections on the Law of Copyright, 45 Columbia Law Review 503, 506–11 (1945)

We should start by reminding ourselves that copyright is a monopoly. Like other monopolies, it is open to many objections; it burdens both competitors and the public. Unlike most other monopolies, the law permits and even encourages it because of its peculiar great advantages. Still, remembering that it is a monopoly, we must be sure that the burdens do not outweigh the benefits. So it becomes desirable for us to examine who is benefited and how much and at whose expense.

The primary purpose of copyright is, of course, to benefit the author.

> ... [I]ntellectual property is, after all, the only absolute possession in the world.... The man who brings out of nothingness some child of his thought has rights therein which cannot belong to any other sort of property....

As Macaulay said in his first speech on the bill which led to the English Act of 1842:[9]

> It is desirable that we should have a supply of good books: we cannot have such a supply unless men of letters are liberally remunerated; and the least objectionable way of remunerating them is by means of copyright.

We do not expect that much of the literature and art which we desire can be produced by men who possess independent means or who derive their living from other occupations and make literature a by-product of their leisure hours. Support by the government or by patrons on which authors used to depend, is today no good substitute for royalties. So we resort to a monopoly, in spite of the plain disadvantage which Macaulay forcefully points out:

> The principle of copyright is this. It is a tax on readers for the purpose of giving a bounty to writers. The tax is an exceedingly bad one; it is a tax on one of the most innocent and most salutary of human pleasures....

Here, as in the case of patents, the Constitution takes the unusual course of expressly sanctioning a gain by private persons. Authors, musicians, and painters are among the greatest benefactors of the race. So we incline to protect them. Yet the very effect of protecting them is to make the enjoyment of their creations more costly and hence to limit the

---

9. Macaulay, Copyright (1841 speech in House of Commons), in 8 Works (Trevelyan   ed. 1879) 195, 197.

possibility of that enjoyment especially by persons of slender purses. Moreover, a monopoly, here as always, makes it possible for the wares to be kept off the market altogether. Therefore, we must be sure that a particular provision of the Copyright Act really helps the author—that it does not impose a burden on the public substantially greater than the benefit it gives to the author.

If we were dealing with only authors and readers, this adjustment of conflicting interests would be fairly simple. But the problem is greatly complicated by the intervention of two other groups who may also be heavily benefited by copyright.

There is the author's surviving family. It often happens that the author does not receive the full benefit of a copyright because he dies before it expires. The benefit and the monopoly may then pass to his widow and children, or to more remote relatives. So far as the widow and minor children go, we all recognize this result as eminently desirable. It goes against the conscience of society that destitution should seize on the family of a man who has made possible great public good. Furthermore, the wish to provide for one's widow and children is one of the strongest incentives to work for all human beings. Erskine, after his maiden argument at the bar, was asked how he had the courage to stand up so boldly before Lord Mansfield, and answered: "I could feel my little children tugging at my gown." ... [But] the benefit becomes dubious when it is conferred on the author's remote relatives; then the tax on the public is less justifiable.

Still another possible beneficiary of copyright has to be considered. Often neither the author nor his family owns the copyright. It belongs to the publisher. (I use the word to include other marketing agencies such as motion-picture companies.) Historically, it was not authors who got the Statute of Anne, but publishers—the London booksellers of those days. A publisher may own the copyright free and clear, and take all the gross income; or he may pay royalties, and take most of the gross income. Either way, he usually gets more from a copyrighted book than when he is subject to open competition. Therefore, much of the tax which the Copyright Act imposes on readers goes directly to publishers.

Then is not the talk of helping authors just a pretense? A vigorous attack of this sort has been widely made on the patent system. Most patents are not owned by the inventors, but by manufacturers, who are often very big corporations. Consequently, it is said that we are betraying the purpose of the Constitution, which was to secure to "Inventors the exclusive Right to their ... Discoveries." Big business is hiding behind the inventor's skirts. This reasoning seems to me unsound. After the inventor makes his invention *work,* an immense expenditure of money is usually necessary to make it *sell.* The inventor is rarely in a position to finance this great development expense himself.... Consequently, the inventor is indirectly benefited by the assignability of his patent.

Similar reasoning applies to copyrights. Although the development expense is not so huge for a book as for a machine or a process, it does cost a good deal to print a book and to attract buyers. Even if an author could afford to publish his own book, he would not do the job well. And if the publishers did not get the benefit of the copyright monopoly, it would be hard for an author to find a publisher to bring out the book. Once the book was launched and became a success, any authorized competitor would eagerly jump into the market because his advertising would be low. He could reap where he had not sown. Both authors and readers would be helpless without publishers. As the poet Wither quaintly said of the good publisher:

> He is the caterer that gathers together provision to satisfy the curious appetite of the soule....

One reason, therefore, for protecting the copyright in the hands of the publisher is to give an indirect benefit to authors by enabling them to get royalties or to sell the manuscript outright for a higher price. A second reason is, that it is only equitable that the publisher should obtain a return on his investment. No doubt the return to a publisher from a particular book which becomes a bestseller may be far above the customary six per cent. But we mustn't concentrate our gaze on this one book. Publishing is close to gambling. Many of the same publisher's books never pay back his original outlay. Only an occasional killing makes it possible for us to read a number of less popular but perhaps more valuable books. If we look at the rate of return on *all* books published by any firm, it does not seem excessive. Few publishers become millionaires. Thus copyright is necessary to make good publishers possible....

———

Mazer v. Stein, 347 U.S. 201 (1954): "The copyright law, like the patent statutes, makes reward to the owner a secondary consideration." *United States v. Paramount Pictures*, 334 U.S. 131, 158. However, it is "intended definitely to grant valuable enforceable rights to authors, publishers, etc., without burdensome requirements; 'to afford greater encouragement to the production of literary [or artistic] works of lasting benefit to the world.'" *Washingtonian Pub. Co. v. Pearson*, 306 U.S. 30.

"The economic philosophy behind the clause empowering Congress to grant patents and copyrights is the conviction that encouragement of individual effort by personal gain is the best way to advance public welfare through the talents of authors and inventors in 'Science and useful Arts.' Sacrificial days devoted to such creative activities deserve rewards commensurate with the services rendered."

Sony Corp. of America v. Universal City Studios, 464 U.S. 417 (1984): "The monopoly privileges that Congress may authorize are neither unlimited nor primarily designed to provide a special private benefit. Rather, the limited grant is a means by which an important public purpose may be achieved. It is intended to motivate the creative activity of authors and inventors by the provision of a special reward, and to allow the public access to the products of their genius after the limited period of exclusive control has expired.''

American Geophysical Union v. Texaco, Inc., 802 F.Supp. 1 (S.D.N.Y.1992), *aff'd*, 60 F.3d 913 (2d Cir.1994): "[The] attempt to deprecate the interest of the copyright owner by reason of profits it has realized through its copyrights is directly contrary to the theory on which the copyright law is premised. The copyright law *celebrates* the profit motive, recognizing that the incentive to profit from the exploitation of copyrights will redound to the public benefit by resulting in the proliferation of knowledge.''

ECONOMIC ANALYSIS OF COPYRIGHT DOCTRINE

The economic analysis of law, which has become an influential school of thinking about legal doctrine and institutions, found its way relatively early into the area of copyright. One would think that the fields of intellectual property generally, and copyright in particular, would lend themselves to economic analysis, because they have at their foundation the assumption that economic incentives for creative activity will contribute to society's welfare (i.e., will "promote the progress of science and the useful arts"). In a sense, the drafters of the constitutional patent and copyright clause were engaging in a bit of armchair economic analysis.

Some seventy years ago, scholars interested in law and economics began to question whether it was indeed necessary to provide to prospective authors a monopoly over the distribution and derivative exploitation of their writings in order to coax them to produce works of literature, art and music that would enrich society. A number of scholarly writers asserted that authors have a variety of incentives to write, apart from royalties, and that adequate royalties can in any event be obtained—with publishers quite willing to publish—by virtue of the "headstart" (accompanied by prestige and by some degree of economic leverage) that comes from a publisher's being first to print and distribute a book. *See* A. Plant, *The Economic Aspects of Copyright in Books,* 1 Economica (n.s.) 167 (1934); R. Hurt & R. Schuchman, *The Economic Rationale of Copyright,* 56 Am. Econ. Rev. Papers & Proc. 42 (1966); S. Breyer, *The Uneasy Case for Copyright: A Study of Copyright in Books, Photocopies, and Computer Programs,* 84 Harv. L. Rev. 281 (1970).

Hurt and Schuchman, for example, conjectured that copyright might well provide unnecessary and excessive incentives for persons whose energies might otherwise be put to use in more socially beneficial ways: "We can intuitively discern books which are less meritorious than given alternative products under any conventional value standard. Even if literature is an intrinsically superior product, it still does not follow that copyright protection is the best device for inducing the optimal number of books." (56 Am. Econ. Rev. Papers & Proc. at 429.) They acknowledge that "some works with high costs of creation, as well as literary creation induced by the expectation of incremental income from subsidiary and reprint rights" might not be produced without "some device to assist authors in receiving compensation for their services," but they suggest that this might be done more aptly and timely (i.e., during the period of creative production) "through private patronage by tax-exempt foundations, universities, and the like, or even by government support for desired literary creation." (*Id.* at 426.)

Professor Breyer (now Associate Justice of the United States Supreme Court) also argued that "copyright is not the only way to resolve the conflict between revenues high enough to secure adequate production and prices low enough not to interfere with widespread dissemination." (84 Harv. L. Rev. at 282.) After examining some data and patterns in book publishing and speculating on alternatives to copyright, he concluded that "the case for copyright rests not on proven need, but rather upon uncertainty as to what would happen if protection were removed." (*Id.* at 322.)

These not altogether charitable assessments of the need for and wisdom of copyright were promptly rebutted; particular attacks were leveled at the assumption that a "headstart" in the publishing marketplace could promise adequate economic rewards to induce publication of most new works. *See* 56 Am. Econ. Rev. Papers & Proc. 435–38 (1966) (Frase rebuttal to Hurd & Schuchman); B. Tyerman, *The Economic Rationale for Copyright Protection for Published Books: A Reply to Professor Breyer,* 18 UCLA L. Rev. 1100 (1971); Breyer, *Copyright: A Rejoinder,* 20 UCLA L. Rev. (1972).

The student should consider both the proposed alternatives to copyright protection (and others you might imagine) and particularly the tenability of the "headstart" proposition (especially in a world of electronic access and downloading, optical scanning, and desktop publishing, and the vast increase in subsidiary markets such as foreign distribution and translation, along with derivative media, character and merchandising rights, and the like). The student should also consider the argument often made by copyright proponents (particularly book publishers and motion picture producers) that exclusive rights must be of a duration more than momentary, not only so that subsidiary markets may be exploited, turning losses into profits for many works, but also so that profitable works can be made as profitable as possible, thus subsidizing the creation and distribution of works whose success is more speculative and whose market is narrower, and whose publication will in fact not be profitable; many of the latter works can make a particularly worthwhile contribution to our fund of knowledge, culture and entertainment, and would otherwise go undisseminated.

The literature exploring the economic underpinnings of copyright—and of a wide array of copyright doctrines—markedly expanded in the past 20 years. *See, e.g., Symposium on the Law and Economics of Intellectual Property,* 78 Va. L. Rev. 1–419 (1992). The doctrine of fair use has been especially well scrutinized through the use of economic analysis. The seminal work was W. Gordon, *Fair Use as Market Failure: A Structural and Economic Analysis of the Betamax Case and Its Predecessors,* 82

Colum. L. Rev. 1600 (1982). *See also* W. Fisher, *Reconstructing the Fair Use Doctrine,* 101 Harv. L. Rev. 1659 (1988); R. Posner, *When Is Parody Fair Use?,* 21 J. Legal Stud. 67 (1992); W. Landes, *Copyright Protection of Letters, Diaries, and Other Unpublished Works: An Economic Approach,* 21 J. Legal Stud. 79 (1992); Robert P. Merges, *Are You Making Fun of Me? Notes on Market Failure and the Parody Defense in Copyright,* 21 Am. Intel. Prop. L. Ass'n Q.J. 305 (1993); Trotter Hardy, *Property (and Copyright) in Cyberspace,* 1996 U. Chi. Legal F. 217 (1996); Tom Bell, *Fair Use v. Fared Use: The Impact of Automated Rights Management on Copyright's Fair Use Doctrine,* 76 N.C. L. Rev. 557 (1998). If many of the initial wave of law and economics articles about copyright law seemed to justify legal protection of works of authorship, several more recent articles employ economic analysis to criticize copyright protection. *See, e.g.,* Julie H. Cohen, *Lochner in Cyberspace: The New Economic Orthodoxy of "Rights Management,"* 97 Mich. L. Rev. 462 (1998); Lydia Pallas Loren, *Redefining the Market Failure Approach to Fair Use in an Era of Copyright Permissions Systems,* 5 J. Intel. Prop. L. 1 (1997); Anastasia P. Winslow, *Rapping on a Revolving Door: An Economic Analysis of Parody in Campbell v. Acuff–Rose Music, Inc.,* 69 S. Cal. L. Rev. 767 (1996).

Perhaps the most comprehensive application of economic analysis to a variety of copyright doctrines—and to the principle of copyright itself—is by Professor William M. Landes and Judge–Professor Richard A. Posner. The following excerpts are from that article, *An Economic Analysis of Copyright Law,* 18 J. Legal Stud. 325 (1989). *See also* R. Posner, Law and Literature, 389–412 (rev. ed. 1998).

Landes & Posner, An Economic Analysis of Copyright, 18 J. Legal Stud. 325–33, 344–46 (1989)

... A distinguishing characteristic of intellectual property is its "public good" aspect. While the cost of creating a work subject to copyright protection—for example, a book, movie, song, ballet, lithograph, map, business directory, or computer software program—is often high, the cost of reproducing the work, whether by the creator or by those to whom he has made it available, is often low. And once copies are available to others, it is often inexpensive for these users to make additional copies. If the copies made by the creator of the work are priced at or close to marginal cost, others may be discouraged from making copies, but the creator's total revenues may not be sufficient to cover the cost of creating the work. Copyright protection—the right of the copyright's owner to prevent others from making copies—trades off the costs of limiting access to a work against the benefits of providing the incentives to create the work in the first place. Striking the correct balance between access and incentives is the central problem in copyright law. For copyright law to promote economic efficiency, its principal legal doctrines must, at least approximately, maximize the benefits from creating additional works minus both the losses from limiting access and the costs of administering copyright protection....

I. The Basic Economics of Copyright

A. *Number of Works as a Function of Copyright and Other Factors*

1. General Considerations

The cost of producing a book or other copyrightable work (we start by talking just about books and later branch out to other forms of expression) has two components. The first is the cost of creating the work. We assume that it does not vary with the number of copies produced or sold, since it consists primarily of the author's time and effort plus the cost to the publisher of soliciting and editing the manuscript and setting it in type. Consistent with copyright usage we call the sum of these costs the "cost of expression."

To simplify the analysis, we ignore any distinction between costs incurred by authors and by publishers, and therefore use the term "author" (or "creator") to mean both author and publisher....

The second component of the cost of producing a work increases with the number of copies produced, for it is the cost of printing, binding, and distributing individual copies. The cost of expression does not enter into the making of copies because, once the work is created, the author's efforts can be incorporated into another copy virtually without cost.

For a new work to be created, the expected return—typically, and we shall assume exclusively, from the sales of copies—must exceed the expected cost.... Since the decision to create the work must be made before the demand for copies is known, the work will be created only if the difference between expected revenues and the cost of making copies equals or exceeds the cost of expression....

This description of the market for copies and the number of works created assumes the existence of copyright protection. In its absence anyone can buy a copy of the book when it first appears and make and sell copies of it. The market price of the book will eventually be bid down to the marginal cost of copying, with the unfortunate result that the book probably will not be produced in the first place, because the author and publisher will not be able to recover their costs of creating the work. The problem is magnified by the fact that the author's cost of creating the work, and many publishing costs (for example, editing costs), are incurred before it is known what the demand for the work will be. Uncertainty about demand is a particularly serious problem with respect to artistic works, such as books, plays, movies, and recordings. Even with copyright protection, sales may be insufficient to cover the cost of expression and may not even cover the variable cost of making copies. Thus, the difference between the price and marginal cost of the successful work must not only cover the cost of expression but also compensate for the risk of failure. If a copier can defer making copies until he knows whether the work is a success, the potential gains from free riding on expression will be even greater, because the difference between the price and marginal cost of the original work will rise to compensate for the uncertainty of demand, thus creating a bigger profit potential for copies. So uncertainty generates an additional disincentive to create works in the absence of copyright protection.

Practical obstacles limit copying the original works of others even in the absence of any copyright protection. But these obstacles, while serious in some cases, can easily be exaggerated. When fully analyzed, they do not make a persuasive case for eliminating copyright protection.

1. *The copy may be of inferior quality, and hence not a perfect substitute for the original.* In the case of books and other printed matter, the copier may not be able to match the quality of paper or binding of the original or the crispness of the printing, and there may be errors in transcription. None of these is an important impediment to good copies any longer, but in the case of works of art—such as a painting by a famous artist—a copy, however accurate, may be such a poor substitute in the market that it will have no negative effects on the price of the artist's work. Indeed, the copy may have a positive effect on that price, by serving as advertising for his works. On the other hand, it may also deprive him of income from selling derivative works—the copies of his paintings—himself. (More on derivative works shortly.) To generalize, when either the cost of making equivalent copies is higher for the copier than for the creator or the copier's product is a poor substitute for the original, the originator will be able to charge a price greater than his marginal cost, even without legal protection. And obviously, the greater the difference in the costs of making copies and in the quality of copies between creator and copier (assuming the latter's cost is higher or quality lower), the less need there is for copyright protection.

2. *Copying may involve some original expression—as when the copy is not a literal copy but involves paraphrasing, deletions, marginal notes, and so on—and so a positive cost of expression.* The copier may incur fixed costs as well, for example costs of rekeying the words from the copy he bought or of photographing them. Still, we would expect the copier's average cost to be lower than the creator's because it will not include the author's time or the cost of soliciting and editing the original manuscript. Nevertheless, when the copier cannot take a complete free ride on the creator's investment in expression and his other fixed costs, the need for copyright protection is reduced....

3. *Copying takes time, so there will be an interval during which the original publisher will not face competition.* This point, which is related to the first because generally the cost of production is inverse to time, has two implications for the analysis of copyright law. First, because modern technology has reduced the time it takes to make copies as well as enabled more perfect copies to be made at low cost, the need for copyright protection has increased over time. Second, for works that are faddish— where demand is initially strong but falls sharply after a brief period— copyright protection may not be as necessary in order to give the creator of the work a fully compensatory return.

4. *There are contractual alternatives to copyright protection for limiting copying.* One is licensing the original work on condition that the

licensee not make copies of it or disclose it to others in a way that would enable them to make copies. But contractual prohibitions on copying may, like trade secrets, be costly to enforce and feasible only if there are few licensees. Where widespread distribution is necessary to generate an adequate return to the author or where the work is resold or publicly performed, contractual prohibitions may not prevent widespread copying. Thus, the greater the potential market for a work, the greater the need for copyright protection. The development of radio, television, and the phonograph has expanded the market for copies and thereby increased the value of copyright protection.

5. *Since a copier normally must have access to a copy in order to make copies, the creator may be able to capture some of the value of copies made by charging a high price for the copies he makes and sells.* For example, a publisher of academic journals may be able to capture part of the value that individuals obtain from copying articles by charging a higher price for the journal—especially to libraries; or a record company may be able to charge a higher price because of home taping. Although this possibility limits the need for copyright protection, it does not eliminate it. If one can make many copies of the first copy, and many copies of subsequent copies, the price of copies will be driven down to marginal cost and the creator will not be able to charge a sufficiently higher price for his copy to capture its value in allowing others to make more copies; no one (except the first copier and the most impatient readers) will buy from him rather than from a copier.

6. *Many authors derive substantial benefits from publication that are over and beyond any royalties.* This is true not only in terms of prestige and other nonpecuniary income but also pecuniary income in such forms as a higher salary for a professor who publishes than for one who does not, or greater consulting income. Publishing is an effective method of self-advertisement and self-promotion. The norms against plagiarism (that is, against copying without giving the author credit) reinforce the conferral of prestige by publishing; to the extent that those norms are effective, they ensure that the author will obtain recognition, if not always royalties, from the works he publishes.

Such points have convinced some students of copyright law that there is no need for copyright protection. Legal rights are costly to enforce—rights in intangibles especially so—and the costs may outweigh the social gains in particular settings. Perhaps copyright in books is one of them. After all, the first copyright law in England dates from 1710 (and gave much less protection than modern copyright law), yet publishing had flourished for hundreds of years in England despite censorship and widespread illiteracy. The point is a little misleading, however. In the old days, the costs of making copies were a higher fraction of total cost than they are today, so the problem of appropriability was less acute. Also, there were alternative institutions for internalizing the benefits of expression. And before freedom of expression became generally applauded, publishing was often believed to impose negative externalities—so there was less, sometimes no, desire to encourage it. Finally, while it may be difficult to determine whether, on balance, copyright is a good thing, it is easy to note particular distortions that a copyright law corrects. Without copyright protection, authors, publishers, and copiers would have inefficient incentives with regard to the timing of various decisions. Publishers, to lengthen their head start, would have a disincentive to engage in prepublication advertising and even to announce publication dates in advance, and copiers would have an incentive to install excessively speedy production lines. There would be increased incentives to create faddish, ephemeral, and otherwise transitory works because the gains from being first in the market for such works would be likely to exceed the losses from absence of copyright protection. There would be a shift toward the production of works that are difficult to copy; authors would be more likely to circulate their works privately rather than widely, to lessen the risk of copying; and contractual restrictions on copying would multiply.

A neglected consideration—one that shows not that copyright protection may be unnecessary but that beyond some level copyright protection may actually be counterproductive by raising the cost of expression—will play an important role both in our model and in our efforts to explain the salient features of copyright law. Creating a new work typically involves borrowing or building on material from a prior body of works, as well as adding original expression to it. A new work of fiction, for example, will contain the author's expressive contribution but also characters, situations, plot details, and so on, invented by previous authors. Similarly, a new work of music may borrow tempo changes and chord progressions from earlier works. The less extensive copyright protection is, the more an author, composer, or other creator can borrow from previous works without infringing copyright and the lower, therefore, the costs of creating a new work. Of course, even if copyright protection effectively prevented all unauthorized copying from a copyrighted work, authors would still copy. But they would copy works whose copyright protection had run out, or they would disguise their copying, engage in costly searches to avoid copying protected works, or incur licensing and other transaction costs to obtain permission to copy such works. The effect would be to raise the cost of creating new works—the cost of expression, broadly defined—and thus, paradoxically, perhaps lower the number of works created.

Copyright holders might, therefore, find it in their self-interest, ex ante, to limit copyright protection. To the extent that a later author is free to borrow material from an earlier one, the later author's cost of expression is reduced; and, from an ex ante viewpoint, every author is both an earlier author from whom a later author might want to borrow material and the later author himself. In the former role, he desires maximum copyright protection for works he creates; in the latter, he prefers minimum protection for works created earlier by others. In principle, there is a level of copyright protection that balances these two competing interests optimally—although notice that the first generation of authors, having no one to borrow from, will have less incentive to strike the optimal balance than later ones. We shall see in Section II that various doctrines of copyright law, such as the distinction between idea and expression and the fair use doctrine, can be understood as attempts to promote economic efficiency by balancing the effect of greater copyright protection—in encouraging the creation of new works by reducing copying—against the effect of less protection—in encouraging the creation of new works by reducing the cost of creating them.

. . .

II.   Applications

A.   *The Nature of Copyright Protection*

. . . We begin with the nature of the protection that a copyright gives its owner. In contrast to a patent, a copyright merely gives protection against copying; independent (that is, accidental) duplication of the copyrighted work is not actionable as such. In speaking of "independent [accidental, inadvertent] duplication" we are addressing only the problem of an independent *recreation* of the original copyrighted work. The accidental *use* of someone else's work might be thought of as duplication, but in that context liability for infringement is strict, much as it is for the trespass on a neighbor's land made by a person who thinks that he owns it.

The more difficult question is to explain why duplication in the sense of independent recreation is not actionable. Our analysis suggests two possible explanations. The first is the added cost to the author of checking countless numbers of copyrighted works to avoid inadvertent duplication. The costs (if actually incurred—a qualification whose significance will become apparent shortly) would . . . lower social welfare because both net welfare per work . . . and the number of works created would fall. True, the author's gross revenues might rise if the reduction in the amount of accidental duplication raised the demand for copies or made the demand less elastic. But since accidental duplication of copyrighted works is rare (except in the area of popular music, discussed below), the net effect of making it unlawful would be to lower social welfare.

In contrast to copyright, accidental infringements of patents are actionable, and the difference makes economic sense. A patent is issued only after a search by the applicant and by the Patent Office of prior patented inventions. This procedure is feasible because it is possible to describe an invention compactly and to establish relatively small classes of related inventions beyond which the searchers need to go. The procedure makes it relatively easy for an inventor to avoid accidentally duplicating an existing patent.

No effort is made by the Copyright Office to search copyrighted works before issuing a copyright, so copyright is not issued but is simply asserted by the author or publisher. There are billions of pages of copyrighted material, any one page of which might contain a sentence or paragraph that a later writer might, by pure coincidence, duplicate so closely that he would be considered an infringer if he had actually copied the words in question or if copying were not required for liability. What is infeasible for the Copyright Office is also infeasible for the author. He cannot read all the copyrighted literature in existence (in all languages, and including unpublished works!) in order to make sure that he has not accidentally duplicated some copyrighted material.

The cost of preventing accidental duplication would be so great, and the benefits in terms of higher revenues (and so the amount of damages if such duplication were actionable) so slight because such duplication is rare, that even if it were actionable no writer or publisher would make much effort to avoid accidental duplication, so the increase in the cost of expression would probably be slight. But social welfare would be reduced somewhat. At best we would have a system of strict liability that had no significant allocative effect; and as explained in the literature on negligence and strict liability in tort law, the costs of enforcing such a regime are socially wasted because their only product is an occasional redistribution of wealth (here that would be from the accidental "infringer" to the first author or publisher of the material duplicated).

The second reason we expect accidental duplication not to be made unlawful derives from the economic rationale for copyright protection, which is to prevent free-riding on the author's expression. Accidental duplication does not involve free-riding. Since the second work is independently created, its author incurs the full cost of expression. If the works are completely identical—a remote possibility, to say the least[30]—competition between the two works could drive the price of copies down to marginal cost and prevent either author from recovering his cost of creating the work. It is more likely that significant differences between the two works will remain, so that both authors may be able to earn enough to cover their respective costs of expression—particularly if neither author is the marginal author, whose gross revenues would just cover the cost of expression in the absence of accidental duplication.

Although for simplicity our analysis focuses on copyright protection for literature and other written works, it is applicable, *mutatis mutandis*, to other forms of expression as well. A significant difference between literary and musical copyright is that courts hold that accidental duplication may infringe a songwriter's copyright if his song has been widely performed[31] Since most popular songs have simple melodies and the number of melodic

---

30. Recall Learned Hand's remark in Sheldon v. Metro–Goldwyn Pictures, 81 F.2d 49 (2d Cir.1936), that "if by some magic a man who had never known it were to compose anew Keats' Ode on a Grecian Urn, he would be an author, and if he copyrighted it, others might not copy that poem, though they might of course copy Keats." Hand, of course, thought such accidental duplication a remote possibility. The probability of accidental duplication of Keats' poem word for word is too small to justify courts in treating it as a litigable question, that is, one fairly open to doubt.

31. For example, in ABKCO Music, Inc. v. Harrisongs Music, Ltd., 722 F.2d 988, 998–99 (2d Cir.1983), the court found that George Harrison's "My Sweet Lord" had infringed "He's So Fine," recorded by the Chiffons. "He's So Fine" had been one of the most popular songs in the United States and England during the same year that Harrison (a former member of the Beatles) composed "My Sweet Lord." The court found an infringement even though it also found that Harrison had copied the Chiffons' song unconsciously rather than deliberately.

variations is limited, the possibility of accidental duplication of several bars is significant. Widespread playing of these songs on the radio makes it likely that the second composer will have had access to the original work, which both increases the likelihood of accidental duplication and reduces the costs of avoiding it. If proof of intentional duplication were required for infringement, composers of popular songs would have little copyright protection and social welfare would fall. . . .

———

David Ladd, the Register of Copyrights from 1980 through January 1985, took issue with the characterization of copyright as a "monopoly" begrudgingly tolerated only to the extent necessary to induce authors to produce works that will enrich human knowledge. He also disputed the perceived tension between copyright and society's interest in full dissemination of ideas and information. Mr. Ladd criticized those who would limit copyright protection to cases in which competitive economic harm has been suffered by the author. He stated that "the notion of economic 'harm' as a prerequisite for copyright protection is mischievous because it disserves the basic constitutional design which embraces both copyright and the First Amendment." Excerpts from his article follow.

Ladd, The Harm of the Concept of Harm in Copyright, 30 Journal of the Copyright Society 421 (1983)

The twenty-seven words in Art. I, § 8, which give Congress the power to legislate copyrights and patents are plain and straightforward (and, incidentally, contain the only use of the word "right" in the entire main body of the Constitution). . . .

Proponents of the harm argument insist that a showing of harm is virtually required as a constitutional limitation: if there is no harm to the copyright owner, there is no demonstrated need for rewards under copyright to motivate the creation and dissemination of the work, and thus "to promote the progress of science." The argument is not only unhistoric, but specious. It paves the way for government interference with information, speech, and discourse which, however indirect, is quite as unlovely as prior restraint. . . .

The framers of the Constitution were men to whom the right to hold property was enormously important. They were not far removed from Locke. His ideas pervaded their debates and decision. Property was seen not as opposed to liberty, but indispensable to it; for men with property would be independent of the power of the State, in that rough-and-tumble roiling of opinion and power which marks freedom.

. . .

That rights of the author are thus of a special kind, rooted both in utility and felt justice, has long been recognized in our country. This has rarely been recalled with greater eloquence than in a statement by Professor Nathaniel Shaler of Harvard, presented to Congress in 1936 by Thorvald Solberg, one of my predecessors in this office:

> When we come to weigh the rights of the several sorts of property which can be held by man, and in this judgment take into consideration only the absolute question of justice, leaving out the limitations of expediency and prejudice, it will be clearly seen that intellectual property is, after all, the only absolute possession in the world. . . . The man who brings out of the nothingness some child of his thought has rights therein which cannot belong to any other sort of property. . . . The inventor of a book or other contrivance of thought holds his property, as a god holds it, by right of creation. . . . Whatever tends to lower the protection given to intellectual property is so much taken from the forces which have been active in securing the advances of society during the last centuries.

. . .

The purpose of copyright is to reward authors as a matter of justice, yes; but only as a beginning. Copyright also is intended to support a system, a macrocosm, in which authors and publishers complete for the attention and favor of the public, independent of the political will of the majority, the powerful, and above all the government, no matter how unorthodox, disturbing, or revolutionary their experience, views, or visions.

The argument for copyright here, to be sure, is an argument of utility—but not mere economic utility. Utility is found in the fostering of a pluralism of opinion, experience, vision, and utterance within the world of authors. . . . [O]ur freedom depends not only on freedom for a few, but also on variety, regardless of the ultimate commingling of truth and error. Copyright fosters that variety.

The marketplace of ideas which the First Amendment nurtures is, then, and must be more widely understood to be, essentially a *copyright* marketplace. . . . Just as we are best served by many visions and visionaries speaking from and to the breadth of human experience, so also do we require a vibrant, heterogeneous, and dissonant community of publishers. The greater their number and variety, the more likely is any author to find a publisher. And while this is of special importance in the areas of thought and political opinion, it is likewise crucial in the fine arts. Joyce and Proust, Beethoven and Stravinsky were all at one time scorned for works for which they later became immortal, but each found the publisher he needed. Those who pioneer, and thereby often disturb, cannot be silenced by anyone if publishers are numerous and the mail delivers the royalty checks.

. . .

By limiting potential rewards in the copyright market—whether by capping them with a compulsory license, or barring them with a complete exemption, or refusing to extend copyright to new uses, or curtailing them in any way under arguments of "harm"—the entrepreneurial calculus which precedes risk-taking in authorship and publishing is shifted in the direction of not taking a chance, i.e., not writing or publishing a "risky" work, whether ideologically or economically risky. Every limitation on copyright is a kind of rate-setting. And however high-minded, every person who thus sets rates applies a value-judgment: how much the author or publisher should receive. Whoever makes this judgment regulates—i.e., controls—how successful a class of authors, works, or publishers shall be. This control of idea-laden copyrighted works is more wisely left with the people than vested in a government tribunal, a statutory license fee, or even a sincere judge searching a record for undefined harm. . . .

[The Supreme Court has echoed Register Ladd's evocation of the beneficial interdependence of copyright and the First Amendment. In *Harper & Row Publishers, Inc. v. Nation Enters.*, 471 U.S. 539 (1985), Justice O'Connor emphasized, "it should not be forgotten that the Framers intended copyright itself to be the engine of free expression. By establishing a marketable right to the use of one's expression, copyright supplies the economic incentive to create and disseminate ideas."]

Burrow–Giles Lithographic Co. v. Sarony

111 U.S. 53 (1884).

■ MR. JUSTICE MILLER delivered the opinion of the court.

This is a writ of error to the Circuit Court for the Southern District of New York.

Plaintiff is a lithographer and defendant a photographer, with large business in those lines in the city of New York.

The suit was commenced by an action at law in which Sarony was plaintiff and the lithographic company was defendant, the plaintiff charging the defendant with violating his copyright in regard to a photograph, the title of which is "Oscar Wilde No. 18." A jury being waived, the court made a finding of facts on which a judgment in favor of the plaintiff was rendered for the sum of $600 for the plates and 85,000 copies sold and exposed to sale, and $10 for copies found in his possession, as penalties under section 4965 of the Revised Statutes.

[The] findings leave no doubt that plaintiff had taken all the steps required by the act of Congress to obtain copyright of this photograph; and section 4952 names photographs among other things for which the author, inventor, or designer may obtain copyright, which is to secure him the sole privilege of reprinting, publishing, copying and vending the same. That defendant is liable under that section and section 4965 there can be no question, if those sections are valid as they relate to photographs.

Accordingly, the two assignments of error in this court by plaintiff in error, are:

Oscar Wilde—the Sarony photograph

1. That the court below decided that Congress had and has the constitutional right to protect photographs and negatives thereof by copyright.

The second assignment related to the sufficiency of the words "Copyright, 1882, by N. Sarony," in the photographs, as a notice of the copyright of Napoleon Sarony under the act of Congress on that subject.

.   .   .

The constitutional question is not free from difficulty.

The eighth section of the first article of the Constitution is the great repository of the powers of Congress, and by the eighth clause of that section Congress is authorized:

> "To promote the progress of science and useful arts, by securing, for limited times to authors and inventors, the exclusive right to their respective writings and discoveries."

The argument here is, that a photograph is not a writing nor the production of an author. Under the acts of Congress designed to give effect to this section, the persons who are to be benefited are divided into two classes, authors and inventors. The monopoly which is granted to the former is called a copyright, that given to the latter, letters patent, or, in the familiar language of the present day, *patent right*.

We have, then, copyright and patent right, and it is the first of these under which plaintiff asserts a claim for relief.

It is insisted in argument, that a photograph being a reproduction on paper of the exact features of some natural object or of some person, is not a writing of which the producer is the author.

Section 4952 of the Revised Statutes places photographs in the same class as things which may be copyrighted with "books, maps, charts, dramatic or musical compositions, engravings, cuts, prints, paintings, drawings, statues, statuary, and models or designs intended to be perfected as works of the fine arts." "According to the practice of legislation in England and America," says Judge Bouvier, 2 Law Dictionary, 363, "the copyright is confined to the exclusive right secured to the author or proprietor of a writing or drawing which may be multiplied by the arts of printing in any of its branches."

The first Congress of the United States, sitting immediately after the formation of the Constitution, enacted that the "author or authors of any map, chart, book or books, being a citizen or resident of the United States, shall have the sole right and liberty of printing, reprinting, publishing and vending the same for the period of fourteen years from the recording of the title thereof in the clerk's office, as afterwards directed." 1 Stat. 124, 1.

This statute not only makes maps and charts subjects of copyright, but mentions them before books in the order of designation. The second section of an act to amend this act, approved April 29, 1802, 2 Stat. 171, enacts that from the first day of January thereafter, he who shall invent and design, engrave, etch or work, or from his own works shall cause to be designed and engraved, etched or worked, any historical or other print or prints shall have the same exclusive right for the term of fourteen years from recording the title thereof as prescribed by law.

By the first section of the act of February 3rd, 1831, 4 Stat. 436, entitled an act to amend the several acts respecting copyright, musical compositions and cuts, in connection with prints and engravings, are added, and the period of protection is extended to twenty-eight years. The caption or title of this act uses the word copyright for the first time in the legislation of Congress.

The construction placed upon the Constitution by the first act of 1790, and the act of 1802, by the men who were contemporary with its formation, many of whom were members of the convention which framed it, is of itself entitled to very great weight, and when it is remembered that the rights thus established have not been disputed during a period of nearly a century, it is almost conclusive.

Unless, therefore, photographs can be distinguished in the classification on this point from the maps, charts, designs, engravings, etchings, cuts, and other prints, it is difficult to see why Congress cannot make them the subject of copyright as well as the others.

These statutes certainly answer the objection that books only, or writing in the limited sense of a book and its author, are within the constitutional provision. Both these words are susceptible of a more enlarged definition than this. An author in that sense is "he to whom anything owes its origin; originator; maker; one who completes a work of science or literature." Worcester. So, also, no one would now claim that the word writing in this clause of the Constitution, though the only word used as to subjects in regard to which authors are to be secured, is limited to the actual script of the author, and excludes books and all other printed matter. By writings in that clause is meant the literary productions of those authors, and Congress very properly has declared these to include all forms of writing, printing, engraving, etching, & c., by which the ideas in the mind of the author are given visible expression. The only reason why photographs were not included in the extended list in the act of 1802 is probably that they did not exist, as photography as an art was then unknown, and the scientific principle on which it rests, and the chemicals and machinery by which it is operated, have all been discovered long since that statute was enacted.

Nor is it to be supposed that the framers of the Constitution did not understand the nature of copyright and the objects to which it was commonly applied, for copyright, as the exclusive right of a man to the production of his own genius or intellect, existed in England at that time....

We entertain no doubt that the Constitution is broad enough to cover an act authorizing copyright of photographs, so far as they are representatives of original intellectual conceptions of the author.

But it is said that an engraving, a painting, a print, does embody the intellectual conception of its author, in which there is novelty, invention, originality, and therefore comes within the purpose of the Constitution in securing its exclusive use or sale to its author, while the photograph is the mere mechanical reproduction of the physical features or outlines of some object animate or inanimate, and involves no originality of thought or any novelty in the intellectual operation connected with its visible reproduction in shape of a picture. That while the effect of light on the prepared plate may have been a discovery in the production of these pictures, and patents could properly be obtained for the combination of the chemicals, for their application to the paper or other surface, for all the machinery by which the light reflected from the object was thrown on the prepared plate, and for all the improvements in this machinery, and in the materials, the remainder of the process is merely mechanical, with no place for novelty, invention or originality. It is simply the manual operation, by the use of these instruments and preparations, of transferring to the plate the visible representation of some existing object, the accuracy of this representation being its highest merit.

This may be true in regard to the ordinary production of a photograph, and, further, that in such case a copyright is no protection. On the question as thus stated we decide nothing.

In regard, however, to the kindred subject of patents for invention, they cannot by law be issued to the inventor until the novelty, the utility, and the actual discovery or invention by the claimant have been established by proof before the Commissioner of Patents; and when he has secured such a patent, and undertakes to obtain redress for a violation of his right in a court of law, the question of invention, of novelty, of originality, is always open to examination. Our copyright system has no such provision for previous examination by a proper tribunal as to the originality of the book, map, or other matter offered for copyright. A deposit of two copies of the article or work with the Librarian of Congress, with the name of the author and its title page, is all that is necessary to secure a copyright. It is, therefore, much more important that when the supposed author sues for a violation of his copyright, the existence of those facts of originality, of intellectual production, of thought, and conception on the part of the author should be proved, than in the case of a patent right.

In the case before us we think this has been done.

The third finding of facts says, in regard to the photograph in question, that it is a "useful, new, harmonious, characteristic, and graceful picture, and that plaintiff made the same ... entirely from his own original mental conception, to which he gave visible form by posing the said Oscar Wilde in front of the camera, selecting and arranging the costume, draperies, and other various accessories in said photograph, arranging the subject so as to present graceful outlines, arranging and disposing the light and shade, suggesting and evoking the desired expression, and from such disposition, arrangement, or representation, made entirely by plaintiff, he produced the picture in suit."

These findings, we think, show this photograph to be an original work of art, the product of plaintiff's intellectual invention, of which plaintiff is the author, and of a class of inventions for which the Constitution intended that Congress should secure to him the exclusive right to use, publish and sell, as it has done by section 4952 of the Revised Statutes.

The judgment of the Circuit Court is accordingly affirmed.

Bleistein v. Donaldson Lithographing Co.

188 U.S. 239 (1903).

■ MR. JUSTICE HOLMES delivered the opinion of the court.

. . . The alleged infringements consisted in the copying in reduced form of three chromolithographs prepared by employes of the plaintiffs for advertisements of a circus owned by one Wallace. Each of the three contained a portrait of Wallace in the corner and lettering bearing some slight relation to the scheme of decoration, indicating the subject of the design and the fact that the reality was to be seen at the circus. One of the designs was of an ordinary ballet, one of a number of men and women, described as the Stirk family, performing on bicycles, and one of groups of men and women whitened to represent statues. The Circuit Court directed a verdict for the defendant on the ground that the chromolithographs were not within the protection of the copyright law, and this ruling was sustained by the Circuit Court of Appeals. *Courier Lithographing Co. v. Donaldson Lithographing Co.,* 104 Fed. Rep. 993.

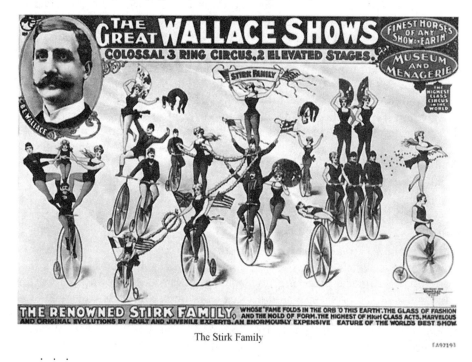

The Stirk Family

. . .

We shall do no more than mention the suggestion that painting and engraving unless for a mechanical end are not among the useful arts, the progress of which Congress is empowered by the Constitution to promote. The Constitution does not limit the useful to that which satisfies immediate bodily needs. *Burrow–Giles Lithographic Co. v. Sarony,* 111 U.S. 53. It is obvious also that the plaintiffs' case is not affected by the fact, if it be one, that the pictures represent actual groups—visible things. They seem from the testimony to have been composed from hints or description, not from sight of a performance. But even if they had been drawn from the life, that fact would not deprive them of protection. The opposite proposition would mean that a portrait by Velasquez or Whistler was common property because others might try their hand on the same face. Others are free to copy the original. They are not free to copy the copy. *Blunt v. Patten,* 2 Paine, 397, 400. See *Kelly v. Morris,* L. R. 1 Eq. 697; *Morris v. Wright,* L. R. 5 Ch. 279. The copy is the personal reaction of an individual upon nature. Personality always contains something unique. It expresses its singularity even in handwriting, and a very modest grade of art has in it something irreducible, which is one man's alone. That something he may copyright unless there is a restriction in the words of the act.

If there is a restriction it is not to be found in the limited pretensions of these particular works. The least pretentious picture has more originality in it than directories and the like, which may be copyrighted. Drone, Copyright, 153. See *Henderson v. Tomkins,* 60 Fed. Rep. 758, 765. The amount of training required for humbler efforts than those before us is well indicated by Ruskin. "If any young person, after being taught what is, in polite circles, called 'drawing,' will try to copy the commonest piece of real *work,*—suppose a lithograph on the title page of a new opera air, or a woodcut in the cheapest illustrated newspaper of the day—they will find themselves entirely beaten." Elements of Drawing, 1st ed. 3. There is no reason to doubt that these prints in their *ensemble* and in all their details, in their design and particular combinations of figures, lines and colors, are the original work of the plaintiffs' designer. If it be necessary, there is express testimony to that effect. It would be pressing the defendant's right to the verge, if not beyond, to leave the question of originality to the jury upon the evidence in this case, as was done in *Hegeman v. Springer,* 110 Fed. Rep. 374.

We assume that the construction of Rev. Stat. § 4952, allowing a copyright to the "author, inventor, designer, or proprietor ... of any engraving, cut, print ... [or] chromo" is affected by the act of 1874, c. 301, § 3, 18 Stat. 78, 79. That section provides that "in the construction of this act the words 'engraving,' 'cut' and 'print' shall be applied only to pictorial illustrations or works connected with the fine arts." We see no reason for taking the words "connected with the fine arts" as qualifying anything except the word "works," but it would not change our decision if we should assume further that they also qualified "pictorial illustrations," as the defendant contends.

These chromolithographs are "pictorial illustrations." The word "illustrations" does not mean that they must illustrate the text of a book, and that the etchings of Rembrandt or Steinla's engraving of the Madonna di

San Sisto could not be protected today if any man were able to produce them. Again, the act however construed, does not mean that ordinary posters are not good enough to be considered within its scope. The antithesis to "illustrations or works connected with the fine arts" is not works of little merit or of humble degree, or illustrations addressed to the less educated classes; it is "prints or labels designed to be used for any other articles of manufacture." Certainly works are not the less connected with the fine arts because their pictorial quality attracts the crowd and therefore gives them a real use—if use means to increase trade and to help to make money. A picture is none the less a picture and none the less a subject of copyright that it is used for an advertisement. And if pictures may be used to advertise soap, or the theatre, or monthly magazines, as they are, they may be used to advertise a circus. Of course, the ballet is as legitimate a subject for illustration as any other. A rule cannot be laid down that would excommunicate the paintings of Degas.

Finally, the special adaptation of these pictures to the advertisement of the Wallace shows does not prevent a copyright. That may be a circumstance for the jury to consider in determining the extent of Mr. Wallace's rights, but it is not a bar. Moreover, on the evidence, such prints are used by less pretentious exhibitions when those for whom they were prepared have given them up.

It would be a dangerous undertaking for persons trained only to the law to constitute themselves final judges of the worth of pictorial illustrations, outside of the narrowest and most obvious limits. At the one extreme some works of genius would be sure to miss appreciation. Their very novelty would make them repulsive until the public had learned the new language in which their author spoke. It may be more than doubted, for instance, whether the etchings of Goya or the paintings of Manet would have been sure of protection when seen for the first time. At the other end, copyright would be denied to pictures which appealed to a public less educated than the judge. Yet if they command the interest of any public, they have a commercial value—it would be bold to say that they have not an aesthetic and educational value—and the taste of any public is not to be treated with contempt. It is an ultimate fact for the moment, whatever may be our hopes for a change. That these pictures had their worth and their success is sufficiently shown by the desire to reproduce them without regard to the plaintiffs' rights. See *Henderson v. Tomkins,* 60 Fed. Rep. 758, 765. We are of opinion that there was evidence that the plaintiffs have rights entitled to the protection of the law.

The judgment of the Circuit Court of Appeals is reversed; the judgment of the Circuit Court is also reversed and the cause remanded to that court with directions to set aside the verdict and grant a new trial.

■ MR. JUSTICE HARLAN, with whom concurred MR. JUSTICE McKENNA, dissenting.

. . . [I]f a chromo, lithograph, or other print, engraving, or picture has no other use than that of a mere advertisement, and no value aside from this function, it would not be promotive of the useful arts, within the meaning of the constitutional provision, to protect the "author" in the exclusive use thereof, and the copyright statute should not be construed as including such a publication.... [The work] must have some connection with the fine arts to give it intrinsic value.... We are unable to discover anything useful or meritorious in the design copyrighted by the plaintiffs in error other than as an advertisement of acts to be done or exhibited to the public in Wallace's show....

Mr. Justice McKenna authorizes me to say that he also dissents.

QUESTIONS

Consider the following issues in connection with the copyright clause of the United States Constitution:

1. Why, in establishing a new federal government, did the founding fathers repose this power in the central government, rather than in the separate states? More generally, why give this power to *any* government unit? More specifically, would state copyright control be effectual, and would it be constitutional after the adoption of the copyright clause?

2. Does the copyright monopoly promote "the Progress of Science" or does it promote "the useful Arts"? *How* does such an exclusive right promote one or the other? Can a specific copyright be struck down because it does *not* promote science or the useful arts? Who would so decide? Is a comic strip constitutionally subject to copyright protection? A design for a flag? A pornographic work? An unpublished work kept in a desk drawer? Does the purpose of promoting progress make for broader or narrower protection in particular cases?

3. Could Congress extend the period of copyright protection to 1000 years? Ninety-nine years from publication? Life of the author plus 70 years? Why is the "property" interest in works of literature, music and art limited in time, when the "property" interest in real and personal property is typically of indefinite duration? Could a *state* grant perpetual copyright protection?

4. Does the reference in the copyright clause to "Authors" have substantive import regarding the nature and amount of work necessary to secure valid copyright protection? Can Congress give such protection to one who copies the work of another? To one who, although not copying, "originates" a work exactly identical to one already written? Or is there a requirement, such as in the patent law, that the work in order to secure copyright protection must be "novel"? If an "Author" is necessary, can Congress extend copyright protection to music, photographs and sculpture?

5. Can Congress constitutionally provide that under certain circumstances, all persons are free, without the prior consent of the copyright owner, to make copies of a copyrighted work upon the payment of a statutorily specified royalty?

6. Is the definition of "Writings" to be limited to the conventional understanding, or to the understanding in 1789? In either case, may Congress constitutionally grant copyright protection of a map, a painting, a photograph, a motion picture, a choreographed dance, a puppet, a sculp-ture, a Frank Lloyd Wright building? Can a work which is reduced to form only in a phonograph record or a tape be given copyright protection? A computer program? A completely unrecorded work, such as a conversation or an improvised "live" performance? If a work is treated as a "non-writing," may the states grant copyright protection?

C.   OVERVIEW OF COPYRIGHT LAW

1.   NATURE OF COPYRIGHT

A copyright is essentially a set of exclusive rights in literary, musical, choreographic, dramatic and artistic works. The rights under copyright pertain to the reproduction, adaptation, public distribution, and public display or performance of the work. The copyright owner's exclusive rights, however, are limited in several important respects. There are three basic limitations:

(a) Because a copyright protects only against copying (or paraphrasing or "colorable alterations" of) the copyrighted work, a copyright does not prohibit another author from *independently* producing the same or a similar work. (Thus, to use a familiar simian example, if one hundred monkeys sat down at one hundred typewriters, and one of them eventually produced *Hamlet,* this remarkable result could not be copyright infringe-ment.)

(b) Anyone may copy the *ideas* from a copyrighted work; copyright protects only the particular expression of ideas. Frequently, however, this "idea/expression dichotomy" is easier to state than to apply. The often hair-splitting, and even hair-rending, exercise of separating ideas from their protected expression will be the subject of considerable attention in later chapters of the casebook. For the moment, an example may suffice to illustrate the difference. The idea that remorse may overwhelm the subcon-scious is not protectible; Lady Macbeth's sleepwalking scene (to stick with Shakespeare) is a particular expression of that idea, and would be subject to protection, were Shakespeare's works not already in the public domain (i.e., copyrights in such works have expired).

(c) A copyright extends neither to systems explained in a work, nor to discrete facts contained within a work. Like the idea/expression dichotomy, the distinction between facts and their expression can be elusive. By way of example, consider the copyrightability of this Overview. The overall presen-tation of the topic and the specific words chosen would be protectible, but the facts the reader learns are not. Thus there is no copyright protection for the *fact* that the Copyright Act covers choreographic works, even though the reader may have ascertained this only by perusing this discus-sion.

2. SUBJECT MATTER OF COPYRIGHT

Copyright is available for "original works of authorship fixed in any tangible medium of expression, now known or later developed from which they can be perceived, reproduced or otherwise communicated, either directly or with the aid of a machine or device." 17 U.S.C.A. § 102(a). This formulation includes several ingredients. First, in accordance with the provision in art. I, sec. 8, cl. 8 of the Constitution, which grants authors the exclusive right to their "writings," fixation in a tangible medium is a prerequisite. For example, an extemporaneous speech or a completely improvised dramatic or musical work would not be within the subject matter of copyright. It should be noted, however, that, under its Commerce Clause authority, Congress has granted performing artists the right to control the fixation, live transmission and distribution of their live musical performances. *See* 17 U.S.C.A. § 1101. Moreover, such creations might be protected under other legal theories, such as "common-law copyright," "unfair competition," or "right of publicity."

In addition to being "fixed," a protected work must reflect "originality" and "authorship." These requirements also follow the constitutional provision for protection for the "writings" of "authors." The legislative history of the 1976 Copyright Act makes clear that the standards for satisfying these requirements are intended to be pretty much what they have been throughout the years. These standards have not been high. An author need not have made an objective contribution to society. (Such a contribution *would* be required of an inventor in order to earn a patent.) Similarly, an author need not produce a work of recognized intellectual or artistic merit. It suffices if the author refrains from copying from prior works and contributes more than a minimal amount of creativity. Courts have often stated that neither judges nor administrators may appropriately act as the arbiters of merit. Rather, a *system* of protection will promote knowledge even if particular works do not.

Although works copied from other works do not qualify for protection, many works are consciously based on earlier works. They may incorporate part of the earlier work but significantly add to it. Examples would be translations, revisions, or adaptations. These are called "derivative works." They can be protected, but only to the extent of the new material that is added. The same principle applies to a "compilation," which is defined as "a work formed by the collection and assembling of preexisting materials or of data that are selected, coordinated, or arranged in such a way that the resulting work as a whole constitutes an original work of authorship." Thus a compilation ranges from a collection of unadorned facts, such as the names and addresses in a college alumni directory, to subjective listings, such as a food critic's choice of the ten best restaurants in New York City, to highly elaborated works, such as an anthology of poetry with accompanying critical essays. It would also include, in this electronic era, computerized data bases. Copyright protection for the compilation extends only to the material newly contributed by the compiler, particularly the selection and arrangement of the component elements; it will not, for example in the last illustration, affect the copyright status—or the public-domain status—of the poetry incorporated in the compilation.

3. DURATION, OWNERSHIP, AND FORMALITIES

a. DURATION OF COPYRIGHT

When copyright protection begins and ends depends on when the work was created. As to works created today or in the future, copyright attaches automatically as soon as the work is put down on paper, tape, digital disk, or some other tangible medium. 17 U.S.C.A. § 102(a). Its duration depends on whether its author was one individual; more than one individual; or someone creating the work in the employ of or at the direction of some other person or organization. The last situation may result in a so-called "work made for hire." To take, at this time, only the example of a literary, musical or artistic work created by an individual after January 1, 1978, copyright lasts for a period of 70 years from the death of the author. This contrasts with the two-term format that has characterized our copyright law since its beginnings and that was in place under the 1909 Act—an initial term of 28 years, starting typically with the work's publication with copyright notice, followed by a 28–year renewal term if timely application were made to the Copyright Office.

The period of copyright protection for a work that was created before the present law became effective on January 1, 1978, depends on a number of factors: whether it was "published" (a term of art that was elaborated under the prior statutes) and whether it was on January 1, 1978 protected in its initial or renewal term of copyright under the 1909 Act. The elaborate provisions of the present statute will be explored below. It suffices to say that, for the most part, unpublished works (e.g., manuscripts and personal letters) will be protected until 70 years after the author's death, or at least through the year 2002. (If the work is published before the end of 2002, it will be protected through the end of 2047.) Works published before 1978 will be protected for 95 years from publication. Works published before 1923 are in the public domain.

b. OWNERSHIP

The Copyright Act gives initial copyright ownership to the author (or authors who jointly create a work). 17 U.S.C.A. § 201(a). In the case of "works made for hire"—a work prepared by an employee within the scope of his employment and certain works commissioned from independent contractors—the employer is considered the author. As "intangible property," a copyright can be transferred from the author to another, *inter vivos* or by will or by intestate succession, in whole or in part. To be an effective transfer, a grant of "exclusive" rights must be in writing and signed by the grantor; a "non-exclusive" grant may be valid even though oral. The grant may cover the entire scope of copyright, or be limited to a particular time period or territory (e.g., a one-year license to perform a copyrighted play in New York City) or medium of expression (e.g., only the right to print a novel but not the right to serialize it in a magazine or prepare a screenplay based on it). A grant need not be recorded in the U.S. Copyright Office, but there are significant advantages in doing so.

In addition to the considerable flexibility afforded the copyright owner to subdivide his or her copyright and otherwise exploit it, the 1976 Act confers a special protective privilege on author-transferors and their families. Because of the highly speculative value of literary, artistic and musical works—at least shortly after they are created—an author who grants an interest in a copyright, after January 1, 1978, may terminate that grant, upon complying with certain procedures, effective 35 years after the grant was made. (There is also a termination right with respect to a narrow category of copyright transfers made prior to January 1, 1978.) This termination option cannot be contracted away or waived in advance.

Finally, one should note the distinction between ownership of a copyright, or of any of the exclusive rights under a copyright, and ownership of "any material object in which the work is embodied." Suppose an artist paints a work, and sells the finished canvas. Unless the artist has made specific provision otherwise, he or she retains all exploitation rights in the work. Thus the artist would have the sole right to create postcards—a derivative work—based on the painting. But the artist cannot prevent the buyer from selling, renting, or making certain public displays (for example, in an art gallery) of the physical object—the canvas—which the buyer now owns. *See* 17 U.S.C.A. §§ 109, 202.

c. NOTICE AND REGISTRATION OF COPYRIGHT

The role of the copyright notice has been sharply reduced since United States adherence to the Berne Convention, which forbids conditioning the enjoyment of copyright upon compliance with formalities. Nonetheless, because adherence does not affect the status of works published before the effective date of the ratification, familiarity with pre-Berne notice requirements remains important. These requirements, in turn, differ depending on whether the work is governed by the 1976 Act or by its predecessor the 1909 Act.

Before January 1, 1978, in order to enjoy a copyright, published works had to bear a copyright notice, which would follow a prescribed form. If the notice was not properly affixed upon publication, the work went into the public domain. These rules remain important even after 1978 if a pre–1978 work is at issue.

The 1976 Act liberalized the notice rules for works published on or after January 1, 1978. As originally written, the 1976 Act continued to prescribe the use of a copyright notice on all copies and phonorecords publicly distributed (anywhere in the world) under authority of the copyright owner. The notice consisted of the three familiar elements—a copyright word or symbol, the name of the copyright owner, and the year of first publication. But the formal requirements were made more flexible, both with respect to location of the notice and the consequences of error in, or total lack of, notice.

Most recently, after 200 years of requiring some form of notice as a condition of a valid copyright, our law was changed effective March 1, 1989. Notice is no longer necessary on copies and phonorecords publicly distributed after that date. Nonetheless, copyright notice continues to be routinely used; there are modest statutory incentives to do so, and in any event the notice is an effective and inexpensive way for the copyright owner to call its claim to the attention of potential users.

A common misunderstanding is that registration with the Copyright Office is a condition to a valid copyright. In fact, registration of claims to copyright is optional. But the advantages of registration are very significant. Among other things, it is generally a prerequisite to an action for infringement; and it provides a number of advantages in proving a case and securing remedies. *See* 17 U.S.C.A. §§ 408–12. Accordingly, it is most advisable to register promptly in the case of any work of significance. The registration procedure is relatively simple. A short application form states the required information regarding authorship, year in which the work was created, and the like—and is to be accompanied by deposit of one or two copies of the work (as prescribed by regulation) and a $30 fee. The Copyright Office examines the application and deposit copies to see that they are generally in proper form. The Office does not compare the deposit copies to earlier material or judge their worth.

4.   SCOPE OF EXCLUSIVE RIGHTS UNDER COPYRIGHT

a.   EXCLUSIVE RIGHTS

Among the exclusive rights comprised within a copyright, the **reproduction** right, or right to produce copies, is the most basic of all. The right protects against copying in any medium, including within the temporary memory of a computer. The right also protects against paraphrasing. But the right prohibits only actual use of the copyright owner's work as a model, either directly or indirectly; it does not cover coincidental similarities in a work created independently and without reference to the first. Moreover, the second author must have copied protected material. As explained earlier, a second author may freely copy a copyrighted work's ideas and discrete facts, so long as he or she does not also copy the expression or particular manner in which the first author set forth these ideas and facts. In addition, to violate the exclusive right of reproduction, the second author's copying must be "substantial." No set rule or formula can determine when the defendant's copying has been substantial; even a small extract from a larger work may be found to infringe, depending on the nature of the copyrighted work and of the portion copied.

The adaptation right, or right to make **derivative works**, overlaps somewhat with the reproduction right. Thus, a poster containing a photograph of a copyrighted painting is in a sense a "copy." But, whether or not a translation or a motion picture version of a copyrighted novel is comfortably thought of as a "copy," they too will infringe if unauthorized—for they are "derivative works." A derivative work "is a work based upon one or more pre-existing works," and includes "any . . . form in which a work may be recast, transformed, or adapted."

The copyright owner also has the exclusive right to **distribute** the work to the public "by sale or other transfer of ownership, or by rental, lease, or lending." The distribution right covers both traditional hard copies and digital copies, including those disseminated over digital networks, such as the Internet. The right clearly prohibits sales of unlawfully produced copies of a work. Whether the right also protects the copyright owner against sale of licensed copies at a time or place or under circumstances that the copyright owner did not authorize depends principally on whether the accused act was the first or a subsequent distribution of the copy involved. The copyright owner has the right to control only the *first* public distribution of a particular copy of the work, whether by rental or sale. After first distribution, it is not infringement (although it may be breach of contract) for the owner of particular copies within the United States to rent or sell them without authority of the copyright owner. An important exception to this so-called "first sale doctrine" is the unauthorized rental for profit of phonograph records or computer programs—even though those records or programs were lawfully manufactured and lawfully purchased by the commercial renter; the purpose of course is to inhibit those who would make a profit inducing retail patrons to engage in home copying.

The rights of **public performance and display** are of great importance to dramatic, musical, and audiovisual works. This last category includes both conventional works such as motion pictures, and works in newer media such as computer videogames. The display right also covers pictorial, graphic, and sculptural works, although the copyright proprietor may not, absent an appropriate contractual provision, prevent the owner of a particular copy (including the original) from displaying it in a museum, art gallery, or other public place.

The statute defines a public performance or display as one presented at a place open to the public or where a substantial number of persons outside of a normal circle of a family or its social acquaintances is gathered, or presented by a transmission, such as a radio or television broadcast. Thus, absent the consent of the copyright owner, reading a copyrighted lecture or poem aloud in a public auditorium, or showing a painting or sculpture on a television program (or a computer network), will constitute respectively an infringing public performance and public display.

How can the copyright owner of, say, a popular song monitor all of the possible infringements of his or her musical work through public performances in nightclubs, concert halls, and radio and television broadcasts? That is the task of the so-called performing rights societies, most notably the American Society of Composers, Authors and Publishers (ASCAP) and Broadcast Music Incorporated (BMI). These societies license the performance rights in nondramatic musical compositions, pursue unlicensed users, and distribute royalties to their composer, lyricist, and publisher members. Performing rights societies are the most well-established examples of collective licensing entities in the United States—and are serving as a model for licensing arrangements for the photocopying of books and periodicals. By representing the interests of large numbers of copyright holders, the performing rights societies are able to secure better enforcement and compensation than could individual claimants. The collective nature of the licensing also benefits users: rather than seek out individual authors, a party wishing to perform quantities of copyrighted music may obtain all the requisite authorizations from one or two sources.

Amendments introduced in 1995 and 1998 extend the public performance right to the copyright owners of sound recordings, but only with respect to digital transmissions. Thus, when a sound recording is played in a discotheque or over traditional broadcast radio, the composers of the underlying music are entitled to performance right royalties, but the performing artists and record producer are not. By contrast, if the performance derives from an interactive digital transmission, the performance rights in the sound recording apply.

b. COPYRIGHT LITIGATION

28 U.S.C.A. § 1338(a) vests exclusive jurisdiction over copyright (and patent) claims in the federal courts. A party seeking to prove the infringement of exclusive rights under copyright, and particularly of the reproduction and derivative works rights, must make out the following **elements of a claim**: (1) *Ownership* of a valid copyright (or of an exclusive right under copyright). If registration occurs within five years of first publication of the work, the certificate of registration serves as *prima facie* evidence of the validity of the copyright. (2) *Copying* of plaintiff's work by the defendant. Because copyright protects against reproduction, but not against independent generation of the same or similar work, there can be no copyright infringement unless defendant came into contact with and in fact copied plaintiff's work. Copying is ordinarily proved through circumstantial evidence: did the defendant have access to the plaintiff's work and are there similarities of expression (i.e., the sequence of words or notes) that are probative of copying rather than independent origination. The copying need not have been intentional: subconscious or unconscious copying of a work can constitute infringing copying. The kind of similarity that permits an inference of copying is called *probative similarity*. (3) As a result of the copying, defendant's work is *substantially similar* to plaintiff's. Substantial similarity may be determined with respect to either the quantity or the quality of the copying. Copying a small, but central, portion of plaintiff's original work can constitute substantial and infringing copying.

If plaintiff succeeds in the above demonstration, it has made out a *prima facie* case of copyright infringement. The burden now shifts to the defendant to justify its conduct, if it can, by application of a relevant statutory exception to copyright infringement (discussed immediately below).

If the copyright owner prevails, the available **remedies** include preliminary and permanent injunctions against further infringements, impoundment and destruction of infringing articles, and damages. Damages can either be actual, as determined by the plaintiff's actual damages and the defendant's profits, or can take the form of what is known as "statutory damages"; the latter measure, with a largely deterrent objective, is to be determined by the jury under the circumstances of the case, and typically fits within a minimum of $500 and a maximum of $20,000 for each work infringed (with a possible assessment as high as $100,000 where the infringement is willful). The court also has discretion to award the prevailing party its attorney's fees.

5. Limitations on the Exclusive Rights Under Copyright

a. EXEMPTIONS AND COMPULSORY LICENSES

The exclusive rights of copyright proprietors to reproduce, adapt, distribute, and publicly perform and display their works encounter manifold and complicated statutory limitations. For example, the Copyright Act permits many classroom, religious, and charitable performances and displays of copyrighted works. The statute exempts most live classroom uses, including the performance of copyrighted dramatic works. Songs may be sung, and other musical compositions played, in most school settings—and also in a number of other noncommercial settings. Instructional broadcasts are also exempted from copyright liability if they meet statutory requirements. The Act also provides that a public performance or display of a work through a transmission on a "home-type receiving apparatus" is not an infringement, if there is no direct charge to see or hear the transmission, and if there is no further public transmission. Essentially, this provision concerns the use by small commercial establishments of a radio to provide background music.

In other instances, the Act removes certain reproductions, performances, and displays from the copyright owner's exclusive control and substitutes a "compulsory licensing" scheme. This compromise provision permits certain uses of the copyrighted work without the copyright owner's consent, but requires the user to adhere to statutory formalities, and to pay specified fees to the copyright owner. The most important and longstanding example of the compulsory license—incorporated in our law since the 1909 Act—relates to making recordings of nondramatic musical works. The current statute provides that once the copyright owner of a nondramatic musical composition has authorized distribution to the public in the United States of a "phonorecord" embodying the composition, another producer may make and distribute phonorecords of the composition to the public. The compulsory licensee may not, without authorization, simply duplicate a preexisting recording; it must produce an independent sound recording with its own musical performers and arrangement. Therefore, the statute permits the compulsory licensee some leeway to arrange the music (technically, the making of a derivative work).

The 1976 Act, as originally written, extended the compulsory-license format to other situations as well: performances of music in jukeboxes, certain retransmissions of television programs by cable services, and certain uses of music and art by public broadcasting stations. The jukebox compulsory license has since been displaced by negotiated arrangements between jukebox operators and performing rights societies, so as to comply with the pertinent provisions of the Berne Convention.

b. FAIR USE

Perhaps the best known, most important, and most elusive exception to the exclusive rights of the copyright owner is embodied in the doctrine known as fair use. The doctrine, a feature of our copyright law since the middle of the nineteenth century through judicial creation and elaboration, was developed in order to allow unauthorized uses that the courts thought were reasonable and that did not unduly deprive the plaintiff's work of a market. Fair use is now expressly incorporated in the statute for the first time, in Section 107.

That section lists several kinds of illustrative uses subject to the defense, including criticism, comment, news reporting, teaching, scholarship, and research. Nonetheless, a defendant who has reproduced, adapted, or publicly distributed, performed, or displayed a copyrighted work without authorization must do more than invoke one of the above socially beneficent purposes. The statute also enumerates four factors to be reviewed in the disposition of the defense. These factors are: the nature of the defendant's use; the nature of the copyrighted work; the amount and substantiality of the portions taken from the copyrighted work; and the effect of the taking upon the potential market for the copyrighted work. These four factors are not exhaustive. Because the fair-use doctrine is still "an equitable rule of reason," courts are free to consider other factors, or to give greater weight to some factors than to others, depending on the given case. A defendant invoking the fair-use defense must establish that the balance of the statutory and any additional judicial criteria weighs in his or her favor.

Fair use has been characteristically invoked as a defense in cases involving historical and biographical works that have quoted from or paraphrased earlier such works or original source materials still in copyright. It has also been invoked by parodists who have borrowed from an earlier work, to poke fun either at that work or at some extrinsic social or political phenomenon. Among the most perplexing applications of the fair use doctrine has been to the relatively new copying technologies, such as audiotaping, videotaping, and photocopying. The Supreme Court has held, for example, that home videotaping of copyrighted television programs, to facilitate later viewing, is a fair use. Lower courts continue to wrestle with the question of photocopying for a variety of purposes, both commercial and nonprofit. A factor that some courts have considered in assessing the fairness of certain photocopying practices is the existence of the Copyright Clearance Center, an international consortium of publishers of general and also scientific and technical books and journals, which undertakes collective licensing efforts, much as ASCAP and BMI do for music copyright holders. Fair use questions are also arising with increasing frequency in connection with the duplication and use of copyrighted material in digital form, such as computer programs and more conventional literary and musical works transmitted over the Internet.

When the photocopying is by a library—whether for internal purposes such as the preservation of archival material or the replacement of a lost copy, or for service to library users engaged in research—the Copyright Act does not rely on the elusive and generalized treatment of fair use in § 107. Rather, one must turn to the much more detailed provisions in § 108. This section, reflecting a hard-fought adjustment of interests between libraries and researchers on the one hand and authors and publishers on the other, allows the making of a strictly limited number of photocopies (and, since 1998, digital copies) of certain kinds of works under certain stipulated circumstances. It does not govern the "systematic" making of multiple photocopies that in effect substitute for subscriptions or purchases; nor does it exempt photocopying done by library users at photocopy machines made available by the library for their convenience.

Several commentators have contended that the First Amendment affords a privilege, separate from statutory exemptions or limitations, to make otherwise infringing reproductions, adaptations, performances, or displays of a copyrighted work. Courts, however, have generally declined to recognize a First Amendment-copyright conflict. The Supreme Court, in fact, has held that two features inherent in copyright law amply secure protection of free speech interests. First, copyright does not prevent the free dissemination of the author's facts and ideas. Second, even "expression" may be copied, by virtue of the fair-use doctrine, in many instances in which there is a compelling societal justification for doing so.

6. STRUCTURE AND OPERATIONS OF THE COPYRIGHT OFFICE

The Copyright Office, a department of the Library of Congress, has for a century been charged with the registration of claims to copyright and with related duties. The copies of works that have been deposited in conjunction with such registration have been used to enrich the holdings of the Library. Beyond that most important day-to-day task, the Office also exercises the power to promulgate regulations (as is true of federal administrative agencies generally). Section 702 of the Copyright Act provides: "The Register of Copyrights is authorized to establish regulations not inconsistent with law for the administration of the functions and duties made the responsibility of the Register under this title. All regulations established by the Register under this title are subject to the approval of the Librarian of Congress." Excerpts from the regulations of the Copyright Office are set forth in Appendix C to this casebook. These regulations cover a variety of subjects, from the kinds of works that are ineligible for registration to the details of copyright notice and of registration and deposit. Because these regulations reflect the Register's interpretation of the statute, they are always subject to challenge in a court for their consistency with the Act (as provided in § 702).

In addition to its power to issue regulations, the Copyright Office has also with increasing frequency—both at congressional direction and on its own initiative—prepared a variety of reports on significant policy issues relating to copyright. In addition, throughout the various copyright reform efforts since the turn of the century, the Register of Copyrights—the head of the Copyright Office—has been a major voice for change and improvement of our copyright law.

While registration has important procedural, and even substantive ramifications, it must be emphasized that the Copyright Office does not grant copyrights; copyright subsists in a work as soon as that work is "created," i.e., "fixed in a copy or phonorecord for the first time." (Even under the 1909 Act, copyright attached to a work when it was publicly disseminated with an appropriate notice; registration could follow later). Copyright is to be distinguished in this respect from the functions of the Patent and Trademark Office, in the Department of Commerce, which issues patents (the effectiveness of which dates only from the date of issuance, the claim of "patent pending" to the contrary notwithstanding). *See* 35 U.S.C.A. § 131. *Compare* § 7(a) of the Lanham Trademark Act, 15 U.S.C.A. § 1057(a) (registration of trademarks).

When an application for copyright registration is filed, however, the function of the Examining Division, though modest, is not altogether nonexistent. It has commonly been assumed that the Register of Copyrights has the power to decline to register a work, a power of some significance since registration—while not a condition of copyright itself—has long been a condition to suing for infringement. Registration has been denied for works deemed by the Register to lack sufficient originality, or to be solely utilitarian in design, or to be obscene. (*But see Mitchell Bros. Film Group v. Cinema Adult Theater, infra.*) This power to deny registration has been controversial and has been exercised sparingly; the Register, in fact, adheres to a policy that, in cases of doubt, dictates registration. (This policy was, for example, employed beginning in 1964 to explain the Register's willingness to register computer programs.) If registration is denied, and a copyright claimant wishes to sue for infringement, he or she is not barred from doing so; but the plaintiff must give notice of the lawsuit to the Register, who is empowered to intervene with respect to the issue of registrability. Recordation of assignments, mortgages and other transactions involving copyright has long complemented the basic examining and registration function of the office.

The Copyright Office has a number of divisions which carry out the various functions necessary to implement the statute. Among those divisions are: the Deposits and Acquisitions Division, which establishes controls over the collections of the Library of Congress through implementation of the statute's deposit requirements; the Examining Division, which examines all applications and material presented to the Copyright Office for registration of original and renewal copyright claims and which determines whether the material deposited constitutes copyrightable subject matter and whether the other legal and formal requirements of the statute have been met; and the Information and Reference Division, which, among other things, educates staff and the public on the copyright law, issues and distributes informational materials, responds to reference requests regarding copyright matters, and prepares search reports based upon copyright records. The interested student can obtain on-line access to copyright registration records dating from 1978.

D.   DISTINCTIONS: PATENTS

Patent Statute

35 U.S.C. 101–03, 112, 154, 171, 173, 271.

§ 101.   *Inventions patentable*

Whoever invents or discovers any new and useful process, machine, manufacture, or composition of matter, or any new and useful improvement thereof, may obtain a patent therefor, subject to the conditions and requirements of this title.

§ 102.   *Conditions for patentability; novelty and loss of right to patent*

A person shall be entitled to a patent unless

(a) the invention was known or used by others in this country, or patented or described in a printed publication in this or a foreign country, before the invention thereof by the applicant for patent, or

(b) the invention was patented or described in a printed publication in this or a foreign country or in public use or on sale in this country, more than one year prior to the date of the application for patent in the United States, or

(c) he has abandoned the invention, or

(d) the invention was first patented or caused to be patented, or was the subject of an inventor's certificate, by the applicant or his legal representatives or assigns in a foreign country prior to the date of the application for patent in this country on an application for patent or inventor's certificate filed more than twelve months before the filing of the application in the United States, or

(e) The invention was described in—

(1) an application for patent, published, under section 122(b), by another filed in the United States before the invention by the applicant for patent . . . ; or

(2) a patent granted on an application for patent by another filed in the United States before the invention by the applicant for patent; or

(f) he did not himself invent the subject matter sought to be patented, or (g)(1) during the course of an interference conducted under section 135 or section 291, another inventor involved therein establishes, to the extent permitted in section 104, that before such person's invention thereof the invention was made by such other inventor and not abandoned, suppressed, or concealed, or (2) before such person's invention thereof, the invention was made in this country by another inventor who had not abandoned, suppressed, or concealed it. In determining priority of invention under this subsection, there shall be considered not only the respective dates of conception and reduction to practice of the invention, but also the reasonable diligence of one who was first to conceive and last to reduce to practice, from a time prior to conception by the other.

§ 103.   *Conditions for patentability; non-obvious subject matter*

(a) A patent may not be obtained though the invention is not identically disclosed or described as set forth in section 102 of this title, if the differences between the subject matter sought to be patented and the prior art are such that the subject matter as a whole would have been obvious at the time the invention was made to a person having ordinary skill in the art to which said subject matter pertains....

(c) Patentability shall not be negatived by the manner in which the invention was made....

§ 112.   *Specification*

The specification shall contain a written description of the invention, and of the manner and process of making and using it, in such full, clear, concise, and exact terms as to enable any person skilled in the art to which it pertains, or with which it is most nearly connected, to make and use the same, and shall set forth the best mode contemplated by the inventor of carrying out his invention.

The specification shall conclude with one or more claims particularly pointing out and distinctly claiming the subject matter which the applicant regards as his invention....

§ 154.   *Contents and term of patent*

(a) In general.—

(1) Contents.—Every patent shall contain a short title of the invention and a grant to the patentee, his heirs or assigns, of the right to exclude others from making, using, offering for sale, or selling the invention throughout the United States or importing the invention into the United States, and, if the invention is a process, of the right to exclude others from using, offering for sale or selling throughout the United States, or importing into the United States, products made by that process, referring to the specification for the particulars thereof.

(2) Term.—Subject to the payment of fees under this title, such grant shall be for a term beginning on the date on which the patent

issues and ending 20 years from the date on which the application was filed in the United States. . . .

§ 171.   *Patents for designs*

Whoever invents any new, original and ornamental design for an article of manufacture may obtain a patent therefor, subject to the conditions and requirements of this title.

The provisions of this title relating to patents for inventions shall apply to patents for designs, except as otherwise provided.

§ 173.   *Term of design patent*

Patents for designs shall be granted for the term of fourteen years from the date of grant.

§ 271.   *Infringement of patent*

(a) Except as otherwise provided in this title, whoever without authority makes, uses, offers to sell, or sells any patented invention, within the United States or imports into the United States any patented invention during the term of the patent therefor, infringes the patent.

(b) Whoever actively induces infringement of a patent shall be liable as an infringer.

(c) Whoever offers to sell or sells within the United States or imports into the United States a component of a patented machine, manufacture, combination or composition, or a material or apparatus for use in practicing a patented process, constituting a material part of the invention, knowing the same to be especially made or especially adapted for use in an infringement of such patent, and not a staple article or commodity of commerce suitable for substantial noninfringing use, shall be liable as a contributory infringer.

. . .

QUESTIONS

1. Note that it is not sufficient, in order to secure a patent, that the invention be "new" and never before known or used. It must also be "non-obvious." Do you understand the difference? Is not the fact that a device is altogether novel rather convincing evidence that it was non-obvious as well? What other elements of proof would you, as the patent claimant, introduce in a litigation challenging the validity of your patent? Why have the non-obviousness requirement?

2. The administration of the patent statute involves a fairly rigorous examination of patent applications by a government official, and a comparison with the prior art. Are there significant differences in the field of copyright so as to explain why there is no comparable examining system? There is, as noted previously, an Examining Division within the Copyright Office. What do you suppose it does?

3. Note that § 171 of the Patent Act extends the entire patent regime—novelty, nonobviousness, examining system, etc.—to ornamental designs for manufactured articles. How would the standard of nonobviousness be applied to determine whether a design patent should be granted, for example, to an attractively shaped dress or piece of furniture? Should the examiner, or court, consider the reaction of the skilled dress or furniture designer, or of the average consumer?

4. Would it be constitutional for Congress to accord protection to dress and furniture designs under the law of copyright? That is, are they "writings"? Does the availability of design patent protection—with strict standards of patentability and a relatively short period of protection—indicate that Congress intends to exclude these designs from the scope of copyright? (These issues will be explored in greater detail in Chapter 2.F, *infra.*)

Alfred Bell & Co. v. Catalda Fine Arts

191 F.2d 99 (2d Cir.1951).

[Plaintiff sought protection for certain reproductions of public-domain paintings by the old masters. These were produced by plaintiff through a tedious and exacting form of engraving known as the "mezzotint method." Among its detailed findings, the district court stated: "The work of the engraver upon the plate requires the individual conception, judgment and execution by the engraver on the depth and shape of the depressions in the plate to be made by the scraping process in order to produce in this other medium the engraver's concept of the effect of the oil painting. No two engravers can produce identical interpretations of the same oil painting."]

■ FRANK, CIRCUIT JUDGE. 1. Congressional power to authorize both patents and copyrights is contained in Article 1, § 8 of the Constitution. In passing on the validity of patents, the Supreme Court recurrently insists that this constitutional provision governs. On this basis, pointing to the Supreme Court's consequent requirement that, to be valid, a patent must disclose a high degree of uniqueness, ingenuity and inventiveness, the defendants assert that the same requirement constitutionally governs copyrights. As several sections of the Copyright Act—e.g., those authorizing copyrights of "reproductions of works of art," maps, and compilations—plainly dispense with any such high standard, defendants are, in effect, attacking the constitutionality of those sections. But the very language of the Constitution differentiates (a) "authors" and their "writings" from (b) "inventors" and their "discoveries." Those who penned the Constitution, of course, knew the difference. The pre-revolutionary English statutes had made the distinction. In 1783, the Continental Congress had passed a resolution recommending that the several states enact legislation to "secure" to authors the "copyright" of their books. Twelve of the thirteen states (in 1783–1786) enacted such statutes. Those of Connecticut and North Carolina covered books, pamphlets, maps, and charts.

Moreover, in 1790, in the year after the adoption of the Constitution, the first Congress enacted two statutes, separately dealing with patents and copyrights. The patent statute, enacted April 10, 1790, 1 Stat. 109, provided that patents should issue only if the Secretary of State, Secretary of War and the Attorney General, or any two of them "shall deem the invention or discovery sufficiently useful and important"; the applicant for a patent was obliged to file a specification "so particular" as "to distinguish the invention or discovery from other things before known and used ...''; the patent was to constitute *prima facie* evidence that the patentee was "the first and true inventor or ... discoverer ... of the thing so specified." The Copyright Act, enacted May 31, 1790, 1 Stat. 124, covered "maps, charts, and books." A printed copy of the title of any map, chart or book was to be recorded in the Clerk's office of the District Court, and a copy of the map, chart or book was to be delivered to the Secretary of State within six months after publication. Twelve years later, Congress in 1802, 2 Stat. 171, added, to matters that might be copyrighted, engravings, etchings and prints.

Thus legislators peculiarly familiar with the purpose of the Constitutional grant, by statute, imposed far less exacting standards in the case of copyrights. They authorized the copyrighting of a mere map which, patently, calls for no considerable uniqueness. They exacted far more from an inventor. And, while they demanded that an official should be satisfied as to the character of an invention before a patent issued, they made no such demand in respect of a copyright. In 1884, in *Burrow–Giles Lithographic Co. v. Sarony*, 111 U.S. 53, 57, the Supreme Court, adverting to these facts said: "The construction placed upon the constitution by the first act of 1790 and the act of 1802, by the men who were contemporary with its formation, many of whom were members of the convention which framed it, is of itself entitled to very great weight, and when it is remembered that the rights thus established have not been disputed during a period of nearly a century, it is almost conclusive." Accordingly, the Constitution, as so interpreted, recognizes that the standards for patents and copyrights are basically different.

The defendants' contention apparently results from the ambiguity of the word "original." It may mean startling, novel or unusual, a marked departure from the past. Obviously this is not what is meant when one speaks of "the original package," or the "original bill," or (in connection with the "best evidence" rule) an "original" document; none of those things is highly unusual in creativeness. "Original" in reference to a copyrighted work means that the particular work "owes its origin" to the "author." No large measure of novelty is necessary....

In *Bleistein v. Donaldson Lithographing Co.*, 183 U.S. 239, 250, 252, the Supreme Court cited with approval *Henderson v. Tompkins, C.C.*, 60 F. 758, where it was said, 60 F. at page 764: "There is a *very broad distinction between what is implied in the word 'author,' found in the constitution, and the word 'inventor.' The latter carries an implication which excludes the results of only ordinary skill, while nothing of this is necessarily involved in the former.* Indeed, the statutes themselves make broad distinctions on this point. So much as relates to copyrights ... is expressed, so far as this particular is concerned, by the mere words, 'author, inventor, designer or proprietor,' with such aid as may be derived from the words 'written, composed or made,'. . . . But a *multitude of books rest safely under copyright, which show only ordinary skill and diligence in their preparation.* Compilations are noticeable examples of this fact. With reference to this subject, the courts have not undertaken to assume the functions of critics, or to measure carefully the degree of originality, or literary skill or training involved."

It is clear, then, that nothing in the Constitution commands that copyrighted matter be strikingly unique or novel. Accordingly, we were not ignoring the Constitution when we stated that a "copy of something in the public domain" will support a copyright if it is a "distinguishable variation"; or when we rejected the contention that "like a patent, a copyrighted work must be not only original, but new," adding, "That is not . . . the law as is obvious in the case of maps or compendia, where later works will necessarily be anticipated." All that is needed to satisfy both the Constitution and the statute is that the "author" contributed something more than a "merely trivial" variation, something recognizably "his own." Originality in this context "means little more than a prohibition of actual copying."[13] No matter how poor artistically the "author's" addition, it is enough if it be his own. *Bleistein v. Donaldson Lithographing Co.,* 188 U.S. 239, 47 L. Ed. 460.

On that account, we have often distinguished between the limited protection accorded a copyright owner and the extensive protection granted a patent owner. So we have held that "independent reproduction of a copyrighted . . . work is not infringement," whereas it is *vis-à-vis* a patent. Correlative with the greater immunity of a patentee is the doctrine of anticipation which does not apply to copyrights: The alleged inventor is chargeable with full knowledge of all the prior art, although in fact he may be utterly ignorant of it. The "author" is entitled to a copyright if he independently contrived a work completely identical with what went before; similarly, although he obtains a valid copyright, he has no right to prevent another from publishing a work identical with his, if not copied from his. A patentee, unlike a copyrightee, must not merely produce something "original"; he must also be "the first inventor or discoverer." "Hence it is possible to have a plurality of valid copyrights directed to closely identical or even identical works. Moreover, none of them, if

13. Hoague–Sprague Corp. v. Frank C. Meyer, Inc., D.C.N.Y., 31 F.2d 583, 586. See also as to photographs Judge Learned Hand in Jewelers Circular Publishing Co. v. Keystone Pub. Co., D.C.N.Y., 274 F. 932, 934.

The English doctrine is the same. See Copinger, The Law of Copyrights 40–44 (7th ed. 1936): "Neither original thought nor original research is essential"; he quotes the English courts to the effect that the statute "does not require that the expression must be in an original or novel form, but that the work must not be copied from another work—that it should originate from the author," but only that "though it may be neither novel or ingenious, [it] is the claimant's original work in that it originates from him, and is not copied."

independently arrived at without copying, will constitute an infringement of the copyright of the others."[16]

. . .

2. We consider untenable defendants' suggestion that plaintiff's mezzotints could not validly be copyrighted because they are reproductions of works in the public domain. Not only does the Act include "Reproductions of a work of art," but—while prohibiting a copyright of "the original text of any work ... in the public domain"—it explicitly provides for the copyrighting of "translations, or other versions of works in the public domain." The mezzotints were such "versions." They "originated" with those who made them, and—on the trial judge's findings well supported by the evidence—amply met the standards imposed by the Constitution and the statute[22] There is evidence that they were not intended to, and did not, imitate the paintings they reproduced. But even if their substantial departures from the paintings were inadvertent, the copyrights would be valid.[23]

---

16. *Id.* See Lawrence v. Dana, 15 Fed. Cas. 26, 60 No. 8,136: "Persons making, using or vending to others to be used, the patented article are guilty of infringing the letters-patent, even though they may have subsequently invented the same thing without any knowledge of the existence of the letters-patent; but the recomposition of the same book without copying, though not likely to occur, would not be an infringement." See also Fred Fisher, Inc. v. Dillingham, D.C.N.Y., 298 F. 145, 147.

The English doctrine is the same. See Copinger, The Law of Copyrights 2 (7th ed. 1936): "It is not infrequently urged as an objection to granting copyright protection for a long term, that the effect is to create a monopoly, but at least, it is not a monopoly of knowledge. The grant of a patent does prevent full use being made of knowledge, but the reader of a book is not by the copyright laws prevented from making full use of any information he may acquire from his reading. He is only prohibited from disseminating that information or knowledge by multiplying copies of the book or of material portions of it: or, possibly, by reading the book aloud in public. Copyright is, in fact, only a negative right to prevent the appropriation of the labours of an author by another. If it could be shown that two precisely similar works were in fact produced wholly independently of one another, the author of the work that was published first would have no right to restrain the publication by the other author of that author's independent and original work. A patentee, on the other hand, has the right

to prevent another from using his invention if it in fact infringes the former's patent, notwithstanding that the latter's invention was the subject of independent investigation on his part."

22. See Copinger, The Law of Copyrights 46 (7th ed. 1936): "Again, an engraver is almost invariably a copyist, but although his work may infringe copyright in the original painting if made without the consent of the owner of the copyright therein, his work may still be original in the sense that he has employed skill and judgment in its production. He produces the resemblance he is desirous of obtaining by means very different from those employed by the painter or draughtsman from whom he copies; means which require great labour and talent. The engraver produces his effects by the management of light and shade, or, as the term of his art expresses it, the *chiarooscuro*. The due degrees of light and shade are produced by different lines and dots; he who is the engraver must decide on the choice of the different lines or dots for himself, and on his choice depends the success of his print."

23. See Kallen, Art and Freedom 977 (1942) to the effect that "the beauty of the human singing voice, as the western convention of music hears it, depends upon a physiological dysfunction of the vocal cords...."

Plutarch tells this story: A painter, enraged because he could not depict the foam that filled a horse's mouth from champing at the bit, threw a sponge at his painting; the sponge splashed against the wall—and achieved the desired result.

A copyist's bad eyesight or defective musculature, or a shock caused by a clap of thunder, may yield sufficiently distinguishable variations. Having hit upon such a variation unintentionally, the "author" may adopt it as his and copyright it.

. . .

QUESTIONS

1. How is the "progress of science and the useful arts" advanced by sustaining copyright in a work that is the same, although unknowingly and independently created, as an earlier work? How is it advanced by a knowing adaptation of an earlier work, such as an engraving of an old master, or a translation of a great novel?

2. If the plaintiff's engraving in the *Catalda* case had been based not on an old master but on a copyrighted painting, should it be eligible for copyright? Is it eligible for copyright under the 1976 Copyright Act?

3. Do you agree that a stroke of the pen resulting from "bad eyesight or defective musculature" is copyrightable? Can you distinguish from such a situation the results of "a shock caused by a clap of thunder"? How would dropping globs of paint from a ladder be treated by the *Catalda* court?

4. When Judge Frank quotes from an earlier opinion that notes that "originality in this context means little more than a prohibition of actual copying," what does he mean by "little more"?

5. Three standards (at least) might be applied to determine eligibility for copyright: (a) *Originality,* in the sense of independent origination or non-copying; (b) *Creativity,* in the sense of some modest level of imagination or "escape from the commonplace"; or (c) *Novelty and Invention,* in the sense (like a patent) of a "leap" beyond the "prior art," which would represent a major development in that art (and one that would not be obvious to a person skilled in that art). What are the arguments for and against the application of one or more of these standards? Which standard would Judge Frank apply on the basis of the *Catalda* case?

E.   DISTINCTIONS: TRADEMARKS

Trade–Mark Cases

100 U.S. 82 (1879).

■ MR. JUSTICE MILLER delivered the opinion of the court.

The three cases whose titles stand at the head of this opinion are criminal prosecutions for violations of what is known as the trade-mark legislation of Congress. The first two are indictments in the southern district of New York, and the last is an information in the southern district of Ohio. In all of them the judges of the circuit courts in which they are pending have certified to a difference of opinion on what is substantially the same question; namely, are the acts of Congress on the subject of trademarks founded on any rightful authority in the Constitution of the United States?

The entire legislation of Congress in regard to trade-marks is of very recent origin. It is first seen in sects. 77 to 84, inclusive, of the act of July 8, 1870, entitled "An Act to revise, consolidate, and amend the statutes relating to patents and copyrights." 16 Stat. 198. The part of this act relating to trade-marks is embodied in chap. 2, tit. 60, sects. 4937 to 4947, of the Revised Statutes.

It is sufficient at present to say that they provide for the registration in the Patent Office of any device in the nature of a trade-mark to which any person has by usage established an exclusive right, or which the person so registering intends to appropriate by that act to his exclusive use; and they make the wrongful use of a trade-mark, so registered, by any other person, without the owner's permission, a cause of action in a civil suit for damages. Six years later we have the act of Aug. 14, 1876 (19 Stat. 141), punishing by fine and imprisonment the fraudulent use, sale, and counterfeiting of trade-marks registered in pursuance of the statutes of the United States, on which the informations and indictments are founded in the cases before us.

The right to adopt and use a symbol or a device to distinguish the goods or property made or sold by the person whose mark it is, to the exclusion of use by all other persons, has been long recognized by the common law and the chancery courts of England and of this country, and by the statutes of some of the States. It is a property right for the violation of which damages may be recovered in an action at law, and the continued violation of it will be enjoined by a court of equity, with compensation for past infringement. This exclusive right was not created by the act of Congress, and does not now depend upon it for its enforcement. The whole system of trade-mark property and the civil remedies for its protection existed long anterior to that act, and have remained in full force since its passage.

As the property in trade-marks and the right to their exclusive use rest on the laws of the States, and, like the great body of the rights of person and of property, depend on them for security and protection, the power of Congress to legislate on the subject, to establish the conditions on which these rights shall be enjoyed and exercised, the period of their duration, and the legal remedies for their enforcement, if such power exist at all, must be found in the Constitution of the United States, which is the source of all the powers that Congress can lawfully exercise.

In the argument of these cases this seems to be conceded, and the advocates for the validity of the acts of Congress on this subject point to two clauses of the Constitution, in one or in both of which, as they assert, sufficient warrant may be found for this legislation.

The first of these is the eighth clause of sect. 8 of the first article. That section, manifestly intended to be an enumeration of the powers expressly granted to Congress, and closing with the declaration of a rule for the ascertainment of such powers as are necessary by way of implication to carry into efficient operation those expressly given, authorizes Congress, by the clause referred to, "to promote the progress of science and useful arts, by securing for limited times, to authors and inventors, the exclusive right to their respective writings and discoveries."

As the first and only attempt by Congress to regulate the *right of trade-marks* is to be found in the act of July 8, 1870, to which we have referred, entitled "An Act to revise, consolidate and amend the statutes relating to *patents and copyrights,*" terms which have long since become technical, as referring, the one to inventions and the other to the writings of authors, it is a reasonable inference that this part of the statute also was, in the opinion of Congress, an exercise of the power found in that clause of the Constitution.

Any attempt, however, to identify the essential characteristics of a trade-mark with inventions and discoveries in the arts and sciences, or with the writings of authors, will show that the effort is surrounded with insurmountable difficulties.

The ordinary trade-mark has no necessary relation to invention or discovery. The trade-mark recognized by the common law is generally the growth of a considerable period of use, rather than a sudden invention. It is often the result of accident rather than design, and when under the act of Congress it is sought to establish it by registration, neither originality, invention, discovery, science, nor art is any way essential to the right conferred by that act. If we should endeavor to classify it under the head of writings of authors, the objections are equally strong. In this, as in regard to inventions, originality is required. And while the word *writings* may be liberally construed, as it has been, to include original designs for engravings, prints, & c., it is only such as are *original,* and are founded in the creative powers of the mind. The writings which are to be protected are *the fruits of intellectual labor,* embodied in the form of books, prints, engravings, and the like. The trade-mark may be, and generally is, the adoption of something already in existence as the distinctive symbol of the party using it. At common law the exclusive right to it grows out of its *use,* and not its mere adoption. By the act of Congress this exclusive right attaches upon registration. But in neither case does it depend upon novelty, invention, discovery, or any work of the brain. It requires no fancy or imagination, no genius, no laborious thought. It is simply founded on priority of appropriation. We look in vain in the statute for any other qualification or condition. If the symbol, however plain, simple, old, or well-known, has been first appropriated by the claimant as his distinctive trade-mark, he may by registration secure the right to its exclusive use. While such legislation may be a judicious aid to the common law on the subject of trade-marks, and may be within the competency of legislatures whose general powers embrace that class of subjects, we are unable to see any such power in the constitutional provision concerning authors and inventors, and their writings and discoveries.

The other clause of the Constitution supposed to confer the requisite authority on Congress is the third of the same section, which, read in connection with the granting clause, is as follows: "The Congress shall have power to regulate commerce with foreign nations, and among the several States, and with the Indian tribes."

The argument is that the use of a trade-mark—that which alone gives it any value—is to identify a particular class or quality of goods as the manufacture, produce, or property of the person who puts them in the general market for sale; that the sale of the article so distinguished is commerce; that the trade-mark is, therefore, a useful and valuable aid or instrument of commerce, and its regulation by virtue of the clause belongs to Congress, and that the act in question is a lawful exercise of this power.

[The Court found that the statutes in question were not limited to interstate transactions and were accordingly invalid. The Court expressly left undecided the question "whether the trade-mark bears such a relation to commerce in general terms as to bring it within congressional control, when used or applied to classes of commerce which fall within that control."]

QUESTIONS

1.   Are there weaknesses in the Court's distinction of trademark and patent? Are there any additional weaknesses in its distinction of trademark and copyright?

2.   Does this case hold that trademarks are per se not copyrightable?

3.   Can the title of a book or song be protected by copyright?

4.   If Congress enacted a copyright law pursuant to the Commerce Clause, what additional restrictions on its power would be imposed? What restrictions would be lifted?

TRADEMARKS AND THE LANHAM ACT

When used in connection with goods or services, certain words, phrases, designs or pictures come to identify in the mind of the public the source of those goods or services. The word "Ivory," for example, when used in marketing soap or soap-related products will normally be understood by the purchasing public to stand for a specific manufacturer (even though the purchasing public may not be aware of the identity of the manufacturer, i.e., Procter & Gamble). The same is true for the use of a small knit alligator in connection with sportswear, or a tiger in connection with breakfast cereals or automotive fuel. When such a word or picture identifies the source of goods or services, rather than merely the goods or services themselves, it is said to function as a trademark or a service mark. It is a symbol that represents the reputation or goodwill of the manufacturer or provider, and signifies the quality of its goods or services. The mark provides useful information for the consumer and aids in marketplace competition.

The law has long recognized the commercial value of the trademark (or service mark) and has protected it against unauthorized confusing use by others. Another person who improperly uses, say, the word "Ivory" in the merchandising of skin cream will surely be found to have created the misleading impression that its cream was manufactured by the same company that produces the well-known soap. An injunction will protect Procter & Gamble against the possible sullying of its reputation, and will protect the consumer against being misled about source and quality. The common law of the various states has traditionally afforded protection against "unfair competition" that takes the form of the unauthorized "passing off" of the defendant's product under the guise of another's mark. The two key elements of the claim for passing off are that the copied word, phrase, design or picture identify the plaintiff as source (i.e., that it have "secondary meaning"), and that the defendant's use will cause confusion among a substantial number of persons in the marketplace. To help "warn off" persons from making potentially confusing uses of such marks, states have supplemented their common-law remedies with systems for the registration and publication of such marks.

Obviously, in a national economy in which goods and services routinely cross state lines, the protection of trademarks and service marks would be significantly encumbered by the need to register and enforce claims on a state-by-state basis. The *Trade–Mark Cases* show that Congress enacted federal trademark-registration legislation in 1870. The present-day version of that legislation is known as the Lanham Act of 1946. It provides for the registration of distinctive marks (i.e., those with secondary meaning) on a Principal Register, and the protection of registered marks by actions in federal court against unauthorized confusing uses. The basic substantive doctrines and protections under the Lanham Act are essentially congruent to those afforded by the states (and do not purport to preempt state unfair competition laws). Registration under the federal act provides certain additional substantive and procedural rights not necessarily available under state law. In the very important § 43(a) of the Lanham Act, Congress has gone beyond the protection of registered marks to afford federal relief against more general kinds of false representations in interstate commerce.

The most significant provisions of the Lanham Act follow.

Lanham Act

15 U.S.C. §§ 1051, 1052, 1114, 1125, 1127.

Sec. 1 (15 U.S.C. § 1051). Registration; application ....

(a) The owner of a trademark used in commerce may register his trademark under this Chapter on the principal register hereby established:

(1) By filing in the Patent and Trademark Office—

(A) a written application, in such form as may be prescribed by the Commissioner, verified by the applicant, or by a member of the firm or an officer of the corporation or association applying, specifying applicant's domicile and citizenship, the date of applicant's first use of the mark, the date of applicant's first use of the mark in commerce, the goods in connection with which the mark is used and the mode or manner in which the mark is used in connection with such goods, . . .

(B) a drawing of the mark; and

(C) such number of specimens or facsimiles of the mark as actually used as may be required by the Commissioner.

. . .*

Sec. 2 (15 U.S.C. § 1052). Trademarks registrable on the principal register; concurrent registration

No trademark by which the goods of the applicant may be distinguished from the goods of others shall be refused registration on the principal register on account of its nature unless it—

(a) consists of or comprises immoral, deceptive, or scandalous matter; or matter which may disparage or falsely suggest a connection with persons, living or dead, institutions, beliefs, or national symbols, or bring them into contempt, or disrepute . . .

(b) consists of or comprises the flag or coat of arms or other insignia of the United States, or of any State or municipality, or of any foreign nation, or any simulation thereof.

(c) consists of or comprises a name, portrait, or signature identifying a particular living individual except by his written consent, or the name, signature, or portrait of a deceased President of the United States during the life of his widow, if any, except by the written consent of the widow.

(d) consists of or comprises a mark which so resembles a mark registered in the Patent Office or a mark or trade name previously used in the United States by another and not abandoned, as to be likely, when applied to the goods of the applicant, to cause confusion, or to cause mistake, or to deceive . . . [subject to a proviso which specifies the circumstances under which the same mark may be registered concurrently by different persons].

(e) Consists of a mark which (1) when used on or in connection with the goods of the applicant is merely descriptive or deceptively misdescriptive of them, (2) when used on or in connection with the goods of the applicant is primarily geographically descriptive of them, except as indications of regional origin may be registrable under section 4, (3) when used on or in connection with the goods of the applicant is primarily geographically deceptively misdescriptive of them, (4) is primarily merely a surname, or (5) comprises any matter that, as a whole, is functional.

(f) except as expressly excluded in subsections (a), (b), (c), (d), (e)(3), and (e)(5) of this section, nothing in this chapter shall prevent the

* [Editor's note: Section 1(b), (c) and (d) of the Lanham Act provides for registration on the basis of an intent to use the mark in commerce.]

registration of a mark used by the applicant which has become distinctive of the applicant's goods in commerce. The Director may accept as prima facie evidence that the mark has become distinctive, as used on or in connection with the applicant's goods in commerce, proof of substantially exclusive and continuous use thereof as a mark by the applicant in commerce for the five years before the date on which the claim of distinctiveness is made. . . .

Sec. 32(1) (15 U.S.C. § 1114(1)). Remedies; infringement . . .

Any person who shall, without the consent of the registrant—

(a) use in commerce any reproduction, counterfeit, copy, or colorable imitation of a registered mark in connection with the sale, offering for sale, distribution, or advertising of any goods or services on or in connection with which such use is likely to cause confusion, or to cause mistake, or to deceive; or

(b) reproduce, counterfeit, copy or colorably imitate a registered mark and apply such reproduction, counterfeit, copy, or colorable imitation to labels, signs, prints, packages, wrappers, receptacles or advertisements intended to be used in commerce upon or in connection with the sale, offering for sale, distribution, or advertising of goods or services on or in connection with which such use is likely to cause confusion, or to cause mistake, or to deceive;

shall be liable in a civil action by the registrant for the remedies hereinafter provided. Under subsection (b) of this section, the registrant shall not be entitled to recover profits or damages unless the acts have been committed with knowledge that such imitation is intended to be used to cause confusion, or to cause mistake, or to deceive.

Sec. 43 (15 U.S.C. § 1125). False designations of origin and false descriptions forbidden

(a)(1) Any person who, on or in connection with any goods or services, or any container for goods, uses in commerce any word, term, name, symbol, or device, or any combination thereof, or any false designation of origin, false or misleading description of fact, or false or misleading representation of fact, which—

(A) is likely to cause confusion, or to cause mistake, or to deceive as to the affiliation, connection, or association of such person with another person, or as to the origin, sponsorship, or approval of his or her goods, services, or commercial activities by another person, or

(B) in commercial advertising or promotion, misrepresents the nature, characteristics, qualities, or geographic origin of his or her or another person's goods, services, or commercial activities,

shall be liable in a civil action by any person who believes that he or she is or is likely to be damaged by such act.

. . .

(c)(1) The owner of a famous mark shall be entitled, subject to the principles of equity and upon such terms as the court deems reasonable, to an injunction against another person's commercial use in commerce of a mark or trade name, if such use begins after the mark has become famous and causes dilution of the distinctive quality of the mark. . . .

Sec. 45 (15 U.S.C. § 1127). Construction and definitions; intent of chapter

In the construction of this Act, unless the contrary is plainly apparent from the context:

. . .

The word "commerce" means all commerce which may lawfully be regulated by Congress.

. . .

The term "trademark" includes any word, name, symbol, or device, or any combination thereof—

(1) used by a person, or

(2) which a person has a bona fide intention to use in commerce and applies to register on the principal register established by this Act,

to identify and distinguish his or her goods, including a unique product, from those manufactured or sold by others and to indicate the source of the goods, even if that source is unknown.

The term "service mark" means any word, name, symbol, or device, or any combination thereof—

(1) used by a person, or

(2) which a person has a bona fide intention to use in commerce and applies to register on the principal register established by this Act,

to identify and distinguish the services of one person, including a unique service, from the services of others and to indicate the source of the services, even if that source is unknown. Titles, character names, and other distinctive features of radio or television programs may be registered as service marks notwithstanding that they, or the programs, may advertise the goods of the sponsor.

. . .

The term "mark" includes any trademark, service mark, collective mark, or certification mark.

The term "use in commerce" means the bona fide use of a mark in the ordinary course of trade, and not made merely to reserve a right in a mark. For purposes of this Act, a mark shall be deemed to be in use in commerce—

(1) on goods when—

(A) it is placed in any manner on the goods or their containers or the displays associated therewith or on the tags or labels affixed thereto, or if the nature of the goods makes such placement impracticable, then on documents associated with the goods or their sale, and

(B) the goods are sold or transported in commerce, and

(2) on services when it is used or displayed in the sale or advertising of services and the services are rendered in commerce, or the services are rendered in more than one State or in the United States and a foreign country and the person rendering the services is engaged in commerce in connection with the services.

QUESTIONS

1.   Could an author secure a trademark for a character name in a popular story or series of stories (e.g., James Bond or Sam Spade)? Could an author secure a trademark for a character apart from the name, e.g., the physical appearance of a character or the personality traits of a character? What would be the scope of protection afforded by trademark for such a name or character?

2.   Could a copyright be secured for such a name or character? (Consider both the Constitution and the Copyright Act.) What would be the scope of copyright protection?

3.   The famous children's book author Dr. Seuss created a number of cartoons for Liberty Magazine in 1932. The copyrights were owned by Liberty. More than thirty years later, Liberty authorized Don Poynter to make three-dimensional dolls based on these cartoons. Dr. Seuss, finding these dolls to be "tasteless, unattractive and of an inferior quality," sought to enjoin the use of his name and to recover damages therefor. Should he succeed with respect to the following hang-tag?

See Geisel v. Poynter Prods., Inc., 283 F.Supp. 261 (S.D.N.Y.1968).

Does the following tag call for a different answer (*see* 295 F.Supp. 331 (S.D.N.Y.1968))?

Frederick Warne & Co. v. Book Sales, Inc.

481 F.Supp. 1191 (S.D.N.Y.1979).

■ SOFAER, DISTRICT JUDGE. Frederick Warne & Co., Inc. ("Warne"), brings this trademark infringement action against Book Sales, Inc. ("BSI") under Sections 32(1) and 43(a) of the Lanham Act, 15 U.S.C. § 1114(1) and § 1125(a) respectively, as well as under the New York Anti–Dilution Statute, General Business Law § 368–d. The case is before the court on cross motions for summary judgment filed pursuant to Rule 56 of the Federal Rules of Civil Procedure.

[Plaintiff Warne has, since 1902, been the publisher of the "Original Peter Rabbit Books," a well-known series of children's books written and illustrated by Beatrix Potter. Seven books in the series are no longer, or never were, covered by United States copyright, and several new editions of Miss Potter's works have been marketed in competition with the Warne editions. Although Warne concedes that the seven works are in the public domain, it claims exclusive rights in the cover illustrations (and character marks derived therefrom) originally created by Miss Potter; it also claims exclusive trademark rights in a "sitting rabbit" illustration that appeared within the text of *The Tale of Peter Rabbit*. Warne registered three of the covers under the Lanham Act as book trademarks, and also claims protection for the unregistered marks under § 43(a) of that Act, which permits proof of validity of a trademark even without the benefit of the presumption of validity that registration confers. Warne has used, and licensed others to use, the eight illustrations on a variety of commercial products, including book packaging, other original Warne publications (including a cookbook and coloring book), and toys and clothing; licensed products have generated sales of $5 million per year, with royalties to Warne in the amount of $250,000.

[The defendant has since 1977 marketed copies of the seven Potter stories now in the public domain, bound as a single colorful volume. It has photographically reproduced the original Potter text illustrations; it also has redrawn the Potter cover illustrations, and the "sitting rabbit," and relocated them at the beginning and end of the appropriate stories, and has placed photographic reproductions of the original Warne covers as corner ornaments on most of the pages of the seven stories.

[Warne contends that BSI's use of all eight illustrations constitutes trademark infringement, and seeks injunctive relief as well as damages and an accounting. Both parties moved for summary judgment, which the court denied because of genuine issues of material fact.]

I. *Plaintiff's Claim to Trademark Protection*

To succeed in this action, plaintiff must first establish that it has valid trademark rights in the eight character illustrations as used on its books and other products. Section 45 of the Lanham Act defines a trademark as any "word, name, symbol, or device ... adopted and used by a manufacturer or merchant to identify his goods and distinguish them from those manufactured or sold by others." 15 U.S.C. § 1127. Although the illustrations here are *capable* of distinguishing Warne's books from those of others, it cannot be said that they are so arbitrary, unique, and non-descriptive as to constitute "technical trademarks," which are presumed valid as soon as they are affixed to the goods and the goods are sold. *Blisscraft of Hollywood v. United Plastics Co.,* 294 F.2d 694 (2d Cir.1961). Accordingly, plaintiff has the burden of establishing that these illustrations have acquired secondary meaning, defined as "[t]he power of a name or other configuration to symbolize a particular business, product or company." *Dallas Cowboys Cheerleaders, Inc. v. Pussycat Cinema, Ltd.,* 604 F.2d 200, 203, n. 5 (2d Cir.1979), *quoting Ideal Toy Corp. v. Kenner Products Division of General Mills Fun Group, Inc.,* 443 F. Supp. 291, 305 n. 14 (S.D.N.Y.1977).

In the instant case, it would not be enough that the illustrations in question have come to signify Beatrix Potter as author of the books; plaintiff must show that they have come to represent its goodwill and reputation as *publisher* of those books. Whether or not the illustrations have acquired that kind of secondary meaning is a question of fact, which may be proven by either direct or circumstantial evidence. As to those marks registered under the Lanham Act, the registration constitutes prima facie evidence of trademark validity. *See* Section 33(a), 15 U.S.C. § 1115(a); *see generally* McCarthy, *supra,* § 11:16, § 15:12.

In addition, plaintiff must establish that defendant's use of the eight illustrations is trademark infringement. Under Section 32(1) of the Act, a cause of action for infringement of a registered mark exists where a person uses the mark "in connection with the sale ... or advertising of any goods ... [where] such use is likely to cause confusion, or to cause mistake, or to deceive." 15 U.S.C. § 1114(1). With respect to the unregistered illustrations, plaintiff may succeed under Section 43(a), a broadly worded provision which creates a federal cause of action for false designation of origin or false representation of goods or services. As a general rule, the same facts which support an action for trademark infringement—facts indicating likelihood of confusion—will support an action for unfair competition under Section 43(a). *Dallas Cap, supra,* 510 F.2d at 1010; *see American Footwear*

Corp. v. General Footwear Co., Ltd., 609 F.2d 655, 665 (2d Cir.1979). Likelihood of confusion is a factual inquiry, depending on a host of factors, no one of which is controlling. *E.g., Mushroom Makers, Inc. v. R. G. Barry Corporation,* 580 F.2d 44 (2d Cir.1978), *cert. denied,* 439 U.S. 1116 (1979).

Contrary to what the parties suggested in their motion papers, and even though some of plaintiff's illustrations have been registered under the Lanham Act, defendant is unwilling to concede that any of the illustrations in issue are valid trademarks. Nor is defendant prepared to admit that there would be a likelihood of confusion arising from its use of those illustrations and marks in connection with its own Peter Rabbit publication. Because the present record does not permit a finding that the necessary elements of trademark infringement—secondary meaning and likelihood of confusion—exist, the plaintiff's motion for summary judgment must be denied.

II. *Defendant's Claim to Publish Freely*

Defendant contends that the disputed questions of fact requiring denial of plaintiff's motion need not be reached to find in defendant's favor. Defendant argues that its use of the illustrations and marks is legally protected because they are part of copyrightable works now in the public domain. This argument is not persuasive. The fact that a copyrightable character or design has fallen into the public domain should not preclude protection under the trademark laws so long as it is shown to have acquired independent trademark significance, identifying in some way the source or sponsorship of the goods. *See Wyatt Earp Enterprises v. Sackman, Inc.,* 157 F. Supp. 621 (S.D.N.Y.1958). Because the nature of the property right conferred by copyright is significantly different from that of trademark, trademark protection should be able to co-exist, and possibly to overlap, with copyright protection without posing preemption difficulties. As the Fifth Circuit persuasively reasoned in *Boston Professional Hockey Association, Inc. v. Dallas Cap & Emblem Manufacturing, Inc.,* 510 F.2d 1004, 1014 (5th Cir.), *cert. denied,* 423 U.S. 868 (1975):

> A trademark is a property right which is acquired by use. *Trade–Mark Cases,* 100 U.S. 82 (1879). It differs substantially from a copyright, in both its legal genesis and its scope of federal protection. The legal cornerstone for the protection of copyrights is Article I, section 8, clause 8 of the Constitution. In the case of a copyright, an individual creates a unique design and, because the Constitutional fathers saw fit to encourage creativity, he can secure a copyright for his creation for a [limited period of time]. After the expiration of the copyright, his creation becomes part of the public domain. In the case of a trademark, however, the process is reversed. An individual selects a word or design that might otherwise be in the public domain to represent his business or product. If that word or design comes to symbolize his product or business in the public mind, the individual acquires a property right in the mark. The acquisition of such a right through use represents the passage of a word or design out of the public domain into the protective

ambits of trademark law. Under the provisions of the Lanham Act, the owner of a mark acquires a protectable property interest in his mark through registration and use.

Dual protection under copyright and trademark laws is particularly appropriate for graphic representations of characters. A character deemed an artistic creation deserving copyright protection, *see Walt Disney Productions v. Air Pirates,* 581 F.2d 751 (9th Cir.1978), *cert. denied,* 439 U.S. 1132 (1979), may also serve to identify the creator, thus meriting protection under theories of trademark or unfair competition. Indeed, because of their special value in distinguishing goods and services, names and pictorial representations of characters are often registered as trademarks under the Lanham Act. 5 U.S.C. §§ 1052 & 1053.[3]

. . . If any of these illustrations, including the "sitting rabbit" design, has come to identify Warne publications, defendant's use of it may lead the public to believe that defendant's different, and allegedly inferior, publication has been published by or is somehow associated with plaintiff. This kind of danger of misrepresentation as to the source of copied public domain material may establish a claim for unfair competition. *See Desclee & Cie, S. A. v. Nemmers,* 190 F. Supp. 381, 390 (E.D.Wis.1961).

Defendant argues, however, that it has the right to copy the covers as well as the contents of the original books. Relying on *Triangle Publications, Inc. v. Knight–Ridder Newspapers, Inc.,* 445 F. Supp. 875 (S.D.Fla.1978), and *Nimmer on Copyright,* defendant contends that a book cover should be deemed a copyrightable component of the copyrighted book. Once copyright protection ends, it contends, the entire book should be free to copy.

In principle, defendant seems correct. Covers of books as well as their contents may be entitled to copyright protection. But defendant exaggerates the significance of its logic. None of the authorities it relies upon suggests that trademark and copyright protection are mutually exclusive or that the fate of a book cover is necessarily wedded to the fate of the underlying work.

Furthermore, the rule urged by defendant—that copyrightable book covers may not obtain trademark or unfair competition protection—would permit incongruous results: a book cover lacking sufficient originality to warrant copyright protection could be protected for a potentially unlimited duration under the trademark laws, while covers revealing great artistry or ingenuity would be limited to the duration of the copyright. The better rule would protect all book covers according to the same standards that govern traditional trade dress or packaging cases. Thus, the proper factual inquiry in this case is not whether the cover illustrations were once copyrightable and have fallen into the public domain, but whether they have acquired

3. Some commentators have suggested that trademark and unfair competition theories might serve to protect a character beyond the term of copyright applicable to the underlying work. This provocative question need not be reached, since plaintiff does not seek to establish exclusive trademark rights in the characters themselves but only to protect its limited right to use specific illustrations of those characters.

secondary meaning, identifying Warne as the publisher or sponsor of goods bearing those illustrations, and if so, whether defendant's use of these illustrations in "packaging" or "dressing" its editions is likely to cause confusion. Summary judgment is an inappropriate vehicle for determining these questions.

Defendant's "fair use" defense based on Section 33(b)(4) of the Lanham Act, 15 U.S.C. § 1115(b)(4), is also unpersuasive[4]. . . . [It is not] clear that defendant's use of these illustrations is necessary to the full and effective exploitation of the public domain works. Defendant twice changed the cover of its Peter Rabbit book, suggesting that the "sitting rabbit"—which has been abandoned—was never necessary for its cover. With respect to the seven original cover illustrations, the fact that other publishers have reproduced Miss Potter's stories without copying the covers suggests they may not be crucial to the successful exploitation of the works. And, contrary to what defendant contends, the cover illustrations are not analogous to titles of public domain works, which, Professor Nimmer suggests, may be essential to effective distribution of the works. 1 Nimmer on Copyright § 2.16. A title is generally the primary identifier of a literary work; the cover illustrations are not. Of course, as noted at the outset, if the illustrations merely identify Miss Potter and her works, plaintiff will have no claim to trademark protection. If, however, plaintiff can establish a specialized secondary meaning—that the illustrations represent Warne's goodwill and reputation as the source of children's books and other products—it will have a protectible trademark interest, except to the extent that the covers contain material necessary to identify the book itself. Resolution of these questions must await trial.

The foregoing should not be construed to suggest that plaintiff will have an easy task at trial. Because the claimed marks are derived from or are similar in appearance to the illustrations in the text of the books, they may well prove to be "weak" marks. As a general rule, weak or descriptive marks are accorded less protection than inherently distinctive marks. *See generally* McCarthy, *supra,* § 11.24. Plaintiff must, however, be given an opportunity to meet this relatively greater burden by producing evidence of consumer recognition and likelihood of confusion with respect to each of the marks in dispute.

The motions for summary judgment are denied.

———

For a discussion of the different policies underlying copyright and trademarks, in the context of awarding damages for violations of both rights, see *Nintendo of Am., Inc. v. Dragon Pac., Int'l,* 40 F.3d 1007 (9th Cir.1994), *cert. denied sub nom. Sheng v. Nintendo of Am., Inc.,* 515 U.S.

---

4. Section 33(b)(4) provides a defense to a charge of infringement if the use is "otherwise than as a trade or service mark . . . of a term or device which is descriptive of and used fairly and in good faith only to describe to users the goods or services of such party, or their geographic origin." 15 U.S.C. § 1115(b)(4).

1107 (1995). See also *Lyons Partnership L.P. v. AAA Entertainment Inc.*, 53
U.S.P.Q.2d 1397 (S.D.N.Y.1999), in which the defendants were found to
have infringed both the copyright and trademark in the well-known "Barney" dinosaur character by selling unauthorized costumes; the court found
no duplication in ordering disgorgement of profits as a trademark remedy
along with statutory damages as a copyright remedy, the latter being
"designed to serve a variety of purposes other than compensation, including both deterrence and punishment."

QUESTIONS

1. The copyright on the story "Alice in Wonderland" by Lewis Carroll has
expired. Is there any legal obstacle (which would be interposed by the
Carroll literary estate) to using that title on a play or a song that has
absolutely nothing to do with the bizarre and beloved characters and story
line in the Carroll book? Is there any legal obstacle to the use of that title
by, say, the Walt Disney Company, should it make an animated motion
picture version of the Alice story? If Disney may use the title, and its film is
extremely successful, may it prevent another "lesser" company from producing and distributing its own version of the Alice story under the title
"Alice in Wonderland"? *See Walt Disney Productions v. Souvaine Selective
Pictures*, 98 F.Supp. 774 (S.D.N.Y.), *aff'd*, 192 F.2d 856 (2d Cir.1951).

2. In a recent motion picture, "The Long Kiss Goodnight," the actors
were shown in a room in which a Three Stooges movie was playing on a
television set in the background for 30 seconds. The copyright in the Three
Stooges film (appropriately enough titled "Disorder in the Court") had
expired. A company claiming all rights to the Three Stooges characters has
brought an action against the producers of "The Long Kiss Goodnight,"
claiming infringement of trademark. First, evaluate their arguments for
trademark infringement. Second, consider whether the court was correct
when it said the following about the significance of the expiration of
copyright: "If material covered by copyright law has passed into the public
domain, it cannot then be protected by the Lanham Act without rendering
the Copyright Act a nullity." *See Comedy III Prods., Inc. v. New Line
Cinema*, 200 F.3d 593 (9th Cir.2000).

F. DISTINCTIONS: CHATTELS

Forward v. Thorogood
985 F.2d 604 (1st Cir.1993).

■ BOUDIN, CIRCUIT JUDGE.

This is an appeal from a final judgment determining the copyright
ownership of certain unpublished tape recordings of the musical group
George Thorogood and the Destroyers (the "Band"). The district court
ruled that the Band held the copyright to the tapes and enjoined appellant
John Forward from making commercial use of the recordings. We affirm.

The basic facts can be briefly stated. Forward is a music aficionado and record collector with a special interest in blues and country music. In 1975, Forward was working as a bus driver when he first met Thorogood at a Boston nightclub where the Band was performing. Forward was immediately taken with the Band's act and struck up a friendship with Thorogood. Thorogood and his fellow band members, a drummer and a guitar player, had been playing together at East Coast colleges and clubs since 1973. Upon learning that the Band had yet to release its first album, Forward began a campaign to persuade his friends at Rounder Records to sign the Band to a recording contract. Rounder Records is a small, Boston based record company specializing in blues and folk music. As part of this effort, Forward arranged and paid for two recording sessions for the Band in 1976. The purpose of the sessions was to create a "demo" tape that would capture Rounder Records' interest. At Forward's invitation, one of the principals of Rounder Records attended the Band's second recording session. Other than requesting specific songs to be recorded, Forward's contribution to the sessions was limited to arranging and paying for them.

Rounder Records was impressed by what it heard; the day after the second session, it arranged to sign the Band to a contract. The Band agreed that Forward could keep the tapes for his own enjoyment, and they have remained in his possession ever since. In 1977, the Band's first album was released under the Rounder Records label. Forward was singled out for "special thanks" in the album's acknowledgements. Since then, Thorogood and the Destroyers have released a number of records and gone on to achieve success as a blues/rock band.

The dispute between the parties arose in early 1988, when Forward told the Band that he intended to sell the 1976 tapes to a record company for commercial release. The Band objected, fearing that release of the tapes would harm its reputation; they were, the district court found, of "relatively primitive quality" compared to the Band's published work. On July 5, 1988, Forward filed suit in the district court, seeking a declaratory judgment that he held the common law copyright to the tapes. Determination of copyright ownership is governed by the common law of copyright because the tapes are unpublished and were recorded in 1976, prior to the January 1, 1978, effective date of the Copyright Act of 1976, 17 U.S.C. § 101 et seq.[1] The Band responded with a counterclaim for declaratory and injunctive relief.

In the district court, Forward advanced a number of theories in support of his claim to copyright ownership. After a five-day bench trial, the district court filed its findings of fact and conclusions of law, ruling that Forward did not hold the copyright under any of the theories he advanced. *Forward v. Thorogood*, 758 F. Supp. 782 (D.Mass.1991). The court entered

---

1. *See* M. Nimmer & D. Nimmer, 1 Nimmer on Copyright, § 2.10[A] n.18, at 2–147 (1992) ("Nimmer"). *See also* Roth v. Pritikin, 710 F.2d 934, 938 (2d Cir.) (1976 Act, which preempts the common law of copyright as of January 1, 1978, determines the rights but not the identity of the copyright owners of works created prior to that date), *cert. denied,* 464 U.S. 961, 104 S. Ct. 394, 78 L. Ed. 2d 337 (1983).

judgment for the Band, declaring Thorogood and other Band members to be the copyright owners and permanently enjoining Forward from commercially exploiting the tapes. Forward now appeals.

On this appeal, Forward's first theory in support of his claim of copyright ownership is based on his ownership and possession of the tapes. According to Forward, ownership of a copyrightable work carries with it ownership of the copyright. Alternatively, he argues that the evidence mandated a finding that the copyright was implicitly transferred to him along with the demo tapes. We find no merit in either claim.

The creator of a work is, at least presumptively, its author and the owner of the copyright, *Community for Creative Non–Violence v. Reid,* 490 U.S. 730, 737, 109 S. Ct. 2166, 2171, 104 L. Ed. 2d 811 (1989). The performer of a musical work is the author, as it were, of the performance. 1 Nimmer, § 2.10[A](2)(a), at 2–149. The courts, in applying the common law of copyright, did in a number of cases infer from an unconditional sale of a manuscript or painting an intent to transfer the copyright. 3 Nimmer § 10.09[B], at 10–76.1. This doctrine, often criticized and subject to various judicial and statutory exclusions, *id.,* is the source of Forward's principal claim. The difficulty for Forward is that even under the doctrine this physical transfer merely created a presumption and the ultimate question was one of intent. *Id.*

In this case, the district court found that "[n]either the band nor any of its members ever conveyed, or agreed to convey, their copyright interest in the tapes to Forward." 758 F. Supp. at 784. Rather the Band allowed Forward to keep the tapes solely for his personal enjoyment. *Id.* Forward's disregard of this central finding is premised on a highly artificial attempt to claim "constructive possession" of the tapes from the outset and then to argue that any reservation by the Band at the end of the sessions was an invalid attempt to reconvey or qualify his copyright. The reality is that the Band never surrendered the copyright in the first place and the transfer of the tapes' ownership to Forward was not a sharply defined event distinct from the reservation of the Band's rights. . . .

———

§ 202. Ownership of Copyright as Distinct From Ownership of Material Object

Ownership of a copyright, or of any of the exclusive rights under a copyright, is distinct from ownership of any material object in which the work is embodied. Transfer of ownership of any material object, including the copy or phonorecord in which the work is first fixed, does not of itself convey any rights in the copyrighted work embodied in the object; nor, in the absence of an agreement, does transfer of ownership of a copyright or of any exclusive rights under a copyright convey property rights in any material object.

QUESTIONS

1. The court in the *Forward* case referred to "common law copyright." Throughout our copyright history, until 1978, the right to make copies of an unpublished work was governed typically by state law, known as common-law copyright (whether or not the state copyright law was manifested in court opinions or in a statute). Common-law copyright was potentially perpetual in duration; it lasted until the work was first "published" with the author's consent. As stated in *Forward*, it was generally understood that an author who unconditionally transferred ownership of the chattel embodying the creative work was presumed to have transferred the right of first publication as well. This was often referred to as the "*Pushman* presumption," based on *Pushman v. New York Graphic Soc'y,* 287 N.Y. 302 (1942), in which New York's highest court held that an artist who had sold a painting to the University of Illinois—with no mention of copyright—could not prevent the University from authorizing another to make copies of it.

The *Forward* court observes that the *Pushman* presumption was often criticized. What would you assume was the basis for the presumption? (Does it likely reflect the intentions of the parties? Does it reflect a broader social policy?) What would you assume were the criticisms?

2. If, in your historical researches, you were to unearth a letter written in 1625 by Miles Standish to Priscilla Alden, would you feel free to publish it without concern for copyright infringement? (You would have to ascertain, first, whether such an old letter was still protected by copyright. Is it?) If copyright infringement were a concern, how would you go about securing legal immunity for your publication? (You would have to ascertain whether Miles' transfer of the letter to Priscilla was governed by the *Pushman* presumption. Do you think it was?)

3. The present Copyright Act became effective on January 1, 1978—after the recording session in the *Forward* case but before the litigation. Consult § 202 of the Act. What impact does it have upon the *Pushman* presumption? Would you have supported it had you been in the 1976 Congress that enacted the statute? Can it be applied retroactively to transactions that preceded its effective date, such as that in *Forward*? Had it been applied, would the result or reasoning have been changed? (The student can begin to appreciate the current importance of understanding the law that developed under the 1909 Copyright Act, in addition to the provisions of the 1976 Copyright Act.)

––––––

§ 109. Limitations on Exclusive Rights: Effect of Transfer of Particular Copy or Phonorecord

(a) Notwithstanding the provisions of section 106(3), the owner of a particular copy or phonorecord lawfully made under this title, or any person authorized by such owner, is entitled, without the authority of the copyright owner, to sell or otherwise dispose of the possession of that copy or phonorecord.

QUESTIONS

1. Section 109(a) effectively distinguishes the intellectual property rights in a work and the tangible property rights in a "copy or phonorecord" of a work. It allows the owner of the latter to "sell or otherwise dispose," and apparently even to destroy. Should the copyright law be interpreted—in order better to protect the right of the copyright owner and indeed of the public—to impose on the chattel owner the duty to make it available to the person who is entitled to make copies? For example, if a sculptor retains the copyright while the sculpture is owned by another, should a court require the latter to return the sculpture for a reasonable time in order to allow the sculptor to make copies? Or is copyright no more than the "negative" right to prevent *others* from making reproductions (or to demand compensation in exchange for a license)? *See Community for Creative Non-Violence v. Reid*, 1992 CCH Copyr. L. Dec. ¶ 26,860 (D.D.C. 1991) (on remand from the Supreme Court decision at Chapter 3.A.2, *infra;* later vacated pursuant to consent order); *Baker v. Libbie*, 210 Mass. 599 (1912); *Frasier v. Adams–Sandler, Inc.,* 94 F.3d 129 (4th Cir.1996) (no infringement of photographs when slides are merely withheld from copyright owner; there must be reproduction, printing or other use itemized in § 106).

2. Should copyright, or some other body of law, provide—perhaps in the interest of preserving our cultural and aesthetic heritage—that *all* works of art must be preserved, and must not physically be mutilated or altered, or destroyed? As a result of amendments to the Copyright Act in 1990, a "work of visual art" can in fact be afforded such protection. *See* §§ 101 and 106A of the Act, and Chapter 6.B, *infra.*

CHAPTER 2

COPYRIGHTABLE SUBJECT MATTER

A. IN GENERAL

§ 102. Subject Matter of Copyright: In General

(a) Copyright protection subsists, in accordance with this title, in original works of authorship fixed in any tangible medium of expression, now known or later developed, from which they can be perceived, reproduced, or otherwise communicated, either directly or with the aid of a machine or device. Works of authorship include the following categories:

    (1) literary works;

    (2) musical works, including any accompanying words;

    (3) dramatic works, including any accompanying music;

    (4) pantomimes and choreographic works;

    (5) pictorial, graphic, and sculptural works;

    (6) motion pictures and other audiovisual works;

    (7) sound recordings; and

    (8) architectural works.

1. ORIGINAL WORKS OF AUTHORSHIP

House Report

H.R. Rep. No. 94–1476, 94th Cong., 2d Sess. 51–52 (1976).

The two fundamental criteria of copyright protection—originality and fixation in tangible form—are restated in the first sentence of this cornerstone provision. The phrase "original works of authorship," which is purposely left undefined, is intended to incorporate without change the standard of originality established by the courts under the present copyright statute. This standard does not include requirements of novelty, ingenuity, or esthetic merit, and there is no intention to enlarge the standard of copyright protection to require them. . . .

Feist Publications, Inc. v. Rural Telephone Service, 499 U.S. 340 (1991): "The *sine qua non* of copyright is originality. To qualify for copyright protection, a work must be original to the author. . . . Original, as the term is used in copyright, means only that the work was independently created by the author (as opposed to copied from other works), and that it possesses at least some minimal degree of creativity. . . . To be sure, the requisite level of creativity is extremely low; even a slight amount will suffice. The vast majority of works make the grade quite easily, as they possess some creative spark, 'no matter how crude, humble or obvious' it might be. [Nimmer on Copyright § 1.08[C][1].] Originality does not signify novelty; a work may be original even though it closely resembles other works so long as the similarity is fortuitous, not the result of copying. To illustrate, assume that two poets, each ignorant of the other, compose identical poems. Neither work is novel, yet both are original and, hence, copyrightable.... Originality is a constitutional requirement."

——

In the passage just quoted, the Supreme Court clearly treats "originality" as a twofold requirement: "independent creation" as well as "some minimal degree of creativity." Most of the pertinent court decisions, including those that follow, and the regulations of the Copyright Office, focus principally upon the question of minimal creativity, or at least fail to distinguish the two elements. On occasion, a court will conclude or suggest that material claimed to be infringed is uncopyrightable because it is copied from others. Recently, for example, a court denied protection to the phrase "You've got to stand for something or you'll fall for anything," in the plaintiff's song; the defendant, in its advertisements for class rings, used the slogan "The song says it best: If you don't stand for something, you'll fall for anything." The defendant presented evidence ascribing the plaintiff's phrase to earlier sources including the Bible, Abraham Lincoln, Martin Luther King Jr., and a song recorded by John Cougar Mellencamp. *Acuff–Rose Music, Inc. v. Jostens, Inc.*, 155 F.3d 140 (2d Cir.1998). Another court of appeals suggested that the plaintiff, a T-shirt maker and seller, had copied from others her slogan "Someone went to Boston and got me this shirt because they love me very much." *Matthews v. Freedman*, 157 F.3d 25 (1st Cir.1998). (T-shirts are displayed *infra* page 140.) For an example of a deft avoidance of the question whether the plaintiff copied or independently originated, see the decision of Judge Learned Hand in *Nichols v. Universal Pictures Corp.*, at Chapter 6.A, *infra*.

Magic Marketing v. Mailing Services of Pittsburgh

634 F.Supp. 769 (W.D.Pa.1986).

■ ZIEGLER, DISTRICT JUDGE.

[Defendant] American Paper now moves for summary judgment on the issue of copyrightability. We hold that the envelopes allegedly manufactured by American Paper cannot be accorded copyright protection. We will grant the motion for summary judgment in part.

I. *Facts*

Plaintiff, Magic Marketing, Inc., designs and markets mass mailing advertising campaigns for businesses. In December 1983, plaintiff and defendant, Mailing Services of Pittsburgh, Inc., entered into a contract whereby Mailing Services agreed to supply certain letters, forms and envelopes to plaintiff. Mailing Services subcontracted a portion of the printing work to American Paper. American Paper admits that it supplied envelopes pursuant to orders dated December 11, 1983, May 4, 1984 and June 6, 1984. Affidavit of John E. Gill dated February 13, 1986. However, it denies supplying any forms or letters. *Id.*

Plaintiff alleges that it holds a valid copyright in the relevant letters, forms and envelopes pursuant to an application filed July 23, 1985. According to plaintiff, Mailing Services infringed its copyright by selling copies of the materials to other customers. Plaintiff complains that American Paper manufactured and supplied infringing copies of the letters, forms and envelopes with knowledge of plaintiff's copyright.

Copies of the envelopes in question are contained in Exhibits A and F. *See* Complaint at Exhibits A, F. Both envelopes are conventional in size and contain standard instructions to the postmaster printed on the front. A solid black stripe runs horizontally across the middle of one envelope. Complaint at Exhibit A. The words "PRIORITY MESSAGE: CONTENTS REQUIRE IMMEDIATE ATTENTION" are printed in large white letters within the stripe. A shorter black stripe encasing the word "TELEGRAM" lies at the bottom right corner of the envelope. The other envelope has no stripe. Complaint at Exhibit F. Printed in bold-faced letters just above the window are the words "GIFT CHECK ENCLOSED." The copyright mark, "© 1984 Magic Marketing Inc." is imprinted on the backs of both envelopes.

II.   *Copyrightability of the Envelopes*

A.   Resolution by Summary Judgment

American Paper contends that the envelopes lack the level of originality to warrant copyright protection. We agree. Since a copyright infringement action cannot be maintained without a valid copyright, American Paper's attack is lethal to plaintiff's claim that the envelopes infringe its copyright. *Towle Manufacturing Co. v. Godinger Silver Art Co.,* 612 F. Supp. 986, 992 (S.D.N.Y.1985).

The issue of copyrightability is typically resolved by a motion for summary judgment. Very often no issues of material fact are in dispute and the only task for the court is to analyze the allegedly copyrightable item in light of applicable copyright law....

B.   Originality

Section 102 of the Copyright Act provides that copyright protection subsists in "original works of authorship." 17 U.S.C. § 102. Originality is the "one pervading element" essential for copyright protection regardless of the form of the work. *L. Batlin & Sons, Inc. v. Snyder,* 536 F.2d 486, 489–90 (2d Cir.), *cert. denied,* 429 U.S. 857, 97 S. Ct. 156, 50 L. Ed. 2d 135 (1976); 1 Nimmer on Copyright § 2.01 (1985). Originality is distinct from novelty. To be original, a work must be the product of independent creation. *L. Batlin,* 536 F.2d at 490. While the test for originality is a "low threshold," the "author" must contribute more than a trivial variation of a previous work, i.e., the work must be recognizably "his own." *Id.* There is a narrow class of cases where even admittedly independent efforts may be deemed too trivial or insignificant to support copyright protection. 1 Nimmer on Copyright § 2.01[B] at 2–13.

This class is illustrated by case authority denying copyright protection to "fragmentary words and phrases" and to "forms of expression dictated solely by functional considerations." 1 Nimmer on Copyright § 2.01[B] at 2–13–14. Such material does not exhibit the minimal level of creativity necessary to warrant copyright protection. Indeed, regulations promulgated pursuant to the Copyright Act list the following works as not subject to copyright:

> Words and short phrases such as names, titles, and slogans; familiar symbols or designs; mere variations of typographic ornamentation, lettering or coloring; mere listing of ingredients or contents.

37 C.F.R. § 202.1(a) (1985). Moreover, clichéd language and expressions communicating an idea which may only be conveyed in a more or less stereotyped manner are not copyrightable.

We hold that the envelopes do not exhibit a sufficient degree of creativity to be copyrightable. The terse phrases on the envelopes describe their contents: "TELEGRAM," "GIFT CHECK," and "PRIORITY MESSAGE." The listing of the contents of an envelope or package, like a listing of ingredients, is not protected under the copyright regulations. 37 C.F.R. § 202.1(a). We note that even more colorful descriptions, such as advertising slogans, are not accorded copyright protection. For example, the phrase "most personal sort of deodorant" on a feminine hygiene product is not copyrightable. *Alberto–Culver Co. v. Andrea Dumon, Inc.*, 466 F.2d 705, 711 (7th Cir.1972).

The phrase "CONTENTS REQUIRE IMMEDIATE ATTENTION" merely exhorts the recipient to open the envelope immediately upon delivery. It is nothing more than a direction or instruction for use. As such, it is unprotected. More complex directions, such as the serving directions on a frozen dessert package, are not copyrightable. *Kitchens of Sara Lee, Inc. v. Nifty Foods Corp.*, 266 F.2d 541 (2d Cir.1959). *See also* 1 Nimmer on Copyright § 2.08[G] at 2–117. In sum, the phrases printed on the envelopes are generic in nature and lack the minimal degree of creativity necessary for copyright protection.

C.   "Pictorial, graphic or sculptural" works

The protection accorded "pictorial, graphic or sculptural" works under the Copyright Act is inapplicable. . . .

Initially we note that the envelopes cannot be considered a "pictorial, graphic or sculptural" work if they fail to embody a minimal level of creativity. 37 C.F.R. § 202.10(c). We held above that the envelopes lack this requisite level of creativity.

Furthermore, no part of the envelope constitutes a "pictorial, graphic or sculptural" work. No pictures or designs are imprinted on the face of the envelopes except the solid black stripe. Solid black stripes are not copyrightable. The printing within the stripe is nothing more than a distinctive typeface, which is not protected. 37 C.F.R. § 202.1(a); *Alberto-Culver, supra,* 466 F.2d at 711. . . .

. . .

IT IS ORDERED that the motion of defendant, American Paper Products Company, for summary judgment be and hereby is granted on the issue of the copyrightability of the allegedly infringing envelopes.

————

Compare Tin Pan Apple Inc. v. Miller Brewing Co., 30 U.S.P.Q.2d 1791 (S.D.N.Y.1994), in which the court declined to hold, as a matter of law, that the words "Hugga–Hugga" and "Brr"—as discrete elements of the lyrics of a rap song—lacked sufficient creativity to merit copyright. "These sounds are more complex than [a] single drum beat and . . . in that complexity lies, arguably at least, the fruit of creativity." To the same effect, see *Santrayll v. Burrell,* 39 U.S.P.Q.2d 1052 (S.D.N.Y.1996) (distinctive rhythmic repetition of phrase "uh oh" held sufficiently original to survive motion for summary judgment).

————

Sebastian Int'l, Inc. v. Consumer Contact (PTY) Ltd., 664 F.Supp. 909 (D.N.J.1987), *rev'd on other grounds,* 847 F.2d 1093 (3d Cir.1988). The plaintiff manufactures and markets beauty products including shampoos, conditioners and hair sprays, which are available in the United States only in professional hair care salons. The plaintiff shipped certain of its products to a purchaser in South Africa, who promptly reshipped them to the United States for public sale here. An action was brought to prevent disposing of the products here, relying on theories of contract, trademark infringement, and copyright infringement. In considering the issuance of a preliminary injunction, the court rejected the defendants' claim that the labels on the plaintiff's products (including a product known as WET 4) were not copyrightable. The court of appeals reversed the injunction issued by the district court but did not address the correctness of that court's conclusion that the labels were indeed copyrightable. The lower court's analysis follows.

It is well established that labels are subject to copyright protection, see *Kitchens of Sara Lee, Inc. v. Nifty Foods Corp.,* 266 F.2d 541 (2d Cir.1959), if the label manifests the necessary modicum of creativity. *See, e.g., Drop Dead Co. v. S.C. Johnson & Son, Inc.,* 326 F.2d 87 (9th Cir.1963) (copyright in PLEDGE label is valid); *Abli Inc. v. Standard Brands Paint Co.,* 323 F.Supp. 1400 (C.D.Cal.1970) (label was copyrightable when it contained such phrases as 'Cut to desired length . . . Will not run . . . Simply slide top bead into rod as illustrated)'. Catch phrases, mottos, slogans and short advertising expressions are not copyrightable. *See, e.g., Perma Greetings Inc. v. Russ Berrie & Co.,* 598

F.Supp. 445 (E.D.Mo.1984) (expressions such as 'hang in there' and 'along the way take time to smell the flowers' not copyrightable). But, of course, the length of a sentence is not dispositive of whether it is subject to protection. *Rockford Map Publishers, Inc. v. Directory Service Co. of Colorado,* 768 F.2d 145, 148 (7th Cir.1985).

The following, taken from a WET 4 container is an example of text being challenged in this case.

> Hair stays wet-looking as long as you like. Brushes out to full-bodied dry look. WET 4 is one step-four choice (finishing) in Sebastian's four step program for a healthy scalp and head of hair. WET is not oily, won't flake and keeps hair wet-looking for hours, allowing you to sculpture, contour, wave or curl. It stays looking wet until it's brushed out. When brushed, hair looks and feels thicker, extra full. Try brushing partly, leaving some parts wet for a different look.

This language is more than simply a list of ingredients, directions, or a catchy phrase. No one can seriously dispute that if plaintiff were to discover that a competitor's package utilized the exact language as above with the exception of the product's name, plaintiff would be entitled to protection. While this text tries the limits of the modicum of creativity necessary for a work to be copyrightable, I find that taken as a whole it comes within the purview of the Copyright Act.

QUESTION

Is the following logo, for the New York Arrows soccer team, copyrightable?

See John Muller & Co. v. New York Arrows Soccer Team, 802 F.2d 989 (8th Cir.1986).

B. Kaplan, An Unhurried View of Copyright 45–46 (1967)

Are there compositions which though original are too small to qualify for copyright or to figure as the subjects of actionable infringement? Some of Holmes's language suggests that any emanation of personality, however slight, any uncopied collocation, however slim, should be protected, and his abnegation of judicial responsibility for passing on the merit of intellectual productions points in the same direction.[25] So also does the appearance in the [1909] statute of so mean a category as "prints or labels used for articles of merchandise"—though we must always beware of a false development of copyright law by a process of treating extreme applications as being normal, thus inviting applications even more extreme. There are, on the other hand, definite indications of some rule *de minimis.*

Some have thought it inherent in the very notion of "personality," of spontaneity, that a copyright claimant must exceed the utterly stilted or trite, must satisfy some threshold requirement of "creativity." And though Judge Frank pushed hard in the *Alfred Bell* case to show the theoretical protectibility of any original production, he still admitted that a variation, say, on a public domain work must be more than "trivial" to support copyright. Courts are disinclined to permit copyright to attach to short word sequences or to find plagiarism in the copying of such sequences; this lies close to the slogan that "titles" are not protected through copyright. We can, I think, conclude that to make the copyright turnstile revolve, the author should have to deposit more than a penny in the box, and some like measure ought to apply to infringement. Surely there is danger in trying to fence off small quanta of words or other collocations; these pass quickly into the idiom; to allow them copyright, particularly if aided by a doctrine of "unconscious" plagiarism, could set up untoward barriers to expression.

QUESTIONS

1. Are the following works copyrightable under the Copyright Act of 1976?

(a) A design of a cross (with arms of equal length) inside a circle.

(b) The rearrangement of the three color bars upon a flag.

(c) A drawing of the University Law School (to be used for display in the law building or in an advertising brochure for applicants).

(d) A snapshot of the Law School on a cloudy day.

(e) The Zapruder films of the assassination of President Kennedy.

(f) A Picasso "re-treatment" of a Velasquez painting of the members of the royal family in Spain.

(g) A three-dimensional replica, as statues, of the Velasquez painting.

(h) A black-and-white photocopy of the Velasquez painting.

(i) A printing of a long-lost play by Shakespeare (published and performed in Shakespeare's time but only recently discovered after years of search and analysis by Professor Falstaff of the University's English Department).

---

25. *See* Bleistein v. Donaldson Lithographing Co., 188 U.S. 239 (1903).

(j) A translation of a Molière play.

(*l*) A chart containing, in headings and columns, information about Latin American countries (e.g., capital, population, principal products, square miles), gathered from one encyclopedia.

(m) An article in *Time* magazine about a current news event, derived from original investigation (or derived from other published news reports).

2. The stand-up comedian Henny Youngman (who died in 1998) was known as "The King of the One–Liner"; he typically delivered rapid-fire jokes at the rate of eight jokes per minute. Assuming that he created them all, are they copyrightable? "I was so ugly when I was born that the doctor slapped my mother." "I will never forget my school days. I was teacher's pet. She couldn't afford a dog." "My wife has a nice, even disposition. Miserable all the time." "I miss my wife's cooking—as often as I can." "A man is incomplete until he's married—then he's really finished." "I'm not overweight. I'm just six inches too short." "Take my wife. Please!"

House Report

H.R. Rep. No. 94–1476, 94th Cong., 2d Sess. 53–56 (1976).

Categories of copyrightable works

The second sentence of section 102 lists seven broad categories which the concept of "works of authorship" is said to "include." The use of the word "include," as defined in section 101, makes clear that the listing is "illustrative and not limitative," and that the seven categories do not necessarily exhaust the scope of "original works of authorship" that the bill is intended to protect.... Of the seven items listed, four are defined in section 101. The three undefined categories—"musical works," "dramatic works," and "pantomimes and choreographic works"—have fairly settled meanings. There is no need, for example, to specify the copyrightability of electronic or concrete music in the statute since the form of a work would no longer be of any importance, nor is it necessary to specify that "choreographic works" do not include social dance steps and simple routines.

The four items defined in section 101 are "literary works," "pictorial, graphic, and sculptural works," "motion pictures and audiovisual works," and "sound recordings." In each of these cases, definitions are needed not only because the meaning of the term itself is unsettled but also because the distinction between "work" and "material object" requires clarification. The term "literary works" does not connote any criterion of literary merit or qualitative value: it includes catalogs, directories, similar factual, reference, or instructional works and compilations of data. It also includes computer data bases, and computer programs to the extent that they incorporate authorship in the programmer's expression of original ideas, as distinguished from the ideas themselves.

. . .

Enactment of Public Law 92–140 in 1971 marked the first recognition in American copyright law of sound recordings as copyrightable works. As defined in section 101, copyrightable "sound recordings" are original works of authorship comprising an aggregate of musical, spoken, or other sounds that have been fixed in tangible form. The copyrightable work comprises the aggregation of sounds and not the tangible medium of fixation. Thus, "sound recordings" as copyrightable subject matter are distinguished from "phonorecords," the latter being physical objects in which sounds are fixed. They are also distinguished from any copyrighted literary, dramatic, or musical works that may be reproduced on a "phonorecord."

As a class of subject matter, sound recordings are clearly within the scope of the "writings of an author" capable of protection under the Constitution, and the extension of limited statutory protection to them was too long delayed. Aside from cases in which sounds are fixed by some purely mechanical means without originality of any kind, the copyright protection that would prevent the reproduction and distribution of unauthorized phonorecords of sound recordings is clearly justified.

The copyrightable elements in a sound recording will usually, though not always, involve "authorship" both on the part of the performers whose performance is captured and on the part of the record producer responsible for setting up the recording session, capturing and electronically processing the sounds, and compiling and editing them to make the final sound recording. There may, however, be cases where the record producer's contribution is so minimal that the performance is the only copyrightable element in the work, and there may be cases (for example, recordings of bird calls, sounds of racing cars, et cetera) where only the record producer's contribution is copyrightable.

Sound tracks of motion pictures, long a nebulous area in American copyright law, are specifically included in the definition of "motion pictures," and excluded in the definition of "sound recordings." ... [T]he bill equates audiovisual materials such as filmstrips, slide sets, and sets of transparencies with "motion pictures" rather than with "pictorial, graphic, and sculptural works." Their sequential showing is closer to a "performance" than to a "display," and the definition of "audiovisual works," which applies also to "motion pictures," embraces works consisting of a series of related images that are by their nature, intended for showing by means of projectors or other devices.

QUESTION

Are the categories in § 102(a) discrete or overlapping? Can you think of creative endeavors that do not fall within the § 102(a) categories? Watch for the substantive significance of these categories as you proceed through your study of the statute.

2. Fixation in Tangible Form

House Report

H.R. Rep. No. 94–1476, 94th Cong., 2d Sess. 52–53 (1976).

As a basic condition of copyright protection, the bill perpetuates the existing requirement that a work be fixed in a "tangible medium of expression," and adds that this medium may be one "now known or later developed," and that the fixation is sufficient if the work "can be perceived, reproduced, or otherwise communicated, either directly or with the aid of a machine or device." This broad language is intended to avoid the artificial and largely unjustifiable distinctions, derived from cases such as *White-Smith Music Publishing Co. v. Apollo Co., 209 U.S. 1 (1908)*, under which statutory copyrightability in certain cases has been made to depend upon the form or medium in which the work is fixed. Under the bill it makes no difference what the form, manner, or medium of fixation may be—whether it is in words, numbers, notes, sounds, pictures, or any other graphic or symbolic indicia, whether embodied in a physical object in written, printed, photographic, sculptural, punched, magnetic, or any other stable form, and whether it is capable of perception directly or by means of any machine or device "now known or later developed."

Under the bill, the concept of fixation is important since it not only determines whether the provisions of the statute apply to a work, but it also represents the dividing line between common law and statutory protection. As will be noted in more detail in connection with section 301, an unfixed work of authorship, such as an improvisation or an unrecorded choreographic work, performance, or broadcast, would continue to be subject to protection under State common law or statute, but would not be eligible for Federal statutory protection under section 102.

The bill seeks to resolve, through the definition of "fixation" in section 101, the status of live broadcasts—sports, news coverage, live performances of music, etc.—that are reaching the public in unfixed form but that are simultaneously being recorded. When a football game is being covered by four television cameras, with a director guiding the activities of the four cameramen and choosing which of their electronic images are sent out to the public and in what order, there is little doubt that what the cameramen and the director are doing constitutes "authorship." The further question to be considered is whether there has been a fixation. . . . [T]he content of a live transmission should be accorded statutory protection if it is being recorded simultaneously with its transmission. On the other hand, the definition of "fixation" would exclude from the concept purely evanescent or transient reproductions such as those projected briefly on a screen, shown electronically on a television or other cathode ray tube, or captured momentarily in the "memory" of a computer.

Under this definition "copies" and "phonorecords" together will comprise all of the material objects in which copyrightable works are capable of being fixed. The definitions of these terms in section 101, together with their usage in section 102 and throughout the bill, reflect a fundamental distinction between the "original work" which is the product of "authorship" and the multitude of material objects in which it can be embodied. Thus, in the sense of the bill, a "book" is not a work of authorship, but is a particular kind of "copy." Instead, the author may write a "literary work," which in turn can be embodied in a wide range of "copies" and "phonorecords," including books, periodicals, computer punch cards, microfilm, tape recordings, and so forth. It is possible to have an "original work of authorship" without having a "copy" or "phonorecord" embodying it, and it is also possible to have a "copy" or "phonorecord" embodying something that does not qualify as an "original work of authorship." The two essential elements—original work and tangible object—must merge through fixation in order to produce subject matter copyrightable under the statute.

FIXATION IN DIGITAL MEDIA

Despite the 1976 House Report's suggestion that "transient reproductions ... captured momentarily in the 'memory' of a computer" should not be deemed "fixed," subsequent legislation appears to adopt the principle that entry of a work into the random access memory of a computer makes a "copy" (and thus a "fixation") of the work. This was the position endorsed by the Commission on New Technological Uses [CONTU], appointed by Congress in 1976 to study and make recommendations regarding the copyrightability of computer programs. CONTU issued its Final Report in 1978. Its conclusions as to copying in both permanent and temporary memory follow. (Although CONTU's principal concern here was whether computer input produced a "copy" for purposes of defining an infringement under § 106, the conclusion clearly follows that such a "copy" is a form of "fixation" under § 102.)

The Input Issue

. . .

The protection afforded by section 106 of the new law seemingly would prohibit the unauthorized storage of a work within a computer memory, which would be merely one form of reproduction, one of the exclusive rights granted by copyright.[164]

Considering the act of storing a computerized data base in the memory of a computer as an exclusive right of the copyright proprietor appears consistent both with accepted copyright principles and with considerations of fair treatment for potentially affected parties. Making a copy of an entire work would normally, subject to some possible exception for fair use, be considered exclusively within the domain of the copyright proprietor. One would have to assume, however, that fair use would apply rarely to the reproduction in their entirety of such compendious works as data bases.

. . .

---

164. It may be that the use of the term *input* to describe the act to which copyright liability attaches has been misleading. A more accurate description of the process by which a work may be stored in a computer memory would indicate that a reproduction is created within the computer memory to make the work accessible by means of the computer.

Accordingly, the Commission believes that the application of principles already embodied in the language of the new copyright law achieves the desired substantive legal protection for copyrighted works which exist in machine-readable form. The introduction of a work into a computer memory would, consistent with the new law, be a reproduction of the work, one of the exclusive rights of the copyright proprietor.

. . .

The 1976 Act, without change, makes it clear that the placement of any copyrighted work into a computer is the preparation of a copy and, therefore, a potential infringement of copyright. . . .

————

Congress' subscription to the principle that entry into temporary memory "fixes" the work in a copy may be inferred from Congress' adoption in 1980 of a new section 117 of the Copyright Act, specifying that it is not copyright infringement for an owner of a copy of a computer program to make or authorize the making of another copy or adaptation of that computer program, so long as "such a new copy or adaptation is created as an essential step in the utilization of the computer program in conjunction with a machine and that it is used in no other manner." Since a computer program cannot be "used" in conjunction with the computer unless it is loaded into temporary memory, this exemption is necessary to avoid an impasse between copyright owners and computer program users. Were entry of the program into temporary memory not considered to effect a copy, this exemption would not be necessary.

In 1998 Congress again enacted an amendment necessitated by the doctrine that "RAM [random access memory] copying" is indeed copying (and thus fixes the work in temporary memory). Because the computer automatically loads the programs constituting the operating system into RAM when the computer is turned on, Congress, in Title III of the Digital Millennium Copyright Act, amended section 117 to permit owners and lessees of computer hardware "to make or to authorize the making of a copy of a computer program if such copy is made solely by virtue of the activation of a machine that lawfully contains an authorized copy of the computer program, for purposes only of maintenance or repair of that machine. . . ."

Courts, too, have equated temporary, even transient, storage of a digitally-expressed work with creation of fixed copies. Several decisions concerning liability for communication of works over digital networks have held not only that the storage of works on a web page constitutes a reproduction residing on the server that hosts the webpage, but that making the work available to users to download from the webpage is a distribution of copies to the users' computers. *See, e.g., Playboy Enters. v. Sanfilippo*, 46 U.S.P.Q.2d 1350 (S.D.Cal.1998); *Playboy Enters. v. Webbworld, Inc.*, 991 F.Supp. 543 (N.D.Tex.1997); *Marobie–Fl v. NAFED*, 983 F.Supp. 1167 (N.D.Ill.1997); *Playboy Enters. v. Frena*, 839 F.Supp. 1552

(M.D.Fla.1993). *But see Religious Tech. Center v. Netcom On–Line Commun. Servs.*, 907 F.Supp. 1361 (N.D.Cal.1995) (online access providers who serve as mere conduits for communications initiated by others lack the element of volition implicitly required to make a "reproduction"). Most recently, the Copyright Office in a report submitted on August 29, 2001 (see http://www.loc.gov/copyright/reports/studies/dmca/sec–104–report-vol–1.pdf), reviewed the text of the Copyright Act and the caselaw, and unambiguously concluded that reproductions in RAM are "copies for copyright purposes."

The above-cited authorities on digital distribution of copies address the characterization of a work as "fixed" when its presence on a given computer may be transient. What if the content of the work, as distinguished from its location, is changeable as well? Suppose, for example, that users who access a visual art work on a webpage can also alter the work's appearance: does the work's dynamic character make it unfixed, and therefore outside the scope of federal copyright? The question recalls an earlier controversy concerning the "fixation" of video games, then typically found in "video arcades." The visual images and synthesized sounds that make up these familiar action games are generated by computer programs that are stored in different kinds of memory devices; the patterns of sights and sounds are repetitive in the so-called "attract mode" (when the game is not being played but the customer is being enticed to do so) and are subject to variation during the "play mode" by virtue of human intervention. Relying upon some of the language in the House Report set forth above, defendants in a number of cases claimed that they were free to copy the plaintiffs' games, classified as "audiovisual works," because they were not fixed in a tangible medium of expression but were rather merely ephemeral projections of sight and sound on a cathode ray tube. It was also argued that the inevitable variations in the appearance and sound of the games that result from the differing skill and judgment of the persons playing them prevent any kind of consistent pattern necessary for a "fixation."

These contentions have been uniformly rejected. *See, e.g., M. Kramer Mfg. Co. v. Andrews,* 783 F.2d 421 (4th Cir.1986). In *Stern Elecs., Inc. v. Kaufman,* 669 F.2d 852 (2d Cir.1982), it was held that the audiovisual game was "permanently embodied in a material object, the memory devices, from which it can be perceived with the aid of the other components of the game." And in *Midway Mfg. Co. v. Dirkschneider,* 543 F.Supp. 466 (D.Neb.1981), the court concluded that "The printed circuit boards are tangible objects from which the audiovisual works may be perceived for a period of time more than transitory. The fact that the audiovisual works cannot be viewed without a machine does not mean the works are not fixed." As to the claim that the player's participation prevents the fixing of particular audiovisual patterns, the court in *Williams Elecs., Inc. v. Artic Int'l, Inc.,* 685 F.2d 870 (3d Cir.1982), concluded:

> Although there is player interaction with the machine during the play mode which causes the audiovisual presentation to change in some respects from one game to the next in response to the player's varying

participation, there is always a repetitive sequence of a substantial portion of the sights and sounds of the game, and many aspects of the display remain constant from game to game regardless of how the player operates the controls. . . . Furthermore, there is no player participation in the attract mode which is displayed repetitively without change.

Would the same analysis apply to a dynamic work, such as real-time interactive graphics, that lacked an "attract mode" and whose patterns were more random than the plays of a video game?

QUESTIONS

1. Assume that you send an extended e-mail message (or a message via a digital chatroom among your classmates in Constitutional Law) dealing with the historical antecedents and the philosophical underpinnings of the role of the U.S. President. Is the text of your message automatically protected by federal copyright? (Distinguish the question whether there might be an implied permission for the recipients to make copies of your message. Do you think that there is?)

2. Is a live performance of music in a small nightclub, simultaneously being tape recorded by the performer, within the coverage of the federal Copyright Act? As to the possibility of protection under common-law copyright, compare *Estate of Hemingway v. Random House,* 23 N.Y.2d 341, 244 N.E.2d 250, 296 N.Y.S.2d 771 (1968), with *Falwell v. Penthouse Int'l,* 521 F.Supp. 1204 (W.D.Va.1981).

3. Is a lecture in a law school classroom protected under the federal Act? What if it is being tape recorded without the consent of the instructor? What if students are taking copious (but not verbatim) written notes?

4. Your friends, Bill Blaze and Dorothy Dazzle, are in the business of designing and producing fireworks displays. Depending upon the nature of the celebration, and the amount paid them, they can design any length and complexity of program utilizing fireworks of various colors, exploding patterns, sounds, and the like. The precise timing and sequence of the fireworks display are written first on paper; ultimately, the fireworks are set off through the use of a computer, which of course must be programmed to do so. They have completed their work designing a display for the next Fourth of July, to be "ignited" along the Delaware River waterfront in Philadelphia. They are eager to protect themselves against competing companies copying their newly developed visual displays, both individual "bursts" and the full program. Blaze and Dazzle have consulted you about the possibility of securing protection under the copyright law. What is your advice?

5. Study the definitions of "copy" and "phonorecord" and "fixed" in § 101. What is the difference between a copy and a phonorecord? Can a copyrightable work be embodied in a material object other than these two formats?

PERFORMERS' RIGHT OF FIXATION

As part of the legislation implementing the Agreement on Trade Related Aspects of Intellectual Property (TRIPs), Congress, on December 8, 1994 enacted a new Chapter 11 to Title 17 of the U.S. Code (the title that contains the Copyright Act). The chapter concerns "unauthorized fixation and trafficking in sound recordings and music videos," and establishes a federal right of fixation of live musical performances.

17 U.S.C. § 1101(a) grants to performers of live musical performances rights against:

(1) the unauthorized fixation of their performances; the reproduction of the unauthorized fixation in copies or phonorecords;

(2) the transmission or other communication to the public of the sounds or sounds and images of a live musical performance; and

(3) the distribution, sale, rental or offering to distribute, sell or rent copies or phonorecords of the unauthorized fixation, wherever the unauthorized fixation occurred.

These rights "shall apply to any act or acts that occur on or after the date of the Uruguay Round Amendments Act" (Dec. 8, 1994) 17 U.S.C. § 1101(c). State antibootlegging protection, moreover, is not preempted. *Id.* § 1101(d). Because sale of an unauthorized fixation is an act prohibited by § 1101, it would appear that post–1994 sales of pre–1994 fixations fall within the scope of the new federal enactment. This feature, combined with the Act's prohibition on U.S. sales of copies or phonorecords of unauthorized fixations, wherever the latter occurred, gives the Act very broad reach. For example, consider a surreptitious recording of a live opera performance in Paris in 1979, with subsequent sales of audio cassettes throughout the world. Post–1994 U.S. sales of the bootlegged Paris opera tape would now be actionable in the United States.

This recently created right fits only uncomfortably within Title 17 of the U.S. Code. First, rather than protecting works that are already fixed in a tangible medium, i.e., works within the subject matter of copyright under § 102, what is protected by § 1101 (the only section in Chapter 11 of the Act) is an unfixed musical performance: in effect, Congress has created a "right to fix" an otherwise evanescent work. This has historically been the province of state common-law copyright, but is now the business of federal law as well. How does this square with the constitutional directive to Congress to protect "writings"? In the first court decision on the matter, it was held that Congress indeed has the power under the Commerce Clause to protect "unfixed" works that are ineligible for copyright protection. *United States v. Moghadam*, 175 F.3d 1269 (11th Cir.1999).

Second, just as there appears to be no limit on how far back in time the unauthorized recording was made, § 1101 appears to have no time limit on the future enforcement of rights thereunder. Will a sale of phonorecords in the year 2101, derived from an unauthorized fixation occurring in 1995, still be actionable? How does this square with the "limited times" language in the Constitution?

Finally, note that § 1101(a) makes a violator "subject to the remedies provided in §§ 502 through 505, *to the same extent as an infringer of copyright.*" Congress treats this "right to fix" as similar to copyright, but different from it. Can Congress avoid the restrictions in the Copyright Clause of the Constitution by basing its legislative authority on the Commerce Clause instead? (By the way, are there also constitutional problems in extending the protections of § 1101 to live *musical* performers only, and not, say, to improvisers of poetry or of drama?)

B.   THE "IDEA/EXPRESSION DICHOTOMY"

§ 102.   Subject Matter of Copyright: In General

. . .

(b) In no case does copyright protection for an original work of authorship extend to any idea, procedure, process, system, method of operation, concept, principle, or discovery, regardless of the form in which it is described, explained, illustrated, or embodied in such work.

House Report

H.R. Rep. No. 94–1476, 94th Cong., 2d Sess. 56–57 (1976).

Copyright does not preclude others from using the ideas or information revealed by the author's work. It pertains to the literary, musical, graphic, or artistic form in which the author expressed intellectual concepts.... Some concern has been expressed lest copyright in computer programs should extend protection to the methodology or processes adopted by the programmer, rather than merely to the "writing" expressing his ideas. Section 102 (b) is intended, among other things, to make clear that the expression adopted by the programmer is the copyrightable element in a computer program, and that the actual processes or methods embodied in the program are not within the scope of the copyright law.

Section 102 (b) in no way enlarges or contracts the scope of copyright protection under the present law. Its purpose is to restate, in the context of the new single Federal system of copyright, that the basic dichotomy between expression and idea remains unchanged.

Baker v. Selden

101 U.S. 99 (1879).

■ MR. JUSTICE BRADLEY delivered the opinion of the court.

Charles Selden, the testator of the complainant in this case, in the year 1859 took the requisite steps for obtaining the copyright of a book, entitled "Selden's Condensed Ledger, or Bookkeeping Simplified," the object of which was to exhibit and explain a peculiar system of book-keeping. In 1860 and 1861, he took the copyright of several other books, containing additions to and improvements upon the said system. The bill of complaint was filed against the defendant, Baker, for an alleged infringement of these copyrights. The latter, in his answer, denied that Selden was the author or designer of the books, and denied the infringement charged, and contends on the argument that the matter alleged to be infringed is not a lawful subject of copyright.

CONDENSED LEDGER.

Bro't Forw'd.		ON TIME.		DATE:		SUNDRIES to SUNDRIES.	DISTRIBU-TION.		TOTAL.		BALANCE.	
DR.	CR.	DR.	CR.	DR.	CR.		DR.	CR.	DR.	CR.	DR.	CR.
						CASH. DR. $ CR. $						
						Carried Forward....						

The account book ledger design in which
Selden claimed a copyright

The parties went into proofs, and the various books of the complainant, as well as those sold and used by the defendant, were exhibited before the examiner, and witnesses were examined on both sides. A decree was rendered for the complainant, and the defendant appealed.

The book or series of books of which the complainant claims the copyright consists of an introductory essay explaining the system of book-keeping referred to, to which are annexed certain forms or blanks, consisting of ruled lines, and headings, illustrating the system and showing how it is to be used and carried out in practice. This system effects the same results as book-keeping by double entry; but, by a peculiar arrangement of columns and headings, presents the entire operation, of a day, a week, or a month, on a single page, or on two pages facing each other, in an account-book. The defendant uses a similar plan so far as results are concerned; but makes a different arrangement of the columns, and uses different headings. If the complainant's testator had the exclusive right to the use of the system explained in his book, it would be difficult to contend that the defendant does not infringe it, notwithstanding the difference in his form of arrangement; but if it be assumed that the system is open to public use, it seems to be equally difficult to contend that the books made and sold by the defendant are a violation of the copyright of the complainant's book considered merely as a book explanatory of the system. Where the truths of a science or the methods of an art are the common property of the whole world, any author has the right to express the one, or explain and use the other, in his own way. As an author, Selden explained the system in a particular way. It may be conceded that Baker makes and uses account-books arranged on substantially the same system; but the proof fails to show that he has violated the copyright of Selden's book, regarding the latter merely as an explanatory work; or that he has infringed Selden's right in any way, unless the latter became entitled to an exclusive right in the system.

The evidence of the complainant is principally directed to the object of showing that Baker uses the same system as that which is explained and illustrated in Selden's books. It becomes important, therefore, to determine whether, in obtaining the copyright of his books, he secured the exclusive right to the use of the system or method of book-keeping which the said books are intended to illustrate and explain. It is contended that he has secured such exclusive right, because no one can use the system without using substantially the same ruled lines and headings which he has appended to his books in illustration of it. In other words, it is contended that the ruled lines and headings, given to illustrate the system, are a part of the book, and, as such, are secured by the copyright; and that no one can make or use similar ruled lines and headings, or ruled lines and headings made and arranged on substantially the same system, without violating the copyright. And this is really the question to be decided in this case. Stated in another form, the question is, whether the exclusive property in a system of book-keeping can be claimed, under the law of copyright, by means of a book in which that system is explained? The complainant's bill, and the case made under it, are based on the hypothesis that it can be.

There is no doubt that a work on the subject of book-keeping, though only explanatory of well-known systems, may be the subject of a copyright; but, then, it is claimed only as a book. Such a book may be explanatory either of old systems, or of an entirely new system; and, considered as a book, as the work of an author, conveying information on the subject of book-keeping, and containing detailed explanations of the art, it may be a very valuable acquisition to the practical knowledge of the community. But there is a clear distinction between the book, as such, and the art which it is intended to illustrate. The mere statement of the proposition is so evident, that it requires hardly any argument to support it. The same distinction may be predicated of every other art as well as that of book-keeping. A treatise on the composition and use of medicines, be they old or new; on the construction and use of ploughs, or watches, or churns; or on the mixture and application of colors for painting or dyeing; or on the mode of drawing lines to produce the effect of perspective,—would be the subject of copyright; but no one would contend that the copyright of the treatise would give the exclusive right to the art or manufacture described therein. The copyright of the book, if not pirated from other works, would be valid without regard to the novelty, or want of novelty, of its subject-matter. The novelty of the art or thing described or explained has nothing to do with the validity of the copyright. To give to the author of the book an exclusive property in the art described therein, when no examination of its novelty has ever been officially made, would be a surprise and a fraud upon the public. That is the province of letters-patent, not of copyright. The claim to an invention or discovery of an art or manufacture must be subjected to the examination of the Patent Office before an exclusive right therein can be obtained; and it can only be secured by a patent from the government.

The difference between the two things, letters-patent and copyright, may be illustrated by reference to the subjects just enumerated. Take the case of medicines. Certain mixtures are found to be of great value in the healing art. If the discoverer writes and publishes a book on the subject (as regular physicians generally do), he gains no exclusive right to the manufacture and sale of the medicine; he gives that to the public. If he desires to acquire such exclusive right, he must obtain a patent for the mixture as a new art, manufacture, or composition of matter. He may copyright his book, if he pleases; but that only secures to him the exclusive right of printing and publishing his book. So of all other inventions or discoveries. . . .

The copyright of a work on mathematical science cannot give to the author an exclusive right to the methods of operation which he propounds, or to the diagrams which he employs to explain them, so as to prevent an engineer from using them whenever occasion requires. The very object of publishing a book on science or the useful arts is to communicate to the world the useful knowledge which it contains. But this object would be frustrated if the knowledge could not be used without incurring the guilt of piracy of the book. And where the art it teaches cannot be used without employing the methods and diagrams used to illustrate the book, or such as are similar to them, such methods and diagrams are to be considered as necessary incidents to the art, and given therewith to the public; not given for the purpose of publication in other works explanatory of the art, but for the purpose of practical application.

Of course, these observations are not intended to apply to ornamental designs, or pictorial illustrations addressed to the taste. Of these it may be said, that their form is their essence, and their object, the production of pleasure in their contemplation. This is their final end. They are as much the product of genius and the result of composition, as are the lines of the poet or the historian's periods. On the other hand, the teachings of science and the rules and methods of useful art have their final end in application and use; and this application and use are what the public derive from the publication of a book which teaches them. But as embodied and taught in a literary composition or book, their essence consists only in their statement. This alone is what is secured by the copyright. The use by another of the same methods of statement, whether in words or illustrations, in a book published for teaching the art, would undoubtedly be an infringement of the copyright.

Recurring to the case before us, we observe that Charles Selden, by his books, explained and described a peculiar system of book-keeping, and illustrated his method by means of ruled lines and blank columns, with proper headings on a page, or on successive pages. Now, whilst no one has a right to print or publish his book, or any material part thereof, as a book intended to convey instruction in the art, any person may practice and use the art itself which he has described and illustrated therein. The use of the art is a totally different thing from a publication of the book explaining it. The copyright of a book on book-keeping cannot secure the exclusive right to make, sell, and use account-books prepared upon the plan set forth in such book. Whether the art might or might not have been patented, is a question which is not before us. It was not patented, and is open and free to the use of the public. And, of course, in using the art, the ruled lines and headings of accounts must necessarily be used as incident to it.

. . . The description of the art in a book, though entitled to the benefit of copyright, lays no foundation for an exclusive claim to the art itself. The object of the one is explanation; the object of the other is use. The former may be secured by copyright. The latter can only be secured, if it can be secured at all, by letters-patent.

. . .

The conclusion to which we have come is, that blank account-books are not the subject of copyright; and that the mere copyright of Selden's book did not confer upon him the exclusive right to make and use account-books, ruled and arranged as designated by him and described and illustrated in said book.

The decree of the Circuit Court must be reversed, and the cause remanded with instructions to dismiss the complainant's bill; and it is

So ordered.

QUESTIONS

1.   What is the precise holding of this case: that the accounting forms were copyrightable (and copyrighted) but that such copyright was not infringed? Or that the accounting forms were not eligible for copyright? What practical difference would it make?

2.   What would be the proper analysis of the case if the defendant had been an accountant and had photocopied (assuming that was possible at the time the case arose) the plaintiff's forms? What if the defendant, instead, was in the printing business, and had printed thousands of copies of the forms, which he then sold in a retail store to accountants (along with ledger pads, electronic calculators, accounting magazines, and the like)?

3.   If the defendant had written a book describing, in his own words, plaintiff's accounting system, would that be an infringement of copyright? If, in that book, the defendant had included exact copies of the plaintiff's forms in an appendix for the purpose of illustrating the system described in the book, would that be an infringement? If the former question is answered no, doesn't that compel the same answer to the latter question?

Morrissey v. Procter & Gamble Co.

379 F.2d 675 (1st Cir.1967).

■ ALDRICH, CHIEF JUDGE. This is an appeal from a summary judgment for the defendant. The plaintiff, Morrissey, is the copyright owner of a set of rules for a sales promotional contest of the "sweepstakes" type involving the social security numbers of the participants. Plaintiff alleges that the defendant, Procter & Gamble Company, infringed, by copying, almost precisely, Rule 1. In its motion for summary judgment, based upon affidavits and depositions, defendant denies that plaintiff's Rule 1 is copyrightable material, and denies access. The district court held for the defendant on both grounds.

[The court held that the parties' dispute as to whether defendant had in fact had access to plaintiff's contest rules precluded summary judgment.]

The second aspect of the case raises a more difficult question. Before discussing it we recite plaintiff's Rule 1, and defendant's Rule 1, the italicizing in the latter being ours to note the defendant's variations or changes.

> 1.   Entrants should print name, address and social security number on a boxtop, or a plain paper. Entries must be accompanied by . . . boxtop or by plain paper on which the name . . . is copied from any source. Official rules are explained on . . . packages or leaflets obtained from dealer. If you do not have a social security number you may use the name and number of any member of your immediate family living with you. Only the person named on the entry will be deemed an entrant and may qualify for prize.
>
> Use the correct social security number belonging to the person named on entry . . . wrong numbers will be disqualified.

(Plaintiff's Rule)

1.   Entrants should print name, address and Social Security number on a Tide boxtop, or *on* [a] plain paper. Entries must be accompanied by Tide boxtop *(any size)* or by plain paper on which the name "Tide" is copied from any source. Official rules are *available* on Tide Sweepstakes packages, or *on* leaflets *at* Tide dealers, *or you can send a stamped, self-addressed envelope to:* Tide "Shopping Fling" Sweepstakes, P.O. Box 4459, Chicago 77, Illinois.

If you do not have a Social Security number, you may use the name and number of any member of your immediate family living with you. Only the person named on the entry will be deemed an entrant and may qualify for a prize.

Use the correct Social Security number, belonging to the person named on *the* entry—wrong numbers will be disqualified.

(Defendant's Rule)

.   .   .

[W]e must hold for the defendant. When the uncopyrightable subject matter is very narrow, so that "the topic necessarily requires," *Sampson & Murdock Co. v. Seaver–Radford Co.,* 1 Cir., 1905, 140 F. 539, 541; cf. Kaplan, An Unhurried View of Copyright, 64–65 (1967), if not only one form of expression, at best only a limited number, to permit copyrighting would mean that a party or parties, by copyrighting a mere handful of forms, could exhaust all possibilities of future use of the substance. In such circumstances it does not seem accurate to say that any particular form of expression comes from the subject matter. However, it is necessary to say that the subject matter would be appropriated by permitting the copyrighting of its expression. We cannot recognize copyright as a game of chess in which the public can be checkmated. Cf. *Baker v. Selden, supra.*

Upon examination the matters embraced in Rule 1 are so straightforward and simple that we find this limiting principle to be applicable. Furthermore, its operation need not await an attempt to copyright all possible forms. It cannot be only the last form of expression which is to be condemned, as completing defendant's exclusion from the substance. Rather, in these circumstances, we hold that copyright does not extend to the subject matter at all, and plaintiff cannot complain even if his particular expression was deliberately adopted.

Affirmed.

Continental Casualty Co. v. Beardsley, 253 F.2d 702 (2d Cir.), *cert. denied,* 358 U.S. 816 (1958). The copyright owner (Beardsley) developed a new kind of insurance, covering lost securities. He published a pamphlet describing the policy and including forms (bond, affidavit of loss, indemnity agreement, instruction letter and board resolutions). A competitor (Continental) copied the forms, but not the description. The court rejected Continental's contention that principles derived from *Baker v. Selden* forbade a copyright in the forms. Unlike the essentially blank forms in *Baker,* Beardsley's forms contained prose that was "explanatory" of his insurance plan. The court also found that nothing in the Constitution barred such copyright.

The difficult question for the Second Circuit was not the *existence* of copyright, but its *scope.* The court recognized that

> in the fields of insurance and commerce the use of specific language in forms and documents may be so essential to accomplish a desired result and so integrated with the use of a legal or commercial conception that the proper standard of infringement is one which will protect as far as possible the copyrighted language and yet allow free use of the thought beneath the language.

The court concluded, in effect, that the copyright on the forms may protect against only the exact rendition of the precise wording employed by the copyright owner. (This is commonly referred to as a "thin" copyright.) It acknowledged that its ruling "comes near to invalidating the copyright," but concluded that this was necessary in order to make available the "practical use of the art." To require a second-comer in such cases to generate different words and phrases which mean the same thing "borders on the preposterous."

The court found the evidence to support the conclusion that the language of Beardsley's forms was being used by Continental "only as incidental to its use of the underlying idea," and thus that the valid copyright was not infringed.

QUESTIONS

1. The *Beardsley* case involved business and legal forms. Because such forms must frequently be drafted to conform to the "terms of art" that have been held by courts to be essentially necessary to implement certain legal transactions, the opportunities for fanciful variation in authoring such forms are quite limited. Using the analysis of the court in *Morrissey,* would that not likely compel the conclusion that such business and legal forms are ineligible for copyright? (Indeed, should not legal forms be far less susceptible to copyright protection than contest rules?) *See Donald v. Zack Meyer's T.V. Sales & Serv.,* 426 F.2d 1027 (5th Cir.1970), *cert. denied,* 400 U.S. 992 (1971); *Financial Control Assocs. v. Equity Bldrs. Inc.,* 799 F.Supp. 1103 (D.Kan.1992).

2. Is there any practical difference between allowing copying because (as in *Morrissey*) the forms are not copyrightable and allowing copying because (as in *Beardsley*) the copyrightable forms were not infringed? For example, if a legal publisher prints a compendium of forms for various business transactions, does copyright on the formbook protect only the compilation (i.e., the selection and arrangement) or does it also protect the text of individual forms? Would it infringe to make an unauthorized copy of: (a) the entire formbook? (b) individual forms for purposes of servicing clients? (c) individual forms in order to sell them to attorneys for a profit?

Lotus Development Corp. v. Borland International, Inc.

49 F.3d 807 (1st Cir. 1995), *aff'd by an equally divided Court,* 516 U.S. 233 (1996).

■ STAHL, CIRCUIT JUDGE:

This appeal requires us to decide whether a computer menu command hierarchy is copyrightable subject matter. In particular, we must decide whether, as the district court held, plaintiff-appellee Lotus Development Corporation's copyright in Lotus 1–2–3, a computer spreadsheet program, was infringed by defendant-appellant Borland International, Inc., when Borland copied the Lotus 1–2–3 menu command hierarchy into its Quattro and Quattro Pro computer spreadsheet programs. . . .

I

Background

Lotus 1–2–3 is a spreadsheet program that enables users to perform accounting functions electronically on a computer. Users manipulate and control the program via a series of menu commands, such as "Copy," "Print," and "Quit." Users choose commands either by highlighting them on the screen or by typing their first letter. In all, Lotus 1–2–3 has 469 commands arranged into more than 50 menus and submenus.

Lotus 1–2–3, like many computer programs, allows users to write what are called "macros." By writing a macro, a user can designate a series of command choices with a single macro keystroke. Then, to execute that series of commands in multiple parts of the spreadsheet, rather than typing the whole series each time, the user only needs to type the single pre-programmed macro keystroke, causing the program to recall and perform the designated series of commands automatically. Thus, Lotus 1–2–3 macros shorten the time needed to set up and operate the program.

Borland released its first Quattro program to the public in 1987, after Borland's engineers had labored over its development for nearly three years. Borland's objective was to develop a spreadsheet program far superior to existing programs, including Lotus 1–2–3. In Borland's words, "from the time of its initial release ... Quattro included enormous innovations over competing spreadsheet products."

The district court found, and Borland does not now contest, that Borland included in its Quattro and Quattro Pro version 1.0 programs "a *virtually identical* copy of the entire 1–2–3 menu tree." *Borland III,* 831 F. Supp. at 212 (emphasis in original). In so doing, Borland did not copy any of Lotus's underlying computer code; it copied only the words and structure of Lotus's menu command hierarchy. Borland included the Lotus menu command hierarchy in its programs to make them compatible with Lotus 1–2–3 so that spreadsheet users who were already familiar with Lotus 1–2–3 would be able to switch to the Borland programs without having to learn new commands or rewrite their Lotus macros.

In its Quattro and Quattro Pro version 1.0 programs, Borland achieved compatibility with Lotus 1–2–3 by offering its users an alternate user interface, the "Lotus Emulation Interface." By activating the Emulation Interface, Borland users would see the Lotus menu commands on their screens and could interact with Quattro or Quattro Pro as if using Lotus 1–2–3, albeit with a slightly different looking screen and with many Borland options not available on Lotus 1–2–3. In effect, Borland allowed users to choose how they wanted to communicate with Borland's spreadsheet programs: either by using menu commands designed by Borland, or by using the commands and command structure used in Lotus 1–2–3 augmented by Borland-added commands. . . .

Lotus and Borland filed cross motions for summary judgment. . . .

On July 31, 1992, the district court denied Borland's motion and granted Lotus's motion in part. The district court ruled that the Lotus menu command hierarchy was copyrightable expression because

> [a] very satisfactory spreadsheet menu tree can be constructed using different commands and a different command structure from those of Lotus 1–2–3. In fact, Borland has constructed just such an alternate tree for use in Quattro Pro's native mode. Even if one holds the arrangement of menu commands constant, it is possible to generate literally millions of satisfactory menu trees by varying the menu commands employed.

Borland II, 799 F. Supp. at 217. The district court demonstrated this by offering alternate command words for the ten commands that appear in Lotus's main menu. *Id.* For example, the district court stated that "the 'Quit' command could be named 'Exit' without any other modifications," and that "the 'Copy' command could be called 'Clone,' 'Ditto,' 'Duplicate,' 'Imitate,' 'Mimic,' 'Replicate,' and 'Reproduce,' among others." *Id.* Because so many variations were possible, the district court concluded that the Lotus developers' choice and arrangement of command terms, reflected in the Lotus menu command hierarchy, constituted copyrightable expression.

In granting partial summary judgment to Lotus, the district court held that Borland had infringed Lotus's copyright in Lotus 1–2–3. . . .

Immediately following the district court's summary judgment decision, Borland removed the Lotus Emulation Interface from its products. Thereafter, Borland's spreadsheet programs no longer displayed the Lotus 1–2–3 menus to Borland users, and as a result Borland users could no longer communicate with Borland's programs as if they were using a more sophisticated version of Lotus 1–2–3. Nonetheless, Borland's programs continued to be partially compatible with Lotus 1–2–3, for Borland retained what it called the "Key Reader" in its Quattro Pro programs. Once turned on, the Key Reader allowed Borland's programs to understand and perform some Lotus 1–2–3 macros. With the Key Reader on, the Borland programs used Quattro Pro menus for display, interaction, and macro execution, except when they encountered a slash ("/") key in a macro (the starting key for any Lotus 1–2–3 macro), in which case they interpreted the macro as having been written for Lotus 1–2–3. Accordingly, people who wrote or purchased macros to shorten the time needed to perform an operation in

Lotus 1–2–3 could still use those macros in Borland's programs. The district court permitted Lotus to file a supplemental complaint alleging that the Key Reader infringed its copyright.

The parties agreed to try the remaining liability issues without a jury. . . .

This appeal concerns only Borland's copying of the Lotus menu command hierarchy into its Quattro programs and Borland's affirmative defenses to such copying. Lotus has not cross-appealed; in other words, Lotus does not contend on appeal that the district court erred in finding that Borland had not copied other elements of Lotus 1–2–3, such as its screen displays.

II
Discussion

On appeal, Borland does not dispute that it factually copied the words and arrangement of the Lotus menu command hierarchy. Rather, Borland argues that it "lawfully copied the unprotectible menus of Lotus 1–2–3." Borland contends that the Lotus menu command hierarchy is not copyrightable because it is a system, method of operation, process, or procedure foreclosed from protection by 17 U.S.C. § 102(b). Borland also raises a number of affirmative defenses.

. . .

B. *Matter of First Impression*

Whether a computer menu command hierarchy constitutes copyrightable subject matter is a matter of first impression in this court. While some other courts appear to have touched on it briefly in dicta, see, e.g., *Autoskill, Inc. v. National Educ. Support Sys., Inc.,* 994 F.2d 1476, 1495 n. 23 (10th Cir.), *cert. denied,* 126 L. Ed. 2d 254, 114 S. Ct. 307 (1993), we know of no cases that deal with the copyrightability of a menu command hierarchy standing on its own (i.e., without other elements of the user interface, such as screen displays, in issue). Thus we are navigating in uncharted waters.

Borland vigorously argues, however, that the Supreme Court charted our course more than 100 years ago when it decided *Baker v. Selden,* 101 U.S. 99, 25 L. Ed. 841 (1879). In *Baker v. Selden,* the Court held that Selden's copyright over the textbook in which he explained his new way to do accounting did not grant him a monopoly on the use of his accounting system. Borland argues:

> The facts of *Baker v. Selden,* and even the arguments advanced by the parties in that case, are identical to those in this case. The only difference is that the "user interface" of Selden's system was implemented by pen and paper rather than by computer.

To demonstrate that *Baker v. Selden* and this appeal both involve accounting systems, Borland even supplied this court with a video that, with special effects, shows Selden's paper forms "melting" into a computer screen and transforming into Lotus 1–2–3.

We do not think that *Baker v. Selden* is nearly as analogous to this appeal as Borland claims. Of course, Lotus 1–2–3 is a computer spreadsheet, and as such its grid of horizontal rows and vertical columns certainly resembles an accounting ledger or any other paper spreadsheet. Those grids, however, are not at issue in this appeal for, unlike Selden, Lotus does not claim to have a monopoly over its accounting system. Rather, this appeal involves Lotus's monopoly over the commands it uses to operate the computer. Accordingly, this appeal is not, as Borland contends, "identical" to *Baker v. Selden.*

. . .

D. *The Lotus Menu Command Hierarchy: A "Method of Operation"*

Borland argues that the Lotus menu command hierarchy is uncopyrightable because it is a system, method of operation, process, or procedure foreclosed from copyright protection by 17 U.S.C. § 102(b). Section 102(b) states: "In no case does copyright protection for an original work of authorship extend to any idea, procedure, process, system, method of operation, concept, principle, or discovery, regardless of the form in which it is described, explained, illustrated, or embodied in such work." Because we conclude that the Lotus menu command hierarchy is a method of operation, we do not consider whether it could also be a system, process, or procedure.

We think that "method of operation," as that term is used in § 102(b), refers to the means by which a person operates something, whether it be a car, a food processor, or a computer. Thus a text describing how to operate something would not extend copyright protection to the method of operation itself; other people would be free to employ that method and to describe it in their own words. Similarly, if a new method of operation is used rather than described, other people would still be free to employ or describe that method.

We hold that the Lotus menu command hierarchy is an uncopyrightable "method of operation." The Lotus menu command hierarchy provides the means by which users control and operate Lotus 1–2–3. If users wish to copy material, for example, they use the "Copy" command. If users wish to print material, they use the "Print" command. Users must use the command terms to tell the computer what to do. Without the menu command hierarchy, users would not be able to access and control, or indeed make use of, Lotus 1–2–3's functional capabilities.

The Lotus menu command hierarchy does not merely explain and present Lotus 1–2–3's functional capabilities to the user; it also serves as the method by which the program is operated and controlled. The Lotus menu command hierarchy is different from the Lotus long prompts, for the long prompts are not necessary to the operation of the program; users could operate Lotus 1–2–3 even if there were no long prompts.[9] The Lotus

---

9. As the Lotus long prompts are not before us on appeal, we take no position on their copyrightability, although we do note that a strong argument could be made that

menu command hierarchy is also different from the Lotus screen displays, for users need not "use" any expressive aspects of the screen displays in order to operate Lotus 1–2–3; because the way the screens look has little bearing on how users control the program, the screen displays are not part of Lotus 1–2–3's "method of operation."[10] The Lotus menu command hierarchy is also different from the underlying computer code, because while code is necessary for the program to work, its precise formulation is not. In other words, to offer the same capabilities as Lotus 1–2–3, Borland did not have to copy Lotus's underlying code (and indeed it did not); to allow users to operate its programs in substantially the same way, however, Borland had to copy the Lotus menu command hierarchy. Thus the Lotus 1–2–3 code is not an uncopyrightable "method of operation."[11]

The district court held that the Lotus menu command hierarchy, with its specific choice and arrangement of command terms, constituted an "expression" of the "idea" of operating a computer program with commands arranged hierarchically into menus and submenus. *Borland II,* 799 F. Supp. at 216. Under the district court's reasoning, Lotus's decision to employ hierarchically arranged command terms to operate its program could not foreclose its competitors from also employing hierarchically arranged command terms to operate their programs, but it did foreclose them from employing the specific command terms and arrangement that Lotus had used. . . .

Accepting the district court's finding that the Lotus developers made some expressive choices in choosing and arranging the Lotus command terms, we nonetheless hold that that expression is not copyrightable because it is part of Lotus 1–2–3's "method of operation." . . . "[M]ethods of operation" . . . are the means by which a user operates something. If specific words are essential to operating something, then they are part of a "method of operation" and, as such, are unprotectible. This is so whether they must be highlighted, typed in, or even spoken, as computer programs no doubt will soon be controlled by spoken words.

The fact that Lotus developers could have designed the Lotus menu command hierarchy differently is immaterial to the question of whether it is a "method of operation." In other words, our initial inquiry is not whether the Lotus menu command hierarchy incorporates any expression.

---

the brief explanations they provide "merge" with the underlying idea of explaining such functions. See *Morrissey v. Procter & Gamble Co.,* 379 F.2d 675, 678–79 (1st Cir.1967) (when the possible ways to express an idea are limited, the expression "merges" with the idea and is therefore uncopyrightable; when merger occurs, identical copying is permitted).

10. As they are not before us on appeal, we take no position on whether the Lotus 1–

2–3 screen displays constitute original expression capable of being copyrighted.

11. Because the Lotus 1–2–3 code is not before us on appeal, we take no position on whether it is copyrightable. We note, however, that original computer codes generally are protected by copyright. See, e.g., *Altai,* 982 F.2d at 702 ("It is now well settled that the literal elements of computer programs, i.e., their source and object codes, are the subject of copyright protection.") (citing cases).

Rather, our initial inquiry is whether the Lotus menu command hierarchy is a "method of operation." Concluding, as we do, that users operate Lotus 1–2–3 by using the Lotus menu command hierarchy, and that the entire Lotus menu command hierarchy is essential to operating Lotus 1–2–3, we do not inquire further whether that method of operation could have been designed differently. The "expressive" choices of what to name the command terms and how to arrange them do not magically change the uncopyrightable menu command hierarchy into copyrightable subject matter.

... Lotus wrote its menu command hierarchy so that people could learn it and use it. Accordingly, it falls squarely within the prohibition on copyright protection established in *Baker v. Selden* and codified by Congress in § 102(b).

In many ways, the Lotus menu command hierarchy is like the buttons used to control, say, a video cassette recorder ("VCR"). A VCR is a machine that enables one to watch and record video tapes. Users operate VCRs by pressing a series of buttons that are typically labelled "Record, Play, Reverse, Fast Forward, Pause, Stop/Eject." That the buttons are arranged and labeled does not make them a "literary work," nor does it make them an "expression" of the abstract "method of operating" a VCR via a set of labeled buttons. Instead, the buttons are themselves the "method of operating" the VCR.

When a Lotus 1–2–3 user chooses a command, either by highlighting it on the screen or by typing its first letter, he or she effectively pushes a button. Highlighting the "Print" command on the screen, or typing the letter "P," is analogous to pressing a VCR button labeled "Play."

Just as one could not operate a buttonless VCR, it would be impossible to operate Lotus 1–2–3 without employing its menu command hierarchy. Thus the Lotus command terms are not equivalent to the labels on the VCR's buttons, but are instead equivalent to the buttons themselves. Unlike the labels on a VCR's buttons, which merely make operating a VCR easier by indicating the buttons' functions, the Lotus menu commands are essential to operating Lotus 1–2–3. Without the menu commands, there would be no way to "push" the Lotus buttons, as one could push unlabeled VCR buttons. While Lotus could probably have designed a user interface for which the command terms were mere labels, it did not do so here. Lotus 1–2–3 depends for its operation on use of the precise command terms that make up the Lotus menu command hierarchy....

That the Lotus menu command hierarchy is a "method of operation" becomes clearer when one considers program compatibility. Under Lotus's theory, if a user uses several different programs, he or she must learn how to perform the same operation in a different way for each program used. For example, if the user wanted the computer to print material, then the user would have to learn not just one method of operating the computer such that it prints, but many different methods. We find this absurd. The fact that there may be many different ways to operate a computer program, or even many different ways to operate a computer program using a set of hierarchically arranged command terms, does not make the actual method of operation chosen copyrightable; it still functions as a method for operating the computer and as such is uncopyrightable.

Consider also that users employ the Lotus menu command hierarchy in writing macros. Under the district court's holding, if the user wrote a macro to shorten the time needed to perform a certain operation in Lotus 1–2–3, the user would be unable to use that macro to shorten the time needed to perform that same operation in another program. Rather, the user would have to rewrite his or her macro using that other program's menu command hierarchy. This is despite the fact that the macro is clearly the user's own work product. We think that forcing the user to cause the computer to perform the same operation in a different way ignores Congress's direction in § 102(b) that "methods of operation" are not copyrightable. That programs can offer users the ability to write macros in many different ways does not change the fact that, once written, the macro allows the user to perform an operation automatically. As the Lotus menu command hierarchy serves as the basis for Lotus 1–2–3 macros, the Lotus menu command hierarchy is a "method of operation." . . .

Our holding that methods of operation are not limited to abstractions goes against *Autoskill,* 994 F.2d at 1495 n.23, in which the Tenth Circuit rejected the defendant's argument that the keying procedure used in a computer program was an uncopyrightable "procedure" or "method of operation" under § 102(b). The program at issue, which was designed to test and train students with reading deficiencies, *id.* at 1481, required students to select responses to the program's queries "by pressing the 1, 2, or 3 keys." *Id.* at 1495 n.23. The Tenth Circuit held that, "for purposes of the preliminary injunction, . . . the record showed that [this] keying procedure reflected at least a minimal degree of creativity," as required by *Feist* for copyright protection. *Id.* As an initial matter, we question whether a programmer's decision to have users select a response by pressing the 1, 2, or 3 keys is original. More importantly, however, we fail to see how "a student selecting a response by pressing the 1, 2, or 3 keys," *id.,* can be anything but an unprotectible method of operation.

III
Conclusion

Because we hold that the Lotus menu command hierarchy is uncopyrightable subject matter, we further hold that Borland did not infringe Lotus's copyright by copying it. . . . The judgment of the district court is Reversed.

■ BOUDIN, CIRCUIT JUDGE, concurring:

The importance of this case, and a slightly different emphasis in my view of the underlying problem, prompt me to add a few words to the majority's tightly focused discussion.

I

Most of the law of copyright and the "tools" of analysis have developed in the context of literary works such as novels, plays, and films. In this milieu, the principal problem—simply stated, if difficult to resolve—is to stimulate creative expression without unduly limiting access by others to the broader themes and concepts deployed by the author. The middle of the spectrum presents close cases; but a "mistake" in providing too much protection involves a small cost: subsequent authors treating the same themes must take a few more steps away from the original expression.

The problem presented by computer programs is fundamentally different in one respect. The computer program is a means for causing something to happen; it has a mechanical utility, an instrumental role, in accomplishing the world's work. Granting protection, in other words, can have some of the consequences of patent protection in limiting other people's ability to perform a task in the most efficient manner. Utility does not bar copyright (dictionaries may be copyrighted), but it alters the calculus.

Of course, the argument for protection is undiminished, perhaps even enhanced, by utility: if we want more of an intellectual product, a temporary monopoly for the creator provides incentives for others to create other, different items in this class. But the "cost" side of the equation may be different where one places a very high value on public access to a useful innovation that may be the most efficient means of performing a given task. Thus, the argument for extending protection may be the same; but the stakes on the other side are much higher.

It is no accident that patent protection has preconditions that copyright protection does not—notably, the requirements of novelty and nonobviousness—and that patents are granted for a shorter period than copyrights. This problem of utility has sometimes manifested itself in copyright cases, such as *Baker v. Selden,* 101 U.S. 99, 25 L. Ed. 841 (1879), and been dealt with through various formulations that limit copyright or create limited rights to copy. But the case law and doctrine addressed to utility in copyright have been brief detours in the general march of copyright law.

Requests for the protection of computer menus present the concern with fencing off access to the commons in an acute form. A new menu may be a creative work, but over time its importance may come to reside more in the investment that has been made by users in learning the menu and in building their own mini-programs—macros—in reliance upon the menu. Better typewriter keyboard layouts may exist, but the familiar QWERTY keyboard dominates the market because that is what everyone has learned to use. See P. David, *CLIO and the Economics of QWERTY,* 75 Am. Econ. Rev. 332 (1985). The QWERTY keyboard is nothing other than a menu of letters.

Thus, to assume that computer programs are just one more new means of expression, like a filmed play, may be quite wrong. The "form"—the written source code or the menu structure depicted on the screen—looks hauntingly like the familiar stuff of copyright; but the "substance" probably has more to do with problems presented in patent law or, as already noted, in those rare cases where copyright law has confronted industrially useful expressions. Applying copyright law to computer programs is like assembling a jigsaw puzzle whose pieces do not quite fit. . . .

II

. . .

The present case is an unattractive one for copyright protection of the menu. The menu commands (e.g., "print," "quit") are largely for standard procedures that Lotus did not invent and are common words that Lotus cannot monopolize. What is left is the particular combination and sub-grouping of commands in a pattern devised by Lotus. This arrangement may have a more appealing logic and ease of use than some other configurations; but there is a certain arbitrariness to many of the choices.

If Lotus is granted a monopoly on this pattern, users who have learned the command structure of Lotus 1–2–3 or devised their own macros are locked into Lotus, just as a typist who has learned the QWERTY keyboard would be the captive of anyone who had a monopoly on the production of such a keyboard. Apparently, for a period Lotus 1–2–3 has had such sway in the market that it has represented the de facto standard for electronic spreadsheet commands. So long as Lotus is the superior spreadsheet—either in quality or in price—there may be nothing wrong with this advantage.

But if a better spreadsheet comes along, it is hard to see why customers who have learned the Lotus menu and devised macros for it should remain captives of Lotus because of an investment in learning made by the users and not by Lotus. Lotus has already reaped a substantial reward for being first; assuming that the Borland program is now better, good reasons exist for freeing it to attract old Lotus customers: to enable the old customers to take advantage of a new advance, and to reward Borland in turn for making a better product. If Borland has not made a better product, then customers will remain with Lotus anyway.

Thus, for me the question is not whether Borland should prevail but on what basis. Various avenues might be traveled, but the main choices are between holding that the menu is not protectible by copyright and devising a new doctrine that Borland's use is privileged. No solution is perfect and no intermediate appellate court can make the final choice.

To call the menu a "method of operation" is, in the common use of those words, a defensible position. After all, the purpose of the menu is not to be admired as a work of literary or pictorial art. It is to transmit directions from the user to the computer, i.e., to operate the computer. The menu is also a "method" in the dictionary sense because it is a "planned way of doing something," an "order or system," and (aptly here) an "orderly or systematic arrangement, sequence or the like." Random House Webster's College Dictionary 853 (1991).

A different approach would be to say that Borland's use is privileged because, in the context already described, it is not seeking to appropriate the advances made by Lotus' menu; rather, having provided an arguably more attractive menu of its own, Borland is merely trying to give former Lotus users an option to exploit their own prior investment in learning or in macros. The difference is that such a privileged use approach would not automatically protect Borland if it had simply copied the Lotus menu (using different codes), contributed nothing of its own, and resold Lotus under the Borland label. . . .

But a privileged use doctrine would certainly involve problems of its own. It might more closely tailor the limits on copyright protection to the reasons for limiting that protection; but it would entail a host of administrative problems that would cause cost and delay, and would also reduce the ability of the industry to predict outcomes. Indeed, to the extent that Lotus' menu is an important standard in the industry, it might be argued that any use ought to be deemed privileged.

In sum, the majority's result persuades me and its formulation is as good, if not better, than any other that occurs to me now as within the reach of courts. Some solutions (e.g., a very short copyright period for menus) are not options at all for courts but might be for Congress. In all events, the choices are important ones of policy, not linguistics, and they should be made with the underlying considerations in view.

———

In a similar case involving the menu structure of a computer program intended for engineering purposes, the Court of Appeals for the Eleventh Circuit held that the work was an uncopyrightable "process" under § 102(b), that there was a "merger" between its idea and the limited number of ways in which it could be expressed, and that the work lacked originality. *See Mitek Holdings, Inc. v. ArcE Eng'g Co.*, 89 F.3d 1548 (11th Cir.1996).

By contrast, in **Mitel, Inc. v. Iqtel, Inc.**, 124 F.3d 1366 (10th Cir.1997), the Tenth Circuit took a different view of the protectibility of command codes:

> As its initial basis for finding Mitel's command codes unprotectable, the district court applied the literal language of section 102(b) and concluded that Mitel's set of command codes is an unprotected method of operation or "a method for achieving a particular result." *Gates Rubber*, 9 F.3d at 836 n.13. The court based its conclusion upon the finding that Mitel's command codes comprise the method by which a long distance carrier matches the call controller's functions, the carrier's technical demands, and the telephone customer's choices.
>
> The First Circuit reached a similar conclusion in *Lotus Development Corp. v. Borland Int'l, Inc.*, 49 F.3d 807 (1st Cir.1995), *aff'd by an evenly divided court*, 116 S.Ct. 804 (1996). . . . [T]he First Circuit concluded that the "menu command hierarchy" was not protected by copyright because the hierarchy and its components constituted a "method of operation" unprotectable under 17 U.S.C. § 102(b). *Id.*

The *Lotus* court concluded that the question whether a work is excluded from protection under section 102(b) logically precedes consideration of whether the individual components of the work are "expressive." *Id.* Most significantly, the *Lotus* court held that otherwise protectable expression that is embodied in a method of operation is excluded under section 102(b) from copyright protection because it is part of the method of operation. . . .

We conclude that although an element of a work may be characterized as a method of operation, that element may nevertheless contain expression that is eligible for copyright protection. Section 102(b) does not extinguish the protection accorded a particular expression of an idea merely because that expression is embodied in a method of operation at a higher level of abstraction. Rather, sections 102(a) & (b) interact to secure ideas for [the] public domain and to set apart an author's particular expression for further scrutiny to ensure that copyright protection will "promote the . . . useful Arts." U.S. Const. Art. I, § 8, cl. 8.

QUESTIONS

1. The Copyright Act defines a "computer program" as "a set of statements or instructions to be used directly or indirectly in a computer in order to bring about a certain result." Does that make a "computer program" a "method of operation" excluded from copyright protection under § 102(b)?

2. If the commands of a user interface are an unprotected "method of operation," the initial programmer would be unsuccessful in its infringement claim not only if the second-comer adopted the commands as a means of bridging users to the second-comer's own interface (as Borland ultimately did), but also if the second-comer simply replicated the interface. Does this make sense? *Cf. Lotus Dev. Corp. v. Paperback Software*, 740 F.Supp. 37 (D.Mass.1990).

3. All members of the court of appeals in *Lotus v. Borland* appear rather clearly to have been influenced by the fact that the Lotus commands had become a "standard" in the computer-spreadsheet field, and that it would be extremely inefficient if the vast population familiar with Lotus would have to learn a new set of commands for different spreadsheet programs. (Compare the judges' references to the QWERTY typewriter keyboard.) How compelling is that argument, and is it more or less convincing than the conclusion reached by Judge Keeton in the district court, which follows?

> [O]ne object of copyright law is to protect expression in order to encourage innovation. It follows, then, that the more innovative the expression of an idea is, the more important is copyright protection for that expression. By arguing that 1–2–3 was so innovative that it occupied the field and set a *de facto* industry standard, and that, therefore, defendants were free to copy plaintiff's expression, defendants have flipped copyright on its head. Copyright protection would be

perverse if it only protected mundane increments while leaving unprotected as part of the public domain those advancements that are more strikingly innovative.

———

American Dental Ass'n v. Delta Dental Plans Ass'n, 126 F.3d 977 (7th Cir.1997). The American Dental Association (ADA) creates and publishes a taxonomy of dental procedures. Its Code on Dental Procedures and Nomenclatures classifies all dental procedures into groups; each procedure receives a number, a short description, and a long description. For example, number 04267 has been assigned to the short description "guided tissue regeneration—nonresorbable barrier, per site, per tooth (includes membrane removal)," which is classified with other surgical periodontic services. Delta Dental, an insurance company, publishes Universal Coding and Nomenclature, which includes most of the numbering system and short descriptions from the ADA Code.

The court of appeals rejected the conclusion of the district court that the taxonomy was uncopyrightable as a useful catalogue of a field of knowledge. This, said Circuit Judge Easterbrook, would bar copyright for "the West Key Number System, which is designed as a comprehensive index to legal topics, and A Uniform System of Citation (the Bluebook), a taxonomy of legal sources," to the tests and answers devised by the Educational Testing Service, and to almost all computer programs which are inherently useful. The dental-procedure taxonomy satisfies the minimal standards of creativity to secure copyright:

> Facts do not supply their own principles of organization. Classification is a creative endeavor.... Dental procedures could be classified by complexity, or by the tools necessary to perform them, or by the parts of the mouth involved, or by the anesthesia employed, or in any of a dozen different ways. The Code's descriptions don't "merge with the facts" any more than a scientific description of butterfly attributes is part of a butterfly.... There can be multiple, and equally original, biographies of the same person's life, and multiple original taxonomies of a field of knowledge. Creativity marks the expression even after the fundamental scheme has been devised.

The court found the long descriptions clearly to be copyrightable, and "even the short description and the number are original works of authorship." The record showed that the ADA committees that prepared the taxonomy debated and disagreed about the best ways to draft the descriptions; and "the number assigned to any one of the three descriptions could have had four or six digits rather than five; guided tissue regeneration could have been placed in the 2500 series rather than the 4200 series; again any of these choices is original to the author of a taxonomy, and another author could do things differently." Delta could have written its own classification of dental procedures.

Finally, the court addressed Delta's invocation of *Baker v. Selden* and its claim that the ADA was attempting to protect an uncopyrightable "system." It concluded:

> So far as the ADA is concerned, any dentist, any insurer, anyone at all, may devise and use [blank] forms into which the Code's descriptions may be entered. The ADA encourages this use; standardization of language promotes interchange among professionals.... Section 102(b) precludes the ADA from suing, for copyright infringement, a dentist whose office files record treatments using the Code's nomenclature. No field of practice has been or can be monopolized, given this constraint. Section 102(b) permits Delta Dental to disseminate forms inviting dentists to use the ADA's Code when submitting bills to insurers. But it does not permit Delta to copy the Code itself, or make and distribute a derivative work based on the Code, any more than Baker could copy Selden's book.

QUESTIONS

1. Wasn't Baker permitted to copy Selden's book, at least in order to execute the system therein explained? How is Delta Dental's copying different?

2. A "taxonomy" or classification entails a method of presenting information; is it therefore a "method of operation"? Is the "Uniform *System* of Citation" [emphasis supplied] protectible under copyright? Should it be?

3. In *Publications Int'l, Ltd. v. Meredith Corp.*, 88 F.3d 473 (7th Cir.1996), the court held that recipes contained in a cookbook of yogurt dishes were not copyrightable. "The recipes comprise the lists of required ingredients and the directions for combining them to achieve the final products. The recipes contain no expressive elaboration upon either of these functional components, as opposed to recipes that might spice up functional directives by weaving in creative narrative." The list of ingredients lacked originality (the court noted the Copyright Office regulation, 37 CFR § 202.1) and the procedure for preparing the various dishes was an uncopyrightable "process" or "system" under § 102(b). Suppose each recipe presented only one of a variety of ways of producing the same dish, for example, pot roast: would the recipe still be a "process"? Suppose there were many different kinds of pot roast, from Yankee pot roast to "Daube de boeuf;" if each recipe's steps were necessary to produce a particular kind of pot roast, but there were an infinite variety of kinds of pot roast, would each recipe still be a "process?"

(Check around your home and see if you can find a cookbook whose recipes would satisfy the requirements for copyrightability.)

Bibbero Systems, Inc. v. Colwell Systems, Inc.

893 F.2d 1104 (9th Cir.1990).

■ GOODWIN, CHIEF JUDGE:

This case requires us to examine the scope of the blank forms rule, 37 C.F.R. § 202.1(c) (1982), which provides that blank forms are not copyrightable. Plaintiff Bibbero Systems, Inc. (Bibbero) contends that Colwell Systems, Inc. (Colwell) infringed upon its copyright by duplicating its medical insurance claim form.

Bibbero designs and markets blank forms known as "superbills" which doctors use to obtain reimbursement from insurance companies. Each

---

JOHN R. JOHNNSON, M.D.
Type of Practice or Specialty
1000 MAIN STREET, SUITE 10
SOME PLACE, USA 70000

STATE LIC. # 123456789
SOC. SEC. # 000-11-0000

TELEPHONE: (123) 234-5678

☐PRIVATE ☐BLUE CROSS ☐BLUE SHIELD ☐IND. ☐MEDICAID ☐MEDICARE ☐GOV'T.

PATIENT INFORMATION

PATIENT'S LAST NAME	FIRST		INITIAL	BIRTHDATE / /	SEX [ ] MALE [ ] FEMALE		TODAY'S DATE / /
ADDRESS	CITY	STATE	ZIP	RELATION TO SUBSCRIBER	REFERRING PHYSICIAN		
SUBSCRIBER OR POLICYHOLDER				INSURANCE CARRIER			
ADDRESS – IF DIFFERENT	CITY	STATE	ZIP	INS. ID	COVERAGE CODE		GROUP

DISABILITY RELATED TO:
{ }ILLNESS [ ]ACCIDENT [ ]IND.
[ ]PREGNANCY [ ]

DATE SYMPTOMS APPEARED, INCEPTION OF PREGNANCY, OR ACCIDENT OCCURRED: / /

OTHER HEALTH COVERAGE? - [ ]NO [ ]YES - IDENTIFY

ASSIGNMENT: I hereby assign my insurance benefits to be paid directly to the undersigned physician. I am financially responsible for non-covered services.
SIGNED: (Patient or Parent If Minor)   Date:

RELEASE: I authorize the undersigned physician to release any information acquired in the course of my examination or treatment.
SIGNED: (Patient or Parent If Minor)   Date:

Family Practice

✓	DESCRIPTION		CPT4/MO	FEE	✓	DESCRIPTION		CPT4/MO	FEE	✓	DESCRIPTION	CPT4/MO	FEE
	1. OFFICE VISIT	NEW	EST.			3. HOSP. SERVICES	NEW	EST.			9. LABORATORY — IN OFFICE		
	Minimal		90030			Interm.(days)	90215	90260			Urine	81000	
	Brief	90000	90040			Extended		90270			Occult Blood	89205	
	Limited	90010	90050			Comprehensive	90220				ECG	93000	
	Intermediate	90015	90060			Discharge 30 min. - 1 hr.							
	Extended		90070			Detention Time 30 min.-1hr.	99150						
	Comprehensive	90020	90080			Detention Time ___ Hrs.	99151						
											10. SURGERY		
						4. SPECIAL SERVICES					Anoscopy	46600	
	2. INJECTIONS & IMMUNIZATIONS					Called to ER -during ofc. hrs.	99065				Sigmoidoscopy	45355	
	Surgical Injection		206			Night Call - before 10 pm	99050						
	DPT		90701			Night Call - after 10 pm	99052				Surgery Assist	-80	
	DT		90702			Sundays or Holidays	99054						
	Tetanus		90703			5. EMERGENCY ROOM					11. MISCELLANEOUS		
	OPV		90712				905				Booklets	99071	
	MMR		90707			6. HOUSE CALLS					Special Reports	99080	
							901				Supplies, Ace Bandage	99070	
						7. EXTENDED CARE FACILITY							
							903				X-Ray		
						8. CONSULTATION							
							906						

DIAGNOSIS ICD-9

☐ Abscess	682.9	☐ Chonyloma Accuminate	078.1	☐ Hemorrhoids	455.6	☐ Paroxysmal Atrial Tachy.	427.2
☐ Abrasion-sup. Injury	919	☐ Conjunctivits	372	☐ Hypertension	401.9	☐ Pediculosis Pubis-Scabies	133.0
☐ Allergic Reaction	995.3	☐ Contusion, Hematoma	924.9	☐ Influenza	487.1	☐ Pelvic Congertion	625.5
☐ Amenorrhea	626.0	☐ Coronary Artery Dis.	414.9	☐ Ingrown Toenail	703.0	☐ Pharyngitis, Tonsil.-Acute	462
☐ Anemia	285.9	☐ Cystitis-Pyeloneph. 595.9/590.80		☐ Insomnia	780.52	☐ Pigmented Nevus	M8720/0
☐ Anxiety-Stress-Depression	309	☐ Cephalgia-Migraine Tension 784.0		☐ Irritable Colon	564.1	☐ Post Nasal Drip	473.9
☐ Arteriosclerosis	440.9	☐ Dermatitis	692.0	☐ Jaundice-Hepatitis	782.4	☐ Pneumonitis-Pleuritis	486
☐ Arthralgia	719.4	☐ Diabetes Mellitus	250.0	☐ Labyrinth.-Vertigo 386.30/780.4		☐ P.I.D.	614.9
☐ Arthrit.-Osteo Rheum. 716/714		☐ Duodenal Ulcer	532.9	☐ Laryngo-Tracheitis	464	☐ Prostatitis	601.9
☐ Asthma Hayfever	493.0	☐ Duodenitis-Gas	535.6	☐ Lipoma	214.9	☐ Puncture Wound	879.8
☐ Bleeding Internal	626.6	☐ Dysmenorrhea	625.3	☐ Lipid Cholesterol Ab	272.7	☐ Renal Stone	592.0
☐ Bleeding Post Men	627.1	☐ Emphysema-COPD	496	☐ Low Back Pain	724.2	☐ Sebaceous Cyst.	706.2
☐ Boil-Casbuncle/ Furuncle	680	☐ Epicondylitis	726.32	☐ Lymphadenitis	289.3	☐ Seizure Disorder	780.3
☐ Bronchitis-Acute/Chronic	490	☐ Epilepsy	345.9	☐ Lymphangitis	457.2	☐ Sinusitis	473.9
☐ Bronchopneumonitis	485	☐ Eustachian Tube Congest.	381.50	☐ Memorrhagia	626.2	☐ Thyroid Disorder	246.9
☐ Bursitis	727	☐ Exogenous Obesity	278.0	☐ Menopausal Syndrome	627.2	☐ Tinea Corpus-Pedis	110.5
☐ Cellulitis-Impetigo	682	☐ Fatigue	780.7	☐ Myofascitis-Tendonitis	729.1	☐ URI-Viral Syndrome	460
☐ Cerebral Con.	850.9	☐ Foreign Body	879.8	☐ Muscle Strain/Sprain	848.9	☐ Urethritis-Cystitis	599.0
☐ Cervicitis	616.0	☐ Gastroenteritis	558.9	☐ Otitis-External Cerumen	382.9	☐ Vaginitis	616.10
☐ Cholecyst. & Cholelith. 575/574		☐ Heart Failure	428.0	☐ Otitis-Media Acute	382.9	☐ Weight Loss	783.2
		☐ Hiatal Hernia	553.3	☐ Pain		☐	

| DIAGNOSIS: (IF NOT CHECKED ABOVE) | SERVICES PERFORMED AT: [ ]Office [ ] Johnnson's Hospital [ ]E.R. 100 Main St. [ ]N.H. Some Place, USA 70000 | LAB SENT TO: [ ] State Hospital 200 State St. Some Place, USA 70001 | DATES DISABLED: FROM: / / TO: / / OK TO RETURN TO WORK/SCHOOL / / |

RETURN APPOINTMENT INFORMATION:
5 - 10 - 15 - 20 - 30 - 45 - 60

| DAYS | WKS. | MOS. | PRN | PX. |

NEXT APPOINTMENT:
M – T – W – TH – F – S
DATE: / /   TIME: ___ AM / PM

DOCTOR'S SIGNATURE/DATE

INSTRUCTIONS TO PATIENT FOR FILING INSURANCE CLAIMS

1. COMPLETE UPPER PORTION OF THIS FORM.
2. SIGN & DATE.
3. MAIL THIS FORM DIRECTLY TO YOUR INSURANCE COMPANY. YOU MAY ATTACH YOUR OWN INSURANCE COMPANY'S FORM IF YOU WISH, ALTHOUGH IT IS NOT NECESSARY.

ACCEPT ASSIGNMENT? [ ]YES [ ]NO

REC'D BY:	
[ ]CASH	TOTAL TODAY'S FEE
[ ]CR. CD.	OLD BALANCE
	TOTAL
[ ]CHECK	AMT. REC'D. TODAY
•_____	NEW BALANCE

INSUR-A-BILL® • BIBBERO SYSTEMS, INC. • PETALUMA, CA. • © 3/84 superbill contains simple instructions to the patient for filing insurance claims; boxes for patient information; simple clauses assigning insurance benefits to the doctor and authorizing release of patient information; and two lengthy checklists for the doctor to indicate the diagnosis and any services performed, as well as the applicable fee. All entries on the checklists are categories specified by the American Medical Association (AMA) or government publications, as are the code numbers accompanying each entry. The superbills differ according to specialty, to reflect the illnesses and treatments most relevant to the individual doctor.

The forms are personalized to include the doctor's name and address, the nature of the doctor's practice, and the hospitals or clinics at which services may be performed. Doctors may use either the checklists provided on the sample form, or may create their own checklists of the most relevant diagnoses, treatments and procedures. Bibbero encourages doctors to create their own checklists, which most doctors choose to do.

Bibbero includes approximately 25 or 30 sample superbills in its catalog. Bibbero claims a copyright in each of these forms, as well as in the forms designed by its customers. Bibbero has supplied the family practice superbill at issue in this case since 1984. The superbill contains a notice of copyright. In its fall 1987 catalog, Colwell featured a superbill which was nearly identical to Bibbero's superbill, except for slightly different typefaces and shading, as well as a different sample doctor's name and address. Bibbero saw Colwell's superbill in Colwell's catalog. Bibbero then submitted an application to register its superbill with the Copyright Office, and a certificate of copyright was issued effective October 13, 1987. Upon the issuance of the certificate, Bibbero demanded that Colwell cease infringing upon its copyright in the superbill. Colwell refused to comply with Bibbero's demand, and Bibbero brought suit in district court. Bibbero moved for a preliminary injunction to prevent Colwell from distributing its fall 1987 catalog or future catalogs containing the infringing superbill, and from selling superbills which infringe upon Bibbero's copyright.

After taking the deposition of Bibbero's president, Michael Buckley, Colwell moved for summary judgment on the basis that Bibbero's superbill was not copyrightable because the work was a "blank form" among other reasons.

The district court granted summary judgment to Colwell, denied Bibbero's motion for a preliminary injunction, and dismissed Bibbero's complaint. The district court held that Bibbero's superbill is a blank form which, under the doctrine of *Baker v. Selden,* 101 U.S. 99, 25 L. Ed. 841 (1879), now codified at 37 C.F.R. § 202.1(c) (1982), is not copyrightable.

1. *Is Bibbero's Blank Form "Superbill" Copyrightable?*

Bibbero contends that the district court erroneously granted summary judgment to Colwell because the superbill is not an uncopyrightable blank form, but instead a form which conveys information. Specifically, Bibbero contends that the superbill contains concise descriptions of medical procedures and diagnoses to ensure fair and accurate billing, provisions for assignment of claims and release of information, and instructions for completion.

Bibbero obtained a certificate of registration for its superbill from the Copyright Office. In judicial proceedings, a certificate of copyright registration constitutes prima facie evidence of copyrightability and shifts the burden to the defendant to demonstrate why the copyright is not valid. 17 U.S.C. § 410(c).

It is well-established that blank forms which do not convey information are not copyrightable. *John H. Harland Co. v. Clarke Checks, Inc.,* 711 F.2d 966, 971 (11th Cir.1983). The blank forms rule, first articulated in *Baker v. Selden,* 101 U.S. 99, is codified at 37 C.F.R. § 202.1(c) (1982):

> The following are examples of works not subject to copyright:
>
> . . .
>
> (c) Blank forms, such as time cards, graph paper, account books, diaries, bank checks, scorecards, address books, report forms, order forms and the like, which are designed for recording information and do not in themselves convey information.

Although blank forms are generally not copyrightable, there is a well-established exception where text is integrated with blank forms. Where a work consists of text integrated with blank forms, the forms have explanatory force because of the accompanying copyrightable textual material. *See Edwin K. Williams & Co. v. Edwin K. Williams & Co.—East,* 542 F.2d 1053, 1061 (9th Cir.1976) (combination of instruction book and blank forms constituting an integrated work held to be copyrightable), *cert. denied,* 433 U.S. 908, 97 S. Ct. 2973, 53 L. Ed. 2d 1092 (1977); *Continental Casualty Co. v. Beardsley,* 253 F.2d 702, 704 (2d Cir.) (form with inseparable instructions copyrightable), *cert. denied,* 358 U.S. 816, 79 S. Ct. 25, 3 L. Ed. 2d 58 (1958); *Januz Marketing Communications, Inc. v. Doubleday & Co.,* 569 F. Supp. 76, 79 (S.D.N.Y.1982) (same).

We agree with the district court that cases interpreting the blank forms rule do not yield a consistent line of reasoning. In support of its contention that the superbill is copyrightable, Bibbero relies on *Norton Printing Co. v. Augustana Hospital,* 155 U.S.P.Q. 133 (N.D.Ill.1967), in which the court found copyrightable a medical laboratory test form containing a checklist of possible laboratory tests. The court determined that "the format and arrangement used, together with the different boxes and terms, can ... serve to convey information as to the type of tests to be conducted and the information which is deemed important." Bibbero also relies on *Harcourt Brace & World, Inc. v. Graphic Controls Corp.,* 329 F. Supp. 517 (S.D.N.Y.1971) which held that test answer sheets were copyrightable because the sheets were "designed to guide the student in recording his answer" and thus conveyed information. *Id.* at 524. Bibbero similarly claims that its superbill conveys information.

Norton cannot be distinguished from this case. We agree with Colwell, however, that it should be disapproved. *Norton* indicates a dislike for the blank forms rule, asserting that the rule "has been strongly criticized and would appear to be without foundation." 155 U.S.P.Q. at 134. *Harcourt*

Brace is arguably distinguishable because the answer sheets at issue in that case contained unique symbols to guide students in recording their answers and explanations and answers appeared on some of the answer sheets. *Id.* at 524. To the extent that *Harcourt Brace* contravenes the principles established in *Baker,* however, we decline to follow it.

The Copyright Office recently reaffirmed *Baker v. Selden,* decided not to revise the blank forms regulation, and cited *John H. Harland Co. v. Clarke Checks,* 207 U.S.P.Q. 664 (N.D.Ga.1980) (declining to follow *Harcourt Brace*), *aff'd,* 711 F.2d 966, 972 n. 8 (11th Cir.1983) (agreeing that *Harcourt Brace* should not be followed), as a proper interpretation of the regulation. *See* Notice of Termination of Inquiry Regarding Blank Forms, 45 Fed. Reg. 63297–63300 (September 24, 1980). Despite extensive comments from blank-form suppliers favoring revision of the blank forms rule, the Copyright Office found "no persuasive arguments against the validity of regulation 37 C.F.R. § 202.1(c)." *Id.* at 63299.

We agree with the Eleventh Circuit's "bright-line" approach to the blank forms rule in *Clarke Checks. Norton*'s holding that a medical laboratory test form "conveyed information" because it contained some of the possible categories of information but not others, thus indicating which information was important, is potentially limitless. All forms seek only certain information, and, by their selection, convey that the information sought is important. This cannot be what the Copyright Office intended by the statement "convey information" in 37 C.F.R. § 202.1(c). The purpose of Bibbero's superbill is to record information. Until the superbill is filled out, it conveys no information about the patient, the patient's diagnosis, or the patient's treatment. Doctors do not look to Bibbero's superbill in diagnosing or treating patients. The superbill is simply a blank form which gives doctors a convenient method for recording services performed. The fact that there is a great deal of printing on the face of the form—because there are many possible diagnoses and treatments—does not make the form any less blank.

We also find that the "text with forms" exception to the blank forms rule is inapplicable here. It is true, as Bibbero notes, that the superbill includes some simple instructions to the patient on how to file an insurance claim using the form, such as "complete upper portion of this form."[2] These instructions are far too simple to be copyrightable as text in and of themselves, unlike the instructions in other "text with forms" cases. *See, e.g., Williams,* 542 F.2d at 1060–61 (account books with several pages of instructions on the use of the forms and advice on the successful management of a service station conveyed information and were therefore copyrightable). We therefore affirm the district court's holding that Bibbero's superbill is not copyrightable.[3]

---

2. The complete instructions read as follows: 1. Complete upper portion of this form. 2. Sign and date. 3. Mail this form directly to your insurance company. You may attach your own insurance company's form if you wish, although it is not necessary.

3. Bibbero also contends that its superbill is copyrightable as a compilation. Our

ABR Benefits Services Inc. v. NCO Group, 52 U.S.P.Q.2d 1119 (E.D.Pa.1999), the court noted the view of the Court of Appeals for the Third Circuit that "blank forms may be copyrighted if they are sufficiently innovative that their arrangement of information is itself informative." The court concluded that in that Circuit the blank-form rule announced in *Baker v. Selden* is to be interpreted narrowly, so as to allow for copyright protection for blank forms that organize information in a way that "conveys" information. The defendant's request for summary judgment was thus denied, because of a genuine issue of material fact, when the plaintiff had designed (and registered with the Copyright Office) a multi-paged, multi-purpose Notification Form intended to be used by health insurance companies seeking to comply with the Consolidated Omnibus Budget Reconciliation Act (COBRA). Among other things, the court found that the defendant had specifically set out to copy the ABR forms because of their clear advantage over other COBRA forms. (Wasn't that no doubt equally true in the *Bibbero* case?)

QUESTIONS

1. Note that the court in *Bibbero* begins its opinion by stating that it is required to interpret Copyright Office Regulation 202.1(c), which announces the so-called blank form rule. *Is* the court so required? Isn't it rather obliged to interpret § 102(a) of the Copyright Act, or *Baker v. Selden* and its statutory counterpart in § 102(b)? Recall that the regulations of the Copyright Office are simply the Register's best effort to interpret the statute, and that their consistency with the Act (see § 702) is definitively to be determined by the federal courts. (Is it not odd that the court, in attempting to apply the blank form rule as fashioned by the Copyright Office, did not make very much of the fact that the Office had accepted the *Bibbero* form for registration?!)

2. Is, indeed, the blank form rule a proper reading of § 102(a), and of *Baker v. Selden? See Januz Mktg. Commun., Inc. v. Doubleday & Co.,* 569 F.Supp. 76 (S.D.N.Y.1982). Why should it be necessary, to secure copyright, that the words or graphic images on a form be designed to communicate information rather than to record it? And, even assuming the form is "blank" rather than explanatory, does the court in *Bibbero* properly dispose of the plaintiff's "compilation" claim?

holding that the superbill falls within the blank forms rule precludes it from being copyrightable as a compilation. A "compilation" is a work formed by the collection and assembling of preexisting materials or data that are selected, coordinated or arranged in such a way that the work as a whole constitutes an original work of authorship, and may consist entirely of uncopyrightable elements. 17 U.S.C. § 101; *Harper House, Inc. v.* *Thomas Nelson, Inc.,* 889 F.2d 197, 204 (9th Cir.1989). For example, a collection of common property and blank forms, although not individually copyrightable, may be selected, coordinated or arranged in such a way that they are copyrightable as a compilation. *Harper House,* 204–07. Here, however, the superbill consists in its entirety of one uncopyrightable blank form and hence cannot be copyrightable as a compilation.

C.   FACTS AND COMPILATIONS

§ 101.   Definitions

A "compilation" is a work formed by the collection and assembling of preexisting materials or of data that are selected, coordinated, or arranged in such a way that the resulting work as a whole constitutes an original work of authorship. The term "compilation" includes collective works.

§ 103.   Subject Matter of Copyright: Compilations and Derivative Works

(a) The subject matter of copyright as specified by section 102 includes compilations and derivative works, but protection for a work employing preexisting material in which copyright subsists does not extend to any part of the work in which such material has been used unlawfully.

(b) The copyright in a compilation or derivative work extends only to the material contributed by the author of such work, as distinguished from the preexisting material employed in the work, and does not imply any exclusive right in the preexisting material. The copyright in such work is independent of, and does not affect or enlarge the scope, duration, owner-ship, or subsistence of, any copyright protection in the preexisting material.

House Report

H.R. Rep. No. 94–1476, 94th Cong., 2d Sess. 57–58 (1976).

Between them the terms "compilations" and "derivative works" which are defined in section 101, comprehend every copyrightable work that employs preexisting material or data of any kind. There is necessarily some overlapping between the two, but they basically represent different con-cepts. A "compilation" results from a process of selecting, bringing togeth-er, organizing, and arranging previously existing material of all kinds, regardless of whether the individual items in the material have been or ever could have been subject to copyright. A "derivative work," on the other hand, requires a process of recasting, transforming, or adapting "one or more preexisting works"; the "preexisting work" must come within the general subject matter of copyright set forth in section 102, regardless of whether it is or was ever copyrighted....

... [T]he criteria of copyrightable subject matter stated in section 102 apply with full force to works that are entirely original and to those containing preexisting material.... The most important point [made in § 103(b)] is one that is commonly misunderstood today: copyright in a "new version" covers only the material added by the later author, and has no effect one way or the other on the copyright or public domain status of the preexisting material....

Feist Publications, Inc. v. Rural Telephone Service

499 U.S. 340, 111 S.Ct. 1282, 113 L.Ed.2d 358 (1991).

■ JUSTICE O'CONNOR delivered the opinion of the Court.

This case requires us to clarify the extent of copyright protection available to telephone directory white pages.

I

Rural Telephone Service Company is a certified public utility that provides telephone service to several communities in northwest Kansas. It is subject to a state regulation that requires all telephone companies operating in Kansas to issue annually an updated telephone directory. Accordingly, as a condition of its monopoly franchise, Rural publishes a typical telephone directory, consisting of white pages and yellow pages. The white pages list in alphabetical order the names of Rural's subscribers, together with their towns and telephone numbers. The yellow pages list Rural's business subscribers alphabetically by category and feature classified advertisements of various sizes. Rural distributes its directory free of charge to its subscribers, but earns revenue by selling yellow pages advertisements.

Feist Publications, Inc., is a publishing company that specializes in area-wide telephone directories. Unlike a typical directory, which covers only a particular calling area, Feist's area-wide directories cover a much larger geographical range, reducing the need to call directory assistance or consult multiple directories. The Feist directory that is the subject of this litigation covers 11 different telephone service areas in 15 counties and contains 46,878 white pages listings—compared to Rural's approximately 7,700 listings. Like Rural's directory, Feist's is distributed free of charge and includes both white pages and yellow pages. Feist and Rural compete vigorously for yellow pages advertising.

As the sole provider of telephone service in its service area, Rural obtains subscriber information quite easily. Persons desiring telephone service must apply to Rural and provide their names and addresses; Rural then assigns them a telephone number. Feist is not a telephone company, let alone one with monopoly status, and therefore lacks independent access to any subscriber information. To obtain white pages listings for its area-wide directory, Feist approached each of the 11 telephone companies operating in northwest Kansas and offered to pay for the right to use its white pages listings.

Of the 11 telephone companies, only Rural refused to license its listings to Feist. Rural's refusal created a problem for Feist, as omitting these listings would have left a gaping hole in its area-wide directory, rendering it less attractive to potential yellow pages advertisers. In a decision subsequent to that which we review here, the District Court determined that this was precisely the reason Rural refused to license its listings. The refusal was motivated by an unlawful purpose "to extend its monopoly in telephone service to a monopoly in yellow pages advertising." *Rural Telephone Service Co. v. Feist Publications, Inc.,* 737 F. Supp. 610, 622 (Kan. 1990).

Unable to license Rural's white pages listings, Feist used them without Rural's consent. Feist began by removing several thousand listings that fell outside the geographic range of its area-wide directory, then hired personnel to investigate the 4,935 that remained. These employees verified the data reported by Rural and sought to obtain additional information. As a result, a typical Feist listing includes the individual's street address; most of Rural's listings do not. Notwithstanding these additions, however, 1,309 of the 46,878 listings in Feist's 1983 directory were identical to listings in Rural's 1982–1983 white pages. App. 54 (para. 15–16), 57. Four of these were fictitious listings that Rural had inserted into its directory to detect copying.

Rural sued for copyright infringement in the District Court for the District of Kansas taking the position that Feist, in compiling its own directory, could not use the information contained in Rural's white pages. Rural asserted that Feist's employees were obliged to travel door-to-door or conduct a telephone survey to discover the same information for themselves. Feist responded that such efforts were economically impractical and, in any event, unnecessary because the information copied was beyond the scope of copyright protection. The District Court granted summary judgment to Rural, explaining that "courts have consistently held that telephone directories are copyrightable" and citing a string of lower court decisions. 663 F. Supp. 214, 218 (1987). In an unpublished opinion, the Court of Appeals for the Tenth Circuit affirmed "for substantially the reasons given by the district court." App. to Pet. for Cert. 4a, judgt. order reported at 916 F.2d 718 (1990). We granted certiorari, 498 U.S. ___ (1990), to determine whether the copyright in Rural's directory protects the names, towns, and telephone numbers copied by Feist.

II

A

This case concerns the interaction of two well-established propositions. The first is that facts are not copyrightable; the other, that compilations of facts generally are. Each of these propositions possesses an impeccable pedigree. That there can be no valid copyright in facts is universally understood. The most fundamental axiom of copyright law is that "no author may copyright his ideas or the facts he narrates." *Harper & Row, Publishers, Inc. v. Nation Enterprises,* 471 U.S. 539, 556 (1985). Rural wisely concedes this point, noting in its brief that "facts and discoveries, of course, are not themselves subject to copyright protection." Brief for Respondent 24. At the same time, however, it is beyond dispute that compilations of facts are within the subject matter of copyright. Compilations were expressly mentioned in the Copyright Act of 1909, and again in the Copyright Act of 1976.

There is an undeniable tension between these two propositions. Many compilations consist of nothing but raw data—i.e., wholly factual information not accompanied by any original written expression. On what basis may one claim a copyright in such a work? Common sense tells us that 100 uncopyrightable facts do not magically change their status when gathered together in one place. Yet copyright law seems to contemplate that compilations that consist exclusively of facts are potentially within its scope.

The key to resolving the tension lies in understanding why facts are not copyrightable. The *sine qua non* of copyright is originality. To qualify for copyright protection, a work must be original to the author. *See Harper & Row, supra,* at 547–549. Original, as the term is used in copyright, means only that the work was independently created by the author (as opposed to copied from other works), and that it possesses at least some minimal degree of creativity. 1 M. Nimmer & D. Nimmer, Copyright §§ 2.01[A], [B] (1990) (hereinafter Nimmer). To be sure, the requisite level of creativity is extremely low; even a slight amount will suffice. The vast majority of works make the grade quite easily, as they possess some creative spark, "no matter how crude, humble or obvious" it might be. *Id.,* § 1.08[C][1]. Originality does not signify novelty; a work may be original even though it closely resembles other works so long as the similarity is fortuitous, not the result of copying. To illustrate, assume that two poets, each ignorant of the other, compose identical poems. Neither work is novel, yet both are original and, hence, copyrightable. *See Sheldon v. Metro–Goldwyn Pictures Corp.,* 81 F.2d 49, 54 (C.A.2 1936).

Originality is a constitutional requirement. The source of Congress' power to enact copyright laws is Article I, § 8, cl. 8, of the Constitution, which authorizes Congress to "secure for limited Times to Authors ... the exclusive Right to their respective Writings." In two decisions from the late 19th Century—*The Trade–Mark Cases,* 100 U.S. 82 (1879); and *Burrow-Giles Lithographic Co. v. Sarony,* 111 U.S. 53 (1884)—this Court defined the crucial terms "authors" and "writings." In so doing, the Court made it unmistakably clear that these terms presuppose a degree of originality.... Leading scholars agree on this point. As one pair of commentators succinctly puts it: "The originality requirement is *constitutionally mandated* for all works." Patterson & Joyce, *Monopolizing the Law: The Scope of Copyright Protection for Law Reports and Statutory Compilations,* 36 UCLA L. Rev. 719, 763, n. 155 (1989) (emphasis in original) (hereinafter Patterson & Joyce). *Accord id.,* at 759–760, and n. 140; Nimmer § 1.06[A] ("originality is a statutory as well as a constitutional requirement"); *id.,* § 1.08[C][1] ("a modicum of intellectual labor ... clearly constitutes an essential constitutional element").

It is this bedrock principle of copyright that mandates the law's seemingly disparate treatment of facts and factual compilations. "No one may claim originality as to facts." *Id.,* § 2.11[A], p. 2–157. This is because facts do not owe their origin to an act of authorship. The distinction is one between creation and discovery: the first person to find and report a particular fact has not created the fact; he or she has merely discovered its existence. To borrow from *Burrow-Giles,* one who discovers a fact is not its "maker" or "originator." 111 U.S., at 58. "The discoverer merely finds and records." Nimmer § 2.03[E].... The same is true of all facts—scientific, historical, biographical, and news of the day. "They may not be copyrighted and are part of the public domain available to every person." Miller, *supra,* at 1369.

Factual compilations, on the other hand, may possess the requisite originality. The compilation author typically chooses which facts to include, in what order to place them, and how to arrange the collected data so that they may be used effectively by readers. These choices as to selection and arrangement, so long as they are made independently by the compiler and entail a minimal degree of creativity, are sufficiently original that Congress may protect such compilations through the copyright laws. Nimmer §§ 2.11[D], 3.03; Denicola 523, n. 38. Thus, even a directory that contains absolutely no protectible written expression, only facts, meets the constitutional minimum for copyright protection if it features an original selection or arrangement. *See Harper & Row,* 471 U.S., at 547. *Accord* Nimmer § 3.03.

This protection is subject to an important limitation. The mere fact that a work is copyrighted does not mean that every element of the work may be protected. Originality remains the *sine qua non* of copyright; accordingly, copyright protection may extend only to those components of a work that are original to the author. Patterson & Joyce 800–802; Ginsburg, *Creation and Commercial Value: Copyright Protection of Works of Information,* 90 Colum. L. Rev. 1865, 1868, and n.12 (1990) (hereinafter Ginsburg). Thus, if the compilation author clothes facts with an original collocation of words, he or she may be able to claim a copyright in this written expression. Others may copy the underlying facts from the publication, but not the precise words used to present them. In *Harper & Row,* for example, we explained that President Ford could not prevent others from copying bare historical facts from his autobiography, see 471 U.S., at 556–557, but that he could prevent others from copying his "subjective descriptions and portraits of public figures." *Id.,* at 563. Where the compilation author adds no written expression but rather lets the facts speak for themselves, the expressive element is more elusive. The only conceivable expression is the manner in which the compiler has selected and arranged the facts. Thus, if the selection and arrangement are original, these elements of the work are eligible for copyright protection. *See* Patry, *Copyright in Compilations of Facts (or Why the "White Pages" Are Not Copyrightable),* 12 Com. & Law 37, 64 (Dec. 1990) (hereinafter Patry). No matter how original the format, however, the facts themselves do not become original through association. *See* Patterson & Joyce 776.

This inevitably means that the copyright in a factual compilation is thin. Notwithstanding a valid copyright, a subsequent compiler remains free to use the facts contained in another's publication to aid in preparing a competing work, so long as the competing work does not feature the same selection and arrangement. As one commentator explains it: "No matter how much original authorship the work displays, the facts and ideas it exposes are free for the taking.... The very same facts and ideas may be divorced from the context imposed by the author, and restated or reshuffled by second comers, even if the author was the first to discover the facts or to propose the ideas." Ginsburg 1868.

It may seem unfair that much of the fruit of the compiler's labor may be used by others without compensation. As Justice Brennan has correctly observed, however, this is not "some unforeseen byproduct of a statutory scheme." *Harper & Row,* 471 U.S., at 589 (dissenting opinion). It is, rather, "the essence of copyright," *ibid.,* and a constitutional requirement. The primary objective of copyright is not to reward the labor of authors, but "to promote the Progress of Science and useful Arts." Art. I, § 8, cl. 8. *Accord Twentieth Century Music Corp. v. Aiken,* 422 U.S. 151, 156 (1975). To this end, copyright assures authors the right to their original expression, but encourages others to build freely upon the ideas and information conveyed by a work. *Harper & Row, supra,* at 556–557. This principle, known as the idea/expression or fact/expression dichotomy, applies to all works of authorship. As applied to a factual compilation, assuming the absence of original written expression, only the compiler's selection and arrangement may be protected; the raw facts may be copied at will. This result is neither unfair nor unfortunate. It is the means by which copyright advances the progress of science and art. . . .

This, then, resolves the doctrinal tension: Copyright treats facts and factual compilations in a wholly consistent manner. Facts, whether alone or as part of a compilation, are not original and therefore may not be copyrighted. A factual compilation is eligible for copyright if it features an original selection or arrangement of facts, but the copyright is limited to the particular selection or arrangement. In no event may copyright extend to the facts themselves.

B

As we have explained, originality is a constitutionally mandated prerequisite for copyright protection. The Court's decisions announcing this rule predate the Copyright Act of 1909, but ambiguous language in the 1909 Act caused some lower courts temporarily to lose sight of this requirement.

The 1909 Act embodied the originality requirement, but not as clearly as it might have. *See* Nimmer § 2.01. The subject matter of copyright was set out in § 3 and § 4 of the Act. Section 4 stated that copyright was available to "all the writings of an author." 35 Stat. 1076. By using the words "writings" and "author"—the same words used in Article I, § 8 of the Constitution and defined by the Court in *The Trade–Mark Cases* and *Burrow-Giles*— the statute necessarily incorporated the originality requirement articulated in the Court's decisions. It did so implicitly, however, thereby leaving room for error.

Section 3 was similarly ambiguous. It stated that the copyright in a work protected only "the copyrightable component parts of the work." It thus stated an important copyright principle, but failed to identify the specific characteristic—originality—that determined which component parts of a work were copyrightable and which were not.

Most courts construed the 1909 Act correctly, notwithstanding the less-than-perfect statutory language. They understood from this Court's decisions that there could be no copyright without originality....

But some courts misunderstood the statute. *See, e.g., Leon v. Pacific Telephone & Telegraph Co.,* 91 F.2d 484 (C.A.9 1937); *Jeweler's Circular Publishing Co. v. Keystone Publishing Co.,* 281 F. 83 (C.A.2 1922). These courts ignored § 3 and § 4, focusing their attention instead on § 5 of the Act. Section 5, however, was purely technical in nature: it provided that a person seeking to register a work should indicate on the application the type of work, and it listed 14 categories under which the work might fall. One of these categories was "books, including composite and cyclopedic works, directories, gazetteers, and other compilations." § 5(a). Section 5 did not purport to say that all compilations were automatically copyrightable. Indeed, it expressly disclaimed any such function, pointing out that "the subject-matter of copyright is defined in section four." Nevertheless, the fact that factual compilations were mentioned specifically in § 5 led some courts to infer erroneously that directories and the like were copyrightable *per se,* "without any further or precise showing of original—personal—authorship." Ginsburg 1895.

Making matters worse, these courts developed a new theory to justify the protection of factual compilations. Known alternatively as "sweat of the brow" or "industrious collection," the underlying notion was that copyright was a reward for the hard work that went into compiling facts. The classic formulation of the doctrine appeared in *Jeweler's Circular Publishing Co.,* 281 F., at 88:

> "The right to copyright a book upon which one has expended labor in its preparation does not depend upon whether the materials which he has collected consist or not of matters which are *publici juris,* or whether such materials show literary skill *or originality,* either in thought or in language, or anything more than industrious collection. The man who goes through the streets of a town and puts down the names of each of the inhabitants, with their occupations and their street number, acquires material of which he is the author" (emphasis added).

The "sweat of the brow" doctrine had numerous flaws, the most glaring being that it extended copyright protection in a compilation beyond selection and arrangement—the compiler's original contributions—to the facts themselves. Under the doctrine, the only defense to infringement was independent creation. A subsequent compiler was "not entitled to take one word of information previously published," but rather had to "independently work out the matter for himself, so as to arrive at the same result from the same common sources of information." *Id.,* at 88–89 (internal quotations omitted). "Sweat of the brow" courts thereby eschewed the most fundamental axiom of copyright law—that no one may copyright facts or ideas....

Decisions of this Court applying the 1909 Act make clear that the statute did not permit the "sweat of the brow" approach. The best example is *International News Service v. Associated Press,* 248 U.S. 215 (1918). In that decision, the Court stated unambiguously that the 1909 Act conferred copyright protection only on those elements of a work that were original to the author. Associated Press had conceded taking news reported by International News Service and publishing it in its own newspapers. Recognizing that § 5 of the Act specifically mentioned "periodicals, including newspapers," § 5(b), the Court acknowledged that news articles were copyrightable. *Id.,* at 234. It flatly rejected, however, the notion that the copyright in an article extended to the factual information it contained: "The news element—the information respecting current events contained in the literary production—is not the creation of the writer, but is a report of matters that ordinarily are *publici juris;* it is the history of the day." *Ibid.**

Without a doubt, the "sweat of the brow" doctrine flouted basic copyright principles. Throughout history, copyright law has "recognized a greater need to disseminate factual works than works of fiction or fantasy." *Harper & Row,* 471 U.S., at 563. *Accord* Gorman, *Fact or Fancy: The Implications for Copyright,* 29 J. Copyright Soc. 560, 563 (1982). But "sweat of the brow" courts took a contrary view; they handed out proprietary interests in facts and declared that authors are absolutely precluded from saving time and effort by relying upon the facts contained in prior works. In truth, "it is just such wasted effort that the proscription against the copyright of ideas and facts ... [is] designed to prevent." *Rosemont Enterprises, Inc. v. Random House, Inc.,* 366 F.2d 303, 310 (C.A.2 1966), *cert. denied,* 385 U.S. 1009 (1967). "Protection for the fruits of such research ... may in certain circumstances be available under a theory of unfair competition. But to accord copyright protection on this basis alone distorts basic copyright principles in that it creates a monopoly in public domain materials without the necessary justification of protecting and encouraging the creation of 'writings' by 'authors.'" Nimmer § 3.04, p. 3–23 (footnote omitted).

C

... In enacting the Copyright Act of 1976, Congress dropped the reference to "all the writings of an author" and replaced it with the phrase "original works of authorship." 17 U.S.C. § 102(a). In making explicit the originality requirement, Congress announced that it was merely clarifying existing law: "The two fundamental criteria of copyright protection [are] originality and fixation in tangible form.... The phrase 'original works of authorship,' which is purposely left undefined, is intended to incorporate without change *the standard of originality established by the courts under the present [1909] copyright statute.*" H.R. Rep. No. 94–1476, p. 51 (1976) (emphasis added) (hereinafter H.R. Rep.).

---

* The Court ultimately rendered judgment for International News Service [sic] on noncopyright grounds that are not relevant here. *See* 248 U.S., at 235, 241–242.

To ensure that the mistakes of the "sweat of the brow" courts would not be repeated, Congress took additional measures. For example, § 3 of the 1909 Act had stated that copyright protected only the "copyrightable component parts" of a work, but had not identified originality as the basis for distinguishing those component parts that were copyrightable from those that were not. The 1976 Act deleted this section and replaced it with § 102(b), which identifies specifically those elements of a work for which copyright is not available: "In no case does copyright protection for an original work of authorship extend to any idea, procedure, process, system, method of operation, concept, principle, or discovery, regardless of the form in which it is described, explained, illustrated, or embodied in such work." § 102(b) is universally understood to prohibit any copyright in facts. *Harper & Row, supra,* at 547, 556. *Accord* Nimmer § 2.03[E] (equating facts with "discoveries"). As with § 102(a), Congress emphasized that § 102(b) did not change the law, but merely clarified it: "Section 102(b) in no way enlarges or contracts the scope of copyright protection under the present law. Its purpose is to restate . . . that the basic dichotomy between expression and idea remains unchanged." H.R. Rep., at 57; S. Rep., at 54.

Congress took another step to minimize confusion by deleting the specific mention of "directories . . . and other compilations" in § 5 of the 1909 Act. As mentioned, this section had led some courts to conclude that directories were copyrightable *per se* and that every element of a directory was protected. In its place, Congress enacted two new provisions. First, to make clear that compilations were not copyrightable per se, Congress provided a definition of the term "compilation." Second, to make clear that the copyright in a compilation did not extend to the facts themselves, Congress enacted 17 U.S.C. § 103.

The definition of "compilation" is found in § 101 of the 1976 Act. It defines a "compilation" in the copyright sense as "a work formed by the collection and assembly of preexisting materials or of data *that* are selected, coordinated, or arranged *in such a way that* the resulting work as a whole constitutes an original work of authorship" (emphasis added).

The purpose of the statutory definition is to emphasize that collections of facts are not copyrightable *per se*. It conveys this message through its tripartite structure, as emphasized above by the italics. The statute identifies three distinct elements and requires each to be met for a work to qualify as a copyrightable compilation: (1) the collection and assembly of pre-existing material, facts, or data; (2) the selection, coordination, or arrangement of those materials; and (3) the creation, by virtue of the particular selection, coordination, or arrangement, of an "original" work of authorship. "This tripartite conjunctive structure is self-evident, and should be assumed to 'accurately express the legislative purpose.' " Patry 51, quoting *Mills Music,* 469 U.S., at 164.

At first glance, the first requirement does not seem to tell us much. It merely describes what one normally thinks of as a compilation—a collection of pre-existing material, facts, or data. What makes it significant is that it is not the *sole* requirement. It is not enough for copyright purposes that an author collects and assembles facts. To satisfy the statutory definition, the work must get over two additional hurdles. In this way, the plain language indicates that not every collection of facts receives copyright protection. Otherwise, there would be a period after "data."

The third requirement is also illuminating. It emphasizes that a compilation, like any other work, is copyrightable only if it satisfies the originality requirement ("an *original* work of authorship"). Although § 102 states plainly that the originality requirement applies to all works, the point was emphasized with regard to compilations to ensure that courts would not repeat the mistake of the "sweat of the brow" courts by concluding that fact-based works are treated differently and measured by some other standard. As Congress explained it, the goal was to "make plain that the criteria of copyrightable subject matter stated in section 102 apply with full force to works ... containing preexisting material." H.R. Rep., at 57; S. Rep., at 55.

The key to the statutory definition is the second requirement. It instructs courts that, in determining whether a fact-based work is an original work of authorship, they should focus on the manner in which the collected facts have been selected, coordinated, and arranged. This is a straightforward application of the originality requirement. Facts are never original, so the compilation author can claim originality, if at all, only in the way the facts are presented. To that end, the statute dictates that the principal focus should be on whether the selection, coordination, and arrangement are sufficiently original to merit protection.

Not every selection, coordination, or arrangement will pass muster. This is plain from the statute. It states that, to merit protection, the facts must be selected, coordinated, or arranged "in such a way" as to render the work as a whole original. This implies that some "ways" will trigger copyright, but that others will not. *See* Patry 57, and n. 76.... [W]e conclude that the statute envisions that there will be some fact-based works in which the selection, coordination, and arrangement are not sufficiently original to trigger copyright protection.

As discussed earlier, however, the originality requirement is not particularly stringent. A compiler may settle upon a selection or arrangement that others have used; novelty is not required. Originality requires only that the author make the selection or arrangement independently (i.e., without copying that selection or arrangement from another work), and that it display some minimal level of creativity. Presumably, the vast majority of compilations will pass this test, but not all will. There remains a narrow category of works in which the creative spark is utterly lacking or so trivial as to be virtually nonexistent. *See generally Bleistein v. Donaldson Lithographing Co.,* 188 U.S. 239, 251 (1903) (referring to "the narrowest and most obvious limits"). Such works are incapable of sustaining a valid copyright. Nimmer § 2.01[B].

Even if a work qualifies as a copyrightable compilation, it receives only limited protection. This is the point of § 103 of the Act. Section 103 explains that "the subject matter of copyright ... includes compilations,"

§ 103(a), but that copyright protects only the author's original contributions—not the facts or information conveyed:

> "The copyright in a compilation ... extends only to the material contributed by the author of such work, as distinguished from the preexisting material employed in the work, and does not imply any exclusive right in the preexisting material." § 103(b).

As § 103 makes clear, copyright is not a tool by which a compilation author may keep others from using the facts or data he or she has collected. "The most important point here is one that is commonly misunderstood today: copyright ... has no effect one way or the other on the copyright or public domain status of the preexisting material." H.R. Rep., at 57; S. Rep., at 55. The 1909 Act did not require, as "sweat of the brow" courts mistakenly assumed, that each subsequent compiler must start from scratch and is precluded from relying on research undertaken by another. *See, e.g., Jeweler's Circular Publishing Co.,* 281 F., at 88–89. Rather, the facts contained in existing works may be freely copied because copyright protects only the elements that owe their origin to the compiler—the selection, coordination, and arrangement of facts.

In summary, the 1976 revisions to the Copyright Act leave no doubt that originality, not "sweat of the brow," is the touchstone of copyright protection in directories and other fact-based works. Nor is there any doubt that the same was true under the 1909 Act. The 1976 revisions were a direct response to the Copyright Office's concern that many lower courts had misconstrued this basic principle, and Congress emphasized repeatedly that the purpose of the revisions was to clarify, not change, existing law. The revisions explain with painstaking clarity that copyright requires originality, § 102(a); that facts are never original, § 102(b); that the copyright in a compilation does not extend to the facts it contains, § 103(b); and that a compilation is copyrightable only to the extent that it features an original selection, coordination, or arrangement, § 101.

The 1976 revisions have proven largely successful in steering courts in the right direction....

III

There is no doubt that Feist took from the white pages of Rural's directory a substantial amount of factual information. At a minimum, Feist copied the names, towns, and telephone numbers of 1,309 of Rural's subscribers. Not all copying, however, is copyright infringement. To establish infringement, two elements must be proven: (1) ownership of a valid copyright, and (2) copying of constituent elements of the work that are original. *See Harper & Row,* 471 U.S., at 548. The first element is not at issue here; Feist appears to concede that Rural's directory, considered as a whole, is subject to a valid copyright because it contains some foreword text, as well as original material in its yellow pages advertisements. *See* Brief for Petitioner 18; Pet. for Cert. 9.

The question is whether Rural has proved the second element. In other words, did Feist, by taking 1,309 names, towns, and telephone numbers from Rural's white pages, copy anything that was "original" to Rural? Certainly, the raw data does not satisfy the originality requirement. Rural may have been the first to discover and report the names, towns, and telephone numbers of its subscribers, but this data does not " 'owe its origin' " to Rural. *Burrow-Giles,* 111 U.S., at 58. Rather, these bits of information are uncopyrightable facts; they existed before Rural reported them and would have continued to exist if Rural had never published a telephone directory.... Section 103(b) states explicitly that the copyright in a compilation does not extend to "the preexisting material employed in the work."

The question that remains is whether Rural selected, coordinated, or arranged these uncopyrightable facts in an original way. As mentioned, originality is not a stringent standard; it does not require that facts be presented in an innovative or surprising way. It is equally true, however, that the selection and arrangement of facts cannot be so mechanical or routine as to require no creativity whatsoever. The standard of originality is low, but it does exist....

The selection, coordination, and arrangement of Rural's white pages do not satisfy the minimum constitutional standards for copyright protection. As mentioned at the outset, Rural's white pages are entirely typical. Persons desiring telephone service in Rural's service area fill out an application and Rural issues them a telephone number. In preparing its white pages, Rural simply takes the data provided by its subscribers and lists it alphabetically by surname. The end product is a garden-variety white pages directory, devoid of even the slightest trace of creativity.

Rural's selection of listings could not be more obvious: it publishes the most basic information—name, town, and telephone number—about each person who applies to it for telephone service. This is "selection" of a sort, but it lacks the modicum of creativity necessary to transform mere selection into copyrightable expression. Rural expended sufficient effort to make the white pages directory useful, but insufficient creativity to make it original.

We note in passing that the selection featured in Rural's white pages may also fail the originality requirement for another reason. Feist points out that Rural did not truly "select" to publish the names and telephone numbers of its subscribers; rather, it was required to do so by the Kansas Corporation Commission as part of its monopoly franchise. *See* 737 F. Supp., at 612. Accordingly, one could plausibly conclude that this selection was dictated by state law, not by Rural.

Nor can Rural claim originality in its coordination and arrangement of facts. The white pages do nothing more than list Rural's subscribers in alphabetical order. This arrangement may, technically speaking, owe its origin to Rural; no one disputes that Rural undertook the task of alphabetizing the names itself. But there is nothing remotely creative about arranging names alphabetically in a white pages directory. It is an age-old practice, firmly rooted in tradition and so commonplace that it has come to be expected as a matter of course. *See* Brief for Information Industry Association et al. as Amici Curiae 10 (alphabetical arrangement "is universally observed in directories published by local exchange telephone companies"). It is not only unoriginal, it is practically inevitable. This time-honored tradition does not possess the minimal creative spark required by the Copyright Act and the Constitution.

We conclude that the names, towns, and telephone numbers copied by Feist were not original to Rural and therefore were not protected by the copyright in Rural's combined white and yellow pages directory. As a constitutional matter, copyright protects only those constituent elements of a work that possess more than a *de minimis* quantum of creativity. Rural's white pages, limited to basic subscriber information and arranged alphabetically, fall short of the mark. As a statutory matter, 17 U.S.C. § 101 does not afford protection from copying to a collection of facts that are selected, coordinated, and arranged in a way that utterly lacks originality. Given that some works must fail, we cannot imagine a more likely candidate. Indeed, were we to hold that Rural's white pages pass muster, it is hard to believe that any collection of facts could fail.

Because Rural's white pages lack the requisite originality, Feist's use of the listings cannot constitute infringement. This decision should not be construed as demeaning Rural's efforts in compiling its directory, but rather as making clear that copyright rewards originality, not effort. As this Court noted more than a century ago, " 'great praise may be due to the plaintiffs for their industry and enterprise in publishing this paper, yet the law does not contemplate their being rewarded in this way.' " *Baker v. Selden,* 101 U.S., at 105.

The judgment of the Court of Appeals is

Reversed.

■ JUSTICE BLACKMUN concurs in the judgment.

QUESTIONS

1. If the *Feist* Court has now told us what is not original in a compilation of information, it has failed to tell us what is. How far beyond the "obvious" and "commonplace" must a compilation's selection and arrangement stretch to be "original"? If, for example, a telephone directory publisher includes unusual information—such as marital status, religion, and educational level—do the listings thereby become copyrightable? Or, because the unusual facts (and their conjunction) are still "facts," does it not follow that they too may be copied?

2. Suppose that a compiler selects an unconventional "universe" to survey, such as all American museums whose collections include works by Andy Warhol. Seeking to make the compilation as comprehensive as possible, she eschews "selection" and follows an alphabetical arrangement. Is the compilation then by definition not original? (Does this accord with the "incentive" rationale for copyright?)

3. In light of the decision in *Feist* and its rationale, could a state prohibit copying a white-page directory? Could Congress do so through the enactment of some federal law other than the Copyright Act?

———

The *Feist* court made clear that the expenditure of "sweat" alone no longer justifies copyright protection of the fruits of labor; there must be a "modicum of creativity." But even if "sweat" is no longer a *sufficient* condition, is it nonetheless a *necessary* condition—i.e., together with minimal creativity must the author also have demonstrated minimal effort or enterprise? Consider the following:

Rockford Map Publishers, Inc. v. Directory Service Co., 768 F.2d 145 (7th Cir.1985), *cert. denied,* 474 U.S. 1061. Defendant challenged copyright protection for plaintiff's map, which was drawn principally from numerical information in public land-title record books; the defense was that plaintiff expended little time and effort in compiling the map that defendant copied. Judge Easterbrook rejected defendant's theory:

> The copyright laws protect the work, not the amount of effort expended. A person who produces a short new work or makes a small improvement in a few hours gets a copyright for that contribution fully as effective as that on a novel written as a life's work. Perhaps the smaller the effort the smaller the contribution; if so, the copyright simply bestows fewer rights. Others can expend the same effort to the same end. Copyright covers, after all, only the incremental contribution and not the underlying information. *Mazer v. Stein,* 347 U.S. 201, 74 S.Ct. 460, 98 L.Ed. 630 (1954).

> The input of time is irrelevant. A photograph may be copyrighted, although it is the work of an instant and its significance may be accidental. *Burrow-Giles Lithographic Co. v. Sarony,* 111 U.S. 53, 4 S.Ct. 279, 28 L.Ed. 349 (1884); *Bleistein v. Donaldson Lithographing Co.,* 188 U.S. 239, 23 S.Ct. 298, 47 L.Ed. 460 (1903); *Time, Inc. v. Bernard Geis Assoc.,* 293 F.Supp. 130 (S.D.N.Y.1968) (Zapruder film of Kennedy assassination). In 14 hours Mozart could write a piano concerto, J.S. Bach a cantata, or Dickens a week's installment of *Bleak House.* The Laffer Curve, an economic graph prominent in political debates, appeared on the back of a napkin after dinner, the work of a minute. All of these are copyrightable.

1. FACTUAL NARRATIVES

Nash v. CBS

899 F.2d 1537 (7th Cir.1990).

■ EASTERBROOK, CIRCUIT JUDGE.

John Dillinger, Public Enemy No. 1, died on July 22, 1934, at the Biograph Theater in Chicago. He emerged from the air conditioned movie palace into a sweltering evening accompanied by two women, one wearing a bright red dress. The "lady in red," Anna Sage, had agreed to betray his presence for $10,000. Agents of the FBI were waiting. Alerted by Polly Hamilton, the other woman, Dillinger wheeled to fire, but it was too late. A hail of bullets cut him down, his .45 automatic unused. William C. Sullivan, The Bureau 30–33 (1979). Now a national historic site, the Biograph bears a plaque commemorating the event. It still shows movies, and the air conditioning is no better now than in 1934.

Jay Robert Nash believes that Dillinger did not die at the Biograph. In *Dillinger: Dead or Alive?* (1970), and *The Dillinger Dossier* (1983), Nash maintains that Dillinger learned about the trap and dispatched Jimmy Lawrence, a small-time hoodlum who looked like him, in his stead. The FBI, mortified that its set-up had no sting, kept the switch quiet. Nash points to discrepancies between Dillinger's physical characteristics and those of the corpse: Dillinger had a scar on his upper lip and the corpse did not; Dillinger lacked a tooth that the corpse possessed; Dillinger had blue eyes, the corpse brown eyes; Dillinger's eyebrows were thicker than those of the corpse. Although Dillinger's sister identified the dead man, Nash finds the circumstances suspicious, and he is struck by the decision of Dillinger's father to encase the corpse in concrete before burial. As part of the cover-up, according to Nash, the FBI planted Dillinger's fingerprints in the morgue. After interviewing many persons connected with Dillinger's gang and the FBI's pursuit of it, Nash tracked Dillinger to the west coast, where Dillinger married and lay low. Nash believes that he survived at least until 1979. The *Dillinger Dossier* contains pictures of a middle-aged couple and then an elderly man who, Nash believes, is Dillinger in dotage. Nash provides capsule versions of his conclusions in his *Bloodletters and Badmen: A Narrative Encyclopedia of American Criminals from the Pilgrims to the Present* (1973), and his expose *Citizen Hoover* (1972).

Nash's reconstruction of the Dillinger story has not won adherents among historians—or the FBI. Someone in Hollywood must have read *The Dillinger Dossier,* however, because in 1984 CBS broadcast an episode of its Simon and Simon series entitled The Dillinger Print. Simon and Simon featured brothers Rick and A.J. Simon, private detectives in San Diego. [The challenged episode was full of plot intricacies and twists, involving a murdered retired FBI agent (who before his death was heard to speculate that Dillinger was not shot dead at the Biograph), a mysterious bank robber wearing clothing from the 1930s and using a gun once belonging to Dillinger and bearing a fresh fingerprint of his, the suggestion by A.J. Simon that Dillinger is alive (relying upon several physical discrepancies between Dillinger and the corpse described in the 1934 autopsy, as did Nash in his book), a shooting by the 1930s-style gangster directed at A.J. while he is playing racquetball, a police tip that Dillinger is living in the home of a San Diego dentist, other intimations that Dillinger lives, another shooting in a closed-down movie theater, a solution of the crime against the retired FBI agent that began the show, and an assertion by Rick Simon that Dillinger is probably alive and well in Oregon.]

Nash filed this suit seeking damages on the theory that The Dillinger Print violates his copyrights in the four books setting out his version of Dillinger's escape from death and new life on the west coast. The district court determined that the books' copyrighted material consists in Nash's presentation and exposition, not in any of the historical events. 691 F. Supp. 140 (N.D.Ill.1988). CBS then moved for summary judgment, conceding for this purpose both access to Nash's books and copying of the books' factual material. The court granted this motion, 704 F. Supp. 823, holding that The Dillinger Print did not appropriate any of the material protected by Nash's copyrights.

. . . CBS's concession . . . leaves the questions whether the copier used matter that the copyright law protects and, if so, whether it took "too much." . . .

Intellectual (and artistic) progress is possible only if each author builds on the work of others. No one invents even a tiny fraction of the ideas that make up our cultural heritage. Once a work has been written and published, any rule requiring people to compensate the author slows progress in literature and art, making useful expressions "too expensive" forcing authors to re-invent the wheel, and so on. Every work uses scraps of thought from thousands of predecessors, far too many to compensate even if the legal system were frictionless, which it isn't. Because any new work depends on others even if unconsciously, broad protection of intellectual property also creates a distinct possibility that the cost of litigation—old authors trying to get a "piece of the action" from current successes—will prevent or penalize the production of new works, even though the claims be rebuffed. Authors as a group therefore might prefer limited protection for their writings—they gain in the ability to use others' works more than they lose in potential royalties. *See* William M. Landes & Richard A. Posner, *An Economic Analysis of Copyright Law,* 18 J. Legal Studies 325, 332–33, 349–59 (1989).

Yet to deny authors all reward for the value their labors contribute to the works of others also will lead to inefficiently little writing, just as surely as excessively broad rights will do. The prospect of reward is an important stimulus for thinking and writing, especially for persons such as Nash who are full-time authors. Before the first work is published, broad protection of intellectual property seems best; after it is published, narrow protection seems best. At each instant some new works are in progress, and every author is simultaneously a creator in part and a borrower in part. In these roles, the same person has different objectives. Yet only one rule can be in force. This single rule must achieve as much as possible of these inconsistent demands. Neither Congress nor the courts has the information that would allow it to determine which is best. Both institutions must muddle through, using not a fixed rule but a sense of the consequences of moving dramatically in either direction.

If Nash had written a novel that another had translated into a screenplay, this would be a difficult case. Although The Dillinger Print is substantially original, it does not matter that almost all of the second author's expression is new. "[N]o plagiarist can excuse the wrong by showing how much of his work he did not pirate." *Sheldon v. Metro–Goldwyn Pictures Corp.,* 81 F.2d 49, 56 (2d Cir.1936) (L. Hand, J.). The TV drama took from Nash's works the idea that Dillinger survived and retired to the west coast, and employed many of the ingredients that Nash used to demonstrate that the man in the Cook County morgue was not Dillinger. . . .

Nash does not portray *The Dillinger Dossier* and its companion works as fiction, however, which makes all the difference. The inventor of Sherlock Holmes controls that character's fate while the copyright lasts; the first person to conclude that Dillinger survived does not get dibs on history. If Dillinger survived, that fact is available to all. Nash's rights lie in his expression: in his words, in his arrangement of facts (his deployment of narration interspersed with interviews, for example), but not in the naked "truth." The Dillinger Print does not use any words from *The Dillinger Dossier* or Nash's other books; it does not take over any of Nash's presentation but instead employs a setting of its own invention with new exposition and development. Physical differences between Dillinger and the corpse, planted fingerprints, photographs of Dillinger and other gangsters in the 1930s, these and all the rest are facts as Nash depicts them. . . .

The cases closest to ours are not plays translated to the movie screen but movies made from speculative works representing themselves as fact. For example, Universal made a motion picture based on the premise that an idealistic crewman planted a bomb that destroyed the dirigible Hindenburg on May 6, 1937. The theory came straight from A.A. Hoehling's *Who Destroyed the Hindenburg?* (1962), a monograph based on exhaustive research. The motion picture added sub-plots and development, but the thesis and the evidence adduced in support of it could be traced to Hoehling. Nonetheless, the Second Circuit concluded that this did not infringe Hoehling's rights, because the book placed the facts (as opposed to Hoehling's exposition) in the public domain. *Hoehling v. Universal City Studios, Inc.,* 618 F.2d 972 (1980). *See also Miller v. Universal City Studios* (facts about a notorious kidnapping are not protected by copyright). . . .

Hoehling suggested that "[t]o avoid a chilling effect on authors who contemplate tackling an historical issue or event, broad latitude must be granted to subsequent authors who make use of historical subject matter, including theories or plots." 618 F.2d at 978. As our opinion in *Toksvig* [*v. Bruce Publishing Co.,* 181 F.2d 664 (7th Cir.1950)] shows, we are not willing to say that "anything goes" as long as the first work is about history. *Toksvig* held that the author of a biography of Hans Christian Andersen infringed the copyright of the author of an earlier biography by using portions of Andersen's letters as well as some of the themes and structure. *Hoehling* rejected *Toksvig,* see 618 F.2d at 979, concluding that "[k]nowledge is expanded . . . by granting new authors of historical works a relatively free hand to build upon the work of their predecessors." *Id.* at 980 (footnote omitted). With respect for our colleagues of the east, we think this goes to the extreme of looking at incentives only *ex post.* The authors in *Hoehling* and *Toksvig* spent years tracking down leads. If all of their work, right down to their words, may be used without compensation, there will be too few original investigations, and facts will not be available on which to build.

In *Toksvig* the first author, who knew Danish, spent three years learning about Andersen's life; the second author, who knew no Danish, wrote her biography in less than a year by copying out of the first book scenes and letters that the original author discovered or translated. Reducing the return on such effort, by allowing unhindered use, would make the initial leg-work less attractive and so less frequent. Copyright law does not protect hard work (divorced from expression), and hard work is not an essential ingredient of copyrightable expression (see *Rockford Map*); to the extent *Toksvig* confuses work or ideas with expression, it has been justly criticized.... We need not revisit *Toksvig* on its own facts to know that it is a mistake to hitch up at either pole of the continuum between granting the first author a right to forbid all similar treatments of history and granting the second author a right to use anything he pleases of the first's work....

... Long before the 1976 revision of the statute [including § 102(b)], courts had decided that historical facts are among the "ideas" and "discoveries" that the statute does not cover. *International News Service v. Associated Press*, 248 U.S. 215, 234 (1918). This is not a natural law; Congress could have made copyright broader (as patent law is). But it is law, which will come as no surprise to Nash. His own books are largely fresh expositions of facts looked up in other people's books. Consider the introduction to the bibliography in *Murder, America: Homicide in the United States from the Revolution to the Present* 447 (1980): The research for this book was done in libraries and archives throughout the United States, in addition to interviews and lengthy correspondence. The author's own files, exceeding more than a quarter of a million separate entries and a personal crime library of more than 25,000 volumes, were heavily employed. The producers of Simon and Simon used Nash's work as Nash has used others': as a source of facts and ideas, to which they added their distinctive overlay. As the district court found, CBS did no more than § 102(b) permits. Because The Dillinger Print uses Nash's analysis of history but none of his expression, the judgment is

Affirmed.

———

Wainwright Securities v. Wall Street Transcript Corp., 558 F.2d 91 (2d Cir.1977), *cert. denied,* 434 U.S. 1014 (1978). Plaintiff, in the institutional research and brokerage business, prepares in-depth analytical reports on industrial, financial, utility and railroad corporations. These reports, which may run as many as forty pages in length, are used by nearly 1,000 Wainwright clients, including major banks, insurance companies and mutual funds. The Wainwright analysts examine a company's financial characteristics, trends in an industry, major developments at a company, growth prospects, and profit expectations, and highlight both corporate strengths and weaknesses. The defendant publishes the Wall Street Transcript, a weekly newspaper—available by subscription and at some newsstands—concerned with economic, business, and financial news. One of the Transcript's major features is the "Wall Street Roundup," a column consisting almost exclusively of abstracts of institutional research reports; advertisements for the Transcript expressly promise its readers "a fast-reading, pinpointed account of heavyweight reports from the top institutional research firms." The following is a typical abstract by the defendant of a Wainwright report:

> W.D. Williams of H.C. Wainwright & Co. says in a Special Report (April 13—7 pp) on FMC CORP. that 1976 prospects are strengthened by the magnitude of the increase in industrial and agricultural chemical earnings in last year's recessionary environment. And second, he says that likely to aid comparisons this year was the surprisingly limited extent to which the Fiber Division's losses shrank last year.
>
> His estimated earnings for 1976 is [sic] $3.76 per share compared with earnings of $3.24 per share in 1975.
>
> According to Williams, one of the most hopeful developments in recent years was the decision by management last year to attempt to negotiate sale of the Fiber Division. He says the company could wind up with possibly $100 million, plus a tax writeoff and a sizable one-time charge against earnings. And, concerning the tanker situation, he writes that the company is now far enough along on the learning curve that additional cost overruns, if any, will be small, the major incremental financial cost to FMC will lie in the determination of what share of the present unreserved overrun is the company's responsibility.

Despite protests from Wainwright, Transcript continued to publish these abstracts, contending among other things that the Wainwright reports were essentially news events and that the Transcript's abstracts were simply financial news coverage. The Court of Appeals for the Second Circuit rejected these contentions.

> It is, of course, axiomatic that "news events" may not be copyrighted.... But in considering the copyright protections due a report of news events or factual developments, it is important to differentiate between the substance of the information contained in the report, i.e., the event itself, and "the particular form or collocation of words in which the writer has communicated it." ... What is protected is the manner of expression, the author's analysis or interpretation of events, the way he structures his material and marshals facts, his choice of words, and the emphasis he gives to particular developments....
>
> Here, the appellants did not bother to distinguish between the events contained in the reports and the manner of expression used by the Wainwright analysts.... Rather, the Transcript appropriated almost verbatim the most creative and original aspects of the reports,

the financial analyses and predictions, which represent a substantial investment of time, money and labor....

The court pointed out a number of side-by-side paraphrases, the defendant's recurrent use of the Wainwright reports, and its apparent efforts to fulfill the demand for the original work, and concluded that "This was not legitimate coverage of a news event; instead it was, and there is no other way to describe it, chiseling for personal profit."

QUESTIONS

1. Should the "facts" as they are comprehensively recounted in an historical narrative be entitled, in whole or in part, to copyright protection? The Supreme Court decision in the *Feist* case may explain why single discrete facts are unprotectible because of their preexistence and the absence of human authorship. But in the writing of a comprehensive history, does not the historian "select, coordinate and arrange" from among a potentially unlimited number of such "facts" so as to create a compilation that should not lawfully be recounted by another, even in freshly generated sentences?

2. In *Hoehling v. Universal City Studios, Inc.*, discussed in *Nash*, the defendant's film incorporated from the plaintiff's historical account of the explosion of the German dirigible Hindenburg his speculation that the Hindenburg had been deliberately sabotaged by a member of its crew to embarrass the Nazi regime. The Court of Appeals for the Second Circuit held that such "explanatory hypotheses" (i.e., speculative historical reconstructions regarding unknowable occurrences and motivations) are just as much in the public domain as are "documented facts." To what extent does the *Nash* court disagree? Did it mean to suggest that the scenes from Hans Christian Andersen's life, uncovered by plaintiff Toksvig after arduous research, were subject to copyright protection? (It disclaims the "sweat of the brow" theory, but how else could such protection be justified?) Which court is correct?

3. The court in *Hoehling* also denied copyright protection to certain sequences of events, such as pre-voyage scenes of the Hindenburg crew in a German beer hall, the singing of songs such as the German national anthem, and the mandatory "Heil Hitler" exchange of greetings. These, the court referred to as *scenes a faire,* i.e., "incidents, characters or settings which are as a practical matter indispensable, or at least standard, in the treatment of a given topic." The court concluded: "Because it is virtually impossible to write about a particular historical era or fictional theme without employing certain 'stock' or standard literary devices, we have held that *scenes a faire* are not copyrightable as a matter of law." Do you see any difficulty with the court's analysis?

For discussions of the concept of "expression" in works of history and of the *Hoehling* decision, compare Gorman, *Fact or Fancy: The Implications for Copyright,* 29 J. Copyright Soc'y 560 (1982), with Ginsburg, *Sabotaging and Reconstructing History: A Comment on the Scope of Copyright Protection in Works of History After Hoehling v. Universal City Studios,* 29 J. Copyright Soc'y 647 (1982).

4. Not too long ago, a journalist on the staff of the Washington Post wrote a lengthy story about the travails of a young African–American boy growing up in an urban ghetto. After she was awarded the Pulitzer Prize for news reporting, it gradually became clear that the journalist's story was totally fabricated; she ultimately admitted so, to the consternation of her newspaper (which accepted her resignation) and the Pulitzer panel (to which the prize was relinquished). If, believing the news story to be truthful, a screen writer prepared a motion picture script based on the life of the youngster as depicted in detail in the Washington Post, and a television or theatrical film were produced and widely exhibited, would the Post (assuming it to be the copyright owner in the underlying article) have a successful claim for infringement? Would it have such a claim if the motion picture were produced *after* the exposure of the hoax? *Compare Houts v. Universal City Studios, Inc.,* 603 F.Supp. 26 (C.D.Cal.1984), *and Huie v. National Broadcasting Co.,* 184 F.Supp. 198 (S.D.N.Y.1960) *with De Acosta v. Brown,* 146 F.2d 408 (2d Cir.1944), *cert. denied,* 325 U.S. 862 (1945), *and Belcher v. Tarbox,* 486 F.2d 1087 (9th Cir.1973).

2. COMPILATIONS

Roth Greeting Cards v. United Card Co., 429 F.2d 1106 (9th Cir.1970). The plaintiff, designer and distributor of greeting cards, claimed infringement on seven cards. These cards consisted of a simple drawing (e.g., a cute moppet suppressing a smile or a forlorn boy sitting on a curb) on the cover and a prosaic phrase on the inside. The trial court found that the artwork, although copyrightable, was not copied by the defendant, and that the text was prosaic and not protectible.

A divided appeals court accepted these conclusions but nonetheless found that the copyright on the card had been infringed. All the judges agreed that the text was indeed too commonplace to be copyrighted, and could have been freely copied alone. The majority stated: "However, proper analysis of the problem requires that all elements of each card, including text, arrangement of text, art work, and association between art work and text, be considered as a whole. Considering all of these elements together, the Roth cards are, in our opinion, both original and copyrightable." To prove infringement, a plaintiff must show that the defendant copied protectible material (a factual conclusion that the appeals court found to be compelled by the record) to the extent that the works in question are substantially similar. "It appears to us that in total concept and feel the cards of United are the same as the copyrighted cards of Roth. [T]he characters depicted in the art work, the mood they portrayed, the combination of art work conveying a particular mood with a particular message, and the arrangement of the words on the greeting card are substantially the same as in Roth's cards. In several instances the lettering is also very similar." Although in each case, the defendant's art work was "somewhat different" from the plaintiff's, the overall cards would be recognizable by an ordinary observer as having been taken from the copyrighted works. (One example given by the court was the plaintiff's card showing a weeping boy, with "I miss you already" on the front of the card, and "and You Haven't even Left" on the inside, and the defendant's card with the same text showing a weeping man.)

The dissenting judge stated: "I cannot ... follow the logic of the majority in holding that the uncopyrightable words and the imitated, but not copied art work, constitutes such total composition as to be subject to protection under the copyright laws. The majority concludes that in the overall arrangement of the text, the art work and the association of the art work to the text, the cards were copyrightable and the copyright infringed. This conclusion, as I view it, results in the whole becoming substantially greater than the sum total of its parts. With this conclusion, of course, I cannot agree.... Feeling, as I do, that the copyright act is a grant of limited monopoly to the authors of creative literature and art, I do not think that we should extend a 56–year monopoly in a situation where neither infringement of text, nor infringement of art work can be found. On these facts, we should adhere to our historic philosophy requiring freedom of competition."

What makes a group of items a "compilation"? The definition of a "compilation" specifies a "work *formed* by the collection and assembling of preexisting materials or of data...." (Emphasis supplied). This implies that the assemblage of the items must have some coherence, that the items must bear some relationship to each other as components of a larger work. In **Sem–Torq, Inc. v. K Mart Corp.,** 936 F.2d 851 (6th Cir.1991), the court confronted the problem of determining whether the items at issue indeed formed a compilation. The plaintiff designed placards with simple phrases on both sides, such as "For Rent" and "For Sale." It decided on the phrases, their pairing, and the lettering and coloring. It marketed such signs in sets of five to stores such as K–Mart, the defendant, which placed them in slotted display stands in its stores; customers could buy single signs apart from the set. The plaintiff learned that a competitor was copying the sets, at K–Mart's suggestion, and was also selling them at K–Mart. Although the plaintiff acknowledged that its individual signs could not be separately copyrighted, it forwarded the set of signs to the Copyright Office for registration as a group; its registration application claimed authorship in selection and arrangement. The Copyright Office registered the copyright, but only after informing the plaintiff that the matter was a close one and that it was relying on its "rule of doubt."

The district court found that the set did not qualify as a compilation; the set of signs "is not an independent work; it is incapable of existing separately from its components. Rather, the plaintiff has created five individual works for which the copyright laws provide no protection." The court of appeals agreed. "Because [a] compilation is protected, while its individual components may not be, '[t]he whole of a compilation is thus greater than the sum of its parts.' ... The set here, however, is no greater than the sum of its individual unprotected parts. The five double-sided signs comprising the set are not sold as a set.... In contrast, copyrightable compilations usually involve a work whose value to consumers is in the combination of its individual parts: a baseball card price guide ... a daily organizer ... and a gardening directory.... The signs are displayed together as a set, but there is no value to the consuming public in this arrangement.... The resulting work, then, is the individual unprotected signs, not the set.''

————

Atari Games Corp. v. Oman, 979 F.2d 242 (D.C.Cir.1992). The Register of Copyrights had previously declined to register as an audiovisual work the videogame called Breakout, and the court of appeals had remanded so that the Register could articulate the standard he had used in finding the game uncopyrightable. Although the district court found that the Register's reiterated denial of registration was not an abuse of discretion, the court of appeals reversed (again), noting the *Feist* Court's statement that "the requisite level of creativity [for copyrightability] is extremely low."

Breakout involves competitive play using paddles to strike a ball against and through a wall, composed of strips of colored rectangular bricks (red, amber, green, yellow), with the paddle changing size, the ball changing speed, and four musical tones sounding. In his second refusal to register Breakout, the Register characterized the representations of the wall, ball, and paddle as "simple geometric shapes and coloring" which "per se are not copyrightable." Even viewing the game "as a whole," the Register found "no original authorship in either the selection or arrangement of the images or their components." He explained: "If the Copyright Office were to examine a painting consisting entirely of rectangles and find it copyrightable, it is important to understand that this decision would be based on creative elements such as depth, perspective, shading, texture of brushstroke, etc. and not on the geometric shapes per se."

The court, however, stated that "[r]ecalling the creativity of the work of Mondrian and Malevich, for example, we note that arrangement itself may be indicative of authorship." Invoking the statutory definitions of a compilation and of an audiovisual work (requiring, among other things, "a series of related images"), the court stated that even if the individual graphic elements of each screen are not copyrightable, "[e]ven so, Breakout would be copyrightable if the requisite level of creativity is met by either the individual screens or the relationship of each screen to the other and/or the accompanying sound effects." The court noted the Register's apparent failure to assess "the flow of the game as a whole," "the entire effect of the game as it appears and sounds," "the sequential aspect of the work." Among the elements that contributed to the "creativity" of the audiovisual elements of the game, the court mentioned the square ball, the rectangular shrinking paddles, "the choice of colors (not the solid red, brown, or white of most brick walls), the placement and design of the scores, the changes in speed, the use of sounds, and the synchronized graphics and sounds which accompany the ball's bounces behind the wall."

The court reversed, for a second time, the summary judgment for the Register, and remanded so that the Register, for a third time, could consider Atari's registration application in a manner consistent with the court's opinion.

QUESTIONS

1. Does the arrangement of three-dimensional elements in physical space create an original work of authorship? Is a stage set copyrightable? The arrangement of paintings and sculpture in an art gallery or museum? The arrangement of furniture in a showroom? In a private home? *See, e.g., Baldine v. Furniture Comfort Corp.,* 956 F.Supp. 580 (M.D.N.C.1996) (arrangement of furniture in showroom).

2. Consider the image below: Is it a compilation? Is it copyrightable?

Swimmer of Liberty, postcard collage by Michael Langenstein
© Michael Langenstein 1977

3. Nostalgia Records is releasing an "oldies" CD, "Disco Queens of the Seventies." Assuming that others hold the copyrights in the songs, and in the separate recorded performances, what would be the basis of any copyright Nostalgia might enjoy in "Disco Queens"?

4. If the designer of T-shirt A brought an action for infringement against the designer of T-shirt B, the court would determine which elements of design A were original and whether design B substantially copied those elements. Assuming that design B was indeed knowingly derived from design A, has there been an unlawful appropriation of copyrightable material? *See Matthews v. Freedman,* 157 F.3d 25 (1st Cir.1998).

T-shirt A

T-shirt B

5. Fred Cantor wrote and published a 60–page book entitled "The Graduates: They Came Out of New York's Public Schools." It contained 57 old high school yearbook photographs of celebrities, selected from among hundreds of thousands of such photographs and organized alphabetically. Maggie Haberman wrote a four-page article for the newspaper *The New York Post*, titled "The Graduates: How Celebs Looked in Their City HS Yearbooks," in which she showed 38 old high school yearbook photographs and matched them with current photos. To save time in compiling her book, 16 of Haberman's photos were taken from the Cantor book. Has Haberman infringed Cantor's copyright? (Are there any other persons who can legitimately complain of copyright infringement?) See *Cantor v. NYP Holdings, Inc.,* 51 F.Supp.2d 309 (S.D.N.Y.1999).

———

Matthew Bender & Co. v. West Pub. Co., 158 F.3d 674 (2d Cir.1998). HyperLaw, Inc. intervened as plaintiff in this declaratory judgment action initiated by the Bender Company. HyperLaw noted its intention to publish certain Supreme Court and federal court of appeals decisions on a compact disc-read only memory (CD–ROM), copying them from the Supreme Court Reporter and the Federal Reporter, which are compiled and published by the West Publishing Company. West incorporates case syllabi (summaries), headnotes and topical key numbers, all authored by its own staff, but HyperLaw intended not to copy those. Rather, HyperLaw intended to copy the text of court opinions (which West acknowledged to be in the public domain), and certain "editorial enhancements" in which West claimed copyright. The trial judge determined that those enhancements—basically factual, and thus protectible if at all as compilations—lacked the "modicum of creativity" required under the *Feist* case. The court of appeals panel (one judge dissenting) agreed, concluding: "In light of accepted legal conventions and other external constraining factors, West's choices on selection and arrangement can reasonably be viewed as obvious, typical, and lacking even minimal creativity."

West claimed copyright, singly and as a group, in four elements in its case reports: (1) the arrangement of information specifying the parties, court and date of decision (e.g., abbreviating parties' names, and the sequencing of the caption, court, docket number and date); (2) the selection and arrangement of attorney information (e.g., naming those on brief as well as those arguing, listing law firm, city and state); (3) the arrangement of information relating to subsequent procedural developments such as amendments to judgment and denials of rehearing; and (4) the selection and inclusion of "parallel and alternative citations" to other published case reports. In all such instances, the West "enhancements" added to or revised the official texts as furnished by the courts. Nonetheless, the Court of Appeals for the Second Circuit concluded that these elements lacked creative authorship and were uncopyrightable.

As to the first category, the court found the case-identification information "insubstantial, unoriginal, and uncreative," dictated by the well-known "Bluebook" governing citation form, and "elementary items, [whose] inclusion is a function of their importance, not West's judgment."

The second category was thought to resemble the directory material declared uncopyrightable in the *Feist* case. As to the third, although subsequent court amendments or orders can indeed be printed in a number of different places, the choices are few and warrant little judgment. And, when a court omits a case citation, or cites to a source that is not readily accessible, and West provides the citation—typically to a West-published reporter (such as the Atlantic Second reports)—"there are few options to begin with, and West's case reporters and Westlaw have the widest availability and have essentially become the standard citation to case law."

> One way of saying that West's "choices" are obvious and typical is that a competitor would have difficulty creating a useful case report without using many of the same citations. Affording these decisions copyright protection could give West an effective monopoly over the commercial publication of case reports....

Nor were the individual parallel and alternative citations rendered protectible through their combination throughout a court opinion:

> The cumulative effect of these citation decisions is a piling up of things that are essentially obvious or trivial (albeit helpful), each in its discrete way in its discrete spot. The whole does not disclose or express an overall creative insight or purpose.... The combined effect of West's non-creative citation decisions cannot be said to be creative....

Finally, the court concluded that West's "overall decision" to group all of the above-described four elements in its case reports "exhibits little, if any, creative insight," even though its editorial work "entails considerable scholarly labor and care." "[F]or West or any other editor of judicial opinions for legal research, faithfulness to the public-domain original is the dominant editorial value, so that the creative is the enemy of the true."

The dissenting judge concluded that West's "selection and arrangement of factual annotations to public domain judicial opinions, considered as a whole, is copyrightable." He criticized the panel majority for applying a creativity standard that exceeded the "modicum" and "non-trivial" standard set out in the *Feist* decision. West makes "dozens of multi-part, variable judgments" that are based on its "assessments of readability, clarity, completeness, availability (present and future) of sources, and other subjective considerations related to making the reports more useful." West's several enhancements should not be "atomized"; the "cumulative and collective originality manifest in West's case reports satisfies the '*de minimis*' level needed for the work as a whole to be copyrightable." "The copyright granted West is thin, but it is sufficient to protect against the verbatim digital copying proposed by Hyperlaw," lest "the economic incentive to engage in this kind of original and productive enterprise would largely evaporate."

QUESTIONS

1. Review each of the various editorial "enhancements" inserted by West into the official text of court opinions, and assess the number of different options that West could have utilized. For example, what kinds of information about the lawyers involved in the case might West have incorporated, and what form and placement might it have used? Was the court correct, on each issue, in characterizing the West choice among options as trivial and commonplace? Would your conclusion be affected if West could prove that it devised certain enhancements before they were incorporated in the Bluebook and thus became widely adopted as the editorial standards?

2.   Apart from each individual "enhancement" viewed separately, are you satisfied that the incorporation by West of all of its enhancements in their totality does not constitute a copyrightable compilation? Is the court correct in stating that individual enhancements that are trivial in isolation gain no greater protectibility when considered in the aggregate? Could not West reasonably have decided to "select" other bits of information for inclusion, or to "select out" certain bits that it regularly includes? Would the protection against copying of the collection of West enhancements create a significant risk of interference with the socially useful dissemination of judicial decisions by others?

————

Matthew Bender & Co. v. West Publishing Co., 158 F.3d 693 (2d Cir.1998). In a companion case to the one just set forth, the Court of Appeals for the Second Circuit confronted yet another declaratory-judgment action brought by legal publishers Bender and Hyperlaw. Here, however, the declaratory plaintiffs challenged West's claim that their insertion, into their CD–ROM products containing court decisions, of the page-break numbers in the West hard-copy law reporters infringed West's copyright in its case compilations. The court affirmed the grant of summary judgment for Bender and Hyperlaw. Its principal emphasis was upon its conclusion that the incorporation of such "star pagination" did not—given the nature and uses of a CD–ROM—constitute a "copy" of the sequence or arrangement of court decisions as organized and published in the West hard-copy reporters. The court also ruled against West on the issue of the copyrightability of its case arrangement as reflected in its pagination. The court gave short shrift to West's argument:

> West concedes that insertion of parallel citations (identifying the volume and first page numbers on which a particular case appears) to West's case reporters in plaintiffs' products (as well as any other compilations of judicial opinions) is permissible under the fair use doctrine.... West admitted at oral argument ... that these parallel citations already allow a user of plaintiffs' CD–ROM discs to perceive West's arrangements with the aid of a machine and that plaintiff's CD–ROM discs therefore already have created a lawful "copy" of West's arrangement on their CD–ROM discs—as West defines "copy."

Once the copy of West's arrangement of cases has thus been created through parallel citation—assuming that anyone would wish to avail themselves of the capability of perceiving this copy—the only incremental data made perceivable (through the aid of a machine) by star pagination is the location of page breaks within each judicial opinion. But since page breaks do not result from any original creation by West, their location may be lawfully copied. We therefore conclude that star pagination's volume and page numbers merely convey unprotected information, and that their duplication does not infringe West's copyright.... Prohibiting star pagination would simply allow West to protect unoriginal elements of its compilation that have assumed importance and value....

The court acknowledged that its conclusion was contrary to two decisions in the Eighth Circuit, but concluded that those cases were incorrectly decided. The dissenting judge, however, found them persuasive.

West Publishing Co. v. Mead Data Central, Inc., 799 F.2d 1219 (8th Cir.1986). This was one of those contrary decisions. There, the defendant MDC was the developer, owner and operator of Lexis, a computerized on-line legal research service; it had announced its intention to insert star-paging into its database and resulting screen display of judicial decisions, thus reiterating the page breaks in the West hard-copy reporters. The court concluded that West's arrangement of cases into its various geographic reporters was copyrightable ("West has used sufficient talent and industry in compiling and arranging cases to entitle it to copyright protection ... "); that Mead/Lexis star-paging would infringe that arrangement ("[T]he copyright we recognize here is in West's arrangement, not in its numbering system; MDC's use of West's page numbers is problematic because it infringes West's copyrighted arrangement, not because the numbers themselves are copyrighted."); and that a preliminary injunction should issue. The parties ultimately entered into an agreement settling and dismissing the case, with Mead agreeing to pay West undisclosed license fees for the right to incorporate star-paging into the Lexis on-line case reports. The decision in this case was followed in *Oasis Pub'g Co. v. West Pub. Co.*, 924 F.Supp. 918 (D.Minn.1996).

Since the decision and settlement in the *Lexis* case, legal and business developments have reshaped both the parties and the issues that were before the Eighth Circuit Court of Appeals. The major legal development, of course, has been the Supreme Court decision in the *Feist* case; many have viewed that decision as undermining not only the emphasis of the *Lexis* court upon West's "industry" in compiling judicial opinions but also West's claim of "originality" in the sequencing and arranging of those opinions. The major business development has been a dramatic change in the structure of the law publishing industry, through mergers and acquisitions. In seeking judicial approval for the acquisition of the West Publishing Company by the Thomson Publishing Company, those companies agreed to make licenses available to any interested publisher, on financial terms approved by the court, for star-pagination keyed to the West page breaks.

QUESTIONS

1. The student should examine a West advance sheet or bound volume, perhaps of the Federal (Third) Reporter, the Federal Supplement (Second) Reporter, or the regional reporter in his or her state. Is the sequencing principle discernible, and is it original under the law of copyright? Of course, West makes the initial decision to "coordinate" cases in a particular reporter series, such as the Federal Rules Decisions and the Northeast Reporter (which includes Illinois); it then sequences decisions through a mix of alphabetical, geographic and chronological criteria (making exceptions for certain anomalies, such as companion cases and reheard cases). Does this satisfy the pertinent requirements for "creativity"?

2. Why did West concede that Lexis, Matthew Bender and Hyperlaw were free to incorporate the first page of a West-reported decision into their digital on-line or CD–ROM products? Why did West, however, challenge their incorporation of its page breaks? Was the *Matthew Bender* court correct in holding that the former concession altogether undermined the latter contention?

3. The *Matthew Bender* court also concluded that the West page breaks were unoriginal, apparently because they were a fortuitous product of the decision about the layout and format of the page in the West reporters. First, if West decides on such matters as whether the text is to run across the page or to be in two vertical columns, and what size type to use, why should that not be sufficient to justify protection of its page breaks? Second, and more fundamentally, why should originality and copyright protection turn upon the subjective process of generating page numbers? (Should a publisher of public-domain musical scores for string quartet players get copyright in its page breaks, if it decides where to "break" the pages so as to minimize haste and inconvenience to the instrumentalists?)

CCC Information Services v. Maclean Hunter Market Reports, Inc.

44 F.3d 61 (2d Cir.1994).

■ LEVAL, CIRCUIT JUDGE:

The appellant, publisher of a compendium of its projections of used car valuations, seeks to establish copyright infringement on the part of a competitor, which copied substantial portions of appellant's compendium into the computer data base of used car valuations it offers to its customers. Arising in the wake of the Supreme Court's decision in *Feist Publications, Inc. v. Rural Telephone Serv. Co.*, 499 U.S. 340 (1991), this appeal raises the question of the scope of protection afforded by the copyright law to such compilations of informational matter. Finding no infringement, the district court granted summary judgment to the appellee. In our view, the copyright law offers more substantial protection to such compilations than envisioned in the district court's ruling. We therefore reverse.

Background

The Red Book. The appellant is Maclean Hunter Market Reports, Inc. ("Maclean"). Since 1911, Maclean, or its predecessors, have published the Automobile Red Book—Official Used Car Valuations (the "Red Book"). The Red Book, which is published eight times a year, in different versions for each of three regions of the United States (as well as a version for the State of Wisconsin), sets forth the editors' projections of the values for the next six weeks of "average" versions of most of the used cars (up to seven years old) sold in that region. These predicted values are set forth separately for each automobile make, model number, body style, and engine type. [The] Red Book also provides predicted value adjustments for various options and for mileage in 5,000 mile increments.

The valuation figures given in the Red Book are not historical market prices, quotations, or averages; nor are they derived by mathematical formulas from available statistics. They represent, rather, the Maclean editors' predictions, based on a wide variety of informational sources and their professional judgment, of expected values for "average" vehicles for the upcoming six weeks in a broad region. The introductory text asserts, "You, the subscriber, must be the final judge of the actual value of a particular vehicle. Any guide book is a supplement to and not a substitute for expertise in the complex field of used vehicle valuation."

CCC's computer services. Appellee CCC Information Services, Inc. ("CCC"), is also in the business of providing its customers with information as to the valuation of used vehicles. Rather than publishing a book, however, CCC provides information to its customers through a computer data base. Since at least 1988, CCC has itself been systematically loading major portions of the Red Book onto its computer network and republishing Red Book information in various forms to its customers.

CCC utilizes and resells the Red Book valuations in several different forms. CCC's "VINguard Valuation Service" ("VVS") provides subscribers with the average of a vehicle's Red Book valuation and its valuation in the NADA Official Used Car Guide (the "Bluebook"), the other leading valuation book, published by the National Automobile Dealers Association ("NADA"). The offer of this average of Red Book and Bluebook satisfies a market because the laws of certain states use that average figure as a minimum for insurance payments upon the "total loss" of a vehicle. CCC's "Computerized Valuation Service" ("CVS"), while it primarily provides its subscribers with CCC's independent valuation of used cars, also provides customers with the Red Book/Bluebook average and the Red Book values standing alone.

It is uncontested that CCC earns significant revenues through the sale of its services, in which it both directly and indirectly resells the figures it copies every few weeks from the Red Book. As the court found below, since 1988 numerous Red Book customers have canceled their subscriptions, opting instead to purchase CCC's services.

Proceedings below. CCC brought this action in 1991, seeking, *inter alia*, a declaratory judgment that it incurred no liability to Maclean under the copyright laws by taking and republishing material from the Red Book. Maclean counterclaimed alleging infringement. [The district judge entered summary judgment in favor of CCC, agreeing with the conclusions of a magistrate that the Redbook lacked creativity in selection, coordination and arrangement; that its valuations were uncopyrightable facts; that there was "merger" of the idea of valuing cars and the dollar figures set forth; and that the Redbook was placed in the public domain by being "incorporated into governmental regulations" for insurance-claim purposes.]

Discussion

1. *Does the Red Book manifest originality so as to be protected by the copyright laws?* The first significant question raised by this appeal is whether Maclean holds a protected copyright interest in the Red Book. CCC contends, and the district court held, that the Red Book is nothing more than a compilation of unprotected facts, selected and organized without originality or creativity, and therefore unprotected under the Supreme Court's teachings in *Feist*. We disagree. . . .

The protection of compilations is consistent with the objectives of the copyright law, which are, as dictated by the Constitution, to promote the advancement of knowledge and learning by giving authors economic incentives (in the form of exclusive rights to their creations) to labor on creative, knowledge-enriching works. Compilations that devise new and useful selections and arrangements of information unquestionably contribute to public knowledge by providing cheaper, easier, and better organized access to information. Without financial incentives, creators of such useful compilations might direct their energies elsewhere, depriving the public of their creations and impeding the advance of learning. The grant of such monopoly protection to the original elements of a compilation, furthermore, imposes little cost or disadvantage to society. The facts set forth in the compilation are not protected and may be freely copied; the protection extends only to those aspects of the compilation that embody the original creation of the compiler. For these reasons, the copyright law undertakes to guarantee the exclusive rights of compilers, like other authors, to whatever is original and creative in their works, even where those original contributions are quite minimal.

The thrust of the Supreme Court's ruling in *Feist* was not to erect a high barrier of originality requirement. It was rather to specify, rejecting the strain of lower court rulings that sought to base protection on the "sweat of the brow," that some originality is essential to protection of authorship, and that the protection afforded extends only to those original elements. Because the protection is so limited, there is no reason under the policies of the copyright law to demand a high degree of originality. To the contrary, such a requirement would be counterproductive. The policy embodied into law is to encourage authors to publish innovations for the common good—not to threaten them with loss of their livelihood if their works of authorship are found insufficiently imaginative. . . .

The district court gave several reasons for its ruling that the Red Book failed the test for originality. First, the court stated, "Maclean Hunter has not persuasively demonstrated that the values published in the Red Book are anything more than interpretations or analyses of factual information. . . . While Maclean Hunter may have been the first to discover and report this material, the material does not 'owe its origin' to Maclean Hunter."

The district court was simply mistaken in its conclusion that the Red Book valuations were, like the telephone numbers in *Feist,* pre-existing facts that had merely been discovered by the Red Book editors. To the contrary, Maclean's evidence demonstrated without rebuttal that its valuations were neither reports of historical prices nor mechanical derivations of historical prices or other data. Rather, they represented predictions by the Red Book editors of future prices estimated to cover specified geographic regions. According to Maclean's evidence, these predictions were based not only on a multitude of data sources, but also on professional judgment and expertise. The testimony of one of Maclean's deposition witnesses indicated that fifteen considerations are weighed; among the considerations, for example, is a prediction as to how traditional competitor vehicles, as defined by Maclean, will fare against one another in the marketplace in the coming period. The valuations themselves are original creations of Maclean.

Recognizing that "originality may also be found in the selection and ordering of particular facts or elements," the district court concluded that none had been shown. This was because the Red Book's selection and arrangement of data represents "a logical response to the needs of the vehicle valuation market." In reaching this conclusion, the district court applied the wrong standard. The fact that an arrangement of data responds logically to the needs of the market for which the compilation was prepared does not negate originality. To the contrary, the use of logic to solve the problems of how best to present the information being compiled is independent creation. See *Feist,* 499 U.S. at 359 (originality is to be found unless the creative spark is so utterly lacking as to be "virtually nonexistent").

We find that the selection and arrangement of data in the Red Book displayed amply sufficient originality to pass the low threshold requirement to earn copyright protection. This originality was expressed, for example, in Maclean's division of the national used car market into several regions, with independent predicted valuations for each region depending on conditions there found. A car model does not command the same value throughout a large geographic sector of the United States; used car values are responsive to local conditions and vary from place to place. A 1989 Dodge Caravan will not command the same price in San Diego as in Seattle. In furnishing a single number to cover vast regions that undoubtedly contain innumerable variations, the Red Book expresses a loose judgment that values are likely to group together with greater consistency within a defined region than without. The number produced is necessarily both approximate and original. Several other aspects of the Red Book listings also embody sufficient originality to pass *Feist*'s low threshold. These include: (1) the selection and manner of presentation of optional features for inclusion;[7] (2) the adjustment for mileage by 5,000 mile increments (as opposed to using some other breakpoint and interval); (3) the use of the abstract concept of the "average" vehicle in each category as the subject of the valuation; and (4) the selection of the number of years' models to be included in the compilation.

We conclude for these reasons that the district court erred in ruling that the Red Book commands no copyright protection by reason of lack of originality.

2. *The idea-expression dichotomy and the merger of necessary expression with the ideas expressed.* CCC's strongest argument is that it took nothing more than ideas, for which the copyright law affords no protection to the author. According to this argument, (1) each entry in the Red Book expresses the authors' idea of the value of a particular vehicle; (2) to the extent that "expression" is to be found in the Red Book's valuations, such expression is indispensable to the statement of the idea and therefore merges with the idea, so that the expression is also not protectible, and; (3) because each of Red Book's valuations could freely be taken without infringement, all of them may be taken without infringement. This was one of the alternate bases of the district court's ruling in CCC's favor.

The argument is not easily rebutted, for it does build on classically accepted copyright doctrine. It has been long accepted that copyright protection does not extend to ideas; it protects only the means of expression employed by the author....

It is also well established that, in order to protect the immunity of ideas from private ownership, when the expression is essential to the statement of the idea, the expression also will be unprotected, so as to insure free public access to the discussion of the idea....

[I]f CCC's argument prevails, for reasons explained below, virtually nothing will remain of the protection accorded by the statute to compilations, notwithstanding the express command of the copyright statute.

Given the nature of compilations, it is almost inevitable that the original contributions of the compilers will consist of *ideas*. Originality in *selection*, for example, will involve the compiler's idea of the utility to the consumer of a limited selection from the particular universe of available data. One compiler might select out of a universe of all businesses those that he believes will be of interest to the Chinese–American community, see *Key Publications*, 945 F.2d at 514, another will select those statistics as to racehorses or pitchers that are believed to be practical to the consumer in

---

7. This selection includes far fewer than all extant options, and presents them in a manner that furnishes a single valuation to cover the particular option in numerous different vehicles. The editors make these choices to accommodate the practical space limitations imposed by the book's format, while providing the information most likely to satisfy customers' needs.

helping to pick winners, see *Kregos,* 937 F.2d at 706–07; *Wabash Publishing Co. v. Flanagan,* No. 89 Civ. 1923, 1989 U.S. Dist. LEXIS 3546 (N.D. Ill. Mar. 31, 1989) (particular selection and arrangement of information relevant to horse races found copyrightable); *Triangle Publishing, Inc. v. New England Newspaper Publications Co.,* 46 F. Supp. 198, 201–02 (D.Mass.1942) (same); another will offer a list of restaurants he suggests are the best, the most elegant, or offer the best value within a price range. Each of these exercises in selection represents an idea.

In other compilations, the original contribution of the compiler will relate to ideas for the coordination, or arrangement of the data. Such ideas for arrangement are generally designed to serve the consumers' needs, making the data more useful by increasing the ease of access to those data that answer the needs of the targeted customers, or dividing the data in ways that will efficiently serve the needs of more diverse groups of customers. For example, a listing of New York restaurants might be broken down by geographic areas of the city, specialty or type (e.g., seafood, steaks and chops, vegetarian, kosher, Chinese, Indian); price range; handicapped accessibility, etc.

It is apparent that virtually any independent creation of the compiler as to selection, coordination, or arrangement will be designed to add to the usefulness or desirability of his compendium for targeted groups of potential customers, and will represent an idea. In the case of a compilation, furthermore, such structural ideas are likely to be expressed in the most simple, unadorned, and direct fashion. If, as CCC argues, the doctrine of merger permits the wholesale copier of a compilation to take the individual expression of such ideas, so as to avoid the risk that an idea will improperly achieve protection, then the protection explicitly conferred on compilations by Section 103 of the U.S. Copyright Act will be illusory.

We addressed precisely this problem in *Kregos,* 937 F.2d 700. The plaintiff Kregos had created a form to be used to help predict the outcome of a baseball game by filling in nine statistics of the competing pitchers. The defendant contended, in terms similar to CCC's argument, that the copyright owner's idea was the utility of the nine selected statistics in helping a fan predict the outcome, and that the idea was merged in the expression of it—in the copyrighted form that listed those nine statistics. Judge Newman wrote:

> In one sense, every compilation of facts can be considered to represent a merger of an idea with its expression. Every compiler of facts has the idea that his particular selection of facts is useful. If the compiler's idea is identified at that low level of abstraction, then the idea would always merge into the compiler's expression of it. Under that approach, there could never be a copyrightable compilation of facts.

Kregos, 937 F.2d at 706.

Recognizing that the purpose of the doctrine of merger of expression with idea is to insure that protection not extend to ideas, the *Kregos* opinion went on to describe different categories of ideas. It distinguished between, on the one hand, those ideas that undertake to advance the understanding of phenomena or the solution of problems, such as the identification of the symptoms that are the most useful in identifying the presence of a particular disease; and those, like the pitching form there at issue, that do not undertake to explain phenomena or furnish solutions, but are infused with the author's taste or opinion. *Kregos* postulated that the importance of keeping ideas free from private ownership is far greater for ideas of the first category, directed to the understanding of phenomena or the solving of problems, than for those that merely represent the author's taste or opinion and therefore do not materially assist the understanding of future thinkers. . . .

Because Kregos's idea was of the soft type infused with taste or opinion, the court withheld application of the merger doctrine, permitting Kregos to exercise ownership. It accomplished this by assigning to the idea a different level of abstraction from the expression of it, so that the merger doctrine would not apply and the copyright owner would not lose protection.[23] ("His 'idea,' for purposes of the merger doctrine, remains the general idea that statistics can be used to assess pitching performance rather than the precise idea that his selection yields a determinable probability of outcome." 937 F.2d at 707.) . . .

Application of the *Kregos* approach to our facts leads us to the conclusion that the district court should, as in *Kregos,* have "withheld" the merger doctrine. As a matter of copyright policy, this was not an appropriate instance to apply the merger doctrine so as to deprive [the] Red Book of copyright protection. The consequences of giving CCC the benefit of the merger doctrine are too destructive of the protection the Act intends to confer on compilations, without sufficient benefit to the policy of copyright that seeks to preserve public access to ideas.

In the first place, the takings by CCC from the Red Book are of virtually the entire compendium. This is not an instance of copying of a few entries from a compilation. This copying is so extensive that CCC effectively offers to sell its customers Maclean's Red Book through CCC's data base. CCC's invocation of the merger doctrine to justify its contention that it has

---

23. Professor Robert Gorman has written that protection of compilations is more strongly suggested where the "works are more fanciful than functional, and where the selection criteria are driven by subjective and evaluative judgment. . . ." Robert A. Gorman, *The Feist Case: Reflections on a Pathbreaking Copyright Decision,* 18 Rutgers Computer & Tech. L.J. 731, 751 (1992). *See also* Ginsburg, *No "Sweat"? Copyright and Other Protection of Works of Information After Feist v. Rural Telephone,* 92 Colum. L. Rev. 338, 345 (1992). *Compare Hoehling v. Universal City Studios, Inc.,* 618 F.2d 972 (2d Cir.), *cert. denied,* 449 U.S. 841, 66 L. Ed. 2d 49, 101 S. Ct. 121 (1980) (denying protection to historical theory explaining destruction of Hindenburg dirigible) *with Eckes,* 736 F.2d at 863 (granting protection to identification of "premium" baseball cards because of personal subjectivity of the selection). The *Hoehling* opinion justified the denial of protection to historical analysis on the theory that "knowledge is expanded . . . by granting new authors of historical works a relatively free hand to build upon the work of their predecessors." 618 F.2d at 980.

taken no protectible matter would effectively destroy all protection for Maclean's compilation.[26]

Secondly, the valuations copied by CCC from the Red Book are not ideas of the first, building-block, category described in *Kregos,* but are rather in the category of approximative statements of opinion by the Red Book editors. To the extent that protection of the Red Book would impair free circulation of any ideas, these are ideas of the weaker category, infused with opinion; the valuations explain nothing, and describe no method, process or procedure. . . . Because the ideas contained in the Red Book are of the weaker, suggestion-opinion category, a withholding of the merger doctrine would not seriously impair the policy of the copyright law that seeks to preserve free public access to ideas. If the public's access to Red Book's valuations is slightly limited by enforcement of its copyright against CCC's wholesale copying, this will not inflict injury on the opportunity for public debate, nor restrict access to the kind of idea that illuminates our understanding of the phenomena that surround us or of useful processes to solve our problems. In contrast, if the merger doctrine were applied so as to bar Maclean's enforcement of its copyright against CCC's wholesale takings, this would seriously undermine the protections guaranteed by section 103 of the Copyright Act to compilations that employ original creation in their selection, coordination, or arrangement. It would also largely vitiate the inducements offered by the copyright law to the makers of original useful compilations.

3. *Public domain.* We disagree also with the district court's ruling sustaining CCC's affirmative defense that the Red Book has fallen into the public domain. The district court reasoned that, because the insurance statutes or regulations of several states establish Red Book values as an alternative standard, i.e., by requiring that insurance payments for total losses be at least equal either to Red Book value or to an average of Red Book and Bluebook values (unless another approved valuation method is employed), the Red Book has passed into the public domain. The argument is that the public must have free access to the content of the laws that govern it; if a copyrighted work is incorporated into the laws, the public need for access to the content of the laws requires the elimination of the copyright protection. . . .

We are not prepared to hold that a state's reference to a copyrighted work as a legal standard for valuation results in loss of the copyright. While there are indeed policy considerations that support CCC's argument, they

---

26. In this circuit, consideration of the merger doctrine takes place in light of the alleged copying to determine if infringement has occurred, rather than in analyzing the copyrightability of the original work. *Kregos,* 937 F.2d at 705; *Durham Industries, Inc. v. Tomy Corp.,* 630 F.2d 905, 916 (2d Cir.1980). This approach is applauded by Nimmer as the "better view." 13.03[B] at 13–76 to 78. As we noted in *Kregos,* "assessing merger in the context of alleged infringement will normally provide a more detailed and realistic basis for evaluating the claim that protection of expression would inevitably accord protection to an idea." *Kregos,* 937 F.2d at 705. In the instant case, for example, it is of consequence that we are confronted with wholesale copying of a compilation rather than some more limited copying *from* a compilation.

are opposed by countervailing considerations. For example, a rule that the adoption of such a reference by a state legislature or administrative body deprived the copyright owner of its property would raise very substantial problems under the Takings Clause of the Constitution. We note also that for generations, state education systems have assigned books under copyright to comply with a mandatory school curriculum. It scarcely extends CCC's argument to require that all such assigned books lose their copyright—as one cannot comply with the legal requirements without using the copyrighted works. Yet we think it unlikely courts would reach this conclusion. Although there is scant authority on CCC's argument, Nimmer's treatise opposes such a suggestion as antithetical to the interests sought to be advanced by the Copyright Act. See Nimmer § 5.06[C] at 5–60.[30]

Conclusion

Because Maclean has demonstrated a valid copyright, and an infringement thereof, we direct the entry of judgment in Maclean's favor. We remand to the district court for further proceedings.

BellSouth Advertising & Publishing Corp. v. Donnelley Information Publishing, Inc., 999 F.2d 1436 (11th Cir. en banc 1993). BellSouth (BAPCO) publishes a yellow-page directory covering the Miami, Florida area. All parties concede that, in light of the wide range of materials included, the directory is copyrightable. Donnelley, employing a computer key-punch company to extract information from the BAPCO directory, created a computer database containing the name, address, and telephone number of the telephone subscribers placing advertisements, along with an alphanumeric code indicating the size and type of advertisement, and a similar code indicating the type of business (based on the classified page headings in the BAPCO directory). Donnelley used this database to produce printed lists of this information ("lead sheets"), which it used to contact these BAPCO subscribers to sell them advertising space in the competing Donnelley yellow-page directory. BAPCO sued for copyright infringement. Donnelley admitted to copying the material from BAPCO (including certain erroneous entries purposely inserted by BAPCO in its directory), but asserted that this material was not copyrightable; BAPCO, however, argued that its selection, coordination and arrangement of data satisfied the originality requirement as elaborated by the Supreme Court two years before in *Feist v. Rural Tel. Service.* A divided en banc court of appeals granted Donnelley summary judgment.

30. Nimmer argues that the adoption of a private work into law might well justify a fair use defense for personal use, but should not immunize a competitive commercial publisher from liability since this would "prove destructive of the copyright interest in encouraging creativity in connection with the increasing trend toward state and federal adoptions of model codes." Nimmer, § 5.06[C] at 5–60.

The court held that BAPCO's choice of a geographic area and a closing date for its yellow-page listings was not copyrightable, relying on implications from *Feist* itself and the fact that any collection of facts must have such parameters. Most fundamentally, the court held that "BAPCO's arrangement and coordination is 'entirely typical' for a business directory" and "practically inevitable." It concluded that organizing businesses alphabetically under alphabetical classified headings is "the one way to construct a useful business directory," so that the arrangement has "merged" with the idea of such a directory. The coordination of a particular business with a particular classified heading was an uncopyrightable fact; in any event, Donnelley "selected a somewhat different category of headings" for those listings. Nor did the BAPCO structure of headings contain original expression; headings such as "Attorneys" or "Banks" are obvious, just as BAPCO could not claim copyright in its division of churches by denomination or attorneys by practice specialty. Also, "many of BAPCO's headings result from certain standard industry practices, such as the recommendations of the National Yellow Pages Sales Association (NYPSA), with regard to the selection and phrasing of headings in business directories." And it is the subscriber itself, not BAPCO, which selects where to list its name among alternative available headings. Nor did Donnelley copy "the text or graphic material from the advertisements in the BAPCO directory, the positioning of these advertisements, the typeface, or the textual material included by BAPCO to assist the user." Donnelley copied a great deal quantitatively, but it did not "appropriate whatever original elements might arguably inhere in the BAPCO directory."

The lone dissenting judge disagreed with the majority at almost every point. He did acknowledge that the alphabetical sequencing of headings and of included business listings, and the linkage of name, address and telephone number, were not protectible. But he would have found originality in BAPCO's selection of classified headings (7,000 from the nearly 40,000 headings listed in the BAPCO headings book), and in its departure from the menu of classified headings used in NYPSA publications. Even Donnelley had conceded that heading selection is shaped by the local marketing picture. Moreover, the dissenting judge concluded that it was the representatives of BAPCO, rather than of the subscriber-advertiser, who decided where among alternative headings a company should be listed: with some 106,000 business listings grouped under 7,000 headings, this selection-coordination process was not "obvious" or "mechanical." As to the selection decision regarding "geographic scoping," the dissenter agreed with BAPCO that its selection of a geographic area is not determined simply based on the scope of a white-page directory for the same community, but is instead selected based on BAPCO's evaluation of the shopping habits and desired shopping areas of consumers within a white-pages community. These were not "obvious" decisions relating to the selection and coordination of data, and Donnelley copied them—when it stored the data in its computerized database on magnetic tapes (linking by code number the subscriber's name, address and telephone number with its classified heading and information about its advertisement), when it printed out its lead sheets, and when Donnelley then generated "a directory substantially similar in both content and format."

QUESTIONS

1. The plaintiff compiled a reference guidebook of information designed for companies that own and operate pay telephones. Of its 160 pages, 51 (one for each state and one for the District of Columbia) summarized state tariffs regulating the fees payable to telephone utilities. The plaintiff employed several attorneys to comb the state tariffs and "collapse" them into a simple and readable format. The defendant has copied the 51 pages into its own book on the same subject. Has it infringed? See *U.S. Payphone, Inc. v. Executives Unlimited,*, 931 F.2d 888 (4th Cir.1991).

2. A law school publishes an alumni directory containing three parts. In the first, the names of alumni (along with their home and business addresses and telephone numbers) are organized alphabetically; in the second, they are organized by graduating classes (and alphabetically within those); and, in the third, they are organized by state and city (and alphabetically within those). You have been asked whether the directory is copyrightable. Are there any additional elements of "authorship" that the law school might contribute in order to provide greater assurance of copyrightability? See *Skinder-Strauss Assocs. v. Massachusetts Continuing Legal Ed., Inc.,* 914 F.Supp. 665 (D.Mass.1995).

3. Is the Dow Jones Industrial Index copyrightable? This index is based upon 30 selected stocks, representing a variety of major business corporations, whose collective performance, in the belief of the compilers of the Index, affords a good indication of stock market trends. *See Dow Jones & Co. v. Board of Trade*, 546 F.Supp. 113 (S.D.N.Y.1982).

EXTRA–COPYRIGHT PROTECTION OF DATABASES

In March 1996, the European Parliament and the Council of the European Union issued Directive 96/9/EC on the legal protection of databases. O.J.E.C. No. L 777/20 (23.3.96). The Directive instructs the 15 member nations of the European Union to harmonize their laws to a uniform standard of copyright protection for databases, defined as "a collection of independent works, data or other materials arranged in a systematic or methodical way and individually accessible by electronic or other means." Art. 1.2. The Directive's standard of copyright protection appears to be equivalent to the U.S.-law *Feist* standard. *See* Art. 3.

But the Directive goes beyond copyright protection. Recognizing that copyright does not protect the compiled information against rearrangement or partial selection, the EC Commission created a new *sui generis* right to prevent "extraction" and "reutilization" of a "substantial part" of databases manifesting "qualitatively or quantitatively a substantial investment in either the obtaining, verification or presentation of the contents...." Art. 7.1.

The Directive specifies that the *sui generis* right "shall apply irrespective of the eligibility of that database for protection by copyright or by other rights. Moreover, it shall apply irrespective of eligibility of the contents of that database for protection by copyright or by other rights." In U.S. terms, the E.C. Directive protects the compiler's "sweat of the brow." For example, under the Directive, a comprehensive, alphabetically-arranged telephone book would be protected, not only as an unoriginal whole, but also with respect to substantial portions of its listings. As a result, the Directive supplies an answer to the "thin copyright" problem. The beneficiaries of the *sui generis* right are EC nationals, residents, and companies incorporated or having their principal place of business within the Community. (Art. 11.) Non–E.C. databases will not receive *sui generis* protection against extraction or reutilization of their contents in the E.C. unless, upon the Commission's recommendation, the European Council concludes an agreement with the foreign database's source country. (Art. 11.) The Commission is not likely to recommend concluding an agreement unless the foreign country extends "comparable" protection to E.C. databases.

In the aftermath of *Feist*, it is clear that U.S. copyright law does not protect the compiler's investment. Yet databases and other information compilations are an important object of international, as well as domestic, American trade. The E.C.'s reciprocity requirement thus puts considerable pressure on the U.S. and other database-producing countries outside the E.U. to provide additional protection outside of copyright for compilations. Indeed, passage of the E.C. Directive has spurred legislative activity in the U.S., and a draft treaty by the World Intellectual Property Organization (WIPO). The latter document was scheduled for discussion at the WIPO diplomatic conference held in Geneva in December 1996, but was tabled.

As for U.S. domestic initiatives, in May 1996, Representative Moorhead introduced H.R. 3531, 104th Cong., 2d Sess., the "Database Investment and Intellectual Property Antipiracy Act of 1996." Representative Moorhead's introductory remarks refer to the E.C. measure, and stress that "[w]hen fully implemented in 1998, the European Directive could place U.S. firms at an enormous competitive disadvantage throughout the entire European market." The 104th Congress terminated without enacting database legislation.

In the 105th Congress, a new database protection bill, H.R. 2652, the "Collections of Information Antipiracy Act," passed the House but failed in the Senate. The House Bill was reintroduced in the 106th Congress, H.R. 354, but failed to pass. At the time this edition went to press, no bills had yet been introduced in the 107th Congress, though some were in prospect. The "Collections of Information Antipiracy Act" departs somewhat from the European Union model: instead of articulating a *sui generis* property right in databases, the bill grants information collectors a tort claim against certain forms of misappropriation.

Pertinent provisions of H.R. 354, as initially introduced, follow. As you review them, consider whether they afford effective protection for information compilations. Is the protection excessive? What other interests should

Congress take into account? Has it? Finally, recall that *Feist* declared originality to be a "constitutional requirement." Does Congress have power to enact a statute of the kind set forth below? *Compare United States v. Moghadam*, 175 F.3d 1269 (11th Cir.1999) (constitutionality of § 1101 protecting unfixed musical performances).

Collections of Information Antipiracy Act

H.R. 354, 106th Cong., 1st Sess. (1998).

§ 1401. *Definitions*

As used in this chapter:

(1) COLLECTION OF INFORMATION: The term "collection of information" means information that has been collected and has been organized for the purpose of bringing discrete items of information together in one place or through one source so that users may access them.

(2) INFORMATION: The term "information" means facts, data, works of authorship, or any other intangible material capable of being collected and organized in a systematic way.

(3) POTENTIAL MARKET: The term "potential market" means any market that a person claiming protection under section 1202 has current and demonstrable plans to exploit or that is commonly exploited by persons offering similar products or services incorporating collections of information.

(4) COMMERCE: The term "commerce" means all commerce which may be lawfully regulated by the Congress.

§ 1402. *Prohibition against misappropriation*

Any person who extracts, or uses in commerce, all or a substantial part, measured either quantitatively or qualitatively, of a collection of information gathered, organized, or maintained by another person through the investment of substantial monetary or other resources, so as to cause harm to the actual or potential market of that other person, or a successor in interest of that other person, for a product or service that incorporates that collection of information and is offered or intended to be offered for sale or otherwise in commerce by that other person, or a successor in interest of that person, shall be liable to that person or successor in interest for the remedies set forth in section 1406.

§ 1403. *Permitted acts*

(a) EDUCATIONAL SCIENTIFIC, RESEARCH, AND ADDITIONAL REASONABLE USES.—

(1) CERTAIN NONPROFIT EDUCATIONAL, SCIENTIFIC, OR RESEARCH USES— Notwithstanding section 1402, no person shall be restricted from extracting or using information for nonprofit educational, scientific, or research purposes in a manner that does not harm directly the actual market for the product or service referred to in section 1402.

(2) ADDITIONAL REASONABLE USES—

(A) IN GENERAL—Notwithstanding section 1402, an individual act of use or extraction of information done for the purpose of illustration, explanation, example, comment, criticism, teaching, research, or analysis, in an amount appropriate and customary for that purpose, is not a violation of this chapter, if it is reasonable under the circumstances. In determining whether such an act is reasonable under the circumstances, the following factors shall be considered:

(i) The extent to which the use or extraction is commercial or nonprofit.

(ii) The good faith of the person making the use or extraction.

(iii) The extent to which and the manner in which the portion used or extracted is incorporated into an independent work or collection, and the degree of difference between the collection from which the use or extraction is made and the independent work or collection.

(iv) Whether the collection from which the use or extraction is made is primarily developed for or marketed to persons engaged in the same field or business as the person making the use or extraction.

In no case shall a use or extraction be permitted under this paragraph if the used or extracted portion is offered or intended to be offered for sale or otherwise in commerce and is likely to serve as a market substitute for all or part of the collection from which the use or extraction is made.

(B) DEFINITION—For purposes of this paragraph, the term "individual act" means an act that is not part of a pattern, system, or repeated practice by the same party, related parties, or parties acting in concert with respect to the same collection of information or a series of related collections of information.

(b) INDIVIDUAL ITEMS OF INFORMATION AND OTHER INSUBSTANTIAL PARTS: Nothing in this chapter shall prevent the extraction or use of an individual item of information, or other insubstantial part of a collection of information, in itself. An individual item of information, including a work of authorship, shall not itself be considered a substantial part of a collection of information under section 1402. Nothing in this subsection shall permit the repeated or systematic extraction or use of individual items or insubstantial parts of a collection of information so as to circumvent the prohibition contained in section 1402.

(c) GATHERING OR USE OF INFORMATION OBTAINED THROUGH OTHER MEANS: Nothing in this chapter shall restrict any person from independently gathering information or using information obtained by means other than extracting it from a collection of information gathered, organized, or maintained by another person through the investment of substantial monetary or other resources.

(d) USE OF INFORMATION FOR VERIFICATION: Nothing in this chapter shall restrict any person from extracting information, or from using information within any entity or organization, for the sole purpose of verifying the accuracy of information independently gathered, organized, or maintained by that person. Under no circumstances shall the information so extracted or used be made available to others in a manner that harms the actual or potential market for the collection of information from which it is extracted or used.

(e) NEWS REPORTING: Nothing in this chapter shall restrict any person from extracting or using information for the sole purpose of news reporting, including news gathering, dissemination, and comment, unless the information so extracted or used is time sensitive, has been gathered by a news reporting entity, and the extraction or use is part of a consistent pattern engaged in for the purpose of direct competition.

(f) TRANSFER OF COPY: Nothing in this chapter shall restrict the owner of a particular lawfully made copy of all or part of a collection of information from selling or otherwise disposing of the possession of that copy.

§ 1404. *Exclusions*

(a) GOVERNMENT COLLECTIONS OF INFORMATION.—

(1) EXCLUSION: Protection under this chapter shall not extend to collections of information gathered, organized, or maintained by or for a government entity, whether Federal, State, or local, including any employee or agent of such entity, or any person exclusively licensed by such entity, within the scope of the employment, agency, or license. Nothing in this subsection shall preclude protection under this chapter for information gathered, organized, or maintained by such an agent or licensee that is not within the scope of such agency or license, or by a Federal or State educational institution in the course of engaging in education or scholarship.

. . .

§ 1405. *Relationship to other laws*

(a) OTHER RIGHTS NOT AFFECTED: . . . [N]othing in this chapter shall affect rights, limitations, or remedies concerning copyright, or any other rights or obligations relating to information, including laws with respect to patent, trademark, design rights, antitrust, trade secrets, privacy, access to public documents, and the law of contract.

. . .

(c) RELATIONSHIP TO COPYRIGHT.—Protection under this chapter is independent of, and does not affect or enlarge the scope, duration, ownership, or subsistence of, any copyright protection or limitation, including, but not limited to, fair use, in any work of authorship that is contained in or consists in whole or part of a collection of information. . . .

(d) ANTITRUST.—Nothing in this chapter shall limit in any way the constraints on the manner in which products and services may be provided to the public that are imposed by Federal and State antitrust laws, including those regarding single suppliers of products and services.

. . .

[Section 1406 provides for civil remedies, including injunction, damages and profits. Monetary relief is to be reduced or remitted entirely if the defendant is an employee of a nonprofit educational, scientific, library or research institution, acted within the scope of employment, and reasonably believed that his or her conduct was permissible. Section 1407 provides for criminal liability for willful violation of section 1402. Section 1408 provides for a three-year statute of limitations for both civil and criminal actions.]

§ 1408.   Limitations on Actions

. . .

(c) ADDITIONAL LIMITATION.—No criminal or civil action shall be maintained under this chapter for the extraction or use of all or a substantial part of a collection of information that occurs more than 15 years after the portion of the collection that is extracted or used was first offered for sale of otherwise in commerce, following the investment of resources that qualified that portion of the collection for protection under this chapter. In no case shall any protection under this chapter resulting from a substantial investment of resources in maintaining a preexisting collection prevent any use or extraction of information from a copy of the preexisting collection after the 15 years have expired with respect to the portion of that preexisting collection that is so used or extracted, and no liability shall thereafter attach to such acts of use or extraction.

Mason v. Montgomery Data, Inc.

967 F.2d 135 (5th Cir.1992).

■ REAVLEY, CIRCUIT JUDGE:

Hodge E. Mason, Hodge Mason Maps, Inc., and Hodge Mason Engineers, Inc. (collectively Mason) sued Montgomery Data, Inc. (MDI), Landata, Inc. of Houston (Landata), and Conroe Title & Abstract Co. (Conroe Title), claiming that the defendants infringed Mason's copyrights on 233 real estate ownership maps of Montgomery County, Texas. The district court initially held that Mason cannot recover statutory damages or attorney's fees for any infringement of 232 of the copyrights. The court later held that Mason's maps are not copyrightable under the idea/expression merger doctrine, and granted summary judgment for the defendants. We agree with Mason that the maps are copyrightable, so we reverse the district court's judgment and remand the case. But we agree with the district court that, if Mason proves that the defendants infringed his copyrights, he can only recover statutory damages and attorney's fees for the infringements of one of the 233 maps.

I. BACKGROUND

Between August 1967 and July 1969, Mason created and published 118 real estate ownership maps that, together, cover all of Montgomery County. The maps, which display copyright notices, pictorially portray the location, size, and shape of surveys, land grants, tracts, and various topographical features within the county. Numbers and words on the maps identify deeds, abstract numbers, acreage, and the owners of the various tracts. Mason obtained the information that he included on the maps from a variety of sources.[3] Relying on these sources, Mason initially determined the location and dimensions of each survey in the county, and then drew the corners and lines of the surveys onto topographical maps of the county that were published by the United States Geological Survey (USGS).[4] He then determined the location of the property lines of the real estate tracts within each survey and drew them on the USGS maps. Finally, Mason traced the survey and tract lines onto transparent overlays, enlarged clean USGS maps and the overlays, added names and other information to the overlays, and combined the maps and overlays to print the final maps. Mason testified that he used substantial judgment and discretion to reconcile inconsistencies among the various sources, to select which features to include in the final map sheets, and to portray the information in a manner that would be useful to the public. From 1970 to 1980, Mason revised the original maps and eventually published 115 new maps with copyright notices, for a total of 233 maps. Mason sold copies of his maps individually and in sets.

Mason's infringement claims are based on the defendants' use of his maps as part of a geographical indexing system that Landata created to continuously organize and store ever-changing title information on each tract in Montgomery County. [Landata used Mason's maps, in a reconfigured format, to prepare its own overlays and other copies, on which it recorded continuously updated information about land grants; it keyed these copies to land-title data that it stored in its computers. Landata, by contractual arrangements with a company known as MDI, made these copies and data available to several title-insurance companies, which had jointly incorporated MDI. Landata had asked Mason for permission to use his maps as part of its system, but when Mason denied the request because Landata refused to pay a licensing fee, Landata used the Mason maps anyway. Landata prepared updated overlays and copies, using the Mason maps, between 1982 and 1989.]

---

3. These sources included tax, deed, and survey records from Montgomery County; data provided by the San Jacinto River Authority; survey records, maps, and abstracts of land titles from the Texas General Land Office; title data and subdivision information provided by Conroe Title; a map from the City of Conroe, Texas; and maps from the United States Coast and Geodetic Survey.

4. The USGS has mapped much of the United States, including Montgomery County. Most private mapmakers, like Mason, use USGS topographical maps as starting points for their own maps. *See* David B. Wolf, *Is There Any Copyright Protection for Maps after Feist?,* 39 J. Copyright Soc'y USA 224, 226 (1992).

[Mason registered the copyright for one of the original 118 maps in October 1968. After learning of Landata's use of his maps, Mason registered the copyrights for the remaining 117 original maps and the 115 revised maps between October and December 1987. On motions for summary judgment, the district court dismissed Mason's claims, finding that his maps were uncopyrightable, because the "idea" embodied in them was inseparable from the maps' "expression" of that idea.]

II.   DISCUSSION

A.   *The Copyrightability of Mason's Maps*

1.   *The Idea/Expression Merger Doctrine*

.   .   .

We agree with Mason that the district court erred in applying the merger doctrine in this case. To determine whether the doctrine is applicable in any case, the court must "focus on whether the idea is capable of various modes of expression." *Apple Computer,* 714 F.2d at 1253. Thus, the court must first identify the idea that the work expresses, and then attempt to distinguish that idea from the author's expression of it. If the court concludes that the idea and its expression are inseparable, then the merger doctrine applies and the expression will not be protected. Conversely, if the court can distinguish the idea from its expression, then the expression will be protected because the fact that one author has copyrighted one expression of that idea will not prevent other authors from creating and copyrighting their own expressions of the same idea. In all cases, "[t]he guiding consideration in drawing the line is the preservation of the balance between competition and protection reflected in the patent and copyright laws." *Herbert Rosenthal Jewelry,* 446 F.2d at 742.

The district court determined that Mason's idea, "which includes drawing the abstract and tract boundaries, indicating the ownership name, the tract size, and the other factual information" on a map of Montgomery County, was "to create the maps, based on legal and factual public information." *Mason,* 765 F. Supp. at 356. Mason argues that the court clearly erred in finding that this idea can be expressed in only one or a limited number of ways. We agree. The record in this case contains copies of maps created by Mason's competitors that prove beyond dispute that the idea embodied in Mason's maps is capable of a variety of expressions. Although the competitors' maps and Mason's maps embody the same idea, they differ in the placement, size, and dimensions of numerous surveys, tracts, and other features. The record also contains affidavits in which licensed surveyors and experienced mapmakers explain that the differences between Mason's maps and those of his competitors are the natural result of each mapmaker's selection of sources, interpretation of those sources, discretion in reconciling inconsistencies among the sources, and skill and judgment in depicting the information.[6]

6. One of the experts, Pliny M. Gale, examined Mason's maps and the competitors' maps and concluded that: the assembly, graphic representation, and positioning of

MDI argues that this evidence is irrelevant because there is no proof that Mason and his competitors obtained their information from the same sources. But the fact that different mapmakers with the same idea could reach different conclusions by relying on different sources only supports our result. Whether Mason and his competitors relied on different sources, or interpreted the same sources and resolved inconsistencies among them differently, or made different judgments as to how to best depict the information from those sources, the differences in their maps confirm the fact that the idea embodied in Mason's maps can be expressed in a variety of ways. By selecting different sources, or by resolving inconsistencies among the same sources differently, or by coordinating, arranging, or even drawing the information differently, other mapmakers may create—and indeed have created—expressions of Mason's idea that differ from those that Mason created.

. . .

We focus in this case on an earlier point in the mapping process, a point prior to the selection of information and decisions where to locate tract lines. The idea here was to bring together the available information on boundaries, landmarks, and ownership, and to choose locations and an effective pictorial expression of those locations. That idea and its final expression are separated by Mason's efforts and creativity that are entitled to protection from competitors.... Extending protection to that expression will not grant Mason a monopoly over the idea, because other mapmakers can express the same idea differently. The protection that each map receives extends only to its original expression, and neither the facts nor the idea embodied in the maps is protected. "[T]he facts and ideas ... are free for the taking.... [T]he very same facts and ideas may be divorced from the context imposed by the author, and restated or reshuffled by second comers, even if the author was the first to discover the facts or to propose the ideas." *Feist,* 111 S. Ct. at 1289 (quoting Jane C. Ginsburg,

various records and features involves considerable skill, judgment and originality.... The differences I note between the Mason maps and the other maps which I have examined are to be expected because of the numerous interpretations of records, individual judgments, and map base selection which must be taken into account when producing an ownership map based on a large number of instruments spanning over 100 years of development.... In my inspection of the maps, I found that the Mason map includes many features which are unique to the graphic representations selected by Mason, and which do not appear in any public record information. Gale Aff. at 2–4. Another mapmaker, Milton R. Hanks, stated: In compiling a map as detailed and complex as the Mason maps of Montgomery County, the mapmaker will necessarily make many individual judgments in placing various features from various sets of records onto a single map.... When the Mason map is overlaid with the Tobin map at the same scale ..., many differences in placement of various features and surveys are readily observed. The differences between the two maps are exactly the sort of differences that I would expect to observe between two independently produced maps based on the same ancient records. The reason for the differences is that a large number of independent judgments must be made in any large-scale mapping project of this type. Hanks Aff. at 2, 5.

Creation and Commercial Value: Copyright Protection of Works of Information, 90 Colum. L. Rev. 1865, 1868 (1990)).

For these reasons, we conclude that the district court erred by applying the merger doctrine in this case. Because the idea embodied in Mason's maps can be expressed in a variety of ways, the merger doctrine does not render Mason's expression of that idea uncopyrightable.

2. *The "Originality" Requirement*

Landata contends that, even if the merger doctrine does not apply, Mason's maps are uncopyrightable because they are not "original" under *Feist.* Although the district court applied the merger doctrine to hold that Mason's maps are not copyrightable, it found that "the problem with the Hodge Mason maps is not a lack of originality." *Mason,* 765 F. Supp. at 355. We agree that Mason's maps are original. Originality does not require "novelty, ingenuity, or aesthetic merit." H.R. Rep. No. 1476, 94th Cong., 2d Sess. 51 (1976), reprinted in 1976 U.S.C.C.A.N. 5659, 5664; *see also Feist,* 111 S. Ct. at 1287. Instead, originality "means only that the work was independently created by the author (as opposed to copied from other works), and that it possesses at least some minimal degree of creativity." *Feist,* 111 S. Ct. at 1287 (citing 1 M. Nimmer & D. Nimmer, Copyright § 2.01[A]-[B] (1990)). The parties do not dispute Mason's claim that he independently created his maps, but Landata contends that they do not possess the degree of creativity necessary to qualify them as original under *Feist.*

.   .   .

[T]he evidence in this case demonstrates that Mason exercised sufficient creativity when he created his maps. In his deposition and affidavit, Mason explained the choices that he independently made to select information from numerous and sometimes conflicting sources, and to depict that information on his maps. Mason's compilation of the information on his maps involved creativity that far exceeds the required minimum level.

Mason's maps also possess sufficient creativity to merit copyright protection as pictorial and graphic works of authorship. Historically, most courts have treated maps solely as compilations of facts. *See* Wolf, *supra* note 4, at 227. The Copyright Act, however, categorizes maps not as factual compilations but as "pictorial, graphic, and sculptural works"—a category that includes photographs and architectural plans. 17 U.S.C.A. § 101 (West Supp. 1992). Some courts have recognized that maps, unlike telephone directories and other factual compilations, have an inherent pictorial or photographic nature that merits copyright protection. *See, e.g., Rockford Map Publishers, Inc. v. Directory Service Co.,* 768 F.2d 145, 149 (7th Cir.1985) ("Teasing pictures from the debris left by conveyancers is a substantial change in the form of the information. The result is copyrightable...."), *cert. denied,* 474 U.S. 1061, 106 S. Ct. 806, 88 L. Ed. 2d 781 (1986); *United States v. Hamilton,* 583 F.2d 448, 451 (9th Cir.1978) ("Expression in cartography is not so different from other artistic forms seeking to touch upon external realities that unique rules are needed to judge whether the authorship is original."). We agree with these courts.

The level of creativity required to make a work of authorship original "is extremely low; even a slight amount will suffice." *Feist,* 111 S. Ct. at 1287. We think that the process by which Mason, using his own skill and judgment, pictorially portrayed his understanding of the reality in Montgomery County by drawing lines and symbols in particular relation to one another easily exceeds that level.

Because Mason's maps possess sufficient creativity in both the selection, coordination, and arrangement of the facts that they depict, and the pictorial, graphic nature of the way that they do so, we find no error in the district court's determination that Mason's maps are original.

———

For a decision on similar issues of "merger" with respect to architectural plans for a site-specific building, see *CSM Investors, Inc. v. Everest Dev., Ltd.,* 840 F.Supp. 1304 (D.Minn.1994).

QUESTIONS

1. Are you convinced that the plaintiff's claim is not fatally undermined by the *Feist* case, which finds a lack of authorship in works that are commonplace, time-honored, garden-variety, and practically inevitable? On the other hand, would reference by the plaintiff to the 1790 Copyright Act, protecting "maps, charts [nautical maps], and books," be altogether conclusive in his favor?

2. Would a person using Mason's maps infringe—i.e., would it be copying copyrightable material—if it used his painstakingly detailed information about land boundaries to devise a chart with columns, names and numbers, repeating in tabular form the data that Mason had inscribed in pictorial form? *Compare Rand McNally & Co. v. Fleet Mgt. Sys.,* 634 F.Supp. 604 (N.D.Ill.1986).

D. DERIVATIVE WORKS

L. Batlin & Son v. Snyder
536 F.2d 486 (2d Cir. *en banc* 1976).

■ OAKES, CIRCUIT JUDGE: [The trial court issued an injunction directed against Jeffrey Snyder and his company, the distributor of a plastic "Uncle Sam bank," cancelling their recordation of copyright with the U.S. Customs Service and restraining them from enforcing that copyright.]

Uncle Sam mechanical banks have been on the American scene at least since June 8, 1886, when Design Patent No. 16,723, issued on a toy savings bank of its type. The basic delightful design has long since been in the public domain. The banks are well documented in collectors' books and known to the average person interested in Americana. A description of the bank is that Uncle Sam, dressed in his usual stove pipe hat, blue full dress coat, starred vest and red and white striped trousers, and leaning on his umbrella, stands on a four-or five-inch wide base, on which sits his carpetbag. A coin may be placed in Uncle Sam's extended hand. When a lever is pressed, the arm lowers, and the coin falls into the bag, while Uncle Sam's whiskers move up and down. The base has an embossed American eagle on it with the words "Uncle Sam" on streamers above it, as well as the word "Bank" on each side. Such a bank is listed in a number of collectors' books, the most recent of which may be F. H. Griffith, Mechanical Banks (1972 ed.) where it was listed as No. 280, and is said to be not particularly rare.

[Snyder traveled to Hong Kong to arrange for the design and manufacture of plastic replicas of a cast iron Uncle Sam bank. He arranged for Unitoy to manufacture a bank shortened from 11 to 9 inches, with a narrower and shorter base than the metal bank; the bank was so designed to fit within the desired price range and the quantity and quality of material. The shape of the carpet bag was changed, and the umbrella—detached from the leg of the iron bank—was included in a one-piece mold to facilitate manufacture. The Unitoy representative drew a sketch from the iron bank and then designed a plastic prototype which Snyder approved. The Snyder bank was manufactured, had a copyright notice, and copyright was registered with the Copyright Office. Appellee Batlin also arranged for the manufacture of a plastic Uncle Sam bank in Hong Kong,

Original Cast Iron Bank

Snyder Plastic Bank

but the U.S. Customs Service refused to allow importation because of alleged infringement of Snyder's copyright. Batlin sought a judgment declaring Snyder's copyright void, and the Second Circuit concluded that the trial judge did not abuse his discretion in issuing a preliminary injunction.]

This court has examined both the appellants' plastic Uncle Sam bank made under Snyder's copyright and the uncopyrighted model cast iron mechanical bank which is itself a reproduction of the original public domain Uncle Sam bank. Appellant Snyder claims differences not only of size but also in a number of other very minute details: the carpetbag shape of the plastic bank is smooth, the iron bank rough; the metal bank bag is fatter at its base; the eagle on the front of the platform in the metal bank is holding arrows in his talons while in the plastic bank he clutches leaves, this change concededly having been made, however, because "the arrows did not reproduce well in plastic on a smaller size." The shape of Uncle Sam's face is supposedly different, as is the shape and texture of the hats, according to the Snyder affidavit. In the metal version the umbrella is hanging loose while in the plastic item it is included in the single mold. The texture of the clothing, the hairline, shape of the bow tie and of the shirt collar and left arm as well as the flag carrying the name on the base of the statue are all claimed to be different, along with the shape and texture of the eagles on the side. Many of these differences are not perceptible to the casual observer. Appellants make no claim for any difference based on the plastic mold lines in the Uncle Sam figure which are perceptible.

Our examination of the banks results in the same conclusion as that of Judge Metzner in *Etna Products,* the earlier case enjoining Snyder's copyright, that the Snyder bank is "extremely similar to the cast iron bank, save in size and material" with the only other differences, such as the shape of the satchel and the leaves in the eagle's talons being "by all appearances, minor." Similarities include, more importantly, the appearance and number of stripes on the trousers; buttons on the coat, and stars on the vest and hat, the attire and pose of Uncle Sam, the decor on his base and bag, the overall color scheme, the method of carpetbag opening, to name but a few. [The court below saw the banks and heard] conflicting testimony from opposing expert witnesses as to the substantiality or triviality of the variations and as to the skill necessary to make the plastic model. . . .

. . . The substance of appellee's expert's testimony on which the district judge evidently relied was that the variations found in appellants' plastic bank were merely "trivial" and that it was a reproduction of the metal bank made as simply as possible for the purposes of manufacture. In other words, there were no elements of difference that amounted to significant alteration or that had any purpose other than the functional one of making a more suitable (and probably less expensive) figure in the plastic medium.

. . . It has been the law of this circuit for at least 30 years that in order to obtain a copyright upon a reproduction of a work of art under 17 U.S.C.

§ 5(h) that the work "contain some substantial, not merely trivial originality...." *Chamberlin v. Uris Sales Corp., supra,* 150 F.2d at 513.

Originality is, however, distinguished from novelty; there must be independent creation, but it need not be invention in the sense of striking uniqueness, ingeniousness, or novelty, since the Constitution differentiates "authors" and their "writings" from "inventors" and their "discoveries."

   . . .

[We] follow the school of cases in this circuit and elsewhere supporting the proposition that to support a copyright there must be at least some substantial variation, not merely a trivial variation such as might occur in the translation to a different medium.

Nor can the requirement of originality be satisfied simply by the demonstration of "physical skill" or "special training" which, to be sure, Judge Metzner found was required for the production of the plastic molds that furnished the basis for appellants' plastic bank. A considerably *higher* degree of skill is required, true artistic skill, to make the reproduction copyrightable. Thus in *Alfred Bell & Co. v. Catalda Fine Arts, Inc., supra,* 191 F.2d at 104–05 n.22, Judge Frank pointed out that the mezzotint engraver's art there concerned required "great labour and talent" to effectuate the "management of light and shade ... produced by different lines and ...," means "very different from those employed by the painter or draughtsman from whom he copies...." *See also Millworth Converting Corp. v. Slifka, supra* (fabric designer required one month of work to give three-dimensional color effect to flat surface). Here on the basis of appellants' own expert's testimony it took the Unitoy representative "[a]bout a day and a half, two days work" to produce the plastic mold sculpture from the metal Uncle Sam bank. If there be a point in the copyright law pertaining to reproductions at which sheer artistic skill and effort can act as a substitute for the requirement of substantial variation, it was not reached here.

Appellants rely heavily upon *Alva Studios, Inc. v. Winninger* [177 F. Supp. 265 (S.D.N.Y.1959)] the "Hand of God" case, where the court held that "great skill and originality [were required] to produce a scale reduction of a great work with exactitude." 177 F. Supp. at 267. There, the original sculpture was, "one of the most intricate pieces of sculpture ever created" with "[i]nnumerable planes, lines and geometric patterns ... interdependent in [a] multi-dimensional work." *Id.* Originality was found by the district court to consist primarily in the fact that "[i]t takes 'an extremely skilled sculptor' many hours working directly in front of the original" to effectuate a scale reduction. *Id.* at 266. The court, indeed, found the exact replica to be so original, distinct, and creative as to constitute a work of art in itself. The complexity and exactitude there involved distinguishes that case amply from the one at bar. As appellants themselves have pointed out, there are a number of trivial differences or deviations from the original public domain cast iron bank in their plastic reproduction. Thus concededly the plastic version is not, and was scarcely meticulously produced to be, an exactly faithful reproduction. Nor is the creativity in the underlying work of art of the same order of magnitude as in the case of the "Hand of God." Rodin's sculpture is, furthermore, so unique and rare, and adequate public access to it such a problem that a significant public benefit accrues from its precise, artistic reproduction. No such benefit can be imagined to accrue here from the "knock-off" reproduction of the cast iron Uncle Sam bank. Thus appellants' plastic bank is neither in the category of exactitude required by *Alva Studios* nor in a category of substantial originality; it falls within what has been suggested by the amicus curiae is a copyright no-man's land.

Absent a genuine difference between the underlying work of art and the copy of it for which protection is sought, the public interest in promoting progress in the arts—indeed, the constitutional demand, *Chamberlin v. Uris Sales Corp., supra*— could hardly be served. To extend copyrightability to minuscule variations would simply put a weapon for harassment in the hands of mischievous copiers intent on appropriating and monopolizing public domain work. . . .

Judgment affirmed.

■ MESKILL, CIRCUIT JUDGE (dissenting) (with whom TIMBERS and VAN GRAAFEILAND, CIRCUIT JUDGES, concur): I respectfully dissent.

In the instant case the author has contributed substantially more than a merely trivial variation. "Any 'distinguishable variation' of a prior work will constitute sufficient originality to support a copyright if such variation is the product of the author's independent efforts, and is more than merely trivial." 1 Nimmer on Copyright § 10.1 at 34.2. In accord with the purposes of the copyright law to promote progress by encouraging individual effort through copyright protection, we should require only minimal variations to find copyrightability. The independent sculpting of the mold for the plastic bank and the aggregated differences in size and conformation of the figurine should satisfy this standard.

The plastic bank in question admittedly is based on a work now in the public domain. This does not render it uncopyrightable since "[i]t is hornbook [law] that a new and original plan or combination of existing materials in the public domain is sufficiently original to come within the copyright protection. . . ." *Alva Studios, Inc. v. Winninger,* 177 F. Supp. 265, 267 (S.D.N.Y.1959). The courts have repeatedly emphasized that only a modest level of originality is necessary to be eligible for a copyright. . . . *Dan Kasoff, Inc. v. Novelty Jewelry Co., Inc.,* 309 F.2d 745, 746 (2d Cir.1962), where this Court required only a "faint trace of originality" to support a copyright. . . .

Finally, there are also cases where *no* changes were required because the process of reproduction itself required great skill. . . .

Turning to the case at bar, Judge Metzner made a factual finding that the plastic bank embodied only trivial variations from the bank in the public domain. . . . I make no claim that the process of sculpting involved here is as complex as in *Alva·Studios* (scaled version of Rodin sculpture) or in *Alfred Bell* (mezzotint engravings of art classics). However, those cases depended solely on difficulty of process to establish originality, since there was no attempt to alter or improve upon the underlying work.

The most obvious differences between the two exhibits in this case are size and medium. While these factors alone may not be sufficient to render a work copyrightable, they surely may be considered along with the other variations. On the other hand, the author's reasons for making changes should be irrelevant to a determination of whether the differences are trivial. As noted in *Alfred Bell, supra,* 191 F.2d at 105, even an inadvertent variation can form the basis of a valid copyright. After the fact speculation as to whether Snyder made changes for aesthetic or functional reasons should not be the basis of decision.

The primary variations between the two banks involve height; medium; anatomical proportions of the Uncle Sam figure, including shape and expression of face; design of the clothing (hat, tie, shirt, collar, trousers); detail around the eagle figure on the platform; placement of the umbrella; and the shape and texture of the satchel. Granting Snyder a copyright protecting these variations would ensure only that no one could copy his particular version of the bank now in the public domain, i.e., protection from someone using Snyder's figurine to slavishly copy and make a mold....

This approach seems quite in accord with the purpose of the copyright statute—to promote progress by encouraging individual effort through copyright protection. The relatively low standard of originality required for copyrightability is derived from this purpose....

Accordingly, I would reverse the district court decision.

ORIGINALITY IN DERIVATIVE WORKS

Recall *Bell v. Catalda*, Chapter 1, *supra*, in which the Second Circuit held plaintiff's mezzotint engravings of Old Master paintings to be original, emphasizing the skill, labor and judgment necessary to make a quality art reproduction. *Alva Studios, Inc. v. Winninger*, 177 F.Supp. 265 (S.D.N.Y. 1959), takes this principle one step further, finding originality in the "extreme skill" and "many hours" required to make a scale reduction of Auguste Rodin's sculpture, "The Hand of God." Does this suggest that reproductions of artworks will qualify for protection as derivative works only if their creation required a great deal of skill and labor? What does this suggest about photographic reproductions of works of art? *See, e.g., Bridgeman Art Library, Ltd. v. Corel Corp.*, 36 F.Supp.2d 191 (S.D.N.Y. 1999). Does it, or should it, matter if the photograph portrays a work that was originally in two or in three dimensions?

Whether or not a derivative work, to be protectible, requires expenditure of more "sweat" than would a work not based on a prior work (a debatable proposition, post-*Feist*), it may need to manifest more creativity. The *Batlin* case endorses a standard of "originality" for authorized derivative works that is arguably stiffer than that which obtains for copyrightable works generally. It cannot be said with confidence that *Batlin* announces the prevailing view regarding derivative works, and the decisions even within the Second Circuit are somewhat difficult to reconcile with one another. That court reaffirmed the *Batlin* approach in *Durham Indus., Inc. v. Tomy Corp.*, 630 F.2d 905 (2d Cir.1980), involving Tomy's authorized wind-up plastic figures based upon the Disney characters Mickey Mouse, Donald Duck, and Pluto Dog; those figures were admittedly copied by Durham without consent. The court found that "the three Tomy figures are instantly identifiable as embodiments of the Disney characters in yet another form," and rejected the contention "that the originality requirement of copyrightability can be satisfied by the mere reproduction of a work of art in a different medium, or by the demonstration of some 'physical' as opposed to 'artistic' skill." The court found "no independent creation, no distinguishable variation from preexisting works, nothing recognizably the author's own contribution that sets Tomy's figures apart from the prototypical Mickey, Donald, and Pluto." The court observed that persons whom Disney licensed to copy its characters might otherwise, in order to avoid lawsuits by prior licensees, have to make substantial changes in the Disney characters; "In theory, of course, there would be no infringement of Tomy's rights if Durham copied Disney's characters and not Tomy's figures, ... but because proof of access plus substantial similarity can support a finding of infringement, Durham would at the very least be vulnerable to harassment. Yet any significant changes made by Durham to avoid liability would carry it away from the original Disney characters, in which Tomy concededly has no copyrights, and Disney's right to copy (or to permit others to copy) its own creations would, in effect, be circumscribed."

The same court, however, in *Eden Toys, Inc. v. Florelee Undergarment Co.*, 697 F.2d 27 (2d Cir.1982), purporting to apply *Batlin* and *Durham*, reversed a finding of insufficient originality for the plaintiff's drawing of Paddington Bear that was an authorized derivation of an earlier copyrighted illustration. The underlying work is illustration A below, the plaintiff's work is illustration B, and the defendant's drawing (held by the court to be an infringement) is illustration C. The court of appeals concluded that the district court had applied an improperly stiff standard of originality, and that it had mistakenly concluded that similarities of appearance in derivative pictorial works sufficient to justify an infringement finding must necessarily undermine a copyrightability finding. Even a work having the "same aesthetic appeal" as an underlying work such as to constitute an infringement if unauthorized, might incorporate "non-trivial contributions" to the underlying work and thus be copyrightable if authorized. The court found the plaintiff's illustration B to incorporate "original and substantial" variations upon illustration A, citing "the changed proportions of the hat, the elimination of individualized fingers and toes, the overall smoothing of lines" that provided a "different, cleaner" look than the illustration on which it was based. For a similar favorable treatment of Raggedy Ann and Raggedy Andy dolls, on the defendant's motion for summary judgment, see *Knickerbocker Toy Co. v. Winterbrook Corp.,* 554 F.Supp. 1309 (D.N.H.1982).

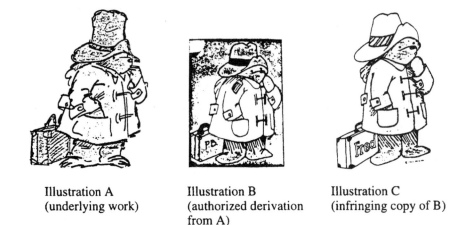

| Illustration A (underlying work) | Illustration B (authorized derivation from A) | Illustration C (infringing copy of B) |

The Paddington Bear case was distinguished in *Sherry Mfg. Co. v. Towel King of Florida, Inc.,* 753 F.2d 1565 (11th Cir.1985). There the plaintiff had marketed without copyright notice towels bearing the design of palm trees at the water's edge; it later changed the design slightly, affixed copyright notice, and brought an action for infringement of the design. The trial court noted the differences between the public domain design and the revised design: the surface of the seawater was painted differently; the amount of sand was increased so as to make the land look more like a beach than merely an island; the palm leaves "are sharper and more lifelike"; the clouds were shaped differently; the effect of the wind is diminished; the water level was lowered so that the drooping palm leaves no longer touch the water; and the palm leaves of the small tree to the right are shortened. The court of appeals held, however—stating that the "clearly erroneous" standard of review was not appropriate when the reviewing court has the opportunity to view the same tangible exhibits as did the trial court—that "the majority of those distinguishing details are so minor that they are virtually unnoticeable upon a cursory comparison of the two towels." The court stated that a cursory side-by-side comparison of the pertinent Paddington Bear drawings, however, showed immediately discernible differences. It also pointed out that "the primary purpose of making the changes [in the towel design] was to make the work copyrightable, and not to make it more aesthetically appealing." (Do you regard this as a pertinent observation?)

The concern of the *Batlin* court regarding potential harassment by claimants of derivative-work copyrights was exalted into the very rationale for the originality requirement by another court of appeals in *Gracen v. Bradford Exch.,* 698 F.2d 300 (7th Cir.1983). There, the plaintiff had prepared an authorized painting of Judy Garland portraying Dorothy in the motion picture "The Wizard of Oz"; this was done in connection with a

SHERRY'S ORIGINAL DESIGN   SHERRY'S NEW DESIGN

contest that was intended to lead to the production by the defendant Bradford of a series of collectors' plates based on the film. Although Gracen's painting was selected as the one that best captured the "essence" of the Dorothy character, she could not come to terms with Bradford, and the task of creating designs for the plates was given to one Auckland, who proceeded to copy Ms. Gracen's painting. The court found that her painting—reproduced below as illustration 1, and based upon "stills" from the motion picture (illustrations 2 and 3)—lacked sufficient originality for copyright. The court viewed the originality standard as designed, especially as applied to derivative works, to prevent overlapping claims; it gave as an example an artist who makes immaterial modifications in a reproduction of the Mona Lisa and who then sues another artist who copied from the da Vinci original. "[I]f the difference between the original and *A*'s reproduction is slight, the difference between *A*'s and *B*'s reproduction will also be slight, so that if *B* had access to *A*'s reproductions the trier of fact will be hard-pressed to decide whether *B* was copying *A* or copying the Mona Lisa itself." The court concluded that the painting of the Dorothy character as superimposed upon a rendition of the movie set of Oz was insufficiently original, "always bearing in mind that the purpose of the term in copyright law is not to guide aesthetic judgments but to assure a sufficiently gross difference between the underlying and the derivative work to avoid entangling subsequent artists depicting the underlying work in copyright problems"; were originality construed too broadly "it would paradoxically inhibit rather than promote the creation of such works."

The Gracen Painting

The concern reflected in the *Durham* and *Gracen* cases for the copyright owner of the underlying work, and for the potential ''entangling'' of that person and of other licensees in disputes, served as the core of the court's decision in *Entertainment Research Group, Inc. v. Genesis Creative Group, Inc.*, 122 F.3d 1211 (9th Cir.1997). There, the plaintiff Entertainment Research Group (ERG) lawfully designed and manufactured inflatable costumes that were based on two-dimensional cartoon characters such as the Pillsbury Doughboy, Cap'n Crunch and Toucan Sam. In converting these images into costumes, ERG obviously had to shape the figures in three dimensions and alter the dimensions somewhat so as to be wearable by humans; choices were also made as to surface texture, and facial expressions were also changed somewhat from the cartoon drawings. Genesis (originally under contract with ERG, but subsequently on its own) also sold such inflatable costumes, patterned after those of ERG, and the court

A Photograph From *The Wizard of Oz*

Film still Gracen followed for background

sustained the defense that the ERG derivative-work costumes lacked sufficient originality.

The court found the differences between the plaintiff's inflatable costumes and the underlying cartoons to be too insignificant to warrant copyright protection. It emphasized the language in § 103(b) which provides that copyright in the derivative work is not to "affect" the copyright in the underlying work, and concluded that the owner of the underlying cartoons would effectively be prevented from permitting others to copy its work (particularly in the form of costumes) if ERG's copyright were to be upheld. Moreover, copyright was not to be extended to the creative decisions that may have enabled ERG to manufacture the costumes successfully, nor to the thought and effort invested by ERG in converting from one medium to another. The court concluded that differences in the derivative work in form, texture and proportionality all stemmed from "functional considerations," which are not within the scope of copyright protection.

Finally, although the court acknowledged that ERG's costumes featured facial expressions that may have been more than trivially different from those of the cartoon characters on which they were based, it was still proper to grant Genesis's motion for summary judgment, for "no reasonable trier of fact would see anything but the underlying copyrighted character when looking at ERG's costumes.... [B]ecause ERG's costumes are 'instantly identifiable as embodiments' of the underlying copyrighted characters in 'yet another form,' no reasonable juror could conclude that there are any 'nontrivial' artistic differences between the underlying cartoon characters and the immediately recognizable costumes that ERG has designed and manufactured."

Is the court's conclusion soundly based? For example, are there not minimally creative decisions made in converting a flat cartoon figure into a sculptural shape? Could there not be a variety of minimally creative ways to re-shape the proportions of a cartoon figure so as to generate an inflatable costume to be worn by children or adults? Would an original facial expression on the plaintiff's costumes be ineligible for copyright because an observer will recognize the overall cartoon character anyway? Are these matters appropriate for resolution by summary judgment? *See generally Medallic Art Co. v. Washington Mint, LLC*, 208 F.3d 203 (table), 2000 WL 298253 (text of unpub. opinion) (2d Cir.2000) (silver coins imitating design of treasury notes are copyrightable, while silver coin imitating coin is not).

The judicial view that there is a higher standard of creativity required for copyrightability of derivative works has culminated in disputes, in two recent cases, as to whether particular photographs of manufactured articles are or are not derivative works. Is, for example, a photograph of a vodka bottle, or of a decorative mirror, a derivative work, in which case there must apparently be more substantial originality to justify copyright protection than if the photograph is "non-derivative"? This somewhat curious approach is well illustrated by the divided decision of the Court of Appeals for the Ninth Circuit in *Ets-Hokin v. Skyy Spirits, Inc.*, 225 F.3d 1068 (9th Cir.2000). The plaintiff photographer, at the request of the defendant vodka distributor, had taken straight-on photographs of a distinctively blue-colored bottle of Skyy Vodka, against a plain white or yellow backdrop with backlighting. When Skyy was dissatisfied with the photos, and had another person take new ones (which were rather like Ets–Hokin's), the first photographer sued. The district judge held his photographs to be derivative works and to lack sufficient originality. The court of appeals reversed.

After an extended and useful review of the history of copyright in photographs, the court noted that Ets–Hokin's photos manifested creativity in his decisions about lighting, shading, angle and background. Whether more was necessary turned, in the court's view, on whether the photos were derivative works—which in turn required a determination whether the vodka bottle was itself a copyrightable work (an issue on which the court divided, 2 to 1). The court concluded that the bottle was a useful article lacking in any "separable" pictorial or sculptural elements, that the label itself was uncopyrightable, and that any possible protectibility of the bottle under the trademark laws was irrelevant to its status under the Copyright Act. Thus, because not "based upon" a preexisting work within the subject matter of copyright, the photograph was not a derivative work, and was copyrightable. The dissenting judge would have found the photos to be derivative works—and uncopyrightable even under the usual standards, because of unoriginality and the merger doctrine. *See also SHL Imaging, Inc. v. Artisan House, Inc.*, 117 F.Supp.2d 301 (S.D.N.Y.2000) (commercial photographs of mirrored picture frames are not derivative works because they do not "recast, transform or adapt" the frames; extensive treatment of copyright protection for photographs).

Are such exegeses into the derivative-work status of a photograph justified? Are they responsive to the kinds of concerns expressed in cases such as *Batlin* and *Gracen*? In assessing copyrightability of photographs, should it really matter whether they are of a painting or of a mountain or of restaurant food? *See Oriental Art Printing, Inc. v. Goldstar Printing Corp.*, 58 U.S.P.Q.2d 1843 (S.D.N.Y.2001) (photographs of familiar Chinese dishes, and their placement on restaurant menu, lack creativity).

QUESTIONS

1. In the field of art reproductions, presumably the aesthetic and educational value of the work derives from its being as exact a reproduction as possible. Is it therefore proper—either under the Constitution or the statute—for a court to deny copyright to such a reproduction unless there is a substantial variation from the original? Would it run afoul of the Supreme Court decision in *Feist* to extend copyright protection to art reproductions that are painstakingly exact?

2. Would a photograph of the public domain cast-iron bank (in the *Batlin* case) be a proper subject of copyright? If so, then why is not Snyder's rendition in plastic?

3. Is there a constitutional or philosophical justification for the court's suggestion that copyright may be used to protect reproductions when the underlying work is "unique and rare" and not readily accessible to the public? Does copyright make works more or less accessible to the public?

4. Had the Snyder plastic bank been granted copyright, would that effectively remove the cast-iron original from the public domain so that others would be forbidden to copy it?

5. Consider the reasoning in the *Gracen* case. First, do you agree that the principal function of the "originality" requirement in copyright generally, and in derivative works in particular, is to eliminate harassing litigation? Second, was it consistent for the court to strike down Ms. Gracen's claim for that reason while concluding—on the basis of Auckland's admission that Bradford had given him Ms. Gracen's painting with directions to "clean it up" and Bradford's failure to attach a copy of Auckland's painting to its motion for summary judgment—that Auckland had indeed copied directly from Ms. Gracen? Third, does the court's approach really provide incentives to *B* to make reproductions of the Mona Lisa? Consider whether *B* will have any recourse when a new hypothetical reproducer, *C,* comes on the scene and makes a direct copy of *B*'s reproduction.

6. What, if anything, is copyrightable in a painting consisting of a faithful reproduction of the Mona Lisa, with the addition of a moustache? Could someone freely copy the reproduction while omitting the moustache? *See Millworth Converting Corp. v. Slifka,* 276 F.2d 443 (2d Cir.1960).

7. When a songwriter composes a tune with a single melodic line (with or without lyrics), the addition of harmonic chords to accompany that tune can be said to generate an independently copyrightable derivative work. Is the preparation of such a series of chords so routine an exercise as to lack sufficient originality to secure copyright protection, or even to constitute a derivative work? (If you know little about music, ask a knowledgeable friend.)

In what appear to be the first two cases, at least in recent times, to address this question—and to decide it barely a month apart—different judges sitting on the same district court came to different conclusions, although their decisions are reconcilable on procedural grounds. *See Tempo Music, Inc. v. Famous Music Corp.,* 838 F.Supp. 162 (S.D.N.Y.1993) (Duke Ellington's jazz classic, *Satin Doll;* subsequent addition of musical elements may constitute protectible expression), *and Woods v. Bourne Co.,* 841 F.Supp. 118 (S.D.N.Y.1994), *aff'd,* 60 F.3d 978 (2d Cir.1995) (the well-known 'Twenties tune, *When the Red, Red Robin Comes Bob–Bob–Bob-bin' Along*; addition of chords to words and a simple melodic line does not create a protectible derivative work).

———

Maljack Productions, Inc. v. UAV Corp., 964 F.Supp. 1416 (C.D.Cal.1997), *aff'd on other grounds sub nom. Batjac Prods. v. Good-Times Home Video Corp.,* 160 F.3d 1223 (9th Cir.1998). A motion picture entitled "McClintock!" (starring John Wayne) was released in 1963 and fell into the public domain at the end of 1991 for lack of renewal. The original producer released a new version of "McClintock!" in 1993. The 1993 version was different in only two respects. First, it was "panned and scanned" for the videocassette market so that its proportions fit onto the standard television screen. The "aspect ratio" (i.e., the ratio of screen length to screen height) was adjusted, which required that certain selected portions of the images on the original full-screen film be deleted. Second, the film's monaural soundtrack was digitized, remixed, "sweetened, equalized and balanced," and converted into upgraded and stereo sound.

The district court held that there was sufficient creativity in both elements such that the 1993 version was copyrightable. Among other things, the court acknowledged—invoking the *Gracen* decision—that extending copyright to the panned-and-scanned version might inhibit those who lawfully wish to base their own derivative version of "McClintock!" on the original public domain film, for fear of unwarranted litigation by the plaintiff Maljack. The court nonetheless concluded that such a concern did not authorize it to depart from the standard modest "creativity" requirement in assessing copyright for a derivative work.

If you sat on the court of appeals, would you affirm the court's decision?

E. COMPUTER PROGRAMS

The omnibus revision of U.S. copyright law that led to the 1976 Act did not specifically address the question of the copyrightability of computer programs. The Copyright Office had, since 1964, been registering computer programs under its "rule of doubt." No judicial decisions under the 1909 Act ruled on the Copyright Office practice of registering claims to copyright in computer programs. Toward the end of the revision process, Congress established a National Commission on New Technological Uses of Copyrighted Works ("CONTU") to study computers and copyright and to make specific recommendations to Congress. Pub. L. No. 93–573, 93d Cong., 2d Sess. (1974). The House Report to the 1976 Act nonetheless suggested quite clearly that Section 102 of the Act was to be understood to provide protection for computer programs. CONTU, consisting of distinguished individuals selected, pursuant to congressional directive, from authors and other copyright owners, copyright users, and "the public," and assisted by an expert staff, produced a Final Report on July 31, 1978. A majority of the commissioners concluded that computer programs were, and should remain, within the subject of copyright. Excerpts from the majority report follow.

FINAL REPORT OF THE NATIONAL COMMISSION ON NEW TECHNOLOGICAL USES OF COPYRIGHTED WORKS (1978)

Computer Programs

Computer programs are a form of writing virtually unknown twenty-five years ago. They consist of sets of instructions which, when properly drafted, are used in an almost limitless number of ways to release human beings from such diverse mundane tasks as preparing payrolls, monitoring aircraft instruments, taking data readings, making calculations for research, setting type, operating assembly lines, and taking inventory. Computer programs are prepared by the careful fixation of words, phrases, numbers, and other symbols in various media. The instructions that make up a program may be read, understood, and followed by a human being. . . .

Great changes have occurred in the construction of computers, as well as in the media in which programs are recorded. Periodic progress has seen the development, utilization, and, in some cases, passage into obsolescence of bulky plug boards, punched paper cards and tape, magnetic tapes and disks, and semiconductor chips. It should be emphasized that these developments reflect differences only in the media in which programs are stored and not in the nature of the programs themselves.

. . .

Just as there was little need to protect the ridged brass wheel in a nineteenth-century music box, so too was there little reason to protect the wired circuit or plug boards of early computers. The cost of making the wheel was inseparable from the cost of producing the ridged final product. The cost of copying a reel of magnetic tape, whether it contains a Chopin étude or a computer program, is small. Thus, the following proposition seems sound: if the cost of duplicating information is small, then it is simple for a less than scrupulous person to duplicate it. This means that legal as well as physical protection for the information is a necessary incentive if such information is to be created and disseminated.

. . .

As the number of computers has increased dramatically, so has the number of programs with which they may be used. While the first computers were designed and programmed to perform one or a few specific tasks, an ever increasing proportion of all computers are general-purpose machines which perform diverse tasks, depending in part upon the programs with which they are used. Early programs were designed by machine manufacturers to be used in conjunction with one model or even one individual computer. Today, many programs are designed to operate on any number of machines from one or more manufacturers. In addition, and perhaps even more importantly, there is a growing proportion of programs created by persons who do not make machines. These people may be users or they may be—and increasingly are—programmers or small firms who market their wares for use by individual machine owners who are not in a position to write their own programs. Just as Victrola once made most of the first record players and records, so too did early machine manufacturers write most of the first programs. Victrola's successor, RCA, still produces sound recordings (but, interestingly enough, not phonographs), but so do hundreds of other firms. If present computer industry trends continue, it is all but certain that programs written by nonmachine manufacturers will gain an increasing share of the market, not only because writing programs and building machines are two very different skills that need not necessarily occur simultaneously, but also because program writing requires little capital investment.

The cost of developing computer programs is far greater than the cost of their duplication. Consequently, computer programs, as the previous discussion illustrates, are likely to be disseminated only if:

1. the creator may recover all of its costs plus a fair profit on the first sale of the work, thus leaving it unconcerned about the later publication of the work; or

2. the creator may spread its costs over multiple copies of the work with some form of protection against unauthorized duplication of the work; or

3. the creator's costs are borne by another, as, for example, when the government or a foundation offers prizes or awards; or

4. the creator is indifferent to cost and donates the work to the public.

The consequence of the first possibility would be that the price of virtually any program would be so high that there would necessarily be a drastic reduction in the number of programs marketed. In this country, possibilities three and four occur, but rarely outside of academic and government-sponsored research. Computer programs are the product of great intellectual effort and their utility is unquestionable. The Commission is, therefore, satisfied that some form of protection is necessary to encourage the creation and broad distribution of computer programs in a competitive market.

The Commission's conclusion is that the continued availability of copyright protection for computer programs is desirable. This availability is in keeping with nearly two centuries' development of American copyright doctrine, during which the universe of works protectable by statutory copyright has expanded along with the imagination, communications media, and technical capabilities of society. Copyright, therefore, protects the program so long as it remains fixed in a tangible medium of expression but does not protect the electro-mechanical functioning of a machine. The way copyright affects games and game-playing is closely analogous: one may not adopt and republish or redistribute copyrighted game rules, but the copyright owner has no power to prevent others from playing the game.

. . .

Copyright and Other Methods Compared

The purpose of copyright is to grant authors a limited property right in the form of expression of their ideas. The other methods used to protect property interests in computer programs have different conceptual bases and, not surprisingly, work in different ways. An appreciation of those differences has contributed to the Commission's recommendation that copyright protection not be withdrawn from programs. Patents are designed to give inventors a short-term, powerful monopoly in devices, processes, compositions of matter, and designs which embody their ideas. The doctrine of trade secrecy is intended to protect proprietors who use a "formula, pattern, device or compilation of information" in their business "which gives [them] an opportunity to obtain an advantage over competitors who do not know or use it." Unfair competition is a legal theory which, among other things, proscribes misrepresentation about the nature and origin of products in commerce. Each of these forms of protection may inhibit the dissemination of information and restrict competition to a greater extent than copyright.

In certain circumstances, proprietors may find patent protection more attractive than copyright, since it gives them the right not only to license and control the use of their patented devices or processes but also to prevent the use of such devices or processes when they are independently developed by third parties. Such rights last for seventeen years. The acquisition of a patent, however, is time consuming and expensive, primarily because a patentee's rights are great and the legal hurdles an applicant must overcome are high. A work must be useful, novel, and nonobvious to those familiar with the state of the art in which the patent is sought. The applicant must prove these conditions to the satisfaction of the Patent and Trademark Office or, failing that, to the Court of Customs and Patent Appeals or the Supreme Court.

Even if patents prove available in the United States, only the very few programs which survive the rigorous application and appeals procedure could be patented. Once such protection attached, of course, all others would be barred from using the patented process, even if independently developed.

Trade secrecy is a doctrine known in every American jurisdiction. As a creature of state statute or common law it differs somewhat from state to state. The premise on which trade secrecy is based is this: if a business maintains confidentiality concerning either the way in which it does something or some information that it has, then courts should protect the business against the misappropriation of that secret. Although many proprietors feel secure when using trade secrecy, there are several problems they must face with respect to its use in protecting programs. Because secrecy is paramount, it is inappropriate for protecting works that contain the secret and are designed to be widely distributed. Although this matters little in the case of unique programs prepared for large commercial customers, it substantially precludes the use of trade secrecy with respect to programs sold in multiple copies over the counter to small businesses, schools, consumers, and hobbyists. Protection is lost when the secret is disclosed, without regard to the circumstances surrounding the disclosure. The lack of uniform national law in this area may also be perceived by proprietors as reducing the utility of this method of protection.

From the user's standpoint, there are additional drawbacks. Users must cover the seller's expenses associated with maintaining a secure system through increased prices. Their freedom to do business in an unencumbered way is reduced, since they may need to enter into elaborate nondisclosure contracts with employees and third parties who have access to the secrets and to limit that access to a very small number of people. Since secrets are by definition known to only a few people, there is necessarily a reduced flow of information in the marketplace, which hinders the ability of potential buyers to make comparisons and hence leads to higher prices.

Experts in the computer industry state that a further problem with respect to trade secrecy is that there is much human effort wasted when people do for themselves that which others have already done but are keeping secret. This was emphasized in the reports to the Commission prepared by the Public Interest Economics Center and the New York University economists.

The availability of copyright for computer programs does not, of course, affect the availability of trade secrecy protection. Under the Act of 1976 only those state rights that are equivalent to the exclusive rights granted therein (generally, common law copyright) are preempted. Any decline in use of trade secrecy might be based not upon preemption but on the rapid increase in the number of widely distributed programs in which trade secret protection could not be successfully asserted.

The common law doctrine of unfair competition of the misappropriation variety is based upon the principle that one may not appropriate a competitor's skill, expenditure, and labor. It prohibits false advertising and the "passing off" of another's work as one's own. While there is a small body of federal unfair competition law, it is largely a state doctrine with the same lack of national uniformity that besets trade secrecy. Although unfair competition may provide relief ancillary to copyright in certain situations, its scope is not as broad, and it seems unlikely that it alone could provide sufficient protection against the misappropriation of programs. For example, the unauthorized copying of any work for any purpose could be a copyright infringement without amounting to unfair competition.

The answers to such economic questions as the effect of protection on the market and the opportunity it creates for an uncompetitive rate of return tend to show that, of the various potential modes of protection, copyright has the smallest negative impact.

. . .

Computer–Authored Works

On the basis of its investigations and society's experience with the computer, the Commission believes that there is no reasonable basis for considering that a computer in any way contributes authorship to a work produced through its use. The computer, like a camera or a typewriter, is an inert instrument, capable of functioning only when activated either directly or indirectly by a human. When so activated it is capable of doing only what it is directed to do in the way it is directed to perform.

Computers may be employed in a variety of ways in creating works that may be protected by copyright. Works of graphic art may consist of designs, lines, intensities of color, and the like selected and organized with the assistance of a computer. A computer may be used to assist an artist in filling in numerous frames in an animation sequence, thus reducing the amount of time and effort otherwise needed to prepare an animated work.

In the case of computer music, a program may be designed to select a series of notes and arrange them into a musical composition, employing various tonal qualities and rhythmic patterns. The computer may also be used to simulate musical instruments and perform the music so composed.

In other instances, a computer may be used to manipulate statistical information to produce an analysis of that information. The resulting work may bear little similarity to the original form or arrangement of the work being analyzed, as in the case of an economic forecast produced by the manipulation of raw economic data. A computer may, on the other hand, be employed to extract and reproduce portions of a work. In every case, the work produced will result from the contents of the data base, the instructions indirectly provided in the program, and the direct discretionary intervention of a human involved in the process.

To be entitled to copyright, a work must be an original work of authorship. It must be a writing within the meaning of that term as used in the Copyright Clause of the Constitution. The Supreme Court has interpreted this requirement to include "any physical rendering of the fruits of creative intellectual or aesthetic labor." The history of the development of the concept of originality shows that only a modicum of effort is required. . . .

Thus, it may be seen that although the quantum of originality needed to support a claim of authorship in a work is small, it must nevertheless be present. If a work created through application of computer technology meets this minimal test of originality, it is copyrightable. The eligibility of any work for protection by copyright depends not upon the device or devices used in its creation, but rather upon the presence of at least minimal human creative effort at the time the work is produced.

Computers are enormously complex and powerful instruments which vastly extend human powers to calculate, select, rearrange, display, design, and do other things involved in the creation of works. However, it is a human power they extend. The computer may be analogized to or equated with, for example, a camera, and the computer affects the copyright status of a resultant work no more than the employment of a still or motion-picture camera, a tape recorder, or a typewriter. Hence, it seems clear that the copyright problems with respect to the authorship of new works produced with the assistance of a computer are not unlike those posed by the creation of more traditional works.

. . .

Recommendations for Statutory Change

[CONTU recommended, *inter alia*, that section 101 be amended to add the following definition:

A "computer program" is a set of statements or instructions to be used directly or indirectly in a computer in order to bring about a certain result.]

In 1980, Congress amended the Copyright Act, adding to § 101 the definition recommended by CONTU. In view of the dearth of legislative history accompanying the 1980 amendments, it has been stated that "it is fair to conclude, since Congress adopted [CONTU's] recommendations without alteration, that the CONTU report reflects the Congressional intent." *Midway Mfg. Co. v. Strohon*, 564 F.Supp. 741, 750 n. 6 (N.D.Ill. 1983).

Apple Computer, Inc. v. Franklin Computer Corp.

714 F.2d 1240 (3d Cir.1983).

■ SLOVITER, CIRCUIT JUDGE.

I. *Introduction*

Apple Computer, Inc. appeals from the district court's denial of a motion to preliminarily enjoin Franklin Computer Corp. from infringing the copyrights Apple holds on fourteen computer programs.... [T]he district court denied the preliminary injunction, *inter alia*, because it had "some doubt as to the copyrightability of the programs." *Apple Computer, Inc. v. Franklin Computer Corp.*, 545 F. Supp. 812, 812 (E.D.Pa.1982). This legal ruling is fundamental to all future proceedings in this action and, as the parties and amici curiae seem to agree, has considerable significance to the computer services industry. Because we conclude that the district court proceeded under an erroneous view of the applicable law, we reverse the denial of the preliminary injunction and remand.

II. *Facts and Procedural History*

Apple, one of the computer industry leaders, manufactures and markets personal computers (microcomputers), related peripheral equipment such as disk drives (peripherals), and computer programs (software). It presently manufactures Apple II computers and distributes over 150 programs. Apple has sold over 400,000 Apple II computers, employs approximately 3,000 people, and had annual sales of $335,000,000 for fiscal year 1981. One of the byproducts of Apple's success is the independent development by third parties of numerous computer programs which are designed to run on the Apple II computer.

Franklin, the defendant below, manufactures and sells the ACE 100 personal computer and at the time of the hearing employed about 75 people and had sold fewer than 1,000 computers. The ACE 100 was designed to be "Apple compatible," so that peripheral equipment and software developed for use with the Apple II computer could be used in conjunction with the

ACE 100. Franklin's copying of Apple's operating system computer programs in an effort to achieve such compatibility precipitated this suit.

Like all computers both the Apple II and ACE 100 have a central processing unit (CPU) which is the integrated circuit that executes programs. In lay terms, the CPU does the work it is instructed to do. Those instructions are contained on computer programs.

. . .

The CPU can only follow instructions written in object code. However, programs are usually written in source code which is more intelligible to humans. Programs written in source code can be converted or translated by a "compiler" program into object code for use by the computer. Programs are generally distributed only in their object code version stored on a memory device.

A computer program can be stored or fixed on a variety of memory devices, two of which are of particular relevance for this case. The ROM (Read Only Memory) is an internal permanent memory device consisting of a semi-conductor or "chip" which is incorporated into the circuitry of the computer. A program in object code is embedded on a ROM before it is incorporated in the computer. Information stored on a ROM can only be read, not erased or rewritten[3].... The other device used for storing the programs at issue is a diskette or "floppy disk," an auxiliary memory device consisting of a flexible magnetic disk resembling a phonograph record, which can be inserted into the computer and from which data or instructions can be read.

Computer programs can be categorized by function as either application programs or operating system programs. Application programs usually perform a specific task for the computer user, such as word processing, checkbook balancing, or playing a game. In contrast, operating system programs generally manage the internal functions of the computer or facilitate use of application programs. The parties agree that the fourteen computer programs at issue in this suit are operating system programs.

Apple filed suit in the United States District Court for the Eastern District of Pennsylvania pursuant to 28 U.S.C. § 1338 on May 12, 1982, alleging that Franklin was liable for copyright infringement of the fourteen computer programs, patent infringement, unfair competition, and misappropriation. Franklin's answer in respect to the copyright counts included the affirmative defense that the programs contained no copyrightable subject matter. Franklin counterclaimed for declaratory judgment that the copyright registrations were invalid and unenforceable, and sought affirmative relief on the basis of Apple's alleged misuse....

After expedited discovery, Apple moved for a preliminary injunction to restrain Franklin from using, copying, selling, or infringing Apple's copy-

---

3. In contrast to the permanent memory devices a RAM (Random Access Memory) is a chip on which volatile internal memory is stored which is erased when the computer's power is turned off.

rights. The district court held a three day evidentiary hearing limited to the copyright infringement claims. Apple produced evidence at the hearing in the form of affidavits and testimony that programs sold by Franklin in conjunction with its ACE 100 computer were virtually identical with those covered by the fourteen Apple copyrights. The variations that did exist were minor, consisting merely of such things as deletion of reference to Apple or its copyright notice.

   .   .   .

Franklin did not dispute that it copied the Apple programs. Its witness admitted copying each of the works in suit from the Apple programs. Its factual defense was directed to its contention that it was not feasible for Franklin to write its own operating system programs. David McWherter, now Franklin's vice-president of engineering, testified he spent 30–40 hours in November 1981 making a study to determine if it was feasible for Franklin to write its own Autostart ROM program and concluded it was not because "there were just too many entry points in relationship to the number of instructions in the program." Entry points at specific locations in the program can be used by programmers to mesh their application programs with the operating system program. McWherter concluded that use of the identical signals was necessary in order to ensure 100% compatibility with application programs created to run on the Apple computer. He admitted that he never attempted to rewrite Autostart ROM and conceded that some of the works in suit (i.e., Copy, Copy A, Master Create, and Hello) probably could have been rewritten by Franklin. Franklin made no attempt to rewrite any of the programs prior to the lawsuit except for Copy, although McWherter testified that Franklin was "in the process of redesigning" some of the Apple programs and that "[w]e had a fair degree of certainty that that would probably work." Apple introduced evidence that Franklin could have rewritten programs, including the Autostart ROM program, and that there are in existence operating programs written by third parties which are compatible with Apple II.

Franklin's principal defense at the preliminary injunction hearing and before us is primarily a legal one, directed to its contention that the Apple operating system programs are not capable of copyright protection.

   .   .   .

IV.   *Discussion*

A.   *Copyrightability of a Computer Program Expressed in Object Code*

Certain statements by the district court suggest that programs expressed in object code, as distinguished from source code, may not be the proper subject of copyright. We find no basis in the statute for any such concern. . . .

Although section 102(a) does not expressly list computer programs as works of authorship, the legislative history suggests that programs were considered copyrightable as literary works. *See* H.R. Rep. No. 1476, 94th

Cong., 2d Sess. 54, *reprinted in* 1976 U.S. Code Cong. & Ad. News 5659, 5667 ("'literary works' ... includes ... computer programs")....

The 1980 amendments added a definition of a computer program:

> A "computer program" is a set of statements or instructions to be used directly or indirectly in a computer in order to bring about a certain result.

17 U.S.C. § 101. The amendments also substituted a new section 117 which provides that "it is not an infringement for the owner of a copy of a computer program to make or authorize the making of another copy or adaptation of that computer program" when necessary to "the utilization of the computer program" or "for archival purposes only." 17 U.S.C. § 117. The parties agree that this section is not implicated in the instant lawsuit. The language of the provision, however, by carving out an exception to the normal proscriptions against copying, clearly indicates that programs are copyrightable and are otherwise afforded copyright protection.

> . . .

The district court here questioned whether copyright was to be limited to works "designed to be 'read' by a human reader [as distinguished from] read by an expert with a microscope and patience," 545 F. Supp. at 821. The suggestion that copyrightability depends on a communicative function to individuals stems from the early decision of *White-Smith Music Publishing Co. v. Apollo Co.,* 209 U.S. 1 (1908), which held a piano roll was not a copy of the musical composition because it was not in a form others, except perhaps for a very expert few, could perceive. See 1 Nimmer on Copyright § 2.03[B][1] (1983). However, it is clear from the language of the 1976 Act and its legislative history that it was intended to obliterate distinctions engendered by *White-Smith.* H.R. Rep. No. 1476, *supra,* at 52, *reprinted in* 1976 U.S. Code Cong. & Ad. News at 5665.

Under the statute, copyright extends to works in any tangible means of expression *"from which they can be perceived,* reproduced, or otherwise communicated, either directly or *with the aid of a machine or device."* 17 U.S.C. § 102(a) (emphasis added). Further, the definition of "computer program" adopted by Congress in the 1980 amendments is "sets of statements or instructions to be used *directly or indirectly* in a computer in order to bring about a certain result." 17 U.S.C. § 101 (emphasis added). As source code instructions must be translated into object code before the computer can act upon them, only instructions expressed in object code can be used "directly" by the computer. *See Midway Manufacturing Co. v. Strohon,* 564 F. Supp. 741 at 750–751 (N.D.Ill.1983). This definition was adopted following the CONTU Report in which the majority clearly took the position that object codes are proper subjects of copyright. *See* CONTU Report at 21. The majority's conclusion was reached although confronted by a dissent based upon the theory that the "machine-control phase" of a program is not directed at a human audience. *See* CONTU Report at 28–30 (dissent of Commissioner Hersey).

> . . .

The district court also expressed uncertainty as to whether a computer program in object code could be classified as a "literary work." However, the category of "literary works," one of the seven copyrightable categories, is not confined to literature in the nature of Hemingway's *For Whom the Bell Tolls*. The definition of "literary works" in section 101 includes expression not only in words but also "numbers, or other ... numerical symbols or indicia," thereby expanding the common usage of "literary works." *Cf. Harcourt, Brace & World, Inc. v. Graphic Controls Corp.*, 329 F. Supp. 517, 523–24 (S.D.N.Y.1971) (the symbols designating questions or response spaces on exam answer sheets held to be copyrightable "writings" under 1909 Act); *Reiss v. National Quotation Bureau, Inc.*, 276 F. 717 (S.D.N.Y.1921) (code book of coined words designed for cable use copyrightable). Thus a computer program, whether in object code or source code, is a "literary work" and is protected from unauthorized copying, whether from its object or source code version. *Accord Midway Mfg. Co. v. Strohon*, 564 F. Supp. at 750–751; *see also GCA Corp. v. Chance*, 217 U.S.P.Q. at 719–20.

B. *Copyrightability of a Computer Program Embedded on a ROM*

Just as the district court's suggestion of a distinction between source code and object code was rejected by our opinion in *Williams* issued three days after the district court opinion, so also was its suggestion that embodiment of a computer program on a ROM, as distinguished from in a traditional writing, detracts from its copyrightability. In *Williams* we rejected the argument that "a computer program is not infringed when the program is loaded into electronic memory devices (ROMs) and used to control the activity of machines." 685 F.2d at 876. Defendant there had argued that there can be no copyright protection for the ROMs because they are utilitarian objects or machine parts. We held that the statutory requirement of "fixation," the manner in which the issue arises, is satisfied through the embodiment of the expression in the ROM devices. *Id.* at 874, 876; *see also Midway Mfg. Co. v. Strohon*, 564 F. Supp. at 751–752; *Tandy Corp. v. Personal Micro Computers, Inc.*, 524 F. Supp. at 173. *cf. Stern Electronics, Inc. v. Kaufman*, 669 F.2d 852, 855–56 (2d Cir.1982) (audiovisual display of video game "fixed" in ROM). Therefore we reaffirm that a computer program in object code embedded in a ROM chip is an appropriate subject of copyright. *See also* Note, *Copyright Protection of Computer Program Object Code*, 96 Harv. L. Rev. 1723 (1983); Note, *Copyright Protection for Computer Programs in Read Only Memory Chips*, 11 Hofstra L. Rev. 329 (1982).

C. *Copyrightability of Computer Operating System Programs*

We turn to the heart of Franklin's position on appeal which is that computer operating system programs, as distinguished from application programs, are not the proper subject of copyright "regardless of the language or medium in which they are fixed." Brief of Appellee at 15 (emphasis deleted).

. . . .

Franklin contends that operating system programs are *per se* excluded from copyright protection under the express terms of section 102(b) of the Copyright Act, and under the precedent and underlying principles of *Baker v. Selden,* 101 U.S. 99 (1879). These separate grounds have substantial analytic overlap.

. . .

1.   *"Process," "System" or "Method of Operation"*

Franklin argues that an operating system program is either a "process," "system," or "method of operation" and hence uncopyrightable. Franklin correctly notes that underlying section 102(b) and many of the statements for which *Baker v. Selden* is cited is the distinction which must be made between property subject to the patent law, which protects discoveries, and that subject to copyright law, which protects the writings describing such discoveries. However, Franklin's argument misapplies that distinction in this case. Apple does not seek to copyright the method which instructs the computer to perform its operating functions but only the instructions themselves. The method would be protected, if at all, by the patent law, an issue as yet unresolved. *See Diamond v. Diehr,* 450 U.S. 175 (1981).

Franklin's attack on operating system programs as "methods" or "processes" seems inconsistent with its concession that application programs are an appropriate subject of copyright. Both types of programs instruct the computer to do something. Therefore, it should make no difference for purposes of section 102(b) whether these instructions tell the computer to help prepare an income tax return (the task of an application program) or to translate a high level language program from source code into its binary language object code form (the task of an operating system program such as "Applesoft"). Since it is only the instructions which are protected, a "process" is no more involved because the instructions in an operating system program may be used to activate the operation of the computer than it would be if instructions were written in ordinary English in a manual which described the necessary steps to activate an intricate complicated machine. There is, therefore, no reason to afford any less copyright protection to the instructions in an operating system program than to the instructions in an application program.

Franklin's argument, receptively treated by the district court, that an operating system program is part of a machine mistakenly focuses on the physical characteristics of the instructions. But the medium is not the message. We have already considered and rejected aspects of this contention in the discussion of object code and ROM. The mere fact that the operating system program may be etched on a ROM does not make the program either a machine, part of a machine or its equivalent. Furthermore, as one of Franklin's witnesses testified, an operating system does not have to be permanently in the machine in ROM, but it may be on some other medium, such as a diskette or magnetic tape, where it could be readily transferred into the temporary memory space of the computer. In fact, some of the operating systems at issue were on diskette. As the CONTU majority stated,

> Programs should no more be considered machine parts than videotapes should be considered parts of projectors or phonorecords parts of sound reproduction equipment.... That the words of a program are used ultimately in the implementation of a process should in no way affect their copyrightability.

CONTU Report at 21.

Franklin also argues that the operating systems cannot be copyrighted because they are "purely utilitarian works" and that Apple is seeking to block the use of the art embodied in its operating systems. This argument stems from the following dictum in *Baker v. Selden:*

> The very object of publishing a book on science or the useful arts is to communicate to the world the useful knowledge which it contains. But this object would be frustrated if the knowledge could not be used without incurring the guilt of piracy of the book. And where the art it teaches cannot be used without employing the methods and diagrams used to illustrate the book, or such as are similar to them, such methods and diagrams are to be considered as necessary incidents to the art, and given therewith to the public; not given for the purpose of publication in other works explanatory of the art, but for the purpose of practical application.

101 U.S. at 103. We cannot accept the expansive reading given to this language by some courts, ...

Although a literal construction of this language could support Franklin's reading that precludes copyrightability if the copyright work is put to a utilitarian use, that interpretation has been rejected by a later Supreme Court decision. In *Mazer v. Stein,* 347 U.S. 201, 218 (1954), the Court stated: "We find nothing in the copyright statute to support the argument that the intended use or use in industry of an article eligible for copyright bars or invalidates its registration. We do not read such a limitation into the copyright law." *Id.* at 218. The CONTU majority also rejected the expansive view some courts have given *Baker v. Selden,* and stated, "That the words of a program are used ultimately in the implementation of a process should in no way affect their copyrightability." *Id.* at 21. It referred to "copyright practice past and present, which recognizes copyright protection for a work of authorship regardless of the uses to which it may be put." *Id.* The Commission continued: "The copyright status of the written rules for a game *or a system for the operation of a machine* is unaffected by the fact that those rules direct the actions of those who play the game or *carry out the process." Id.* (emphasis added). [W]e can consider the CONTU Report as accepted by Congress since Congress wrote into the law the majority's recommendations almost verbatim....

Perhaps the most convincing item leading us to reject Franklin's argument is that the statutory definition of a computer program as a set of instructions to be used in a computer in order to bring about a certain result, 17 U.S.C. § 101, makes no distinction between application programs and operating programs. Franklin can point to no decision which adopts the distinction it seeks to make. . . .

2. *Idea/Expression Dichotomy*

Franklin's other challenge to copyright of operating system programs relies on the line which is drawn between ideas and their expression. *Baker v. Selden* remains a benchmark in the law of copyright for the reading given it in *Mazer v. Stein, supra,* where the Court stated, "Unlike a patent, a copyright gives no exclusive right to the art disclosed; protection is given only to the expression of the idea—not the idea itself." 347 U.S. at 217 (footnote omitted).

The expression/idea dichotomy is now expressly recognized in section 102(b) which precludes copyright for "any idea." This provision was not intended to enlarge or contract the scope of copyright protection but "to restate . . . that the basic dichotomy between expression and idea remains unchanged." H.R. Rep. No. 1476, *supra,* at 57, *reprinted in* 1976 U.S. Code Cong. & Ad. News at 5670. The legislative history indicates that section 102(b) was intended "to make clear that the expression adopted by the programmer is the copyrightable element in a computer program, and that the actual processes or methods embodied in the program are not within the scope of the copyright law." *Id.*

Many of the courts which have sought to draw the line between an idea and expression have found difficulty in articulating where it falls. *See, e.g., Nichols v. Universal Pictures Corp.,* 45 F.2d 119, 121 (2d Cir.1930) (L. Hand, J.); *see* discussion in 3 Nimmer on Copyright § 13.03[A]. We believe that in the context before us, a program for an operating system, the line must be a pragmatic one, which also keeps in consideration "the preservation of the balance between competition and protection reflected in the patent and copyright laws." *Herbert Rosenthal Jewelry Corp. v. Kalpakian,* 446 F.2d 738, 742 (9th Cir.1971). As we stated in *Franklin Mint Corp. v. National Wildlife Art Exchange, Inc.,* 575 F.2d 62, 64 (3d Cir.), *cert. denied,* 439 U.S. 880 (1978), "Unlike a patent, a copyright protects originality rather than novelty or invention." In that opinion, we quoted approvingly the following passage from *Dymow v. Bolton,* 11 F.2d 690, 691 (2d Cir. 1926):

> Just as a patent affords protection only to the means of reducing an inventive idea to practice, so the copyright law protects the means of expressing an idea; and it is as near the whole truth as generalization can usually reach that, *if the same idea can be expressed in a plurality of totally different manners, a plurality of copyrights may result,* and no infringement will exist.

(emphasis added).

We adopt the suggestion in the above language and thus focus on whether the idea is capable of various modes of expression. If other programs can be written or created which perform the same function as an Apple's operating system program, then that program is an expression of the idea and hence copyrightable. In essence, this inquiry is no different than that made to determine whether the expression and idea have merged, which has been stated to occur where there are no or few other ways of expressing a particular idea. *See, e.g., Morrissey v. Procter & Gamble Co.,* 379 F.2d 675, 678–79 (1st Cir.1967); *Freedman v. Grolier Enterprises, Inc.,* 179 U.S.P.Q. 476, 478 (S.D.N.Y.1973) ("[c]opyright protection will not be given to a form of expression necessarily dictated by the underlying subject matter"); CONTU Report at 20.

The district court made no findings as to whether some or all of Apple's operating programs represent the only means of expression of the idea underlying them. Although there seems to be a concession by Franklin that at least some of the programs can be rewritten, we do not believe that the record on that issue is so clear that it can be decided at the appellate level. Therefore, if the issue is pressed on remand, the necessary finding can be made at that time.

Franklin claims that whether or not the programs can be rewritten, there are a limited "number of ways to arrange operating systems to enable a computer to run the vast body of Apple-compatible software," Brief of Appellee at 20. This claim has no pertinence to either the idea/expression dichotomy or merger. The idea which may merge with the expression, thus making the copyright unavailable, is the idea which is the subject of the expression. The idea of one of the operating system programs is, for example, how to translate source code into object code. If other methods of expressing that idea are not foreclosed as a practical matter, then there is no merger. Franklin may wish to achieve total compatibility with independently developed application programs written for the Apple II, but that is a commercial and competitive objective which does not enter into the somewhat metaphysical issue of whether particular ideas and expressions have merged.

In summary, Franklin's contentions that operating system programs are *per se* not copyrightable is unpersuasive. The other courts before whom this issue has been raised have rejected the distinction. Neither the CONTU majority nor Congress made a distinction between operating and application programs. We believe that the 1980 amendments reflect Congress' receptivity to new technology and its desire to encourage, through the copyright laws, continued imagination and creativity in computer programming. Since we believe that the district court's decision on the preliminary injunction was, to a large part, influenced by an erroneous view of the availability of copyright for operating system programs and unnecessary concerns about object code and ROMs, we must reverse the denial of the preliminary injunction and remand for reconsideration....

———

Data General Corp. v. Grumman Systems, 825 F.Supp. 340, 354–55 (D.Mass.1993). Data General registered its computer programs with the Copyright Office in source code, and Grumman copied only their object-code versions. The court rejected Grumman's defense that it had therefore not copied protected material:

> Grumman argues that it is entitled to judgment in its favor because Data General failed to prove that the MV/ADEX computer programs admittedly copied and used by Grumman were the same works in which Data General held copyrights. More specifically, Grumman asserts that Data General was required to prove the *object code* programs copied by Grumman are the same as the *source code* programs registered with the Copyright Office. Since Data General did not produce the source code for any version of MV/ADEX, it is argued that Data General could not prove that Grumman's admitted use of the object code programs infringed the source code programs registered with the Copyright Office. As I explained in my October 9, 1992 ruling, Grumman's argument is flawed.

> Contrary to Grumman's understanding, the materials deposited with the Copyright Office do not define the substantive protection extended to the registered work. Indeed, the Copyright Act expressly provides that copyright "registration is not a condition of copyright protection," and may be obtained at any time during the subsistence of the copyright. 17 U.S.C.A. § 408(a). Since copyright protection exists without regard to copyright registration, it follows that the deposit that accompanies a registration cannot by itself define the copyrighted work. In this case, the source code deposits that were made with the Copyright Office were merely symbols, rather than definitions, of the protected work. *See Midway Mfg. Co. v. Artic Int'l, Inc.*, 211 U.S.P.Q. (BNA) 1152, 1158 (N.D.Ill.1981) ("It is the work that cannot be copied or incorporated and not the specific tangible expression on file in the Copyright Office."). Thus, Data General held copyrights on the various versions of the computer program MV/ADEX, not the source code version of MV/ADEX.

> Similarly, Grumman misconceives as three separate programs the registered computer program, source code version of that program, and object code version of that program. Though Grumman has admittedly used MV/ADEX in its object code form, it claims there was no proof that it infringed the "registered source code program." The Copyright Office, however, "considers source code and object code as two representations of the same computer program. For registration purposes, the claim is in the *computer program* rather than in any particular representation of the program." Copyright Office, Compendium II of Copyright Office Practices § 321.03 (1984) (emphasis in original); *e.g., Apple Computer, Inc., v. Franklin Computer Corp.*, 714 F.2d 1240, 1249 (3d Cir. 1983), *cert. dismissed,* 464 U.S. 1033, 104 S.Ct. 690, 79 L.Ed.2d 158 (1984). Accordingly, while Data General had the burden of proving that Grumman copied MV/ADEX in one of its protected forms, Data General could meet that burden by showing infringement of either the source code or the object code version of the MV/ADEX.

QUESTIONS

1. Do you agree with the court in *Apple v. Franklin* that a copyrightable work need not be "intended as a medium of communication to human beings"? Should there be a distinction between computer programs that communicate directly to the computer, but that nonetheless also yield a communication to a human being, and programs that perform no function other than to instruct the computer to perform internal operations themselves and do not produce further communications to human beings?

2. Is there any distinction pertinent to copyright between a program that instructs a computer to perform a process (such as translating statements from source code to object code), and a literary work that instructs humans to perform a process (such as baking a cake)?

F. PICTORIAL, GRAPHIC AND SCULPTURAL WORKS

INTRODUCTION

Despite the general principle that a work's useful purpose does not detract from its copyrightability, *see, e.g., Bleistein, supra*, Chapter 1, we have already seen that functionality can disqualify a work or limit its protection if, for example, the work or some part of it is considered a "process," or "method of operation." The problem of a work's utility is particularly pronounced in the field of applied art, in which an aesthetically pleasing design may be married to a useful object. As the following materials reveal, the availability of copyright protection for the design of useful objects has evolved from the uncertain to the incoherent. As you review these materials, consider what might be a more workable test than the one Congress adopted in the 1976 Act, and what would be the results of its application.

Draft, Second Supplementary Report of the Register of Copyrights on the General Revision of the U.S. Copyright Law, Chapter VII, 4–13 (1975)

Legislative History of Section 113 and Title II

Until 1954 it had been widely assumed that the only statutory protection for the designs of utilitarian articles was that available under the design patent law, which dated back to 1842. That patents have proved inadequate as a practical form of protection for designs is something on which most people will agree. The main arguments usually advanced against the patent law as a means of protecting designs are:

1) *Inappropriateness.* Patentable designs must be more than "original" (created independently without copying); they must also be "novel" (new in the absolute sense of never having existed before anywhere) and "non-obvious" (the product of a creative act going

beyond mere talent or artistry). A patented design that meets these extraordinarily high standards gets more than rights against copying; a design patent consists of a complete monopoly over the use of the design in any manner.

2) *Judicial hostility.* Because the standards of protection are so high and the scope of protection is so broad, the mortality rate of those design patents that have been tested in the courts has been extremely high.

3) *Cost.* Obtaining a design patent is expensive, in some cases prohibitively so. Nearly all applicants are required to retain an attorney, and the substantial costs of filing and pursuing an application through the searching process often operate as a deterrent, especially since the chances of issuance are problematical. An applicant with several new designs has no way of knowing which will be popular, but in most cases cannot afford to apply for design patents on all of them.

4) *Delay.* The patent examining process consists of searching the "prior art" to determine novelty in an absolute sense. Whatever realistically may be the effectiveness of prior-art searching in the case of designs, the process is inevitably a slow one. In the design patent area, the Patent and Trademark Office now has a backlog of about 7 months, and the average time lag between filing and issuance for a design patent is about 21 months. It must be emphasized that protection under a patent starts only upon issuance, so that a design may be vulnerable to copying during the time a patent application is pending.

Beginning around 1914, the growth and economic impact of design piracy, and the nearly total failure of the patent law as a method to combat it, led to a variety of alternative efforts to protect original designs. The attempts to stop design piracy by industry self-regulation ... combined with a form of boycott, were quite effective for a time during the 1930's, but were eventually struck down by the courts. Judicial actions aimed at getting the courts to declare design piracy illegal on any one of a number of theories—Federal copyright, State common law copyright, Federal and State trademarks, unfair competition (including claims of "passing off" and "misappropriation"), fraud and breach of confidence, implied contract, etc.—were almost entirely unsuccessful.

During this period there were constant and frequently intense efforts to obtain Congressional enactment of separate design legislation. Between 1914 and 1957 nearly 50 design protection bills were introduced, and a number of hearings were held. Some of the bills were closer to copyright than patent; some leaned the other way; most of them took the form of special protection based on copyright principles but considerably more limited in scope and duration than traditional copyright. Several of the bills came close to enactment, but none made it all the way through both Houses.

In 1952, a successful program for the general revision of the patent laws resulted in comprehensive new patent legislation in which the design patent provisions were deliberately left untouched. The basic reason for leaving the design provisions alone was an agreement among the sponsors of the legislation that the patent law was not the place to deal with design protection.... [Soon after, the Copyright Office joined with the Patent Office and other patent experts in the development and drafting of a design-protection bill that became, in the early 1960s, a proposed Title II to the comprehensive copyright revision bill.] ...

A radical change in the legal status of original designs in the United States occurred on March 8, 1954. On that date the United States Supreme Court, by a seven-to-two majority in *Mazer v. Stein,* 347 U.S. 201 (1954), upheld the copyrightability of "works of art" that had been incorporated as the designs of useful articles. The Court strongly endorsed a Copyright Office Regulation accepting as copyrightable "works of artistic craftsmanship, in so far as their form but not their mechanical or utilitarian aspects are concerned, such as artistic jewelry, enamels, glassware, and tapestries, as well as all works belonging to the fine arts, such as paintings, drawings and sculpture...."

THE STATUETTE IN MAZER v. STEIN.

The *Mazer* case involved identical copies of lamp bases in the form of statuettes representing human figures. The figurines had been registered for copyright as "works of art." The majority of the Court, with Justices Douglas and Black dissenting, held that works of art are copyrightable as the "writings of an author," that original works of art do not cease to be copyrightable, as works of art, when they are embodied in useful articles, and that for this purpose the following factors make no difference whatever:

1) the potential availability of design patent protection for the same subject matter; on this point Justice Reed said:

We ... hold that the patentability of the statuettes, fitted as lamps or unfitted, does not bar copyright as works of art. Neither the Copyright Statute nor any other says that because a thing is patentable it may not be copyrighted. We should not so hold.... The dichotomy of protection for the aesthetic is not beauty and utility but art for the copyright and the invention of original and ornamental design for design patents. We find nothing in the copyright statute to support the argument that the intended use or use in industry of an article eligible for copyright bars or invalidates its registration. We do not read such a limitation into the copyright law.

2) the intention of the artist as to commercial application and mass production of the design.

3) the aesthetic value of the design, or its total lack thereof; the majority opinion on this point states:

The successive acts, the legislative history of the 1909 Act and the practice of the Copyright Office unite to show that "works of art" and "reproductions of works of art" are terms that were intended by Congress to include the authority to copyright these statuettes. Individual perception of the beautiful is too varied a power to permit a narrow or rigid concept of art.... They must be original, that is, the author's tangible expression of his ideas.... Such expression, whether meticulously delineating the model or mental image or conveying the meaning by modernistic form or color, is copyrightable.

4) the fact that the design, in its useful embodiment, was mass-produced and merchandised commercially on a nation-wide scale....

The revolutionary impact of the *Mazer* decision upon design protection took some time to sink in. Its reach clearly went beyond lamp base designs, but did it go so far as to cover all original industrial designs (machinery, automobiles, refrigerators, etc.)?

[Editors' note: The issue raised by the Register at this point in her Report was initially addressed, soon after the *Mazer* decision, by detailed regulations of the Copyright Office. These regulations were incorporated, with little change, in the 1976 Act; the principal sections are 101 and 113, to be discussed shortly.]

DESIGN–PROTECTION LEGISLATION

As noted in the Report of Register Barbara Ringer, design-protection legislation has never been far from the congressional agenda since the beginning of the twentieth century. Because such legislation is meant to protect against the copying of the attractive contours of useful articles, its underlying policies are anchored partly in copyright and partly in patent. A major obstacle to enactment has been the concern that the unauthorized manufacture of copied functional articles should not be curtailed hastily, or for an extended period of time, given the demanding standards for patentability. This concern is reinforced by the fact that even aesthetically pleasing elements of useful articles are often not readily separable from the elements that contribute to their utility.

Congress came close to finally enacting design-protection legislation as Title II of the bill that ultimately became the Copyright Act of 1976; that Title was in fact passed by the Senate as part of the revision bill, S. 22, 94th Cong., 2d Sess. (Feb. 1976). Title II was, however, stricken in its entirety by the House Judiciary Committee and was not restored by the conference committee after the bill passed the full House. For some 15 years thereafter, almost every Congress witnessed the introduction of design-protection bills—but never their enactment. Among the most entrenched opponents were automotive insurance companies, and manufacturers and sellers of discounted replacement auto parts. Can you articulate their likely objections?

The design bills that were introduced from the mid–1970s to the early 1990s generally contained the following key provisions:

(1) The design of a useful article can be protected if it is the original creation of its author (i.e., not copied), regardless of whether it is novel or non-obvious; it cannot, however, be "staple or commonplace" or be "dictated solely by a utilitarian function of the article that embodies it."

(2) The original designer is protected only against the unauthorized copying of the substance of the design; independent creation of a similar design will not infringe.

(3) Protection begins when the design is "made public" by public exhibition, sale or offering, and continues for a term of ten years.

(4) A claim to protection must be registered in a Government office within one year after the design is made public, or protection is lost. The Government official undertakes no search or comparison with earlier designs, but must register the design if it "on its face appears to be subject to protection" under the bill. Proceedings may be initiated by third parties to cancel the registration of a design not subject to protection.

(5) There are flexible requirements for placing notice on the design; failure to comply does not forfeit protection but may sharply limit remedies against infringers.

(6) Major remedies are injunctions and compensatory damages (which the court in its discretion may increase to $1.00 per copy or $50,000, whichever is greater).

(7) Certain accommodations are made with the Copyright Act, the Design Patent Act, and state common law.

After some years of quiescence on the design-protection front, Congress enacted a very narrow piece of legislation—protecting the design of boat hulls—as Title V of the Digital Millennium Copyright Act, signed by President Clinton in October 1998. In 1989, the Supreme Court, in *Bonito Boats Inc. v. Thunder Craft Inc.*, 489 U.S. 141 (1989) (see page 855, *infra*), had declared that such designs could not be given legal protection by state law. Boat-hull designers persisted, and in the Vessel Hull Design Protection Act (VHDPA) a new Chapter 13 has been added to Title 17. Earlier design bills were borrowed whole cloth, with the term "useful article" simply being redefined to mean a vessel hull! A design is protected under the VHDPA as soon as a useful article embodying the design is made public or a registration for the design is published. Protection is lost if an application for registration is not made within two years after the design is first made public; once the design is registered, protection continues for ten years from the date that it begins. The creator of the design will enjoy the right to make, have made, import, sell or distribute for sale or for use in trade, useful articles embodying the design. A D-in-a-circle notice affixed to the boat hull so as to give reasonable notice will perfect the design owner's rights.

As will be seen, U.S. law now gives essentially full protection against copying the three-dimensional shape of only three kinds of useful articles: architectural works, vessel hulls, and computer "mask works." The vague and limited nature of copyright protection for other useful articles is explained immediately below.

----

§ 101. Definitions

"Pictorial, graphic, and sculptural works" include two-dimensional and three-dimensional works of fine, graphic, and applied art, photographs, prints and art reproductions, maps, globes, charts, diagrams, models, and technical drawings, including architectural plans. Such works shall include works of artistic craftsmanship insofar as their form but not their mechanical or utilitarian aspects are concerned; the design of a useful article, as defined in this section, shall be considered a pictorial, graphic, or sculptural work only if, and only to the extent that, such design incorporates pictorial, graphic, or sculptural features that can be identified separately from, and are capable of existing independently of, the utilitarian aspects of the article.

A "useful article" is an article having an intrinsic utilitarian function that is not merely to portray the appearance of the article or to convey information. An article that is normally part of a useful article is considered a "useful article."

§ 113. Scope of Exclusive Rights in Pictorial, Graphic, and Sculptural Works

(a) Subject to the provisions of subsections (b) and (c) of this section, the exclusive right to reproduce a copyrighted pictorial, graphic, or sculptural work in copies under section 106 includes the right to reproduce the work in or on any kind of article, whether useful or otherwise.

(b) This title does not afford, to the owner of copyright in a work that portrays a useful article as such, any greater or lesser rights with respect to the making, distribution, or display of the useful article so portrayed than those afforded to such works under the law, whether title 17 or the common law or statutes of a State, in effect on December 31, 1977, as held applicable and construed by a court in an action brought under this title.

(c) In the case of a work lawfully reproduced in useful articles that have been offered for sale or other distribution to the public, copyright does not include any right to prevent the making, distribution, or display of pictures or photographs of such articles in connection with advertisements or commentaries related to the distribution or display of such articles, or in connection with news reports.

House Report

H.R. Rep. No. 94–1476, 94th Cong., 2d Sess. 105 (1976).

Section 113 deals with the extent of copyright protection in "works of applied art." The section takes as its starting point the Supreme Court's decision in *Mazer v. Stein,* 347 U.S. 201 (1954), and the first sentence of subsection (a) restates the basic principle established by that decision. The rule of *Mazer,* as affirmed by the bill, is that copyright in a pictorial, graphic or sculptural work will not be affected if the work is employed as the design of a useful article, and will afford protection to the copyright owner against the unauthorized reproduction of his work in useful as well as nonuseful articles. The terms "pictorial, graphic, and sculptural works" and "useful article" are defined in section 101....

The broad language of section 106(1) and of subsection (a) of section 113 raises questions as to the extent of copyright protection for a pictorial, graphic, or sculptural work that portrays, depicts, or represents an image of a useful article in such a way that the utilitarian nature of the article can be seen. To take the example usually cited, would copyright in a drawing or model of an automobile give the artist the exclusive right to make automobiles of the same design?

The 1961 Report of the Register of Copyrights stated, on the basis of judicial precedent, that "copyright in a pictorial, graphic, or sculptural work, portraying a useful article as such, does not extend to the manufacture of the useful article itself," and recommended specifically that "the distinctions drawn in this area by existing court decisions" not be altered by the statute. The Register's Supplementary Report, at page 48, cited a number of these decisions, and explained the insuperable difficulty of finding "any statutory formulation that would express the distinction satisfactorily." Section 113(b) reflects the Register's conclusion that "the real need is to make clear that there is no intention to change the present law with respect to the scope of protection in a work portraying a useful article as such.''

Is the application of copyright to the design of useful articles consistent with the Constitution, which grants Congress the power to protect "writings" and "authors"? In a concurring opinion in *Mazer v. Stein,* Justice Douglas observed:

> The Copyright Office has supplied us with a long list of such articles which have been copyrighted—statuettes, book ends, clocks, lamps, door knockers, candlesticks, inkstands, chandeliers, piggy banks, sundials, salt and pepper shakers, fish bowls, casseroles, and ash trays. Perhaps these are all "writings" in the constitutional sense. But to me, at least, they are not obviously so. It is time that we came to the problem full face.

In *Goldstein v. California,* 412 U.S. 546 (1973), involving the question whether states could bar the duplication of musical performances from phonograph records, the Court noted that the terms in the copyright clause of the Constitution "have not been construed in their narrow literal sense but, rather, with the reach necessary to reflect the broad scope of constitutional principles"; it interpreted the word "writings" to "include any physical rendering of the fruits of creative intellectual or aesthetic labor."

1.   WHAT IS A "USEFUL ARTICLE"?

In **Masquerade Novelty Inc. v. Unique Industries,** 912 F.2d 663 (3d Cir.1990), the Third Circuit reversed the trial court's holding that masks designed to resemble the noses of a pig, an elephant, or a parrot, were unprotectible "useful articles." The appellate court found that "the only utilitarian function of the nose masks is in their portrayal of animal noses.... [N]ose masks have no utility that does not derive from their appearance."

What if Masquerade's nose masks could also serve to keep the wearer's nose warm in winter? Should this additional, albeit improbable, utility recast the article as "useful" in the sense of the copyright statute? What about theatrical costumes, or Halloween disguises? Should these items be considered merely "depictive" or should they also be considered articles of clothing? For example, in *Whimsicality, Inc. v. Rubie's Costume Co.,* 891 F.2d 452 (2d Cir.1989), the court rejected plaintiff's characterization of Halloween costumes as "soft sculptures," finding them to be uncopyright-able clothing. More recently, the ever-persistent Whimsicality, Inc. again failed to persuade a court that its costumes' utility of enabling its wearer to portray an animal did not make them "useful articles." *See Whimsicality, Inc. v. Maison Joseph Battat,* 27 F.Supp.2d 456 (S.D.N.Y.1998).

Subsequent to the first *Whimsicality* decision, the Copyright Office issued a Policy Decision on the Registrability of Costume Designs, 56 FR

56530 (November 5, 1991), stating: "Under the adopted practices, masks will be registrable on the basis of pictorial and/or sculptural authorship. Costumes will be treated as useful articles, and will be registrable only upon a finding of separable artistic authorship." The Copyright Office determined that "Since masks generally portray their own appearance, this subject matter appears to fall outside of the definition of 'useful article.'" By contrast, according to the Copyright Office, "Costumes serve a dual purpose of clothing the body and portraying their appearance. Since clothing the body serves as a useful function, costumes fall within the literal definition of useful article."

Does this make sense? If a costume does "clothe the body," it does so in order to permit the wearer to "portray the appearance" of the character depicted by the costume. Although a costume may also be worn for warmth or modesty, those are generally not its purposes. On the other hand, the statute defines a "useful article" as one having "*an* intrinsic utilitarian function." Thus, a subsidiary utilitarian purpose, such as keeping the trick-or-treater warm as well as looking like a dinosaur, might suffice to characterize a Halloween Stegosaurus costume as "useful," no matter how unlikely it is to be used to "clothe the body" at times other than those at which the wearer seeks to portray the extinct reptile. (Of course, under the Policy Decision, the Stegosaurus mask, not being "useful," would be protectible, leaving the determination of the copyrightability of the decapitated remainder of the costume to assessment under the "separability" test, discussed *infra*.)

2. SEPARABILITY

Kieselstein–Cord v. Accessories by Pearl, Inc.

632 F.2d 989 (2d Cir.1980).

■ OAKES, CIRCUIT JUDGE: This case is on a razor's edge of copyright law. It involves belt buckles, utilitarian objects which as such are not copyrightable. But these are not ordinary buckles; they are sculptured designs cast in precious metals—decorative in nature and used as jewelry is, principally for ornamentation. We say "on a razor's edge" because the case requires us to draw a fine line under applicable copyright law and regulations. Drawing the line in favor of the appellant designer, we uphold the copyrights granted to him by the Copyright Office and reverse the district court's grant of summary judgment, 489 F. Supp. 732, in favor of the appellee, the copier of appellant's designs.

Facts

Appellant Barry Kieselstein–Cord designs, manufactures exclusively by handcraftsmanship, and sells fashion accessories. To produce the two buckles in issue here, the "Winchester" and the "Vaquero," he worked from original renderings which he had conceived and sketched. He then carved by hand a waxen prototype of each of the works from which molds were made for casting the objects in gold and silver. Difficult to describe, the buckles are solid sculptured designs, in the words of district court Judge Goettel, "with rounded corners, a sculpted surface, . . . a rectangular cut-out at one end for the belt attachment," and "several surface levels."

. . .

The Vaquero buckle, created in 1978, was part of a series of works that the designer testified was inspired by a book on design of the art nouveau school and the subsequent viewing of related architecture on a trip to Spain. . . . Explaining why he named the earlier buckle design "Winchester," the designer said that he saw "in [his] mind's eye a correlation between the art nouveau period and the butt of an antique Winchester rifle" and then "pulled these elements together graphically." The registration, which is recorded on a form used for works of art, or models or designs for works of art, specifically describes the nature of the work as "sculpture."

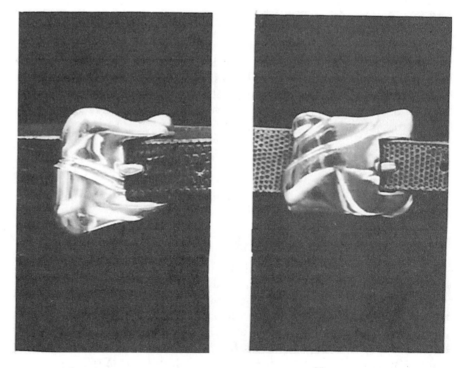

Winchester   Vaquero

The Winchester buckle in particular has had great success in the marketplace: more than 4,000 belts with Winchester buckles were sold from 1976 to early 1980, and in 1979 sales of the belts amounted to 95% of appellant's more than $300,000 in jewelry sales. A small women's size in silver with "double truncated triangle belt loops" sold, at the time this lawsuit commenced, at wholesale for $147.50 and a larger silver version for men sold at wholesale with loops for $662 and without loops for $465.

Lighter-weight men's versions in silver wholesaled for $450 and $295, with and without loops respectively. The gold versions sold at wholesale from $1,200 to $6,000. A shortened version of the belt with the small Winchester buckle is sometimes worn around the neck or elsewhere on the body rather than around the waist. Sales of both buckles were made primarily in high fashion stores and jewelry stores, bringing recognition to appellant as a "designer." This recognition included a 1979 Coty American Fashion Critics' Award for his work in jewelry design as well as election in 1978 to the Council of Fashion Designers of America. Both the Winchester and the Vaquero buckles, donated by appellant after this lawsuit was commenced, have been accepted by the Metropolitan Museum of Art for its permanent collection.

As the court below found, appellee's buckles "appear to be line-for-line copies but are made of common metal rather than" precious metal. Appellee admitted to copying the Vaquero and selling its imitations, and to selling copies of the Winchester. Indeed some of the order blanks of appellee's customers specifically referred to "Barry K Copy," "BK copy," and even "Barry Kieselstein Knock-off." . . .

We . . . only reach the question whether the buckles may be copyrighted.

Discussion

We commence our discussion by noting that no claim has been made that the appellant's work here in question lacks originality or creativity, elements necessary for copyrighting works of art. The thrust of appellee's argument, as well as of the court's decision below, is that appellant's buckles are not copyrightable because they are "useful articles" with no "pictorial, graphic, or sculptural features that can be identified separately from, and are capable of existing independently of, the utilitarian aspects" of the buckles. The 1976 copyright statute does not provide for the copyrighting of useful articles except to the extent that their designs incorporate artistic features that can be identified separately from the functional elements of the articles. *See* 17 U.S.C. §§ 101, 102. With respect to this question, the law adopts the language of the longstanding Copyright Office regulations, 37 C.F.R. § 202.10(c) (1977) (revoked Jan. 5, 1978, 43 Fed. Reg. 965, 966 (1978)).

The regulations in turn were adopted in the mid–1950's, under the 1909 Act, in an effort to implement the Supreme Court's decision in *Mazer v. Stein,* 347 U.S. 201 (1954). . . .

Ultimately, as Professor Nimmer concludes, none of the authorities— the *Mazer* opinion, the old regulations, or the statute—offer any "ready answer to the line-drawing problem inherent in delineating the extent of copyright protection available for works of applied art." *Id.* at 2–89. . . .

Appellee argues that the belt buckles are merely useful objects, which include decorative features that serve an aesthetic as well as a utilitarian purpose. And the copyright laws, appellee points out, were never intended to nor would the Constitution permit them to protect monopolies on useful articles. But appellee goes too far by further arguing that "copyrightability cannot adhere in the 'conceptual' separation of an artistic element." Brief for Defendant–Appellee at 17. This assertion flies in the face of the legislative intent as expressed in the House Report, which specifically refers to elements that "physically or conceptually, can be identified as separable from the utilitarian aspects of" a useful article. *House Report* at 55, [1976] U.S. Code Cong. & Admin. News at 5668.

We see in appellant's belt buckles conceptually separable sculptural elements, as apparently have the buckles' wearers who have used them as ornamentation for parts of the body other than the waist. The primary ornamental aspect of the Vaquero and Winchester buckles is conceptually separable from their subsidiary utilitarian function. This conclusion is not at variance with the expressed congressional intent to distinguish copyrightable applied art and uncopyrightable industrial design. *House Report* at 55, [1976] U.S. Code Cong. & Admin. News at 5668. Pieces of applied art, these buckles may be considered jewelry, the form of which is subject to copyright protection. . . .

Appellant's designs are not, as the appellee suggests in an affidavit, mere variations of "the well-known western buckle." As both the expert witnesses for appellant testified and the Copyright Office's action implied, the buckles rise to the level of creative art.

> . . .

■ WEINSTEIN, DISTRICT JUDGE (dissenting): The trial judge was correct on both the law and the facts for the reasons given in his excellent opinion holding that plaintiff was not entitled to copyright protection. *Kieselstein-Cord v. Accessories by Pearl, Inc.,* 489 F. Supp. 732 (S.D.N.Y.1980). The works sued on are, while admirable aesthetically pleasing examples of modern design, indubitably belt buckles and nothing else; their innovations of form are inseparable from the important function they serve—helping to keep the tops of trousers at waist level.

The conclusion that affirmance is required is reached reluctantly. The result does deny protection to designers who use modern three-dimensional abstract works artfully incorporated into a functional object as an inseparable aspect of the article while granting it to those who attach their independent representational art, or even their trite gimmickry, to a useful object for purposes of enhancement. Moreover, this result enables the commercial pirates of the marketplace to appropriate for their own profit, without any cost to themselves, the works of talented designers who enrich our lives with their intuition and skill. The crass are rewarded, the artist who creates beauty is not. All of us are offended by the flagrant copying of another's work. This is regrettable, but it is not for this court to twist the law in order to achieve a result Congress has denied.

> . . .

The statute follows the decision of the Supreme Court in *Mazer v. Stein,* 347 U.S. 201, *rehearing denied,* 347 U.S. 949 (1954). In *Mazer,* the

Court held that independent works of art may be copyrighted even if they are incorporated into useful articles—"nothing in the copyright statute . . . support[s] the argument that the intended use or use in industry of an article eligible for copyright bars or invalidates its registration." *Id.* at 218. But the copyright protection covered only that aspect of the article that was a separately identifiable work of art independent of the useful article, in that instance a statuette used as part of a lamp.

Among recent decisions making this same distinction is *Esquire v. Ringer,* 591 F.2d 796 (D.C.Cir.), *cert. denied,* 440 U.S. 908, *rehearing denied,* 441 U.S. 917 (1979). *Esquire* denied copyright protection to the overall shape of a lighting fixture because of its integration of the functional aspects of the entire lighting assembly. The "overall design or configuration of a utilitarian object, even if it is determined by aesthetic as well as functional considerations, is not eligible for copyright." *Id.* at 804.

While the distinction is not precise, the courts, both before and after *Mazer,* have tried to follow the principle of the copyright act permitting copyright to extend only to ornamental or superfluous designs contained within useful objects while denying it to artistically designed functional components of useful objects. Generally they have favored representational art as opposed to non-representation[al] artistic forms which are embodied in, and part of the structure of, a useful article [citations omitted]. The relative certainty that has developed in this area of the law should not be disturbed absent some compelling development—and none has thus far been presented.

Interpretation and application of the copyright statute is facilitated by House Report No. 94–1476, U.S. Code Cong. & Admin. News 1976, p. 5658, by the Committee on the Judiciary. It explicitly indicated that the rule of *Mazer* was incorporated.

> In accordance with the Supreme Court's decision in *Mazer v. Stein,* 347 U.S. 201, 74 S. Ct. 460, 98 L. Ed. 630 (1954), works of "applied art" encompass all original pictorial, graphic, and sculptural works that are intended to be or have been embodied in useful articles, regardless of factors such as mass production, commercial exploitation, and the potential availability of design patent protection. . . .

> The Committee has added language to the definition of "pictorial, graphic, and sculptural works" in an effort to make clearer the distinction between works of applied art protectable under the bill and industrial designs not subject to copyright protection. The declaration that "pictorial, graphic, and sculptural works" include "works of artistic craftsmanship insofar as their form but not their mechanical or utilitarian aspects are concerned" is classic language: it is drawn from Copyright Office regulations promulgated in the 1940's and expressly endorsed by the Supreme Court in the *Mazer* case.

>   . . .

> In adopting this amendatory language, the Committee is seeking to draw as clear a line as possible between copyrightable works of applied

art and uncopyrighted works of industrial design. A two-dimensional painting, drawing, or graphic work is still capable of being identified as such when it is printed on or applied to utilitarian articles such as textile fabrics, wallpaper, containers, and the like. The same is true when a statue or carving is used to embellish an industrial product or, as in the *Mazer* case, is incorporated into a product without losing its ability to exist independently as a work of art. On the other hand, *although the shape of an industrial product may be aesthetically satisfying and valuable, the Committee's intention is not to offer it copyright protection under the bill.* Unless the shape of an automobile, airplane, ladies' dress, food processor, television set, or any other industrial product contains some element that, physically or conceptually, can be identified as separable from the utilitarian aspects of that article, the design would not be copyrighted under the bill. The test of separability and independence from "the utilitarian aspects of the article" does not depend upon the nature of the design—that is, even if the appearance of an article is determined by aesthetic (as opposed to functional) considerations, only elements, if any, which can be identified separately from the useful article as such are copyrightable. *And, even if the three-dimensional design contains some such element (for example, a carving on the back of a chair or a floral relief design on silver flatware), copyright protection would extend only to that element, and would not cover the overall configuration of the utilitarian article as such.*

1976 U.S. Code Cong. & Admin. News, pp. 5667–5668. (Emphasis supplied.)

Congress considered and declined to enact legislation that would have extended copyright protection to "[t]he 'design of a useful article' ... including its two-dimensional or three-dimensional features of shape and surface, which make up the appearance of the article." H.R. 2223, Title II, § 201(b)(2), 94th Cong., 1st Sess. (January 28, 1975). Passage of this provision was recommended by the Register of Copyrights, ... and the United States Department of Commerce.... It was opposed by the Department of Justice on policy grounds.... The Justice Department noted the important substantive objections to the proposal—primarily it would charge the public a fee for the use of improved and pleasing new designs and styles in useful articles.

. . .

While the protection period as proposed for the new type of ornamental design protection is only a maximum of 10 years as compared with the maximum of 14 years available for a design patent, it is granted without the need of meeting the novelty and unobviousness requirements of the patent statute. A threshold consideration before finding that the needs are such that this new type of protection should be available *is whether the benefits to the public of such protection outweigh the burdens. We believe that insufficient need has been shown to date to justify removing from the public domain and possible use by others of the rights and benefits proposed under the present bill for such ornamental designs.* We believe that design patents, as are granted today, are as far as the public should go to grant exclusive rights for ornamental designs of useful articles in the absence of an adequate showing that the new protection will provide substantial benefits to the general public which outweigh removing such designs from free public use.

While it has been said that the examination procedure in the Patent Office results in serious delays in the issuance of a design patent so as to be a significant problem and damaging to "inventors" of ornamental designs of useful articles, *the desirable free use of designs which do not rise to patentable invention of ornamental designs of useful articles are believed* to be paramount.

If the contribution made to the public by the creation of an ornamental design of a useful article is insufficient to rise to patentable novelty, the design should not be protected by the law. The Department of Justice has consistently opposed legislation of this character.

To omit Federal statutory protection for the form of a useful object is not to deny the originator of that form any remedy whatsoever. If he can prove that competitors are passing their goods as the originator's by copying the product's design, he may bring an unfair competition action against such copyists.

Id. at 139–140. (Emphasis supplied.)

No additional testimony was received with respect to this aspect of the House bill. The Joint Senate–House Conference Committee deleted the design protection section to give further consideration to its administrative difficulties and to the benefits and burdens created by limiting the free public domain. 1976 U.S. Code Cong. & Admin. News, pp. 5663, 5832. . . .

Interestingly, even if the design protection section proposed by the Department of Commerce . . . had been passed, appellant's buckles might still have been excluded under the following subsection excluding three-dimensional features of apparel:

Designs Not Subject to Protection

§ 202. *Protection under this title shall not be available for a design that is—*

. . .

(e) *composed of three-dimensional features of shape and surface with respect to men's, women's and children's apparel,* including undergarments and outerwear.

(Emphasis supplied.) . . .

The distinctions between copyrightable "pictorial, graphic and sculptural works" and noncopyrightable industrial "designs" reflect serious concerns about the promotion of competition, the widespread availability of quality products and the advancement of technology through copying and modification. *See, e.g.,* G. Nelson, Design, 170 (1979) (experience suggests that free copying results in more rapid development). . . .

Important policies are obviously at stake. Should we encourage the artist and increase the compensation to the creative? Or should we allow cheap reproductions which will permit our less affluent to afford beautiful artifacts? Appellant sold the original for $600.00 and up. Defendant's version went for one-fiftieth of that sum.

Thus far Congress and the Supreme Court have answered in favor of commerce and the masses rather than the artists, designers and the well-to-do. Any change must be left to those higher authorities. The choices are legislative not judicial.

QUESTIONS

1. Was the ornamental belt buckle in the principal case also protectible, as an initial matter, under the design patent laws? Now that the court has held that it is protectible under copyright, must Kieselstein–Cord opt for protection under one or the other statute, or may he claim protection under both? Can you formulate any argument, based upon the Constitution or otherwise, that would in effect require "preemption" as between the copyright and patent laws? See Appendix C, Regulation § 202.10(a).

2. In the *Esquire* case (discussed in the principal case), the claimant of copyright in the street-light design, reproduced just below, argued that, for the better part of the day, the fixture had no utilitarian function at all but was in fact exclusively a publicly displayed work of sculpture. If you agree, does this not make *Esquire* an even more appealing case for copyright protection than *Kieselstein-Cord* (despite their opposite results)?

3. It has been argued that the view of the dissenting judge in the *Kieselstein-Cord* case would work an impermissible discrimination against designs that emphasize line and shape rather than the ornate, thus ignoring the admonition of Justice Holmes in *Bleistein v. Donaldson Lithographing Co.,* at Chapter 1.B, *supra* that judges must not sit as arbiters of national taste. Do you agree?

4. On the other hand, do you agree with the claim of the Register of Copyrights (set forth by the Court of Appeals for the District of Columbia Circuit in *Esquire, Inc. v. Ringer*) that protection of such designs as those in the principal case would mean that "the whole realm of consumer products—garments, toasters, refrigerators, furniture, bathtubs, automobiles, etc.—and industrial products designed to have aesthetic appeal—subway cars, computers, photocopying machines, typewriters, adding machines, etc." would also qualify for copyright protection?

Carol Barnhart Inc. v. Economy Cover Corp.

773 F.2d 411 (2d Cir.1985).

■ Mansfield, Circuit Judge:

Carol Barnhart Inc. ("Barnhart"), which sells display forms to department stores, distributors, and small retail stores, appeals from a judgment of the Eastern District of New York, Leonard D. Wexler, Judge, granting a motion for summary judgment made by defendant Economy Cover Corporation ("Economy"), which sells a wide variety of display products primarily to jobbers and distributors. Barnhart's complaint alleges that Economy has infringed its copyright and engaged in unfair competition by offering for sale display forms copied from four original "sculptural forms" to which Barnhart holds the copyright. Judge Wexler granted Economy's motion for summary judgment on the ground that plaintiff's mannequins of partial human torsos used to display articles of clothing are utilitarian articles not containing separable works of art, and thus are not copyrightable. We affirm.

The bones of contention are four human torso forms designed by Barnhart, each of which is life-size, without neck, arms, or a back, and made of expandable white styrene. Plaintiff's president created the forms in 1982 by using clay, buttons, and fabric to develop an initial mold, which she then used to build an aluminum mold into which the polystyrene is poured to manufacture the sculptural display form. There are two male and two female upper torsos. One each of the male and female torsos is unclad for the purpose of displaying shirts and sweaters, while the other two are sculpted with shirts for displaying sweaters and jackets. All the forms, which are otherwise life-like and anatomically accurate, have hollow backs designed to hold excess fabric when the garment is fitted onto the form. Barnhart's advertising stresses the forms' uses to display items such as sweaters, blouses, and dress shirts, and states that they come "[p]ackaged in UPS-size boxes for easy shipping and [are] sold in multiples of twelve."

. . .

Since the four Barnhart forms are concededly useful articles, the crucial issue in determining their copyrightability is whether they possess artistic or aesthetic features that are physically or conceptually separable from their utilitarian dimension. . . .

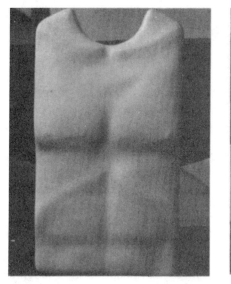

Figure 1

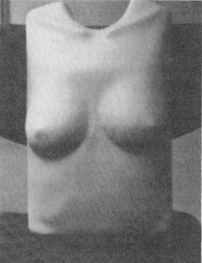

Figure 2

Figure 3

Figure 4

[The court reviewed the legislative history, since 1909, of protection for pictorial and sculptural works and traced the development of the "separability" principle.]

The legislative history thus confirms that, while copyright protection has increasingly been extended to cover articles having a utilitarian dimension, Congress has explicitly refused copyright protection for works of applied art or industrial design which have aesthetic or artistic features that cannot be identified separately from the useful article. Such works are not copyrightable regardless of the fact that they may be "aesthetically satisfying and valuable." H.R. Rep. No. 1476, *supra*, at 55, 1976 U.S. Code Cong. & Admin. News at 5668.

Applying these principles, we are persuaded that since the aesthetic and artistic features of the Barnhart forms are inseparable from the forms' use as utilitarian articles the forms are not copyrightable. Appellant emphasizes that clay sculpting, often used in traditional sculpture, was used in making the molds for the forms. It also stresses that the forms have been responded to as sculptural forms, and have been used for purposes other than modeling clothes, e.g., as decorating props and signs without any clothing or accessories. While this may indicate that the forms are "aesthetically satisfying and valuable," it is insufficient to show that the forms possess aesthetic or artistic features that are physically or conceptually separable from the forms' use as utilitarian objects to display clothes. On the contrary, to the extent the forms possess aesthetically pleasing features, even when these features are considered in the aggregate, they cannot be conceptualized as existing independently of their utilitarian function.

. . . Appellant suggests that since the Barnhart forms fall within the traditional category of sculpture of the human body, they should be subjected to a lower level of scrutiny in determining [their] copyrightability. We disagree. We find no support in the statutory language or legislative history for the claim that merely because a utilitarian article falls within a traditional art form it is entitled to a lower level of scrutiny in determining its copyrightability. Recognition of such a claim would in any event conflict with the anti-discrimination principle Justice Holmes enunciated in *Bleistein v. Donaldson Lithographing Co., supra*, 188 U.S. at 251–52, 23 S. Ct. at 300.

Nor do we agree that copyrightability here is dictated by our decision in *Kieselstein-Cord v. Accessories by Pearl, Inc.*, 632 F.2d 989 (2d Cir. 1980). . . . What distinguishes those buckles from the Barnhart forms is that the ornamented surfaces of the buckles were not in any respect required by their utilitarian functions; the artistic and aesthetic features could thus be conceived of as having been added to, or superimposed upon, an otherwise utilitarian article. The unique artistic design was wholly unnecessary to performance of the utilitarian function. In the case of the Barnhart forms, on the other hand, the features claimed to be aesthetic or artistic, e.g., the life-size configuration of the breasts and the width of the shoulders, are inextricably intertwined with the utilitarian feature, the display of clothes. Whereas a model of a human torso, in order to serve its utilitarian function, must have some configuration of the chest and some width of shoulders, a belt buckle can serve its function satisfactorily without any ornamentation of the type that renders the *Kieselstein-Cord* buckles distinctive.[5]

The judgment of the district court is affirmed.

■ JON O. NEWMAN, CIRCUIT JUDGE, dissenting:

. . . I would grant summary judgment to the plaintiff as to two of the objects in question and remand for trial of disputed issues of fact as to the other two objects in question.

. . . [T]he issue becomes whether the designs of these useful articles have "sculptural features that can be identified separately from, and are capable of existing independently of, the utilitarian aspects" of the forms.

This elusive standard was somewhat clarified by the House Report accompanying the bill that became the 1976 Act. The Report states that the article must contain "some element that, *physically or conceptually,* can be identified as separable from the utilitarian aspects of that article." H.R. Rep. No. 1476, 94th Cong., 2d Sess. 55, reprinted in 1976 U.S. Code Cong. & Admin. News 5668 (emphasis added). In this Circuit it is settled, and the majority does not dispute, that "conceptual separability" is distinct from "physical separability" and, when present, entitles the creator of a useful article to a copyright on its design. . . .

What must be carefully considered is the meaning and application of the principle of "conceptual separability." Initially, it may be helpful to make the obvious point that this principle must mean something other than "physical separability." That latter principle is illustrated by the numerous familiar examples of useful objects ornamented by a drawing, a

5. Our learned colleague, Judge Newman, would have copyrightability of a utilitarian article turn on "whether visual inspection of the article and consideration of all pertinent evidence would engender in the [ordinary] observer's mind a separate non-utilitarian concept that can displace, at least temporarily, the utilitarian aspect." (Dissenting Op. p. 423). The difficulty with this proposal is that it uses as its yardstick a standard so ethereal as to amount to a "non-test" that would be extremely difficult, if not impossible, to administer or apply. Whether a utilitarian object could temporarily be conceived of as a work of art would require a judicial investigation into the ways in which it might on occasion have been displayed and the extent of the displays. It might involve expert testimony and some kind of survey evidence, as distinguished from reliance upon the judge as an ordinary observer.

Almost any utilitarian article may be viewed by some separately as art, depending on how it is displayed (e.g., a can of Campbell Soup or a pair of ornate scissors affixed to the wall of a museum of modern art). But it is the object, not the form of display, for which copyright protection is sought. Congress has made it reasonably clear that copyrightability of the object should turn on its ordinary use as viewed by the average observer, not by a temporary flight of fancy that could attach to any utilitarian object, including an automobile engine, depending on how it is displayed.

. . . We disagree with the proposition that the mannequins here, when viewed as hollowed-out three-dimensional forms (as presented for copyright) as distinguished from two-dimensional photographs, could be viewed by the ordinary observer as anything other than objects having a utilitarian function as mannequins. It would only be by concealing the open, hollowed-out rear half of the object, which is obviously designed to facilitate pinning or tucking in of garments, that an illusion of a sculpture can be created. In that case (as with the photos relied on by the dissent) the subject would not be the same as that presented for copyright.

carving, a sculpted figure, or any other decorative embellishment that could physically appear apart from the useful article. Professor Nimmer offers the example of the sculptured jaguar that adorns the hood of and provides the name for the well-known British automobile. . . .

A somewhat related approach, suggested by a sentence in Judge Oakes' opinion in *Kieselstein-Cord,* is to uphold the copyright whenever the decorative or aesthetically pleasing aspect of the article can be said to be "primary" and the utilitarian function can be said to be "subsidiary." 632 F.2d at 993. This approach apparently does not focus on frequency of utilitarian and non-utilitarian usage since the belt buckles in that case were frequently used to fasten belts and less frequently used as pieces of ornamental jewelry displayed at various locations other than the waist. The difficulty with this approach is that it offers little guidance to the trier of fact, or the judge endeavoring to determine whether a triable issue of fact exists, as to what is being measured by the classifications "primary" and "subsidiary."

. . .

Some might suggest that "conceptual separability" exists whenever the design of a form has sufficient aesthetic appeal to be appreciated for its artistic qualities. That approach has plainly been rejected by Congress. The House Report makes clear that, if the artistic features cannot be identified separately, the work is not copyrightable even though such features are "aesthetically satisfying and valuable." H.R. Rep. No. 1476, *supra,* at 55, 1976 U.S. Code Cong. & Admin. News at 5668. A chair may be so artistically designed as to merit display in a museum, but that fact alone cannot satisfy the test of "conceptual separateness." The viewer in the museum sees and apprehends a well-designed chair, not a work of art with a design that is conceptually separate from the functional purposes of an object on which people sit.

How, then, is "conceptual separateness" to be determined? In my view, the answer derives from the word "conceptual." For the design features to be "conceptually separate" from the utilitarian aspects of the useful article that embodies the design, the article must stimulate in the mind of the beholder a concept that is separate from the concept evoked by its utilitarian function. The test turns on what may reasonably be understood to be occurring in the mind of the beholder or, as some might say, in the "mind's eye" of the beholder. This formulation requires consideration of who the beholder is and when a concept may be considered "separate."

. . . [Judge Newman concluded that the "relevant beholder must be that most useful legal personage—the ordinary, reasonable observer."] The "separateness" of the utilitarian and non-utilitarian concepts engendered by an article's design is itself a perplexing concept. I think the requisite "separateness" exists whenever the design creates in the mind of the ordinary observer two different concepts that are not inevitably entertained simultaneously. Again, the example of the artistically designed chair displayed in a museum may be helpful. The ordinary observer can be expected to apprehend the design of a chair whenever the object is viewed. He may, in addition, entertain the concept of a work of art, but, if this second concept is engendered in the observer's mind simultaneously with the concept of the article's utilitarian function, the requisite "separateness" does not exist. The test is not whether the observer fails to recognize the object as a chair but only whether the concept of the utilitarian function can be displaced in the mind by some other concept. That does not occur, at least for the ordinary observer, when viewing even the most artistically designed chair. It may occur, however, when viewing some other object if the utilitarian function of the object is not perceived at all; it may also occur, even when the utilitarian function is perceived by observation, perhaps aided by explanation, if the concept of the utilitarian function can be displaced in the observer's mind while he entertains the separate concept of some non-utilitarian function. The separate concept will normally be that of a work of art.

. . .

In endeavoring to draw the line between the design of an aesthetically pleasing useful article, which is not copyrightable, and the copyrightable design of a useful article that engenders a concept separate from the concept of its utilitarian function, courts will inevitably be drawn into some minimal inquiry as to the nature of art. The need for the inquiry is regrettable, since courts must not become the arbiters of taste in art or any other aspect of aesthetics. However, as long as "conceptual separability" determines whether the design of a useful article is copyrightable, some threshold assessment of art is inevitable since the separate concept that will satisfy the test of "conceptual separability" will often be the concept of a work of art. Of course, courts must not assess the *quality* of art, but a determination of whether a design engenders the concept of a work of art, separate from the concept of an article's utilitarian function, necessarily requires some consideration of whether the object *is* a work of art.

... Our case involving the four styrene chest forms seems to me a much easier case than *Kieselstein-Cord.* An ordinary observer, indeed, an ordinary reader of this opinion who views the two unclothed forms depicted in figures 1 and 2 below, would be most unlikely even to entertain, from visual inspection alone, the concept of a mannequin with the utilitarian function of displaying a shirt or a blouse. The initial concept in the observer's mind, I believe, would be of an art object, an entirely understandable mental impression based on previous viewing of unclad torsos displayed as artistic sculptures. Even after learning that these two forms are used to display clothing in retail stores, the only reasonable conclusion that an ordinary viewer would reach is that the forms have both a utilitarian function and an entirely separate function of serving as a work of art. I am confident that the ordinary observer could reasonably conclude only that these two forms are not simply mannequins that happen to have sufficient aesthetic appeal to qualify as works of art, but that the conception in the mind is that of a work of art *in addition to and capable of being entertained separately from* the concept of a mannequin, if the latter concept is entertained at all. As appellant contends, with pardonable hyperbole, the design of Michelangelo's "David" would not cease to be copyrightable simply because cheap copies of it were used by a retail store to display clothing.

. . . The two forms depicted in figures 1 and 2, however, if perceived as mannequins at all, clearly engender an entirely separable concept of an art object, one that can be entertained in the mind without simultaneously perceiving the forms as mannequins at all.

. . .

Of course, appellant's entitlement to a copyright on the design of the unclothed forms would give it only limited, though apparently valuable, protection. The copyright would not bar imitators from designing human chests. It would only bar them from copying the precise design embodied in appellant's forms.

As for the two forms, depicted in figures 3 and 4 [above], of chests clothed with a shirt or a blouse, I am uncertain what concept or concepts would be engendered in the mind of an ordinary observer.

. . . [The ordinary] observer might always perceive them as manne-quins or perhaps as devices advertising for sale the particular style of shirt or blouse sculpted on each form. I think a reasonable trier could conclude either way on the issue of "conceptual separability" as to the clothed forms. That issue is therefore not amenable to summary judgment and should, in my view, be remanded for trial. In any event, I do not agree that the only reasonable conclusion a trier of fact could reach is that the clothed forms create no concept separable from the concept of their utilitarian function.

I would grant summary judgment to the copyright proprietor as to the design of the two nude forms and remand for trial with respect to the two clothed forms.

QUESTION

Is it so clear that the and human-form mannequins used for displaying clothing in *Carol Barnhart* were "useful articles"? What is the nature of their utility? Compare *Superior Form Bldrs., Inc. v. Dan Chase Taxidermy Supply Co.,* 74 F.3d 488 (4th Cir.1996), *cert. denied,* 519 U.S. 809 (1996) and *Hart v. Dan Chase Taxidermy Supply Co.,* 86 F.3d 320 (2d Cir.1996), in which animal mannequins used by taxidermists to mount animal skins were not deemed "useful articles" within the meaning of the Copyright Act. "[T]hese animal mannequins were designed to portray the appearance of animals through artistic features introduced by the author in their creation . . . ."

The Second Circuit has continued to struggle with conceptual separability. Judge Oakes, *Kieselstein-Cord's* majority author, attempted to harmonize that decision with *Carol Barnhart* in a controversy concerning the copyrightability of a bicycle rack (see photograph below). In **Brandir Int'l v. Cascade Pac. Lumber Co.,** 834 F.2d 1142 (2d Cir.1987), the panel majority held the form of an undulating tubed bicycle rack inseparable from its function. According to the majority, if functional concerns influenced the work's aesthetically pleasing appearance, the sculptural features would be deemed inseparable under § 101. (The court gave credit to Denicola, *Applied Art and Industrial Design: A Suggested Approach to Copyright in Useful Articles,* 67 Minn. L. Rev. 707 (1983), for devising the test.) The majority indicated that the inquiry into whether form follows function in the work under scrutiny would relieve judges of the improper burden of evaluating the aesthetic merits of nonfunctional art. In dissent, Judge Winter contended that the majority's approach virtually eliminated "conceptual separability." Worse, rather than protecting judges from art criticism, the majority's emphasis on the influence of utilitarian concerns in the design process would in fact require too much inquiry into the creative processes.

Reproduced with permission
Photograph by Joanne Gere

QUESTIONS

1. Suppose copyright protection is sought for an abstract horizontal shapeembodied in plaster and entitled "Repose." Would embodiment of this shape in a bed or other piece of furniture disqualify the design as the kind of "overall shape or configuration of a utilitarian article" excluded from protection under the language of the House Report, or would it still be protectible?

2. Which of the following pictured works (on pages 219–20), if any, are copyrightable?*

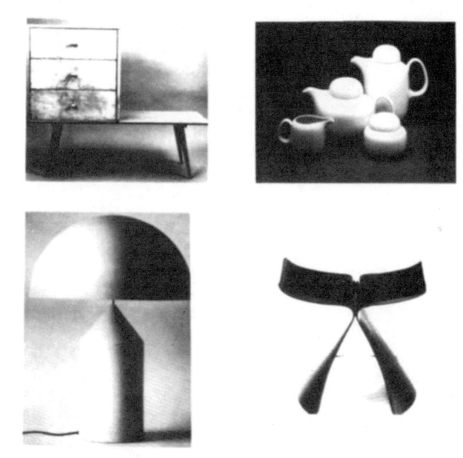

* All of the works in the photographs on this page and page 241 were displayed in the exhibition "Design Since 1945" at the Philadelphia Museum of Art, from October 1983 to January 1984. The designer, title, and date of each work is as follows: *This page.* Top left: P. McCobb, "Planner Group" components (1949). Top right: H.T. Baumann, "Brasilia" coffee and tea service (1975). Bottom left: V. Magistretti, "Atollo" table lamp (1977). Bottom right: S. Yanagi, "Butterfly" stool (1956). *Page 241.* Top: DePas, D'Urbino, Lomazzi, "Joe" chair (1970). Bottom: F.O. Gehry, "Easy Edges" rocking chair (1972). These works are reproduced with the permission of the Philadelphia Museum of Art (and, for the "Joe" chair, the permission of Stendig, Inc.).

COPYRIGHTABILITY OF TYPEFACE DESIGNS

A troubling issue of design protection that was raised in the debates leading to the enactment of the 1976 Copyright Act concerned typeface design. The House Report (at page 55) included the following passage:

> The Committee has considered, but chosen to defer, the possibility of protecting the design of typefaces. A "typeface" can be defined as a set of letters, numbers, or other symbolic characters, whose forms are related by repeating design elements consistently applied in a notational system and are intended to be embodied in articles whose intrinsic utilitarian function is for use in composing text or other cognizable combinations of characters. The Committee does not regard the design of typeface, as thus defined, to be a copyrightable "pictorial, graphic, or sculptural work" within the meaning of this bill and the application of the dividing line in section 101.

The issue of typeface protection had become particularly heated by the early 1970's, as a result of the development of new photocomposition techniques that made it possible readily to make unauthorized copies of typeface designs. Register Barbara Ringer, on November 6, 1974, held the first rulemaking hearing in the history of the Copyright Office, for the purpose of determining whether to modify an existing Office regulation that was generally understood to bar copyright for typeface designs. Proponents of protection contended—at the Copyright Office hearing and at concurrent congressional hearings on the pending revision bill—that original designs for fonts of type are "writings of an author" under both the Constitution and the 1909 statute, that caselaw was not inconsistent with such protection, that registration would impose no burden on authors and reprinters, and that protection should be made available under both copyright and the projected new design legislation (at that time, title II of the copyright bill, ultimately deleted before passage). Opponents claimed, among other things, that design protection would simply invite the major typeface manufacturers to engage in behavior violative of the antitrust laws and would lead to suits to enjoin publication of printed matter. The Copyright Office chose ultimately to decline registration for typeface designs, and a mandamus action was brought to compel such registration. In *Eltra Corp. v. Ringer,* 579 F.2d 294 (4th Cir.1978), mandamus was denied, the court concluding that typeface was not a "work of art" within the subject matter covered by the 1909 Act. Should that result be controlling today? How dispositive is the pertinent passage from the House Report quoted above? While considering these questions, study the typeface samples reproduced below.

In view of the fact that type fonts are regularly designed and reproduced by computer program, efforts have been made to circumvent the *Eltra* decision by registering the pertinent computer program, which will provide relief at least against another who copies that program directly (as distinguished from the typeface that it generates). At least one court has held that copyright extends to such a computer program, which digitally reflects the x and y coordinates for typeface and the "on-curve and off-curve" reference points interpolated by an editor. The instructions in the computer program were held to embody sufficient originality. *Adobe Sys. Inc. v. Southern Software Inc.,* 45 U.S.P.Q.2d 1827 (N.D.Cal.1998). This distinction between uncopyrightable typeface and the underlying copyrightable computer program explains the otherwise unfathomable reference in Copyright Office Regulation 202.1(e) to "typeface as typeface."

Lightline LIGHTLINE
LINCOLN GOTHIC
Lubalin Graph LUBALI
Lubalin Graph LUBA
Lubalin Graph LUB
Lubalin Graph LUI
Lubalin Graph LU
Lubalin Graph LU
Lucifer LUCIFER
Lys Calligraph L
Macbeth MACBETH macbe
MACHINE
MACHINE
MADISON MADISON
Madisonian MADISO
Manchester MANCHE
MANDARIN
Mandate MANDATE
Manhattan MANHATT
MANUSCRIPT INITIAL
MARBLEHEART

Marten Roman MART
Mastodon MASTOD
Maxie MAXIE
Melior MELIOR
Melior MELIOR
Melior MELIOR
MICHELANGELO
MICROGRAMMA
MICROGRAMM
MICROGRAMM
Milano Roman MILAN
Mistral MISTRAL
Modern No 20 MODE
Modernique MODI
Modernique MODI
Moonshadow MOONSHA
MOORE COMPUTER
MOORE LIBERTY
Musketeer MUSKETEER
Musketeer MUSKETEE
Musketeer MUSKETEE

ROBERT MERGES, OVERVIEW OF DESIGN PATENTS*

Due to a lengthy processing time, high application cost, strict and wavering standards, and a long history of judicial hostility, the design patent system has been criticized as ineffective and in need of reform. J.H. Reichman, *Design Protection and the New Technologies: The United States Experience in a Transnational Perspective*, 19 U. Balt. L. Rev. 6, 23 (1991). As the courts have recently become more receptive to design patents, interest has been renewed in this form of intellectual property protection. This section provides a basic introduction to the design patent system.

* The following materials are excerpted from *Patent Law and Policy, Cases and Materials*, 1289–94 (2d ed. 1997), by Robert P. Merges. The editors wish to thank Professor Merges for authorizing the inclusion of this excerpt from his book, a new edition of which will be published in 2002.

A design may consist of surface ornamentation, configuration, or both. The Design Patent Act was codified under the Patent Act of 1954 in 35 U.S.C. § 171, which allows a design patent to be obtained for "any new, original and ornamental design for an article of manufacture ..." and provides that all provisions relating to patents for inventions also apply to design patents. Design patents are issued for a fourteen-year term.

I. *Requirements for Patentability*

A. *Novelty*

Novelty is established if no prior art shows exactly the same design. A design is novel if the "ordinary observer," viewing the new design as a whole, would consider it to be different from, rather than a modification of, an already existing design.

B. *Nonobviousness*

Because Section 171 provides that the provisions of Title 35 relating to utility patents also apply to design patents, a design must be nonobvious, which requires the "exercise of the inventive or originative faculty." *Smith v. Whitman*, 148 U.S. 674, 679 (1893).

Prior to the adoption of a uniform standard to determine nonobviousness in design patents, the courts were in conflict over whether to use an "ordinary designer" standard or that of an "ordinary intelligent man." *See In re Laverne*, 356 F.2d 1003 (C.C.P.A.1966). Determining the nonobviousness of a design patent, as opposed to a utility patent, is unpredictable, as it is an inherently subjective inquiry, depending largely on personal taste. In evaluating nonobviousness of utility patents, judges can measure the distance between the prior art and a new invention on the basis of uniform scientific criteria and technical data, while the evaluation of the distance between an appearance design and its predecessors necessarily involves "value judgments that are hard to quantify and unreliable at best." Reichman, *supra*, at 33 n.164. The Federal Circuit's liberalization of the nonobviousness requirement has lowered the invalidation rate of design patents from seventy-five to one hundred percent only a few years ago, to thirty-eight percent today. *Id*. at 37.

In 1981, the Court of Customs and Patent Appeals held that the *Graham* test applies to design patents, and that nonobviousness should be measured in terms of a "designer of ordinary capability who designs articles of the type presented in the application." *In re Nalbandian*, 661 F.2d 1214, 1216 (C.C.P.A.1981). The new standard allows for objective evidence of expert testimony from designers in the field to be used to prove nonobviousness. *Id*. at 1217. The Federal Circuit subsequently adopted this standard. While this approach appears more evenhanded and has led to more patents being upheld as valid, it may not solve the problem of unpredictability, because the opinions of different designers can vary considerably. William T. Fryer, III, *Industrial Design Protection in the United*

States of America—Present Situation and Plans for Revision, 70 J. Pat. & Trademark Off. Soc'y 821, 829 (1988).

The Federal Circuit emphasized the presumptive validity of a design patent and placed the burden on the challenger to come forward with clear and convincing proof of obviousness.... Most significantly, the Federal Circuit held that objective secondary considerations, such as commercial success and copying, which apply to utility patents, are relevant to determining nonobviousness of design patents. *See, e.g., Litton,* 728 F.2d at 1441; *Avia,* 853 F.2d at 1564. The theory supporting the consideration of commercial success is that the purpose of a design patent is to increase salability, so if a design has been a success it "must have been sufficiently novel and superior to attract attention." *Robert W. Brown & Co. v. De Bell,* 243 F.2d 200, 202 (9th Cir.1957); *see also* 1 Donald S. Chisum, Patents § 1.04[2][f], at 1–208 (1992). Evidence of commercial success must be related to the patented design rather than to factors such as functional improvement or advertising. *See, e.g., Litton,* 728 F.2d at 1443; *Avia,* 853 F.2d at 1564.

C. *Ornamentality*

A patentable design must be ornamental—it must create a pleasing appearance. To satisfy the requirement of ornamentality, a design "must be the product of aesthetic skill and artistic conception." *Blisscraft of Hollywood v. United Plastics Co.,* 294 F.2d 694, 696 (2d Cir.1961). This requirement has been met by articles which are outside the realm of traditional "art." *See In re Koehring,* 37 F.2d 421, 422 (C.C.P.A.1930) (determining a design for a cement mixer to be ornamental because it "possessed more grace and pleasing appearance" than prior art)....

D. *Functionality*

If a design is "primarily functional rather than ornamental," or is "dictated by functional considerations," it is not patentable. *Power Controls Corp. v. Hybrinetics, Inc.,* 806 F.2d 234, 238 (Fed.Cir.1986). The functionality rule furthers the purpose of the design patent statute, which is to promote the decorative arts. In addition, the rule prevents granting in essence a monopoly to functional features that do not meet the requirements of a utility patent. Recognizing that strict application of the functionality rule would invalidate the majority of modern designs, the Federal Circuit validated designs with a higher functionality factor than had been tolerated by the courts previously. If the functional aspect of a design may be achieved by other design techniques, then it is not primarily functional. This more flexible approach reflects a recognition by the court that the majority of valuable industrial designs that should be granted protection in order to stimulate economic growth are a combination of functional and aesthetic features.

II. *Claim Requirements and Procedure*

Two major criticisms of the design patent system in the United States are that it is too expensive and that protection takes too long to obtain....

In 1988, the cost of a design patent application was estimated at $1,000. Fryer, *supra*, at 835. A large part of this cost is the expense of preparing the drawings which constitute the claim. The drawings "must contain a sufficient number of views to constitute a complete disclosure of the appearance of the article." 37 C.F.R. § 1.152. All that is required in writing is a very brief description of the drawings. The adequate disclosure and definiteness of the claim required by Section 112 are accomplished by the drawings. . . .

Design patents normally issue two to three years after filing. Saidman, *supra*, at 861. This leaves a design patent applicant without any protection from copiers during this long waiting period, as opposed to copyright protection which requires no initial procedural requirement and takes only a few months for registration to be issued. Fryer, *supra*, at 840, 835. It has been noted that the current system is "unsuited to the fast-moving but short-lived product cycle characteristic of today's market for mass-produced consumer goods." Reichman, *supra*, at 24. While there is general agreement that a new form of protection for industrial design is needed, Congress has yet to adopt any of the proposed legislation. An example of proposed legislation that would afford better protection for designs is Design Copyright Protection, which employs a modified copyright form of protection as an alternative to the design patent. *See* Fryer, *supra*, at 839–46. Alternatively, proposed legislation would protect functional industrial designs, including those that are neither aesthetically nor technically innovative. Reichman, *supra*, at 121–22.

III. *Infringement*

The standard for finding infringement of a design patent was defined in *Gorham Mfg. Co. v. White*, where the Supreme Court held that "if in the eye of an ordinary observer, giving such attention as a purchaser usually gives, two designs are substantially the same, if the resemblance is such as to deceive such an observer, inducing him to purchase one supposing it to be the other, the first one patented is infringed by the other." 81 U.S. (14 Wall.) 511, 528 (1872).

The "eye of the ordinary observer" standard continues to be the rule. *See Oakley, Inc. v. International Tropic–Cal, Inc.*, 923 F.2d 167, 169 (Fed.Cir.1991). The ordinary observer is one who has "reasonable familiarity" with the object in question and is capable of making a comparison to other objects which have preceded it. *Applied Arts Corp. v. Grand Rapids Metalcraft Corp.*, 67 F.2d 428, 430 (6th Cir.1933). The key factor is similarity, rather than consumer confusion. *Unette*, 785 F.2d at 1029 (holding that "likelihood of confusion as to the source of goods is not a necessary or appropriate factor for determining infringement of a design patent.").

The second prong of the infringement analysis is the "point of novelty" test, which is distinct from the issue of similarity. Under the "point of novelty" test, the similarity found by the ordinary observer must be attributable to the novel elements of the patented design which distinguish it from prior art. . . .

After determining the scope of the patented claim, the infringement inquiry focuses only on the protectable aesthetic components of a patented design. *See Lee v. Dayton–Hudson Corp.*, 838 F.2d 1186, 1188 (Fed.Cir. 1988) (holding that "it is the non-functional, design aspects that are pertinent to determinations of infringement"). Thus, this test permits strong similarities to be excused if the defendant can prove that she borrowed "only commonplace or generic ideas, functional features, or other nonprotectable matter" while adding sufficient variation to protectable elements of the design. Reichman, *supra*, at 44.

Whether a design is infringed when it is used on an entirely different type of article than the patented one has not been settled. . . .

G. ARCHITECTURAL WORKS

One of the creative art forms that we encounter daily, and that has historically had an ill-defined coverage by our copyright laws, is architecture. As was recently stated in a congressional committee report accompanying proposed legislation (which ultimately became the Architectural Works Copyright Protection Act of 1990) that was designed to expand the scope of copyright protection for architectural works:

> . . . All copyright legislation is premised on Article I, section 8, clause 8 of the Constitution, which grants Congress the power to protect the "writings" of authors in order to "promote the progress of science." The proposed legislation must (and the Committee believes does) further this constitutional goal. Architecture plays a central role in our daily lives, not only as a form of shelter or as an investment, but also as a work of art. It is an art form that performs a very public, social purpose. As Winston Churchill is reputed to have once remarked: "We shape our buildings and our buildings shape us." We rarely appreciate works of architecture alone, but instead typically view them in conjunction with other structures and the environment at large, where, at their best, they serve to express the goals and aspirations of the entire community. Frank Lloyd Wright aptly observed: "buildings will always remain the most valuable aspect in a people's environment, the one most capable of cultural reaction."

> . . . [T]he Committee concluded that the design of a work of architecture is a "writing" under the Constitution and fully deserves protection under the Copyright Act. Protection for works of architecture should stimulate excellence in design, thereby enriching our public environment in keeping with the constitutional goal.

(H.R. Rep. No. 101–735, 101st Cong. 2d Sess. 12–13 (1990).)

PROTECTION UNDER THE 1976 COPYRIGHT ACT

In the 1976 Copyright Act, as originally enacted, architecture could be protected, if at all, as a "pictorial, graphic, or sculptural work," which, as defined in § 101, included "technical drawings, diagrams, and models"; as a gesture toward greater protection for architecture, but with uncertain implications, the definition was altered in 1988 to include "diagrams, models, and technical drawings, including architectural plans." Of course, most architecture would also fall within the definition in § 101 of a "useful article," i.e., "an article having an intrinsic utilitarian function." As such, copyright protection for a work of architecture would be subject to the usual limitations for PGS works generally—it would extend only to features "that can be identified separately from, and are capable of existing independently of, the utilitarian aspects of the article." Thus, detachable decorative features such as friezes or gargoyles would most likely have been protectible by copyright; the building as a whole would probably not. Indeed, the less exuberant the architecture, the less likely the building would be to meet the definition in the 1976 Act. This was, of course, the fate of all useful articles, be they furniture, street lighting fixtures or automobiles. Despite the cryptic notion of "conceptual separability" articulated in the House Report, it was generally understood that the overall shape of a residential or office building was not likely to be protectible by copyright; "eyeballing" a building while constructing its likeness across the street, although generally thought worthy of professional and moral condemnation, would probably not have given rise to a substantial copyright infringement claim.

A similar limitation under the original 1976 Act affected copyrighted architectural plans and drawings. These were not "useful articles," because their purpose was "merely to portray the appearance of the article or to convey information" (§ 101); no "separability" limitation was pertinent. But there was another obstacle. Unauthorized copying of the two-dimensional plan would infringe, but would constructing a three-dimensional building based on those plans? Courts almost uniformly found that the unauthorized construction was not an infringement of the plans. It was held either that the plagiarizing structure embodied merely the "ideas" of the plan rather than the "expression" (was that likely so?)—or, more tenably, that *Baker v. Selden* barred a copyright claim for converting the plan into its functional counterpart, a building.

Perhaps the most thorough exploration of the issue is to be found in the following case.

Demetriades v. Kaufmann, 680 F.Supp. 658 (S.D.N.Y.1988). In somewhat simplified terms, the plaintiff designed the plans for an expensive "one of a kind" residence in Scarsdale; the defendant couple secured unauthorized access to the plans, had their architect *trace* the plaintiff's plans, and began to build essentially the same house—a few doors down the street! The plaintiff sought an injunction against the completion of the house, claiming copyright infringement of his architectural plans. He conceded that, had the defendants based their construction on photographs or drawings that they had made of his house, they would not have infringed; he argued, however, that basing their house directly on his copyrighted plans did. The court disagreed.

The court found that the traced plans infringed; but it held that the construction of the offending residence did not. Invoking § 113(b) of the 1976 Act, which "froze" the law as it was in 1977 with respect to the "making" of a useful article depicted in a drawing, the court found the key element of that earlier law to be the Supreme Court decision in *Baker v. Selden*. The court read that decision to hold that although copyright protection extends to the particular *explanation* of an art or work, it does not protect against *use* of the art or work described by the copyrighted document. Thus, "although an owner of copyrighted architectural plans is granted the right to prevent the unauthorized copying of those plans, that individual, without benefit of a design patent, does not obtain a protectible interest in the useful article depicted by those plans."

The *Demetriades* court also relied upon an often-discussed case, *Muller v. Triborough Bridge Auth.*, 43 F.Supp. 298 (S.D.N.Y.1942), in which the owner of copyright in plans depicting an approach to the Cross Bay Parkway Bridge alleged that the defendant had infringed by constructing a similar approach to its bridge; the court had concluded that the plaintiff's copyrighted drawing, "showing a novel bridge approach to unsnarl traffic congestion, does not prevent any one from using and applying the system of traffic separation therein set forth."

The preliminary relief ultimately issued by the *Demetriades* court, however, gave the plaintiff essentially what he had sought. The court enjoined the defendants from any further unauthorized copying of the architectural plans, and "from relying on any infringing copies of those plans" in constructing their house; it also ordered that all infringing copies within the defendants' control be impounded.

As will be noted immediately below, the Copyright Act was amended in 1990 so as to extend protection to "architectural works" that goes beyond the protection accorded by the 1976 Act in its original form. However, the amendments do not apply to buildings constructed before the effective date of the legislation, December 1, 1990. Therefore it is necessary to be familiar with the pre–1990 law just recounted, for it applies to most of the buildings we see around us (regardless of the date on which any alleged infringement might take place).

Given the economic-incentive rationale underlying the law of copyright, is it justifiable to give the architect protection only against unauthorized two-dimensional copies of his or her plan, while freely allowing the unauthorized construction of the depicted building? Which is the exclusive right that truly has economic value to the architect? Is it sensible to make infringement turn upon whether the defendant, in constructing the building, photocopies the plaintiff's plans (which would infringe) or steals them (which would not)?

THE ARCHITECTURAL WORKS COPYRIGHT PROTECTION ACT OF 1990

A principal incentive for expanding copyright protection for architectural works is the Berne Convention, which the United States ratified in October 1988. Article 2.1 of the Convention includes "works of architecture" among copyrightable subject matter which member countries must protect. The 1990 amendments to the 1976 Copyright Act—signed by President Bush on December 1, 1990 and immediately effective—added "architectural works" as protectible subject matter under § 102(a), defined that term in § 101, and set forth certain limitations on protection in § 120. The importance of creating a separate category for architectural works, apart from pictorial, graphic and sculptural works, is that the "separability" requirement that applies to the latter works does not apply to the former. The new provisions cover any architectural work created on or after December 1, 1990, and any such work that on that date "is unconstructed and embodied in unpublished plans or drawings" (with protection to terminate on December 31, 2002 unless the work is constructed by that date) (Pub. L. No. 101–650, § 706). The Court of Appeals for the Second Circuit has held that an architectural work is not to be protected under the 1990 Act if it was "substantially constructed" before December 1 of that year. Among other things, it relied upon 37 C.F.R. § 202.11(d)(3) of the Copyright Office Regulations, which excludes from protection works "constructed or otherwise published" before that date; and upon its belief that "substantially constructed" is more practically understandable than the test of "sufficiently finished to be habitable" (as suggested by the plaintiff architect). *Zitz v. Pereira*, 232 F.3d 290 (2d Cir.2000).

§ 101. Definitions

An "architectural work" is the design of a building as embodied in any tangible medium of expression, including a building, architectural plans, or drawings. The work includes the overall form as well as the arrangement and composition of spaces and elements in the design, but does not include individual standard features.

§ 120. Scope of Exclusive Rights in Architectural Works

(a) *Pictorial Representations Permitted*— The copyright in an architectural work that has been constructed does not include the right to prevent the making, distributing, or public display of pictures, paintings, photographs, or other pictorial representations of the work, if the building in which the work is embodied is located in or ordinarily visible from a public place.

(b) *Alteration to and Destruction of Buildings*— Notwithstanding the provisions of section 106(2), the owners of a building embodying an architectural work may, without the consent of the author or copyright owner of the architectural work, make or authorize the making of alterations of such building, and destroy or authorize the destruction of such building.

House Report

H.R. Rep. No. 101–735, 101st Cong. 2d Sess. 18–21, 24 (1990).

Definitions

. . . The protected work is the design of a building. The term "design" includes the overall form as well as the arrangement and composition of spaces and elements in the design. The phrase "arrangement and composition of spaces and elements," recognizes that: (1) creativity in architecture frequently takes the form of a selection, coordination, or arrangement of unprotectible elements into an original, protectible whole; (2) an architect may incorporate new, protectible design elements into otherwise standard, unprotectible building features; and (3) interior architecture may be protected.

Consistent with other provisions of the Copyright Act and Copyright Office regulations, the definition makes clear that protection does not extend to individual standard features, such as common windows, doors, and other staple building components. A grant of exclusive rights in such features would impede, rather than promote, the progress of architectural innovation. The provision is not, however, intended to exclude from the copyright in the architectural work any individual features that reflect the architect's creativity.

. . .

The Subcommittee made a second amendment in the definition of architectural work: the deletion of the phrase "or three-dimensional structure." This phrase was included in [an earlier bill] to cover cases where architectural works are embodied in innovative structures that defy easy classification. Unfortunately, the phrase also could be interpreted as covering interstate highway bridges, cloverleafs, canals, dams, and pedestrian walkways. The Subcommittee examined protection for these works, some of which form important elements of this nation's transportation system, and determined that copyright protection is not necessary to stimulate creativity or prohibit unauthorized reproduction.

The sole purpose of legislating at this time is to place the United States unequivocally in compliance with its Berne Convention obligations. Protection for bridges and related nonhabitable three-dimensional structures is not required by the Berne Convention. Accordingly, the question of copyright protection for these works can be deferred to another day. As a consequence, the phrase "or other three-dimensional structures" was deleted from the definition of architectural work and from all other places in the bill.

This deletion, though, raises more sharply the question of what is meant by the term "building." Obviously, the term encompasses habitable structures such as houses and office buildings. It also covers structures that are used, but not inhabited, by human beings; such as churches, pergolas, gazebos, and garden pavilions.

. . .

Subject Matter of Copyright

This provision amends section 102, title 17, United States Code, to create a new category of protected subject matter: "architectural works." By creating a new category of protectible subject matter in new section 102(a)(8), and, therefore, by deliberately not encompassing architectural works as pictorial, graphic, or sculptural works in existing section 102(a)(5), the copyrightability of architectural works shall not be evaluated under the separability test applicable to pictorial, graphic, or sculptural works embodied in useful articles. There is considerable scholarly and judicial disagreement over how to apply the separability test, and the principal reason for not treating architectural works as pictorial, graphic, or sculptural works is to avoid entangling architectural works in this disagreement.

The Committee does not suggest, though, that in evaluating the copyrightability or scope of protection for architectural works, the Copyright Office or the courts should ignore functionality. A two-step analysis is envisioned. First, an architectural work should be examined to determine whether there are original design elements present, including overall shape and interior architecture. If such design elements are present, a second step is reached to examine whether the design elements are functionally required. If the design elements are not functionally required, the work is protectible without regard to physical or conceptual separability. As a consequence, contrary to the Committee's report accompanying the 1976 Copyright Act with respect to industrial products, the aesthetically pleasing overall shape of an architectural work would be protected under this bill.

———

DECISIONS APPLYING THE ARCHITECTURAL WORKS COPYRIGHT PROTECTION ACT

There are, as yet, very few decisions that apply the Architectural Works amendment and determine the extent to which it has expanded protection previously accorded to architectural designs. For a full discussion of such matters (as well as of remedies and attorneys' fees), see *Richmond Homes Mgt., Inc. v. Raintree, Inc.*, 862 F.Supp. 1517 (W.D.Va. 1994) (defendant's Rockford model substantially copied its exterior and interior features from the plaintiff's Louisa model; copyright protection extended to the dimensions and location of the family room, the placement of doors and windows, and the sizes and locations of rooms and closets), *modified on other grounds*, 66 F.3d 316 (4th Cir.1995). *See also Yankee Candle Co. v. New England Candle Co.*, 14 F.Supp.2d 154 (D.Mass.1998) (an enclosed shopping mall may be a "building" the design of which is protected under the Architectural Works Act, but the individual units within are not; two-dimensional store plans, however, may furnish a basis for an infringement action).

In *Hunt v. Pasternack*, 179 F.3d 683 (9th Cir.1999), the court of appeals held—as clearly required by the definition of "architectural work" in sec.101—that such a work is protectable against infringement even though it exists only in the form of two-dimensional plans and has not yet been constructed. The court had stated otherwise in an earlier decision, which it disavowed.

That judgments of infringement may be difficult to obtain with respect to architectural works, particularly in light of their functional attributes, is shown in *Attia v. Society of N.Y. Hospital*, 201 F.3d 50 (2d Cir.1999) (assuming copying, there was no infringement of preliminary sketches for renovated hospital building on platform over highway, which showed placement of building, use of truss technology, alignment of floor heights and corridors and other spaces, continuous traffic loop through hospital complex, placement of emergency services and ambulance parking, and location of pedestrian area and mechanical equipment); and *Walter Sedovic Architect, P.C. v. Alesandro*, 2000 CCH Copyr. L. Dec. para. 28,012 (S.D.N.Y. 1999) (no infringement of church renovation plans, when there were differences in building size, roof features, and location of an entrance, and only similarities were that both churches had a tall vertical main door and both buildings were in the shape of a cross).

QUESTIONS

1. Think of a strikingly designed architectural work with which you are familiar—a residence, an office building, a place of worship, or a museum. Can you identify features that are "physically or conceptually separable" and are therefore copyrightable under the pre-December 1990 tests? Is the overall shape of the building copyrightable?

Articulate the differences between the functionality limitation on the copyrightability of works of architecture (discussed in the House Report, *supra*), and the various statements of the "conceptual separability" standard for the copyrightability of pictorial, graphic and sculptural works.

2. Is the structure depicted below copyrightable under the 1990 Amendments? Would it have been protectible as a "pictorial, graphic or sculptural work" before the 1990 amendments?

3. Daring Development Company has built an unusual office building in Los Angeles. It used the services of Samuel Sculpt, who designed a series of towers that are incorporated into one of the perimeter walls and that extend to the adjacent sidewalk. The towers depict different objects that have played a role in the history of the city, such as a drill bit to evoke the water that had to be transported to the California desert. Mogul Motion Pictures Company, in filming *Son of Wonderman*, has done some filming on the streets near Daring Development's office building; the film portrays action in front of the towers and connecting wall. Mogul is also selling Batman merchandise that incorporates replicas of the wall and towers. Sculpt has brought an action for copyright infringement of his towers. Among the issues that have been raised are Sculpt's ownership of the copyright, whether the towers have "separable" artistic elements protectible by copyright, and whether the "public place" exemption in section 120(a) extends to Mogul's activities. Would you grant Mogul's motion for summary judgment? (What, if any, additional facts would you need to know?) *See Leicester v. Warner Bros.*, 232 F.3d 1212 (9th Cir. 2000).

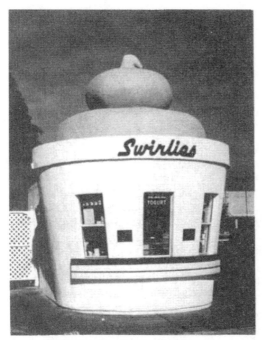

Reproduced with permission of
Dennis A. Rocha

4. Is there an aesthetic, economic or pragmatic reason—as distinguished from the desire to comply with the Berne Convention—for extending copyright protection to the overall shape of architectural works, but denying such protection to other forms of useful sculptural works such as furniture, dresses, automobiles, silverware, vacuum cleaners, and the like? Can designers of buildings make a convincing distinctive claim for protection?

H. CHARACTERS

Nichols v. Universal Pictures Corp., 45 F.2d 119, 121 (2d Cir.1930) (L. Hand, J.): "[W]e do not doubt that two plays may correspond in plot closely enough for infringement. How far that correspondence must go is another matter. Nor need we hold that the same may not be true as to the characters, quite independently of the 'plot' proper, though, as far as we know, such a case has never arisen. If Twelfth Night were copyrighted, it is quite possible that a second comer might so closely imitate Sir Toby Belch or Malvolio as to infringe, but it would not be enough that for one of his characters he cast a riotous knight who kept wassail to the discomfort of the household, or a vain and foppish steward who became amorous of his mistress. These would be no more than Shakespeare's 'ideas' in the play, as little capable of monopoly as Einstein's Doctrine of Relativity, or Darwin's theory of the Origin of Species. It follows that the less developed the characters, the less they can be copyrighted; that is the penalty an author must bear for marking them too indistinctly."

[Editors' note: The Court of Appeals for the Second Circuit has indicated, without elaboration, that the Hopalong Cassidy and Amos & Andy characters, in their textual description, meet Judge Hand's test. *See Filmvideo Releasing Corp. v. Hastings*, 668 F.2d 91 (2d Cir.1981); *Silverman v. CBS Inc.*, 870 F.2d 40 (2d Cir.), *cert. denied*, 492 U.S. 907 (1989)].

Warner Bros. Pictures v. Columbia Broadcasting System, 216 F.2d 945 (9th Cir.1954), *cert. denied*, 348 U.S. 971 (1955). [Long before litigation about rights to use characters in films and on television became routine, this case was the preeminent one in the genre; its influence has been somewhat narrowed by later events.] The well-known mystery-detective story, "The Maltese Falcon," was written by Dashiell Hammett, and was published serially in a magazine and then in a book by the publisher Knopf, which held the copyright. In 1930, Hammett and Knopf conveyed to Warner Brothers, for $8,500, certain defined exclusive rights (along with a copyright assignment) to the use of The Maltese Falcon in moving pictures, radio, and television. Warner's highly successful motion picture, starring Humphrey Bogart as the detective protagonist Sam Spade, was released in 1941 (it was a new version of a Warner Brothers film made in 1931). In 1946, Hammett granted to CBS the right to use the Sam Spade character and name, along with the names and characters of others in The Maltese Falcon, on radio programs—except their use in the Falcon story; CBS broadcast weekly half-hour Sam Spade radio programs from 1946 to 1950. Warner sued CBS, Hammett, and Knopf, claiming that the programs infringed its rights to the Falcon story and characters under copyright and unfair competition law.

The court interpreted the 1930 grants to Warner and held that they could not properly be read to have conveyed rights to the characters outside of the Falcon story. The court pointed out that Warner was a "large, experienced moving picture producer," that ambiguities in the contract should be construed against it, that rights to characters and their names were nowhere expressly mentioned in the agreement, and that these—given their value particularly in detective sequels, as was customary in the genre (citing among others Sir Arthur Conan Doyle)—should not be interpreted as falling within the general grants made to Warner. The court also noted that Warner had not objected to Hammett's publication in 1932 of three stories using the Falcon characters, nor to the use by CBS of those characters in a radio program, "The Kandy Tooth," after negotiations between CBS and Warner for the Falcon had broken down. The court also observed that Warner's purchase price of $8,500 "would seem inadequate compensation for the complete surrender of the characters made famous" in the Falcon book. It concluded that the intention of the parties was not to deprive Hammett of using, and licensing others to use, the Falcon characters in other stories.

Having in effect fully decided the case, the court went on, however, "to consider whether it was ever intended by the copyright statute that characters with their names should be under its protection."

> ... If Congress had intended that the sale of the right to publish a copyrighted story would foreclose the author's use of its characters in subsequent works for the life of the copyright, it would seem Congress would have made specific provision therefor. Authors work for the love of their art no more than other professional people work in other lines of work for the love of it. There is the financial motive as well. The characters of an author's imagination and the art of his descriptive talent, like a painter's or like a person with his penmanship, are always limited and always fall into limited patterns. The restriction argued for is unreasonable, and would effect the very opposite of the statute's purpose which is to encourage the production of the arts....

> It is conceivable that the character really constitutes the story being told, but if the character is only the chessman in the game of telling the story he is not within the area of the protection afforded by the copyright.... We conclude that even if the owners assigned their complete rights in the copyright to the Falcon, such assignment did not prevent the author from using the characters used therein, in other stories. The characters were vehicles for the story told, and the vehicles did not go with the sale of the story.

Anderson v. Stallone

11 U.S.P.Q.2D 1161 (C.D.Cal.1989).

■ WILLIAM D. KELLER, UNITED STATES DISTRICT JUDGE.

. . .

FACTUAL BACKGROUND

The movies Rocky I, II, and III were extremely successful motion pictures. Sylvester Stallone wrote each script and played the role of Rocky Balboa, the dominant character in each of the movies. In May of 1982, while on a promotional tour for the movie Rocky III, Stallone informed members of the press of his ideas for Rocky IV. Although Stallone's description of his ideas would vary slightly in each of the press conferences, he would generally describe his ideas as follows:

> I'd do it [Rocky IV] if Rocky himself could step out a bit. Maybe tackle world problems. So what would happen, say, if Russia allowed her boxers to enter the professional ranks? Say Rocky is the United States' representative and the White House wants him to fight with the Russians before the Olympics. It's in Russia with everything against him. It's a giant stadium in Moscow and everything is Russian Red. It's

a fight of astounding proportions with 50 monitors sent to 50 countries. It's the World Cup—a war between 2 countries.

Waco Tribune Herald, May 28, 1982; Section D, pg. 1 (EX 168). In June of 1982, after viewing the movie Rocky III, Timothy Anderson wrote a thirty-one page treatment entitled "Rocky IV" that he hoped would be used by Stallone and MGM/UA Communications Co. (hereinafter "MGM") as a sequel to Rocky III. The treatment incorporated the characters created by Stallone in his prior movies and cited Stallone as a co-author.

[Anderson later discussed it with the President and/or members of the Board of MGM.]

On April 22, 1984, Anderson's attorney wrote MGM requesting compensation for the alleged use of his treatment in the forthcoming Rocky IV movie. On July 12, 1984, Stallone described his plans for the Rocky IV script on the Today Show before a national television audience. Anderson, in his deposition, states that his parents and friends called him to tell him that Stallone was telling "his story" on television. In a diary entry of July 12, 1984, Anderson noted that Stallone "explained my story" on national television.

Stallone completed his Rocky IV script in October of 1984. Rocky IV was released in November of 1985. The complaint in this action was filed on January 29, 1987.

CONCLUSIONS OF LAW

[The court first held that Anderson's claim for breach of confidence, under state law, was barred by the statute of limitations; and that his state-law claims for unjust enrichment and unfair competition were equivalent to copyright infringement and were thus preempted by the federal Copyright Act as provided in § 301. The court also held that Stallone and his co-defendants were entitled to summary judgment on Anderson's copyright infringement claim, because Anderson's film treatment was not copyrightable. To reach that conclusion, the court found that the "Rocky characters developed in Rocky I, II and III constitute expression protected by copyright independent from the story in which they are contained"; that Anderson's treatment was an infringing derivative work based on those copyrightable characters; and that the unlawful use of those characters forfeited the plaintiff's copyright by virtue of § 103(a) of the Copyright Act. In holding the Rocky characters copyrightable, the court found them to meet both the "specificity" test of Learned Hand and the "story being told" test in the *Sam Spade* (Warner Brothers) case. Finally, the court held that the story elements in the Rocky IV film were not substantially similar to those in the plaintiff's treatment. What follows is the court's discussion of the copyrightability of the Rocky characters.]

. . .

The Rocky characters are one of the most highly delineated groups of characters in modern American cinema. The physical and emotional characteristics of Rocky Balboa and the other characters were set forth in tremendous detail in the three Rocky movies before Anderson appropriated the characters for his treatment. The interrelationships and development of Rocky, Adrian, Apollo Creed, Clubber Lang, and Paulie are central to all three movies. Rocky Balboa is such a highly delineated character that his name is the title of all four of the Rocky movies and his character has become identified with specific character traits ranging from his speaking mannerisms to his physical characteristics. This Court has no difficulty ruling as a matter of law that the Rocky characters are delineated so extensively that they are protected from bodily appropriation when taken as a group and transposed into a sequel by another author. Plaintiff has not and cannot put before this Court any evidence to rebut the defendants' showing that the Rocky characters are so highly delineated that they warrant copyright protection.

Plaintiff's unsupported assertions that Rocky is merely a stock character, made in the face of voluminous evidence that the Rocky characters are copyrightable, do not bar this Court from granting summary judgment on this issue. If any group of movie characters is protected by copyright, surely the Rocky characters are protected from bodily appropriation into a sequel which merely builds on the relationships and characteristics which these characters developed in the first three Rocky movies. No reasonable jury could find otherwise.

This Court need not and does not reach the issue of whether any single character alone, apart from Rocky, is delineated with enough specificity so as to garner copyright protection. Nor does the Court reach the issue of whether these characters are protected from less than bodily appropriation. *See* I M. Nimmer, § 2.12, pg. 2–171 (copyrightability of characters is "more properly framed as relating to the degree of substantial similarity required to constitute infringement rather than in terms of copyrightability per se").

This Court also finds that the Rocky characters were so highly developed and central to the three movies made before Anderson's treatment that they "constituted the story being told." All three Rocky movies focused on the development and relationships of the various characters. The movies did not revolve around intricate plots or story lines. Instead, the focus of these movies was the development of the Rocky characters. The same evidence which supports the finding of delineation above is so extensive that it also warrants a finding that the Rocky characters—Rocky, Adrian, Apollo Creed, Clubber Lang, and Paulie—"constituted the story being told" in the first three Rocky movies. . . .

QUESTIONS

1. Articulate the features that make each of the "Rocky" characters sufficiently well developed to meet Judge Hand's standard. For example, how would you delineate in detail the character attributes of Rocky's wife Adrian? (Be sure to separate her character attributes from the details of plot in which she is involved. Is that possible?) And would it infringe to prepare an unauthorized film for television featuring a shy monosyllabic underdog amateur prizefighter (wrestler? chess player? karate kid?) who trains in the gyms and on the streets of Baltimore or Boston? Does each of the Rocky characters—even Rocky himself—satisfy the "story being told" test? Are Rocky and Adrian more fully developed than the "chessmen" Sam Spade and Brigid O'Shaughnessey from *The Maltese Falcon*? Which of the two tests is the easier to satisfy?

2. Did the *Stallone* court find infringement not of the individual Rocky characters but of the several of them as a group? (If so, is that really character protection, or story protection?)

3. Is it fair to permit Stallone now to copy Anderson's entire detailed story? Is that not the consequence of the court's holding?

4. "The Amos 'n Andy Show" was a popular radio comedy program that was broadcast from 1928 to 1955, depicting a number of African–American characters. It also became a network television program from 1951 to 1953 and was shown in non-network syndication until 1966. Your client is interested in adapting some of the old radio programs for use in a Broadway-style musical comedy. You have ascertained that all of the pertinent radio scripts are now in the public domain. Your client asks whether, even assuming he can use the text of those scripts in his show, he is free without the consent of the Columbia Broadcasting System (the owner of copyright in the television programs) to use the characters of Amos, Andy, and others portrayed on the television programs, and particularly whether his performers can be chosen so as to resemble those on the programs. What advice do you give? *See Silverman v. CBS Inc.,* 870 F.2d 40 (2d Cir.), *cert. denied,* 492 U.S. 907 (1989).

Wincor, Book Review of Kaplan, An Unhurried View of Copyright, 76 Yale Law Journal 1473, 1478–83 (1967)*

How far should the bounds of protection extend? *An Unhurried View of Copyright* sets out many of the standards used in measuring traditional copyrights. Professor Kaplan relies on existing case law, which is a reasonable road for a lawyer to travel. But it is not the way life is lived in the communications industries.

There a dynamic world is making ground rules for current contracts and future laws. If the genius of the common law is its ability to catch up with the market place, it had better look twice at the communications field. As suggested earlier, "copyright" is the wrong word—wrong chiefly in being incomplete—for describing the exotic new plants that grow in this surrealist garden.

Consider the following passage, introduced less in the hope of affording readers innocent amusement than of bringing out a point:

> Florienbad was burning. The world's espionage capital, on the outskirts of Bucharest, was half destroyed. Among the ruins strolled tall, indifferent Secret Agent Leverett Lowell (Harvard, '42) wearing as

* Reprinted by permission of the Yale Law Journal Co. and Fred B. Rothman & Co.

always his Black Belt, Fifth Degree for Kiaijutsu (Zen combat by Screaming), puffing casually on a consciousness-expanding cigarette and followed by Alec, his lame ocelot who had figured so gallantly in the Tower of London Demolition Case. Lowell was flanked, as always, by two of his luscious Eurasian girl bodyguards.

A small man disguised as a passerby stood by a burning building, watching the flames with satisfaction. Lowell recognized him as Q 50, a medium-ranking agent of the dreaded ACL, Arson Consultants, Ltd. Q 50's eyes glistened as he turned from the conflagration and addressed Lowell.

"That's one for the insurance company, mate," observed Q 50.

"Touché," Lowell replied indifferently.

That deeply affecting passage, by this reviewer, appears in Vol. IV, *Television Quarterly,* Fall, 1965. Its want of literary excellence makes it thoroughly part of a tradition in copyright cases.

Leverett Lowell and his bizarre entourage may actually constitute property. Taken together, they are a sort of compound of elements that the public values. Taken separately, each element may have value in its own right, even in a different setting. As things actually happen, especially in television, one of the girl bodyguards, with or without the lame ocelot, may be extracted from a series about Leverett Lowell and star in her own series without Lowell next season.

Television is the most voracious consumer of literary property on a repeating basis. It serves, accordingly, as the ideal subject for the study of new theories, new forms of legal life, new property concepts. Snobbishness has no place in such studies. Judge Learned Hand's concern was not confined to *Twelfth Night.*

In television the Leverett Lowell extract might be the subject of protracted negotiation and sale. Probably but not inevitably the character would in fact have been more fully developed in successive episodes without appreciable enrichment. Be that as it may, Lowell and his entourage might be dealt with as a commodity.

They might originate in a spy novel, or a film, or a series "presentation" designed specifically for television. Typically an independent production company acquires an option, sometimes on the text of Leverett Lowell stories, sometimes merely on the character himself and his attendant props. The most elaborate negotiations accompany such acquisitions. Does one remember to secure rights to Mrs. Hudson besides Holmes and Watson? How much does the original owner receive per new program episode if the series is one hour, how much if the series is half-hour? To what extent does he share in proceeds from a sound track album, or Leverett Lowell figurines, or theatrical exhibition of two program segments stuck together as a feature film? Does he share "spin-off" proceeds when one of the minor characters goes into a different series? All of it sounds fantastic, but it happens.

... The spin-off concept is crucial. It means the transplant of one or more fictitious elements into new settings. It describes extraction in business terms, and it comes up in nearly all contracts for the acquisition of television rights. There is no use pretending it will all go away if we ignore it.

Professor Kaplan and others who decry excessive protection may have a plausible rebuttal to the argument that real life has outrun their law. They may suggest that purchasers in this field merely buy quit-claims to avoid lawsuits. Sometimes that will be true; television moves quickly, and there is no time for test cases. Some of the fictitious elements that command royalties probably are nothing but ideas with names, and belong in the public domain. Certainly a slight shift in presentation, a change of name, a different occupation or nationality is sufficient to avoid legal trouble in many instances of copying. Still, there is more to it. Once in a long time we find fictitious elements such as characters that are both original and valuable, even under a different name, even snipped off and planted in a new garden. The point is that conceptually protection for elements such as these is all quite possible.

If trade custom means anything, the broadcasting industry has created standards that the common law must consider. Industry-wide collective bargaining agreements between management and the Writers Guild of America contain royalty provisions for the use of characters. Some day they may encompass additional elements, at least in general language.

Nevertheless trade custom is not everything, and Professor Kaplan is entitled to legal analysis in support of our new heresies.

In supplying it, one comes back to the question of names again. Fictitious characters are not "copyrights." Neither are fictitious eras, languages or battles. If Shakespeare were under copyright today, another's piracy of Falstaff might be a crucial factor in determining copyright infringement of particular plays, but Sir John is no copyright. He is something else, something without a name.

And yet not entirely without a name. The right name is "literary service mark protected against dilution." It lacks grace, but perhaps we shall coin something better after examining what lies behind it.

The trademark, sibling concept to the service mark, began as a liability and became an asset. In this happy course it ran parallel to the copyright. One originated as a device for policing measures and standards in the medieval guilds. The other began (in England, at any rate) as a device to record heretical authors and publishers. Then the trademark became a sales badge identifying the source of products, and the copyright turned into an economic *res,* a legal claim to rights in a work of art.

The two doctrines have different rules. Trademark is of uncertain duration; its geography is not fixed, and there are sometimes restrictions on its transfer so as to avoid deceiving the public. It depends largely on facts postulated at a given moment. Such and such a name is well known in Hawaii this year as a device for identifying pineapples, but not in Bonn, where it was famous a decade ago as a name for bicycles. Copyright is quite different. The owner has the security of fixed time periods, and his protection is national, often international, in scope. Trademark is the more flexible, copyright the more certain. The trouble with copyright is that it leaves off too soon, and fails to protect characters and related imaginings by Lovecraft and Tolkien.

Here trademark is a useful supplement—or service mark to be more exact about it, since the author's creations identify his services. These services are literary, hence the term "literary service mark." Dilution in turn is a German doctrine, adopted by several states including New York and Massachusetts, that protects marks against "whittling away" by use on disparate products, even where there is no likelihood of public confusion. In this doctrine the medieval mark ripens fully into an asset without any of the old hurdles in the way of protection. Rolls–Royce shoes, theoretically, would be enjoined under the dilution doctrine. With this concept we round out the translation of that awkward phrase for Sir John Falstaff: "literary service mark protected against dilution." Today that is what Falstaff would be in law.

. . .

An Unhurried View of Copyright is a way of looking at things in terms of franchises and grants from the sovereign. It has on its side American copyright history, with its concern for the public interest in free or cheap communications and its unconcern for authors. At least it has American history on its side as far as it goes.

Against this Kaplanesque view is a different way of looking at things, more as writers and publishers and producers do. A good statement of this second view is what G. K. Chesterton wrote in *Charles Dickens* (Methuen, 1906) at p. 81:

> Ordinary men would understand you if you referred currently to Sherlock Holmes. Sir Arthur Conan Doyle would no doubt be justified in rearing his head to the stars, remembering that Sherlock Holmes is the only really familiar figure in modern fiction. But let him droop that head again with a gentle sadness, remembering that if Sherlock Holmes is the only familiar figure in modern fiction, Sherlock Holmes is also the only familiar figure in the Sherlock Holmes Tales. Not many people could say offhand what was the name of the owner of Silver Blaze, or whether Mrs. Hudson was dark or fair. But if Dickens had written the Sherlock Holmes stories, every character in them would have been equally arresting and memorable. A Sherlock Holmes would have cooked the dinner for Sherlock Holmes; a Sherlock Holmes would have driven his cab. If Dickens brought in a man merely to carry a letter, he had time for a touch or two, and made him a giant.

The touch that creates giants, there perhaps is the point Professor Kaplan forgets. It appears only occasionally, and not even the most avid protectionist wants to dignify stock characters and mere ideas with property attributes. By all means enlarge the public domain with unworthy artifice, but recognize too that there are magicians among us.

———

Imagine a television commercial for a sports car, in which a young, well-dressed couple are being chased by a high-tech helicopter, from which a grotesque villain with metal-encased arms jumps onto the car roof; the male driver, flirtatiously eyeing his companion, releases the detachable roof and sends the villain flying off into space, allowing the couple to drive off to safety. As originally produced, the commercial had the characters speaking with a British accent, and James Bond-type music on the soundtrack; these were subsequently altered (e.g., an American accent was used). Is this an infringement of either the James Bond films or the James Bond character?

In **Metro–Goldwyn–Mayer, Inc. v. American Honda Motor Co.,** 900 F.Supp. 1287 (C.D.Cal.1995), the court rejected the defendants' contention that the commercial depicted merely a generic action scene with a generic hero. It found that the various dramatic elements of the commercial were copied from and substantially similar to several copyrighted James Bond films; among other things, the court noted the handsome hero and beautiful companion, the high-speed escape from a grotesque villain with the aid of intelligence and gadgetry, the high-tech effects and loud exciting music, the dry wit and subtle humor of the dialogue. (Consider later whether these are copyrightable dramatic elements.)

Viewing the male characters in isolation from their respective stories, the court found an infringing use of the James Bond character (even though, in contrast to the borrowed character discussed in the Wincor excerpt, no name was used in the commercial).

The court concluded that both of the standard tests for character-copyright—the "story being told" and the "fully delineated" tests—were satisfied by the James Bond character, with "characters visually depicted in a television series or in a movie" being entitled to more protection than purely literary characters. As to the former test, the court compared Bond with the Tarzan, Superman and Sherlock Holmes characters who attract an audience not to see the surrounding story but to see their heroes at work. As to the latter test, the court noted similarities in the way the heroes looked and acted: both are young, tuxedo-clad, British-looking, uncannily calm under pressure, and attracted (and attractive) to their female companions. Can it be that the court would find a character thus "delineated" an infringement of the James Bond character, had the former been placed in an altogether different milieu?

———

DeCarlo v. Archie Comic Publications, Inc., 127 F.Supp.2d 497 (S.D.N.Y.2001). The plaintiff created, in the 1950s, the cartoon character of Josie, who led a musical group "The Pussycats," and he transferred certain rights to the defendant comic book publisher. With the increasing 21st century popularity of Josie in merchandise and motion pictures, the plaintiff attempted to formulate a number of state claims (based on old and unpublished sketches) that would allow him to secure compensation. The defendant argued, among other things, that those claims were preempted by federal law. The court stated the following (citations omitted):

> Plaintiff nevertheless argues that his claim does not arise under the Copyright Act because comic strip characters are not susceptible of federal copyright protection. But he misconstrues the law. While the copyrightability of literary characters can present a troublesome question, "there has been no doubt that copyright protection is available for characters portrayed in cartoons...." This is so, explained one court, because the difficulties of distinguishing distinct attributes of a literary character from its embodiment of more general ideas and themes (the test for copyrightability offered by the Second Circuit in *Nichols v. Universal Pictures Corp.*) do not arise, at least to the same degree, with visual images. "While many literary characters may embody little more than a protected idea, a comic book character, which has physical as well as conceptual qualities, is more likely to contain some unique elements of expression." Such elements have been held to include "what the character thinks, feels, says and does and the descriptions conveyed by the author through the comments of other characters in the work," as well as "the visual perception ... [which] tends to create a dominant impression...." Moreover, the protectible attributes in an animated character "extend ... not merely to the physical appearance of the animated figure, but also to the manner in which it moves, acts and portrays a combination of ... characteristics." In consequence, DeCarlo's contention that cartoon characters are not protectible under the Copyright Act is, at best, a vast oversimplification.

King Features Syndicate v. Fleischer, 299 F. 533 (2d Cir.1924). The plaintiff was engaged in the creation and syndication to daily newspapers of a copyrighted comic strip known as "Barney Google and Spark Plug." "Spark Plug" (sometimes referred to as "Sparky") was, in the court's language, "a new grotesque and comic race horse." The defendant manufactured and sold a toy which was an exact reproduction of "Sparky." The district court denied a preliminary injunction, but the court of appeals reversed. The court concluded that, even though the defendant had not plagiarized all of the comic strip or all of its principal characters, it had infringed by copying "Sparky": "We do not think it avoids the infringement of the copyright to take the substance or idea, and produce it through a different medium.... Differences which relate merely to size and material are not important." "The concept of beauty expressed in the materials of statuary or drawing, is the thing which is copyrighted. That is what the infringer copies. The Copyright Act was intended to prohibit the taking of this conception. The Copyright Act protects the conception of humor which a cartoonist may produce, as well as the conception of genius which an artist or sculptor may use. . . ." [The court's language was surely broader than it had to be?]

   Detective Comics v. Bruns Publications, 111 F.2d 432 (2d Cir. 1940). Plaintiff owned the copyright in the comic book "Action Comics," which portrayed "Superman," while the defendants published and distributed a "Wonderman" comic book. The court affirmed the conclusion of the district court that the defendants had infringed plaintiff's copyright by copying the pictures in "Action Comics." Both Superman and Wonderman are men "of miraculous strength and speed"; their "attributes and antics . . . are closely similar"; each sheds his ordinary clothing to stand "revealed in full panoply in a skin-tight acrobatic costume," the only real difference being that Superman's is blue and Wonderman's is red; each can crush a gun in his powerful hands and can deflect bullets without injury; Superman is shown leaping over buildings while Wonderman leaps from roof to roof, and each is described as being the strongest man in the world and an enemy of evil and injustice. The court rejected the defendant's argument that Superman's attributes were general and unoriginal, with prototypes among heroes of literature and mythology. "[I]f the author of 'Superman' has portrayed a comic Hercules, yet if his production involves more than the presentation of a general type he may copyright it and say of it 'A poor thing but mine own.' Perhaps the periodicals of the complainant are foolish rather than comic, but they embody an original arrangement of incidents and a pictorial and literary form which preclude the contention that Bruns was not copying the antics of 'Superman' portrayed in 'Action Comics.' We think it plain that the defendants have used more than general types and ideas and have appropriated the pictorial and literary details embodied in the complainant's copyrights." Although plaintiff is not entitled to a monopoly "of the mere character of a 'Superman' who is a blessing to mankind," it may invoke copyright protection to the extent its work embodies "an arrangement of incidents and literary expressions original with the author." The court's injunction forbade, among other things, printing or distributing any cartoon or book "portraying any of the feats of strength or powers performed by 'Superman' or closely imitating his costume or appearance in any feat whatever."

QUESTIONS

1. Doesn't the injunction in the "Wonderman" case overreach the breadth of the court's analysis and of the defendant's infringement? Has the court properly limited itself to protecting the plaintiff's "expression" rather than its "idea"?

2. If the defendant in the "Wonderman" case were subsequently to publish a prose book, without pictures, describing Wonderman engaging in the same heroic feats that it had depicted in its comic books, would it be in contempt of court? Should it be?

3. If a literary character were sufficiently well-delineated to qualify for copyright protection, would unauthorized pictorial representations of the character infringe the copyright?

I.   GOVERNMENT WORKS AND OTHER PUBLIC POLICY ISSUES

§ 105.   Subject Matter of Copyright: United States Government Works

Copyright protection under this title is not available for any work of the United States Government, but the United States Government is not precluded from receiving and holding copyrights transferred to it by assignment, bequest, or otherwise.

House Report

H.R. Rep. No. 94–1476, 94th Cong., 2d Sess. 58–59 (1976).

Scope of the prohibition

The general prohibition against copyright in section 105 applies to "any work of the United States Government," which is defined in section 101 as "a work prepared by an officer or employee of the United States Government as part of that person's official duties." Under this definition a Government official or employee would not be prevented from securing copyright in a work written at that person's own volition and outside his or her duties, even though the subject matter involves the Government work or professional field of the official or employee. Although the wording of the definition of "work of the United States Government" differs somewhat from that of the definition of "work made for hire," the concepts are intended to be construed in the same way.

A more difficult and far-reaching problem is whether the definition should be broadened to prohibit copyright in works prepared under U.S. Government contract or grant. As the bill is written, the Government agency concerned could determine in each case whether to allow an independent contractor or grantee to secure copyright in works prepared in whole or in part with the use of Government funds. The argument that has been made against allowing copyright in this situation is that the public should not be required to pay a "double subsidy," and that it is inconsistent to prohibit copyright in works by Government employees while permitting private copyrights in a growing body of works created by persons who are paid with Government funds. Those arguing in favor of potential copyright protection have stressed the importance of copyright as an incentive to creation and dissemination in this situation and the basically different policy considerations applicable to works written by Government employees and those applicable to works prepared by private organizations with the use of Federal funds.

The bill deliberately avoids making any sort of outright, unqualified prohibition against copyright in works prepared under Government contract or grant. There may well be cases where it would be in the public interest to deny copyright in the writings generated by Government research contracts and the like; it can be assumed that, where a Government agency commissions a work for its own use merely as an alternative to having one of its own employees prepare the work the right to secure a private copyright would be withheld. However, there are almost certainly many other cases where the denial of copyright protection would be unfair or would hamper the production and publication of important works. Where, under the particular circumstances, Congress or the agency involved finds that the need to have work freely available outweighs the need of the private author to secure copyright, the problem can be dealt with by specific legislation, agency regulations, or contractual restrictions.

QUESTIONS

1. Examine the official reports of the United States Supreme Court and the volumes in the Federal Third series. What parts of these volumes, if any, are eligible for copyright?

2. Is the *Scott Stamp Catalogue*—which reproduces all United States stamps and lists such accompanying information as perforations, watermarks and value new and used—an infringement of copyright? Can United States stamps be freely reproduced as part of a fabric design for curtains or clothing? The House Report states (at page 60) that § 105 "does not apply to works created by employees of the United States Postal Service" because of its separate status under the 1970 Postal Reorganization Act. The Postal Service "could, if it chooses, use the copyright law to prevent the reproduction of postage stamp designs for private or commercial non-postal services (for example, in philatelic publications and catalogs, in general advertising, in art reproductions, in textile designs, and so forth)." Is this exclusion from § 105 tenable?

3. Hyman Rickover was Vice Admiral in the Navy Department as Assistant Chief of the Bureau of Ships for Nuclear Propulsion. During his tenure in that position, Admiral Rickover prepared a number of speeches on a wide range of subjects, such as "Nuclear Power and the Navy," "Engineering and Scientific Education," "The Education of Our Talented Children," "Nuclear Power—Challenge to Industry," "Energy Resources and Our Future," "Revolution at Sea," and "European Secondary Schools." These speeches were delivered at such places as chambers of commerce, the Minnesota State Medical Association, the Detroit Engineering Society, the Nuclear Power Training School, and the Columbia University Forum. In all instances, the locations were near places where Rickover had duties of supervision and inspection, so that no transportation costs were borne by him; he made the speeches in free or off-duty hours. The final drafts of the speeches were typed by his Navy secretary on his office typewriter, and copies were made with Navy photocopy machines on the paper stock used for press releases by the Department of Defense. (Assume that all copies bore a copyright notice in the name of Admiral Rickover.) An educational publishing company has compiled many of the Rickover speeches and is about to publish them in hard-cover form. Rickover has brought an action to enjoin this publication, but the publishing company has asserted that his speeches are in the public domain. Should the injunction be granted? *See*

Public Affairs Assocs. v. Rickover, 177 F.Supp. 601 (D.D.C.1959), *rev'd & remanded,* 284 F.2d 262 (D.C.Cir.1960), *vacated for further proceedings,* 369 U.S. 111 (1962), *on remand,* 268 F.Supp. 444 (D.D.C.1967).

4. The United States Mint recently decided to issue a dollar coin to replace the Susan B. Anthony coin, and it held a competition to select a designer; the competition was open to designers employed by the Mint as well as to outsiders. The competition winner, selected anonymously, was Glenda Goodyear (not an employee of the Mint), who submitted a plaster sculpture of Sacagawea, a native American who played a key role in the Lewis and Clark Expedition into the early western territories. Goodyear was paid $10,000 for her design and its copyright, and the Mint registered copyright in the plaster sculpture. The coin was subsequently issued and promoted by the U.S. Mint (including in larger metallic replicas). The Minnetonka Mint, a private company, has issued silver replicas—three inches in diameter—of the Sacagawea dollar coin. The U.S. Mint has brought an action against the Minnetonka Mint for copyright infringement. The defendant has invoked section 105 to challenge the right of the U.S. government to assert copyright in the sculpture, and it contends, in any event, that any preexisting copyright is lost when the sculptural image is incorporated in official U.S. coinage. How should the court rule on these issues? (The latter issue is illuminated by the material that immediately follows.) *See United States v. Washington Mint, LLC,* 115 F.Supp.2d 1089 (D.Minn.2000).

THE COPYRIGHT STATUS OF STATE–AUTHORED MATERIALS

It is clear that section 105 of the Copyright Act addresses only the question of works of the United States Government. What is the copyright status of primary legal documents generated by *state* governments? For example, are state statutes and court decisions eligible for federal copyright protection? It might be contended that copyright is appropriate not only so that the state government can defray the expense of its lawmaking and other operations but also in order to assure that others do not distort or misquote official texts. On the other hand, however, one may question whether the "incentive" rationale that underlies copyright is pertinent to the product of state and municipal authorities, both because there are other obvious incentives to write laws and judicial decisions and the like and because the public has already been taxed to support these activities and should not be expected to pay again in the event copyright is invoked to bar copying. Even more forcefully, it is argued that the state laws, regulations, court opinions and the like are designed to regulate the conduct of the state's citizens—often accompanied by penalties for noncompliance—so that all members of the public should be given free access to these texts and permitted to copy and disseminate them widely.

Although section 105 does not purport to resolve this question, the Supreme Court did so more than a century ago, at least with regard to state judicial opinions. In Banks v. Manchester, 128 U.S. 244 (1888), the

Court denied copyright to a compilation of those opinions, prepared by a private reporter, on the grounds that judicial opinions are publicly owned by virtue of the fact that the judges who render them are paid with public funds, and that as a matter of public policy the public interest is served by free access to the law. This view has come to be taken for granted in copyright jurisprudence, and is generally formulated as an element of "due process of law," i.e., that citizens who are expected to comply with the law and to be subject to its penalties must be accorded free access to it, which implies the right to make copies (by citizens and by publishers).

Two significant issues have been highlighted in recent cases, as litigation has pushed beyond the "core" example of state legislative codes and court opinions. One issue is whether the principle of noncopyrightability extends to other kinds of official state and municipal documents, such as government reports, informational documents and compilations, and maps. If, for example, a state or county prepares detailed maps showing all of the properties that are subject to taxes, and stores these maps for public inspection in an official government office, is an individual entitled to make copies of those maps, either for personal use or for public distribution among his neighbors (perhaps on an internet website)? Do the same policies that dictate denying copyright to municipal codes apply here as well? That is the issue addressed in the following case.

County of Suffolk, N.Y. v. First American Real Estate Solutions, 261 F.3d 179 (2d Cir.2001). Since 1974, Suffolk County has compiled and designed a series of official "tax maps" showing the ownership, size and location of real property parcels in each of its political subdivisions. These maps are revised annually, and are by state law made available to the public. Currently, there are 12 albums containing over 4,600 tax maps, which show over 500,000 parcels of land. Each map, and each album, contains a copyright notice, and they are registered with the Copyright Office. The defendant reproduced those maps in both hardcopy and CD–ROM form and, after persisting despite a number of cease-and-desist letters from the County, it was sued for copyright infringement, the County seeking an injunction and damages.

The Court of Appeals concluded that the maps displayed sufficient original authorship in selection and compilation of information. It also held, despite an advisory opinion to the contrary by the New York State Committee on Open Government, that the state's Freedom of Information Law (FOIL, N.Y. Pub. Off. Law § 84)—which requires that public documents be "ma[d]e available for public inspection and copying" by citizens— does not override the County's federal rights under the Copyright Act. "It is one thing to read this provision [FOIL] to permit a member of the public to copy a public record, but it is quite another to read into it the right of a private entity to distribute commercially what it would otherwise, under copyright law, be unable to distribute. . . . Moreover, First American ignores the fact that the free press or an individual seeking to use the state agency records to educate others or to criticize the state or the state agency may be protected by the Copyright Act's fair use doctrine. *See* 17 U.S.C.

§ 107 ... Therefore, we conclude that the Legislature, by enacting FOIL, did not abrogate Suffolk County's copyright." On this issue, the court continued:

> Suffolk County is not attempting to restrict initial access but is attempting to restrict only the subsequent redistribution of its copyrighted works. There is nothing inconsistent between fulfilling FOIL's goal of access and permitting a state agency to place reasonable restrictions on the redistribution of its copyrighted works....
>
> It is true that Suffolk County's tax maps, because they are used in "making up the assessment rolls," N.Y. Real Prop. Tax Law § 503(1)(a), go to the heart of the purposes of FOIL: providing the public access to the operation or decision-making functions of government. A commercial publisher may be an effective means for distributing those records as widely as possible. One could thus attempt to draw a distinction between copyrighted materials such as the tax maps and those copyrighted materials that do not directly impact the governmental agency's decision-making. But this distinction ignores the fact that FOIL, by its text, simply does not distinguish among governmental functions that are performed in the exercise of the government's public role, its proprietary role, or as a hybrid of both roles....

The court then addressed the question whether the governmental authorship of the maps rendered them *ab initio* public domain materials, like judicial opinions and statutes, which the defendant was free to copy and publically distribute. The court first pointed out that by barring copyright, in Section 105, only for works of the federal government, the Act contemplates copyright ownership by states and their subdivisions. It continued:

> The determination that no one may own a copyright in statutes and opinions arises not from a specific provision of the Copyright Act, but from a "judicial gloss" on the Act. Building Officials & Code Adm. v. Code Tech., Inc., 628 F.2d 730, 735 (1st Cir.1980) ("BOCA"). In *Banks*, for example, the Supreme Court held that as a matter of public policy judges may not own a copyright in the fruits of their judicial labor. See 128 U.S. at 253. Because judges "receive from the public treasury a stated annual salary ... and can themselves have no pecuniary interest or proprietorship, as against the public at large," they cannot own a copyright. Id. Considerations of due process and fair notice also motivated the *Banks* Court: the "whole work done by the judges constitutes the authentic exposition and interpretation of the law, which, binding every citizen, is free for publication to all...." Id. If judges owned a copyright in their opinions, theoretically, they could restrict dissemination of the law. Thus, two considerations influence whether a particular work may be properly deemed in the public domain: (1) whether the entity or individual who created the work needs an economic incentive to create or has a proprietary interest in creating the work and (2) whether the public needs notice of this particular work to have notice of the law. See Practice Mgmt. Info.

Corp. v. American Med. Assoc., 121 F.3d 516, 518–19 (9th Cir.1997); *BOCA*, 628 F.2d at 734–35. We consider each factor in turn.

1. Incentive to Create

Copyright benefits the public by providing an incentive to stimulate artistic creativity through the grant of a temporary monopoly to a copyright owner. See Twentieth Century Music Corp. v. Aiken, 422 U.S. 151, 156 (1975). The *Banks* Court found such an incentive for the creation of judicial opinions unnecessary. But *Banks*, to us, represents more than the simple syllogism concluding that the public owns works produced by government employees merely because it pays their salaries. Rather, *Banks* is properly read as requiring a determination whether the particular governmental entity or employee has adequate incentive to create the work absent copyright protections.... Judges and legislators [because of salaries] do not need additional economic incentives to, respectively, write opinions or enact legislation.

Many works of government, however, due to their expense, may require additional incentives in order to justify their creation.... Thus, we are unable to declare a general rule that works by state governmental authors are automatically in the public domain from their inception. Some of the evidence relevant in determining whether the tax maps are original will also be relevant in determining whether Suffolk County required an additional incentive to create those maps. For example, if the existence and content of Suffolk County's maps are purely dictated by law, it is likely that Suffolk County needed no additional incentive to create them.... [W]e cannot say as a matter of law whether the tax maps are such that no additional incentive for their creation is necessary. What we can say, however, is that Suffolk County is entitled to present evidence whether it needed the additional incentives provided by copyright law to create its maps....

2. Notice

Due process requires that before a criminal sanction or significant civil or administrative penalty attaches, an individual must have fair warning of the conduct prohibited by the statute or the regulation that makes such a sanction possible....

Here, the tax maps themselves do not create the legal obligation to pay property taxes but are merely a means by which the government assesses a pre-existing obligation. The "fair warning" required under the Due Process Clause is satisfied through the notice provided by the statute that establishes the obligation to pay property taxes. There is no allegation that notice of this statute is not generally available.... Moreover, there is no allegation that any individual required to pay the applicable property tax has any difficulty in obtaining access to either the law or the relevant tax map, for Suffolk County is required by FOIL to disclose such a map on request.... Notice concerns simply are not present here.

In sum, on the record before us, we cannot conclude as a matter of law that Suffolk County's tax maps are in the public domain since their inception. We do conclude that Suffolk County has stated a valid claim upon which relief could be granted. Therefore, Suffolk County is entitled to present evidence in support of its copyright infringement claim. . . .

————

A second issue that has arisen with increasing frequency derives from the fact that many legislative codes are initially drafted not by a state or municipal agency but rather by private bodies and later adopted as law by official bodies. Another form in which the issue arises is when a legislative or administrative body simply makes reference to privately copyrighted material as furnishing a standard that is to be used in regulating societal activity. It has been seen, for example, in CCC Information Servs. v. Maclean Hunter Market Reports, Inc., ch. 2C *supra*, that the court upheld the copyrightability of compiled automobile values even though several states had, in their insurance statutes or regulations, established those values as a standard for determining insurance payments. Although noting the importance of free public access to the governing laws, the court opined that there would be serious constitutional questions if such state reference would result in the immediate taking of property rights under the Copyright Act.

In **Practice Mgt. Info. Corp. v. American Medical Ass'n**, 121 F.3d 516 (9th Cir.1997), another federal court of appeals addressed a claim concerning the Physician's Current Procedural Terminology (CPT), a coding system developed by the American Medical Association (AMA) to identify medical procedures; these codes are particularly useful for insurance forms. Subsequently, Congress directed the federal Health Care Financing Administration (HCFA) to establish a code to identify physicians' services; instead of creating its own code, the HCFA obtained the AMA's authorization to "adopt and use" the AMA's codes. The declaratory judgment plaintiff in this action sought to publilsh books of the AMA codes, and therefore endeavored to obtain a declaration of the codes' public domain status. The court ruled that the HCFA's incorporation of the AMA codes did not convert the codes into an unprotectable government document:

> The copyright system's goal of promoting the arts and sciences by granting temporary monopolies to copyrightholders was not at stake in *Banks* because judges' salaries provided adequate incentive to write opinions. In contrast, copyrightability of the CPT provides the economic incentive for the AMA to produce and maintain the CPT. "To vitiate copyright, in such circumstances, could, without adequate justification, prove destructive of the copyright interest, in encouraging creativity," a matter of particular significance in this context because of "the increasing trend toward state and federal adoptions of model codes." 1 Melville B. Nimmer & David Nimmer, *Nimmer on Copyright* § 5.06[C],

at 5–92 (1996). As the AMA points out, invalidating its copyright on the ground that the CPT entered the public domain when HCFA required its use would expose copyrights on a wide range of privately authored model codes, standards, and reference works to invalidation. Non-profit organizations that develop these model codes and standards warn they will be unable to continue to do so if the codes and standards enter the public domain when adopted by a public agency.

This issue is being addressed by yet another Circuit Court of Appeals as this book goes to press. In *Veeck v. Southern Bldg. Code Congress Int'l Inc.*, the plaintiff (seeking a declaratory judgment) had posted certain model codes, written and registered for copyright by the defendant SBCCI, on the internet without permission. SBCCI is a nonprofit organization that develops and promotes the adoption of model building codes, such as a standard plumbing code, gas code, fire prevention code and mechanical code; these are often enacted into law by reference by local governments, allegedly resulting in cost savings to the government. These codes are typically available in certain government offices and libraries. Plaintiff Veeck secured from SBCCI the building codes of certain Texas towns, on computer disks, and used his personal computer to upload these texts onto his website (without getting permission from, or giving credit to, SBCCI). A divided court of appeals affirmed a summary judgment for SBCCI. The majority concluded that the *Banks* case was not pertinent when the text of a code is initially drafted by a private organization (in need of the financial rewards provided by copyright) and that due-process concerns were satisfied so long as the texts were available in government offices to concerned individuals. It also rejected the argument that the "fact" of the legislative text had merged with the "expression" of the SBCCI code, so that copyright was immediately destroyed when the code was enacted into law. The dissenting judge endorsed the "merger" argument, and would have held that due process concerns warrant public access and dissemination of public laws regardless whether they are drafted initially by the state or by a private body. The full court of appeals has granted rehearing en banc, 241 F.3d 398 (5th Cir.2001), and has vacated the decision of the panel.

QUESTIONS

1. In the *Suffolk County* case, what sort of evidence would you, representing the County, introduce on remand in order to show the need for an "economic incentive" to produce the tax maps? Under this standard, can citizens or publishers ever know in advance of acting whether they are entitled to make copies of comparable public documents for broader distribution?

2. Are both the *Veeck* and *Suffolk* decisions correct in concluding that the needs of public access to laws and other official documents are satisfied by making them available at city halls and the like? Are the benefits of the "electronic revolution" in our "information society" unacceptably negated by forbidding unauthorized dissemination of public documents to the citizenry—conveniently, and free or inexpensively—through the internet and CD–ROMs?

3. If public taxation produces the revenues to pay public officials for doing their work, including producing laws and tax maps and the like, should the public be expected to pay again, through license fees, by virtue of copyright? Should it matter whether the public officials draft these materials themselves, or subcontract the task to private organizations?

4. Recall that in the *CCC* case, at Ch. 2C *supra*, the compiler of automobile-value information was a private company that undertook its evaluation for private purposes (to assist car buyers)—and then found its information "coopted" by a government agency without compensation. There, it is understandable that this should not strip the compilation of copyright protection. Is the case as appealing for the code-drafting organizations, whose reason for being is to prepare official texts for the sole purpose of adoption and promulgation by governmental entities?

Mitchell Bros. Film Group v. Cinema Adult Theater

604 F.2d 852 (5th Cir.1979).

■ Godbold, Circuit Judge: This is a copyright infringement suit, arising under the now-superseded Copyright Act of 1909. But it is more than the usual commercial contest between copyright holder and alleged infringer. The infringers asserted as an affirmative defense that the copyrighted material—a movie—was obscene, and that, therefore, under the equitable rubric of "unclean hands" plaintiffs were barred from relief. After viewing the film the court found it obscene, adopted the unclean hands rationale, and denied relief to the copyright owners. . . .

Plaintiffs-appellants owned a properly registered copyright on a motion picture titled "Behind the Green Door," issued under the 1909 Act, 17 U.S.C. § 34 (1970) (repealed). Two groups of defendants, each group consisting of a theater and several individuals, obtained copies of the movie without plaintiffs' permission and infringed the copyright by exhibiting the film at the theaters. . . .

We hold that the district court erred in permitting the assertion of obscenity as an affirmative defense to the claim of infringement, and, accordingly, reverse without reaching the question whether the film is obscene.

I. *The Statutory Language*

The statutory provision that controls in this case reads:

The works for which copyright may be secured under this title shall include all the writings of an author.

17 U.S.C. § 4 (1970) (repealed). Motion pictures are unquestionably "writings" under the Copyright Act.

The district court did not base its decision on standards found within the Act, which it described as "silent as to works which are subject to registration and copyright." The Act is not "silent." Rather, the statutory language "all the writings of an author" is facially all-inclusive, within itself admitting of no exceptions. There is not even a hint in the language of § 4 that the obscene nature of a work renders it any less a copyrightable "writing." There is no other statutory language from which it can be inferred that Congress intended that obscene materials could not be copyrighted.

Moreover, there is good reason not to read an implied exception for obscenity into the copyright statutes. The history of content-based restrictions on copyrights, trademarks, and patents suggests that the absence of such limitations in the Copyright Act of 1909 is the result of an intentional policy choice and not simply an omission. *See generally* 74 Colum. L. Rev. 1351, 1354 n.27 (1974). From the first copyright act in 1790, Congress has seldom added restrictions on copyright based on the subject matter of the work, and in each instance has later removed the content restriction. These congressional additions and subsequent deletions, though certainly not conclusive, suggest that Congress has been hostile to content-based restrictions on copyrightability. In contrast Congress has placed explicit content-related restrictions in the current statutes governing the related areas of trademarks and patents. The Lanham Act prohibits registration of any trademark that "[c]onsists of or comprises immoral, deceptive, or scandalous matter," 15 U.S.C. § 1052(a), and inventions must be shown to be "useful" before a patent is issued. *See* 35 U.S.C. § 101.

The legislative history of the 1976 Act reveals that Congress intends to continue the policy of the 1909 Act of avoiding content restrictions on copyrightability. In recommending passage of the 1976 Act, the House Judiciary Committee stated:

> The phrase "original works of authorship," [§ 102] which is purposely left undefined, is intended to incorporate without change the standard of originality established by the courts under the present copyright statute. This standard does not include requirements of novelty, ingenuity, or *esthetic merit,* and there is no intention to enlarge the standard of copyright protection to require them.

H.R. Rep. No. 1476, 94th Cong., 2d Sess., 51, *reprinted in* [1976] U.S. Code Cong. & Admin. News pp. 5659, 5664 (emphasis added).

It appears to us that Congress has concluded that the constitutional purpose of its copyright power, "[t]o promote the Progress of Science and useful Arts," U.S. Const. art. I, § 8, cl. 8, is best served by allowing all creative works (in a copyrightable format) to be accorded copyright protection regardless of subject matter or content, trusting to the public taste to reward creators of useful works and to deny creators of useless works any reward....

[The Ninth Circuit recently rejected the defense of fraudulent content in copyright infringement actions, saying]:

> There is nothing in the Copyright Act to suggest that the courts are to pass upon the truth or falsity, the soundness or unsoundness, of the

views embodied in a copyrighted work. The gravity and immensity of the problems, theological, philosophical, economic and scientific, that would confront a court if this view were adopted are staggering to contemplate. It is surely not a task lightly to be assumed, and we decline the invitation to assume it.

Belcher v. Tarbox, 486 F.2d 1087, 1088 (C.A.9, 1973).

In our view, the absence of content restrictions on copyrightability indicates that Congress has decided that the constitutional goal of encouraging creativity would not be best served if an author had to concern himself not only with the marketability of his work but also with the judgment of government officials regarding the worth of the work.

Further, if Congress were receptive to subject matter restrictions on copyright, there are many reasons why it would be unlikely to choose obscenity as one of those restrictions. . . . Such restraints, if imposed, would be antithetical to promotion of creativity. The pursuit of creativity requires freedom to explore into the gray areas, to the cutting edge, and even beyond. Obscenity, on the other hand, is a limiting doctrine constricting the scope of acceptability of the written word.

. . .

Denying copyright protection to works adjudged obscene by the standards of one era would frequently result in lack of copyright protection (and thus lack of financial incentive to create) for works that later generations might consider to be not only non-obscene but even of great literary merit. *See* Phillips, *Copyright in Obscene Works: Some British and American Problems,* 6 Anglo–Am. L. Rev. 138, 168–69 (1977). Many works that are today held in high regard have been adjudged obscene in previous eras. . . .

Further, Congress in not enacting an obscenity exception to copyrightability avoids substantial practical difficulties and delicate First Amendment issues. Since what is obscene in one local community may be non-obscene protected speech in another, *see Miller v. California,* 413 U.S. 15 (1973), and the copyright statute does not in other respects vary in its applicability from locality to locality, Congress in enacting an obscenity exception would create the dilemma of choosing between using community standards that would (arguably unconstitutionally) fragment the uniform national standards of the copyright system and venturing into the uncharted waters of a national obscenity standard. We can only conclude that we must read the facially all-inclusive 1909 copyright statute as containing no explicit or implicit bar to the copyrighting of obscene materials, and as therefore providing for the copyright of all creative works, obscene or non-obscene, that otherwise meet the requirements of the Copyright Act.

II. *Constitutionality of the Copyright Statute*

The conclusion that the 1909 Act was all-inclusive and did not provide an exception for obscenity does not end our inquiry, however. We must consider whether the statute, in allowing copyright of obscene material, was constitutional and whether despite congressional intent the courts should take it upon themselves to permit the defense of obscenity in copyright infringement cases. We first turn to the question of constitutionality.

The Copyright and Patent Clause of the Constitution provides that "The Congress shall have Power ... To promote the Progress of Science and useful Arts, by securing for limited Times to Authors and Inventors the exclusive Right to their respective Writings and Discoveries...." U.S. Const. art. I, § 8, cl. 8. The district court construed this clause to limit the congressional power to grant copyrights solely to works that promote the sciences and useful arts. If one carries the district court's reasoning to its necessary conclusion, Congress acted unconstitutionally in enacting an all-inclusive statute that allows copyrighting of non-useful works (such as, arguably, obscenity) as well as useful works. Several lower courts and commentators have agreed with this construction of the Copyright and Patent Clause.... In our view the district court's reading of the Copyright and Patent Clause is unduly restrictive of Congress' power and is inconsistent with the Supreme Court's broad view of the congressional powers granted by this Clause. As one commentator has pointed out,

> The words of the copyright clause of the constitution do not require that *writings* shall promote science or useful arts: they require that *Congress* shall promote those ends. It could well be argued that by passing general laws to protect all works, Congress better fulfills its designated ends than it would by denying protection to all books the contents of which were open to real or imagined objection.

Phillips, *op. cit. supra* note 15, at 165–66 (emphasis original).

. . .

... [I]t is obvious that although Congress could require that each copyrighted work be shown to promote the useful arts (as it has with patents), it need not do so. As discussed in the previous section, Congress could reasonably conclude that the best way to promote creativity is not to impose any governmental restrictions on the subject matter of copyrightable works. By making this choice Congress removes the chilling effect of governmental judgments on potential authors and avoids the strong possibility that governmental officials (including judges) will err in separating the useful from the non-useful. Moreover, unlike patents, the grant of a copyright to a non-useful work impedes the progress of the sciences and the useful arts only very slightly, if at all, for the possessor of a copyright does not have any right to block further dissemination or use of the ideas contained in his works. *See Baker v. Selden,* 101 U.S. 99 (1879).

The all-inclusive nature of the 1909 Act reflects the policy judgment that encouraging the production of wheat also requires the protection of a good deal of chaff. We cannot say this judgment was so unreasonable as to exceed congressional power. We conclude that the protection of all writings, without regard to their content, is a constitutionally permissible means of promoting science and the useful arts.

III. *Judicially-Created Defenses to Infringement Actions
Involving Immoral or Obscene Works*

Some courts have denied legal redress in infringement suits to holders of copyrights on immoral or obscene works by applying judicially-created doctrines. . . .

. . .

Assuming for the moment that the equitable doctrine of unclean hands has any field of application in this case, it should not be used as a conduit for asserting obscenity as a limit upon copyright protection. Creating a defense of obscenity—in the name of unclean hands or through any other vehicle—adds a defense not authorized by Congress that may, as discussed above, actually frustrate the congressional purpose underlying an all-inclusive copyright statute. It will discourage creativity by freighting it with a requirement of judicial approval. Requiring authors of controversial, unpopular, or new material to go through judicial proceedings to validate the content of their writings is antithetical to the aim of copyrights. If the copyright holder cannot obtain financial protection for his work because of actual or possible judicial objections to the subject matter, the pro-creativity purpose of the copyright laws will be undercut.

. . .

Reversed and remanded.

————

Devils Films, Inc. v. Nectar Video, 29 F.Supp.2d 174 (S.D.N.Y. 1998). Devils Films produces adult films in California and distributes them, among other places, to New York. After viewing a few of those videos, the trial judge determined that they were unquestionably obscene, so that their interstate transportation was a crime, making the films subject to forfeiture. In this infringement action against Nectar, which was selling unauthorized copies of plaintiff's films, Devils sought a court order directing the U.S. Marshal to seize the infringing films, along with all of Nectar's business records, and to freeze the defendant's assets. The court refrained from deciding whether the Second Circuit—contrary to the decision of the Fifth Circuit in the *Mitchell Bros.* case—might hold that the obscene nature of a copyright claimant's works can properly be asserted as a defense in an infringement action. Here, the court was being asked to issue a temporary restraining order, and it concluded that it had the equitable discretion to withhold such an order given the plaintiff's "unclean hands" in the circumstances of the case; it was empowered to give less weight to plaintiff's lost sales "than the potential ramifications of ordering the U.S. Marshal to aid in a violation of state and federal law. . . . It strains credulity that Congress intended to extend the protection of the copyright law to contraband." The court also noted that its holding—which followed upon its own conclusion about the violation of obscenity laws—did not require an examiner in the Copyright Office to make an obscenity determination as a precondition to registration, which could raise First Amendment questions concerning the prior restraint of protected speech.

QUESTION

The *Mitchell Bros.* court rejects the argument that each work must individually promote the progress of knowledge. Should courts adopt a similar position with respect to another feature of the constitutional copyright clause: while copyright is conceived as an incentive to the production of works of authorship, must it be demonstrated in each case that it was copyright protection that spurred each author to create the work at issue? *Compare Hutchinson Tel. Co. v. Fronteer Directory Co.,* 770 F.2d 128 (8th Cir.1985), *with Feist Pubs., Inc. v. Rural Tel. Serv.,* Section A.1, *supra* this chapter: in both cases, the obligation to publish a telephone directory in order to secure the telephone service franchise afforded a significant incentive to creation of the compilation; the *Hutchinson* court found that this fact did not compromise plaintiff's copyright, while the *Feist* court observed that plaintiff had other incentives than copyright to create its directory.

The *Mitchell Bros.* decision seems consistent with the longstanding copyright policy of refraining from assessing the aesthetic merit of the work. *See Bleistein v. Donaldson Lithographing Co., supra.* Would avoidance of inquiry into specific economic incentives be as well-founded? *Should* a court attempt to discern what role the prospect of copyright protection played in the creation or elaboration of the work? What problems do you see with such an inquiry?

CHAPTER 3

OWNERSHIP

A. INITIAL OWNERSHIP

1. AUTHORSHIP STATUS

Lindsay v. R.M.S. Titanic

52 U.S.P.Q.2D 1609 (S.D.N.Y.1999).

■ HAROLD BAER, JR., DISTRICT JUDGE.

The plaintiff, Alexander Lindsay, commenced this lawsuit in 1997, seeking damages based upon his share of the revenues generated by the salvage operations conducted at the wreck site of the famous sunken vessel, the R.M.S. Titanic. Defendants R.M.S. Titanic, Inc. ("RMST") and Suarez Corporation Inc. ("SCI") answered and asserted counterclaims against the plaintiff for copyright infringement. The plaintiff's amended complaint joined defendant Discovery Communications, Inc. ("DCI") and added claims of copyright infringement against RMST, SCI and DCI. [The plaintiff moved for summary judgment, and the defendants for dismissal, on Lindsay's copyright claims.]

[The plaintiff is an independent documentary film maker engaged in the business of creating, producing, directing, and filming documentaries. In 1993, RMST was awarded exclusive status as salvor-in-possession of the Titanic wreck site and is therefore authorized to carry on salvage operations there. Lindsay filmed a documentary in 1994 that depicted RMST's third salvage expedition, and he there conceived of yet another film project for the Titanic wreck using high illumination lighting equipment. Negotiations followed for Lindsay's work on a film of the 1996 expedition, but no written agreement was executed. Lindsay planned in detail the filming of the wreckage, both in advance and during the 1996 expedition, in ways that are described below by the court; he did not, however, operate the film cameras himself. In this action, he seeks compensation for his services, and he claims that the defendants are "unlawfully profiting from the exploitation" of the film project at issue.]

III. DISCUSSION

. . .

B. Copyright Claims

. . .

2. Authorship

The defendants first argue that the plaintiff cannot have any protectable right in the illuminated footage since he did not dive to the ship and thus did not himself actually photograph the wreckage. This argument, however, does not hold water.

The Copyright Act of 1976 provides that copyright ownership "vests initially in the author or authors of the work." 17 U.S.C. sec. 201(a). Generally speaking, the author of a work is the person "who actually creates the work, that is, the person who translates an idea into a fixed, tangible expression entitled to copyright protection." *Community for Creative Non–Violence v. Reid*, 490 U.S. 730, 737(1989) (citing 17 U.S.C. sec. 102). In the context of film footage and photography, it makes intuitive sense that the "author" of a work is the individual or individuals who took the pictures, i.e. the photographer. However, the concept is broader than as argued by the defendants.

For over 100 years, the Supreme Court has recognized that photographs may receive copyright protection in "so far as they are representatives of original intellectual conceptions of the author." *Burrow-Giles Lithographic Co. v. Sarony*, 111 U.S. 53, 58 (1884). An individual claiming to be an author for copyright purposes must show "the existence of those facts of originality, of intellectual production, of thought, and conception." *Feist*. Some elements of originality in a photograph include "posing the subjects, lighting, angle, selection of film and camera, evoking the desired expression, and almost any variant involved." *Rogers v. Koons*, 960 F.2d 301, 307 (2d Cir.), cert. denied, 506 U.S. 934 (1992). Taken as true, the plaintiff's allegations meet this standard. Lindsay's alleged storyboards and the specific directions he provided to the film crew regarding the use of the lightowers and the angles from which to shoot the wreck all indicate that the final footage would indeed be the product of Lindsay's "original intellectual conceptions."

The fact that Lindsay did not literally perform the filming, i.e. by diving to the wreck and operating the cameras, will not defeat his claims of having "authored" the illuminated footage. The plaintiff alleges that as part of his pre-production efforts, he created so-called "storyboards," a series of drawings which incorporated images of the Titanic by identifying specific camera angles and shooting sequences. During the expedition itself, Lindsay claims to have been "the director, producer and cinematographer" of the underwater footage. As part of this role, Lindsay alleges that he directed daily planning sessions with the film crew to provide them with "detailed instructions for positioning and utilizing the light towers." Moreover, the plaintiff actually "directed the filming" of the Titanic from on board the Ocean Voyager, the salvage vessel that held the crew and equipment. Finally, Lindsay screened the footage at the end of each day to "confirm that he had obtained the images he wanted."

All else being equal, where a plaintiff alleges that he exercised such a high degree of control over a film operation—including the type and amount of lighting used, the specific camera angles to be employed, and other detail-intensive artistic elements of a film—such that the final product duplicates his conceptions and visions of what the film should look like, the plaintiff may be said to be an "author" within the meaning of the Copyright Act.

Indeed, the instant case is analogous to *Andrien v. Southern Ocean County Chamber of Commerce*, 927 F.2d 132 (3d Cir.1991). There, the Third Circuit recognized that "a party can be considered an author when his or her expression of an idea is transposed by mechanical or rote transcription into tangible form under the authority of the party." Id. at 135. The plaintiff in *Andrien* had received a copyright for a map of Long Beach Island, New Jersey which was created from a compilation of pre-existing maps and the plaintiff's personal survey of the island. To transform his concepts and the information he had gathered into the final map, the plaintiff hired a printing company to print the map in final form. The plaintiff testified that the maps were made by the printer "with me at her elbow practically" and that he spent time each day at the print shop during the weeks the map was made, directing the map's preparation in specific detail. In reversing the lower court's granting of summary judgment against the plaintiff, the court noted that the printers had not "intellectually modified or technically enhanced the concept articulated by Andrien," nor did they "change the substance of Andrien's original expression." Id. at 135. See also *Lakedreams v. Taylor*, 932 F.2d 1103, 1108 (5th Cir.1991) (noting that authors may be entitled to copyright protection even if they do not "perform with their own hands the mechanical tasks of putting the material into the form distributed to the public"). It is too early to tell whether the allegations of the plaintiff here satisfy the copyright laws, but crediting his story as I must, dismissal is unwarranted at this stage of the litigation.

The defendants' argue that *Geshwind v. Garrick*, 734 F. Supp. 644 (S.D.N.Y.1990), vacated in part, 738 F. Supp. 792 (S.D.N.Y.1990), aff'd, 927 F.2d 594 (2d Cir.), cert. denied, 502 U.S. 811 (1991), mandates dismissal. That case, however, is inapposite. The plaintiff there, a producer of computer graphics animation and special effects, had contracted to produce a 15–second animation piece. The plaintiff hired Digital, a computer graphics company to, in essence, produce the animated piece. The court in *Geshwind* found that Digital, by its employee, was the "author" within the meaning of the Copyright Act. In ruling that the plaintiff was not an "author," Judge Patterson found that the plaintiff there had made only minimal contributions to the final product and had only some, if any, of his "suggestions" incorporated into the final product. Id. at 650. This is in stark contrast to the case at bar where Lindsay alleges that his contributions—not suggestions—were anything but minimal, and he describes himself as the driving force behind the final film product at issue here.

. . . .

QUESTION

In the *Andrien* case, discussed by the court, reference was made to the words of the Supreme Court: "As a general rule, the author is the party who actually creates the work, that is, the person who translates an idea into a fixed, tangible expression entitled to copyright protection." (The quotation is from *CCNV v. Reid*, which follows soon below.) But the courts in both *Andrien* and *Lindsay* effectively modified that rule by pointing out the difference between a "work" and the "tangible medium" in which it is embodied; one person can be an author of a literary or musical work, without writing it down himself, by dictating to another who "fixes" the words or notes. The former is the "author" while the latter is not and is merely what the *Andrien* court labeled an amanuensis.

If an amanuensis is not an "author," what of a person who claims to have transcribed a work of divine revelation? See, e.g., *Urantia Foundation v. Maaherra*, 114 F.3d 955 (9th Cir.1997); *Penguin Books v. New Christian Church*, 55 U.S.P.Q.2d 1680 (S.D.N.Y.2000) (in the latter case, the transcriber stated that "the Voice" [of Jesus] not only dictated the book to her, but directed her to obtain a copyright registration for the work). See also Cummins v. Bond, [1927] 1 Ch. 167 (addressing whether "authorship and copyright rest with some one already domiciled on the other side of the inevitable river.")

———

The *Andrien* and *Lindsay* decisions elect between two competing concepts of authorship: one based on conception, the other based on execution. The *Andrien* and *Lindsay* courts' view, certainly today the dominant one, prefers the intellectual to the muscular contribution to creation. But it would be an overstatement to claim that U.S. copyright today rests entirely on an intellectual characterization of authorship. There is another competing concept of authorship in our copyright law, an economic one. Under this conception, the "author" is the person or entity who finances the work's creation and dissemination, including covering the cost of the persons actually creating the work. This person's or entity's assumption of all economic risks entitles it to be treated as the "author." This is the concept sustaining the "works made for hire" rule of U.S. copyright law. As you review the following materials, consider the differences in philosophy and result between the various concepts of authorship.

2.   AUTHORSHIP AS AN ECONOMIC CONCEPT: WORKS MADE FOR HIRE

The Constitution authorizes Congress to "secur[e] to *Authors* . . . the exclusive Right to their . . . Writings," Art. I, § 1, cl. 8 (emphasis added). In determining who is an "author" for constitutional purposes, one might conclude that the text reserves to the actual creators of works the initial entitlement to copyright. However, the United States copyright statute does not limit authorship status to human beings. The Copyright Act permits corporate entities to claim the "author" title: the "work made for hire" doctrine (*see infra,* part a) designates as "authors" employers and certain commissioning parties.

Is conferring authorship status on corporations and on other persons who did not create the work (certain commissioning parties) any more than a formalistic, but substantively inadequate, compliance with the language of the Constitutional copyright clause? What kinds of efforts make one an "author" in the Constitutional sense? Doesn't the Constitutional text imply a closer connection between "Author" and "Writing" (money may talk, but it doesn't write)? On the other hand, if the United States conception of copyright, as expressed in the copyright clause, is primarily economic, is it not consonant with the Constitution to award the limited monopoly to the person or entity who finances the work's creation and takes the risk of bringing it to market? If "Author" signifies not one who is merely a payor, but one "to whom anything owes its origin; originator; maker; one who completes a work of science or literature," *Burrow-Giles v. Sarony, supra* Chapter 1, does Congress' recognition of any other person or entity as an "author" contravene the Constitution?

§ 101. Definitions

As used in this title, the following terms and their variant forms mean the following:

A "work made for hire" is—

(1) a work prepared by an employee within the scope of his or her employment; or

(2) a work specially ordered or commissioned for use as a contribution to a collective work, as a part of a motion picture or other audiovisual work, as a translation, as a supplementary work, as a compilation, as an instructional text, as a test, as answer material for a test, or as an atlas, if the parties expressly agree in a written instrument signed by them that the work shall be considered a work made for hire.

§ 201. Ownership of Copyright

. . .

(b) *Works Made For Hire*—In the case of a work made for hire, the employer or other person for whom the work was prepared is considered the author for purposes of this title, and, unless the parties have expressly agreed otherwise in a written instrument signed by them, owns all of the rights comprised in the copyright.

a. EMPLOYEE–CREATED WORKS

Community for Creative Non–Violence v. Reid

490 U.S. 730, 109 S.Ct. 2166, 104 L.Ed.2d 811 (1989).

■ JUSTICE MARSHALL delivered the opinion of the Court.

In this case, an artist and the organization that hired him to produce a sculpture contest the ownership of the copyright in that work. To resolve this dispute, we must construe the "work made for hire" provisions of the Copyright Act of 1976 (Act or 1976 Act), 17 U.S.C. §§ 101 and 201(b), and in particular, the provision in § 101, which defines as a "work made for hire" a "work prepared by an employee within the scope of his or her employment" (hereinafter § 101(1)).

I

Petitioners are the Community for Creative Non–Violence (CCNV), a nonprofit unincorporated association dedicated to eliminating homelessness in America, and Mitch Snyder, a member and trustee of CCNV. In the fall of 1985, CCNV decided to participate in the annual Christmastime Pageant of Peace in Washington, D.C., by sponsoring a display to dramatize the plight of the homeless. As the District Court recounted:

> "Snyder and fellow CCNV members conceived the idea for the nature of the display: a sculpture of a modern Nativity scene in which, in lieu of the traditional Holy Family, the two adult figures and the infant would appear as contemporary homeless people huddled on a streetside steam grate. The family was to be black (most of the homeless in Washington being black); the figures were to be life-sized, and the steam grate would be positioned atop a platform 'pedestal,' or base, within which special-effects equipment would be enclosed to emit simulated 'steam' through the grid to swirl about the figures. They also settled upon a title for the work—'Third World America'—and a legend for the pedestal: 'and still there is no room at the inn.' " 652 F. Supp. 1453, 1454 (DC 1987).

Reproduced with permission of CCNV

Snyder made inquiries to locate an artist to produce the sculpture. He was referred to respondent James Earl Reid, a Baltimore, Maryland, sculptor. In the course of two telephone calls, Reid agreed to sculpt the three human figures. CCNV agreed to make the steam grate and pedestal for the statue. Reid proposed that the work be cast in bronze, at a total cost of approximately $100,000 and taking six to eight months to complete.... [After deciding that a synthetic substance could be used instead of bronze, the] parties agreed that the project would cost no more than $15,000, not including Reid's services, which he offered to donate. The parties did not sign a written agreement. Neither party mentioned copyright.

After Reid received an advance of $3,000, he made several sketches of figures in various poses. At Snyder's request, Reid sent CCNV a sketch of a proposed sculpture showing the family in a crechelike setting: the mother seated, cradling a baby in her lap; the father standing behind her, bending over her shoulder to touch the baby's foot. Reid testified that Snyder asked for the sketch to use in raising funds for the sculpture. Snyder testified that it was also for his approval.... While Reid was in Washington, Snyder took him to see homeless people living on the streets. Snyder pointed out that they tended to recline on steam grates, rather than sit or stand, in order to warm their bodies. From that time on, Reid's sketches contained only reclining figures.

Throughout November and the first two weeks of December 1985, Reid worked exclusively on the statue, assisted at various times by a dozen different people who were paid with funds provided in installments by CCNV. On a number of occasions, CCNV members visited Reid to check on his progress and to coordinate CCNV's construction of the base. CCNV rejected Reid's proposal to use suitcases or shopping bags to hold the family's personal belongings, insisting instead on a shopping cart. Reid and CCNV members did not discuss copyright ownership on any of these visits.

On December 24, 1985, 12 days after the agreed-upon date, Reid delivered the completed statue to Washington. There it was joined to the steam grate and pedestal prepared by CCNV and placed on display near the site of the pageant.

Snyder paid Reid the final installment of the $15,000. The statue remained on display for a month. In late January 1986, CCNV members returned it to Reid's studio in Baltimore for minor repairs. Several weeks later, Snyder began making plans to take the statue on a tour of several cities to raise money for the homeless. Reid objected, contending that the Design Cast 62 material was not strong enough to withstand the ambitious itinerary. He urged CCNV to cast the statue in bronze at a cost of $35,000, or to create a master mold at a cost of $5,000. Snyder declined to spend more of CCNV's money on the project.

In March 1986, Snyder asked Reid to return the sculpture. Reid refused. He then filed a certificate of copyright registration for "Third World America" in his name and announced plans to take the sculpture on a more modest tour than the one CCNV had proposed. Snyder, acting in his capacity as CCNV's trustee, immediately filed a competing certificate of copyright registration.

Snyder and CCNV then commenced this action against Reid and his photographer, Ronald Purtee, seeking return of the sculpture and a determination of copyright ownership. The District Court granted a preliminary injunction, ordering the sculpture's return. After a 2–day bench trial, the District Court declared that "Third World America" was a "work made for hire" under § 101 of the Copyright Act and that Snyder, as trustee for CCNV, was the exclusive owner of the copyright in the sculpture. 652 F. Supp., at 1457. The court reasoned that Reid had been an "employee" of CCNV within the meaning of § 101(1) because CCNV was the motivating force in the statue's production. Snyder and other CCNV members, the court explained, "conceived the idea of a contemporary Nativity scene to contrast with the national celebration of the season," and "directed enough of [Reid's] effort to assure that, in the end, he had produced what they, not he, wanted." *Id.*, at 1456.

The Court of Appeals for the District of Columbia Circuit reversed and remanded, holding that Reid owned the copyright because "Third World America" was not a work for hire.

We granted certiorari to resolve a conflict among the Courts of Appeals over the proper construction of the "work made for hire" provisions of the Act. 488 U.S. 940 (1988). We now affirm.

II

A

The Copyright Act of 1976 provides that copyright ownership "vests initially in the author or authors of the work." 17 U.S.C. § 201(a). As a general rule, the author is the party who actually creates the work, that is, the person who translates an idea into a fixed, tangible expression entitled to copyright protection. § 102. The Act carves out an important exception, however, for "works made for hire." If the work is for hire, "the employer or other person for whom the work was prepared is considered the author" and owns the copyright, unless there is a written agreement to the contrary. § 201(b). Classifying a work as "made for hire" determines not only the initial ownership of its copyright, but also the copyright's duration, § 302(c), and the owners' renewal rights, § 304(a), termination rights, § 203(a), and right to import certain goods bearing the copyright, § 601(b)(1). *See* 1 M. Nimmer & D. Nimmer, Nimmer on Copyright § 5.03[A], pp. 5–10 (1988). The contours of the work for hire doctrine therefore carry profound significance for freelance creators—including artists, writers, photographers, designers, composers, and computer programmers—and for the publishing, advertising, music, and other industries which commission their works.[4]

---

4. As of 1955, approximately 40 percent of all copyright registrations were for works for hire, according to a Copyright Office study....

... The petitioners do not claim that the statue satisfies the terms of § 101(2). Quite clearly, it does not. Sculpture does not fit within any of the nine categories of "specially ordered or commissioned" works enumerated in that subsection, and no written agreement between the parties establishes "Third World America" as a work for hire.

The dispositive inquiry in this case therefore is whether "Third World America" is "a work prepared by an employee within the scope of his or her employment" under § 101(1). The Act does not define these terms. In the absence of such guidance, four interpretations have emerged. The first holds that a work is prepared by an employee whenever the hiring party retains the right to control the product. *See Peregrine v. Lauren Corp.*, 601 F. Supp. 828, 829 (Colo. 1985); *Clarkstown v. Reeder*, 566 F. Supp. 137, 142 (S.D.N.Y.1983). Petitioners take this view. Brief for Petitioners 15; Tr. of Oral Arg. 12. A second, and closely related, view is that a work is prepared by an employee under § 101(1) when the hiring party has actually wielded control with respect to the creation of a particular work. This approach was formulated by the Court of Appeals for the Second Circuit, *Aldon Accessories Ltd. v. Spiegel, Inc.*, 738 F.2d 548, *cert. denied*, 469 U.S. 982, 105 S. Ct. 387, 83 L. Ed. 2d 321 (1984), and adopted by the Fourth Circuit, *Brunswick Beacon, Inc. v. Schock–Hopchas Publishing Co.*, 810 F.2d 410 (1987), the Seventh Circuit, *Evans Newton, Inc. v. Chicago Systems Software*, 793 F.2d 889, *cert. denied*, 479 U.S. 949, 107 S. Ct. 434, 93 L. Ed. 2d 383 (1986), and, at times, by petitioners, Brief for Petitioners 17. A third view is that the term "employee" within § 101(1) carries its common law agency law meaning. This view was endorsed by the Fifth Circuit in *Easter Seal Society for Crippled Children and Adults of Louisiana, Inc. v. Playboy Enterprises*, 815 F.2d 323 (1987), and by the Court of Appeals below. Finally, respondent and numerous *amici curiae* contend that the term "employee" only refers to "formal, salaried" employees. *See, e.g.*, Brief for Respondents 23–24; Brief for Register of Copyrights as *Amicus Curiae* 7. The Court of Appeals for the Ninth Circuit recently adopted this view. *See Dumas v. Gommerman*, 865 F.2d 1093 (1989).

The starting point for our interpretation of a statute is always its language. *Consumer Product Safety Comm'n v. GTE Sylvania, Inc.*, 447 U.S. 102, 108, 100 S. Ct. 2051, 2056, 64 L. Ed. 2d 766 (1980). The Act nowhere defines the terms "employee" or "scope of employment." ... In the past, when Congress has used the term "employee" without defining it, we have concluded that Congress intended to describe the conventional master-servant relationship as understood by common law agency doctrine.... Nothing in the text of the work for hire provisions indicates that Congress used the words "employee" and "employment" to describe anything other than " 'the conventional relation of employer and employee.' " ... On the contrary, Congress' intent to incorporate the agency law definition is suggested by § 101(1)'s use of the term, "scope of employment," a widely used term of art in agency law. *See* Restatement (Second) of Agency § 228 (1958) (hereinafter Restatement).

In past cases of statutory interpretation, when we have concluded that Congress intended terms such as "employee," "employer," and "scope of employment" to be understood in light of agency law, we have relied on the general common law of agency, rather than on the law of any particular State, to give meaning to these terms....

In contrast, neither test proposed by petitioners is consistent with the text of the Act.... Section 101 plainly creates two distinct ways in which a work can be deemed for hire: one for works prepared by employees, the other for those specially ordered or commissioned works which fall within one of the nine enumerated categories and are the subject of a written agreement. The right to control the product test ignores this dichotomy by transforming into a work for hire under § 101(1) any "specially ordered or commissioned" work that is subject to the supervision and control of the hiring party. Because a party who hires a "specially ordered or commissioned" work by definition has a right to specify the characteristics of the product desired, at the time the commission is accepted, and frequently until it is completed, the right to control the product test would mean that many works that could satisfy § 101(2) would already have been deemed works for hire under § 101(1). Petitioners' interpretation is particularly hard to square with § 101(2)'s enumeration of the nine specific categories of specially ordered or commissioned works eligible to be works for hire, e.g., "a contribution to a collective work," "a part of a motion picture," and "answer material for a test." The unifying feature of these works is that they are usually prepared at the instance, direction, and risk of a publisher or producer. By their very nature, therefore, these types of works would be works by an employee under petitioners' right to control the product test.

The actual control test, articulated by the Second Circuit in *Aldon Accessories,* fares only marginally better when measured against the language and structure of § 101.... Section 101 clearly delineates between works prepared by an employee and commissioned works. Sound though other distinctions might be as a matter of copyright policy, there is no statutory support for an additional dichotomy between commissioned works that are actually controlled and supervised by the hiring party and those that are not.

We therefore conclude that the language and structure of § 101 of the Act do not support either the right to control the product or the actual control approaches.[8] The structure of § 101 indicates that a work for hire can arise through one of two mutually exclusive means, one for employees and one for independent contractors, and ordinary canons of statutory interpretation indicate that the classification of a particular hired party should be made with reference to agency law.

---

8. We also reject the suggestion of respondent and *amici* that the § 101(1) term "employee" refers only to formal, salaried employees. While there is some support for such a definition in the legislative history, see Varmer, Works Made for Hire 130; *infra* at n. 11, the language of § 101(1) cannot support it. The Act does not say "formal" or "salaried" employee, but simply "employee." ...

This reading of the undefined statutory terms finds considerable support in the Act's legislative history. *Cf. Diamond v. Chakrabarty,* 447 U.S. 303, 315, 100 S. Ct. 2204, 2210–11, 65 L. Ed. 2d 144 (1980). The Act, which almost completely revised existing copyright law, was the product of two decades of negotiation by representatives of creators and copyright-using industries, supervised by the Copyright Office and, to a lesser extent, by Congress. *See Mills Music, Inc. v. Snyder,* 469 U.S. 153, 159, 105 S. Ct. 638, 642–43, 83 L. Ed. 2d 556 (1985); Litman, *Copyright, Compromise, and Legislative History,* 72 Cornell L. Rev. 857, 862 (1987)....

. . .

In 1961, the Copyright Office's first legislative proposal retained the distinction between works by employees and works by independent contractors. After numerous meetings with representatives of the affected parties, the Copyright Office issued a preliminary draft bill in 1963. Adopting the Register's recommendation, it defined "work made for hire" as "a work prepared by an employee within the scope of the duties of his employment, but not including a work made on special order or commission."

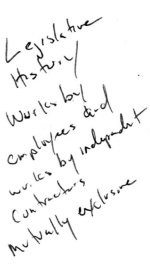

In response to objections by book publishers that the preliminary draft bill limited the work for hire doctrine to "employees," the 1964 revision bill expanded the scope of the work for hire classification to reach, for the first time, commissioned works. The bill's language, proposed initially by representatives of the publishing industry, retained the definition of work for hire insofar as it referred to "employees," but added a separate clause covering commissioned works, without regard to the subject matter, "if the parties so agree in writing." Those representing authors objected that the added provision would allow publishers to use their superior bargaining position to force authors to sign work for hire agreements, thereby relinquishing all copyright rights as a condition of getting their books published. *See* Supplementary Report, at 67.

In 1965, the competing interests reached an historic compromise which was embodied in a joint memorandum submitted to Congress and the Copyright Office, incorporated into the 1965 revision bill, and ultimately enacted in the same form and nearly the same terms 11 years later, as § 101 of the 1976 Act. The compromise retained as subsection (1) the language referring to "a work prepared by an employee within the scope of his or her employment." However, in exchange for concessions from publishers on provisions relating to the termination of transfer rights, the authors consented to a second subsection which classified four categories of commissioned works as works for hire if the parties expressly so agreed in writing: works for use "as a contribution to a collective work, as a part of a motion picture, as a translation, or as supplementary work." S. 1006, H.R. 4347, H.R. 5680, H.R. 6835, 89th Cong., 1st Sess., § 101 (1965). The interested parties selected these categories because they concluded that these commissioned works, although not prepared by employees and thus not covered by the first subsection, nevertheless should be treated as works for hire because they were ordinarily prepared "at the instance, direction, and risk of a publisher or producer." Supplementary Report, at 67. The

Supplementary Report emphasized that only the "four special cases specifically mentioned" could qualify as works made for hire; "[o]ther works made on special order or commission would not come within the definition." *Id.*, at 67–68.

In 1966, the House Committee on the Judiciary endorsed this compromise in the first legislative report on the revision bills. *See* H.R. Rep. No. 2237, 89th Cong., 2d Sess., 114, 116 (1966). Retaining the distinction between works by employees and commissioned works, the House Committee focused instead on "how to draw a statutory line between those works written on special order or commission that should be considered as works made for hire, and those that should not." *Id.*, at 115. The House Committee added four other enumerated categories of commissioned works that could be treated as works for hire: compilations, instructional texts, tests, and atlases. *Id.*, at 116. With the single addition of "answer material for a test," the 1976 Act, as enacted, contained the same definition of works made for hire as did the 1966 revision bill, and had the same structure and nearly the same terms as the 1966 bill.[13] Indeed, much of the language of the 1976 House and Senate Reports was borrowed from the Reports accompanying the earlier drafts.

Thus, the legislative history of the Act is significant for several reasons. First, the enactment of the 1965 compromise with only minor modifications demonstrates that Congress intended to provide two mutually exclusive ways for works to acquire work for hire status: one for employees and the other for independent contractors. Second, the legislative history underscores the clear import of the statutory language: only enumerated categories of commissioned works may be accorded work for hire status. The hiring party's right to control the product simply is not determinative. . . .

We do not find convincing petitioners' contrary interpretation of the history of the Act. They contend that Congress, in enacting the Act, meant to incorporate a line of cases decided under the 1909 Act holding that an employment relationship exists sufficient to give the hiring party copyright ownership whenever that party has the right to control or supervise the artist's work. In support of this position, petitioners note: "[n]owhere in the 1976 Act or in the Act's legislative history does Congress state that it intended to jettison the control standard or otherwise to reject the pre-Act

---

13. An attempt to add "photographic or other portrait[s]," S. Rep. No. 94–473, p. 4 (1975), to the list of commissioned works eligible for work for hire status failed after the Register of Copyrights objected:

The addition of portraits to the list of commissioned works that can be made into "works made for hire" by agreement of the parties is difficult to justify. Artists and photographers are among the most vulnerable and poorly protected of all the beneficiaries of the copyright law, and it seems clear that, like serious composers and choreographers, they were not intended to be treated as "employees" under the carefully negotiated definition in section 101.

Second Supplementary Report of the Register of Copyrights on the General Revision of the U.S. Copyright Law: 1975 Revision Bill, Chapter XI, pp. 12–13.

judicial approach to identifying a work for hire employment relationship." Brief for Petitioners 20, citing *Aldon Accessories,* 738 F.2d, at 552.

We are unpersuaded. Ordinarily, "Congress' silence is just that— silence." *Alaska Airlines, Inc. v. Brock,* 480 U.S. 678, 686, 107 S. Ct. 1476, 1481, 94 L. Ed. 2d 661 (1987). Petitioners' reliance on legislative silence is particularly misplaced here because the text and structure of § 101 counsel otherwise. Furthermore, the structure of the work for hire provisions was fully developed in 1965 and the text was agreed upon in essentially final form by 1966. At that time, however, the courts had applied the work for hire doctrine under the 1909 Act exclusively to traditional employees. Indeed, it was not until after the 1965 compromise was forged and adopted by Congress that a federal court for the first time applied the work for hire doctrine to commissioned works. *See, e.g., Brattleboro Publishing Co.* [*v. Winwill Publishing Corp.,* 369 F.2d 565 (2d Cir.1966)]. Congress certainly could not have "jettisoned" a line of cases that had not yet been decided.

Finally, petitioners' construction of the work for hire provisions would impede Congress' paramount goal in revising the 1976 Act of enhancing predictability and certainty of copyright ownership. . . .

To the extent that petitioners endorse an actual control test, CCNV's construction of the work for hire provisions prevents such planning. Because that test turns on whether the hiring party has closely monitored the production process, the parties would not know until late in the process, if not until the work is completed, whether a work will ultimately fall within § 101(1). Under petitioners' approach, therefore, parties would have to predict in advance whether the hiring party will sufficiently control a given work to make it the author. "If they guess incorrectly, their reliance on 'work for hire' or an assignment may give them a copyright interest that they did not bargain for." *Easter Seal Society,* 815 F.2d, at 333; *accord Dumas,* 865 F.2d, at 1103. This understanding of the work for hire provisions clearly thwarts Congress' goal of ensuring predictability through advance planning. Moreover, petitioners' interpretation "leaves the door open for hiring parties, who have failed to get a full assignment of copyright rights from independent contractors falling outside the subdivision (2) guidelines, to unilaterally obtain work-made-for-hire rights years after the work has been completed as long as they directed or supervised the work, a standard that is hard not to meet when one is a hiring party." Hamilton, *Commissioned Works as Works Made for Hire Under the 1976 Copyright Act: Misinterpretation and Injustice,* 135 U. Pa. L. Rev. 1281, 1304 (1987).

. . . To determine whether a work is for hire under the Act, a court first should ascertain, using principles of general common law of agency, whether the work was prepared by an employee or an independent contractor. After making this determination, the court can apply the appropriate subsection of § 101.

B

We turn, finally, to an application of § 101 to Reid's production of "Third World America." In determining whether a hired party is an

Factors

employee under the general common law of agency, we consider the hiring party's right to control the manner and means by which the product is accomplished. Among the other factors relevant to this inquiry are the skill required; the source of the instrumentalities and tools; the location of the work; the duration of the relationship between the parties; whether the hiring party has the right to assign additional projects to the hired party; the extent of the hired party's discretion over when and how long to work; the method of payment; the hired party's role in hiring and paying assistants; whether the work is part of the regular business of the hiring party; whether the hiring party is in business; the provision of employee benefits; and the tax treatment of the hired party. *See* Restatement § 220(2) (setting forth a non-exhaustive list of factors relevant to determining whether a hired party is an employee). No one of these factors is determinative. *See Ward,* 362 U.S., at 400, 80 S. Ct., at 792; *Hilton Int'l Co. v. NLRB,* 690 F.2d 318, 321 (C.A.2 1982).

Examining the circumstances of this case in light of these factors, we agree with the Court of Appeals that Reid was not an employee of CCNV but an independent contractor. 270 U.S. App. D.C., at 35, n. 11, 846 F.2d, at 1494, n. 11. True, CCNV members directed enough of Reid's work to ensure that he produced a sculpture that met their specifications. 652 F. Supp., at 1456. But the extent of control the hiring party exercises over the details of the product is not dispositive. Indeed, all the other circumstances weigh heavily against finding an employment relationship. Reid is a sculptor, a skilled occupation. Reid supplied his own tools. He worked in his own studio in Baltimore, making daily supervision of his activities from Washington practicably impossible. Reid was retained for less than two months, a relatively short period of time. During and after this time, CCNV had no right to assign additional projects to Reid. Apart from the deadline for completing the sculpture, Reid had absolute freedom to decide when and how long to work. CCNV paid Reid $15,000, a sum dependent on "completion of a specific job, a method by which independent contractors are often compensated." *Holt v. Winpisinger,* 258 U.S. App. D.C. 343, 351, 811 F.2d 1532, 1540 (1987). Reid had total discretion in hiring and paying assistants. "Creating sculptures was hardly 'regular business' for CCNV." 270 U.S. App. D.C., at 35, n. 11, 846 F.2d, at 1494, n. 11. Indeed, CCNV is not a business at all. Finally, CCNV did not pay payroll or social security taxes, provide any employee benefits, or contribute to unemployment insurance or workers' compensation funds.

Because Reid was an independent contractor, whether "Third World America" is a work for hire depends on whether it satisfies the terms of § 101(2). This petitioners concede it cannot do. Thus CCNV is not the author of "Third World America" by virtue of the work for hire provisions of the Act. However, as the Court of Appeals made clear, CCNV nevertheless may be a joint author of the sculpture if, on remand, the District Court so determines that CCNV and Reid prepared the work "with the intention that their contributions be merged into inseparable or interdependent parts of a unitary whole." 17 U.S.C. § 101. In that case, CCNV and Reid would be co-owners of the copyright in the work. *See* § 201(a).

For the aforestated reasons, we affirm the judgment of the Court of Appeals for the District of Columbia.

It is so ordered.

———

Taking the case on remand on the issue of joint authorship, the district court persuaded both CCNV and Reid to submit that issue to mediation. The mediation resulted in a mutually satisfactory resolution which was reflected in a consent judgment entered on January 7, 1991. Under the terms of that agreement, CCNV is awarded sole ownership of the original sculpture (i.e., the physical chattel) while Reid is to be recognized as the sole "author" of the work. Reid is to have the exclusive right to make three-dimensional reproductions of the statue. Both CCNV and Reid are given the right to make two-dimensional reproductions of the statue: but Reid is to omit the base and inscription in the reproductions he makes, and CCNV is to give credit to Reid as sculptor in its reproductions. Each party is to be sole owner of any income derived from exercising its own reproduction rights.

The agreement was apparently silent about the issue of Reid's access to the original statue. That issue came to a head when Reid sought possession of that statue in order to make a master mold so that he could in fact make three-dimensional reproductions as contemplated by the mediated agreement, but CCNV refused. The district court ruled that "Reid is entitled to a limited possessory right of his own, in the nature of an implied easement of necessity, to cause a master mold to be made of the sculpture, whereupon it shall be returned promptly to CCNV." 1992 CCH Copyr. Dec. ¶ 26,860 (D.D.C. 1991). (That order was later vacated when the parties reached yet another agreement that was adopted by the court in an unpublished order.)

QUESTIONS

1. Why should employees and commissioned persons who create works for hire be deprived of the status of an "author" by virtue of § 201(b)? Why should the hiring party be deemed the initial owner of copyright? Why should the "life plus seventy years" period of protection not apply to works made for hire? Why should the power given to an "author" to terminate certain long-term grants of copyright (to be studied below) not also apply to creators of works made for hire?

2. Articulate the difference between the rejected "right to supervise and control" test of employment and the approved agency test of "right to control the manner and means by which the product is accomplished."

3. Dan's Department Store decided to place an advertisement in one of the local newspapers, The Brunswick Beacon. Because Dan's had no advertising layout to supply to The Beacon—other than Dan's slogan—original advertising copy was prepared by The Beacon's staff, which designed both text and graphic work. Shortly after the advertisement was paid for and run in The Beacon, several competing local newspapers ran the same ad; Dan's had authorized them to do so. The Beacon has brought an action against Dan's Department Store and the other newspapers. Decide the case. Deal, in particular, with the defendant's contention that it would be absurd to hold that The Beacon is copyright owner, because then advertisers like Dan's would be forbidden to make use of the advertisement—which is obviously useful only to them—in any other media. *Compare Brunswick Beacon, Inc. v. Schock–Hopchas Pub. Co.,* 810 F.2d 410 (4th Cir.1987), *with Canfield v. The Ponchatoula Times,* 759 F.2d 493 (5th Cir.1985).

4. Note that even if, in cases like *Brunswick* and *CCNV*, the relationship between a person doing work for another and the person requesting the work is that of independent contract (and not of conventional employment), the latter person is not at a loss for theories to justify copyright ownership. As noted in W. Patry, The Copyright Law 124–25 (1986):

> If the hiring party contributes significant artistic effort, that party is a joint author along with the independent contractor. Where the hiring party has contributed all of the expression and the independent contractor acts as a mere amanuensis, the hiring party should be considered the sole author. Where, however, the hiring party contributes only ideas or generalized expression incapable of copyright protection, copyright vests in the independent contractor regardless of "whether the alleged employer has the right to direct and supervise the manner in which the writer performs his work." Yet the hiring party under such circumstances may still obtain a transfer of all rights from the independent contractor as a condition to the creation of the work.

In light of these ways to protect the commissioning party, are you convinced of the need to place *any* commissioned works within the definition of works made for hire, as in § 101(2)? Do you see the justification behind each of the nine categories of works listed in that definition?

5. When a current litigation involves a work created pursuant to a particular relationship formed, or a transaction undertaken, prior to 1978, are the governing definitions of "work for hire" to be those under the 1909 Act or those provided in the 1976 Act? *Compare Meltzer v. Zoller,* 520 F.Supp. 847 (D.N.J.1981) *with Roth v. Pritikin,* 710 F.2d 934 (2d Cir.), *cert. denied,* 464 U.S. 961 (1983).

———

Aymes v. Bonelli, 980 F.2d 857 (2d Cir.1992). At the request of Bonelli, the President and CEO of Island Company—which owned stores selling swimming pools and other such items—Aymes created a series of computer programs. The programs maintained records of cash receipts, physical inventory, sales figures, purchase orders, merchandise transfers and price changes. There was no written agreement between Aymes and Bonelli dealing with the ownership of copyright in the programs. Aymes generally worked alone in the Island office, but Bonelli was sometimes there to instruct him on what he wanted from the programs; Bonelli was not himself skilled enough to write such a program. Aymes left when Bonelli cut his hours and was in arrears some $15,000 in Aymes's pay. Aymes registered his copyright in his own name and sued for infringement; representing himself. Aymes secured a reversal by the court of appeals of the finding of "work made for hire" by the trial court. Excerpts from the Second Circuit's opinion follow:

> We begin our analysis by noting that the *Reid* test can be easily misapplied, since it consists merely of a list of possible considerations that may or may not be relevant in a given case. *Reid* established that no one factor was dispositive, but gave no direction concerning how the factors were to be weighed. It does not necessarily follow that because no one factor is dispositive all factors are equally important, or indeed that all factors will have relevance in every case. The factors should not merely be tallied but should be weighed according to their significance in the case. . . .

> Some factors will often have little or no significance in determining whether a party is an independent contractor or an employee. In contrast, there are some factors that will be significant in virtually every situation. These include: (1) the hiring party's right to control the manner and means of creation; (2) the skill required; (3) the provision of employee benefits; (4) the tax treatment of the hired party; and (5) whether the hiring party has the right to assign additional projects to the hired party. These factors will almost always be relevant and should be given more weight in the analysis, because they will usually be highly probative of the true nature of the employment relationship.

> Although the *Reid* test has not yet received widespread application, other courts that have interpreted the test have in effect adopted this weighted approach by only addressing those factors found to be significant in the individual case. . . .

> The importance of the [employee benefits and tax treatment] factors is underscored by the fact that every case since *Reid* that has applied the test has found the hired party to be an independent contractor where the hiring party failed to extend benefits or pay social security taxes. . . .

Carter v. Helmsley–Spear, Inc., 71 F.3d 77 (2d Cir.1995), *cert. denied,* 517 U.S. 1208 (1996). Plaintiff sculptors sought an injunction under the recently-enacted Visual Artists' Rights Act [VARA] against altering, defacing, modifying, mutilating or removing the large "walk-through sculpture" that they were erecting in a building in Queens, New York City, that was owned and managed by the defendants. The contract between the parties provided that the sculptors had full authority in design, creation and installation, that they would receive design credit, and that they would retain the copyright. When ownership of the building changed hands, the new owners ordered the sculptors to leave the property, and made statements indicating that the work would be removed or materially altered.

The court acknowledged that no one of the thirteen factors mentioned by the Supreme Court in *CCNV v. Reid* was dispositive in determining whether a sculpture was a work made for hire—and thus expressly outside of VARA's statutory definition of "work of visual art"—but observed, as it did in *Aymes v. Bonelli*, that five factors are relevant in nearly all cases: (1) The sculptors controlled the manner and means of producing the work; (2) the sculptural work required great skill; (3) the building owner could and did assign additional projects (without additional pay); (4) the defendants paid payroll and social security taxes; and (5) they also paid the sculptors a weekly salary (on a 40-hour per week basis) and provided benefits such as life, health, and liability insurance, paid vacations, and contributed to unemployment insurance and workers' compensation funds on plaintiffs' behalf. These last two factors weighed strongly in favor of employee status, as did other *CCNV* factors: defendants provided most of the supplies used in creating the sculpture, plaintiffs were employed for more than two years with no set date for termination, and they could hire paid assistants only with defendants' approval. The court of appeals therefore overturned an injunction that had been issued by the trial court.

The sculptors relied heavily upon the fact that their contract with the building owner and manager reserved copyright in the sculpture to the plaintiffs; this, they said, evidenced independent-contractor status. The court reserved consideration of this issue. If you were among the appellate judges, how would you deal with it?

QUESTION

Various groups representing creative free-lance authors—particularly photographers and graphic artists—have supported proposed legislation that would drastically constrict the "work for hire" definitions presently in § 101. Among the proposed changes would be the requirement, in order to make out an "employment" relationship under § 101(1), that federal income taxes be withheld from the compensation of the putative employee; and a reduction of the categories of works in § 101(2) to only one, the motion picture. *See* S. 1223, 100th Cong., 1st Sess. (1987). Would you support such legislation?

"WITHIN THE SCOPE OF EMPLOYMENT"

The first prong of the statutory definition of "work made for hire" assumes both that the creative individual is an employee *and* that the work is prepared "within the scope" of that person's employment. Although most of the pertinent decided cases since *CCNV v. Reid* have dealt with the question whether an employer-employee relationship exists, a few cases have treated the "scope of employment" issue. Here as well, the matter typically turns upon a careful assessment of the facts of each case; the trial court's fact findings will be sustained if not clearly erroneous, but the appellate court is free to decide *de novo* whether these facts in their totality satisfy the "scope of employment" test. It is the Restatement (Second) of

Agency to which the courts turn not only in distinguishing the employee from the independent contractor but also for defining the "scope of employment." Under the Restatement, the putative employer has the burden to show that: (1) the work was of the type which the individual was hired to perform; (2) his or her creation of the work occurred "substantially within the authorized time and space limits" of the job; and (3) the work was "actuated, at least in part, by a purpose to serve" the interests of the putative employer. *Avtec Sys., Inc. v. Peiffer*, 21 F.3d 568 (4th Cir.1994).

In two cases involving the development of computer programs, largely at the employee's home after normal working hours, the Court of Appeals for the Fourth Circuit reached differing results. At a later stage of the *Avtec* litigation, the court of appeals reached a conclusion favoring the employee, observing among other things that:

> He was not salaried, and the Program was not directly related to any specific task he was performing during duty hours. The fact that he later received a minuscule amount of compensation and direction from Avtec when temporarily refining the Program for a demonstration is irrelevant; copyright ownership is determined at the moment that the work is created ... and there is no question that Peiffer created the Program outside the time and space constraints of his employment.

Moreover, Peiffer "was not working on a way to improve the efficiency of his job or Avtec's business." *Avtec Sys., Inc. v. Peiffer*, 67 F.3d 293 (4th Cir.1995) (per curiam, table; full opinion at 38 U.S.P.Q.2d 1922). *See also City of Newark v. Beasley*, 883 F.Supp. 3 (D.N.J.1995) (police officer developed educational material to deter juvenile auto theft; it was not the kind of work he was hired to perform and the work was done at home during off hours).

But in *Cramer v. Crestar Fin. Corp.*, 67 F.3d 294 (4th Cir.1995) (per curiam, table; full opinion at 38 U.S.P.Q.2d 1684), the same court on the same day ruled that a computer program developed by a bank's director of the information systems department was a work made for hire. The creation of the software system to deliver innovative bank services fell within the employee's area of responsibility, and he was "motivated at least in part" by a purpose to serve the bank's interests. The work was done "within the authorized time and space limits of his job—even if he did so at home, outside regular work hours, on his own initiative, and using his own equipment.... Cramer admitted that his job required him to work long hours, on weekends, and at home, so he can hardly claim now that work he did at home was by definition not within the scope of his employment."

The scope of employment issue arose more recently in an unusual context. ABC News reporters posing and hired as supermarket employees surreptitiously filmed allegedly unsanitary practices at a Food Lion supermarket. Food Lion sought to prevent the broadcast of the tapes on the ground that the tapes were employee-created works for hire to which Food Lion owned the copyright. The district court rejected Food Lion's ownership claim, holding that videotaping was not normally part of meatwrappers' and similar employees' jobs, nor was it "motivated ... [by] a desire to serve the employer." *Food Lion, Inc. v. Capital Cities/ABC, Inc.,* 946 F.Supp. 420 (M.D.N.C.1996), *aff'd per curiam,* 116 F.3d 472 (4th Cir.1997) (table).

WORK FOR HIRE UNDER THE 1976 ACT AND THE "TEACHER EXCEPTION"

Two decisions from the Seventh Circuit, *Weinstein v. University of Illinois,* 811 F.2d 1091 (7th Cir.1987), and *Hays v. Sony Corp. of Am.,* 847 F.2d 412 (7th Cir.1988), authored by two former law professors, Judges Easterbrook and Posner, considered whether, under the 1976 Act, academic writings were works made for hire whose copyrights belonged to the schools and universities employing the teacher or professor writers.

Addressing a written university policy which purported to claim copyright ownership of works created pursuant to a university "requirement or duty," Judge Easterbrook concluded that the academic writing at issue was not produced under the kind of compulsion implicit in a work for hire employment relationship.

A University "requires" all of its scholars to write. Its demands—especially the demands of departments deciding whether to award tenure—will be "the motivating factor in the preparation of" many a scholarly work. When [plaintiff's dean] told [plaintiff] to publish or perish he was not simultaneously claiming for the University a copyright on the ground that the work had become a "requirement or duty" within the meaning of [the university policy]. The University concedes in this court that a professor of mathematics who proves a new theorem in the course of his employment will own the copyright to his article containing that proof. This has been the academic tradition since copyright law began.

The tradition Judge Easterbrook cited is indeed venerable—proponents of the doctrine that professors own the copyright in their works include great figures in the common law. According to Lord Eldon, Sir William Blackstone owned the copyright in his lectures on law; this precedent warranted Eldon's recognition of a litigant's claim to ownership of his lectures on medicine. *See Abernethy v. Hutchinson,* 3 L.J. 209, 214–15 (Ch.) (1825). A slim, but apparently unanimous, common-law copyright caselaw in the United States follows the English tradition. *See, e.g., C.O. Sherrill v. L.C. Grieves,* 57 Wash. L. Rep. 286, 20 C.O. Bull. 675 (1929) ("the court does not know of any authority holding that a professor is obliged to reduce his lectures to writing or if he does so they become the property of the institution employing him"); *Williams v. Weisser,* 78 Cal.Rptr. 542 (Cal. App.1969) (lectures delivered in class are the professor's common-law copyright property). *Compare Manasa v. University of Miami,* 320 So.2d 467 (Fla.App.1975) (university owns copyright in funding proposal written by administrative officer).

For Judge Posner in the *Hays* case, this tradition deserved deference, despite possibly contradictory statutory language in the 1976 Act:

Until 1976, the statutory term "work made for hire" was not defined, and some courts had adopted a "teacher exception" whereby academic writing was presumed not to be work made for hire.... [V]irtually no one questioned that the academic author was entitled to copyright his writings. Although college and university teachers do academic writing as a part of their employment responsibilities and use their employer's paper, copier, secretarial staff, and (often) computer facilities in that writing, the universal assumption and practice was that (in the absence of an explicit agreement as to who had the right to copyright) the right to copyright such writing belonged to the teacher rather than to the college or university. There were good reasons for the assumption. A college or university does not supervise its faculty in the preparation of academic books and articles, and is poorly equipped to exploit their writings, whether through publication or otherwise; we may set to one side cases where a school directs a teacher to prepare teaching materials and then directs its other teachers to use the materials too.

The reasons for a presumption against finding academic writings to be work made for hire are as forceful today as they ever were. Nevertheless it is widely believed that the 1976 Act abolished the teacher exception, though, if so, probably inadvertently, for there is no discussion of the issue in the legislative history, and no political or other reasons come to mind as to why Congress might have wanted to abolish the exception. To a literalist of statutory interpretation, the conclusion that the Act abolished the exception may seem inescapable. The argument would be that academic writing, being within the scope of academic employment, is work made for hire, per se; so, in the absence of an express written and signed waiver of the academic employer's rights, the copyright in such writing must belong to the employer. But considering the havoc that such a conclusion would wreak in the settled practices of academic institutions, the lack of fit between the policy of the work-for-hire doctrine and the conditions of academic production, and the absence of any indication that Congress meant to abolish the teacher exception, we might, if forced to decide the issue, conclude that the exception had survived the enactment of the 1976 Act....

Judge Posner's decision also indicated a further reason academic writings may not be works for hire: while they may have been "prepared by an employee within the scope of his employment," § 101, they may not have been prepared "*for*" the educational institution. *See* § 201(b). That is, while professors are expected to produce scholarly works, it does not follow that these works have been created at the school's or university's behest for its own use. The proposition that academics do not write "*for*" their institutions rests on two premises: academic freedom, and a sense of personal independence recalling the medieval model of the professor as autonomous, even itinerant, scholar; *see, e.g.,* Abelard, *History of My Troubles* (describing Peter Abelard's glorious, but brief, association with the University of Paris); *NLRB v. Yeshiva Univ.*, 444 U.S. 672, 680 (1980) ("guilds of scholars were responsible only to themselves").

A recent departure from the "teacher exception" principle can be found in *Vanderhurst v. Colorado Mountain College Dist.*, 16 F.Supp.2d 1297 (D.Colo.1998), in which—after an extended treatment of the faculty member's academic freedom in the context of sexual harassment claims against him—the court granted summary judgment against him on his claim against his school for copyright infringement of his Veterinary Technology Outline, prepared by him in connection with his teaching. The College defined course development and preparation as within the "professional service duties" of a faculty member. The court held that "Vanderhurst's creation of the Outline was connected directly with the work [he] was employed to do and was fairly and reasonably incidental to his employment," and that it was therefore a work made for hire.

QUESTIONS

1. Is the "teacher exception" limited to teachers? What of scholars employed at think tanks, such as the Brookings Institution? What about leaders of religious congregations who regularly deliver sermons? If these persons exercise unfettered discretion in research and writing, do they benefit from the exception as well? Should they? Is there a good rationale for a specific "teacher" exception, apart from tradition (and, perhaps, self-interest on the part of former academics now on the bench)?

2. Judge Posner suggested that one basis of the teacher exception was that the academic institution "is poorly equipped to exploit [professorial] writings." Is this persuasive? Might analysis of the exception change if the kinds of works at issue, for example, computer software and instructional materials for distance learning, could be exploited to produce substantial rewards? (Many colleges and universities have created "technology transfer" offices for the precise purpose of marketing faculty-generated intellectual property, principally patents but also broadly enough construed to embrace copyrights.) Assume that you are General Counsel to Franklin University, and you have learned that the well-known Law School professor there, Donna Prima, is using her class notes as a basis for videotaped lectures that have been produced by and are being distributed by Long-range Distance Education, Inc. Professor Prima is paid well for her taped lectures and Longrange has entered into lucrative contracts to license the videotapes at other colleges and universities. Advise Franklin University on its rights against Prima and Longrange.

3. If the university is indeed deemed to be the author and copyright owner of works prepared by its faculty, what would you advise a faculty member—who has prepared her lecture notes while an assistant professor at University A—about freely using and updating them for her lecture notes at University B, where she has just begun to teach as an associate professor? What about revising and publishing them as a book?

4. Even if there is a serious question about how the work-for-hire doctrine should apply to professorial writings, it is generally understood that it does apply to other full-time university employees such as administrative staff, for example, a dean of admissions or placement. Another example would be a staff photographer hired for the purpose of taking photographs of university buildings, faculty and students, events and activities, and the like, for various university publications. Suppose that Parkland College has recently published a copyright policy manual which provides: "Members of the College staff who develop materials shall have copyrights in such materials." Suppose too that staff are covered by a collective bargaining agreement which incorporates the copyright policy manual by reference, and which is signed by the union representing all staff members. Phyllis Photo, who took photographs at college events over the past year, has just been terminated by the College. She seeks your advice on whether she or the College owns copyright in those photos. How would you advise her? (Be sure to consider Section 201(b) of the Act.) *See Manning v. Parkland College*, 109 F.Supp.2d 976 (C.D.Ill.2000).

b. SPECIALLY ORDERED OR COMMISSIONED WORKS

THE NINE STATUTORY CATEGORIES FOR A COMMISSIONED WORK

As the Supreme Court noted in *CCNV v. Reid*, the legislative history behind the definition of "work made for hire" took a number of twists and turns, particularly in connection with the categories of commissioned works to be included within the statutory definition. Usually, there is no dispute over the question whether a commissioned work being litigated falls within one of the nine statutory categories.

Such an issue was, however, raised in *Lulirama Ltd. v. Axcess Broadcast Servs., Inc.*, 128 F.3d 872 (5th Cir.1997). There, Lulirama agreed in writing to provide Axcess with fifty advertising jingles, which Axcess in turn intended to sell to sponsors of radio or television programs. The so-called jingle writing agreement, signed by both parties, contained a notation by Axcess that the works were "for hire." Lulirama provided only seven jingles under that contract, and there were subsequent dealings and contracts between the parties, which ultimately ended in a dispute; Axcess used the jingles and Lulirama sued for copyright infringement.

Although the court (by implying licenses from Lulirama) ultimately concluded that Axcess did not infringe any copyrights, it rejected the claim that the jingles were works for hire owned by Axcess. Axcess asserted that the jingles were commissioned for use "as a part of a motion picture or other audiovisual work." The court of appeals, however, held that the jingles were "audio" works only and lacked the accompanying "images" that are necessary to constitute an "audiovisual" work under the definition in § 101 of the Copyright Act. Because of the lack of any visual component, the jingles failed to fall into any of the statutory "work for hire" categories, so that Axcess's written reference to "for hire" was unavailing. Even considering that the jingles might ultimately be marketed by Axcess to television clients, the record did not conclusively show which jingles might be used on television and which might be used only on radio.

At the end of 1999, Congress passed an omnibus intellectual property bill, one of whose provisions added "a sound recording" to the section 101 list of commissioned works for hire. This late and unadvertised addition sparked much criticism, and in May 2000, the House Subcommittee on Courts and Intellectual Property held hearings on the expansion of the categories to include sound recordings. Performing artists in particular expressed outrage at their deprivation of statutory authorship status. Record producers insisted the change was merely a technical amendment because commissioned sound recordings, as parts of compilations or collective works, were already capable of being works for hire. (Consult the pertinent statutory definitions, and see whether you agree.) The outcry provoked by the 1999 change in the statute, the legal arguments arrayed in response, and perhaps some public mood adverse to the record producers who were in the midst of resisting "peer-to-peer file sharing" in the Napster dispute—all contributed to an acquiescence by the recording industry in the deletion of the "sound recording" phrase from the work-for-hire definition. The record companies did, however, secure substitute language designed to ensure that the repeal would not cast a cloud on their assertions that sound recordings were works for hire anyway. The added language in section 101—approved by Congress on October 27, 2000, less than a year after the insertion of the "sound recording" phrase—is designed to restore the matter to where it was at the outset, without prejudice to any of the parties. (It is otherwise quite incomprehensible without this background.)

IF A WORK IS "SPECIALLY ORDERED OR COMMISSIONED" WITHIN § 101(2), AT WHAT POINT IN THE PARTIES' RELATIONSHIP MUST A CONTRACT MAKING IT A "WORK FOR HIRE" BE EXECUTED?

In providing for certain kinds of contractually created commissioned works for hire, § 101(2) mandates that "the parties expressly agree in a written instrument signed by them" that the specially ordered or commissioned work shall be a work for hire. But § 101(2) does not say *when* the parties must so agree. At the outset of the commission? In the course of the work's creation? When the work is delivered to the commissioning party? When the commissioning party pays the creator? One might anticipate that a hiring party could compensate for a failure to negotiate the authorship status of the work at the outset of the commission, were it to make subsequent receipt of payment conditional upon signing a work for hire agreement. One might also imagine that such a scheme, capitalizing on the absence of a specific provision, takes advantage of the letter (or its lack), but clashes with the spirit of the work for hire provision, particularly as interpreted by the Supreme Court in *CCNV*.

A decision by Judge Posner reaches a similar conclusion. In *Schiller & Schmidt, Inc. v. Nordisco Corp.*, 969 F.2d 410 (7th Cir.1992), the publisher of a catalogue claimed to be the employer for hire of a photographer whose work appeared in the catalogue. Judge Posner wrote:

> Bertel [the photographer] made the 18 photos, but Schiller [the catalogue publisher] owned the copyrights in them if they were "works for hire," or if Bertel assigned the copyrights to Schiller. 17 U.S.C. §§ 101(1), (2), 201(b), (d). Since no one could suppose after *Community for Creative Non–Violence v. Reid* that Bertel was an employee of Schiller, they were works for hire only if they fell in one or more of the categories of intellectual property enumerated in section 101(2), as they did, and were specially commissioned by Schiller, as they were, and the parties had signed a statement to that effect—which they had not. What is true is that in 1988, long after this suit had begun, Bertel obligingly signed a statement in which he "agreed that Schiller and Schmidt has owned the copyright [in the photos], and I hereby assign any remaining copyright which I may own in any photographs which I took for Schiller and Schmidt, and any right to maintain actions, now or hereafter existing, for alleged infringement thereof" to Schiller. The statement was not signed by Schiller, however, as the statute required if the photos were to be works for hire. The statutory language is "signed by them," that is, by both parties, and it means what it says.
>
> The statement also came too late. The requirement of a written statement regarding the copyright on a specially commissioned work is not merely a statute of frauds, although that is the purpose emphasized by the cases [citations omitted]. That is, it is not only designed to protect people against false claims of oral agreements. If it were, then it might not matter when the statement had been made or signed, although there is authority that it must be signed before suit is brought.... We need not try to resolve the question here. For the signed-statement requirement in section 101(2) has a second purpose— to make the ownership of property rights in intellectual property clear and definite, so that such property will be readily marketable. The creator of the property is the owner, unless he is an employee creating the property within the scope of his employment or the parties have agreed in a writing signed by both that the person who commissioned the creation of the property is the owner. The writing must precede the creation of the property in order to serve its purpose of identifying the (noncreator) owner unequivocally. It did not precede it here.

The Court of Appeals for the Second Circuit has concluded to the contrary. In *Playboy Enters., Inc. v. Dumas,* 53 F.3d 549 (2d Cir.1995), the court held that, for a commissioned work to be a work made for hire, the parties indeed must so *agree* before the commissioned work is in fact created; that agreement may, however, be oral or implied, and the written document that manifests that agreement may be executed *after* the work is begun or is completed. The court therefore found the writing requirement to be satisfied—with regard to many paintings prepared by an artist and published in Playboy Magazine—when the artist, after the paintings were completed and sent to Playboy, endorsed checks bearing a legend that contained "work made for hire" language. See also the opinion of the district court on remand, 960 F.Supp. 710 (S.D.N.Y.1997).

Another court has held that the contract commissioning the work need not even specify that the work is to be "for hire," so long as it is clear from the contract that the commissioning party is to own all rights. *See Armento v. Laser Image, Inc.*, 950 F.Supp. 719 (W.D.N.C.1996). This ruling is open to question, however, as it appears to equate a work for hire agreement with an assignment of all rights. There is an important practical difference between the two: an assignment may be terminated and the copyright recaptured, but not if there is a work made for hire. See Chapter 4.C, *infra*.

3. AUTHORSHIP AS AN INTELLECTUAL CONCEPT: JOINT WORKS

§ 101. Definitions

A joint work is a work prepared by two or more authors with the intention that their contributions be merged into inseparable or interdependent parts of a unitary whole.

Thomson v. Larson

147 F.3d 195 (2d Cir.1998).

■ CALABRESI, CIRCUIT JUDGE:

Plaintiff-appellant Lynn Thomson claims that, along with principal playwright Jonathan Larson, she co-authored a "new version" of the critically acclaimed Broadway musical Rent. Since Thomson and Larson did not specify their respective rights by contract, this case raises two issues: (1) whether Rent qualifies as a statutory "joint work," co-authored by Thomson; and (2) whether, even if Thomson is not deemed a co-author, she automatically retains exclusive copyright interests in the material she contributed to the work. The first question is squarely answered by the nuanced co-authorship test announced in *Childress v. Taylor*, 945 F.2d 500 (2d Cir.1991), and, on that basis, we affirm the district court's conclusion that Thomson is not a co-author of Rent. The second question—ownership of a copyright (in the absence of any written contract) in a "non-co-author's" contribution to a work—was not addressed in *Childress*. Because Thomson did not plead infringement of any such putative copyright interest, however, this issue is not properly before us, and so we do not decide it.

BACKGROUND

The facts given below and found by the district court are essentially uncontested.

Rent, the Pulitzer Prize and Tony Award-winning Broadway modern musical based on Puccini's opera La Boheme, began in 1989 as the joint project of Billy Aronson and composer Jonathan Larson. Aronson and Larson collaborated on the work until their amicable separation in 1991. At that time, Larson obtained Aronson's permission to develop the play on his own. By written agreement, Larson promised that the title would always be "RENT a rock opera by Jonathan Larson. Original concept and additional lyrics by Billy Aronson." In return, Aronson agreed that he would "not . . . be considered [an] active collaborator or co-author of RENT."

In the summer of 1992, Larson's Rent script was favorably received by James Nicola, Artistic Director of the New York Theatre Workshop ("NYTW"), a non-profit theater company in the East Village. Larson continued to develop and revise the "workshop version" of his Rent script. In the spring of 1993, Nicola urged Larson to allow the NYTW to hire a playwright or a bookwriter to help revamp the storyline and narrative structure of the play. But Larson "absolutely, vehemently and totally rejected [Nicola's] suggestion of hiring a bookwriter" and "was insistent on making RENT entirely his own project." Larson received a grant in the spring of 1994 to pay for a workshop production of Rent, which was presented to the public in the fall of 1994 in a series of ten staged performances produced by the NYTW and directed by Michael Greif. "[T]he professional consensus concerning the show, after the studio production, was that it was, at a minimum, very promising and that it needed a great deal of work." Artistic Director Nicola once again suggested to Larson that he consider working with a bookwriter, which Larson "adamantly and steadfastly refused, consistently emphasizing his intention to be the only author of RENT."

In May 1995, in preparation for Rent's off-Broadway opening scheduled for early 1996, Larson agreed to the NYTW's hiring of Lynn Thomson, a professor of advanced playwrighting at New York University, as a dramaturg[5] to assist him in clarifying the storyline of the musical. Thomson signed a contract with the NYTW, in which she agreed to provide her services with the workshop production from May 1, 1995, through the press opening, scheduled for early February of 1996. The agreement stated that Thomson's "responsibilities shall include, but not be limited to: Providing dramaturgical assistance and research to the playwright and director." In exchange, the NYTW agreed to pay "a fee" of $2000, "[i]n full consideration of the services to be rendered" and to provide for billing credit for Thomson as "Dramaturg." The Thomson/NYTW agreement was silent as to any copyright interests or any issue of ownership with respect to the final work.

In the summer and fall of 1995, Thomson and Larson worked extremely intensively together on the show. For the most part, the two worked on the script alone in Larson's apartment. Thomson testified that revisions to the text of Rent didn't begin until early August 1995. Larson himself entered all changes directly onto his computer, where he kept the script,

5. Dramaturgs provide a range of services to playwrights and directors in connection with the production and development of theater pieces. According to Thomson's testimony, the role of the dramaturg "can include any number of the elements that go into the crafting of a play," such as "actual plot elements, dramatic structure, character details, themes, and even specific language."

and Thomson made no contemporaneous notes of her specific contributions of language or other structural or thematic suggestions. Thomson alludes to the "October Version" of Rent as the culmination of her collaborative efforts with Larson. That new version was characterized by experts as "a radical transformation of the show."

A "sing-through" of the "October Version" of Rent took place in early November 1995. And on November 3, 1995, Larson signed a contract with the NYTW for ongoing revisions to Rent. This agreement identified Larson as the "Author" of Rent and made no reference to Thomson. The contract incorporated by reference an earlier draft author's agreement that set forth the terms that would apply if the NYTW opted to produce Rent. The earlier draft author's agreement gave Larson approval rights over all changes in text, provided that any changes in text would become his property, and assured him billing as "sole author."

The final dress rehearsal was held on January 24, 1996. Just hours after it ended, Larson died suddenly of an aortic aneurysm. Over the next few weeks, Nicola, Greif, Thomson, and musical director Tim Weil worked together to fine-tune the script. The play opened off-Broadway on February 13, 1996, to rave reviews. On February 23, Rent's move to Broadway was announced. Since its opening on Broadway on April 29, 1996, the show has been "an astounding critical, artistic, and commercial success."

Before the Broadway opening, Thomson, in view of her contributions to Rent, sought compensation and title page dramaturgical credit from the Broadway producers. And on April 2, 1996, she signed a contract in which the producers agreed to pay her $10,000 plus a nominal $50/week for her dramaturgical services. Around the same time, upon the producers' advice, Thomson approached Allan S. Larson, Nanette Larson, and Julie Larson McCollum ("Larson Heirs"), the surviving members of Jonathan Larson's family, to request a percentage of the royalties derived from the play. In a letter to the Larson family, dated April 8, 1996, Thomson stated that she believed Larson, had he lived, would have offered her a "small percentage of his royalties to acknowledge the contribution I made." In reply, the Larson Heirs offered Thomson a gift of 1% of the author's royalties. Negotiations between Thomson and the Larson Heirs, however, broke down.

After the parties failed to reach a settlement, Thomson brought suit against the Larson Heirs, claiming that she was a co-author of Rent[10] and that she had never assigned, licensed, or otherwise transferred her rights. Thomson sought declaratory relief and a retroactive and on-going accounting under the Copyright Act. Specifically, she asked that the court declare her a "co-author" of Rent and grant her 16% of the author's share of the royalties.[11]

10. Thomson's amended complaint alleges that "she developed the plot and theme, contributed extensively to the story, created many character elements, wrote a significant portion of the dialogue and song lyrics, and made other copyrightable contributions to the Work."

11. Thomson claims that she seeks 16% of the proceeds "because of her respect for Larson's role as the principal creator of the

... In a decision rendered from the bench, [District] Judge Kaplan concluded that Thomson was not a joint author of Rent and dismissed the remainder of Thomson's complaint....

[T]he focus of Thomson's appeal is on whether the district court correctly applied the *Childress* test of co-authorship, and, secondarily, whether the district court's declaration that Thomson is not a co-author nevertheless means that she retains exclusive copyright interests in any material that she contributed to the work.

. . .

I. THOMSON'S CO-AUTHORSHIP CLAIM

A. Statutory Definition of "Joint Work"

Thomson's request for a declaratory judgment establishing her co-authorship under the Copyright Act of 1976, 17 U.S.C. § 101 et seq., requires us to interpret and apply the copyright ownership provisions of the Act. The Copyright Act defines a "joint work" as "a work prepared by two or more authors with the intention that their contributions be merged into inseparable or interdependent parts of a unitary whole." 17 U.S.C. § 101 (1994). The touchstone of the statutory definition "is the intention at the time the writing is done that the parts be absorbed or combined into an integrated unit." H.R. Rep. No. 1476, 94th Cong. 120, 121 (1976), *reprinted in* 1976 U.S. Code Cong. & Admin. News 5659, 5735.

Joint authorship entitles the co-authors to equal undivided interests in the whole work—in other words, each joint author has the right to use or to license the work as he or she wishes, subject only to the obligation to account to the other joint owner for any profits that are made....

B. *Childress* Requirements

In *Childress v. Taylor*, our court interpreted this section of the Act and set forth "standards for determining when a contributor to a copyrighted work is entitled to be regarded as a joint author" where the parties have failed to sign any written agreement dealing with coauthorship. 945 F.2d at 501. While the Copyright Act states only that co-authors must intend that their contributions "be merged into ... a unitary whole," in *Childress*, Judge Newman explained why a more stringent inquiry than the statutory language would seem to suggest is required:

> [A]n inquiry so limited would extend joint author status to many persons who are not likely to have been within the contemplation of Congress. For example, a writer frequently works with an editor who

work." Thomson derives the 16% figure in the following way: she alleges that 48% of the Rent script is new in relation to the 1994 Workshop version (prior to her involvement); as co-author, she is, therefore, entitled to 50% of this part (or 24% of the total revenues); but since there are three components to Rent (book, lyrics, and music) and she did not contribute to one (music), she is entitled to 2/3, or 16% of the total revenues. Brief for Plaintiff–Appellant at 49–50. Thomson also sought the right to quote freely from various versions of Rent in a book that she planned to write.

makes numerous useful revisions to the first draft, some of which will consist of additions of copyrightable expression. Both intend their contributions to be merged into inseparable parts of a unitary whole, yet very few editors and even fewer writers would expect the editor to be accorded the status of joint author, enjoying an undivided half interest in the copyright in the published work.

Id. at 507.

The facts of *Childress* highlighted this concern with "overreaching" contributors. Actress Clarice Taylor wrote a script based on the life of legendary comedienne Jackie "Moms" Mabley, but Taylor was unable to get it produced as a play. Taylor convinced playwright Alice Childress to rescue the project by writing a new script. After Childress' completion of the script, Taylor took a copy of Childress' copyrighted play and produced it at another theater without permission. See *id.* at 503. Childress sued Taylor for copyright infringement, and Taylor asserted a defense of co-authorship.[12] *See id.* at 504.

The court concluded that there was "no evidence that [Taylor's contribution] ever evolved into more than the helpful advice that might come from the cast, the directors, or the producers of any play."[13] *Id.* at 509. On that basis, the court upheld a grant of summary judgment for Childress. *See id.*

The potential danger of allowing anyone who makes even a minimal contribution to the writing of a work to be deemed a statutory co-author— as long as the two parties intended the contributions to merge—motivated the court to set forth a two-pronged test. A co-authorship claimant bears the burden of establishing that each of the putative co-authors (1) made independently copyrightable contributions to the work; and (2) fully intended to be co-authors. *See id.* at 507–08. The court attempted to strike a balance between "ensur[ing] that true collaborators in the creative process are accorded the perquisites of co-authorship," *id.* at 504, while at the same time, "guard[ing] against the risk that a sole author is denied exclusive authorship status simply because another person render[s] some form of assistance." *Id.*

1.   Independently Copyrightable Contributions

Childress held that collaboration alone is not sufficient to establish joint authorship. Rather, the contribution of each joint author must be independently copyrightable. See 945 F.2d at 507. It noted that this is "the position taken by the case law and endorsed by the agency administering the Copyright Act." *Id.*; *see Seshadri v. Kasraian*, 130 F.3d 798, 803 (7th

---

12. Taylor alleged joint authorship, notwithstanding the fact that, as she conceded, her major role had been researching the historical background for the script. *See Childress*, 945 F.2d at 502.

13. The court stated that Childress had "always insisted upon her status as the sole author," noting that Childress had registered the copyrights in her own name and had refused to sign an agreement proposed by Taylor that provided that the play would be jointly owned.

Cir.1997); *M.G.B. Homes, Inc. v. Ameron Homes, Inc.*, 903 F.2d 1486, 1493 (11th Cir.1990).

Without making specific findings as to any of Thomson's claims regarding lyrics or other contributions, the district court concluded that Thomson "made at least some non-*de minimis* copyrightable contribution," and that Thomson's contributions to the Rent libretto were "certainly not zero." Once having said that, the court decided the case on the second *Childress* prong—mutual intent of co-authorship. It hence did not reach the issue of the individual copyrightability of Thomson's varied alleged contributions (plot developments, thematic elements, character details, and structural components).

2. Intent of the Parties

a. Mutual Intent Requirement

Childress mandates that the parties "entertain in their minds the concept of joint authorship." 945 F.2d at 508. This requirement of mutual intent recognizes that, since coauthors are afforded equal rights in the co-authored work, the "equal sharing of rights should be reserved for relationships in which all participants fully intend to be joint authors." *Id.* at 509.[15]

. . . [T]he *Childress* rule of mutual co-authorship intent has subsequently been followed in this circuit and elsewhere. . . . *Childress* and its progeny, however, do not explicitly define the nature of the necessary intent to be co-authors. The court stated that "[i]n many instances, a useful test will be whether, in the absence of contractual arrangements concerning listed authorship, each participant intended that all would be identified as co-authors." *Childress*, 945 F.2d at 508. But it is also clear that the intention standard is not strictly subjective. In other words, co-authorship intent does not turn solely on the parties' own words or professed state of mind. *See id.* ("[J]oint authorship can exist without any explicit discussion of this topic by the parties."). Rather, the *Childress* court suggested a more nuanced inquiry into factual indicia of ownership and authorship, such as how a collaborator regarded herself in relation to the work in terms of billing and credit, decisionmaking, and the right to enter into contracts. *See id.* at 508–09. In this regard, the court stated that "[t]hough joint authorship does not require an understanding by the co-authors of the legal consequences of their relationship, obviously some distinguishing characteristic of the relationship must be understood for it to be the subject of their intent." *Id.* at 508.

Finally, the *Childress* court emphasized that the requirement of intent is particularly important where "one person . . . is indisputably the dominant author of the work and the only issue is whether that person is the sole author or she and another . . . are joint authors." *Id.* "Care must be

---

15. The court added that "[t]he sharing of benefits in other relationships involving assistance in the creation of a copyrightable work can be more precisely calibrated by the participants in their contract negotiations regarding division of royalties or assignment of shares of ownership of the copyright." *Childress*, 945 F.2d at 509 (citing 17 U.S.C. § 201(d)).

taken ... to guard against the risk that a sole author is denied exclusive authorship status simply because another person render[s] some form of assistance." *Id.* at 504; *see also Erickson,* 13 F.3d at 1069 ("Those seeking copyrights would not seek further refinement that colleagues may offer if they risked losing their sole authorship.").

Thomson intimates that *Childress'* stringent mutual intent standard is properly limited, by its facts, to cases involving claimants who have made "minimal contribution[s] to the writing of a work." Brief for Appellant at 30. And she asserts that her purported major contribution of copyrightable expression to Rent, by itself, is evidence of Larson's intent that she be a co-author. Indeed, Thomson goes further and claims that this proof is enough to give her relationship with Larson the "distinguishing characteristics" needed to establish co-authorship. But *Childress* makes clear that the contribution even of significant language to a work does not automatically suffice to confer co-author status on the contributor. Under *Childress,* a specific finding of mutual intent remains necessary.[19] *See* 945 F.2d at 508. We therefore turn to an examination of the factual indicia of ownership and authorship relevant to this inquiry, as they are defined in prior cases.

  b. Evidence of Larson's Intent[20]

  i. Decisionmaking Authority

An important indicator of authorship is a contributor's decisionmaking authority over what changes are made and what is included in a work. *See, e.g., Erickson,* 13 F.3d at 1071–72 (an actor's suggestion of text does not support a claim of co-authorship where the sole author determined whether and where such contributions were included in the work); *see also Maurel,* 271 F. at 214–15 (claimant had a contractual right to control the contents of the opera).

The district court determined that Larson "retained and intended to retain at all times sole decision-making authority as to what went into

---

19. Thomson asserts that the instant case is "the first case in which a contributor of non-*de minim[i]s* copyrightable material has co-created a joint work within the statutory definition, yet has been denied the rights of joint authorship." Brief for Appellant at 16. The Larson Heirs counter this contention by citing *Clogston v. American Academy of Orthopaedic Surgeons,* 930 F. Supp. 1156 (W.D.Tex.1996). In *Clogston,* a district court granted summary judgment in favor of the defendant sole author of a medical textbook and rejected the plaintiff photographer's claim that he was a co-author on the basis of having contributed more than ninety percent of the photographs. We do not go as far as the *Clogston* court, which stated that "the importance of [a claimant's] contribution" to a work "is simply not a relevant inquiry" under *Childress. Id.* at 1162. And we, there-

fore, do not embrace *Clogston's* holding that the "extent of ... contribution alone is inadequate to create a genuine issue of material fact." *Id.* We believe, however, that in *Childress,* the limited contribution made by Taylor was not the only, or even the dominant, factor in the determination that co-authorship intent was missing.

20. Under *Childress,* each putative co-author must intend to be a co-author in order to give rise to a co-author relationship. *See* 945 F.2d at 508. The Larson Heirs suggest that "Thomson's lack of co-authorship intent provides a second and independent basis for affirming the decision below." ... Because we affirm the district court's conclusion that Larson lacked co-authorship intent, we too will refrain from addressing Ms. Thomson's intent, except as it may seem to bear on Larson's.

[Rent]." In support of its conclusion, the court relied upon Thomson's statement that she was "flattered that [Larson] was asking [her] to contribute actual language to the text" and found that this statement demonstrated that even Thomson understood "that the question whether any contribution she might make would go into the script was within Mr. Larson's sole and complete discretion." Moreover, as the court recognized, the November agreement between Larson and the NYTW expressly stated that Larson had final approval over all changes to Rent and that all such changes would become Larson's property.[22]

ii. Billing

In discerning how parties viewed themselves in relation to a work, *Childress* also deemed the way in which the parties bill or credit themselves to be significant. *See* 945 F.2d at 508 ("Though 'billing' or 'credit' is not decisive in all cases ... consideration of the topic helpfully serves to focus the fact-finder's attention on how the parties implicitly regarded their undertaking."). As the district court noted, "billing or credit is ... a window on the mind of the party who is responsible for giving the billing or the credit." And a writer's attribution of the work to herself alone is "persuasive proof ... that she intended this particular piece to represent her own individual authorship" and is "prima facie proof that [the] work was not intended to be joint." *Weissmann*, 868 F.2d at 1320.

Thomson claims that Larson's decision to credit her as "dramaturg" on the final page of Rent scripts reflected some co-authorship intent. Thomson concedes that she never sought equal billing with Larson, but argues that she did not need to do so in order to be deemed a statutory co-author.

The district court found, instead, that the billing was unequivocal: Every script brought to [the court's] attention says "Rent, by Jonathan Larson."[24] In addition, Larson "described himself in the biography he submitted for the playbill in January 1996, nine days before he died, as the author/composer, and listed Ms. Thomson on the same document as dramaturg." And while, as Ms. Thomson argues, it may indeed have been highly unusual for an author/composer to credit his dramaturg with a byline, we fail to see how Larson's decision to style her as "dramaturg" on the final page in Rent scripts reflects a co-authorship intent on the part of Larson. The district court properly concluded that "the manner in which [Larson]

---

22. In this respect, the district court also credited a telephone interview Larson gave in October 1995 to a high school student, in which Larson "said, in substance, that he wrote everything in Rent and distinguished writers in the theater from writers in the other media by saying that in the theater the writer is the king." ("In theater, as opposed to film and television, dramatists retain copyright to their work, [and] are inde-pendent contractors...." Brief for Amicus Curiae The Dramatists Guild, Inc. at 15 n.3.) The district court found this statement significant because it "evidences Mr. Larson's view that Rent in all respects was his, he was the king."

24. Similarly, both the Off–Broadway and the Broadway playbills identify Rent as being "by Jonathan Larson," while Thomson is listed as "Dramaturg."

listed credits on the scripts strongly supports the view that he regarded himself as the sole author."

iii.   Written Agreements with Third Parties

Just as the parties' written agreements with each other can constitute evidence of whether the parties considered themselves to be co-authors, *see Gilliam v. American Broad. Cos.*, 538 F.2d 14, 22 (2d Cir.1976) (written screenwriters' agreement between the parties indicate that they did not consider themselves joint authors of a single work); *Erickson*, 13 F.3d at 1072 (licensing agreement evidences lack of co-authorship intent); *see also Maurel v. Smith*, 271 F. at 214–15 (contracts evidence co-authorship relationship), so the parties' agreements with outsiders also can provide insight into co-authorship intent, albeit to a somewhat more attenuated degree.

The district court found that Larson "listed himself or treated himself as the author in the November 1995 revisions contract that he entered into with the NYTW, which in turn incorporated the earlier draft author's agreement that had not been signed." That agreement identifies Larson as Rent's "Author" and does not mention Thomson. It also incorporates the terms of a September 1995 draft agreement (termed "Author's Agreement") that states that Larson "shall receive billing as sole author." The district court commented, moreover, that "[t]he fact that [Larson] felt free to enter into the November 1995 contract on his own, without the consent of and without any reference to Ms. Thomson quite apart from whatever the terms of the agreements are, indicates that his intention was to be the sole author."

iv.   Additional Evidence

Besides relying on evidence that Larson retained decisionmaking authority over the final work, that he was billed as sole author, and that he entered into written agreements with third parties as sole author, the district court found much other evidence that indicated a lack of intent on Larson's part to make Thomson a co-author.

Thus, at various times during the development of Rent (once shortly before Thomson was hired as dramaturg in the summer of 1995), Artistic Director Nicola suggested to Larson that he work with a bookwriter to assist him in the refinement of the script. Larson, however, "absolutely, vehemently and totally" rejected the idea of a bookwriter and was steadfast in his determination to make Rent "entirely his own project." The district court found that Larson's "rejection of a book writer ... speaks to Mr. Larson's intent[ ] ... [and] is part of a broader pattern that persuades me that Mr. Larson never intended the joint authorship relationship."

... Finally, the court relies on "an explicit discussion on the topic of co-authorship" that Thomson claims she and Larson had. Brief for Appellant at 9. According to Thomson's written trial testimony, the conversation was as follows: I told him I was flattered that he was asking me to contribute actual language to the text. He responded by saying "Of course I want you to do that!" ... He then told me the following: "I'll always acknowledge your contribution," and "I would never say that I wrote what you did."

The district court found that the alleged conversation was "entirely consistent with Mr. Larson's view that he was the sole author and that Ms. Thomson ... was the dramaturg, which he conceived to be a different role."

c. Conclusion

... We believe that the district court correctly applied the *Childress* standards to the evidence before it and hold that its finding that Larson never intended co-authorship was not clearly erroneous.

II. THOMSON'S ALLEGED COPYRIGHT INTERESTS

... Thomson argues that, if she is not deemed to be a joint author of Rent, then "she must have all of the rights of a sole author with respect to her own contribution." Brief for Plaintiff–Appellant at 17. On appeal, she asserts for the first time that the only alternative to finding co-authorship is to split a co-created work into its components—i.e., she must be entitled to withdraw her purported contributions. The National Writers Union, a trade union of freelance writers, and Literary Managers and Dramaturgs of the Americas, Inc., a professional association, as amici curiae in support of Thomson, further suggest that Thomson has grounds to file an infringement suit relating to the same material on which her co-authorship claim is premised. . . .

The Larson Heirs contend that "[u]nder *Childress*, copyrightable contributions by an editor or other person retained to assist an author belong to the author, absent mutual co-authorship intent." Brief for Defendants–Appellees at 46. They conclude that "[b]ecause she is not a joint author, Thomson has no rights." *Id.* at 47. In the alternative, the Larson Heirs claim that "even if, despite *Childress*, the sole author is not the copyright owner of the materials contributed by others, the suggestions proffered by Thomson were impliedly or expressly licensed to Larson for use in Rent." *Id.* . . .

Our circuit has not decided whether a person who makes a non-*de minimis* copyrightable contribution but cannot meet the mutual intent requirement of co-authorship, retains, in the absence of a work-for-hire agreement or of any explicit contractual assignment of the copyright, any rights and interests in his or her own contribution. This issue, however, was not presented to the district court by the parties. . . . Accordingly, the district court had no occasion to rule on: (1) whether Thomson, if not deemed a co-author, nevertheless had copyright interests in the material that she contributed to Rent or, alternatively, (2) whether Thomson granted Larson a license to use the material that she purportedly contributed to Rent, and if so on what terms. Because these issues were not raised below and therefore are not properly before us, we express no opinion on them. . . .

Aalmuhammed v. Lee, 202 F.3d 1227 (9th Cir.2000). Under contract with Warner Brothers, Spike Lee co-wrote, co-produced, and directed the motion picture *Malcolm X*, starring Denzel Washington in the title role. At the request of Washington, one Jefri Aalmuhammed—who was very knowledgeable about the life of Malcolm X, particularly about his religious conversion to Islam—assisted Washington and contributed to the film. Aalmuhammed suggested extensive script revisions, some of which were included, to ensure religious and historical accuracy; he directed Washington and other actors while on the set, created some new scenes with new characters, and edited parts of the film during post-production. Despite never having a written contract with Warner Brothers or with Lee, Aalmuhammed was ultimately paid $25,000 by Lee and $100,000 by Washington. His request for a credit as a co-writer of the film was rejected, but the film when released credited Aalmuhammed (far down the list) as an "Islamic Technical Consultant." He filed an application with the Copyright Office (as Warner had done previously), listing himself as co-creator, co-writer and co-director of *Malcolm X*, and he brought an action against Warner, Lee and others seeking declaratory relief and an accounting. He claimed that the motion picture was a joint work of which he was co-owner of copyright. The court, on a motion for summary judgment, dismissed his action.

The court examined the statutory definition of "joint work" and concluded that the term "requires each author to make an independently copyrightable contribution." Aalmuhammed "made substantial and valuable contributions to the movie, including technical help, . . . scholarly and creative help . . . and script changes." These were "independently copyrightable," and intended by all involved to be "merged into a unitary whole." Yet the court concluded that although Aalmuhammed made such substantial contributions to the film, he was not one of the authors of the film, which requires more. "Everyone from the producer and director to casting director, costumer, hairstylist, and 'best boy' gets listed in the movie credits because all of their creative contributions really do matter." In the absence of a contract to the contrary, the author of a joint work is the person "who superintended the whole work, the 'master mind' "—and for a motion picture, this is generally "someone at the top of the screen credits . . . someone who has artistic control." The court viewed its test as very much like that in *Thomson v. Larson*, which requires objective evidence that both parties intended each other to be joint authors.

Aalmuhammed "made extremely helpful recommendations, but Spike Lee was not bound to accept any of them"; Warner Brothers and Lee superintended the film, and Aalmuhammed did not. None of the three made any objective manifestation of an intent to be coauthors: Lee signed a "work for hire" agreement for Warner Brothers, and it would be illogical to conclude that Warner intended to share ownership with individuals like Aalmuhammed who worked under Lee's control. There was no evidence that Aalmuhammed was the "inventive or master mind" of the movie. Progress in the arts "would be retarded rather than promoted, if an author could not consult with others and adopt their useful suggestions without sacrificing sole ownership of the work. . . . Spike Lee could not consult a scholarly Muslim to make a movie about a religious conversion to Islam, and the arts would be the poorer for that.... Claim jumping by research assistants, editors, and former spouses, lovers and friends would endanger authors who talked with people about what they were doing, if creative copyrightable contribution [sic] were all that authorship required."

QUESTIONS

1. The statutory definition of "joint work" focuses on the intention of both parties to merge their contributions into a unitary work; the court in *Thomson v. Larson* adds a requirement that, in effect, focuses on the intention of one of the parties (in the "dominant-subsidiary" collaboration) to share ownership. Is this an inappropriate judicial "amendment" of the statute? Are there strong reasons for adding this requirement? (Consider, in particular, the contributions of the student research assistant and the book editor—and the fact that, absent other negotiated arrangements, joint authors share income 50–50.)

2. Are the courts requiring that would-be co-authors show greater creativity than a sole author need demonstrate? Cf. Chapter 2D (querying whether more creativity is required of the creator of a derivative work). Are the courts, by emphasizing (in applying the joint-work definition) the creative dominance of a given individual, collapsing the distinction between the joint work and the work for hire?

3. Is the added "intention" requirement practicable and fair to implement? For example, how should a court deal with those many situations in which collaborators simply have no intention about copyright ownership at all? And what of those cases, such as *Thomson v. Larson*, in which the intention of the dominant party is based on communications to third parties (such as the NYTW or a high school interviewer), about which the subsidiary party knows nothing?

4. After studying the materials immediately below on Transfer of Copyright Ownership, how would you resolve the issues left unresolved at the end of the opinion in the *Thomson v. Larson* case?

5. John Q. Homeowner has consulted and retained an architect to prepare plans to be used in the construction of a house. Homeowner has informed Architect that he wishes to have a two-story colonial with four bedrooms and two bathrooms upstairs, and a kitchen, family room (with fireplace), library, laundry room and bathroom downstairs. He also provided Architect with a rough pencil sketch of the layout he had been inspired to draw by examining several floor plans reproduced in home-decorating magazines. Architect prepared her first sketches and showed them to Homeowner, who made several suggestions about the shape (to accommodate certain items of furniture) and dimensions of the rooms; he also suggested changes in the angles of roof and windows. These suggestions were then incorporated by Architect in a final set of detailed plans, which Homeowner approved. Homeowner paid Architect $10,000 for her services and had the house built for $200,000. Nothing was said either orally or in writing between Homeowner and Architect about the ownership of the architectural plans. Homeowner has just learned that Architect has used essentially the same plans in designing a house to be built across town. He has consulted you and wishes to know whether he may stop Architect from doing so, or at least be compensated for the use of his plans. What is your advice? *See Joseph J. Legat Architects, P.C. v. United States Dev. Corp.,* 625 F.Supp. 293 (N.D.Ill. 1985); *Meltzer v. Zoller,* 520 F.Supp. 847 (D.N.J.1981); *M.G.B. Homes, Inc. v. Ameron Homes, Inc.,* 903 F.2d 1486 (11th Cir.1990).

6. Alfonse and Gaston have collaborated on several editions of a manual of proper deportment, originally titled *Etiquette for the Eighties,* and later titled *Etiquette for the Nineties.* Following a falling-out with Gaston, Alfonse prepared the update, *Etiquette for the Millennium,* on his own. *Etiquette for the Millennium* includes new material by Alfonse, but also incorporates substantial portions of the prior co-authored editions. Is *Etiquette for the Millennium* a joint work? *See Weissmann v. Freeman,* 868 F.2d 1313 (2d Cir.), *cert. denied,* 493 U.S. 883 (1989).

7. High school and college students are, with increasing frequency, creating personalized home pages on the World Wide Web as a means of fun, notoriety and communication. Of course, an attractive Web page must have a photograph. A professional photographer, hired to photograph students singly and in groups for yearbooks and the like, has learned that several students have digitally scanned onto their Web pages photographs that she has taken. She wishes to know whether she has a tenable claim of copyright infringement. Assess in particular the claim being made by some of the students that—by wearing certain clothing and a certain expression on their face—they have contributed joint authorship to their class and graduation photographs, so that they are free to use them in this manner, without any permission from or compensation to the photographer. *See Olan Mills, Inc. v. Eckerd Drug of Tex., Inc.,* 1989 CCH Copyr. L. Dec. ¶ 26,420 (N.D.Tex.1989). *Compare Natkin v. Winfrey,* 111 F.Supp.2d 1003 (N.D.Ill.2000) (producers of "Oprah" TV show claim joint authorship of photographs taken on production set by virtue of Oprah's facial expressions and attire, choice of guests, staging of show).

———

A claim of co-authorship and co-ownership of a "joint" work is considered to present an issue of federal law. The test for whether a claim arises under the Copyright Act or under state law is whether the claim asserts a remedy expressly granted by the Act, or requires construction of the Act, or at least implicates federal copyright policy. *See T.B. Harms v. Eliscu,* 339 F.2d 823 (2d Cir.1964), *cert. denied,* 381 U.S. 915 (1965). A claim of co-authorship of a joint work requires construction and application of the statutory definition of a joint work, and seeks the remedy of a declaration of an undivided one-half interest in the work, as contemplated in 17 U.S.C. § 201(a). *See Lieberman v. Estate of Chayefsky,* 535 F.Supp. 90 (S.D.N.Y. 1982). *Compare Royal v. Leading Edge Prods., Inc.,* 833 F.2d 1 (1st Cir.1987). In effect, the Act's requirement of a demonstration of intent to create a joint work may result in articulation of a federal law definition of the requisite intent. *See, e.g., Merchant v. Levy,* 92 F.3d 51 (2d Cir.1996), *cert. denied,* 519 U.S. 1108 (1997) (action to declare co-ownership as joint authors is one "arising under" U.S. Copyright Act); *Zuill v. Shanahan,* 80 F.3d 1366 (9th Cir.1996) (same).

B.   TRANSFER OF COPYRIGHT OWNERSHIP

1.   DIVISIBILITY AND FORMAL REQUIREMENTS

§ 101.   Definitions

... A "transfer of copyright ownership" is an assignment, mortgage, exclusive license, or any other conveyance, alienation, or hypothecation of a copyright or of any of the exclusive rights comprised in a copyright whether or not it is limited in time or place of effect, but not including a nonexclusive license.

§ 201.   Ownership of Copyright

. . .

(d) *Transfer of Ownership.—*

(1) The ownership of a copyright may be transferred in whole or in part by any means of conveyance or by operation of law, and may be bequeathed by will or pass as personal property by the applicable laws of intestate succession.

(2) Any of the exclusive rights comprised in a copyright, including any subdivision of any of the rights specified by section 106, may be transferred as provided by clause (1) and owned separately. The owner of any particular exclusive right is entitled, to the extent of that right, to all of the protection and remedies accorded to the copyright owner by this title.

§ 204.   Execution of Transfers of Copyright Ownership

(a) A transfer of copyright ownership, other than by operation of law, is not valid unless an instrument of conveyance, or a note or memorandum of the transfer, is in writing and signed by the owner of the rights conveyed or such owner's duly authorized agent.

DIVISIBILITY

The 1976 Act contains "the first explicit statutory recognition of the principle of divisibility of copyright in our law." H.R. Rep. No. 94–1476 at 123. Repudiation of the concept of indivisibility, a concept of long standing in the prior law, was long an important objective of authors and other groups.

The indivisibility concept mandated a single owner or proprietor of copyright at any one time; all others having an interest under the copyright were deemed licensees. The ramifications of indivisibility reached such questions as notice, ownership, recordation of transfers, standing to sue, and taxes. For example, under the 1909 Act the name of the copyright "proprietor" was to be placed in the notice inscribed upon all publicly distributed copies; the failure to do so would usually thrust the work into the public domain. Thus, the indivisibility doctrine made it advisable for contributing authors and periodicals to structure their arrangement so that a complete transfer or "assignment" to the magazine was effected. A single notice in the name of the magazine would thus secure copyright. *Cf. Kaplan v. Fox Film Corp.,* 19 F.Supp. 780 (S.D.N.Y.1937). The author would frequently accompany the assignment with a provision for a future reconveyance of the copyright in his or her contribution. *See Geisel v. Poynter Prods., Inc.,* 295 F.Supp. 331, 337–42 (S.D.N.Y.1968).

The 1976 Act expressly contemplates a divisible copyright by providing: " 'Copyright owner', with respect to any one of the exclusive rights comprised in a copyright, refers to the owner of that particular right." § 101. This definition underlies § 201(d)(2), which provides that "[a]ny of the exclusive rights comprised in a copyright, including any subdivision of any of the rights specified by section 106 [the provision enumerating protected rights], may be transferred . . . and owned separately." In line with the definition quoted immediately above, this subsection then provides that "[t]he owner of any particular exclusive right is entitled, to the extent of that right, to all of the protection and remedies accorded to the copyright owner by this title."

The committee reports indicate that this provision may be taken literally. The House Report states:

> It is thus clear, for example, that a local broadcasting station holding an exclusive license to transmit a particular work within a particular geographic area and for a particular period of time, could sue, in its own name as copyright owner, someone who infringed that particular exclusive right.

H.R. Rep. No. 94–1476, *supra* at 123.

One of the rights that can be exercised by an exclusive licensee is the right to bring an action for copyright infringement. Thus § 501(b) provides: "The legal or beneficial owner of an exclusive right under a copyright is entitled . . . to institute an action for any infringement of that particular right committed while he or she is the owner of it." It follows that a person holding a nonexclusive license to one or more of the rights in § 106 may not properly sue for infringement.

This principle was applied in *Broadcast Music, Inc. v. CBS, Inc.,* 421 F.Supp. 592 (S.D.N.Y.1976), rather startlingly a case of first impression as applied to the plaintiff, one of the two major performing-rights societies for musical compositions (the other being the American Society of Composers, Authors and Publishers). BMI and ASCAP are given nonexclusive licenses by copyright owners of popular music (some being composers and some being music publishers) to license others, such as radio and television broadcasters, publicly to perform that music. BMI and ASCAP have an elaborate system of granting permissions to broadcasters, night clubs, restaurants, and the like, and of policing those who publicly perform copyrighted music without permission, and of collecting and distributing royalties to the copyright owners. In *BMI v. CBS*, the defendant—apparently for the first time in the history of the many lawsuits brought by BMI and ASCAP—pressed to decision the question of BMI's capacity to sue for infringement of the public-performance right. The court held that, because BMI was only a nonexclusive licensee, it had no standing to sue. Nonetheless, recognizing that joining a large number of publishers when many different songs are at issue may be burdensome for BMI, the court suggested that BMI might seek to have the publishers declared a plaintiff class under Fed. R. Civ. P. 23(b).

Effects Associates v. Cohen

908 F.2d 555 (9th Cir.1990), *cert. denied*, 498 U.S. 1103 (1991).

■ KOZINSKI, CIRCUIT JUDGE.

What we have here is a failure to compensate. Larry Cohen, a low-budget horror movie mogul, paid less than the agreed price for special effects footage he had commissioned from Effects Associates. Cohen then used this footage without first obtaining a written license or assignment of the copyright; Effects sued for copyright infringement. We consider whether a transfer of copyright without a written agreement, an arrangement apparently not uncommon in the motion picture industry, conforms with the requirements of the Copyright Act.

Facts

This started out as a run-of-the-mill Hollywood squabble. Defendant Larry Cohen wrote, directed and executive produced "The Stuff," a horror movie with a dash of social satire: Earth is invaded by an alien life form that looks (and tastes) like frozen yogurt but, alas, has some unfortunate side effects—it's addictive and takes over the mind of anyone who eats it. Marketed by an unscrupulous entrepreneur, the Stuff becomes a big hit. An industrial spy hired by ice cream manufacturers eventually uncovers the terrible truth; he alerts the American people and blows up the yogurt factory, making the world safe once again for lovers of frozen confections.

In cooking up this gustatory melodrama, Cohen asked Effects Associates, a small special effects company, to create footage to enhance certain action sequences in the film. In a short letter dated October 29, 1984, Effects offered to prepare seven shots, the most dramatic of which would depict the climactic explosion of the Stuff factory. Cohen agreed to the deal orally, but no one said anything about who would own the copyright in the footage.

Cohen was unhappy with the factory explosion Effects created, and he expressed his dissatisfaction by paying Effects only half the promised amount for that shot. Effects made several demands for the rest of the money (a little over $8,000), but Cohen refused. Nevertheless, Cohen incorporated Effects's footage into the film and turned it over to New World Entertainment for distribution. Effects then brought this copyright infringement action, claiming that Cohen (along with his production company and New World) had no right to use the special effects footage unless he paid Effects the full contract price. . . .

. . . [T]he district court granted summary judgment to Cohen on the infringement claim, holding that Effects had granted Cohen an implied license to use the shots. Accordingly, the court dismissed the remaining state law claims, allowing Effects to pursue them in state court. We review the district court's grant of summary judgment de novo.

Discussion

A. *Transfer of Copyright Ownership*

The law couldn't be clearer: The copyright owner of "a motion picture or other audiovisual work" has the exclusive rights to copy, distribute or display the copyrighted work publicly. 17 U.S.C. § 106 (1988). While the copyright owner can sell or license his rights to someone else, section 204 of the Copyright Act invalidates a purported transfer of ownership unless it is in writing. 17 U.S.C. § 204(a) (1988). Here, no one disputes that Effects is the copyright owner of the special effects footage used in "The Stuff," and that defendants copied, distributed and publicly displayed this footage without written authorization.

Cohen suggests that section 204's writing requirement does not apply to this situation, advancing an argument that might be summarized, tongue in cheek, as: Moviemakers do lunch, not contracts. Cohen concedes that "in the best of all possible legal worlds" parties would obey the writing requirement, but contends that moviemakers are too absorbed in developing "joint creative endeavors" to "focus upon the legal niceties of copyright licenses." Appellees' Brief at 16, 18. Thus, Cohen suggests that we hold section 204's writing requirement inapplicable here because "it is customary in the motion picture industry . . . not to have written licenses." *Id.* at 18. To the extent that Cohen's argument amounts to a plea to exempt moviemakers from the normal operation of section 204 by making implied transfers of copyrights "the rule, not the exception," *id.*, we reject his argument.

Common sense tells us that agreements should routinely be put in writing. This simple practice prevents misunderstandings by spelling out the terms of a deal in black and white, forces parties to clarify their thinking and consider problems that could potentially arise, and encourages them to take their promises seriously because it's harder to backtrack on a written contract than on an oral one. Copyright law dovetails nicely with common sense by requiring that a transfer of copyright ownership be in writing. Section 204 ensures that the creator of a work will not give away his copyright inadvertently and forces a party who wants to use the copyrighted work to negotiate with the creator to determine precisely what rights are being transferred and at what price. Cf. *Community for Creative Non–Violence v. Reid,* 109 S. Ct. 2166, 2177–78 (1989) (describing purpose of writing requirement for works made for hire). Most importantly, section 204 enhances predictability and certainty of copyright ownership—"Congress' paramount goal" when it revised the Act in 1976. *Community for Creative Non–Violence,* 109 S. Ct. at 2177; see also *Dumas v. Gommerman,* 865 F.2d 1093, 1103–04 (9th Cir.1989). Rather than look to the courts every time they disagree as to whether a particular use of the work violates their mutual understanding, parties need only look to the writing that sets out their respective rights.

Section 204's writing requirement is not unduly burdensome; it necessitates neither protracted negotiations nor substantial expense. The rule is really quite simple: If the copyright holder agrees to transfer ownership to another party, that party must get the copyright holder to sign a piece of paper saying so. It doesn't have to be the Magna Charta; a one-line pro forma statement will do.

Cohen's attempt to exempt moviemakers from the requirements of the Copyright Act is largely precluded by recent Supreme Court and circuit authority construing the work-for-hire doctrine.[4] ... [W]here a non-employee contributes to a book or movie, as Effects did here, the exclusive rights of copyright ownership vest in the creator of the contribution, unless there is a written agreement to the contrary....

Thus, section 101 specifically addresses the movie and book publishing industries, affording moviemakers a simple, straightforward way of obtaining ownership of the copyright in a creative contribution—namely, a written agreement. The Supreme Court and this circuit, while recognizing the custom and practice in the industry, have refused to permit moviemakers to sidestep section 204's writing requirement. Accordingly, we find unpersuasive Cohen's contention that section 204's writing requirement, which singles out no particular group, somehow doesn't apply to him. As section 204 makes no special allowances for the movie industry, neither do we.

B. *Nonexclusive Licenses*

Although we reject any suggestion that moviemakers are immune to section 204, we note that there is a narrow exception to the writing requirement that may apply here. Section 204 provides that all transfers of copyright ownership must be in writing; section 101 defines transfers of ownership broadly, but expressly removes from the scope of section 204 a "nonexclusive license." See note 2 *supra.* The sole issue that remains, then,

---

4. Because Effects is not an employee and there is no written agreement stating that plaintiff's footage is a work made for hire, Cohen can't take advantage of this doctrine....

is whether Cohen had a nonexclusive license to use plaintiff's special effects footage.

The leading treatise on copyright law states that "[a] nonexclusive license may be granted orally, or may even be implied from conduct." 3 M. Nimmer & D. Nimmer, Nimmer on Copyright § 10.03[A], at 10–36 (1989). Cohen relies on the latter proposition; he insists that, although Effects never gave him a written or oral license, Effects's conduct created an implied license to use the footage in "The Stuff."

Cohen relies largely on our decision in *Oddo v. Ries,* 743 F.2d 630 (9th Cir.1984). There, we held that Oddo, the author of a series of articles on how to restore Ford F–100 pickup trucks, had impliedly granted a limited non-exclusive license to Ries, a publisher, to use plaintiff's articles in a book on the same topic. We relied on the fact that Oddo and Ries had formed a partnership to create and publish the book, with Oddo writing and Ries providing capital. *Id.* at 632 & n. 1. Oddo prepared a manuscript consisting partly of material taken from his prior articles and submitted it to Ries. *Id.* at 632. Because the manuscript incorporated pre-existing material, it was a derivative work; by publishing it, Ries would have necessarily infringed the copyright in Oddo's articles, unless Oddo had granted him a license. *Id.* at 634. We concluded that, in preparing and handing over to Ries a manuscript intended for publication that, if published, would infringe Oddo's copyright, Oddo "impliedly gave the partnership a license to use the articles insofar as they were incorporated in the manuscript, for without such a license, Oddo's contribution to the partnership venture would have been of minimal value." *Id.*

The district court agreed with Cohen, and we agree with the district court: *Oddo* controls here. Like the plaintiff in *Oddo,* Effects created a work at defendant's request and handed it over, intending that defendant copy and distribute it. To hold that Effects did not at the same time convey a license to use the footage in "The Stuff" would mean that plaintiff's contribution to the film was "of minimal value," a conclusion that can't be squared with the fact that Cohen paid Effects almost $56,000 for this footage. Accordingly, we conclude that Effects impliedly granted nonexclusive licenses to Cohen and his production company to incorporate the special effects footage into "The Stuff" and to New World Entertainment to distribute the film.

Conclusion

We affirm the district court's grant of summary judgment in favor of Cohen and the other defendants. We note, however, that plaintiff doesn't leave this court empty-handed. Copyright ownership is comprised of a bundle of rights; in granting a nonexclusive license to Cohen, Effects has given up only one stick from that bundle—the right to sue Cohen for copyright infringement. It retains the right to sue him in state court on a variety of other grounds, including breach of contract. Additionally, Effects may license, sell or give away for nothing its remaining rights in the special effects footage. Those rights may not be particularly valuable, of course:

"The Stuff" was something less than a blockbuster, and it remains to be seen whether there's a market for shots featuring great gobs of alien yogurt oozing out of a defunct factory. On the other hand, the shots may have much potential for use in music videos. See generally Kozinski & Banner, *Who's Afraid of Commercial Speech?*, 76 Va. L. Rev. 627, 641 (1990). In any event, whatever Effects chooses to do with the footage, Cohen will have no basis for complaining. And that's an important lesson that licensees of more versatile film properties may want to take to heart.

QUESTIONS

1. Why heed the court's cautionary tale about the § 204(a) requirement of a writing if a course of conduct will imply a license anyway? *See I.A.E. Inc. v. Shaver*, 74 F.3d 768 (7th Cir.1996).

2. Dr. Payne paid Dora Digital to design and furnish computer software that would keep track of the doctor's billings and collections, and his inventory of pharmaceutical products. Digital developed two programs, and both parties signed a simple written document in which Dr. Payne transferred $15,000 and Ms. Digital acknowledged that the programs were "your property." When Dr. Payne learned that Dora was marketing the same software to other physicians, he brought an action for copyright infringement. In defense, Dora asserted that all she had conveyed was the physical material containing the software, and that she had no intention of transferring the copyright. The trial court denied Ms. Digital's motion for summary judgment, ruling that: (a) the language used in the writing was sufficient to convey copyright to Dr. Payne, and (b) even if that language was ambiguous, the parol evidence rule applied so that Dr. Payne should be permitted to introduce evidence about his subjective intention, his course of dealings with Dora, her agreements with third parties, and commercial practices in the medical-software trade. On appeal, what would your decision be? *See Friedman v. Stacey Data Processing Servs.*, 17 U.S.P.Q.2d 1858 (N.D.Ill. 1990).

3. Medical Publications, Inc., publishes and owns the copyright to a best-selling home medical book, *Heal Thyself*. Last year, it orally agreed with Book Placement Company (BPC) that BPC would have the right to place the book in all bookstores not then being supplied by Medical Publications. Within a matter of months, however, Medical Publications began to distribute *Heal Thyself* to the nationwide Dalton chain of bookstores, a new account. BPC has brought an action against Medical Publications for breach of contract. The defendant has moved for summary judgment, claiming that the oral exclusive license is void because not in writing. BPC, however, claims that its license was not an exclusive license, because Medical Publications retained the right to distribute *Heal Thyself* to its old accounts. Rule on the defendant's motion. *See Library Pubs., Inc. v. Medical Economics Co.*, 548 F.Supp. 1231 (E.D.Pa.1982), *aff'd without opinion*, 714 F.2d 123 (3d Cir.1983).

4. Al Artist prepared paintings for Playboy Magazine over a period of several years after 1980; he sent in one original painting each month, and

Playboy sent him a check for each. Each such check bore a legend adjacent to the endorsement line, reading "By endorsement of this check, Payee acknowledges payment in full for assignment to Playboy Enterprises of all rights, title and interest in and to" the particular painting. Playboy recently began to market reproductions of Al's artwork, and Al has brought an action for copyright infringement, claiming that it was his intention to convey only a one-time right to print reproductions in the magazine, but not to convey the copyright; he also claims, in any event, that the check endorsement does not satisfy the requirements of § 204. How would you rule? *See Playboy Enters., Inc. v. Dumas,* 53 F.3d 549 (2d Cir.1995). Would it make a difference if the check endorsement formula stated: "In consideration of the transfer of any and all copyrighted ownership in the materials described above. Endorsement signifies consent." *See National Ass'n of Freelance Photographers v. Associated Press,* 45 U.S.P.Q.2d 1321 (S.D.N.Y. 1997). *Compare Arthur Rutenberg Homes v. Drew Homes,* 29 F.3d 1529 (11th Cir.1994).

5. Is an exchange of faxes confirming a transfer, but failing to give information about the transfer, sufficient to meet the section 204(a) requirement of a "note or memorandum of the transfer"? See *Radio Television Espanola S.A. v. New World Entertainment, Ltd.,* 183 F.3d 922 (9th Cir.1999). What about an exchange of e-mails?

RECORDATION OF TRANSFERS AND OTHER DOCUMENTS

The recordation system established by the 1976 Act expressly provides that, in addition to transfers of copyright ownership, any signed document pertaining to a copyright—for example, a will—may be recorded (§ 205(a)). Its operation as constructive notice is also expressly provided, subject to two conditions: (1) specific identification of the work and (2) registration of a claim to copyright in the work (§ 205(c)).

Such recordation of a transfer affords the transferee priority over any subsequent transfer later so recorded. *See, e.g., Quality Records, Inc. v. Coast to Coast Music Inc.,* Copyr. L. Rep. (CCH) ¶ 29,924 (9th Cir.1997). The first transferee is also granted a one-month grace period (two months, if the transfer was executed abroad) in which he or she will in any event prevail. Even without observing these time limits, the first transferee may prevail if the subsequent transferee had notice of the earlier transfer or otherwise was not in good faith or had not taken his or her transfer "for valuable consideration or on the basis of a binding promise to pay royalties" or failed to record. (§ 205(d).)

The 1976 Act also tackles the difficult problem of priority between conflicting transfers and nonexclusive licenses. It will be recalled that such licenses, being excluded from the definition of a "transfer of copyright ownership," need not even be in writing much less recorded. (Of course, they *may* be recorded.) But written, signed nonexclusive licenses, whether or not recorded, prevail over conflicting transfers if the license was taken either before the transfer or in good faith before recordation of the transfer and without notice of it. (§ 205(f).)

In a case of first instance, it was decided in **National Peregrine, Inc. v. Capitol Fed. Sav. & Loan Ass'n,** 116 Bankr. 194, 16 U.S.P.Q.2d 1017 (C.D.Cal.1990) (Kozinski, Circuit Judge, sitting by designation), that § 205 of the Copyright Act, providing for recordation of transfers in the Copyright Office and a priority for timely recorders over conflicting claimants, preempts state laws (i.e., the Uniform Commercial Code) providing for recording of security interests in various state offices. In that case, the plaintiff, NPI, was a debtor-in-possession in a bankruptcy proceeding, and it sought to preserve for the benefit of the bankruptcy estate some 145 copyrighted films and the licensing income therefrom. NPI's predecessor had earlier obtained a $6 million loan from the defendant Capitol Federal Savings, and that bank took the film library and future income as security or collateral for the loan. Capitol filed a UCC–1 financing statement in three states, pursuant to their respective state laws, but it did not record the transfer of the security interest in the Copyright Office.

The district court stated the question for decision to be: "Is a security interest in a copyright perfected by an appropriate filing with the Copyright Office or by a UCC–1 financing statement with the relevant secretary of state?" and concluded that the former was the correct answer. It held that a security interest in copyrights as collateral for a loan is a "transfer" of the copyrights (as defined in § 101) that may be recorded in the Copyright Office under § 205(a). The court went on to conclude that the comprehensive scope of the recording provisions of the Act, along with the unique federal interests implicated, supports the view that federal law preempts state methods of perfecting security interests in copyrights and related accounts receivable. If state methods of perfection were valid, lenders would be forced to search for security interests in a variety of states, leading to expense and delay; this "could hinder the purchase and sale of copyrights, frustrating Congress's policy that copyrights be readily transferable in commerce." The court also found that Article 9 of the UCC itself had a "step back" provision which displaced the state recording system in the face of a federal recording system such as that provided under the Copyright Act.

Because under the Bankruptcy Act, NPI was to be treated as a "hypothetical lien creditor" taking its interest in good faith for valuable consideration and without notice—and also treated as recording its interest with the Copyright Office in a timely manner—the priority provisions of § 205(d) of the Copyright Act thus entitled NPI to avoid Capitol Federal's interest and capture the disputed copyright interests for the benefit of the bankruptcy estate.

An apparent consequence of the court's decision is that a person, typically a bank, taking a security interest in the copyrights in many works—for example, the 145 films involved in the case itself—will in order to protect its interest have to record separately in the Copyright Office the transfers to each of those 145 films. Moreover, under § 205(c)(2), the bank would have to take steps to assure that the copyright in each work is registered. A filing under the UCC instead, in the name of the borrower and showing a security interest in "a library of 145 copyrighted films," accompanied by a list of the names of the films, would of course be much more conveniently done by the bank. Reliance on the single filing by a secured creditor under the UCC would particularly facilitate lending that is secured by copyright interests to be acquired by the borrower in the future. Security interests in such "after-acquired property" are routinely perfected with a single filing in a single place under the Code. But under the Copyright Act, the lender is required constantly to monitor the borrower's development or acquisition of new copyrights, along with the individualized registration of new works and the individualized recordation of transferred security interests.

Proposed legislation introduced in early 1993 (S. 373 and H.R. 897) would have, among other things, overturned the *Peregrine* decision and later decisions of bankruptcy courts reaching the same conclusion. *See In re AEG Acquisition Corp.*, 127 B.R. 34 (Bkrtcy.C.D.Cal.1991), *aff'd*, 161 B.R. 50 (9th Cir.1993); *In re Avalon Software, Inc.*, 209 B.R. 517 (Bkrtcy.D.Ariz. 1997). One of the bill's sponsors, Congressmen Hughes, had this to say: "These decisions have turned a relatively simple business transaction into a nightmare for businesses and lenders. Moreover, given that a number of lenders have, in the past, only made UCC filings, there is considerable uncertainty about past transactions. This uncertainty is heightened by lenders' inability to register the work. Congress' intent in enacting the relevant provisions in section 205 was to provide a system for ordering the priority between conflicting transfers, not to preempt state procedures for ensuring that a secured creditor's rights are protected. There is no reason the Federal and State systems cannot coexist in this area."

Such legislative efforts continue. Various approaches have been suggested, most prominently the amendment of either § 205(e) or § 301(b) of the Copyright Act so as to make clear that state law will govern with respect to the registration, perfection and enforceability of competing security interests (especially against the borrower's trustee in bankruptcy), while federal law will govern the transfer and recordation of copyright interests other than consensual security interests. (For example, bona fide transferees of the copyright will prevail over an intervening security-interest holder unless the latter has registered in the Copyright Office.)

2. SCOPE OF GRANT

Cohen v. Paramount Pictures Corp.

845 F.2d 851 (9th Cir.1988).

■ HUG, CIRCUIT JUDGE.

This case involves a novel issue of copyright law: whether a license conferring the right to exhibit a film "by means of television" includes the right to distribute videocassettes of the film. We hold it does not.

Facts

Herbert Cohen is the owner of the copyright in a musical composition entitled "Merry–Go–Round" (hereinafter "the composition"). On May 12, 1969, Cohen granted H & J Pictures, Inc., a "synchronization" license, which gave H & J the right to use the composition in a film called "Medium Cool" and to exhibit the film in theatres and on television. Subsequently, H & J assigned to Paramount Pictures all of its rights, title, and interest in the movie "Medium Cool," including all of the rights and interests created by the 1969 license from Cohen to H & J. Sometime later, Paramount furnished a negative of the film to a videocassette manufacturer, who made copies of the film—including a recording of the composition—and supplied these copies to Paramount. Paramount, in turn, sold approximately 2,725 videocassettes of the film, receiving a gross revenue of $69,024.26 from the sales.

On February 20, 1985, Cohen filed suit against Paramount in federal district court alleging copyright infringement. Cohen contended that the license granted to H & J did not confer the right to use the composition in a videocassette reproduction of the film. The parties stipulated to the facts and both filed motions for summary judgment. The district court entered judgment in favor of Paramount, and Cohen appeals....

. . .

To resolve this case, we must examine the terms of the license, in order to determine whether the license conveyed the right to use the composition in videocassette reproductions of "Medium Cool." The document begins by granting the licensee the "authority ... to record, in any manner, medium, form or language, the words and music of the musical composition ... with ['Medium Cool'], *all in accordance* with the terms, conditions, and limitations hereinafter set forth...." (Emphasis added.) Paragraph 4 states, "The ... license herein granted to perform ... said musical composition is granted for: (a) The exhibition of said motion picture ... to audiences in motion picture theatres.... (b) The exhibition of said motion picture ... *by means of television* ..., including 'pay television', 'subscription television' and 'closed circuit into homes' television...." (Emphasis added.) Finally, paragraph 6 of the license reserves to the grantor "all rights and uses in and to said musical composition, except those herein granted to the Licensee...."

Notably, the license does not expressly grant rights to use the composition in connection with a videocassette reproduction of "Medium Cool." Paramount argues that this right is conferred by the language granting the licensee the authority to record "in any manner, medium, form or language" the composition with the film. This seemingly broad grant, however, is expressly subject to the limitations set forth thereafter. The authority to present the composition as part of the film is found in paragraph 4, and that paragraph expressly limits such presentation to two mediums: theatre and television. Unless videocassette production falls into either of those categories, the license does not authorize Paramount's actions, because paragraph 6 expressly reserves to the licensor all rights not granted by the terms of the license.

Not surprisingly, Paramount argues that videocassette display is the equivalent of "exhibition ... by means of television." We cannot agree. Though videocassettes may be displayed by using a television monitor, it does not follow that, for copyright purposes, videocassettes constitute "exhibition by television." Exhibition of a film on television differs fundamentally from exhibition by means of a videocassette recorder ("VCR"). Television requires an intermediary network, station, or cable to send the television signals into consumers' homes. The menu of entertainment appearing on television is controlled entirely by the intermediary and, thus, the consumer's selection is limited to what is available on various channels. Moreover, equipped merely with a conventional television set, a consumer has no means of capturing any part of the television display; when the program is over it vanishes, and the consumer is powerless to replay it. Because they originate outside the home, television signals are ephemeral and beyond the viewer's grasp.

Videocassettes, of course, allow viewing of a markedly different nature. Videocassette entertainment is controlled within the home, at the viewer's complete discretion. A consumer may view exactly what he or she wants (assuming availability in the marketplace) at whatever time he or she chooses. The viewer may even "fast forward" the tape so as to quickly pass over parts of the program he or she does not wish to view. By their very essence, then, videocassettes liberate viewers from the constraints otherwise inherent in television, and eliminate the involvement of an intermediary, such as a network.

. . .

Perhaps the primary reason why the words "exhibition by means of television" in the license cannot be construed as including videocassette reproduction is that, although in use by the networks, VCRs for home use were not invented or known in 1969, when the license was executed. The parties both acknowledge this fact and it is noted in the order of the district judge. Thus, in 1969—long before the market for videocassettes burgeoned—Cohen could not have assumed that the public would have free and virtually unlimited access to the film in which the composition was played; instead, he must have assumed that viewer access to the film "Medium Cool" would be largely controlled by theatres and networks. By the same token, the original licensee could not have bargained for, or paid for, the rights associated with videocassette reproduction. *See* Comment, *Past Copyright Licenses and the New Video Software Medium*, 29 U.C.L.A. L. Rev. 1160, 1184 (1982). The holder of the license should not now "reap the entire windfall" associated with the new medium. *See id.* As noted above, the license reserved to the grantor "all rights and uses in and to said musical composition, except those herein granted to the licensee...." This language operates to preclude uses not then known to, or contemplated by the parties.

Moreover, the license must be construed in accordance with the purpose underlying federal copyright law. Courts have repeatedly stated that the Copyright Act was "intended definitively to grant valuable, enforceable rights to authors, publishers, etc., . . . 'to afford greater encouragement to the production of literary works of lasting benefit to the world.' " . . . We would frustrate the purposes of the Act were we to construe this license—with its limiting language—as granting a right in a medium that had not been introduced to the domestic market at the time the parties entered into the agreement.

Paramount directs our attention to two district court cases, which, it contends, compel the opposite result. Both, however, involve licenses that contain language markedly different from the language in the license at hand.

Platinum Record Co., Inc. v. Lucasfilm, Ltd., 566 F. Supp. 226 (D.N.J. 1983), involved an agreement executed in 1973 in which plaintiff's predecessor in interest granted Lucasfilm, a film producer, the right to use four popular songs on the soundtrack of the motion picture *American Graffiti*. The agreement expressly conferred the right to "exhibit, distribute, exploit, market and perform said motion picture, its air, screen and television trailers, perpetually throughout the world *by any means or methods now or hereafter known*." *Id.* at 227 (emphasis added). Lucasfilm produced *American Graffiti* under a contract with Universal. *Id.* The film was shown in theatres and on cable, network, and local television. In 1980, a Universal affiliate released the film for sale and rental to the public on videocassettes. *Id.* Plaintiffs brought suit against Universal and its affiliate, alleging that the agreement did not give them the right to distribute the film on videocassettes.

The district court granted summary judgment in favor of the defendants. *Id.* at 226. It reasoned that the language in the agreement conferring the right to exhibit the film " 'by any means or methods now or hereafter known' " was "extremely broad and completely unambiguous, and precludes any need in the Agreement for an exhaustive list of specific potential uses of the film. . . . It is obvious that the contract in question may 'fairly be read' as including newly developed media, and the absence of any specific mention in the Agreement of videotapes and video cassettes is thus insignificant." *Id.* at 227.

Similarly, the district court in *Rooney v. Columbia Pictures Industries, Inc.*, 538 F. Supp. 211 (S.D.N.Y.1982), *aff'd*, 714 F.2d 117 (2d Cir.1982), *cert. denied*, 460 U.S. 1084 (1983) found that the contracts in question, which granted rights to exhibit certain films, also gave defendants the right to sell videocassettes of the films. *Id.* at 228. Like the contract in *Platinum*, the contracts in *Rooney* contained sweeping language, granting, for example, the right to exhibit the films "by any present or *future* methods or means," and by "any other means *now known or unknown*." *Id.* at 223 (emphasis added). The court stated, "The contracts in question gave defendants extremely broad rights in the distribution and exhibition of [the films], plainly intending that such rights would be without limitation unless otherwise specified and further indicating that future technological advances in methods of reproduction, transmission, and exhibition would inure to the benefit of defendants." *Id.* at 228.

In contrast to the contracts in *Platinum* and *Rooney,* the license in this case lacks such broad language. The contracts in those cases expressly conferred the right to exhibit the films by methods yet to be invented. Not only is this language missing in the license at hand, but the license also expressly reserves to the copyright holder all rights not expressly granted. We fail to find the *Rooney* and *Platinum* decisions persuasive.

Conclusion

We hold that the license did not give Paramount the right to use the composition in connection with videocassette production and distribution of the film "Medium Cool." The district court's award of summary judgment in favor of Paramount is reversed.

Reversed and remanded.

Boosey & Hawkes Music Publishers, Ltd. v. Walt Disney Co.

145 F.3d 481 (2d Cir.1998).

■ LEVAL, Circuit Judge:

Boosey & Hawkes Music Publishers Ltd., an English corporation and the assignee of Igor Stravinsky's copyrights for "The Rite of Spring," brought this action alleging that the Walt Disney Company's foreign distribution in video cassette and laser disc format ("video format") of the film "Fantasia," featuring Stravinsky's work, infringed Boosey's rights. In 1939 Stravinsky licensed Disney's distribution of The Rite of Spring in the motion picture. Boosey, which acquired Stravinsky's copyright in 1947, contends that the license does not authorize distribution in video format.

The district court (Duffy, J.) granted partial summary judgment to Boosey, declaring that Disney's video format release was not authorized by the license agreement. Disney appeals from that ruling. . . .

We hold that . . . material issues of fact barred the . . . grant of summary judgment [with respect to the scope of the contract]. . . .

I. BACKGROUND

During 1938, Disney sought Stravinsky's authorization to use The Rite of Spring (sometimes referred to as the "work" or the "composition") throughout the world in a motion picture. Because under United States law the work was in the public domain, Disney needed no authorization to record or distribute it in this country, but permission was required for distribution in countries where Stravinsky enjoyed copyright protection. In January 1939 the parties executed an agreement (the "1939 Agreement") giving Disney rights to use the work in a motion picture in consideration of a fee to Stravinsky of $6000.

The 1939 Agreement provided that

In consideration of the sum of Six Thousand ($6,000) Dollars, receipt of which is hereby acknowledged, [Stravinsky] does hereby give and grant unto Walt Disney Enterprises, a California corporation ... the nonexclusive, irrevocable right, license, privilege and authority to record in any manner, medium or form, and to license the performance of, the musical composition hereinbelow set out: ....

Under "type of use" in ¶ 3, the Agreement specified that

the music of said musical composition may be used in one motion picture throughout the length thereof or through such portion or portions thereof as The Purchaser shall desire. The said music may be used in whole or in part and may be adapted, changed, added to or subtracted from, all as shall appear desirable to the Purchaser in its uncontrolled discretion.... The title "Rites of Spring" or "Le Sacre de Printemps," or any other title, may be used as the title of said motion picture and the name of [Stravinsky] may be announced in or in connection with said motion picture.

The Agreement went on to specify in ¶ 4 that Disney's license to the work "is limited to the use of the musical composition in synchronism or timed-relation with the motion picture."

Paragraph Five of the Agreement provided that

The right to record the musical composition as covered by this agreement is conditioned upon the performance of the musical work in theatres having valid licenses from the American Society of Composers, Authors and Publishers, or any other performing rights society having jurisdiction in the territory in which the said musical composition is performed.

We refer to this clause, which is of importance to the litigation, as "the ASCAP Condition."

Finally, ¶ 7 of the Agreement provided that "the licensor reserves to himself all rights and uses in and to the said musical composition not herein specifically granted" (the "reservation clause").

Disney released Fantasia, starring Mickey Mouse, in 1940. The film contains no dialogue. It matches a pantomime of animated beasts and fantastic creatures to passages of great classical music, creating what critics celebrated as a "partnership between fine music and animated film." The soundtrack uses compositions of Bach, Beethoven, Dukas, Schubert, Tchaikovsky, and Stravinsky, all performed by the Philadelphia Orchestra under the direction of Leopold Stokowski. As it appears in the film soundtrack, The Rite of Spring was shortened from its original 34 minutes to about 22.5; sections of the score were cut, while other sections were reordered. For more than five decades Disney exhibited The Rite of Spring in Fantasia under the 1939 license. The film has been re-released for theatrical distribution at least seven times since 1940, and although Fantasia has never appeared on television in its entirety, excerpts including portions of The

Rite of Spring have been televised occasionally over the years. Neither Stravinsky nor Boosey has ever previously objected to any of the distributions.

In 1991 Disney first released Fantasia in video format. The video has been sold in foreign countries, as well as in the United States. To date, the Fantasia video release has generated more than $360 million in gross revenue for Disney.

Boosey brought this action in February 1993. The complaint sought (1) a declaration that the 1939 Agreement did not include a grant of rights to Disney to use the Stravinsky work in video format. . . .

On cross-motions for summary judgment the district court made the rulings described above. In determining that the license did not cover the distribution of a video format, the district court found that while the broad language of the license gave Disney "the right to record [the work] on video tape and laser disc," the ASCAP Condition "prevents Disney from distributing video tapes or laser discs directly to consumers." *Boosey & Hawkes Music Publishers Ltd. v. Walt Disney Co.*, 934 F. Supp. 119, 123 (S.D.N.Y. 1996). The court therefore concluded that Disney's video format sales exceeded the scope of the license.

. . .

II. DISCUSSION

. . . Disney challenges the summary judgment which declared that the 1939 Agreement does not authorize video distribution of The Rite of Spring. . . .

A. *Declaratory Judgment on the Scope of the License.*

Boosey's request for declaratory judgment raises two issues of contract interpretation: whether the general grant of permission under the 1939 Agreement licensed Disney to use The Rite of Spring in the video format version of Fantasia (on which the district court found in Disney's favor); and, if so, whether the ASCAP Condition barred Disney from exploiting the work through video format (on which the district court found for Boosey).

1. *Whether the "motion picture" license covers video format.* Boosey contends that the license to use Stravinsky's work in a "motion picture" did not authorize distribution of the motion picture in video format, especially in view of the absence of an express provision for "future technologies" and Stravinsky's reservation of all rights not granted in the Agreement. Disputes about whether licensees may exploit licensed works through new marketing channels made possible by technologies developed after the licensing contract—often called "new-use" problems—have vexed courts since at least the advent of the motion picture. See 3 Melville B. Nimmer and David Nimmer, Nimmer on Copyright, § 10.10[A] at 10–86 (hereinafter "Nimmer"); *Kirke La Shelle Co. v. Paul Armstrong Co.*, 263 N.Y. 79, 188 N.E. 163 (1933) (deciding whether a license for a stage production also conveyed rights in sound motion pictures).

In *Bartsch v. Metro–Goldwyn–Mayer, Inc.*, we held that "licensees may properly pursue any uses which may reasonably be said to fall within the medium as described in the license." 391 F.2d 150, 155 (2d Cir.1968) (Friendly, J.) (quoting Nimmer). We held in *Bartsch* that a license of motion picture rights to a play included the right to telecast the motion picture. We observed that "if the words are broad enough to cover the new use, it seems fairer that the burden of framing and negotiating an exception should fall on the grantor," at least when the new medium is not completely unknown at the time of contracting. *Id.* at 154, 155.

The 1939 Agreement conveys the right "to record [the composition] in any manner, medium or form" for use "in [a] motion picture." We believe this language is broad enough to include distribution of the motion picture in video format. At a minimum, *Bartsch* holds that when a license includes a grant of rights that is reasonably read to cover a new use (at least where the new use was foreseeable at the time of contracting), the burden of excluding the right to the new use will rest on the grantor. 391 F.2d at 155; see also *Bloom v. Hearst Entertainment Inc.*, 33 F.3d 518, 524–25 (5th Cir.1994) (applying *Bartsch* to hold that a grant of movie and television rights to a book encompassed video rights as well). The license "to record in any manner, medium or form" doubtless extends to videocassette recording and we can see no reason why the grant of "motion picture" reproduction rights should not include the video format, absent any indication in the Agreement to the contrary. See *Bourne v. Walt Disney Co.*, 68 F.3d 621, 630 (2d Cir.1995); *Bloom*, 33 F.3d at 525. If a new-use license hinges on the foreseeability of the new channels of distribution at the time of contracting—a question left open in *Bartsch*—Disney has proffered unrefuted evidence that a nascent market for home viewing of feature films existed by 1939. The *Bartsch* analysis thus compels the conclusion that the license for motion picture rights extends to video format distribution.

We recognize that courts and scholars are not in complete accord on the capacity of a broad license to cover future developed markets resulting from new technologies. The Nimmer treatise describes two principal approaches to the problem. According to the first view, advocated here by Boosey, "a license of rights in a given medium (e.g., 'motion picture rights') includes only such uses as fall within the unambiguous core meaning of the term (e.g., exhibition of motion picture film in motion picture theaters) and exclude any uses that lie within the ambiguous penumbra (e.g., exhibition of motion picture on television)." Nimmer, § 10.10[B] at 10–90; see also *Cohen v. Paramount Pictures Corp.*, 845 F.2d 851, 853–54 (9th Cir.1988) (holding that license to use musical score in television production does not extend to use in videocassette release); *Rey v. Lafferty*, 990 F.2d 1379, 1390–91 (1st Cir.1993) (holding that license to portray Curious George in animations for "television viewing" does not extend to videocassette release). Under this approach, a license given in 1939 to "motion picture" rights would include only the core uses of "motion picture" as understood in 1939—presumably theatrical distribution—and would not include subsequently developed methods of distribution of a motion picture such as television videocassettes or laser discs. See Nimmer § 10.10[b] at 10–90.

The second position described by Nimmer is "that the licensee may properly pursue any uses that may reasonably be said to fall within the medium as described in the license." *Id.* at 10–91. Nimmer expresses clear preferences for the latter approach on the ground that it is "less likely to prove unjust." *Id.* As Judge Friendly noted in *Bartsch*, "So do we." 391 F.2d at 155.

We acknowledge that a result which deprives the author-licensor of participation in the profits of new unforeseen channels of distribution is not an altogether happy solution. Nonetheless, we think it more fair and sensible than a result that would deprive a contracting party of the rights reasonably found in the terms of the contract it negotiates. This issue is too often, and improperly, framed as one of favoritism as between licensors and licensees. Because licensors are often authors—whose creativity the copyright laws intend to nurture—and are often impecunious, while licensees are often large business organizations, there is sometimes a tendency in copyright scholarship and adjudication to seek solutions that favor licensors over licensees. Thus in *Cohen*, 845 F.2d at 854, the Ninth Circuit wrote that a "license must be construed in accordance with the purpose underlying federal copyright law," which the court construed as the granting of valuable, enforceable rights to authors and the encouragement of the production of literary works. Asserting that copyright law "is enacted for the benefit of the composer," (quoting *Jondora Music Publish[ing] Co. v. Melody Recordings, Inc.*, 506 F.2d 392, 395 (3d Cir.1975) (as amended)), the court concluded that it would "frustrate the purposes of the [Copyright] Act" to construe the license as encompassing video technology, which did not exist when the license was granted. *Id.*; see also *Warner Bros. Pictures v. Columbia Broadcasting System*, 216 F.2d 945, 949 (9th Cir.1954) ("Such doubt as there is should be resolved in favor of the composer. The clearest language is necessary to divest the author from the fruit of his labor."); William F. Patry, 1 Copyright Law and Practice 392 (1994) (arguing that "agreements should, wherever possible, be construed in favor of the copyright transferor," to reflect Congress's "policy judgment that copyright owners should retain all rights unless specifically transferred").

In our view, new-use analysis should rely on neutral principles of contract interpretation rather than solicitude for either party. Although *Bartsch* speaks of placing the "burden of framing and negotiating an exception ... on the grantor," 391 F.2d at 155, it should not be understood to adopt a default rule in favor of copyright licensees or any default rule whatsoever.[3] What governs under *Bartsch* is the language of the contract. If

---

3. We note that commentators and courts have misinterpreted *Bartsch* in just this way. See, e.g., *Film Video Releasing Corp. v. Hastings*, 426 F. Supp. 690, 695 (S.D.N.Y.1976) (interpreting *Bartsch* to mean that "the words of the grant are to be construed against the grantor"); James W. Dabney, Licenses and New Technology: Apportioning and Benefits, C674 ALI–ABA 85, 89, 96 (characterizing *Bartsch* as a "pro-licensee" decision that articulates a rule of contract construction favoring licensees in new-use cases). We emphasize that *Bartsch* favors neither party and announces no special rule of contract interpretation for the new-use context. Rather, it instructs courts to rely on the language of the license contract and basic principles of interpretation.

the contract is more reasonably read to convey one meaning, the party benefitted by that reading should be able to rely on it; the party seeking exception or deviation from the meaning reasonably conveyed by the words of the contract should bear the burden of negotiating for language that would express the limitation or deviation. This principle favors neither licensors nor licensees. It follows simply from the words of the contract.

The words of Disney's license are more reasonably read to include than to exclude a motion picture distributed in video format. Thus, we conclude that the burden fell on Stravinsky, if he wished to exclude new markets arising from subsequently developed motion picture technology, to insert such language of limitation in the license, rather than on Disney to add language that reiterated what the license already stated.

Other significant jurisprudential and policy considerations confirm our approach to new-use problems. We think that our view is more consistent with the law of contract than the view that would exclude new technologies even when they reasonably fall within the description of what is licensed. Although contract interpretation normally requires inquiry into the intent of the contracting parties, intent is not likely to be helpful when the subject of the inquiry is something the parties were not thinking about. See Nimmer, § 10.10[B] at 10–90 (noting that usually "there simply was no intent at all at the time of execution with respect to . . . whether the grant includes a new use developed at a later time"). Nor is extrinsic evidence such as past dealings or industry custom likely to illuminate the intent of the parties, because the use in question was, by hypothesis, new, and could not have been the subject of prior negotiations or established practice. See Michael R. Fuller, *Hollywood Goes Interactive: Licensing Problems Associated with Re–Purposing Motion Pictures into Interactive Multimedia Video-games*, 15 Loy. L.A. Ent. L.J. 599, 607 (1985). Moreover, many years after formation of the contract, it may well be impossible to consult the principals or retrieve documentary evidence to ascertain the parties' intent, if any, with respect to new uses. On the other hand, the parties or assignees of the contract should be entitled to rely on the words of the contract. Especially where, as here, evidence probative of intent is likely to be both scant and unreliable, the burden of justifying a departure from the most reasonable reading of the contract should fall on the party advocating the departure.[4]

---

4. We note also that an approach to new-use problems that tilts against licensees gives rise to antiprogressive incentives. Motion picture producers would be reluctant to explore and utilize innovative technologies for the exhibition of movies if the consequence would be that they would lose the right to exhibit pictures containing licensed works. See *Bartsch*, 391 F.2d at 155.

Nor do we believe that our approach disadvantages licensors. By holding contracting parties accountable to the reasonable interpretation of their agreements, we encourage licensors and licensees to anticipate and bargain for the full value of potential future uses. Licensors reluctant to anticipate future developments remain free to negotiate language that clearly reserves the rights to future uses. But the creation of exceptional principles of contract construction that places doubt on the capacity of a license to transfer new technologies is likely to harm licensors together with licensees, by placing a significant percentage of the profits they might have shared in the hands of lawyers instead.

Neither the absence of a future technologies clause in the Agreement nor the presence of the reservation clause alters that analysis. The reservation clause stands for no more than the truism that Stravinsky retained whatever he had not granted. It contributes nothing to the definition of the boundaries of the license. See *Bartsch* 391 F.2d at 154 n.1. And irrespective of the presence or absence of a clause expressly confirming a license over future technologies, the burden still falls on the party advancing a deviation from the most reasonable reading of the license to insure that the desired deviation is reflected in the final terms of the contract. As we have already stated, if the broad terms of the license are more reasonably read to include the particular future technology in question, then the licensee may rely on that language.

Bartsch therefore continues to articulate our "preferred" approach to new-use questions, Nimmer, § 10.10[B] at 10–91, and we hold that the district court properly applied it to find that the basic terms of Disney's license included the right to record and distribute Fantasia in video format.

2. *The ASCAP Condition.* Boosey further contends that distribution of Fantasia in video format violated the ASCAP Condition. The district court agreed. It granted summary judgment to Boosey declaring that the ASCAP Condition "prevents Disney from distributing video tapes and laser discs directly to consumers." *Boosey & Hawkes*, 934 F. Supp. at 123. We disagree with the district court's analysis.

The ASCAP Condition provides that

The right to record the musical composition as covered by this agreement is conditioned upon the performance of the musical work in theaters having valid licenses from the American Society of Composers, Authors and Publishers, or any other performing rights society having jurisdiction in the territory in which the said musical composition is performed.

The court apparently believed, as Boosey argues, that the ASCAP Condition unambiguously limited Disney's exploitation of its motion picture to theaters operating under a license from ASCAP or similar performing rights society. This interpretation treats the clause as if it stated explicitly either that the license extends only to performances in theaters licensed by ASCAP, or that Disney commits itself to exploit the license only in such theaters. But that is not what the clause says.

The terms of the provision condition Disney's right to record the work only "upon the performance of the ... work in theaters" having ASCAP (or similar) licenses. Read literally, this language requires no more of Disney than that it expose the motion picture in two or more ASCAP-certified theaters, a condition surely long ago satisfied. Whatever may have been the intention, the ASCAP Condition does not unambiguously prohibit Disney from exhibiting the composition in non-ASCAP theaters, or from distributing the film directly to consumers.

Apart from the fact that the language of the Condition does not compel Boosey's interpretation, there is also good reason to regard that construction as improbable. Because the work was in the public domain in the United States, the license pertained only to foreign rights, which the contract described as world wide. Construing the Condition as Boosey argues would mean that the film could not be shown at all in any country where the work was protected and theaters did not employ ASCAP-type licenses.

. . .

We find that neither party's interpretation is compelled by the plain terms of the provision. Accord Kohn [on Music Licensing, 2d ed. 1996], at 838–39 (classifying a hypothetical provision identical to the ASCAP Condition as a license whose scope is unclear). The Condition is sufficiently unclear on its face to justify consideration of extrinsic evidence. See *Shann v. Dunk*, 84 F.3d 73, 80 (2d Cir.1996).

Boosey argues that any ambiguity regarding the meaning of the ASCAP Provision is dissipated by extrinsic evidence showing Disney knew that the 1939 Agreement permitted use of the composition only in ASCAP-licensed motion picture theaters. We do not find this evidence persuasive.

Boosey first points to the parties' limited post-contract course of dealing. In 1941, Boosey notes, Disney acknowledged that the Agreement did not license use of The Rite of Spring on radio. In 1969, Disney negotiated and paid for the right to release the soundtrack recording of "The Rite of Spring" as part of a complete Fantasia album. And in 1990, Disney unsuccessfully sought Boosey's permission to use sections of the composition "in a new performance by . . . Pink Floyd to be filmed at the Great Pyramid of Giza, while imagery from 'Fantasia' is projected across the entire face of the Pyramid." Boosey would have us infer that these requests for permission demonstrate Disney's awareness that its right to the composition was limited to exploitation in licensed motion picture theaters.

However, those exploitations of the composition seem clearly beyond the scope of the 1939 Agreement. None of the proposed uses involved "the use of the musical composition in synchronism or timed-relation" with Fantasia, as required by ¶ 4 of the Agreement; the 1941 and 1969 requests did not even envision use of the composition in a motion picture, as required by ¶ 3 of the Agreement. Because the Agreement could not reasonably be interpreted to cover these uses, Disney's decision to seek supplemental permission for them reveals nothing regarding its view as to whether it was authorized to license Fantasia otherwise than in theaters with ASCAP licenses.

Indeed, there is course of dealing evidence that supports the opposite conclusion—that Disney did not view the license as restricted to performance in ASCAP-licensed theaters. Without seeking Boosey's permission, Disney appears to have sold Fantasia directly to consumers in at least two foreign markets and telecast the composition in excerpts from "Fantasia" several times. That Disney sought permission for uses of the composition not involving the motion picture Fantasia, but did not seek permission for direct distribution of Fantasia in alternative motion picture formats, arguably rebuts Boosey's argument that Disney's conduct shows it agreed with Boosey's interpretation.

. . .

Neither the plain terms of the 1939 Agreement nor the sparse and contradictory extrinsic evidence require the conclusion that Disney's license is limited to theatrical performance of the composition. Summary judgment is therefore inappropriate. We vacate the summary grant of declaratory judgment in Boosey's favor and remand for a trial to determine whether Disney's video format release violated the ASCAP Condition.

[Editors' Note: The court of appeals also held that Boosey could bring an action against Disney in the New York City federal court for copyright infringement in 18 foreign nations, despite Disney's invocation of the doctrine of forum non conveniens. *See* p. 930, *infra*. In January 2001, Disney announced that it had agreed to pay $3 million to Boosey & Hawkes in settlement of this case. Boosey was seeking $200 million.]

QUESTIONS

1. Are *Cohen v. Paramount Pictures* and *Boosey v. Disney* consistent? Do the different results depend on the terms of the respective contracts? On the respectively then-applicable copyright laws? On the state of the pertinent technologies when the contracts were made?

2. Reread the quoted clauses of the *Cohen* and *Boosey* synchronization licenses: do you see the word "distribute"? Where does the license explicitly authorize the distribution of copies of the motion picture to the public for home viewing?

3. A familiar canon of contract interpretation requires ambiguities to be interpreted against the drafter. Does the Second Circuit follow this canon? Who drafted the "Disney license"?

4. Note the presumption by the *Boosey* court that a grant of rights to exploit a work should be construed in a reasonably all-embracing manner. In § 202 of the Copyright Act, in a not dissimilar setting, Congress adopted a different presumption with regard to transfers of a material object, which are to be treated as not transferring the copyright as well, even though that might limit the reproduction and exploitation of the work and generate conflicts between the owners of the two different rights. Does this suggest that the court's presumption in *Boosey* is unsound?

5. If you were contracting for a transfer of copyright interests, how, in light of *Cohen* and *Boosey,* would you draft the document to insure that you (the grantee) received the right to unknown future uses? If you were the grantor, how would you draft the contract to preserve your rights to future modes of exploitation?

Random House, Inc. v. Rosetta Books, LLC

150 F.Supp.2d 613 (S.D.N.Y.2001).

[William Styron, Kurt Vonnegut, Jr., and Robert Parker all published novels with Random House, signing publishing contracts in the 1960s, 1970s, and 1980s, respectively. The contracts gave Random House the exclusive right to publish the works "in book form." The authors also signed a clause promising not to use any rights they retained in a way that would compete with Random House's exercise of the rights the authors conveyed. The authors later granted Rosetta Books, an eBook publisher, the exclusive right to publish electronic versions of their works. Random House, their original publisher, claimed that the authors did not have those rights to give: an eBook, said Random House, is still a "book," and therefore comes within the "in book form" grant. Random House also claimed that even were an eBook not "in book form," it would come within the "noncompete" clause. The authors responded that Random House did not begin contractually to claim electronic rights explicitly until 1994. The authors also stressed that publishing contracts contained distinct and closely-worded subsidiary rights clauses covering paperback versions, book club versions, magazine excerpts, audio-books; eBooks, they urged, are no more in "book form" than these other variant presentations of the works. The court analyzed Random House's claim within the framework of "old license/new media" cases, including *Boosey* and *Bartsch*. It denied Random House's motion for a preliminary injunction against Rosetta's eBook publication]

■ Sidney H. Stein, U.S. District Judge

. . . Relying on "the language of the license contract and basic principles of interpretation," *Boosey,* 145 F.3d at 487 n.3, as instructed to do so by *Boosey* and *Bartsch*, this Court finds that the most reasonable interpretation of the grant in the contracts at issue to "print, publish and sell the work in book form" does not include the right to publish the work as an ebook. At the outset, the phrase itself distinguishes between the pure content—i.e. "the work"—and the format of display—"in book form." The Random House Webster's Unabridged Dictionary defines a "book" as "a written or printed work of fiction or nonfiction, usually on sheets of paper fastened or bound together within covers" and defines "form" as "external appearance of a clearly defined area, as distinguished from color or material; the shape of a thing or person."

Manifestly, paragraph #1 of each contract—entitled either "grant of rights" or "exclusive publication right"—conveys certain rights from the author to the publisher. In that paragraph, separate grant language is used to convey the rights to publish book club editions, reprint editions, abridged forms, and editions in Braille. This language would not be necessary if the phrase "in book form" encompassed all types of books. That paragraph specifies exactly which rights were being granted by the author to the publisher. Indeed, many of the rights set forth in the publisher's form contracts were in fact not granted to the publisher, but rather were reserved by the authors to themselves. For example, each of the authors specifically reserved certain rights for themselves by striking out phrases, sentences, and paragraphs of the publisher's form contract. This evidences an intent by these authors not to grant the publisher the broadest rights in their works.

Random House contends that the phrase "in book form" means to faithfully reproduce the author's text in its complete form as a reading experience and that, since ebooks concededly contain the complete text of the work, Rosetta cannot also possess those rights. While Random House's definition distinguishes "book form" from other formats that require separate contractual language—such as audio books and serialization rights—it does not distinguish other formats specifically mentioned in paragraph #1 of the contracts, such as book club editions and reprint editions. Because the Court must, if possible, give effect to all contractual language in order to "safeguard against adopting an interpretation that would render any individual provision superfluous," Random House's definition cannot be adopted.

Random House points specifically to the clause requiring it to "publish the work at its own expense and in such a style and manner and at such a price as [Random House] deems suitable" as support for its position. However, plaintiff takes this clause out of context. It appears in paragraph #2, captioned "Style, Price and Date of Publication," not paragraph #1, which includes all the grants of rights. In context, the phrase simply means that Random House has control over the appearance of the formats granted to Random House in the first paragraph; i.e., control over the style of the book.

Random House also cites the non-compete clauses as evidence that the authors granted it broad, exclusive rights in their work. Random House reasons that because the authors could not permit any material that would injure the sale of the work to be published without Random House's consent, the authors must have granted the right to publish ebooks to Random House.... [E]ven if the authors did violate this provision of their Random House agreements by contracting with Rosetta Books—a point on which this Court does not opine—the remedy is a breach of contract action against the authors, not a copyright infringement action against Rosetta Books.

The photocopy clause—giving Random House the right to "Xerox and other forms of copying, either now in use or hereafter developed"—similarly does not bolster Random House's position. Although the clause does appear in the grant language paragraph, taken in context, it clearly refers only to new developments in xerography and other forms of photocopying. Stretching it to include new forms of publishing, such as ebooks, would make the rest of the contract superfluous because there would be no reason for authors to reserve rights to forms of publishing "now in use." This interpretation also comports with the publishing industry's trade usage of the phrase.

Not only does the language of the contract itself lead almost ineluctably to the conclusion that Random House does not own the right to publish the works as ebooks, but also a reasonable person "cognizant of the customs, practices, usages and terminology as generally understood in the particular trade or business," would conclude that the grant language does not include ebooks. "To print, publish and sell the work in book form" is understood in the publishing industry to be a "limited" grant.

In Field v. True Comics, the court held that "the sole and exclusive right to publish, print and market in book form"—especially when the author had specifically reserved rights for himself—was "much more limited" than "the sole and exclusive right to publish, print and market *the book*." 89 F. Supp. at 612 (emphasis added). In fact, the publishing industry generally interprets the phrase "in book form" as granting the publisher "the exclusive right to publish a hardcover trade book in English for distribution in North America." 1 Lindey on Entertainment, Publishing and the Arts Form 1.01–1 (2d ed. 2000) (using the Random House form contract to explain the meaning of each clause) [other citations omitted].

3. Comparison to Prior "New Use" Caselaw

The finding that the five licensing agreements at issue do not convey the right to publish the works as ebooks accords with Second Circuit and New York case law. Indeed, the two leading cases ... that found that a particular new use was included within the grant language—*Boosey,* 145 F.3d 481 (2d Cir.1998), and *Bartsch,* 391 F.2d 150 (2d Cir.1968)—can be distinguished from this case on four grounds.

First, the language conveying the rights in *Boosey* and *Bartsch* was far broader than here. Second, the "new use" in those cases—i.e. display of a motion picture on television or videocassette—fell squarely within the same medium as the original grant. See *Boosey,* 145 F.3d at 486 (describing videocassettes and laser discs as "subsequently developed methods of distribution of a motion picture"); *Bourne,* 68 F.3d at 630 ("The term 'motion picture' reasonably can be understood to refer to 'a broad genus whose fundamental characteristic is a series of related images that impart an impression of motion when shown in succession. . . . Under this concept the physical form in which the motion picture is fixed—film, tape, discs, and so forth—is irrelevant.' ").

In this case, the "new use"—electronic digital signals sent over the internet—is a separate medium from the original use—printed words on paper. Random House's own expert concludes that the media are distinct because information stored digitally can be manipulated in ways that analog information cannot. Ebooks take advantage of the digital medium's ability to manipulate data by allowing ebook users to electronically search the text for specific words and phrases, change the font size and style, type notes into the text and electronically organize them, highlight and bookmark, hyperlink to specific parts of the text, and, in the future, to other sites on related topics as well, and access a dictionary that pronounces words in the ebook aloud. The need for a software program to interact with the data in order to make it usable, as well as the need for a piece of hardware to enable the reader to view the text, also distinguishes analog formats from digital formats. See *Greenberg v. National Geographic Soc'y,* 244 F.3d 1267, 1273 n. 12 (11th Cir.2001) (Digital format is not analogous to reproducing the magazine in microfilm or microfiche because it "requires the interaction of a computer program in order to accomplish the useful reproduction involved with the new medium.").

Therefore, *Boosey* and *Bartsch*, which apply to new uses within the same medium, do not control this case. See, e.g., ... *Tele–Pac, Inc. v. Grainger,* 168 A.D.2d 11, 570 N.Y.S.2d 521 (1st Dep't 1991) (distinguishing Second Circuit "new use" doctrine by holding that right to "broadcast[] by television or any other similar device now known or hereafter to be made known" was so dissimilar from display on videocassette and videodisc "as to preclude consideration of video rights as even falling within the 'ambiguous penumbra' of the terms used in the agreement").

The third significant difference between the licensee in the motion picture cases cited above and the book publisher in this action is that the licensees in the motion picture cases have actually created a new work based on the material from the licensor. Therefore, the right to display that new work—whether on television or video—is derivative of the right to create that work. In the book publishing context, the publishers, although they participate in the editorial process, display the words written by the author, not themselves.

Fourth, the courts in *Boosey* and *Bartsch* were concerned that any approach to new use problems that "tilts against licensees [here, Random House] gives rise to antiprogressive incentives" insofar as licensees "would be reluctant to explore and utilize innovative technologies." However, in this action, the policy rationale of encouraging development in new technology is at least as well served by finding that the licensors—i.e., the authors—retain these rights to their works. In the 21st century, it cannot be said that licensees such as book publishers and movie producers are ipso facto more likely to make advances in digital technology than start-up companies....

QUESTIONS

1. Phil Phlash, a professional photographer, owns the copyright in certain photographs he took of the America's Cup yacht race. He entered into a license agreement with Winterland Productions, in which he conveyed "the exclusive license to use the photographs as guides, models, and examples, for illustrations to be used on screen printed T-shirts or other sportswear." Although Winterland typically has its artists produce hand-made drawings with which it decorates its apparel, in this instance it has scanned Phlash's America's Cup photographs into a computer, and has manipulated the digitized image so as to reverse from right to left the image of the two competing boats and to intensify the colors of the sails and the water; it has then transferred the altered image to shirts and other sportswear. Phlash has brought an action for copyright infringement, asserting that Winterland's images are not licensed "illustrations." Advise the court on whether Winterland has produced authorized illustrations or unauthorized photographs. *See Mendler v. Winterland Prod., Ltd.*, 207 F.3d 1119 (9th Cir. 2000).

2. A songwriter and recording artist, Jack Sprat, authorized his record producer, Manny Motown, to license to others certain rights in Sprat's recording of his song "Funky Soul." The producer was authorized in writing to "license in any and all fields of use, by any method now or hereafter known, throughout the world, records embodying my performance of Funky Soul." Another recording artist, Gee Whiz, wished to incorporate a six and one-half second "digital sample" from the Sprat recording of "Funky Soul" in Whiz's new recording "So On and So On." Manny Motown licensed such sampling. Sprat has brought an action against Motown and Whiz for copyright infringement. Would you grant the defendants' motion for summary judgment? *See Batiste v. Island Records Inc.*, 179 F.3d 217 (5th Cir.1999).

3. Kennedy was hired as a consultant by the National Juvenile Rights Center to prepare a report about juvenile justice in various judicial districts in the United States. The consulting agreement authorized the Center, among other things, to "reproduce, publish and use" the material contained in the report. After Kennedy submitted his final draft (and was paid therefor), the Center concluded that it was incomplete and distorted in its analysis and conclusions, and it used the services of another consultant to revise and expand the report—in the course of which different conclusions were reached and recommendations made. Kennedy has sued the Center for copyright infringement. The Center contends that the word "use" in its contract with Kennedy embraces the preparation of a derivative work; Kennedy contends otherwise. Who has the more convincing case? *See Kennedy v. National Juvenile Detention Ass'n.*, 187 F.3d 690 (7th Cir.1999).

"ARISING UNDER" COPYRIGHT OR CONTRACT LAW?

In *Boosey & Hawkes*, as in the *Bartsch* decision it discusses, the Second Circuit deemed the question of the scope of the contractual transfer of copyright to be a matter of state contract law, rather than of federal copyright law. The author's (or his successor's) claim that the author had not granted the rights the defendant sought to exercise therefore arose under the state law of contract. Not every claim involving copyright and contracts is properly considered to arise under state law, however. For example, where the Copyright Act requires that transfers be made in writing, it is for federal law to determine what satisfies the section 204(a) "note or memorandum of the transfer" standard. Or where the author claims that her grantee exceeded the scope of the license, and therefore infringed her copyright, the claim arises under federal copyright law. (How different is this claim from one disputing copyright ownership?) As the following decision illustrates, courts have had some difficulty articulating when a claim "arises under" federal copyright or state contract law.

Bassett v. Mashantucket Pequot Tribe, 204 F.3d 343 (2d Cir. 2000). The plaintiff entered into a letter agreement to produce a motion picture (about the Pequot War of 1636–38) to be exhibited in the Native American tribe's museum. She provided the tribe with a copy of her proposed script, but the tribe terminated the agreement, claiming that she had failed to perform her duties. The tribe completed the film using another motion picture production company. The plaintiff's action for copyright infringement—for using her copyrighted script without her consent or license—and contract breach was dismissed below for lack of subject matter jurisdiction; the district court concluded, under the governing law of *Schoenberg v. Shapolsky Pubs., Inc.*, 971 F.2d 926 (2d Cir.1992), that the plaintiff's copyright claim was "incidental to" her contract claim and thus did not "arise under" federal law.

The Court of Appeals for the Second Circuit, however, found the *Schoenberg* approach to be unworkable and vague, and reverted to the earlier prevailing standard in *T.B. Harms Co. v. Eliscu*, 339 F.2d 823 (2d Cir.1964). These kinds of cases involve a license to exploit a copyright, along with a breach of the contract terms by the licensee that forfeits the license and results in copyright infringement. *T.B. Harms* had itself abandoned an earlier approach which was to assess whether copyright was the "essence" of the dispute or was "merely incidental" to the contract issue; it held instead that a suit "arises under" the Copyright Act if: (1) the complaint seeks a remedy expressly granted by the statute, or (2) the complaint asserts a claim requiring construction of the statute. This standard looks to the complaint, rather than to the defense that might be proffered, i.e., whether the defendant refers to state law to claim a contractual entitlement or refers to a defense under the Copyright Act.

The court in *Bassett* found that the "essence"/"incidental" standard had several flaws. The distinction is vague. The *Schoenberg* test denies access to a federal forum and federal remedies for copyright claims that are found to be incidental to a contract dispute, thus frustrating the purposes of Congress and of the federal statute. Because that test rests more upon the defenses than upon the demands asserted in the complaint, the plaintiff's attorney can have no way of telling whether the action should be filed in a federal or state court—and the court's threshold determination on jurisdictional grounds will often have to rest on complex factual determinations (such as whether the defendant's alleged breach is substantial, allowing the plaintiff to rescind) that relate to the merits of the case. The court, applying the *T.B. Harms* test, concluded that Bassett's claims "arise under" the Copyright Act, because the complaint alleged an infringing use of Bassett's script to produce the movie and sought injunctive relief under the statute.

Foad Consulting Group, Inc. v. Musil Govan Azzalino, 270 F.3d 821 (9th Cir.2001), the Ninth Circuit ruled that "while federal law answers [affirmatively] the threshold question of whether an implied, nonexclusive copyright license can be granted ..., state law determines the contract question: whether a copyright holder has, in fact, granted such a license." According to the majority, federal law imposes certain requirements regarding the validity of exclusive transfers of rights, but, by remaining silent as to non exclusive grants, Congress leaves the validity of those agreements to state law. Under California law, a court may, even in the absence of textual ambiguity, admit parol evidence to ascertain the existence and scope of a grant; the court found no conflict between state contract law and federal copyright policy. Judge Kosinski disputed the characterization of the implied license as a matter of state contract law: "an implied contract is not a contract at all; it is a legal obligation the law imposes between certain parties where there is no actual agreement between them. . . . it is an incident of the copyright and is therefore governed by law."

§ 201. Ownership of Copyright

. . .

(c) *Contributions to Collective Works.*—Copyright in each separate contribution to a collective work is distinct from copyright in the collective work as a whole, and vests initially in the author of the contribution. In the absence of an express transfer of the copyright or of any rights under it, the owner of copyright in the collective work is presumed to have acquired only the privilege of reproducing and distributing the contribution as part of that particular collective work, any revision of that collective work, and any later collective work in the same series.

New York Times Company, Inc. v. Tasini
___ U.S. ___, 121 S.Ct. 2381 (2001).

■ JUSTICE GINSBURG delivered the opinion of the Court.

This copyright case concerns the rights of freelance authors and a presumptive privilege of their publishers. The litigation was initiated by six freelance authors and relates to articles they contributed to three print periodicals (two newspapers and one magazine). Under agreements with the periodicals' publishers, but without the freelancers' consent, two computer database companies placed copies of the freelancers' articles—along with all other articles from the periodicals in which the freelancers' work appeared—into three databases. Whether written by a freelancer or staff member, each article is presented to, and retrievable by, the user in isolation, clear of the context the original print publication presented.

The freelance authors' complaint alleged that their copyrights had been infringed by the inclusion of their articles in the databases. The publishers, in response, relied on the privilege of reproduction and distribution accorded them by § 201(c) of the Copyright Act . . . 17 U.S.C. § 201(c).

. . . [W]e hold that § 201(c) does not authorize the copying at issue here. The publishers are not sheltered by § 201(c), we conclude, because the databases reproduce and distribute articles standing alone and not in context, not "as part of that particular collective work" to which the author contributed, "as part of . . . any revision" thereof, or "as part of . . . any later collective work in the same series." Both the print publishers and the electronic publishers, we rule, have infringed the copyrights of the freelance authors.

I

A

Respondents Jonathan Tasini, Mary Kay Blakely, Barbara Garson, Margot Mifflin, Sonia Jaffe Robbins, and David S. Whitford are authors

(Authors). Between 1990 and 1993, they wrote the 21 articles (Articles) on which this dispute centers.... The Authors registered copyrights in each of the Articles. The Times, Newsday, and Time (Print Publishers) registered collective work copyrights in each periodical edition in which an Article originally appeared. The Print Publishers engaged the Authors as independent contractors (freelancers) under contracts that in no instance secured consent from an Author to placement of an Article in an electronic database.

At the time the Articles were published, all three Print Publishers had agreements with petitioner LEXIS/NEXIS (formerly Mead Data Central Corp.), owner and operator of NEXIS, a computerized database that stores information in a text-only format. NEXIS contains articles from hundreds of journals (newspapers and periodicals) spanning many years. The Print Publishers have licensed to LEXIS/NEXIS the text of articles appearing in the three periodicals. The licenses authorize LEXIS/NEXIS to copy and sell any portion of those texts.

Pursuant to the licensing agreements, the Print Publishers regularly provide LEXIS/NEXIS with a batch of all the articles published in each periodical edition. The Print Publisher codes each article to facilitate computerized retrieval, then transmits it in a separate file. After further coding, LEXIS/NEXIS places the article in the central discs of its database.

Subscribers to NEXIS, accessing the system through a computer, may search for articles by author, subject, date, publication, headline, key term, words in text, or other criteria. Responding to a search command, NEXIS scans the database and informs the user of the number of articles meeting the user's search criteria. The user then may view, print, or download each of the articles yielded by the search. The display of each article includes the print publication (*e.g.*, The New York Times), date (September 23, 1990), section (Magazine), initial page number (26), headline or title ("Remembering Jane"), and author (Mary Kay Blakely). Each article appears as a separate, isolated "story"—without any visible link to the other stories originally published in the same newspaper or magazine edition. NEXIS does not contain pictures or advertisements, and it does not reproduce the original print publication's formatting features such as headline size, page placement (*e.g.*, above or below the fold for newspapers), or location of continuation pages.

The Times (but not Newsday or Time) also has licensing agreements with petitioner University Microfilms International (UMI). The agreements authorize reproduction of Times materials on two CD–ROM products, the New York Times OnDisc (NYTO) and General Periodicals OnDisc (GPO).

Like NEXIS, NYTO is a text-only system. Unlike NEXIS, NYTO, as its name suggests, contains only the Times. Pursuant to a three-way agreement, LEXIS/NEXIS provides UMI with computer files containing each article as transmitted by the Times to LEXIS/NEXIS. Like LEXIS/NEXIS, UMI marks each article with special codes. UMI also provides an index of all the articles in NYTO. Articles appear in NYTO in essentially the same way they appear in NEXIS, *i.e.*, with identifying information (author, title, etc.), but without original formatting or accompanying images.

GPO contains articles from approximately 200 publications or sections of publications. Unlike NEXIS and NYTO, GPO is an image-based, rather than a text-based, system. The Times has licensed GPO to provide a facsimile of the Times' Sunday Book Review and Magazine. UMI "burns" images of each page of these sections onto CD–ROMs. The CD–ROMs show each article exactly as it appeared on printed pages, complete with photographs, captions, advertisements, and other surrounding materials. UMI provides an index and abstracts of all the articles in GPO.

Articles are accessed through NYTO and GPO much as they are accessed through NEXIS. The user enters a search query using similar criteria (*e.g.*, author, headline, date). The computer program searches available indexes and abstracts, and retrieves a list of results matching the query. The user then may view each article within the search result, and may print the article or download it to a disc. The display of each article provides no links to articles appearing on other pages of the original print publications.[2]

. . .

II

[The Court described how, under the 1909 Act, the provisions on copyright notice and the doctrine of "indivisibility" often resulted in individual authors transferring copyright in their articles to the magazine publisher—as a safeguard against losing the copyright because of lack of proper notice. In the 1976 Act, Congress sought to correct the situation by providing for a "divisible" copyright and by allowing the magazine's copyright notice to protect authors who retain copyright in their individual contributions. In those latter situations, section 201(c) allocates the respective rights of author and collective-work publisher, in the absence of a written agreement.]

Section 201(c) both describes and circumscribes the "privilege" a publisher acquires regarding an author's contribution to a collective work. . . .

A newspaper or magazine publisher is thus privileged to reproduce or distribute an article contributed by a freelance author, absent a contract otherwise providing, only "as part of" any (or all) of three categories of collective works: (a) "that collective work" to which the author contributed her work, (b) "any revision of that collective work," or (c) "any later collective work in the same series." In accord with Congress' prescription, a "publishing company could reprint a contribution from one issue in a later issue of its magazine, and could reprint an article from a 1980 edition of an encyclopedia in a 1990 revision of it; the publisher could not revise the contribution itself or include it in a new anthology or an entirely different magazine or other collective work." H. R. Rep. 122–123.

2. For example, the GPO user who retrieves Blakely's "Remembering Jane" article will see the entirety of Magazine page 26, where the article begins, and Magazine page 78, where the article continues and ends. The NYTO user who retrieves Blakely's article will see only the text of the article and its identifying information (author, headline, publication, page number, etc.). Neither the GPO retrieval nor the NYTO retrieval produces any text on page 27, page 79, or any other page. The user who wishes to see other pages may not simply "flip" to them. She must conduct a new search.

Essentially, § 201(c) adjusts a publisher's copyright in its collective work to accommodate a freelancer's copyright in her contribution. If there is demand for a freelance article standing alone or in a new collection, the Copyright Act allows the freelancer to benefit from that demand; after authorizing initial publication, the freelancer may also sell the article to others. It would scarcely "preserve the author's copyright in a contribution" as contemplated by Congress, H. R. Rep. 122, if a newspaper or magazine publisher were permitted to reproduce or distribute copies of the author's contribution in isolation or within new collective works. See Gordon, Fine–Tuning *Tasini*: Privileges of Electronic Distribution and Reproduction, 66 Brooklyn L. Rev. 473, 484 (2000).

III

In the instant case, the Authors wrote several Articles and gave the Print Publishers permission to publish the Articles in certain newspapers and magazines. It is undisputed that the Authors hold copyrights and, therefore, exclusive rights in the Articles. It is clear, moreover, that the Print and Electronic Publishers have exercised at least some rights that § 106 initially assigns exclusively to the Authors: LEXIS/NEXIS' central discs and UMI's CD–ROMs "reproduce ... copies" of the Articles, § 106(1); UMI, by selling those CD–ROMs, and LEXIS/NEXIS, by selling copies of the Articles through the NEXIS Database, "distribute copies" of the Articles "to the public by sale," § 106(3); and the Print Publishers, through contracts licensing the production of copies in the Databases, "authorize" reproduction and distribution of the Articles, § 106.[8]

Against the Authors' charge of infringement, the Publishers do not here contend the Authors entered into an agreement authorizing reproduction of the Articles in the Databases.... Instead, the Publishers rest entirely on the privilege described in § 201(c). Each discrete edition of the periodicals in which the Articles appeared is a "collective work," the Publishers agree. They contend, however, that reproduction and distribution of each Article by the Databases lie within the "privilege of reproducing and distributing the [Articles] as part of ... [a] revision of that collective work," § 201(c). The Publishers' encompassing construction of the § 201(c) privilege is unacceptable, we conclude, for it would diminish the Authors' exclusive rights in the Articles.

In determining whether the Articles have been reproduced and distributed "as part of" a "revision" of the collective works in issue, we focus on the Articles as presented to, and perceptible by, the user of the Databases. See § 102 (copyright protection subsists in original works fixed in any medium "from which they can be perceived, reproduced, or otherwise

---

8. Satisfied that the Publishers exercised rights § 106 initially assigns exclusively to the Author, we need resolve no more on that score. Thus, we do not reach an issue the Register of Copyrights has argued vigorously. The Register maintains that the Data- bases publicly "display" the Articles, § 106(5); because § 201(c) does not privilege "display," the Register urges, the § 201(c) privilege does not shield the Databases. See Peters Letter E182–E183.

communicated"); see also § 101 (definitions of "copies" and "fixed"); Haemmerli, Commentary: *Tasini v. New York Times Co.*, 22 Colum.-VLA. J. L. & Arts 129, 142–143 (1998). In this case, the three Databases present articles to users clear of the *context* provided either by the original periodical editions or by any revision of those editions. The Databases first prompt users to search the universe of their contents: thousands or millions of files containing individual articles from thousands of collective works (*i.e.,* editions), either in one series (the Times, in NYTO) or in scores of series (the sundry titles in NEXIS and GPO). When the user conducts a search, each article appears as a separate item within the search result. In NEXIS and NYTO, an article appears to a user without the graphics, formatting, or other articles with which the article was initially published. In GPO, the article appears with the other materials published on the same page or pages, but without any material published on other pages of the original periodical. In either circumstance, we cannot see how the Database perceptibly reproduces and distributes the article "as part of 'either the original edition' or a 'revision' of that edition."

One might view the articles as parts of a new compendium—namely, the entirety of works in the Database. In that compendium, each edition of each periodical represents only a miniscule fraction of the ever-expanding Database. The Database no more constitutes a "revision" of each constituent edition than a 400–page novel quoting a sonnet in passing would represent a "revision" of that poem. "Revision" denotes a new "version," and a version is, in this setting, a "distinct form of something regarded by its creators or others as one work." Webster's Third New International Dictionary 1944, 2545 (1976). The massive whole of the Database is not recognizable as a new version of its every small part.

Alternatively, one could view the Articles in the Databases "as part of" no larger work at all, but simply as individual articles presented individually. That each article bears marks of its origin in a particular periodical (less vivid marks in NEXIS and NYTO, more vivid marks in GPO) suggests the article was *previously* part of that periodical. But the markings do not mean the article is *currently* reproduced or distributed as part of the periodical. The Databases' reproduction and distribution of individual Articles—simply *as individual Articles*—would invade the core of the Authors' exclusive rights under § 106.

The Publishers press an analogy between the Databases, on the one hand, and microfilm and microfiche, on the other. We find the analogy wanting. Microforms typically contain continuous photographic reproductions of a periodical in the medium of miniaturized film. Accordingly, articles appear on the microforms, writ very small, in precisely the position in which the articles appeared in the newspaper. The Times, for example, printed the beginning of Blakely's "Remembering Jane" Article on page 26 of the Magazine in the September 23, 1990, edition; the microfilm version of the Times reproduces that same Article on film in the very same position, within a film reproduction of the entire Magazine, in turn within a reproduction of the entire September 23, 1990, edition. True, the microfilm roll contains multiple editions, and the microfilm user can adjust the machine lens to focus only on the Article, to the exclusion of surrounding material. Nonetheless, the user first encounters the Article in context. In the Databases, by contrast, the Articles appear disconnected from their original context.... In short, unlike microforms, the Databases do not perceptibly reproduce articles as part of the collective work to which the author contributed or as part of any "revision" thereof.

Invoking the concept of "media neutrality," the Publishers urge that the "transfer of a work between media" does not "alter the character of" that work for copyright purposes. Brief for Petitioners 23. That is indeed true. See 17 U.S.C. § 102(a) (copyright protection subsists in original works "fixed in any tangible medium of expression"). But unlike the conversion of newsprint to microfilm, the transfer of articles to the Databases does not represent a mere conversion of intact periodicals (or revisions of periodicals) from one medium to another. The Databases offer users individual articles, not intact periodicals. In this case, media neutrality should protect the Authors' rights in the individual Articles to the extent those Articles are now presented individually, outside the collective work context, within the Databases' new media.[11] ...

IV

The Publishers warn that a ruling for the Authors will have "devastating" consequences. The Databases, the Publishers note, provide easy access to complete newspaper texts going back decades. A ruling for the Authors, the Publishers suggest, will punch gaping holes in the electronic record of history. The Publishers' concerns are echoed by several historians, see Brief for Ken Burns et al. as Amici Curiae, but discounted by several other historians, see Brief for Ellen Schrecker et al. as Amici Curiae; Brief for Authors' Guild, Jacques Barzun et al. as Amici Curiae.

Notwithstanding the dire predictions from some quarters, it hardly follows from today's decision that an injunction against the inclusion of these Articles in the Databases (much less all freelance articles in any databases) must issue. See 17 U.S.C. § 502(a) (court "may" enjoin infringement); *Campbell v. Acuff–Rose Music, Inc.*, 510 U.S. 569, 578, n. 10 (1994) (goals of copyright law are "not always best served by automatically granting injunctive relief"). The parties (Authors and Publishers) may enter into an agreement allowing continued electronic reproduction of the Authors' works; they, and if necessary the courts and Congress, may draw on numerous models for distributing copyrighted works and remunerating authors for their distribution. See, e.g., 17 U.S.C. § 118(b); *Broadcast Music, Inc. v. Columbia Broadcasting System, Inc.*, 441 U.S. 1, 4–6, 10–12 (1979) (recounting history of blanket music licensing regimes and consent decrees governing their operation).[13] In any event, speculation about future

---

11. ... [I]t bears reminder here and throughout that these Publishers and all others can protect their interests by private contractual arrangement.

13. Courts in other nations, applying their domestic copyright laws, have also concluded that Internet or CD–ROM reproduction and distribution of freelancers' works

harms is no basis for this Court to shrink authorial rights Congress established in § 201(c). Agreeing with the Court of Appeals that the Publishers are liable for infringement, we leave remedial issues open for initial airing and decision in the District Court.

. . . .

It is so ordered.

■ JUSTICE STEVENS, with whom JUSTICE BREYER joins, dissenting.

. . . .

. . . Because I do not think it is at all obvious that the decision the majority reaches today is a result clearly intended by the 1976 Congress, I disagree with the Court's conclusion that a ruling in petitioners' favor would "shrink authorial rights" that "*Congress* [has] established."

II

. . . Like the majority, I believe that the crucial inquiry is whether the article appears within the "context" of the original collective work. But this question simply raises the further issue of precisely how much "context" is enough.

The record indicates that what is sent from the New York Times to the Electronic Databases (with the exception of General Periodicals on Disc (GPO)) is simply a collection of ASCII text files representing the editorial content of the New York Times for a particular day. Each individual ASCII file contains the text of a single article as well as additional coding intended to help readers identify the context in which the article originally appeared and to facilitate database searches. Thus, for example, to the original text of an article, the New York Times adds information on the article's "headline, byline and title," "the section of the paper in which the article had originally appeared," and "the page in the paper or periodical on which the article had first appeared."

I see no compelling reason why a collection of files corresponding to a single edition of the New York Times, standing alone, cannot constitute a "revision" of that day's New York Times. It might be argued, as respondents appear to do, that the presentation of each article within its own

---

violate the copyrights of freelancers. See, *e.g.*, *Union Syndicale des Journalistes Franais* v. *SDV Plurimdia* (T.G.I., Strasbourg, Fr., Feb. 3, 1998), in Lodging of International Federation of Journalists (IFJ) as *Amicus Curiae*; S. C. R. L. *Central Station* v. *Association Generale des Journalistes Professionnels de Belgique* (CA, Brussels, Belg., 9e ch., Oct. 28, 1997), transl. and ed. in *22 Colum.-VLA J. L. & Arts 195 (1998); Heg* v. *De Volskrant B. V.* (Dist. Ct., Amsterdam, Neth., Sept. 24, 1997),

transl. and ed. in *22 Colum.-VLA J. L. & Arts, at 181.* After the French *Plurimdia* decision, the journalists' union and the newspaper-defendant entered into an agreement compensating authors for the continued electronic reproduction of their works. See *FR3* v. *Syndicats de Journalistes* (CA, Colmar, Sept. 15, 1998), in Lodging of IFJ as Amicus Curiae. In Norway, it has been reported, a similar agreement was reached. See Brief for IFJ as Amicus Curiae 18.

electronic file makes it impossible to claim that the collection of files as a whole amounts to a "revision." But the conversion of the text of the overall collective work into separate electronic files should not, by itself, decide the question. After all, one of the hallmarks of copyright policy, as the majority recognizes, is the principle of media neutrality.

No one doubts that the New York Times has the right to reprint its issues in Braille, in a foreign language, or in microform, even though such revisions might look and feel quite different from the original. Such differences, however, would largely result from the different medium being employed. Similarly, the decision to convert the single collective work newspaper into a collection of individual ASCII files can be explained as little more than a decision that reflects the different nature of the electronic medium. . . .

. . . I think that a proper respect for media neutrality suggests that the New York Times, reproduced as a collection of individual ASCII files, should be treated as a "revision" of the original edition, as long as each article explicitly refers to the original collective work and as long as substantially the rest of the collective work is, at the same time, readily accessible to the reader of the individual file. In this case, no one disputes that the first pieces of information a user sees when looking at an individual ASCII article file are the name of the publication in which the article appeared, the edition of that publication, and the location of the article within that edition. . . .

In addition to the labels, the batch of electronic files contains the entire editorial content of the original edition of the New York Times for that day. That is, while I might agree that a single article, standing alone, even when coded with identifying information (*e.g.*, publication, edition date, headline, etc.), should not be characterized as a "part of" a larger collective work, I would not say the same about an individual article existing as "part of" a collection of articles *containing all the editorial content of that day's New York Times*. This is all the more true because . . . it is the Print Publishers' *selection* process, the editorial process by which the staff of the New York Times, for example, decides which articles will be included in "All the News That's Fit to Print," that is the most important creative element they contribute to the collective works they publish. While such superficial features as page placement and column width are lost in ASCII format, the Print Publishers' all-important editorial selection is wholly preserved in the collection of individual article-files sent to the Electronic Databases.

. . .

It is true that, once the revision of the October 31, 2000, New York Times is surrounded by the additional content, it can be conceptualized as existing as part of an even larger collective work (*e.g.*, the entire NEXIS database). The question then becomes whether this ability to conceive of a revision of a collective work as existing within a larger "collective work" changes the status of the original revision. Section 201(c)'s requirement that the article be published only as "part of . . . any revision of *that collective work*" does not compel any particular answer to that question. A microfilm of the New York Times for October 31, 2000, does not cease to be a revision of that individual collective work simply because it is stored on the same roll of film as other editions of the Times or on a library shelf containing hundreds of other microfilm periodicals. Nor does § 201(c) compel the counterintuitive conclusion that the microfilm version of the Times would cease to be a revision simply because its publishers might choose to sell it on rolls of film that contained a year's editions of both the New York Times *and* the Herald–Tribune. Similarly, the placement of our hypothetical electronic revision of the October 31, 2000, New York Times within a larger electronic database does nothing to alter either the nature of our original electronic revision or the relationship between that revision and the individual articles that exist as "part of" it.

. . .

. . . [I]n resolving ambiguities in the relevant text of the statute, we should be mindful of the policies underlying copyright law.

Macaulay wrote that copyright is "a tax on readers for the purpose of giving a bounty to writers." T. Macaulay, Speeches on Copyright 11 (A. Thorndike ed. 1915) That tax restricts the dissemination of writings, but only insofar as necessary to encourage their production, the bounty's basic objective. See U.S. Const., Art. I, § 8, cl. 8. In other words, "the primary purpose of copyright is not to reward the author, but is rather to secure 'the general benefits derived by the public from the labors of authors.' " The majority's decision today unnecessarily subverts this fundamental goal of copyright law in favor of a narrow focus on "authorial rights." Although the desire to protect such rights is certainly a laudable sentiment, copyright law demands that "private motivation must ultimately serve the cause of promoting *broad public availability* of literature, music, and the other arts." *Twentieth Century Music Corp. v. Aiken*, 422 U.S. 151, 156 (1975) (emphasis added).

The majority discounts the effect its decision will have on the availability of comprehensive digital databases, but I am not as confident. As petitioners' amici have persuasively argued, the difficulties of locating individual freelance authors and the potential of exposure to statutory damages may well have the effect of forcing electronic archives to purge freelance pieces from their databases. "The omission of these materials from electronic collections, for any reason on a large scale or even an occasional basis, undermines the principal benefits that electronic archives offer historians—efficiency, accuracy and comprehensiveness." Brief for Ken Burns et al. as Amici Curiae 13.

. . .

Nor is it clear that [authors] will gain any prospective benefits from a victory in this case. As counsel for petitioners represented at oral argument, since 1995, the New York Times has required freelance authors to grant the Times "electronic rights" to articles. And the inclusion of such a term has had *no effect* on the compensation authors receive. This is understandable because, even if one accepts the majority's characterization of the Electronic Databases as collections of freestanding articles, demand for databases like NEXIS probably does not reflect a "demand for a freelance article standing alone," to which the publishers are greedily helping themselves. Cf. *Ryan v. Carl Corp.*, 23 F. Supp. 2d 1146, 1150–1151 (N.D.Cal.1998) ("The value added by the publisher to a reproduced article is significant").

Instead, it seems far more likely that demand for the Electronic Databases reflects demand for a product that will provide a user with the means to quickly search through scores of complete periodicals....

. . .

Users ... do not go to NEXIS because it contains a score of individual articles by Jonathan Tasini.[20] Rather, they go to NEXIS because it contains a comprehensive and easily searchable collection of (intact) periodicals.

... I would reverse the judgment of the Court of Appeals. The majority is correct that we cannot know in advance the effects of today's decision on the comprehensiveness of electronic databases. We can be fairly certain, however, that it will provide little, if any, benefit to either authors or readers.

QUESTIONS

1. In light of the Court's decision, what would you advise a magazine client regarding electronic republication of articles for which your client has not explicitly obtained electronic rights? Has the Court foreclosed all electronic republication under sec. 201(c)?

2. Assume that you represent the National Geographic Mazagine, which has proposed that 50 years of issues are to be placed onto CD–ROMs for sale to the public. The pages of the magazine are stored on the CD–ROM in such a fashion as to preserve their precise appearance, so that the user will see the exact text, photographs and advertisements in precisely the configuration in which they appeared in the original hardcopy issues. The CD–

---

20. Even assuming, as the majority does, see *ante*, at 12, n. 6, that the existence of databases like NEXIS may have some adverse effect on the market for stand-alone compilations of authors' contributions to collective works, I fail to see how, on that basis, electronic databases are any different from microform. With respect to effects on the market for stand-alone works, the only difference between the two products is the speed with which digital technology allows NEXIS users to retrieve the desired data. But the 1976 Act was not intended to bar the use of every conceivable innovation in technology that might " 'give[] publishers [new] opportu-nities to exploit authors' works.' " *Ibid.* Copyright law is not an insurance policy for authors, but a carefully struck balance between the need to create incentives for authorship and the interests of society in the broad accessibility of ideas. See U.S. Const., Art. I, § 8, cl. 8 (in order to promote production, Congress should allow authors and inventors to enjoy "exclusive Rights," but only "for *limited* Times" (emphasis added)); see also *supra*, at 15. The majority's focus on authorial incentive comes at the expense of the equally important (at least from the perspective of copyright policy) public interest....

ROMs also contain a program that allows the user to search for articles and photographs by subject matter, author, date, etc. The articles can be printed out, but they cannot be disengaged on the monitor screen from the surrounding material. A single CD–ROM contains many years of issues. On behalf of National Geographic, do you believe that you are free to use in the above-described manner photographs submitted for past issues (without express provision regarding copyright) by free-lance photographers? See *Greenberg v. National Geographic Soc'y*, 244 F.3d 1267 (11th Cir. 2001).

3. Compare the *Tasini* dissenters' concern that a victory for authors would hobble "history," with the *Random House v. Rosetta Books* court's determination that authors' retention of their electronic publishing rights would not foster "antiprogressive incentives." Who has the better of the argument? Why?

COPYRIGHT TRANSFER "BY OPERATION OF LAW"

What does a transfer of ownership "by operation of law," as contemplated in §§ 201(d) and 204(a), encompass? Can a copyright be the subject of an exercise of eminent domain? Section 201(e) would appear to preclude that result. On the other hand, that same section explicitly contemplates transfers of copyright as part of a bankruptcy sale or reorganization. Section 201(d) explicitly accommodates transfers of the decedent's copyright under state intestacy rules. What, if any, role in designating copyright ownership may state law play when the initial copyright holder is alive? May state community property laws step in to enforce a sharing of the copyright, or would application of such laws contravene § 201(e)?

A California appellate court, in deciding *In re Marriage of Susan M. & Frederick L. Worth,* 241 Cal.Rptr. 135, 195 Cal.App.3d 768 (1st Dist.1987), held that copyrights in works written during the marriage are community property; that § 201(d)(1) accommodates transfer of the copyright "by operation of law" from the husband, in whom the copyright initially vested, to the community; and that the federal copyright act does not preempt the application of state community property laws. The consequences of this result may be quite broad. If copyrights are community property, then a former (or, indeed, a present) spouse is entitled not merely to half of any royalties the community's copyrighted works may earn; the spouse is also, as a joint owner, as fully entitled as is the author to license or assign rights in the work, without first securing the author's agreement to the alienation of the rights under copyright. While the licensing spouse must account to the other co-owner (i.e., the author) for sums earned through the grant of rights, absent written agreement to the contrary the author has no independent right to veto or control the terms of the grant.

More recently, in a community-property dispute arising in Louisiana, the Court of Appeals for the Fifth Circuit stated that "we do not necessarily disapprove" of the decision in the *Worth* case—although it based its own decision on somewhat different and narrower grounds. In *Rodrigue v. Rodrigue*, 218 F.3d 432 (5th Cir. 2000), an artist who had been married for

27 years encountered a claim by his wife after their divorce that she was joint owner not only of the copyrights in works produced by him during the marriage but also of his post-divorce works that incorporated certain images (a blue dog) he had created during the marriage. She sought, among other relief, an accounting of income from the derivative works created by his continued use of those images after the divorce. Although the district court ruled for the husband, because an involuntary transfer to the wife would conflict with the ownership rules of the federal Copyright Act, the Court of Appeals reversed. It stated that it was not necessary to go as far as did the court in *Worth*, which actually divested the husband of half his copyright interest. Rather, the court examined the pertinent Louisiana community property law, which divided ownership into a number of components including the right to transfer or encumber and the right to enjoy the economic fruits. It held that the author-spouse consistent with section 201(a) would continue to hold the copyright, i.e., the exclusive rights in section 106 and the right to transfer them, but that his wife was to share equally in the "earnings and profits" from the copyrighted work (and derivative works based thereon) during and after the marriage. Is this result consistent with the ownership provisions of the Copyright Act, especially section 201(e)? For a more detailed discussion of the *Rodrigue* case, see Chapter 9C, *infra*.

Although a transfer of copyright divests the transferor of what might be called legal title, situations have arisen in which the transferor claims to continue to have "beneficial ownership." The 1976 Copyright Act, in § 501(b), gives explicit recognition to the concept of beneficial ownership, and gives such owner the right to sue for infringement: "The legal or beneficial owner of an exclusive right under a copyright is entitled ... to institute an action for any infringement of that particular right committed while he or she is the owner of it." The following case illustrates the most common kind of beneficial ownership; how far the concept goes beyond this core example is difficult to say.

Fantasy, Inc. v. Fogerty, 654 F.Supp. 1129 (N.D.Cal.1987): John Fogerty in 1970 wrote the song "Run Through the Jungle" ("Jungle") and granted exclusive rights in the copyright to plaintiff's predecessors, Cireco Music and Galaxy Records. In return, Fogerty was to receive a sales percentage and other royalties. In 1984, Fogerty wrote the song "The Old Man Down the Road" ("Old Man") and authorized Warner Bros. Records to make recordings of his performance of that song. Believing that the music of Old Man was essentially the same as that of Jungle, Fantasy sued for copyright infringement. Warner—which admitted that the plaintiff was the "legal owner" of the Jungle copyright—argued that Fogerty was a "beneficial owner" and should be treated as a co-owner who thus cannot infringe.

The court agreed with the proposition that one joint copyright owner cannot sue his co-owner for infringement. It went on to define a "beneficial owner" as including (in the language of the House Report) "an author who had parted with legal title to the copyright in exchange for percentage royalties based on sales or license fees." A beneficial owner may bring an infringement action under § 501(b) to protect his economic interest in the copyright from being diluted by a wrongdoer's infringement. Plaintiff agreed that Fogerty was such a "beneficial owner."

But the court concluded that, unlike joint owners or co-owners—who have an independent right to use or license the use of the copyright and so cannot infringe—beneficial owners have given up their exclusive rights in exchange for royalties derived from the exploitation of the copyright by another. "A beneficial owner then has only an *economic interest* in the copyright ... which extends merely to the proceeds derived from *the use of the copyright by its legal owner*. Since a beneficial owner has no independent right to use or license the copyright, the beneficial owner can infringe upon the legal owner's exclusive rights. A copyright owner can infringe upon any exclusive right which he transfers or grants to another." Here, Fogerty transferred all of his exclusive rights to the plaintiff's predecessor, which became the sole owner of the copyright. "Therefore, if Fogerty's Old Man is a derivative work of Jungle, then Fogerty has exercised one of the exclusive rights that he previously granted to plaintiff [who] could sue Fogerty for copyright infringement," as it also could sue Warner, Fogerty's licensee. The court therefore denied Warner's motion for summary judgment.

QUESTIONS

1. Author writes a scientific text in 1980, and in that year he assigns the copyright to Publisher in exchange for the payment of $10,000 (paid in two installments six months apart). In the publishing agreement, Publisher promises to reconvey the copyright to Author in the event all copies of the book are sold and Publisher decides not to reprint. (As the student will learn shortly, the 1980 transfer of copyright will be terminable by Author effective in 2015.) If Author learns today that the Pirate Publishing Company is making unauthorized copies of his book, may he bring a copyright infringement action as "beneficial owner"? *See Hearn v. Meyer,* 664 F.Supp. 832 (S.D.N.Y.1987).

2. Author assigns copyright to Publisher in exchange for payment of royalties. Publisher, in need of a substantial loan, assigns the copyright (and Publisher's anticipated income therefrom) as security to Bank. It has been discovered that unauthorized copies of the book are being made and distributed. Who may sue for infringement? *See Hearst Corp. v. Stark,* 639 F.Supp. 970 (N.D.Cal.1986).

CHAPTER 4

DURATION AND RENEWAL, AND TERMINATION OF TRANSFERS

A. DURATION AND RENEWAL

1. THE POLICY DEBATE

Chafee, Reflections on the Law of Copyright, 45 Columbia Law Review 719–21, 725–27, 729–30 (1945)

a. A long or a short monopoly? Recall that our primary purpose is to benefit the author.* One's first impression is, that the longer the monopoly, the better for him. How far this is from being true was pointed out by Macaulay in 1841:[1]

[T]he evil effects of the monopoly are proportioned to the length of its duration. But the good effects for the sake of which we bear with the evil effects are by no means proportioned to the length of its duration. A monopoly of sixty years produces twice as much evil as a monopoly of thirty years, and thrice as much evil as a monopoly of twenty years. But it is by no means the fact that a posthumous monopoly of sixty years gives to an author thrice as much pleasure and thrice as strong a motive as a posthumous monopoly of twenty years. On the contrary, the difference is so small as to be hardly perceptible. We all know how faintly we are affected by the prospect of very distant advantages, even when they are advantages which we may reasonably hope that we shall ourselves enjoy. But an advantage that is to be enjoyed more than half a century after we are dead, by somebody, we know not by whom, perhaps by somebody unborn, by somebody utterly unconnected with us, is really no motive at all to action.... Considered as a boon to [authors, long posthumous duration of the copyright monopoly] is a mere nullity; but, considered as an impost on the public, it is no nullity, but a very serious and pernicious reality. I will take an example. Dr. Johnson died fifty-six years ago. If the law [prolonged the copyright for sixty years after the author's death], somebody would now have the monopoly of Dr. Johnson's works. Who that somebody would be it is impossible to say; but we may venture to guess. I guess, then, that it would have been some bookseller, who was the assign of another bookseller, who was the grandson of a third bookseller, who

---

* *But see* the excerpts at pages 17–18, *supra.*—Eds.

1. 8 Macaulay, Works (Trevelyan ed. 1879) 199–201 (hereafter cited as Works).

338

had bought the copyright from Black Frank, the Doctor's servant and residuary legatee, in 1785 or 1786. Now, would the knowledge that this copyright would exist in 1841 have been a source of gratification to Johnson? Would it have stimulated his exertions? Would it have once drawn him out of his bed before noon? Would it have once cheered him under a fit of the spleen? Would it have induced him to give us one more allegory, one more life of a poet, one more imitation of Juvenal? I firmly believe not.... Considered as a reward to him, the difference between a twenty years' term and a sixty years' term of posthumous copyright would have been nothing or next to nothing. But is the difference nothing to us? I can buy Rasselas for sixpence; I might have had to give five shillings for it. I can buy the Dictionary, the entire genuine Dictionary, for two guineas, perhaps for less; I might have had to give five or six guineas for it. Do I grudge this to a man like Dr. Johnson? Not at all. Show me that the prospect of this boon roused him to any vigorous effort, or sustained his spirits under depressing circumstances, and I am quite willing to pay the price of such an object, heavy as that price is. But what I do complain of is that my circumstances are to be worse, and Johnson's none the better; that I am to give five pounds for what to him was not worth a farthing.

. . . Plainly the kind of pecuniary bargain which the author makes with his publisher is a vital fact in determining whether a long monopoly is of value to the author or not. If the author makes a royalty agreement for the life of the copyright, then he and his family will gain, the longer it is. But if the author sells his rights for a lump sum, the only value to him from length depends on whether it enhances the price which the publisher pays. Given the speculative nature of publishing, the price is not likely to be affected by the difference between fifty-six years, let us say, and life plus fifty years. How much more would any publisher pay for the right to monopolize after fifty-six years a book brought out in 1945? As Birrell says, "The money market takes short views." A businessman remarked to J. M. Maguire that for him "fifteen years was eternity." The publisher must have always shaped his lump-sum offer according to his expectation of sales within the first few years of the copyright. That is when he makes his killing. This is probably truer today than ever, because of the rapid waning of most books and songs. Where are the Hit Parades of yesteryear? Leave out classics and lawbooks—how many books published before 1940 did lawyers read during 1944? Good publishing accounting writes off all books within three years after publication as no longer an asset. Rudy Vallee keeps *The Maine Stein Song* alive and the current motion picture *To The Victor* is drawn from a dog-story of 1898, but such resurrections are too problematical to raise the lump-sum price for a new book or song. Royalties, however, reflect the ups-and-downs of sales....

Therefore, the last part of a long copyright does no good to the author who sells all his rights at once. It really taxes the readers for the benefit of the publisher. He gets a windfall for which he paid practically nothing. A long term is desirable only if the author and his family are sure to get the benefit of the latter years. The law can accomplish this in various ways. It can require a royalty contract, at least for the latter years; or it can make rights in those years revert to the author and limit the effect of an outright sale to the early part of the copyright. The Act of 1909 attempts to use the second method. . . .

House Report

H.R. Rep. No. 94–1476, 94th Cong., 2d Sess. 133–36 (1976).

The debate over how long a copyright should last is as old as the oldest copyright statute and will doubtless continue as long as there is a copyright law. With certain exceptions, there appears to be strong support for the principle, as embodied in the bill, of a copyright term consisting of the life of the author and 50 years after his death. In particular, the authors and their representatives stressed that the adoption of a life-plus–50 term was by far their most important legislative goal in copyright law revision. The Register of Copyrights now regards a life-plus–50 term as the foundation of the entire bill.

Under the present law statutory copyright protection begins on the date of publication (or on the date of registration in unpublished form) and continues for 28 years from that date; it may be renewed for a second 28 years, making a total potential term of 56 years in all cases.[2] The principal elements of this system—a definite number of years, computed from either publication or registration, with a renewal feature—have been a part of the U.S. copyright law since the first statute in 1790. The arguments for changing this system to one based on the life of the author can be summarized as follows:

    1.   The present 56–year term is not long enough to insure an author and his dependents the fair economic benefits from his works. Life expectancy has increased substantially, and more and more authors are seeing their works fall into the public domain during their lifetimes, forcing later works to compete with their own early works in which copyright has expired.

    2.   The tremendous growth in communications media has substantially lengthened the commercial life of a great many works. A short term is particularly discriminatory against serious works of music, literature, and art, whose value may not be recognized until after many years.

    3.   Although limitations on the term of copyright are obviously necessary, too short a term harms the author without giving any substantial benefit to the public. The public frequently pays the same for works in the public domain as it does for copyrighted works, and the only result is a commercial windfall to certain users at the author's

2. Under Public Laws 87–668, 89–142, 90–141, 90–416, 91–147, 91–555, 92–170, 92–566, and 93–573, copyrights that were subsisting in their renewal term on September 19, 1962, and that were scheduled to expire before Dec. 31, 1976, have been extended to that later date, in anticipation that general revision legislation extending their terms still further will be enacted by then.

expense. In some cases the lack of copyright protection actually re-strains dissemination of the work, since publishers and other users cannot risk investing in the work unless assured of exclusive rights.

4. A system based on the life of the author would go a long way toward clearing up the confusion and uncertainty involved in the vague concept of "publication," and would provide a much simpler, clearer method for computing the term. The death of the author is a definite, determinable event, and it would be the only date that a potential user would have to worry about. All of a particular author's works, includ-ing successive revisions of them, would fall into the public domain at the same time, thus avoiding the present problems of determining a multitude of publication dates and of distinguishing "old" and "new" matter in later editions. The bill answers the problems of determining when relatively obscure authors died, by establishing a registry of death dates and a system of presumptions.

5. One of the worst features of the present copyright law is the provision for renewal of copyright. A substantial burden and expense, this unclear and highly technical requirement results in incalculable amounts of unproductive work. In a number of cases it is the cause of inadvertent and unjust loss of copyright. Under a life-plus–50 system the renewal device would be inappropriate and unnecessary.

6. Under the preemption provisions of section 301 and the single Federal system they would establish, authors will be giving up perpet-ual, unlimited exclusive common law rights in their unpublished works, including works that have been widely disseminated by means other than publication. A statutory term of life-plus–50 years is no more than a fair recompense for the loss of these perpetual rights.

7. A very large majority of the world's countries have adopted a copyright term of the life of the author and 50 years after the author's death. Since American authors are frequently protected longer in foreign countries than in the United States, the disparity in the duration of copyright has provoked considerable resentment and some proposals for retaliatory legislation. Copyrighted works move across national borders faster and more easily than virtually any other economic commodity, and with the techniques now in common use this movement has in many cases become instantaneous and effortless. The need to conform the duration of U.S. copyright to that prevalent throughout the rest of the world is increasingly pressing in order to provide certainty and simplicity in international business dealings. Even more important, a change in the basis of our copyright term would place the United States in the forefront of the international copyright community. Without this change, the possibility of future United States adherence to the Berne Copyright Union would evapo-rate, but with it would come a great and immediate improvement in our copyright relations. All of these benefits would accrue directly to American and foreign authors alike.

... A point that has concerned some educational groups arose from the possibility that, since a large majority (now about 85 percent) of all copyrighted works are not renewed, a life-plus–50 year term would tie up a substantial body of material that is probably of no commercial interest but that would be more readily available for scholarly use if free of copyright restrictions. A statistical study of renewal registrations made by the Copyright Office in 1966 supports the generalization that most material which is considered to be of continuing or potential commercial value is renewed. Of the remainder, a certain proportion is of practically no value to anyone, but there are a large number of unrenewed works that have scholarly value to historians, archivists, and specialists in a variety of fields. This consideration lay behind the proposals for retaining the renewal device or for limiting the term for unpublished or unregistered works.

It is true that today's ephemera represent tomorrow's social history, and that works of scholarly value, which are now falling into the public domain after 29 [sic] years, would be protected much longer under the bill. Balanced against this are the burdens and expenses of renewals, the near impossibility of distinguishing between types of works in fixing a statutory term, and the extremely strong case in favor of a life-plus–50 system. Moreover, it is important to realize that the bill would not restrain scholars from using any work as source material or from making "fair use" of it. . . .

SONNY BONO COPYRIGHT TERM EXTENSION ACT

In 1998, in the "Sonny Bono Copyright Term Extension Act," Congress extended the term of copyright from 50 to 70 years following the death of the author. In the case of anonymous and pseudonymous works, and works made for hire, the copyright term has increased from 75 years from publication to 95 years from publication. Congress has also added 20 years to subsisting copyrights, so that a copyright originally secured under the 1909 Copyright Act, and extended to 75 years from publication under the 1976 Act, will now endure for 95 years from publication. Which, if any, of the reasons advanced in the House Report to the 1976 Act would apply to this extension?

The term extension act provides that the additional 20–year term is to vest in the current rights holder; there is a provision for termination of transfers and recapture of that new term by the author or by the owner of the termination right (provided he or she has not previously exercised a termination right covering an earlier period of the copyright term). Thus, if the author or surviving spouse, or children, or grandchildren (or if none of these survive, the author's executor, administrator, personal representative or trustee) terminated a pre–1978 transfer of the renewal term—as thereafter extended by 19 years—and later transferred those added years to another person (typically, a publisher), that latter person will be entitled to the benefits of the proposed new 20–year extension (a windfall?), without any additional termination right by the author's heirs. Do you see any problem with this?

In an effort to ease the objections of academics and librarians to the 20–year extension, the term extension act provides that a library in a nonprofit educational institution may freely reproduce, distribute, display and perform a published work during the newly added 20 years, for purposes of preservation, scholarship, or research, provided the library has first determined that a copy of the work is not available "at a reasonable price" and that the work is not "subject to normal commercial exploitation." Is this a satisfactory accommodation of the interests of the academic and library community?

Was term extension desirable? The 1998 law delays the reception into the public domain not only of future but of pre-existing works. Because the public domain is a crucial counterpart to the copyright system—the Constitution authorizes Congress to secure copyright for "limited Times"— compelling reasons should be required to revise the 1976 Copyright Act's balance between protected and expired works. It is not clear that those reasons have been demonstrated.

The considerations favoring term extension fall into two categories: promotion of authors' rights, and promotion of U.S. interests in international trade of copyrighted works. While the latter may afford a convincing justification, the former is highly doubtful. Assess the following lines of argument.

Regarding the promotion of authors' rights, the 'incentive' rationale traditionally offered for copyright simply does not apply to extension of the term of *preexisting* works; the prior statutory incentives have been adequate to induce creation of those works, and keeping them from the public for an additional generation will only inhibit the creation of new derivative works that they might otherwise inspire. As to whether the additional 20 years of protection will create incentives for *new* works in the future, the prospect of an additional 20 years of protection commencing 50 years after the author's death (with no statutory entitlement to those 20 years for family descendants) seems too remote to impel additional authorial activity.

THE CONSTITUTIONALITY OF THE COPYRIGHT TERM EXTENSION ACT: *ELDRED v. RENO*

In January 1999, the Eldridge press, an online publisher of public domain works, filed a complaint seeking to enjoin the Attorney General from enforcing the term extension act, on the grounds that the extension violates both the First Amendment and the constitutional provision for "limited Times," particularly with respect to already-created works. The District Court dismissed the complaint, in an opinion so succinct as to suggest small regard for its contentions. The District Court rejected the First Amendment claim on the ground that the First Amendment did not extend to free use of other people's speech. It rejected the "limited Times" claim on the ground that so long as the term was limited, Congress enjoyed discretion as to its length. The Court of Appeals for the District of Columbia affirmed, 2-to-1. Eldred v. Reno, 239 F.3d 372 (D.C.Cir.2001).

The First Amendment claim fared poorly before the Court of Appeals. Citing its prior decisions, the court stated, "copyrights are categorically immune from challenges under the First Amendment." On the merits of the "limited Times" challenge, the plaintiffs sought to interpret that phrase in light of the Patent–Copyright Clause's preamble, "Congress shall have Power ... to promote the Progress of Science ..." Under this construction, Congress has power to legislate in the copyright area only so long as its enactments promote the progress of knowledge. The "limited Times" constraint makes clear, according to this argument, that Congress is to grant copyright for no more time than is necessary to supply the incentive to create works that promote knowledge. If the prior term limit furnished sufficient incentive (hard to know how one would prove this one way or the other), then any further protection is surplusage, and surplusage is not only wasteful but unconstitutional. The D.C. Circuit rejected the argument that the preamble constrains Congress's power. Even granting, arguendo, the preamble operative force, the majority found that extension of existing copyrights was consistent with Constitutional goals, because it "promotes Progress" by furnishing an incentive to preserve older works, especially "motion pictures in need of restoration" which "would otherwise disappear."

The majority also pointed out the benefits of harmonizing the U.S. term of copyright with that in force in the European Union, which had extended the term to life-plus-70 in 1993. Under the "rule of the shorter term" posed by article 7 of the Directive, an E.U. country is not obliged to grant national treatment with respect to copyright duration, if the work's term of protection in the country of origin is shorter. As a result, unless the U.S. term of protection was extended, many U.S. works would not enjoy the full duration of copyright available to domestic works in the European Union. U.S. term extension will generally, therefore, put U.S. works on an equal footing with European works. Since the balance of trade in copyrighted works between Europe and the U.S. heavily favors the U.S., term extension would benefit U.S. copyright industries.

The dissenting judge departed from the majority's analysis with respect to the constitutionality of extending the term of copyright in already-existing works. Judge Sentelle read the Preamble to the Copyright Clause as limiting Congress's power to enacting laws that promote the progress of knowledge by supplying an incentive to create. Extension of the term of copyright of pre-existing works cannot promote the progress of knowledge in this way because there is no incentive to supply to create a work that has already been created. Excerpts from the dissent follow:

> Th[e patent-copyright] clause empowers the Congress to do one thing, and one thing only. That one thing is "to promote the progress of science and useful arts." How may Congress do that? "By securing for limited times to authors and inventors the exclusive right to their

respective writings and discoveries." The clause is not an open grant of power to secure exclusive rights. It is a grant of a power to promote progress. The means by which that power is to be exercised is certainly the granting of exclusive rights—not an elastic and open-ended use of that means, but only a securing for limited times. See Stewart v. Abend, 495 U.S. 207, 228, 110 S.Ct. 1750, 109 L.Ed.2d 184 (1990) ("The copyright term is limited so that the public will not be permanently deprived of the fruits of an artist's labors."). The majority acknowledges that "if the Congress were to make copyright protection permanent, then it surely would exceed the power conferred upon it by the Copyright Clause." Maj. Op. at 10. However, there is no apparent substantive distinction between permanent protection and permanently available authority to extend originally limited protection. The Congress that can extend the protection of an existing work from 100 years to 120 years; can extend that protection from 120 years to 140; and from 140 to 200; and from 200 to 300; and in effect can accomplish precisely what the majority admits it cannot do directly. This, in my view, exceeds the proper understanding of enumerated powers ... requiring some definable stopping point.

Returning to the language of the clause itself, it is impossible that the Framers of the Constitution contemplated permanent protection, either directly obtained or attained through the guise of progressive extension of existing copyrights. The power granted by the clause again is the power "to promote the progress of science and useful arts." As stated above, Congress is empowered to accomplish this by securing for limited times exclusive rights. Extending existing copyrights is not promoting useful arts, nor is it securing exclusivity for a limited time.

The government has offered no tenable theory as to how retrospective extension can promote the useful arts. As the Supreme Court [has noted], that Congress concluded a given piece of legislation serves a constitutional purpose "does not necessarily make it so." [citation omitted] Pressed at oral argument, counsel for the government referred to keeping the promise made in the original grant of exclusivity for a limited time. The easy answer to this assertion is that Congress is not empowered to "make or keep promises" but only to do those things enumerated in Article I. The second problem with the government's assertion is that Congress made no promise to commit [sic] such an extension but only to secure the exclusive rights for the original limited period. Thirdly, the means employed by Congress here are not the securing of the exclusive rights for a limited period, but rather are a different animal altogether: the extension of exclusivity previously secured. This is not within the means authorized by the Copyright Clause, and it is not constitutional.

Here follow excerpts from the majority's response to the dissent's contentions:

Even were we to proceed as urged by ... the dissent, however, we would only review the CTEA [Copyright Term Extension Act] as we would any other exercise of a power enumerated in Article I. That is we would ask, following *McCulloch v. Maryland*, 17 U.S. 316, 421, 4 L.Ed. 579 (1819), whether the CTEA is a "necessary and proper" exercise of the power conferred upon the Congress by the Copyright Clause; assuming Judge Sentelle is correct ... about the relationship of the preamble to the rest of that Clause, this would require that the CTEA be an "appropriate" means, and "plainly adapted" to the end prescribed in the preamble, "promoting Progress of Science and useful Arts." The Congress found that extending the duration of copyrights on existing works would, among other things, give copyright holders an incentive to preserve older works, particularly motion pictures in need of restoration. See S. REP. NO. 104–315, at 12 (1996). If called upon to do so, therefore, we might well hold that the application of the CTEA to subsisting copyrights is "plainly adapted" and "appropriate" to "promoting progress." See Ladd v. Law & Technology Press, 762 F.2d 809, 812 (9th Cir.1985) (upholding the deposit requirement of the Copyright Act of 1976 as "necessary and proper" because the purpose was "to enforce contributions of desirable books to the Library of Congress").

Judge Sentelle concludes otherwise only because he sees a categorical distinction between extending the term of a subsisting copyright and extending that of a prospective copyright. This distinction is not to be found in the Constitution itself, however. The dissent identifies nothing in text or in history that suggests that a term of years for a copyright is not a "limited Time" if it may later be extended for another "limited Time." Instead, the dissent suggests that the Congress—or rather, many successive Congresses—might in effect confer a perpetual copyright by stringing together an unlimited number of "limited Times," although that clearly is not the situation before us. The temporal thrust of the CTEA is a good deal more modest: The Act matches United States copyrights to the terms of copyrights granted by the European Union, see Council Directive 93/98, art. 7, 1993 O.J. (L 290) 9; in an era of multinational publishers and instantaneous electronic transmission, harmonization in this regard has obvious practical benefits for the exploitation of copyrights. This is a powerful indication that the CTEA is a "necessary and proper" measure to meet contemporary circumstances rather than a step on the way to making copyrights perpetual; the force of that evidence is hardly diminished because, as the dissent correctly points out, the EU is not bound by the Copyright Clause of our Constitution. As for the dissent's objection that extending a subsisting copyright does nothing to "promote Progress," we think that implies a rather crabbed view of progress: Preserving access to works that would otherwise disappear—not enter the public domain but disappear—"promotes Progress" as surely as does stimulating the creation of new works.

. . .

"As the text of the Constitution makes plain, it is Congress that has been assigned the task of defining the scope of the limited monopoly that should be granted to authors or to inventors in order to give the appropriate public access to their work product;" that "task involves a difficult balance between [competing interests]" as reflected in the frequent modifications of the relevant statutes. And still more recently: "The evolution of the duration of copyright protection tellingly illustrates the difficulties Congress faces [in exercising its copyright power].... It is not our role to alter the delicate balance Congress has labored to achieve." Stewart v. Abend, 495 U.S. 207, 230, 110 S.Ct. 1750, 109 L.Ed.2d 184 (1990).

The majority and dissent thus differ in their premises as to the scope of Congress's constitutional authority to devise copyright laws. If Congress's sole power were to enact laws that supply incentives to create, then a term extension law that applies to works currently under copyright would seem vulnerable, as it cannot provide an incentive to create an already-created work. But there are several reasons to doubt whether the Preamble should be read in the way the dissent urged. First, as the majority pointed out, the progress of knowledge is not promoted only by spurring the creation of new works; fostering preservation and availability of crumbling old works also promotes knowledge. According to the Constitutional text, the progress of knowledge is promoted by "securing for limited Times to Authors the exclusive Right to their Writings"; the text does not say that the Writings must be newly-created. The Supreme Court in *Feist* held that a "Writing" must be minimally creative, but it did not say when the creativity had to occur. In fact, up until the effective date of the 1976 Act, federal copyright (with modest exceptions) applied only to already-created works, because it did not attach until publication. Under the regime from 1790–1978, then, the incentive that copyright furnished was principally one to disseminate, rather than to create, works of authorship. If one shifts focus from creation to dissemination, the objection loses much force. One can create a work only once, but one can disseminate it many times. If term extension is seen as part of a scheme to foster further communication of works of authorship by making it worthwhile to undertake the costs of making works usable and available, then the incentive rationale still holds.

2.   COPYRIGHT DURATION UNDER THE 1976 ACT, AS AMENDED IN 1998

a.   WORKS CREATED OR UNPUBLISHED AFTER 1977

§ 302.   Duration of Copyright: Works Created on or After January 1, 1978

(a) *In General*—Copyright in a work created on or after January 1, 1978, subsists from its creation and, except as provided by the following subsections, endures for a term consisting of the life of the author and 70 years after the author's death.

(b) *Joint Works*—In the case of a joint work prepared by two or more authors who did not work for hire, the copyright endures for a term consisting of the life of the last surviving author and 70 years after such last surviving author's death.

(c) *Anonymous Works, Pseudonymous Works, and Works Made for Hire*—In the case of an anonymous work, a pseudonymous work, or a work made for hire, the copyright endures for a term of 95 years from the year of its first publication, or a term of 120 years from the year of its creation, whichever expires first. . . .

(d) *Records Relating to Death of Authors*—Any person having an interest in a copyright may at any time record in the Copyright Office a statement of the date of death of the author of the copyrighted work, or a statement that the author is still living on a particular date. . . .

(e) *Presumption as to Author's Death*—After a period of 95 years from the year of first publication of a work, or a period of 120 years from the year of its creation, whichever expires first, any person who obtains from the Copyright Office a certified report that the records provided by subsection (d) disclose nothing to indicate that the author of the work is living, or died less than 70 years before, is entitled to the benefit of a presumption that the author has been dead for at least 70 years. Reliance in good faith upon this presumption shall be a complete defense to any action for infringement under this title.

§ 303. Duration of Copyright: Works Created but not Published or Copyrighted Before January 1, 1978

Copyright in a work created before January 1, 1978, but not theretofore in the public domain or copyrighted, subsists from January 1, 1978, and endures for the term provided by section 302. In no case, however, shall the term of copyright in such a work expire before December 31, 2002; and, if the work is published on or before December 31, 2002, the term of copyright shall not expire before December 31, 2047.

House Report

H.R. Rep. No. 94–1476, 94th Cong., 2d Sess. 138–39 (1976).

Theoretically, at least, the legal impact of section 303 would be far reaching. . . . Its basic purpose is to substitute statutory for common law copyright for everything now protected at common law, and to substitute reasonable time limits for the perpetual protection now available. In general, the substituted time limits are those applicable to works created after the effective date of the law; for example, an unpublished work written in 1945 whose author dies in 1980 would be protected under the statute from the effective date through [2050 (70 years after the author's death)].

A special problem under this provision is what to do with works whose ordinary statutory terms will have expired or will be nearing expiration on the effective date. The committee believes that a provision taking away subsisting common law rights and substituting statutory rights for a reasonable period is fully in harmony with the constitutional requirements of due process, but it is necessary to fix a "reasonable period" for this purpose. Section 303 provides that under no circumstances would copyright protection expire before December 31, 2002, and also attempts to encourage publication by providing [45] years more protection (through [2047]) if the work were published before the end of 2002.

QUESTIONS

1. By virtue of the renewal format under the 1909 Act, a great many copyrights terminated a mere 28 years after publication. Indeed, it was probably a contemplated benefit in the public interest thus to shorten the copyright term. Has Congress, then, provided adequate justification for extending copyright protection for almost all works created after January 1, 1978 to the life of the author plus 70 years?

2. In a trunk purchased at a flea market, you have discovered an unpublished letter written by (fictitious) Mayflower passenger Goodspeak Brown, who died in Massachusetts Bay Colony in 1650. When may you publish the letter?

Unlike the 1909 Act, which dated its 28–year and 56–year periods from the precise date of publication (and, in connection with certain unpublished works, the date of registration in the Copyright Office)—including the day and month—the 1976 Act provides, in § 305: "All terms of copyright provided by sections 302 through 304 run to the end of the calendar year in which they would otherwise expire." The purpose, as stated in the House Report, was to "make the duration of copyright much easier to compute." This was a matter of particular pertinence in determining when an application for renewal of copyright had to be filed with the Copyright Office; it is considerably less significant today, for reasons that will appear below, but it still remains of some importance.

b. 1976 ACT TREATMENT OF WORKS FIRST PUBLISHED UNDER THE 1909 ACT

RENEWAL

A distinctive feature of our copyright law since its inception until 1978 was the renewal term, which the copyright owner could secure after a relatively short initial term upon timely re-registration. The Statute of Anne of 1710 provided, for works to be published thereafter, an initial term of 14 years and a renewal term of equal length. Initial and renewal terms of 14 years were also featured in the first United States Copyright Act of 1790. In both that statute and its British antecedent, renewal was not available unless the author survived through the first copyright term. In 1831, the initial term was expanded to 28 years, and under the 1909 Act both the initial and renewal terms ran for 28 years. To secure the benefit of the renewal term, an application had to be filed within the last year of the initial term. The purposes of the renewal format will be explored presently, but it should be noted here that its effect, because of the significant proportion of copyrighted works for which renewal was not sought, was a rather short period of copyright protection for many works. While almost all copyright laws in the world were adopting a lengthy period of protection, usually measured by the life of the author plus 50 years, the United States, all but alone, retained the renewal format until 1978.

Under the 1909 Act, it was provided that the renewal term could be claimed by the author if he or she survived the initial term (or at least until the date in the 28th year when renewal was sought; the statute was altogether silent about such details). If the author had died, then the right to claim the renewal passed successively to three other statutory beneficiaries—the surviving spouse or children, or for lack of those the author's executor, or in the absence of a will the author's next of kin. Exceptions to this statutory sequence were provided for a limited number of categories of works. The details, purposes and implications of these provisions are discussed in the following study prepared in connection with the revision of the 1909 Act.

Although that act was in almost all significant respects superseded by the 1976 Act, renewal of copyright for pre–1978 works—in precisely the manner, and by precisely the same person, as provided by § 24 of the 1909 Act—remained a central feature of the 1976 Act, in § 304(a) as originally enacted. The 28–year duration of the renewal term was, however, increased to 47 years, so that timely renewal would lead to copyright protection for 75 years rather than 56. As was true under the 1909 Act, the renewal term came into being only if an application for renewal registration was filed with the Copyright Office. That feature of the law was, however, significantly changed in 1992, when Congress provided for automatic renewal of works whose first term would expire following passage of the amendment. Thus, renewal at the initiative of a copyright claimant is no longer required for pre–1978 works published in or after 1964 (but, as we shall see, *infra*, whether the renewal is automatic or voluntary still carries important consequences for, *inter alia*, ownership of renewal term rights).

Ringer, Renewal of Copyright, in Studies on Copyright (Fisher mem. ed. 1960) (Study No. 31)

. . .

The Nature and Theoretical Basis of Renewal Copyright

The renewal copyright established in the Act of 1831 and elaborated in the Act of 1909 is a unique form of property whose nature and theoretical basis are still unclear. The courts and the commentators have repeatedly characterized a renewal as a "new estate" or a "new grant" rather than a mere continuation or extension. Renewals are said to be separate from and independent of the original copyright, to be "free and clear of any rights, interests, or licenses attached to the copyright for the initial term," and to have "absolutely all of the attributes of a new work copyrighted at the time the renewal is effected." The right of renewal is considered a personal right given directly to certain named beneficiaries; it "does not follow the author's estate but . . . is derived directly from the statute." . . .

The legislative history shows that, in retaining the reversionary aspect of renewals, Congress was trying to accomplish two things:

1) If the author were still living, Congress wanted to give him an opportunity to benefit from the success of his work and to renegotiate disadvantageous bargains. It has often been said that the renewal provision was based on "the familiar imprudence of authors in commercial matters." While superficially logical, there is nothing in the legislative history to support this supposition. There is more evidence of a Congressional recognition that author-publisher contracts must frequently be made at a time when the value of the work is unknown or conjectural and the author (regardless of his business ability) is necessarily in a poor bargaining position.

2) If the author were dead, Congress wanted to insure that his "dependent relatives" would receive the benefits of the renewal, regardless of any agreements the author had entered into.

To attain these results Congress had to depart from ordinary concepts of property in two important respects:

1) *Reversion.* The statute had to break the continuity of title at the end of the first term and provide for a reversion of ownership to the author, if living.

2) *Statutory designation of beneficiaries.* To make sure that the renewal benefits went to "those naturally dependent upon the deceased author's bounty," something more than a reversion to the author's "executors, administrators, or heirs" had to be provided. If the renewal reverted to the author's estate, it was entirely possible that legatees and creditors might gain the benefits at the expense of the author's family and dependents. Apparently in a deliberate effort to avoid this result, Congress set up a schedule of successive classes of persons who were entitled to take the renewal as "a new personal grant of a right."

These features made renewals so unusual that, immediately after the 1909 Act came into effect, there was uncertainty whether this could really be what Congress intended. Within a few years, however, it had been firmly established that a proprietor or assignee, as such, had no right in a renewal copyright, that the right was a personal one, and that a renewal is not "really and truly an extension to the author, his assigns, executors, and administrators, but a new grant to the author or others enumerated."

Acceptance of these basic principles still left open some important questions:

1) *Is a future copyright assignable?* Assuming that assignment of the first term does not carry with it the renewal copyright, can the author or

any other statutory beneficiary make a valid separate assignment of his potential renewal copyright before he has secured it? This turned out to be a very close question, which the Supreme Court finally settled in favor of alienability.[135]

2) *Whom does the executor represent?* The executor is different from the author's widow, children, and next of kin, since he obviously cannot take the renewal for his own personal benefit. Does he take it as representative of (1) the author, (2) the corpus of the author's estate, or (3) the legatees? The cases have now established that the executor represents neither the author[136] nor the author's estate,[137] but that he takes the renewal as personal representative or trustee of the author's legatees; since the renewal does not become part of the author's estate, an assignment by the author of his renewal rights would be invalidated at the author's death, and the executor would take the renewal for the benefit of the author's legatees rather than his assignees. . . .

It is now well-established that, even though the author can assign away his own renewal expectancy, he cannot cut off, defeat, or diminish the independent statutory renewal rights of his widow and children or next of kin. . . . It is clear that the rights of the author's assignees are dependent on his survival and fail if he dies before the renewal year.

At the same time it is settled that the widow, children, and next of kin can also assign their own rights in the renewal expectancy, no matter how contingent or fragmentary. They can join the author in his assignment or execute an independent transfer, although in either case a separate consideration for each assignor would probably be needed for validity.

The renewal assignee stands in the shoes of his assignor, and takes the renewal only if the assignor is the beneficiary entitled under the statute. . . .

THE STATUTORY RENEWAL PROVISIONS

As originally drafted in the 1976 Copyright Act, § 304(a) provided that the copyright in a work which was in its initial term of protection on January 1, 1978 would last for only 28 years, unless an application for renewal was made to and registered by the Copyright Office in the 28th year. This was true under the 1909 Act as well; the only change from the earlier law, and it was quite significant, was that if renewal was secured in a timely manner, the renewal term was to last not for 28 years but for 47 years. As a result of the 1998 Sonny Bono Act, the renewal term now lasts for 67 years. The same categories of persons entitled to own the renewal under the 1909 Act were so entitled under the 1976 Act.

135. *Fred Fisher Music Co. v. Witmark & Sons*, 318 U.S. 643 (1943).

136. *Fox Film Corp. v. Knowles*, 261 U.S. 326 (1923).

137. *Miller Music Corp. v. Charles N. Daniels, Inc.*, 158 F.Supp. 188 (1957), *aff'd mem.*, 265 F.2d 925 (1959), *aff'd*, 362 U.S. 373, 125 U.S.P.Q. 147 (1960).

Section 304(b) as originally enacted provided, simply, that works already in their renewal term in 1977 would have that term automatically extended from 28 years to 47 years. (Beginning in 1962, Congress—in anticipation of imminent copyright reform that would predictably extend the term of copyright—in a series of "interim renewal extension" laws prolonged the life of renewal copyrights that would have otherwise expired; thus, when the new law came into effect in 1978, a work copyrighted in 1906 and renewed in 1934 would still have been in its renewal term, so that its new overall 75–year copyright would last through 1981.)

In the House Report that accompanied the original §§ 304(a) and (b), it was stated: "The arguments in favor of lengthening the duration of copyright apply to subsisting as well as future copyrights. The bill's basic approach is to increase the present 56–year term to 75 years in the case of copyrights subsisting in both their first and their renewal terms." Do you agree with the proposition stated in the first quoted sentence? If Congress was intent on extending the life of existing copyrights, why did it choose not to apply the "life plus 50" measure to such works rather than retain the cumbersome and unique renewal format?

For all of their importance and complexity, the renewal provisions of both the 1909 and 1976 Acts have been the subject of infrequent judicial interpretation. Among the most significant decisions, already mentioned in the Ringer study, *supra,* was *Fred Fisher Music Co. v. M. Witmark & Sons,* 318 U.S. 643 (1943), in which the Supreme Court held—despite the obvious purpose of the renewal format to protect the author against unremunerative copyright transfers during the initial term—that an author could validly assign in the initial term of copyright his or her interest in the renewal term. (The student should consider how much money the author would likely receive for assignment of the renewal interest, as distinguished from payment by the assignee for the right to market the work for the balance of the initial 28–year term, particularly when the assignment is made early in the initial term.)

The Court of Appeals for the Second Circuit was confronted with the question whether the songwriter of the popular song, "Desafinado," which contributed to the initial popularity of the bossa nova in the United States, had effectively assigned his renewal interest in the song. In 1958 and 1960, Antonio Carlos Jobim—in a contract written in Portuguese in Brazil—assigned to a music publisher (Arapua) the United States copyright in five songs, one of which was "Desafinado." Through successive assignments from Arapua, the copyright came into the hands of Hollis (and its affiliate Songways). In 1987 and 1988, apparently believing that he was entitled to the renewal copyright in the U.S., Jobim purported to assign the renewal to Corcovado. Because Hollis continued to collect royalties and claim copyright at the start of the renewal term, Corcovado brought an action for copyright infringement. *Corcovado Music Corp. v. Hollis Music, Inc.,* 981 F.2d 679 (2d Cir.1993).

The court of appeals concluded that despite the 1958 Desafinado contract's specification that all litigation thereunder should be in Brazil, this was a copyright infringement action rather than one for breach of contract, all of the parties to the action were in New York so that New York was a proper forum, and that U.S. law rather than the law of Brazil should be used in construing Jobim's grant of copyright in order to determine whether it embraced the renewal term. There were slight differences in the parties' translation of the Portuguese; the defendant's interpretation was: "The Authors assign and transfer to the Publisher, the full property, for the exercise of the corresponding rights in all the countries of the world, of their ownership rights in the musical composition . . . in the form, scope and application which they hold by virtue of the laws and treaties in force and those which become effective hereinafter."

The Court of Appeals for the Second Circuit, after reciting the author-protective purposes of the renewal provisions of the 1909 Copyright Act, stated that "there is a strong presumption against the conveyance of renewal rights: 'In the absence of language which expressly grants rights in 'renewals of copyright' or 'extensions of copyright' the courts are hesitant to conclude that a transfer of copyright (even if it includes a grant of 'all right, title and interest') is intended to include a transfer with 'respect to the renewal expectancy.' " The court noted that in *Fisher v. Witmark,* the Supreme Court had held that "an assignment by the author of his 'copyright' in general terms did not include conveyance of his renewal interest." The court of appeals concluded: "The presumption against conveyance of renewal rights serves the congressional purpose of protecting authors' entitlement to receive new rights in the 28th year of the original term. In the present case, Jobim's 1958 and 1960 contracts with Arapua were silent as to renewal rights. Accordingly, under federal copyright law Jobim retained renewal rights to the Five Songs and could validly assign them to Corcovado." The court distinguished an earlier case in which the author had agreed to convey his "exclusive right . . . forever," and not to convey it "at any time hereafter." Would a grant of the "perpetual" right to distribute a copyrighted work, made during the initial term of copyright, also transfer that right during the renewal term? *See P.C. Films Corp. v. Turner Entertainment Co.,* 138 F.3d 453 (2d Cir.1998), for an affirmative answer. And what of a grant of all "existing or future" interest in the copyright, along with rights "hereafter arising or acquired"? See Hayes v. Carlin America, Inc., 2001 WL 1242270 (S.D.N.Y.2001).

Of course, an author who purports to assign the renewal term can assign only the interest that he himself possesses—which is a right to own the renewal interest only if the author survives until the renewal term vests (at some unspecified point in the 28th year of the initial term.) Absent such survival, the 1909 Act provided for succession to renewal ownership by the surviving spouse and children—who would take in preference to the assignee, who took only a conditional interest.

In a case decided under § 304(a) as originally written in the 1976 Copyright Act, *Saroyan v. William Saroyan Found.,* 675 F.Supp. 843 (S.D.N.Y.1987), it was held that the author's children, who would otherwise be entitled to succeed to the renewal term, would not be foreclosed from doing so by virtue of their long-term estrangement from their author-father. The noted author William Saroyan wrote and copyrighted in 1958 a play titled The Cave Dwellers. On his death in 1981, he left a will which purported to give "all copyrights" to the William Saroyan Foundation, which was to maintain his writings and disburse the income therefrom to charitable and educational entities. The court found in the statute a "non-discretionary order of renewal rights" that gave priority to the surviving children over persons named in an author's will, and it rejected the defendant's argument that its charitable purposes should prevail over the private interests of the children (especially in view of their "stormy relationship" with their father). It quoted from earlier authorities to the effect that "[e]ach of these named classes is separated in the statute by a condition precedent to the passing of renewal rights, namely, that the persons named in the preceding class be deceased," and that "[a]n author in effect is required by statutory mandate to leave the right to obtain renewals to his widow and children if he has any." The court concluded that "the bequest of renewal rights to the Foundation was without effect because the renewal rights never became part of the estate.... This result is fortified by court decisions holding that widows who re-marry and illegitimate children meet the statutory definition, thereby precluding executors' renewal rights."

Finally, one must take note of the somewhat odd segment of the renewal provisions that departs from the standard four-tier allocation of renewal rights (i.e., author if alive, then widow, widower or children, etc.) in connection with a limited number of works, the most important being works made for hire and posthumous works. (As was usual with the 1909 Act, neither of those important terms was defined.) As to those works, the renewal term is owned by the then copyright owner, and not by the author's family, legatee, or next of kin. *See Epoch Producing Corp. v. Killiam Shows, Inc.,* 522 F.2d 737 (2d Cir.1975); *Bartok v. Boosey & Hawkes, Inc.,* 523 F.2d 941 (2d Cir.1975).

The present § 304(a) carries over from § 24 of the 1909 Act the provision for renewal of "posthumous works" by the then copyright owner, but the act continues to have no definition of that phrase. The pertinent legislative history, however, demonstrates that the drafters have endorsed the narrow interpretation given to that phrase in *Bartok v. Boosey & Hawkes, Inc.,* 523 F.2d 941 (2d Cir.1975), where the great modern composer died before his composition, Concerto for Orchestra, was published. *See* H.R. Rep. No. 94–1476, 94th Cong., 2d Sess. 139–40 (1976): "[T]he Committee intends that the reference to a 'posthumous work' in this section has the meaning given to it in [the *Bartok* case]—one as to which no copyright assignment or other contract for exploitation of the work has occurred during an author's lifetime, rather than one which is simply first published after the author's death."

The student may appropriately wonder why Congress chose to make several exceptions—including works for hire and posthumous works—to the generally prevailing principle of "author renewal." The sad truth is that the exceptions were a product of nothing more than inadvertent and mangled draftsmanship in the shaping of the 1909 Act, and offer up no plausible rationale. The depressing tale is recounted in Ringer, *Renewal of Copyright,* in Studies on Copyright (Study No. 31, 1960).

QUESTIONS

1. Assuming that works were first published and copyrighted in the following years, when did or will copyright terminate? 1920, 1925, 1950, 1970, 2000. What further facts, if any, would you have to know to answer this question?

2. Author writes a novel in 1975, and in 1976 he assigns "all of my copyright interest" to Publisher for $10,000. Publisher prints and distributes the book and secures copyright in its own name, in 1976. In the year 2004, both Author and Publisher apply for renewal of the copyright. Whose claim should prevail? (Note that under the 1992 amendments to § 304—see the note immediately below—it will not be necessary for either the Author or the Publisher to take the initiative to apply for renewal; renewal will be automatic. But the issue of ownership will remain.)

3. Assume instead that Author had in 1976 conveyed "both the initial and renewal terms of copyright" to Publisher, which published and copyrighted the work that year. If Author is alive throughout the year 2004, who is entitled to the enjoyment of the renewal term? If Author dies before the year 2004, leaving a widow and two children (who are alive in 2004), who is entitled to the enjoyment of the renewal term? Assume the widow and children take; what are their respective shares? (Could Publisher in 1976 have fully protected itself against the eventuality of Author's early death, by taking assignments of the renewal term not only from him but also from his wife and children?)

AUTOMATIC RENEWAL OF PRE–1978 WORKS NOW IN THEIR FIRST TERM

At the time of U.S. adherence to the Berne Convention in 1989, Congress took no steps to amend the 1976 Act to remove the formalities of an initial and renewal registration as prerequisites to the second term of copyright, despite the probable inconsistency between the renewal requirement and Berne's prohibition upon formalities. Persistence of the renewal obligation has, through the years, been a trap for all authors (even large corporate copyrightholders have neglected to renew works), but especially so for foreign authors whose own countries' copyright laws contain no similar requirement. As was stated on the floor of the House of Representatives: "The renewal requirements are highly technical and have resulted in the unintended loss of valuable copyrights. In addition to countless individuals who do not have knowledge of the requirements, even famous directors such as Frank Capra have fallen victim. Capra's 'It's a Wonderful Life,' starring Jimmy Stewart and Donna Reed, went into the public domain when the film production company that owned the copyright went bankrupt and no one was around to file the renewal application."

This concern was finally addressed (after 200 years) through an amendment of the Copyright Act, enacted in June 1992, that provided for the automatic renewal of pre–1978 works then in their first term of copyright. The law, Pub. L. 102–307, 106 Stat. 264, substituted the equivalent of a single 75–year term for the prior dual terms, by making the second term (28 plus 19 years) vest without filing for renewal. Then, in 1998, the Sonny Bono Term Extension Act added another 20 years, for a total of 95. This means that pre–1978 works then in their first term of copyright, i.e., works first published between 1964 and 1977 (inclusive), will enjoy the full 95–year copyright term, without having to register and then to renew the registration during the 28th year following publication.

However, the automatic renewal law includes certain incentives to renewal registration. A registration issuing from an application made within one year before expiration of the first term will "constitute prima facie evidence as to the validity of the copyright during its renewal and extended term and of the facts stated in the certificate." § 304(a)(4)(B). This benefit may be most significant to copyright owners of works that never were registered during the first term of copyright. The law as passed does not require a first term registration as a prerequisite to automatic vesting of the renewal term.

The automatic renewal amendment also resolves an issue that had divided the courts: When must the deceased author have died to prevent vesting of the expectancy of the renewal term in the author's grantee? Assume that in the initial term of copyright A assigns the renewal term to B, and that renewal is applied for early in the 28th year but that A dies before the end of the year, leaving a widow. B claims that its renewal interest vested on the date of renewal registration (to be enjoyed beginning with the 29th year), while the widow claims that vesting does not occur unless and until A survives to the end of the 28th year, so that she takes the renewal term rather than the assignee. Courts reached different conclusions. *Compare Marascalco v. Fantasy Inc.*, 953 F.2d 469 (9th Cir. 1991), *with Frederick Music Co. v. Sickler*, 708 F.Supp. 587 (S.D.N.Y.1989).

This confusion is now resolved by the amended § 304(a)(2)(B). If renewal is secured by "voluntary" application and registration in the 28th year, then ownership of the renewal vests at that time (to be enjoyed in the 29th year and thereafter); in the hypothetical above, B will enjoy the renewal. If, however, the renewal is effected not voluntarily but "automatically" by virtue of the statutory amendment, then rights to the renewal term will not vest until the last day of the 28th year, and the spouse will take.

For the effect of the "automatic renewal" amendment upon derivative works created by an assignee during the initial term of the underlying work, see page 370 *infra*.

———

§ 304.   Duration of Copyright: Subsisting Copyrights

(a) *Copyrights in Their First Term on January 1, 1978.*

(1)(A) Any copyright, the first term of which is subsisting on January 1, 1978, shall endure for 28 years from the date it was originally secured.

(B) In the case of—

(i) any posthumous work or . . .

(ii) any work copyrighted . . . by an employer for whom such work is made for hire,

the proprietor of such copyright shall be entitled to a renewal and extension of the copyright in such work for the further term of 67 years.

(C) In the case of any other copyrighted work, including a contribution by an individual author to a periodical or to a cyclopedic or other composite work—

(i) the author of such work, if the author is still living,

(ii) the widow, widower, or children of the author, if the author is not living,

(iii) the author's executors, if such author, widow, widower, or children are not living, or

(iv) the author's next of kin, in the absence of a will of the author,

shall be entitled to a renewal and extension of the copyright in such work for a further term of 67 years.

(2) . . . (B) At the expiration of the original term of copyright in a work specified in paragraph (1)(C) of this subsection, the copyright shall endure for a renewed and extended further term of 67 years, which—

(i) if an application to register a claim to such further term has been made to the Copyright Office within 1 year before the expiration of the original term of copyright, and the claim is registered, shall vest, upon the beginning of such further term, in any person who is entitled under paragraph (1)(C) to the renewal and extension of the copyright at the time the application is made; or

(ii) if no such application is made or the claim pursuant to such application is not registered, shall vest, upon the beginning of such further term, in any person entitled under paragraph (1)(C), as of the last day of the original term of copyright, to the renewal and extension of the copyright.

(3)(A) An application to register a claim to the renewed and extended term of copyright in a work may be made to the Copyright Office—

(i) within 1 year before the expiration of the original term of copyright by any person entitled under paragraph (1)(B) or (C) to such further term of 67 years; and

(ii) at any time during the renewed and extended term by any person in whom such further term vested, under paragraph (2)(A) or (B). . . .

(B) Such an application is not a condition of the renewal and extension of the copyright in a work for a further term of 67 years.

(4) . . . (B) If an application to register a claim to the renewed and extended term of copyright in a work is made within 1 year before its expiration, and the claim is registered, the certificate of such registration shall constitute prima facie evidence as to the validity of the copyright during its renewed and extended term and of the facts stated in the certificate. . . .

(b) *Copyrights in Their Renewal Term at time of the effective date of the Sonny Bono Copyright Term Extension Act.*

Any copyright still in its renewal term at the time that the Sonny Bono Copyright Term Extension Act becomes effective [October 27, 1998] shall have a copyright term of 95 years from the date copyright was originally secured.

WORKS IN THE PUBLIC DOMAIN PRIOR TO JANUARY 1, 1978 (AND THEREAFTER)

None of the statutory sections treated above deals with the duration of copyright protection for works that were already in the public domain when the Copyright Act became effective on January 1, 1978. As the student might assume, Congress intended to leave all such works in the public domain, available for copying and other forms of use by anyone interested in doing so. Congress enacted a number of "transitional and supplementary provisions" in addition to the substantive provisions of the 1976 Act, and T & S § 103 provides, in pertinent part: "This Act does not provide copyright protection for any work that goes into the public domain before January 1, 1978."

The question of recapture of works from the public domain remains a lively one, however. As the student is already aware, among the world's copyright regimes, the U.S. 28–year term was peculiarly short. As the student will learn in Chapter 5, another peculiarity of U.S. copyright, the notice requirement, also could cause a work's early demise into the public domain. As a result, pressure has been brought from time to time to revive the copyrights in foreign works that fell prey to the draconian features of the U.S. copyright system. Finally, in 1994, as a result of U.S. adherence to the agreement on Trade Related Aspects of Intellectual Property (TRIPs), Congress enacted detailed provisions restoring copyright protection to (non-U.S.) works from qualifying countries. Under a new § 104A, works still protected in their source countries that had been denied protection in the U.S. as a result, for example, of failure to comply with notice or renewal formalities, retrieved U.S. copyright protection as of January 1, 1996.

Protection attached automatically, and copyright may be enforced without formalities against all exploiters other than "reliance parties."

A reliance party is defined as "any person who with respect to a particular work, engages in acts [before January 1, 1995] which would have violated § 106 if the restored work had been subject to copyright protection, and who, after [January 1, 1995] continues to engage in such acts." The enactment gives reliance parties a grace period of 12 months following notification by the owner of the restored copyright in which to continue to exploit the work. The owner of the restored copyright may notify the reliance party either directly, or constructively by filing, within 24 months of the effective date of the restoration (January 1, 1996), a notice of intent with the Copyright Office. In that case, the 12–month grace period runs from publication of the notice by the Copyright Office in the Federal Register. The owner of the restored copyright is defined as the author "as determined by the law of the source country of the work."

Does Congress have power to reanimate dead copyrights? Arguably, retrieval of works from the public domain would violate the constitutional restriction of copyright to "limited Times." On the other hand, one might contend that the Constitution merely forbids *perpetual* copyright protection; as long as the duration is limited, there is no requirement that the period of protection be single and uninterrupted. Indeed, Congress has in the past authorized the President to issue proclamations reinstating lapsed copyrights. The Act of Dec. 18, 1919, 41 Stat. 368, and the Act of Sept. 25, 1941, subsequently codified in § 9 of the 1909 Copyright Act, provided for the revival of copyrights of foreign works that would have fallen into the public domain due to the authors' inability (due principally to the World Wars) to comply with U.S. formalities.

Note that the "Sonny Bono Term Extension Act" does not restore copyright to any work already in the public domain as of the act's enactment in 1998. Thus, while the term of protection for 1909 Act works is extended to 95 years from publication, the extension only applies to works that were still under copyright in 1998, i.e., works initially published in or after 1923 and timely renewed (or restored pursuant to the TRIPs implementation act).

THE TRANSITION FROM 1909 TO 1976 ACT AND ITS AMENDMENTS

The following table may help the student review the applicable duration periods.

Date of Work	When Protection Attaches	First Term	Renewal Term
Created in 1978 or later	Upon being fixed in a tangible medium	Unitary term of life + 70 (or, if anonymous or pseudonymous work, or work for hire, 95 years from publication, or 120 years from creation, whichever is first)	

| *Published* 1964–1977 | Upon publication with notice | 28 years | 67 years, second term now commences automatically; renewal registration optional |

| *Published* between 1923 and 1963, inclusive | Upon publication with notice | 28 years | 67 years, if renewal was sought, otherwise these works are in the public domain (note that even as to works whose first terms expired after 1977, it remained necessary to effect a renewal registration) |

| *Published* before 1923 | The work is now in the public domain | | |

| *Created, but not published*, before 1978 | On 1/1/1978, when federal copyright displaced state copyright | | Unitary term of at least life + 70, earliest expiration dates 12/31/2002 (if work remains unpublished) or 12/31/2047 (if work is published by the end of 2002) |

B.   RENEWALS AND DERIVATIVE WORKS

A number of vexing issues generated by the renewal format in the 1909 Act, and still with us, concern the ownership and use of derivative works after the end of the initial copyright term on the underlying work. For example, assume that *A*, the author of a copyrighted novel, conveys to *B* during the initial term of copyright in the novel the exclusive right to produce a play or motion picture based upon the novel. *B* produces such a play or motion picture and secures copyright for it. Twenty-eight years after the publication and copyrighting of the underlying novel, *A* (or *A*'s statutory successor) renews the copyright. What are the respective rights of *A* and *B*?

A number of possible situations come to mind.

(1) Is *A* free to perform *B*'s play or publicly exhibit *B*'s motion picture without *B*'s consent? That would surely be an infringement of *B*'s copyright to the extent *B* has contributed as an "author" some "original" elements in the play or motion picture.

(2) Is *A* free to grant to a third person, *C*, the right to produce an altogether new play or motion picture based on *A*'s underlying novel? At least to that extent, the renewal term has been said to create a "new estate" in *A* (or *A*'s statutory successor) that is not encumbered by *A*'s

promise during the initial term of the underlying copyright not to grant such derivative rights to persons other than *B*. After all, the principal purpose of the renewal format was to permit *A* to benefit, through the right to make new grants and licenses, from the unanticipated popularity of his underlying novel.

(3) Is *B* free (assuming *A*'s initial grant to have made no mention of the renewal term) to make an altogether new version of a play or motion picture based on *A*'s novel? Here, too, it has been generally assumed that *A*'s renewal, and the "new estate" created thereby, empowers *A* to prevent *B* from indefinitely exploiting *A*'s underlying novel, during its renewal term, in the form of wholly new plays and motion pictures. To the extent such plays and films borrow from *A*'s novel without *A*'s consent, this would be an infringement of the renewal copyright.

(4) Is *B* free, however, to continue to perform *B*'s own play, or exhibit *B*'s own motion picture, exactly as written by him, during the renewal term of *A*'s underlying novel, without *A*'s consent? Strict application of the "new estate" theory might suggest that *A* takes the renewal free and clear of all licenses granted earlier, all of which terminate and revert to *A*, so that *A* can renegotiate the license with *B* and thus directly benefit from the success of *A*'s underlying novel (as a component in *B*'s play or motion picture). If so, *B* would infringe. *B*'s equities in this situation are, however, weighty, especially if the grant of derivative rights and the preparation of his derivative work came late in the initial copyright term of the underlying work, and particularly if the success of the play or motion picture is largely attributable to the literary or artistic contributions of *B* (and if *B* is indeed making no changes in the derivative work he has previously been performing or exhibiting).

This fourth variation is the issue that is presented in the Supreme Court's recent decision in *Stewart v. Abend*, which is featured immediately below.

(5) Assume that not only does the initial copyright term of the underlying work expire, and that a renewal is secured, but also that the initial copyright term of the derivative play or motion picture expires—and that it is *not* renewed. Is a third person free to publish, publicly perform, or publicly exhibit the derivative play or motion picture? Is *A* free to do so? Strict application of copyright theory would suggest that because *B*'s copyright protects only those elements he authored in the play or motion picture, only those discrete elements fall into the public domain when no renewal copyright is secured for the derivative work; the publication, performance, or exhibition of the derivative work would therefore infringe the elements of *A*'s underlying novel that are still being protected by *A*'s renewal copyright. Thus a third person so using *B*'s work would infringe *A*'s. *A*, however, would be free so to use *B*'s work. One difficulty with such a conclusion is that it appears to undermine the public-domain policy of the Copyright Act, for it would prevent all persons (except *A*) from exploiting *B*'s work despite the termination of its copyright; and it places in jeopardy

those third persons who exploit *B*'s work in reliance on the apparent expiration of protection.

This dilemma is raised and explored in *Russell v. Price, infra.*

Stewart v. Abend

495 U.S. 207, 110 S.Ct. 1750, 109 L.Ed.2d 184 (1990).

■ JUSTICE O'CONNOR delivered the opinion of the Court.

The author of a pre-existing work may assign to another the right to use it in a derivative work. In this case the author of a pre-existing work agreed to assign the rights in his renewal copyright term to the owner of a derivative work, but died before the commencement of the renewal period. The question presented is whether the owner of the derivative work infringed the rights of the successor owner of the pre-existing work by continued distribution and publication of the derivative work during the renewal term of the pre-existing work.

I

Cornell Woolrich authored the story "It Had to Be Murder," which was first published in February 1942 in Dime Detective Magazine. The magazine's publisher, Popular Publications, Inc., obtained the rights to magazine publication of the story and Woolrich retained all other rights. Popular Publications obtained a blanket copyright for the issue of Dime Detective Magazine in which "It Had to Be Murder" was published.

The Copyright Act of 1909, 35 Stat. 1075, 17 U.S.C. § 1 *et seq.* (1976 ed.) (1909 Act), provided authors a 28–year initial term of copyright protection plus a 28–year renewal term. See 17 U.S.C. § 24 (1976 ed.). In 1945, Woolrich agreed to assign the rights to make motion picture versions of six of his stories, including "It Had to Be Murder," to B. G. De Sylva Productions for $9,250. He also agreed to renew the copyrights in the stories at the appropriate time and to assign the same motion picture rights to De Sylva Productions for the 28–year renewal term. In 1953, actor Jimmy Stewart and director Alfred Hitchcock formed a production company, Patron, Inc., which obtained the motion picture rights in "It Had to Be Murder" from De Sylva's successors in interest for $10,000.

In 1954, Patron, Inc., along with Paramount Pictures, produced and distributed, "Rear Window," the motion picture version of Woolrich's story "It Had to Be Murder." Woolrich died in 1968 before he could obtain the rights in the renewal term for petitioners as promised and without a surviving spouse or child. He left his property to a trust administered by his executor, Chase Manhattan Bank, for the benefit of Columbia University. On December 29, 1969, Chase Manhattan Bank renewed the copyright in the "It Had to Be Murder" story pursuant to 17 U.S.C. § 24 (1976 ed.). Chase Manhattan assigned the renewal rights to respondent Abend for $650 plus 10% of all proceeds from exploitation of the story.

"Rear Window" was broadcast on the ABC television network in 1971. Respondent then notified petitioners Hitchcock (now represented by co-trustees of his will), Stewart, and MCA Inc., the owners of the "Rear Window" motion picture and renewal rights in the motion picture, that he owned the renewal rights in the copyright and that their distribution of the motion picture without permission infringed his copyright in the story. Hitchcock, Stewart, and MCA nonetheless entered into a second license with ABC to rebroadcast the motion picture. In 1974, respondent filed suit against these same petitioners, and others, in the United States District Court for the Southern District of New York, alleging copyright infringement. Respondent dismissed his complaint in return for $25,000.

Three years later, the United States Court of Appeals for the Second Circuit decided *Rohauer v. Killiam Shows, Inc.,* 551 F.2d 484, *cert. denied,* 431 U.S. 949 (1977), in which it held that the owner of the copyright in a derivative work may continue to use the existing derivative work according to the original grant from the author of the pre-existing work even if the grant of rights in the pre-existing work lapsed. 551 F.2d, at 494. Several years later, apparently in reliance on *Rohauer,* petitioners re-released the motion picture in a variety of media, including new 35 and 16 millimeter prints for theatrical exhibition in the United States, videocassettes, and videodiscs. They also publicly exhibited the motion picture in theaters, over cable television, and through videodisc and videocassette rentals and sales.

[Respondent Abend brought the instant infringement action against Hitchcock, Stewart, MCA and Universal Film Exchange (the distributor of the motion picture). Abend alleged that the petitioners could not re-release the film because Woolrich's death before being able to register for the renewal term of the story resulted in the lapsing of their right to use it. Abend also alleged that his rights in the story's renewal copyright were impaired by the petitioners' threatening him against using the name "Rear Window" or "It Had to Be Murder" on any newly produced television program based on the story, and by themselves attempting to make a television sequel. The trial court granted summary judgment for Hitchcock, Stewart, et al., invoking the *Rohauer* decision and the fair use doctrine, but the Court of Appeals for the Ninth Circuit reversed. It concluded that the use of the preexisting story incorporated in the film was infringing unless the owner of the derivative film held a valid grant of rights in the renewal term; and it held that Woolrich's statutory successor, Chase Manhattan Bank, took the renewal term unencumbered by the earlier, contingent, grant to the petitioners. The Supreme Court granted certiorari to resolve the conflict between the two circuit decisions.]

II

A

Petitioners would have us read into the Copyright Act a limitation on the statutorily created rights of the owner of an underlying work. They argue in essence that the rights of the owner of the copyright in the derivative use of the pre-existing work are extinguished once it is incorporated into the derivative work, assuming the author of the pre-existing work has agreed to assign his renewal rights. Because we find no support for such a curtailment of rights in either the 1909 Act, the 1976 Act, or the legislative history of either, we affirm the judgment of the Court of Appeals.

. . .

The right of renewal found in § 24 [of the 1909 Act] provides authors a second opportunity to obtain remuneration for their works. . . .

Since the earliest copyright statute in this country, the copyright term of ownership has been split between an original term and a renewal term. Originally, the renewal was intended merely to serve as an extension of the original term; at the end of the original term, the renewal could be effected and claimed by the author, if living, or by the author's executors, administrators or assigns. See Copyright Act of May 31, 1790, ch. XV, § 1, 1 Stat. 124. In 1831, Congress altered the provision so that the author could assign his contingent interest in the renewal term, but could not, through his assignment, divest the rights of his widow or children in the renewal term. See Copyright Act of February 3, 1831, ch. XVI, 4 Stat. 436; see also G. Curtis, Law of Copyright 235 (1847). The 1831 renewal provisions created "an entirely new policy, completely dissevering the title, breaking up the continuance ... and vesting an absolutely new title *eo nomine* in the persons designated." *White–Smith Music Publishing Co. v. Goff,* 187 F. 247, 250 (C.A.1 1911). In this way, Congress attempted to give the author a second chance to control and benefit from his work. Congress also intended to secure to the author's family the opportunity to exploit the work if the author died before he could register for the renewal term. See Bricker, *Renewal and Extension of Copyright,* 29 S. Cal. L. Rev. 23, 27 (1955) ("The renewal term of copyright is the law's second chance to the author and his family to profit from his mental labors"). "The evident purpose of [the renewal provision] is to provide for the family of the author after his death. Since the author cannot assign his family's renewal rights, [it] takes the form of a compulsory bequest of the copyright to the designated persons." *De Sylva v. Ballentine,* 351 U.S. 570, 582 (1956). See *Fred Fisher Music Co. v. M. Witmark & Sons,* 318 U.S. 643, 651 (1943) (if at the end of the original copyright period, the author is not living, "his family stand[s] in more need of the only means of subsistence ordinarily left to them" (citation omitted)).

In its debates leading up to the Copyright Act of 1909, Congress elaborated upon the policy underlying a system comprised of an original term and a completely separate renewal term. See *G. Ricordi & Co. v. Paramount Pictures, Inc.,* 189 F.2d 469, 471 (CA2) (the renewal right "creates a new estate, and the ... cases which have dealt with the subject assert that the new estate is clear of all rights, interests or licenses granted under the original copyright"), *cert. denied,* 342 U.S. 849 (1951). "It not infrequently happens that the author sells his copyright outright to a publisher for a comparatively small sum." H.R. Rep. No. 2222, 60th Cong. 2d Sess., 14 (1909). The renewal term permits the author, originally in a poor bargaining position, to renegotiate the terms of the grant once the value of the work has been tested. "[U]nlike real property and other forms of personal property, [a copyright] is by its very nature incapable of accurate monetary evaluation prior to its exploitation." 2 M. Nimmer & D. Nimmer, Nimmer on Copyright, § 9.02, p. 9–23 (1989) (hereinafter Nimmer). "If the work proves to be a great success and lives beyond the term of twenty-eight years, . . . it should be the exclusive right of the author to take the renewal term, and the law should be framed . . . so that [the author] could not be deprived of that right." H.R. Rep. No. 2222, *supra*, at 14. With these purposes in mind, Congress enacted the renewal provision of the Copyright Act of 1909, 17 U.S.C. § 24 (1976 ed.). With respect to works in their original or renewal term as of January 1, 1978, Congress retained the two-term system of copyright protection in the 1976 Act. See 17 U.S.C. §§ 304(a) and (b) (1988 ed.) (incorporating language of 17 U.S.C. § 24 (1976 ed.)).

Applying these principles in *Miller Music Corp. v. Charles N. Daniels, Inc.*, 362 U.S. 373 (1960), this Court held that when an author dies before the renewal period arrives, his executor is entitled to the renewal rights, even though the author previously assigned his renewal rights to another party. "An assignment by an author of his renewal rights made before the original copyright expires is valid against the world, if the author is alive at the commencement of the renewal period. *[Fred] Fisher Co. v. Witmark & Sons*, 318 U.S. 643, so holds." *Id.*, at 375. If the author dies before that time, the "next of kin obtain the renewal copyright free of any claim founded upon an assignment made by the author in his lifetime. These results follow not because the author's assignment is invalid but because he had only an expectancy to assign; and his death, prior to the renewal period, terminates his interest in the renewal which by § 24 vests in the named classes." *Ibid.* The legislative history of the 1909 Act echoes this view: "The right of renewal is contingent. It does not vest until the end [of the original term]. If [the author] is alive at the time of renewal, then the original contract may pass it, but his widow or children or other persons entitled would not be bound by the contract." 5 Legislative History of the 1909 Copyright Act, part K, p. 77 (E. Brylawski & A. Goldman eds. 1976) (statement of Mr. Hale).[2] Thus, the renewal provisions were intended to give the author a second chance to obtain fair remuneration for his creative efforts and to provide the author's family a "new estate" if the author died before the renewal period arrived.

An author holds a bundle of exclusive rights in the copyrighted work, among them the right to copy and the right to incorporate the work into derivative works. By assigning the renewal copyright in the work without limitation, as in *Miller Music,* the author assigns all of these rights. After *Miller Music,* if the author dies before the commencement of the renewal period, the assignee holds nothing. If the assignee of all of the renewal rights holds nothing upon the death of the assignor before arrival of the

---

2. Neither *Miller Music* nor *Fred Fisher* decided the question of when the renewal rights vest, i.e., whether the renewal rights vest upon commencement of the registration period, registration, or the date on which the original term expires and the renewal term begins. We have no occasion to address the issue here.

renewal period, then *a fortiori,* the assignee of a portion of the renewal rights, e.g., the right to produce a derivative work, must also hold nothing. See also Brief for Register of Copyrights as Amicus Curiae 22 (*"[A]ny* assignment of renewal rights made during the original term is void if the author dies before the renewal period"). Therefore, if the author dies before the renewal period, then the assignee may continue to use the original work only if the author's successor transfers the renewal rights to the assignee. This is the rule adopted by the Court of Appeals below and advocated by the Register of Copyrights. See 863 F.2d, at 1478; Brief for Register of Copyrights as Amicus Curiae 22. Application of this rule to this case should end the inquiry. Woolrich died before the commencement of the renewal period in the story, and, therefore, petitioners hold only an unfulfilled expectancy. Petitioners have been "deprived of nothing. Like all purchasers of contingent interests, [they took] subject to the possibility that the contingency may not occur." *Miller Music, supra,* at 378.

B

The reason that our inquiry does not end here, and that we granted certiorari, is that the Court of Appeals for the Second Circuit reached a contrary result in *Rohauer v. Killiam Shows, Inc.,* 551 F.2d 484 (1977). Petitioners' theory is drawn largely from *Rohauer.* The Court of Appeals in *Rohauer* attempted to craft a "proper reconciliation" between the owner of the pre-existing work, who held the right to the work pursuant to *Miller Music,* and the owner of the derivative work, who had a great deal to lose if the work could not be published or distributed. 551 F.2d, at 490. Addressing a case factually similar to this case, the court concluded that even if the death of the author caused the renewal rights in the pre-existing work to revert to the statutory successor, the owner of the derivative work could continue to exploit that work. The court reasoned that the 1976 Act and the relevant precedents did not preclude such a result and that it was necessitated by a balancing of the equities:

> "[The] equities lie preponderantly in favor of the proprietor of the derivative copyright. In contrast to the situation where an assignee or licensee has done nothing more than print, publicize and distribute a copyrighted story or novel, a person who with the consent of the author has created an opera or a motion picture film will often have made contributions literary, musical and economic, as great as or greater than the original author.... [T]he purchaser of derivative rights has no truly effective way to protect himself against the eventuality of the author's death before the renewal period since there is no way of telling who will be the surviving widow, children or next of kin or the executor until that date arrives." 551 F.2d, at 493.

. . .

Petitioners maintain that the creation of the "new," i.e., derivative, work extinguishes any right the owner of rights in the pre-existing work might have had to sue for infringement that occurs during the renewal term.

We think, as stated in Nimmer on Copyright, that "[t]his conclusion is neither warranted by any express provision of the Copyright Act, nor by the rationale as to the scope of protection achieved in a derivative work. It is moreover contrary to the axiomatic copyright principle that a person may exploit only such copyrighted literary material as he either owns or is licensed to use." 1 Nimmer § 3.07[A], pp. 3–23 to 3–24 (footnotes omitted). The aspects of a derivative work added by the derivative author are that author's property, but the element drawn from the pre-existing work remains on grant from the owner of the pre-existing work. See *Russell v. Price,* 612 F.2d 1123, 1128 (C.A.9 1979) (reaffirming "well-established doctrine that a derivative copyright protects only the new material contained in the derivative work, not the matter derived from the underlying work"), *cert. denied,* 446 U.S. 952 (1980). . . . So long as the pre-existing work remains out of the public domain, its use is infringing if one who employs the work does not have a valid license or assignment for use of the pre-existing work. *Russell v. Price, supra,* at 1128. . . . It is irrelevant whether the pre-existing work is inseparably intertwined with the derivative work. . . .

> "The copyright in a compilation or derivative work extends only to the material contributed by the author of such work, as distinguished from the preexisting material employed in the work, and does not imply any exclusive right in the preexisting material. The copyright in such work is independent of, and does not affect or enlarge the scope, duration, ownership, or subsistence of, any copyright protection in the pre-existing material." 17 U.S.C. § 103(b).

. . . [W]e conclude that neither the 1909 Act nor the 1976 Act provides support for the theory set forth in *Rohauer.* And even if the theory found some support in the statute or the legislative history, the approach set forth in *Rohauer* is problematic. Petitioners characterize the result in *Rohauer* as a bright-line "rule." The Court of Appeals in *Rohauer,* however, expressly implemented policy considerations as a means of reconciling what it viewed as the competing interests in that case. See 551 F.2d, at 493–494. While the result in *Rohauer* might make some sense in some contexts, it makes no sense in others. In the case of a condensed book, for example, the contribution by the derivative author may be little, while the contribution by the original author is great. Yet, under the *Rohauer* "rule," publication of the condensed book would not infringe the pre-existing work even though the derivative author has no license or valid grant of rights in the pre-existing work. . . . Thus, even if the *Rohauer* "rule" made sense in terms of policy in that case, it makes little sense when it is applied across the derivative works spectrum.

Finally, petitioners urge us to consider the policies underlying the Copyright Act. They argue that the rule announced by the Court of Appeals will undermine one of the policies of the Act—the dissemination of creative works—by leading to many fewer works reaching the public. Amicus Columbia Pictures asserts that "[s]ome owners of underlying work renewal copyrights may refuse to negotiate, preferring instead to retire their copyrighted works, and all derivative works based thereon, from public use. Others may make demands—like respondent's demand for 50% of petitioners' future gross proceeds in excess of advertising expenses . . .—which are so exorbitant that a negotiated economic accommodation will be impossible." Brief for Columbia Pictures et al. as Amicus Curiae 21. These arguments are better addressed by Congress than the courts.

In any event, the complaint that the respondent's monetary request in this case is so high as to preclude agreement fails to acknowledge that an initially high asking price does not preclude bargaining. Presumably, respondent is asking for a share in the proceeds because he wants to profit from the distribution of the work, not because he seeks suppression of it.

Moreover, although dissemination of creative works is a goal of the Copyright Act, the Copyright Act creates a balance between the artist's right to control the work during the term of the copyright protection and the public's need for access to creative works. The copyright term is limited so that the public will not be permanently deprived of the fruits of an artist's labors. . . . But nothing in the copyright statutes would prevent an author from hoarding all of his works during the term of the copyright. In fact, this Court has held that a copyright owner has the capacity arbitrarily to refuse to license one who seeks to exploit the work. See *Fox Film Corp. v. Doyal,* 286 U.S. 123, 127 (1932).

. . . When an author produces a work which later commands a higher price in the market than the original bargain provided, the copyright statute is designed to provide the author the power to negotiate for the realized value of the work. That is how the separate renewal term was intended to operate. . . . At heart, petitioners' true complaint is that they will have to pay more for the use of works they have employed in creating their own works. But such a result was contemplated by Congress and is consistent with the goals of the Copyright Act.

. . . Absent an explicit statement of congressional intent that the rights in the renewal term of an owner of a pre-existing work are extinguished upon incorporation of his work into another work, it is not our role to alter the delicate balance Congress has labored to achieve.

. . .

III

Petitioners assert that even if their use of "It Had to Be Murder" is unauthorized, it is a fair use and, therefore, not infringing. . . .

The Court of Appeals determined that the use of Woolrich's story in the petitioners' motion picture was not fair use. . . . The record supports the Court of Appeals' conclusion that re-release of the film impinged on the ability to market new versions of the story. Common sense would yield the same conclusion. Thus, all four factors point to unfair use. "This case presents a classic example of an unfair use: a commercial use of a fictional story that adversely affects the story owner's adaptation rights." 863 F.2d, at 1482.

For the foregoing reasons, the judgment of the Court of Appeals is affirmed and the case is remanded for further proceedings consistent with this opinion.

It is so ordered.

[The concurring opinion of Justice White and the dissent of Justice Stevens are omitted.]

QUESTIONS

1. Didn't the Supreme Court avoid the thorniest issue regarding renewals and derivative works: apportionment of control and/or compensation when the immense success of the derivative work owes much to the "new matter"? How would you resolve the question?

2. If you were the owner of the copyright in a motion picture that had been based on a previously published story, must you stop exhibiting and distributing it to the public once the copyright in the underlying work has been renewed? What information would you need in order to decide that question, and how would you go about securing such information?

3. If you were the owner of the copyright in a motion picture that had been based on a completely original screenplay but that incorporates a three-minute song written by a well-known songwriter (who had assigned copyright in the song to the motion picture producer), must you stop exhibiting and distributing the film to the public once the copyright in the song has been renewed?

———

The amendment to § 304(a), which provides for automatic renewal of copyrighted works published between 1964 and 1977 (see pages 356–57, *supra*), would partly limit the effect of the *Rear Window* decision. If a renewal registration is filed, the author's heirs would take a "new estate" despite the author's grant, as in *Rear Window*. But, under § 304(a)(4)(A) of the new law, if no filing is made, and renewal simply occurs by operation of law, then even if the author has died before the renewal term vested, "a derivative work prepared under authority of a grant or transfer or license of copyright that is made before the expiration of the original term of copyright may continue to be used during the renewed and extended term of copyright without infringing the copyright, except that such use does not extend to the preparation during such renewed and extended term of other derivative works based upon the copyrighted work covered by such grant." *Cf.* 17 U.S.C. § 203(b)(1) (implementing a similar solution for derivative works prepared under the authority of a terminated grant).

Russell v. Price

612 F.2d 1123 (9th Cir.1979).

■ GOODWIN, CIRCUIT JUDGE: Defendants distributed copies of the film "Pygmalion," the copyright for which had expired. They were sued by the owners of the renewal copyright in the George Bernard Shaw play upon which the film was based. Defendants appeal the resulting judgment for damages and attorney fees. . . . We affirm.

In 1913 Shaw registered a copyright on his stage play "Pygmalion." The renewal copyright on the play, obtained in 1941 and originally scheduled to expire in 1969, was extended by Congressional action to the year 1988. Shaw died in 1950 and the plaintiffs, except for Janus Films, are current proprietors of the copyright. Janus Films is a licensee.

In 1938 a derivative version of the play, a motion picture also entitled "Pygmalion," was produced under a license from Shaw; neither the terms nor the licensee's identity appear in the record. The film was produced by Gabriel Pascal, copyrighted by Loew's, and distributed by Metro–Goldwyn–Mayer ("MGM"). For undisclosed reasons, the film's copyright was allowed to expire in 1966. When and if the original film rights agreement expired is also not disclosed.

In 1971 the play's copyright proprietors licensed Janus Films to be the exclusive distributor of the film "Pygmalion." Shortly after discovering in 1972 that Budget Films was renting out copies of the 1938 film, Janus brought an action against Budget. . . .

II. *Infringement*

Defendants' main contention on the primary issue in this litigation is simply stated: Because the film copyright on "Pygmalion" has expired, that film is in the public domain, and, consequently, prints of that film may be used freely by anyone. Thus, they argue that their renting out of the film does not infringe the statutory copyright on Shaw's play.

. . .

. . . [W]e reaffirm, without finding it necessary to repeat the rationale, the well-established doctrine that a derivative copyright protects only the new material contained in the derivative work, not the matter derived from the underlying work. 1 Nimmer on Copyright § 3.04 (1979). Thus, although the derivative work may enter the public domain, the matter contained therein which derives from a work still covered by statutory copyright is not dedicated to the public. [Citations omitted.] The established doctrine prevents unauthorized copying or other infringing use of the underlying work or any part of that work contained in the derivative product so long as the underlying work itself remains copyrighted. Therefore, since exhibition of the film "Pygmalion" necessarily involves exhibition of parts of Shaw's play, which is still copyrighted, plaintiffs here may prevent defendants from renting the film for exhibition without their authorization.

. . . The underlying statutory copyright in the instant case will expire in 1988. After that time Budget may freely distribute its copies of the 1938 film. . . .

For the foregoing reasons, we conclude that defendants' activities here infringed the subsisting copyright in Shaw's play and were properly enjoined.

. . .

Affirmed.

———

Three circuits have addressed the relationship of the subsisting copyright in an *unpublished* screenplay to the resulting motion picture, whose copyright has expired. *See Shoptalk, Ltd. v. Concorde–New Horizons Corp.,* 168 F.3d 586 (2d Cir.1999); *Batjac Prods. v. GoodTimes Home Video Corp.,* 160 F.3d 1223 (9th Cir.1998); *Classic Film Museum, Inc. v. Warner Bros., Inc.,* 597 F.2d 13 (1st Cir.1979), *aff'g* 453 F.Supp. 852 (D.Me.1978). The First Circuit had resisted, on public policy grounds, the motion picture producer's argument that the underlying unpublished screenplay enjoyed a separate copyright (which would in effect prolong the protection of the otherwise expired motion picture). The Second and Ninth Circuits reached the same result, but by holding that the publication of the motion picture published as much of the underlying screenplay as was incorporated in the film. The Second Circuit rejected the district court's determination that the film was a derivative work whose copyright term was independent of the underlying work's. *See* 897 F.Supp. 144 (S.D.N.Y.1995). Under the district court's reasoning, the expiration of the film's copyright removed the consideration for a license agreement requiring payment of royalties for exploitation of the film; nonetheless, the subsistence of copyright in the underlying screenplay entitled the film-rights licensor, as joint owner of the screenplay, to receive royalties for the use of the screenplay (through the exhibition of the film). Under the Second Circuit's approach, if the film published the relevant portions of the screenplay, then those portions were now in the public domain, and there could no longer be any consideration for licensing rights in those portions of the screenplay.

As we will see in the next chapter, many courts have held that publication of a derivative work does not effect a divestive publication of the underlying work. The *Shoptalk* district court's ruling is therefore consistent with the general principle of the independence of underlying and derivative works. *See* 17 U.S.C. § 103(b). But the problem may be less in the analysis of the effect on the underlying work of publication of a derivative work than in the characterization of the films as derivative works. On the one hand, it might be argued that the motion picture is indeed a derivative work with a "separate life" from the underlying script; the film, after all, typically contains visual elements and directorial contributions that are not a part of the screenplay. Similarly, a song that is written for and incorporated in the motion picture is sufficiently discrete that it is questionable that the film should be regarded as a derivative work whose loss of copyright should automatically carry with it the loss of the copyright in the song. On the other hand, how really distinctive from one another is a screenplay and the resulting film? Should it not make a difference, in assessing whether the copyright in the "underlying work" is divested by publication, if it is prepared as a preliminary version of the final work? Is the first draft of a novel the "underlying work," of which the published version is a "derivative work"? What about a composer's piano sketch of a work she will develop into an orchestral composition? A screenplay for a motion picture?

C. TERMINATION OF TRANSFERS

Under the 1909 Copyright Act and its predecessors, the principal purpose of the renewal format was to assure that a transferred copyright, when the transfer was made in the initial term, could be recaptured by the author (or his surviving family, or legatee, or next of kin) after a reasonable time. The economic rewards during the renewal term could thus be fully enjoyed by the author, unencumbered by any rights, interests, or licenses previously contracted away. The author, or her statutory successors, was to have a "new estate," a second chance to license or assign for a new consideration.

Once Congress decided to abandon the two-part renewal format and to endorse a single term of copyright—beginning with the work's creation and ending 50 years (as originally enacted in 1978) after the author's death—it had to determine whether, and how, to structure a "right of recapture" of the copyright comparable to that provided under the earlier statutes. This was not only an issue with respect to works created after January 1, 1978, to which the "life plus 50" yardstick applied. It was even more of an issue for works that were already in copyright under the 1909 Act, as to which the author (or statutory successor) had conveyed the renewal term—at a time (prior to January 1, 1978) when that term was understood by the parties to last for only 28 years. In such a case, who should benefit from the 39 years that Congress added to the renewal term subsequent to the grant, the author or the assignee?—and if the former, how should the recapture be effected?

In these two situations, Congress provided for a termination of copyright transfer. Section 203 governs transfers made after the effective date of the 1976 Act, and § 304(c) governs transfers of renewal interests made before that date.

House Report

H.R. Rep. No. 94–1476, 94th Cong., 2d Sess. 124–28 (1976).

The problem in general

The provisions of section 203 are based on the premise that the reversionary provisions of the present section on copyright renewal (17 U.S.C. sec. 24) should be eliminated, and that the proposed law should substitute for them a provision safeguarding authors against unremunerative transfers. A provision of this sort is needed because of the unequal bargaining position of authors, resulting in part from the impossibility of determining a work's value until it has been exploited. Section 203 reflects a practical compromise that will further the objectives of the copyright law while recognizing the problems and legitimate needs of all interests involved.

Scope of the provision

Instead of being automatic, as is theoretically the case under the present renewal provision, the termination of a transfer or license under section 203 would require the serving of an advance notice within specified time limits and under specified conditions. However, although affirmative action is needed to effect a termination, the right to take this action cannot be waived in advance or contracted away. Under section 203(a) the right of termination would apply only to transfers and licenses executed after the effective date of the new statute, and would have no retroactive effect.

The right of termination would be confined to inter vivos transfers or licenses executed by the author, and would not apply to transfers by the author's successors in interest or to the author's own bequests. The scope of the right would extend not only to any "transfer of copyright ownership," as defined in section 101, but also to nonexclusive licenses. The right of termination would not apply to "works made for hire," which is one of the principal reasons the definition of that term assumed importance in the development of the bill.

Who can terminate a grant

Two issues emerged from the disputes over section 203 as to the persons empowered to terminate a grant: (1) the specific classes of beneficiaries in the case of joint works; and (2) whether anything less than unanimous consent of all those entitled to terminate should be required to make a termination effective. The bill to some extent reflects a compromise on these points, including a recognition of the dangers of one or more beneficiaries being induced to "hold out" and of unknown children or grandchildren being discovered later. The provision can be summarized as follows:

> 1. In the case of a work of joint authorship, where the grant was signed by two or more of the authors, majority action by those who signed the grant, or by their interests, would be required to terminate it.

> 2. There are three different situations in which the shares of joint authors, or of a dead author's widow or widower, children, and grandchildren, must be divided under the statute: (1) The right to effect a termination; (2) the ownership of the terminated rights; and (3) the right to make further grants of reverted rights. The respective shares of the authors, and of a dead author's widow or widower, children, and grandchildren, would be divided in exactly the same way in each of these situations. The terms "widow," "widower," and

"children" are defined in section 101 in an effort to avoid problems and uncertainties that have arisen under the present renewal section.

3. The principle of *per stirpes* representation would also be applied in exactly the same way in all three situations. Take for example, a case where a dead author left a widow, two living children, and three grandchildren by a third child who is dead. The widow will own half of the reverted interests, the two children will each own 16 2/3 percent, and the three grandchildren will each own a share of roughly 5 1/2 percent. But who can exercise the right of termination? Obviously, since she owns 50 percent, the widow is an essential party, but suppose neither of the two surviving children is willing to join her in the termination; is it enough that she gets one of the children of the dead child to join, or can the dead child's interest be exercised only by the action of a majority of his children? Consistent with the *per stirpes* principle, the interest of a dead child can be exercised only as a unit by majority action of his surviving children. Thus, even though the widow and one grandchild would own 55 1/2 percent of the reverted copyright, they would have to be joined by another child or grandchild in order to effect a termination or a further transfer of reverted rights. This principle also applies where, for example, two joint authors executed a grant and one of them is dead; in order to effect a termination, the living author must be joined by a *per stirpes* majority of the dead author's beneficiaries. The notice of termination may be signed by the specified owners of termination interests or by "their duly authorized agents," which would include the legally appointed guardians or committees of persons incompetent to sign because of age or mental disability.

When a grant can be terminated

Section 203 draws a distinction between the date when a termination becomes effective and the earlier date when the advance notice of termination is served. With respect to the ultimate effective date, section 203(a)(3) provides, as a general rule, that a grant may be terminated during the 5 years following the expiration of a period of 35 years from the execution of the grant. As an exception to this basic 35–year rule, the bill also provides that "if the grant covers the right of publication of the work, the period begins at the end of 35 years from the date of publication of the work under the grant or at the end of 40 years from the date of execution of the grant, whichever term ends earlier." This alternative method of computation is intended to cover cases where years elapse between the signing of a publication contract and the eventual publication of the work.

The effective date of termination, which must be stated in the advance notice, is required to fall within the 5 years following the end of the applicable 35–or 40–year period, but the advance notice itself must be served earlier. Under section 203(a)(4)(A), the notice must be served "not less than two or more than ten years' before the effective date stated in it."

As an example of how these time-limit requirements would operate in practice, we suggest two typical contract situations:

Case 1: Contract for theatrical production signed on September 2, 1987. Termination of grant can be made to take effect between September 2, 2022 (35 years from execution) and September 1, 2027 (end of 5 year termination period). Assuming that the author decides to terminate on September 1, 2022 (the earliest possible date) the advance notice must be filed between September 1, 2012 and September 1, 2020.

Case 2: Contract for book publication executed on April 10, 1980; book finally published on August 23, 1987. Since contract covers the right of publication, the 5–year termination period would begin on April 10, 2020 (40 years from execution) rather than April 10, 2015 (35 years from execution) or August 23, 2022 (35 years from publication). Assuming that the author decides to make the termination effective on January 1, 2024, the advance notice would have to be served between January 1, 2014, and January 1, 2022.

Effect of termination

Section 203(b) makes clear that, unless effectively terminated within the applicable 5–year period, all rights covered by an existing grant will continue unchanged, and that rights under other Federal, State, or foreign laws are unaffected. However, assuming that a copyright transfer or license is terminated under section 203, who are bound by the termination and how are they affected?

Under the bill, termination means that ownership of the rights covered by the terminated grant reverts to everyone who owns termination interests on the date the notice of termination was served, whether they joined in signing the notice or not. In other words, if a person could have signed the notice, that person is bound by the action of the majority who did; the termination of the grant will be effective as to that person, and a proportionate share of the reverted rights automatically vests in that person. Ownership is divided proportionately on the same *per stirpes* basis as that provided for the right to effect termination under section 203(a) and, since the reverted rights vest on the date notice is served, the heirs of a dead beneficiary would inherit his or her share.

Under clause (3) of subsection (b), majority action is required to make a further grant of reverted rights. A problem here, of course, is that years may have passed between the time the reverted rights vested and the time the new owners want to make a further transfer; people may have died and children may have been born in the interim. To deal with this problem, the bill looks back to the date of vesting; out of the group in whom rights vested on that date, it requires the further transfer or license to be signed by "the same number and proportion of the owners" (though not necessarily the same individuals) as were then required to terminate the grant under subsection (a). If some of those in whom the rights originally vested have died, their "legal representatives, legatees, or heirs at law" may represent them for this purpose and, as in the case of the termination itself, any one of the minority who does not join in the further grant is nevertheless bound by it.

An important limitation on the rights of a copyright owner under a terminated grant is specified in section 203(b)(1). This clause provides that, notwithstanding a termination, a derivative work prepared earlier may "continue to be utilized" under the conditions of the terminated grant; the clause adds, however, that this privilege is not broad enough to permit the preparation of other derivative works. In other words, a film made from a play could continue to be licensed for performance after the motion picture contract had been terminated but any remake rights covered by the contract would be cut off. . . .

Nothing contained in this section or elsewhere in this legislation is intended to extend the duration of any license, transfer or assignment made for a period of less than thirty-five years. If, for example, an agreement provides an earlier termination date or lesser duration, or if it allows the author the right of cancelling or terminating the agreement under certain circumstances, the duration is governed by the agreement. . . .

Section 203(b)(6) provides that, unless and until termination is effected under this section, the grant, "if it does not provide otherwise," continues for the term of copyright. This section means that, if the agreement does not contain provisions specifying its term or duration, and the author has not terminated the agreement under this section, the agreement continues for the term of the copyright, subject to any right of termination under circumstances which may be specified therein. . . .

COMPARISON OF TERMINATION PROVISIONS

The key distinctions between termination rights under § 304(c) and § 203 may be summarized as follows:

§ 304(c)   *§ 203*

1. *Grants Covered*

(a) before Jan. 1, 1978	(a) on or after Jan. 1, 1978
(b) by author or other person designated by § 304(a)(1)(C) and § 304(c)(2)	(b) by author
(c) of renewal right in statutory copyright; of 19–year extended renewal term (or, if owner of the termination right failed to exercise the right to terminate, of the 20–year second extension of the renewal term)	(c) of any right under any copyright

2. *Persons Who May Exercise*

Author or majority interest of his statutory beneficiaries (*per stirpes*) to the extent of that author's share	Author or majority of granting authors or majority of their respective beneficiaries, voting as a unit for each author and *per stirpes*

or

in case of grant by others, all surviving grantors

§ 304(c) | *§ 203*

3. *Beginning of Five–Year Termination Period*

End of 56 years of copyright or January 1, 1978, whichever is later; if owner of termination right failed to exercise the right at the end of 56 years, s/he has another opportunity at the end of 75 years of copyright	End of 35 years from grant, or if covering publication right, either 35 years from publication or 40 years from grant whichever is earlier

4. *Further Grants*

Generally tenants in common with right to deal separately, except where dead author's rights are shared, then majority action (*per stirpes*) as to that author's share	Requires same number and proportion as required for termination

QUESTION

In 1939, Ernestine Hamingweigh submitted a manuscript to the publishing house of Scriveners & Daughters. The manuscript showed promise, but required substantial editorial revisions. These were carried out by Maximillian Parsons, Scriveners' lead literary editor. The fruits of the editorial process were published in 1940 under the title *Ding Dong Bell*. Hamingweigh transferred the first and second terms of copyright to Scriveners. In 1995, Hamingweigh's statutory successors served Scriveners with a notice of termination of the extended renewal period in *Ding Dong Bell*. Scriveners claims that the original work was Hamingweigh's manuscript and that *Ding Dong Bell* as published is a derivative work, and therefore exempt from termination. Who should prevail? *See Woods v. Bourne Co.*, 841 F.Supp. 118 (S.D.N.Y.1994), *aff'd.*, 60 F.3d 978 (2d Cir.1995).

TRANSFERS, RENEWALS AND TERMINATIONS

1. Work is created, published and copyrighted in 1960. In 1960, Author (hereinafter *A*) assigns the initial and renewal terms to *B*. If *A* lives through 1988, the assignment to *B* is effective and *A* will take the renewal on behalf of *B*. If *A* dies before 1988, leaving Surviving Spouse (hereinafter *S*), *S* is entitled to claim the renewal, and *B* will have no rights in the renewal term. (These results flow from § 304(a), as embellished (in its earlier form as § 24 of the 1909 Act) by *Fred Fisher Music Co. v. M. Witmark & Sons*, 318 U.S. 643 (1943).)

However, the 39 years added to the renewal term by the 1976 Act (taking account as well of the 1998 Sonny Bono Act) can be recaptured by the giving of timely notice to *B*. If, when notice is given, *A* is alive, then it is *A* who is entitled to give the notice. If, when notice is given, *A* is dead and *S* is alive, then it is *S* who is entitled to give the notice. The right to give this notice and recapture the added 39 years of the renewal term cannot be waived or assigned in advance by either A or S. (These results flow from § 304(c).)

2. Work is created (and therefore automatically copyrighted) by A in 1980. A transfers inter vivos the copyright (which will last for A's life plus 70 years) to B the same year. That transfer may be terminated effective 35 to 40 years thereafter (i.e., beginning in 2015) by timely notice. If, when notice of termination is given, A is alive, then it is A who is entitled to give the notice and claim the "reversion." If, when notice is given, A is dead and S is alive, then it is S who is entitled to give the notice and claim the "reversion." Neither A nor S can waive or assign in advance that power to terminate. (These results flow from § 203(a).)

3. As in case 2, work is created by A in 1980, but A transfers the copyright to B by a will upon A's death in 1980, rather than inter vivos. The transfer may *not* be terminated and the copyright may *not* be recaptured by S, at any date in the future. (*See* § 203(a).) Is there any sense to the different outcomes in case 2 and case 3?

4. Work is created, published, and copyrighted in 1960 by A. In 1980, A assigns the initial and renewal terms to B.

If A lives into 1988, the assignment to B of the renewal term will be effective: Under *Fisher v. Witmark*, A will apply for the renewal but B will really own it. A will not be able to recapture the added 39 years of the renewal term pursuant to § 304(c), since that section governs only transfers executed *prior* to January 1, 1978, and this transfer was made by A in 1980. Therefore, B will be entitled to ownership of the renewal term throughout its duration, 1989 through 2055.

However, § 203 *will* govern, since the transfer by A to B was executed *after* January 1, 1978. Therefore, A may "recapture" the copyright 35 years after the 1980 transfer, or in 2015, even though at that time there are still 40 years remaining in B's renewal term. And, if A dies between 1988 when the copyright was renewed and 2015, then S can exercise the termination right under § 203. In short, although S cannot oust B of B's right to claim the renewal under these facts, S can shorten the renewal term enjoyed by B, simply by a timely termination.

5. As in case 4, the work is created, published and copyrighted by A in 1960, and the initial and renewal terms are assigned by A to B in 1980. However, A dies before 1988. Under § 304(a), the assignment of the renewal term is ineffective, and S will be entitled to secure the renewal term, to the exclusion of B.

6. Finally, as in the above two cases, the work is created, published, and copyrighted by A in 1960. A dies in 1980, and by will transfers the initial and renewal terms to B. S will not be able to terminate that transfer in 2015, pursuant to § 203, because the transfer by A was not inter vivos. But do not anguish for S just yet. Although A can, in 1980, assign the remaining eight years of the initial term—either inter vivos or by will—A's death before 1988 makes *S* the proper claimant of the renewal term, to the exclusion of *B*.

QUESTIONS

1. Author secures copyright in her novel in 1950, and in 1970 she executes a will in which she purports to devise the initial and renewal terms of the copyright to Princeton University. In 1978 she applies for and secures a renewal of the copyright. Author dies in 1980, leaving three daughters. In the year 2006 (56 years from the date of the initial copyright, and 28 years from the beginning of the renewal term) the daughters seek to join together to terminate the transfer of the renewal term in order to enjoy the remaining 39 years of that term. May they do so?

2. Section 203(a)(5) explicitly seeks to assure that the termination right will not be bargained away by the author and his family at the same time (or later) as they transfer their interest in the copyright itself. As attorney for the transferee of the copyright, is there a contract provision you can draft that would permit you, in effect, to prolong the transfer for more than thirty-five years? For example, would it be effective to provide that the grant shall terminate in thirty years and that the author (and any spouse and children making the initial grant) shall be obligated to re-transfer the copyright for an additional thirty years at a stipulated price? (Even assuming some such provision to comply technically with the statute, would you as counsel conclude that this so frustrates the spirit of § 203(a)(5) that it would be improper for you to insert this in the contract of transfer?)

3. Is a termination right available in the following situations: (a) Work is created, published, and copyrighted in 1975. In 1980, *both* the author and his wife assign original and renewal copyrights to *B*. *A* dies in 1985 and *W* renews in 2003. (b) In 1974, *A* enters into a contract with Publisher *P* assigning to *P* the copyright in a future book, which *A* completes in 1976. The work is published in 1978.

4. Author creates a musical composition and assigns the copyright in the composition to Publishing Company in 1980. Publishing Company subsequently licenses Record Company to create a sound recording of the composition, and Record Company makes and distributes the sound recording. Effective 2015, Author terminates the assignment to Publishing Company. Is Record Company's license also terminated by the termination of the assignment to Publishing Company? If the rights of Record Company are not terminated, should Record Company pay royalties for continued distribution of the sound recording to Publishing Company, or to Author? *See Mills Music, Inc. v. Snyder*, 469 U.S. 153 (1985).

5. Does the § 203 termination right in effect impose a *minimum* 35-year term on any copyright license or assignment which is silent on the matter of termination, or may the transferor terminate earlier? Compare *Rano v. Sipa Press, Inc.*, 987 F.2d 580 (9th Cir.1993), with *Walthal v. Rusk*, 172 F.3d 481 (7th Cir.1999), and *Korman v. HBC Florida, Inc.*, 182 F.3d 1291(11th Cir.1999), and see Ch. 9C *infra*.

TERMINATION TIME LINE

The following outline may assist the student in calculating when a grant may be terminated:

Work published before 1978

Reversion of renewal term rights

For works published before 1964: renewal term reversion of rights vested automatically (upon proper application and registration): in the author, if the author did not grant renewal term rights; in the author's surviving spouse or children if the author granted renewal term rights but died before the renewal term vested.

No deadline was imposed on the renewal term rights holder's exercise of the reverted rights. Thus, for example, in *Rohauer v. Killiam Shows*, 551 F.2d 484 (2d Cir.1977), the author's widow effected the renewal in 1952, but did not assign the rights to Rohauer until 1965.

For works published between 1964 and 1977, inclusive: if the author did not grant the renewal term, or if the author died before the renewal term vested, then renewal term rights will revert *if the renewal is effected during the 28th year of copyright*. (If the author, or survivor, does not renew, then the term of copyright will be automatically renewed, *but* the transferee may continue to use already-created derivative works.)

Reversion of extended renewal term rights

Five-year period beginning at the end of 56 years from publication (with a minimum of two years, and a maximum of 10 years, advance notice; but the transferee may continue to use already-created derivative works).

Five-year period beginning at the end of 75 years from publication (with a minimum of two years, and a maximum of 10 years, advance notice), *if* the author or her heirs did not terminate at the end of 56 years; the transferee may continue to use already-created derivative works.

Grant of exclusive or non-exclusive rights made after 1977 (regardless of the work's date of publication)

Five-year period beginning 35 years from execution of the grant (or, if a grant of publication rights, 35 years from publication or 40 years from execution, whichever is earlier), with a minimum of two years, and a maximum of 10 years, advance notice; the transferee may continue to use already-created derivative works.

PROBLEMS

1. Hundreds of manuscripts of songs, many of them previously unknown, by popular American composers, including George Gershwin, Jerome Kern, Cole Porter, Richard Rodgers, and Victor Herbert, have recently been discovered in a Warner Brothers warehouse in Secaucus, New Jersey. Many of these songs were never included in the depression-era movie musicals, such as *Showboat,* for which they had been composed.

Following national news coverage of the find, many claimants of rights in the songs are expected to come forward. You are counsel to Warner Brothers. What issues do you see regarding ownership of rights in the songs, and how would you resolve them?

2.   Nora Novelist published a short story, *Saskatchewan*, in 1940. In 1965, Mort Mogul produced a film, *Canadian Rockies*, which was based on Nora's story. Your client, Cindy Cinemix, wants to make a remake of the film. What information do you need to know in order to determine whether there are subsisting copyrights and from whom you would need to acquire rights?

CHAPTER 5

FORMALITIES

Perhaps no feature of United States copyright law has been more controversial than our requirement that, as a condition of protection, a work that has been "published" must contain a notice of copyright. Nor has any feature of our law been as subject to as frequent statutory change in the past 25 years. A notice requirement had been a feature of every United States copyright statute since the original Act of 1790. Although the placing of notice on published copies can serve as a warning to the unauthorized user, and can provide useful information, there is no *a priori* reason why the inclusion of a copyright notice need be required as a condition of protection. Indeed, for more than a century most of the major publishing nations of the world—with the principal exception of the United States—have had no notice requirements. This liberal approach toward the grant of copyright protection has been in large measure fostered by the dominant international copyright convention, the Berne Convention. Article 5(2) of Berne states that "the enjoyment and the exercise of [copyright] shall not be subject to any formality." Nonetheless, the United States throughout the twentieth century, even in the 1976 amendments effective on January 1, 1978, continued strictly to impose a notice requirement and thereby rendered itself ineligible for participation in the Berne Convention.

As will be noted below, the 1909 Act—although it failed to define the term "publication," the very significant behavior that gave rise to the notice requirement—provided detailed rules regarding the form and placement of the copyright notice. Failure of the copyright owner to comply with the notice requirements of the 1909 Act generally caused the work to fall into the public domain. Careless or inadvertent oversights thus resulted in many cases of loss of copyright. These consequences, and the desire to bring United States law closer to that contemplated by the Berne Convention, induced Congress in 1976 to make its first significant liberalization of the notice requirement. As will be noted further below, placement of notice on all copies of published works was still required, but omission was no longer fatal; most significantly, it could be cured by registration of the copyright and other action by the copyright owner within five years after publication.

Because the uncured failure to meet the statutory notice requirements continued even after January 1, 1978 to result in the loss of copyright protection, our law still failed to comport with Article 5(2) of the Berne Convention. A vigorous campaign in and out of Congress to amend our law to make it Berne-compatible resulted in the enactment of the Berne Convention Implementation Act of 1988, which became effective on March

1, 1989. For the first time in our history, notice on published copies and phonorecords is now no longer a condition of copyright protection. It remains, however, an option that is afforded to the copyright owner, an option that Congress continues to seek to promote.

What must be emphasized is that the recent changes in our law regarding copyright notice give no reason for the student to ignore the more strict requirements that prevailed under the 1909 Act or during the pre-Berne years of the 1976 Act (i.e., between January 1, 1978 and February 28, 1989). As Congress stated at the time of enacting the 1976 Act, the new law "does not provide copyright protection for any work that goes into the public domain before January 1, 1978." (Trans. & Suppl. sec. 103, 90 Stat. 2599.) Thus, the statutory rules regarding copyright notice that were in effect at the time of the first publication of a work determine the copyright status of that work; failure to comply with those rules would thrust the work into the public domain. For example, a court reviewing an alleged infringement committed in the year 2010, with respect to a work arguably first "published" in 1975 (or in 1935), will have to examine the statutory conditions of protection in those earlier years to determine whether or not the work was in the public domain on January 1, 1978. *See* Nimmer, *Preface—The Old Copyright Act as a Part of the New Act,* 22 N.Y.L.S. L. Rev. 471 (1977). It is thus not accurate to say that the provisions of the 1909 Act concerning publication and proper copyright notice, and the many court decisions interpreting those provisions, were "displaced" by the 1976 Act.

A. PUBLICATION AND NOTICE BEFORE THE 1976 ACT

The pivot of the 1909 law was the concept of "publication." This event was generally the dividing line between common-law protection on the one hand and either statutory or no protection on the other. Thus the traditional litany was that publication with the prescribed copyright notice secured statutory copyright, while publication without such notice placed a work in the public domain.

This rule was anchored in the text of § 10 of the 1909 Act, which provided: "Any person entitled thereto by this title may secure copyright for his work by publication thereof with the notice of copyright required by this title." (For certain categories of works, however, the 1909 Act did allow, in § 12, for securing statutory protection through registration even in the absence of publication.) Publication, as the traditional requirement for statutory protection in this country, results from the legendary bargain between the public and the author reflected in a statutory system of copyright as construed by *Donaldson v. Becket,* 4 Burrows 2303, 98 Eng. Rep. 257 (1774). In order to induce the author to disclose his work to the public notwithstanding the resulting loss of his common-law protection, the statute substitutes new rights, albeit limited in time. As a corollary, the term of copyright was measured from "the date of first publication" according to § 24 of the statute.

The concept of "publication" as utilized in § 10 developed into a rather technical construct; it is not always coterminous with the general notion of "making public," nor even with the act that divests the author of common-law rights.

Definition of "Publication." The 1909 Act did not expressly define "publication." This omission was apparently based on the assumption that a general definition of this concept was too difficult. *Hearings on S. 6330 and H.R. 19853 Before Committee on Patents,* 59th Cong., 1st Sess. 71 (June 1906). In § 26, however, we are told that in the case of a work "of which copies are reproduced for sale or distribution," "the 'date of publication' shall ... be held to be the earliest date when copies of the first authorized edition were placed on sale, sold or publicly distributed by the proprietor of the copyright or under his authority." As noted by the court in *Cardinal Film Corp. v. Beck,* 248 F. 368 (S.D.N.Y.1918), the section was evidently intended to fix the date from which the term of copyright should begin to run for such a work, rather than to provide a general definition of what should constitute publication in all cases.

Despite how crucial it was to have a clear understanding of the concept of "publication" under the 1909 Act, a number of rather arbitrary distinctions emerged in giving content to that term. Among the most well known, and most important, was the generally accepted rule that the public performance of a spoken drama did not constitute publication. This rule was established under the pre–1909 law. *Ferris v. Frohman,* 223 U.S. 424 (1912). The *Ferris* rule was applied by analogy to the exhibition of a motion picture, *De Mille v. Casey,* 121 Misc. 78 (N.Y.Sup.Ct.1923); the public performance of a musical composition, whether for profit or not, *McCarthy v. White,* 259 F. 364 (S.D.N.Y.1919); and the oral delivery of a lecture or address, *Nutt v. National Institute, Inc.,* 31 F.2d 236 (2d Cir.1929), all irrespective of the methods employed, including radio broadcasting. *Uproar Co. v. National Broadcasting Co.,* 81 F.2d 373 (1st Cir.1936).

There was considerable uncertainty whether, under the 1909 Act, the general distribution of phonograph records of a musical or a literary work constituted a publication that forfeited common-law protection and required use of a copyright notice in order to secure statutory protection. A key influence in contributing to this uncertainty was a Supreme Court decision, under the pre–1909 law, which held that a perforated "pianola" music roll was not a "copy" of a musical composition and therefore did not infringe the copyright in the composition. *White–Smith Music Pub'g Co. v. Apollo Co.,* 209 U.S. 1 (1908). While Congress directly remedied this situation in 1909 by giving the copyright owner control in § 1(e) over mechanical reproduction of music, it did so without equating mechanical reproduction with "copy."

Accordingly, for more than half a century, it was generally accepted in a number of contexts that a recording is not a "copy" of the work recorded, and in particular that the sale of records of a song did not oust common-law copyright and did not require the use of a copyright notice. *See Rosette v. Rainbo Record Mfg. Corp.,* 354 F.Supp. 1183 (S.D.N.Y.1973), *aff'd per curiam*, 546 F.2d 461 (2d Cir.1976). But to the surprise of many—particularly those in the music publishing and recording industries—a directly contrary result was reached in 1995 by the Court of Appeals for the Ninth Circuit, in *La Cienega Music Co. v. ZZ Top,* 53 F.3d 950 (9th Cir.1995). Congress did not wait long before it enacted a statutory amendment to overturn the result in that case, which threatened the loss of copyright in thousands of songs recorded and distributed (without copyright notice on the record) before 1978. Pub. L. No. 105–80, 111 Stat. 1534 (1997). Section 303(b) was added to the Act: "The distribution before January 1, 1978, of a phonorecord shall not for any purpose constitute a publication of the musical work embodied therein."

Under the 1909 Act, considerable uncertainty was also created as to the effect of publication of a derivative work—such as a reproduction of a work of art, or the motion picture based on a novel—on the status of the underlying work on which it is based. *Compare Rushton v. Vitale,* 218 F.2d 434 (2d Cir.1955), *with Leigh v. Gerber,* 86 F.Supp. 320 (S.D.N.Y.1949). In *Batjac Prods. v. GoodTimes Home Video Corp.,* 160 F.3d 1223 (9th Cir. 1998), the Ninth Circuit held that "a common law copyright in the underlying screenplay does not survive the motion picture's loss of copyright and falls into the public domain due to a failure to renew the movie's copyright." *Accord, Shoptalk, Ltd. v. Concorde–New Horizons Corp.,* 168 F.3d 586 (2d Cir.1999) (publication of motion picture "The Little Shop of Horrors" published as much of the film's screenplay as was disclosed in the film); *Harris Custom Builders, Inc. v. Hoffmeyer,* 92 F.3d 517, 520 (7th Cir.1996), *cert. denied,* 519 U.S. 1114 (1997) (publication of architectural drawings publishes underlying plans); *Classic Film Museum, Inc. v. Warner Bros., Inc.,* 597 F.2d 13 (1st Cir.1979) (publication of motion picture publishes underlying screenplay to the extent the movie incorporates the screenplay).

Limited Publication. It should be apparent from the above discussion that disclosure or communication of a work to another person does not always amount to "publication" under the copyright law. Restricted communication of the contents of a work was generally held not to be a publication of the work. Distribution with limitation by the proprietor of the persons to whom the work is communicated and of the purpose of the disclosure was long known as "limited," "restricted," or "private" publication, but is, more accurately, no publication at all. *See White v. Kimmell,* 193 F.2d 744 (9th Cir.), *cert. denied,* 343 U.S. 957 (1952).

The absence of any effort to limit distribution or use of copies of speeches by a public official could result in a finding of publication with divestive effect. In *Public Affairs Assocs. v. Rickover,* 284 F.2d 262 (D.C.Cir. 1960), *judgment vacated,* 369 U.S. 111 (1962), *on remand,* 268 F.Supp. 444 (D.D.C.1967), Justice Reed (sitting by designation) stated:

> Certainly when all of Admiral Rickover's acts of distribution are considered together—performance, distribution to the press, the copies sent to individuals at the recipient's request and those sent unsolicited, the copies sent in batches of 50 for distribution by the sponsors of

speeches—it is difficult to avoid the conclusion that these acts, in their totality, constitute publication of the speeches and their dedication to the public domain.

284 F.2d at 271. The court remanded for further hearing, but its judgment was vacated by the Supreme Court for a more adequate record.

The *Rickover* case was distinguished in *King v. Mister Maestro, Inc.,* 224 F.Supp. 101 (S.D.N.Y.1963), in which distribution in a press kit of "advance copies" of Rev. Martin Luther King Jr.'s famous "I Have a Dream" speech was held to be a limited publication because the copies were not offered *to the public.*

The distinction between limited and general publication under the 1909 Act was complicated even further by the distinction between "divestive" and "investive" publication. The former described dissemination that lost common law copyright; the latter described dissemination, with copyright notice, that triggered statutory copyright—and, out of concern for forfeitures, courts more readily found the latter than the former. *E.g.,* *Atlantic Monthly Co. v. Post Pub'g Co.,* 27 F.2d 556 (D.Mass.1928) (sale of proof copy of magazine to publisher's treasurer held investive publication "insofar as the statutory formalities are concerned").

The Notice Requirement. Once a determination was made that a work was "published," the 1909 Act—as did most of its forebears— required the placement of a copyright notice in a specified location. This requirement was rooted in § 10: "Any person entitled thereto by this title may secure copyright for his work by publication thereof with the notice of copyright required by this title; and such notice shall be affixed to each copy thereof published or offered for sale in the United States by authority of the copyright proprietor." The required form of notice was set forth in § 19, which (with some minor exceptions) provided for the word "copyright" (or abbreviation) or the familiar copyright symbol, the name of the copyright proprietor and the year of publication. That section also mandated the location of the notice—for a book, "upon its title page or the page immediately following"; for a periodical, "either upon the title page or upon the first page of text of each separate number or under the title heading"; and for a musical work "either upon its title page or the first page of music."

Some courts were prepared to overlook minor departures from the form and location requirements of the 1909 Act, provided there was substantial compliance. This was particularly true if a technically inaccurate corporate or partnership name was used, but it was close enough to the name of the true copyright proprietor (e.g., a company with identical officers) such that no one could reasonably claim to have been misled. But other courts were more punctilious, operating on the theory that the copyright was a special legislative privilege that could be secured only through full compliance with formalities. Although a notice accompanying the masthead of a periodical (typically on the editorial page of a newspaper) was commonly regarded as satisfactory, it was, for example, held that it was improper to place the copyright notice on the back cover of a 28–page pamphlet; such a defect was regarded as fatal, and the work was thrust into the public domain. *J.A. Richards, Inc. v. New York Post*, 23 F.Supp. 619 (S.D.N.Y.1938). Similarly, courts could be strict about the placement of the notice on a journal or other collective work, holding that such notice would not protect included works that were authored by others and that did not carry a separate copyright notice. *E.g., Sanga Music Inc. v. EMI Blackwood Music, Inc.*, 55 F.3d 756 (2d Cir.1995).

Inaccuracies in the year date placed in the notice could also be fatal to the copyright. The general rule that developed, through judicial decisions and Copyright Office regulations, was that an inaccurately *early* date was not fatal, but the beginning of the statutory term would be reckoned from that year (so as to shorten the term of protection, for the benefit of the public); while a notice that was *postdated* by more than one year (thus allowing for end-of-the-year slippage in publication schedules) was regarded as fatally defective.

Of course, if the required notice was altogether omitted, that too was fatal. The statute itself, however, in § 21, allowed of one exception: when the copyright owner had "sought to comply" with the notice provisions but "by accident or mistake" had omitted the notice "from a particular copy or copies." That oversight would not invalidate the copyright, but would "prevent the recovery of damages against an innocent infringer who has been misled by the omission of the notice." This statutory exception, however, was held not to apply if the omission of notice was through "neglect or oversight," *Sieff v. Continental Auto Supply*, 39 F.Supp. 683 (D.Minn.1941), or through a mistake of law, *Wildman v. New York Times Co.*, 42 F.Supp. 412 (S.D.N.Y.1941).

Another issue that has divided the courts is whether U.S. copyright is lost, under the 1909 Act, when a work is first published without a notice of copyright outside of the U.S. The Court of Appeals for the Ninth Circuit recently answered that question in the negative—thought by many to be the correct view—in *Twin Books Corp. v. Walt Disney Co.*, 83 F.3d 1162 (9th Cir.1996), which involved the beloved story of Bambi the deer. "Bambi, A Life in the Woods" was first published without notice in Germany in 1923, and then republished with notice in 1926 (and registered for U.S. copyright). The copyright owner renewed the copyright in 1954, which would have been too late had the work's first publication been in 1923. The court noted some early decisions which indicated that publication abroad without notice forfeits the possibility of securing copyright through a later U.S. publication, but the court concluded that such a view conflicted with the prevailing doctrine of "territoriality" of the copyright law. The Ninth Circuit relied upon *Heim v. Universal Pictures Co.*, 154 F.2d 480 (2d Cir.1946), for the proposition that publication abroad without notice—in a nation that does not place the work in the public domain for that reason— will not prevent subsequently obtaining a valid U.S. copyright. (When enacted in 1976, however, the revised Copyright Act, in § 401(a), did require notice "whenever a work protected under this title is published in the United States *or elsewhere* by authority of the copyright owner...."

(Emphasis added.) It was held in *Hasbro Bradley, Inc. v. Sparkle Toys, Inc.*, see *infra*, that a toy published by a Japanese copyright owner in Japan, without notice, fell short of the requirement in § 401(a). Of course, as will be noted below, this notice requirement was eliminated through an amendment of the 1976 Copyright Act, effective March 1, 1989.)

Estate of Martin Luther King, Jr., Inc. v. CBS, Inc.

194 F.3d 1211 (11th Cir.1999).

■ ANDERSON, CHIEF JUDGE

The Estate of Martin Luther King, Jr., Inc. brought this copyright infringement action against CBS, Inc. after CBS produced a video documentary that used, without authorization, portions of civil rights leader Dr. Martin Luther King's famous "I Have a Dream" speech at the March on Washington on August 28, 1963. The district court granted summary judgment to CBS on the ground that Dr. King had engaged in a general publication of the speech, placing it into the public domain. See Estate of Martin Luther King, Jr., Inc. v. CBS, Inc., 13 F.Supp.2d 1347 (N.D.Ga. 1998). We now reverse.

I. Facts

The facts underlying this case form part of our national heritage and are well-known to many Americans. On the afternoon of August 28, 1963, the Southern Christian Leadership Conference ("SCLC") held the March on Washington ("March") to promote the growing civil rights movement. The events of the day were seen and heard by some 200,000 people gathered at the March, and were broadcast live via radio and television to a nationwide audience of millions of viewers. The highlight of the March was a rousing speech that Dr. Martin Luther King, Jr., the SCLC's founder and president, gave in front of the Lincoln Memorial ("Speech"). The Speech contained the famous utterance, "I have a dream" which became symbolic of the civil rights movement. The SCLC had sought out wide press coverage of the March and the Speech, and these efforts were successful; the Speech was reported in daily newspapers across the country, was broadcast live on radio and television, and was extensively covered on television and radio subsequent to the live broadcast.

On September 30, 1963, approximately one month after the delivery of the Speech, Dr. King took steps to secure federal copyright protection for the Speech under the Copyright Act of 1909, and a certificate of registration of his claim to copyright was issued by the Copyright Office on October 2, 1963. Almost immediately thereafter, Dr. King filed suit in the Southern District of New York to enjoin the unauthorized sale of recordings of the Speech and won a preliminary injunction on December 13, 1963. See King v. Mister Maestro, Inc., 224 F.Supp. 101 (S.D.N.Y.1963).

For the next twenty years, Dr. King and the Estate enjoyed copyright protection in the Speech and licensed it for a variety of uses, and renewed the copyright when necessary. In 1994, CBS entered into a contract with the Arts & Entertainment Network to produce a historical documentary series entitled "The 20th Century with Mike Wallace." One segment was devoted to "Martin Luther King, Jr. and The March on Washington." That episode contained material filmed by CBS during the March and extensive footage of the Speech (amounting to about 60% of its total content). CBS, however, did not seek the Estate's permission to use the Speech in this manner and refused to pay royalties to the Estate. The instant litigation ensued.

On summary judgment, the district court framed the issue as "whether the public delivery of Dr. King's speech ... constituted a general publication of the speech so as to place it in the public domain." 13 F.Supp.2d at 1351. After discussing the relevant case law, the district court held that Dr. King's "performance coupled with such wide and unlimited reproduction and dissemination as occurred concomitant to Dr. King's speech during the March on Washington can be seen only as a general publication which thrust the speech into the public domain." Id. at 1354. Thus, the district court granted CBS's motion for summary judgment. The Estate now appeals to this Court.[2]

II. Discussion

* * * * Because of the dates of the critical events, the determinative issues in this case are properly analyzed under the Copyright Act of 1909 ("1909 Act"), rather than the Copyright Act of 1976 ("1976 Act") that is currently in effect. See Brown v. Tabb, 714 F.2d 1088, 1091 (11th Cir.1983) ("[T]he determination whether a work entered the public domain prior to the effective date of the 1976 Act must be made according to the copyright law as it existed before that date."). The question is whether Dr. King's attempt to obtain statutory copyright protection on September 30, 1963 was effective, or whether it was a nullity because the Speech had already been forfeited to the public domain via a general publication.

Under the regime created by the 1909 Act, an author received state common law protection automatically at the time of creation of a work. This state common law protection persisted until the moment of a general publication. When a general publication occurred, the author either forfeited his work to the public domain, see, e.g., White v. Kimmell, 193 F.2d 744 (9th Cir.1952), or, if he had therebefore complied with federal statutory requirements, converted his common law copyright into a federal statutory copyright. See Mister Maestro, 224 F.Supp. at 105 ("The [statutory] copyright may be obtained before publication of such works but as soon as publication occurs there must be compliance with the requirements as to published works.") ...

---

2. If Dr. King and the Estate had a valid copyright in the Speech under the 1909 Act, that copyright was carried forward under the 1976 Act pursuant to the provisions of 17 U.S.C. § 304. In 1991, the copyright in the Speech was duly renewed.

In order to soften the hardship of the rule that publication destroys common law rights, courts developed a distinction between a "general publication" and a "limited publication." Brown, 714 F.2d at 1091 (citing American Vitagraph, Inc. v. Levy, 659 F.2d 1023, 1026–27 (9th Cir.1981)). Only a general publication divested a common law copyright. See id. A general publication occurred "when a work was made available to members of the public at large without regard to their identity or what they intended to do with the work." Id. (citing Burke v. National Broadcasting Co., 598 F.2d 688, 691 (1st Cir.1979)). Conversely, a non-divesting limited publication was one that communicated the contents of a work to a select group and for a limited purpose, and without the right of diffusion, reproduction, distribution or sale. The issue before us is whether Dr. King's delivery of the Speech was a general publication.

Numerous cases stand for the proposition that the performance of a work is not a general publication. See, e.g., Ferris v. Frohman, 223 U.S. 424, 433, 32 S.Ct. 263, 265, 56 L.Ed. 492 (1912) ("The public representation of a dramatic composition, not printed and published, does not deprive the owner of his common-law right.... [T]he public performance of the play is not an abandonment of it to the public use."); * * * Columbia Broad. Sys., Inc. v. Documentaries Unlimited, Inc., 42 Misc.2d 723, 248 N.Y.S.2d 809, 811 (Sup.Ct.1964) (holding with respect to news anchor's famous announcement of the death of President Kennedy that "[t]he rendering of a performance before the microphone does not constitute an abandonment of ownership or a dedication of it to the public at large"); * * * see generally Nimmer & sect; & ensp;4.08, at 4–43 ("[T]he oral dissemination or performance of a literary, dramatic, or musical work does not constitute a publication of that work.").

It appears from the case law that a general publication occurs only in two situations. First, a general publication occurs if tangible copies of the work are distributed to the general public in such a manner as allows the public to exercise dominion and control over the work. * * * Second, a general publication may occur if the work is exhibited or displayed in such a manner as to permit unrestricted copying by the general public. See * * * Letter Edged in Black Press, Inc. v. Public Bldg. Comm'n of Chicago, 320 F.Supp. 1303, 1311 (N.D.Ill.1970) (invoking this exception where "there were no restrictions on copying [of a publicly displayed sculpture] and no guards preventing copying" and "every citizen was free to copy the maquette for his own pleasure and camera permits were available to members of the public"). However, the case law indicates that restrictions on copying may be implied, and that express limitations in that regard are deemed unnecessary. See American Tobacco, 207 U.S. at 300, 28 S.Ct. at 77 (holding that there is no general publication where artwork is exhibited and "there are bylaws against copies, or where it is *tacitly* understood that no copying shall take place, and the public are admitted ... on the *implied understanding* that no improper advantage will be taken of the privilege" (emphasis added)) * * *.

The case law indicates that distribution to the news media, as opposed to the general public, for the purpose of enabling the reporting of a contemporary newsworthy event, is only a limited publication. For example, in Public Affairs Assoc., Inc. v. Rickover, 284 F.2d 262 (D.C.Cir.1960), vacated on other grounds, 369 U.S. 111, 82 S.Ct. 580, 7 L.Ed.2d 604 (1962), the court said that general publication occurs only when there is "a studied effort not only to secure publicity for the contents of the addresses through the channels of information, but to *go beyond customary sources of press or broadcasting* in distributing the addresses to any interested individual." Id. at 270 (emphasis added). Although the *Rickover* court ultimately held that a general publication had occurred, it contrasted the "limited use of the addresses by the press for fair comment," i.e., limited publication, with "the unlimited distribution to anyone who was interested," i.e., general publication. Id. at 271. See also *Mister Maestro*, 224 F.Supp. at 107 (taking the position that solicitation of news coverage and distribution to the media amounts to only a limited publication); cf. *Documentaries Unlimited, Inc.*, 248 N.Y.S.2d at 810–11 (news anchor's announcement concerning the assassination of President Kennedy was not generally published by virtue of the broadcast over the radio as newsworthy material). This rule comports with common sense; it does not force an author whose message happens to be newsworthy to choose between obtaining news coverage for his work and preserving his common-law copyright. * * *

With the above principles in mind, in the summary judgment posture of this case and on the current state of this record, we are unable to conclude that CBS has demonstrated beyond any genuine issue of material fact that Dr. King, simply through his oral delivery of the Speech, engaged in a general publication making the Speech "available to members of the public at large without regard to their identity or what they intended to do with the work." *Brown*, 714 F.2d at 1091. A performance, no matter how broad the audience, is not a publication; to hold otherwise would be to upset a long line of precedent. This conclusion is not altered by the fact that the Speech was broadcast live to a broad radio and television audience and was the subject of extensive contemporaneous news coverage. We follow the above cited case law indicating that release to the news media for contemporary coverage of a newsworthy event is only a limited publication.[4]

---

4. We emphasize the summary judgment posture of this case, which necessitates that we disregard evidence that may be important or even dispositive at trial. In other words, in this summary judgment posture, we consider only the evidence with respect to which there is no genuine issue of material fact. This evidence includes only the fact of the oral delivery of the Speech to a large audience and the fact that the sponsors of the event including Dr. King sought and successfully obtained live broadcasts on radio and television and extensive contemporary coverage in the news media. In this regard, we do not consider at this stage of the litigation two potentially important pieces of evidence brought to our attention by CBS. First, an advance text of the Speech was apparently available in a press tent on the day of the speech. According to an eyewitness affidavit submitted by CBS, members of the public at large—not merely the press—were permitted access to the press tent and were given copies of the advance text. However, the Estate has proffered affidavits which contradict the statements of the CBS witness, and suggest

* * * The district court held that "the circumstances in this case take the work in question outside the parameters of the 'performance is not a publication' doctrine." 13 F.Supp.2d at 1351. These circumstances included "the overwhelmingly public nature of the speech and the fervent intentions of the March organizers to draw press attention." Id. Certainly, the Speech was one of a kind—a unique event in history.[5]

However, the features that make the Speech unique—e.g., the huge audience and the Speech's significance in terms of newsworthiness and history—are features that, according to the case law, are not significant in the general versus limited publication analysis. With respect to the huge audience, the case law indicates that the general publication issue depends, not on the number of people involved, but rather on the fact that the work is made available to the public without regard to who they are or what they propose to do with it. * * * In the instant case, the district court acknowledged that "[t]he size of the audience before which a work is performed cannot be the basis for a court's finding that a general publication has occurred." 13 F.Supp.2d at 1352.

With respect to the significance of the Speech in terms of newsworthiness and history, the case law again suggests that this feature should not play a substantial role in the analysis. As noted above, the D.C. Circuit in Rickover indicated that the wide press distribution of the speeches at issue there would not alone have constituted a general publication. Indeed, *Mister Maestro* so held with respect to the very Speech at issue before us. Also supporting this proposition is the case law above cited to the effect that size of the audience is not significant.

The district court cited Letter Edged in Black Press, Inc. v. Public Bldg. Comm'n of Chicago, 320 F.Supp. 1303 (N.D.Ill.1970), CBS's best case,

that access was controlled by the SCLC within reasonable means. Moreover, the Estate argues that much of the content of the Speech was generated extemporaneously by Dr. King and was not contained in this advance text—an argument that we do not consider but that can be explored by the district court. Finding genuine issues of material fact with respect to the availability of the advance text to the general public, the district court disregarded CBS's allegations in this regard, 13 F.Supp.2d at 1353 n. 5. We agree, and do likewise.

Second, CBS has produced a September 1963 issue of the SCLC's newsletter in which the text of the Speech was reprinted in its entirety, with no copyright notice. The newsletter was widely circulated to the general public. Indeed, at oral argument, the Estate conceded that this reprinting of the Speech and wide distribution of the newsletter would constitute a general publication, if it were authorized by Dr. King. However, the Estate

has raised the issue that Dr. King did not authorize this reprinting and distribution of the Speech. Finding genuine issues of fact in this regard, the district court disregarded this evidence. We agree, and do likewise.

Finally, we note that the opinion in *Mister Maestro*, 224 F.Supp. at 104, suggests that there may have been evidence of subsequent rebroadcasts of the Speech in movie houses and sales of phonograph records. We do not consider any such evidence because CBS has not argued in this appeal that such evidence is relevant at this stage. Moreover, the opinion in *Mister Maestro* suggests that there may be genuine issues of material fact (e.g., authorization) with respect to such evidence.

5. The district court stated that "as one of the most public and most widely disseminated speeches in history, [the Speech] could be the poster child for general publications." 13 F.Supp.2d at 1353.

in support of its reasoning, see 13 F.Supp.2d at 1353–54, and that case warrants some exploration. In *Letter Edged in Black*, the question was whether the city had dedicated a Picasso sculpture (located in front of the Chicago Civic Center) to the public domain by general publication. The city had done the following: it carried out a massive campaign to publicize the monumental sculpture; it placed a maquette (portable model of the sculpture) on exhibition at a local museum; it gave photographs to the public upon request; it arranged for pictures of the sculpture to appear in several magazines of large national circulation; it sold a postcard featuring the sculpture; and it distributed numerous publications and reports containing photographs of the sculpture. See *Letter Edged in Black*, 320 F.Supp. at 1306–07. After stating the controlling legal principles with regard to general and limited publication, the *Letter Edged in Black* court stated its view that the cumulation of these various acts by the city equated to general publication. * * *

The district court likened the instant case to *Letter Edged in Black* on the ground that there was a lack of restriction on copying and free allowance of reproduction by the press. However, we do not believe the analogy fits—at least not at this summary judgment stage. Significantly, in *Letter Edged in Black* there were manifestations of the city's intent to distribute generally among the public at large that have no parallels in the evidence we can consider in the instant summary judgment posture. The city gave photographs of the sculpture to the public, not merely the press, upon request. The city commercially sold a postcard featuring the sculpture. Copying was apparently widespread at an exhibit of the sculpture, and the city took no action to curtail copying and photographing by the public. At trial, CBS may well produce evidence that brings the instant case on all fours with *Letter Edged in Black*,[6] but the present state of the record does not support the analogy; to the contrary, the performance of the Speech in the instant case is more like the exhibition of the painting in the gallery in *American Tobacco [Co. v. Werckmeister*, 207 U.S. 284 (1907), where the copying of exhibited paintings was forbidden].[7]

---

6. For example, if the SCLC's reprinting of the text of the Speech in the September 1963 newsletter was authorized, see supra note 4, that reprinting might be analogous to the public distribution of photographs in *Letter Edged in Black*. Similarly, if CBS were to adduce evidence that Dr. King or his agents offered copies of the Speech indiscriminately to any member of the public who requested them, e.g., through the availability of the advance text in the press tent, that would make the facts of the instant case closer to those of *Letter Edged in Black*.

7. *Public Affairs Associates, Inc. v. Rickover*, where the D.C. Circuit found a general publication by virtue of Admiral Rickover's distribution to the public of copies of his speeches, is also factually distinguishable. " 'In distributing the speeches, Admiral Rickover mailed some [copies] to individuals who had requested copies or who[m] Admiral Rickover believed would be interested in the subject. Some were sent by Admiral Rickover, approximately 50 in each case, to the sponsor of the speech to be made available to the press and others at the place where the speech was to be delivered.' " *Rickover*, 284 F.2d at 266 (emphasis added) (quoting the parties' agreed statement of facts). In short, as the court observed, "[a]nyone was welcome to a copy." Id. at 271. The present state of the record in the instant case does not allow us to draw similar conclusions with respect to Dr. King's Speech.

Because there exist genuine issues of material fact as to whether a general publication occurred, we must reverse the district court's grant of summary judgment for CBS. * * * *

■ Cook, Senior District Judge, concurring in part and dissenting in part:

I concur in the result that was reached by my distinguished colleague, Chief Judge Anderson. Nevertheless, I write separately to express my own thoughts about this very complicated area of the law. To summarize, I agree with the proposition that this case is controlled by the 1909 Copyright Act, under which Dr. King did not lose copyright protection over his "I Have A Dream Speech" by placing it into the public domain based on the factors considered below. However, my reading of the law leads me to believe that a distinction between works that are performed and those that are not is crucial to a proper resolution of this dispute. . . .

* * * While agreeing with Chief Judge Anderson that the speech was not placed into the public domain on the basis of these factors [Dr. King's delivery of the speech, the contemporaneous wide dissemination by broadcast and print media through efforts of the March organizers, and the absence of restrictions on copying by press and public], I do not reach this conclusion because of the limited publication rule. Rather, I rely upon the more fundamental principle that, in the context of performed works, none of these factors may be properly considered as having contributed to a general or limited publication in the absence of an authorized dissemination of a tangible copy of the work without copyright notice.

. . . [I]t is my view that the trial court erred by failing to recognize the special nature of performed works such as speeches which was recognized by the principle under the common law and the 1909 Act that performance does not constitute publication in the absence of an authorized distribution of tangible copies without a copyright notice or a reservation of rights . . .

The trial court ruled that the widespread dissemination of the speech, which was due in large measure to the efforts of the March organizers, supported the conclusion that it had been placed into the public domain. In my opinion, this reasoning is incorrect because the size of the audience before whom a work is performed is irrelevant to the issue of publication. * * *

The logical result of the rule that performance cannot constitute a publication regardless of audience size is that an affirmative effort to obtain press coverage does not constitute an exception because media coverage does nothing more than increase the size of the audience, which is irrelevant to the issue of publication. Thus, I am of the opinion that the trial court erroneously found that a general publication existed in part because of the widespread dissemination of the speech that had been implemented by the concerted efforts of the March organizers to maximize press coverage. * * *

■ Roney, Senior Circuit Judge, dissenting:

I respectfully dissent on the ground that the district court correctly held there was a general publication. I would affirm on the basis of the district court opinion. See Estate of Martin Luther King, Jr., Inc. v. CBS, Inc., 13 F.Supp.2d 1347 (N.D.Ga.1998).

Academy of Motion Picture Arts & Sciences v. Creative House Promotions, Inc., 944 F.2d 1446 (9th Cir.1991). The defendant, a manufacturer and distributor of advertising specialty items, commissioned and sold trophies shaped almost identically to the well-known Oscar statuette, except that the gold male figure was shorter and held a star rather than a sword. Most of the defendant's customers were corporate buyers who purchased the awards as gifts for employees. The Academy, which was founded in 1927 and had held its annual awards ceremony since 1929, insisted that Creative House discontinue or significantly change its star award; upon the refusal to do so, the Academy sued for copyright infringement. The trial court held that the distribution of the Oscar statuettes without any copyright notice, prior to 1941, was a "general publication" that divested common law copyright (under the 1909 Act) and thrust the statuette into the public domain. The court of appeals reversed.

From 1929 through 1941, the Academy awarded 159 Oscars, each bearing the winner's name but no copyright notice. In 1941, the Academy registered the Oscar with the Copyright Office as an unpublished work of art, and all Oscars since then have borne the copyright notice; copyright was renewed in 1968. The court of appeals stated that the registration created a rebuttable presumption of copyright validity, i.e., that the Oscar was an unpublished work in 1941. It also stated that common law copyright was not lost when a work was shown or distributed "to a limited class of persons for a limited purpose"; this doctrine of "limited publication" reflected "an attempt by the courts to mitigate the harsh forfeiture effects of a divesting general publication." The court held that the display and presentation of the Oscar statuettes at the annual award ceremonies was such a limited publication, even though there was no express restriction on the use or sale of the award. So too, "publishing pictures of the Oscar in books, newspapers, and magazines did not thrust the award into the public domain, because publishing two-dimensional pictures does not constitute a divesting publication of three-dimensional objects."

The court found compliance with the several prerequisites for a "limited publication." (1) The Oscar was awarded "only to a *select group of persons.*" (2) The *purpose* of distributing the award was limited: Oscars have never been sold to anyone and have been distributed only to award recipients, for the limited purpose "of advancing the motion picture arts and sciences." (The court referred to one case in which business cards featuring a reproduced photograph were distributed for employment purposes, and another case in which 2000 copies of a song were distributed to broadcasting stations and musicians for "plugging" purposes; both found only a limited purpose and thus a limited publication.) (3) Oscar recipients have had *no right of sale or further distribution*; restrictions on recipients' use or distribution, although not express, were implied, and "neither the Academy nor any living Oscar recipient has ever offered to transfer an Oscar to the general public." In sum, "the Academy's actions constituted a limited publication that did not divest the Oscar of its common law protection." The court remanded to allow the Academy to present evidence of copyright infringement.

QUESTIONS

1.   What was the policy that underlay the divesting of perpetual common law copyright once a work was "published"? Should common law copyright be divested when a Broadway play runs for three years before capacity audiences, but is not marketed in book form? When a painting is exhibited indefinitely in a public museum?

2.   The Court of Appeals for the Ninth Circuit, in the "Oscar" case, held that publication of a two-dimensional representation of a three-dimensional work—for example, distribution of photographs of a sculpture—does not publish the three-dimensional work. (The case cited by the court involved the wide distribution of toy catalogues, without copyright notice, showing photographs of an "E.T." doll.) Why is that so? Under the court's analysis, would the Academy's marketing of three-dimensional miniature Oscar statuettes divest common law copyright? Is that not just as much a "derivative work" of the original statue as is a photograph? (If you *wished* to publish a sculpture, how would you do it?)

B.   1976 ACT SOLUTIONS AS TO PUBLICATION AND NOTICE

1.   "PUBLICATION": DEFINITION AND CONTEXTS

Section 101 defines publication as:

The distribution of copies or phonorecords of a work to the public by sale or other transfer of ownership, or by rental, lease, or lending. The offering to distribute copies or phonorecords to a group of persons for purposes of further distribution, public performance, or public display, constitutes publication. A public performance or display of a work does not itself constitute publication.

This definition resolves many of the problems that arose by virtue of the definitional vacuum in the 1909 Act, particularly by providing that a public performance or display of a work is not a "publication" that bears upon the use of a copyright notice; but that the public distribution of phonograph records does constitute publication of the recorded work (as well as of the sound recording).

Not all confusion or uncertainty is dispelled, however. For example, almost 70 years after *White–Smith Music Pub'g Co. v. Apollo Co.*, 209 U.S. 1 (1908), Congress still declined to equate recordings with copies. Thus, in this definition and throughout the statute, one notes the refrain "copies or phonorecords." And, as will be noted below, there is no provision for use of a © copyright notice on phonorecords pertaining to the underlying recorded work. (There *is* a provision for a Ⓟ notice pertaining to the recorded *performance* under § 402.) And, while the statute uses "copies" and "phonorecords" in the plural, the committee reports state that under this definition "a work is 'published' if *one or more* copies or phonorecords embodying it are distributed to the public." (Emphasis added.) S. Rep. No. 94–473 at 121; H.R. Rep. No. 94–1476 at 138. But Chairman Kastenmeier of the House subcommittee stated on the House Floor that "in the case of a work of art, such as a painting or statue, that exists in only one copy . . . [i]t is not the committee's intention that such a work should be regarded as 'published' when the single existing copy is sold or offered for sale in the traditional way—for example, through an art dealer, gallery, or auction house." 122 Cong. Rec. H10875 (Sept. 22, 1976).

When one hears the overstatement that the 1976 Act "does away with" publication, one should consider at least the following statutory provisions in which the concept of publication is significant: under § 104, unpublished works are protected irrespective of the nationality of the author, while with respect to published works such nationality at the time of first publication is relevant; under § 107, the fair use doctrine is generally applied less generously to unpublished works; under § 108, libraries are given wider exemptions in the photocopying of unpublished works; under § 302(c) and (e), the duration of protection for anonymous and pseudonymous works and works made for hire is measured from publication or creation, and under § 303, works created before 1978 but not yet published are given statutory protection for a term of life-plus–50 (or 70, depending upon the dates involved); and under § 407 deposit for Library of Congress purposes is mandatory for works once they are published.

Over and above the foregoing, publication was most integrally connected under the 1976 Act before U.S. adherence to the Berne Convention (just as it had been under the 1909 Act) with the question of *notice* covered in Chapter 4 of the Act.

QUESTIONS

Which of the following acts amount to "publication" under the 1976 Copyright Act:

1. A professor, in class, distributes outlines and questions to her students in "hardcopy" form. At other times, she distributes this information by an e-mail message; and at other times, on her webpage.

2. An architect distributes blueprints to a municipal agency and subcontractors. *See Kunycia v. Melville Realty Co.,* 755 F.Supp. 566 (S.D.N.Y.1990).

3. An author, or her agent, offers copies of a manuscript to five publishers for their consideration.

4. A producer of computer hardware and software leases programs, encoded on magnetic tape, under a restrictive licensing agreement to purchasers of the producer's hardware. *See Hubco Data Prods. Corp. v. Management Assistance, Inc.,* 219 U.S.P.Q. 450 (D.Idaho 1983).

5. An artist offers an original oil painting to a museum for exhibition.

6. A record company distributes a "single" of a song; the song has not yet been sold as sheet music or otherwise distributed. *See, e.g., Greenwich Film Prods. v. DRG Records, Inc.*, 25 U.S.P.Q.2d 1435 (S.D.N.Y. 1992).

2.   THE NOTICE REQUIREMENT: 1978 TO MARCH 1989

Among the issues that were hotly debated during the comprehensive revision of the 1909 Copyright Act was the continued imposition of a requirement to place copyright notice on "published" works and the sanction for a failure to do so. Congress decided to retain the notice requirement but to make less draconian the consequences of an error or omission. The reasons are set forth in the House Report.

House Report

H.R. Rep. No. 94–1476, 94th Cong., 2d Sess. 143–44 (1976).

A requirement that the public be given formal notice of every work in which copyright is claimed was a part of the first U.S. copyright statute enacted in 1790, and since 1802 our copyright laws have always provided that the published copies of copyrighted works must bear a specified notice as a condition of protection. Under the present law the copyright notice serves four principal functions:

(1) It has the effect of placing in the public domain a substantial body of published material that no one is interested in copyrighting;

(2) It informs the public as to whether a particular work is copyrighted;

(3) It identifies the copyright owner; and

(4) It shows the date of publication.

Ranged against these values of a notice requirement are its burdens and unfairness to copyright owners. One of the strongest arguments for revision of the present statute has been the need to avoid the arbitrary and unjust forfeitures now resulting from unintentional or relatively unimportant omissions or errors in the copyright notice. It has been contended that the disadvantages of the notice requirement outweigh its values and that it should therefore be eliminated or substantially liberalized.

The fundamental principle underlying the notice provisions of the bill is that the copyright notice has real values which should be preserved, and that this should be done by inducing use of notice without causing outright forfeiture for errors or omissions. Subject to certain safeguards for innocent infringers, protection would not be lost by the complete omission of copyright notice from large numbers of copies or from a whole edition, if registration for the work is made before or within 5 years after publication. Errors in the name or date in the notice could be corrected without forfeiture of copyright.

The notice requirements were set forth in §§ 401 and 402 of the 1976 Act. Section 401 applied to "copies" of published works, and Section 402 to "phonorecords." The text of § 401 follows as originally written. (The principal change in its current text, as a result of an amendment in 1989, is that the word "shall" in the first sentence of § 401(a) has been replaced by the word "may.")

§ 401. Notice of Copyright: Visually Perceptible Copies

(a) *General Requirement.*—Whenever a work protected under this title is published in the United States or elsewhere by authority of the copyright owner, a notice of copyright as provided by this section shall be placed on all publicly distributed copies from which the work can be visually perceived, either directly or with the aid of a machine or device.

(b) *Form of Notice.*—The notice appearing on the copies shall consist of the following three elements:

(1) the symbol © (the letter C in a circle), or the word "Copyright," or the abbreviation "Copr."; and

(2) the year of first publication of the work; in the case of compilations or derivative works incorporating previously published material, the year date of first publication of the compilation or derivative work is sufficient. The year date may be omitted where a pictorial, graphic, or sculptural work, with accompanying text matter, if any, is reproduced in or on greeting cards, postcards, stationery, jewelry, dolls, toys, or any useful articles; and

(3) the name of the owner of copyright in the work, or an abbreviation by which the name can be recognized, or a generally known alternative designation of the owner.

(c) *Position of Notice.*—The notice shall be affixed to the copies in such manner and location as to give reasonable notice of the claim of copyright. The Register of Copyrights shall prescribe by regulation, as examples, specific methods of affixation and positions of the notice on various types of works that will satisfy this requirement, but these specifications shall not be considered exhaustive.

NOTICE FOR SOUND RECORDINGS, GOVERNMENT WORKS, AND COLLECTIVE WORKS

In § 402 as enacted in 1976 (and effective January 1, 1978), Congress provided for a different notice for sound recordings that were embodied in publicly distributed phonorecords. Congress thought it appropriate to afford a means for signaling a claim of copyright in the sound recording, as distinct from a claim of copyright in the literary or musical work that is performed in the sound recording.

Because the phonorecord (i.e., the vinyl or compact disc, or the audiotape) in which a song is embodied is not a "copy" of that song under § 101 of the Copyright Act, no © notice was required under § 401 in order to protect copyright in the song. But to protect copyright in the sound recording—so that it would be an infringement to make an unauthorized duplication of the recorded sounds—the 1976 Act required that a ℗ notice be placed on each phonorecord publicly distributed "in the United States or elsewhere by authority of the copyright owner." The form of notice was, in all respects, similar to the form of the © notice; and "the notice shall be placed on the surface of the phonorecord, or on the phonorecord label or container, in such manner and location as to give reasonable notice of the claim of copyright." (These provisions apply today as well, but on a permissive rather than required basis.) The use of the ℗ notice for the sound recording not only permits a clear claim of copyright to the sound recording as distinguished from the underlying literary or musical work; it also effects a distinction from the claim of any copyright in the printed text or art work appearing on the record label, album cover, or liner notes on the record jacket or tape container.

Section 403 deals with a work, published in copies or phonorecords, that consists "preponderantly of one or more works of the United States Government." For such works, the notice under § 401 or 402 is to include "a statement identifying, either affirmatively or negatively, those portions of the copies or phonorecords embodying any work or works protected under this title." The 1976 Congress thereby expected those who, for example, marketed commercially a public-domain government report or federal judicial opinions—and merely added an introduction or illustrations or commentary—to include a copyright notice that would avoid misleading the public into believing that the entire work was protected by the publisher's copyright and thus could not be copied. (You might wish to consult volumes of the West reporter system published between 1978 and 1989, to see whether they contained a proper copyright notice.) The more detailed copyright notice in section 403 has not been a requirement since 1989. As the court held in Matthew Bender & Co. v. West Pub. Co., 240 F.3d 116, 123 (2d Cir. 2001), although the section provides for a defense to certain remedies when the stipulated notice is missing, it "does not impose any affirmative obligation on a copyright holder" to use that notice.

Finally, § 404 of the 1976 Act drew a distinction between the copyright notice for a collective work and the distinct notice for separate articles or other contributions included therein. It provided that a separate contribution could bear its own notice, but also that the notice requirements of the statute for that contribution could be satisfied by using a single notice that was applicable to the collective work as a whole, even though the copyright owners of the collective work and the individual contribution were not the same. Because of the possible resulting confusion that might flow, Congress provided that a person misled by such a confusion—and who dealt with the wrong person in seeking permission to use an individual contribution—could have the defenses set forth in § 406(a), which deals with mistakes in the name placed in a copyright notice. Consult section 406 as presently written, to see how this issue is addressed with respect to material that was distributed before 1989—and material that has been distributed since.

QUESTIONS

1. Your client had a short story published in 1985 in *Science Fiction Magazine*. What copyright notice should be affixed, and where? (What significant information will the notice give the reader, and what will be omitted?)

2. Assume that it is 1986, and your client wishes to reprint her story, as written, in a paperback edition. What notice should the story bear? (What is the consequence of the notice bearing the date 1980? What is the consequence of the notice bearing the date 1990?)

3. *A,* an author, grants book rights to *B,* a publisher, which in turn grants paperback rights to *C.* Whose name should appear in the notice on the paperback edition?

4. You represent Pineapple Records, Inc., a manufacturer of phonograph records and tapes. A song composed by Alan Robert in 1985 is recorded by your client in 1986. The recording is released in 1987. (a) What copyright notice should be affixed and where? (b) Would your answer be any different if there were original artwork on the labels and jacket and textual notes on the jacket? (c) Sheet music embodying this song is distributed in 1988. What copyright notice should be affixed? Is this answer affected by the identity or lack of identity of the material embodied on the recording and on the sheet music?

————

§ 405. Notice of Copyright: Omission of Notice [Effective January 1, 1978 Through February 28, 1989]

(a) *Effect of Omission on Copyright.*—The omission of the copyright notice prescribed by sections 401 through 403 from copies or phonorecords publicly distributed by authority of the copyright owner does not invalidate the copyright in a work if—

(1) the notice has been omitted from no more than a relatively small number of copies or phonorecords distributed to the public; or

(2) registration for the work has been made before or is made within five years after the publication without notice, and a reasonable effort is made to add notice to all copies or phonorecords that are distributed to the public in the United States after the omission has been discovered; or

(3) the notice has been omitted in violation of an express requirement in writing that, as a condition of the copyright owner's authorization of the public distribution of copies or phonorecords, they bear the prescribed notice.

(b) *Effect of Omission on Innocent Infringers.*—Any person who innocently infringes a copyright, in reliance upon an authorized copy or phonorecord from which the copyright notice has been omitted, incurs no liability for actual or statutory damages under section 504 for any infringing acts committed before receiving actual notice that registration for the work has been made under section 408, if such person proves that he or she was misled by the omission of notice. In a suit for infringement in such a case the court may allow or disallow recovery of any of the infringer's profits attributable to the infringement, and may enjoin the continuation of the infringing undertaking or may require, as a condition of permitting the continuation of the infringing undertaking, that the infringer pay the copyright owner a reasonable license fee in an amount and on terms fixed by the court.

(c) *Removal of Notice.*—Protection under this title is not affected by the removal, destruction, or obliteration of the notice, without the authorization of the copyright owner, from any publicly distributed copies or phonorecords.

House Report
H.R. Rep. No. 94–1476, 94th Cong., 2d Sess. 146–48 (1976).

Effect of omission on copyright protection

The provisions of section 405(a) make clear that the notice requirements of sections 401, 402, and 403 are not absolute and that, unlike the law now in effect, the outright omission of a copyright notice does not automatically forfeit protection and throw the work into the public domain. This not only represents a major change in the theoretical framework of American copyright law, but it also seems certain to have immediate practical consequences in a great many individual cases. Under the proposed law a work published without any copyright notice will still be subject to statutory protection for at least 5 years, whether the omission was partial or total, unintentional or deliberate.

. . .

Effect of omission on innocent infringers

In addition to the possibility that copyright protection will be forfeited under section 405(a) (2) if the notice is omitted, a second major inducement to use of the notice is found in subsection (b) of section 405. That provision, which limits the rights of a copyright owner against innocent infringers under certain circumstances, would be applicable whether the notice has been omitted from a large number or from a "relatively small number" of copies. The general postulates underlying the provision are that a person acting in good faith and with no reason to think otherwise should ordinarily be able to assume that a work is in the public domain if there is no notice on an authorized copy or phonorecord and that, if he relies on this assumption, he should be shielded from unreasonable liability.

Under section 405(b) an innocent infringer who acts "in reliance upon an authorized copy or phonorecord from which the copyright notice has been omitted," and who proves that he was misled by the omission, is shielded from liability for actual or statutory damages with respect to "any infringing acts committed before receiving actual notice" of registration.

Thus, where the infringement is completed before actual notice has been served—as would be the usual case with respect to relatively minor infringements by teachers, librarians, journalists, and the like—liability, if any, would be limited to the profits the infringer realized from the act of infringement. On the other hand, where the infringing enterprise is one running over a period of time, the copyright owner would be able to seek an injunction against continuation of the infringement, and to obtain full monetary recovery for all infringing acts committed after he had served notice of registration. Persons who undertake major enterprises of this sort should check the Copyright Office registration records before starting, even where copies have been published without notice. . . .

Hasbro Bradley, Inc. v. Sparkle Toys, Inc., 780 F.2d 189 (2d Cir.1985). The plaintiff's predecessor (Takara) marketed certain toys in Japan but neglected to place any copyright notice on them. This was held not to comply with the notice requirement of § 401(a) as then written ("published in the United States or elsewhere"). The court held that this omission could, however, be excused or cured "under certain circumstances, in which case the copyright is valid from the moment the work was created, just as if no omission had occurred. . . . In effect, § 405(a)(2) allows a person who publishes a copyrightable work without notice to hold a kind of incipient copyright in the work for five years thereafter: if the omission is cured in that time through registration and the exercise of 'a reasonable effort . . . to add notice to all copies . . . that are distributed to the public in the United States after the omission has been discovered,' the copyright is perfected and valid retroactively for the entire period after cure; if the omission is not cured in that time, the incipient copyright never achieves enforceability."

The defendant argued that Hasbro had no power to cure under § 405(a)(2) because that section allows cure only when the omission is inadvertent and Takara's omission of notice was deliberate. The court rejected that reading of the section, and held that cure could be effected even when the initial omission of notice was deliberate. It relied, among other things, upon a statement in the House Report that "under the proposed law a work published without any copyright notice will still be subject to statutory protection for at least 5 years, whether the omission was partial or total, unintentional or deliberate," and a contemporaneous statement by the Register of Copyrights that "we concluded that questions involving the subjective state of mind of one or more persons and their ignorance or knowledge of the law should be avoided if at all possible . . . we decided that the bill should drop any distinction between 'deliberate' and 'inadvertent' or 'unintentional' omission and, subject to certain conditions, should preserve the copyright in all cases."

The court held that its conclusion was not inconsistent with the requirement in the cure provisions of § 405(a)(2) that there be reasonable efforts made to add the notice to all copies distributed to the public in the U.S. "after the omission has been discovered." The court explained: "No violence is done to the statutory language by saying that the omission, though deliberate on the part of the assignor or licensor, was 'discovered' by the person later attempting to cure it. Similarly, a deliberate omission at a lower level of a corporate hierarchy might well be 'discovered,' in all realistic terms, by someone at a higher level. Instances like these at least indicate that the 'discovered' language does not reveal a plain intent to exclude all deliberate omissions."

———

§ 406.   Notice of Copyright: Error in Name or Date [Effective January 1, 1978 Through February 28, 1989]

(a) *Error in Name.*—Where the person named in the copyright notice on copies or phonorecords publicly distributed by authority of the copyright owner is not the owner of copyright, the validity and ownership of the copyright are not affected. In such a case, however, any person who innocently begins an undertaking that infringes the copyright has a complete defense to any action for such infringement if such person proves that he or she was misled by the notice and began the undertaking in good faith under a purported transfer or license from the person named therein, unless before the undertaking was begun—

(1) registration for the work had been made in the name of the owner of copyright; or

(2) a document executed by the person named in the notice and showing the ownership of the copyright had been recorded.

The person named in the notice is liable to account to the copyright owner for all receipts from transfers or licenses purportedly made under the copyright by the person named in the notice.

(b) *Error in Date.*—When the year date in the notice on copies or phonorecords distributed by authority of the copyright owner is earlier than the year in which publication first occurred, any period computed from the year of first publication under section 302 is to be computed from the year in the notice. Where the year date is more than one year later than the year in which publication first occurred, the work is considered to have been published without any notice and is governed by the provisions of section 405.

(c) *Omission of Name or Date.*—Where copies or phonorecords publicly distributed by authority of the copyright owner contain no name or no date that could reasonably be considered a part of the notice, the work is considered to have been published without any notice and is governed by the provisions of section 405.

[*Editors' Note:* When the notice provisions in §§ 401 and 402 were made optional rather than mandatory, effective March 1, 1989, the text of

§§ 405 and 406 was amended so as to preserve their force and effect with respect to copies and phonorecords "publicly distributed by authority of the copyright owner before the effective date of the Berne Convention Implementation Act of 1988," that is, between January 1, 1978 and February 28, 1989 inclusive.]

QUESTIONS

1. Recall the publication of your client's short story in *Science Fiction Magazine* in 1985. Assume that the issue in which your client's story appears lacks any copyright notice, either on the masthead or on the story itself. Are there any steps your client could have taken (by what date?) to prevent copyright from being forfeited? Would a motion picture producer who saw the story in 1989 be free to base a script on it and produce a film?

2. Recall (yet again) the publication of your client's short story in *Science Fiction Magazine*. Assume that the only copyright notice in *Science Fiction* when your client's story was printed was the "masthead notice" in the name of *Science Fiction*. (Consult § 404.) Assume, too, that a motion picture producer buys the motion picture rights to the story from *Science Fiction* for $20,000; that one month later, he hires a scriptwriter; that two months later, he hires stars; that five months later, he begins production; and that the movie, when released, quickly nets $5 million. When your client learns of this, what are her rights (if any) against *Science Fiction* and the producer?

When Author brings an action against Magazine for the unauthorized (indeed fraudulent) transfer of copyright to Movie Producer, will Author's recovery be limited to $20,000?

What steps would you recommend that your client have taken at the outset to avoid this problem? What steps should the producer have taken?

3.   OPTIONAL NOTICE UNDER THE BERNE–IMPLEMENTATION ACT

As noted above, the major change required in the 1976 Act in order to permit United States adherence to the Berne Convention has been the elimination of the copyright notice as a precondition to copyright protection (even allowing for the five-year grace period for registration as a cure for omission of notice). In part because it is difficult to break with such a longstanding practice as the use of copyright notice, and in part because Congress and the Copyright Office continue to believe that notice serves useful purposes in warning unauthorized users and in conveying information, the Berne–Implementation amendments to the 1976 Act continue to provide incentives to the copyright owner to avail himself of what is now—since March 1, 1989—merely a discretionary option to use the notice on published works.

For works first published on or after March 1, 1989—and also for copies or phonorecords distributed after that date of works that had been published previously—§§ 401(a) and 402(a) no longer require placement of notice on publicly distributed copies and phonorecords, but instead provide that the © notice "may" be placed on copies and the Ⓟ notice "may" be placed on phonorecords of sound recordings. The form and placement of the optional notice are as they were previously when the notice was mandated. The incentive provided for use of the notice is set forth in a new subsection (d) to §§ 401 and 402. Section 401(d) now provides:

> *Evidentiary Weight of Notice.*—If a notice of copyright in the form specified by this section appears on the published copy or copies to which a defendant in a copyright infringement suit had access, then no weight shall be given to such a defendant's interposition of a defense based on innocent infringement in mitigation of actual or statutory damages, except as provided in the last sentence of section 504(c)(2).

Will that be a sufficient inducement to use the now optional copyright notice? Will there be any other inducements to do so, other than inertia? *See* H.R. Rep. No. 100–609, 100th Cong., 2d Sess. 26–67 (1988): "It is entirely possible that elimination of the notice formality may not in the end curtail its use. Old habits die hard; it remains useful under the Universal Copyright Convention; and, it is, in all probability, the cheapest deterrent to infringement which a copyright holder may take."

The question has arisen as to the "retroactive" import of the Berne Implementation amendments concerning notice. Assume, for example, that copies of a work were distributed without notice for a period shortly before March 1, 1989, and that the omission was discovered by the copyright owner before that date. Is it necessary, in order to avoid forfeiture of copyright, that there be registration within five years of initial publication? Is it also necessary to make reasonable efforts to add notice to after-distributed copies? One court has held that § 405 of the pre–1989 law governs those questions, which must therefore be answered in the affirmative. *Garnier v. Andin Int'l, Inc.*, 36 F.3d 1214 (1st Cir.1994). (Do you agree?)

C.   DEPOSIT AND REGISTRATION

Sections 407 through 412 of the 1976 Act enact a modernized administrative scheme with the dual purpose of enriching the resources of the Library of Congress and securing a comprehensive record of copyright claims. The former is achieved in § 407, which prescribes a mandatory system of deposit as to published works for Library purposes with administrative flexibility as to implementation and realistic sanctions for noncompliance under § 407(d) (not including forfeiture of copyright). The latter is embodied in a "permissive" registration provision, § 408. The Library deposit under § 407 may do double duty as the deposit required for registration under § 408. Moreover, the incentives for registration are quite strong. Accordingly, the dichotomy between these two deposit provisions may not be quite as sharp as initially thought.

1.   DEPOSIT FOR LIBRARY OF CONGRESS

The § 407 deposit, which "shall" be made by "the owner of copyright or of the exclusive right of publication" within three months after publication in the United States, is to consist of "two complete copies of the best edition" or, if the work is a sound recording, two complete phonorecords of the best edition, together with all accompanying printed material. The term "best edition" is defined in § 101 as "the edition, published in the United States at any time before the date of deposit, that the Library of Congress determines to be most suitable for its purposes." The Library has issued a policy statement on what constitutes such a "best edition," and this is now referred to in the implementing Copyright Office regulations. *See* 37 C.F.R. § 202.19(b)(1). The deposit requirement has been judicially sustained against a variety of constitutional attacks in *Ladd v. Law & Technology Press*, 762 F.2d 809 (9th Cir.1985).

The material for use or disposition of the Library of Congress under § 407(b) of the 1976 Act is to be deposited in the Copyright Office. The Register of Copyrights is given authority to issue regulations exempting categories of material from the deposit requirements of this section, reducing the required copies or phonorecords to one, or, in the case of certain pictorial, graphic, or sculptural works, providing for exemptions or alternative forms of deposit. § 407(c). The Register is also empowered, under § 408(c), to specify classes of works for purposes of deposit and to permit the deposit of "identifying material instead of copies or phonorecords." Acting pursuant to this provision, the Copyright Office has promulgated what is known as a "secure test" regulation, 37 C.F.R. § 202.20, which covers such examinations as the SAT, the LSAT, and the Multistate Bar Examination, and permits the Copyright Office to retain only a small identifying portion of the examination.

2.   REGISTRATION

a.   PROCEDURE

Registration under § 408 contrasts with the Library deposit provision under § 407 in the following respects: (1) it may be made by not only the owner of copyright but also the owner of any exclusive right thereunder rather than by the owner of the exclusive right of publication; (2) it applies to unpublished as well as published works; (3) it includes works published abroad; and (4) it may be made "at any time" during the subsistence of copyright. If the Library deposit under § 407 is accompanied by a prescribed application for registration along with a fee (currently $30 for most works), it may be used to satisfy the deposit requirements of registration.

The purpose of the registration fee is to defray the expenses of operating the Copyright Office. The income from registration fees represents roughly one-half of the budget of the Copyright Office, with Government appropriations constituting the other half.

The application for registration includes various items of information potentially required for computation of duration, e.g., dates of death, year of creation, and year of publication if any, as well as the basis of ownership for persons other than authors and a brief, general statement of preexisting and added material used in any derivative work or compilation. See § 409. The TX form, for nondramatic literary works, is shown immediately below.

FEE CHANGES
Fees are effective through June 30, 2002. After that date, check the Copyright Office Website at www.loc.gov/copyright or call (202) 707-3000 for current fee information.

FORM TX
For a Nondramatic Literary Work
UNITED STATES COPYRIGHT OFFICE

REGISTRATION NUMBER

TX   TXU

EFFECTIVE DATE OF REGISTRATION

Month   Day   Year

DO NOT WRITE ABOVE THIS LINE. IF YOU NEED MORE SPACE, USE A SEPARATE CONTINUATION SHEET.

1

TITLE OF THIS WORK ▼

PREVIOUS OR ALTERNATIVE TITLES ▼

PUBLICATION AS A CONTRIBUTION If this work was published as a contribution to a periodical, serial, or collection, give information about the collective work in which the contribution appeared. Title of Collective Work ▼

If published in a periodical or serial give: Volume ▼   Number ▼   Issue Date ▼   On Pages ▼

2 a

NAME OF AUTHOR ▼

DATES OF BIRTH AND DEATH
Year Born ▼   Year Died ▼

Was this contribution to the work a "work made for hire"?
☐ Yes
☐ No

AUTHOR'S NATIONALITY OR DOMICILE
Name of Country
OR { Citizen of ▶
Domiciled in ▶

WAS THIS AUTHOR'S CONTRIBUTION TO THE WORK
Anonymous? ☐ Yes ☐ No
Pseudonymous? ☐ Yes ☐ No
If the answer to either of these questions is "Yes," see detailed instructions.

NATURE OF AUTHORSHIP Briefly describe nature of material created by this author in which copyright is claimed. ▼

NOTE
Under the law, the "author" of a "work made for hire" is generally the employer, not the employee (see instructions). For any part of this work that was "made for hire" check "Yes" in the space provided, give the employer (or other person for whom the work was prepared) as "Author" of that part, and leave the space for dates of birth and death blank.

b

NAME OF AUTHOR ▼

DATES OF BIRTH AND DEATH
Year Born ▼   Year Died ▼

Was this contribution to the work a "work made for hire"?
☐ Yes
☐ No

AUTHOR'S NATIONALITY OR DOMICILE
Name of Country
OR { Citizen of ▶
Domiciled in ▶

WAS THIS AUTHOR'S CONTRIBUTION TO THE WORK
Anonymous? ☐ Yes ☐ No
Pseudonymous? ☐ Yes ☐ No
If the answer to either of these questions is "Yes," see detailed instructions.

NATURE OF AUTHORSHIP Briefly describe nature of material created by this author in which copyright is claimed. ▼

c

NAME OF AUTHOR ▼

DATES OF BIRTH AND DEATH
Year Born ▼   Year Died ▼

Was this contribution to the work a "work made for hire"?
☐ Yes
☐ No

AUTHOR'S NATIONALITY OR DOMICILE
Name of Country
OR { Citizen of ▶
Domiciled in ▶

WAS THIS AUTHOR'S CONTRIBUTION TO THE WORK
Anonymous? ☐ Yes ☐ No
Pseudonymous? ☐ Yes ☐ No
If the answer to either of these questions is "Yes," see detailed instructions.

NATURE OF AUTHORSHIP Briefly describe nature of material created by this author in which copyright is claimed. ▼

3 a

YEAR IN WHICH CREATION OF THIS WORK WAS COMPLETED This information must be given ◀ Year in all cases.

b DATE AND NATION OF FIRST PUBLICATION OF THIS PARTICULAR WORK
Complete this information Month ▶ _____ Day ▶ _____ Year ▶ _____
ONLY if this work has been published. ◀ Nation

4

See instructions before completing this space.

COPYRIGHT CLAIMANT(S) Name and address must be given even if the claimant is the same as the author given in space 2. ▼

TRANSFER If the claimant(s) named here in space 4 is (are) different from the author(s) named in space 2, give a brief statement of how the claimant(s) obtained ownership of the copyright. ▼

DO NOT WRITE HERE OFFICE USE ONLY
APPLICATION RECEIVED
ONE DEPOSIT RECEIVED
TWO DEPOSITS RECEIVED
FUNDS RECEIVED

MORE ON BACK ▶ • Complete all applicable spaces (numbers 5-9) on the reverse side of this page.
• See detailed instructions.   • Sign the form at line 8.

DO NOT WRITE HERE
Page 1 of _____ pages

EXAMINED BY		FORM TX
CHECKED BY		
☐ CORRESPONDENCE		FOR COPYRIGHT OFFICE USE ONLY
Yes		

DO NOT WRITE ABOVE THIS LINE. IF YOU NEED MORE SPACE, USE A SEPARATE CONTINUATION SHEET.

PREVIOUS REGISTRATION Has registration for this work, or for an earlier version of this work, already been made in the Copyright Office?

☐ Yes ☐ No If your answer is "Yes," why is another registration being sought? (Check appropriate box.) ▼

a. ☐ This is the first published edition of a work previously registered in unpublished form.

b. ☐ This is the first application submitted by this author as copyright claimant.

c. ☐ This is a changed version of the work, as shown by space 6 on this application.

If your answer is "Yes," give: **Previous Registration Number** ▶   **Year of Registration** ▶

5

DERIVATIVE WORK OR COMPILATION

Preexisting Material Identify any preexisting work or works that this work is based on or incorporates. ▼

a **6**

Material Added to This Work Give a brief, general statement of the material that has been added to this work and in which copyright is claimed. ▼

b

See instructions before completing this space.

DEPOSIT ACCOUNT If the registration fee is to be charged to a Deposit Account established in the Copyright Office, give name and number of Account.
Name ▼   **Account Number** ▼

a **7**

CORRESPONDENCE Give name and address to which correspondence about this application should be sent.   Name/Address/Apt/City/State/ZIP ▼

b

Area code and daytime telephone number ▶   Fax number ▶

Email ▶

CERTIFICATION* I, the undersigned, hereby certify that I am the

Check only one ▶

☐ author
☐ other copyright claimant
☐ owner of exclusive right(s)
☐ authorized agent of _____

8

of the work identified in this application and that the statements made by me in this application are correct to the best of my knowledge.

Name of author or other copyright claimant, or owner of exclusive right(s) ▲

Typed or printed name and date ▼ If this application gives a date of publication in space 3, do not sign and submit it before that date.

_____   Date ▶ _____

Handwritten signature (X) ▼

X _

Certificate will be mailed in window envelope to this address:	Name ▼	**YOU MUST** • Complete all necessary spaces • Sign your application in space 8	**9**
	Number/Street/Apt ▼	**SEND ALL 3 ELEMENTS IN THE SAME PACKAGE** 1. Application form 2. Nonrefundable filing fee in check or money order payable to Register of Copyrights 3. Deposit material	As of July 1, 1999,
	City/State/ZIP ▼	**MAIL TO** Library of Congress Copyright Office 101 Independence Avenue, S.E. Washington, D.C. 20559-6000	the filing fee for Form TX is $30.

*17 U.S.C. § 506(e): Any person who knowingly makes a false representation of a material fact in the application for copyright registration provided for by section 409, or in any written statement filed in connection with the application, shall be fined not more than $2,500.

June 1999—200.000
WEB REV: June 1999   ◉ PRINTED ON RECYCLED PAPER   ☆U.S. GOVERNMENT PRINTING OFFICE: 1999-454-879/49

b. REGISTER'S AUTHORITY AND EFFECT OF REGISTRATION

The 1976 Act, in § 410(b), expressly provides that the Register may refuse registration upon his or her determination that a claim is invalid. Under the 1909 Act, actual registration, rather than merely application for registration, was required as a prerequisite for an infringement action. But this result has been reversed by § 411(a), which permits an infringement suit even where registration has been refused, provided that the deposit, application, and fee are in proper form *and* notice is given to the Register who is given the right to intervene. *See Nova Stylings, Inc. v. Ladd,* 695

F.2d 1179 (9th Cir.1983) (mandamus no longer available to compel registration).

Although the Berne Convention Implementation Act of 1988 has as one of its objectives the elimination of the need to comply with statutory formalities, its principal focus is upon the elimination of the *notice* requirement for published works; it makes few changes in the sections on *deposit and registration* as they were written in the 1976 Act. The major change in this respect is that registration of copyright is no longer a prerequisite to an action for infringement of copyright "in Berne Convention works whose country of origin is not the United States." Most pertinently, this means that registration remains a prerequisite for an infringement action when the copyrighted work is first published in the United States or when the work, if unpublished, is by a United States author. The 1988 Act thus creates what is known as a two-tier registration system, with works of U.S. origin being on the "lower" tier for purposes of litigation. The requirement of pre-suit registration has been criticized, both because of the inferior position in which it places U.S. authors compared to foreign authors and because the number of incremental registrations it induces is extremely small in comparison with all works published and all works registered.

Although registration of copyright is "permissive," the statute has provided the following incentives for timely registration: (1) Early registration will ensure prima facie proof of validity of the copyright (§ 410(c)); (2) for works of United States origin, registration is a prerequisite to an infringement action (§ 411(a)); (3) statutory damages and attorney's fees may be awarded only if registration is made prior to the commencement of the infringement (§ 412, which makes these remedies available even as to infringements before registration if the latter is made within three months after first publication). Among copyright practitioners, the last-mentioned incentive is regarded as particularly important.

QUESTIONS

1. What are the purposes of the registration system? Would those purposes be significantly frustrated if Congress were to eliminate the incentives found in §§ 411(a) and 412? Even assuming that such elimination would result in diminished registration (and accompanying deposit): (a) Would that be a reasonable loss to bear in light of the alleged unfairness of the present registration regime? and (b) Would there be alternative measures that you would propose in order to promote registrations?

2. S, a songwriter, writes a song and registers the copyright with the Copyright Office. She later adds lyrics, but does not register this derivative work. P then performs S's song with the lyrics, without S's permission. S sues P, who defends with S's failure to register the copyright in the song that P performed. S relies on the initial registration. Should P's motion to dismiss be granted? See Murray Hill Pubs., Inc. v. ABC Communications, Inc., 264 F.3d 622 (6th Cir. 2001). Would it matter if P publicly recited only the lyrics?

3. Alice Author submitted an article to the Sunday Evening Post, which published it in January 2002 under a written agreement giving the Post the exclusive right to print the article in serial (i.e., magazine) form, but retaining the remainder of her rights under copyright. The Post also promptly registered the magazine with the Copyright Office as a collective work; Alice did not register her article separately. When Alice learned that her article had been republished, without her consent, by the Monday Morning Newsletter, she sued for copyright infringement. The Newsletter has moved to dismiss her action for lack of jurisdiction because of non-registration of her copyright. In the alternative, it has moved to exclude recovery for statutory damages and attorneys' fees, for lack of timely registration. How should the court rule? (Consider in particular her claim that the Sunday Evening Post, as exclusive licensee, took a transfer of "copyright ownership" of the article, and that its registration of the magazine also effected a registration of at least the component articles in which it held copyright.) Would it make a difference if the Sunday Evening Post had sued the Monday Morning Newsletter? See Morris v. Business Concepts, Inc., 259 F.3d 65 (2d Cir.2001).

4. What if the unauthorized copying had been by the Sunday Evening Post itself, which revised Alice's article and published the revised version in a book. When Alice sues for infringement, the Post moves to dismiss for lack of her registration, and Alice seeks to rely upon the registration by her own litigative adversary. Should there be any difference in the result?

5. Suppose Alice had granted the Sunday Evening Post exclusive magazine publication rights for a 90–day period? Who should register the copyright in the article? When?

FORMALITIES UNDER 1909 ACT AND UNDER 1976 ACT BEFORE AND AFTER THE BERNE CONVENTION IMPLEMENTATION ACT

The following chart may assist the student in determining whether and which formalities may be applicable:

	Work published before 1978	*Work published 1978– Feb. 1989*	*Work published after Feb. 1989*
Notice	Federal copyright arose upon publication with notice; if no notice, work fell into public domain.*	Affixation of notice perfected protection; five years to cure omissions, otherwise work fell into public domain.	Optional; incentive: unavailability of innocent infringer defense.
Registration	Optional until last year of first term; mandatory for renewal of works first published before 1964**; prerequisite to initiation of infringement suit during *both* terms of copyright.	Optional, *but* prerequisite to initiation of suit. Incentives: statutory damages and attorney fees not available unless work was registered before infringement commenced.***	Optional for non-U.S. Berne and WTO works; remains prerequisite to suit for U.S. and other foreign works. Same incentives apply.

	Work published before 1978	*Work published 1978– Feb. 1989*	*Work published after Feb. 1989*
Deposit	Prerequisite to suit; in addition, fines may be imposed for failure to deposit copies with Library of Congress.	Same.	No longer a prerequisite to suit for non-U.S. Berne works; *but* fines may still be imposed.
Recordation of Transfers	Unrecorded transfer void against subsequent bona fide purchaser for value.	Same, plus a prerequisite to suit.	No longer a prerequisite to suit; unrecorded transfers still void against subsequent b.f.p.v.'s.

* § 104A restores copyright as of 1/1/96 in Berne and WTO works still protected in their countries of origin, but that lost U.S. copyright through failure to affix notice.

** § 104A restores copyright as of 1/1/96 in Berne and WTO works still protected in their countries of origin, but that lost U.S. copyright through failure to renew.

*** Or unless the work is infringed within the first three months of publication, and registration is made before the third month elapses.

CHAPTER 6

Exclusive Rights Under Copyright

§ 106. **Exclusive Rights in Copyrighted Works**

Subject to sections 107 through 121, the owner of copyright under this title has the exclusive rights to do and to authorize any of the following:

(1) to reproduce the copyrighted work in copies or phonorecords;

(2) to prepare derivative works based upon the copyrighted work;

(3) to distribute copies or phonorecords of the copyrighted work to the public by the sale or other transfer of ownership, or by rental, lease, or lending;

(4) in the case of literary, musical, dramatic, and choreographic works, pantomimes, and motion pictures and other audiovisual works, to perform the copyrighted work publicly; and

(5) in the case of literary, musical, dramatic, and choreographic works, pantomimes, and pictorial, graphic, or sculptural works, including the individual images of a motion picture or other audiovisual work, to display the copyrighted work publicly.

(6) in the case of sound recordings, to perform the copyrighted work publicly by means of a digital audio transmission*

A. The Right to Reproduce the Work in Copies and Phonorecords Under § 106(1)

House Report

H.R. Rep. No. 94–1476, 94th Cong., 2d Sess. 61–62 (1976).

Rights of reproduction, adaptation, and publication

The first three clauses of section 106, which cover all rights under a copyright except those of performance and display, extend to every kind of copyrighted work. The exclusive rights encompassed by these clauses, though closely related, are independent; they can generally be character-

---

* Editors' note: § 106(6) was added by the Digital Performance Right in Sound Re- cordings Act of 1995, Pub. L. No. 104–39, 109 Stat. 336.

ized as rights of copying, recording, adaptation, and publishing. A single act of infringement may violate all of these rights at once, as where a publisher reproduces, adapts, and sells copies of a person's copyrighted work as part of a publishing venture. Infringement takes place when any one of the rights is violated: where, for example, a printer reproduces copies without selling them or a retailer sells copies without having anything to do with their reproduction. The references to "copies or phonorecords," although in the plural, are intended here and throughout the bill to include the singular (1 U.S.C. § 1).

Reproduction.—Read together with the relevant definitions in section 101, the right "to reproduce the copyrighted work in copies or phonorecords" means the right to produce a material object in which the work is duplicated, transcribed, imitated, or simulated in a fixed form from which it can be "perceived, reproduced, or otherwise communicated, either directly or with the aid of a machine or device." As under the present law, a copyrighted work would be infringed by reproducing it in whole or in any substantial part, and by duplicating it exactly or by imitation or simulation. Wide departures or variations from the copyrighted works would still be an infringement as long as the author's "expression" rather than merely the author's "ideas" are taken....

"Reproduction" under clause (1) of section 106 is to be distinguished from "display" under clause (5). For a work to be "reproduced," its fixation in tangible form must be "sufficiently permanent or stable to permit it to be perceived, reproduced, or otherwise communicated for a period of more than transitory duration." Thus, the showing of images on a screen or tube would not be a violation of clause (1), although it might come within the scope of clause (5).

———

Section 106 of the 1976 Act states that copyright owners have the "exclusive rights to do and to authorize any of the following...." Does this text recognize that a copyright owner enjoys not only the negative prerogative to prevent others from engaging in acts of reproduction, distribution, etc. (that are not privileged by §§ 107–122), but also the affirmative right to undertake these acts herself, or to designate another to carry them out? Section 501 defines an infringer as "anyone who violates any of the exclusive rights of the copyright owner as provided in sections 106 through 122...." If the copyright owner's rights are not merely the negative rights to prevent third party exploitation but also the affirmative rights to exploit the work herself, it would follow that one violates the copyright owner's rights—and thus commits copyright infringement—by preventing the copyright owner from exercising her exclusive rights. For example, suppose that the owner of the physical copy of a work, such as the original canvas of a painting, or the possessor of photographic negatives, refused to permit the author (who retained the copyright when she transferred the chattel) to obtain access to the work in order to exercise her copyright. The chattel owner has certainly frustrated the author's exercise of copyright; has the chattel owner thus infringed the copyright? The Fourth Circuit recently held that there is no infringement of photographs when the defendant merely withholds slides from the copyright owner; for infringement to occur there must be a reproduction, printing or other use itemized in § 106. *See Frasier v. Adams–Sandler, Inc.,* 94 F.3d 129 (4th Cir.1996) (reading § 501 to define infringement as the commission of an act of reproduction, distribution, etc.).

1.   THE RIGHT TO MAKE COPIES

a.   WHAT IS A "COPY"?

§ 101.   Definitions

"Copies" are material objects, other than phonorecords, in which a work is fixed by any method now known or later developed, and from which the work can be perceived, reproduced, or otherwise directly communicated, either directly or with the aid of a machine or device. The term "copies" includes the material object, other than a phonorecord, in which the work is first fixed.

———

It should be clear from this definition that copyright law is indifferent to the medium in which the copy exists: any medium, now known or later developed, is included. Hence, for example, while fax machines may have been unknown in 1976, the unauthorized "faxing" of a photocopy of a newsletter was later held to create an infringing copy. *See Pasha Pubs., Inc. v. Enmark Gas Corp.,* 22 U.S.P.Q.2d 1076 (N.D.Tex.1992).

As we saw earlier (see Note "Fixation in Digital Media," *supra* Chapter 2.A), a "copy" also includes a fixation in temporary computer memory. The Copyright Office report there referenced (see http://www.loc.gov/copyright/reports/studies/dmca/sec–104–report-vol–1.pdf) analyzes the statutory text and offers several policy considerations favoring the characterization of reproductions in RAM as "copies."

[A] general rule can be drawn from the language of the statute. In establishing the dividing line between those reproductions that are subject to the reproduction right and those that are not, we believe that Congress intended the copyright owner's exclusive right to extend to all reproductions from which economic value can be derived. The economic value derived from a reproduction lies in the ability to copy, perceive or communicate it. Unless a reproduction manifests itself so fleetingly that it cannot be copied, perceived or communicated, the making of that copy should fall within the scope of the copyright owner's exclusive rights. The dividing line, then, can be drawn between reproductions that exist for a sufficient period of time to be capable of being "perceived, reproduced, or otherwise communicated" and those that do not. . . .

Drawing the line with reference to the ability to perceive, reproduce or otherwise communicate a work makes particular sense when one considers the manner in which one important category of digital works—computer programs—are utilized. Computer programs are exploited chiefly through exercise of the rights of reproduction and distribution. In order to utilize a program, it must be copied into RAM. To exercise the right to make that temporary copy in RAM is to realize the economic value of the program. That RAM copy need only exist long enough to communicate the instructions to the computer's processing unit in the proper sequence.

Exploitation of works on digital networks illustrates the same point. Digital networks permit a single disk copy of a work to meet the demands of many users by creating multiple RAM copies. These copies need exist only long enough to be perceived (e.g., displayed on the screen or played through speakers), reproduced or otherwise communicated (e.g., to a computer's processing unit) in order for their economic value to be realized. If the network is sufficiently reliable, users have no need to retain copies of the material. Commercial exploitation in a network environment can be said to be based on selling a right to perceive temporary reproductions of works.

The statute also requires that the work be perceived either directly or with the aid of a machine or device. This implies that there is no "copy" unless the work may be perceived. In most cases, perceptibility is not an issue, but the question has arisen in at least two contexts. First is the problem of "intermediate copying," that is, a copy is made as a step in the creation of an end product that does not itself incorporate the copied work. The public to whom the product is sold thus neither receives nor perceives the intermediate copy. In those circumstances, is there an actionable "copy"? *See Sega Enterprises, Ltd. v. Accolade, Inc., infra* Chapter 7.

Second, if the components of a work are dispersed throughout a larger work so that, without reassembly, the incorporated work is no longer perceptible, does the incorporating work contain a "copy" of the dispersed work? Digital media have brought this issue to the fore. A work communicated over a digital network such as the Internet, may well be divided into many "packets," but these are reassembled on arrival at their destination. Courts have consistently held that the digital dissemination of a work from a website or bulletin board service [BBS] to a user effects a distribution of "copies" by the website or BBS operator. *See, e.g., Playboy Enters. v. Webbworld, Inc.*, 991 F.Supp. 543 (N.D.Tex.1997); *Marobie-Fl v. National Ass'n of Fire Equip. Distribs.*, 983 F.Supp. 1167 (N.D.Ill.1997); *Playboy Enters. v. Frena*, 839 F.Supp. 1552 (M.D.Fla.1993). When the components remain dispersed, however, it is less clear that a "copy" has been made. The following decision addresses this problem.

Matthew Bender & Co. v. West Publishing Co., 158 F.3d 693 (2d Cir.1998). Matthew Bender & HyperLaw manufacture and market compilations of judicial opinions stored on compact disc-read only memory ("CD–ROM") discs, in which opinions they sought to embed citations that show the page location of the particular text in West's printed version of the opinions in the familiar federal and state regional reporters (so-called "star pagination"). Bender and HyperLaw sought a judgment declaring that star pagination will not infringe West's copyrights in its compilations of judicial opinions. The district court granted a judgment of non-infringement, and the Second Circuit affirmed, holding, *inter alia*, that star pagination did not create a "copy" of the West reporters.

> [West argues] that plaintiffs have inserted or will insert *all* of West's volume and page numbers for certain case reporters. West's ... argument is that even though the page numbering is not (by itself) a protectable element of West's compilation, (i) plaintiffs' star pagination to West's case reporters embeds West's arrangement of cases in plaintiffs' CD–ROM discs, thereby allowing a user to perceive West's protected arrangement through the plaintiffs' file-retrieval programs, and (ii) that under the Copyright Act's definition of "copies," 17 U.S.C. § 101, a work that allows the perception of a protectable element of a compilation through the aid of a machine amounts to a copy of the compilation. We reject this argument ...

B

> But our rejection of West's position is even more fundamental. If one browses through plaintiffs' CD–ROM discs from beginning to end, using the computer software that reads and sorts it, the sequence of cases owes nothing to West's arrangement. West's argument is that the CD–ROM discs are infringing copies because a user who manipulates the data on the CD–ROM discs could at will re-sequence the cases (discarding many of them) into the West arrangement. To state West's theory in the statutory words on which West (mistakenly) relies, each of the plaintiffs' CD–ROM discs is a "copy" because West's copyrighted arrangement is "fixed" on the disc in a way that can be "perceived ... with the aid of a machine or device." 17 U.S.C. § 101 (1994).

> For reasons set forth below, we conclude that a CD–ROM disc infringes a copyrighted arrangement when a machine or device that reads it perceives the embedded material in the copyrighted arrangement or in a substantially similar arrangement. At least absent some invitation, incentive, or facilitation not in the record here, a copyrighted arrangement is not infringed by a CD–ROM disc if a machine can perceive the arrangement only after another person uses the machine to re-arrange the material into the copyrightholder's arrangement.

> 1.   Section 101's Definition of "Copies"

> West relies on the statutory definition of "copies." To establish infringement, the copyright holder must demonstrate a violation of an exclusive right. 17 U.S.C. § 501 (1994). One such right is the right "to

reproduce the copyrighted work in copies or phonorecords." 17 U.S.C. § 106(1) (1994) (emphasis added).... § 101's definition ...—intended to clarify that a work stored on a disk or tape can be a copy of the copyrighted work even if it cannot be perceived by human senses without technological aid—means that CD–ROM discs can infringe a copyright even if the information embedded upon them is not perceptible without the aid of a CD–ROM player. In this case, however, the only fixed arrangement is the (non-West) sequence that is embedded on plaintiffs' CD–ROM discs and that appears with the aid of a machine without manipulation of the data.

To recapitulate a bit, West relies on the definition of "copies" to argue that plaintiffs' CD–ROM discs duplicate its copyrighted arrangement of cases because star pagination permits a user to "perceive" the copyrighted element "with the aid of" a computer and the FOLIO retrieval system, i.e., by manipulating the data embedded on a CD–ROM disc to retrieve the cases in the order in which they appear in the West case reporters. West's definition of a copy, as applied to a CD–ROM disc, would expand the embedded work to include all arrangements and rearrangements that could be made by a third-party user who manipulates the data on his or her own initiative. But the relevant statutory wording refers to material objects in which "a work" readable by technology "is fixed," not to another work or works that can be created, unbidden, by using technology to alter the fixed embedding of the work, by rearrangement or otherwise. The natural reading of the statute is that the arrangement of the work is the one that can be perceived by a machine without an uninvited manipulation of the data . . . . .

———

Courts are coming routinely to hold that computer input and manipulation of copyrighted works are violations of either the reproduction right or the derivative-work right. For example, in *Phillips v. Kidsoft, L.L.C.*, 52 U.S.P.Q.2d 1102 (D.Md.1999), the plaintiff was an author and artist who designed mazes and maze theme books, particularly for children. The defendant Kidsoft scanned some 30 of the plaintiff's mazes into a computer, and then "cleaned up" the resulting images and added new colors, textures, perspectives and artwork—while preserving the placement of walls, openings and objects—and then published them in book form as well as on Kidsoft's website. The court held that scanning the maze images into Kidsoft's computer constituted the unauthorized making of an infringing copy, as did their posting to Kidsoft's website (which also constituted an unauthorized distribution of the copyrighted works). The additions of new colors and the like constituted the making of unauthorized derivative works.

Much the same result was reached in *Tiffany Design, Inc. v. Reno–Tahoe Specialty, Inc.*, 55 F.Supp.2d 1113 (D.Nev.1999). There, the plaintiff took aerial photographs of the Las Vegas Strip and retained the services of a graphic artist to make modifications in the appearance and size of buildings and other elements. The defendant scanned those altered images into a computer, for purposes of extracting and manipulating certain elements for inclusion in its own photographic products. The court found that the scanning (or digitizing) produced infringing copies, even though the scanned images resided only temporarily in the random access memory (RAM) of the defendant's computer.

b. PROVING INFRINGEMENT

Arnstein v. Porter

154 F.2d 464 (2d Cir.1946), *cert. denied,* 330 U.S. 851 (1947).

Plaintiff, a citizen and resident of New York, brought this suit, charging infringement by defendant, a citizen and resident of New York, of plaintiff's copyrights to several musical compositions, infringement of his rights to other uncopyrighted musical compositions, and wrongful use of the titles of others. Plaintiff, when filing his complaint, demanded a jury trial. Plaintiff took the deposition of defendant, and defendant, the deposition of plaintiff. Defendant then moved for an order striking out plaintiff's jury demand, and for summary judgment. Attached to defendant's motion papers were the depositions, phonograph records of piano renditions of the plaintiff's compositions and defendant's alleged infringing compositions, and the court records of five previous copyright infringement suits brought by plaintiff in the court below against other persons, in which judgments had been entered, after trials, against plaintiff. Defendant also moved for dismissal of the action on the ground of "vexatiousness."

Plaintiff alleged that defendant's "Begin the Beguine" is a plagiarism from plaintiff's "The Lord Is My Shepherd" and "A Mother's Prayer." Plaintiff testified, on deposition, that "The Lord Is My Shepherd" had been published and about 2,000 copies sold, that "A Mother's Prayer" had been published, over a million copies having been sold. In his depositions, he gave no direct evidence that defendant saw or heard these compositions. He also alleged that defendant's "My Heart Belongs to Daddy" had been plagiarized from plaintiff's "A Mother's Prayer."

Plaintiff also alleged that defendant's "I Love You Madly" is a plagiarism from plaintiff's composition "La Priere," stating in his deposition that the latter composition had been sold. He gave no direct proof that defendant knew of this composition.

He also alleged that defendant's song "Night and Day" is a plagiarism of plaintiff's song "I Love You Madly," which he testified had not been published but had once been publicly performed over the radio, copies having been sent to divers radio stations but none to defendant; a copy of this song, plaintiff testified, had been stolen from his room. He also alleged that "I Love You Madly" was in part plagiarized from "La Priere." He further alleged that defendant's "You'd Be So Nice To Come Home To" is plagiarized from plaintiff's "Sadness Overwhelms My Soul." He testified that this song had never been published or publicly performed but that copies had been sent to a movie producer and to several publishers. He also alleged that defendant's "Don't Fence Me In" is a plagiarism of plaintiff's song "A Modern Messiah" which has not been published or publicly performed; in his deposition he said that about a hundred copies had been sent to divers radio stations and band leaders but that he sent no copy to defendant. Plaintiff said that defendant "had stooges right along to follow me, watch me, and live in the same apartment with me," and that plaintiff's room had been ransacked on several occasions. Asked how he knew that defendant had anything to do with any of these "burglaries," plaintiff said, "I don't know that he had to do with it, but I only know that he could have." He also said " ... many of my compositions had been published. No one had to break in to steal them. They were sung publicly."

Defendant in his deposition categorically denied that he had ever seen or heard any of plaintiff's compositions or had had any acquaintance with any persons said to have stolen any of them.

The prayer of plaintiff's original complaint asked "at least one million dollars out of the millions the defendant has earned and is earning out of all the plagiarism." In his amended complaint the prayer is "for judgment against the defendant in the sum of $1,000,000 as damages sustained by the plagiarism of all the compositions named in the complaint." Plaintiff, not a lawyer, appeared pro se below and on this appeal.

■ FRANK, CIRCUIT JUDGE.

. . .

2. The principal question on this appeal is whether the lower court, under Rule 56, properly deprived plaintiff of a trial of his copyright infringement action. The answer depends on whether "there is the slightest doubt about the facts." [Citations omitted.] In applying that standard here, it is important to avoid confusing two separate elements essential to a plaintiff's case in such a suit: (a) that defendant copied from plaintiff's copyrighted work and (b) that the copying (assuming it to be proved) went so far as to constitute improper appropriation.

As to the first—copying—the evidence may consist (a) of defendant's admission that he copied or (b) of circumstantial evidence—usually evidence of access—from which the trier of the facts may reasonably infer copying. Of course, if there are no similarities, no amount of evidence of access will suffice to prove copying. If there is evidence of access and similarities exist, then the trier of the facts must determine whether the similarities are sufficient to prove copying. On this issue, analysis ("dissection") is relevant, and the testimony of experts may be received to aid the trier of the facts. If evidence of access is absent, the similarities must be so striking as to preclude the possibility that plaintiff and defendant independently arrived at the same result.

If copying is established, then only does there arise the second issue, that of illicit copying (unlawful appropriation). On that issue (as noted more in detail below) the test is the response of the ordinary lay hearer; accordingly, on that issue, "dissection" and expert testimony are irrelevant.

In some cases, the similarities between the plaintiff's and defendant's work are so extensive and striking as, without more, both to justify an inference of copying and to prove improper appropriation. But such double-purpose evidence is not required; that is, if copying is otherwise shown, proof of improper appropriation need not consist of similarities which, standing alone, would support an inference of copying.

Each of these two issues—copying and improper appropriation—is an issue of fact. . . .

3. We turn first to the issue of copying. After listening to the compositions as played in the phonograph recordings submitted by defendant, we find similarities; but we hold that unquestionably, standing alone, they do not compel the conclusion, or permit the inference, that defendant copied. The similarities, however, are sufficient so that, if there is enough evidence of access to permit the case to go to the jury, the jury may properly infer that the similarities did not result from coincidence.

Summary judgment was, then, proper if indubitably defendant did not have access to plaintiff's compositions. Plainly that presents an issue of fact. On that issue, the district judge, who heard no oral testimony, had before him the depositions of plaintiff and defendant. The judge characterized plaintiff's story as "fantastic"; and, in the light of the references in his opinion to defendant's deposition, the judge obviously accepted defendant's denial of access and copying. Although part of plaintiff's testimony on deposition (as to "stooges" and the like) does seem "fantastic," yet plaintiff's credibility, even as to those improbabilities, should be left to the jury. . . . We should not overlook the shrewd proverbial admonition that sometimes truth is stranger than fiction.

But even if we were to disregard the improbable aspects of plaintiff's story, there remains parts by no means "fantastic." On the record now before us, more than a million copies of one of his compositions were sold; copies of others were sold in smaller quantities or distributed to radio stations or band leaders or publishers, or the pieces were publicly performed. If, after hearing both parties testify, the jury disbelieves defendant's denials, it can, from such facts, reasonably infer access. It follows that, as credibility is unavoidably involved, a genuine issue of material fact presents itself. With credibility a vital factor, plaintiff is entitled to a trial where the jury can observe the witnesses while testifying. Plaintiff must not be deprived of the invaluable privilege of cross-examining the defendant—the "crucial test of credibility"—in the presence of the jury. Plaintiff, or a lawyer on his behalf, on such examination may elicit damaging admissions from defendant; more important, plaintiff may persuade the jury, observing defendant's manner when testifying, that defendant is unworthy of belief.

. . .

With all that in mind, we cannot now say—as we think we must say to sustain a summary judgment—that at the close of a trial the judge could properly direct a verdict.

.   .   .

4. Assuming that adequate proof is made of copying, that is not enough; for there can be "permissible copying," copying which is not illicit. Whether (if he copied) defendant unlawfully appropriated presents, too, an issue of fact. The proper criterion on that issue is not an analytic or other comparison of the respective musical compositions as they appear on paper or in the judgment of trained musicians.[19] The plaintiff's legally protected interest is not, as such, his reputation as a musician but his interest in the potential financial returns from his compositions which derive from the lay public's approbation of his efforts. The question, therefore, is whether defendant took from plaintiff's works so much of what is pleasing to the ears of lay listeners, who comprise the audience for whom such popular music is composed, that defendant wrongfully appropriated something which belongs to the plaintiff.

Surely, then, we have an issue of fact which a jury is peculiarly fitted to determine.[22] Indeed, even if there were to be a trial before a judge, it would be desirable (although not necessary) for him to summon an advisory jury on this question.

We should not be taken as saying that a plagiarism case can never arise in which absence of similarities is so patent that a summary judgment for defendant would be correct. Thus, suppose that Ravel's "Bolero" or Shostakovitch's "Fifth Symphony" were alleged to infringe "When Irish Eyes Are Smiling."[23] But this is not such a case. For, after listening to the playing of the respective compositions, we are, at this time, unable to conclude that the likenesses are so trifling that, on the issue of misappropriation, a trial judge could legitimately direct a verdict for defendant.

At the trial, plaintiff may play, or cause to be played, the pieces in such manner that they may seem to a jury to be inexcusably alike, in terms of the way in which lay listeners of such music would be likely to react. The plaintiff may call witnesses whose testimony may aid the jury in reaching its conclusion as to the responses of such audiences. Expert testimony of musicians may also be received, but it will in no way be controlling on the issue of illicit copying, and should be utilized only to assist in determining the reactions of lay auditors. The impression made on the refined ears of musical experts or their views as to the musical excellence of plaintiff's or defendant's works are utterly immaterial on the issue of misappropriation;

---

19. Where plaintiff relies on similarities to prove copying (as distinguished from improper appropriation) paper comparisons and the opinions of experts may aid the court.

22. It would, accordingly, be proper to exclude tone-deaf persons from the jury, cf.

Chatterton v. Cave, 3 A.C. 483, 499–501, 502–504.

23. In such a case, the complete absence of similarity would negate both copying and improper appropriation.

for the views of such persons are caviar to the general—and plaintiff's and defendant's compositions are not caviar.

. . .

Modified in part; otherwise reversed and remanded.

. . .

■ CLARK, CIRCUIT JUDGE (dissenting). While the procedure followed below seems to me generally simple and appropriate, the defendant did make one fatal tactical error. In an endeavor to assist us, he caused to be prepared records of all the musical pieces here involved, and presented these transcriptions through the medium of the affidavit of his pianist.... [A]fter repeated hearings of the records, I could not find therein what my brothers found. The only thing definitely mentioned seemed to be the repetitive use of the note e^2 in certain places by both plaintiff and defendant, surely too simple and ordinary a device of composition to be significant. In our former musical plagiarism cases we have, naturally, relied on what seemed the total sound effect; but we have also analyzed the music enough to make sure of an intelligible and intellectual decision. Thus in *Arnstein v. Edward B. Marks Music Corp.*, 2 Cir., 82 F.2d 275, 277, Judge L. Hand made quite an extended comparison of the songs, concluding, inter alia: " . . . the seven notes available do not admit of so many agreeable permutations that we need be amazed at the re-appearance of old themes, even though the identity extend through a sequence of twelve notes." . . .

It is true that in *Arnstein v. Broadcast Music, Inc.*, 2 Cir., 137 F.2d 410, 412, we considered "dissection" or "technical analysis" not the proper approach to support a finding of plagiarism, and said that it must be "more ingenuous, more like that of a spectator, who would rely upon the complex of his impressions." But in its context that seems to me clearly sound and in accord with what I have in mind. Thus one may look to the total impression to repulse the charge of plagiarism where a minute "dissection" might dredge up some points of similarity. Hence one cannot use a purely theoretical disquisition to supply a total resemblance which does not otherwise exist. Certainly, however, that does not suggest or compel the converse—that one must keep his brain in torpor for fear that otherwise it would make clear differences which do exist....

. . . [Plaintiff] does not and cannot claim extensive copying, measure by measure, of his compositions. He therefore has resorted to a comparative analysis—the "dissection" found unpersuasive in the earlier cases—to support his claim of plagiarism of small detached portions here and there, the musical fillers between the better known parts of the melody. And plaintiff's compositions, as pointed out in the cases cited above, are of the simple and trite character where small repetitive sequences are not hard to discover. It is as though we found Shakespeare a plagiarist on the basis of his use of articles, pronouns, prepositions, and adjectives also used by others. The surprising thing, however, is to note the small amount of even this type of reproduction which plaintiff by dint of extreme dissection has been able to find.

... The usual claim seems to be rested upon a sequence of three, of four, or of five—never more than five—identical notes, usually of different rhythmical values. Nowhere is there anything approaching the twelve-note sequence of the *Marks* case, *supra*....

In the light of these utmost claims of the plaintiff, I do not see a legal basis for the claim of plagiarism. So far as I have been able to discover, no earlier case approaches the holding that a simple and trite sequence of this type, even if copying may seem indicated, constitutes proof either of access or of plagiarism....

[On remand, after jury trial, judgment was entered for the defendant. *See* 158 F.2d 795 (2d Cir. 1946), *cert. denied,* 330 U.S. 851 (1947).]

QUESTIONS

1. Given the limited tonal range that a popular song composer uses, the confinements of conventional harmony, and the frequency with which we observe that many pop songs sound alike, how likely is it that a defendant will ever be able to prevail on a motion for summary judgment after the *Arnstein* decision? Isn't that decision an invitation to litigate frivolous claims, which are almost certain to reach a jury or to force an unfair settlement?

2. Wouldn't it be sensible to have some judicially recognized "rule of thumb" regarding the number of consecutive notes of an earlier copyrighted song that may be duplicated (consciously or not) without fear of liability for infringement? (Judge Clark appears to opt for twelve notes, more or less. Is that too many?) Would it be feasible to formulate such a rule? Would it have to take into account whether the notes were in the accompaniment or in the melody? In the verse (introduction) or chorus (main melody section)? In the main theme or in the "bridge"?

3. Is it relevant in determining infringement that the plaintiff's song ceased to be popular five years ago? Is it relevant that the plaintiff's work is an operatic aria and the defendant's is a jukebox hit with little or no overlapping audience?

4. What should be the role of experts in musical, artistic or literary infringement cases? On what issues can they make the greatest contribution? On what issues should the fact-finder rely primarily on personal observation or on intuition?

———

Dawson v. Hinshaw Music, Inc., 905 F.2d 731 (4th Cir.), *cert. denied,* 498 U.S. 981 (1990). The court held that the determination of "substantial similarity" as the second test under *Arnstein v. Porter* is to be made from the perspective of the audience that was intended by the author to constitute the commercial market. This will often be what *Arnstein* referred to as the "ordinary observer," but it need not be the lay person when the work is designed to appeal to an audience with specialized

[handwritten margin note: Similarity determined from point of view of the intended audience] knowledge. One example is a computer program, which, when being compared with another program, must be scrutinized by an expert. Another example is a toy or a computer game made for children; there, substantial similarity between works should be assessed from a child's perspective. The "ordinary observer" test should be displaced, however, only when the intended audience has "specialized expertise" and not merely when its tastes might differ from those of the lay observer.

The work litigated in the instant case was a musical arrangement of a spiritual. The court of appeals therefore suggested that the trial court should be free (on remand) to determine whether the intended audience was a lay audience or rather choral directors having specialized knowledge of choral music. The court also suggested that if there were indeed a specialized audience for the parties' spirituals and if that audience (i.e., choral directors) would ordinarily compare the works of plaintiff and defendant by examining printed sheet music rather than by listening to recordings of the two arrangements, then it would not be reversible error for the district court to exclude recordings from the trial.

Lyons Partnership, L.P. v. Morris Costumes, Inc., 243 F.3d 789 (4th Cir.2001). This was the case envisaged by the same court years earlier in *Dawson v. Hinshaw*. The defendant company rented and sold costumes to adults; one was named Duffy the Dragon, whose purple color and overall appearance was alleged by the plaintiff to infringe its well-known creation Barney the Dinosaur. The Duffy costume was acquired by adults to be worn to amuse groups of children. Although the district court had concluded that it was the adults who were the "intended audience" to be used in applying the "substantial similarity" test, and that the average adult purchaser or renter would not find Duffy and Barney to be similar in appearance, the court of appeals reversed, and held that the perceptions of a two-to five-year old child should apply.

> The evidence of actual confusion among children, however, which the court disregarded, was substantial. An elementary school administrator testified that her school rented the Duffy costume for a school rally called "Character Counts," because Barney exemplified the qualities that the rally intended to communicate. When the administrator appeared without advance notice before 500 children in the Duffy costume, the children saw Barney. As she testified, "the kids just went wild. They went crazy and they were just going, 'Barney. Barney. Barney.'" Also, various parents testified that they rented Duffy knowing that it would be perceived by children as Barney, and in each case the children so perceived Duffy as Barney. In addition to this evidence of actual confusion among children, Lyons offered over 30 newspaper clippings from around the country in which persons wearing the Duffy costume were depicted but the newspaper reported them as "Barney." None of the papers reported an awareness of its error.... [T]he similarity of child-oriented works "must be viewed from the perspective of the child audience for which the products were intended." ...

The *Dawson* court adopted the "intended audience" rule, as opposed to an "ordinary observer" rule, because copyright law, at its core, is intended only to protect the creator's economic market and resulting financial returns. *See Dawson*, 905 F.2d at 733–34 (citing *Arnstein*, 154 F.2d at 473). Accordingly, the relevant question that courts must ask in determining whether a work has been copied is not whether society as a whole would perceive the works to be similar in an aesthetic sense, but rather whether the works are so similar that the introduction of the alleged copy into the market will have an adverse effect on the demand for the protected work. . . .

In this case, all of the relevant evidence tended to show that the target for both the Barney and Duffy characters was an audience consisting of young children. Lyons states more particularly that it targets children from ages two to five. Accordingly, the economically important views are those of the young children who watch Barney on television, wear t-shirts bearing his likeness, and desperately hope that the purple dinosaur will make an appearance at their birthday parties. Even if adults can easily distinguish between Barney and Duffy, a child's belief that they are one and the same could deprive Barney's owners of profits in a manner that the Copyright Act deems impermissible. . . . The fact that children were not actually present when their parents purchased or rented the costumes did not eliminate the need to consider the children's perspectives because both Morris Costumes and those parents foresaw that the costumes would be used to entertain children.

i. Proof of Copying

Bright Tunes Music Corp. v. Harrisongs Music, Ltd.

420 F.Supp. 177 (S.D.N.Y.1976).

■ OWEN, DISTRICT JUDGE. This is an action in which it is claimed that a successful song, My Sweet Lord, listing George Harrison as the composer, is plagiarized from an earlier successful song, He's So Fine, composed by Ronald Mack, recorded by a singing group called the "Chiffons," the copyright of which is owned by plaintiff, Bright Tunes Music Corp.

He's So Fine, recorded in 1962, is a catchy tune consisting essentially of four repetitions of a very short basic musical phrase, "sol-mi-re," (hereinafter motif A),[1] altered as necessary to fit the words, followed by four repetitions of another short basic musical phrase, "sol-la-do-la-do," (hereinafter motif B).[2] While neither motif is novel, the four repetitions of A, followed by four repetitions of B, is a highly unique pattern.[3] In addition,

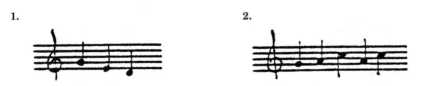

1.   2.

3. All the experts agreed on this.

in the second use of the motif B series, there is a grace note inserted making the phrase go "sol-la-do-la-re-do."[4]

My Sweet Lord, recorded first in 1970, also uses the same motif A (modified to suit the words) four times, followed by motif B, repeated three times, not four. In place of He's So Fine's fourth repetition of motif B, My Sweet Lord has a transitional passage of musical attractiveness of the same approximate length, with the identical grace note in the identical second repetition. The harmonies of both songs are identical.[6]

George Harrison, a former member of The Beatles, was aware of He's So Fine. In the United States, it was No. 1 on the billboard charts for five weeks; in England, Harrison's home country, it was No. 12 on the charts on June 1, 1963, a date upon which one of the Beatle songs was, in fact, in first position. For seven weeks in 1963, He's So Fine was one of the top hits in England.

[According to Harrison, he generated the song "My Sweet Lord" while sitting by himself repeating some simple guitar chords, fitting in the words "Hallelujah" and "Hare Krishna." (These words ultimately were interpolated "responsively" into the lyrics of "My Sweet Lord," just as the Chiffons inserted "dulang" in the equivalent places in "He's So Fine.") Harrison then joined with the members of his band, and played the repeated chord pattern, singing those simple words; and gradually the text of the "My Sweet Lord" lyrics began to develop. Harrison continued to develop the song at home, including motif A. That three-note motif was perfected in a recording session featuring Billy Preston, one of the members of Harrison's group; at trial, Harrison could not precisely recall whether he or Preston played the major role in perfecting the melodic motif. Motif B also developed in that recording session, and apparently it was Preston who interpolated the "grace note." The Billy Preston recording was issued by Apple Records (listing Harrison as composer), and printed music sheets were later prepared and used for U.S. copyright registration.]

.   .   .

Seeking the wellsprings of musical composition—why a composer chooses the succession of notes and the harmonies he does—whether it be George Harrison or Richard Wagner—is a fascinating inquiry. It is apparent from the extensive colloquy between the Court and Harrison covering forty pages in the transcript that neither Harrison nor Preston were conscious of the fact that they were utilizing the He's So Fine theme.

4.

6. Expert witnesses for the defendants asserted crucial differences in the two songs. These claimed differences essentially stem, however, from the fact that different words and number of syllables were involved. This necessitated modest alterations in the repetitions or the places of beginning of a phrase, which, however, has nothing to do whatsoever with the essential musical kernel that is involved.

However, they in fact were, for it is perfectly obvious to the listener that in musical terms, the two songs are virtually identical except for one phrase. There is motif A used four times, followed by motif B, four times in one case, and three times in the other, with the same grace note in the second repetition of motif B.

What happened? I conclude that the composer, in seeking musical materials to clothe his thoughts, was working with various possibilities. As he tried this possibility and that, there came to the surface of his mind a particular combination that pleased him as being one he felt would be appealing to a prospective listener; in other words, that this combination of sounds would work. Why? Because his subconscious knew it already had worked in a song his conscious mind did not remember. Having arrived at this pleasing combination of sounds, the recording was made, the lead sheet prepared for copyright and the song became an enormous success. Did Harrison deliberately use the music of He's So Fine? I do not believe he did so deliberately. Nevertheless, it is clear that My Sweet Lord is the very same song as He's So Fine with different words, and Harrison had access to He's So Fine. This is, under the law, infringement of copyright, and is no less so even though subconsciously accomplished. *Sheldon v. Metro–Goldwyn Pictures Corp.*, 81 F.2d 49, 54 (2d Cir.1936); *Northern Music Corp. v. Pacemaker Music Co., Inc.*, 147 U.S.P.Q. 358, 359 (S.D.N.Y.1965).

Given the foregoing, I find for the plaintiff on the issue of plagiarism, and set the action down for trial on November 8, 1976 on the issue of damages and other relief as to which the plaintiff may be entitled. The foregoing constitutes the Court's findings of fact and conclusions of law.

So ordered.

[The Court of Appeals for the Second Circuit affirmed the holding of infringement, stating that access could be inferred from the top-hit status of the plaintiff's song and explicitly endorsing the principle of subconscious infringement. *ABKCO Music, Inc. v. Harrisongs Music, Ltd.*, 722 F.2d 988 (2d Cir.1983). Protracted litigation over damages finally culminated in *ABKCO Music, Inc. v. Harrisongs Music, Ltd.*, 944 F.2d 971 (2d Cir.1991), more than 20 years after Harrison's subconscious infringement.]

———

A Y2K version of the *Harrisongs* case is *Three Boys Music Corp. v. Bolton*, 212 F.3d 477 (9th Cir.2000), in which the court of appeals sustained as reasonably based a jury verdict to the effect that Michael Bolton had subconsciously infringed a song ("Love is a Wonderful Thing") heard by him as a youngster some 20 years before he wrote his substantially similar song of the same title. The jury awarded $5.4 million.

QUESTIONS

1. It is uniformly held that copyright is infringed when one intentionally makes copies of a copyrighted work, even though the person copying does not know (and has no reason to know) of the copyright. For example, if a book publisher publishes a manuscript that has been represented to be an original work but is in fact a copy of a copyrighted work, the book publisher infringes. *De Acosta v. Brown,* 146 F.2d 408 (2d Cir.1944); *Lipton v. Nature Co.,* 71 F.3d 464 (2d Cir.1995). Is this a sound rule? What are the arguments for and against this rule?

2. Even assuming the above rule to be sound and widely endorsed, is not the case for infringement much more difficult when the defendant does not intend to reproduce any work by another and is unaware that he is copying at all? Why should liability be imposed in such a case?

3. How do you think the court should have ruled had defendant Harrison copied only motif A or motif B?

4. What if Harrison, idly sitting at the piano, purposely played the notes of motifs A and B *backwards* and, finding the resulting tune to be pleasant, added lyrics, and published and performed the new song. Is this an infringement?

CIRCUMSTANTIAL PROOF OF COPYING

In *Arnstein v. Porter,* the Second Circuit stated that the similarities between "Begin the Beguine" and plaintiff's songs, and the sale of one million copies of plaintiff's "A Mother's Prayer" as well as the public performance of others of plaintiff's songs, raised a sufficient possibility that Cole Porter had access to and copied from the songs to permit a trial on the issue. In the "My Sweet Lord" case, George Harrison's access to plaintiff's song was inferred from the song's status as a top hit in England and the United States, when Harrison, then a Beatle, would have had ample opportunity to hear the song.

In other instances, however, access and copying may be less subject to inference. In *Heim v. Universal Pictures Co.,* 154 F.2d 480 (2d Cir.1946), the Second Circuit declined to hold that the similarities between plaintiff's and defendant's songs resulted from access to and copying of plaintiff's song, even though plaintiff's song was included in a motion picture that was widely exhibited throughout the United States, had been publicly performed in major cities, and had been sold in sheet music. The court held that the similarities between the songs derived from their common reference to Dvořák's "Humoresque," and that plaintiff's variations on Dvořák were not sufficiently distinctive to permit a finding that defendant copied from plaintiff rather than from Dvořák.

In *Selle v. Gibb,* 567 F.Supp. 1173 (N.D.Ill.1983), *aff'd,* 741 F.2d 896 (7th Cir.1984), the court affirmed a judgment n.o.v. that defendants, the Bee Gees, did not copy from plaintiff's song in creating "How Deep Is Your Love." Although the two songs contained many similarities, the court held there was no credible evidence of access to plaintiff's song when defendants created their song in France, and plaintiff's song was unpublished and had only been performed by plaintiff at Chicago-area weddings and bar mitzvahs.

The Seventh Circuit stated that striking similarities, indeed even complete identity, between two works will not support a finding of infringement unless there is "at least some other evidence which would establish a reasonable possibility that the complaining work was *available* to the alleged infringer."

By contrast, the Second Circuit has declared its adherence to the original *Arnstein* "striking similarity" rule. In *Gasté v. Kaiserman,* 863 F.2d 1061 (2d Cir.1988), the court reaffirmed its willingness to find copying, even without evidence of access, when the two works are exceptionally close. The court upheld the verdict that defendant's work, the immensely popular song "Feelings," infringed the rather obscure French song "Pour Toi." To the lay ear, the songs were indeed quite similar. Evidence of access was somewhat skimpy: some twenty years before defendant composed his song, plaintiff had sent sheet music of his song to a Brazilian music publisher who ultimately became defendant's music publisher. It was therefore possible that defendant's publisher provided access to plaintiff's work. Even absent that possibility, the trial judge instructed the jury, access could be presumed from striking similarity. In affirming this instruction, the Second Circuit stated:

> Though striking similarity alone can raise an inference of copying, that inference must be reasonable in light of all the evidence. A plaintiff has not proved striking similarity sufficient to sustain a finding of copying if the evidence as a whole does not preclude any possibility of independent creation.

Although the Second and Seventh Circuits appeared to offer divergent approaches to striking similarity, more recent decisions indicate more of a common view in the Second and Seventh Circuits as to the role of "striking similarity" in furnishing circumstantial proof of access to the copyrighted work.

The Court of Appeals for the Second Circuit reiterated its view that similarity can be so "striking" as by itself to constitute proof of access sufficient to withstand summary judgment in *Repp v. Webber,* 132 F.3d 882 (2d Cir.1997). The plaintiff Repp, a composer and performer of liturgical music, wrote his song, "Till You," in 1978. The song was distributed as part of a record album and in sheet music, and performed by Repp in more than 200 concerts in the United States and abroad. The world-renowned popular stage composer, Andrew Lloyd Webber, composed his "Phantom Song" for "The Phantom of the Opera" in 1983. Repp claimed that the "Phantom Song" infringed "Till You," but Webber denied access and also introduced evidence (through the star of "Phantom" and his then-wife, Sarah Brightman) of the circumstances of the independent composition of "Phantom Song." Musical experts testified contradictorily as to whether the two songs were so strikingly similar as to preclude the possibility of independent creation by Webber. Although the district judge, based in part on his own "aural examination," cast his lot against striking similarity, the court of appeals held that there was enough contrary evidence so as to withstand Webber's motion for summary judgment and to create a triable issue of fact. (Webber had filed a counterclaim against Repp, asserting that "Till You" was itself copied from Webber's 1968 song "Close Every Door," part of his musical play "Joseph and the Amazing Technicolor Dreamcoat." The district court, after a five-day trial, found no copying; the court of appeals affirmed.) In the jury trial finally held on Repp's claim against Webber, the jury quickly returned a verdict for the defendant.

The Court of Appeals for the Seventh Circuit, in *Ty, Inc. v. GMA Accessories, Inc.*, 132 F.3d 1167 (7th Cir.1997), essentially reinterpreted its holding in *Selle v. Gibb* so as to allow a plaintiff to base its proof of access solely on striking similarity so long as there is no earlier exemplar, typically in the public domain, that could have independently inspired both works (which was how the court viewed the facts in the earlier case). At issue in the *Ty* case was the well-known Beanie Babies line of stuffed animals; it was alleged that GMA's "Preston the Pig" and "Louie the Cow" infringed Ty's "Squealer" and "Daisy" (see photographs, next page). Although the defendant denied having had access to the copyrighted works, the court found such striking similarity as to justify the conclusion that the copier must have had access to the original.

Selle required that the plaintiff produce evidence of access; but "a similarity that is so close as to be highly unlikely to have been an accident of independent creation *is* evidence of access." "A similarity may be striking without being suspicious" if it is explainable because both works copied the same thing in the public domain. In this case, "GMA's pig is strikingly similar to Ty's pig but not to anything in the public domain—a real pig, for example. . . . Real pigs are not the only pigs in the public domain. But GMA has not pointed to any fictional pig in the public domain that Preston resembles. Preston resembles only Squealer, and resembles him so closely as to warrant an inference that GMA copied Squealer."

The court stated a principle that would resolve the tension between the earlier cases in the Second and Seventh Circuits: "Access (and copying) may be inferred when two works are so similar to each other and not to anything in the public domain that it is likely that the creator of the second work copied the first, but the inference can be rebutted by disproving access or otherwise showing independent creation."

Ty's Squealer

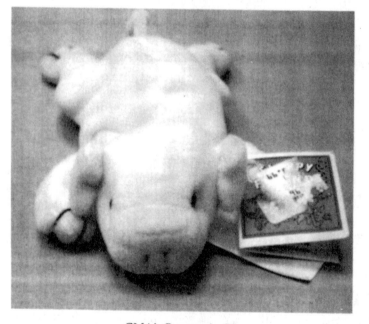

GMA's Preston the Pig

ii. Infringing Copying

ON THE DIFFERENCE BETWEEN PROVING COPYING
AND PROVING INFRINGEMENT

To prove copyright infringement, plaintiff must show not only that defendant copied the work but that the copying was illicit. To this end, plaintiff must demonstrate not only that similarities exist between the works but that these similarities are substantial. One may evaluate the substantiality of the similarities with regard either to their quantity or to their quality. In either event, the substantial similarity between plaintiff's and defendant's works must go to their expression, not merely to their facts or ideas.

The subject matter of substantial similarity illustrates a key difference between proving copying and proving infringement. Similarities of facts or ideas may be probative of the existence of copying. Indeed, publishers of compilations often introduce "false facts" as a way to trace copying. Discovery of plaintiff's invented entry in defendant's work will generally defeat the latter's claim of independent generation of the same material or information. *See, e.g., Feist v. Rural Telephone Serv., supra* Chapter 2.C (publisher of white pages telephone directory, suspecting copying by a competitor, "planted" some false information in its listings; reappearance of this information in defendant's telephone listings demonstrated defendant's copying). Once plaintiff shows copying, however, its demonstration is not complete; the substantial similarity standard requires evaluation of the nature of the correspondence between the two works. If, for example, defendant is shown to have copied only uncopyrightable information, no infringement has occurred. *See, e.g., id.* (while defendant clearly copied from plaintiff, its copying was noninfringing because the white pages lacked sufficient originality to be protected). The materials that follow illustrate methods of and problems in determining whether defendant copied plaintiff's *substantially protectible* expression.

———

Laureyssens v. Idea Group, Inc., 964 F.2d 131 (2d Cir.1992). The court here focused upon the element of "similarity" which appears to be utilized at two different stages of the analysis propounded in *Arnstein v. Porter*. The question in *Laureyssens* was whether the plaintiff's jigsaw-type puzzle, named HAPPY CUBE—which had the unusual feature of being assembleable either in a flat form in a rectangular frame or into a three-dimensional hollow cube—was infringed by the defendant's SNAFOOZ puzzle. Although there was no dispute about the plaintiff's valid copyright in the puzzle design, the district court denied a preliminary injunction based on its conclusion that no serious question of infringement existed. The court of appeals affirmed.

In parsing the *Arnstein* requirements of first finding copying (usually based on access and similarity) and then finding unlawful appropriation ("by demonstrating that substantial similarities relate to protectible material"), the court relied heavily upon an article by the late Professor Latman, titled " 'Probative Similarity' as Proof of Copying: Toward Dispelling Some Myths in Copyright Infringement," and posthumously published at 90 Colum. L. Rev. 1187 (1990). The court stated:

> A common form of indirect proof of copying—but far from the only form—is a showing of defendant's opportunity to come into contact with plaintiff's work and such similarities between the works which, under all the circumstances, make independent creation unlikely. Such similarities may or may not be substantial. They are not, however, offered for their own sake in satisfaction of the requirement that defendant has taken a substantial amount of protected material from the plaintiff's work. Rather, they are offered as probative of the act of copying and may accordingly for the sake of clarity conveniently be called "probative similarity."

Similarity that may be probative of copying—and it may in fact be insubstantial—may properly be uncovered through dissection and expert testimony. The defendant admitted access to the plaintiff's HAPPY CUBE puzzle, and the court found similarities that "are probative of copying and which at least raise a question of actual copying."

In turning to whether there was "substantial similarity as to protectible material," the court invoked the "ordinary observer" standard articulated by Judge Learned Hand in the *Peter Pan Fabrics* case, see *infra,* and stated: "[W]here a design contains both protectible and unprotectible elements, we have held that the observer's inspection must be more 'discerning,' ignoring those aspects of a work that are unprotectible in making the comparison." The court agreed with the trial judge that the similarities in the parties' works were principally in their idea and not in their expressive configuration.

Does "substantial similarity" imply the copying of a substantial *amount* of material? Suppose a defendant proven to have engaged in copying nonetheless asserts that the quantum of copying was *de minimis,* and therefore does not warrant a finding of infringement. The issue of how much copying must be shown to establish an infringement can be considered a matter of the plaintiff's prima facie case, or might be analyzed as part of a "fair use" defense, see *infra,* Chapter 7. Consider the following decision.

Ringgold v. Black Entertainment Television, Inc., 126 F.3d 70 (2d Cir.1997). Plaintiff had authorized the making of a poster featuring her pictorial quilt but had not authorized the inclusion of a copy of the poster as part of the set for a television program. Defendant rejoined that the poster was seen on the screen only fleetingly, scarcely two minutes total in the course of the program, and that any reproduction of the image of the quilt was therefore too trivial to constitute a violation. The Second Circuit addressed the proper characterization of the *de minimis* defense. Excerpts from the court's decision follow.

A. *The De Minimis Concept in Copyright Law*

The legal maxim "de minimis non curat lex" (sometimes rendered, "the law does not concern itself with trifles") insulates from liability those who cause insignificant violations of the rights of others. In the context of copyright law, the concept of *de minimis* has significance in three respects, which, though related, should be considered separately.

First, *de minimis* in the copyright context can mean what it means in most legal contexts: a technical violation of a right so trivial that the law will not impose legal consequences. Understandably, fact patterns are rarely litigated illustrating this use of the phrase, for, as Judge Leval has observed, such circumstances would usually involve "questions that never need to be answered." Pierre N. Leval, *Nimmer Lecture: Fair Use Rescued*, 44 U.C.L.A. L. Rev. 1449, 1457 (1997). He offers the example of a [photocopied] New Yorker cartoon put up on a refrigerator. In *Knickerbocker Toy Co. v. Azrak–Hamway International, Inc.*, 668 F.2d 699, 703 (2d Cir.1982), we relied on the *de minimis* doctrine to reject a toy manufacturer's claim based on a photograph of its product in an office copy of a display card of a competitor's product where the display card was never used. See *id*. at 702.

Second, *de minimis* can mean that copying has occurred to such a trivial extent as to fall below the quantitative threshold of substantial similarity, which is always a required element of actionable copying. . . .

In the pending case, there is no dispute about copying as a factual matter: the "Church Picnic" poster itself, not some poster that was similar in some respects to it, was displayed on the set of defendants' television program. What defendants dispute when they assert that their use of the poster was *de minimis* is whether the admitted copying occurred to an extent sufficient to constitute actionable copying, i.e., infringement. That requires "substantial similarity" in the sense of actionable copying, and it is that sense of the phrase to which the concept of *de minimis* is relevant.

At first glance, it might seem odd to pursue an inquiry as to "substantial similarity" even after copying as a factual matter has been established. However, the superficial anomaly reflects only a lack of appreciation of the difference between factual copying and actionable copying. The former (probative similarity) requires only the fact that the infringing work copies something from the copyrighted work; the latter (substantial similarity) requires that the copying is quantitatively and qualitatively sufficient to support the legal conclusion that infringement (actionable copying) has occurred. The qualitative component concerns the copying of expression, rather than ideas, a distinction that often turns on the level of abstraction at which the works are compared. The quantitative component generally concerns the amount of the copyrighted work that is copied, a consideration that is especially pertinent to exact copying. In cases involving visual works, like the pending one, the quantitative component of substantial similarity also concerns the observability of the copied work—the length of time the copied work is observable in the allegedly infringing work and such factors as focus, lighting, camera angles, and prominence. Thus, as in this case, a copyrighted work might be copied as a factual matter, yet a serious dispute might remain as to whether the copying that occurred was actionable. Since "substantial similarity," properly understood, includes a quantitative component, it becomes apparent why the concept of *de minimis* is relevant to a defendant's contention that an indisputably copied work has not been infringed.

Third, *de minimis* might be considered relevant to the defense of fair use. One of the statutory factors to be assessed in making the fair use determination is "the amount and substantiality of the portion used in relation to the copyrighted work as a whole," 17 U.S.C. § 107(3). A defendant might contend, as the District Court concluded in this case, that the portion used was minimal and the use was so brief and indistinct as to tip the third fair use factor decisively against the plaintiff.

Though the concept of *de minimis* is useful in insulating trivial types of copying from liability (the photocopied cartoon on the refrigerator) and in marking the quantitative threshold for actionable copying, see, e.g., *Vault Corp. v. Quaid Software, Ltd.*, 847 F.2d 255, 267 (5th Cir.1988) (30 characters out of 50 pages of source code held *de minimis*), the concept is an inappropriate one to be enlisted in fair use analysis. The third fair use factor concerns a quantitative continuum. Like all the fair use factors, it has no precise threshold below which the factor is accorded decisive significance. If the amount copied is very slight in relation to the work as a whole, the third factor might strongly favor the alleged infringer, but that will not always be the case. *See, e.g., Iowa State University Research Foundation, Inc. v. American Broadcasting Companies, Inc.*, 621 F.2d 57, 59, 61–62 (2d Cir.1980) (television program's copying of portions of copyrighted film, including an eight second segment). More important, the fair use defense involves a careful examination of many factors, often confronting courts with a perplexing task. If the allegedly infringing work makes such a quantitatively insubstantial use of the copyrighted work as to fall below the threshold required for actionable copying, it makes more sense to reject the claim on that basis and find no infringement, rather than undertake an elaborate fair use analysis in order to uphold a defense.

[handwritten margin note: Insubstantial copying is NOT infringement]

When a court inquires into whether the copying is infringing, it is generally confident that "copying" has occurred; the question is whether the copying is actionable. In the context of the Internet, however, it may not always be apparent that "copying" has occurred at all. In **Ticketmaster Corp. v. Tickets.Com, Inc.**, 54 U.S.P.Q.2d 1344 (C.D.Cal.2000), the court initially determined that hyperlinking was not "copying."

The web site of plaintiffs Ticketmaster Corporation and Ticketmaster Online–CitySearch, Inc. (hereafter collectively, in the singular

Ticketmaster) operates to allow customers to purchase tickets to various events (concerts, ball games, etc.) through an internet connection with its customers. On the Ticketmaster home page, there are instructions and a directory to subsequent pages (one per event). The event pages provide basic information (short description of the event, date, time, place, and price) and a description of how to order tickets by either internet response, telephone, mail, or in person. Each of these subsequent pages is identifiable with an electronic address. The home page further contains (if a customer scrolls to the bottom) "terms and conditions" which proscribe, among other things, copying for commercial use. However, the customer need not view the terms and conditions to proceed straight to the event page which interests him. Ticketmaster has exclusive agreements with the events it carries on its web pages so that tickets are not generally available to those events except through Ticketmaster (or reserved for sale by the event itself, or available from premium ticket brokers who generally charge higher than face value).

Tickets also operates a web site (Tickets.Com) which performs a somewhat different ticketing service. While Tickets does sell some tickets to certain events on its own, it also provides information as to where and how tickets which it does not sell may be purchased. A short factual description as to event, time, date, place and price is listed. Where Tickets does not itself sell the tickets, a place is given the customers to click for a reference to another ticket broker, or to another on-line ticket seller. Here is where the unique feature of this case—hyperlinks or deep linking—comes in. Where the exclusive ticket broker is Ticketmaster, and the customer clicks on "Buy this ticket from another on-line ticketing company", the customer is instantly transferred to the interior web page of Ticketmaster (bypassing the home page) for the particular event in question, where the customer may buy the tickets (from Ticketmaster, not Tickets) on-line. An explanation is generally given by Tickets as follows: "These tickets are sold by another ticketing company. Although we can't sell them to you, the link above will take you directly to the other company's web site where you can purchase them." The interior web page contains the Ticketmaster logo and the customer must know he is dealing with Ticketmaster, not Tickets.

In order to obtain the basic information on Ticketmaster events, Tickets is alleged to copy the interior web pages and extract the basic information (event, place, time, date and price) from them. That information is then placed in Tickets format on its own interior web pages. Tickets no longer (if it once did, as alleged) merely copies the Ticketmaster event page on its own event page. However, by the use of hyper-linking (i.e. electronic transfer to the particularly numbered interior web page of Ticketmaster), the customer is transferred directly to the Ticketmaster interior event page.

... Plaintiff claims that the copying includes printing the factual information derived from the Ticketmaster interior web pages. The court does not accept this argument. A copyright may not be claimed to protect factual data. While the expression, organization, placement, etc., of the factual data may be protected, Tickets is not alleged to have copied the method of presentation, but rather to have extracted the factual data and presented it in its own format. Where Tickets is alleged to have copied is in the making of thousands of copies taken from Ticketmaster's interior web pages for the purpose of extracting the factual data carried thereon and using it to publish its own version containing the factual data. Thus, copying is alleged (albeit not republication of protected material). Thus, the court rejects Ticketmaster's basic contention that it is copyright infringement to take basic facts from its publicly available web pages and use those facts (if the expression and method of presentation [are] not copied). Copying is alleged by transferring the event pages to Ticket's own computer to facilitate extraction of the facts. This is a very different case from merely copying for its customers the Ticketmaster event pages. This falls in the same category of taking historical facts from a work of reference and printing them in different expression. By a similar analogy, the hyperlink to the interior web page ... does not allege copying.

[handwritten margin note: Hyperlink not copying.]

In a subsequent opinion denying entry of an injunction 2000 WL 1887522 (C.D.Cal.2000), *aff'd.mem*, 248 F.3d 1173 (9th Cir. 2001), the district court returned to the issue of copying by Tickets.com:

> [T]here is undeniably copying of the electronic bits which make up the Ticketmaster event pages when projected on the screen. Except for the URL, the copying is transitory and temporary and is not used directly in competition with Ticketmaster, but it is copying and it would violate the Copyright Act if not justified. [Nonetheless, the temporary copying into RAM is] a necessary part of the process by which Tickets.com efficiently takes basic facts from the Ticketmaster websites.

[handwritten margin note: Copying to RAM is necessary to extract unprotected parts.]

The court then determined that the fair use doctrine excused copying necessary to obtain non-protectable information, such as the facts contained in the Ticketmaster webpages. That information included Ticketmaster's web addresses:

> Ticketmaster makes the point that copying the URL (the electronic address to the web pages) which is not destroyed, but retained and used, is copying protected material. The court doubts that the material is protectable because the URL appears to contain functional and factual elements only and not original material.

Peter Pan Fabrics, Inc. v. Martin Weiner Corp.

274 F.2d 487 (2d Cir.1960).

[A copyrighted design, "Byzantium," was imprinted upon bolts of cloth sold to garment manufacturers who later cut them into dresses. In doing so, the manufacturers cut or sewed the cloth so that copyright notices printed into the border or "selvage" of the cloth were no longer visible. The litigation was important in the area of copyrightability (accepting the extension of *Mazer v. Stein* to textile prints) and copyright notice (routine removal of the notice by customers of copyright owners did not forfeit copyright). But the words of Judge Learned Hand on the issue of substantial similarity have often been quoted:]

The test for infringement of a copyright is of necessity vague. In the case of verbal "works" it is well settled that although the "proprietor's" monopoly extends beyond an exact reproduction of the words, there can be no copyright in the "ideas" disclosed but only in their "expression." Obviously, no principle can be stated as to when an imitator has gone beyond copying the "idea," and has borrowed its "expression." Decisions must therefore inevitably be *ad hoc*. In the case of designs, which are addressed to the aesthetic sensibilities of an observer, the test is, if possible, even more intangible. No one disputes that the copyright extends beyond a photographic reproduction of the design, but one cannot say how far an imitator must depart from an undeviating reproduction to escape infringement. In deciding that question one should consider the uses for which the design is intended, especially the scrutiny that observers will give to it as used. In the case at bar we must try to estimate how far its overall appearance will determine its aesthetic appeal when the cloth is made into a garment. Both designs have the same general color, and the arches, scrolls, rows of symbols, etc. on one resemble those on the other though they are not identical. Moreover, the patterns in which these figures are distributed to make up the design as a whole are not identical. However, the ordinary observer, unless he set out to detect the disparities, would be disposed to overlook them, and regard their aesthetic appeal as the same. That is enough; and indeed, it is all that can be said, unless protection against infringement is to be denied because of variants irrelevant to the purpose for which the design is intended.

Herbert Rosenthal Jewelry Corp. v. Kalpakian

446 F.2d 738 (9th Cir.1971).

■ Browning, Circuit Judge: Plaintiff and defendants are engaged in the design, manufacture, and sale of fine jewelry.

Plaintiff charged defendants with infringing plaintiff's copyright registration of a pin in the shape of a bee formed of gold encrusted with jewels.... [A consent decree was entered, including an injunction against infringing the plaintiff's copyright. The plaintiff later moved for an order holding defendants in contempt.] The district court, after an evidentiary hearing, found that while defendants had manufactured and sold a line of jeweled bee pins, they designed their pins themselves after a study of bees in nature and in published works and did not copy plaintiff's copyrighted bee. The court further found that defendant's jeweled bees were "not substantially similar" to plaintiff's bees, except that both "do look like bees." The court concluded that defendants had neither infringed plaintiff's copyright nor violated the consent decree, and entered a judgment order denying plaintiff's motion. We affirm.

. . .

II

Plaintiff contends that its copyright registration of a jeweled bee entitles it to protection from the manufacture and sale by others of any object that to the ordinary observer is substantially similar in appearance. The breadth of this claim is evident. For example, while a photograph of the copyrighted bee pin attached to the complaint depicts a bee with nineteen small white jewels on its back, plaintiff argues that its copyright is infringed by defendants' entire line of a score or more jeweled bees in three sizes decorated with from nine to thirty jewels of various sizes, kinds, and colors.

Although plaintiff's counsel asserted that the originality of plaintiff's bee pin lay in a particular arrangement of jewels on the top of the pin, the elements of this arrangement were never identified. Defendants' witnesses testified that the "arrangement" was simply a function of the size and form of the bee pin and the size of the jewels used. Plaintiff's counsel, repeatedly pressed by the district judge, was unable to suggest how jewels might be placed on the back of a pin in the shape of a bee without infringing plaintiff's copyright. He eventually conceded, "not being a jeweler, I can't conceive of how he might rearrange the design so it is dissimilar."

Impossible to put jewels on a bee without being similar.

If plaintiff's understanding of its rights were correct, its copyright would effectively prevent others from engaging in the business of manufacturing and selling jeweled bees. We think plaintiff confuses the balance Congress struck between protection and competition under the Patent Act and the Copyright Act.

. . .

Obviously a copyright must not be treated as equivalent to a patent lest long continuing private monopolies be conferred over areas of gainful activity without first satisfying the substantive and procedural prerequisites to the grant of such privileges.

Because copyright bars only copying, perhaps this case could be disposed of on the district court's finding that defendants did not copy plaintiff's bee pin. It is true that defendants had access to the plaintiff's pin and that there is an obvious similarity between plaintiff's pin and those of defendants. These two facts constitute strong circumstantial evidence of copying. But they are not conclusive. *Overman v. Loesser*, 205 F.2d 521, 523 (9th Cir.1953); Nimmer on Copyright §§ 139.4, 141.2, and there was substantial evidence to support the trial court's finding that defendants' pin was in fact an independent creation. Defendants testified to independent creation from identified sources other than plaintiff's pin. The evidence established defendants' standing as designers of fine jewelry and reflected that on earlier occasions they had designed jeweled pins in the form of living creatures other than bees, including spiders, dragonflies, and

Access & Similarity not conclusive

Defendants proved independent creation.

other insects, birds, turtles, and frogs. Any inference of copying based upon similar appearance lost much of its strength because both pins were lifelike representations of a natural creature. Moreover, there were differences between defendants' and plaintiff's bees—notably in the veining of the wings.

Although this evidence would support a finding that defendants' bees were their own work rather than copied from plaintiff's, this resolution of the problem is not entirely satisfactory, particularly in view of the principle that copying need not be conscious, but "may be the result of subconscious memory derived from hearing, seeing or reading the copyrighted work at some time in the past." Howell's Copyright Law 129 (4th ed. 1962). *See Sheldon v. Metro–Goldwyn Pictures Corp.,* 81 F.2d 49, 54 (2d Cir.1936); *Harold Lloyd Corp. v. Witwer,* 65 F.2d 1, 16 (9th Cir.1933). It seems unrealistic to suppose that defendants could have closed their minds to plaintiff's highly successful jeweled bee pin as they designed their own.

A finding that defendants "copied" plaintiff's pin in this sense, however, would not necessarily justify judgment against them. A copyright, we have seen, bars use of the particular "expression" of an idea in a copyrighted work but does not bar use of the "idea" itself. Others are free to utilize the "idea" so long as they do not plagiarize its "expression." As the court said in *Trifari, Krussman & Fishel, Inc. v. B. Steinberg–Kaslo Co.,* 144 F. Supp. 577, 580 (S.D.N.Y.1956), where the copyrighted work was a jeweled pin representing a hansom cab, "though an alleged infringer gets the idea of a hansom cab pin from a copyrighted article there can be no infringement unless the article itself has been copied. The idea of a hansom cab cannot be copyrighted. Nevertheless plaintiff's expression of that idea, as embodied in its pin, can be copyrighted." . . .

The critical distinction between "idea" and "expression" is difficult to draw. . . . At least in close cases, one may suspect, the classification the court selects may simply state the result reached rather than the reason for it. In our view, the difference is really one of degree as Judge Hand suggested in his striking "abstraction" formulation in *Nichols v. Universal Pictures Corp.,* 45 F.2d 119, 121 (2d Cir.1930). The guiding consideration in drawing the line is the preservation of the balance between competition and protection reflected in the patent and copyright laws.

What is basically at stake is the extent of the copyright owner's monopoly—from how large an area of activity did Congress intend to allow the copyright owner to exclude others? We think the production of jeweled bee pins is a larger private preserve than Congress intended to be set aside in the public market without a patent. A jeweled bee pin is therefore an "idea" that defendants were free to copy. Plaintiff seems to agree, for it disavows any claim that defendants cannot manufacture and sell jeweled bee pins and concedes that only plaintiff's particular design or "expression" of the jeweled bee pin "idea" is protected under its copyright. The difficulty, as we have noted, is that on this record the "idea" and its "expression" appear to be indistinguishable. There is no greater similarity between the pins of plaintiff and defendants than is inevitable from the use of jewel-encrusted bee forms in both.

When the "idea" and its "expression" are thus inseparable, copying the "expression" will not be barred, since protecting the "expression" in such circumstances would confer a monopoly of the "idea" upon the copyright owner free of the conditions and limitations imposed by the patent law. [*Citations to, inter alia, Baker v. Selden* and *Morrissey v. Procter & Gamble* omitted.]

Affirmed.

[handwritten margin note: When the idea & expression are inseparable, Copying the expression is not barred.]

Educational Testing Services v. Katzman

793 F.2d 533 (3d Cir.1986).

[Plaintiff ETS develops and administers standardized tests, such as the Scholastic Aptitude Test (SAT), which it attempts to keep secret. Defendant, Katzman, operates Princeton Review, which, for a fee, prepares test takers and devises sample questions. The court of appeals first found that the ETS exam questions that were allegedly copied by the Princeton Review in preparing and distributing its "facsimile examinations" were copyrightable: they were not merely "ideas," nor were there so few ways to formulate questions that there was a "merger" of idea and expression so as to destroy copyrightability. The court then turned to the question whether the plaintiff was likely to prevail on its allegation that defendants had copied the ETS questions. It pointed out that "the record shows only rare instances of technically verbatim copying. However, ETS relies on the substantial similarity between its questions and those used by defendant to show copying." The court's discussion of substantial similarity follows.]

A finding of substantial similarity is an ad hoc determination. *See Peter Pan Fabrics, Inc. v. Martin Weiner Corp.*, 274 F.2d 487, 489 (2d Cir.1960). We apply the reasonable person standard, under which

the test is whether the accused work is so similar to the plaintiff's work that an ordinary reasonable person would conclude that the defendant unlawfully appropriated the plaintiff's protectible expression by taking material of substance and value.

.   .   .

This case does not present the exact duplication between copyrighted test questions for medical school admission and those used by a different coaching business that was before the court in *Association of American Medical Colleges v. Mikaelian*, 571 F. Supp. 144 (E.D.Pa.1983). There, the defendant's "facsimile" was an exact image of plaintiff's examination down to typeface and errors, *id.* at 148, and the court found that such similarities could only be explained by copying. *Id.* at 151.

Nonetheless, our examination discloses that at least some of Review's questions are so strikingly similar to those prepared by ETS as to lead to no other conclusion than that they were copied. For example, several of Review's math questions duplicate ETS' except for a change in the variables used. One example from the Math Level I Achievement Test will suffice:

ETS Question	*Review Question*

If $\underline{x} = 3$, then $\sqrt{x} =$
  3 3
	If $\underline{x} = 4$, then $\sqrt{x} =$
	  4 4

(A)⅓ (B) 1 (C) 3 (D)9 (E) 27	(A)¼ (B) 1 (C) 4 (D)16 (E) 64

Other math questions were similarly altered merely by substituting different values for the numbers in ETS' equations, or making other minor alterations.

It is also evident that the Review's "facsimile" used questions copied from the ETS' SAT questions:

	SAT Question	*Princeton Review* *"Facsimile"*
9.	REPROBATE: (A) predecessor (B) antagonist (C) virtuous person (D) temporary ruler (E) strict supervisor	9. REPROBATE: (A) antagonist (B) predecessor (C) virtuous person (D) temporary ruler (E) strict supervisor

* * * *

17.	CONVEYOR BELT: PACKAGES: (A) forklift:warehouse (B) crane:ships (C) escalator:people (D) elevator:penthouse (E) scaffold:ropes	17. CONVEYOR BELT: PACKAGES: (A) crane:ships (B) forklift: warehouse (C) escalator:people (D) parachute:airplane (E) scaffold:ropes

In some of the other questions used by defendants and identified by ETS as infringing, the copying is not apparent, at least without more explanation than appears on this record. For example, ETS claims infringement in the following pair of questions:

ETS Question	*Review Question*
Even though history does not $\quad$ A actually repeat itself, knowledge of $\quad\quad\quad\quad\quad\quad\quad\quad\quad\quad\quad$ B history can give current problems a $\quad\quad\quad\quad$ C familiar, less formidable look. $\quad\quad\quad$ D No error $\quad$ E	President Carter felt that, $\quad\quad\quad\quad\quad\quad\quad\quad\quad$ A by announcing all his $\quad$ B decisions while wearing a cardigan sweater, he would give $\quad\quad\quad\quad\quad\quad\quad\quad\quad\quad$ C his presidency a friendly, less $\quad\quad\quad\quad\quad\quad\quad\quad\quad\quad$ D formidable image. No error $\quad\quad\quad\quad\quad\quad\quad\quad$ E

The substantial similarity between Review's question and ETS' question, which was designed to test whether the applicant knew that there was no grammatical error, eludes us.

We recognize that even in the absence of closely similar language, courts have found copyright infringement on the basis of "recognizable paraphrases." . . .

ETS apparently believes the "recognizable paraphrasing" cases apply to the illustration set forth immediately above. However, in both of the cited cases, there was a striking similarity between the two works. Here, there is nothing comparable. ETS complains that some of defendants' questions copy both the structure and wording of its questions, testing the same points in the same order. We have already sustained its contention with regard to the use of the same wording or substantially similar wording. On the other hand, its claim with respect to the use of the same structure sweeps too broadly. We are not convinced that ETS' copyright in the text of a question precludes a coaching school from testing the same concept in the same order, as long as it does not use the same or substantially similar language. In any event, it is an issue on which more specific district court's findings, based on an adequate record, are essential. However, since the record adequately supports ETS' contention of copying based on nearly verbatim or substantially similar questions, the fact that some questions referred to by ETS may not be infringing does not affect its substantial likelihood of success on the merits.

. . .

QUESTIONS

1. Is idea/expression "merger" a question of law, or a question of fact? The breadth of plaintiff's claim in the bee pin allowed the *Kalpakian* court to rule that the subject matter of bee pins admits of insufficient variation of expression. But did the court *know* that this was the case? (Recall that the district court found defendant's pins *not* "substantially similar.") Should a court hear evidence on the question whether an idea in fact permits a highly limited range of expressions? *See, e.g., Apple Computer, Inc. v. Franklin Computer Corp.,* 714 F.2d 1240 (3d Cir.1983); *Higgins v. Baker,* 309 F.Supp. 635 (S.D.N.Y.1969). *Cf. Eckes v. Card Prices Update,* 736 F.2d 859 (2d Cir.1984). Does it/should it make a difference whether the idea/expression inquiry is conducted at the outset, to determine whether plaintiff's work is copyrightable at all, or at the infringement stage, to determine if what defendant copied was protectible?

2. The *Kalpakian* court offers an economic rationale for the idea/expression dichotomy: "ideas" are subject matter we wish to leave open to competition; "expression" is subject matter we feel comfortable allowing the copyright owner to exclude others from copying. In that light, consider the following:

In copyright law, an "idea" is not an epistemological concept, but a legal conclusion prompted by notions—often unarticulated and unproven—of appropriate competition. Thus, copyright doctrine attaches the label "idea" to aspects of works which, if protected, would (or, we fear, might) preclude, or render too expensive, subsequent authors' endeavors.

Ginsburg, *No "Sweat?" Copyright and Other Protection of Works of Information After Feist v. Rural Telephone,* 92 Colum. L. Rev. 338, 346 (1992). Do you agree?

3. In the *ETS* case, compare the ETS question featuring the fraction X/3 and the Princeton Review question featuring the fraction X/4; consider the multiple-choice answers for each question. Was the court correct in concluding that the similarities in the matched questions and answers were ones of "expression" rather than of "idea"? Does this not in fact come perilously close to granting ETS a monopoly over all questions about square roots and particular algebraic solutions?

Nichols v. Universal Pictures Corp.

45 F.2d 119 (2d Cir.1930).

■ L. HAND, CIRCUIT JUDGE. The plaintiff is the author of a play, "Abie's Irish Rose," which it may be assumed was properly copyrighted under section five, subdivision (d), of the Copyright Act, 17 USCA § 5(d). The defendant produced publicly a motion picture play, "The Cohens and The Kellys," which the plaintiff alleges was taken from it. As we think the defendant's play too unlike the plaintiff's to be an infringement, we may assume, arguendo, that in some details the defendant used the plaintiff's play, as will subsequently appear, though we do not so decide. It therefore becomes necessary to give an outline of the two plays.

"Abie's Irish Rose" presents a Jewish family living in prosperous circumstances in New York. The father, a widower, is in business as a merchant, in which his son and only child helps him. The boy has philandered with young women, who to his father's great disgust have always been Gentiles, for he is obsessed with a passion that his daughter-in-law shall be an orthodox Jewess. When the play opens the son, who has been courting a young Irish Catholic girl, has already married her secretly before a Protestant minister, and is concerned to soften the blow for his father, by securing a favorable impression of his bride, while concealing her faith and race. To accomplish this he introduces her to his father at his home as a Jewess, and lets it appear that he is interested in her, though he conceals the marriage. The girl somewhat reluctantly falls in with the plan; the father takes the bait, becomes infatuated with the girl, concludes that they must marry, and assumes that of course they will, if he so decides. He calls in a rabbi, and prepares for the wedding according to the Jewish rite.

Meanwhile the girl's father, also a widower, who lives in California, and is as intense in his own religious antagonism as the Jew, has been called to New York, supposing that his daughter is to marry an Irishman and a Catholic. Accompanied by a priest, he arrives at the house at the moment when the marriage is being celebrated, but too late to prevent it, and the two fathers, each infuriated by the proposed union of his child to a heretic, fall into unseemly and grotesque antics. The priest and the rabbi become friendly, exchange trite sentiments about religion, and agree that the match is good. Apparently out of abundant caution, the priest celebrates the marriage for a third time, while the girl's father is inveigled away. The second act closes with each father, still outraged, seeking to find some way by which the union, thus trebly insured, may be dissolved.

The last act takes place about a year later, the young couple having meanwhile been abjured by each father, and left to their own resources. They have had twins, a boy and a girl, but their fathers know no more than that a child has been born. At Christmas, each, led by his craving to see his grandchild, goes separately to the young folks' home, where they encounter each other, each laden with gifts, one for a boy, the other for a girl. After some slapstick comedy, depending upon the insistence of each that he is right about the sex of the grandchild, they become reconciled when they learn the truth, and that each child is to bear the given name of a grandparent. The curtain falls as the fathers are exchanging amenities, and the Jew giving evidence of an abatement in the strictness of his orthodoxy.

"The Cohens and The Kellys" presents two families, Jewish and Irish, living side by side in the poorer quarters of New York in a state of perpetual enmity. The wives in both cases are still living, and share in the mutual animosity, as do two small sons, and even the respective dogs. The Jews have a daughter, the Irish a son; the Jewish father is in the clothing business; the Irishman is a policeman. The children are in love with each other, and secretly marry, apparently after the play opens. The Jew, being in great financial straits, learns from a lawyer that he has fallen heir to a large fortune from a great-aunt, and moves into a great house, fitted luxuriously. Here he and his family live in vulgar ostentation, and here the Irish boy seeks out his Jewish bride, and is chased away by the angry father. The Jew then abuses the Irishman over the telephone, and both become hysterically excited. The extremity of his feelings makes the Jew sick, so that he must go to Florida for a rest, just before which the daughter discloses her marriage to her mother.

On his return the Jew finds that his daughter has borne a child; at first he suspects the lawyer, but eventually learns the truth and is overcome with anger at such a low alliance. Meanwhile, the Irish family who have been forbidden to see the grandchild, go to the Jew's house, and after a violent scene between the two fathers in which the Jew disowns his daughter, who decides to go back with her husband, the Irishman takes her back with her baby to his own poor lodgings. The lawyer, who had hoped to marry the Jew's daughter, seeing his plan foiled, tells the Jew that his fortune really belongs to the Irishman, who was also related to the dead woman, but offers to conceal his knowledge, if the Jew will share the loot. This the Jew repudiates, and, leaving the astonished lawyer, walks through the rain to his enemy's house to surrender the property. He arrives in great dejection, tells the truth, and abjectly turns to leave. A reconciliation ensues, the Irishman agreeing to share with him equally. The Jew shows some interest in his grandchild, though this is at most a minor motive in the reconciliation, and the curtain falls while the two are in their cups, the Jew insisting that in the firm name for the business, which they are to carry on jointly, his name shall stand first.

It is of course essential to any protection of literary property, whether at common law or under the statute, that the right cannot be limited literally to the text, else a plagiarist would escape by immaterial variations. That has never been the law, but, as soon as literal appropriation ceases to be the test, the whole matter is necessarily at large, so that, as was recently well said by a distinguished judge, the decisions cannot help much in a new case. *Fendler v. Morosco,* 253 N.Y. 281, 292, 171 N.E. 56. When plays are concerned, the plagiarist may excise a separate scene [*Daly v. Webster,* 56 F. 483 (C.C.A.2); *Chappell v. Fields,* 210 F. 864 (C.C.A.2); *Chatterton v. Cave,* L.R. 3 App. Cas. 483]; or he may appropriate part of the dialogue (*Warne v. Seebohm,* L.R. 39 Ch. D. 73). Then the question is whether the part so taken is "substantial," and therefore not a "fair use" of the copyrighted work; it is the same question as arises in the case of any other copyrighted work. *Marks v. Feist,* 290 F. 959 (C.C.A.2); *Emerson v. Davies,* Fed. Cas. No. 4436, 3 Story, 768, 795–797. But when the plagiarist does not take out a block in situ, but an abstract of the whole, decision is more troublesome. Upon any work, and especially upon a play, a great number of patterns of increasing generality will fit equally well, as more and more of the incident is left out. The last may perhaps be no more than the most general statement of what the play is about, and at times might consist only of its title; but there is a point in this series of abstractions where they are no longer protected, since otherwise the playwright could prevent the use of his "ideas," to which, apart from their expression, his property is never extended. *Holmes v. Hurst,* 174 U.S. 82, 86; *Guthrie v. Curlett,* 36 F.(2d) 694 (C.C.A.2). Nobody has ever been able to fix that boundary, and nobody ever can. In some cases the question has been treated as though it were analogous to lifting a portion out of the copyrighted work (*Rees v. Melville,* MacGillivray's Copyright Cases [1911–1916], 168); but the analogy is not a good one, because, though the skeleton is a part of the body, it pervades and supports the whole. In such cases we are rather concerned with the line between expression and what is expressed. As respects plays, the controversy chiefly centers upon the characters and sequence of incident, these being the substance.

... [W]e do not doubt that two plays may correspond in plot closely enough for infringement. How far that correspondence must go is another matter. Nor need we hold that the same may not be true as to the characters, quite independently of the "plot" proper, though, as far as we know, such a case has never arisen. If Twelfth Night were copyrighted, it is quite possible that a second comer might so closely imitate Sir Toby Belch or Malvolio as to infringe, but it would not be enough that for one of his characters he cast a riotous knight who kept wassail to the discomfort of the household, or a vain and foppish steward who became amorous of his mistress. These would be no more than Shakespeare's "ideas" in the play, as little capable of monopoly as Einstein's Doctrine of Relativity, or Darwin's theory of the Origin of Species. It follows that the less developed the characters, the less they can be copyrighted; that is the penalty an author must bear for marking them too indistinctly.

In the two plays at bar we think both as to incident and character, the defendant took no more—assuming that it took anything at all—than the law allowed. The stories are quite different. One is of a religious zealot who insists upon his child's marrying no one outside his faith; opposed by another who is in this respect just like him, and is his foil. Their difference in race is merely an obbligato to the main theme, religion. They sink their differences through grandparental pride and affection. In the other, zealotry is wholly absent; religion does not even appear. It is true that the parents are hostile to each other in part because they differ in race; but the marriage of their son to a Jew does not apparently offend the Irish family at all, and it exacerbates the existing animosity of the Jew, principally because he has become rich, when he learns it. They are reconciled through the honesty of the Jew and the generosity of the Irishman; the grandchild has nothing whatever to do with it. The only matter common to the two is a quarrel between a Jewish and an Irish father, the marriage of their children, the birth of grandchildren and a reconciliation.

If the defendant took so much from the plaintiff, it may well have been because her amazing success seemed to prove that this was a subject of enduring popularity. Even so, granting that the plaintiff's play was wholly original, and assuming that novelty is not essential to a copyright, there is no monopoly in such a background. Though the plaintiff discovered the vein, she could not keep it to herself; so defined, the theme was too generalized an abstraction from what she wrote. It was only a part of her "ideas."

Nor does she fare better as to her characters. It is indeed scarcely credible that she should not have been aware of those stock figures, the low comedy Jew and Irishman. The defendant has not taken from her more than their prototypes have contained for many decades. If so, obviously so to generalize her copyright, would allow her to cover what was not original with her. But we need not hold this as matter of fact, much as we might be justified. Even though we take it that she devised her figures out of her brain de novo, still the defendant was within its rights.

There are but four characters common to both plays, the lovers and the fathers. The lovers are so faintly indicated as to be no more than stage properties. They are loving and fertile; that is really all that can be said of them, and anyone else is quite within his rights if he puts loving and fertile lovers in a play of his own, wherever he gets the cue. The plaintiff's Jew is quite unlike the defendant's. His obsession is his religion, on which depends such racial animosity as he has. He is affectionate, warm and patriarchal. None of these fit the defendant's Jew, who shows affection for his daughter only once, and who has none but the most superficial interest in his grandchild. He is tricky, ostentatious and vulgar, only by misfortune redeemed into honesty. Both are grotesque, extravagant and quarrelsome; both are fond of display; but these common qualities make up only a small part of their simple pictures, no more than any one might lift if he chose. The Irish fathers are even more unlike; the plaintiff's a mere symbol for religious fanaticism and patriarchal pride, scarcely a character at all. Neither quality appears in the defendant's, for while he goes to get his grandchild, it is rather out of a truculent determination not to be forbidden, than from pride in his progeny. For the rest he is only a grotesque hobbledehoy, used for low comedy of the most conventional sort, which any one might borrow, if he chanced not to know the exemplar.

The defendant argues that the case is controlled by my decision in *Fisher v. Dillingham* (D.C.) 298 F. 145. Neither my brothers nor I wish to throw doubt upon the doctrine of that case, but it is not applicable here. We assume that the plaintiff's play is altogether original, even to an extent that in fact it is hard to believe. We assume further that, so far as it has been anticipated by earlier plays of which she knew nothing, that fact is immaterial. Still, as we have already said, her copyright did not cover everything that might be drawn from her play; its content went to some extent into the public domain. We have to decide how much, and while we are as aware as any one that the line, wherever it is drawn, will seem arbitrary, that is no excuse for not drawing it; it is a question such as courts must answer in nearly all cases. Whatever may be the difficulties a priori, we have no question on which side of the line this case falls. A comedy based upon conflicts between Irish and Jews, into which the marriage of their children enters, is no more susceptible of copyright than the outline of Romeo and Juliet.

The plaintiff has prepared an elaborate analysis of the two plays, showing a "quadrangle" of the common characters, in which each is represented by the emotions which he discovers. She presents the resulting parallelism as proof of infringement, but the adjectives employed are so general as to be quite useless. Take for example the attribute of "love" ascribed to both Jews. The plaintiff has depicted her father as deeply attached to his son, who is his hope and joy; not so, the defendant, whose father's conduct is throughout not actuated by any affection for his daughter, and who is merely once overcome for the moment by her distress when he has violently dismissed her lover. "Anger" covers emotions aroused by quite different occasions in each case; so do "anxiety," "despondency" and "disgust." It is unnecessary to go through the catalogue for emotions are too much colored by their causes to be a test when used so broadly. This is not the proper approach to a solution; it must be more ingenuous, more like that of a spectator, who would rely upon the complex of his impressions of each character.

We cannot approve the length of the record, which was due chiefly to the use of expert witnesses. Argument is argument whether in the box or at the bar, and its proper place is the last. The testimony of an expert upon such issues, especially his cross-examination, greatly extends the trial and contributes nothing which cannot be better heard after the evidence is all submitted. It ought not to be allowed at all; and while its admission is not a ground for reversal, it cumbers the case and tends to confusion, for the more the court is led into the intricacies of dramatic craftsmanship, the less likely it is to stand upon the firmer, if more naive, ground of its considered impressions upon its own perusal. We hope that in this class of cases such evidence may in the future be entirely excluded, and the case confined to the actual issues; that is, whether the copyrighted work was original, and whether the defendant copied it, so far as the supposed infringement is identical.

The defendant, "the prevailing party," was entitled to a reasonable attorney's fee (section 40 of the Copyright Act [17 USCA § 40]).

Decree affirmed.

QUESTIONS

1. The plaintiff had obviously discovered a vein of extremely appealing popular drama—first-generation ethnic combatants reconciled, in the "melting pot" that was early twentieth century America, by the love of the younger generation. Defendant was apparently seeking to "horn in" on that eminently successful (and remunerative) theme. Reasoning from first principles, should that be permitted?

2. In these cases of literary plagiarism, to what extent and for what purposes might a defendant bring to the court's attention literary and dramatic works that preceded that of the plaintiff?

3. When Judge Hand discusses the literal copying of dialogue, he states that takings that are "insubstantial" are allowable. Is "substantiality" to be determined by a quantitative test alone? (This is an example of what Professor Nimmer labeled "fragmented literal similarity," which focuses upon copying of direct quotations or close paraphrasing. He contrasted it with "comprehensive nonliteral similarity," which involves the copying of the structure of a work, and similarities in plot line and the sequence of incidents; this is, of course, the more usual form of alleged literary infringement. This distinction, and the Nimmer phraseology, are often referred to in the decided cases.) *See* Melville Nimmer & David Nimmer, Nimmer on Copyright § 13.03[A].

Sheldon v. Metro–Goldwyn Pictures Corp.

81 F.2d 49 (2d Cir.1936).

■ L. Hand, Circuit Judge. The suit is to enjoin the performance of the picture play, "Letty Lynton," as an infringement of the plaintiffs' copyrighted play, "Dishonored Lady." The plaintiffs' title is conceded, so too the validity of the copyright; the only issue is infringement. The defendants say that they did not use the play in any way to produce the picture; the plaintiffs discredit this denial because of the negotiations between the parties for the purchase of rights in the play, and because the similarities between the two are too specific and detailed to have resulted from chance. The judge thought that, so far as the defendants had used the play, they had taken only what the law allowed, that is, those general themes, motives, or ideas in which there could be no copyright. Therefore he dismissed the bill.

An understanding of the issue involves some description of what was in the public demesne, as well as of the play and the picture. In 1857 a Scotch girl, named Madeleine Smith, living in Glasgow, was brought to trial upon an indictment in three counts; two for attempts to poison her lover, a third for poisoning him. The jury acquitted her on the first count, and brought in a verdict of "Not Proven" on the second and third. The circumstances of the prosecution aroused much interest at the time not only in Scotland but in England; so much indeed that it became a cause célèbre, and that as late as 1927 the whole proceedings were published in book form. An outline of the story so published, which became the original of the play here in suit, is as follows: The Smiths were a respectable middle-class family, able to send their daughter to a "young ladies' boarding school"; they supposed her protected not only from any waywardness of her own, but from the wiles of seducers. In both they were mistaken, for when at the age of twenty-one she met a young Jerseyman of French blood, Emile L'Angelier, ten years older, and already the hero of many amorous adventures, she quickly succumbed and poured out her feelings in letters of the utmost ardor and indiscretion, and at times of a candor beyond the standards then, and even yet, permissible for well-nurtured young women. They wrote each other as though already married, he assuming to dictate her conduct and even her feelings; both expected to marry, she on any terms, he with the approval of her family. Nevertheless she soon tired of him and engaged herself to a man some twenty years older who was a better match, but for whom she had no more than a friendly complaisance. L'Angelier was not, however, to be fobbed off so easily; he threatened to expose her to her father by showing her letters. She at first tried to dissuade him by appeals to their tender memories, but finding this useless and thinking herself otherwise undone, she affected a return of her former passion and invited him to visit her again. Whether he did, was the turning point of the trial; the evidence, though it really left the issue in no doubt, was too indirect to satisfy the jury, perhaps in part because of her advocate's argument that to kill him only insured the discovery of her letters. It was shown that she had several times bought or tried to buy poison—prussic acid and arsenic—and that twice before his death L'Angelier became violently ill, the second time on the day after her purchase. He died of arsenical poison, which the prosecution charged that she had given him in a cup of chocolate. At her trial, Madeleine being incompetent as a witness, her advocate proved an alibi by the testimony of her younger sister that early on the night of the murder as laid in the indictment, she had gone to bed with Madeleine, who had slept with her throughout the night. As to one of the attempts her betrothed swore that she had been with him at the theatre.

This was the story which the plaintiffs used to build their play. As will appear they took from it but the merest skeleton, the acquittal of a wanton young woman, who to extricate herself from an amour that stood in the way of a respectable marriage, poisoned her lover. The incidents, the characters, the mise-en-scène, the sequence of events, were all changed; nobody disputes that the plaintiffs were entitled to their copyright. All that they took from the story they might probably have taken, had it even been copyrighted. Their heroine is named Madeleine Cary; she lives in New York, brought up in affluence, if not in luxury; she is intelligent, voluptuous, ardent and corrupt; but, though she has had a succession of amours, she is capable of genuine affection. Her lover and victim is an Argentinian, named Moreno, who makes his living as a dancer in night-clubs. Madeleine has met him once in Europe before the play opens, has danced with him, has excited his concupiscence; he presses presents upon her. The play opens in his rooms, he and his dancing partner who is also his mistress, are together; Madeleine on the telephone recalls herself to him and says she wishes to visit him, though it is already past midnight. He disposes of his mistress by a device which does not deceive her and receives Madeleine; at once he falls to wooing her, luring her among other devices by singing a Gaucho song. He finds her facile and the curtain falls in season.

The second act is in her home, and introduces her father, a bibulous dotard, who has shot his wife's lover in the long past; Laurence Brennan, a self-made man in the fifties, untutored, self-reliant and reliable, who has had with Madeleine a relation, half paternal, half-amorous since she grew up; and Denis Farnborough, a young British labor peer, a mannikin to delight the heart of well ordered young women. Madeleine loves him; he loves Madeleine; she will give him no chance to declare himself, remembering her mottled past and his supposedly immaculate standards. She confides to Brennan, who makes clear to her the imbecility of her self-denial; she accepts this enlightenment and engages herself to her high-minded paragon after confessing vaguely her evil life and being assured that to post-war generations all such lapses are peccadillo.

In the next act Moreno, who has got wind of the engagement, comes to her house. Disposing of Farnborough, who chances to be there, she admits Moreno, acknowledges that she is to marry Farnborough, and asks him to accept the situation as the normal outcome of their intrigue. He refuses to be cast off, high words pass, he threatens to expose their relations, she raves at him, until finally he knocks her down and commands her to go to his apartment that morning as before. After he leaves full of swagger, her eye lights on a bottle of strychnine which her father uses as a drug; her fingers slowly close upon it; the audience understands that she will kill Moreno. Farnborough is at the telephone; this apparently stiffens her resolve, showing her the heights she may reach by its execution.

The scene then shifts again to Moreno's apartment; his mistress must again be put out, most unwillingly for she is aware of the situation; Madeleine comes in; she pretends once more to feel warmly, she must wheedle him for he is out of sorts after the quarrel. Meanwhile she prepares to poison him by putting the strychnine in coffee, which she asks him to make ready. But in the course of these preparations during which he sings her again his Gaucho song, what with their proximity, and this and that, her animal ardors are once more aroused and drag her, unwillingly and protesting, from her purpose. The play must therefore wait for an hour or more until, relieved of her passion, she appears from his bedroom and while breakfasting puts the strychnine in his coffee. He soon discovers what has happened and tries to telephone for help. He does succeed in getting a few words through, but she tears away the wire and fills his dying ears with her hatred and disgust. She then carefully wipes away all traces of her finger prints and manages to get away while the door is being pounded in by those who have come at his call.

The next act is again at her home on the following evening. Things are going well with her and Farnborough and her father, when a district attorney comes in, a familiar of the household, now in stern mood; Moreno's mistress and a waiter have incriminated Madeleine, and a cross has been found in Moreno's pocket, which he superstitiously took off her neck the night before. The district attorney cross-questions her, during which Farnborough several times fatuously intervenes; she is driven from point to point almost to an avowal when as a desperate plunge she says she spent the night with Brennan. Brennan is brought to the house and, catching the situation after a moment's delay, bears her out. This puts off the district attorney until seeing strychnine brought to relieve the father, his suspicions spring up again and he arrests Madeleine. The rest of the play is of no consequence here, except that it appears in the last scene that at the trial where she is acquitted, her father on the witness stand accounts for the absence of the bottle of strychnine which had been used to poison Moreno.

At about the time that this play was being written an English woman named Lowndes wrote a book called Letty Lynton, also founded on the story of Madeleine Smith. Letty Lynton lives in England; she is eighteen years old, beautiful, well-reared and intelligent, but wayward. She has had a more or less equivocal love affair with a young Scot, named McLean, who worked in her father's chemical factory, but has discarded him, apparently before their love-making had gone very far. Then she chances upon a young Swede—half English—named Ekebon, and their acquaintance quickly becomes a standardized amour, kept secret from her parents, especially her mother, who is an uncompromising moralist, and somewhat estranged from Letty anyway. She and her lover use an old barn as their place of assignation; it had been fitted up as a play house for Letty when she was a child. Like Madeleine Smith she had written her lover a series of indiscreet letters which he has kept, for though he is on pleasure bent Ekebon has a frugal mind, and means to marry his sweetheart and set himself up for life. They are betrothed and he keeps pressing her to declare it to her parents, which she means never to do. While he is away in Sweden Letty meets an unmarried peer considerably older than she, poor, but intelligent and charming; he falls in love with her and she accepts him, more because it is a good match than for any other reason, though she likes him well enough, and will make him suppose that she loves him.

Thereupon Ekebon reappears, learns of Letty's new betrothal, and threatens to disclose his own to her father, backing up his story with her letters. She must at once disown her peer and resume her engagement with him. His motive, like L'Angelier's, is ambition rather than love, though conquest is a flattery and Letty a charming morsel. His threats naturally throw Letty into dismay; she has come to loathe him and at any cost must get free, but she has no one to turn to. In her plight she thinks of her old suitor, McLean, and goes to the factory only to find him gone. He has taught her how to get access to poisons in his office and has told of their effect on human beings. At first she thinks of jumping out the window, and when she winces at that, of poisoning herself; that would be easier. So she selects arsenic which is less painful and goes away with it; it is only when she gets home that she thinks of poisoning Ekebon. Her mind is soon made up, however, and she makes an appointment with him at the barn; she has told her father, she writes, and Ekebon is to see him on Monday, but meanwhile on Sunday they will meet secretly once more. She has prepared to go on a week-end party and conceals her car near the barn. He comes; she welcomes him with a pretense of her former ardors, and tries to get back her letters. Unsuccessful in this she persuades him to drink a cup of chocolate into which she puts the arsenic. After carefully washing the pans and cups, she leaves with him, dropping him from her car near his home; he being still unaffected. On her way to her party she pretends to have broken down and by asking the help of a passing cyclist establishes an alibi. Ekebon dies at his home attended by his mistress; the letters are discovered and Letty is brought before the coroner's inquest and acquitted chiefly through the alibi, for things look very bad for her until the cyclist appears.

The defendants, who are engaged in producing speaking films on a very large scale in Hollywood, California, had seen the play and wished to get the rights. They found, however, an obstacle in an association of motion picture producers presided over by Mr. Will Hays, who thought the play obscene; not being able to overcome his objections, they returned the copy of the manuscript which they had. That was in the spring of 1930, but in the autumn they induced the plaintiffs to get up a scenario, which they hoped might pass moral muster. Although this did not suit them after the plaintiffs prepared it, they must still have thought in the spring of 1931 that they could satisfy Mr. Hays, for they then procured an offer from the plaintiffs to sell their rights for $30,000. These negotiations also proved abortive because the play continued to be objectionable, and eventually they cried off on the bargain. Mrs. Lowndes' novel was suggested to Thalberg, one of the vice-presidents of the Metro–Goldwyn Company, in July, 1931, and again in the following November, and he bought the rights to it in December. At once he assigned the preparation of a play to Stromberg, who had read the novel in January, and thought it would make a suitable play for an actress named Crawford, just then not employed. Stromberg chose Meehan, Tuchock and Brown to help him, the first two with the scenario, the third with the dramatic production. All these four were examined by deposition; all denied that they had used the play in any way whatever; all agreed that they had based the picture on the story of Madeleine Smith and on the novel, "Letty Lynton." All had seen the play, and Tuchock had read the manuscript, as had Thalberg, but Stromberg,

Meehan and Brown swore that they had not; Stromberg's denial being however worthless, for he had originally sworn the contrary in an affidavit. They all say that work began late in November or early in December, 1931, and the picture was finished by the end of March. To meet these denials, the plaintiffs appeal to the substantial identity between passages in the picture and those parts of the play which are original with them.

The picture opens in Montevideo where Letty Lynton is recovering from her fondness for Emile Renaul. She is rich, luxurious and fatherless, her father having been killed by his mistress's husband; her mother is seared, hard, selfish, unmotherly; and Letty has left home to escape her, wandering about in search of excitement. Apparently for the good part of a year she has been carrying on a love affair with Renaul; twice before she has tried to shake loose, has gone once to Rio where she lit another flame, but each time she has weakened and been drawn back. Though not fully declared as an amour, there can be no real question as to the character of her attachment. She at length determines really to break loose, but once again her senses are too much for her and it is indicated, if not declared, that she spends the night with Renaul. Though he is left a vague figure only indistinctly associated with South America somewhere or other, the part was cast for an actor with a marked foreign accent, and it is plain that he was meant to be understood, in origin anyway, as South American, like Moreno in the play. He is violent, possessive and sensual; his power over Letty lies in his strong animal attractions. However, she escapes in the morning while he is asleep, whether from his bed or not is perhaps uncertain; and with a wax figure in the form of a loyal maid—Letty in the novel had one—boards a steamer for New York. On board she meets Darrow, a young American, the son of a rich rubber manufacturer, who is coming back from a trip to Africa. They fall in love upon the faintest provocation and become betrothed before the ship docks, three weeks after she left Montevideo. At the pier she finds Renaul who has flown up to reclaim her. She must in some way keep her two suitors apart, and she manages to dismiss Darrow and then to escape Renaul by asking him to pay her customs duties, which he does. Arrived home her mother gives her a cold welcome and refuses to concern herself with the girl's betrothal. Renaul is announced; he has read of the betrothal in the papers and is furious. He tries again to stir her sensuality by the familiar gambit, but this time he fails; she slaps his face and declares that she hates him. He commands her to come to his apartment that evening; she begs him to part with her and let her have her life; he insists on renewing their affair. She threatens to call the police; he rejoins that if so her letters will be published, and then he leaves. Desperate, she chances on a bottle of strychnine, which we are to suppose is an accoutrement of every affluent household, and seizes it; the implication is of intended suicide, not murder. Then she calls Darrow, tells him that she will not leave with him that night for his parents' place in the Adirondacks as they had planned; she renews to him the pledge of her love, without him she cannot live, an intimation to the audience of her purpose to kill herself.

That evening she goes to Renaul's apartment in a hotel armed with her strychnine bottle, for use on the spot; she finds him cooling champagne, but in bad temper. His caresses which he bestows plentifully enough, again stir her disgust not her passions, but he does not believe it and assumes that she will spend the night with him. Finding that he will not return the letters, she believes herself lost and empties the strychnine into a wine glass. Again he embraces her; she vilifies him; he knocks her down; she vilifies him again. Ignorant of the poison he grasps her glass, and she, perceiving it, lets him drink. He woos her again, this time with more apparent success, for she is terrified; he sings a Gaucho song to her, the same one that has been heard at Montevideo. The poison begins to work and, at length supposing that she has meant to murder him, he reaches for the telephone; she forestalls him, but she does not tear out the wire. As he slowly dies, she stands over him and vituperates him. A waiter enters; she steps behind a curtain; he leaves thinking Renaul drunk; she comes out, wipes off all traces of her fingerprints and goes out, leaving however her rubbers which Renaul had taken from her when she entered.

Next she and Darrow are found at his parents' in the Adirondacks; while there a detective appears, arrests Letty and takes her to New York; she is charged with the murder of Renaul; Darrow goes back to New York with her. The finish is at the district attorney's office; Letty and Darrow, Letty's mother, the wax serving maid are all there. The letters appear incriminating to an elderly rather benevolent district attorney; also the customs slip and the rubbers. Letty begins to break down; she admits that she went to Renaul's room, not to kill him but to get him to release her. Darrow sees that story will not pass, and volunteers that she came to his room at a hotel and spent the night with him. Letty confirms this and her mother, till then silent, backs up their story; she had traced them to the hotel and saw the lights go out, having ineffectually tried to dissuade them. The maid still further confirms them and the district attorney, not sorry to be discomfited, though unbelieving, discharges Letty.

We are to remember that it makes no difference how far the play was anticipated by works in the public demesne which the plaintiffs did not use. The defendants appear not to recognize this, for they have filled the record with earlier instances of the same dramatic incidents and devices, as though, like a patent, a copyrighted work must be not only original, but new. That is not however the law as is obvious in the case of maps or compendia, where later works will necessarily be anticipated.... It is plain beyond peradventure that anticipation as such cannot invalidate a copyright. Borrowed the work must indeed not be, for a plagiarist is not himself *pro tanto* an "author"; but if by some magic a man who had never known it were to compose anew Keats's Ode on a Grecian Urn, he would be an "author," and, if he copyrighted it, others might not copy that poem, though they might of course copy Keats's. *Bleistein v. Donaldson Lithographing Co.*, 188 U.S. 239, 249; *Gerlach-Barklow Co. v. Morris & Bendien, Inc.*, 23 F.(2d) 159, 161 (C.C.A.2); Weil, Copyright Law, p. 234. But though a copyright is for this reason less vulnerable than a patent, the owner's protection is more limited, for just as he is no less an "author" because others have preceded him, so another who follows him, is not a tort-feasor unless he pirates his work. . . . If the copyrighted work is therefore original, the public demesne is important only on the issue of infringement; that is, so far as it may break the force of the inference to be drawn from likenesses between the work and the putative piracy. If the defendant has had access to other material which would have served him as well, his disclaimer becomes more plausible.

In the case at bar there are then two questions: First, whether the defendants actually used the play; second, if so, whether theirs was a[n infringing] use. [I]t is convenient to define such a use by saying that others may "copy" the "theme," or "ideas," or the like, of a work, though not its "expression." At any rate so long as it is clear what is meant, no harm is done. In the case at bar the distinction is not so important as usual, because so much of the play was borrowed from the story of Madeleine Smith, and the plaintiffs' originality is necessarily limited to the variants they introduced. Nevertheless, it is still true that their whole contribution may not be protected; for the defendants were entitled to use, not only all that had gone before, but even the plaintiffs' contribution itself, if they drew from it only the more general patterns; that is, if they kept clear of its "expression." We must therefore state in detail those similarities which seem to us to pass the limits of [licit copying]. Finally, in concluding as we do that the defendants used the play pro tanto, we need not charge their witnesses with perjury. With so many sources before them they might quite honestly forget what they took; nobody knows the origin of his inventions; memory and fancy merge even in adults. Yet unconscious plagiarism is actionable quite as much as deliberate. . . .

The defendants took for their mise-en-scène the same city and the same social class; and they chose a South American villain. The heroines had indeed to be wanton, but Letty Lynton "tracked" Madeleine Cary more closely than that. She is overcome by passion in the first part of the picture and yields after announcing that she hates Renaul and has made up her mind to leave him. This is the same weakness as in the murder scene of the play, though transposed. Each heroine's waywardness is suggested as an inherited disposition; each has had an errant parent involved in scandal; one killed, the other becoming an outcast. Each is redeemed by a higher love. Madeleine Cary must not be misread; it is true that her lust overcomes her at the critical moment, but it does not extinguish her love for Farnborough; her body, not her soul, consents to her lapse. Moreover, her later avowal, which she knew would finally lose her lover, is meant to show the basic rectitude of her nature. Though it does not need Darrow to cure Letty of her wanton ways, she too is redeemed by a nobler love. Neither Madeleine Smith, nor the Letty of the novel, were at all like that; they wished to shake off a clandestine intrigue to set themselves up in the world; their love as distinct from their lust, was pallid. So much for the similarity in character.

Coming to the parallelism of incident, the threat scene is carried out with almost exactly the same sequence of event and actuation; it has no prototype in either story or novel. Neither Ekebon nor L'Angelier went to his fatal interview to break up the new betrothal; he was beguiled by the pretense of a renewed affection. Moreno and Renaul each goes to his sweetheart's home to detach her from her new love; when he is there, she appeals to his better side, unsuccessfully; she abuses him, he returns the abuse and commands her to come to his rooms; she pretends to agree, expecting to finish with him one way or another. True, the assault is deferred in the picture from this scene to the next, but it is the same dramatic trick. Again, the poison in each case is found at home, and the girl talks with her betrothed just after the villain has left and again pledges him her faith. Surely the sequence of these details is pro tanto the very web of the authors' dramatic expression; and copying them is not "fair use."

The death scene follows the play even more closely; the girl goes to the villain's room as he directs; from the outset he is plainly to be poisoned while they are together. (The defendants deny that this is apparent in the picture, but we cannot agree. It would have been an impossible denouement on the screen for the heroine, just plighted to the hero, to kill herself in desperation, because the villain has successfully enmeshed her in their mutual past; yet the poison is surely to be used on some one.) Moreno and Renaul each tries to arouse the girl by the memory of their former love, using among other aphrodisiacs the Gaucho song; each dies while she is there, incidentally of strychnine not arsenic. In extremis each makes for the telephone and is thwarted by the girl; as he dies, she pours upon him her rage and loathing. When he is dead, she follows the same ritual to eradicate all traces of her presence, but forgets tell-tale bits of property. Again these details in the same sequence embody more than the "ideas" of the play; they are its very raiment.

Finally in both play and picture in place of a trial, as in the story and the novel, there is substituted an examination by a district attorney; and this examination is again in parallel almost step by step. A parent is present; so is the lover; the girl yields progressively as the evidence accumulates; in the picture, the customs slip, the rubbers and the letters; in the play, the cross and the witnesses, brought in to confront her. She is at the breaking point when she is saved by substantially the same most unexpected alibi; a man declares that she has spent the night with him. That alibi there introduced is the turning point in each drama and alone prevents its ending in accordance with the classic canon of tragedy; i.e., fate as an inevitable consequence of past conduct, itself not evil enough to quench pity. It is the essence of the authors' expression, the very voice with which they speak.

We have often decided that a play may be pirated without using the dialogue. Were it not so, there could be no piracy of a pantomime, where there cannot be any dialogue; yet nobody would deny to pantomime the name of drama. Speech is only a small part of a dramatist's means of expression; he draws on all the arts and compounds his play from words and gestures and scenery and costume and from the very looks of the actors themselves. The play is the sequence of the confluents of all these means,

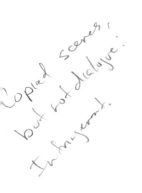

bound together in an inseparable unity; it may often be most effectively pirated by leaving out the speech, for which a substitute can be found, which keeps the whole dramatic meaning. That as it appears to us is exactly what the defendants have done here; the dramatic significance of the scenes we have recited is the same, almost to the letter. True, much of the picture owes nothing to the play; some of it is plainly drawn from the novel; but that is entirely immaterial; it is enough that substantial parts were lifted; no plagiarist can excuse the wrong by showing how much of his work he did not pirate. We cannot avoid the conviction that, if the picture was not an infringement of the play, there can be none short of taking the dialogue.

The decree will be reversed and an injunction will go against the picture together with a decree for damages and an accounting. The plaintiffs will be awarded an attorney's fee in this court and in the court below. . . .

Decree reversed.

QUESTIONS

1. Was there any issue as to "access" in this case? How likely is it that the defendants were being honest in the claims that they did not copy from the plaintiff's play? How likely is it that this affected the decision in the case?

2. Did the court hold that the Letty of the defendant's motion picture so closely tracked the Madeleine Cary of the plaintiff's play as to infringe the copyright in the character?

3. When explaining his conclusion that the crucial scenes in the motion picture infringed the comparable scenes in the plaintiff's play, does Judge Hand closely analyze the literary similarities or does he simply state his result? Is it possible to do much better?

4. Sigmund Freund is a well-known professor of psychology and author of a leading college treatise on the subject. Carl Young, also a psychology professor, has recently published a competing text. Freund was the first writer in the field to adopt a light and easily readable style, utilizing colloquialisms and "homey" examples; Young's treatise has adopted the same style. Psychological theories initially developed by Freund are recounted by Young. There are other similarities: topic selection, chapter headings and organization, "nomenclature" (terms of art and professional definitions), charts and tables, and some problems (although Young writes them in his own words and places them in different sections of his book). Freund has sued Young for copyright infringement. Has Freund, on the above facts, made out a case for the jury on the issue of copying? Has he made out such a case on the issue of infringing similarity? *See Morrison v. Solomons,* 494 F.Supp. 218 (S.D.N.Y.1980); *McMahon v. Prentice–Hall, Inc.,* 486 F.Supp. 1296 (E.D.Mo.1980).

5. The producers of the well-known television game show, *To Tell the Truth,* have brought an action for copyright infringement against the producers of a recent arrival on the game show scene, *Bamboozle*. *To Tell the Truth* is played with a four-person panel of questioners (all celebrities), a panel of three "liars," and a master of ceremonies. The "liars" all pretend to be the same person. For example, one show featured three young men all claiming to be the man who had saved a four-year-old girl from the subway tracks. Each celebrity panelist is given a short period of time to question any of the "liars" to identify the imposters. Each of the panelists then votes; every wrong vote generates money to be split among the "liars." At the end of each of the two sequences on the show, the master of ceremonies asks, "Will the real [contestant's name] please stand up?"

Bamboozle also utilizes a panel of questioners (three rather than four, two of whom are celebrities and one noncelebrity), three "bamboozlers," and a master of ceremonies. Each of the three "bamboozlers" tells a different fantastic story—e.g., owning a turkey that jogs, or a rabbit that surfs, or a dog that bowls; one of these stories is true, and the panel's job is to determine which. The panelists take turns asking the "bamboozlers" questions. Following this, the two celebrity panelists give advice to the noncelebrity, who announces which story he believes true. Depending on the vote, either the panelist or the "bamboozlers" can win money. At the end of the show, the truth teller is revealed and demonstrates the fantastic incident or occurrence. Two such sequences are performed on each *Bamboozle* program.

The producers of both game shows have moved for summary judgment. How would you rule on the motion? *See Barris/Fraser Enters. v. Goodson–Todman Enters.*, 5 U.S.P.Q.2d 1887 (S.D.N.Y.1988).

6.   Because there is copyright infringement only when there is substantial unauthorized copying of "original" material authored by the plaintiff, a case such as *Sheldon* is complicated by the fact that much that is recounted in the plaintiff's novel was derived from historical events that are properly in the public domain. The court concluded that the defendant's motion picture tracked too much of the altogether fictional elements contributed by the plaintiff from her imagination. Essentially the same conclusion was reached more recently in *Burgess v. Chase–Riboud,* 765 F.Supp. 233 (E.D.Pa.1991), which involved a play that was held to infringe a novel about Thomas Jefferson that vividly elaborated on what was at the time regarded as an unproven and speculative amorous relationship between Jefferson and his slave Sally Hemings. In the proceeding for a declaratory judgment of noninfringement, the court summarized a number of scenes in the novel that were altogether fictional and that were followed too closely in the play written by the plaintiff.

Given the importance of uninhibited access to historical fact, at least as much with regard to Thomas Jefferson as Madeleine Smith, should the later author be "given the benefit of the doubt" in determining literary infringement in such cases? Should a burden be placed upon the author of "docudramas" and works of "faction" somehow to delineate at the time of publication what is the author's contribution and what is public-domain historical information? Or should the burden of making the distinction fall upon the later borrower of material?

7. You have been consulted by Tim and Nina Zagat, who compile and publish well-known paperback restaurant guides in cities in the United

| F | D | S | C |

Orrery Restaurant & Bar [S] | 22 | 20 | 20 | £41 |
55 Marylebone High St., W1 (Baker St./Regent's Park), 0171-616 8000
☑ "Small for a Conran" ("conversation is possible"), this recent Marylebone addition to Sir Terence's stable has made an "impressive" debut, earning solid scores for its "excellent" New French fare (a "sublime treat for the taste buds"), "elegant", "airy" setting and "good" service; quibblers call it a "bit of an anticlimax", citing "bland", "overpriced" food in a "flat atmosphere" that's "full of suits", but to the majority it's "a welcome addition" and arguably "the best Conran."

Orsino ◐[S] | 19 | 19 | 16 | £32 |
119 Portland Rd., W11 (Holland Park), 0171-221 3299
☑ "A more polished and relaxing version of Orso" is how partisans appraise this "upbeat" Holland Park sibling with "agreeable" Italian cooking at a "reasonable" price; but whilst many consider it a "fine neighbourhood" place with "nice atmosphere", some suggest that the "uninventive" fare could use "an injection of creativity."

Orso ◐[S] | 20 | 17 | 17 | £33 |
27 Wellington St., WC2 (Covent Garden), 0171-240 5269
☑ It may be "busy" and "rushed", but this basement Italian in Covent Garden satisfies most with "spot-on rustic" cooking that's "always delicious", served in a "stylish, atmospheric" ambience; though there are grumbles of discontent ("brusque service", "overpriced", "lost some of its standard"), just about everyone agrees it's a "great after-theatre standby."

Oslo Court Restaurant | 23 | 17 | 23 | £32 |
Prince Albert Rd., NW8 (St. John's Wood), 0171-722 8795
■ Despite an "odd location" under a block of flats in St. John's Wood, it's "impossible to make a weekend reservation" at this "comfortable, old-fashioned" eaterie that has quite a following for its "consistent" Classic French food, "good value" prix fixe menus and "attentive" service; some think it's "not as good as it has been" and note a prevalence of "geriatrics", but for devotees it's a "favourite" "refuge from the world."

Osteria Antica Bologna [S] | 21 | 15 | 17 | £23 |
23 Northcote Rd., SW11 (Clapham Junction B.R.), 0171-978 4771
■ This "idiosyncratic", "homestyle" Battersea trattoria takes some "back to student days" with its "crowded", "friendly" atmosphere and "big portions" of "truly rustic" Italian food that most find "innovative" and "excellent" (though a few brand it "uneven"); the place gets "cramped" and "noisy" most evenings (reservations suggested) so some feel it's "better at lunchtime when less crowded."

FSA

192 W11   £ 33   ④④●
192 Kensington Pk Rd   229 0482   6–1A
Perennially "trendy" and "easy-going" Portobello spot, which, as always, generates mixed reviews; to its fans, it's still "the very example of what a contemporary English restaurant should be" – to too many, though, it's just "overcrowded" and "overpriced". / 11.30 pm; no smoking area.

L'Oranger SW1   £ 36   ●●●
5 St James's St   839 3774   3–4D
"State of the art" modern French cooking and "well honed service" has made this "comfortable" St James's newcomer (from the same stable as the much-fêted Aubergine) a huge success; we share the reservation that the kitchen is "exact rather than exciting", but that is not to question the exceptional value currently on offer – "watch for the prices going up soon". / 11.15 pm; closed Sun L.

Oriel SW1   £ 26   ●④●
50-51 Sloane Sq   730 2804   5–2D
Sloane Square's prominently located, "casual" brasserie remains a "fun place to meet for drinks or a light dinner", or, of course, for the weekend breakfasts which are its natural forte. i 10.45 pm; no smoking area; no booking.

Orsino W11   £ 37   ④④●
119 Portland Rd   221 3299   6–2A
Chicly furnished and discreetly located Holland Park Italian – the country-cousin of Orso (below) – which is "still not getting there"; some culinary successes are reported, but "overpriced and under-exciting" remains the summary view. / 11 pm; no Switch; no smoking area.

Orso WC2   £ 33   ④④●
27 Wellington St   240 5269   4–3D
Thanks to its late-night buzz, this Covent Garden basement Italian can still make a "good choice after the opera"; but "disappointing" cooking still mars too many visits here, and the loss is keenly felt by the many who remember what a great place it used to be; hold the front page – Orso Now Takes Credit Cards! / Midnight; no smoking area.

Oslo Court NW8   £ 34   ●●●
Prince Albert Rd   722 8795   8–3A
"Perfect in every way", say devoted followers of this supremely old-fashioned International restaurant – at the foot of an anonymous apartment block, north of Regent's Park – which "never varies"; "my mother dotes on this place, and all her bridge-playing cronies are here – every night!" / 11 pm; closed Sun; smart casual.

Zagat Guide   Harden Guide

States and around the world. The guides are based upon surveys taken of restaurant customers, who both comment in prose upon the restaurant's qualities and numerically rate the food, service and decor. The Zagats have learned of a competing paperback, published by Harden's, covering the restaurants in London. The following pages are from the Zagat's Guide to London Restaurants and the Harden's London Restaurant Guide. (Some of the same restaurants are shown on these comparison pages.) In the front of the London Zagat's, there is a list of the five top-rated restaurants under each of a number of headings for types of food, e.g., Indian, Italian, Japanese, Vegetarian; Harden's has similar lists under similar headings (although their customer-based ratings are somewhat different). Zagat's also lists restaurants under headings that reflect certain special features, e.g., Cigar–Friendly, Late Opening, Pre–Theater, Romantic, Watch the Passing Scene; Harden's likewise lists special features, many of which are essentially the same as those in Zagat's (and once again, there is considerable overlap in the restaurants listed). Zagat's has been on the London market since 1990, and Harden's only within the last two years. How strong is Zagat's claim for copyright infringement?

————

It is not unusual to find claims of infringement against novelists and motion picture production companies involving their successful books and films; more often than not, summary judgment is granted against the plaintiff. Four recent examples are: *Chase–Riboud v. Dreamworks, Inc.*, 987 F.Supp. 1222 (C.D.Cal.1997) (film "Amistad" does not infringe novel "Echo of Lions" about the "Amistad" slaveship revolt; similarities mainly attributable to common historical facts, or to "ideas" such as the inclusion of a fictional Black abolitionist who assists the Africans); *Towler v. Sayles*, 76 F.3d 579 (4th Cir.1996) (John Sayles film "Passion Fish" does not infringe screenplay; only similarity is "idea" of black woman and white woman who are friends); *Nelson v. Grisham*, 942 F.Supp. 649 (D.D.C.1996) (John Grisham novel "The Chamber" does not infringe nonfiction book about a lawyer's representation of a serial killer; major similarity is representation of death-row convict); *Arden v. Columbia Pictures Indus., Inc.*, 908 F.Supp. 1248 (S.D.N.Y.1995) (film "Groundhog Day" with Bill Murray does not infringe novel; only similarity is "idea" of a man trapped in a repeating day). In the world of television commercials, see *Reed-Union Corp. v. Turtle Wax, Inc.*, 77 F.3d 909 (7th Cir.1996) (competitive car-polish commercial copies only the *scène à faire* of a beat-up car that is revived with new polish and then lasts through a year of car washes). For a rare exception, see *Zervitz v. Hollywood Pictures*, 989 F.Supp. 727 (D.Md.1995), 995 F.Supp. 596 (D.Md.1996) (judgment in excess of $1.2 million against producer and distributor of film "The Air Up There," held to have been based on plaintiff's six-page treatment for a movie about a basketball star recruited from an African tribe).

APPROACHES TO "SUBSTANTIAL SIMILARITY"

Some lack of uniformity prevails in judicial application of the substantial-similarity test. In essence, courts differ over the subject matter to which the test is applied. Under one view, the fact-finder judges substantial similarity with respect to the whole of the copied portions of the plaintiff's work, including portions that viewed in isolation might not be eligible for copyright. Under another view, the fact-finder first removes from consideration the uncopyrightable elements of the copied material. Such elements include facts, ideas, and "scènes à faire"—trite, stock scenes or treatments of facts and ideas. The application of one or the other approach will frequently affect the outcome of the case, for any copyrighted literary work is likely to contain some, if not all, of these individually unprotectible elements.

For example, in *Sheldon v. Metro–Goldwyn Pictures Corp., supra,* the episodes that were apparently copied from the plaintiff's play, "Dishonored Lady," included factual detail drawn from the life of the historical Madeleine Smith, such as incriminating letters and a poisoning; and featured a number of arguably "stock" dramatic devices, such as the heroine's vilification of the villain, wiping away fingerprints, and leaving behind tell-tale evidence. Judge Hand, however, declined the defendants' invitation to review these discrete elements against the backdrop of an alleged common repertory of dramatic scenes. In effect, such an analysis treats the selection and sequencing of these elements, perhaps unprotectible in isolation, as though they were a copyrightable compilation.

Another court has expressed dissatisfaction with the "dissection" approach. In a thoughtful opinion, the judge in *Apple Computer, Inc. v. Microsoft Corp.,* 779 F.Supp. 133 (N.D.Cal.1991), discussed the "variations on the substantial similarity of expression test":

> ... Removing unprotectible elements prior to the substantial similarity of expression test would preclude copyright protection for factual compilations containing an innovative selection or arrangement of elements because each element would be eliminated and nothing would be left for purposes of determining substantial similarity.
>
> Some dissection of elements and the application of merger, functionality, scènes à faire, and unoriginality theories are necessary to determine which elements can be used freely by the public in creating new works, so long as those works do not incorporate the same selection or arrangement as that of the plaintiff's work. Because there ought to be copyright protection for an innovative melding of elements from preexisting works, elements which have been deemed "unprotectible" should not be eliminated prior to the substantial similarity of expression analysis. Suppose defendant copied plaintiff's abstract painting composed entirely of geometric forms arranged in an original pattern. The alleged infringer could argue that each expressive element (i.e., the geometric forms) is unprotectible under the functionality, merger, scènes à faire, and unoriginality theories and, thus, all elements should be excluded prior to the substantial similarity of expression analysis. Then, there would be nothing left for purposes of determining substantial similarity of expression.
>
> In this example, elimination of "unprotectible" elements would result in a finding of no copyright infringement, which would be clearly

inconsistent with the copyright law's purpose of providing incentives to authors of original works.

Accordingly, the court concludes that even if elements are found "unprotectible," they should not be eliminated from the substantial similarity of expression analysis. Instead, if it is determined that the defendant used the unprotectible elements in an arrangement which is not substantially similar to the plaintiff's work, then no copyright infringement can be found. If, on the other hand, the works are deemed substantially similar, then copyright infringement will be established even though the copyrighted work is composed of unprotectible elements. There is simply no other logical way of protecting an innovative arrangement or "look and feel" of certain works.

In contrast to the approach in the *Sheldon* case is the analysis employed in a decision involving alleged infringement by Alex Haley's "Roots." There, the trial court held that most of the alleged similarities between the plaintiff's and the defendant's novels concerned scenes that were commonplace to depictions of slavery in the Old South. Once these scenes were eliminated from consideration, the works could not be deemed substantially similar. *See Alexander v. Haley,* 460 F.Supp. 40 (S.D.N.Y. 1978).

This dissection and disqualification of uncopyrightable elements from a plaintiff's work has gained favor among some courts, especially when the court is leery of a result that would suggest monopolization of a common theme, or when the work at issue is a nonfiction work. *See, e.g., Hoehling v. Universal City Studios, Inc.,* 618 F.2d 972 (2d Cir.), *cert. denied,* 449 U.S. 841 (1980), *supra.* In *Computer Assocs. Int'l, Inc. v. Altai, Inc.,* 982 F.2d 693 (2d Cir.1992), set forth immediately below, the court adopted, in the context of computer software protection, a "filtration" analysis that separates out "unprotectible" elements before comparing plaintiff's and defendant's works.

Computer Associates International, Inc. v. Altai, Inc.

982 F.2d 693 (2d Cir.1992).

■ WALKER, CIRCUIT JUDGE.

. . . [T]his case deals with the challenging question of whether and to what extent the "non-literal" aspects of a computer program, that is, those aspects that are not reduced to written code, are protected by copyright. While a few other courts have already grappled with this issue, this case is one of first impression in this circuit. As we shall discuss, we find the results reached by other courts to be less than satisfactory. Drawing upon long-standing doctrines of copyright law, we take an approach that we think better addresses the practical difficulties embedded in these types of cases. In so doing, we have kept in mind the necessary balance between creative incentive and industrial competition.

[The District] Judge found that defendant Altai, Inc.'s ("Altai"), OSCAR 3.4 computer program had infringed plaintiff Computer Associates'

("CA"), copyrighted computer program entitled CA–SCHEDULER. With respect to CA's second claim for copyright infringement, Judge Pratt found that Altai's OSCAR 3.5 program was not substantially similar to a portion of CA–SCHEDULER called ADAPTER, and thus denied relief....

BACKGROUND

. . .

II. *Facts*

CA is a Delaware corporation, with its principal place of business in Garden City, New York. Altai is a Texas corporation, doing business primarily in Arlington, Texas. Both companies are in the computer software industry—designing, developing and marketing various types of computer programs.

The subject of this litigation originates with one of CA's marketed programs entitled CA–SCHEDULER. CA–SCHEDULER is a job scheduling program designed for IBM mainframe computers. Its primary functions are straightforward: to create a schedule specifying when the computer should run various tasks, and then to control the computer as it executes the schedule. CA–SCHEDULER contains a sub-program entitled ADAPTER, also developed by CA. ADAPTER is not an independently marketed product of CA; it is a wholly integrated component of CA–SCHEDULER and has no capacity for independent use.

Nevertheless, ADAPTER plays an extremely important role. It is an "operating system compatibility component," which means, roughly speaking, it serves as a translator. An "operating system" is itself a program that manages the resources of the computer, allocating those resources to other programs as needed. The IBM's System 370 family of computers, for which CA–SCHEDULER was created, is, depending upon the computer's size, designed to contain one of three operating systems: DOS/VSE, MVS, or CMS. As the district court noted, the general rule is that "a program written for one operating system, e.g., DOS/VSE, will not, without modification, run under another operating system such as MVS." ADAPTER's function is to translate the language of a given program into the particular language that the computer's own operating system can understand.

The district court succinctly outlined the manner in which ADAPTER works within the context of the larger programs. In order to enable CA–SCHEDULER to function on different operating systems, CA divided the CA–SCHEDULER into two components:

> a first component that contains only the task-specific portions of the program, independent of all operating system issues, and

> a second component that contains all the interconnections between the first component and the operating system.

In a program constructed in this way, whenever the first, task-specific, component needs to ask the operating system for some resource through a "system call," it calls the second component instead of calling the operating system directly.

The second component serves as an "interface" or "compatibility component" between the task-specific portion of the program and the operating system. It receives the request from the first component and translates it into the appropriate system call that will be recognized by whatever operating system is installed on the computer, e.g., DOS/VSE, MVS, or CMS. Since the first, task-specific component calls the adapter component rather than the operating system, the first component need not be customized to use any specific operating system. The second interface component insures that all the system calls are performed properly for the particular operating system in use. ADAPTER serves as the second, "common system interface" component referred to above.

A program like ADAPTER, which allows a computer user to change or use multiple operating systems while maintaining the same software, is highly desirable. It saves the user the costs, both in time and money, that otherwise would be expended in purchasing new programs, modifying existing systems to run them, and gaining familiarity with their operation. The benefits run both ways. The increased compatibility afforded by an ADAPTER-like component, and its resulting popularity among consumers, makes whatever software in which it is incorporated significantly more marketable.

[In 1982, defendant Altai began marketing its own job scheduling program entitled ZEKE, which was designed for use in conjunction with a VSE operating system; later, Altai decided to rewrite ZEKE to run in an MVS operating system. An Altai employee, Williams (soon to become Altai president) induced a longtime friend, Arney, to leave CA and come to work for Altai. Williams knew of CA–SCHEDULER and ADAPTER, but did not know that the latter was a component of the former; nor had he seen the codes of either program. Arney, however, was fully familiar with various aspects of ADAPTER—and when he left CA for Altai in January 1984, Arney took with him copies of the source code for both the VSE and MVS versions of ADAPTER, in knowing violation of his employment agreement with CA. Arney convinced Williams that the best way to make ZEKE compatible with the MVS operating system was to introduce a "common system interface" component into ZEKE; this new component was to be named OSCAR. Arney quickly completed the OSCAR/VSE and OSCAR/MVS versions, in the process copying approximately 30% of OSCAR's code from CA's ADAPTER program—this was not known to anyone at Altai, including Williams.

[The first generation of OSCAR programs was known as OSCAR 3.4; it was used for some three years as a component of the ZEKE product, when CA first learned that Altai may have appropriated parts of ADAPTER and brought this action for copyright infringement and trade secret misappropriation. For the first time, Williams learned that Arney had copied much of the OSCAR code from ADAPTER, and he had Arney point out the tainted sections of the OSCAR code. Williams initiated OSCAR's rewrite;

the goal was to excise all portions copied from ADAPTER and save as much of OSCAR 3.4 as legitimately could be used. None of the programmers had been involved in the initial development of OSCAR 3.4, and Arney was entirely excluded from the process. Williams gave the programmers a description of the ZEKE operating system, and the OSCAR rewrite project was completed after six months in November 1989; the resulting program was entitled OSCAR 3.5. From then on, Altai shipped only OSCAR 3.5 to its customers. In the court's words, "While Altai and Williams acted responsibly to correct what Arney had wrought, the damage was done. CA's lawsuit remained."]

DISCUSSION

We address only CA's appeal from the district court's rulings that: Altai was not liable for copyright infringement in developing OSCAR 3.5....

CA contends that the district court applied an erroneous method for determining whether there exists substantial similarity between computer programs, and thus, erred in determining that OSCAR 3.5 did not infringe the copyrights held on the different versions of its CA–SCHEDULER program. CA asserts that the test applied by the district court failed to account sufficiently for a computer program's non-literal elements.

I. *Copyright Infringement*

For the purpose of analysis, the district court assumed that Altai had access to the ADAPTER code when creating OSCAR 3.5. Thus, in determining whether Altai had unlawfully copied protected aspects of CA's ADAPTER, the district court narrowed its focus of inquiry to ascertaining whether Altai's OSCAR 3.5 was substantially similar to ADAPTER. Because we approve Judge Pratt's conclusions regarding substantial similarity, our analysis will proceed along the same assumption.

As a general matter, and to varying degrees, copyright protection extends beyond a literary work's strictly textual form to its non-literal components. As we have said, "it is of course essential to any protection of literary property ... that the right cannot be limited literally to the text, else a plagiarist would escape by immaterial variations." *Nichols v. Universal Pictures Co.,* 45 F.2d 119, 121 (2d Cir.1930) (L. Hand, J.), *cert. denied,* 282 U.S. 902 (1931). Thus, where "the fundamental essence or structure of one work is duplicated in another," courts have found copyright infringement. [The court cited precedents involving ballet, motion pictures, television programs, and plays.] *Accord Stewart v. Abend,* 495 U.S. 207, 238 (1990) (recognizing that motion picture may infringe copyright in book by using its "unique setting, characters, plot, and sequence of events"). This black letter proposition is the springboard for our discussion.

A. *Copyright Protection for the Non-literal Elements of Computer Programs*

It is now well settled that the literal elements of computer programs, i.e., their source and object codes, are the subject of copyright protection.

See Whelan (source and object code); *CMS Software Design Sys., Inc. v. Info Designs, Inc.,* 785 F.2d 1246, 1249 (5th Cir.1986) (source code); *Apple Computer, Inc. v. Franklin Computer Corp.,* 714 F.2d 1240, 1249 (3d Cir.1983), *cert. dismissed,* 464 U.S. 1033 (1984) (source and object code); *Williams Electronics, Inc. v. Artic Int'l, Inc.,* 685 F.2d 870, 876–77 (3d Cir.1982) (object code). Here, as noted earlier, Altai admits having copied approximately 30% of the OSCAR 3.4 program from CA's ADAPTER source code, and does not challenge the district court's related finding of infringement.

In this case, the hotly contested issues surround OSCAR 3.5. As recounted above, OSCAR 3.5 is the product of Altai's carefully orchestrated rewrite of OSCAR 3.4. After the purge, none of the ADAPTER source code remained in the 3.5 version; thus, Altai made sure that the literal elements of its revamped OSCAR program were no longer substantially similar to the literal elements of CA's ADAPTER.

. . .

CA argues that, despite Altai's rewrite of the OSCAR code, the resulting program remained substantially similar to the structure of its ADAPTER program. As discussed above, a program's structure includes its non-literal components such as general flow charts as well as the more specific organization of inter-modular relationships, parameter lists, and macros. In addition to these aspects, CA contends that OSCAR 3.5 is also substantially similar to ADAPTER with respect to the list of services that both ADAPTER and OSCAR obtain from their respective operating systems. We must decide whether and to what extent these elements of computer programs are protected by copyright law.

. . . While computer programs are not specifically listed as part of the above statutory definition, the legislative history leaves no doubt that Congress intended them to be considered literary works. *See* H.R. Rep. No. 1476, 94th Cong., 2d Sess. 54, *reprinted in* 1975 U.S.C.C.A.N. 5659, 5667 (hereinafter *"House Report"*); *Whelan,* 797 F.2d at 1234; *Apple Computer,* 714 F.2d at 1247.

The syllogism that follows from the foregoing premises is a powerful one: if the non-literal structures of literary works are protected by copyright; and if computer programs are literary works, as we are told by the legislature; then the non-literal structures of computer programs are protected by copyright. *See Whelan,* 797 F.2d at 1234 ("By analogy to other literary works, it would thus appear that the copyrights of computer programs can be infringed even absent copying of the literal elements of the program."). We have no reservation in joining the company of those courts that have already ascribed to this logic [citations omitted]. However, that conclusion does not end our analysis. We must determine the scope of copyright protection that extends to a computer program's non-literal structure.

As a caveat, we note that our decision here does not control infringement actions regarding categorically distinct works, such as certain types of screen displays. These items represent products of computer programs, rather than the programs themselves, and fall under the copyright rubric of audiovisual works.... In this case, however, we are concerned not with a program's display, but the program itself, and then with only its non-literal components. In considering the copyrightability of these components, we must refer to venerable doctrines of copyright law.

(1) *Idea vs. Expression Dichotomy*

It is a fundamental principle of copyright law that a copyright does not protect an idea, but only the expression of the idea. *See Baker v. Selden,* 101 U.S. 99 (1879); *Mazer v. Stein,* 347 U.S. 201, 217 (1954). This axiom of common law has been incorporated into the governing statute.... Congress made no special exception for computer programs. To the contrary, the legislative history explicitly states that copyright protects computer programs only "to the extent that they incorporate authorship in programmer's expression of original ideas, as distinguished from the ideas themselves."

The essentially utilitarian nature of a computer program further complicates the task of distilling its idea from its expression. In order to describe both computational processes and abstract ideas, its content "combines creative and technical expression." The variations of expression found in purely creative compositions, as opposed to those contained in utilitarian works, are not directed towards practical application. For example, a narration of Humpty Dumpty's demise, which would clearly be a creative composition, does not serve the same ends as, say, a recipe for scrambled eggs—which is a more process oriented text. Thus, compared to aesthetic works, computer programs hover even more closely to the elusive boundary line described in § 102(b).

The doctrinal starting point in analyses of utilitarian works, is the seminal case of *Baker v. Selden,* 101 U.S. 99 (1879)....

To the extent that an accounting text and a computer program are both "a set of statements or instructions ... to bring about a certain result," 17 U.S.C. § 101, they are roughly analogous. In the former case, the processes are ultimately conducted by human agency; in the latter, by electronic means. In either case, as already stated, the processes themselves are not protectable. But the holding in *Baker* goes farther. The Court concluded that those aspects of a work, which "must necessarily be used as incident to" the idea, system or process that the work describes, are also not copyrightable. *Selden*'s ledger sheets, therefore, enjoyed no copyright protection because they were "necessary incidents to" the system of accounting that he described. From this reasoning, we conclude that those elements of a computer program that are necessarily incidental to its function are similarly unprotectable.

While *Baker v. Selden* provides a sound analytical foundation, it offers scant guidance on how to separate idea or process from expression, and moreover, on how to further distinguish protectable expression from that expression which "must necessarily be used as incident to" the work's underlying concept. In the context of computer programs, the Third Circuit's noted decision in *Whelan* has, thus far, been the most thoughtful attempt to accomplish these ends.

The court in *Whelan* faced substantially the same problem as presented by this case. There, the defendant was accused of making off with the non-literal structure of the plaintiff's copyrighted dental lab management program, and employing it to create its own competitive version. In assessing whether there had been an infringement, the court had to determine which aspects of the program involved were ideas, and which were expression.... The "idea" of the program at issue in *Whelan* was identified by the court as simply "the efficient management of a dental laboratory."

So far, in the courts, the *Whelan* rule has received a mixed reception. While some decisions have adopted its reasoning [citations omitted], others have rejected it [citations omitted].

Whelan has fared even more poorly in the academic community, where its standard for distinguishing idea from expression has been widely criticized for being conceptually overbroad [citations omitted]. The leading commentator in the field has stated that, "the crucial flaw in [*Whelan*'s] reasoning is that it assumes that only one 'idea,' in copyright law terms, underlies any computer program, and that once a separable idea can be identified, everything else must be expression." 3 Nimmer § 13.03[F], at 13–62.34. This criticism focuses not upon the program's ultimate purpose but upon the reality of its structural design. As we have already noted, a computer program's ultimate function or purpose is the composite result of interacting subroutines. Since each subroutine is itself a program, and thus, may be said to have its own "idea," *Whelan*'s general formulation that a program's overall purpose equates with the program's idea is descriptively inadequate.

. . .

(2) *Substantial Similarity Test for Computer Program Structure: Abstraction–Filtration–Comparison*

We think that *Whelan*'s approach to separating idea from expression in computer programs relies too heavily on metaphysical distinctions and does not place enough emphasis on practical considerations. As the cases that we shall discuss demonstrate, a satisfactory answer to this problem cannot be reached by resorting, a priori, to philosophical first principles.

As discussed herein, we think that district courts would be well-advised to undertake a three-step procedure, based on the abstractions test utilized by the district court, in order to determine whether the non-literal elements of two or more computer programs are substantially similar. This approach breaks no new grounds; rather, it draws on such familiar copyright doctrines as merger, scènes à faire, and public domain....

In ascertaining substantial similarity under this approach, a court would first break down the allegedly infringed program into its constituent structural parts. Then, by examining each of these parts for such things as incorporated ideas, expression that is necessarily incidental to those ideas, and elements that are taken from the public domain, a court would then be able to sift out all non-protectable material. Left with a kernel, or possibly kernels, of creative expression after following this process of elimination, the court's last step would be to compare this material with the structure of an allegedly infringing program. The result of this comparison will determine whether the protectable elements of the programs at issue are substantially similar so as to warrant a finding of infringement. It will be helpful to elaborate a bit further.

Step One: Abstraction

As the district court appreciated, the theoretic framework for analyzing substantial similarity expounded by Learned Hand in the *Nichols* case is helpful in the present context. In *Nichols,* we enunciated what has now become known as the "abstractions" test for separating idea from expression. While the abstractions test was originally applied in relation to literary works such as novels and plays, it is adaptable to computer programs. In contrast to the *Whelan* approach, the abstractions test "implicitly recognizes that any given work may consist of a mixture of numerous ideas and expressions."

As applied to computer programs, the abstractions test will comprise the first step in the examination for substantial similarity. Initially, in a manner that resembles reverse engineering on a theoretical plane, a court should dissect the allegedly copied program's structure and isolate each level of abstraction contained within it. This process begins with the code and ends with an articulation of the program's ultimate function. Along the way, it is necessary essentially to retrace and map each of the designer's steps—in the opposite order in which they were taken during the program's creation.

As an anatomical guide to this procedure, the following description is helpful:

> At the lowest level of abstraction, a computer program may be thought of in its entirety as a set of individual instructions organized into a hierarchy of modules. At a higher level of abstraction, the instructions in the lowest-level modules may be replaced conceptually by the functions of those modules. At progressively higher levels of abstraction, the functions of higher-level modules conceptually replace the implementations of those modules in terms of lower-level modules and instructions, until finally, one is left with nothing but the ultimate function of the program. . . . A program has structure at every level of abstraction at which it is viewed. At low levels of abstraction, a program's structure may be quite complex; at the highest level it is trivial.

Step Two: Filtration

Once the program's abstraction levels have been discovered, the substantial similarity inquiry moves from the conceptual to the concrete. Professor Nimmer suggests, and we endorse, a "successive filtering method" for separating protectable expression from non-protectable material. *See generally* 3 Nimmer § 13.03[F]. This process entails examining the structural components at each level of abstraction to determine whether their particular inclusion at that level was "idea" or was dictated by considerations of efficiency, so as to be necessarily incidental to that idea; required by factors external to the program itself; or taken from the public domain and hence is non-protectable expression. The structure of any given program may reflect some, all, or none of these considerations. Each case requires its own fact specific investigation.

Strictly speaking, this filtration serves "the purpose of defining the scope of plaintiff's copyright." *Brown Bag Software v. Symantec Corp.*, No. 89–16239, slip op. 3719, 3738 (9th Cir. April 7, 1992) (endorsing "analytic dissection" of computer programs in order to isolate protectable expression). By applying well developed doctrines of copyright law, it may ultimately leave behind a "core of protectable material." 3 Nimmer § 13.03[F][5], at 13–72. Further explication of this second step may be helpful.

(a) *Elements Dictated by Efficiency*

The portion of *Baker v. Selden*, discussed earlier, which denies copyright protection to expression necessarily incidental to the idea being expressed, appears to be the cornerstone for what has developed into the doctrine of merger. *See Morrissey v. Procter & Gamble Co.*, 379 F.2d 675, 678–79 (1st Cir.1967) (relying on *Baker* for the proposition that expression embodying the rules of a sweepstakes contest was inseparable from the idea of the contest itself, and therefore were not protectable by copyright); *see also Digital Communications*, 659 F. Supp. at 457. The doctrine's underlying principle is that "when there is essentially only one way to express an idea, the idea and its expression are inseparable and copyright is no bar to copying that expression." *Concrete Machinery Co. v. Classic Lawn Ornaments, Inc.*, 843 F.2d 600, 606 (1st Cir.1988). Under these circumstances, the expression is said to have "merged" with the idea itself. In order not to confer a monopoly of the idea upon the copyright owner, such expression should not be protected. *See Herbert Rosenthal Jewelry Corp. v. Kalpakian*, 446 F.2d 738, 742 (9th Cir.1971).

CONTU recognized the applicability of the merger doctrine to computer programs. In its report to Congress it stated that:

> Copyrighted language may be copied without infringing when there is but a limited number of ways to express a given idea.... In the computer context, this means that when specific instructions, even though previously copyrighted, are the only and essential means of accomplishing a given task, their later use by another will not amount to infringement.

CONTU Report at 20. While this statement directly concerns only the application of merger to program code, that is, the textual aspect of the program, it reasonably suggests that the doctrine fits comfortably within the general context of computer programs.

Furthermore, when one considers the fact that programmers generally strive to create programs "that meet the user's needs in the most efficient manner," the applicability of the merger doctrine to computer programs becomes compelling. In the context of computer programs design, the concept of efficiency is akin to deriving the most concise logical proof or formulating the most succinct mathematical computation. Thus, the more efficient a set of modules are, the more closely they approximate the idea or process embodied in that particular aspect of the program's structure.

While, hypothetically, there might be a myriad of ways in which a programmer may effectuate certain functions within a program,—i.e., express the idea embodied in a given subroutine—efficiency concerns may so narrow the practical range of choice as to make only one or two forms of expression workable options. *See also Whelan,* 797 F.2d at 1243 n.43 ("It is true that for certain tasks there are only a very limited number of file structures available, and in such cases the structures might not be copyrightable ... "). Of course, not all program structure is informed by efficiency concerns. It follows that in order to determine whether the merger doctrine precludes copyright protection to an aspect of a program's structure that is so oriented, a court must inquire "whether the use of this particular set of modules is necessary efficiently to implement that part of the program's process" being implemented. If the answer is yes, then the expression represented by the programmer's choice of a specific module or group of modules has merged with their underlying idea and is unprotected.

Another justification for linking structural economy with the application of the merger doctrine stems from a program's essentially utilitarian nature and the competitive forces that exist in the software marketplace. Working in tandem, these factors give rise to a problem of proof which merger helps to eliminate.

Efficiency is an industry-wide goal. Since, as we have already noted, there may be only a limited number of efficient implementations for any given program task, it is quite possible that multiple programmers, working independently, will design the identical method employed in the allegedly infringed work. Of course, if this is the case, there is no copyright infringement.

Under these circumstances, the fact that two programs contain the same efficient structure may as likely lead to an inference of independent creation as it does to one of copying. Thus, since evidence of similarly efficient structure is not particularly probative of copying, it should be disregarded in the overall substantial similarity analysis.

We find support for applying the merger doctrine in cases that have already addressed the question of substantial similarity in the context of computer program structure. Most recently, in *Lotus Dev. Corp.,* 740 F. Supp. at 66, the district court had before it a claim of copyright infringement relating to the structure of a computer spreadsheet program. The court observed that "the basic spreadsheet screen display that resembles a rotated 'L' ..., if not present in every expression of such a program, is present in most expressions." Similarly, the court found that "an essential detail present in most if not all expressions of an electronic spreadsheet—is the designation of a particular key that, when pressed, will invoke the menu command system." *Id.* Applying the merger doctrine, the court denied copyright protection to both program elements.

In *Manufacturers Technologies, Inc. v. Cams, Inc.,* 706 F. Supp. 984, 995–99 (D.Conn.1989), the infringement claims stemmed from various alleged program similarities "as indicated in their screen displays." Stressing efficiency concerns in the context of a merger analysis, the court determined that the program's method of allowing the user to navigate within the screen displays was not protectable because, in part, "the process or manner of navigating internally on any specific screen displays ... is limited in the number of ways it may be simply achieved to facilitate user comfort." ...

We agree with the approach taken in these decisions, and conclude that application of the merger doctrine in this setting is an effective way to eliminate non-protectable expression contained in computer programs.

(b) *Elements Dictated by External Factors*

We have stated that where "it is virtually impossible to write about a particular historical era or fictional theme without employing certain 'stock' or standard literary devices," such expression is not copyrightable. *Hoehling v. Universal City Studios, Inc.,* 618 F.2d 972, 979 (2d Cir.), *cert. denied,* 449 U.S. 841 (1980). For example, the *Hoehling* case was an infringement suit stemming from several works on the Hindenburg disaster. There we concluded that similarities in representations of German beer halls, scenes depicting German greetings such as "Heil Hitler," or the singing of certain German songs would not lead to a finding of infringement because they were " 'indispensable, or at least standard, in the treatment of' " life in Nazi Germany. *Id.* (*quoting Alexander v. Haley,* 460 F. Supp. 40, 45 (S.D.N.Y.1978)). This is known as the scènes à faire doctrine, and like "merger," it has its analogous application to computer programs. *Cf. Data East USA,* 862 F.2d at 208 (applying scènes à faire to a home computer video game).

Professor Nimmer points out that "in many instances it is virtually impossible to write a program to perform particular functions in a specific computing environment without employing standard techniques." This is a result of the fact that a programmer's freedom of design choice is often circumscribed by extrinsic considerations such as (1) the mechanical specifications of the computer on which a particular program is intended to run; (2) compatibility requirements of other programs with which a program is designed to operate in conjunction; (3) computer manufacturers' design standards; (4) demands of the industry being serviced; and (5) widely accepted programming practices within the computer industry.

Courts have already considered some of these factors in denying copyright protection to various elements of computer programs. In the *Plains Cotton* case, the Fifth Circuit refused to reverse the district court's denial of a preliminary injunction against an alleged program infringer because, in part, "many of the similarities between the . . . programs [were] dictated by the externalities of the cotton market."

In *Manufacturers Technologies,* the district court noted that the program's method of screen navigation "is influenced by the type of hardware that the software is designed to be used on." Because, in part, "the functioning of the hardware package impacted and constrained the type of navigational tools used in plaintiff's screen displays," the court denied copyright protection to that aspect of the program. . . .

. . .

Building upon this existing case law, we conclude that a court must also examine the structural content of an allegedly infringed program for elements that might have been dictated by external factors.

(c) *Elements Taken From the Public Domain*

Closely related to the non-protectability of scènes à faire, is material found in the public domain. Such material is free for the taking and cannot be appropriated by a single author even though it is included in a copyrighted work. *See E.F. Johnson Co. v. Uniden Corp. of America,* 623 F. Supp. 1485, 1499 (D.Minn. (1985)); *see also Sheldon,* 81 F.2d at 54. We see no reason to make an exception to this rule for elements of a computer program that have entered the public domain by virtue of freely accessible program exchanges and the like. *See Brown Bag Software,* slip op. at 3732 (affirming the district court's finding that " 'plaintiffs may not claim copyright protection of an . . . expression that is, if not standard, then commonplace in the computer software industry.' "). Thus, a court must also filter out this material from the allegedly infringed program before it makes the final inquiry in its substantial similarity analysis.

Step Three: Comparison

The third and final step of the test for substantial similarity that we believe appropriate for non-literal program components entails a comparison. Once a court has sifted out all elements of the allegedly infringed program which are "ideas" or are dictated by efficiency or external factors, or taken from the public domain, there may remain a core of protectable expression. In terms of a work's copyright value, this is the golden nugget. At this point, the court's substantial similarity inquiry focuses on whether the defendant copied any aspect of this protected expression, as well as an assessment of the copied portion's relative importance with respect to the plaintiff's overall program. *See Data East USA,* 862 F.2d at 208 ("To determine whether similarities result from unprotectable expression, analytic dissection of similarities may be performed. If . . . all similarities in expression arise from use of common ideas, then no substantial similarity can be found.")

(3) *Policy Considerations*

. . .

CA and some amici argue against the type of approach that we have set forth on the grounds that it will be a disincentive for future computer program research and development. At bottom, they claim that if programmers are not guaranteed broad copyright protection for their work, they will not invest the extensive time, energy and funds required to design and improve program structures. While they have a point, their argument cannot carry the day. The interest of the copyright law is not in simply conferring a monopoly on industrious persons, but in advancing the public welfare through rewarding artistic creativity, in a manner that permits the free use and development of non-protectable ideas and processes.

Recently, the Supreme Court has emphatically reiterated that "the primary objective of copyright is not to reward the labor of authors...." *Feist Publications, Inc. v. Rural Telephone Service Co., Inc.,* 111 S. Ct. 1282, 1290 (1991)....

Feist teaches that substantial effort alone cannot confer copyright status on an otherwise uncopyrightable work. As we have discussed, despite the fact that significant labor and expense often goes [sic] into computer program flow-charting and debugging, that process does not always result in inherently protectable expression. Thus, *Feist* implicitly undercuts the *Whelan* rationale, "which allowed copyright protection beyond the literal computer code ... [in order to] provide the proper incentive for programmers by protecting their most valuable efforts." We note that *Whelan* was decided prior to *Feist* when the "sweat of the brow" doctrine still had vitality. In view of the Supreme Court's recent holding, however, we must reject the legal basis of CA's disincentive argument.

Furthermore, we are unpersuaded that the test we approve today will lead to the dire consequences for the computer program industry that plaintiff and some amici predict. To the contrary, serious students of the industry have been highly critical of the sweeping scope of copyright protection engendered by the *Whelan* rule, in that it "enables first comers to 'lock up' basic programming techniques as implemented in programs to perform particular tasks."

To be frank, the exact contours of copyright protection for non-literal program structure are not completely clear. We trust that as future cases are decided, those limits will become better defined. Indeed, it may well be that the Copyright Act serves as a relatively weak barrier against public access to the theoretical interstices behind a program's source and object codes. This results from the hybrid nature of a computer program, which, while it is literary expression, is also a highly functional, utilitarian component in the larger process of computing.

Generally, we think that copyright registration—with its indiscriminating availability—is not ideally suited to deal with the highly dynamic technology of computer science. Thus far, many of the decisions in this area reflect the courts' attempt to fit the proverbial square peg in a round hole. The district court, and at least one commentator, has suggested that patent registration, with its exacting up-front novelty and non-obviousness requirements, might be the more appropriate rubric of protection for intellectual property of this kind.... *See also Lotus Dev. Corp. v. Borland Int'l, Inc.* (discussing the potentially supplemental relationship between patent and copyright protection in the context of computer programs). In any event, now that more than 12 years have passed since CONTU issued its final report, the resolution of this specific issue could benefit from further legislative investigation—perhaps a CONTU II.

In the meantime, Congress has made clear that computer programs are literary works entitled to copyright protection. Of course, we shall abide by these instructions, but in so doing we must not impair the overall integrity of copyright law. While incentive based arguments in favor of broad copyright protection are perhaps attractive from a pure policy perspective, ultimately, they have a corrosive effect on certain fundamental tenets of copyright doctrine. If the test we have outlined results in narrowing the scope of protection, as we expect it will, that result flows from applying, in accordance with Congressional intent, long-standing principles of copyright law to computer programs. Of course, our decision is also informed by our concern that these fundamental principles remain undistorted.

B.   *The District Court Decision*

We turn now to our review of the district court's decision in this particular case.

The district court had to determine whether Altai's OSCAR 3.5 program was substantially similar to CA's ADAPTER....

. . .

The district court took the first step in the analysis set forth in this opinion when it separated the program by levels of abstraction. The district court stated:

> As applied to computer software programs, this abstractions test would progress in order of "increasing generality" from object code, to source code, to parameter lists, to services required, to general outline. In discussing the particular similarities, therefore, we shall focus on these levels.

While the facts of a different case might require that a district court draw a more particularized blueprint of a program's overall structure, this description is a workable one for the case at hand.

Moving to the district court's evaluation of OSCAR 3.5's structural components, we agree with Judge Pratt's systematic exclusion of non-protectable expression. With respect to code, the district court observed that after the rewrite of OSCAR 3.4 to OSCAR 3.5, "there remained virtually no lines of code that were identical to ADAPTER." Accordingly, the court found that the code "presented no similarity at all."

Next, Judge Pratt addressed the issue of similarity between the two programs' parameter lists and macros. He concluded that, viewing the conflicting evidence most favorably to CA, it demonstrated that "only a few of the lists and macros were similar to protected elements in ADAPTER;

the others were either in the public domain or dictated by the functional demands of the program." As discussed above, functional elements and elements taken from the public domain do not qualify for copyright protection. With respect to the few remaining parameter lists and macros, the district court could reasonably conclude that they did not warrant a finding of infringement given their relative contribution to the overall program. In any event, the district court reasonably found that, for lack of persuasive evidence, CA failed to meet its burden of proof on whether the macros and parameter lists at issue were substantially similar.

The district court also found that the overlap exhibited between the list of services required for both ADAPTER and OSCAR 3.5 was "determined by the demands of the operating system and of the applications program to which it [was] to be linked through ADAPTER or OSCAR." *Id.* In other words, this aspect of the program's structure was dictated by the nature of other programs with which it was designed to interact and, thus, is not protected by copyright.

Finally, in his infringement analysis, Judge Pratt accorded no weight to the similarities between the two programs' organizational charts, "because [the charts were] so simple and obvious to anyone exposed to the operation of the program[s]." CA argues that the district court's action in this regard "is not consistent with copyright law"—that "obvious" expression is protected, and that the district court erroneously failed to realize this. However, to say that elements of a work are "obvious," in the manner in which the district court used the word, is to say that they "follow naturally from the work's theme rather than from the author's creativity." This is but one formulation of the scènes à faire doctrine, which we have already endorsed as a means of weeding out unprotectable expression.

Since we accept Judge Pratt's factual conclusions and the results of his legal analysis, we affirm his dismissal of CA's copyright infringement claim based upon OSCAR 3.5. We emphasize that, like all copyright infringement cases, those that involve computer programs are highly fact specific. The amount of protection due structural elements, in any given case, will vary according to the protectable expression found to exist within the program at issue.

QUESTIONS

1. Evaluate the approach of the *Altai* court toward what it calls "abstraction-filtration-comparison." Is that analytical process properly to be applied in assessing infringement of novels (or dramatic works or motion pictures) as well? For example, should a court "filter" out all material in a plaintiff's novel that is in the public domain because factual, and elements that are abstract enough to be considered "ideas," and elements that are routine in the genre so as to be considered "scènes à faire," and other elements that are thought insufficiently original—*before* making a comparison with the defendant's work as to substantial similarity?

2. If it can be said that the court's analysis in *Altai* is perhaps stricter on the plaintiff than is true in literary cases generally, is that justified by the "functionality" of the programs claimed by Computer Associates? Consider other functional works, and the application of the court's method of separating unprotectible idea from protectible expression, i.e., splitting the overall program into its component modules and subroutines. How would that analysis be applied to such "functional" works as cookbooks? Or manuals for the assembly of a machine or for the playing of a game? Or law school casebooks?

3. What *was* the "idea" of ADAPTER: (1) to translate the language of a given program into the particular language that the computer's own operating system can understand? (2) to allow a computer user to change or use multiple operating systems while maintaining the same software? (3) to communicate between programs through a two-stage process involving a first component that contains only the task-specific portions of the program, independent of all operating system issues, and a second component that contains all the interconnections between the first component and the operating system? What difference does it make? Did the Second Circuit identify the "idea"?

Steinberg v. Columbia Pictures Industries

663 F.Supp. 706 (S.D.N.Y.1987).

■ STANTON, DISTRICT JUDGE.

In these actions for copyright infringement, plaintiff Saul Steinberg is suing the producers, promoters, distributors and advertisers of the movie "Moscow on the Hudson" ("Moscow"). Steinberg is an artist whose fame derives in part from cartoons and illustrations he has drawn for *The New Yorker* magazine. Defendant Columbia Pictures Industries, Inc. (Columbia) is in the business of producing, promoting and distributing motion pictures, including "Moscow." Defendant RCA Corporation (RCA) was involved with Columbia in promoting and distributing the home video version of "Moscow," and defendant Diener Hauser Bates Co. (DHB) acted as an advertising agent for "Moscow." ...

. . .

Plaintiff alleges that defendants' promotional poster for "Moscow" infringes his copyright on an illustration that he drew for *The New Yorker* [see illustrations on pages 482–83] and that appeared on the cover of the March 29, 1976 issue of the magazine, in violation of 17 U.S.C. §§ 101–810. . . .

Defendants have moved, and plaintiff has cross-moved, for summary judgment. For the reasons set forth below, this court rejects defendants' asserted defenses and grants summary judgment on the issue of copying to plaintiff.

. . .

II

The essential facts are not disputed by the parties despite their disagreements on nonessential matters. On March 29, 1976, *The New*

Yorker published as a cover illustration the work at issue in this suit, widely known as a parochial New Yorker's view of the world. The magazine registered this illustration with the United States Copyright Office and subsequently assigned the copyright to Steinberg. Approximately three months later, plaintiff and *The New Yorker* entered into an agreement to print and sell a certain number of posters of the cover illustration.

. . .

Defendants' illustration was created to advertise the movie "Moscow on the Hudson," which recounts the adventures of a Muscovite who defects in New York. In designing this illustration, Columbia's executive art director, Kevin Nolan, has admitted that he specifically referred to Steinberg's poster, and indeed, that he purchased it and hung it, among others, in his office. Furthermore, Nolan explicitly directed the outside artist whom he retained to execute his design, Craig Nelson, to use Steinberg's poster to achieve a more recognizably New York look. Indeed, Nelson acknowledged having used the facade of one particular edifice, at Nolan's suggestion that it would render his drawing more "New York-ish." Curtis Affidavit ¶ 28(c). While the two buildings are not identical, they are so similar that it is impossible, especially in view of the artist's testimony, not to find that defendants' impermissibly copied plaintiff's.

To decide the issue of infringement, it is necessary to consider the posters themselves. Steinberg's illustration presents a bird's eye view across a portion of the western edge of Manhattan, past the Hudson River and a telescoped version of the rest of the United States and the Pacific Ocean, to a red strip of horizon, beneath which are three flat land masses labeled China, Japan and Russia. The name of the magazine, in *The New Yorker*'s usual typeface, occupies the top fifth of the poster, beneath a thin band of blue wash representing a stylized sky.

The parts of the poster beyond New York are minimalized, to symbolize a New Yorker's myopic view of the centrality of his city to the world. The entire United States west of the Hudson River, for example, is reduced to a brown strip labeled "Jersey," together with a light green trapezoid with a few rudimentary rock outcroppings and the names of only seven cities and two states scattered across it. The few blocks of Manhattan, by contrast, are depicted and colored in detail. The four square blocks of the city, which occupy the whole lower half of the poster, include numerous buildings, pedestrians and cars, as well as parking lots and lamp posts, with water towers atop a few of the buildings. The whimsical, sketchy style and spiky lettering are recognizable as Steinberg's.

Illustration 1 — Steinberg's cover illustration
for The New Yorker

Illustration 2 — Columbia Pictures' promotional poster

The "Moscow" illustration depicts the three main characters of the film on the lower third of their poster, superimposed on a bird's eye view of New York City, and continues eastward across Manhattan and the Atlantic Ocean, past a rudimentary evocation of Europe, to a clump of recognizably Russian-styled buildings on the horizon, labeled "Moscow." The movie credits appear over the lower portion of the characters. The central part of the poster depicts approximately four New York City blocks, with fairly detailed buildings, pedestrians and vehicles, a parking lot, and some water towers and lamp posts. Columbia's artist added a few New York landmarks at apparently random places in his illustration, apparently to render the locale more easily recognizable. Beyond the blue strip labeled "Atlantic Ocean," Europe is represented by London, Paris and Rome, each anchored by a single landmark (although the landmark used for Rome is the Leaning Tower of Pisa).

The horizon behind Moscow is delineated by a red crayoned strip, above which are the title of the movie and a brief textual introduction to the plot. The poster is crowned by a thin strip of blue wash, apparently a stylization of the sky. This poster is executed in a blend of styles: the three characters, whose likenesses were copied from a photograph, have realistic faces and somewhat sketchy clothing, and the city blocks are drawn in a fairly detailed but sketchy style. The lettering on the drawing is spiky, in block-printed handwritten capital letters substantially identical to plaintiff's while the printed texts at the top and bottom of the poster are in the typeface commonly associated with *The New Yorker* magazine.[2]

III

. . .

Defendants' access to plaintiff's illustration is established beyond peradventure. Therefore, the sole issue remaining with respect to liability is whether there is such substantial similarity between the copyrighted and accused works as to establish a violation of plaintiff's copyright. . . .

The definition of "substantial similarity" in this circuit is "whether an average lay observer would recognize the alleged copy as having been appropriated from the copyrighted work." *Ideal Toy Corp. v. Fab–Lu Ltd.*, 360 F.2d 1021, 1022 (2d Cir.1966); *Silverman v. CBS, Inc.*, 632 F. Supp. at 1351–52. . . .

Moreover, it is now recognized that "[t]he copying need not be of every detail so long as the copy is substantially similar to the copyrighted work." . . .

There is no dispute that defendants cannot be held liable for using the *idea* of a map of the world from an egocentrically myopic perspective. No rigid principle has been developed, however, to ascertain when one has gone beyond the idea to the expression, and "[d]ecisions must therefore

2. The typeface is not a subject of copyright, but the similarity reinforces the impression that defendants copied plaintiff's illustration.

inevitably be ad hoc." *Peter Pan Fabrics, Inc. v. Martin Weiner Corp.*, 274 F.2d 487, 489 (2d Cir.1960) (L. Hand, J.)....

Even at first glance, one can see the striking stylistic relationship between the posters, and since style is one ingredient of "expression," this relationship is significant. Defendants' illustration was executed in the sketchy, whimsical style that has become one of Steinberg's hallmarks. Both illustrations represent a bird's eye view across the edge of Manhattan and a river bordering New York City to the world beyond. Both depict approximately four city blocks in detail and become increasingly minimalist as the design recedes into the background. Both use the device of a narrow band of blue wash across the top of the poster to represent the sky, and both delineate the horizon with a band of primary red.[3]

The strongest similarity is evident in the rendering of the New York City blocks. Both artists chose a vantage point that looks directly down a wide two-way cross street that intersects two avenues before reaching a river. Despite defendants' protestations, this is not an inevitable way of depicting blocks in a city with a grid-like street system, particularly since most New York City cross streets are one-way. Since even a photograph may be copyrighted because "no photograph, however simple, can be unaffected by the personal influence of the author," *Time Inc. v. Bernard Geis Assoc.*, 293 F. Supp. 130, 141 (S.D.N.Y.1968), *quoting Bleistein, supra*, one can hardly gainsay the right of an artist to protect his choice of perspective and layout in a drawing, especially in conjunction with the overall concept and individual details. Indeed, the fact that defendants changed the names of the streets while retaining the same graphic depiction weakens their case: had they intended their illustration realistically to depict the streets labeled on the poster, their four city blocks would not so closely resemble plaintiff's four city blocks....

While not all of the details are identical, many of them could be mistaken for one another; for example, the depiction of the water towers, and the cars, and the red sign above a parking lot, and even many of the individual buildings. The shapes, windows, and configurations of various edifices are substantially similar. The ornaments, facades and details of Steinberg's buildings appear in defendants', although occasionally at other locations. In this context, it is significant that Steinberg did not depict any buildings actually erected in New York; rather, he was inspired by the general appearance of the structures on the West Side of Manhattan to create his own New York-ish structures. Thus, the similarity between the

---

3. Defendants claim that since this use of thin bands of primary colors is a traditional Japanese technique, their adoption of it cannot infringe Steinberg's copyright. This argument ignores the principle that while "[o]thers are free to copy the original ... [t]hey are not free to copy the copy." *Bleistein v. Donaldson Lithographing Co.*, 188 U.S. 239, 250, 23 S. Ct. 298, 300, 47 L. Ed. 460 (1903) (Holmes, J.). *Cf. Dave Grossman Designs, Inc. v. Bortin*, 347 F. Supp. 1150, 1156–57 (N.D.Ill.1972) (an artist may use the same subject and style as another "so long as the second artist does not *substantially copy* [the first artist's] specific expression of his idea.")

buildings depicted in the "Moscow" and Steinberg posters cannot be explained by an assertion that the artists happened to choose the same buildings to draw. The close similarity can be explained only by the defendants' artist having copied the plaintiff's work. Similarly, the locations and size, the errors and anomalies of Steinberg's shadows and streetlight, are meticulously imitated.

In addition, the Columbia artist's use of the childlike, spiky block print that has become one of Steinberg's hallmarks to letter the names of the streets in the "Moscow" poster can be explained only as copying. There is no inherent justification for using this style of lettering to label New York City streets as it is associated with New York only through Steinberg's poster.

While defendants' poster shows the city of Moscow on the horizon in far greater detail than anything is depicted in the background of plaintiff's illustration, this fact alone cannot alter the conclusion. "Substantial similarity" does not require identity, and "duplication or near identity is not necessary to establish infringement." *Krofft,* 562 F.2d at 1167. Neither the depiction of Moscow, nor the eastward perspective, nor the presence of randomly scattered New York City landmarks in defendants' poster suffices to eliminate the substantial similarity between the posters. As Judge Learned Hand wrote, "no plagiarist can excuse the wrong by showing how much of his work he did not pirate." *Sheldon v. Metro–Goldwyn Pictures Corp.,* 81 F.2d 49, 56 (2d Cir.), *cert. denied,* 298 U.S. 669, 56 S. Ct. 835, 80 L. Ed. 1392 (1936).

Defendants argue that their poster could not infringe plaintiff's copyright because only a small proportion of its design could possibly be considered similar. This argument is both factually and legally without merit. "[A] copyright infringement may occur by reason of a substantial similarity that involves only a small portion of each work." *Burroughs v. Metro–Goldwyn–Mayer, Inc.,* 683 F.2d 610, 624 n. 14 (2d Cir.1982). Moreover, this case involves the entire protected work and an iconographically, as well as proportionately, significant portion of the allegedly infringing work. *Cf. Mattel, Inc. v. Azrak–Hamway Intern., Inc.,* 724 F.2d 357, 360 (2d Cir.1983); *Elsmere Music, Inc. v. National Broadcasting Co.,* 482 F. Supp. 741, 744 (S.D.N.Y.), *aff'd,* 623 F.2d 252 (2d Cir.1980) (taking small part of protected work can violate copyright).

. . .

I also reject defendants' argument that any similarities between the works are unprotectible *scènes à faire,* or "incidents, characters or settings which, as a practical matter, are indispensable or standard in the treatment of a given topic." *Walker,* 615 F. Supp. at 436. *See also Reyher,* 533 F.2d at 92. It is undeniable that a drawing of New York City blocks could be expected to include buildings, pedestrians, vehicles, lamp posts and water towers. Plaintiff, however, does not complain of defendants' mere use of these elements in their poster; rather, his complaint is that defendants copied his *expression* of those elements of a street scene.

[The defendant also asserted the defenses of fair use (parody), estoppel (failure to protest the use of the Steinberg poster by other artists), and laches. The court rejected them all.]

QUESTION

Below are some further variations on the theme of the *New Yorker* poster. Assuming neither was produced with Steinberg's permission, does either infringe his copyright? Why or why not?

Kisch v. Ammirati & Puris Inc.

657 F.Supp. 380 (S.D.N.Y.1987).

[Plaintiff had taken a photograph of a woman seated in the Village Vanguard, a Manhattan nightclub; the woman was holding a concertina, and behind her was a large mural on the wall. Defendants were two companies marketing beverages, an advertising agency and a photographer hired by the agency. The allegedly infringing photograph was taken at the Village Vanguard and showed a man, seated in front of the same mural, holding a saxophone, with a bottle of lime juice on a table nearby. Defendants moved for summary judgment, conceding for purposes of the motion that they had had access to plaintiff's photograph. The court denied the motion, finding that there was sufficient evidence from which a reasonable conclusion might be reached that the defendants had copied the plaintiff's photograph and that the works would be regarded as substantially similar by an ordinary observer. The operative passages from the court's opinion follow.]

The Court has found no precedent, and the parties have cited none, which is substantively and procedurally on all fours with the instant case. It has been recognized, however, that where a photographer "in choosing subject matter, camera angle, lighting, etc., copies and attempts to duplicate all of such elements as contained in a prior photograph," then even though "the second photographer is photographing a live subject rather than the first photograph ... [s]uch an act would constitute an infringement of the first photograph...." 1 Nimmer § 2.08[E][1] at 2–112.... On the other hand, if the elements of an earlier photograph are "by chance" duplicated subsequently by another photographer, the new photograph will not be held to infringe the earlier one because others are "entirely free to form [their] own conception" of the subject matter. *Id. Cf.* 1 Nimmer § 2.08[E][1] at 2–112.

Turning to a comparison of the two photographs involved in this case, there are differences between the works, to be sure. For example, plaintiff's photograph is in black and white while defendants' is in color. Plaintiff's photograph is of an unidentified woman while defendants' is of musician John Lurie. The woman in plaintiff's photograph is holding a concertina while John Lurie is holding a saxophone. A bottle of lime juice and a portion of a table appear only in defendants' photograph. There are also many similarities. Most noticeably, the two photographs were taken in the same small corner of the Village Vanguard nightclub. The same striking mural appears as the background for each photograph. Both John Lurie and the woman in plaintiff's photograph are seated and holding a musical instrument. In addition, the lighting, camera angle, and camera position appear to be similar in each photograph. The Court concludes that a rational trier of fact could find sufficient similarities to prove "copying." *See Arnstein,* 154 F.2d at 468, *quoted in Walker,* 784 F.2d at 51.

A closer question is posed with respect to the issue of "illicit copying (unlawful appropriation)" under the "ordinary observer" test. *See id.* Still, the Court is unable to conclude that a rational trier of fact would not be permitted to find substantial similarity relating to protectible material. *See Walker*, 784 F.2d at 48; *Durham Industries, Inc.*, 630 F.2d at 918. Significantly, a rational trier of fact would be permitted to find that the underlying tone or mood of defendants' photograph was similar to the original conception expressed in plaintiff's work. Accordingly, defendants' motion to dismiss plaintiff's claim for copyright infringement is denied.

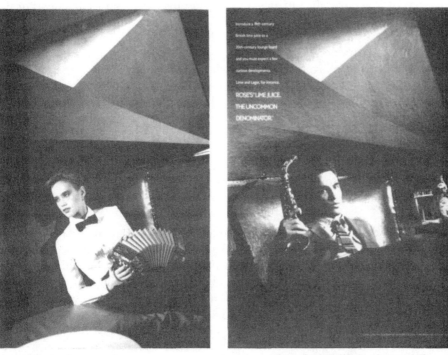

Kisch photograph   Ammirati & Puris photograph
Reproduced with permission   Reproduced with permission

QUESTIONS

1.   The court in *Steinberg* stated that "substantial similarity" means that "an average lay observer would recognize the alleged copy as having been appropriated from the copyrighted work." Is this too lenient a standard? For example, would not most persons familiar with the Steinberg *New Yorker* cover affirm that the Paris and Florence renditions, *supra* had been "appropriated" from Steinberg? Does that alone warrant a finding of infringement? Would the same visual process, and conclusion about legality, obtain if the fact-finder were instead to use the formula announced by Learned Hand in *Peter Pan* for determining whether two works are substantially similar, i.e., whether the ordinary observer "unless he set out to detect the disparities, would be disposed to overlook them, and regard their aesthetic appeal as the same"?

2.   The *Steinberg* court stated that although the plaintiff's graphic "style" was not protectible, it was a significant ingredient in determining whether "expression" was copied. It stated the same about such things as the "childlike, spiky block print" used in delineating the street names. Is it possible to separate out these unprotectible elements in determining whether the defendant has copied too much protectible detail from the plaintiff? Is it analytically proper to separate them out?

3.   In *Steinberg* and *Kisch*, the defendant may well have "based" its work on that of the plaintiff, but it also made a purposeful effort to incorporate changes in order to distance itself from the expressive details of the plaintiff's work. Courts sometimes speak of that effort disparagingly, counting it against the defendant on the issues of copying and illicit similarity. Even if not counted against the defendant, such an effort is commonly said not to cut in the defendant's favor. For example, the late Professor Nimmer has stated: "It is entirely immaterial that in many respects plaintiff's and defendant's work are dissimilar if in other respects similarity as to a substantial element of plaintiff's work can be shown." 3 Nimmer on Copyright § 13.03[B]. On the other hand, Professor Nimmer also states: "A defendant may legitimately avoid infringement by intentionally making sufficient changes in a work that would otherwise be regarded as substantially similar to that of the plaintiff's." *Id.* How would you reconcile these principles?

4.   Blore Advertising Agency has brought an infringement action against 20/20 Advertising Agency, claiming that the latter's television commercial for eyewear is a substantial copy of its own television commercial for a local newspaper. Blore's advertisement features Deborah Shelton, an actress best known for her work in the *Dallas* television series. The commercial lasts thirty seconds. It begins with a close-up of Ms. Shelton and the word "Deborah" in the lower left of the screen. Then follows a series of rapid-edits of twenty close-ups of Shelton's face; she wears a white shirt with blue stripes. With each line of text the camera cuts to a new close-up of Shelton in a different pose, with a different hairstyle and expression. The script is as follows:

> What do the Daily News and a hot bubble bath have in common? . . . Me. . . . I just love them both. . . . Everybody knows about the Daily News' commitment to the Valley . . . and its commitment to excellence. . . . There is another paper that says it covers the Valley. . . . But everybody knows. . . . They're over the hill. . . . Can you imagine living in the Valley and not reading the Daily News? . . . That's like wearing all new underwear and not getting hit by a bus. . . . What a waste. . . . Daily . . . News. . . . Daily . . . And Sundays. . . . You . . . Ought to look into that.

The 20/20 advertisement, prepared for Duling Optical Company, also uses the services of Ms. Shelton, who is captured in fourteen different poses over thirty seconds. It also begins with a close-up and the words "Deborah Shelton" on the lower right of the screen. There are a series of close-up and medium-range shots, in which Ms. Shelton wears a blue-striped blouse. In each shot, she is featured in a new pose with a different pair of glasses or no glasses at all as well as a different hairstyle. Her pose changes with each phrase of text:

> There are some things in life that should take . . . more than an hour. . . . But making your glasses isn't one of them. . . . Duling Optical Super Store . . . Has thousands of designer frames . . . And contact lenses to choose from. . . . I can have my eyes examined . . . And have my new glasses and . . . Contact lenses in about an hour. . . . And they're guaranteed to be . . . Prescription perfect. . . . The Duling Optical Super Store . . . The one-stop shopping . . . That allows me more time for . . . Other things.

Blore claims that 20/20 has copied the expressive elements of the Blore commercials. 20/20 claims that the plaintiff cannot use the copyright law to monopolize the rapid-edit montage style involving close-ups of a particular celebrity (with whom 20/20 entered into a lawful contract). What supporting arguments should each party make? How should the court rule? *See Chuck Blore & Don Richman Inc. v. 20/20 Adv., Inc.,* 674 F.Supp. 671 (D.Minn.1987).

CONCEPT AND FEEL

The student may recall that the "concept and feel" formula was introduced by the Court of Appeals for the Ninth Circuit in the *Roth Greeting Cards* case, Chap. 2(C)(2), *supra*, involving simple greeting cards with simple drawings on the front and standard phrases inside. The *Kisch* decision uses something of the same approach when it states that a jury could reasonably find that the "underlying tone or mood" of the defendant's photograph was "similar to the original conception" expressed in the plaintiff's. By the same token, one might inquire whether the *Steinberg* decision, although not using the "concept and feel" formula, may not be extending protection to the plaintiff's conceptual ingenuity, rather than his expressive artistry.

If two works are similar only in "concept and feel" or "tone or mood," can it properly be said that there is an illicit copying of "expression" rather than "idea"? Indeed, is not the "concept and feel" standard facially inconsistent with the exclusion of "concepts" from the subject matter of copyright under § 102(b)? Or does the phrase, however unhappily worded, attempt to capture the point at which defendant has gone beyond mere mimicry of general style to capture elements of plaintiff's work which, however ill-defined, are particularly "expressive." Is there a better way to identify that point? (*Can* it be identified?)

The "concept and feel" standard seems to find its way more into cases of pictorial copyright than literary copyright, probably because the pictorial work can be viewed in a single glance as a totality. If applied to literary works, some might argue, the "concept and feel" approach could result in protecting plot ideas and stock devices. Does application of the standard to art works present a similar potential for overprotection?

QUESTIONS

1. Itzchak Tarkay is an Israeli artist of international renown; two of his works, in poster format, are shown below. Patricia Govezensky has de-

signed and distributed the other two posters shown below. Has she infringed Tarkay's copyright? Has she arguably violated any other of Tarkay's legal rights? *See Romm Art Creations, Ltd. v. Simcha Int'l, Inc.,* 786 F.Supp. 1126 (E.D.N.Y.1992).

2. Photograph A below depicts a Santa Claus statuette designed and marketed by Kurt Adler. It includes a hidden mechanism that lowers and raises Santa's arm, which dips a wand into a container of liquid soap and thus produces floating bubbles. Photograph B depicts a statuette designed and marketed by World Bazaars, which acknowledged access to Adler's Santa, at a trade show, but denied copying and infringement. Would you find copyright infringement? *See Kurt S. Adler, Inc. v. World Bazaars, Inc.,* 897 F.Supp. 92 (S.D.N.Y.1995).

Photograph A (Adler)

Photograph B (World Bazaars)

AUTHORS REPRODUCING WORKS IN WHICH THEY
NO LONGER OWN THE COPYRIGHT

In *Gross v. Seligman*, 212 F. 930 (2d Cir.1914), a photographer posed a nude young woman for a photograph entitled "Grace of Youth." He then sold all rights in the photograph to plaintiff. Two years later he posed the same young woman for another photograph entitled "Cherry Ripe." Apart from a minor variation of background (and, the court noted, slight changes in the contours of the woman's figure resulting from the passage of two years), the sole difference between the two photographs was that the first showed her face in repose and the second had the woman smiling with a cherry stem between her teeth.

The court stressed that where the photographer, as well as the model, pose, light and shade were the same in both photographs, there is a very strong indication that the second photograph was merely a copy of the first. The exercise of artistic talent, the sine qua non of the first photograph's copyrightability, was used in the second photograph to create not a new independently copyrightable photograph, but a copy of the first photograph. Accordingly, infringement was found. By contrast, the court stated that another artist would be free to photograph the same young woman and create his own work, even though striking similarities might exist between this new photograph and the old, but that the original artist in this case had not created a new photograph, but copied the original.

More recently, in *Franklin Mint Corp. v. National Wildlife Art Exchange, Inc.*, 575 F.2d 62 (3d Cir.1978), a court was again faced with the situation whereby, in a later work, an artist had allegedly infringed the copyright that he no longer owned in one of his earlier works. This time the ruling was in favor of the artist, as the court resorted to the idea-expression distinction in finding that no infringement had occurred.

A nationally recognized wildlife artist, Albert Earl Gilbert, was commissioned to paint a watercolor of cardinals for subsequent commercial exploitation by National Wildlife Art Exchange. Using slides, photographs, sketches and two stuffed cardinals as source material, the artist completed "Cardinals on Apple Blossom" and, as previously agreed, sold it, along with all its attendant rights, to National. Three years later, as part of a series of bird life watercolors done for Franklin Mint, the artist painted "The Cardinal," using some of the same source materials he had used to create "Cardinals on Apple Blossom." In addition, however, in painting "The Cardinal" he used new slides, photographs and sketches that had not been available to him earlier. (The two watercolors are reproduced below; a major difference is the switch in location of the male and female cardinals. To buttress his claim of non-copying, the artist painted—in open court, during the course of the trial—yet a third rendering of two cardinals on blossomed branches, without reference to the earlier works; it looked remarkably the same as the other two.) The court held that an artist is free to use the same source material he has already used in creating a painting to create a different painting depicting the same subject matter.

In ruling for Franklin Mint, the court cited readily apparent dissimilarities between the two paintings in the area of color, body attitude and positioning of birds, linear effect, background, and composition. This "pattern of differences" was held sufficient to establish that the second painting represented "diversity of expression rather than only an echo."

Can these seemingly conflicting resolutions of similar problems be explained on the basis of the relative similarities and differences in the pair

National Wildlife Watercolor   Franklin Mint Watercolor

of works in each case? Can the complete identity of the source materials in *Gross* be contrasted with the lesser degree of overlap in *Franklin* to explain the different judgments? Or does the explanation for the opposite results reached in these two cases lie in the differences between the media of photography and watercolor painting? The *Franklin* court talked around this in a paragraph discussing the effect of the artist's style on the protectibility of a copyright in an artistic work. (The *Gross* case is cited in a footnote to the discussion's conclusion.) The discussion concludes that a painting or drawing of photograph-like clarity and accuracy will be less protectible than a more abstract or impressionistic work where the expression is more personal and distinctive.

Both courts skirted an issue raised by cases of this kind: Does a lawsuit against an artist for infringement of a copyright in a work he has created possibly inhibit him from continuing to operate in his own style? In *Gross* the court ignored the possibility, and in *Franklin* the court merely noted that "an artist is free to consult the same source for another original painting." Compare the problems created when a songwriter transfers copyright and continues to write "reminiscent" music in his usual style, or when a novelist transfers copyright and continues to write in a comfortable genre using character types he has used before. *See Fantasy, Inc. v. Fogerty,* supra *Chapter 3.B, and* Warner Bros. v. CBS, *supra* Chapter 2.H.

Regarding the above issues, consider the following observations by Judge Posner in *Schiller & Schmidt, Inc. v. Nordisco Corp.,* 969 F.2d 410, 414 (7th Cir.1992):

We might still suppose the evidence of copying of the layouts compelling were it not that the creator of the copyrighted work and the infringer were the same person. Although one can and often does copy one's own work (and so may be an infringer if one doesn't own the copyright on it), one is also more likely to duplicate one's own work without copying than another person would be likely to do. If Cezanne painted two pictures of Mont St. Victoire, we should expect them to look more alike than if Matisse had painted the second, even if Cezanne painted the second painting from life rather than from the first painting.

2. THE RIGHT TO MAKE PHONORECORDS

What is a "phonorecord"?

§ 101. Definitions

"Phonorecords" are material objects in which sounds, other than those accompanying a motion picture or other audiovisual work, are fixed by any method now known or later developed, and from which the sounds can be perceived, reproduced, or otherwise communicated, either directly or with the aid of a machine or device. The term "phonorecords" includes the material object in which the sounds are first fixed.

———

In lay terms, a "phonorecord" is a copy of a sound recording. But the 1976 Act has retained the historical distinction between "copies" (material objects in which works of authorship *other* than sound recordings are reproduced) and "phonorecords" (material objects in which sound recordings are reproduced). Hence this rather cumbersome term. Another way to understand the terms is that a "copy" generally communicates a work to the eye, while a "phonorecord" generally communicates a work to the ear. You may also encounter the term "phonogram" used, particularly in other countries, for material objects in which sound recordings are reproduced.

It is important to distinguish the sound recording (and its fixation in phonorecords) from the work of authorship that is recorded. The phonorecord often embodies *two* copyrighted works: (1) a "musical composition" or a "literary work," whose performance and recording creates (2) a "sound recording." In the materials that follow, we will consider: (a) with respect to copyright owners of *musical compositions*, the scope of their rights to reproduce the work in phonorecords; and (b) with respect to copyright owners of *sound recordings*, the scope of their right to reproduce the work in phonorecords.

a. MUSICAL COMPOSITIONS: THE COMPULSORY LICENSE UNDER § 115

Note first that authors of literary works and dramatic musical compositions (such as operas and musicals) enjoy full rights to authorize or prohibit the creation of recorded performances of their works. In the case of nondramatic musical compositions (e.g., popular songs), however, a compulsory license limits the composers' reproduction rights.

The concept of a compulsory license was introduced into our copyright law in 1909. The Supreme Court had already decided in *White-Smith Music Pub'g Co. v. Apollo Co.,* 209 U.S. 1 (1908), that piano rolls (and by analogy phonograph records and the like) did not embody a system of notation that could be read and hence were not "copies" of the musical composition within the meaning of the law, but constituted merely parts of devices for mechanically performing the music. The exclusive right of the copyright owner to public performance already existed under the Act of 1897, and this undoubtedly included such *performance* by mechanical instruments. It was the right to *make* such devices that was lacking, and so Congress undertook to grant such right, but without intending to extend the right of copyright to the mechanical devices themselves. H.R. Rep. No. 2222, 60th Cong., 2d Sess. 9 (1909).

Because of what seemed at the time a well-grounded fear of monopolistic control of music for recording purposes, *id.,* Congress saw fit to qualify the right of mechanical control by providing in subsection (e) of § 1 that if the copyright proprietor himself used or sanctioned the use of his composition in this way, any other person was free to do so upon paying a royalty of two cents for each part (each roll or record) manufactured. A corresponding infringement provision was inserted in § 101(e). Mechanisms were provided for the filing of notices by the compulsory licensor (notice of use) and licensee (notice of intention to use) and for payment.

These verbose and internally inconsistent provisions left many questions unanswered. However, the remarkable adjustment of the music industry to this unique provision resulted in its retention in 1976, but with changes designed to balance anew the competing interests and to answer some of these questions. *See generally* Rosenlund, *Compulsory Licensing of Musical Compositions for Phonorecords Under the Copyright Act of 1976,* 30 Hastings L.J. 683 (1979).

House Report

H.R. Rep. No. 94–1476, 94th Cong., 2d Sess. 107–09 (1976).

The provisions of sections 1(e) and 101(e) of the present law, establishing a system of compulsory licensing for the making and distribution of phonorecords of copyrighted music, are retained with a number of modifications in section 115 of the bill. Under these provisions, which represented a compromise of the most controversial issue of the 1909 act, a musical composition that has been reproduced in phonorecords with the permission of the copyright owner may generally be reproduced in phonorecords by another person, if that person notifies the copyright owner and pays a specified royalty. . . .

Availability and scope of compulsory license

. . .

The present law, though not altogether clear, apparently bases compulsory licensing on the making or licensing of the first recording, even if no authorized records are distributed to the public. The first sentence of section 115(a)(1) would change the basis for compulsory licensing to authorized public distribution of phonorecords (including disks and audio tapes but not the sound tracks or other sound records accompanying a motion picture or other audiovisual work). Under the clause, a compulsory license would be available to anyone as soon as "phonorecords of a nondramatic musical work have been distributed to the public in the United States under the authority of the copyright owner."

The second sentence of clause (1), which has been the subject of some debate, provides that "a person may obtain a compulsory license only if his or her primary purpose in making phonorecords is to distribute them to the public for private use." ... The committee concluded ... that the purpose of the compulsory license does not extend to manufacturers of phonorecords that are intended primarily for commercial use, including not only broadcasters and jukebox operators but also background music services.

... The basic intent of [the final sentence of clause (1)] is to make clear that a person is not entitled to a compulsory license of copyrighted musical works for the purpose of making an unauthorized duplication of a musical sound recording originally developed and produced by another. It is the view of the Committee that such was the original intent of the Congress in enacting the 1909 Copyright Act, and it has been so construed by the 3d, 5th, 9th and 10th Circuits....

The second clause of subsection (a) is intended to recognize the practical need for a limited privilege to make arrangements of music being used under a compulsory license, but without allowing the music to be perverted, distorted, or travestied. Clause (2) permits arrangements of a work "to the extent necessary to conform it to the style or manner of interpretation of the performance involved," so long as it does not "change the basic melody or fundamental character of the work." The provision also prohibits the compulsory licensee from claiming an independent copyright in his arrangement as a "derivative work" without the express consent of the copyright owner.

———

ABKCO Music, Inc. v. Stellar Records, Inc., 96 F.3d 60 (2d Cir.1996). Defendant (Performance Tracks, Inc., or "Tracks"), which recorded plaintiff's music onto the soundtrack of a karaoke CD–ROM whose video portion showed the lyrics scrolling across the screen, claimed that its audio rendition of the copyrighted songs and video display of the lyrics was a "phonorecord" of the song covered by the compulsory license. The copyright owners contended that the karaoke disc—known as a CD + G ("Compact Disc + Graphics")—was an audiovisual work not subject to the compulsory license: the relevant license was not the compulsory "mechanical" license to make phonorecords, but the "synchronization" license to record onto the soundtrack of an audiovisual work. Synchronization licenses are voluntarily negotiated. In ruling for the copyright owners, the court clarified the scope of the section 115 compulsory license as well as the meaning of a "phonorecord" under the 1976 Act:

> In granting the preliminary injunction, the court below properly found that Tracks' compulsory licenses do not give it the right to publish the compositions' lyrics on a screen. Song lyrics enjoy independent copyright protection as "literary works," 1 Nimmer § 2.05[B], and the right to print a song's lyrics is exclusively that of the copyright holder under 17 U.S.C. § 106(1). Thus, while a compulsory license permits the recording of a "cover" version of a song, it does not permit the inclusion of a copy of the lyrics. That requires the separate permission of the copyright holder.
>
> . . .
>
> A time-honored method of facilitating singing along with music has been to furnish the singer with a printed copy of the lyrics. Copyright holders have always enjoyed exclusive rights over such copies. While projecting lyrics on a screen and producing printed copies of the lyrics, of course, have their differences, there is no reason to treat them differently for purposes of the Copyright Act.
>
> While we hardly need go further to affirm, we deal briefly with Tracks' contention that the court below, applying *Bourne,* was in error because its CD + G's are "phonorecords," not copies, within the meaning of the Copyright Act, and therefore its compulsory licenses include the right to its limited video display. While the court below did not reach this contention, we do so hereafter and conclude that it is both factually and legally flawed.
>
> Tracks' contention that CD + G's are "phonorecords" and thus the video aspect is within the grant of its compulsory licenses can be disposed of quickly. The plain language of the Copyright Act refutes Tracks' view. Phonorecords are defined as objects on which "sounds" are fixed; CD + G's, however, are objects on which sounds and visual representations of song lyrics are fixed. Moreover, the term phonorecord expressly excludes "audiovisual works," yet CD + G's constitute "audiovisual works," since they "consist of a series of related images"—the lyrics—"together with accompanying sounds"—the music. 17 U.S.C. § 101.
>
> Tracks does not claim that the actual definition of "phonorecord" in Section 101 includes the visual capabilities of its CD + G's, but rather contends that the Copyright Act has not kept pace with new technology, and that Congress, in view of its definition of "digital music recording" in the Audio Home Recording Act of 1992, 17 U.S.C.A. § 1001 et seq. ("AHRA") would include Tracks' entire CD + G capability within the definition of "phonorecords" if it were to redefine "phonorecord" today. It would, however, seem to be a sufficient answer to Tracks' contention to observe that Tracks' product is not

within the statutory definition of "phonorecord," and what Congress may or may not do in the future to redefine the term is not for us to speculate.

THE ROYALTY RATE AND THE COPYRIGHT ARBITRATION ROYALTY PANELS

Under § 115, a person wishing to obtain a compulsory license must file with the copyright owner a "notice of intention" to distribute phonorecords of the copyrighted work, and is to pay a royalty for each record of the work that is "made and distributed." One of the most heated issues in the revision process was the amount of the per-record royalty to be paid by record manufacturers (the compulsory licensees) to the owners of musical copyrights. The latter, although not arguing that the two-cent rate set in 1909 should mechanically be indexed to the increased cost-of-living in the subsequent 65 years, did urge that the royalty rate should be markedly increased beyond two cents—particularly in light of the significant increase in the price of phonograph records during that period.

The recording companies, contending that no increase beyond the two-cent royalty was warranted, emphasized among other things the fact that the aggregate royalties paid to copyright owners in the preceding decade had doubled due to increased record sales and the introduction of the long-playing multi-song recording, and the fact that the two-cent royalty represented roughly the same percentage of the manufacturers' wholesale selling price in 1970 as it did in 1909. They also argued that an increase in the royalty rate even to three cents per song would have to be reflected in increased record prices to the public, a result opposed not only by consumers but also by recording artists, record distributors and retailers, and jukebox operators. If, on the other hand, record prices were not raised, the higher royalty would result in the demise of many marginal record companies as well as many wholesalers and retailers; this would lead to a reduction in the recording of new music and to greater concentration in the recording industry. The songwriters and publishing companies challenged the accuracy of the manufacturers' economic data, claimed that the recording industry was more than capable of absorbing a very minor increase in mechanical royalties without financial disasters, and asserted that (quoting again from the Senate Report) "they see no reason why an industry which has more than doubled the price per recorded selection over the last decade should be excused from paying fair compensation to those who created the music."

Weighing all of these arguments, the two Houses and ultimately the Conference Committee decided to increase the statutory royalty rate to 2.75 cents per recording. The legislative history made it explicit that the publishers and composers would be able to take their case, beginning in 1980, to a newly created agency, the Copyright Royalty Tribunal, for review of the statutory royalty rate in light of current economic evidence.

In its 1980 proceedings, the Tribunal increased the royalty rate under § 115 from 2.75 cents (or .5 cent per minute, whichever is larger) to 4 cents for each recording of a copyrighted work (or .75 cent per minute, whichever is larger); the increase was made applicable to phonorecords made and distributed on or after July 1, 1981. In subsequent years, the Copyright Royalty Tribunal further increased the per-recording royalty. Effective January 1, 1986, the rate to be paid by phonorecord manufacturers became five cents for each recording (made and distributed) of a song (or .95 cents per minute, whichever was larger). The Tribunal declared that thereafter the rate would increase biannually in automatic correspondence to changes in the Consumer Price Index.

In 1993, Congress terminated the existence of the Copyright Royalty Tribunal. The Copyright Royalty Tribunal Reform Act of 1993, Pub. L. No. 103–198, 107 Stat. 2304, transferred the functions of the Tribunal to ad hoc arbitration panels convened by the Librarian of Congress (but whose costs are borne by the parties rather than through Government salaries). Royalty rate and distribution decisions by the arbitration panels are subject to review by the Librarian for arbitrariness, and his or her decision is in turn reviewable by the District of Columbia Circuit Court of Appeals. *See* 17 U.S.C.A. §§ 801–03.

The Copyright Office promptly adopted, essentially unchanged, the substantive rules and regulations of the defunct Tribunal, but also promulgated new rules and regulations of its own to implement new procedures for rate-setting and royalty distribution.

Compulsory Recording Royalty Rate. Pursuant to § 803(a)(3) of the Act, the compulsory license royalty was subject to comprehensive reassessment in 1997. In that year, at the invitation of the Copyright Office, a joint proposal was agreed upon by the National Music Publishers' Association and the Songwriters Guild of America (both representing owners of copyright in musical works) and the Recording Industry Association of America. The Copyright Office embraced this industry proposal after it conducted a rulemaking proceeding, so that beginning January 1, 2000, the rate was increased to 7.55 cents per song (or 1.45 cents per minute); in 2002–03, it will be 8.0 cents per song (or 1.55 cents per minute); in 2004–05, 8.5 cents per song (or 1.65 cents per minute); and beginning January 1, 2006, the rate will be 9.1 cents per song (or 1.75 cents per minute). In sum, over the next decade, the typical multi-track musical compact disc will move toward generating a total of roughly one dollar for all of the copyrighted songs embodied therein. *See* 37 C.F.R. § 255 (set forth in Appendix C of the Casebook).

When must a compulsory licensee obtain the license? According to § 115(b), the party wishing to make and distribute phonorecords incorporating the nondramatic musical composition must serve the copyright owner with notice of its intention to obtain a compulsory license "before or within thirty days after making, and before distributing any phonorecords of the work." Timely service is crucial: if the party makes and distributes the phonorecords before serving notice, it is too late to obtain a compulsory license thereafter—and the "making and distribution of phonorecords [thereby become] actionable as acts of infringement under section 501 and fully subject to" copyright remedies.

A recent decision underscores the serious consequences of failure to comply with § 115(b). In *Cherry River Music v. Simitar Entertainment*, 38 F.Supp.2d 310 (S.D.N.Y.1999), the defendant produced a recording of copyrighted music performed at wrestling matches, but failed to obtain from the music publisher a negotiated license to make the phonorecords. Although the defendant also allowed the period to obtain compulsory licenses to expire, it nonetheless recorded and shipped 370,000 phonorecords incorporating 13 musical compositions associated with famous wrestling personalities. The court granted a preliminary injunction against further distribution of the phonorecords, and, more significantly, ordered a recall of those phonorecords already shipped to distributors and retailers.

Digital Phonorecord Deliveries. On November 1, 1995, President Clinton signed the Digital Performance Right in Sound Recordings Act of 1995. That act made needed adjustments, principally by expanding rights held by owners of copyright in sound recordings, in light of dramatic technological innovations in digital radio transmissions. One such innovation permits what the act refers to as a "digital phonorecord delivery," which is equivalent to the sale and distribution of a musical recording. The act extends the compulsory license—covering nondramatic musical works (as distinguished from sound recordings)—to such "deliveries"; the compulsory-licensee recording company must pay royalties for each such "digital phonorecord delivery" that is made with its authorization.

As was stated by one of the supporters of the new law in the House of Representatives: "By passing this legislation, Congress will open the door to a golden age of digital technology where ... consumers may never have to set foot in a record store, yet have the ability to choose a musical selection from everything ever recorded without fear that it is out of stock, and be able to copy the album, at any time of the day or night, over a fiber optic cable by using a remote control while sitting in the comfort of their living rooms." Cong. Rec. H10103 (Oct. 17, 1995) (remarks of Rep. Conyers). The Librarian of Congress has declared that the royalty rate for each digital phonorecord delivery is to be the same as that for more conventional phonorecords.

For more details about the 1995 act, see Section D.4 of this chapter, *infra*.

QUESTIONS

1. It can probably be demonstrated that the fears of economic monopoly that justified the compulsory license in 1909 were unwarranted in 1976, when the new Copyright Act was passed. Given the control normally allowed by law to the copyright owner over the commercial exploitation of his or her work, is the fact that the recording industry is accustomed to operating under the compulsory license sufficient reason to preserve it in the current law? Are there other reasons that counsel retention of the compulsory license?

2.   Assume that a raunchy recording ensemble (whom we shall call 3 Dead Rats) records its version of a successful love ballad, which incorporates speed-ups, hiccoughs and more scatological sounds, ambulance sirens, and the like; this version becomes quite popular, and many phonorecords are sold and considerable airtime given. If Rats tender the statutory royalty for each record sold, have they infringed? If so, is that a sound result? If the infringement is outside the statutory license granted by § 115, is there some other section or principle on which Rats might rely? *See Campbell v. Acuff–Rose, infra* Chapter 7.B. (Consider later whether the radio stations which play the Rats' record are liable for infringement.)

THE "HARRY FOX LICENSE"

A large number of music publishers/copyright owners have authorized an organization called the Harry Fox Agency to issue licenses on their own behalf for recording their musical compositions onto phonorecords (this recording right, as it developed under the 1909 Act, came to be known as the "mechanical" right). These licenses incorporate variations of the § 115 compulsory license. Harry Fox also licenses other reproduction rights, including synchronization with motion pictures and other audiovisual works (recall that recording a musical composition onto a soundtrack does *not* create a "phonorecord" subject to § 115), and recordings of dramatico-musical material, both of which involve a variety of contractual terms and conditions.

In late 1995, a settlement agreement was announced between, on the one side, the National Music Publishers' Association, Inc. and the Harry Fox Agency, Inc. (which collects "mechanical royalties" on their behalf under § 115), and CompuServe. Internet services provided by such companies as CompuServe, America On–Line and Prodigy had made it possible for subscribers to reproduce and distribute copyrighted music (live or prerecorded) in digital form, to upload that music "file" to bulletin boards for the benefit of other subscribers, and then for those subscribers to download such files and to play them. Since 1998, the music publishers have entered into numerous agreements regarding "digital phonorecord deliveries" (see § 115 as amended in 1995) with websites, authorizing their on-line distribution of musical compositions.

In 2001, the music publishers and the record producers reached an agreement to extend the mechanical recording license to cover copies made as part of an on-demand digital audio stream or time-limited download. The copies covered include the "server copy" from which the audio stream emanates, as well as transient copies made in the course of communicating the music to the user, and the "buffer copies" made in the user's computer as part of the transmission. The license agreement states that the parties agree that the section 115 compulsory license applies to on-demand streaming music services; do you agree with this interpretation? What does it imply about the characterization of this kind of communication? See *infra*, this chapter, subsection D.6: "When Is a Public Performance/Display (Not) Also a Reproduction and Distribution of Copies?"

b.   REPRODUCTION RIGHTS IN SOUND RECORDINGS

Returning to the distinction between a recorded composition (usually musical) and the recorded performance of such composition, let us now consider the scope of the reproduction right of the copyright owner of a sound recording.

Section 114 expressly limits the rights of the owner in such works to protection against recordings "that directly or indirectly recapture the actual sounds fixed in the [protected] recording." The provision does not prevent a recording "that consists entirely of an independent fixation of other sounds, even though such sounds imitate or simulate those in the copyrighted sound recording." Thus imitation through an independent recording is permitted, but capturing the fixed sounds by re-recording—even with some technical changes—can still amount to infringement.

One prominent example of recapture of a sound recording's actual fixed sounds is the practice of "sound sampling." Sound sampling involves the exact duplication of portions (often very small portions, for example, a few beats of music played on a saxophone) of a sound recording for inclusion with other similarly acquired sounds into a new sound recording, or in a live performance. The resulting effect can be like an aural collage. Another form of sound sampling involves the reproduction through digital recording of small portions of a sound recording, followed by their analysis and reconstruction by computer. The computer synthesizer can extrapolate full musical or percussive lines from just a few sounds.

Although sound sampling techniques may subsequently alter the quality of the sounds recorded, this alone should not excuse the sound sampler from any copyright liability that would otherwise exist. Section 114 affords the sound recording copyright holder exclusive rights both over exact reproductions and over works "in which the actual sounds fixed are rearranged, remixed, or otherwise altered in sequence or quality." Of course, digital-sampling litigation—particularly when what is sampled is arguably *de minimis*—will likely raise such questions as whether the plaintiff has contributed original authorship and whether the defendant has made a fair use. One court has held that the repetition of three sampled words and their accompanying music constituted qualitatively significant copying and, therefore, infringement. See *Grand Upright Music Ltd. v. Warner Bros. Records, Inc.*, 780 F.Supp. 182 (S.D.N.Y.1991) (sampling the phrase and tune "Alone Again, Naturally" as performed by Gilbert O'Sullivan.); *see also Williams v. Broadus*, 60 U.S.P.Q.2d 1051 (S.D.N.Y.2001) (question of fact whether sampling 2 of 54 musical measures, consisting of opening 10 notes, is "substantial" copying). *See generally* Carl A. Falstrom, *Thou Shalt Not Steal: Grand Upright Music Ltd. v. Warner Bros. Records Inc. and the Future of Digital Sound Sampling in Popular Music,* 45 Hastings L.J. 359 (1994); Bruce McGiverin, Note,

Digital Sound Sampling, Copyright and Publicity: Protecting Against the Electronic Appropriation of Sounds, 87 Colum. L. Rev. 1723 (1987); James P. Allen, *Look What They've Done to My Song Ma—Digital Sampling in the '90s: A Legal Challenge for the Music Industry,* 9 U. Miami Ent. & Sports L. Rev. 179 (1992).

Until 1995, the scope of copyright in a sound recording excluded the public performance right, i.e., the right to control or be compensated for broadcast or other public performance of a genuine sound recording. With the Digital Performance Right in Sound Recordings Act of 1995, and its expansion by the 1998 Digital Millennium Copyright Act, sound recording copyright owners now enjoy the rights to receive compensation for certain digital performances, and to prohibit others. We will examine the details of this legislation *infra* Section D of this chapter, on the public performance right.

QUESTION

Is a sound recording a "writing" subject to protection by Congress under the copyright clause of the Constitution? Is there an "author" of a sound recording, for purposes of the Constitution? Who is the owner of copyright in a sound recording? (This will determine such matters as the duration of protection and whose name is placed in the notice of copyright. Review the appropriate sections of the Act.)

PRIVATE COPYING OF SOUND RECORDINGS

For the first time in U.S. copyright law, Congress in October 1992 enacted legislation specifically addressing the problem of private copying. The legislation is limited in scope, but may afford a first step toward broader regulation of reproductions of copyrighted works by individuals for their private enjoyment. The legislation was spurred by the development of a new private copying medium, digital audiotape, whose superior recording capabilities prompted songwriters and sound-recording producers to fear that private copies would substantially displace sales of authorized recordings. Unlike analog tape, digital tape permits an apparently infinite number of "generations" of copies (copies from copies from copies), without loss of sound quality from copy to copy.

The Audio Home Recording Act of 1992 [AHRA] both adapts copyright law and imposes a "technological fix." It contains three main features: First, it expressly prohibits infringement actions "based on the noncommercial use by a consumer of a [digital audio recording device or an analog recording] device or medium for making digital or analog musical recordings." *See* § 1008. The Act defines a "digital audio recording device" as one "the digital recording function of which is designed or marketed for the primary purpose of, and that is capable of, making a digital audio copied recording for private use . . ." *See* § 1001(3).

Second, in return, it imposes royalty charges upon sales of digital audiotape recorders and recording media (i.e., blank tapes), to be paid by manufacturers and importers. *See* §§ 1003–1004 (Note that there is no such surcharge on analog recording equipment or media.) Those royalties are then to be divided between two "Funds." *See* § 1006(b). One-third of the sums collected are marked for the "Musical Works Fund," for the benefit of "writers" (composers and lyricists) and music publishers, and the remaining two-thirds for the "Sound Recordings Fund," for record producers and performers. Royalties in the Musical Works Fund are divided evenly between writers and publishers. Within the Sound Recordings Fund, an initial 4% of the revenues will go to nonfeatured musicians and vocalists; the remaining sums will be divided 40% to featured performers and 60% to record producers. The beneficiaries of the Funds receive the royalties not only for digital recordings, but for analog recordings as well.

The first distribution of royalties pursuant to the AHRA consolidated the royalties from 1992 through 1994 and was determined principally by settlement among the parties and in small part by a proceeding before a Copyright Arbitration Royalty Panel, which was in turn reviewed (for arbitrariness) by the Copyright Office and finally by the Librarian of Congress. The total amount of royalties distributed for those years was not overwhelming: some $350,000 to the Musical Works Fund and slightly more than $1 million to the Sound Recordings Fund. By the year 2000, the total distribution of AHRA royalties had increased to some $5.4 million. (Sales of digital recording machines and blank tapes have been less than initially projected.)

The third principal feature of the AHRA is that the Act obliges manufacturers and importers to include in all consumer digital audio recording devices a "serial copy management system" (SCMS) that would disable the machines from recording a copy from a prior copy (but would permit unlimited "first generation" recordings from the original recorded source). The law also prohibits selling devices or offering services to override the SCMS. *See* § 1002.

In what appears to be the first case to arise under the AHRA's SCMS requirement, the Recording Industry Association of America (RIAA) sought to restrain the dissemination of the "Rio" digital recording device. The Rio is a handheld playback device that permits the storage of up to 60 minutes of compressed music files that are on the hard drive of a personal computer, and then transferred (by a cable) to the Rio's memory. Some of the files on the hard drive may have been "ripped" from CDs that the user records into her computer, others may have been downloaded from recorded music that has been placed—some lawfully and some unlawfully—on the Internet. The Rio is incapable of receiving audio files from anything other than a personal computer, and its sole output is an analog audio signal sent to the user via headphones. The Rio cannot make duplicates of any digital audio file it stores, nor can it transfer or upload such a file to a computer or to another device (including another Rio).

The RIAA asserted that the Rio was a "digital audio recording device" under the AHRA, which unlawfully neglects to incorporate a Serial Copy Management System and whose manufacturer and distributor failed to pay the royalties for each device sold. The district judge found the Rio to be a "digital audio recording device," defined in § 1001(3) as "any machine or device . . . the digital recording function of which is designed or marketed for the primary purpose of, and that is capable of, making a digital audio copied recording for private use." She nonetheless declined to issue an injunction principally because of the inability of the Rio to make further recordings (whether or not encoded with an SCMS).

The Court of Appeals for the Ninth Circuit, however, concluded—more favorably to the manufacturer Diamond Multimedia Systems, Inc.—that the Rio was not a "digital audio recording device" at all. The principal focus was on the Rio's capability to record only from a computer hard drive. The court held the latter not to be a "digital musical recording" (§ 1005(1)(A)), so that the musical sounds that are transferred to the Rio are not "digital audio copied recordings" (§ 1001(1)), so that in turn the Rio is not a "digital audio recording device." (The student should carefully examine the pertinent definitions, and should attempt to assess whether the court correctly interpreted them all.) The court also pointed out that the purpose of the AHRA was to restrict generations of copied digital music, and that "the Rio does not permit such further copies to be made because it simply cannot download or transmit the files that it stores to any other device. Thus, The Rio without SCMS inherently allows less copying than SCMA permits." Moreover, the Rio fosters the main purpose of the Act, the facilitation of personal use of recorded music: "The Rio merely makes copies in order to render portable, or 'space-shift,' those files that already reside on a user's hard drive. . . . Such copying is paradigmatic noncommercial personal use." *Recording Indus. Ass'n of Am. v. Diamond Multimedia Sys., Inc.*, 180 F.3d 1072 (9th Cir.1999).

When a song recording that unlawfully resides on the Internet is downloaded to the hard drive of a personal computer, is there an infringement? Must the computer incorporate an SCMS, or generate a royalty payment to the song copyright owners and performers? If the Rio cannot make additional phonorecords of recorded music, why should the RIAA seek to prevent its dissemination? (Reconsider this question after reviewing the note *infra* on "Digital Phonorecord Deliveries.")

Is making a personal digital copy by "ripping" a CD to a user's hard drive an activity shielded by AHRA § 1008? What about sending the ripped file to a friend? What about making the file available to participants in a file-sharing program, such as Napster? (For more on the Napster controversy, see *infra* Chapters 7 and 8.)

————

In the 1998 "Digital Millennium Copyright Act," Congress returned to the AHRA's approach to technological responses to private copying. Under the DMCA, the works at issue are not sound recordings, but audiovisual works. A new § 1201(k) addresses the problem of home videotaping by prohibiting the manufacture and distribution of certain analog videocassette recorders unless the recorders are equipped with a designated copy control technology.*

The copy control technology will work in tandem with audiovisual works and transmissions that have been encoded to prevent or limit consumer copying. Section 1201(k), however, restricts the circumstances under which a copyright owner or other person may encode the audiovisual work or transmission. These are limited to: transmissions of live events; transmissions of audiovisual works delivered on a pay-per-view basis; copies of transmissions of live events or of audiovisual works made available through a subscription to a television channel (be it herzian, cable, or satellite); "physical media containing one or more prerecorded audiovisual works"; and copies of transmissions of live events or of pay-per-view motion picture transmissions, or copies made from a physical medium containing prerecorded audiovisual works.** This means, for example, that the producer of the (fictitious) motion picture "It Came From the Titanic" may distribute encoded copies of videocassettes, and if a purchasing or renting consumer attempts to make an extra copy using a videocassette recorder that conforms to § 1202(k), then the anticopying technology incorporated in the recorder will produce an extremely degraded quality copy. It also means that if "It Came From the Titanic" is transmitted on pay-per-view, the producer may encode the transmission so that the consumer will be able to view the film at the time requested, but if she attempts to use a conforming videocassette machine to tape the film as it is being transmitted, the quality of the resulting copy will be too low to be worth viewing. By contrast, the copyright owner or broadcaster may *not* encode programs broadcast over television stations to which access is available without payment. Thus, consumers may continue to time-shift (or even retain) copies of "free" television programming. A good deal of home taping (particularly that which most competes with the marketing of the audiovisual work) will no longer be possible.

DIGITAL PHONORECORD DELIVERIES

Communication of recorded musical and other works over digital networks, for example the Internet, results in a "digital phonorecord delivery." *See* 17 U.S.C.A. § 115(c)(3). Where the communication of a musical work is authorized, the 1995 and 1998 amendments to the Copyright Act extend the § 115 compulsory license to digital transmissions of a recorded musical work under circumstances that we will explore in Subchapter D, *infra*, in connection with the public performance right. (As we

---

* *See* § 1201(k)(1)(A) (18 months from the Digital Millennium Copyright Act's effective date (Oct. 28, 1998), all affected devices must be equipped with "automatic gain control"); § 1201(k)(1)(B) (as of Oct. 28, 2000, the manufacturers of any extant devices that currently conform to automatic gain control or "four-line colorstripe copy control technol-ogy" must not modify devices so that they no longer so conform, and any affected device manufactured or sold as of DMCA's effective date must conform to four-line colorstripe technology).

** § 1201(k)(2).

shall see, digital media tend to merge copyright rights, such as reproduction and public performance, that once were thought distinct.) Where the communication is not authorized, however, the availability of the work for downloading through the Internet implicates copyright claims not only in the musical (or other recorded) works but also in the copyrighted sound recordings. For example, consider a website that, without authorization, catalogues and delivers full recordings of high quality to subscribers with appropriate software. In this situation, the recordings are stored on the website's computer file server (i.e., an unauthorized reproduction), from which the user can download recordings (another reproduction) and to which the user may upload recordings (another reproduction) not already in the website catalogue. This scenario implicates more than the reproduction right; as we will see in Subchapters C and D *infra*, the exclusive rights to distribute the work in copies or phonorecords under § 106(3), and to publicly perform the works under § 106(4) are also called into play. Because the same act of digital communication of works can implicate formerly distinct rights under copyright, it may become increasingly necessary to determine whether all those rights must be cleared. In addition to requiring an assessment of which exclusive rights are most properly at issue in a given communication, this scenario poses the practical problem of determining how, and against whom, the copyright owner may enforce its exclusive rights. We will defer further consideration of these problems to Subchapters C and D, and to Chapter 8 on Enforcement of Copyright.

B. THE RIGHT TO PREPARE DERIVATIVE WORKS UNDER § 106(2)

§ 106. Exclusive Rights in Copyrighted Works

Subject to sections 107 through 121, the owner of copyright under this title has the exclusive rights to do and to authorize any of the following:

. . .

(2) to prepare derivative works based upon the copyrighted work: . . . .

House Report

H.R. Rep. No. 94–1476, 94th Cong., 2d Sess. 62 (1976).

Preparation of derivative works.—The exclusive right to prepare derivative works, specified separately in clause (2) of section 106, overlaps the exclusive right of reproduction to some extent. It is broader than that right, however, in the sense that reproduction requires fixation in copies or phonorecords, whereas the preparation of a derivative work, such as a ballet, pantomime, or improvised performance, may be an infringement even though nothing is ever fixed in tangible form.

To be an infringement the "derivative work" must be "based upon the copyrighted work," and the definition in section 101 refers to "a translation, musical arrangement, dramatization, fictionalization, motion picture version, sound recording, art reproduction, abridgment, condensation, or any other form in which a work may be recast, transformed, or adapted." Thus, to constitute a violation of section 106(2), the infringing work must incorporate a portion of the copyrighted work in some form; for example, a detailed commentary on a work or a programmatic musical composition inspired by a novel would not normally constitute infringements under this clause.

Chafee, Reflections on Copyright Law, 45 Columbia Law Review 503, 511 (1945)

The protection given the copyright-owner should not stifle independent creation by others. Nobody else should *market* the author's book, but we refuse to say nobody else should *use* it. The world goes ahead because each of us builds on the work of our predecessors. "A dwarf standing on the shoulders of a giant can see farther than the giant himself." Progress would be stifled if the author had a complete monopoly of everything in his book for fifty-six years or any other long period. Some use of its contents must be permitted in connection with the independent creation of other authors. The very policy which leads the law to encourage his creativeness also justifies it in facilitating the creativeness of others.

In the late eighteenth century, this ideal of the encouragement of independent creation was pushed so far as to allow translations and abridgments without the author's consent, on the ground that the new man had put in a great deal of his own work. Thus Lord Apsley, backed by Blackstone, gave immunity to an abridgment of Hawksworth's *Voyages,* calling it "a new and meritorious work," less expensive and more convenient to handle than the original; he said it could be read in a quarter of the time with all the substance preserved in language as good as Hawksworth's or better and in a more agreeable and useful manner. This sort of reasoning made Dr. Johnson's blood boil. During the *Tour to the Hebrides,* Boswell mentioned Lord Monboddo's opinion, that if a man could get a work by heart, he might print it, as by such an act "the mind is exercised."

> Johnson: "No, sir, a man's repeating it no more makes it his property than a man may sell a cow which he drives home."

> I said printing an abridgment of a work was allowed, which was only cutting the horns and tail off the cow.

> Johnson: "No, sir, 'tis making the cow have a calf."

... The author should not lose a large portion of his market so easily. Fortunately, our copyright law has abandoned its early tolerance of unauthorized abridgments and translations. They are ways for the author to reach the public and properly belong to him, as the 1909 Act expressly recognizes.

Even when there is access, the precise boundaries of this defensive ideal of independent creation are hard to fix. Everybody agrees that the ideas in the copyrighted book are not protected. Another physicist can read Einstein's book and write about relativity. But he must not tell about it in Einstein's words. Should protection be limited to the precise words? If so, a translation, which uses entirely different words, would not infringe. Yet, if we protect more than precise words, where shall we stop? The line is sometimes drawn between an idea and its expression. This does not solve the problem, because "expression" has too wide a range. To some extent, the expression of an abstract idea should be free for use by others. No doubt, the line does lie somewhere between the author's idea and the precise form in which he wrote it down. I like to say that the protection covers the "pattern" of the work. This is not a solution, but I find it helpful as an imaginative description of what should not be imitated. For example, the idea of an Irish–Jewish marriage in a play may be borrowed. With this theme, some resemblance in characters and situations is inevitable, but the line of infringement may not yet be crossed. On the other hand, the pattern of the play—the sequence of events and the development of the interplay of the characters—must not be followed scene by scene. Such a correspondence of pattern would be an infringement although every word of the spoken dialogue was changed.

Even the first user of a plot or a human situation should not have a monopoly of it. The public should have the opportunity to see what other artists will do with the same plot or situation, after the fashion set by the Greek tragedians. Yet we want to encourage originality and not slavishness. There comes a point where the use of material is so close as not to give the public anything really new. At that point, the ideal of encouraging independent creation ceases to operate.

1.   THE SCOPE OF THE DERIVATIVE WORKS RIGHT

Horgan v. Macmillan, Inc.

789 F.2d 157 (2d Cir.1986).

[The plaintiff is executrix of the estate of George Balanchine, a giant in the field of twentieth-century choreography, who died in April 1983. Balanchine co-founded the New York City Ballet in 1948, and was its director, ballet master and chief choreographer. In 1954, he choreographed his version of the ballet, The Nutcracker, set to music by Tchaikovsky; the ballet is an adaptation of a nineteenth century folk tale and an earlier choreographic version by the Russian Ivanov. The "Balanchine Nutcracker" has been performed to great popular acclaim by the New York City Ballet Company and other ballet companies throughout the world; royalties were paid to Balanchine for these performances. The defendants in this action are the publisher Macmillan, two photographers, and an author (Switzer); all collaborated on a book titled "The Nutcracker: A Story and a Ballet." The book tells of the origins of The Nutcracker as a story and as a ballet, and devotes most of its pages to what is labeled "The Balanchine Ballet." It contains sixty color photographs of scenes from the Company's production of The Nutcracker, following the sequence of the ballet's story and dances; a text is interspersed providing the story including those portions not portrayed visually. The defendants were authorized by the New York City Ballet to create and publish the book. No consent, however, was secured from the Balanchine estate, which brought this action for copyright infringement, seeking preliminary and permanent injunctive relief.

District court:
Pictures don't
infringe choreography/

[The district judge ruled against the Balanchine estate. He found no infringement of the ballet because "choreography has to do with the flow of the steps in a ballet. The still photographs in the Nutcracker book, numerous though they are, catch dancers in various attitudes at specific instants of time; they do not, nor do they intend to, take or use the underlying choreography. The staged performance could not be recreated from them." The court drew an analogy to the inability to recreate a Beethoven symphony from a document containing only every twenty-fifth chord of the symphony.

From Switzer, The Nutcracker: A Story and a Ballet (1985)

[The court of appeals reversed and remanded. It reiterated the plaintiff's claim that the book was either a "copy" of the Balanchine choreographic work or a derivative work based thereon; and that in either case the test was whether there was "substantial similarity" and not whether the ballet could be reconstructed from the plaintiff's book. The defendants argued that the book could not possibly be substantially similar to the ballet because the essence of choreography is movement, which cannot be reproduced from pictures capturing only a fraction of an instant in time. Noting that this was a case of first impression, the court of appeals agreed with the plaintiff. The central part of its discussion follows.]

[T]he standard for determining copyright infringement is not whether the original could be recreated from the allegedly infringing copy, but whether the latter is "substantially similar" to the former. The test, as stated by Judge Learned Hand in *Peter Pan,* is whether "the ordinary observer, unless he set out to detect the disparities, would be disposed to overlook them, and regard their aesthetic appeal as the same."

When the allegedly infringing material is in a different medium, as it is here, recreation of the original from the infringing material is unlikely if not impossible, but that is not a defense to infringement. It surely would not be a defense to an infringement claim against the movie version of "Gone With The Wind" that a viewer of the movie could not recreate the book. Even a small amount of the original, if it is qualitatively significant, may be sufficient to be an infringement, although the full original could not be recreated from the excerpt. See, e.g., *Roy Export Co. Establishment v. Columbia Broadcasting System, Inc.,* 503 F. Supp. 1137, 1145 (S.D.N.Y. 1980), *aff'd,* 672 F.2d 1095 (2d Cir.), *cert. denied,* 459 U.S. 826, 103 S. Ct. 60, 74 L. Ed. 2d 63 (1982), and *Elsmere Music, Inc. v. National Broadcasting Co.,* 482 F. Supp. 741, 744 (S.D.N.Y.), *aff'd,* 623 F.2d 252 (2d Cir.1980). In the former case, short film clips used in a film memorial to Charlie Chaplin were held to infringe full length films. In the latter, the use of four notes from a musical composition containing one hundred measures was held sufficient to infringe the copyrighted original.

Moreover, the district judge took a far too limited view of the extent to which choreographic material may be conveyed in the medium of still photography. A snapshot of a single moment in a dance sequence may communicate a great deal. It may, for example, capture a gesture, the composition of dancers' bodies or the placement of dancers on the stage. Such freezing of a choreographic moment is shown in a number of the photographs in the Switzer book, e.g., at pp. 30, 38, 42, 66–67, 68, 69, 74, 75, 78, 80, and 81. A photograph may also convey to the viewer's imagination the moments before and after the split second recorded. On page 76–77 of the Switzer book, for example, there is a two-page photograph of the "Sugar Canes," one of the troupes that perform in The Nutcracker. In this photograph, the Sugar Canes are a foot or more off the ground, holding large hoops above their heads. One member of the ensemble is jumping through a hoop, which is held extended in front of the dancer. The dancer's legs are thrust forward, parallel to the stage and several feet off the ground. The viewer understands instinctively, based simply on the laws of gravity, that the Sugar Canes jumped up from the floor only a moment earlier, and came down shortly after the photographed moment. An ordinary observer, who had only recently seen a performance of The Nutcracker, could probably perceive even more from this photograph. The single instant thus communicates far more than a single chord of a Beethoven symphony—the analogy suggested by the district judge.

It may be that all of the photographs mentioned above are of insufficient quantity or sequencing to constitute infringement; it may also be that they do copy but also are protected as fair use. But that is not what the district judge said in denying a preliminary injunction. The judge errone-ously held that still photographs cannot infringe choreography. Since the judge applied the wrong test in evaluating appellant's likelihood of success on the preliminary injunction, we believe that a remand is appropriate. . . .

QUESTIONS

Are the following uses of a copyrighted work an infringement? If so, under what subsection of the 1976 Act?

1. *X* secures a copy of the copyrighted motion picture film of the assassination of President Kennedy, taken at the scene by Abraham Zapru-der, and makes a direct copy of the film.

2. *X*, a few feet away from Mr. Zapruder at the time of the assassina-tion, films exactly the same sequence of events with his own motion picture camera.

3. *X* re-poses Oscar Wilde to match the Sarony photograph and takes his own still photograph, this one in color. (Assume for the purpose of the example that Wilde is alive and that the Sarony photograph is still in copyright.)

4. *X*, seeing an attractive copyrighted photograph of the Golden Gate Bridge at sunset, positions himself at the same location and time and takes his own still photograph.

5. An artist paints a cubistic version of the (copyrighted) Sarony photograph of Oscar Wilde.

6. A sculptor makes a three-dimensional version of a copyrighted painting.

7. A novelist sees a copyrighted silent motion picture and writes a novel recounting all of the incidents in the film (and, obviously, supplying original dialogue).

8. A journalist writing for a competing news weekly takes a news story from *Time* magazine and rewrites it for publication in his own words.

9. An artist creates unauthorized illustrations for a book, giving visual form to, while closely following, the meticulous verbal descriptions of the characters and scenery.

10. A writer creates a detailed verbal description of a painting.

11. Assume that, without authorization, a company runs the illustra-tions below in an advertisement. The ad is inspired by the lyrics to the Rodgers and Hammerstein song "My Favorite Things," from their well-known musical show *The Sound of Music*. ("Raindrops on roses, and whiskers on kittens. Bright copper kettles and warm woolen mittens. Brown paper packages tied up with strings. These are a few of my favorite things.") The illustrations are accompanied by text stating: "If these are a few of your favorite things, then you'll love shopping at Country Home

Furniture Stores.'' Assess the claim of the Rodgers and Hammerstein licensing organization for copyright infringement.

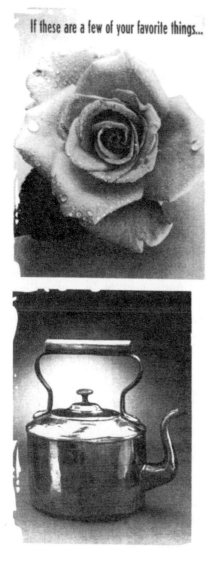

...Then you'll love shopping at
Country Home Furniture Stores!

12.   Paramount Pictures Corporation produces motion pictures and distributes them by means that include videocassettes sold and rented by stores to retail customers. These videos contain several feet of tape as "lead-ins" to the featured film. Paramount places on those lead-ins warnings against use of the film in a manner that would violate the Copyright Act, as well as advertisements for others of its films and for commercial products. It has brought an action against Video Ads, a company that produces audiovisual advertising material for its clients and inserts that advertising onto the lead-ins of videocassettes supplied to Video Ads by local video stores; the client pays Video Ads, which in turn pays a smaller amount to the stores that turn over the videocassettes (which have been lawfully purchased by the stores). Paramount claims that the inserted commercials at the beginning of the tapes of its copyrighted motion pictures constitute a copyright infringement. How would you decide the case? *See Paramount Pictures Corp. v. Video Broadcasting Sys.*, 724 F.Supp. 808 (D.Kan.1989).

Micro Star v. Formgen Inc.

154 F.3d 1107 (9th Cir.1998).

■ KOZINSKI, CIRCUIT JUDGE.

Duke Nukem routinely vanquishes Octabrain and the Protozoid Slimer. But what about the dreaded Micro Star?

I

FormGen Inc., ... made, distributed and own the rights to Duke Nukem 3D (D/N–3D), an immensely popular (and very cool) computer game. D/N–3D is played from the first-person perspective; the player assumes the personality and point of view of the title character, who is seen on the screen only as a pair of hands and an occasional boot, much as one might see oneself in real life without the aid of a mirror. Players explore a futuristic city infested with evil aliens and other hazards. The goal is to zap them before they zap you, while searching for the hidden passage to the next level. The basic game comes with twenty-nine levels, each with a different combination of scenery, aliens, and other challenges. The game also includes a "Build Editor," a utility that enables players to create their own levels. With FormGen's encouragement, players frequently post levels they have created on the Internet where others can download them. Micro Star, a computer software distributor, did just that: It downloaded 300 user-created levels and stamped them onto a CD, which it then sold commercially as Nuke It (N/I). . . .

Micro Star filed suit in district court, seeking a declaratory judgment that N/I did not infringe on any of FormGen's copyrights. FormGen counterclaimed, seeking a preliminary injunction barring further production and distribution of N/I. Relying on *Lewis Galoob Toys, Inc. v. Nintendo of Am., Inc.*, 964 F.2d 965 (9th Cir.1992), the district court held that N/I was not a derivative work and therefore did not infringe FormGen's copyright. . . .

According to FormGen, the audiovisual displays generated when D/N–3D is run in conjunction with the N/I CD MAP files are derivative works that infringe this exclusivity. Is FormGen right? The answer is not obvious.

. . . The statutory language [defining a derivative work] is hopelessly overbroad, . . . for "every book in literature, science and art, borrows and must necessarily borrow, and use much which was well known and used before." *Emerson v. Davies*, 8 F. Cas. 615, 619 (C.C.D.Mass.1845) (No. 4436), quoted in 1 Nimmer on Copyright, § 3.01, at 3–2 (1997). To narrow the statute to a manageable level, we have developed certain criteria a work must satisfy in order to qualify as a derivative work. One of these is that a derivative work must exist in a "concrete or permanent form," *Galoob*, 964 F.2d at 967 (internal quotation marks omitted), and must substantially incorporate protected material from the preexisting work, see *Litchfield v. Spielberg*, 736 F.2d 1352, 1357 (9th Cir.1984). Micro Star argues that N/I is not a derivative work because the audiovisual displays generated when D/N–3D is run with N/I's MAP files are not incorporated in any concrete or permanent form, and the MAP files do not copy any of D/N–3D's protected expression. It is mistaken on both counts.

The requirement that a derivative work must assume a concrete or permanent form was recognized without much discussion in *Galoob*. There, we noted that all the Copyright Act's examples of derivative works took some definite, physical form and concluded that this was a requirement of the Act. . . . Obviously, N/I's MAP files themselves exist in a concrete or permanent form; they are burned onto a CD–ROM. . . . But what about the audiovisual displays generated when D/N–3D runs the N/I MAP files—i.e., the actual game level as displayed on the screen? Micro Star argues that, because the audiovisual displays in *Galoob* didn't meet the "concrete or permanent form" requirement, neither do N/I's.

[handwritten margin note: Criteria for Derivative Work: 1) Fixed 2) substantially Incorporate protected material.]

In *Galoob*, we considered audiovisual displays created using a device called the Game Genie, which was sold for use with the Nintendo Entertainment System. The Game Genie allowed players to alter individual features of a game, such as a character's strength or speed, by selectively "blocking the value for a single data byte sent by the game cartridge to the [Nintendo console] and replacing it with a new value." Players chose which data value to replace by entering a code; over a billion different codes were possible. The Game Genie was dumb; it functioned only as a window into the computer program, allowing players to temporarily modify individual aspects of the game.

Nintendo sued, claiming that when the Game Genie modified the game system's audiovisual display, it created an infringing derivative work. We rejected this claim because "[a] derivative work must incorporate a protected work in some concrete or permanent form." The audiovisual displays generated by combining the Nintendo System with the Game Genie were not incorporated in any permanent form; when the game was over, they were gone. Of course, they could be reconstructed, but only if the next player chose to reenter the same codes.[4]

Micro Star argues that the MAP files on N/I are a more advanced version of the Game Genie, replacing old values (the MAP files in the original game) with new values (N/I's MAP files). But, whereas the audiovisual displays created by Game Genie were never recorded in any permanent form, the audiovisual displays generated by D/N–3D from the N/I MAP files are—in the MAP files themselves. In *Galoob*, the audiovisual display was defined by the original game cartridge, not by the Game Genie; no one could possibly say that the data values inserted by the Game Genie described the audiovisual display. In the present case the audiovisual display that appears on the computer monitor when a N/I level is played is described—in exact detail—by a N/I MAP file.

This raises the interesting question whether an exact, down to the last detail, description of an audiovisual display (and—by definition—we know that MAP files do describe audiovisual displays down to the last detail) counts as a permanent or concrete form for purposes of *Galoob*. We see no reason it shouldn't. What, after all, does sheet music do but describe in precise detail the way a copyrighted melody sounds? ... Similarly, the N/I MAP files describe the audiovisual display that is to be generated when the player chooses to play D/N–3D using the N/I levels. Because the audiovisual

[handwritten margin note: Audiovisual display comes from defendants CD. (MAP files)]

---

4. A low-tech example might aid understanding. Imagine a product called the Pink Screener, which consists of a big piece of pink cellophane stretched over a frame. When put in front of a television, it makes everything on the screen look pinker. Someone who manages to record the programs with this pink cast (maybe by filming the screen) would have created an infringing derivative work. But the audiovisual display observed by a person watching television through the Pink Screener is not a derivative work because it does not incorporate the modified image in any permanent or concrete form. The Game Genie might be described as a fancy Pink Screener for video games, changing a value of the game as perceived by the current player, but never incorporating the new audiovisual display into a permanent or concrete form.

displays assume a concrete or permanent form in the MAP files, *Galoob* stands as no bar to finding that they are derivative works.

. . .

Micro Star further argues that the MAP files are not derivative works because they do not, in fact, incorporate any of D/N–3D's protected expression. In particular, Micro Star makes much of the fact that the N/I MAP files reference the source art library, but do not actually contain any art files themselves. Therefore, it claims, nothing of D/N–3D's is reproduced in the MAP files. In making this argument, Micro Star misconstrues the protected work. The work that Micro Star infringes is the D/N–3D story itself—a beefy commando type named Duke who wanders around post-Apocalypse Los Angeles, shooting Pig Cops with a gun, lobbing hand grenades, searching for medkits and steroids, using a jetpack to leap over obstacles, blowing up gas tanks, avoiding radioactive slime. A copyright owner holds the right to create sequels, see *Trust Co. Bank v. MGM/UA Entertainment Co.*, 772 F.2d 740 (11th Cir.1985), and the stories told in the N/I MAP files are surely sequels, telling new (though somewhat repetitive) tales of Duke's fabulous adventures. A book about Duke Nukem would infringe for the same reason, even if it contained no pictures. . . .

[handwritten margin note: Infringes the story.]

QUESTIONS

1. The Ninth Circuit has ruled that to be a "derivative work," the alteration to the underlying work "must exist in a concrete or permanent form." Does the 1976 Act compel this requirement? The House Report? Is the requirement good policy?

2. In *Galoob*, discussed in *Micro Star*, the Ninth Circuit offered the following as a reason for determining that the "Game Genie" did not create a derivative work when used in conjunction with Nintendo's games:

> In holding that the audiovisual displays created by the Game Genie are not derivative works, we recognize that technology often advances by improvement rather than replacement. Some time ago, for example, computer companies began marketing spell-checkers that operate within existing word processors by signalling the writer when a word is misspelled. These applications, as well as countless others, could not be produced and marketed if courts were to conclude that the audiovisual display of a word processor and spell-checker combination is a derivative work based on the display of the word processor alone. The Game Genie is useless by itself; it can only enhance, and cannot duplicate, a Nintendo game's output. Such innovations rarely will constitute derivative works under the Copyright Act.

Do you see any problems with this reasoning?

3. To create Nuke It (N/I), Micro Star "downloaded 300 user-created Duke Nukem levels and stamped them onto a CD which it then sold commercially. . . . " In addition to the matters discussed in the Ninth Circuit's opinion, do any other infringement issues occur to you?

4. Assume that a highly regarded teacher of high school physics prepares a book with text and problems which quickly becomes the bestselling work in the field. Another teacher publishes a pamphlet advertised as a book of solutions to the problems in the copyrighted text. In the pamphlet, the problems are not copied; the solutions consist of arithmetic equations, which show how the problem should be solved (utilizing, of course, the numbers used in the copyrighted textbook problems), and they are accompanied where possible with diagrams (also utilizing the same numbers). Do the solutions infringe the copyright on the problem book? *See Addison–Wesley Pub'g Co. v. Brown*, 223 F.Supp. 219 (E.D.N.Y.1963).

5. Plaintiff Worlds of Wonder, Inc. manufactures the Teddy Ruxpin doll. The doll, shaped like a bear, has inside it a tape-playing mechanism attached to certain motors in the doll's eyes, nose and mouth. Audiotapes manufactured by W.O.W. and sold with Teddy have two tracks, one with sound and the other with digital information transmitted to the motors that move Teddy's face so that its movements are synchronized with the stories and songs emanating from the tape. The tape communicates a high-pitched male voice purporting to be that of Teddy Ruxpin. The doll has been enormously successful and in its first year has topped 1.5 million sales, or $93 million.

Defendant Veritel manufactures audiotapes for the exclusive purpose of utilization of the innards of Teddy Ruxpin. On the audio track, a high-pitched male voice tells stories (based on fairy tales) altogether different from those told on the W.O.W. tapes. Electromechanical impulses from the other track activate the Teddy Ruxpin bear in the same manner as do the W.O.W. tapes. When the Veritel tapes are inserted, Teddy's voice and movements are very much the same as when the W.O.W. tapes are used.

W.O.W. has placed proper copyright notice on its Teddy Ruxpin dolls and has registered them in the Copyright Office. (What category of work in § 102 is appropriate?) It has sued to enjoin Veritel from marketing tapes as described above. Who should prevail? *See Worlds of Wonder, Inc. v. Vector Intercontinental, Inc.*, 653 F.Supp. 135 (N.D.Ohio 1986); *Worlds of Wonder, Inc. v. Veritel Learning Sys.*, 658 F.Supp. 351 (N.D.Tex.1986).

Lee v. A.R.T. Co.

125 F.3d 580 (7th Cir.1997).

■ EASTERBROOK, Circuit Judge.

Annie Lee creates works of art, which she sells through her firm Annie Lee & Friends. Deck the Walls, a chain of outlets for modestly priced art, is among the buyers of her works, which have been registered with the Register of Copyrights. One Deck the Walls store sold some of Lee's notecards and small lithographs to A.R.T. Company, which mounted the works on ceramic tiles (covering the art with transparent epoxy resin in the process) and resold the tiles. Lee contends that these tiles are derivative works, which under 17 U.S.C.A. § 106(2) may not be prepared without the permission of the copyright proprietor. She seeks both monetary and injunctive relief. Her position has the support of two cases holding that A.R.T.'s business violates the copyright laws. *Munoz v. Albuquerque A.R.T. Co.*, 38 F.3d 1218 (9th Cir.1994), *aff'g without published opinion*, 829 F. Supp. 309 (D.Alaska 1993); *Mirage Editions, Inc. v. Albuquerque A.R.T. Co.*, 856 F.2d 1341 (9th Cir.1988). *Mirage Editions*, the only full appellate discussion, dealt with pages cut from books and mounted on tiles; the court of appeals' brief order in *Munoz* concludes that the reasoning of *Mirage Editions* is equally applicable to works of art that were sold loose. Our district court disagreed with these decisions and entered summary judgment for the defendant. 925 F. Supp. 576 (N.D.Ill.1996).

Now one might suppose that this is an open and shut case under the doctrine of first sale, codified at 17 U.S.C. § 109(a). A.R.T. bought the work legitimately, mounted it on a tile, and resold what it had purchased. Because the artist could capture the value of her art's contribution to the finished product as part of the price for the original transaction, the economic rationale for protecting an adaptation as "derivative" is absent. *See* William M. Landes & Richard A. Posner, *An Economic Analysis of Copyright Law*, 17 J. Legal Studies 325, 353–57 (1989). An alteration that includes (or consumes) a complete copy of the original lacks economic significance. One work changes hands multiple times, exactly what § 109(a) permits, so it may lack legal significance too. But § 106(2) creates a separate exclusive right, to "prepare derivative works", and Lee believes that affixing the art to the tile is "preparation," so that A.R.T. would have violated § 106(2) even if it had dumped the finished tiles into the Marianas Trench. For the sake of argument we assume that this is so and ask whether card-on-a-tile is a "derivative work" in the first place. . . .

[margin note: First Sale]

The district court concluded that A.R.T.'s mounting of Lee's works on tile is not an "original work of authorship" because it is no different in form or function from displaying a painting in a frame or placing a medallion in a velvet case. No one believes that a museum violates § 106(2) every time it changes the frame of a painting that is still under copyright, although the choice of frame or glazing affects the impression the art conveys, and many artists specify frames (or pedestals for sculptures) in detail. *Munoz* and *Mirage Editions* acknowledge that framing and other traditional means of mounting and displaying art do not infringe authors' exclusive right to make derivative works. Nonetheless, the Ninth Circuit held, what A.R.T. does creates a derivative work because the epoxy resin bonds the art to the tile. Our district judge thought this a distinction without a difference, and we agree. If changing the way in which a work of art will be displayed creates a derivative work, and if Lee is right about what "prepared" means, then the derivative work is "prepared" when the art is mounted; what happens later is not relevant, because the violation of the § 106(2) right has already occurred. If the framing process does not create a derivative work, then mounting art on a tile, which serves as a flush frame, does not create a derivative work. . . .

Lee wages a vigorous attack on the district court's conclusion that A.R.T.'s mounting process cannot create a derivative work because the change to the work "as a whole" is not sufficiently original to support a copyright. Cases such as *Gracen v. The Bradford Exchange, Inc.*, 698 F.2d 300 (7th Cir.1983), show that neither A.R.T. nor Lee herself could have obtained a copyright in the card-on-a-tile, thereby not only extending the period of protection for the images but also eliminating competition in one medium of display. After the Ninth Circuit held that its mounting process created derivative works, A.R.T. tried to obtain a copyright in one of its products; the Register of Copyrights sensibly informed A.R.T. that the card-on-a-tile could not be copyrighted independently of the note card itself. But Lee says that this is irrelevant—that a change in a work's appearance may infringe the exclusive right under § 106(2) even if the alteration is too trivial to support an independent copyright. Pointing to the word "original" in the second sentence of the statutory definition, the district judge held that "originality" is essential to a derivative work. This understanding has the support of both cases and respected commentators. *E.g., L. Batlin & Son, Inc. v. Snyder*, 536 F.2d 486 (2d Cir.1976); Melville B. Nimmer & David Nimmer, 1 Nimmer on Copyright § 3.03 (1997). Pointing to the fact that the first sentence in the statutory definition omits any reference to originality, Lee insists that a work may be derivative despite the mechanical nature of the transformation. This view, too, has the support of both cases and respected commentators. E.g., *Lone Ranger Television, Inc. v. Program Radio Corp.*, 740 F.2d 718, 722 (9th Cir.1984); Paul Goldstein, Copyright: Principles, Law and Practice § 5.3.1 (2d ed. 1996) (suggesting that a transformation is covered by § 106(2) whenever it creates a "new work for a different market").

Fortunately, it is not necessary for us to choose sides. Assume for the moment that the first sentence recognizes a set of non-original derivative works. To prevail, then, Lee must show that A.R.T. altered her works in one of the ways mentioned in the first sentence. The tile is not an "art reproduction"; A.R.T. purchased and mounted Lee's original works. That leaves the residual clause: "any other form in which a work may be recast, transformed, or adapted." None of these words fits what A.R.T. did. Lee's works were not "recast" or "adapted". "Transformed" comes closer and gives the Ninth Circuit some purchase for its view that the permanence of the bond between art and base matters. Yet the copyrighted note cards and lithographs were not "transformed" in the slightest. The art was bonded to a slab of ceramic, but it was not changed in the process. It still depicts exactly what it depicted when it left Lee's studio. See William F. Patry, Copyright Law and Practice 823–24 (1994) (disapproving *Mirage Editions* on this ground). If mounting works a "transformation," then changing a painting's frame or a photograph's mat equally produces a derivative work. Indeed, if Lee is right about the meaning of the definition's first sentence, then any alteration of a work, however slight, requires the author's permission. We asked at oral argument what would happen if a purchaser jotted a note on one of the note cards, or used it as a coaster for a drink, or cut it in half, or if a collector applied his seal (as is common in Japan); Lee's counsel replied that such changes prepare derivative works, but that as a practical matter artists would not file suit. A definition of derivative work that makes criminals out of art collectors and tourists is jarring despite Lee's gracious offer not to commence civil litigation.

. . .

Affirmed.

QUESTIONS

1. Review the pertinent statutory definitions. Does the "originality" requirement apply not only for the purpose of determining the copyrightability of the tiled artwork but also for the purpose of determining whether it infringes? Has the Seventh Circuit clearly answered this question?

2. How would you analyze the infringement claim when one of Lee's cards is used, without authorization, as a coaster? What about the scribbling of notes on the card? What about the entry of your notes in the margins of this casebook?

3. Subsequent to the trial court's decision in *Lee v. A.R.T.*, a district court in California (within the Ninth Circuit, and thus bound by the *Mirage* decision) held that the defendant infringed the copyright in a book of art prints (and the prints themselves) by cutting out the prints, mounting each on a canvas and placing them in frames for hanging on the wall. *See Greenwich Workshop, Inc. v. Timber Creations, Inc.*, 932 F.Supp. 1210 (C.D.Cal.1996). The court concluded that this was a "recasting" and "transformation" rather than merely a method of display, and that it was not saved by the first-sale doctrine. Would you affirm this decision on appeal?

4. Fancy Fabrics, Inc. designs and distributes rolls of fabric that are imprinted with attractive abstract patterns in vivid colors. Lovely Linens, Inc. buys hundreds of feet of these rolls, and cuts and sews them into bedsheets and pillow cases. Fancy Fabrics has insisted that Lovely Linens cease and desist, to no avail, and has initiated an action for copyright infringement, claiming a violation of § 106(2). How should the court rule? *See Precious Moments, Inc. v. La Infantil, Inc.*, 971 F.Supp. 66 (D.P.R. 1997).

5. The *Lee v. A.R.T.* court alluded to the role of a frame in altering the perception of a work, but seemed to take it for granted that framing does not create a derivative work. Does it make a difference if the "frame" is electronic, such as an Internet link and frame? Consider the following decision.

Futuredontics, Inc. v. Applied Anagramics, Inc., 45 U.S.P.Q.2d 2005 (C.D.Cal.1998). Plaintiff operates a dental referral business, which it publicizes by, among other means, a website. Applied Anagramics, Inc.'s (AAI) website "links" to Futuredontics', surrounding Futuredontics' information with a "frame" that identifies AAI and links to AAI's other webpages. Futuredontics did not authorize the linking and framing, and initiated this suit for copyright and trademark infringement. Regarding the copyright claim, the court determined that the outcome of AAI's motion to dismiss would turn on whether the framing yielded an unauthorized derivative work. The court stated:

> The parties sharply dispute what function AAI's framed link serves. Defendants contend that AAI's window or frame provides a "lens" which enables Internet users to view the information that Plaintiff itself placed on the Internet. Plaintiff's complaint, however, alleges that defendants reproduce its copyrighted web page by combining AAI material and Plaintiff's web site.
>
> The parties cite to several cases which purportedly support their interpretation of the function AAI's framed link serves. None of these cases, however, is directly on point.
>
> The parties discuss the applicability of *Mirage Editions.... Mirage* is distinguishable from the present case. In this case, AAI has not affixed an image to a ceramic tile; rather AAI appears to have placed an electronic frame or border around Plaintiff's webpage.
>
> Defendants primarily rely on *Louis Galoob.... Galoob* did distinguish *Mirage* and noted that the *Mirage* decision would have been different had the plaintiff "distributed lenses that merely enabled users to view several works of art simultaneously."
>
> Nevertheless, *Galoob*, like *Mirage*, is distinguishable from the instant case. *Galoob* does not foreclose Plaintiff from establishing that AAI's web page incorporates Futuredontics' web page in some "concrete or permanent form" or that AAI's framed link duplicates or recasts Plaintiff's web page.
>
> For these reasons, the Court finds that the cases cited by the parties do not conclusively determine whether Defendants' frame page constitutes a derivative work. Therefore, the Court determines that Plaintiff's Third Claim for Relief sufficiently alleges a claim for copyright infringement.

————

National Geographic Society v. Classified Geographic, Inc., 27 F.Supp. 655 (D.Mass.1939). The well-known plaintiff, a nonprofit organization devoted to gathering and disseminating geographic knowledge, publishes the National Geographic Magazine. It also publishes books, such as "The Book of Birds," "The Book of Fishes," and "Horses of the World"; these books are formed by selecting and compiling articles published in the magazine. The defendant is in the business of arranging and compiling articles from the National Geographic Magazine (without the plaintiff's consent) and selling them in book form to the public; its books cover such topics as Birds, Fish, Domestic Animals, and Insects. The defendant does not reprint any of the plaintiff's copyrighted articles but obtains all of its material by purchasing copies of the National Geographic Magazine, tearing the magazines apart, bringing together articles of related subject matter, binding them in a substantial backing, and offering them for sale as original compilations of National Geographic articles.

The court held the defendant's activities to constitute copyright infringement. It pointed out that the statute also gave the plaintiff the exclusive right to compile, adapt or arrange its copyrighted articles, and held that the defendant's use of lawfully purchased National Geographic Magazines constituted an unlawful compilation, adaptation or arrangement. Although the defendant was the owner of the physical material on which the copyrighted works were printed, it was not the owner of the right to make these kinds of unauthorized uses. The court distinguished cases holding that the purchaser of a second-hand book could, without the consent of the copyright owner, place it within a new cover and binding.

QUESTIONS

1. Is the court's decision in the *National Geographic* case convincing? If the defendant there had purchased and then resold the back issues separately, or resold individual torn-out articles, presumably that would not have infringed the copyright (by virtue of the "first sale" doctrine soon to be discussed). Precisely what different economic interest of the plaintiff is implicated by the conduct in which the defendant actually engaged, and should that interest be protected by copyright?

2. The defendant in *National Geographic* was held to have engaged in the unauthorized act of "compiling" the plaintiff's articles. Is there a "compilation" right granted by § 106(2) of the Copyright Act?

2. MORAL RIGHTS

Gilliam v. American Broadcasting Cos.

538 F.2d 14 (2d Cir.1976).

■ LUMBARD, CIRCUIT JUDGE:

[Plaintiffs, the British comedy writers and performers known as Monty Python, sought a preliminary injunction to restrain the broadcasting by ABC network of edited versions of three programs originally written and performed by Monty Python for the British Broadcasting Corporation (BBC). Under their agreement with the BBC, Monty Python delivers scripts for use in their television series; the contract reserves to them maximum control over the scripts and the BBC may make only minor changes thereafter; once the program is recorded, nothing in the agreement allows BBC to alter it. BBC is given the right to license the transmission of the recorded programs in any overseas territory; when shown in the U.S. on public broadcasting stations, and on a small number of commercial stations, the programs have been shown in their entirety and without commercial interruption. In October 1973, Time–Life Films acquired from BBC the right to distribute Monty Python programs, and were given the right to edit for only, inter alia, the insertion of commercials; no similar clause was included in the Python–BBC agreement. Time–Life in turn licensed ABC in July 1975 to broadcast two Monty Python programs. ABC broadcast a 90–minute program in October 1975, and edited out some 24 minutes, either for commercials or (according to ABC) to delete offensive or obscene matter. When they saw that version in November, Monty Python was "appalled" at the discontinuity and "mutilation" that had resulted from the editing done by Time–Life for ABC.]

[Monty Python's request for a preliminary injunction of the December showing (one week later) of the next 90–minute special was denied by the trial court because of Python's delay and the financial loss to ABC; the judge did, however, find damage caused to the plaintiffs by the "impairment of the integrity of their work." The court of appeals held that ABC should accompany its broadcast with a legend to the effect that the program had been edited by ABC, and subsequently enjoined ABC preliminarily from any further broadcast of edited Monty Python programs.]

I

[The court concluded that the denial of injunctive relief would likely seriously injure the reputation of the plaintiffs, and that the grant of such relief against future ABC broadcasts (there having been no scheduling or advertising of such) would not harm defendant's relations with its affiliates or with the public.]

We then reach the question whether there is a likelihood that appellants will succeed on the merits. In concluding that there is a likelihood of infringement here, we rely especially on the fact that the editing was substantial, i.e., approximately 27 per cent of the original program was omitted, and the editing contravened contractual provisions that limited the right to edit Monty Python material. . . .

Judge Lasker denied the preliminary injunction in part because he was unsure of the ownership of the copyright in the recorded program. Appellants first contend that the question of ownership is irrelevant because the recorded program was merely a derivative work taken from the script in which they hold the uncontested copyright. Thus, even if BBC owned the copyright in the recorded program, its use of that work would be limited by the license granted to BBC by Monty Python for use of the underlying script. We agree. [The court of appeals found the television program to be a "dramatization" (a term used in the 1909 Copyright Act) of the script, and thus independently copyrightable to the extent of its newly added material; but also held that this did not affect the force or validity of the copyright in the underlying script.] . . .

Since the copyright in the underlying script survives intact despite the incorporation of that work into a derivative work, one who uses the script, even with the permission of the proprietor of the derivative work, may infringe the underlying copyright.

. . .

One who obtains permission to use a copyrighted script in the production of a derivative work ... may not exceed the specific purpose for which permission was granted.... [Appellants] claim that revisions in the script, and ultimately in the program, could be made only after consultation with Monty Python, and that ABC's broadcast of a program edited after recording and without consultation with Monty Python exceeded the scope of any license that BBC was entitled to grant.

The rationale for finding infringement when a licensee exceeds time or media restrictions on his license—the need to allow the proprietor of the underlying copyright to control the method in which his work is presented to the public—applies equally to the situation in which a licensee makes an unauthorized use of the underlying work by publishing it in a truncated version. Whether intended to allow greater economic exploitation of the work, as in the media and time cases, or to ensure that the copyright proprietor retains a veto power over revisions desired for the derivative work, the ability of the copyright holder to control his work remains paramount in our copyright law. We find, therefore, that unauthorized editing of the underlying work, if proven, would constitute an infringement of the copyright in that work similar to any other use of a work that exceeded the license granted by the proprietor of the copyright.

... Since a grantor may not convey greater rights than it owns, BBC's permission to allow Time–Life, and hence ABC, to edit appears to have been a nullity.

. . .

Finally, ABC contends that appellants must have expected that deletions would be made in the recordings to conform them for use on commercial television in the United States. ABC argues that licensing in the United States implicitly grants a license to insert commercials in a program and to remove offensive or obscene material prior to broadcast. According to the network, appellants should have anticipated that most of the excised material contained scatological references inappropriate for American television and that these scenes would be replaced with commercials, which presumably are more palatable to the American public.

The proof adduced up to this point, however, provides no basis for finding any implied consent to edit. Prior to the ABC broadcasts, Monty Python programs had been broadcast on a regular basis by both commercial and public television stations in this country without interruption or deletion. Indeed, there is no evidence of any prior broadcast of edited Monty Python material in the United States. These facts, combined with the persistent requests for assurances by the group and its representatives that the programs would be shown intact belie the argument that the group knew or should have known that deletions and commercial interruptions were inevitable.

Several of the deletions made for ABC, such as elimination of the words "hell" and "damn," seem inexplicable given today's standard television fare.[8] If, however, ABC honestly determined that the programs were obscene in substantial part, it could have decided not to broadcast the specials at all, or it could have attempted to reconcile its differences with appellants. The network could not, however, free from a claim of infringement, broadcast in a substantially altered form a program incorporating the script over which the group had retained control.

. . . We therefore conclude that there is a substantial likelihood that, after a full trial, appellants will succeed in proving infringement of their copyright by ABC's broadcast of edited versions of Monty Python programs. . . .

II

It also seems likely that appellants will succeed on the theory that, regardless of the right ABC had to broadcast an edited program, the cuts made constituted an actionable mutilation of Monty Python's work. This cause of action, which seeks redress for deformation of an artist's work, finds its roots in the continental concept of *droit moral*, or moral right, which may generally be summarized as including the right of the artist to have his work attributed to him in the form in which he created it. See 1 M. Nimmer, *supra*, at § 110.1.

American copyright law, as presently written, does not recognize moral rights or provide a cause of action for their violation, since the law seeks to vindicate the economic, rather than the personal, rights of authors. Nevertheless, the economic incentive for artistic and intellectual creation that serves as the foundation for American copyright law, *Goldstein v. California,* 412 U.S. 546 (1973); *Mazer v. Stein,* 347 U.S. 201 (1954), cannot be reconciled with the inability of artists to obtain relief for mutilation or misrepresentation of their work to the public on which the artists are financially dependent. Thus courts have long granted relief for misrepresentation of an artist's work by relying on theories outside the statutory law of copyright, such as contract law, *Granz v. Harris,* 198 F.2d 585 (2d Cir.1952) (substantial cutting of original work constitutes misrepresentation), or the tort of unfair competition, *Prouty v. National Broadcasting Co.,* 26 F. Supp. 265 (D.Mass.1939). See Strauss, *The Moral Right of the Author* 128–138, in Studies on Copyright (1963). Although such decisions are clothed in terms of proprietary right in one's creation, they also properly vindicate the author's personal right to prevent the presentation of his work to the public in a distorted form. See *Gardella v. Log Cabin Products Co.,* 89 F.2d 891, 895–96 (2d Cir.1937); Roeder, *The Doctrine of Moral Right,* 53 Harv. L. Rev. 554, 568 (1940).

Here, the appellants claim that the editing done for ABC mutilated the original work and that consequently the broadcast of those programs as the creation of Monty Python violated the Lanham Act § 43(a), 15 U.S.C.

---

8. We also note that broadcast of the Monty Python specials was scheduled by ABC for an 11:30 p.m. to 1:00 a.m. time slot.

§ 1125(a).[10] This statute, the federal counterpart to state unfair competition laws, has been invoked to prevent misrepresentations that may injure plaintiff's business or personal reputation, even where no registered trademark is concerned. See *Mortellito v. Nina of California,* 335 F. Supp. 1238, 1294 (S.D.N.Y. 1972). It is sufficient to violate the Act that a representation of a product, although technically true, creates a false impression of the product's origin. See *Rich v. RCA Corp.,* 390 F. Supp. 530 (S.D.N.Y.1975) (recent picture of plaintiff on cover of album containing songs recorded in distant past held to be a false representation that the songs were new); *Geisel v. Poynter Products, Inc.,* 283 F. Supp. 261, 267 (S.D.N.Y.1968).

These cases cannot be distinguished from the situation in which a television network broadcasts a program properly designated as having been written and performed by a group, but which has been edited, without the writer's consent, into a form that departs substantially from the original work. "To deform his work is to present him to the public as the creator of a work not his own, and thus makes him subject to criticism for work he has not done." Roeder, *supra,* at 569. In such a case, it is the writer or performer, rather than the network, who suffers the consequences of the mutilation, for the public will have only the final product by which to evaluate the work. Thus, an allegation that a defendant has presented to the public a "garbled," *Granz v. Harris, supra* (Frank, J., concurring), distorted version of plaintiff's work seeks to redress the very rights sought to be protected by the Lanham Act, 15 U.S.C. § 1125(a), and should be recognized as stating a cause of action under that statute. . . .

During the hearing on the preliminary injunction, Judge Lasker viewed the edited version of the Monty Python program broadcast on December 26 and the original, unedited version. After hearing argument of this appeal, this panel also viewed and compared the two versions. We find that the truncated version at times omitted the climax of the skits to which appellants' rare brand of humor was leading and at other times deleted essential elements in the schematic development of a story line.[12] We therefore agree with Judge Lasker's conclusion that the edited version broadcast by ABC impaired the integrity of appellants' work and represented to the public as the product of appellants what was actually a mere caricature of their talents. We believe that a valid cause of action for such

---

10. That statute provides in part:

Any person who shall affix, apply, or annex, or use in connection with any goods or services, . . . a false designation of origin, or any false description or representation . . . and shall cause such goods or services to enter into commerce . . . shall be liable to a civil action by any person . . . who believes that he is or is likely to be damaged by the use of any such false description or representation.

12. A single example will illustrate the extent of distortion engendered by the edit-

ing. In one skit, an upper class English family is engaged in a discussion of the tonal quality of certain words as "woody" or "tinny." The father soon begins to suggest certain words with sexual connotations as either "woody" or "tinny," whereupon the mother fetches a bucket of water and pours it over his head. The skit continues from this point. The ABC edit eliminates this middle sequence so that the father is comfortably dressed at one moment and, in the next moment, is shown in a soaked condition without any explanation for the change in his appearance.

distortion exists and that therefore a preliminary injunction may issue to prevent repetition of the broadcast prior to final determination of the issues.[13] . . .

QUESTIONS

1. What copyright was considered infringed in the "Monty Python" case? Under the court's analysis, is the BBC an infringer?

Assume that Monty Python, prior to the initiation of their lawsuit, had assigned to Book Publisher all of their rights in all of the scripts written by them. Would Book Publisher have been a proper plaintiff in an action for copyright infringement? In an action for a Lanham Act violation? In an action to recover damages for "mutilation and distortion" of the script? In *Boosey & Hawkes Music Pubs. Ltd. v. Walt Disney Co.*, 53 U.S.P.Q.2d 2021 (S.D.N.Y.2000), the court held that an assignee has no standing to assert such a claim on behalf of a well-known classical composer (Igor Stravinsky) whose music was allegedly distorted in a well-known animated motion picture (Fantasia), because "moral rights are inalienable and unassignable. As such, they are only assertable by the author/composer, or his heirs." Why not by an assignee? Why by his heirs?

2. Some years ago, a computer-facilitated technique was developed to add color to motion picture films originally made in black-and-white. (The original films are in the public domain or, if they are still protected by copyright, permission to colorize has been given by the copyright owner, typically a production company or its assignee.) Certain frames of the film are identified for colorization; decisions are made about what colors to incorporate in the frames, based upon research as to such matters as the color of an actor's hair or an adjacent building, and judgments are frequently made about appealing color combinations, about shading, etc.; and a computer is then used to "color" the remaining film frames in the pertinent scene sequences.

(a) Is the colorized version of the motion picture copyrightable as a derivative work?

(b) Does such colorization violate any rights of the director or other leading artistic contributors to the black-and-white original? (Recall that, in most instances, the motion picture will have been prepared as a work made for hire.)

---

13. Judge Gurfein's concurring opinion suggests that since the gravamen of a complaint under the Lanham Act is that the origin of goods has been falsely described, a legend disclaiming Monty Python's approval of the edited version would preclude violation of that Act. We are doubtful that a few words could erase the indelible impression that is made by a television broadcast, especially since the viewer has no means of comparing the truncated version with the complete work in order to determine for himself the talents of plaintiffs. Furthermore, a disclaimer such as the one originally suggested by Judge Lasker in the exigencies of an impending broadcast last December would go unnoticed by viewers who tuned into the broadcast a few minutes after it began.

We therefore conclude that Judge Gurfein's proposal that the district court could find some form of disclaimer would be sufficient might not provide appropriate relief.

a. FEDERAL LAW PROTECTION OF MORAL RIGHTS

The *Gilliam* court alluded to the continental concept of moral rights, and to the author's prerogatives to secure proper attribution for her work and to preserve the work in the form in which it was created. These rights of attribution (also known as the right of "paternity") and of integrity are among the guarantees that nations party to the Berne Convention for the Protection of Literary and Artistic Works must afford authors from other member countries (Art. 6bis). The effective date of U.S. adherence to the Berne Convention was March 1, 1989.

The theory of moral rights holds that these rights inhere in and protect the personality of the author. While, according to the continental view, the author enjoys *both* moral and economic rights "by the sole fact of creating the work" (France, copyright law [law of March 11, 1957], art. 1), moral rights are conceptually separate from economic exploitation rights. Indeed, in many countries, moral rights are considered inalienable: the author retains them even after, or despite, transfer of economic rights. The Berne Convention, however, does not prohibit waiver or alienation of these rights, so long as a transfer of economic rights is not deemed of itself to effect a transfer of moral rights.

The extent to which U.S. copyright or other doctrines assimilate or simulate moral rights was hotly debated at the time of Berne adherence. *See generally Final Report of the Ad Hoc Working Group on U.S. Adherence to the Berne Convention*, 10 Colum.-VLA J.L. & Arts 513, 547–57 (1986) (concluding that, on the whole, U.S. law affords meaningful equivalents to moral rights). Since then, Congress has enacted explicit protections for the attribution and integrity interests of a limited class of visual artists. *See* Visual Artists Rights Act of 1990, P.L. 101–650, Title VI, 104 Stat. 5089 (1990).

Visual Artists Rights Act of 1990

17 U.S.C. §§ 101, 106A.

§ 101. Definitions.

. . .

A "work of visual art" is—

(1) a painting, drawing, print, or sculpture, existing in a single copy, in a limited edition of 200 copies or fewer that are signed and consecutively numbered by the author, or in the case of a sculpture, in multiple cast, carved, or fabricated sculptures of two hundred or fewer that are consecutively numbered by the author and bear the signature or other identifying mark of the author; or

(2) a still photographic image produced for exhibition purposes only, existing in a single copy that is signed by the author, or in a limited edition of 200 copies or fewer that are signed and consecutively numbered by the author.

A work of visual art does not include—

(A)(i) any poster, map, globe, chart, technical drawing, diagram, model, applied art, motion picture or other audiovisual work, book, magazine, newspaper, periodical, data base, electronic information service, electronic publication, or similar publication;

(ii) any merchandising item or advertising, promotional, descriptive, covering, or packaging material or container;

(iii) any portion or part of any item described in clause (i) or (ii);

(B) any work made for hire; or

(C) any work not subject to copyright protection under this title.

. . .

§ 106A.   Rights of Certain Authors to Attribution and Integrity

(a) RIGHTS OF ATTRIBUTION AND INTEGRITY. —Subject to section 107 and independent of the exclusive rights provided in section 106, the author of a work of visual art—

(1) shall have the right—

(A) to claim authorship of that work, and

(B) to prevent the use of his or her name as the author of any work of visual art which he or she did not create;

(2) shall have the right to prevent the use of his or her name as the author of the work of visual art in the event of a distortion, mutilation, or other modification of the work which would be prejudicial to his or her honor or reputation and

(3) subject to the limitations set forth in section 113(d), shall have the right—

(A) to prevent any intentional distortion, mutilation, or other modification of that work which would be prejudicial to his or her honor or reputation, and any intentional distortion, mutilation, or modification of that work is a violation of that right, and

(B) to prevent any destruction of a work of recognized stature, and any intentional or grossly negligent destruction of that work is a violation of that right.

(b) SCOPE AND EXERCISE OF RIGHTS. —Only the author of a work of visual art has the rights conferred by subsection (a) in that work, whether or not the author is the copyright owner. The authors of a joint work of visual art are coowners of the rights conferred by subsection (a) in that work.

(c) EXCEPTIONS. —(1) The modification of a work of visual art which is a result of the passage of time or the inherent nature of the materials is not a distortion, mutilation, or other modification described in subsection (a)(3)(A).

(2) The modification of a work of visual art which is the result of conservation, or of the public presentation, including lighting and place-

ment, of the work is not a destruction, distortion, mutilation, or other modification described in subsection (a)(3) unless the modification is caused by gross negligence.

(3) The rights described in paragraph (1) and (2) of subsection(a) shall not apply to any reproduction, depiction, portrayal, or other use of a work in, upon, or in any connection with any item described in subparagraph (A) or (B) of the definition of "work of visual art" in section 101, and any such reproduction, depiction, portrayal, or other use of a work is not a destruction, distortion, mutilation, or other modification described in paragraph (3) of subsection (a)....

(d) TRANSFER AND WAIVER. —(1) The rights conferred by subsection (a) may not be transferred, but those rights may be waived if the author expressly agrees to such waiver in a written instrument signed by the author. Such instrument shall specifically identify the work, and uses of that work to which the waiver applies, and the waiver shall apply only to the work and uses so identified. In the case of a joint work prepared by two or more authors, a waiver of rights under this paragraph made by one such author waives such rights for all such authors....

Editors' Note—The student should also consult §§ 113(d) (works incorporated in buildings) and 301(f) (preemption of state law), also enacted in 1990 and set forth in Appendix A to the Casebook.

WORKS OF VISUAL ART

There have been a number of recent cases testing the coverage of the Visual Artists Rights Act; they evidence a judicial inclination to construe the Act generously. In *Carter v. Helmsley–Spear, Inc.*, 71 F.3d 77 (2d Cir.1995), a site-specific sculpture that had been commissioned to fill the lobby of a building was removed by the new building owner; the previous owner had not obtained from the artists a signed agreement waiving their rights (under § 113(d)). Although the Court of Appeals ultimately concluded that the sculpture was not protected by VARA because it was a work made for hire, the court considered and rejected the argument of the building owner that the sculpture should be deemed "applied art" which is also excluded from the Act. The court stated:

> "Applied art" describes "two-and three-dimensional ornamentation or decoration that is affixed to otherwise utilitarian objects." ... Defendants' assertion that at least parts of the work are applied art appears to rest on the fact that some of the sculptural elements are affixed to the lobby's floor, walls, and ceiling—all utilitarian objects. Interpreting applied art to include such works would render meaningless VARA's protection for works of visual art installed in buildings. A court should not read one part of a statute so as to deprive another part of meaning.
>
> Appellants do not suggest the entire work is applied art. The district court correctly stated that even if components of the work

standing alone were applied art, "nothing in VARA proscribes protection of works of visual art that incorporate elements of, rather than constitute, applied art." ... VARA's legislative history leaves no doubt that "a new and independent work created from snippets of [excluded] materials, such as a collage, is of course not excluded" from the definition of a work of visual art. H.R. Rep. No. 514 at 14. The trial judge correctly ruled the work is not applied art precluded from protection under the Act.

The definition of "work of visual art" excludes, among other things, "chart, technical drawing, diagram [and] model." In *Flack v. Friends of Queen Catherine Inc.*, 139 F.Supp.2d 526 (S.D.N.Y.2001), the court had to determine the meaning of the word "model." The plaintiff artist had won a competition to sculpt a 35–foot bronze statue of a mid–17th century Queen of England and Princess of Portugal, but after she had begun work on a clay enlargement of the head and face, the project was interrupted by the sponsor. The company that was to fabricate the bronze sculpture had possession of the clay head and stored it outdoors in what the plaintiff called its "garbage dump," where it was damaged; efforts by others to repair it did not satisfy the sculptor. She sued the sponsor and fabricator for copyright infringement and violation of VARA, to which the defense was asserted that the clay head was only a "model" that was excluded from VARA's protection. The district court noted the absence of any statutory definition of that word, but also the reference in the legislative history to using common sense and generally accepted standards of the artistic community in determining VARA's coverage. The court concluded—because the artistic community considers models such as the clay sculpture to be independent works of art, and because preliminary drawings and sketches of painters are surely covered by VARA—that the clay head and face were not meant to be excluded as "models" from VARA's coverage.

Another expansive construction was given to VARA in determining whether a large stainless steel sculpture by a hobbyist sculptor was a "work of recognized stature" which VARA protected against destruction. In *Martin v. City of Indianapolis*, 192 F.3d 608 (7th Cir.1999), the City reclaimed the real property on which the sculpture was located and had it torn down for some $330 (after being told by the sculptor that it could be disassembled and preserved for some $8,000), and he sued for a violation of VARA. The federal court of appeals divided on the question whether the sculpture was a "work of recognized stature." The sculptor introduced no live testimony from art experts or museum directors or gallery owners; rather, he introduced articles and letters from newspapers and magazines containing compliments (but no assessments of "stature") from a local art critic and a college museum director. Over the dissenter's objections, the majority stated that, although usually live testimony (at least, sworn documentary evidence) is required on the issue so that the defendant may cross-examine, the special circumstances of the case (which were not delineated) justified reliance on the articles and letters, and a finding of "recognized stature."

QUESTIONS

1. Among the works excluded from coverage by VARA are "works made for hire." If an artist hires assistants to work on a painting or sculpture—for example, welders for a large-scale steel sculpture—is the resulting work "for hire?" Do you suppose Congress intended to remove these kinds of works from the Act's protections? Can one resolve this anomaly by considering the work not "for hire" if the persons engaged by the artist would not be considered "authors"? Is this a sufficient solution?

2. In 1999 Phoebe Photographer created several fashion photographs which were published in magazines like *Vogue* and *GQ*. These photographs have since become prized as works of art. Responding to the popularity of her photos, Ms. Photographer, who has retained the original negatives of her work, creates limited editions of 200 of each of the fashion photographs, which she signs and numbers. Are these editions protected under the Visual Artists Rights Act?

3. Artemis Artist has displayed her recent canvasses and lithographs at the Gallery. Gallery has issued a catalogue depicting Artist's work. However, on the walls and in the catalogue, Gallery has failed to attribute any of the work to Artist. Which, if any, of Gallery's conduct violates the Visual Artists Rights Act?

4. Are works of architecture covered by VARA? Are works of literature or music? If not, should they be? Are motion pictures or other audiovisual works, as in the *Gilliam* case? Why are creators of classic motion pictures accorded no moral rights? Does it relate to the medium of film, or to the identity of those who would claim moral rights, or to the prevailing methods for commercially marketing (and editing and exhibiting) motion pictures?

5. Suppose a property owner erects a building in front of a wall bearing a mural that was painted, with authorization, after 1991. The mural remains intact, but is no longer visible. Does the muralist have a VARA claim against the owner/builder of the obstructing structure? *See English v. CFC&R East 11th Street LLC*, 1997 WL 746444 (S.D.N.Y.1997).

6. Molly Matisse has painted a mural on paper measuring 10 feet by 30 feet, with the intention that it will be affixed to a metal supporting frame and exhibited at a convention dealing with the problems of the poor. The night before the convention, the mural was attached temporarily to the frame; but by the next morning, the organizers of the convention had removed the painting from the frame, tearing it in the process, because of Molly's failure to secure the needed permissions for displaying her mural. Later that day she observed the mural crumpled in the corner of an office, and she has sued the organizers for unlawful destruction under VARA. The defendants have moved for summary judgment, contending that a work cannot, as a matter of law, be of "recognized stature" if it has never been displayed to or seen by members of the public. Molly, however, claims that a work can be of recognized stature immediately upon its creation; she states that even an "undiscovered Picasso" can be such a work, and its destruction a violation of law, before it is publicly seen. She offers the testimony of two art critics, who base their opinion on Molly's artistic reputation and photos of the mural prior to its destruction. Should the court deny the defendant's motion to exclude such evidence? What interpretation would make most sense in light of the goals of VARA? *See Pollara v. Seymour*, 150 F.Supp.2d 393 (N.D.N.Y.2001).

———

Does VARA apply to works of visual arts that were created prior to its June 1, 1991 effective date? Section 106A(d)(2) answers "yes," but only if title to the work had not been transferred from the author before that date. What if such a work was altered or mutilated before June 1991 but is kept on public display in that form thereafter? Is VARA violated?

In **Pavia v. 1120 Avenue of the Americas Assocs.**, 901 F.Supp. 620 (S.D.N.Y.1995), a sculptor was commissioned in 1963 to create a sculpture to be displayed in a New York City hotel lobby; he created a large four-piece geometric work, title to which was not transferred by the artist. In 1988, the hotel owners dismantled the work and moved two of the pieces, displaying them at a commercial warehouse (while removing the other two pieces altogether). After making numerous requests from 1992 to 1994 to display the work properly, the sculptor brought an action claiming unlawful alteration, causing prejudice to his reputation, that constituted a "continuing violation" of VARA (as well as of the New York State Arts and Cultural Affairs Law) that persisted after VARA's 1991 effective date.

The court pointed out that, although the New York statute outlaws the unauthorized display of an altered or mutilated work (which is improperly attributed to the sculptor), VARA outlaws only the act of alteration itself and states nothing about continued display of the altered work. The court therefore concluded that the sculptor had stated a claim under the New York act, which it also held not to be preempted by VARA or by other provisions of the Copyright Act. But it dismissed the VARA claim because the only offending act under that statute, the dismantling, had taken place before the statute's effective date. The district judge rejected the argument that the continued display, after June 1991, constituted an ongoing mutilation:

> In according these new [moral rights to artists under VARA], Congress sought to balance them against the prior expectations of other parties.... Among these prior understandings, and at the root of VARA's passage, was the cession by an artist of the right to prevent alteration of his work. By including [a transition provision declaring that acts occurring before VARA's effective date are not within its proscription] and avoiding retroactivity, Congress allowed those who had commissioned works before its effective date to maintain their privilege to alter those works, in line with the understanding of all parties to the pre-VARA transaction. The same intent is evident in [§ 106A(d)(2)], which gave moral rights to artists for works created

before the effective date only if they had not already transferred title. Congress, then, could not have intended to give artists the right to prevent the continued display after VARA's effective date of works distorted, mutilated, or modified before that date.

b. STATE PROTECTION OF MORAL RIGHTS

Before enactment of the federal Visual Artists Rights Act, several states, including California, New York, Massachusetts, New Jersey, Maine, Connecticut, Louisiana, New Mexico, Pennsylvania and Rhode Island, adopted laws protecting rights of integrity and of attribution in "works of fine art." These state law protections proved an important element in the argument advanced by some observers, and embraced by Congress in 1988, that the overall combination of federal and state laws together afforded sufficient coverage of moral rights to permit U.S. adherence to the Berne Convention without further specific federal legislation regarding moral rights.

Although the overall "fine arts" subject matter covered by the state laws is often similar, the rationales for and the terms of protection are not always identical. For example, the preamble to the California act, Cal. Civ. Code § 987(a), states:

> The Legislature hereby finds and declares that the physical alteration or destruction of fine art, which is an expression of the artist's personality, is detrimental to the artist's reputation, and artists therefore have an interest in protecting their works of fine art against such alteration or destruction; and that there is also a public interest in preserving the integrity of cultural and artistic creations.

The attribution and integrity rights (including the right not to have the work intentionally destroyed) are granted for the life of the artist plus 50 years; but the rights can be waived in an express writing signed by the artist.

The New York statute, N.Y. Arts & Cultural Affairs Law 14.03, is somewhat different. Its principal articulated concern is with the reasonable likelihood of "damage to the artist's reputation" resulting from an alteration, defacement, mutilation or other modified form. Accordingly, the New York statute does not outlaw this offensive conduct as such, but only the publishing or the public display of a work (or a reproduction of a work) in such altered form, when the work would reasonably be attributed to the artist and "damage to the artist's reputation is reasonably likely to result therefrom." There are several exceptions to the rights accorded to the artist:

> (1) The act does not apply "to work prepared under contract for advertising or trade unless the contract so provides";

> (2) the act expressly excludes motion pictures from its coverage;

> (3) alteration or other modification of a work "resulting from the passage of time or the inherent nature of the materials" will not violate the act;

(4) a modification of a work in the course of reproducing it "that is an ordinary result of the medium of reproduction" will not violate the act; and

(5) destruction of a work is not expressly outlawed.

The New York statute is silent on the question whether the artist may waive the statutory rights in writing or otherwise. It is also silent as to the duration of those rights.

While the state laws and the federal statute now overlap to some extent, they are not completely congruent with respect to either subject matter covered or conduct prohibited. The following decision, applying the New York statute, illustrates some of the differences in purpose and scope between federal and state rights.

Wojnarowicz v. American Family Ass'n

745 F.Supp. 130 (S.D.N.Y.1990).

■ CONNER, DISTRICT JUDGE.

Multimedia artist David Wojnarowicz brings this action to enjoin the publication of a pamphlet by defendants American Family Association ("AFA") and Donald E. Wildmon, Executive Director of AFA, and for damages based upon claims of copyright infringement, defamation, and violations of the Lanham Act and the New York Artists' Authorship Rights Act....

... Having reviewed the record and considered counsels' post-trial briefs, the Court concludes that plaintiff is entitled to judgment for defendants' violation of New York's Artists' Authorship Rights Act....

[Plaintiff is an artist, working in various media, whose artworks focus upon the AIDS epidemic within the gay community; much of his work has earned critical acclaim and is exhibited in galleries and museums. The National Endowment for the Arts (NEA) awarded $15,000 to the University Galleries at Illinois State University to help pay for an exhibit (titled "Tongues of Flame") and catalogue of the plaintiff's work; several of the works in the exhibit—copyrights to which were held by the plaintiff—depicted sexual acts and a few portrayed Christ with a hypodermic needle in his arm. The defendant AFA is chartered for the purpose of promoting decency and Judeo–Christian values in American society. It widely distributed—to members of Congress and to Christian leaders and media—a pamphlet that contained unauthorized reproductions of 14 fragments of the plaintiff's exhibited works, and criticized the use of government funds to subsidize such art.]

. . .

Defendants next argue that the distribution of a photocopy of cropped images extracted from plaintiff's work is not a violation of the statute because it did not alter, deface, mutilate or modify plaintiff's original work. This Court does not agree. A literal reading of section 14.03(1) of the [New York Artists'] Authorship Rights Act, N.Y. Cultural Affairs Law Section

14.03, clearly demonstrates that the statute guards against alterations of reproductions as well as of the original works:

> 1. [N]o person ... shall knowingly display in a place accessible to the public or publish a work of fine art ... *or a reproduction thereof* in an altered, defaced, mutilated or modified form if the work is displayed, published or *reproduced* as being the work of the artist.[3]

See Damich, *A Comparative Critique,* 84 Colum. L. Rev. at 1740 ("A more plausible interpretation of the reproduction provision—and one supported by statutory language—is that unfaithful reproductions activate the protection of the statute if publicly displayed so as to damage the reputation of the author of the original."). Moreover, section 14.03(3)(b) of the Act confirms its applicability to altered reproductions of artworks in which no physical change has been made in the original work. That subsection—by which 14.03 is expressly limited—states that:

> In the case of a reproduction, a change that is an ordinary result of the medium of reproduction does not by itself create a violation of subdivision one of this section or a right to disclaim authorship under subdivision two of this section.

Sections 14.03(1) and 14.03(3)(b), read together, suggest that deliberate alterations (such as selective cropping), as distinguished from those that ordinarily result from the reproduction process (such as reduction in overall size or loss of detail), would constitute violations. See Damich, *A Comparative Critique,* 84 Colum. L. Rev. at 1740.

Defendants maintain that the statute's legislative history supports their contention that the display or publication envisioned is the altered original or limited edition multiple by a subsequent owner.... It is evident that the statute was intended to protect the integrity of the original artworks and the artist's limited edition multiples after they were sold or transferred to new owners. The statute prevents the new owner from displaying or publishing and attributing to the creator an altered version of that creator's work. However, nothing in the legislative history suggests that the New York legislature intended to limit the Act's protection to that scenario. To the contrary, because the intent of the bill was to protect not only the integrity of the artwork, but the reputation of the artist, the spirit of the statute is best served by prohibiting the attribution to an artist of a published or publicly displayed altered reproduction of his original artwork. From a photographic reproduction, it cannot be seen whether the alteration was effected on the original or the copy, and both may cause the same harm to the artist's reputation when the altered version is published with attribution to him. In fact, the mass mailing of an altered photographic reproduction is likely to reach a far greater audience and cause greater harm to the artist than the display of an altered original, which may reach

---

3. " 'Reproduction' means a copy, in any medium, of a work of fine art, that is displayed or published under circumstances that, reasonably construed, evince an intent that it be taken as a representation of a work of fine art as created by the artist." N.Y. Arts & Cultural Affairs Law § 11.01(16) (McKinney's 1990).

only a limited audience. While this situation may not have been expressly contemplated by the drafters, the wording of the statute literally covers it, and the spirit of the statute would be contravened by it.

Second, this Court rejects defendants' claim that the reproduction and publication of minor, unrepresentative segments of larger works, printed wholly without context, does not constitute an alteration, defacement, mutilation or modification of plaintiff's artworks. By excising and reproducing only small portions of plaintiff's work, defendants have largely reduced plaintiff's multi-imaged works of art to solely sexual images, devoid of any political and artistic context. Extracting fragmentary images from complex, multi-imaged collages clearly alters and modifies such work.

. . .

Defendants next claim that plaintiff has failed to demonstrate that the alteration, modification, defacement or mutilation has caused or is reasonably likely to result in damage to his reputation. Defendants urge that plaintiff's reputation has not been diminished in the eyes of his peers or gallery directors, dealers and potential buyers who determine his livelihood but, to the contrary, the increased exposure and publicity has enhanced his reputation. However, the trial testimony of Philip Yenawine, an expert on contemporary art, employed by the Modern Museum of Art in New York, established that there is a reasonable likelihood that defendants' actions have jeopardized the monetary value of plaintiff's works and impaired plaintiff's professional and personal reputation.

Yenawine testified that because the details in the pamphlet imply that plaintiff's work consists primarily of explicit images of homosexual sex activity, plaintiff's name will be "anathema" to museums. Museums unfamiliar with plaintiff's work, believing the pamphlet to be representative of his work, may fail to review his work, even though many of plaintiff's art works do not contain sexual images. Even museums familiar with plaintiff's work may be reluctant to show his work due to his perceived association with pornography.

... Additionally, the public may associate plaintiff with only the sexually explicit images which were taken out of his intended political and artistic context, resulting in a reasonable likelihood of harm to his reputation and to the market for his work. . . .

. . .

Defendants next assert that where the speech involves matters of public concern allegedly injuring the reputation of a public figure, actual malice must be proven to defeat First Amendment protection. While agreeing with the quotations submitted by defendants eloquently extolling the virtues of the First Amendment, this Court cannot agree that the alteration, defacement, mutilation or modification of artwork is protected speech, entitling defendants to immunity where they acted without actual malice. . . . [S]uch deception serves no socially useful purpose. The New York Statute does not impede truthful speech, but rather prevents false attribution, requiring only accurate labeling to permit dissemination of the desired message. Such labeling in no way diminishes the force of the message. Defendants remain free to criticize and condemn plaintiff's work if they so choose. They may present incomplete reproductions labeled as such or, alternatively, without attribution of such images to plaintiff. However, they may not present as complete works by plaintiff, selectively cropped versions of his originals. . . .

Accordingly, defendants and all those in privity with them are hereby enjoined and restrained from further publication or distribution of the pamphlet in controversy. . . .

. . .

Under New York's Artists' Authorship Rights Act, an artist is also entitled to legal relief, i.e. damages, for a violation of the Act. N.Y. Art & Cult. Aff. Law § 14.03(4)(a) (McKinney's Supp. 1990). Even though plaintiff has established that defendants' actions were reasonably likely to result in damage to his reputation, he has proven no actual damages. So far as the record shows, not one gallery or museum currently scheduled to exhibit plaintiff's work has canceled; nor has one planned sale been cancelled. Plaintiff presented no evidence that he has been harmed in any other specific, quantifiable way. Accordingly, the Court hereby awards plaintiff nominal damages in the amount of $1.00.

. . . [Editors' Note: The court, however, dismissed the claim for copyright infringement, sustaining the defense of fair use.]

QUESTION

Would defendant have escaped liability under the New York statute had his brochure not attributed the fragments to any particular artist, but had simply asserted that the fragments were illustrative of the kind of art that defendant's association deplored?

C. The Right to Distribute Under § 106(3)

House Report

H.R. Rep. No. 94–1476, 94th Cong., 2d Sess. 62 (1976).

Public distribution.—Clause (3) of section 106 establishes the exclusive right of publication: The right "to distribute copies or phonorecords of the copyrighted work to the public by sale or other transfer of ownership, or by rental, lease, or lending." Under this provision the copyright owner would have the right to control the first public distribution of an authorized copy or phonorecord of his work, whether by sale, gift, loan, or some rental or lease arrangement. Likewise, any unauthorized public distribution of copies or phonorecords that were unlawfully made would be an infringement. As section 109 makes clear, however, the copyright owner's rights under section 106(3) cease with respect to a particular copy or phonorecord once he has parted with ownership of it.

[*Editors' Note.*—Section 109(a) provides: "Notwithstanding the provisions of section 106(3), the owner of a particular copy or phonorecord lawfully made under this title, or any person authorized by such owner, is entitled, without authority of the copyright owner, to sell or otherwise dispose of the possession of that copy or phonorecord."]

1.   THE PURPOSE AND APPLICATION OF THE DISTRIBUTION RIGHT

While the exclusive right to distribute copies or phonorecords of a work is often considered in light of the "first sale doctrine" that limits it, see *infra*, subsection 2, it is appropriate first to consider the right itself. Often implicated in copyright infringement cases, the distribution right rarely receives separate attention, since the principal question tends to be whether the copies defendant sold were infringing. If the reproduction right is violated, then the sale (distribution) of the infringing copies is infringing as well. By the same token, if making the copies entails no violation, then distributing them will often be licit as well. There are instances, however, in which only the distribution right is at issue. For example, in *Columbia Pictures Indus., Inc. v. Garcia*, 996 F.Supp. 770 (N.D.Ill.1998), the defendant purchased unauthorized videocassette copies of motion pictures, which he then rented to his video store's customers. Since Garcia did not reproduce the videocassettes, he could not be charged with violating the reproduction right. But the court held that he infringed the distribution right by renting the unauthorized copies to the public. In *Psihoyos v. Liberation Inc.*, 42 U.S.P.Q.2d 1947 (S.D.N.Y.1997), the plaintiff photographer alleged that an Austrian publisher reproduced his photograph in the pages of its magazine, copies of which were distributed in the U.S. The Austrian defendant contended that there was no violation of the U.S. Copyright Act because the reproduction had occurred in Austria. Even so, held the court, the distribution of copies of the magazine in the U.S. brought the photographer's U.S. distribution right into play.

PUBLIC DISTRIBUTION THROUGH DIGITAL TECHNOLOGIES

Although the prototypical form of public distribution of copies of a work is the physical transfer of possession of tangible books, journals and the like, it has recently become routine to place texts "into the hands" of others through transmissions over computer networks. The text of a newspaper article, for example, can be placed into the storage unit of a computer (by typing or scanning), "uploaded" to an individual by e-mail or more widely to a listserver or bulletin board, viewed by the recipients and then "downloaded" by them into portable form. Under the Copyright Act, there has been a "transmission" of the text from one place to another; this leads to a "display" on the recipient's monitor screen and a "reproduction" when printed out (indeed, the antecedent scanning and uploading have already generated "reproductions"). Does it also lead to a "public distribution" under § 106(3) of the Act? And, if the transmitter uses a lawfully made and lawfully purchased copy of the protected work (i.e., he or she buys the morning's newspaper), does the first-sale doctrine apply so as to exempt the digital transmissions?

It is easy to understand why copyright owners would not be prepared to treat these digital transmissions of text (or music, or art) as within the shelter of the first-sale doctrine. The prototypical "distribution" under the Copyright Act involves one person parting with ownership or possession so that another might acquire it. The described electronic transmission allows the transmitter to retain the original while multiple transmission-recipients end up with copies of their own. The copyright owner's market is adversely affected to the same degree as with the making (either in multiples by the initiating party or singly by each of the recipients) of many unauthorized copies.

When, in 1995, the report, *Intellectual Property and the National Information Infrastructure* (also known as the "White Paper"), was published by the Information Infrastructure Task Force (a group of high-level representatives of U.S. government agencies, chaired by the Secretary of Commerce), the application of § 106(3) to digital dissemination appeared uncertain. As a result, bills were submitted in the 104th Congress (S. 1284, H.R. 2441, 104th Cong., 1st Sess.) adopting the White Paper's recommendations to add to the § 106(3) right the phrase "or by transmission" after the phrase "by rental, lease, or lending." The bills also would have expanded the definition of "publication" in § 101 to include "by transmission"; and would have added to the definition of "transmit" in that section the concept of "transmitting a reproduction," i.e., "to distribute it by any device or process whereby a copy or phonorecord of the work is fixed beyond the place from which it was sent." Unlawful importation under § 602 would also be expanded to include not only "carriage of tangible goods" but also "by transmission."

Congress did not enact these bills, responding in part to the criticisms of many who believed that the White Paper and related legislative proposals exalted the interests of copyright owners while ignoring the vast potential benefits to be derived from Internet access as a means of disseminating information and facilitating public discourse.

In the absence of legislative action, the federal courts appear to have resolved the issue squarely in favor of characterizing as a "distribution" under § 106(3) the affirmative act of making a work available through an electronic network for end-user downloading. Two early decisions concerning digital distributions, one rendered before the White Paper's publication, the other after, ruled that the dissemination of copyrighted works over digital networks effects a distribution of copies. In *Playboy Enters., Inc. v. Frena*, 839 F.Supp. 1552 (M.D.Fla.1993), defendant operated a bulletin board service onto which subscribers had uploaded images scanned from *Playboy* magazine, and which other subscribers could access by downloading from the bulletin board. The court held that, by making the images available for downloading, the bulletin board operator was "supplying a product," and thus engaged in an unauthorized distribution of copies to subscribers.

Similarly, the district court in *Playboy Enters., Inc. v. Chuckleberry Pub'g, Inc.*, 939 F.Supp. 1032 (S.D.N.Y.1996), held that the operator of an Italian website accessible to U.S. users, and featuring "Playmen" magazine, effected a distribution of copies of "Playmen" in the U.S., in violation of *Playboy*'s trademark rights. The website operator had argued that its role was passive: rather than distributing copies in the U.S., the website was simply making it possible for U.S. readers to make a "virtual voyage" to Italy, where they would collect and repatriate their copies. The court found the website's role to be more active: "That the local user 'pulls' these images from [defendant's] computer in Italy, as opposed to [defendant] 'sending' them to this country, is irrelevant. By inviting United States users to download these images, [defendant] is causing and contributing to their distribution in the United States." 939 F.Supp. at 1044.

More recently, other decisions, many of them also involving Playboy Enterprises, have followed or elaborated on *Frena* in holding that a website operator "distributes" copyright works "by allowing its users to download and print copies of electronic image files." *Playboy Enters., Inc. v. Webbworld, Inc.*, 991 F.Supp. 543 (N.D.Tex.1997). *See also Playboy Enters., Inc. v. Russ Hardenburgh, Inc.*, 982 F.Supp. 503 (N.D.Ohio 1997) ("Defendants disseminated unlawful copies of PEI photographs to the public by adopting a policy in which Rusty 'N' Edie's BBS employees moved those copies to the generally available files [for public downloading] instead of discarding them.").

By contrast, in *Religious Tech. Ctr. v. Netcom*, 907 F.Supp. 1361 (N.D.Cal.1995), the court held that the online service provider's role in making allegedly infringing material available to the public was truly passive: "Only the [uploading] subscriber should be liable for causing the distribution of plaintiff's work, as the contributing actions of the BBS provider are automatic and indiscriminate.... Unlike the BBS in [*Playboy v. Frena*], Netcom ... cannot be said to be 'supplying a product.' ... Netcom does not create or control the content of the information available to its subscribers; it merely provides access to the Internet.... " 907 F.Supp. at 1372. *Accord, Marobie-Fl, Inc. v. National Ass'n of Fire Equip. Distribs.*, 983 F.Supp. 1167 (N.D.Ill.1997) (holding that the webserver host of a webpage containing infringing copies of plaintiff's works had violated plaintiff's exclusive distribution right, but also holding that the online service provider who merely "automatically serves up a copy of the requested file" to Internet users, should not be liable for violation of the distribution, display, or reproduction rights).

Together, these decisions indicate that a bulletin board or webpage operator or online service that, like the "Playmen" webpage, *originates* infringing content may be held to have effected a "distribution of copies" in violation of § 106(3). Moreover, a digital entrepreneur who, like Frena or "Rusty and Edie," operates a BBS or website whose content it can supervise or control (and perhaps even invites), may also be "distributing" copies. On the other hand, the more the digital service resembles a "mere conduit" for material originated or controlled by others, the less likely its simple, "automatic and indiscriminate" relaying of content from one server to another is to be deemed a "distribution of copies" (or, for that matter, a direct violation of any of the § 106 rights).

On the liability of online service providers, see also *infra* Chapter 8.F.

2. The First Sale Doctrine (Exhaustion of the Distribution Right), and its Exceptions

Fawcett Publications v. Elliot Publishing Co.

46 F.Supp. 717 (S.D.N.Y.1942).

■ Clancy, District Judge.

The plaintiff is engaged in the magazine publishing business as is the defendant. The plaintiff, on or about April 18, 1941, being then the author and proprietor of a publication known as "Wow Comics, No. 2 Summer Edition," copyrighted it and was, therefore, entitled to the exclusive right to print, reprint, publish, copy and vend it. Subsequent to this publication's issuance the defendant purchased secondhand copies of it and of another copyrighted publication of the plaintiff, which he makes the subject of the second cause of action, and bound them together with other comic publications not owned or copyrighted by the plaintiff within one copyrighted cover of its own with the words "Double Comics" thereon.

Section 1 of Title 17, U.S.C.A. grants to the copyright owner the exclusive right "to print, reprint, publish, copy, and vend the copyrighted work.... " The alleged infringement as set forth in the complaint is that the defendant published and placed upon the market said "Double Comics" containing the complete issue of plaintiff's publication, without its consent or approval, so that as thus limited, it must be determined whether the defendant violated the plaintiff's admitted exclusive right to publish and secondly to vend. The decisions appear to be uniform that the purpose and effect of the copyright statute is to secure to the owner thereof the exclusive right to multiply copies. *Bobbs-Merrill Co. v. Straus*, 210 U.S. 339; *Jeweler's Circular Pub. Co. v. Keystone Pub. Co.*, 281 F. 83 (C.C.A.2d.), *cert. denied*, 259 U.S. 581. It is conceded here that the defendant has not multiplied copies but merely resold the plaintiff's under a different cover. The exclusive right to vend is limited. It is confined to the first sale of any one copy and exerts no restriction on the future sale of that copy. *Bureau of National Literature v. Sells*, 211 F. 379; *Strauss v. American Publishers Ass'n*, 231 U.S. 222; *Bentley v. Tibbals*, 223 F. 247 (C.C.A.2d.). The defendant is not charged with copying, reprinting or rearranging the copyrighted material of the plaintiff or any of its component parts nor has it removed the plaintiff's copyright notice....

The [plaintiff's] motion [for summary judgment] is denied.

QUESTIONS

1. If the defendant had in fact been charged with the acts enumerated in the court's last sentence, what would the outcome have been?

2. Suppose a bookstore receives from a publisher copyrighted prints picturing the mansion that is the setting of a novel. The bookstore is to distribute the print only as a premium with the purchase of copies of the novel, but instead it sells the prints. Does the publisher have a claim for copyright infringement, or for anything else? *Compare Burke & Van Heusen, Inc. v. Arrow Drug, Inc.,* 233 F.Supp. 881 (E.D.Pa.1964) *with U.S. Naval Inst. v. Charter Commun., Inc.,* 936 F.2d 692 (2d Cir.1991).

For a more modern version of this problem, see *Microsoft Corp. v. Harmony Computers & Elec., Inc.,* 846 F.Supp. 208 (E.D.N.Y.1994). There, Microsoft distributed software by way of license (rather than sale) to persons using single-user computer systems; the license was accompanied by warranties and a product-support system. Certain licensees sold the software to Harmony Electronics, which in turn distributed it to the public in "stand-alone form" or loaded onto computer hard disks. As a defense to Microsoft's lawsuit for unauthorized public distribution, Harmony asserted rights under the first-sale doctrine. Does it have such rights (i.e., has there been the kind of "first sale" to Harmony that gives it rights in turn to sell to others)? *See also Adobe Systems Inc. v. One Stop Micro, Inc.,* 84 F.Supp.2d 1086 (N.D.Cal.2000).

A "DIGITAL FIRST SALE DOCTRINE"?

As we have seen (Note, "Public Distribution through Digital Technologies," *supra*), distribution of digital copies entails the making of additional copies. While the seller or giver of a physical copy parts with her copy in order to confer it on the recipient, one who communicates a copy digitally is in fact not parting with her copy, but is making another copy appear in the RAM or hard drive of the recipient (along with transient copies made in the course of the communication through computer networks). Because "giving" a digital copy in fact yields new copies, the first sale doctrine, which derives from the analog copy owner's chattel rights, does not apply. But one might contend that those who communicate a digital copy should be able to claim the shelter of the first sale doctrine, so long as they erase their own copies. If the recipient obtains a copy, while the sender no longer has hers, then this approach would approximate the situation underlying the first sale doctrine scenario. Digital copy owners would then enjoy the same autonomy as analog copy owners, and copyright owners would not be harmed because, in effect, only one copy would circulate.

In its report issued August 29, 2001 (see Note on "What is a Copy?" *supra*, subchapter 6A), the Copyright Office, however, declined to endorse a "digital first sale doctrine," which would modify the Copyright Act to exempt a digital copy forwarded to one recipient so long as the original were deleted. (See *http://www.loc.gov/copyright/reports/studies/dmca/sec–104–report–vol–1.pdf*) Although proponents of this exemption claimed that it is the digital equivalent of giving away a book—an activity squarely covered by the current first sale doctrine—the Copyright office articulated several pragmatic distinctions. The Office first noted that the urged doctrine in fact involved creating a new exception to the *reproduction* right, rather than a new application of the exhaustion doctrine which centers on physical objects. It then stressed that software currently in use does not include a forward-and-delete function, and that one cannot expect that senders will systematically delete their copies themselves. The Office also rejected the claimed equivalence between forward-and-delete and the first sale doctrine, on the ground that a "digital first sale doctrine's" impact on normal exploitation of the work is far greater than a physical-copy first sale doctrine. For example, the Office pointed out that a library (commercial or non-commercial) would need fewer copies of a work that is "lent" out digitally, because its delivery and return are instantaneous, while physical copies require more time going out and coming back. Fewer copies can satisfy the same or greater demand when physical-copy travel time is eliminated.

THE RECORD RENTAL AND COMPUTER–SOFTWARE RENTAL AMENDMENTS OF 1984 AND 1990

On October 4, 1984, Congress made a significant departure from the first-sale doctrine initially codified in the 1909 Act and endorsed in § 109(a). In the Record Rental Amendment of 1984, Pub. L. No. 98–450, Congress in a new § 109(b) declared:

> [U]nless authorized by the owners of copyright in the sound recording and in the musical works embodied therein, the owner of a particular phonorecord may not, for purposes of direct or indirect commercial advantage, dispose of, or authorize the disposal of, the possession of that phonorecord by rental, lease, or lending.

The obvious target of the new legislation was the record-rental store, which came upon the retail marketing scene in 1981 and by mid–1984 had grown to about 200 in number. These stores rented phonorecords to their customers for anywhere from 24 to 72 hours, at rates ranging from 99 cents to $2.50 per disc; most such stores also stocked blank cassette tapes, often sold at discount to customers renting albums. In the words of the Senate Report: "The Committee has no doubt that the purpose and result of record rentals is to enable and encourage customers to tape their rented albums at home.... Thus, a record rental and a blank tape purchase is now an alternative way of obtaining a record without having to buy one. The rental is a direct displacement of a sale." S. Rep. No. 98–162, 98th Cong., 1st Sess. 2 (1983). The Report referred to the proliferation of record-rental stores in Japan, numbering at the time approximately 1700, as well as the spread of the phenomenon to Canada and a number of countries in Western Europe. It also mentioned the recent development of the digital compact disc, scanned by a laser and nearly indestructible, thus permitting the record-rental shop to rent each disc hundreds of times.

The legislative reports made it clear that the new law would constitute only a minor modification of the first-sale doctrine. It would not restrict the right of the purchaser of a phonorecord to sell it or give it away. The amended § 109(b) explicitly provides that the record-renting ban is not to apply "to the rental, lease, or lending of a phonorecord for nonprofit purposes by a nonprofit library or nonprofit educational institution." Section 115(c) was amended so as to permit record rental or leasing for profit by a record manufacturer operating under that section's compulsory-license provision, so long as it shared its income from the rental or leasing with the copyright owner of the musical composition.

In 1990 Congress again modified the first-sale doctrine, this time by enacting the Computer Software Rental Amendments of 1990, Pub. L. No. 101–650, Title VII, 104 Stat. 5089 (1990). This amendment grants authors or producers of software the right to authorize or to prohibit the rental of copies, even after their initial sale. However, the scope of the right is more limited than that of the 1984 record rental amendment, for Congress included even more exceptions to the computer program rental right than it had imposed on the record rental right. The 1990 law excepts non-remunerative transfers of copies of programs within libraries, universities and schools. Moreover, software copyright owners may not prohibit the rental of copies contained within computer hardware when the programs are not normally susceptible to copying. As a result, the law does not hinder the rental of hardware, even when it contains chips or other fixations of programs. Thus, for example, this exemption permits untrammeled rental of cars containing computer voice programs that remind the driver that the seat belt is unbuckled or that "a door is ajar."

Finally, the 1990 amendment allows noncommercial libraries to lend copies of computer programs to the public, so long as these copies bear a copyright notice.

In *Central Point Software, Inc. v. Global Software & Accessories, Inc.,* 880 F.Supp. 957 (S.D.N.Y.1995), the court interpreted the statute's prohibition of "any other act or practice in the nature of rental, lease or lending" to condemn a deferred billing program through which defendant's customers could purchase a computer program and then return the program thereafter, incurring merely a service charge for the temporary possession of the program.

QUESTIONS

1. You have been consulted by a bookstore, seeking advice on whether permission must be sought to engage in either of the following activities: (a) It wishes to rent, for a nightly charge of $1.99, "audiobooks"—audiocassettes containing full or abridged texts of books as read by authors or actors—that it has purchased from legitimate wholesale sources. (b) It wishes to rent, for the same nightly charge, computerized videogames, i.e., game cartridges to be used in conjunction with a device attached to a home television set or computer monitor. What advice would you give?

2. It has been suggested that there be a statutory ban on renting not only phonorecords and computer programs but also on videocassettes of motion pictures. Would you support such a ban (or perhaps a compulsory license)? Do the same policies and principles apply?

PUBLIC LENDING RIGHT

Because public libraries purchase only a few copies of a book and yet disseminate that work to a large number of people who might otherwise buy it, some countries (mostly European) have developed an alternative form of compensation to the author called a "public lending right." Generally, in these countries, an author receives a "royalty" based upon the circulation (actual or potential) of the work. In some countries, the royalty is correlated directly to the number of times the book is loaned to a library user. In others, the royalty is calculated on the basis of the library's holdings, regardless of how often a particular work is loaned to users. Finally, some countries provide for a one-time payment to the author at the time of acquisition, as a sort of "surcharge." Public lending right schemes are often enacted outside of the country's copyright laws. This is because many countries, the U.K., for example, consider the public lending right royalty as a kind of payment for services, rather than a traditional license for exploitation. *See* Brigid Brophy, A Guide to the Public Lending Right [U.K.] 53 (1983). In 1992, the European Union harmonized the rental and public lending rights, instructing member States to afford authors at least the right to receive remuneration for public lending (defined as "not for direct or indirect economic or commercial advantage ... made through establishments which are accessible to the public"). *See* Council Directive 92/100, O.J.E.D. No. L. 346/61 (Nov. 27, 1992), arts. 1.2, 1.3, 5.1.

DROIT DE SUITE

Another manifestation of the belief that authors should share in the subsequent profitable disposition of lawfully owned copies of their works is the so-called *droit de suite,* which provides that an artist shall share in the profits accruing to subsequent purchasers from the appreciation in value of the artist's works. Although the *droit de suite* exists in a number of European countries, California is the only state that has enacted a resale-royalties statute. It provides that:

> Whenever a work of fine art is sold and the seller resides in California or the sale takes place in California, the seller or his agent shall pay to the artist of such work of fine art or to such artist's agent 5 percent of the amount of such sale.

The artist's right is non-waivable and may be enforced by an action for damages with a three-year period of limitations; moneys payable to the artist will be paid to the state Arts Council if the seller cannot locate the artist within 90 days, and all moneys due the artist are exempt from attachment or execution of judgment by creditors of the seller. Among those sales exempted from the statute are resales for a gross price of less than $1,000, resales made more than 20 years after the death of the artist, and resales for a gross sales price less than the purchase price paid by the seller.

On the federal level, proponents of the *droit de suite* have made several attempts to incorporate the concept into the Copyright Act, most recently as a provision in the Visual Artists Rights Act of 1990, Pub. L. No. 101–650, Title VI, 104 Stat. 5089 (1990). Though the 1990 provision was ultimately deleted from the final bill, the effort was more successful than its predecessors: Congress did direct the Register of Copyrights to conduct a study examining the feasibility of adopting a resale-rights program in the United States.

On December 1, 1992, the Register reported that, based on the record developed through the inquiry, he had found insufficient justification for the adoption of the system in the U.S. copyright law. *See generally* U.S. Copyright Office, *Droit de Suite*: The Artists Resale Royalty (1992) [Report]. However, the Register's negative assessment was explicitly qualified by both the lack of conclusive data and the possibility that a harmonization of policy within the European Community countries might dictate a different conclusion. The Report concluded by proposing alternatives to *droit de suite,* such as creating a commercial rental right, and expanding the public display right (by amending § 109) to provide for an artist's right to license the work for public display even after the work has been sold. These alternatives might not in fact provide greater income for the artist, but would at least expand an artist's control over her work.

Ultimately, in the event that Congress were to override the Register's suggestion to reject *droit de suite,* the Report offered a model for the implementation of *droit de suite.* Drawing on several features from several sources, the Report suggested that the U.S. *droit de suite*: cover all works covered by the Visual Artists Rights Act (except those created in more than 10 copies); endure as long as the copyright term; apply only to works sold at public auction; be calculated as three to five percent of the sale price with no minimum threshold; be collected by a private collecting society. Additionally, the right would extend prospectively, i.e., only to works created after passage of the law, and would cover foreign authors on the basis of reciprocity rather than national treatment. For a critical analysis of the Report, see Shira Perlmutter, *Resale Royalties for Artists: An Analysis of the Register of Copyrights' Report,* 16 Colum.-VLA J. L. & Arts 395 (1993).

QUESTIONS

1. Do you favor a general public lending right? How would you provide for such a right by amendment of the Copyright Act? For example, would it apply to all classes of works in § 102, or only to certain classes, such as literary works or audiovisual works? (Or only sound recordings?) Would it apply to all lending transactions (including public libraries) or only those for commercial purposes? Would your bill provide for an absolute ban on such lending or would it provide for a compulsory license? If the latter, how would the rates be established?

2. Do you favor a ban (or a compulsory license) regarding the subsequent sales of certain kinds of works, such as used textbooks? Doesn't the California resale royalties statute in effect create a compulsory license governing the resale of works of fine art? Is the statute an unconstitutional encumbrance upon the rights granted by the Copyright Act? *See Morseburg v. Balyon,* 621 F.2d 972 (9th Cir.), *cert. denied,* 449 U.S. 983 (1980). Should Congress amend the Act to provide for such resale royalties?

3. THE § 602(a) IMPORTATION RIGHT, AND ITS RELATIONSHIP TO THE DISTRIBUTION RIGHT

§ 602. Infringing Importation of Copies or Phonorecords

(a) Importation into the United States, without the authority of the owner of copyright under this title, of copies or phonorecords of a work that have been acquired outside the United States is an infringement of the exclusive right to distribute copies or phonorecords under Section 106, actionable under Section 501....

§ 501. Infringement of Copyright

(a) Anyone who violates any of the exclusive rights of the copyright owner as provided by sections 106 through 119, or who imports copies or phonorecords into the United States in violation of section 602, is an infringer of the copyright.

———

The relationship among the § 106(3) distribution right, its limitation by § 109(a), and the § 602(a) importation right has proved controversial under the 1976 Act. The cases arose in the context of the "grey market": the distribution in the United States of genuine goods (usually lawfully manufactured abroad, but sometimes manufactured in the U.S. for shipment overseas) imported into the United States without the authorization of the United States copyright holder. A strong dollar often underlies the grey market; as a result of disparities in currency values, it can be cheaper for a distributor to purchase the goods abroad and import them to the United States (to undersell the authorized United States dealer) than to purchase the goods here.

Quality King Distributors, Inc. v. L'anza Research International, Inc.

523 U.S. 135 (1998).

■ JUSTICE STEVENS delivered the opinion of the Court.

Section 106(3) of the Copyright Act of 1976 (Act), 17 U.S.C. § 106(3), gives the owner of a copyright the exclusive right to distribute copies of a copyrighted work. That exclusive right is expressly limited, however, by the provisions of §§ 107 through 120. Section 602(a) gives the copyright owner the right to prohibit the unauthorized importation of copies. The question presented by this case is whether the right granted by § 602(a) is also limited by §§ 107 through 120. More narrowly, the question is whether the "first sale" doctrine endorsed in § 109(a) is applicable to imported copies.

I

Respondent, L'anza Research International, Inc. (L'anza), is a California corporation engaged in the business of manufacturing and selling shampoos, conditioners, and other hair care products. L'anza has copyrighted the labels that are affixed to those products. In the United States, L'anza sells exclusively to domestic distributors who have agreed to resell within limited geographic areas and then only to authorized retailers such as barber shops, beauty salons, and professional hair care colleges. L'anza has found that the American "public is generally unwilling to pay the price charged for high quality products, such as L'anza's products, when they are sold along with the less expensive lower quality products that are generally carried by supermarkets and drug stores." App. 54 (declaration of Robert Hall). L'anza promotes the domestic sales of its products with extensive advertising in various trade magazines and at point of sale, and by providing special training to authorized retailers.

L'anza also sells its products in foreign markets. In those markets, however, it does not engage in comparable advertising or promotion; its prices to foreign distributors are 35% to 40% lower than the prices charged to domestic distributors. In 1992 and 1993, L'anza's distributor in the United Kingdom arranged the sale of three shipments to a distributor in Malta; each shipment contained several tons of L'anza products with copyrighted labels affixed. The record does not establish whether the initial purchaser was the distributor in the United Kingdom or the distributor in Malta, or whether title passed when the goods were delivered to the carrier or when they arrived at their destination, but it is undisputed that the goods were manufactured by L'anza and first sold by L'anza to a foreign purchaser.

It is also undisputed that the goods found their way back to the United States without the permission of L'anza and were sold in California by unauthorized retailers who had purchased them at discounted prices from Quality King Distributors, Inc. (petitioner). There is some uncertainty about the identity of the actual importer, but for the purpose of our decision we assume that petitioner bought all three shipments from the Malta distributor, imported them, and then resold them to retailers who were not in L'anza's authorized chain of distribution.

After determining the source of the unauthorized sales, L'anza brought suit against petitioner and several other defendants. The complaint alleged that the importation and subsequent distribution of those products bearing copyrighted labels violated L'anza's "exclusive rights under 17 U.S.C. §§ 106, 501 and 602 to reproduce and distribute the copyrighted material in the United States." App. 32. The District Court rejected petitioner's defense based on the "first sale" doctrine recognized by § 109 and entered summary judgment in favor of L'anza. Based largely on its conclusion that § 602 would be "meaningless" if § 109 provided a defense in a case of this kind, the Court of Appeals affirmed. 98 F.3d 1109, 1114 (C.A.9 1996). Because its decision created a conflict with the Third Circuit, see *Sebastian Int'l, Inc. v. Consumer Contacts (PTY) Ltd.*, 847 F.2d 1093 (1988), we granted the petition for certiorari. 520 U.S. ___ (1997).

II

This is an unusual copyright case because L'anza does not claim that anyone has made unauthorized copies of its copyrighted labels. Instead, L'anza is primarily interested in protecting the integrity of its method of marketing the products to which the labels are affixed. Although the labels themselves have only a limited creative component, our interpretation of the relevant statutory provisions would apply equally to a case involving more familiar copyrighted materials such as sound recordings or books. Indeed, we first endorsed the first sale doctrine in a case involving a claim by a publisher that the resale of its books at discounted prices infringed its copyright on the books. *Bobbs-Merrill Co. v. Straus*, 210 U.S. 339 (1908).

In that case, the publisher, Bobbs–Merrill, had inserted a notice in its books that any retail sale at a price under $1.00 would constitute an infringement of its copyright. The defendants, who owned Macy's department store, disregarded the notice and sold the books at a lower price without Bobbs–Merrill's consent. We held that the exclusive statutory right to "vend" applied only to the first sale of the copyrighted work:

> What does the statute mean in granting "the sole right of vending the same"? Was it intended to create a right which would permit the holder of the copyright to fasten, by notice in a book or upon one of the articles mentioned within the statute, a restriction upon the subsequent alienation of the subject-matter of copyright after the owner had parted with the title to one who had acquired full dominion over it and had given a satisfactory price for it? It is not denied that one who has sold a copyrighted article, without restriction, has parted with all right to control the sale of it. The purchaser of a book, once sold by authority of the owner of the copyright, may sell it again, although he could not publish a new edition of it.

> In this case the stipulated facts show that the books sold by the appellant were sold at wholesale, and purchased by those who made no agreement as to the control of future sales of the book, and took upon themselves no obligation to enforce the notice printed in the book, undertaking to restrict retail sales to a price of one dollar per copy. *Id.*, at 349–350.

The statute in force when *Bobbs-Merrill* was decided provided that the copyright owner had the exclusive right to "vend" the copyrighted work.

Congress subsequently codified our holding in *Bobbs-Merrill* that the exclusive right to "vend" was limited to first sales of the work. Under the 1976 Act, the comparable exclusive right granted in 17 U.S.C. § 106(3) is the right "to distribute copies . . . by sale or other transfer of ownership." The comparable limitation on that right is provided not by judicial interpretation, but by an express statutory provision. Section 109(a) provides:

> Notwithstanding the provisions of section 106(3), the owner of a particular copy or phonorecord lawfully made under this title, or any person authorized by such owner, is entitled, without the authority of the copyright owner, to sell or otherwise dispose of the possession of that copy or phonorecord. . . .

The *Bobbs-Merrill* opinion emphasized the critical distinction between statutory rights and contract rights. In this case, L'anza relies on the terms of its contracts with its domestic distributors to limit their sales to authorized retail outlets. . . . L'anza [claims], however, that contractual provisions are inadequate to protect it from the actions of foreign distributors who may resell L'anza's products to American vendors unable to buy from L'anza's domestic distributors, and that § 602(a) of the Act, properly construed, prohibits such unauthorized competition. To evaluate that submission, we must, of course, consider the text of § 602(a).

III

The most relevant portion of § 602(a) provides:

> Importation into the United States, without the authority of the owner of copyright under this title, of copies or phonorecords of a work that have been acquired outside the United States is an infringement of the exclusive right to distribute copies or phonorecords under section 106, actionable under section 501. . . .

It is significant that this provision does not categorically prohibit the unauthorized importation of copyrighted materials. Instead, it provides that such importation is an infringement of the exclusive right to distribute copies "under section 106." Like the exclusive right to "vend" that was construed in Bobbs–Merrill, the exclusive right to distribute is a limited right. The introductory language in § 106 expressly states that all of the exclusive rights granted by that section—including, of course, the distribution right granted by subsection (3)—are limited by the provisions of §§ 107 through 120. One of those limitations, as we have noted, is provided by the terms of § 109(a), which expressly permit the owner of a lawfully made copy to sell that copy "notwithstanding the provisions of section 106(3)."

After the first sale of a copyrighted item "lawfully made under this title," any subsequent purchaser, whether from a domestic or from a foreign reseller, is obviously an "owner" of that item. Read literally, § 109(a) unambiguously states that such an owner "is entitled, without the authority of the copyright owner, to sell" that item. Moreover, since § 602(a) merely provides that unauthorized importation is an infringement of an exclusive right "under section 106," and since that limited right does not encompass resales by lawful owners, the literal text of § 602(a) is simply inapplicable to both domestic and foreign owners of L'anza's products who decide to import them and resell them in the United States.[14]

Notwithstanding the clarity of the text of §§ 106(3), 109(a), and 602(a), L'anza argues that the language of the Act supports a construction of the right granted by § 602(a) as "distinct from the right under Section 106(3) standing alone," and thus not subject to § 109(a)....

IV

L'anza advances two primary arguments based on the text of the Act: (1) that § 602(a), and particularly its three exceptions, are superfluous if limited by the first sale doctrine; and (2) that the text of § 501 defining an "infringer" refers separately to violations of § 106, on the one hand, and to imports in violation of § 602. The short answer to both of these arguments is that neither adequately explains why the words "under section 106" appear in § 602(a)....

The Coverage of § 602(a)

The argument that the statutory exceptions to § 602(a) are superfluous if the first sale doctrine is applicable rests on the assumption that the coverage of that section is co-extensive with the coverage of § 109(a). But since it is, in fact, broader because it encompasses copies that are not subject to the first sale doctrine—e.g., copies that are lawfully made under the law of another country—the exceptions do protect the traveler who may have made an isolated purchase of a copy of a work that could not be imported in bulk for purposes of resale. As we read the Act, although both the first sale doctrine embodied in § 109(a) and the exceptions in § 602(a) may be applicable in some situations, the former does not subsume the latter; those provisions retain significant independent meaning.

Section 501's Separate References to §§ 106 and 602

The text of § 501 does lend support to L'anza's submission. In relevant part, it provides:

> (a) Anyone who violates any of the exclusive rights of the copyright owner as provided by sections 106 through 118 or of the author as provided in section 106A(a), or who imports copies or phonorecords into the United States in violation of section 602, is an infringer of the copyright or right of the author, as the case may be....

The use of the words "or who imports," rather than words such as "including one who imports," is more consistent with an interpretation that a violation of § 602 is distinct from a violation of § 106 (and thus not

---

14. Despite L'anza's contention to the contrary, see Brief for Respondent 26–27, the owner of goods lawfully made under the Act is entitled to the protection of the first sale doctrine in an action in a United States court even if the first sale occurred abroad. Such protection does not require the extraterritorial application of the Act any more than § 602(a)'s "acquired abroad" language does.

subject to the first sale doctrine set out in § 109(a)) than with the view that it is a species of such a violation. Nevertheless, the force of that inference is outweighed by other provisions in the statutory text.

Most directly relevant is the fact that the text of § 602(a) itself unambiguously states that the prohibited importation is an infringement of the exclusive distribution right "under section 106, actionable under section 501." ... [T]hat phrase ... identifies § 602 violations as a species of § 106 violations....

Of even greater importance is the fact that the § 106 rights are subject not only to the first sale defense in § 109(a), but also to all of the other provisions of "sections 107 through 120." If § 602(a) functioned independently, none of those sections would limit its coverage. For example, the "fair use" defense embodied in § 107 would be unavailable to importers if § 602(a) created a separate right not subject to the limitations on the § 106(3) distribution right. Under L'anza's interpretation of the Act, it presumably would be unlawful for a distributor to import copies of a British newspaper that contained a book review quoting excerpts from an American novel protected by a United States copyright.[23] Given the importance of the fair use defense to publishers of scholarly works, as well as to publishers of periodicals, it is difficult to believe that Congress intended to impose an absolute ban on the importation of all such works containing any copying of material protected by a United States copyright.

In the context of this case, involving copyrighted labels, it seems unlikely that an importer could defend an infringement as a "fair use" of the label. In construing the statute, however, we must remember that its principal purpose was to promote the progress of the "useful Arts," U.S. Const., Art. I, § 8, cl. 8, by rewarding creativity, and its principal function is the protection of original works, rather than ordinary commercial products that use copyrighted material as a marketing aid. It is therefore appropriate to take into account the impact of the denial of the fair use defense for the importer of foreign publications. As applied to such publications, L'anza's construction of § 602 "would merely inhibit access to ideas without any countervailing benefit." *Sony Corp. of America v. Universal City Studios, Inc.*, 464 U.S. 417, 450–451 (1984).

. . . .

V

The parties and their amici have debated at length the wisdom or unwisdom of governmental restraints on what is sometimes described as either the "gray market" or the practice of "parallel importation." In *K-Mart Corp. v. Cartier, Inc.*, 486 U.S. 281 (1988), we used those terms to refer to the importation of foreign-manufactured goods bearing a valid United States trademark without the consent of the trademark holder. *Id.*,

---

23. The § 602(a) exceptions, which are substantially narrower than § 107, would not   permit such importation.

at 285–286. We are not at all sure that those terms appropriately describe the consequences of an American manufacturer's decision to limit its promotional efforts to the domestic market and to sell its products abroad at discounted prices that are so low that its foreign distributors can compete in the domestic market. But even if they do, whether or not we think it would be wise policy to provide statutory protection for such price discrimination is not a matter that is relevant to our duty to interpret the text of the Copyright Act. . . .

The judgment of the Court of Appeals is reversed.

■ Justice Ginsburg, concurring.

This case involves a "round trip" journey, travel of the copies in question from the United States to places abroad, then back again. I join the Court's opinion recognizing that we do not today resolve cases in which the allegedly infringing imports were manufactured abroad. *See* W. Patry, Copyright Law and Practice 166–170 (1997 Supp.) (commenting that provisions of Title 17 do not apply extraterritorially unless expressly so stated, hence the words "lawfully made under this title" in the "first sale" provision, 17 U.S.C. § 109(a), must mean "lawfully made in the United States"); *see generally* P. Goldstein, Copyright § 16.0, pp. 16:1–16:2 (2d ed. 1998) ("Copyright protection is territorial. The rights granted by the United States Copyright Act extend no farther than the nation's borders.").

QUESTIONS

1. What *does* "lawfully made under this title" mean? Does Title 17 apply to reproductions made outside the U.S.?

2. If § 109(a) applies to "round trip" copies, but not to copies made abroad and then imported to the U.S., what might one anticipate about where a producer, who seeks to price-discriminate among different national or regional markets, might manufacture the copies?

D. Rights of Public Performance and Display Under § 106(4), (5), (6)

Public performing rights came relatively late in statutory copyright development. The right was first recognized as to dramatic compositions by the amendatory Act of 1856, and as to musical compositions by the Act of 1897. At the turn of the twentieth century, the main source of revenue for the composer had long been by way of royalties from the sale of copies of his or her work in the form of sheet music, and sometimes these ran into large sums: before radio, an average hit song may have sold over a million copies of sheet music. The increasing use of popular music through performances—in theaters (both in live musical revues and to accompany silent motion pictures) and by radio broadcasts—and the contemporaneous decline in revenue from the sale of copies, at last awakened composers to the possibilities inherent in the performing right.

In 1909, the Copyright Act—which retained the right of public performance of dramatic works—was amended to give to the owner of copyright in a musical composition the exclusive right to perform it "publicly for profit." As was not unusual with the 1909 Act, none of the central terms—such as perform, public or profit—was defined, and it fell to the courts to give meaning to this language, not an easy task as new technologies and industries developed for the use and dissemination of music. A landmark decision of the Supreme Court was *Herbert v. Shanley*, 242 U.S. 591 (1917), which held that a musical performance by a small orchestra in a restaurant was "for profit" despite the fact that no separate admission charge was made to hear the music. Lower courts also interpreted the phrase liberally over time, so as to make it clear that live music accompanying silent motion pictures required a license from the copyright owner, *M. Witmark & Sons v. Pastime Amusement Co.*, 298 F. 470 (E.D.S.C.), aff'd, 2 F.2d 1020 (4th Cir.1925); as did the broadcast of music, on a commercial-free program, by a nonprofit radio station which paid for one-third of its airtime by accepting commercial advertising, *Associated Music Pubs. v. Debs Mem. Radio Fund, Inc.*, 141 F.2d 852 (2d Cir.1944).

The question whether certain face-to-face performances were "public"—such as at a social club or summer camp—was left uncertain by the decided cases under the 1909 Act. And, once "talkies" were invented, the question whether showings in movie houses were "public" performances was left unanswered after it was held that the flashing of a film upon the screen generated an infringing "copy" under the 1909 Act, requiring a license regardless of the public or private character of the performance. *See Patterson v. Century Prods.*, 93 F.2d 489 (2d Cir.1937). It became clear, however, that a radio broadcast was a "public" performance, even though the members of the public who received the broadcast on their sets were in their private homes and in separate locations. *See, e.g., Jerome H. Remick & Co. v. American Auto. Accessories Co.*, 5 F.2d 411 (6th Cir.1925).

New technologies, which allowed for intermediate re-transmissions of radio and television broadcasts, further compounded the definitional complexities confronted by the courts under the 1909 Act—even concerning the most fundamental question whether these re-transmissions constitute "performances." In a somewhat controversial decision in 1931, the Supreme Court held that a hotel proprietor "performed" music by making the sounds of radio broadcasts audible by placing receivers and loudspeakers in public and private rooms in the hotel. *Buck v. Jewell–LaSalle Realty Co.*, 283 U.S. 191 (1931). (On the precise facts, the broadcasts of the neighboring radio station were themselves unauthorized, which later Supreme Court decisions emphasized in explaining the hotel's liability.) The Court's approach came to be known as the "multiple performance" doctrine.

In the early days of cable television, indeed when it was better known as community antenna television ("CATV"), the Supreme Court held that unauthorized re-transmissions of television broadcasts did not require licenses from the copyright owners of the broadcast programs, because the cable systems did not "perform" those works. This was true whether the cable stations were showing local programs that could not be clearly viewed because of obstacles such as mountains or tall buildings, *Fortnightly Corp.*

v. United Artists T.V., Inc., 392 U.S. 390 (1968), or were showing programs re-transmitted from hundreds of miles away into distant television markets in which those programs were otherwise inaccessible, *Teleprompter Corp. v. Columbia Broadcasting Sys.*, 415 U.S. 394 (1974). On the theory that broadcasters "perform" but home viewers do not, a divided Court treated the cable technology as merely facilitating reception by the homeowner.

It therefore came as little surprise when the Court held, on the eve of the enactment of the 1976 Act, that a fast-food restaurant owner who played radio programs through four small speakers he had installed in the ceiling of his shop did not "perform"; he was doing little more than turning on the radio, and "those who listen to the broadcast through the use of radio receivers do not perform the composition." *Twentieth Century Music Corp. v. Aiken*, 422 U.S. 151 (1975).

The Court endorsed this principle of statutory interpretation of the Copyright Act: "Creative work is to be encouraged and rewarded, but private motivation must ultimately serve the cause of promoting broad public availability of literature, music, and the other arts. . . . When technological change has rendered its literal terms ambiguous, the Copyright Act must be construed in light of this basic purpose."

Congress soon stepped in to clarify the scope of the public-performance right.

§ 106.   Exclusive Rights in Copyrighted Works

Subject to sections 107 through 121, the owner of copyright under this title has the exclusive rights to do and to authorize any of the following:

. . .

(4) in the case of literary, musical, dramatic and choreographic works, pantomimes, and motion pictures and other audiovisual works, to perform the copyrighted work publicly;

. . .

(6) in the case of sound recordings, to perform the copyrighted work publicly by means of a digital audio transmission.

[*Editors' Note:* The 1976 Act, subject to certain specified limitations, extended the copyright monopoly to public performances without regard to whether the performance is "for profit." In reviewing the cases and materials addressing the 1976 Act right of public performance, keep in mind the following questions: (1) Is the act at issue a "performance"? (2) Is the performance "public"? (3) Is there an applicable exemption from liability?]

1.   The Meaning of "Perform" Under the 1976 Act

§ 101.   Definitions

As used in this title, the following terms and their variant forms mean the following:

. . .

To "perform" a work means to recite, render, play, dance, or act it, either directly or by means of any device or process or, in the case of a motion picture or other audiovisual work, to show its images in any sequence or to make the sounds accompanying it audible.

House Report

H.R. Rep. No. 94–1476, 94th Cong., 2d Sess. 64 (1976).

Definitions

Under the definitions of "perform," "display," "publicly," and "transmit" in section 101, the concepts of public performance and public display cover not only the initial rendition or showing, but also any further act by which that rendition or showing is transmitted or communicated to the public. Thus, for example: a singer is performing when he or she sings a song; a broadcasting network is performing when it transmits his or her performance (whether simultaneously or from records); a local broadcaster is performing when it transmits the network broadcast; a cable television system is performing when it re-transmits the broadcast to its subscribers; and any individual is performing whenever he or she plays a phonorecord embodying the performance or communicates the performance by turning on a receiving set. Although any act by which the initial performance or display is transmitted, repeated, or made to recur would itself be a "performance" or "display" under the bill, it would not be actionable as an infringement unless it were done "publicly," as defined in section 101. Certain other performances and displays, in addition to those that are "private," are exempted or given qualified copyright control under sections 107 through 118.

To "perform" a work, under the definition in section 101, includes reading a literary work aloud, singing or playing music, dancing a ballet or other choreographic work, and acting out a dramatic work or pantomime. A performance may be accomplished "either directly or by means of any device or process," including all kinds of equipment for reproducing or amplifying sounds or visual images, any sort of transmitting apparatus, any type of electronic retrieval system, and any other techniques and systems not yet in use or even invented.

QUESTION

Sam Scrabble is a creator of board games having an educational element, and has registered the game board, pieces and rules brochures with the Copyright Office. Sam both markets these games and conducts national tournaments at which the games are played. A nonprofit corporation, Academic Games League of America (AGLOA), has been recently formed to purchase Sam's games, to sell them without profit to school districts, and to conduct student tournaments at which the games are played; the rules of the AGLOA tournaments refer to the rules that accompany Sam's games but do not copy them to any substantial extent. Sam has brought an action to enjoin AGLOA's holding these tournaments, claiming that they constitute infringing public performances of his copyrighted games; he emphasizes the word "play" in the statutory definition. Would you grant AGLOA's motion for summary judgment? *See Allen v. Academic Games League of Am., Inc.,* 89 F.3d 614 (9th Cir.1996).

2.   "Public" Performances Under the 1976 Act

§ 101.   Definitions

. . .

To perform or display a work "publicly" means—

(1) to perform or display it at a place open to the public or at any place where a substantial number of persons outside of a normal circle of a family and its social acquaintances is gathered; or

(2) to transmit or otherwise communicate a performance or display of the work to a place specified by clause (1) or to the public, by means of any device or process, whether the members of the public capable of receiving the performance or display receive it in the same place or in separate places and at the same time or at different times.

To "transmit" a performance or display is to communicate it by any device or process whereby images or sounds are received beyond the place from which they are sent.

. . .

House Report

H.R. Rep. No. 94–1476, 94th Cong., 2d Sess. 64–65 (1976).

Under clause (1) of the definition of "publicly" in section 101, a performance or display is "public" if it takes place "at a place open to the public or at any place where a substantial number of persons outside of a normal circle of a family and its social acquaintances is gathered." One of the principal purposes of the definition was to make clear that, contrary to the decision in *Metro-Goldwyn–Mayer Distributing Corp. v. Wyatt,* 21 C.O. Bull. 203 (D. Md. 1932), performances in "semipublic" places such as clubs, lodges, factories, summer camps, and schools are "public performances" subject to copyright control. The term "a family" in this context would include an individual living alone, so that a gathering confined to the individual's social acquaintances would normally be regarded as private. Routine meetings of business and governmental personnel would be excluded because they do not represent the gathering of a "substantial number of persons."

Clause (2) of the definition of "publicly" in section 101 makes clear that the concepts of public performance and public display include not only performances and displays that occur initially in a public place, but also acts that transmit or otherwise communicate a performance or display of the work to the public by means of any device or process. The definition of "transmit"—to communicate a performance or display "by any device or process whereby images or sound are received beyond the place from which they are sent"—is broad enough to include all conceivable forms and combinations of wired or wireless communications media, including but by no means limited to radio and television broadcasting as we know them. Each and every method by which the images or sounds comprising a performance or display are picked up and conveyed is a "transmission," and if the transmission reaches the public in any form, the case comes within the scope of clauses (4) or (5) of section 106.

Under the bill, as under the present law, a performance made available by transmission to the public at large is "public" even though the recipients are not gathered in a single place, and even if there is no proof that any of the potential recipients was operating his receiving apparatus at the time of the transmission. The same principles apply whenever the potential recipients of the transmission represent a limited segment of the public, such as the occupants of hotel rooms or the subscribers of a cable television service. Clause (2) of the definition of "publicly" is applicable "whether the members of the public capable of receiving the performance or display receive it in the same place or in separate places and at the same time or at different times."

QUESTIONS

Which of the following is a "public" performance?

1. The performance of copyrighted music at a very large wedding in the home of the parents of the bride.

2. The performance of copyrighted music at a very small wedding in a hotel reception room.

3. The performance of copyrighted music at five simultaneous wedding receptions in separate rooms at a catering hall.

Columbia Pictures Industries, Inc. v. Aveco, Inc.

800 F.2d 59 (3d Cir.1986).

■ STAPLETON, CIRCUIT JUDGE.

Plaintiffs, appellees in this action, are producers of motion pictures ("Producers") and bring this copyright infringement action against the defendant, Aveco, Inc. Producers claim that Aveco's business, which includes renting video cassettes of motion pictures in conjunction with rooms in which they may be viewed, violates their exclusive rights under the Copyright Act of 1976, 17 U.S.C. § 101 et seq. The district court agreed and we affirm.

. . .

I

Among their other operations, Producers distribute video cassette copies of motion pictures in which they own registered copyrights. They do so knowing that many retail purchasers of these video cassettes, including

Aveco, rent them to others for profit. Aveco also makes available private rooms of various sizes in which its customers may view the video cassettes that they have chosen from Aveco's offerings. For example, at one location, Lock Haven, Aveco has thirty viewing rooms, each containing seating, a video cassette player, and television monitor. Aveco charges a rental fee for the viewing room that is separate from the charge for the video cassette rental.

Customers of Aveco may (1) rent a room and also rent a video cassette for viewing in that room, (2) rent a room and bring a video cassette obtained elsewhere to play in the room, or (3) rent a video cassette for out-of-store viewing.

Aveco has placed its video cassette players inside the individual viewing rooms and, subject to a time limitation, allows the customer complete control over the playing of the video cassettes. Customers operate the video cassette players in each viewing room and Aveco's employees assist only upon request. Each video cassette may be viewed only from inside the viewing room, and is not transmitted beyond the particular room in which it is being played. Aveco asserts that it rents its viewing rooms to individual customers who may be joined in the room only by members of their families and social acquaintances. Furthermore, Aveco's stated practice is not to permit unrelated groups of customers to share a viewing room while a video cassette is being played. For purposes of this appeal we assume the veracity of these assertions.

II

As the owners of copyrights in motion pictures, Producers possess statutory rights under the Copyright Act of 1976, 17 U.S.C. §§ 101–810. Among these are the exclusive rights set out in Section 106. . . . Producers do not, in the present litigation, allege infringement of their exclusive rights "to do and to authorize [the distribution of] copies or phonorecords of the copyrighted work to the public by sale or other transfer of owner-ship, or by rental, lease, or lending." Thus, Aveco's rental of video cassettes for at-home viewing is not challenged.

Producers' claim in this litigation is based on the alleged infringement of their "exclusive right . . . to perform the copyrighted work publicly" and to "authorize" such performances. Producers assert that Aveco, by renting its viewing rooms to the public for the purpose of watching Producers' video cassettes, is authorizing the public performance of copyrighted motion pictures.

Our analysis begins with the language of the Act. We first observe that there is no question that "performances" of copyrighted materials take place at Aveco's stores. "To perform" a work is defined in the Act as, "in the case of a motion picture or other audiovisual work, to show its images in any sequence or to make the sounds accompanying it audible." Section 101. As the House Report notes, this definition means that an individual is performing a work whenever he does anything by which the work is transmitted, repeated, or made to recur. H.R. Rep. No. 1476, 94th Cong., 2d Sess. 63, *reprinted in* 1976 U.S. Code Cong. & Ad. News 5659, 5676–77.

Producers do not argue that Aveco itself performs the video cassettes. They acknowledge that under the Act Aveco's *customers* are the ones performing the works, for it is they who actually place the video cassette in the video cassette player and operate the controls. As we said in *Columbia Pictures Industries v. Redd Horne*, 749 F.2d 154, 158 (3d Cir.1984), "[p]laying a video cassette … constitute[s] a performance under Section 101." However, if there is a public performance, Aveco may still be responsible as an infringer even though it does not actually operate the video cassette players. In granting copyright owners the exclusive rights to "authorize" public performances, Congress intended "to avoid any questions as to the liability of contributory infringers. For example, a person who lawfully acquires an authorized copy of a motion picture would be an infringer if he or she engages in the business of renting it to others for purposes of an unauthorized public performance." H.R. Rep. No. 1476, 94th Cong., 2d Sess. 61, *reprinted in* 1976 U.S. Code Cong. & Ad. News at 5674; *see* S. Rep. No. 473, 94th Cong., 1st Sess. 57 (1975). In our opinion, this rationale applies equally to the person who knowingly makes available other requisites of a public performance. Accordingly, we agree with the district court that Aveco, by enabling its customers to perform the video cassettes in the viewing rooms, authorizes the performances.[3]

The performances of Producers' motion pictures at Aveco's stores infringe their copyrights, however, only if they are "public." The copyright owners' rights do not extend to control over private performances.

. . .

We recently parsed th[e Act's] definition [of a public performance] in *Redd Horne,* a case similar to the one at bar. The principal factual distinction is that in Redd Horne's operation, known as Maxwell's Video Showcase, Ltd. ("Maxwell's"), the video cassette players were located in the stores' central areas, not in each individual screening room. Maxwell's customers would select a video cassette from Maxwell's stock and rent a room which they entered to watch the motion picture on a television monitor. A Maxwell's employee would play the video cassette for the customers in one of the centrally-located video cassette players and transmit the performance to the monitor located in the room. Thus, unlike Aveco's customers, Maxwell's clientele had no control over the video cassette players.

---

3. Aveco authorizes the performances that occur in the viewing rooms no less when the copyrighted video cassette is obtained from some other source. Aveco encourages the public to make use of its facilities for the purpose of viewing such tapes and makes available its rooms and equipment to customers who bring cassettes with them. By thus knowingly promoting and facilitating public performances of Producers' works, Aveco authorizes those performances even when it is not the source of Producers' copyrighted video cassettes. *RCA Records v. All–Fast Systems, Inc.,* 594 F. Supp. 335 (S.D.N.Y.1984) (provision of facilities used for unlawful copying enjoined as an infringement); *Italian Book Corp. v. Palms Sheepshead Country Club, Inc.,* 186 U.S.P.Q. 326 (E.D.N.Y.1975).

The *Redd Horne* court began its analysis with the observation that the two components of clause (1) of the definition of a public performance are disjunctive. 749 F.2d at 159. "The first category is self-evident; it is 'a place open to the public.' The second category, commonly referred to as a semi-public place, is determined by the size and composition of the audience." *Id.* The court then concluded that the performances were occurring at a place open to the public, which it found to be the entire store, including the viewing rooms.

> Any member of the public can view a motion picture by paying the appropriate fee. The services provided by Maxwell's are essentially the same as a movie theatre, with the additional feature of privacy. The relevant "place" within the meaning of Section 101 is each of Maxwell's two stores, not each individual booth within each store. Simply because the cassettes can be viewed in private does not mitigate the essential fact that Maxwell's is unquestionably open to the public.

749 F.2d at 159.

. . .

. . . Aveco suggests that, in *Redd Horne,* the location of the customers in the private rooms was simply irrelevant, for the *performers* were in a public place, the lobby. In the case at bar, Aveco continues, its employees do not perform anything, the customers do. Unlike Maxwell's employees located in the public lobby, Aveco's customers are in private screening rooms. Aveco argues that while these viewing rooms are available to anyone for rent, they are private during each rental period, and therefore, not "open to the public." The performance—the playing of the video cassette—thus occurs not in the public lobby, but in the private viewing rooms.

We disagree. The necessary implication of Aveco's analysis is that *Redd Horne* would have been decided differently had Maxwell's located its video cassette players in a locked closet in the back of the stores. We do not read *Redd Horne* to adopt such an analysis. The Copyright Act speaks of performances at a place open to the public. It does not require that the public place be actually crowded with people. A telephone booth, a taxi cab, and even a pay toilet are commonly regarded as "open to the public," even though they are usually occupied only by one party at a time. Our opinion in *Redd Horne* turned not on the precise whereabouts of the video cassette players, but on the nature of Maxwell's stores. Maxwell's, like Aveco, was willing to make a viewing room and video cassettes available to any member of the public with the inclination to avail himself of this service. It is this availability that made Maxwell's stores public places, not the coincidence that the video cassette players were situated in the lobby. Because we find *Redd Horne* indistinguishable from the case at bar, we find that Aveco's operations constituted an authorization of public performances of Producers' copyrighted works.

Aveco's reliance on the first sale doctrine is likewise misplaced. The first sale doctrine, codified at 17 U.S.C. § 109(a), prevents the copyright owner from controlling future transfers of a particular copy of a copyrighted work after he has transferred its "material ownership" to another. *Redd Horne,* 749 F.2d at 159. When a copyright owner parts with title to a particular copy of his copyrighted work, he thereby divests himself of his exclusive right to vend that particular copy. *Id. See United States v. Powell,* 701 F.2d 70, 72 (8th Cir.1983); *United States v. Moore,* 604 F.2d 1228, 1232 (9th Cir.1979). Accordingly, under the first sale doctrine, Producers cannot claim that Aveco's rentals or sales of lawfully acquired video cassettes infringe on their exclusive rights to vend those cassettes. . . .

In the case at bar, even assuming, *arguendo,* both a waiver by Producers of their Section 106(3) distribution rights and a valid transfer of ownership of the video cassette during the rental period, the first sale doctrine is nonetheless irrelevant. The rights protected by copyright are divisible and the waiver of one does not necessarily waive any of the others. *See* Section 202. In particular, the transfer of ownership in a particular copy of a work does not affect Producers' Section 106(4) exclusive rights to do and to authorize public performances. *Redd Horne,* 749 F.2d at 160; *Powell,* 701 F.2d at 72; *Moore,* 604 F.2d at 1232. It therefore cannot protect one who is infringing Producers' Section 106(4) rights by the public performance of the copyrighted work.

III

We therefore conclude that Aveco, by renting its rooms to members of the general public in which they may view performances of Producers' copyrighted video cassettes, obtained from any source, has authorized public performances of those cassettes. This is a violation of Producers' Section 106 rights and is appropriately enjoined. We therefore will affirm the order of the district court.

QUESTIONS

1. Presumably, had Aveco's customers taken the rented videotapes home with them, and viewed them there the same evening—and certainly if they had viewed at home videos *purchased* by them—neither the rental nor the viewing would have constituted a copyright infringement. Why should there be any different result when the viewers, for their own convenience, remain on Aveco's premises, in separate rooms, and view the tapes there? *See Opinion of Ohio Att'y Gen. 87–108* (Dec. 29, 1987), 1988 CCH Copyright L. Dec. ¶ 26,240.

2. Sleepwell Motel has television sets in all of its private guest rooms, and attached to each set is a videocassette recorder. Motel guests may rent, for $4 per night, any number of videocassettes that the motel has purchased from a local video store and stocks at the motel registration counter. These cassettes are then taken back to the guest rooms for viewing through the VCRs. Owners of copyrighted motion pictures have brought an action against Sleepwell Motel for copyright infringement. What should the result be? Is the *Aveco* decision distinguishable? *See Columbia Pictures Indus. v. Professional Real Estate Investors, Inc.,* 866 F.2d 278 (9th Cir.1989). Does it make a difference if the motion pictures are transmitted to private rooms, one customer at a time? *See On Command Video Corp. v. Columbia Pictures Indus.*, 777 F.Supp. 787 (N.D.Cal.1991).

3. WebFilmClub.com offers a pay-per-view service to its members. Members, who enter their password and billing information, may individually download films for one-time viewing at home. Has a public performance occurred? Does it matter if members view the film as soon as it is downloaded, or if they download and defer viewing till later?

3.   Performing Rights Societies

When the Copyright Act was amended in 1909 to accord to the owner of copyright in a musical composition the right to perform it "publicly for profit," a group of prominent popular composers—among them Victor Herbert and John Philip Sousa—gathered in 1914 to discuss the formation of an organization that could implement that new right. Thus was formed the American Society of Composers, Authors and Publishers [ASCAP], the first performing rights organization in the United States. The purpose of the organization was to serve as a clearinghouse for performing-rights licensing (thereby reducing the cost of individual licensing) and as an agency to monitor performances and to police infringements. With the aid of their able and dedicated attorney, Nathan Burkan, ASCAP embarked on a litigation campaign to establish their statutory rights. Its earliest and most noteworthy victory came with the Supreme Court decision in *Herbert v. Shanley Co.*, 242 U.S. 591 (1917), in which it was held that the live performance of Victor Herbert's popular song, "Sweethearts" in Shanley's Restaurant in New York City was a public performance "for profit" (as the 1909 Act required, in order to make out an infringement), even in the absence of a separate admission charge for the music. Justice Holmes stated, in his characteristically insightful and pithy style:

> If the rights under the copyright are infringed only by a performance where money is taken at the door, they are very imperfectly protected.... The defendants' performances are not eleemosynary. They are part of a total for which the public pays, and the fact that the price of the whole is attributed to a particular item which those present are expected to order is not important. It is true that the music is not the sole object, but neither is the food, which probably could be got cheaper elsewhere. The object is a repast in surroundings that to people having limited powers of conversation, or disliking the rival noise, give a luxurious pleasure not to be had from eating a silent meal. If music did not pay, it would be given up. If it pays, it pays out of the public's pocket. Whether it pays or not, the purpose of employing it is profit, and that is enough.

Today, public performance is the major source of revenue in the music industry. ASCAP remains one of the two major performing rights organizations in the United States; the other is Broadcast Music, Inc. (BMI), which was formed in 1940 by radio networks and independent radio stations that were concerned about increased licensing royalties charged by ASCAP for broadcast music. ASCAP and BMI license the performance rights of about 200,000 writer and publisher members and affiliates to hundreds of thousands of users—generating about $1 billion in royalties annually. (SESAC, a much smaller, privately owned organization, performs similar functions.) The functions and methods of operation of these organizations are well illustrated in the following case.

Ocasek v. Hegglund

116 F.R.D. 154 (D.Wyo.1987).

■ BRIMMER, CHIEF JUDGE.

. . .

This is an action for copyright infringement brought by four copyright owners against the owner and operator of a dance hall in Douglas, Wyoming. The plaintiffs allege that five (5) musical compositions owned by them were publicly performed at the defendant's establishment on February 1, 1985 and/or February 2, 1985 without their authorization and thus in violation of their copyrights. . . .

[The defendant served notice on the plaintiff songwriters that she intended to take their depositions some six weeks later in Cheyenne, Wyoming. Although the plaintiffs objected to the taking of depositions and sought a protective order, the Magistrate issued an order granting the motion to compel depositions, concluding that anyone electing to sue in the District of Wyoming is obligated to appear there to be deposed. He held that the defendant had an absolute right to discovery on such issues as the identity or substantial similarity of the music at issue, the nature and extent of damages and of future injury to the plaintiffs. On appeal, the court reversed the Magistrate's order.]

The plaintiffs are members of the American Society of Composers, Authors and Publishers (ASCAP). As explained below, due to the difficult nature of enforcing a copyright, copyright owners have ceded to ASCAP certain powers of enforcement such that discovery which is considered reasonable and routine in most situations is not so in copyright infringement actions involving ASCAP or like organizations.[1]

The purpose of ASCAP is to enforce the copyright for the owner. In the area of musical composition copyright, the need for this type of service is particularly acute. As the United States District Court for the Southern District of New York has explained,

> Prior to ASCAP's formation in 1914 there was no effective method by which composers and publishers of music could secure payment for the performance for profit of their copyrighted works. The users of music, such as theaters, dance halls and bars, were so numerous and wide-

---

1. For example, Broadcast Music, Inc. (BMI) provides services similar to AS-CAP. . . .

spread, and each performance so fleeting an occurrence, that no individual copyright owner could negotiate licenses with users of his music, or detect unauthorized uses. On the other side of the coin, those who wished to perform compositions without infringing the copyright were, as a practical matter, unable to obtain licenses from the owners of the works they wished to perform. ASCAP was organized as a "clearinghouse" for copyright owners and users to solve these problems.

Columbia Broad. Sys., Inc. v. American Soc. of Comp., 400 F. Supp. 737, 741 (S.D.N.Y.1975). The Supreme Court has also recognized the copyright owner's need for some other party to enforce its copyright, stating that

> Because a musical composition can be "consumed" by many different people at the same time and without the creator's knowledge, the "owner" has no real way to demand reimbursement for the use of his property except through the copyright laws *and* an effective way to enforce those legal rights. *See Twentieth Century Music Corp. v. Aiken,* 422 U.S. 151, 162, 95 S. Ct. 2040, 2047, 45 L. Ed. 2d 84 (1975). It takes an organization of rather large size to monitor most or all uses and to deal with users on behalf of the composers. Moreover, it is inefficient to have too many such organizations duplicating each other's monitoring of use.

Broadcast Music, Inc. v. CBS, 441 U.S. 1, 19 n. 32, 99 S. Ct. 1551, 1562 n. 32, 60 L. Ed. 2d 1 (1978). Thus it is acknowledged by most, and taken for granted by some, that ASCAP, or some similar organization, will enforce a composer's or publisher's copyright.

Typically, composers enforce their copyright via membership in ASCAP. As part of the terms of the membership agreement, the copyright owner grants to ASCAP a non-exclusive right to license public performances of the member's copyrighted musical compositions. The membership agreement authorizes ASCAP to prevent the infringement of the copyright, to act as the member's attorney-in-fact and to litigate and take all necessary legal actions to prevent unauthorized public performances of the member's copyrighted musical works and to collect damages for infringements.

In order to accomplish this rather formidable task,

> ASCAP provides its members with a wide range of services. It maintains a surveillance system of radio and television broadcasts to detect unlicensed uses, institutes infringement actions, collects revenues from licensees and distributes royalties to copyright owners in accordance with a schedule which reflects the nature and amount of the use of their music and other factors.

Columbia Broad. Sys., Inc. v. American Soc. of Comp., 400 F. Supp. at 742. ASCAP also employs a number of field agents who monitor unlicensed, local entertainment establishments to check for unauthorized uses of its members' compositions. In short, ASCAP handles virtually every aspect of enforcing the member's copyright, from licensing users to litigating unauthorized uses, and the copyright owner is virtually uninvolved with the actual enforcement activities; ASCAP members typically have no personal knowledge of infringements on their copyrights, but are completely dependent on ASCAP to protect their rights.

Yet for all of ASCAP's broad power to enforce its members' copyrights, it cannot bring an infringement suit in its own name....

... The Copyright Act has always specified that only the copyright owner, or the owner of exclusive rights under the copyright, as of the time the acts of infringement occur, has standing to bring an action for infringement of such rights; a non-exclusive licensee does not have standing. 17 U.S.C. § 501(b)....

In this case, as is typical of most ASCAP-assisted infringement suits, two ASCAP investigators visited the defendant's establishment in Douglas, Wyoming, on February 1 and 2, 1985. *See, e.g., Stone City Music v. Thunderbird, Inc.,* 116 F.R.D. 473 (N.D.Miss.1987). They noted which of their members' compositions were performed and subsequently submitted a written report to their regional director. Based on this report and ASCAP's own records that the defendant was not licensed by it, ASCAP initiated this lawsuit for copyright infringement on behalf of their members, the plaintiffs herein.... [Under Federal Rule of Civil Procedure 26(b) and (c), a court is to limit discovery—and may issue a protective order—when discovery is found to be unduly burdensome or expensive.]

[T]he Court finds that the plaintiffs are entitled to a protective order pursuant to Rule 26(c)(3). The reasons for which the magistrate and the defendant assert that the plaintiffs must be deposed constitute information that is either irrelevant, not known by the plaintiffs or discoverable via a less costly or burdensome method.

. . . .

As to proof of the unauthorized public performance of the plaintiffs' songs, it is clear that the plaintiffs have no knowledge of these events. As in most infringement cases enforced by ASCAP, ASCAP investigators actually witness the unauthorized public performance of the plaintiffs' songs. These investigators write a report and submit it to their district manager who then submits it to the ASCAP national director. The Court notes that ASCAP followed this standard operating procedure in this case and that all of these ASCAP employees are available to be deposed in this forum. Significantly, the defendant does not argue that the plaintiffs have knowledge of the actual performance. We find, therefore, that the plaintiffs are not the proper or likely source for this admittedly relevant information and that discovery of this information does not justify deposing the plaintiffs. *See Girlsongs v. J.N.S. Grand, Inc.,* No. 84–C–7890 (N.D. Ill. June 9, 1986).

In light of the foregoing, the Court finds that if there is, in fact, some relevant information which the defendant can discover from the plaintiffs, she may do so by way of written interrogatories. Deposing the plaintiffs in these types of cases is unduly burdensome and expensive.... The very purpose of ASCAP is to relieve the copyright owner of the time-consuming and expensive task of enforcing his rights; requiring that the owner be deposed defeats this purpose. Although this particular case, by itself, may not seem especially burdensome to the plaintiffs, this case must be viewed as part of the aggregate of all cases in which the plaintiffs must enforce their rights. As a general rule, to allow the defendants to depose the plaintiffs in these types of infringement suits would render the enforcement procedure so costly and burdensome as to preclude the vindication of the principle of copyright. Therefore, the Court must grant the plaintiffs' request for a protective order against the taking of their depositions.

. . .

———

Copyright holders—the composers, lyricists and publishers—become members of ASCAP or affiliates of BMI by granting the non-exclusive right to license public performance of their musical compositions in a non-dramatic fashion. These rights are in turn granted to networks, local television stations, radio stations, nightclubs, hotels, and other users in blanket licensing agreements that allow the licensee full use of any licensed works. Licensing fees vary from industry to industry (although similarly situated licensees must be treated equally). Broadcasters (both network and local) pay fees directly or indirectly related to sponsorship receipts (less certain deductions). Fees for "general establishments" depend on a number of factors, such as seating capacity, frequency of music performances, type of rendition, admission charges, etc. Hotel and motel fees are based on total entertainment expenditures; concert rates depend on admission price and seating capacity; background music users such as Muzak® pay a fee based primarily on the number and character of subscribers. Users who contend that a proposed ASCAP or BMI fee is unreasonable may have a reasonable fee determined by the United States District Court for the Southern District of New York. (After nearly 60 years of restricting such fee determinations to the New York federal court, Congress—as part of the so-called Fairness in Music Licensing Act of 1998—decided, by enacting § 513, to allow such challenges to be initiated against ASCAP, BMI or SESAC, as an alternative, by small business licensees in the district court in which the licensee is located; the licensee must be "an individual proprietor who owns or operates fewer than seven non-publicly traded establishments in which nondramatic musical works are performed publicly.")

Collecting the money from users, even with the variety of fee schedules, is relatively simple because of the nature of the blanket licensing, which permits licensees to use any and all music in the repertoire. But the very simplicity of collecting a single fee from a blanket licensee creates difficulties in the apportioning and distributing of the collected royalties. Surveys and logging of broadcasts are conducted by the performing rights organizations, which then apply formulas in order to distribute royalties. Dissatisfied members or affiliates have remedies under the ASCAP and BMI consent decrees. A closer look at the history and provisions of the ASCAP decree is in order.

The increasing importance of the broadcast industry in the late 1930s heightened the importance of performance rights licensing. With ASCAP operating almost alone in the field, a growing antagonism developed between the society and the broadcast users of copyrighted musical works. Finally, angered over what they considered exorbitant licensing fees and unacceptable ASCAP practices, the broadcasters refused to negotiate with ASCAP, forming their own performance rights organization (BMI) and boycotting ASCAP music. "This was the era when 'Jeanie With the Light Brown Hair' was burned in effigy on college campuses and the listening public was surfeited with Latin American rhythms." [Statement of March 13, 1958 of Victor Hansen before the House Select Comm. on Small Business, Subcomm. No. 5, Hearings, Policies of American Society of Composers, Authors, and Publishers 138–141 (March–April 1958)].

On February 25, 1941, the Antitrust Division of the Department of Justice filed a civil complaint against ASCAP, charging Sherman Act violations. A consent agreement was signed one week later. *See* 1940–43 Trade Cases ¶ 56,104 (S.D.N.Y. 1941). That decree was amended in significant respects in 1950, and again ten years later. *See* 1950–51 Trade Cas. ¶ 62,595 (S.D.N.Y. 1950); Timberg, *The Antitrust Aspects of Merchandising Modern Music: The ASCAP Consent Judgment of 1950,* 19 Law & Contemp. Probs. 294 (1954); Garner, *United States v. ASCAP: The Licensing Provisions of the Amended Final Judgment of 1950,* 23 Bull. Copyr. Soc'y 119 (1976). (For the BMI consent decree, see 1966 Trade Cas. ¶ 71,941 (S.D.N.Y. 1966).) The amended ASCAP consent decree has a number of important features: (1) ASCAP is prohibited from discriminating in license rates or terms among similarly situated licensees. (2) ASCAP may not acquire exclusive rights to license members' performance rights; composers, authors and publishers also have the right to negotiate licenses on their own. (3) ASCAP is required to offer broadcasters per-program licenses (in which the fee is based on revenues only from programs containing ASCAP-licensed music) in addition to the blanket licenses. (4) Membership requirements (including withdrawal rights) and voting rights are set forth. (5) Movie theatre licensing is prohibited, i.e., the performance of music is cleared by the producer at the source (the result of *Alden-Rochelle, Inc. v. ASCAP,* 80 F.Supp. 888 (S.D.N.Y.1948)). (6) A procedure for determination of reasonable fees by the District Court for the Southern District of New York is established. (7) Internal governance regulations, such as those relating to Board elections are imposed. (8) Distribution of royalties is to be based primarily on an objective survey system.

Although this history of antitrust consent decrees helped calm the government, certain users subject to ASCAP and BMI licensing—particularly the broadcasters—were still not satisfied. They simply could not accept blanket licensing, which exacted the same fee regardless of the level of use. A decade-long antitrust attack on the blanket license by a television network proved to be unsuccessful.

Under the blanket license, the licensee may use any music in the repertory of the licensor, as often as desired, for a single fee. Payment is either a flat sum or a percentage of the licensee's revenue and is therefore not related to the amount used or the particular works used. CBS claimed, in lawsuits against ASCAP and BMI, that the blanket license was an agreement unlawfully restraining trade (i.e., a price-fixing device that was per se unlawful) in violation of § 1 of the Sherman Act and sought to have both performing rights societies barred from using it, or, alternatively, to require them to charge predetermined amounts each time copyrighted music is used on the air.

Although the Second Circuit Court of Appeals agreed with CBS, its judgment was overturned by the Supreme Court. In *BMI v. CBS*, 441 U.S. 1 (1979), the Court ruled that the blanket license was not a per se violation, and remanded the case to have the licensing practice evaluated using rule-of-reason analysis.

In applying rule-of-reason standards, the Second Circuit held that CBS must first establish that the practice has a restraining effect in the industry. This issue was deemed to have been left unresolved by the Supreme Court's decision. The fact that there is no price competition among songs is not determinative on this question. However, it is crucial that there is the opportunity to obtain individual performing rights. "If the opportunity to purchase performing rights to individual songs is fully available, then it is customer preference for the blanket license, and not the license itself, that causes the lack of price competition among songs." *CBS v. ASCAP*, 620 F.2d 930, 935 (2d Cir.1980), *cert. denied*, 450 U.S. 970 (1981). The issue then is whether direct licensing is feasible. The court of appeals, after reviewing the district court's findings, agreed that CBS had failed to prove the factual predicate of its claim—the nonavailability of alternatives to the blanket license. *See* Hartnick, *The Network Blanket License Triumphant—The Fourth Round of the ASCAP–BMI–CBS Litigation*, 2 Com. & L. 49 (1980).

In a different series of proceedings, the challenge to blanket licensing moved from the network level down to the local broadcasting level. In *Buffalo Broadcasting Corp. v. ASCAP*, 546 F.Supp. 274 (S.D.N.Y.1982), *rev'd*, 744 F.2d 917 (2d Cir.1984), the district court held that requiring local television stations to purchase blanket licenses for the performance of copyrighted music in syndicated programs was an unreasonable restraint of trade in violation of the Sherman Act. The court distinguished *CBS v. ASCAP*, holding that local broadcasters lacked the market power of the networks to obtain licenses directly from the copyright owners. The Second Circuit, however, reversed, holding that the local broadcasters had not demonstrated a lack of power to obtain performance rights through a mechanism other than blanket licenses.

In the 1980s, the attack upon the blanket license was taken up by a cable system, Showtime/The Movie Channel (SMC), which challenged not the overall validity of the blanket-license device but rather the reasonableness of the blanket-license rate charged by ASCAP for the soundtrack music in motion pictures performed on SMC's cable programs. In exercising its jurisdiction to determine the reasonableness of such rates, the District Court in the Southern District of New York (the "rate court") rejected ASCAP's request for a fee of 25 cents per SMC cable subscriber, as well as

SMC's suggested fee of 8 cents per subscriber, and settled instead on a rate of 15 cents; the court of appeals affirmed. *ASCAP v. Showtime/The Movie Channel, Inc.*, 912 F.2d 563 (2d Cir.1990). The local television industry similarly sought a court determination of reasonable blanket and per program license fees. In a 1994 decision, the court again set the fees between those requested by ASCAP and the users. *United States v. ASCAP*, 157 F.R.D. 173 (S.D.N.Y.1994).

"GRAND" AND "SMALL" RIGHTS

The performing rights organizations license only nondramatic musical rights, the so-called "small" rights. The "grand" (dramatic) rights are licensed only by the copyright holders, who have traditionally felt capable of monitoring the more detectable dramatic performances. Little was it realized that this dramatic/non-dramatic distinction generated a definitional problem of increasing significance. For many years, there was a dearth of litigation on this issue. A 1955 case held that a medley of songs from *The Student Prince* performed as part of a ten-scene costumed extravaganza revue was not a dramatic presentation. *April Prods., Inc. v. Strand Enters.*, 221 F.2d 292 (2d Cir.1955). Rather, the performance by Ben Yost and His Royal Guardsmen was an "entr' acte" and contributed nothing to the show's overall plot.

The problem was once again confronted—this time with a different result—in a series of cases involving performances of selections from the rock opera *Jesus Christ Superstar*. In *Rice v. American Program Bureau*, 446 F.2d 685 (2d Cir.1971), a booking agent who had secured an ASCAP license was enjoined from performing either the work in its entirety or even excerpts accompanied by words, pantomime, dance or visual representations of the opera as a whole. In *Robert Stigwood Group, Ltd. v. Sperber*, 457 F.2d 50 (2d Cir.1972), another performance was enjoined. Here, the performance was without costume, but almost all of the songs were presented in identical sequence to the original and performers maintained specific characters throughout the performance. The court held that the performance was dramatic even without scenery, costumes and dialogue and despite the concert setting. The court's injunctive decree, arguably overbroad, forbade:

(1) performing any song in such a way as to follow another song in the same order as in the original *Jesus Christ Superstar* opera;

(2) performing any songs from the opera accompanied by dramatic action, scenic accessory or costumes.

There are differing points of view as to how best to distinguish between dramatic performances (not covered by the ASCAP license to the music user) and non-dramatic performances. One extreme, put forward by ASCAP's late long-time General Counsel Herman Finkelstein, defines non-dramatic performances as "renditions of a song ... without dialogue, scenery or costumes." Finkelstein, *The Composer and the Public Interest— Regulation of Performing Right Societies,* 19 Law & Contemp. Probs. 275,

283 n.32 (1954). This, however, would exclude from the ASCAP license, quite questionably, a song that is sung by a person wearing a pertinent costume or standing in front of a simply decorated flat. At the other extreme is the *April Productions* rule, that "the performance of a noninstrumental musical composition (i.e., lyrics and music) would be dramatic only if it were accompanied by material from the dramatico-musical work of which the composition was a part." Such a rule, however, would unwisely allow an ASCAP licensee to perform, for example, all of the songs from "South Pacific" in sequence with freshly written transition dialogue, so long as no dialogue is borrowed directly from the Hammerstein book.

Although the distinction between grand and small rights is thus rather elusive, practices have developed through the years in the pertinent entertainment industries so that the respective rights of music licensors and licensees are fairly well established. Thus, a performance of a musical revue such as "Ain't Misbehavin'," done with costumes and a set but with no discernible story line, would be treated as a "grand" performance, while a showing on television of the motion picture "South Pacific" would be covered by the license for "small" rights. Similarly, performance rights in music videos are licensed as "small" rights, even though they may depict the performers in a variety of costumed or dramatic routines.

4.   The Right of Public Display

§ 106.   Exclusive Rights In Copyrighted Works

Subject to sections 107 through 121, the owner of copyright under this title has the exclusive rights to do and to authorize any of the following:

. . .

(5) in the case of literary, musical, dramatic, and choreographic works, pantomimes, and pictorial, graphic, or sculptural works, including the individual images of a motion picture or other audiovisual work, to display the copyrighted work publicly.

§ 101.   Definitions

As used in this title, the following terms and their variant forms mean the following:

. . .

To "display" a work means to show a copy of it, either directly or by means of a film, slide, television image, or any other device or process or, in the case of a motion picture or other audiovisual work, to show individual images nonsequentially.

. . .

§ 109.   Limitations on Exclusive Rights: Effect of Transfer of Particular Copy or Phonorecord

. . .

(c) Notwithstanding the provisions of section 106(5), the owner of a particular copy lawfully made under this title, or any person authorized by such owner, is entitled, without the authority of the copyright owner, to display that copy publicly, either directly or by the projection of no more than one image at a time, to viewers present at the place where the copy is located.

(d) The privileges prescribed by subsections (a) and (c) do not, unless authorized by the copyright owner, extend to any person who has acquired possession of the copy or phonorecord from the copyright owner, by rental, lease, loan, or otherwise, without acquiring ownership of it.

NOTE

"Clause (5) of section 106 represents the first explicit statutory recognition in United States copyright law of an exclusive right to show a copyrighted work, or an image of it, to the public. The existence or extent of this right under the present [1909] statute is uncertain and subject to challenge." S. Rep. No. 94–473, at 59; H.R. Rep. No. 94–1476, at 63. A particularly troubling issue was whether the showing of a pictorial work on a television broadcast was an infringing "copy" under the 1909 act; the evanescence of the image helped convince at least one court that it was not. *Mura v. Columbia Broadcasting Sys.*, 245 F.Supp. 587 (S.D.N.Y.1965).

The right of display is limited, in common with the performing right in § 106(4), to *public* presentation, and it applies only to specified types of works. (The student should consult the definition of "publicly" in § 101.) It will be noted that sound recordings are not afforded a statutory right of public display, and that audiovisual works are covered only to the extent of nonsequential presentation of individual images; sequential presentation would amount to a "performance." Moreover, the right to display published pictorial, graphic and sculptural works by public broadcasters on television is covered, if parties fail to agree upon negotiated royalties, by a compulsory license granted in § 118. Finally, the right of public display is limited by the provisions of § 109(c), discussed in the passages from the House Report immediately below. (As originally enacted in 1976, this section was designated as 109(b).)

House Report

H.R. Rep. No. 94–1476, 94th Cong., 2d Sess. 64, 79–80 (1976).

. . . In addition to the direct showings of a copy of a work, "display" would include the projection of an image on a screen or other surface by any method, the transmission of an image by electronic or other means, and the showing of an image on a cathode ray tube, or similar viewing apparatus connected with any sort of information storage and retrieval system.

. . . .

Effect of display of copy

Subsection [(c)] of section 109 deals with the scope of the copyright owner's exclusive right to control the public display of a particular "copy" of a work (including the original or prototype copy in which the work was first fixed). Assuming, for example, that a painter has sold the only copy of an original work of art without restrictions, would it be possible for him to restrain the new owner from displaying it publicly in galleries, shop windows, on a projector, or on television?

Section 109[(c)] adopts the general principle that the lawful owner of a copy of a work should be able to put his copy on public display without the consent of the copyright owner. As in cases arising under section 109(a), this does not mean that contractual restrictions on display between a buyer and seller would be unenforceable as a matter of contract law.

The exclusive right of public display granted by section 106(5) would not apply where the owner of a copy wishes to show it directly to the public, as in a gallery or display case, or indirectly, as through an opaque projector. . . .

On the other hand, section 109[(c)] takes account of the potentialities of the new communications media, notably television, cable and optical transmission devices, and information storage and retrieval devices, for replacing printed copies with visual images. First of all, the public display of an image of a copyrighted work would not be exempted from copyright control if the copy from which the image was derived were outside the presence of the viewers. In other words, the display of a visual image of a copyrighted work would be an infringement if the image were transmitted by any method (by closed or open circuit television, for example, or by a computer system) from one place to members of the public located elsewhere.

Moreover, the exemption would extend only to public displays that are made "either directly or by the projection of no more than one image at a time." Thus, even where the copy and the viewers are located at the same place, the simultaneous projection of multiple images of the work would not be exempted. For example, where each person in a lecture hall is supplied with a separate viewing apparatus, the copyright owner's permission would generally be required in order to project an image of a work on each individual screen at the same time.

The committee's intention is to preserve the traditional privilege of the owner of a copy to display it directly, but to place reasonable restrictions on the ability to display it indirectly in such a way that the copyright owner's market for reproduction and distribution of copies would be affected. Unless it constitutes a fair use under section 107, or unless one of the special provisions of section 110 or 111 is applicable, projection of more than one image at a time, or transmission of an image to the public over television or other communication channels, would be an infringement for the same reasons that reproduction in copies would be. The concept of "the place where the copy is located" is generally intended to refer to a situation in which the viewers are present in the same physical surroundings as the copy, even though they cannot see the copy directly.

QUESTION

Last year, Art Teest donated an abstract geometric canvas painted by him to the Institute of Very Contemporary Art at the Urban University. This year, as the University fell upon hard economic times, it decided to sell certain of its assets, including some paintings at the Institute, Teest's painting among them. When the auction was held at the Institute, it was also shown on a closed-circuit television system to audiences at five separate locations within the University and also at alumni clubs throughout the country. Persons in attendance at those locations could see the artworks being auctioned and could submit their bids. Teest's painting was auctioned off for a price that he regarded as embarrassingly low—and he was also distressed about how quickly the Institute got rid of his painting. He has consulted you and wishes to know whether he has any legal recourse against the Institute and the University. What will you tell him? Consider too, as you study the materials immediately below, whether any exemptions in the Copyright Act apply to the conduct challenged by Teest.

The public display right, long overshadowed by § 109(c), may take on considerable importance as a result of communication of works on digital networks, such as the Internet, and commercial services such as America Online. The transmission of screen displays to subscribers meets the statutory definition of a "public performance or display." *See, e.g., On Command Video Corp. v. Columbia Pictures Indus.*, 777 F.Supp. 787 (N.D.Cal.1991). Several courts considered the liability of services for their subscribers' unauthorized posting of scanned copies of *Playboy* centerfolds to a bulletin board service or a website. The courts have held the services liable for direct infringement of *Playboy*'s display rights, because the service transmitted the scanned images to its other subscribers. *See Playboy Enters., Inc. v. Frena*, 839 F.Supp. 1552 (M.D.Fla.1993); *Playboy Enters. v. Russ Hardenburgh, Inc.*, 982 F.Supp. 503 (N.D.Ohio 1997) (finding infringement of display right where BBS operator allowed subscribers to view copyrighted photographs); *Playboy Enters. v. Webbworld Inc.*, 991 F.Supp. 543 (N.D.Tex.1997) (finding infringement of display right where defendant allowed subscribers to view plaintiff's copyrighted images). But see *Religious Tech. Ctr. v. Netcom On–Line Communication Servs., Inc.*, 907 F.Supp. 1361 (N.D.Cal.1995) (refusing to find internet service provider directly liable for display right infringement when user posted copyrighted works). *See generally*, R. Anthony Reese, *The Public Display Right: The Copyright Act's Neglected Solution to the Controversy Over RAM "Copies,"* 2001 U.Ill.L.Rev. 83.

5. THE DIGITAL PERFORMANCE RIGHT IN SOUND RECORDINGS . . . AND ITS LIMITATIONS

As originally enacted, the 1976 Copyright Act did not extend the public performance right to sound recordings. When, for example, a radio station broadcast a recording of a popular song, the station paid performance royalties to the copyright owners of the musical composition, but not to the performers and producers of the sound recording. Similarly, there was no liability to a stand-up comedian for the radio transmission of his recording of jokes written by other persons (though, presumably, the comedy writers would have had a claim). See *Guedes v. Martinez*, 131 F.Supp.2d 272 (D.P.R.2001). This continues to be the law with respect to analog transmissions. Since 1995, however, producers and performers of sound recordings enjoy public performance rights with respect to digital audio transmissions.

On November 1, 1995, President Clinton signed into law major amendments to §§ 106 and 114 that extend, for the first time in our law, limited public-performance rights to owners of copyright in sound recordings, i.e., to recording artists and companies. A new § 106(6) now adds to the list of exclusive rights: "in the case of sound recordings, to perform the copyrighted work publicly by means of a digital audio transmission."

What precipitated the amendment was the introduction of technology allowing for digital audio transmissions to home subscribers (fully akin to cable-television subscribers) who receive the sounds of top quality digital sound recordings and who may well thus forego the purchase of cassettes and compact discs. In part it was assumed that many digital-audio subscribers would indulge in home taping. It was also understood by the congressional proponents of the legislation that "interactive" audio services would allow subscribers to call up any desired digital recordings at any time (i.e., pay-per-listen or audio-on-demand, the equivalent of pay-for-view for current-day cable subscribers) and thus altogether displace the need to purchase recordings. The "celestial jukebox" would have potentially severe impact upon recording artists and companies (as well as songwriters and publishers owning copyrights in musical works), whose livelihood depends upon recording sales. An appreciation that digital transmissions can displace tape and compact disc purchases is the key to understanding the extremely elaborate and detailed provisions of the Digital Performance Rights in Sound Recordings Act of 1995.

In addition to adding § 106(6), the 1995 amendments added several subsections to § 114. Exempted from the new exclusive digital-audio-transmission right are traditional radio and television broadcasts, background music services such as Muzak®, public radio, and transmissions in business establishments and public places such as restaurants, department stores, hotels and amusement parks. Home transmissions by noninteractive subscription services are subject to compulsory licensing in the event voluntary licenses (given shelter against antitrust challenges) cannot be negotiated; any compulsory license royalties will be set and distributed by the Librarian of Congress with the assistance of arbitration panels. Digital-performance royalties received by recording companies are to be shared with recording artists: 50% to the companies, 45% to "featured" artists, and 5% shared equally by nonfeatured musicians and vocalists. Effective June 1, 1998, a new Copyright Office regulation provides that "the royalty fee for digital performance of sound recording by nonexempt subscription digital services shall be 6.5% of gross revenues resulting from residential services in the United States," to be paid to the Recording Industry Association of America, as agent for the royalty claimants. *See* 37 C.F.R. § 260.2.

Interactive digital audio services, i.e., "celestial jukeboxes," fall outside the compulsory-license format and are thus fully subject to the ban of § 106(6). So too are certain noninteractive transmissions, in particular ones in which the digital transmission service publishes advance program schedules carrying the titles of specific recordings to be played, or when more than a prescribed number of selections from the same phonorecord (the "sound recording performance complement") are played within a limited period of time. In such situations falling within the ban of § 106(6), voluntary negotiations between operators of digital services and representatives of recording companies and artists will presumably result in a royalty structure, akin to the dealings between performing-rights societies such as ASCAP and BMI and those who engage in radio and television broadcasts of musical works.

The final major amendment of the Copyright Act that resulted from the 1995 Digital Performance Rights Act relates to the rights of copyright owners of musical works (as distinguished from the sound recordings). By treating song selections from the celestial jukebox as functional substitutes for home playing of cassettes and compact discs of recorded music—and thus as threatening the displacement of individual purchases of such recordings—Congress concluded that the new interactive digital audio systems should recompense songwriters and music publishers for lost "mechanical royalties" ordinarily forthcoming under § 115 of the Copyright Act. That section has been amended so as to provide for compulsory license payments not only by those who make phonorecords but also by those who make "digital phonorecord deliveries" (defined as "each individual delivery of a phonorecord by digital transmission of a sound recording which results in a specifically identifiable reproduction by or for any transmission recipient of a phonorecord of that sound recording"); this royalty is to be paid by the compulsory licensee (i.e., recording company) that authorized the digital transmission.

In 1998, Congress again amended § 114. The digital transmissions reached by the 1995 expansion of the sound recording copyright turn out to have omitted a principal form of Internet exploitation of sound recordings: audio "streaming" or "webcasting" of recorded performances. These transmissions originate on the Internet, and are generally nonsubscription; the user calls up the "Internet radio" website, much as she or he would seek the channel of a conventional herzian radio station. The difference is that the geographic factors that limit the broadcast area of traditional radio simply do not apply to websites: a webcaster from anywhere in the world can reach a world-wide audience. As original (rather than re-transmitted) transmissions that are neither subscription nor interactive (the listener does not select the content), webcasts were exempted both from the sound recording copyright owner's right of control, and from the obligation to secure a statutory or negotiated license under the 1995 amendments. (By contrast, webcasters remained liable to composers of the underlying music if the recordings were transmitted without a license from the music copyright holders.)

It therefore appeared that an increasingly significant form of digital exploitation of sound recordings would not only elude the copyright owners' control, but would not give rise to a right to remuneration. But a different provision of the Copyright Act, § 112 on "ephemeral recordings," called into question the webcaster's ability to transmit recorded performances free of copyright claims. § 112 permitted a "transmitting organization entitled to transmit to the public a performance or display of a work ..." to make a copy of the program to be transmitted. The ephemeral recording exception makes it possible for radio broadcasters (and analogous actors) to engage in the frequent industry practice of prerecording the transmissions, without having to clear reproduction rights. The ephemeral recording exception, however, was subject to the condition that the recorded program be "used solely for the transmitting organization's own transmissions *within its local service area....*" 17 U.S.C.A. § 112(a)(2). This condition makes perfect sense when the transmitting organization is a local herzian radio station; the confines of the broadcast signal constitute the local service area. The condition makes no sense when the transmitting organization is communicating the program over the Internet: at the point there is no *local* service area, the Internet service reaches the whole world.

The lack of fit between the ephemeral recording exception and webcasting led the sound recording copyright owners to contend that even if the Digital Performance Right in Sound Recordings amendments entitled nonsubscription webcasters to transmit without paying for performance rights, they nonetheless could not transmit prerecorded programming without clearing reproduction rights as well. This impasse set the stage for negotiations between copyright owners and digital transmission services, leading to a substantial revision of the performance right regime established by the 1995 amendments. A detailed examination of the new regime is beyond the scope of this note, but a review of its broader outlines is appropriate.

The new version of the sound recording public performance right retains the three-tier structure of the 1995 amendments, but substantially narrows the category of transmissions that are wholly exempted from the right. Where this category had included nonsubscription digital transmissions in general, and hence on its face exempted most webcasting, this category now is limited to "nonsubscription *broadcast* transmission[s]" (emphasis supplied). That term would not appear to mean point-to-point herzian transmissions ("*broad*casting," as the name implies, means a transmission to multiple simultaneous recipients). The 1998 amendments then subject other digital transmissions, whether subscription or non subscription, to the statutory license, so long as these transmissions meet the act's exceedingly detailed eligibility requirements. Ineligible transmissions, whether subscription or not, are subject to the sound recording copyright owner's full public performance right, including the right to prohibit the transmission.

To simplify, the conditions on applicability of the compulsory license primarily endeavor to ensure that the transmitting organization does not facilitate a user's substitution of the recorded performance for a purchase of a phonorecord. Hence, for example, the amendments retain the "sound recording performance complement;" they bar the transmitting entity from advance announcement of the content of the programs; they oblige the entity to accommodate technological measures imposed by the sound recording copyright owner to protect the works against copying, and to cooperate with the sound recording copyright owner to prevent users or other third parties from scanning the transmissions for the purpose of selecting particular transmissions. *See id.* § 114(d)(2)(A). The last requirement addresses the copyright owners' concern that third parties will develop search engines that will identify and download particular sound recordings from a variety of webcasting sites. Copyright owners apparently feared that a user might employ such a search engine to find and reproduce, for example, any Beatles song transmitted by any webcaster, thus enabling the user to avoid purchasing authorized Beatles recordings.

With respect to the determination of the statutory royalty rate that webcasters must pay, the 1998 legislation modifies the criteria of the 1995 amendments. Under both versions, a copyright arbitration royalty panel, subject to review by the Copyright Office, determines the rates and terms of royalty payments. Under the prior version, however, the panel set the rate according to its determination of what would afford a "fair return" to the copyright owner, and a "fair income" to the copyright user. *Id.* §§ 114(f)(2) [prior to 1998 amendments]; 801(b)(1). The current version instructs the copyright arbitration royalty panel to "establish rates and terms that most clearly represent the rates and terms that would have been negotiated in the marketplace between a willing buyer and a willing seller." *Id.* § 114(f)(1)(C)(iii)(2)(B). Copyright owners anticipate that this should yield a higher royalty rate than the 6.5% announced under the 1995 amendments. *See* 63 Fed. Reg. 25394; the rate is 6.5% of "gross revenues resulting from residential services" 37 C.F.R. 260.2(a).

While the 1998 amendments narrowed the scope of digital transmissions that would be wholly exempt from the performance right, they left the status of analog transmissions (traditional broadcasts) unaltered. Thus, an over-the-air broadcaster paid no royalties to sound recording copyright owners, while webcasters paid at least the compulsory license fees. In the years since 1998, an increasing number of radio broadcasters have simultaneously webcast their programming. The Copyright Office therefore conducted a Rulemaking to determine whether those broadcasters who also webcast their radio transmissions are engaged in a nonsubscription digital transmission under § 114(d)(2), and therefore must pay the statutory royalty for the noninteractive digital public performance of sound recordings, or if all their transmissions should instead fall under the § 114(d)(1)(A) exemption from compulsory license fees to "nonsubscription broadcast transmission[s]." See Copyright Office Rulemaking, "Public Performance of Sound Recordings: Definition of a Service," 65 Fed. Reg. 77292 (December 11, 2000). The broadcasters claimed the exemption extended to all digital transmissions of an AM or FM signal made by broadcasters, whether over the air or via the Internet. Copyright owners and the Digital Media Association (DiMA) contended the exemption was limited to over-the-air transmissions.

The Copyright Office in due course endorsed the latter view. It stated:

> The Copyright Office's determination to read the statutory definition of a "broadcast transmission" as including only over-the-air transmissions made by an FCC-licensed broadcaster under the terms of that license is consistent with Congress' intent in passing the DPRA. This approach preserves the traditional relationship between the record companies and the radio broadcasters as it existed in 1995. In effect, it allows for the continued transmission of an over-the-air radio broadcast signal without regard to whether the transmission is made in an analog or a digital format. Such signals, however, are limited geographically under the licensing standards of the FCC. At the same time, it subjects all other digital transmissions made by a noninteractive, nonsubscription service to the terms and conditions of the statutory license in order to compensate record companies for the increased risk that a listener may make a high-quality unauthorized reproduction of a sound recording directly from the transmission instead of purchasing a legitimate copy in the marketplace, a risk that is clearly greater when the recipient is receiving the transmission on a computer, which can instantly replicate and retransmit the transmission.

> Congress' intent would be thwarted if an FCC-licensed radio broadcaster was allowed to transmit its radio signal over a digital communication network, such as the Internet, without any restrictions on the programming format. For example, as DiMA suggests, an FCC-licensed broadcaster could tailor its program to highlight a particular artist and announce its intent to do so in advance, thereby increasing the likelihood that a listener would be prepared to make a copy of the sound recording at the appointed time. Such a result would violate not only the letter of the law under our interpretation of the statute, but also the very spirit and intent of the law.

In a contemporaneous lawsuit brought by the broadcasters, a federal court held that it would defer to the expertise of the Copyright Office in interpreting section 114 and that, in any event viewing the matter on the merits, the court would reach the same conclusion about the applicability of the compulsory license. Bonneville International Corp. v. Peters, 153 F.Supp.2d 763 (E.D.Pa.2001).

If the 1995 amendments produced a hybrid regime for sound recordings, combining both a reproduction right and a public performance right, the 1998 amendments more closely approach a full fledged performance right, albeit one in which statutory licensing may outweigh a right to prohibit. Fear of unauthorized copying still pervades the text, but the text more fully enables copyright owners to benefit from the public performance right as an independent source of revenue. This marks an important shift in the economics of sound recordings: before these amendments, sound recording artists and producers derived a return only from sales of phonorecords. Radio broadcasts of the sound recordings, albeit uncompensated, in effect advertised the recordings, stimulating sales. In the digital environment, sales of phonorecords may well persist (including via the Internet), but performances of recorded music, whether by on-demand interactive services, or by webcasting, are likely to displace acquisition of retention copies. This is because *having* the recorded performance is likely to matter less to consumers than *hearing* it, and the digital environment may well make it as easy for the user to hear the desired performance via transmission as to play her own copy of it. This observation applies to many kinds of copyrighted works beyond sound recordings. The more easy it becomes to access and experience works of authorship by means of digital transmission, the less necessary, and perhaps also the less desirable, it becomes to possess retention copies. The evolution of the scope of the sound recording copyright thus is just one manifestation of an overall change in the exploitation of works of authorship, a change that also underlies Congress' creation of a right to control "access" to copyrighted works, *see infra*, Chapter 8.

QUESTION

Your client wishes to start a retail website that would distribute digital musical recordings to end-user consumers. The website, to be called CDWeb, would be accessible to all Internet users, without need to purchase a password or other access control. The site would post images of the cover jackets of the CDs offered for sale. Customers would click on an image to hear an excerpt from one song on the CD. If the customer determines that she wishes to purchase CDs from CDWeb, she must fax her credit card number to CDWeb, which will in turn send the user a password that will permit her to access files of complete CDs, and to download the CD(s) designated in the fax.

What rights under copyright are implicated by CDWeb's project? From whom, if anyone, must CDWeb obtain copyright permissions to conduct these activities, and why?

WHEN IS A PUBLIC PERFORMANCE/DISPLAY (NOT) ALSO A REPRODUCTION AND DISTRIBUTION OF COPIES?

We have seen that digital communications can implicate both the reproduction and distribution rights on the one hand, and the public performance/display rights on the other. While once these rights were considered distinct (and were separately licensed), all rights may converge on the Internet. One example that the Copyright Office has recently addressed is audiostreaming of recorded musical compositions. In its August 29, 2001 Report, *http://www.loc.gov/copyright/reports/studies/dmca/sec-104–report–vol–1.pdf*, the Copyright Office acknowledged that, formally, the communication of a musical work by means of audiostreaming could be characterized as both a public performance received by the public in different places and at different times, and also, by virtue of the RAM copying doctrine, as a series of reproductions made in the computer of the audiostream recipient. The Office recommended an amendment to exempt from the reproduction right the buffer copies made in audiostreaming musical works, on the ground that the audiostreaming entrepreneurs are already paying for the works' public performances (communications to the public), and the lawful entrepreneur should not have to get two licenses (often from different entities) for an act whose economic significance is essentially as a performance rather than as a reproduction. In the case of buffer copies, end users are not enjoying those copies as *copies*; the copies are a necessary, automatic, and consumer-imperceptible means to the consumer experience of hearing the work in more-or-less real time. As a result, the Office concluded, the performance-right licensee should not be obliged to pay twice. Indeed, in practice, these licensees would not pay twice but for the separate administration of performance and reproduction rights that characterizes the musical composition industry.

The Report then suggests that it might be appropriate to introduce a "symmetrical" exemption from the performance right when the digital communication is a download. The symmetrical exemption would be justified because separate administration and double dipping remain a problem when the end user is seeking to acquire a copy rather than a real-time performance, as the delivery of the copy could be considered a public performance as well as a digital distribution of a copy. It therefore would follow that the reproduction right is the only one that should be paid for.

This "symmetry" may not be completely persuasive, however. As long as we can tell when the economically significant act is a reproduction as opposed to a public performance (or vice versa), this kind of analysis and result make perfect sense. But will we always be able to tell the difference? Imagine, for example, a subscription service that will enable customers to program their music-hearing day. At noon, the subscriber will hear "I Wanna Hold Your Hand;" at 12:03, "Don't You Want Somebody to Love?;" from 12:07 to 1:00, a further selection of nostalgia, and so on. The subscriber is not receiving these songs in real time, however; the service has sent her hard drive the contents at the lower-traffic time of 4:00 AM, but timed them to "play" at the hours selected. Is this a digital download or a public performance? Does it matter if, obsessed with Jefferson Airplane, the subscriber has programmed "White Rabbit" to play twice an hour all week, so that the copy the service sends stays in the subscriber's hard drive continuously for a week? A month? But the subscriber hears it only at the pre-programmed times. Is this arrangement's economic significance as a public performance? Or as a (temporary) copy? As both, as the subscriber enjoys the "public performance" experience of hearing the work on demand, but the "copy" convenience of having it temporarily on her hard drive?

6. FURTHER LIMITATIONS ON THE RIGHTS OF PUBLIC PERFORMANCE AND DISPLAY

a. CERTAIN NONPROFIT PERFORMANCES AND DISPLAYS

§ 110. Limitations on Exclusive Rights: Exemption of Certain Performances and Displays

Notwithstanding the provisions of section 106, the following are not infringements of copyright:

(1) performance or display of a work by instructors or pupils in the course of face-to-face teaching activities of a nonprofit educational institution, in a classroom or similar place devoted to instruction, unless, in the case of a motion picture or other audiovisual work, the performance, or the display of individual images, is given by means of a copy that was not lawfully made under this title, and that the person responsible for the performance knew or had reason to believe was not lawfully made;

(2) performance of a nondramatic literary or musical work or display of a work, by or in the course of a transmission, if—

(A) the performance or display is a regular part of the systematic instructional activities of a governmental body or a nonprofit educational institution; and

(B) the performance or display is directly related and of material assistance to the teaching content of the transmission; and

(C) the transmission is made primarily for—

(i) reception in classrooms or similar places normally devoted to instruction, or

(ii) reception by persons to whom the transmission is directed because their disabilities or other special circumstances prevent their attendance in classrooms or similar places normally devoted to instruction, or

(iii) reception by officers or employees of governmental bodies as a part of their official duties or employment;

(3) performance of a nondramatic literary or musical work or of a dramatico-musical work of a religious nature, or display of a work, in the course of services at a place of worship or other religious assembly;

(4) performance of a nondramatic literary or musical work otherwise than in a transmission to the public, without any purpose of direct or indirect commercial advantage and without payment of any fee or other compensation for the performance to any of its performers, promoters, or organizers, if—

(A) there is no direct or indirect admission charge; or

(B) the proceeds, after deducting the reasonable costs of producing the performance, are used exclusively for educational, religious, or charitable purposes and not for private financial gain, except where the copyright owner has served notice of objection to the performance under the following conditions;

(i) the notice shall be in writing and signed by the copyright owner or such owner's duly authorized agent; and

(ii) the notice shall be served on the person responsible for the performance at least seven days before the date of the performance, and shall state the reasons for the objection; and

(iii) the notice shall comply, in form, content, and manner of service, with requirements that the Register of Copyrights shall prescribe by regulation;

(5)(A) except as provided in subparagraph (B), communication of a transmission embodying a performance or display of a work by the public reception of the transmission on a single receiving apparatus of a kind commonly used in private homes, unless—

(i) a direct charge is made to see or hear the transmission; or

(ii) the transmission thus received is further transmitted to the public....

[§ 110(5)(B) expands the exception's coverage to any establishment with less than 2000 gross square feet of space, and to any food service or drinking establishment that has less than 3750 gross square feet of space. If the establishment is 2000 gross square feet or more, or if the food service or drinking establishment is 3750 gross square feet or more, the establishment will nonetheless be exempt, if:

the performance of the radio transmission incorporating nondramatic musical compositions is "communicated by means of a total of not more than 6 loudspeakers, of which not more than 4 loudspeakers are located in any 1 room or adjoining outdoor space," or

the performance of a television transmission incorporating nondramatic musical compositions is "communicated by means of a total of not more than 4 audiovisual devices, of which not more than one audiovisual device is located in any 1 room, and no such audiovisual device has a diagonal screen size greater than 55 inches, and any audio portion of the performance or display is communicated by means of a total of not more than 6 loudspeakers, of which not more than 4 loudspeakers are located in any 1 room or adjoining outdoor space."]

. . .

(7) performance of a nondramatic musical work by a vending establishment open to the public at large without any direct or indirect admission charge, where the sole purpose of the performance is to promote the retail sale of copies or phonorecords of the work, or of the audiovisual or other devices utilized in such performance, and the performance is not transmit-

ted beyond the place where the establishment is located and is within the immediate area where the sale is occurring

. . .

House Report

H.R. Rep. No. 94–1476, 94th Cong., 2d Sess. 81–86 (1976).

Face-to-face teaching activities

Clause (1) of section 110 is generally intended to set out the conditions under which performances or displays, in the course of instructional activities other than educational broadcasting, are to be exempted from copyright control. The clause covers all types of copyrighted works, and exempts their performance or display "by instructors or pupils in the course of face-to-face teaching activities of a nonprofit educational institution," where the activities take place "in a classroom or similar place devoted to instruction."

There appears to be no need for a statutory definition of "face-to-face" teaching activities to clarify the scope of the provision. "Face-to-face teaching activities" under clause (1) embrace instructional performances and displays that are not "transmitted." . . . The "teaching activities" exempted by the clause encompass systematic instruction of a very wide variety of subjects, but they do not include performances or displays, whatever their cultural value or intellectual appeal, that are given for the recreation or entertainment of any part of their audience.

Works affected.—Since there is no limitation on the types of works covered by the exemption, teachers or students would be free to perform or display anything in class as long as the other conditions of the clause are met. They could read aloud from copyrighted text material, act out a drama, play or sing a musical work, perform a motion picture or filmstrip, or display text or pictorial material to the class by means of a projector. However, nothing in this provision is intended to sanction the unauthorized reproduction of copies or phonorecords for the purpose of classroom performance or display, and the clause contains a special exception dealing with performances from unlawfully made copies of motion pictures and other audiovisual works. . . .

Instructors or pupils.—To come within clause (1), the performance or display must be "by instructors or pupils," thus ruling out performances by actors, singers, or instrumentalists brought in from outside the school to put on a program. However, the term "instructors" would be broad enough to include guest lecturers if their instructional activities remain confined to classroom situations. In general, the term "pupils" refers to the enrolled members of a class.

Nonprofit educational institution.—Clause (1) makes clear that it applies only to the teaching activities "of a nonprofit educational institution," thus excluding from the exemption performances or displays in profit-making institutions such as dance studios and language schools.

Classroom or similar place.—The teaching activities exempted by the clause must take place "in a classroom or similar place devoted to instruction." For example, performances in an auditorium or stadium during a school assembly, graduation ceremony, class play, or sporting event, where the audience is not confined to the members of a particular class, would fall outside the scope of clause (1), although in some cases they might be exempted by clause (4) of section 110. . . .

. . .

Certain other nonprofit performances

In addition to the educational and religious exemptions provided by clauses (1) through (3) of section 110, clause (4) contains a general exception to the exclusive right of public performance that would cover some, though not all, of the same ground as the present "for profit" limitation.

Scope of exemption.—The exemption in clause (4) applies to the same general activities and subject matter as those covered by the "for profit" limitation today: public performances of nondramatic literary and musical works. However, the exemption would be limited to public performances given directly in the presence of an audience whether by means of living performers, the playing of phonorecords, or the operation of a receiving apparatus, and would not include a "transmission to the public." Unlike the clauses (1) through (3) and (5) of section 110, but like clauses (6) through (8), clause (4) applies only to performing rights in certain works, and does not affect the exclusive right to display a work in public.

No profit motive.—In addition to the other conditions specified by the clause, the performance must be "without any purpose of direct or indirect commercial advantage." This provision expressly adopts the principle established by the court decisions construing the "for profit" limitation: that public performances given or sponsored in connection with any commercial or profit-making enterprises are subject to the exclusive rights of the copyright owner even though the public is not charged for seeing or hearing the performance.

No payment for performance.—An important condition for this exemption is that the performance be given "without payment of any fee or other compensation for the performance to any of its performers, promoters, or organizers." The basic purpose of this requirement is to prevent the free use of copyrighted material under the guise of charity where fees or percentages are paid to performers, promoters, producers, and the like. However, the exemption would not be lost if the performers, directors, or producers of the performance, instead of being paid directly "for the performance," are paid a salary for duties encompassing the performance. Examples are performances by a school orchestra conducted by a music teacher who receives an annual salary, or by a service band whose members and conductors perform as part of their assigned duties and who receive military pay. The committee believes that performances of this type should be exempt, assuming the other conditions in clause (4) are met, and has not adopted the suggestion that the word "salary" be added to the phrase referring to the "payment of any fee or other compensation."

Admission charge.—Assuming that the performance involves no profit motive and no one responsible for it gets paid a fee, it must still meet one of two alternative conditions to be exempt. As specified in subclauses (A) and (B) of section 110(4), these conditions are: (1) that no direct or indirect admission charge is made, or (2) that the net proceeds are "used exclusively for educational, religious, or charitable purposes and not for private financial gain."

Under the second of these conditions, a performance meeting the other conditions of clause (4) would be exempt even if an admission fee is charged, provided any amounts left "after deducting the reasonable costs of producing the performance" are used solely for bona fide educational, religious, or charitable purposes. In cases arising under this second condition and as provided in subclause (B), where there is an admission charge, the copyright owner is given an opportunity to decide whether and under what conditions the copyrighted work should be performed; otherwise, owners could be compelled to make involuntary donations to the fund-raising activities of causes to which they are opposed. The subclause would thus permit copyright owners to prevent public performances of their works under section 110(4)(B) by serving notice of objection, with the reasons therefor, at least seven days in advance.

QUESTIONS

1. By providing in § 110(4)(B) for the serving by the copyright owner of a "notice of objection" to certain nonprofit public performances, does Congress contemplate that advance word of all such performances must be communicated by the promoters or performers to the copyright owner? If not, how often will the copyright owner actually be aware of such performances? Should the copyright owner, in order to deal with this problem, serve a "blanket" notice of objection, covering all of his musical compositions, to all institutions where there is some chance of its performance (e.g., all colleges and all secondary schools)? (Obviously, ASCAP or BMI could much more effectively serve such notices than could individual composers.) Would such a blanket notice, served *in futuro*, be adequate under § 110(4) to remove the exemption? *See* 37 CFR § 201.13, at Appendix C of the casebook.

2. Are any of the following exempted under § 110?

a. Taking advantage of the first fine spring day, a high school English teacher conducts her class in the park, where she and her students read portions of a copyrighted play out loud.

b. A high school teacher shows a video to her class during a lesson. The video was rented, and bore the label "For Private Viewing Only."

c. During a special church service directed at the younger generation, a performance is given of substantial excerpts (in sequence) from the rock musical "Jesus Christ Superstar."

d. Members of a religious sect perform portions of "Jesus Christ Superstar" in Times Square to inattentive passers-by.

e. A law student sings popular copyrighted songs in Times Square, and, passing the hat, requests contributions toward his law school tuition.

DISTANCE EDUCATION AND THE
SECTION 110(2) EXEMPTION

The use of copyrighted materials for purposes of education has generally been favored under the Copyright Act. Section 107 recognizes fair use in teaching (including multiple copies for classroom use), scholarship and research. Section 108 assumes that some photocopying for teachers and students will be lawfully undertaken in school libraries. Section 110(1) exempts performances and displays in face-to-face teaching by teachers and students. When enacted in 1976, Section 110(2) was intended to exempt the transmission of certain kinds of works through what was then known as "instructional television," normally by way of broadcast or "closed circuit" programming. The kinds of uses, however, were limited: "the performance of a nondramatic literary or musical work or display of a work." And the contemplated audience was limited as well: basically, a nonprofit school transmitting to classrooms or to students whose disabilities prevented them from getting to a classroom.

The advent and rapid growth of so-called distance education in the 1990s focused the attention of educators, so-called "content providers" (i.e., publishers and other copyright owners), and legislators on tapping into new technologies for bringing instruction to an expanded demographic audience: students living far from their schools, adults working during the typical class day, and senior citizens. To some extent, distance education could be accomplished by television, the prototype being a professor at one university location teaching students at several other locations, with both teacher and students being visible on large television monitors and being able to communicate with one another "in real time" (i.e., synchronous transmissions). Or asynchronous use of a taped lecture could be made by students at a later time.

But the internet quickly emerged as the more powerful and flexible instructional tool. The instructor, through his own or an institution's website could make available to students—independently logging on from different locations and at different times—a wide range of materials in textual, sound, pictorial and audiovisual formats, along with interactive capabilities.

A comprehensive and thoughtful report published in March 1999 by the Copyright Office pointed out that Section 110(2) was inadequate to allow the use of new technologies such as the internet for its full capacities in distance education. Most significantly, the 1976 provisions did not exempt the transmission of dramatic works or television programs or motion pictures; they did not exempt the transmission of textual material; they did not contemplate transmissions to students, away from the classroom at times and places of their own convenience; and they did not exempt the kinds of "copies" and "distribution" (as distinguished from public performance and display) that computers necessarily make in transmitting material through the internet. Although educational groups were eager to eliminate these restrictions, copyright owners were quick to point out that broad exemptions for internet transmission of copyrighted works, even for education, raised the prospect not only of unjustly uncompensated authors but also of vast uncontrolled "downstream transmissions," in infinitely reproducible digital form, instantaneously and potentially to all corners of the globe.

At the urging of several members of Congress, the various interest groups attempted to address their respective concerns in negotiations, and legislative language emerged that was ultimately incorporated in the so-called TEACH Act (Technology, Education and Copyright Harmonization Act of 2001), which passed the U.S. Senate unanimously in the spring of 2001. It is highly likely that in due time the House will pass a comparable bill, so that Section 110(2) will be replaced by provisions that will promote "digital distance education" while also recognizing the needs of the copyright community. Although some of the congressionally approved uses of copyrighted works through digital transmissions might well be embraced within the fair use doctrine and Section 107, it was the intention of the TEACH Act to articulate several specific conditions which, when satisfied, would provide educators with a "safe harbor" free of concern about infringement liability. Here are the pertinent provisions of the bill, which would strike the language of Section 110(2) as written in 1976 and substitute the following, as *not* an infringement of copyright:

except with respect to a work produced or marketed primarily for performance or display as part of mediated instructional activities transmitted via digital networks, or a performance or display that is given by means of a copy or phonorecord that is not lawfully made and acquired under this title, and the transmitting government body or accredited nonprofit educational institution knew or had reason to believe was not lawfully made and acquired, the performance of a nondramatic literary or musical work or reasonable and limited portions of any other work, or display of a work in an amount comparable to that which is typically displayed in the course of a live classroom session, by or in the course of a transmission, if—

(A) the performance or display is made by, at the direction of, or under the actual supervision of an instructor as an integral part of a class session offered as a regular part of the systematic mediated instructional activities of a governmental body or an accredited nonprofit educational institution;

(B) the performance or display is directly related and of material assistance to the teaching content of the transmission;

(C) the transmission is made solely for, and, to the extent technologically feasible, the reception of such transmission is limited to—

(i) students officially enrolled in the course for which the transmission is made; or (ii) officers or employees of governmental bodies as a part of their official duties or employment; and

(D) the transmitting body or institution—

(i) institutes policies regarding copyright, provides informational materials to faculty, students, and relevant staff members that accurately describe, and promote compliance with, the laws of the United States relating to copyright, and provides notice to students that materials used in connection with the course may be subject to copyright protection; and

(ii) in the case of digital transmissions—

(I) applies technological measures that, in the ordinary course of their operations, prevent—

(aa) retention of the work in accessible form by recipients of the transmission from the transmitting body or institution for longer than the class session; and (bb) unauthorized further dissemination of the work in accessible form by such recipients to others; and

(II) does not engage in conduct that could reasonably be expected to interfere with technological measures used by copyright owners to prevent such retention or unauthorized further dissemination;

In [this paragraph (2)], the term 'mediated instructional activities' with respect to the performance or display of a work by digital transmission under this section refers to activities that use such work as an integral part of the class experience, controlled by or under the actual supervision of the instructor and analogous to the type of performance or display that would take place in a live classroom setting. The term does not refer to activities that use, in 1 or more class sessions of a single course, such works as textbooks, course packs, or other material in any media, copies or phonorecords of which are typically purchased or acquired by the students in higher education for their independent use and retention or are typically purchased or acquired for elementary and secondary students for their possession and independent use....

For purposes of [this paragraph (2)], no governmental body or accredited nonprofit educational institution shall be liable for infringement by reason of the transient or temporary storage of material carried out through the automatic technical process of a digital transmission of the performance or display of that material as authorized under paragraph (2). No such material stored on the system or network controlled or operated by the transmitting body or institution under this paragraph shall be maintained on such system or network in a manner ordinarily accessible to anyone other than anticipated recipients. No such copy shall be maintained on the system or network in a manner ordinarily accessible to such anticipated recipients for a longer period than is reasonably necessary to facilitate the transmissions for which it was made.

(Can you identify any concerns or issues that the bill overlooks? Can you suggest any improvements in the text of the bill?) Section 112, dealing with so-called ephemeral recordings, would also be amended so as to allow the making of copies or phonorecords of copyrighted works, by a nonprofit educational institution, solely for the purpose of implementing its rights under the new Section 110(2).

b.   THE SECTION 110(5) EXEMPTION

Edison Bros. Stores, Inc. v. Broadcast Music, Inc.

954 F.2d 1419 (8th Cir.1992).

■ BOWMAN, CIRCUIT JUDGE.

Broadcast Music, Inc. (BMI), appeals the District Court's decision to grant summary judgment in favor of Edison Brothers Stores, Inc., in Edison's suit for a declaratory judgment that its stores qualify for an exemption from the vesting of exclusive rights of performance in the owners of copyrighted works. *See Edison Bros. Stores, Inc. v. Broadcast Music, Inc.*, 760 F.Supp. 767 (E.D.Mo.1991). We affirm.

The relevant facts are not in dispute. BMI is a performing rights organization that collectively licenses, as assignee of the rights of its copyright-holding clients (primarily publishers and songwriters), the public performance of such clients' copyrighted works.

Edison owns a chain of approximately 2500 retail clothing and shoe stores doing business as Chandlers, Jeans West, Fashion Conspiracy, Size 5–7–9 Shops, J. Riggins, Bakers, the Wild Pair, and others. Most of Edison's stores operate a single radio receiver with two attached shelf speakers to play radio broadcasts in the stores for the enjoyment of employees and customers. The equipment is simple and inexpensive. Edison has promulgated a radio usage policy and requires the adherence of these stores to the rules therein. The District Court summarized the policy as follows:

1.   Only simple, low grade radio-only receivers are to be used.

2.   Only two speakers may be attached to a radio receiver.

3.   The speakers must be placed within 15 feet of the receiver.

4.   Speakers that are built into the walls or ceilings must not be used. Only portable box speakers are allowed.

5.   [Edison will a]dvise each store manager that they are not to use tapes, cassettes, or any other type of recording equipment in their stores. They are to play the radio only.

Edison Bros. Stores, 760 F.Supp. at 769–70, quoted in Brief of Appellee at 7. BMI has submitted no evidence that any of the Edison stores to which the radio usage policy applies have failed to comply with it.

Approximately 220 of Edison's stores have more sophisticated audio and video systems or subscribe to commercial music services. Edison pays license fees to BMI or to commercial services licensed by BMI or other performing rights organizations for the music played in these stores. In recent years BMI approached Edison about licensing the remaining stores in its chain. Negotiations between the two parties evidently broke down, and Edison filed suit in District Court seeking declaratory relief. The court, agreeing with Edison's position, declared that the radio systems in use at Edison's unlicensed stores qualified for the so-called homestyle exemption to the exclusive performance rights that copyright owners enjoy under federal law. BMI appeals. . . .

I.

Under the Copyright Act, the owner of the copyright of a musical work has the exclusive right, among other rights, to perform the copyrighted work publicly. 17 U.S.C.A. § 106(4) (West Supp.1991). The Act, however, provides exemptions for certain performances. 17 U.S.C.A. § 110 (1988). Among the acts that are not "infringements of copyright" is the following:

> communication of a transmission embodying a performance or display of a work by the public reception of the transmission on a single receiving apparatus of a kind commonly used in private homes, un-less—
>
> (A) a direct charge is made to see or hear the transmission; or
>
> (B) the transmission thus received is further transmitted to the pub-lic[.]

Id. § 110(5). The issue before the District Court, and now before us, is whether Edison's 2000–plus radio receivers, each with two attached speak-ers and each operated in a different store, qualify for this homestyle exemption. BMI insists that, for several reasons, the exemption is unavail-able to Edison.

Clearly, each radio in an Edison store is a "single receiving apparatus" and is "communicat[ing] ... a transmission embodying a performance ... of a work by the public reception of the transmission." The receivers in the Edison stores are tuned to local radio stations and play anything and everything, including musical works, that the radio stations broadcast while the stores' receivers are on. No "direct charge is made to see or hear the transmission," and there is no contention that the broadcast is "fur-ther transmitted to the public" beyond the stores.

The sticking point for the parties, and the basis for BMI's first argument, is Edison's multiple locations, each employing a single receiver and two speakers in conformity with the company's radio usage policy. BMI argues that the statutory requirement that the transmission be received "on a single receiving apparatus of a kind commonly used in private homes" is not satisfied by this arrangement; although BMI concedes that an individual receiver and speaker set-up in one store may fit within the exemption, it takes the position that Edison lost section 110(5) protection as soon as it installed the second receiving apparatus in another of its stores. BMI contends that the statute requires that we consider the equipment of any one owner in toto, and not on a per-store basis, when we decide whether or not the exemption applies and find (as of course we would if we did as BMI suggests) that Edison is not in fact operating a "single receiving apparatus" within the meaning of the statute.

We cannot accept BMI's interpretation of section 110(5), as it defies the plain language of the statute. Section 110(5) does not say that a person, company, or other entity must own or operate only a single receiver to qualify for the exemption; it refers to "the communication of *a* transmission embodying *a* performance . . . of *a* work" (emphasis added). We think it obvious that the language refers to a single location. "The statute does not ask how many receiving apparatuses were used to receive a number of different works. The language of the statute thus strongly suggests that the proper analysis should be limited to the area where a single work is performed." *Broadcast Music, Inc. v. Claire's Boutiques*, Inc., 949 F.2d 1482, 1490 (7th Cir.1991). If we were to embrace BMI's argument and reach the result it suggests, the equipment used in any Edison store, including those stores that have more sophisticated equipment, would be attributable to each of the other stores owned by Edison for purposes of the Copyright Act. Such a result does not comport with the statutory language.

We agree with the District Court "that it is not appropriate to focus on the number of stores involved, but rather on whether each store duplicates the requirements of the homestyle exception." *Edison Bros. Stores*, 760 F.Supp. at 770. There is no evidence in the record that any of Edison's unlicensed stores fail to meet the statutory criteria for entitlement to the section 110(5) exemption. . . .

II.

BMI . . . bases its next argument on the legislative history of the enactment. BMI is not asking us to use legislative history to assist in clarifying an ambiguous statute; we are being asked to use legislative history to rewrite the section 110(5) exemption to add new requirements.

BMI contends that the physical size of Edison's stores removes the chain and its individual stores from the protection of the section 110(5) exemption. In order to reach such a result, BMI would have us read into the exemption a requirement that total space in the stores must not exceed 1055 square feet, with the area open to the public not to exceed 620 square feet. Brief of Appellant at 9, 11. The basis for this argument is a Supreme Court decision in a copyright case antedating the enactment of section 110(5) and the Report of the House Judiciary Committee relating to that section.

In *Twentieth Century Music Corp. v. Aiken*, 422 U.S. 151, 95 S.Ct. 2040, 45 L.Ed.2d 84 (1975), the Supreme Court had before it the issue of whether the proprietor of a food shop who installed and played a radio with four speakers on the premises of his business was required to pay licensing fees for the music thus provided for his patrons. The Court, holding that in so using a radio Aiken was not "performing" within the meaning of the Copyright Act, ruled that he was not. The House Report on the 1976 amendments to the Copyright Act suggests that the section 110(5) exemption was added to the Copyright Act in response to the Court's opinion in *Aiken*. H.R.Rep. No. 1476, 94th Cong., 2d Sess. 86–87 (1976), reprinted in 1976 U.S.C.C.A.N. 5659, 5700–01. The Report indicates that the new exemption was intended to supersede the Court's holding in *Aiken* that the playing of a radio in a commercial establishment open to the public is not a "performance," and thus not an infringing act. At the same time, the Report suggests that on the facts of *Aiken* the Court's decision exempting Aiken from the payment of licensing fees was appropriate and deserving of codification.

The language from the Report upon which BMI focuses is this: "the Committee considers this fact situation [in *Aiken*] to represent the outer limit of the [homestyle] exemption, and believes that the line should be drawn at that point." Id. at 87, reprinted in 1976 U.S.C.C.A.N. at 5701. Even accepting arguendo the untenable proposition that we would give greater weight to what a House Committee "considers" than to the text the entire Congress enacts and the President signs, BMI neglects to point out that the "fact situation" described in the Report, which immediately precedes the above-quoted language, makes no mention of square footage: "Under the particular fact situation in the *Aiken* case, assuming a small commercial establishment and the use of a home receiver with four ordinary loudspeakers grouped within a relatively narrow circumference from the set, it is intended that the performances would be exempt under clause (5)." Id. Further, the "fact situation" as described in *Aiken* makes no mention of the square footage of Aiken's shop . . . :

BMI directs our attention to several opinions where, BMI maintains, the square footage of the establishment attempting to qualify for the exemption was discussed.

Having reviewed these cases, we reject as totally inaccurate BMI's assertion that "in virtually every case the excessive square footage of the defendant's store alone was found to disqualify the defendant from invoking the Section 110(5) exemption." Brief of Appellant at 27 n. 14. The fact is that in none of these cases did the court base its decision solely on the square footage of the stores without considering the nature of the equipment, i.e., whether it was "homestyle," nor did any of them declare that they would have reached the same result based only upon the square footage of the infringing stores. Moreover, none of the cases cited has any binding precedential force in this Circuit.

The closest we come to Eighth Circuit precedent on this issue is this Court's dicta in *National Football League v. McBee & Bruno's, Inc.*, 792 F.2d 726 (8th Cir.1986), in which the challenged action was the receipt via satellite antenna of blacked-out NFL games and the playing of the broadcasts on television sets in bars. Although the Court noted that "[t]he factors listed in the legislative history do speak of the size of the area where the transmission will be played," id. at 731, the Court said nothing about a maximum square footage. Further, the Court stated that the 1976 legislative history indicates that "to decide whether an infringement had occurred, the critical question instead would be the type of equipment used by the putative infringer." *Id.* at 730. The Court also quoted this language from the legislative history of the exemption:

> the clause would exempt small commercial establishments whose proprietors merely bring onto their premises standard radio or television equipment and turn it on for their customers' enjoyment, but it would impose liability where the proprietor has a commercial 'sound system' installed or converts a standard home receiving apparatus . . . into the equivalent of a commercial sound system.

Id. at 730–31 (quoting H.R.Rep. No. 1476, 94th Cong., 2d Sess. 87 (1976), reprinted in 1976 U.S.C.C.A.N. 5659, 5701). Clearly, this passage from the legislative history directs attention to the quality of the sound system used, and not to the square footage of the establishment using it.

Although the legislative history is interesting, it is beside the point; we need only look to the statute itself. If Congress intended to impose a physical size limitation on the establishment qualifying for the exemption, it might easily have written it into the statute. But it did not; it did not even qualify the exemption by limiting its availability to a "small commercial establishment," the language of the legislative history. The statute focuses on the equipment being used, and so must we. This Court is not a legislative body, and it has no authority to rewrite the statute.

The same observation applies fully to BMI's next argument: that the legislative history supports its contention that a section 110(5) exemption is available only if "the business [does] not have the ability to pay for its use of music or [is not] of sufficient size to justify, as a practical matter, a subscription to a commercial background music service." Brief of Appellant at 11. The legislative history BMI relies upon is this:

> It is the intent of the conferees that a small commercial establishment of the type involved in Twentieth Century Music Corp. v. Aiken, which merely augmented a home-type receiver and which was not of sufficient size to justify, as a practical matter, a subscription to a commercial background music service, would be exempt.

H.R.Conf.Rep. No. 1733, 94th Cong., 2d Sess. 75 (1976) (citation omitted), reprinted in 1976 U.S.C.C.A.N. 5810, 5816. [FN8]

The intent expressed in the report of the House conferees is irrelevant when the statutory language does not say or even imply that the size or financial wherewithal of the establishment has a bearing on eligibility for the homestyle exemption. As with the square footage requirement that BMI would have us read into the exemption, the opinions of other courts that mention this language do not persuade us that, even though Congress enacted the law without any such requirement, it truly intended a size-and-financial-means test to be a part of the statute. *See Claire's Boutiques*, 949 F.2d at 1492 ("no case has relied solely on the financial size or ability of the defendant as a reason for denying the application of § 110(5)"). Moreover, we surmise that any such requirement would surely run into constitutional problems for vagueness: who would determine when an establishment is "of sufficient size to justify ... a subscription to a commercial background music service," and what criteria would they use?

We hold that 17 U.S.C. § 110(5) does not require that the square footage of a qualifying establishment be less than 1055, with fewer than 620 square feet open to the public; nor does it require that the entity's ability to pay for a commercial background music service be considered. The focus of the statute is on the equipment in use, and as each of Edison's unlicensed stores uses only homestyle equipment each qualifies for the homestyle exemption.

III.

... BMI's argument that this decision interferes with the international treaty obligations of the United States also fails. The treaty in question is the international copyright agreement known as the Berne Convention. Berne Convention for the Protection of Literary and Artistic Works, S. Treaty Doc. No. 27, 99th Cong., 2d Sess. (1986). The Convention, signed on September 9, 1886, as revised at Paris on July 24, 1971, entered into force for the United States on March 1, 1989. See Berne Convention Implementation Act of 1988, Pub.L. No. 100–568, § 13, 102 Stat. 2853, 2861 (1988). Congress then revised the Copyright Act (although section 110(5) was unaffected) and declared that the Act as amended "satisf[ies] the obligations of the United States in adhering to the Berne Convention and no further rights or interests shall be recognized or created for that purpose." Id. § 2(3), 102 Stat. 2853.

BMI asserts that the District Court's interpretation of section 110(5) to provide shelter for Edison under the homestyle exemption expands the scope of the exemption to such a degree that it renders section 110(5) in violation of the United States' treaty obligations under Article 11bis of the Berne Convention. Under that article, authors of artistic works have exclusive rights to authorize "the public communication by loudspeaker or any other analogous instrument transmitting, by signs, sounds or images, the broadcast of the work." Berne Convention, art. 11bis(iii), S. Treaty Doc. No. 27, 99th Cong., 2d Sess. 44 (1986). The flaw in BMI's argument is that the District Court's interpretation of section 110(5) does not expand the homestyle exemption, but merely declares that the statutory language means what it says. We cannot presume that Congress, in enacting this language, intended something else, and we know that Congress declared its handiwork to be consistent with the Berne Convention. Congress thus declared the public policy of the United States and, for us, that is the end of the matter....

QUESTIONS

1. Assume that Edison Brothers, desiring to hide its unsightly radio wires, places its stereo receiver in the stockroom of each of its stores, away from customer view, and runs its wiring from the receiver over the top of a false ceiling in its retail space and through the ceiling to its two speakers, which are attached high on the walls by metal brackets. Will this arrangement forfeit the exemption provided by Section 110(5)(A)? In other words, does Edison use "a single receiving apparatus of a kind commonly used in private homes"? And are the radio transmissions that it receives "further transmitted to the public"? *See Broadcast Music, Inc. v. Claire's Boutiques, Inc.*, 949 F.2d 1482 (7th Cir.1991).

2. You have been consulted by a law firm that wishes to know whether it must seek express permission to make the following uses of copyrighted music: (a) It re-transmits the broadcast signal of a local all-music radio station to telephone callers whom the receptionist puts on "Hold." *See Prophet Music, Inc. v. Shamla Oil Co.*, 26 U.S.P.Q.2d 1554 (D.Minn.1993); (b) It has the receptionist activate a compact-disc player with music CDs to entertain persons waiting in the reception lounge area.

3. As originally enacted in 1976, § 110(5) exempted commercial establishments that communicated radio and television broadcasts to their customers through "a single receiving apparatus of a kind commonly used in private homes." This so-called home-style exemption contemplated the use of simple loudspeakers, and thus a fairly limited square footage for the establishment. Those establishments that used commercial speakers to amplify over a large area had to secure a license from the copyright owner, typically through ASCAP and BMI. As a result of pressures from bars and restaurants and other retailers, Congress in October 1998 enacted the so-called "Fairness in Music Licensing Act," which added what is now § 110(5)(B). That section exempts the transmission of radio and television broadcasts for eating and drinking establishments of less than 3,750 square feet, and other retail establishments of less than 2,000 square feet—as well as larger such establishments based on certain limits as to the number of loudspeakers (even commercial rather than home-style equipment) and television sets.

Music copyright owners assert that this is hardly "fairness in music licensing"—especially when one considers, for example, that the square footage exemption for restaurants covers an establishment that is roughly the size of a three-story, four-bedroom house. Would you have supported such legislation? (The legislation was a *quid pro quo* for the 20–year extension of the copyright term for, among other things, popular music dating back to the 1920s and 1930s.) The legislation has been the subject of a World Trade Organization Dispute Resolution Panel's ruling, see *infra*, subsection f.

c. SECONDARY TRANSMISSIONS, INCLUDING BY CABLE AND SATELLITE—§§ 111, 119

Because of the broad definition of "public performance" in the 1976 Copyright Act, it is a violation of this § 106(4) right for a person, without the consent of the copyright owner, to receive a transmission of the copyrighted work and then to re-transmit it to yet another location (where there are members of the public). Examples would be a hotel's re-transmitting by electrical devices the sounds of a radio broadcast into its lobby, elevators or dining room; or the re-transmission of a television broadcast by cable or satellite to persons well beyond the local viewing area of the broadcast station. Do any of these activities, facially infringements, warrant some sort of protected status—either through a statutory exemption or as the beneficiary of a compulsory license?

Section 111(a)(1) exempts such a "secondary transmission" that takes the form of "relaying, by the management of a hotel, apartment house, or similar establishment, of signals transmitted by a broadcast station licensed by the Federal Communications Commission, within the local service area of such station, to the private lodgings of guests or residents of such establishment, and no direct charge is made to see or hear the secondary transmission." The House Report (at p. 92) points out that the exemption does not extend to "dining rooms, meeting halls, theatres, ballrooms, or similar places that are outside of a normal circle of a family and its social acquaintances." In effect, the hotel is permitted to do what might be regarded as the functional equivalent of placing an ordinary radio or television set in its private rooms. Thus has Congress dealt with the issue so conspicuously addressed by the Supreme Court in *Buck v. Jewell–LaSalle, supra,* and its progeny.

The balance of § 111 of the Copyright Act focuses principally on secondary transmission of television broadcasts by cable services. The provisions attempt to dovetail copyright policy with the regulatory policies of the Federal Communications Commission. The major distinction to be drawn for both FCC and copyright regulation is between cable re-transmission of "local" and "distant" broadcast signals. Local signals are those that reach the viewers in the area where the cable system is located; distant signals are those that are imported from broadcast stations at such a distance that they could not otherwise be received by viewers in the area in which the cable system is located. In general, a broadcast signal is "distant" if it is re-transmitted by a cable system located more than 35 miles from the signal's point of origin.

The FCC regulations governing cable systems have changed significantly over time—reflecting in part the development of cable television from an infant industry to a most profitable one that rivals the popularity of over-the-air television broadcast networks and stations, and in part changes in the regulatory philosophy of the agency. For most of the period since the effective date of the 1976 Copyright Act, FCC regulations have provided that if a cable system is located in the "local service area" of a broadcast station (or within the "area of dominant influence," equivalent to the local TV market), then the system *must* carry that station's programs to the cable subscribers. As will be noted below, such local programming may be re-transmitted without having to pay copyright license fees. If a cable system wishes to re-transmit distant signals, then it *may* do so, subject to conditions imposed by the Commission.

The compulsory-license provisions of § 111 of the Copyright Act are designed to advance the usual copyright policies—providing a fair market return to the copyright owner as an incentive for creative authorship—while accommodating the broadcasting regulatory policies of the FCC. A cable system will be entitled to re-transmit distant signals if, basically, such re-transmission is permitted by the FCC and if the cable system complies with the requirements of § 111(d) requiring the periodic filing of statements of account and payment of royalties (the usual obligations of compulsory licensees under the copyright law). The statute recognizes that—at least in the circumstances of the cable and broadcast industries in 1976—although cable systems derive income from their re-transmissions and should be required to pay the creators of the copyrighted programs they carry, individual royalty negotiations with all copyright owners would be unduly burdensome. In October 1994, Congress extended the provisions of § 111 to cover "wireless" as well as cable re-transmissions (Pub. L. 103–369, amending § 111(f)).

The semi-annual accountings filed by the cable systems identify the broadcast stations whose signals were re-transmitted in the preceding six months, state the total number of subscribers to the cable system and the gross amounts paid for the system's "basic service" (as distinguished from installations and pay channels), and identify the non-network programs carried by the cable system beyond the local service area of the primary transmitter. The latter information is the basis for computing what is known as the "distant signal equivalent," a factor that plays an important role in calculating the royalties to be paid by the compulsory licensee; the other principal factor is the gross receipts from subscribers for the service of providing secondary transmissions. *See Cablevision Systems Development Co. v. Motion Picture Ass'n of Am.*, 836 F.2d 599 (D.C.Cir.1988) (interpretation of "gross receipts" and "basic service" in § 111(d)(2)(B)). Royalty payments must accompany the semi-annual statements of account that are filed with the Register of Copyrights.

The statutory provisions for the computation of royalties are among the lengthiest in the statute. No royalty is exacted for the re-transmission of local signals, because this is assumed not to threaten the existing market for owners of copyrighted programs (whose payment from the broadcast stations takes into account viewers in the "local service area" whether they receive the program off-the-air or by cable). Nor does the compulsory license recompense the copyright owner for re-transmission of network programming, including programs from distant markets; the network compensates the program owner based upon all of the markets served by the network. Copyright liability under § 111 is thus based upon the cable transmission of distant non-network programming, which carries the program to an area beyond which it has been licensed and which thus adversely affects the ability of the copyright owner to exploit the work in that distant market.

The royalty fee is determined by a two-step process. First, a value called a "distant signal equivalent" is assigned to all distant signals carried by the cable system, weighted according to the different amounts of non-network programming carried by the broadcast station. *See* § 111(f). These values are added up, and then a scale of percentages as set forth in § 111(d)(1) of the statute is determined by the cumulative total of DSEs and is then multiplied by the cable system's gross receipts. The 1976 Copyright Act, as originally written, gave the Copyright Royalty Tribunal the power to adjust the statutory percentages to be used in calculating royalty rates. Since the 1994 abolition of the CRT, the power to modify rates and distribute royalties is in the hands of Copyright Arbitration Royalty Panels, subject to limited review by the Librarian of Congress (and, in turn, by the D.C. Circuit Court of Appeals). *See National Ass'n of Broadcasters v. Librarian of Congress*, 146 F.3d 907 (D.C.Cir.1998). The rates—i.e., the applicable percentages of a cable system's gross receipts— are subject to adjustment every five years. Most recently, they were modified by the Copyright Office effective July 1, 2000. The pertinent regulations are 37 C.F.R. §§ 201.17, 256.2.

The Register of Copyrights receives all of these fees from all cable systems operating under the compulsory license, and then after the deduction of administrative costs, they are distributed to copyright owners whose works were included in secondary transmissions of non-network television programs beyond the local service area of the primary transmitter. *See* § 111(d)(3). No royalty fees are to be distributed to copyright owners for the re-transmission of either "local" or "network" programs. The statute encourages claimants to agree among themselves regarding the division of the royalties, and if there is no controversy among the claimants, the Register is to distribute the royalties; if there is a controversy, then the CARPs (or Librarian of Congress) will resolve it.

When distribution decisions are to be made, the Register divides the proceedings into two phases. In Phase I, the Register allocates percentages of the fund to specific groups of claimants; for example, the general pattern has been 55–60% to "program suppliers" (i.e., motion picture companies engaged in production and distribution of programs to television broadcasters, and syndicators of television programs), and some 20–25% to professional sports leagues. In Phase II of the cable-royalty distribution proceedings, the Register makes allocations among the individual claimants within each category (e.g., within the "program supplier" group, the Motion Picture Association of America is entitled to roughly 97–98% of the royalties), although this allocation is usually worked out consensually among the respective claimants.

The overall size of the royalty fund for cable re-transmissions has grown dramatically since the $13 million distributed for the 1978 calendar year. Cable royalties for the year 2000 totaled roughly $113 million.

Section 111, besides identifying the kinds of cable re-transmissions that are subject to a compulsory license, also identifies what re-transmissions will be infringements (subject to various conditions and limitations): when the primary transmission is not by a licensed broadcast station but is, for example, by closed-circuit television or a background music service or a pay-cable program; when signals are re-transmitted without taking the usual steps of filing accounts and paying royalties; when there is willful or repeated re-transmission of signals which a cable system is not permitted by the FCC to carry; when the cable system willfully alters the content of any program in the primary transmission or the advertising therein; or when, rather than re-transmitting a primary transmission simultaneously, the cable system first records it and then transmits the recorded program at a later time.

In 1988, Congress created a new, temporary, compulsory license for secondary transmissions by satellite carriers to certain "earth stations," i.e., household satellite "dishes" capturing signals for private home viewing. Home dishes make possible individuals' direct receipt not only of popular independent "superstations" (such as WTBS and WGN) but also of distant signals from network stations; they provide particular benefits for persons living in remote areas served neither by off-air signals nor by a cable system. Yet they dilute the economic return of copyright owners from transmitted public performances (e.g., by substituting for cable systems).

Inspired by the cable compulsory license under § 111, the satellite compulsory license has a somewhat different rate structure. Pursuant to Section 119(b)(1)(B), the Copyright Office had set a flat fee of 27 cents a month per subscriber for each received superstation signal and for each received network signal. But Congress, wishing to bring those rates closer to those exacted for cable retransmissions under Section 111, amended the statute in 1999; now, § 119(c)(4) reduces that satellite compulsory royalty rate by 30 percent for superstation retransmissions and by 45% for network retransmissions. See 37 C.F.R. § 258.3(c). At the same time, Congress added a new Section 122 to the Copyright Act, which allows satellite carriers for the first time to retransmit local broadcasts, royalty-free.

The compulsory royalties that have been collected from satellite carriers have dramatically increased in the period since Section 119 was enacted, from $2.4 million for 1989 to nearly $68 million for the year 2000. Taking account of the compulsory payments under both Sections 111 and 119, between $180 million to $210 million have been paid to owners of copyrighted television programs for each of the years since 1988, a not inconsiderable sum.

d.   "JUKEBOX" PUBLIC PERFORMANCES—§ 116

The 1909 Act contained an express exemption from liability for unauthorized performance of music by means of coin-operated machines where there was no admission fee to the place of performance. This so-called jukebox exemption, originally designed to insulate the "penny parlor," became a haven for an increasingly profitable jukebox industry. Legislative assaults on the exemption failed for nearly 70 years. The elimination of the exemption in the 1976 Act, and the substitution of a compulsory-license arrangement—with a modest statutory royalty rate, subject to redetermination by the Copyright Royalty Tribunal—were most significant steps in protecting the copyright owner's right of public performance.

Not surprisingly, the precise amount of the statutory royalty was a subject of considerable debate throughout the revision process. As enacted, § 116(b)(1)(A) provided for a royalty fee of $8 per year per jukebox, which would cover all of the musical works placed in that box. Acting pursuant to statutory authorization in §§ 801(b) and 804(a), the Copyright Royalty Tribunal initiated proceedings in January 1980 to determine whether the statutory rates warranted adjustment; hearings were held, with appearances by the three performing rights societies representing copyright owners (ASCAP, BMI and SESAC) and by representatives of the jukebox industry (the Amusement and Music Operators Association). The Tribunal determined that jukebox operators should pay an increased royalty fee of $25 per jukebox in 1982 and 1983, and $50 in subsequent years, with a cost-of-living adjustment to be introduced in 1987. On judicial review, the Tribunal's action was upheld against claims by the performing rights societies that a more reasonable royalty would have been in the range of $70–$140, as well as against claims by AMOA that the $25/$50 fee was inconsistent with Congress's intent and would have a serious adverse impact upon many jukebox operators. *Amusement & Music Operators Ass'n v. Copyright Royalty Tribunal*, 676 F.2d 1144 (7th Cir.), *cert. denied*, 459 U.S. 907 (1982).

In its initial distribution of jukebox royalties in 1978, the Copyright Royalty Tribunal allocated 47.5% of the fund each to ASCAP and BMI, and 5% to SESAC. Since then, the societies have voluntarily settled their claims among themselves. The size of the distributable fund mounted steadily, from $1.12 million in 1978 to $6.2 million in 1988. In the latter year, Congress reviewed the compulsory license provisions to determine whether modification was required in order to render United States law consistent with Berne Convention requirements. The jukebox licensing provisions were found to be inconsistent with Article 11(1) of the Convention.

Since then, there have been two major changes in the jukebox provisions of the Copyright Act. First, as a matter of procedure, the Copyright Royalty Tribunal was abolished effective December 17, 1993, and its functions were transferred to ad hoc arbitration panels convened by the Librarian of Congress. The powers of the Copyright Arbitration Royalty Panels (CARPs)—similar in general outlines to those that had been exercised by the Tribunal—are set forth in §§ 801–803. More pertinently, Congress decided to abandon the compulsory license for jukebox performances and, in light of the practices that had developed since 1978, facilitated continuing efforts at reaching negotiated arrangements for establishing royalty rates and the division of fees; if the parties wish, they may utilize arbitration to do so.

Thus, § 116(b)(1), as now written, provides that owners of copyright in musical works and operators of "coin-operated phonorecord players" (as defined in § 116(d)) "may negotiate and agree upon the terms and rates of royalty payments for the performance of such works and the proportionate division of fees paid among copyright owners," and § 116(b)(2) permits recourse to arbitration. Under § 116(c), any such voluntarily negotiated license agreements "shall be given effect in lieu of any otherwise applicable determination by a copyright arbitration royalty panel." Under § 803(a)(4), if such negotiated licenses expire or are terminated, and are not replaced with other agreements covering an equivalent quantity of musical works, upon petition filed within one year after such expiration or termination the Librarian is to convene a CARP; the rates set by such a panel shall then prevail until superseded by a new negotiated license agreement.

Negotiated agreements have in fact been reached between ASCAP, BMI and SESAC representing copyright owners and the Amusement and Music Operators Association representing jukebox operators. These agreements provide for the payment of $275 per year for the operator's first jukebox, $55 per box for the second through the tenth box, and $48 per year for the eleventh and each box beyond. This royalty structure obviously works to the disadvantage of the person who operates only a small number of jukeboxes.

e. PUBLIC BROADCASTING—§ 118

A limitation on performing rights that was adopted late in the development of the 1976 Act is the compulsory license for public broadcasting. Public broadcasters, while acknowledging that copyright holders should receive payments for their valuable contributions to high-quality programming, emphasized the "multitude of administratively cumbersome and very costly rights 'clearance' problems that cannot help but impair the vitality" of public broadcasting were there to be no compulsory license; the financial and administrative burdens of securing clearances would overwhelm the budgets of the public broadcasters, which are financed by public support and donations. The musical performing rights societies argued against the compulsory license, which it thought wrong in principle even if utilized in three other statutory situations for special historical reasons. Rebutting the argument regarding administrative burden, they emphasized that commercial broadcasters had for many years secured negotiated licenses that were working well, and that even public broadcasters had traditionally negotiated for synchronization (or recording) licenses in the past, for lack of a "for profit" limitation on such synchronization under the 1909 Act. A particularly strong argument against the compulsory license for public broadcasters was the increasing overlap in function between public and commercial broadcasting:

> Public broadcasting has grown and changed significantly in the past decade and will continue to do so. It now competes with commercial broadcasting as a national medium, and its programming contains much of the same types of entertainment and cultural material presented by commercial broadcasters. The revenues of public broadcasting have grown significantly. . . .

As originally enacted in 1976, § 118 provided for a compulsory license with respect to the performance of published nondramatic musical works and the display of published pictorial, graphic and sculptural works. This license was granted to "public broadcasting entities," principally "noncommercial educational broadcast stations" as defined in the Federal Communications Act. Compulsory license fees were to be established by the Copyright Royalty Tribunal.

As has already been noted, the Tribunal was abolished in December 1993, and its powers given to the Librarian of Congress, who can appoint Copyright Arbitration Royalty Panels. And, like the statutory arrangements just described for jukebox performances, § 118 has now abandoned the compulsory-license format and has given preference to license agreements voluntarily negotiated between public broadcasting entities, on the one side, and copyright owners of nondramatic music or of pictorial, graphic and sculptural works, on the other. These negotiated agreements, under § 118(b), may establish "the terms and rates of royalty payments and the proportionate division of fees paid among various copyright owners." Failing such voluntary agreements, the Librarian, under § 118(b)(3), is to convene a CARP "to determine and publish in the Federal Register a schedule of rates and terms." A CARP proceeding in fact took place in 1998, and the Librarian determined (see 37 C.F.R. § 253.3) that "the following annual royalty rates shall apply to the performance of published nondramatic musical compositions within the scope of [section 118]: $3,320,000 to ASCAP, and $2,123,000 to BMI," to be paid semiannually; this regulation covers the period from January 1, 1998 to December 31, 2001. See Part 253 of the Regulations of the Copyright Office, which is set forth in Appendix C of the Casebook.

Upon compliance with negotiated license rates and terms (or, failing those, with the rates and terms declared by the Librarian), the following activities are authorized by § 118(d): performance or display in the course of a broadcast transmission by a noncommercial radio or television station; the production, copying and distribution of a program containing such performance or display solely for the purpose of broadcast by other such stations; and the taping by a public school or other nonprofit institution of such a broadcast for nonprofit face-to-face instructional use within seven days.

f. COMPATIBILITY WITH THE BERNE CONVENTION OF COMPULSORY LICENSES AND OTHER QUALIFICATIONS OF THE PERFORMANCE AND DISPLAY RIGHTS

The previous materials addressed the many limitations that United States copyright law imposes on the exclusive exercise of the public performance and display rights. Some of these limitations are outright exemptions from liability; others, in the form of compulsory licenses, substitute government regulation for free selection of licensees and negotiation of royalty rates. Is this diverse collection of restraints upon the copyright holder's free and full exercise of copyright compatible with the Berne Convention's specification of composers' and dramatists' exclusive rights in "any communication to the public" and to "public performance by any means or process" (Art. 11)?

Although the Berne Convention generally sets a high level of minimum protection, it does tolerate some qualifications to the principle of exclusive right under copyright. Article 13.1 of the treaty explicitly permits member countries to provide for compulsory licenses for the making of sound recordings of musical works. Note that the performance right in sound recordings—limited to digital performances and laden with intricate compulsory licenses—does not contravene the Berne Convention because that treaty does not cover sound recordings. (Another treaty, the Geneva Phonograms Convention, secures international protection for sound recordings, but this convention is limited to reproduction rights.) Article 11bis(2) of the Berne Convention allows member countries to qualify rights to broadcasts and secondary transmissions, subject to a guarantee of equitable remuneration "which, in the absence of agreement, shall be fixed by competent authority." This text appears consistent with the provisions in Title 17 for compulsory licenses for cable and satellite re-transmissions and for royalties sometimes set by government arbitration panels for public broadcasting. In 1988, to conform to Berne Convention norms, Congress modified the compulsory license for jukeboxes to substitute an initial system of negotiated licenses for the former jukebox compulsory license (the compulsory license remains as a residual measure in the event that private negotiations fail).

Finally, with one important exception, most of the § 110 exemptions to the performance and display rights may be accommodated within the Berne Convention's underlying authorization to member countries to maintain "minor reservations" to the general rights of public performance, broadcasting and re-transmission. The drafters of the most recent version of the Berne Convention (Stockholm 1967/Paris 1971) anticipated that these reservations would extend to small-scale or publicly beneficial uses such as "religious ceremonies, performances by military bands and the requirements of education and popularization." *Id.* at 535; *see also* World Intellectual Property Organization, Guide to the Berne Convention ¶ 11.6 (1978).

The exception that seems difficult to square with the mandates of the Berne Convention is the newly-expanded § 110(5)(B) exemption for re-transmissions by restaurants and business establishments, see *supra* subchapter 6.D.7.a. The European Union initiated a proceeding against the U.S. before a World Trade Organization dispute settlement panel on the ground that the incompatibility of § 110(5)(B) with the norms of Article 11 of the Berne Convention violates U.S. obligations under the Trade Related Aspects of Intellectual Property Accord. *See* WT/DS160/1–IP/D/16 (Request for Consultations by the European Communities (Feb. 4, 1999) (panel established on May 26, 1999)).

On June 15, 2000 the WTO dispute resolution panel announced its decision regarding complaint no. WT/DS160/R that § 110(5)(B) violated the U.S. obligations under the TRIPs accord. The Panel concluded that while Subparagraph (A) of Section 110(5), the old "homestyle" exception, was consistent with Articles 11bis(1)(iii) and 11(1)(ii) of the Berne Convention (1971), new subparagraph (B) of Section 110(5) was not. The Panel therefore recommended that the Dispute Settlement Body request the United States to bring subparagraph (B) of Section 110(5) into conformity with its obligations under the TRIPS Agreement. (Persistent non-conformity subjects the U.S. to trade sanctions.)

The panel determined that § 110(5)(B) failed to meet the criteria of art. 13 of the TRIPs Accord, which limits national exceptions to "certain special cases that do not conflict with a normal exploitation of the work. . . ." (These criteria are derived from article 9.2 of the Berne Convention.) The Panel emphasized that § 110(5)(B)'s broad business exception well exceeded "certain special cases" (by contrast, it deemed the "homestyle" exception sufficiently limited to meet this standard); the term "requires that a limitation or exception in national legislation should be clearly defined and should be narrow in its scope and reach." While § 110(5)(B) may be clearly defined, it could hardly be deemed "narrow" when, according to studies quoted by the Panel, 73% of all eating establishments, 70% of all drinking establishments, and 45% of all retail establishments, fall below § 110(5)(B)'s size limits, and therefore benefit from the exemption. By contrast, 16% of eating establishments, 13.5% of drinking establishments, and 18% of retail establishments benefited from the "homestyle" exemption.

The Panel also ruled that § 110(5)(B) was inconsistent with the requirement that a national exception not "conflict with a normal exploitation of the work." In the first attempt by a supranational decisional body to interpret this provision—a provision that is likely to assume paramount importance in international copyright law—the Panel stated:

> We believe that an exception or limitation to an exclusive right in domestic legislation rises to the level of a conflict with a normal exploitation of the work . . . if uses, that in principle are covered by that right but exempted under the exception or limitation, enter into economic competition with the ways that right holders normally extract economic value from that right to the work . . . and thereby deprive them of significant or tangible commercial gains.

Applying this standard, the Panel observed, *inter alia*, that rights owners license business establishments to play live and recorded music, while § 110(5)(B) eliminates the basis for licensing the same establishments with respect to performing works via broadcast radio and television. If the market as a whole is music performed in business establishments, then the exemption of broadcasts significantly compromises the copyright owner's opportunity for commercial gain. Even were the markets separated into live and prerecorded music on the one hand, and broadcasts on the other, the exemption for broadcasts competes with the exploitation of the other market because it provides business establishments an incentive to shift from paying modes of exploitation to exempt modes of exploitation.

The Panel gave the U.S. until July 27, 2001 to comply with its ruling. As this edition goes to press, it appears very unlikely that Congress will amend § 110(5)(B) to conform to international standards; rather the U.S.

may choose to pay damages to WTO member states to compensate for the licensing fees of which the expanded exemption deprives them. [cite]

GENERAL REVIEW QUESTIONS

What, if any, are the copyright infringements in the following cases?

1. *E* exhibits a copyrighted painting, which it owns, in an art gallery, without the consent of *A*, the artist and owner of copyright. *E* exhibits the same painting on a television program.

2. *H* Hotel hires a three-piece band to play copyrighted music at the hotel restaurant; there is no admission charge or entertainment charge. *E* (exclusive) membership social club has a band playing the same music at weekend dances.

3. Michael Jackson plays a copyrighted song in a television studio; ABC television network transmits the performance to its local television affiliates, which broadcast it; a viewer turns on the television set in a room filled with family friends; and a doctor does the same for the patients in her waiting room. (What if the doctor plays a recorded version of the song on a CD player?)

4. *H* Hotel pipes the sound from the Jackson television show into the hotel elevators and private guest rooms. It also plays a different rendition of that song through its Muzak® background-music service system, into private guest rooms.

5. A jukebox operator places a phonorecord of *C*'s song in a coin-operated jukebox, and the record is frequently played; the performance of the song is by *P* and the record is made by the *R* Recording Company.

6. Arthur Miller's "Death of a Salesman" is performed by students in a 12th-grade classroom.

(a) Assume instead that one of the performers is a professional actor, an alumnus of the school.

(b) Assume instead that the student performance is in the school auditorium.

(c) Assume that the student classroom performance is transmitted by closed-circuit television to all high school English classes in the school district.

7. The high school glee club opens an assembly program in the school auditorium with a copyrighted hymn. It also sings the hymn at the beginning of a school football game; tickets are sold to the game, the proceeds being devoted to uniforms and other expenses of the school's athletic teams and musical organizations.

8. The high school glee club makes a recording of the copyrighted song, and publicly distributes the recording. Jolly Roger Records "dubs" the sounds onto its own phonorecords (without any consents) and sells them to the public. A disc jockey plays the glee club record over local radio station WDJ.

9.   Officials within the California prison system have in the past year purchased at retail prices cassettes of copyrighted motion pictures, from stores lawfully selling videotapes and videodiscs. The videotapes bear a legend stating: "This tape is exclusively for viewing in private homes. Any duplication, or any public showing, is a violation of the law." They are kept in a central prison-system library, under the control of prison authorities, from which they are distributed to a number of state prison facilities. At these facilities (e.g., the California state penitentiary), the videotapes are taken to recreational areas containing television sets and are inserted into hooked-up videotape recorders so that the complete film can be viewed upon the television screen. Prison inmates are informed of the time and location of showing of particular films, and are invited to attend. A given prison facility will retain the film, and exhibit it, over a few days and will then return it to the central system library. Because the same tape is shown fairly often, the typical individual viewing is attended by some eight to ten inmates. Upon learning of this use, the copyright owners of the motion pictures in question bring an action against the California Commission of Prisons. Will the action be successful? Why? *Compare* Cal. Att'y Gen. No. 81–503 (Feb. 5, 1982), in 1982 Copyright L. Dec. (CCH) ¶ 25,368, *with* Louisiana Att'y Gen. No. 84–436 (Jan. 10, 1985), in 29 BNA P.T.C.J. 480.

CHAPTER 7

FAIR USE

A. BACKGROUND

Despite the constitutional authorization to Congress to secure to authors "the *exclusive* Right to their ... Writings," Art. 1, § 8, cl. 8 (emphasis added), we have already encountered many statutory limitations upon the author's exclusive rights. *See* Chapter 6.D, *supra*. Together with the idea-expression dichotomy, the "fair use" exception to copyright protection constitutes perhaps the most significant, and the most venerable, limitation on an author's or copyright holder's prerogatives. Originally a judge-made doctrine, the exception is now codified at § 107 of the 1976 Act. In essence, the traditional concept of fair use excused reasonable unauthorized appropriations from a first work, when the use to which the second author put the appropriated material in some way advanced the public benefit, without substantially impairing the present or potential economic value of the first work.

§ 107. Limitations on exclusive rights: Fair use

Notwithstanding the provisions of section 106, the fair use of a copyrighted work, including such use by reproduction in copies or phonorecords or by any other means specified by that section, for purposes such as criticism, comment, news reporting, teaching (including multiple copies for classroom use), scholarship, or research, is not an infringement of copyright. In determining whether the use made of a work in any particular case is a fair use the factors to be considered shall include—

(1) the purpose and character of the use, including whether such use is of a commercial nature or is for nonprofit educational purposes;

(2) the nature of the copyrighted work;

(3) the amount and substantiality of the portion used in relation to the copyrighted work as a whole; and

(4) the effect of the use upon the potential market for or value of the copyrighted work.

The fact that a work is unpublished shall not itself bar a finding of fair use if such finding is made upon consideration of all the above factors.

House Report

H.R. Rep. No. 94–1476, 94th Cong., 2d Sess. 65–66 (1976).

General background of the problem

The judicial doctrine of fair use, one of the most important and well-established limitations on the exclusive right of copyright owners, would be given express statutory recognition for the first time in section 107. The claim that a defendant's acts constituted a fair use rather than an infringement has been raised as a defense in innumerable copyright actions over the years, and there is ample case law recognizing the existence of the doctrine and applying it. The examples enumerated at page 24 of the Register's 1961 Report, while by no means exhaustive, give some idea of the sort of activities the courts might regard as fair use under the circumstances: "quotation of excerpts in a review or criticism for purposes of illustration or comment; quotation of short passages in a scholarly or technical work, for illustration or clarification of the author's observations; use in a parody of some of the content of the work parodied; summary of an address or article, with brief quotations, in a news report; reproduction by a library of a portion of a work to replace part of a damaged copy; reproduction by a teacher or student of a small part of a work to illustrate a lesson; reproduction of a work in legislative or judicial proceedings or reports; incidental and fortuitous reproduction, in a newsreel or broadcast, of a work located in the scene of an event being reported."

Although the courts have considered and ruled upon the fair use doctrine over and over again, no real definition of the concept has ever emerged. Indeed, since the doctrine is an equitable rule of reason, no generally applicable definition is possible, and each case raising the question must be decided on its own facts. On the other hand, the courts have evolved a set of criteria which, though in no case definitive or determinative, provide some gauge for balancing the equities. These criteria have been stated in various ways, but essentially they can all be reduced to the four standards which have been adopted in section 107. . . .

The specific wording of section 107 as it now stands is the result of a process of accretion, resulting from the long controversy over the related problems of fair use and the reproduction (mostly by photocopying) of copyrighted material for educational and scholarly purposes. For example, the reference to fair use "by reproduction in copies or phonorecords or by any other means" is mainly intended to make clear that the doctrine has as much application to photocopying and taping as to older forms of use; it is not intended to give these kinds of reproduction any special status under the fair use provision or to sanction any reproduction beyond the normal and reasonable limits of fair use. Similarly, the newly-added reference to "multiple copies for classroom use" is a recognition that, under the proper circumstances of fairness, the doctrine can be applied to reproductions of multiple copies for the members of a class.

The Committee has amended the first of the criteria to be considered—"the purpose and character of the use"—to state explicitly that this factor includes a consideration of "whether such use is of a commercial nature or is for non-profit educational purposes." This amendment is not intended to be interpreted as any sort of not-for-profit limitation on educational uses of copyrighted works. It is an express recognition that, as under the present law, the commercial or non-profit character of an activity, while not conclusive with respect to fair use, can and should be weighed along with other factors in fair use decisions.

General intention behind the provision

The statement of the fair use doctrine in section 107 offers some guidance to users in determining when the principles of the doctrine apply. However, the endless variety of situations and combinations of circumstances that can arise in particular cases precludes the formulation of exact rules in the statute. The bill endorses the purpose and general scope of the judicial doctrine of fair use, but there is no disposition to freeze the doctrine in the statute, especially during a period of rapid technological change. Beyond a very broad statutory explanation of what fair use is and some of the criteria applicable to it, the courts must be free to adapt the doctrine to particular situations on a case-by-case basis. Section 107 is intended to restate the present judicial doctrine of fair use, not to change, narrow, or enlarge it in any way.

B.   THE APPLICATION OF THE FAIR USE DOCTRINE TO THE CREATION OF NEW WORKS

Campbell v. Acuff–Rose Music, Inc.

510 U.S. 569 (1994).

■ JUSTICE SOUTER delivered the opinion of the Court:

We are called upon to decide whether 2 Live Crew's commercial parody of Roy Orbison's song, "Oh, Pretty Woman," may be a fair use within the meaning of the Copyright Act of 1976, 17 U.S.C. § 107 (1988 ed. and Supp. IV). Although the District Court granted summary judgment for 2 Live Crew, the Court of Appeals reversed, holding the defense of fair use barred by the song's commercial character and excessive borrowing. Because we hold that a parody's commercial character is only one element to be weighed in a fair use enquiry, and that insufficient consideration was given to the nature of parody in weighing the degree of copying, we reverse and remand.

I

In 1964, Roy Orbison and William Dees wrote a rock ballad called "Oh, Pretty Woman" and assigned their rights in it to respondent Acuff–Rose Music, Inc. *See* Appendix A, *infra* .... Acuff–Rose registered the song for copyright protection.

Petitioners Luther R. Campbell, Christopher Wongwon, Mark Ross, and David Hobbs, are collectively known as 2 Live Crew, a popular rap music group.[1] In 1989, Campbell wrote a song entitled "Pretty Woman," which he later described in an affidavit as intended, "through comical lyrics, to satirize the original work...." App. to Pet. for Cert. 80a. On July 5, 1989, 2 Live Crew's manager informed Acuff–Rose that 2 Live Crew had written a parody of "Oh, Pretty Woman," that they would afford all credit for ownership and authorship of the original song to Acuff–Rose, Dees, and Orbison, and that they were willing to pay a fee for the use they wished to make of it. Enclosed with the letter were a copy of the lyrics and a recording of 2 Live Crew's song. See Appendix B, *infra*.... Acuff–Rose's agent refused permission, stating that "I am aware of the success enjoyed by 'The 2 Live Crews,' but I must inform you that we cannot permit the use of a parody of 'Oh, Pretty Woman.' " App. to Pet. for Cert. 85a. Nonetheless, in June or July 1989, 2 Live Crew released records, cassette tapes, and compact discs of "Pretty Woman" in a collection of songs entitled "As Clean As They Wanna Be." The albums and compact discs identify the authors of "Pretty Woman" as Orbison and Dees and its publisher as Acuff–Rose.

[handwritten in margin: Tried to get permission. Permission Denied]

Almost a year later, after nearly a quarter of a million copies of the recording had been sold, Acuff–Rose sued 2 Live Crew and its record company, Luke Skyywalker Records, for copyright infringement. The District Court granted summary judgment for 2 Live Crew, reasoning that the commercial purpose of 2 Live Crew's song was no bar to fair use; that 2 Live Crew's version was a parody, which "quickly degenerates into a play on words, substituting predictable lyrics with shocking ones" to show "how bland and banal the Orbison song" is; that 2 Live Crew had taken no more than was necessary to "conjure up" the original in order to parody it; and that it was "extremely unlikely that 2 Live Crew's song could adversely affect the market for the original." 754 F. Supp. 1150, 1154–1155, 1157–1158 (M.D.Tenn.1991). The District Court weighed these factors and held that 2 Live Crew's song made fair use of Orbison's original. *Id.*, at 1158–1159.

The Court of Appeals for the Sixth Circuit reversed and remanded. 972 F.2d 1429, 1439 (1992). Although it assumed for the purpose of its opinion that 2 Live Crew's song was a parody of the Orbison original, the Court of Appeals thought the District Court had put too little emphasis on the fact that "every commercial use ... is presumptively ... unfair," *Sony Corp. of America v. Universal City Studios, Inc.*, 464 U.S. 417, 451 (1984), and it held that "the admittedly commercial nature" of the parody "requires the conclusion" that the first of four factors relevant under the statute weighs against a finding of fair use. 972 F.2d, at 1435, 1437. Next, the Court of Appeals determined that, by "taking the heart of the original and making it

---

1. Rap has been defined as a "style of black American popular music consisting of improvised rhymes performed to a rhythmic accompaniment." The Norton/Grove Concise Encyclopedia of Music 613 (1988). 2 Live Crew plays "[b]ass music," a regional, hip-hop style of rap from the Liberty City area of Miami, Florida. Brief for Petitioners 34.

the heart of a new work," 2 Live Crew had, qualitatively, taken too much. *Id.*, at 1438. Finally, after noting that the effect on the potential market for the original (and the market for derivative works) is "undoubtedly the single most important element of fair use," *Harper & Row, Publishers, Inc. v. Nation Enterprises,* 471 U.S. 539, 566 (1985), the Court of Appeals faulted the District Court for "refus[ing] to indulge the presumption" that "harm for purposes of the fair use analysis has been established by the presumption attaching to commercial uses." 972 F.2d, at 1438–1439. In sum, the court concluded that its "blatantly commercial purpose ... prevents this parody from being a fair use." *Id.*, at 1439.

We granted certiorari, 507 U.S. 1003 (1993), to determine whether 2 Live Crew's commercial parody could be a fair use.

II

It is uncontested here that 2 Live Crew's song would be an infringement of Acuff–Rose's rights in "Oh, Pretty Woman," under the Copyright Act of 1976, 17 U.S.C. § 106 (1988 ed. and Supp. IV), but for a finding of fair use through parody.[4] From the infancy of copyright protection, some opportunity for fair use of copyrighted materials has been thought necessary to fulfill copyright's very purpose, "[t]o promote the Progress of Science and useful Arts...." U.S. Const., Art. I, § 8, cl. 8.[5] For as Justice Story explained, "[i]n truth, in literature, in science and in art, there are, and can be, few, if any, things, which in an abstract sense, are strictly new and original throughout. Every book in literature, science and art, borrows, and must necessarily borrow, and use much which was well known and used before." *Emerson v. Davies,* 8 F. Cas. 615, 619 (No. 4,436) (CCD Mass. 1845). Similarly, Lord Ellenborough expressed the inherent tension in the need simultaneously to protect copyrighted material and to allow others to build upon it when he wrote, "while I shall think myself bound to secure every man in the enjoyment of his copy-right, one must not put manacles upon science." *Carey v. Kearsley,* 4 Esp. 168, 170, 170 Eng. Rep. 679, 681 (K.B. 1803). In copyright cases brought under the Statute of Anne of 1710, English courts held that in some instances "fair abridgements" would not infringe an author's rights, see W. Patry, The Fair Use Privilege in Copyright Law 6–17 (1985) (hereinafter Patry); Leval, *Toward a Fair Use Standard,* 103 Harv. L. Rev. 1105, 1105 (1990) (hereinafter Leval), and although the First Congress enacted our initial copyright statute, Act of May 31, 1790, 1 Stat. 124, without any explicit reference to "fair use," as it later came to be known, the doctrine was recognized by the American courts nonetheless.

In *Folsom v. Marsh,* Justice Story distilled the essence of law and methodology from the earlier cases: "look to the nature and objects of the

---

4. ... 2 Live Crew concedes that it is not entitled to a compulsory license under 115 because its arrangement changes "the basic melody or fundamental character" of the original. 115(a)(2).

5. The exclusion of facts and ideas from copyright protection serves that goal as well....

selections made, the quantity and value of the materials used, and the degree in which the use may prejudice the sale, or diminish the profits, or supersede the objects, of the original work." 9 F. Cas. 342, 348 (No. 4,901) (CCD Mass. 1841). Thus expressed, fair use remained exclusively judge-made doctrine until the passage of the 1976 Copyright Act, in which Story's summary is discernible. . . . Congress meant § 107 "to restate the present judicial doctrine of fair use, not to change, narrow, or enlarge it in any way" and intended that courts continue the common law tradition of fair use adjudication. H.R. Rep. No. 94–1476, p. 66 (1976) (hereinafter House Report); S. Rep. No. 94–473, p. 62 (1975) U.S. Code Cong. & Admin. News 1976, pp. 5659, 5679 (hereinafter Senate Report). The fair use doctrine thus "permits [and requires] courts to avoid rigid application of the copyright statute when, on occasion, it would stifle the very creativity which that law is designed to foster." *Stewart v. Abend,* 495 U.S. 207, 236 (1990) (internal quotation marks and citation omitted).

The task is not to be simplified with bright-line rules, for the statute, like the doctrine it recognizes, calls for case-by-case analysis. *Harper & Row,* 471 U.S., at 560, 105 S. Ct., at 2230; *Sony,* 464 U.S., at 448, and n.31, 104 S. Ct., at 792, & n.31; House Report, pp. 65–66; Senate Report, p. 62. The text employs the terms "including" and "such as" in the preamble paragraph to indicate the "illustrative and not limitative" function of the examples given, § 101; see *Harper & Row, supra,* 471 U.S., at 561, which thus provide only general guidance about the sorts of copying that courts and Congress most commonly had found to be fair uses. Nor may the four statutory factors be treated in isolation, one from another. All are to be explored, and the results weighed together, in light of the purposes of copyright. *See* Leval 1110–1111; Patry & Perlmutter, *Fair Use Misconstrued: Profit, Presumptions, and Parody,* 11 Cardozo Arts & Ent. L.J. 667, 685–687 (1993) (hereinafter Patry & Perlmutter).[10]

A

The first factor in a fair use enquiry is "the purpose and character of the use, including whether such use is of a commercial nature or is for

---

10. Because the fair use enquiry often requires close questions of judgment as to the extent of permissible borrowing in cases involving parodies (or other critical works), courts may also wish to bear in mind that the goals of the copyright law, "to stimulate the creation and publication of edifying matter," Leval 1134, are not always best served by automatically granting injunctive relief when parodists are found to have gone beyond the bounds of fair use. *See* 17 U.S.C. 502(a) (court "*may* ... grant ... injunctions on such terms as it may deem reasonable to prevent or restrain infringement") (emphasis added); Leval 1132 (while in the "vast majority of cases, [an injunctive] remedy is justified because most infringements are simple piracy," such cases are "worlds apart from many of those raising reasonable contentions of fair use" where "there may be a strong public interest in the publication of the secondary work [and] the copyright owner's interest may be adequately protected by an award of damages for whatever infringement is found"); *Abend v. MCA, Inc.,* 863 F.2d 1465, 1479 (C.A.9 1988) (finding "special circumstances" that would cause "great injustice" to defendants and "public injury" were injunction to issue), *aff'd sub nom. Stewart v. Abend,* 495 U.S. 207, 110 S. Ct. 1750, 109 L. Ed. 2d 184 (1990).

nonprofit educational purposes." § 107(1). This factor draws on Justice Story's formulation, "the nature and objects of the selections made." *Folsom v. Marsh,* 9 F. Cas., at 348. The enquiry here may be guided by the examples given in the preamble to § 107, looking to whether the use is for criticism, or comment, or news reporting, and the like, see § 107. The central purpose of this investigation is to see, in Justice Story's words, whether the new work merely "supersede[s] the objects" of the original creation, *Folsom v. Marsh, supra,* at 348; *accord, Harper & Row, supra,* 471 U.S., at 562 ("supplanting" the original), or instead adds something new, with a further purpose or different character, altering the first with new expression, meaning, or message; it asks, in other words, whether and to what extent the new work is "transformative." Leval 1111. Although such transformative use is not absolutely necessary for a finding of fair use, *Sony, supra,* 464 U.S., at 455, n.40,[11] the goal of copyright, to promote science and the arts, is generally furthered by the creation of transformative works. Such works thus lie at the heart of the fair use doctrine's guarantee of breathing space within the confines of copyright, see, e.g., *Sony, supra,* at 478–480 (Blackmun, J., dissenting), and the more transformative the new work, the less will be the significance of other factors, like commercialism, that may weigh against a finding of fair use.

This Court has only once before even considered whether parody may be fair use, and that time issued no opinion because of the Court's equal division. *Benny v. Loew's Inc.,* 239 F.2d 532 (C.A.9 1956), *aff'd sub nom. Columbia Broadcasting System, Inc. v. Loew's Inc.,* 356 U.S. 43 (1958). Suffice it to say now that parody has an obvious claim to transformative value, as Acuff–Rose itself does not deny. Like less ostensibly humorous forms of criticism, it can provide social benefit, by shedding light on an earlier work, and, in the process, creating a new one. We thus line up with the courts that have held that parody, like other comment or criticism, may claim fair use under § 107. *See, e.g., Fisher v. Dees,* 794 F.2d 432 (C.A.9 1986) ("When Sonny Sniffs Glue," a parody of "When Sunny Gets Blue," is fair use); *Elsmere Music, Inc. v. National Broadcasting Co.,* 482 F. Supp. 741 (S.D.N.Y.), *aff'd,* 623 F.2d 252 (C.A.2 1980) ("I Love Sodom," a "Saturday Night Live" television parody of "I Love New York" is fair use); see also House Report, p. 65; Senate Report, p. 61, U.S. Code Cong. & Admin. News 1976, pp. 5659, 5678 ("[U]se in a parody of some of the content of the work parodied" may be fair use).

. . . For the purposes of copyright law, . . . the heart of any parodist's claim to quote from existing material is the use of some elements of a prior author's composition to create a new one that, at least in part, comments on that author's works. *See, e.g., Fisher v. Dees, supra,* at 437; *MCA, Inc. v. Wilson,* 677 F.2d 180, 185 (C.A.2 1981). If, on the contrary, the commentary has no critical bearing on the substance or style of the original composition, which the alleged infringer merely uses to get attention or to avoid the drudgery in working up something fresh, the claim to fairness in

---

11. The obvious statutory exception to this focus on transformative uses is the straight reproduction of multiple copies for classroom distribution.

borrowing from another's work diminishes accordingly (if it does not vanish), and other factors, like the extent of its commerciality, loom larger. Parody needs to mimic an original to make its point, and so has some claim to use the creation of its victim's (or collective victims') imagination, whereas satire can stand on its own two feet and so requires justification for the very act of borrowing.[15] *See ibid.*; Bisceglia, *Parody and Copyright Protection: Turning the Balancing Act into a Juggling Act*, in ASCAP, Copyright Law Symposium, No. 34, p. 25 (1987).

The fact that parody can claim legitimacy for some appropriation does not, of course, tell either parodist or judge much about where to draw the line. Like a book review quoting the copyrighted material criticized, parody may or may not be fair use, and petitioner's suggestion that any parodic use is presumptively fair has no more justification in law or fact than the equally hopeful claim that any use for news reporting should be presumed fair, see *Harper & Row,* 471 U.S. at 561. The Act has no hint of an evidentiary preference for parodists over their victims, and no workable presumption for parody could take account of the fact that parody often shades into satire when society is lampooned through its creative artifacts, or that a work may contain both parodic and non-parodic elements. Accordingly, parody, like any other use, has to work its way through the relevant factors, and be judged case by case, in light of the ends of the copyright law.

Here, the District Court held, and the Court of Appeals assumed, that 2 Live Crew's "Pretty Woman" contains parody, commenting on and criticizing the original work, whatever it may have to say about society at large. . . .

We have less difficulty in finding that critical element in 2 Live Crew's song than the Court of Appeals did, although having found it we will not take the further step of evaluating its quality. The threshold question when fair use is raised in defense of parody is whether a parodic character may reasonably be perceived. Whether, going beyond that, parody is in good taste or bad does not and should not matter to fair use. As Justice Holmes explained, "[i]t would be a dangerous undertaking for persons trained only to the law to constitute themselves final judges of the worth of [a work], outside of the narrowest and most obvious limits. At the one extreme some works of genius would be sure to miss appreciation. Their very novelty would make them repulsive until the public had learned the new language in which their author spoke." *Bleistein v. Donaldson Lithographing Co.,* 188 U.S. 239, 251 (1903) (circus posters have copyright protection); *cf. Yankee Publishing Inc. v. News America Publishing, Inc.,* 809 F. Supp. 267, 280 (S.D.N.Y.1992) (Leval, J.) ("First Amendment protections do not apply only to those who speak clearly, whose jokes are funny, and whose parodies succeed") (trademark case).

---

15. Satire has been defined as a work "in which prevalent follies or vices are assailed with ridicule," 14 The Oxford English Dictionary 500 (2d ed. 1989), or are "at-tacked through irony, derision, or wit," The American Heritage Dictionary 1604 (3d ed. 1992).

While we might not assign a high rank to the parodic element here, we think it fair to say that 2 Live Crew's song reasonably could be perceived as commenting on the original or criticizing it, to some degree. 2 Live Crew juxtaposes the romantic musings of a man whose fantasy comes true, with degrading taunts, a bawdy demand for sex, and a sigh of relief from paternal responsibility. The later words can be taken as a comment on the naivete of the original of an earlier day, as a rejection of its sentiment that ignores the ugliness of street life and the debasement that it signifies. It is this joinder of reference and ridicule that marks off the author's choice of parody from the other types of comment and criticism that traditionally have had a claim to fair use protection as transformative works.

The Court of Appeals, however, immediately cut short the enquiry into 2 Live Crew's fair use claim by confining its treatment of the first factor essentially to one relevant fact, the commercial nature of the use. The court then inflated the significance of this fact by applying a presumption ostensibly culled from *Sony,* that "every commercial use of copyrighted material is presumptively . . . unfair. . . ." *Sony,* 464 U.S., at 451. In giving virtually dispositive weight to the commercial nature of the parody, the Court of Appeals erred.

The language of the statute makes clear that the commercial or nonprofit educational purpose of a work is only one element of the first factor enquiry into its purpose and character. Section 107(1) uses the term "including" to begin the dependent clause referring to commercial use, and the main clause speaks of a broader investigation into "purpose and character." As we explained in *Harper & Row,* Congress resisted attempts to narrow the ambit of this traditional enquiry by adopting categories of presumptively fair use, and it urged courts to preserve the breadth of their traditionally ample view of the universe of relevant evidence. 471 U.S., at 561; House Report, p. 66, U.S. Code Cong. & Admin. News 1976, pp. 5659, 5679. Accordingly, the mere fact that a use is educational and not for profit does not insulate it from a finding of infringement, any more than the commercial character of a use bars a finding of fairness. If, indeed, commerciality carried presumptive force against a finding of fairness, the presumption would swallow nearly all of the illustrative uses listed in the preamble paragraph of § 107, including news reporting, comment, criticism, teaching, scholarship, and research, since these activities "are generally conducted for profit in this country." *Harper & Row, supra,* at 592 (Brennan, J., dissenting). Congress could not have intended such a rule, which certainly is not inferable from the common-law cases, arising as they did from the world of letters in which Samuel Johnson could pronounce that "[n]o man but a blockhead ever wrote, except for money." 3 Boswell's Life of Johnson 19 (G. Hill ed. 1934).

Sony itself called for no hard evidentiary presumption. . . . Rather, as we explained in *Harper & Row, Sony* stands for the proposition that the "fact that a publication was commercial as opposed to nonprofit is a separate factor that tends to weigh against a finding of fair use." 471 U.S., at 562. But that is all, and the fact that even the force of that tendency will vary with the context is a further reason against elevating commerciality to hard presumptive significance. The use, for example, of a copyrighted work to advertise a product, even in a parody, will be entitled to less indulgence under the first factor of the fair use enquiry, than the sale of a parody for its own sake, let alone one performed a single time by students in school. *See generally* Patry & Perlmutter 679–680; *Fisher v. Dees*, 794 F.2d, at 437; *Maxtone-Graham v. Burtchaell*, 803 F.2d 1253, 1262 (C.A.2 1986); *Sega Enterprises, Ltd. v. Accolade, Inc.*, 977 F.2d 1510, 1522 (C.A.9 1992).[18]

B

The second statutory factor, "the nature of the copyrighted work," § 107(2), draws on Justice Story's expression, the "value of the materials used." *Folsom v. Marsh*, 9 F. Cas., at 348. This factor calls for recognition that some works are closer to the core of intended copyright protection than others, with the consequence that fair use is more difficult to establish when the former works are copied. *See, e.g., Stewart v. Abend*, 495 U.S., at 237–238, 110 S. Ct., at 1768–1769 (contrasting fictional short story with factual works); *Harper & Row*, 471 U.S., at 563–564 (contrasting soon-to-be-published memoir with published speech); *Sony*, 464 U.S., at 455, n.40, (contrasting motion pictures with news broadcasts); *Feist*, 499 U.S., 348–351 (contrasting creative works with bare factual compilations); 3 M. Nimmer & D. Nimmer, Nimmer on Copyright § 13.05–[A][2] (1993) (hereinafter Nimmer); Leval 1116. We agree with both the District Court and the Court of Appeals that the Orbison original's creative expression for public dissemination falls within the core of the copyright's protective purposes. 754 F. Supp., at 1155–1156; 972 F.2d, at 1437. This fact, however, is not much help in this case, or ever likely to help much in separating the fair use sheep from the infringing goats in a parody case, since parodies almost invariably copy publicly known, expressive works.

C

The third factor asks whether "the amount and substantiality of the portion used in relation to the copyrighted work as a whole," § 107(3) (or, in Justice Story's words, "the quantity and value of the materials used," *Folsom v. Marsh, supra,* at 348) are reasonable in relation to the purpose of the copying. Here, attention turns to the persuasiveness of a parodist's justification for the particular copying done, and the enquiry will harken

---

18. Finally, regardless of the weight one might place on the alleged infringer's state of mind, compare *Harper & Row*, 471 U.S., at 562 (fair use presupposes good faith and fair dealing) (quotation marks omitted), with *Folsom v. Marsh*, 9 F. Cas. 342, 349 (No. 4,901) (CCD Mass. 1841) (good faith does not bar a finding of infringement); Leval 1126–1127 (good faith irrelevant to fair use analysis), we reject Acuff–Rose's argument that 2 Live Crew's request for permission to use the original should be weighed against a finding of fair use. Even if good faith were central to fair use, 2 Live Crew's actions do not necessarily suggest that they believed their version was not fair use; the offer may simply have been made in a good faith effort to avoid this litigation. If the use is otherwise fair, then no permission need be sought or granted. Thus, being denied permission to use a work does not weigh against a finding of fair use. *See Fisher v. Dees*, 794 F.2d 432, 437 (C.A.9 1986).

back to the first of the statutory factors, for, as in prior cases, we recognize that the extent of permissible copying varies with the purpose and character of the use. *See Sony,* 464 U.S., at 449–450 (reproduction of entire work "does not have its ordinary effect of militating against a finding of fair use" as to home videotaping of television programs); *Harper & Row,* 471 U.S., at 564 ("[E]ven substantial quotations might qualify as fair use in a review of a published work or a news account of a speech" but not in a scoop of a soon-to-be-published memoir). The facts bearing on this factor will also tend to address the fourth, by revealing the degree to which the parody may serve as a market substitute for the original or potentially licensed derivatives. *See* Leval 1123.

The District Court considered the song's parodic purpose in finding that 2 Live Crew had not helped themselves overmuch. 754 F. Supp., at 1156–1157. The Court of Appeals disagreed, stating that "[w]hile it may not be inappropriate to find that no more was taken than necessary, the copying was qualitatively substantial.... We conclude that taking the heart of the original and making it the heart of a new work was to purloin a substantial portion of the essence of the original." 972 F.2d, at 1438.

The Court of Appeals is of course correct that this factor calls for thought not only about the quantity of the materials used, but about their quality and importance, too. In *Harper & Row,* for example, the Nation had taken only some 300 words out of President Ford's memoirs, but we signaled the significance of the quotations in finding them to amount to "the heart of the book," the part most likely to be newsworthy and important in licensing serialization. 471 U.S., at 564–566, 568 (internal quotation marks omitted). We also agree with the Court of Appeals that whether "a substantial portion of the infringing work was copied verbatim" from the copyrighted work is a relevant question, see *id.,* at 565, for it may reveal a dearth of transformative character or purpose under the first factor, or a greater likelihood of market harm under the fourth; a work composed primarily of an original, particularly its heart, with little added or changed, is more likely to be a merely superseding use, fulfilling demand for the original.

Where we part company with the court below is in applying these guides to parody, and in particular to parody in the song before us. Parody presents a difficult case. Parody's humor, or in any event its comment, necessarily springs from recognizable allusion to its object through distorted imitation. Its art lies in the tension between a known original and its parodic twin. When parody takes aim at a particular original work, the parody must be able to "conjure up" at least enough of that original to make the object of its critical wit recognizable. *See, e.g., Elsmere Music,* 623 F.2d, at 253, n.1; *Fisher v. Dees,* 794 F.2d, at 438–439. What makes for this recognition is quotation of the original's most distinctive or memorable features, which the parodist can be sure the audience will know. Once enough has been taken to assure identification, how much more is reasonable will depend, say, on the extent to which the song's overriding purpose and character is to parody the original or, in contrast, the likelihood that the parody may serve as a market substitute for the original. But using some characteristic features cannot be avoided.

We think the Court of Appeals was insufficiently appreciative of parody's need for the recognizable sight or sound when it ruled 2 Live Crew's use unreasonable as a matter of law. It is true, of course, that 2 Live Crew copied the characteristic opening bass riff (or musical phrase) of the original, and true that the words of the first line copy the Orbison lyrics. But if quotation of the opening riff and the first line may be said to go to the "heart" of the original, the heart is also what most readily conjures up the song for parody, and it is the heart at which parody takes aim. Copying does not become excessive in relation to parodic purpose merely because the portion taken was the original's heart. If 2 Live Crew had copied a significantly less memorable part of the original, it is difficult to see how its parodic character would have come through. *See Fisher v. Dees,* 794 F.2d, at 439.

This is not, of course, to say that anyone who calls himself a parodist can skim the cream and get away scot free. In parody, as in news reporting, see *Harper & Row, supra,* context is everything, and the question of fairness asks what else the parodist did besides go to the heart of the original. It is significant that 2 Live Crew not only copied the first line of the original, but thereafter departed markedly from the Orbison lyrics for its own ends. 2 Live Crew not only copied the bass riff and repeated it, but also produced otherwise distinctive sounds, interposing "scraper" noise, overlaying the music with solos in different keys, and altering the drum beat. *See* 754 F. Supp., at 1155. This is not a case, then, where "a substantial portion" of the parody itself is composed of a "verbatim" copying of the original. It is not, that is, a case where the parody is so insubstantial, as compared to the copying, that the third factor must be resolved as a matter of law against the parodists.

Suffice it to say here that, as to the lyrics, we think the Court of Appeals correctly suggested that "no more was taken than necessary," 972 F.2d, at 1438, but just for that reason, we fail to see how the copying can be excessive in relation to its parodic purpose, even if the portion taken is the original's "heart." As to the music, we express no opinion whether repetition of the bass riff is excessive copying, and we remand to permit evaluation of the amount taken, in light of the song's parodic purpose and character, its transformative elements, and considerations of the potential for market substitution sketched more fully below.

D

The fourth fair use factor is "the effect of the use upon the potential market for or value of the copyrighted work." § 107(4). It requires courts to consider not only the extent of market harm caused by the particular actions of the alleged infringer, but also "whether unrestricted and widespread conduct of the sort engaged in by the defendant ... would result in a substantially adverse impact on the potential market" for the original. Nimmer § 13.05[A][4], p. 13–102.61 (footnote omitted); *accord, Harper &*

Row, 471 U.S., at 569; Senate Report, p. 65; *Folsom v. Marsh,* 9 F. Cas., at 349. The enquiry "must take account not only of harm to the original but also of harm to the market for derivative works." *Harper & Row, supra,* 471 U.S. at 568.

Since fair use is an affirmative defense, its proponent would have difficulty carrying the burden of demonstrating fair use without favorable evidence about relevant markets.[21] In moving for summary judgment, 2 Live Crew left themselves at just such a disadvantage when they failed to address the effect on the market for rap derivatives, and confined themselves to uncontroverted submissions that there was no likely effect on the market for the original. They did not, however, thereby subject themselves to the evidentiary presumption applied by the Court of Appeals. In assessing the likelihood of significant market harm, the Court of Appeals quoted from language in *Sony* that " '[i]f the intended use is for commercial gain, that likelihood may be presumed. But if it is for a noncommercial purpose, the likelihood must be demonstrated.' " 972 F.2d, at 1438 *quoting Sony,* 464 U.S., at 451. The court reasoned that because "the use of the copyrighted work is wholly commercial, ... we presume a likelihood of future harm to Acuff–Rose exists." 972 F.2d, at 1438. In so doing, the court resolved the fourth factor against 2 Live Crew, just as it had the first, by applying a presumption about the effect of commercial use, a presumption which as applied here we hold to be error.

No "presumption" or inference of market harm that might find support in *Sony* is applicable to a case involving something beyond mere duplication for commercial purposes. *Sony*'s discussion of a presumption contrasts a context of verbatim copying of the original in its entirety for commercial purposes, with the non-commercial context of *Sony* itself (home copying of television programming). In the former circumstances, what *Sony* said simply makes common sense: when a commercial use amounts to mere duplication of the entirety of an original, it clearly "supersede[s] the objects," *Folsom v. Marsh,* 9 F. Cas., at 348, of the original and serves as a market replacement for it, making it likely that cognizable market harm to the original will occur. *Sony,* 464 U.S., at 451. But when, on the contrary, the second use is transformative, market substitution is at least less certain, and market harm may not be so readily inferred. Indeed, as to parody pure and simple, it is more likely that the new work will not affect the market for the original in a way cognizable under this factor, that is, by acting as a substitute for it ("supersed[ing] [its] objects"). *See* Leval 1125; Patry & Perlmutter 692, 697–698. This is so because the parody and the

---

21. Even favorable evidence, without more, is no guarantee of fairness. Judge Leval gives the example of the film producer's appropriation of a composer's previously unknown song that turns the song into a commercial success; the boon to the song does not make the film's simple copying fair. Leval, 1124, n.84. This factor, no less than the other three, may be addressed only through a "sensitive balancing of interests." *Sony,* 464 U.S., at 455, n.40. Market harm is a matter of degree, and the importance of this factor will vary, not only with the amount of harm, but also with the relative strength of the showing on the other factors.

original usually serve different market functions. Bisceglia, ASCAP, Copyright Law Symposium, No. 34, p. 23.

We do not, of course, suggest that a parody may not harm the market at all, but when a lethal parody, like a scathing theater review, kills demand for the original, it does not produce a harm cognizable under the Copyright Act. Because "parody may quite legitimately aim at garroting the original, destroying it commercially as well as artistically," B. Kaplan, An Unhurried View of Copyright 69 (1967), the role of the courts is to distinguish between "[b]iting criticism [that merely] suppresses demand [and] copyright infringement[, which] usurps it." *Fisher v. Dees,* 794 F.2d, at 438.

This distinction between potentially remediable displacement and unremediable disparagement is reflected in the rule that there is no protectible derivative market for criticism. The market for potential derivative uses includes only those that creators of original works would in general develop or license others to develop. Yet the unlikelihood that creators of imaginative works will license critical reviews or lampoons of their own productions removes such uses from the very notion of a potential licensing market. "People ask ... for criticism, but they only want praise." S. Maugham, Of Human Bondage 241 (Penguin ed. 1992). Thus, to the extent that the opinion below may be read to have considered harm to the market for parodies of "Oh, Pretty Woman," see 972 F.2d, at 1439, the court erred. *Accord, Fisher v. Dees,* 794 F.2d, at 437; Leval 1125; Patry & Perlmutter 688–691.[22]

In explaining why the law recognizes no derivative market for critical works, including parody, we have, of course, been speaking of the later work as if it had nothing but a critical aspect (i.e., "parody pure and simple," *supra,* at 22). But the later work may have a more complex character, with effects not only in the arena of criticism but also in protectible markets for derivative works, too. In that sort of case, the law looks beyond the criticism to the other elements of the work, as it does here. 2 Live Crew's song comprises not only parody but also rap music, and the derivative market for rap music is a proper focus of enquiry, see *Harper & Row,* 471 U.S., at 568; Nimmer § 13.05[B]. Evidence of substantial harm to it would weigh against a finding of fair use, because the licensing of derivatives is an important economic incentive to the creation of originals. See 17 U.S.C. § 106(2) (copyright owner has rights to derivative works). Of course, the only harm to derivatives that need concern us, as discussed above, is the harm of market substitution. The fact that a parody may impair the market for derivative uses by the very effectiveness of its critical commentary is no more relevant under copyright than the like threat to the original market.

---

22. We express no opinion as to the derivative markets for works using elements of an original as vehicles for satire or amusement, making no comment on the original or criticism of it.

Did they harm the market for a non-parody derivative work?

Although 2 Live Crew submitted uncontroverted affidavits on the question of market harm to the original, neither they, nor Acuff–Rose, introduced evidence or affidavits addressing the likely effect of 2 Live Crew's parodic rap song on the market for a non-parody, rap version of "Oh, Pretty Woman." And while Acuff–Rose would have us find evidence of a rap market in the very facts that 2 Live Crew recorded a rap parody of "Oh, Pretty Woman" and another rap group sought a license to record a rap derivative, there was no evidence that a potential rap market was harmed in any way by 2 Live Crew's parody, rap version. The fact that 2 Live Crew's parody sold as part of a collection of rap songs says very little about the parody's effect on a market for a rap version of the original, either of the music alone or of the music with its lyrics. The District Court essentially passed on this issue, observing that Acuff–Rose is free to record "whatever version of the original it desires," 754 F. Supp., at 1158; the Court of Appeals went the other way by erroneous presumption. Contrary to each treatment, it is impossible to deal with the fourth factor except by recognizing that a silent record on an important factor bearing on fair use disentitled the proponent of the defense, 2 Live Crew, to summary judgment. The evidentiary hole will doubtless be plugged on remand.

III

It was error for the Court of Appeals to conclude that the commercial nature of 2 Live Crew's parody of "Oh, Pretty Woman" rendered it presumptively unfair. No such evidentiary presumption is available to address either the first factor, the character and purpose of the use, or the fourth, market harm, in determining whether a transformative use, such as parody, is a fair one. The court also erred in holding that 2 Live Crew had necessarily copied excessively from the Orbison original, considering the parodic purpose of the use. We therefore reverse the judgment of the Court of Appeals and remand for further proceedings consistent with this opinion.

It is so ordered.

APPENDIX A

"Oh, Pretty Woman" by Roy Orbison and William Dees

Pretty Woman, walking down the street, Pretty Woman, the kind I like to meet, Pretty Woman, I don't believe you, you're not the truth, No one could look as good as you Mercy Pretty Woman, won't you pardon me, Pretty Woman, I couldn't help but see, Pretty Woman, that you look lovely as can be Are you lonely just like me? Pretty Woman, stop a while, Pretty Woman, talk a while, Pretty Woman give your smile to me Pretty woman, yeah, yeah, yeah Pretty Woman, look my way, Pretty Woman, say you'll stay with me 'Cause I need you, I'll treat you right Come to me baby, Be mine tonight Pretty Woman, don't walk on by, Pretty Woman, don't make me cry, Pretty Woman, don't walk away, Hey, O.K. If that's the way it must be, O.K. I guess I'll go on home, it's late There'll be tomorrow night, but wait! What do I see Is she walking back to me? Yeah, she's walking back to me! Oh, Pretty Woman.

APPENDIX B
"Pretty Woman" as Recorded by 2 Live Crew

Pretty woman walkin' down the street Pretty woman girl you look so sweet Pretty woman you bring me down to that knee Pretty woman you make me wanna beg please Oh, pretty woman Big hairy woman you need to shave that stuff Big hairy woman you know I bet it's tough Big hairy woman all that hair it ain't legit 'Cause you look like 'Cousin It' Big hairy woman

Bald headed woman girl your hair won't grow Bald headed woman you got a teeny weeny afro Bald headed woman you know your hair could look nice Bald headed woman first you got to roll it with rice Bald headed woman here, let me get this hunk of biz for ya Ya know what I'm saying you look better than rice a roni Oh bald headed woman Big hairy woman come on in And don't forget your bald headed friend Hey pretty woman let the boys Jump in

Two timin' woman girl you know you ain't right Two timin' woman you's out with my boy last night Two timin' woman that takes a load off my mind Two timin' woman now I know the baby ain't mine Oh, two timin' woman Oh pretty woman

■ Justice Kennedy, concurring:

I agree that remand is appropriate and join the opinion of the Court, with these further observations about the fair use analysis of parody.

... It is not enough that the parody use the original in a humorous fashion, however creative that humor may be. The parody must target the original, and not just its general style, the genre of art to which it belongs, or society as a whole (although if it targets the original, it may target those features as well)....

The fair use factors ... reinforce the importance of keeping the definition of parody within proper limits. More than arguable parodic content should be required to deem a would-be parody a fair use. Fair use is an affirmative defense, so doubts about whether a given use is fair should not be resolved in favor of the self-proclaimed parodist. We should not make it easy for musicians to exploit existing works and then later claim that their rendition was a valuable commentary on the original. Almost any revamped modern version of a familiar composition can be construed as a "comment on the naivete of the original," *ante,* at 1173, because of the difference in style and because it will be amusing to hear how the old tune sounds in the new genre. Just the thought of a rap version of Beethoven's Fifth Symphony or "Achy, Breaky Heart" is bound to make people smile. If we allow any weak transformation to qualify as parody, however, we weaken the protection of copyright. And underprotection of copyright disserves the goals of copyright just as much as overprotection, by reducing the financial incentive to create.

The Court decides it is "fair to say that 2 Live Crew's song reasonably could be perceived as commenting on the original or criticizing it, to some degree." *Ante,* at 1173 (applying the first fair use factor). While I am not so assured that 2 Live Crew's song is a legitimate parody, the Court's treatment of the remaining factors leaves room for the District Court to determine on remand that the song is not a fair use. As future courts apply our fair use analysis, they must take care to ensure that not just any commercial take-off is rationalized *post hoc* as a parody.

With these observations, I join the opinion of the Court.

QUESTIONS

1. As you may infer from the *Campbell* decision, the Supreme Court's prior opinions may have induced lower courts to give undue weight to certain of the § 107 factors, and too little weight to others. (You may judge for yourself: see *Harper & Row v. Nation Enterprises, infra*; *Sony Corp. of America v. Universal Studios, Inc., infra.*) Thus, while *Campbell* concerned the particular problem of parody, its analysis bears on fair use claims in general. Moreover, parody in some respects poses a paradigmatic fair use defense: it is a productive use that comments on or criticizes the copied work (public benefit), and that copyright owners are unlikely to license (lack of economic harm). As you review the ensuing materials, consider how well the § 107 criteria apply to copying that departs from this model.

2. When the Court handed down its opinion, it was a cause for rejoicing by performers such as the Capitol Steps and Mark Russell, who often use copyrighted songs as vehicles for poking fun at personalities and institutions located in Washington, D.C. Would you, had you been their attorney, counseled a more despondent reaction to the Court's opinion? Do you believe that the Court's distinction between parody and satire is well taken? Do you believe that it will be easy to apply? (Do you agree with the Court that the 2 Live Crew rendition could reasonably be regarded as a parody?)

3. The Supreme Court overturned the court of appeals for giving what was in effect conclusive weight to the rap group's commercial motive and their copying of the musical "heart" of the Orbison song. The Court also rejects litmus and bright-line tests for parodic fair use, and holds that all four factors—and all of their various sub-parts—must be carefully weighed one against the other, and their interrelationships noted. As counsel for a potential parodist, what advice can you confidently give about how much can be copied, what amount of parody must be added, and what other original elements can/must be added? As counsel for the copyright owner, what advice can you confidently give about the success of a lawsuit?

The Supreme Court decision in *Acuff-Rose* has since been applied by lower courts in not altogether consistent (or altogether intelligible) rulings. In *Dr. Seuss Enters., L.P. v. Penguin Books USA, Inc.,* 109 F.3d 1394 (9th Cir.1997), the court ruled against the parody defense of the publisher of a book that adapted the image and verse familiar as the Cat in the Hat to tell the tale of the O.J. Simpson trial in a book titled "The Cat NOT in the Hat" as narrated by Dr. Juice. O.J. Simpson was pictorially portrayed many times in the Cat's "distinctively scrunched and somewhat shabby red and white stove-pipe hat," and there were verses such as: "A plea went out to Rob Shapiro, Can you save the fallen hero? And Marcia Clark, hooray, hooray, Was called in with a justice play. A man this famous, never hires, lawyers like, Jacoby–Meyers. When you're accused of a killing scheme, you need to build a real Dream Team." The court found both the drawings and the verse (along with the title, lettering design, etc.) to be infringing, and not saved by the fair use doctrine as a parody. Among other things, the court counted it against the defendants that they did not hold up the Dr. Seuss story and style to ridicule, but simply mimicked it to retell the Simpson tale; nor did the court find any effort to create a transformative work with new expression, meaning or message. The commercial nature of the Simpson story allowed an inference of commercial injury; certainly it impaired the good will associated with the Dr. Seuss work. (In this very brief synopsis, how many dubious assertions can the student identify?)

On the other hand, the well-known 1991 *Vanity Fair* cover photograph (by Annie Leibovitz) of the eight-month pregnant Demi Moore was held to have been lawfully parodied in an advertisement for a comedy movie in the "Naked Gun" series; an eight-month pregnant model was portrayed nude, with the same pose and lighting as the Moore photograph, but with actor Leslie Nielsen's head superimposed. *Leibovitz v. Paramount Pictures Corp.,* 137 F.3d 109 (2d Cir.1998). The court of appeals affirmed a finding that the film advertisement was a parody that was protected under the fair use doctrine. As for the first statutory factor, the court found the ad to be transformative and, with "some concern," as also reasonably to be viewed as a comment upon the seriousness and pretentiousness of the Demi Moore photograph; being different from the copyrighted work (i.e., the serious Moore and the smirking Nielsen) does not necessarily create a "comment" upon it, but "A photographer posing a well known actress in a manner that calls to mind a well known painting [Botticelli's *Birth of Venus*] must expect, or at least tolerate, a parodist's deflating ridicule." In the court's view, even when the parody does not strongly disparage the original, so that the first author might not automatically decline to license it for a fee, a finding of fair use is not automatically negated. So too, that the parody is used in connection with an advertisement may lessen the "indulgence" to which it is entitled, but does not of itself negate fair use.

The court found the artistic nature of the copyrighted work to weigh "slightly" in Leibovitz's favor; but the fact that the advertisement may have copied extensively and duplicated more than necessary to "conjure up" the original did not weigh heavily against Paramount under the third factor, given the lack of adverse impact (acknowledged by Leibovitz) on the market for the copyrighted photograph. The court also concluded that the photographer's claim of lost licensing fees from the film company was unpersuasive, for she was not entitled to such a fee if the advertisement otherwise qualified for the fair use defense.

Suntrust Bank v. Houghton Mifflin Co., 60 U.S.P.Q.2d 1225 (11th Cir. 2001). SunTrust Bank is the trustee of the Mitchell Trust, which holds the copyright in the classic 1936 novel by Margaret Mitchell, *Gone With the Wind (GWTW)*, along with derivative works such as the equally classic motion picture and an authorized literary sequel. Houghton Mifflin sought to publish a novel by Alice Randall, titled *The Wind Done Gone (TWDG)*, which purports to be a parody and critique of *GWTW* and its "romanticized" depiction of slavery and the American South at the time of the Civil War. The district court issued a preliminary injunction, but the court of appeals—at oral argument—reversed that as an unconstitutional "prior restraint." It later filed a full opinion.

Although *TWDG* is told from the perspective of a new fictional character, a slave named Cynara, 18 characters are taken from *GWTW*, and their names (as well as the names of places) are transparently changed (e.g., Rhett Butler becomes R.B., Scarlett O'Hara becomes "Other," and the plantation Tara becomes Tata). The court stated: "*TWDG* copies, often in wholesale fashion, the descriptions and histories of these fictional characters and places from *GWTW*, as well as their relationships and interactions with one another.... [P]articularly in its first half, *TWDG* is largely 'an encapsulation of *GWTW* that exploits its copyrighted characters, story lines, and settings as the palette for the new story.'" However, in *TWDG*, the characteristics of the white and black characters are generally reversed, with the former being depicted as weak and ignorant and the latter being depicted as intelligent, strong, shrewd and heroic—and incidents from *GWTW* are modified accordingly—so that (in the defendant's words) "the institutions and values romanticized in *GWTW* are exposed as corrupt in *TWDG*."

Although Houghton Mifflin contended otherwise, the court of appeals found that *TWDG* is "substantially similar" to *GWTW*, and thus a prima facie infringement of copyright. The principal defense was fair use, which the court unanimously (with a separate concurrence) upheld. The court viewed the fair use doctrine, as developed by the Supreme Court in *Campbell v. Acuff-Rose*, as a vehicle for implementing First Amendment values central to copyright law: "the free flow of ideas—particularly criticism and commentary." Rejecting the claim that fair use parodies must have a "comic" effect, the court held that

> we will treat a work as a parody if its aim is to comment upon or criticize a prior work by appropriating elements of the original in creating a new artistic, as opposed to scholarly or journalistic, work. Under this definition, the parodic character of *TWDG* is clear. *TWDG* is ... a specific criticism of and rejoinder to the depiction of slavery and the relationships between black and whites in *GWTW*. The fact that Randall chose to convey her criticisms of *GWTW* through a work of fiction, which she contends is a more powerful vehicle for her message than a scholarly article, does not, in and of itself, deprive *TWDG* of fair-use protection.

The court turned to an analysis of the four factors set forth in section 107 of the Copyright Act. The fact that *TWDG* is a commercial work is "strongly overshadowed and outweighed in view of its highly transformative use of *GWTW*'s copyrighted elements." Although Randall's book is strongly dependent on the use of characters and incidents from *GWTW*, there are a variety of literary transformations—in the respective attributes of the characters, in the voice (Cynara's) through which the story is told, and in the second half of *TWDG* , which develops a "completely new story that ... features plot elements found nowhere within the covers of *GWTW*." The court concluded that "It is hard to imagine how Randall could have specifically criticized *GWTW* without depending heavily upon copyrighted elements of that book.... Randall has fully employed those conscripted elements from *GWTW* to make war against it."

As to the second statutory factor, *GWTW* is clearly a creative expressive work—but the targets of parodies will almost invariably be so. As to the third factor, the plaintiff contended that Ms. Randall copied far more than was necessary to "conjure up" the extremely well-known novel. The court acknowledged "substantial appropriation," but identified many incidents that were copied in order to be transformed to further the author's parodic purpose. It noted, however, that other copying arguably went beyond seeking to "conjure up" for purposes of specific criticism; but it concluded that the record at this stage of the case was insufficient to allow resolution of this issue. That matter was, however, closely related to the fourth factor, of potential substitution for *GWTW*. The plaintiff offered evidence as to the economic value of the novel, the sequel, the film, and other actual and potential derivative works, including a second sequel then under a lucrative contract. The court found, however, that on the record at this stage, SunTrust "fails to address and offers little evidence or argument to demonstrate that *TWDG* would supplant demand for SunTrust's licensed derivatives."

In vacating the preliminary injunction, the court concluded: "[A] lack of irreparable injury to SunTrust, together with the First Amendment concerns regarding comment and criticism and the likelihood that a fair use defense will prevail, make injunctive relief improper."

The concurring judge, in a thoughtful separate opinion, developed three points. First, *TWDG* is "unequivocally parody" and is "critical by [its] constitution." Second, because Ms. Randall "radically reshapes what she borrows from Mitchell," the "purpose and use" prong of section 107 "is not a close call." Third, the preliminary record suggests that *TWDG* (which aims at a different readership) will not act as a substitute for *GWTW* and its authorized derivatives. Further to this issue, the concurring judge pointed out the persistent refusal on the part of the Mitchell estate to license "the sort of derivative use Randall has undertaken" (including the incorporation of elements of homosexuality and miscegenation).

QUESTIONS

1. Do you agree with the court in the *Suntrust* case that the Supreme Court in *Campbell v. Acuff Rose* meant to embrace serious works, in the same artistic genre as a copyrighted work, within the concept of parody? If so, are there any adjustments that have to be made in a fair use analysis when moving from a comic defendant to a serious one?

2. If you were counsel for the plaintiff, what evidence might you seek to introduce in an attempt to prove, under the fourth fair use factor, that *TWDG* could or would have an adverse impact upon actual or potential markets for *GWTW*? What contrary evidence might you introduce on behalf of *TWDG*? *See Castle Rock Enter., Inc. v. Carol Pub. Group, Inc.,* at p. 654, *infra.*

3. In the case depicted in the adjacent comic book cover, the defendants published a bawdy cartoon magazine which pictorially depicted characters originated by the Walt Disney company (such as Mickey Mouse and Donald Duck) in sexual situations and using drugs and the like. The court rejected the defense of fair use. Walt Disney Prods. v. Air Pirates, 581 F.2d 751 (9th Cir.1978). The court held that, despite the permission given by the fair use doctrine to copy what is necessary to "conjure up" the original copyrighted target, the defendants had taken more than was necessary to recall the Disney characters to the reader. The court emphasized the "widespread public recognition" of the Disney characters, and stated that in a comic book—a graphic work as distinguished from a literary work—a recognizable caricature is easier to draw without close copying. It concluded that the parodist could copy "what is necessary to conjure up the original, and in the absence of a special need for accuracy ... that standard was exceeded here. By copying the images in their entirety, defendants took more than was necessary to place firmly in the reader's mind the parodied work and those specific attributes that are to be satirized." Would the court's reasoning and result likely be any different after the *Acuff–Rose* and *Gone With the Wind* decisions?

4. Do you share the view that the court ought not to consider the alleged pornographic or scatological nature of the defendant's work in analyzing the fair use question? Reexamine the court's opinion in the *Mitchell Brothers* case, *supra* Chapter 2.I, regarding the copyrightability of an allegedly obscene motion picture film. Even assuming that the analysis there is sound, does it follow from the fact that the court should not hold an X-rated film to be uncopyrightable that it should also refrain from weighing the defendant's "X rating" in determining whether its use is "fair"?

Harper & Row Publishers, Inc. v. Nation Enterprises

471 U.S. 539 (1985).

■ JUSTICE O'CONNOR delivered the opinion of the Court.

This case requires us to consider to what extent the "fair use" provision of the Copyright Revision Act of 1976 (hereinafter the Copyright Act), 17 U.S.C. § 107, sanctions the unauthorized use of quotations from a public figure's unpublished manuscript. In March 1979, an undisclosed source provided The Nation Magazine with the unpublished manuscript of "A Time to Heal: The Autobiography of Gerald R. Ford." Working directly from the purloined manuscript, an editor of The Nation produced a short piece entitled "The Ford Memoirs—Behind the Nixon Pardon." The piece was timed to "scoop" an article scheduled shortly to appear in Time Magazine. Time had agreed to purchase the exclusive right to print prepublication excerpts from the copyright holders, Harper & Row Publishers, Inc. (hereinafter Harper & Row), and Reader's Digest Association, Inc. (hereinafter Reader's Digest). As a result of The Nation article, Time canceled its agreement. Petitioners brought a successful copyright action against The Nation. On appeal, the Second Circuit reversed the lower court's finding of infringement, holding that The Nation's act was sanctioned as a "fair use" of the copyrighted material. We granted certiorari, 467 U.S. 1214 (1984), and we now reverse.

I

In February 1977, shortly after leaving the White House, former President Gerald R. Ford contracted with petitioners Harper & Row and Reader's Digest, to publish his as yet unwritten memoirs. The memoirs were to contain "significant hitherto unpublished material" concerning the Watergate crisis, Mr. Ford's pardon of former President Nixon and "Mr. Ford's reflections on this period of history, and the morality and personalities involved." App. to Pet. for Cert. C–14—C–15. In addition to the right to publish the Ford memoirs in book form, the agreement gave petitioners the exclusive right to license prepublication excerpts, known in the trade as "first serial rights." Two years later, as the memoirs were nearing completion, petitioners negotiated a prepublication licensing agreement with Time, a weekly news magazine. Time agreed to pay $25,000, $12,500 in advance and an additional $12,500 at publication, in exchange for the right to excerpt 7,500 words from Mr. Ford's account of the Nixon pardon. The issue featuring the excerpts was timed to appear approximately one week before shipment of the full length book version to bookstores. Exclusivity was an important consideration; Harper & Row instituted procedures designed to maintain the confidentiality of the manuscript, and Time retained the right to renegotiate the second payment should the material appear in print prior to its release of the excerpts.

Two to three weeks before the Time article's scheduled release, an unidentified person secretly brought a copy of the Ford manuscript to Victor Navasky, editor of The Nation, a political commentary magazine. Mr. Navasky knew that his possession of the manuscript was not authorized and that the manuscript must be returned quickly to his "source" to avoid discovery. 557 F. Supp. 1067, 1069 (S.D.N.Y.1983). He hastily put together what he believed was "a real hot news story" composed of quotes, paraphrases, and facts drawn exclusively from the manuscript. *Ibid.* Mr. Navasky attempted no independent commentary, research or criticism, in part because of the need for speed if he was to "make news" by "publish[ing] in advance of publication of the Ford book." App. 416–417. The 2,250–word article, reprinted in the Appendix to this opinion, appeared on April 3, 1979. As a result of The Nation's article, Time canceled its piece and refused to pay the remaining $12,500.

Petitioners brought suit in the District Court for the Southern District of New York, alleging conversion, tortious interference with contract, and violations of the Copyright Act.... [Although the district judge held that The Nation's use of the Ford material was not a fair use, a divided court of appeals panel disagreed.] Examining the four factors enumerated in § 107, see *infra,* at 547, n. 2, the majority found the purpose of the article was "news reporting," the original work was essentially factual in nature, the 300 words appropriated were insubstantial in relation to the 2,250–word piece, and the impact on the market for the original was minimal as "the evidence [did] not support a finding that it was the very limited use of expression *per se* which led to Time's decision not to print the excerpt." The Nation's borrowing of verbatim quotations merely "len[t] authenticity to this politically significant material ... complementing the reporting of the facts." 723 F.2d, at 208. The Court of Appeals was especially influenced by the "politically significant" nature of the subject matter and its conviction that it is not "the purpose of the Copyright Act to impede that harvest of knowledge so necessary to a democratic state" or "chill the activities of the press by forbidding a circumscribed use of copyrighted words." *Id.,* at 197, 209.

II

... The rights conferred by copyright are designed to assure contributors to the store of knowledge a fair return for their labors. *Twentieth Century Music Corp. v. Aiken,* 422 U.S. 151, 156 (1975).

Article I, § 8, of the Constitution provides:

> The Congress shall have Power ... to Promote the Progress of Science and useful Arts, by securing for limited Times to Authors and Inventors the exclusive Right to their respective Writings and Discoveries.

As we noted last Term: "[This] limited grant is a means by which an important public purpose may be achieved. It is intended to motivate the creative activity of authors and inventors by the provision of a special reward, and to allow the public access to the products of their genius after the limited period of exclusive control has expired." *Sony Corp. of America v. Universal City Studios, Inc.,* 464 U.S. 417, 429 (1984). "The monopoly created by copyright thus rewards the individual author in order to benefit the public." *Id.,* at 477 (dissenting opinion). This principle applies equally to works of fiction and nonfiction. The book at issue here, for example, was two years in the making, and began with a contract giving the author's copyright to the publishers in exchange for their services in producing and marketing the work. In preparing the book, Mr. Ford drafted essays and word portraits of public figures and participated in hundreds of taped interviews that were later distilled to chronicle his personal viewpoint. It is evident that the monopoly granted by copyright actively served its intended purpose of inducing the creation of new material of potential historical value.

.   .   .

... The Nation has admitted to lifting verbatim quotes of the author's original language totaling between 300 and 400 words and constituting some 13% of The Nation article. In using generous verbatim excerpts of Mr. Ford's unpublished manuscript to lend authenticity to its account of the forthcoming memoirs, The Nation effectively arrogated to itself the right of first publication, an important marketable subsidiary right. For the reasons set forth below, we find that this use of the copyrighted manuscript, even stripped to the verbatim quotes conceded by The Nation to be copyrightable expression, was not a fair use within the meaning of the Copyright Act.

III

A

Fair use was traditionally defined as "a privilege in others than the owner of the copyright to use the copyrighted material in a reasonable manner without his consent." H. Ball, Law of Copyright and Literary Property 260 (1944) (hereinafter Ball). The statutory formulation of the defense of fair use in the Copyright Act reflects the intent of Congress to codify the common-law doctrine. 3 Nimmer § 13.05. Section 107 requires a case-by-case determination whether a particular use is fair, and the statute notes four nonexclusive factors to be considered. This approach was "intended to restate the [pre-existing] judicial doctrine of fair use, not to change, narrow, or enlarge it in any way." H. R. Rep. No. 94–1476, p. 66 (1976) (hereinafter House Report).

"[T]he author's consent to a reasonable use of his copyrighted works ha[d] always been implied by the courts as a necessary incident of the constitutional policy of promoting the progress of science and the useful arts, since a prohibition of such use would inhibit subsequent writers from attempting to improve upon prior works and thus ... frustrate the very ends sought to be attained." Ball 260. Professor Latman, in a study of the doctrine of fair use commissioned by Congress for the revision effort, see *Sony Corp. of America v. Universal City Studios, Inc.,* 464 U.S., at 462–463,

n. 9 (dissenting opinion), summarized prior law as turning on the "importance of the material copied or performed from the point of view of the reasonable copyright owner. In other words, would the reasonable copyright owner have consented to the use?" ...

As early as 1841, Justice Story gave judicial recognition to the doctrine in a case that concerned the letters of another former President, George Washington.

> [A] reviewer may fairly cite largely from the original work, if his design be really and truly to use the passages for the purposes of fair and reasonable criticism. On the other hand, it is as clear, that if he thus cites the most important parts of the work, with a view, not to criticise, but to supersede the use of the original work, and substitute the review for it, such a use will be deemed in law a piracy.

Folsom v. Marsh, 9 F. Cas. 342, 344–345 (No. 4,901) (CC Mass.) As Justice Story's hypothetical illustrates, the fair use doctrine has always precluded a use that "supersede[s] the use of the original." *Ibid. Accord,* S. Rep. No. 94–473, p. 65 (1975) (hereinafter Senate Report).

Perhaps because the fair use doctrine was predicated on the author's implied consent to "reasonable and customary" use when he released his work for public consumption, fair use traditionally was not recognized as a defense to charges of copying from an author's as yet unpublished works. Under common-law copyright, "the property of the author ... in his intellectual creation [was] absolute until he voluntarily part[ed] with the same." *American Tobacco Co. v. Werckmeister,* 207 U.S. 284, 299 (1907); 2 Nimmer § 8.23, at 8–273. This absolute rule, however, was tempered in practice by the equitable nature of the fair use doctrine. In a given case, factors such as implied consent through *de facto* publication on performance or dissemination of a work may tip the balance of equities in favor of prepublication use.... But it has never been seriously disputed that "the fact that the plaintiff's work is unpublished ... is a factor tending to negate the defense of fair use." *Ibid.* Publication of an author's expression before he has authorized its dissemination seriously infringes the author's right to decide when and whether it will be made public, a factor not present in fair use of published works. Respondents contend, however, that Congress, in including first publication among the rights enumerated in § 106, which are expressly subject to fair use under § 107, intended that fair use would apply *in pari materia* to published and unpublished works. The Copyright Act does not support this proposition.

The Copyright Act represents the culmination of a major legislative reexamination of copyright doctrine. See *Mills Music, Inc. v. Snyder,* 469 U.S. 153, 159–160 (1985); *Sony Corp. of America v. Universal City Studios, Inc.,* 464 U.S., at 462–463, n.9 (dissenting opinion). Among its other innovations, it eliminated publication "as a dividing line between common law and statutory protection," House Report, at 129, extending statutory protection to all works from the time of their creation....

First Publication is subject to fair use

However! First Publication is different. Balance shifts to author

Though the right of first publication, like the other rights enumerated in § 106, is expressly made subject to the fair use provision of § 107, fair use analysis must always be tailored to the individual case. *Id.,* at 65; 3 Nimmer § 13.05[A]. The nature of the interest at stake is highly relevant to whether a given use is fair. From the beginning, those entrusted with the task of revision recognized the "overbalancing reasons to preserve the common law protection of undisseminated works until the author or his successor chooses to disclose them." Copyright Law Revision, Report of the Register of Copyrights on the General Revision of the U.S. Copyright Law, 87th Cong., 1st Sess., 41 (Comm. Print 1961). The right of first publication implicates a threshold decision by the author whether and in what form to release his work. First publication is inherently different from other § 106 rights in that only one person can be the first publisher; as the contract with Time illustrates, the commercial value of the right lies primarily in exclusivity. Because the potential damage to the author from judicially enforced "sharing" of the first publication right with unauthorized users of his manuscript is substantial, the balance of equities in evaluating such a claim of fair use inevitably shifts.

The Senate Report confirms that Congress intended the unpublished nature of the work to figure prominently in fair use analysis. In discussing fair use of photocopied materials in the classroom the Committee Report states:

> ... The applicability of the fair use doctrine to unpublished works is narrowly limited since, although the work is unavailable, this is the result of a deliberate choice on the part of the copyright owner. Under ordinary circumstances, the copyright owner's "right of first publication" would outweigh any needs of reproduction for classroom purposes.

Senate Report, at 64....

Unpublished nature is key

Even if the legislative history were entirely silent, we would be bound to conclude from Congress' characterization of § 107 as a "restatement" that its effect was to preserve existing law concerning fair use of unpublished works as of other types of protected works and not to "change, narrow, or enlarge it." *Id.,* at 66. We conclude that the unpublished nature of a work is "[a] key, though not necessarily determinative, factor" tending to negate a defense of fair use. Senate Report, at 64. See 3 Nimmer § 13.05, at 13–62, n. 2; W. Patry, The Fair Use Privilege in Copyright Law 125 (1985) (hereinafter Patry).

Pre-publication period is key. Author should control.

... The period encompassing the work's initiation, its preparation, and its grooming for public dissemination is a crucial one for any literary endeavor. The Copyright Act, which accords the copyright owner the "right to control the first public distribution" of his work, House Report, at 62, echoes the common law's concern that the author or copyright owner retain control throughout this critical stage.... The author's control of first public distribution implicates not only his personal interest in creative control but his property interest in exploitation of prepublication rights, which are valuable in themselves and serve as a valuable adjunct to publicity and marketing. . . . Under ordinary circumstances, the author's right to control the first public appearance of his undisseminated expression will outweigh a claim of fair use.

First publication wins in ordinary circumstances

B

Respondents, however, contend that First Amendment values require a different rule under the circumstances of this case. The thrust of the decision below is that "[t]he scope of [fair use] is undoubtedly wider when the information conveyed relates to matters of high public concern." *Consumers Union of the United States, Inc. v. General Signal Corp.,* 724 F.2d 1044, 1050 (C.A.2 1983) (construing 723 F.2d 195 (1983) (case below) as allowing advertiser to quote Consumer Reports), *cert. denied,* 469 U.S. 823 (1984). Respondents advance the substantial public import of the subject matter of the Ford memoirs as grounds for excusing a use that would ordinarily not pass muster as a fair use—the piracy of verbatim quotations for the purpose of "scooping" the authorized first serialization. Respondents explain their copying of Mr. Ford's expression as essential to reporting the news story it claims the book itself represents. In respondents' view, not only the facts contained in Mr. Ford's memoirs, but "the precise manner in which [he] expressed himself [were] as newsworthy as what he had to say." Brief for Respondents 38–39. Respondents argue that the public's interest in learning this news as fast as possible outweighs the right of the author to control its first publication.

The Second Circuit noted, correctly, that copyright's idea/expression dichotomy "strike[s] a definitional balance between the First Amendment and the Copyright Act by permitting free communication of facts while still protecting an author's expression." 723 F.2d, at 203. No author may copyright his ideas or the facts he narrates. 17 U.S.C. § 102(b). See, e.g., *New York Times Co. v. United States,* 403 U.S. 713, 726, n. (thus in U.S. Rpts.) (1971) (BRENNAN, J., concurring) (Copyright laws are not restrictions on freedom of speech as copyright protects only form of expression and not the ideas expressed); 1 Nimmer § 1.10[B][2]. . . .

Respondents' theory, however, would expand fair use to effectively destroy any expectation of copyright protection in the work of a public figure. Absent such protection, there would be little incentive to create or profit in financing such memoirs, and the public would be denied an important source of significant historical information. The promise of copyright would be an empty one if it could be avoided merely by dubbing the infringement a fair use "news report" of the book. See *Wainwright Securities Inc. v. Wall Street Transcript Corp.,* 558 F.2d 91 (C.A.2 1977), *cert. denied,* 434 U.S. 1014 (1978).

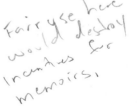

Fair use here would destroy incentives for memoirs.

Nor do respondents assert any actual necessity for circumventing the copyright scheme with respect to the types of works and users at issue here. Where an author and publisher have invested extensive resources in creating an original work and are poised to release it to the public, no legitimate aim is served by pre-empting the right of first publication. The fact that the words the author has chosen to clothe his narrative may of

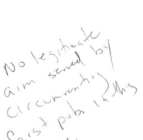

No legitimate aim served by circumventing first pub in this case.

themselves be "newsworthy" is not an independent justification for unauthorized copying of the author's expression prior to publication....

In our haste to disseminate news, it should not be forgotten that the Framers intended copyright itself to be the engine of free expression. By establishing a marketable right to the use of one's expression, copyright supplies the economic incentive to create and disseminate ideas....

It is fundamentally at odds with the scheme of copyright to accord lesser rights in those works that are of greatest importance to the public. Such a notion ignores the major premise of copyright and injures author and public alike. "[T]o propose that fair use be imposed whenever the 'social value [of dissemination] ... outweighs any detriment to the artist,' would be to propose depriving copyright owners of their right in the property precisely when they encounter those users who could afford to pay for it." Gordon, *Fair Use as Market Failure: A Structural and Economic Analysis of the Betamax Case and Its Predecessors,* 82 Colum. L. Rev. 1600, 1615 (1982). And as one commentator has noted: "If every volume that was in the public interest could be pirated away by a competing publisher, ... the public [soon] would have nothing worth reading." Sobel, *Copyright and the First Amendment: A Gathering Storm?,* 19 ASCAP Copyright Law Symposium 43, 78 (1971). See generally Comment, *Copyright and the First Amendment: Where Lies the Public Interest?,* 59 Tulane L. Rev. 135 (1984).

Moreover, freedom of thought and expression "includes both the right to speak freely and the right to refrain from speaking at all." *Wooley v. Maynard,* 430 U.S. 705, 714 (1977) (BURGER, C.J.). We do not suggest this right not to speak would sanction abuse of the copyright owner's monopoly as an instrument to suppress facts. But in the words of New York's Chief Judge Fuld:

> The essential thrust of the First Amendment is to prohibit improper restraints on the *voluntary* public expression of ideas; it shields the man who wants to speak or publish when others wish him to be quiet. There is necessarily, and within suitably defined areas, a concomitant freedom *not* to speak publicly, one which serves the same ultimate end as freedom of speech in its affirmative aspect.

Estate of Hemingway v. Random House, Inc., 23 N.Y.2d 341, 348, 244 N.E.2d 250, 255 (1968). Courts and commentators have recognized that copyright, and the right of first publication in particular, serve this countervailing First Amendment value. See *Schnapper v. Foley,* 215 U.S. App. D.C. 59, 667 F.2d 102 (1981), *cert. denied,* 455 U.S. 948 (1982); 1 Nimmer § 1.10[B], at 1–70, n. 24; Patry 140–142.

In view of the First Amendment protections already embodied in the Copyright Act's distinction between copyrightable expression and uncopyrightable facts and ideas, and the latitude for scholarship and comment traditionally afforded by fair use, we see no warrant for expanding the doctrine of fair use to create what amounts to a public figure exception to copyright. Whether verbatim copying from a public figure's manuscript in a given case is or is not fair must be judged according to the traditional equities of fair use.

IV

Fair use is a mixed question of law and fact. *Pacific & Southern Co. v. Duncan*, 744 F.2d 1490, 1495, n. 8 (C.A.11 1984). Where the district court has found facts sufficient to evaluate each of the statutory factors, an appellate court "need not remand for further factfinding ... [but] may conclude as a matter of law that [the challenged use] do[es] not qualify as a fair use of the copyrighted work." *Id.,* at 1495. Thus whether The Nation article constitutes fair use under § 107 must be reviewed in light of the principles discussed above....

Purpose of the Use. The Second Circuit correctly identified news reporting as the general purpose of The Nation's use. News reporting is one of the examples enumerated in § 107 to "give some idea of the sort of activities the courts might regard as fair use under the circumstances." Senate Report, at 61. This listing was not intended to be exhaustive, see *ibid.*; § 101 (definition of "including" and "such as"), or to single out any particular use as presumptively a "fair" use. The drafters resisted pressures from special interest groups to create presumptive categories of fair use, but structured the provision as an affirmative defense requiring a case-by-case analysis. See H.R. Rep. No. 83, 90th Cong., 1st Sess., 37 (1967); Patry 477, n. 4. "[W]hether a use referred to in the first sentence of section 107 is a fair use in a particular case will depend upon the application of the determinative factors, including those mentioned in the second sentence." Senate Report, at 62. The fact that an article arguably is "news" and therefore a productive use is simply one factor in a fair use analysis.

We agree with the Second Circuit that the trial court erred in fixing on whether the information contained in the memoirs was actually new to the public.... The Nation has every right to seek to be the first to publish information. But The Nation went beyond simply reporting uncopyrightable information and actively sought to exploit the headline value of its infringement, making a "news event" out of its unauthorized first publication of a noted figure's copyrighted expression.

The fact that a publication was commercial as opposed to nonprofit is a separate factor that tends to weigh against a finding of fair use. "[E]very commercial use of copyrighted material is presumptively an unfair exploitation of the monopoly privilege that belongs to the owner of the copyright." *Sony Corp. of America v. Universal City Studios, Inc.,* 464 U.S., at 451. In arguing that the purpose of news reporting is not purely commercial, The Nation misses the point entirely. The crux of the profit/nonprofit distinction is not whether the sole motive of the use is monetary gain but whether the user stands to profit from exploitation of the copyrighted material without paying the customary price. See *Roy Export Co. Establishment v. Columbia Broadcasting System, Inc.,* 503 F. Supp., at 1144; 3 Nimmer § 13.05[A][1], at 13–71, n. 25.3.

In evaluating character and purpose we cannot ignore The Nation's stated purpose of scooping the forthcoming hardcover and Time abstracts. App. to Pet. for Cert. C–27. The Nation's use had not merely the incidental effect but the *intended purpose* of supplanting the copyright holder's commercially valuable right of first publication. See *Meredith Corp. v. Harper & Row, Publishers, Inc.*, 378 F. Supp. 686, 690 (S.D.N.Y.) (purpose of text was to compete with original), *aff'd*, 500 F.2d 1221 (C.A.2 1974). Also relevant to the "character" of the use is "the propriety of the defendant's conduct." 3 Nimmer § 13.05[A], at 13–72. "Fair use presupposes 'good faith' and 'fair dealing.'" *Time Inc. v. Bernard Geis Associates*, 293 F. Supp. 130, 146 (S.D.N.Y.1968), quoting Schulman, *Fair Use and the Revision of the Copyright Act*, 53 Iowa L. Rev. 832 (1968). The trial court found that The Nation knowingly exploited a purloined manuscript. App. to Pet. for Cert. B–1, C–20–C–21, C–28–C–29. Unlike the typical claim of fair use, The Nation cannot offer up even the fiction of consent as justification. . . .

Nature of the Copyrighted Work. Second, the Act directs attention to the nature of the copyrighted work. "A Time to Heal" may be characterized as an unpublished historical narrative or autobiography. The law generally recognizes a greater need to disseminate factual works than works of fiction or fantasy. See Gorman, *Fact or Fancy? The Implications for Copyright*, 29 J. Copyright Soc. 560, 561 (1982).

> [E]ven within the field of fact works, there are gradations as to the relative proportion of fact and fancy. One may move from sparsely embellished maps and directories to elegantly written biography. The extent to which one must permit expressive language to be copied, in order to assure dissemination of the underlying facts, will thus vary from case to case.

Id., at 563. Some of the briefer quotes from the memoirs are arguably necessary adequately to convey the facts; for example, Mr. Ford's characterization of the White House tapes as the "smoking gun" is perhaps so integral to the idea expressed as to be inseparable from it. Cf. 1 Nimmer § 1.10[C]. But The Nation did not stop at isolated phrases and instead excerpted subjective descriptions and portraits of public figures whose power lies in the author's individualized expression. Such use, focusing on the most expressive elements of the work, exceeds that necessary to disseminate the facts.

The fact that a work is unpublished is a critical element of its "nature." 3 Nimmer § 13.05[A]; Comment, 58 St. John's L. Rev., at 613. Our prior discussion establishes that the scope of fair use is narrower with respect to unpublished works. While even substantial quotations might qualify as fair use in a review of a published work or a news account of a speech that had been delivered to the public or disseminated to the press, see House Report, at 65, the author's right to control the first public appearance of his expression weighs against such use of the work before its release. The right of first publication encompasses not only the choice whether to publish at all, but also the choices of when, where, and in what form first to publish a work.

In the case of Mr. Ford's manuscript, the copyright holders' interest in confidentiality is irrefutable.... A use that so clearly infringes the copyright holder's interests in confidentiality and creative control is difficult to characterize as "fair."

Amount and Substantiality of the Portion Used. Next, the Act directs us to examine the amount and substantiality of the portion used in relation to the copyrighted work as a whole. In absolute terms, the words actually quoted were an insubstantial portion of "A Time to Heal." The District Court, however, found that "[T]he Nation took what was essentially the heart of the book." 557 F. Supp., at 1072. We believe the Court of Appeals erred in overruling the District Judge's evaluation of the qualitative nature of the taking. See, e.g., *Roy Export Co. Establishment v. Columbia Broadcasting System, Inc.,* 503 F. Supp., at 1145 (taking of 55 seconds out of 1 hour and 29–minute film deemed qualitatively substantial). A Time editor described the chapters on the pardon as "the most interesting and moving parts of the entire manuscript." Reply Brief for Petitioners 16, n.8. The portions actually quoted were selected by Mr. Navasky as among the most powerful passages in those chapters. He testified that he used verbatim excerpts because simply reciting the information could not adequately convey the "absolute certainty with which [Ford] expressed himself," App. 303; or show that "this comes from President Ford," *id.,* at 305; or carry the "definitive quality" of the original, *id.,* at 306. In short, he quoted these passages precisely because they qualitatively embodied Ford's distinctive expression.

... [T]the fact that a substantial portion of the infringing work was copied verbatim is evidence of the qualitative value of the copied material, both to the originator and to the plagiarist who seeks to profit from marketing someone else's copyrighted expression.

Stripped to the verbatim quotes, the direct takings from the unpublished manuscript constitute at least 13% of the infringing article. See *Meeropol v. Nizer,* 560 F.2d 1061, 1071 (C.A.2 1977) (copyrighted letters constituted less than 1% of infringing work but were prominently featured). The Nation article is structured around the quoted excerpts which serve as its dramatic focal points. See Appendix to this opinion, *post,* p. 570. In view of the expressive value of the excerpts and their key role in the infringing work, we cannot agree with the Second Circuit that the "magazine took a meager, indeed an infinitesimal amount of Ford's original language." 723 F.2d, at 209.

Effect on the Market. Finally, the Act focuses on "the effect of the use upon the potential market for or value of the copyrighted work." This last factor is undoubtedly the single most important element of fair use.[9] See 3

---

9. Economists who have addressed the issue believe the fair use exception should come into play only in those situations in which the market fails or the price the copyright holder would ask is near zero. See, e.g., T. Brennan, *Harper & Row v. The Nation,*

Nimmer § 13.05[A], at 13–76, and cases cited therein. "Fair use, when properly applied, is limited to copying by others which does not materially impair the marketability of the work which is copied." 1 Nimmer § 1.10[D], at 1–87. The trial court found not merely a potential but an actual effect on the market. Time's cancellation of its projected serialization and its refusal to pay the $12,500 were the direct effect of the infringement. The Court of Appeals rejected this fact-finding as clearly erroneous, noting that the record did not establish a causal relation between Time's nonperformance and respondents' unauthorized publication of Mr. Ford's *expression* as opposed to the facts taken from the memoirs. We disagree. Rarely will a case of copyright infringement present such clear-cut evidence of actual damage. . . . [O]nce a copyright holder establishes with reasonable probability the existence of a causal connection between the infringement and a loss of revenue, the burden properly shifts to the infringer to show that this damage would have occurred had there been no taking of copyrighted expression. See 3 Nimmer § 14.02, at 14–7– 14–8.1. Petitioners established a prima facie case of actual damage that respondents failed to rebut. See *Stevens Linen Associates, Inc. v. Mastercraft Corp.*, 656 F.2d 11, 15 (C.A.2 1981). The trial court properly awarded actual damages and accounting of profits. See 17 U.S.C. § 504(b).

More important, to negate fair use one need only show that if the challenged use "should become widespread, it would adversely affect the *potential* market for the copyrighted work." *Sony Corp. of America v. Universal City Studios, Inc.*, 464 U.S., at 451 (emphasis added); *id.*, at 484, and n. 36 (collecting cases) (dissenting opinion). This inquiry must take account not only of harm to the original but also of harm to the market for derivative works. "If the defendant's work adversely affects the value of any of the rights in the copyrighted work (in this case the adaptation [and serialization] right) the use is not fair." 3 Nimmer § 13.05[B], at 13–77– 13–78 (footnote omitted).

It is undisputed that the factual material in the balance of The Nation's article, besides the verbatim quotes at issue here, was drawn exclusively from the chapters on the pardon. The excerpts were employed as featured episodes in a story about the Nixon pardon—precisely the use petitioners had licensed to Time. The borrowing of these verbatim quotes from the unpublished manuscript lent The Nation's piece a special air of authenticity—as Navasky expressed it, the reader would know it was Ford speaking and not The Nation. App. 300c. Thus it directly competed for a share of the market for prepublication excerpts. . . .

Copyrightability and Fair Use, Dept. of Justice Economic Policy Office Discussion Paper 13–17 (1984); Gordon, *Fair Use as Market Failure: A Structural and Economic Analysis of the Betamax Case and Its Predecessors*, 82 Colum. L. Rev. 1600, 1615 (1982). As the facts here demonstrate, there is a fully functioning market that encourages the creation and dissemination of memoirs of public figures. In the economists' view, permitting "fair use" to displace normal copyright channels disrupts the copyright market without a commensurate public benefit.

V

... In sum, the traditional doctrine of fair use, as embodied in the Copyright Act, does not sanction the use made by The Nation of these copyrighted materials. Any copyright infringer may claim to benefit the public by increasing public access to the copyrighted work. See *Pacific & Southern Co. v. Duncan,* 744 F.2d, at 1499–1500. But Congress has not designed, and we see no warrant for judicially imposing, a "compulsory license" permitting unfettered access to the unpublished copyrighted expression of public figures.

The Nation conceded that its verbatim copying of some 300 words of direct quotation from the Ford manuscript would constitute an infringement unless excused as a fair use. Because we find that The Nation's use of these verbatim excerpts from the unpublished manuscript was not a fair use, the judgment of the Court of Appeals is reversed, and the case is remanded for further proceedings consistent with this opinion.

It is so ordered.

■ Justice Brennan, with whom Justice White and Justice Marshall join, dissenting.

The Court holds that The Nation's quotation of 300 words from the unpublished 200,000–word manuscript of President Gerald R. Ford infringed the copyright in that manuscript, even though the quotations related to a historical event of undoubted significance—the resignation and pardon of President Richard M. Nixon. Although the Court pursues the laudable goal of protecting "the economic incentive to create and disseminate ideas," *ante,* at 558, this zealous defense of the copyright owner's prerogative will, I fear, stifle the broad dissemination of ideas and information copyright is intended to nurture. Protection of the copyright owner's economic interest is achieved in this case through an exceedingly narrow definition of the scope of fair use. The progress of arts and sciences and the robust public debate essential to an enlightened citizenry are ill served by this constricted reading of the fair use doctrine. See 17 U.S.C. § 107. I therefore respectfully dissent.

. . .

With respect to a work of history, particularly the memoirs of a public official, the statutorily prescribed analysis cannot properly be conducted without constant attention to copyright's crucial distinction between protected literary form and unprotected information or ideas....

... Protection against only substantial appropriation of literary form does not ensure historians a return commensurate with the full value of their labors. The literary form contained in works like "A Time to Heal" reflects only a part of the labor that goes into the book. It is the labor of collecting, sifting, organizing, and reflecting that predominates in the creation of works of history such as this one. The value this labor produces lies primarily in the information and ideas revealed, and not in the particular collocation of words through which the information and ideas are expressed. Copyright thus does not protect that which is often of most value in a work of history, and courts must resist the tendency to reject the fair use defense on the basis of their feeling that an author of history has been deprived of the full value of his or her labor. A subsequent author's taking of information and ideas is in no sense piratical because copyright law simply does not create any property interest in information and ideas.

The urge to compensate for subsequent use of information and ideas is perhaps understandable. An inequity seems to lurk in the idea that much of the fruit of the historian's labor may be used without compensation. This, however, is not some unforeseen byproduct of a statutory scheme intended primarily to ensure a return for works of the imagination. Congress made the affirmative choice that the copyright laws should apply in this way: "Copyright does not preclude others from using the ideas or information revealed by the author's work. It pertains to the literary ... form in which the author expressed intellectual concepts." H.R. Rep. No. 94–1476, at 56–57. This distinction is at the essence of copyright. The copyright laws serve as the "engine of free expression," *ante,* at 558, only when the statutory monopoly does not choke off multifarious indirect uses and consequent broad dissemination of information and ideas. To ensure the progress of arts and sciences and the integrity of First Amendment values, ideas and information must not be freighted with claims of proprietary right.

In my judgment, the Court's fair use analysis has fallen to the temptation to find a copyright violation based on a minimal use of literary form in order to provide compensation for the appropriation of information from a work of history. The failure to distinguish between information and literary form permeates every aspect of the Court's fair use analysis and leads the Court to the wrong result in this case. Application of the statutorily prescribed analysis with attention to the distinction between information and literary form leads to a straightforward finding of fair use within the meaning of § 107.

. . .

[T]he Court introduces into analysis of this case a categorical presumption against prepublication fair use. See *ante,* at 555 ("Under ordinary circumstances, the author's right to control the first public appearance of his undisseminated expression will outweigh a claim of fair use").

This categorical presumption is unwarranted on its own terms and unfaithful to congressional intent. Whether a particular prepublication use will impair any interest the Court identifies as encompassed within the right of first publication, see *ante,* at 552–555, will depend on the nature of the copyrighted work, the timing of prepublication use, the amount of expression used, and the medium in which the second author communicates. . . .

. . .

Balancing the Interests. Once the distinction between information and literary form is made clear, the statutorily prescribed process of weighing the four statutory fair use factors discussed above leads naturally to a conclusion that The Nation's limited use of literary form was not an infringement. Both the purpose of the use and the nature of the copyrighted work strongly favor the fair use defense here. The Nation appropriated Mr. Ford's expression for a purpose Congress expressly authorized in § 107 and borrowed from a work whose nature justifies some appropriation to facilitate the spread of information. The factor that is perhaps least favorable to the claim of fair use is the amount and substantiality of the expression used. Without question, a portion of the expression appropriated was among the most poignant in the Ford manuscript. But it is difficult to conclude that this taking was excessive in relation to the news reporting purpose. In any event, because the appropriation of literary form—as opposed to the use of information—was not shown to injure Harper & Row's economic interest, any uncertainty with respect to the propriety of the amount of expression borrowed should be resolved in favor of a finding of fair use. In light of the circumscribed scope of the quotation in The Nation's article and the undoubted validity of the purpose motivating that quotation, I must conclude that the Court has simply adopted an exceedingly narrow view of fair use in order to impose liability for what was in essence a taking of unprotected information.

.   .   .

QUESTIONS

1.   Much copyrighted material may be of public interest. Indeed, it may contain considerable news value. When the press's or other authors' claimed need for unfettered (and unpaid) access to copyrighted works encounters the first author's objections, does a copyright/First Amendment conflict arise? The Supreme Court in *Harper & Row* indicated that the assertion of such a conflict evokes a false dichotomy: copyright may in fact promote First Amendment goals.

Similarly, courts and commentators generally agree that the copyright law may accommodate First Amendment concerns by application of two established copyright doctrines: the idea/expression dichotomy, and the fair use doctrine. The idea/expression dichotomy preserves free access to an author's "ideas" and information; the fair use defense aids those second authors who can demonstrate a compelling justification for copying the first author's *expression*. If the use of the first author's expression is not "fair," then neither should it be shielded by the First Amendment. Are you convinced? Even if, for example in the case of excessive quotation of copyrighted materials in a serious critical biography, the court rejects the fair use defense, should First Amendment policies induce the court not to enjoin publication, but rather to limit recovery to money damages? *See Campbell v. Acuff–Rose, supra,* at n. 10.

2.   *Harper & Row* concerned preemptive publication of an about-to-be-published work. Does the fair use analysis change if the author wishes *never* to publish the work from which defendant seeks to quote? *See Salinger v. Random House,* 811 F.2d 90 (2d Cir.1987).

In *Salinger,* defendant biographer had obtained access to Salinger's unpublished letters in libraries where the letters' recipients had deposited them. The libraries made the letters available to researchers on the condition that the letters would not be reproduced. The court quickly dismissed the argument that availability of the Salinger letters in publicly accessible libraries entitled the biographer to copy from the letters. Assuming the library had not imposed conditions on researchers' access to the letters, *should* their public availability affect the fair use analysis? Should a library's imposition of conditions on access make a difference?

Several post-*Harper & Row* decisions regarding unpublished works (*Salinger* was one of these) followed the Supreme Court's indication that unlicensed disclosure of the expression of an unpublished work would rarely be held fair. *See, e.g., New Era Pubs. v. Henry Holt & Co.,* 873 F.2d 576 (2d Cir.1989), *cert. denied,* 493 U.S. 1094 (1990) (quotations and paraphrases from unpublished writings of Church of Scientology founder L. Ron Hubbard; fair use rejected, but preliminary injunction denied on grounds of laches); *but see Wright v. Warner Books, Inc.,* 953 F.2d 731 (2d Cir.1991) (upholding fair use defense of academic's quotations and paraphrases from letters and journals of author Richard Wright). Many publishers (who had previously urged the *Harper & Row* court to recognize strong protection for the first publication right), as well as educational and library groups, lobbied to modify § 107 to specify that a work's unpublished status should not be determinative. The result was a 1992 amendment that added the following sentence to the end of § 107: "The fact that a work is unpublished shall not itself bar a finding of fair use if such finding is made upon consideration of all the above factors."

In one of the earliest decided cases invoking the added language in § 107, the court found fair use of an unpublished literary manuscript. In *Sundeman v. Seajay Soc'y, Inc.,* 142 F.3d 194 (4th Cir.1998), two unauthorized copies were made of a manuscript of the first novel, written in 1928, by Pulitzer Prize winning author Marjorie Kinnan Rawlings and left unpublished at her death. The copies—one to avoid damage to the manuscript and the other for purposes of authentication—were made by Seajay Society, a nonprofit organization dedicated to enhancing public awareness of southern culture. (The manuscript was lawfully in its possession.) One copy was used by an officer of Seajay to prepare a critical analysis of the Rawlings novel. She orally presented her analysis—quoting some 4–6% of the 183–page manuscript, with additional paraphrasing—to some 150–200 persons at a meeting of the Rawlings Society. A printed copy of the oral presentation was not published, and Seajay's request for permission to publish the entire novel was denied by the copyright holder, who sued for copyright infringement stemming from both the manuscript copying and the oral presentation.

The court characterized the copying and quoting as having been made for an essentially noncommercial, educational and transformative purpose, without any prospect of damaging the market for the Rawlings novel and without interfering with the copyright owner's right of first publication. It found—considering the amended § 107 and the decision in *Harper & Row*—that the unpublished status of the novel weighed against fair use but, weighing all of the statutory factors, concluded that the copying was fair use.

Craft v. Kobler, 667 F.Supp. 120 (S.D.N.Y.1987). In this controversy concerning the plaintiff's *published* works, the district court distinguished between copying to achieve literary vividness and copying material that is integral to the second author's argument or analysis. The decision rejected the fair use defense interposed by the author of a biography of composer Igor Stravinsky; the infringement action was brought by Robert Craft, who was Stravinsky's co-author, literary executor, and close colleague. The court determined that the defendant took more quotations and paraphrases from published works by Stravinsky and Craft than were necessary to the task of writing a critical biography. The Stravinsky sentences that the court found properly quoted or closely paraphrased were deemed by the court to be necessary to support analysis by the biographer that "depends on a perception of the style of writing and manner of expression" of Stravinsky, which "could not be made effectively without direct quotation." However, most of Kobler's quotations and paraphrases did not fit within this category. "More common are takings of Stravinsky's radiant, startlingly expressive phrases to make a richer, better portrait of Stravinsky, and to make better reading than a drab paraphrase reduced to bare facts." The court attempted to articulate a standard that fell somewhere between the defendant's liberal proposal and an arguably quite narrow reading of the decision of the Court of Appeals in the then recently decided *Salinger* case.

> In support of Kobler's quotation of such examples of Stravinsky's wit and power of description, the defendants argue that for a biography or critical study of an author, the doctrine of fair use gives latitude to quote protected matter for the purpose of illustrating and communicating the subject's powers of observation and expression.
>
> Surely there is merit to the argument. Nor is it contradicted by the recent admonition of the Court of Appeals in *Salinger*: "This dilemma [of choosing between loss of accuracy and vividness and risking an injunction] is not faced by the biographer who elects to copy only the factual content of letters. The biographer who copies only facts incurs no risk of an injunction; ... [W]hen dealing with copyrighted expression, a biographer ... may frequently have to content himself with reporting only the fact of what the subject did, even if he thereby pens

a 'pedestrian' sentence. The copier is not at liberty to avoid 'pedestrian' reportage by appropriating his subject's literary devices." 811 F.2d at 96–97. Taken out of context this passage appears to bar the biographer of an author from using any of his subject's protected expression whether done to achieve accuracy in the rendition of the subject's idea or to illustrate comments on the subject's writing style, skill and power. The biographer would be restricted to telling his readers, "This Mickey Spillane, boy, he sure can write." He would not be permitted to take examples of protected material to illustrate the point. A full reading of the *Salinger* opinion makes clear, however, that this discussion refers only to takings from unpublished copyrighted material, as to which the court ruled there is little opportunity for fair use.

I agree with the defendants that the fair use doctrine gives latitude to the biographer of an author to quote limited excerpts of published copyrighted work to illustrate the descriptive skill, wit, power, vividness, and originality of the author's writing.

But the license is not unlimited. In assessing claims of fair use, we must consider the number, size and importance of appropriated passages, as well as their individual justifications. . . .

In my view, Kobler's takings are far too numerous and with too little instructional justification to support the conclusion of fair use. Kobler uses Stravinsky's colorful words without restraint throughout the book to describe and comment on the events and personages of Stravinsky's life. Most of these passages do not individually present a compelling justification of fair use. By a conservative count (that includes neither the doubtful rulings, cases of disputed ownership, nor claims based on translations), the appropriations constitute approximately 3% of the volume of Kobler's book. The importance of these passages to the book far exceeds that percentage. Stravinsky's colorful epigrams animate the narrative. I think Kobler might agree that they are the liveliest and most entertaining part of the biography.

QUESTIONS

1. The court seems to accord the second author little latitude to enhance his works by copying the first author's most evocative expressions. On the other hand, use of the first author's vivid language may be permissible to illustrate a second author's argument concerning the authorship or literary style of the prior work. Are you satisfied with a court's ability to discern when a second author is making a critical use of the prior work, as opposed to a merely decorative use? Is there any better alternative?

2. In ruling against the comic book publisher in the *Air Pirates* case, p. 634 *supra*, the court observed that the parodist is not to be afforded the right to make the "best parody" and that this desire of the parodist must be subordinated to the interest of the copyright owner in protecting its own creative expression. Is this not essentially the same as the point made in the *Salinger* and *Craft* cases about the biographer's obligation under the law to content himself with less than the most vivid recreation of the biographical subject? Do you find the point equally convincing in both contexts?

3. Consumers Union (CU) publishes a copyrighted monthly magazine, Consumer Reports (CR), which reports at length on its evaluation, after rigorous testing, of a wide array of consumer products. Although a high rating from CU is of great commercial value to a manufacturer, CU—in an effort to maintain its objectivity and integrity—declines to run any outside advertising in CR and it has steadfastly refused to grant permission to others to use its name or copyrighted materials in advertisements. The July issue of CR contained an article evaluating and comparing eighteen different models of lightweight vacuum cleaners. Four models manufactured by Regina were discussed and rated; the Powerteam 6910 model was judged the best of all models tested by a good margin, while the other three were rated fair to poor.

Regina asked CU for permission to quote its favorable evaluation in an advertising campaign, but CU refused. Regina nonetheless proceeded to prepare and broadcast a television advertisement that featured a voice-over and simultaneous display of the text of several quotations from the CR article, such as: "Far ahead of the pack in cleaning ability.... Of all the lightweights tested, only one worked well.... The 6910 is the only cleaner tested that is an adequate substitute for a full-sized vacuum." While the announcer speaks, the screen notes a disclaimer: "Consumer Reports is not affiliated with Regina and does not endorse Regina products or any other products."

CU has brought an action for copyright infringement and Regina has raised the defense of fair use. Should that defense be sustained? *See Consumers Union of U.S., Inc. v. New Regina Corp.*, 664 F.Supp. 753 (S.D.N.Y.1987). (Is it important to know how lengthy the CR article was? *See Henry Holt & Co. v. Liggett & Myers Tobacco Co.*, 23 F.Supp. 302 (E.D.Pa.1938).)

4. Hustler Magazine ran a parody advertisement based upon the "first time" advertisements of Campari liquor. The parody portrayed the Reverend Jerry Falwell, a nationally known fundamentalist minister, describing his "first time" as being incest with his mother in an outhouse. Falwell reproduced and distributed by mail the Hustler advertisement, along with a request for contributions to aid him in litigation against Hustler, to combat pornography, and to aid religious television stations to reinforce America's moral fiber. The Falwell campaign raised $700,000. Hustler Magazine has sued for copyright infringement, and Falwell has asserted fair use. How should the case be decided? *See Hustler Magazine, Inc. v. Moral Majority, Inc.*, 796 F.2d 1148 (9th Cir.1986).

5. In January 2001, the Reverend Jesse Jackson acknowledged that he had fathered a daughter in an extramarital affair with a former staff member, Karin Stanford. The month before, Ms. Stanford had taken a photograph of herself and her two-year old daughter, and had sent it as a Christmas card to many of her friends, including one Jack White, a writer for Time Magazine. Although other tabloids ran pictures of the child with her face obscured, Time published the Christmas card photograph, unedited, that had been sent by Ms. Stanford to Mr. White. Although Time could have obscured the child's face, it stated that this would have been stigmatizing and dehumanizing. (Do you agree?) Although in real life, the matter was not litigated, assess whether Time Magazine would have had a persuasive fair use defense had it been sued by Ms. Stanford for copyright infringement. Cf. Nunez v. Caribbean International News Corp., 235 F.3d 18 (1st Cir.2000)(nude photographs of Puerto Rican beauty contest winner, circulated as part of her modeling portfolio, reproduced without the photographer's permission on local newspaper front page).

Castle Rock Entertainment, Inc. v. Carol Pub. Group, Inc., 150 F.3d 132 (2d Cir.1998). The plaintiff, which owns the copyright in the Jerry Seinfeld television programs, brought an action against an author and publisher who prepared and sold The Seinfeld Aptitude Test (SAT) devoted to testing its readers' recollection of scenes and events from that TV series. The defendants' 132–page book contained 643 trivia questions, some multiple choice, some matching, and some short answer, at five levels of difficulty. Some questions dealt with incidents, and others with precise text from the shows, e.g., "Who said, 'I don't go for those nonrefundable deals . . . I can't commit to a woman . . . I'm not committing to an airline': Jerry, George or Kramer?" The SAT draws from 84 of the 86 Seinfeld episodes. The defendants asserted fair use, but the court ruled against them.

As to the first factor, the court pointed out that the purpose of the SAT was not to educate, analyze, criticize or comment, but rather to repackage the Seinfeld programs to entertain the reader and to sate their "passion" for Seinfeld. The court conceded that the SAT contained minimally creative elements, such as formulating the questions, generating several incorrect answers in the multiple-choice questions, and creating several levels of difficulty. However, the court concluded that the SAT too minimally altered Seinfeld's expression, and evidenced no transformative purpose. The Seinfeld programs were of course of a fictional nature; and posing 643 questions was far more than necessary to pursue the defendants' purpose of entertainment rather than commentary. As to the fourth fair use factor, the defendants' contended that Castle Rock had evidenced no interest in publishing Seinfeld-related trivia books, so that there was no adverse economic impact. The court, however, concluded that the fourth factor also favored the plaintiff:

> . . . The SAT substitutes for a derivative market that a television program copyright owner such as Castle Rock "would in general develop or license others to develop." Because The SAT borrows exclusively from Seinfeld and not from any other television or entertainment programs, The SAT is likely to fill a market niche that Castle Rock would in general develop. Moreover, as noted by the district

court, this "Seinfeld trivia game is not critical of the program, nor does it parody the program: if anything, SAT pays homage to Seinfeld." ... Although Castle Rock has evidenced little if any interest in exploiting this market for derivative works based on Seinfeld, such as by creating and publishing Seinfeld trivia books, ... the copyright law must respect that creative and economic choice. "It would ... not serve the ends of the Copyright Act—i.e., to advance the arts—if artists were denied their monopoly over derivative versions of their creative works merely because they made the artistic decision not to saturate those markets with variations of their original." ...

See also Worldwide Church of God v. Philadelphia Church of God, 227 F.3d 1110 (9th Cir.2000)(court is divided concerning fourth fair use factor, when plaintiff Church, the copyright owner, sought to suppress the text of a book written by its founder and now thought to be outmoded and racist; held, 2–to–1, publication by former ministers, for new church, is not fair use); Salinger v. Random House, Inc., 811 F.2d 90 (2d Cir.1987)("Even an author who had disavowed any intention to publish his work during his lifetime was entitled to protection of his copyright, first, because the relevant consideration was the 'potential market' and second, because he has the right to change his mind."). But, where the author has refused to exploit a particular market niche, why should third parties not be permitted to occupy that niche, as there is no market harm to the author and the public will benefit from the availability of a new work that the author would not supply? What is the policy that outweighs the public benefit for others to take up where the author leaves off when the author chooses to forego a market?

QUESTION

Consider another claim involving the same defendant as in the *Seinfeld* case, *Paramount Pictures Corp. v. Carol Pub'g Group, Inc.*, 11 F. Supp. 2d 329 (S.D.N.Y.1998), *aff'd*, 181 F.3d 83 (2d Cir.1999)(table). There, the work at issue is a guide to the television show *Star Trek*, promoted as containing everything the uninitiate needs to know about the show before taking a "trekkie" out for a date. The book summarizes plot lines and exposes characters, often in a bantering tone, with ironic asides. Is the sarcasm of its presentation sufficient to justify treating the work as a commentary with a strong claim to fair use? On the one hand, ponderous academic tomes on high art are not the only beneficiaries of the fair use exception: humorous analysis of popular culture may also qualify. On the other hand, shouldn't we be leery of a rule that might permit a second-comer to lace its version with a few jokes, and thereby turn an infringing derivative work into a fair use?

ADDITIONAL FAIR USE CONSIDERATIONS

Under the approach taken by the courts in the above decisions, the four factors delineated in the second sentence of § 107 must be considered in all cases in which fair use is asserted as a defense. But the language does not preclude consideration of other factors. Courts have, in fact, declined to assign an exclusive role to these factors, and have instead regularly introduced additional considerations.

Thus, courts have inquired into the "amount and substantiality of the portion used" not only "in relation to the copyrighted work as a whole," but in relation to *defendant*'s work as well. *See, e.g., Harper & Row v. Nation Enters.*, 471 U.S. 539 (1985) (300 words copied from plaintiff's 450–page book constituted 13% of defendant's article). They have tended to be more lenient when the unauthorized use was "incidental," that is, when the plaintiff's work was captured as part of a larger permissible reproduction or performance. *See, e.g., Italian Book Corp. v. ABC*, 458 F.Supp. 65 (S.D.N.Y.1978) (portion of plaintiff's song performed in "Little Italy" street festival was included in defendant's television news coverage of festival). *But see Schumann v. Albuquerque Corp.*, 664 F.Supp. 473 (D.N.M.1987) (broadcast of entire copyrighted songs played by band at local festival not fair use; because the broadcast had "entertainment value," it was held to be competitive with uses copyright owners would license).

Apart from copyrighted music being "incidentally" incorporated in radio or television broadcasts, a question that has arisen with increasing frequency is the use, in the background of a television program, of a copyrighted artwork that is intended to impart a visual context to a home or business setting. Typically, the artwork is seen on the broadcast for only a short period of time, and often only indistinctly. Courts have taken differing views on whether there is "substantial" copying in such circumstances, and whether, even if there is, it is sheltered by the fair use doctrine. *Compare Ringgold v. Black Entertainment T.V., Inc.*, 126 F.3d 70 (2d Cir.1997) (holding use "decorative" rather than "transformative"; § 118 contemplates royalty payments for the use of art even on noncommercial television, and an "incidental" defense would unfairly permit wholesale appropriation by movie and television users), *with Sandoval v. New Line Cinema Corp.*, 147 F.3d 215 (2d Cir.1998) (artwork is seen indistinctly and for very limited time; under *de minimis* doctrine, the copying is insubstantial, and there is no need to consider fair use), *and Jackson v. Warner Bros.*, 993 F.Supp. 585 (E.D.Mich.1997) (defendant studio did not use the paintings to increase film sales, film would not serve as substitute for paintings, and artist would suffer no demonstrable harm).

In applying the fair use doctrine, courts have tended to be far less lenient when defendant's conduct betrayed callous disregard for plaintiff's interests. Emphasizing the equitable nature of the defense, courts have cautioned, "the fair use doctrine is not a license for corporate theft, empowering a court to ignore a copyright whenever it determines the underlying work contains material of public importance." *Iowa State Univ. Research Found. v. ABC*, 621 F.2d 57, 61 (2d Cir.1980). One court has observed: "Because fair use presupposes 'good faith' and 'fair dealing,' . . . courts may weigh 'the propriety of the defendant's conduct' in the equitable balance of a fair use determination." *Fisher v. Dees*, 794 F.2d 432 (9th

Cir.1986). *See* L. Weinreb, *Fair's Fair: A Comment on the Fair Use Doctrine,* 103 Harv. L. Rev. 1137 (1990).

A similar message can be found in the Supreme Court's references in *Harper & Row Pub'rs, Inc. v. Nation Enterprises,* 471 U.S. 539 (1985), to the "purloined manuscript" of President Ford's memoirs that illicitly came into the hands of the publisher of *Nation Magazine*; and to the illicit photographing, through an illegal entry in the dark of night, of segments of a copyrighted motion picture of the assassination of President Kennedy, undertaken by an author in the course of preparing a serious book about that tragic event, *Time, Inc. v. Bernard Geis Assocs.,* 293 F.Supp. 130 (S.D.N.Y.1968) (although the court found this misbehavior to have been counterbalanced by the author's proffer to the plaintiff of all royalties generated by the sale of his book). Forceful contrary arguments have been made, however, to the effect that any wrongdoing on the part of a defendant asserting fair use, even if constituting a private injury, should be discounted in assessing the more compelling public interests at stake in the fair use analysis. *See* P. Leval, *Toward a Fair Use Standard,* 103 Harv. L. Rev. 1105 (1990). Which of these positions is more compelling? (For consideration of the question whether it counts against fair use that the defendant has placed the borrowed copyrighted work in a pornographic or salacious setting, see the cases set forth above relating to parody.)

Related to the issue of improper conduct as a factor beyond the four listed in § 107 is whether or not the defendant requested permission of the copyright owner before making an unauthorized use. On the one hand, it can be argued that the making and denial of such a request counts against the defendant, who is thereby put on notice of the plaintiff's disapproval and establishes willful misbehavior. On the other hand, such requests should be encouraged, both as a courtesy and as a possible prelude to a negotiated arrangement for compensation—and it might be argued that in any event it is circular to impose on a user an obligation to seek permission, when the very question for the court to decide is whether the use is fair so that no permission need be sought. The decision in the *Acuff-Rose* case (see its note 18, *supra*) appears clearly to support the latter position.

Just as courts have been disinclined to find fair use when they regard the defendant's activity as wrongful or immoral, by the same token, courts may be more inclined to deem defendant's use fair if it suspects the copyright owner of unreasonable conduct. *See, e.g., Rosemont Enters., Inc. v. Random House, Inc.,* 366 F.2d 303 (2d Cir.1966) (Howard Hughes appeared to be invoking copyrights in biographical articles in order to prevent others from writing about his life).

––––––

Fair use claims involving copying from a prior work to create a new work that builds on its predecessor arise in the context of computer programs as well as of more traditional works. The decision that follows also concerns the problem of "intermediate copying" alluded to in Chapter

6.A, *supra*, i.e., is a reproduction actionable if the copy is not made available to the public, but the fruits of that copying, in the form of a new work, are?

Sega Enterprises, Ltd. v. Accolade, Inc.

977 F.2d 1510 (9th Cir.1992).

■ REINHARDT, CIRCUIT JUDGE:

... We are asked to determine ... whether the Copyright Act permits persons who are neither copyright holders nor licensees to disassemble a copyrighted computer program in order to gain an understanding of the unprotected functional elements of the program. In light of the public policies underlying the Act, we conclude that, when the person seeking the understanding has a legitimate reason for doing so and when no other means of access to the unprotected elements exists, such disassembly is as a matter of law a fair use of the copyrighted work....

I.   *Background*

Plaintiff-appellee Sega Enterprises, Ltd. ("Sega"), a Japanese corporation, and its subsidiary, Sega of America, develop and market video entertainment systems, including the "Genesis" console (distributed in Asia under the name "MegaDrive") and video game cartridges. Defendant-appellant Accolade, Inc., is an independent developer, manufacturer, and marketer of computer entertainment software, including game cartridges that are compatible with the Genesis console, as well as game cartridges that are compatible with other computer systems.

Sega licenses its copyrighted computer code and its "SEGA" trademark to a number of independent developers of computer game software. Those licensees develop and sell Genesis-compatible video games in competition with Sega. Accolade is not and never has been a licensee of Sega. Prior to rendering its own games compatible with the Genesis console, Accolade explored the possibility of entering into a licensing agreement with Sega, but abandoned the effort because the agreement would have required that Sega be the exclusive manufacturer of all games produced by Accolade.

Accolade used a two-step process to render its video games compatible with the Genesis console. First, it "reverse engineered" Sega's video game programs in order to discover the requirements for compatibility with the Genesis console. As part of the reverse engineering process, Accolade transformed the machine-readable object code contained in commercially available copies of Sega's game cartridges into human-readable source code using a process called "disassembly" or "decompilation." Accolade purchased a Genesis console and three Sega game cartridges, wired a decompiler into the console circuitry, and generated printouts of the resulting source code. Accolade engineers studied and annotated the printouts in order to identify areas of commonality among the three game programs. They then loaded the disassembled code back into a computer, and experimented to discover the interface specifications for the Genesis console by modifying the programs and studying the results. At the end of the reverse engineering process, Accolade created a development manual that incorporated the information it had discovered about the requirements for a Genesis-compatible game. According to the Accolade employees who created the manual, the manual contained only functional descriptions of the interface requirements and did not include any of Sega's code.

In the second stage, Accolade created its own games for the Genesis. According to Accolade, at this stage it did not copy Sega's programs, but relied only on the information concerning interface specifications for the Genesis that was contained in its development manual. Accolade maintains that with the exception of the interface specifications, none of the code in its own games is derived in any way from its examination of Sega's code. In 1990, Accolade released "Ishido," a game which it had originally developed and released for use with the Macintosh and IBM personal computer systems, for use with the Genesis console. . . .

. . .

. . . Although the question is fairly debatable, we conclude based on the policies underlying the Copyright Act that disassembly of copyrighted object code is, as a matter of law, a fair use of the copyrighted work if such disassembly provides the only means of access to those elements of the code that are not protected by copyright and the copier has a legitimate reason for seeking such access. Accordingly, we hold that Sega has failed to demonstrate a likelihood of success on the merits of its copyright claim. Because on the record before us the hardships do not tip sharply (or at all) in Sega's favor, the preliminary injunction issued in its favor must be dissolved, at least with respect to that claim.

A. *Intermediate Copying*

We have previously held that the Copyright Act does not distinguish between unauthorized copies of a copyrighted work on the basis of what stage of the alleged infringer's work the unauthorized copies represent. *Walker v. University Books,* 602 F.2d 859, 864 (9th Cir.1979). . . . Section 501 provides that "anyone who violates any of the exclusive rights of the copyright owner as provided by sections 106 through 118 . . . is an infringer of the copyright." *Id.* § 501(a). On its face, that language unambiguously encompasses and proscribes "intermediate copying." *Walker,* 602 F.2d at 863–64; *see also Walt Disney Productions v. Filmation Associates,* 628 F. Supp. 871, 875–76 (C.D.Cal.1986).

In order to constitute a "copy" for purposes of the Act, the allegedly infringing work must be fixed in some tangible form, "from which the work can be perceived, reproduced, or otherwise communicated, either directly or with the aid of a machine or device." 17 U.S.C. § 101. The computer file generated by the disassembly program, the printouts of the disassembled code, and the computer files containing Accolade's modifications of the code that were generated during the reverse engineering process all satisfy that

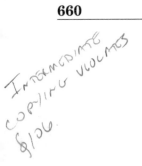

requirement. The intermediate copying done by Accolade therefore falls squarely within the category of acts that are prohibited by the statute....

... Accordingly, we hold that intermediate copying of computer object code may infringe the exclusive rights granted to the copyright owner in section 106 of the Copyright Act regardless of whether the end product of the copying also infringes those rights. If intermediate copying is permissible under the Act, authority for such copying must be found in one of the statutory provisions to which the rights granted in section 106 are subject....

D. *Fair Use*

Accolade contends, finally, that its disassembly of copyrighted object code as a necessary step in its examination of the unprotected ideas and functional concepts embodied in the code is a fair use that is privileged by section 107 of the Act. Because, in the case before us, disassembly is the only means of gaining access to those unprotected aspects of the program, and because Accolade has a legitimate interest in gaining such access (in order to determine how to make its cartridges compatible with the Genesis console), we agree with Accolade. Where there is good reason for studying or examining the unprotected aspects of a copyrighted computer program, disassembly for purposes of such study or examination constitutes a fair use....

In determining that Accolade's disassembly of Sega's object code did not constitute a fair use, the district court treated the first and fourth statutory factors as dispositive, and ignored the second factor entirely. Given the nature and characteristics of Accolade's direct use of the copied works, the ultimate use to which Accolade put the functional information it obtained, and the nature of the market for home video entertainment systems, we conclude that neither the first nor the fourth factor weighs in Sega's favor. In fact, we conclude that both factors support Accolade's fair use defense, as does the second factor, a factor which is important to the resolution of cases such as the one before us.

(a)

With respect to the first statutory factor, we observe initially that the fact that copying is for a commercial purpose weighs against a finding of fair use. *Harper & Row*, 471 U.S. at 562. However, the presumption of unfairness that arises in such cases can be rebutted by the characteristics of a particular commercial use....

Sega argues that because Accolade copied its object code in order to produce a competing product, the *Harper & Row* presumption applies and precludes a finding of fair use. That analysis is far too simple and ignores a number of important considerations. We must consider other aspects of "the purpose and character of the use" as well. As we have noted, the use at issue was an intermediate one only and thus any commercial "exploitation" was indirect or derivative.

The declarations of Accolade's employees indicate, and the district court found, that Accolade copied Sega's software solely in order to discover the functional requirements for compatibility with the Genesis console—aspects of Sega's programs that are not protected by copyright. 17 U.S.C. § 102(b). With respect to the video game programs contained in Accolade's game cartridges, there is no evidence in the record that Accolade sought to avoid performing its own creative work. Indeed, most of the games that Accolade released for use with the Genesis console were originally developed for other hardware systems. Moreover, with respect to the interface procedures for the Genesis console, Accolade did not seek to avoid paying a customarily charged fee for use of those procedures, nor did it simply copy Sega's code; rather, it wrote its own procedures based on what it had learned through disassembly. Taken together, these facts indicate that although Accolade's ultimate purpose was the release of Genesis-compatible games for sale, its direct purpose in copying Sega's code, and thus its direct use of the copyrighted material, was simply to study the functional requirements for Genesis compatibility so that it could modify existing games and make them usable with the Genesis console. Moreover, as we discuss below, no other method of studying those requirements was available to Accolade. On these facts, we conclude that Accolade copied Sega's code for a legitimate, essentially non-exploitative purpose, and that the commercial aspect of its use can best be described as of minimal significance.

We further note that we are free to consider the public benefit resulting from a particular use notwithstanding the fact that the alleged infringer may gain commercially. *See Hustler,* 796 F.2d at 1153 (quoting *MCA, Inc. v. Wilson,* 677 F.2d 180, 182 (2d Cir.1981)). Public benefit need not be direct or tangible, but may arise because the challenged use serves a public interest. *Id.* In the case before us, Accolade's identification of the functional requirements for Genesis compatibility has led to an increase in the number of independently designed video game programs offered for use with the Genesis console. It is precisely this growth in creative expression, based on the dissemination of other creative works and the unprotected ideas contained in those works, that the Copyright Act was intended to promote. *See Feist Publications, Inc. v. Rural Tel. Serv. Co.,* 499 U.S. 340 (1991) (citing *Harper & Row,* 471 U.S. at 556–57). The fact that Genesis-compatible video games are not scholarly works, but works offered for sale on the market, does not alter our judgment in this regard. We conclude that given the purpose and character of Accolade's use of Sega's video game programs, the presumption of unfairness has been overcome and the first statutory factor weighs in favor of Accolade.

(b)

As applied, the fourth statutory factor, effect on the potential market for the copyrighted work, bears a close relationship to the "purpose and character" inquiry in that it, too, accommodates the distinction between the copying of works in order to make independent creative expression possible and the simple exploitation of another's creative efforts. . . .

Unlike the defendant in *Harper & Row,* which printed excerpts from President Ford's memoirs verbatim with the stated purpose of "scooping" a Time magazine review of the book, 471 U.S. at 562, Accolade did not attempt to "scoop" Sega's release of any particular game or games, but sought only to become a legitimate competitor in the field of Genesis-compatible video games. Within that market, it is the characteristics of the game program as experienced by the user that determine the program's commercial success. As we have noted, there is nothing in the record that suggests that Accolade copied any of those elements.

By facilitating the entry of a new competitor, the first lawful one that is not a Sega licensee, Accolade's disassembly of Sega's software undoubtedly "affected" the market for Genesis-compatible games in an indirect fashion. We note, however, that while no consumer except the most avid devotee of President Ford's regime might be expected to buy more than one version of the President's memoirs, video game users typically purchase more than one game. There is no basis for assuming that Accolade's "Ishido" has significantly affected the market for Sega's "Altered Beast," since a consumer might easily purchase both; nor does it seem unlikely that a consumer particularly interested in sports might purchase both Accolade's "Mike Ditka Power Football" and Sega's "Joe Montana Football," particularly if the games are, as Accolade contends, not substantially similar. In any event, an attempt to monopolize the market by making it impossible for others to compete runs counter to the statutory purpose of promoting creative expression and cannot constitute a strong equitable basis for resisting the invocation of the fair use doctrine. Thus, we conclude that the fourth statutory factor weighs in Accolade's, not Sega's, favor, notwithstanding the minor economic loss Sega may suffer.

(c)

The second statutory factor, the nature of the copyrighted work, reflects the fact that not all copyrighted works are entitled to the same level of protection. The protection established by the Copyright Act for original works of authorship does not extend to the ideas underlying a work or to the functional or factual aspects of the work. 17 U.S.C. § 102(b). To the extent that a work is functional or factual, it may be copied, *Baker v. Selden,* 101 U.S. 99, 102–04 (1879), as may those expressive elements of the work that "must necessarily be used as incident to" expression of the underlying ideas, functional concepts, or facts, *id.* at 104. Works of fiction receive greater protection than works that have strong factual elements, such as historical or biographical works, *Maxtone-Graham,* 803 F.2d at 1263 (citing *Rosemont Enterprises, Inc. v. Random House, Inc.,* 366 F.2d 303, 307 (2d Cir.1966), *cert. denied,* 385 U.S. 1009 (1967)), or works that have strong functional elements, such as accounting textbooks, *Baker,* 101 U.S. at 104. Works that are merely compilations of fact are copyrightable, but the copyright in such a work is "thin." *Feist Publications,* 111 S. Ct. at 1289.

Computer programs pose unique problems for the application of the "idea/expression distinction" that determines the extent of copyright protection. To the extent that there are many possible ways of accomplishing a given task or fulfilling a particular market demand, the programmer's choice of program structure and design may be highly creative and idiosyncratic. However, computer programs are, in essence, utilitarian articles—articles that accomplish tasks. As such, they contain many logical, structural, and visual display elements that are dictated by the function to be performed, by considerations of efficiency, or by external factors such as compatibility requirements and industry demands. . . .

. . .

Sega argues that even if many elements of its video game programs are properly characterized as functional and therefore not protected by copyright, Accolade copied protected expression. Sega is correct. The record makes clear that disassembly is wholesale copying. Because computer programs are also unique among copyrighted works in the form in which they are distributed for public use, however, Sega's observation does not bring us much closer to a resolution of the dispute.

The unprotected aspects of most functional works are readily accessible to the human eye. The systems described in accounting textbooks or the basic structural concepts embodied in architectural plans, to give two examples, can be easily copied without also copying any of the protected, expressive aspects of the original works. Computer programs, however, are typically distributed for public use in object code form, embedded in a silicon chip or on a floppy disk. For that reason, humans often cannot gain access to the unprotected ideas and functional concepts contained in object code without disassembling that code—i.e., making copies. *Atari Games Corp. v. Nintendo of America,* 975 F.2d 832 (Fed.Cir.1992).

. . .

[T]he record clearly establishes that humans cannot read object code. Sega makes much of Mike Lorenzen's statement that a reverse engineer can work directly from the zeros and ones of object code but "it's not as fun." In full, Lorenzen's statements establish only that the use of an electronic decompiler is not absolutely necessary. Trained programmers can disassemble object code by hand. Because even a trained programmer cannot possibly remember the millions of zeros and ones that make up a program, however, he must make a written or computerized copy of the disassembled code in order to keep track of his work. See generally Johnson–Laird, *Technical Demonstration of "Decompilation,"* reprinted in Reverse Engineering: Legal and Business Strategies for Competitive Design in the 1990's 102 (Prentice Hall Law & Business ed. 1992). The relevant fact for purposes of Sega's copyright infringement claim and Accolade's fair use defense is that translation of a program from object code into source code cannot be accomplished without making copies of the code. . . .

. . . Those facts dictate our analysis of the second statutory fair use factor. If disassembly of copyrighted object code is per se an unfair use, the

owner of the copyright gains a de facto monopoly over the functional aspects of his work—aspects that were expressly denied copyright protection by Congress. 17 U.S.C. § 102(b). In order to enjoy a lawful monopoly over the idea or functional principle underlying a work, the creator of the work must satisfy the more stringent standards imposed by the patent laws. *Bonito Boats, Inc. v. Thunder Craft Boats, Inc.*, 489 U.S. 141, 159–64, 103 L. Ed. 2d 118, 109 S. Ct. 971 (1989). Sega does not hold a patent on the Genesis console.

Because Sega's video game programs contain unprotected aspects that cannot be examined without copying, we afford them a lower degree of protection than more traditional literary works. See *CAI*, 23 U.S.P.Q.2d at 1257. In light of all the considerations discussed above, we conclude that the second statutory factor also weighs in favor of Accolade.

(d)

As to the third statutory factor, Accolade disassembled entire programs written by Sega. Accordingly, the third factor weighs against Accolade. The fact that an entire work was copied does not, however, preclude a finding [of] fair use. *Sony Corp.*, 464 U.S. at 449–50; *Hustler*, 795 F.2d at 1155 ("*Sony Corp.* teaches us that the copying of an entire work does not preclude fair use per se."). In fact, where the ultimate (as opposed to direct) use is as limited as it was here, the factor is of very little weight. Cf. *Wright v. Warner Books, Inc.*, 953 F.2d 731, 738 (2d Cir.1991).

(e)

In summary, careful analysis of the purpose and characteristics of Accolade's use of Sega's video game programs, the nature of the computer programs involved, and the nature of the market for video game cartridges yields the conclusion that the first, second, and fourth statutory fair use factors weigh in favor of Accolade, while only the third weighs in favor of Sega, and even then only slightly. Accordingly, Accolade clearly has by far the better case on the fair use issue.

We are not unaware of the fact that to those used to considering copyright issues in more traditional contexts, our result may seem incongruous at first blush. To oversimplify, the record establishes that Accolade, a commercial competitor of Sega, engaged in wholesale copying of Sega's copyrighted code as a preliminary step in the development of a competing product. However, the key to this case is that we are dealing with computer software, a relatively unexplored area in the world of copyright law....

In determining whether a challenged use of copyrighted material is fair, a court must keep in mind the public policy underlying the Copyright Act.... [T]he fact that computer programs are distributed for public use in object code form often precludes public access to the ideas and functional concepts contained in those programs, and thus confers on the copyright owner a de facto monopoly over those ideas and functional concepts. That result defeats the fundamental purpose of the Copyright Act—to encourage the production of original works by protecting the expressive elements of those works while leaving the ideas, facts, and functional concepts in the public domain for others to build on. *Feist Publications,* 111 S. Ct. at 1290; see also *Atari Games Corp.,* slip op. at 18–20....

(f)

We conclude that where disassembly is the only way to gain access to the ideas and functional elements embodied in a copyrighted computer program and where there is a legitimate reason for seeking such access, disassembly is a fair use of the copyrighted work, as a matter of law....

. . .

QUESTIONS

1. Can one fairly extract from the court's opinion in *Sega* a principle that "intermediate copying" of a copyrighted work will be strongly favored under fair use analysis when such copying is necessary (useful? convenient?) to extract unprotectable material from the copyrighted work, such as its ideas, facts, processes, etc.?

2. For example, can *Sega* be properly invoked by a scholar who, in preparing a concordance of all of the novels written by a twentieth century novelist, has the full text of those novels scanned into the memory bank of a computer, thus technically making a "reproduction" in the form of a copy? Can the R & D department of a for-profit petrochemical company properly invoke *Sega* to justify photocopying of individual journal articles for its researchers, because original journal issues cannot be safely taken into the laboratory (with exposure to chemicals), where the researchers wish to make use of the intricate mathematical formulas set forth by the journal authors?

———

Sega v. Accolade concerned reverse engineering of the hardware console's operating system by a software producer who sought to sell computer games that would be compatible with the console. The reverse engineering yielded a product that did not compete with the reverse-engineered work, although it did compete with other works produced by the console-maker. Is the fair use analysis any different when an entrepreneur reverse engineers the console's operating system in order to create a rival console? In such a situation, the work produced by reverse engineering substitutes for the reverse-engineered work. Should that matter?

In **Sony Computer Ent., Inc. v. Connectix Corp.,** 203 F.3d 596 (9th Cir.2000), the Court of Appeals for the Ninth Circuit applied the analysis in its *Sega*; decision to uphold the fair use defense of a manufacturer that reverse engineered Sony's PlayStation operating system [basic input-output system, or BIOS], from a console designed to receive a compact-disc game for display on a television monitor; the defendant manufacturer Connectix thereby created the "Virtual Game Station," a program that would enable users to play Sony PlayStation games on their computer (by inserting the Sony game CD into the computer's CD–ROM drive).

Excerpts from the court's discussion of the first and fourth fair use factors follow:

[1.]   Purpose and character of the use

Under the first factor, purpose and character of the use, we inquire into whether Connectix's Virtual Game Station merely supersedes the objects of the original creation, or instead adds something new, with a further purpose or different character, altering the first with new expression, meaning, or message; it asks, in other words, whether and to what extent the new work is "transformative." ...

We find that Connectix's Virtual Game Station is modestly transformative. The product creates a new platform, the personal computer, on which consumers can play games designed for the Sony PlayStation. This innovation affords opportunities for game play in new environments, specifically anywhere a Sony PlayStation console and television are not available, but a computer with a CD–ROM drive is. More important, the Virtual Game Station itself is a wholly new product, notwithstanding the similarity of uses and functions between the Sony PlayStation and the Virtual Game Station. The expressive element of software lies as much in the organization and structure of the object code that runs the computer as it does in the visual expression of that code that appears on a computer screen. *See* 17 U.S.C. § 102(a) (extending copyright protection to original works of authorship that "can be perceived, reproduced, or otherwise communicated, either directly or with the aid of a machine or device"). Sony does not claim that the Virtual Game Station itself contains object code that infringes Sony's copyright. We are therefore at a loss to see how Connectix's drafting of entirely new object code for its VGS program could not be transformative, despite the similarities in function and screen output.

Finally, we must weigh the extent of any transformation in Connectix's Virtual Game Station against the significance of other factors, including commercialism, that militate against fair use. Connectix's commercial use of the copyrighted material was an intermediate one, and thus was only "indirect or derivative." Moreover, Connectix reverse-engineered the Sony BIOS to produce a product that would be compatible with games designed for the Sony PlayStation. We have recognized this purpose as a legitimate one under the first factor of the fair use analysis.... Upon weighing these factors, we find that the first factor favors Connectix.

The district court ruled, however, that the Virtual Game Station was not transformative on the rationale that a computer screen and a television screen are interchangeable, and the Connectix product therefore merely "supplants" the Sony PlayStation console. Order at 15. The district court clearly erred. For the reasons stated above, the

Virtual Game Station is transformative and does not merely supplant the PlayStation console. In reaching its decision, the district court apparently failed to consider the expressive nature of the Virtual Game Station software itself. Sony's reliance on Infinity Broadcast Corp. v. Kirkwood, 150 F.3d 104 (2d Cir.1998), suffers from the same defect. The *Infinity* court reasoned that a "change of format, though useful, is not technically a transformation." But the infringing party in that case was merely taking copyrighted radio transmissions and retransmitting them over telephone lines; there was no new expression. *Id.* at 108. *Infinity* does not change our conclusion; the purpose and character of Connectix's copying points toward fair use.

4. Effect of the use upon the potential market

We also find that the fourth factor, effect of the use upon the potential market, favors Connectix. Under this factor, we consider not only the extent of market harm caused by the particular actions of the alleged infringer, but also "whether unrestricted and widespread conduct of the sort engaged in by the defendant would result in a substantially adverse impact on the potential market" for the original. Whereas a work that merely supplants or supersedes another is likely to cause a substantially adverse impact on the potential market of the original, a transformative work is less likely to do so.

The district court found that "to the extent that such a substitution [of Connectix's Virtual Game Station for Sony PlayStation console] occurs, Sony will lose console sales and profits." Order at 19. We recognize that this may be so. But because the Virtual Game Station is transformative, and does not merely supplant the PlayStation console, the Virtual Game Station is a legitimate competitor in the market for platforms on which Sony and Sony-licensed games can be played. For this reason, some economic loss by Sony as a result of this competition does not compel a finding of no fair use. Sony understandably seeks control over the market for devices that play games Sony produces or licenses. The copyright law, however, does not confer such a monopoly.... This factor favors Connectix....

We reverse the district court's grant of a preliminary injunction on the ground of copyright.[11]

---

11. We do not accept Sony's argument that the downloading of Sony's BIOS from the Internet was itself an infringement justifying the injunction. The evidence of record suggests that the downloaded BIOS played a minimal role, if any, in development of the Virtual Game Station. We conclude that, on this record, the downloading infringement, if such it was, would not justify our upholding the injunction on the development and sale of the Virtual Game Station. The Virtual Game Station itself infringes no copyright. Bearing in mind the goals of the copyright law, "to stimulate artistic creativity for the general public good," we conclude that there is a legitimate public interest in the publication of Connectix's software, and that this interest is not overborne by the record evidence related to the downloaded BIOS. The imposition of an injunction is discretionary. See 17 U.S.C. § 502(a). On this record, we conclude that it would be inappropriate to uphold the injunction because of Connectix's copying and use of the downloaded Sony BIOS; damages would adequately protect Sony's interest with respect to that alleged infringement. *See*

Assuming that reverse engineering of the *Connectix* kind is fair use, is it also fair use to copy from a protected videogame in order to demonstrate how the game appears on the computer screen when played? In **Sony Computer Ent. America, Inc. v. Bleem**, 214 F.3d 1022 (9th Cir.2000), Bleem, like Connectix, produced a "software emulator" that allowed PlayStation games to be played on a personal computer. Advertisements for the Bleem product showed fixed-image "screen shots" of PlayStation games as played on a television screen, through the PlayStation console, and as played on a personal computer screen, through the emulator. The comparison revealed the higher graphic resolution of the computer screen. The district court held that Bleem had copied Sony's protected work, the images from Sony's games, for commercial purposes, and rejected the fair use defense.

The Court of Appeals for the Ninth Circuit reversed. The court held that the purpose of the copying, for comparative advertising, was favored under the fair use doctrine:

> [B]y seeing how the games' graphics look on a television when played on a console as compared to how they look on a computer screen when played with Bleem's emulator, consumers will be most able to make "rational purchase decisions." Sony argues that Bleem can advertise without the screen shots, which is certainly true, but no other way will allow for the clearest consumer decisionmaking. Indeed, Bleem's advertising in this fashion will almost certainly lead to product improvements as Sony responds to this competitive threat and as other emulator producers strive for even better performance.

> The first factor, considered in light of the animating principles of the copyright regime, weighs in Bleem's favor. Although Bleem is most certainly copying Sony's copyrighted material for the commercial purposes of increasing its own sales, such comparative advertising redounds greatly to the purchasing public's benefit with very little corresponding loss to the integrity of Sony's copyrighted material.

The court found that the second factor favored neither party. The third factor "will almost always weigh against the video game manufacturer since a screen shot is such an insignificant portion of the complex copyrighted work as a whole." The court's discussion of the fourth factor addressed the question of the relevant "market" when the copied work is not itself the object of competition:

> The first question in this appeal is what precisely the market is. The market cannot be the video games themselves because it is the emulator that competes in that niche, not the screen shots that adorn the emulator's advertising. We have already ruled that the emulator is not a violation of the copyright laws. See Connectix, 203 F.3d at 607. Sony argues that the market is in the screen shots themselves: Bleem's use of the screen shots impinges upon Sony's ability to use the screen

Acuff–Rose, 510 U.S. at 578 n.10 (discussing factors to be evaluated in deciding whether to enjoin product found to have exceeded bounds of fair use).

shots for promotional purposes in the market. Bleem responds by contending that there is no market in screen shots. Certainly screen shots are a standard device used in the industry to demonstrate video game graphics, but there is not a market for them, or at least not one in which Bleem may participate given Sony's refusal to license to it.

Assuming there is a market for screen shots, however, this factor still weighs in Bleem's favor, not because Bleem does not compete with Sony, as it contends, but because & hellip; this sort of use does not sufficiently impair Sony.... Bleem's use of a handful of screen shots in its advertising will have no noticeable effect on Sony's ability to do with its screen shots what it chooses. If sales of Sony consoles drop, it will be due to the Bleem emulator's technical superiority over the PlayStation console, not because Bleem used screen shots to illustrate that comparison. This fourth factor, like all the others, appears to weigh in Bleem's favor.

C.   THE APPLICATION OF THE FAIR USE DOCTRINE TO NEW TECHNOLOGIES OF COPYING AND DISSEMINATION

Sony Corp. of America v. Universal City Studios, Inc.

464 U.S. 417 (1984).

■ JUSTICE STEVENS delivered the opinion of the Court.

[Plaintiff-respondents own the copyrights on certain publicly broadcast television programs. The principal defendant-petitioner was Sony Corp., manufacturer of the Betamax video tape recorder (VTR), and other defendants were Sony's advertising agency, retail distributors of the Betamax, and a home user. Plaintiffs alleged that home videotaping of their programs constituted an infringement of copyright, and that Sony was liable as a contributory infringer. Plaintiffs sought damages and profits, as well as an injunction against the manufacture and marketing of the Betamax VTR. The record showed that the principal use of the VTR is for "time shifting," i.e. the recording of a program that the VTR owner cannot view as it is being televised and the watching of the taped program at a later time (followed by the erasing of the program). The district court found that time shifting was a fair use of the plaintiffs' copyrighted programs and that Sony was not liable as a contributory infringer. The court of appeals disagreed on both issues. A divided (5–4) Supreme Court reversed the decision of the court of appeals.

[After analyzing the pertinent law regarding contributory infringement (*see* Chapter 8.F, *infra*), the Court concluded that "the sale of copying equipment, like the sale of other articles of commerce, does not constitute contributory infringement if the product is widely used for legitimate, unobjectionable purposes. Indeed, it need merely be capable of substantial noninfringing uses." The Court concluded that there was a substantial number of television-program copyright owners (particularly of sports, religious, and educational programs) who have no objection to the video-tape recording (and then erasure) of their programs for time-shifting purposes. It then turned to the question whether the unauthorized home taping of programs owned by persons such as the plaintiffs constituted fair use, for if it did then the manufacture of the Betamax VTR could not be deemed contributory copyright infringement. The Court began its analysis by considering § 107.]

That section identifies various factors that enable a Court to apply an "equitable rule of reason" analysis to particular claims of infringement. Although not conclusive, the first factor requires that "the commercial or nonprofit character of an activity" be weighed in any fair use decision. If the Betamax were used to make copies for a commercial or profit-making purpose, such use would presumptively be unfair. The contrary presumption is appropriate here, however, because the District Court's findings plainly establish that time-shifting for private home use must be characterized as a noncommercial, nonprofit activity. Moreover, when one considers the nature of a televised copyrighted audiovisual work, see 17 U.S.C. § 107(2), and that time-shifting merely enables a viewer to see such a work which he had been invited to witness in its entirety free of charge, the fact that the entire work is reproduced, see *id.*, at § 107(3), does not have its ordinary effect of militating against a finding of fair use.

This is not, however, the end of the inquiry because Congress has also directed us to consider "the effect of the use upon the potential market for or value of the copyrighted work." *Id.*, at § 107(4). The purpose of copyright is to create incentives for creative effort. Even copying for noncommercial purposes may impair the copyright holder's ability to obtain the rewards that Congress intended him to have. But a use that has no demonstrable effect upon the potential market for, or the value of, the copyrighted work need not be prohibited in order to protect the author's incentive to create. The prohibition of such noncommercial uses would merely inhibit access to ideas without any countervailing benefit.

Thus, although every commercial use of copyrighted material is presumptively an unfair exploitation of the monopoly privilege that belongs to the owner of the copyright, noncommercial uses are a different matter. A challenge to a noncommercial use of a copyrighted work requires proof either that the particular use is harmful, or that if it should become widespread, it would adversely affect the potential market for the copyrighted work. Actual present harm need not be shown; such a requirement would leave the copyright holder with no defense against predictable damage. Nor is it necessary to show with certainty that future harm will result. What is necessary is a showing by a preponderance of the evidence that *some* meaningful likelihood of future harm exists. If the intended use is for commercial gain, that likelihood may be presumed. But if it is for a noncommercial purpose, the likelihood must be demonstrated.

In this case, respondents failed to carry their burden with regard to home time-shifting. . . .

There was no need for the District Court to say much about past harm. "Plaintiffs have admitted that no actual harm to their copyrights has occurred to date." [480 F. Supp.], at 451.

On the question of potential future harm from time-shifting, the District Court offered a more detailed analysis of the evidence. It rejected respondents' "fear that persons 'watching' the original telecast of a program will not be measured in the live audience and the ratings and revenues will decrease," by observing that current measurement technology allows the Betamax audience to be reflected. *Id.*, at 466.[36] It rejected respondents' prediction "that live television or movie audiences will decrease as more people watch Betamax tapes as an alternative," with the observation that "[t]here is no factual basis for [the underlying] assumption." *Ibid.* It rejected respondents' "fear that time-shifting will reduce audiences for telecast reruns," and concluded instead that "given current market practices, this should aid plaintiffs rather than harm them." *Ibid.* And it declared that respondents' suggestion "that theater or film rental exhibition of a program will suffer because of time-shift recording of that program" "lacks merit." 480 F. Supp., at 467.[39]

After completing that review, the District Court restated its overall conclusion several times, in several different ways. "Harm from time-shifting is speculative and, at best, minimal." *Ibid.* "The audience benefits from the time-shifting capability have already been discussed. It is not implausible that benefits could also accrue to plaintiffs, broadcasters, and advertisers, as the Betamax makes it possible for more persons to view their broadcasts." *Ibid.* "No likelihood of harm was shown at trial, and plaintiffs admitted that there had been no actual harm to date."

---

36. "There was testimony at trial, however, that Nielsen Ratings has already developed the ability to measure when a Betamax in a sample home is recording the program. Thus, the Betamax will be measured as a part of the live audience. The later diary can augment that measurement with information about subsequent viewing." 480 F. Supp., at 466.

In a separate section, the District Court rejected plaintiffs' suggestion that the commercial attractiveness of television broadcasts would be diminished because Betamax owners would use the pause button or fast-forward control to avoid viewing advertisements: "It must be remembered, however, that to omit commercials, Betamax owners must view the program, including the commercials, while recording. To avoid commercials during playback, the viewer must fast-forward and, for the most part, guess as to when the commercial has passed. For most recordings, either practice may be too tedious. As defendants' survey showed, 92% of the programs were recorded with commercials and only 25% of the owners fast-forward through them. Advertisers will have to make the same kinds of judgments they do now about whether persons viewing televised programs actually watch the advertisements which interrupt them." *Id.*, at 468.

39. "This suggestion lacks merit. By definition, time-shift recording entails viewing and erasing, so the program will no longer be on tape when the later theater run begins. Of course, plaintiffs may fear that the Betamax will keep the tapes long enough to satisfy all their interest in the program and will, therefore, not patronize later theater exhibitions. To the extent this practice involves librarying, it is addressed in section V.C., *infra*. It should also be noted that there is no evidence to suggest that the public interest in later theatrical exhibitions of motion pictures will be reduced any more by Betamax recording than it already is by the television broadcast of the film." 480 F. Supp., at 467.

The District Court's conclusions are buttressed by the fact that to the extent time-shifting expands public access to freely broadcast television programs, it yields societal benefits. . . .

When these factors are all weighed in the "equitable rule of reason" balance, we must conclude that this record amply supports the District Court's conclusion that home time-shifting is fair use. In light of the findings of the District Court regarding the state of the empirical data, it is clear that the Court of Appeals erred in holding that the statute as presently written bars such conduct.[40]

. . .

■ JUSTICE BLACKMUN, with whom JUSTICE MARSHALL, JUSTICE POWELL, and JUSTICE REHNQUIST join, dissenting.

. . .

There are situations . . . in which strict enforcement of [the copyright] monopoly would inhibit the very "Progress of Science and useful Arts" that copyright is intended to promote. An obvious example is the researcher or scholar whose own work depends on the ability to refer to and to quote the work of prior scholars. Obviously, no author could create a new work if he were first required to repeat the research of every author who had gone

40. The Court of Appeals chose not to engage in any "equitable rule of reason" analysis in this case. Instead, it assumed that the category of "fair use" is rigidly circumscribed by a requirement that every such use must be "productive." It therefore concluded that copying a television program merely to enable the viewer to receive information or entertainment that he would otherwise miss because of a personal scheduling conflict could never be fair use. That understanding of "fair use" was erroneous.

Congress has plainly instructed us that fair use analysis calls for a sensitive balancing of interests. The distinction between "productive" and "unproductive" uses may be helpful in calibrating the balance, but it cannot be wholly determinative. Although copying to promote a scholarly endeavor certainly has a stronger claim to fair use than copying to avoid interrupting a poker game, the question is not simply two-dimensional. For one thing, it is not true that all copyrights are fungible. Some copyrights govern material with broad potential secondary markets. Such material may well have a broader claim to protection because of the greater potential for commercial harm. Copying a news broadcast may have a stronger claim to fair use than copying a motion picture. And, of course, not all uses are fungible. Copying

for commercial gain has a much weaker claim to fair use than copying for personal enrichment. But the notion of social "productivity" cannot be a complete answer to this analysis. A teacher who copies to prepare lecture notes is clearly productive. But so is a teacher who copies for the sake of broadening his personal understanding of his specialty. Or a legislator who copies for the sake of broadening her understanding of what her constituents are watching; or a constituent who copies a news program to help make a decision on how to vote.

Making a copy of a copyrighted work for the convenience of a blind person is expressly identified by the House Committee Report as an example of fair use, with no suggestion that anything more than a purpose to entertain or to inform need motivate the copying. In a hospital setting, using a VTR to enable a patient to see programs he would otherwise miss has no productive purpose other than contributing to the psychological well-being of the patient. Virtually any time-shifting that increases viewer access to television programming may result in a comparable benefit. The statutory language does not identify any dichotomy between productive and nonproductive time-shifting, but does require consideration of the economic consequences of copying.

before him. The scholar, like the ordinary user, of course could be left to bargain with each copyright owner for permission to quote from or refer to prior works. But there is a crucial difference between the scholar and the ordinary user. When the ordinary user decides that the owner's price is too high, and forgoes use of the work, only the individual is the loser. When the scholar forgoes the use of a prior work, not only does his own work suffer, but the public is deprived of his contribution to knowledge. The scholar's work, in other words, produces external benefits from which everyone profits. In such a case, the fair use doctrine acts as a form of subsidy—albeit at the first author's expense—to permit the second author to make limited use of the first author's work for the public good. See Latman, Fair Use Study 31; Gordon, *Fair Use as Market Failure: A Structural Analysis of the Betamax Case and Its Predecessors,* 82 Colum. L. Rev. 1600, 1630 (1982).

A similar subsidy may be appropriate in a range of areas other than pure scholarship. The situations in which fair use is most commonly recognized are listed in § 107 itself; fair use may be found when a work is used "for purposes such as criticism, comment, news reporting, teaching, ... scholarship, or research." The House and Senate Reports expand on this list somewhat, and other examples may be found in the case law. Each of these uses, however, reflects a common theme: each is a *productive* use, resulting in some added benefit to the public beyond that produced by the first author's work.

The fair use doctrine, in other words, permits works to be used for "socially laudable purposes." See Copyright Office, Briefing Papers on Current Issues, reprinted in 1975 House Hearings 2051, 2055. I am aware of no case in which the reproduction of a copyrighted work for the sole benefit of the user has been held to be fair use.

I do not suggest, of course, that every productive use is a fair use.... But when a user reproduces an entire work and uses it for its original purpose, with no added benefit to the public, the doctrine of fair use usually does not apply. There is then no need whatsoever to provide the ordinary user with a fair use subsidy at the author's expense.

. . .

Courts should move with caution ... in depriving authors of protection from unproductive "ordinary" uses. As has been noted above, even in the case of a productive use, § 107(4) requires consideration of "the effect of the use upon the *potential* market for or value of the copyrighted work" (emphasis added). "[A] particular use which may seem to have little or no economic impact on the author's rights today can assume tremendous importance in times to come." Register's Supplementary Report 14. Although such a use may seem harmless when viewed in isolation, "[i]solated instances of minor infringements, when multiplied many times, become in the aggregate a major inroad on copyright that must be prevented." 1975 Senate Report 65.

I therefore conclude that, at least when the proposed use is an unproductive one, a copyright owner need prove only a *potential* for harm to the market for or the value of the copyrighted work. . . .

The Studios have identified a number of ways in which VTR recording could damage their copyrights. VTR recording could reduce their ability to market their works in movie theaters and through the rental or sale of pre-recorded videotapes or videodiscs; it also could reduce their rerun audience, and consequently the license fees available to them for repeated showings. Moreover, advertisers may be willing to pay for only "live" viewing audiences, if they believe VTR viewers will delete commercials or if rating services are unable to measure VTR use; if this is the case, VTR recording could reduce the license fees the Studios are able to charge even for first-run showings. Library-building [i.e., taping copyrighted television programs for indefinite retention and repeated viewings] may raise the potential for each of the types of harm identified by the Studios, and time-shifting may raise the potential for substantial harm as well.

. . .

The District Court's reluctance to engage in prediction in this area is understandable, but, in my view, the court was mistaken in concluding that the Studios should bear the risk created by this uncertainty. The Studios have demonstrated a potential for harm, which has not been, and could not be, refuted at this early stage of technological development. . . .

[T]he Court . . . purports to apply to time-shifting the four factors explicitly stated in the statute. The first is "the purpose and character of the use, including whether such use is of a commercial nature or is for nonprofit educational purposes." § 107(1). The Court confidently describes time-shifting as a noncommercial, nonprofit activity. It is clear, however, that personal use of programs that have been copied without permission is not what § 107(1) protects. The intent of the section is to encourage users to engage in activities the primary benefit of which accrues to others. Time-shifting involves no such humanitarian impulse. It is likewise something of a mischaracterization of time-shifting to describe it as noncommercial in the sense that that term is used in the statute. As one commentator has observed, time-shifting is noncommercial in the same sense that stealing jewelry and wearing it—instead of reselling it—is noncommercial. Purely consumptive uses are certainly not what the fair use doctrine was designed to protect, and the awkwardness of applying the statutory language to time-shifting only makes clearer that fair use was designed to protect only uses that are productive.

The next two statutory factors are all but ignored by the Court—though certainly not because they have no applicability. The second factor—"the nature of the copyrighted work"—strongly supports the view that time-shifting is an infringing use. . . . Thus, for example, informational works, such as news reports, that readily lend themselves to productive use by others, are less protected than creative works of entertainment. Sony's own surveys indicate that entertainment shows account for more than 80 percent of the programs recorded by Betamax owners.

The third statutory factor—"the amount and substantiality of the portion used"—is even more devastating to the Court's interpretation. It is undisputed that virtually all VTR owners record entire works, see 480 F. Supp., at 454, thereby creating an exact substitute for the copyrighted original. Fair use is intended to allow individuals engaged in productive uses to copy small portions of original works that will facilitate their own productive endeavors. Time-shifting bears no resemblance to such activity, and the complete duplication that it involves might alone be sufficient to preclude a finding of fair use. It is little wonder that the Court has chosen to ignore this statutory factor.

The fourth factor requires an evaluation of "the effect of the use upon the potential market for or value of the copyrighted work." This is the factor upon which the Court focuses, but once again, the Court has misread the statute. As mentioned above, the statute requires a court to consider the effect of the use on the *potential* market for the copyrighted work. The Court has struggled mightily to show that VTR use has not *reduced* the value of the Studios' copyrighted works in their *present* markets. Even if true, that showing only begins the proper inquiry. The development of the VTR has created a new market for the works produced by the Studios. That market consists of those persons who desire to view television programs at times other than when they are broadcast, and who therefore purchase VTR recorders to enable them to time-shift. Because time-shifting of the Studios' copyrighted works involves the copying of them, however, the Studios are entitled to share in the benefits of that new market. Those benefits currently go to Sony through Betamax sales. Respondents therefore can show harm from VTR use simply by showing that the value of their copyrights would *increase* if they were compensated for the copies that are used in the new market. The existence of this effect is self-evident.

. . .

QUESTIONS

1. Which opinion within the Court do you find the more convincing? Of the two opinions in the "Betamax case," the dissent seems more closely analyzed and fully articulated than does the majority's opinion. We now know, thanks to the release of the late Justice Thurgood Marshall's papers, that the "Betamax" dissent had initially been drafted as the majority opinion. Justice Stevens's opinion had been a dissent, but he succeeded in attracting enough votes to shift the outcome of the case. For a detailed discussion of the evolution of the "Betamax" opinions, see Jonathan Bank & Andrew J. McLaughlin, *The Marshall Papers: A Peek Behind the Scenes at the Making of Sony v. Universal City Studios*, 17 Colum.-VLA J. L. & Arts 427 (1994). *See also* Paul Goldstein, Copyright's Highway: The Law and Lore of Copyright from Gutenberg to the Celestial Jukebox, 149–57 (1994).

2. Compare the majority and dissenting opinions in *Sony* with the court's later opinion in *Campbell v. Acuff–Rose, supra* Subchapter B. How much of the *Sony* majority opinion do you think is still good law? Does it matter whether the controversy concerns copying to create a new work, or copying for convenience or further dissemination?

3. Should "copying for personal enrichment" (*Sony* at n. 40) be a fair use? Is the proposition inconsistent with *Harper & Row*'s statement that "The crux of the profit/nonprofit distinction is not whether the sole motive of the use is monetary gain but whether the user stands to profit from exploitation of the copyrighted material without paying the customary price."? Does the difficulty in enforcing copyright interests against individual, private users play a role in your evaluation of the "fairness" of the use? *Compare American Geophysical Union v. Texaco, Inc.*, and *A & M Records v. Napster, Inc., infra* this chapter.

4. How different would the Court's analysis be if the record showed that a significant proportion of home videotaping was done for the purpose of "librarying" rather than "time shifting"? (What are the proportions in *your* household, or the households of your friends?)

5. If a small college were about to be favorably featured on a television news program, and it asked you for advice about whether it is lawful to make a videotape of the segment of the program and to distribute the short tape to potential applicants, what advice would you give? Would your answer be different if it merely retained a few copies of the videotape in the college admissions office, to show to potential applicants?

Princeton University Press v. Michigan Document Services, Inc.

99 F.3d 1381 (6th Cir.1996) (en banc), *cert. denied*, 520 U.S. 1156 (1997).

■ DAVID A. NELSON, CIRCUIT JUDGE.*

This is a copyright infringement case. The corporate defendant, Michigan Document Services, Inc., is a commercial copyshop that reproduced substantial segments of copyrighted works of scholarship, bound the copies into "coursepacks," and sold the coursepacks to students for use in fulfilling reading assignments given by professors at the University of Michigan. The copyshop acted without permission from the copyright holders, and the main question presented is whether the "fair use" doctrine codified at 17 U.S.C. § 107 obviated the need to obtain such permission.

Answering this question "no," and finding the infringement willful, the district court entered a summary judgment order in which the copyright holders were granted equitable relief and were awarded damages that may have been enhanced for willfulness. *Princeton Univ. Press v. Michigan*

---

* Editor's note: Judge Nelson wrote for eight judges; the dissenting opinion of Judge Merritt was joined by two judges, one of whom also joined the dissenting opinion of Judge Ryan.

Document Servs., Inc., 855 F. Supp. 905 (E.D.Mich.1994). A three-judge panel of this court reversed the judgment on appeal, but a majority of the active judges of the court subsequently voted to rehear the case en banc. The appeal has now been argued before the full court.

We agree with the district court that the defendants' commercial exploitation of the copyrighted materials did not constitute fair use, and we shall affirm that branch of the district court's judgment. We believe that the district court erred in its finding of willfulness, however, and we shall vacate the damages award because of its possible linkage to that finding.

I

Thanks to relatively recent advances in technology, the coursepack—an artifact largely unknown to college students when the author of this opinion was an undergraduate—has become almost as ubiquitous at American colleges and universities as the conventional textbook. From the standpoint of the professor responsible for developing and teaching a particular course, the availability of coursepacks has an obvious advantage; by selecting readings from a variety of sources, the professor can create what amounts to an anthology perfectly tailored to the course the professor wants to present.

The physical production of coursepacks is typically handled by a commercial copyshop. The professor gives the copyshop the materials of which the coursepack is to be made up, and the copyshop does the rest. Adding a cover page and a table of contents, perhaps, the copyshop runs off as many sets as are needed, does the necessary binding, and sells the finished product to the professor's students.

Ann Arbor, the home of the University of Michigan, is also home to several copyshops. Among them is defendant Michigan Document Services (MDS), a corporation owned by defendant James Smith. We are told that MDS differs from most, if not all, of its competitors in at least one important way: it does not request permission from, nor does it pay agreed royalties to, copyright owners. Mr. Smith has been something of a crusader against the system under which his competitors have been paying agreed royalties, or "permission fees" as they are known in the trade. The story begins in March of 1991, when Judge Constance Baker Motley, of the United States District Court for the Southern District of New York, decided the first reported case involving the copyright implications of educational coursepacks. *See Basic Books, Inc. v. Kinko's Graphics Corp.*, 758 F.Supp. 1522 (S.D.N.Y.1991), holding that a Kinko's copyshop had violated the copyright statute by creating and selling coursepacks without permission from the publishing houses that held the copyrights. After *Kinko's*, we are told, many copyshops that had not previously requested permission from copyright holders began to obtain such permission. Mr. Smith chose not to do so. He consulted an attorney, and the attorney apparently advised him that while it was "risky" not to obtain permission, there were flaws in the *Kinko's* decision. Mr. Smith also undertook his own study of the fair use doctrine, reading what he could find on this subject in a law library. He ultimately concluded that the *Kinko's* case had been wrongly decided, and he publicized this conclusion through speeches, writings, and advertisements. His advertisements stressed that professors whose students purchased his coursepacks would not have to worry about delays attendant upon obtaining permission from publishers.

Not surprisingly, Mr. Smith attracted the attention of the publishing industry. Three publishers—Princeton University Press, Macmillan, Inc., and St. Martin's Press, Inc.—eventually brought the present suit against Mr. Smith and his corporation.

Each of the plaintiff publishers maintains a department that processes requests for permission to reproduce portions of copyrighted works. (In addition, copyshops may request such permission through the Copyright Clearance Center, a national clearinghouse.) Macmillan and St. Martin's, both of which are for-profit companies, claim that they generally respond within two weeks to requests for permission to make copies for classroom use. Princeton, a non-profit organization, claims to respond within two to four weeks. Mr. Smith has not put these claims to the test, and he has not paid permission fees.

The plaintiffs allege infringement of the copyrights on six different works that were excerpted without permission. The works in question, and the statistics on the magnitude of the excerpts, are as follows: Nancy J. Weiss, Farewell to the Party of Lincoln: Black Politics in the Age of FDR (95 pages copied, representing 30 percent of the entire book); Walter Lippmann, Public Opinion (45 pages copied, representing 18 percent of the whole); Robert E. Layne, Political Ideology: Why the American Common Man Believes What He Does (78 pages, 16 percent); Roger Brown, Social Psychology (52 pages, 8 percent); Milton Rokeach, The Nature of Human Values (77 pages, 18 percent); James S. Olson and Randy Roberts, Where the Domino Fell, America and Vietnam, 1945–1950 (17 pages, 5 percent). The extent of the copying is undisputed, and the questions presented by the case appear to be purely legal in nature.

II

The fair use doctrine, which creates an exception to the copyright monopoly, "permits [and requires] courts to avoid rigid application of the copyright statute when, on occasion, it would stifle the very creativity which that law is designed to foster." *Campbell v. Acuff–Rose Music, Inc.*, 510 U.S. 569, 577 (1994), quoting *Stewart v. Abend*, 495 U.S. 207, 236. Initially developed by the courts, the doctrine was codified at 17 U.S.C. § 107 in 1976....

This language does not provide blanket immunity for "multiple copies for classroom use." Rather, "whether a use referred to in the first sentence of Section 107 is a fair use in a particular case ... depend[s] upon the application of the determinative factors." *Campbell*, 510 U.S. at 578 n.9, *quoting* S. Rep. No. 94–473, p. 62.[1]

---

1. Judge Merritt's dissent rejects this proposition and asserts, in effect, that under the plain language of the copyright statute the making of multiple copies for classroom

The four statutory factors may not have been created equal. In determining whether a use is "fair," the Supreme Court has said that the most important factor is the fourth, the one contained in 17 U.S.C. § 107(4).... We take it that this factor, "the effect of the use upon the potential market for or value of the copyrighted work," is at least *primus inter pares*, figuratively speaking, and we shall turn to it first.

The burden of proof as to market effect rests with the copyright holder if the challenged use is of a "noncommercial" nature. The alleged infringer has the burden, on the other hand, if the challenged use is "commercial" in nature. *Sony Corp. v. Universal City Studios, Inc.*, 464 U.S. 417, 451 (1984). In the case at bar the defendants argue that the burden of proof rests with the publishers because the use being challenged is "noncommercial." We disagree.

It is true that the use to which the materials are put by the students who purchase the coursepacks is noncommercial in nature. But the use of the materials by the students is not the use that the publishers are challenging. What the publishers are challenging is the duplication of copyrighted materials for sale by a for-profit corporation that has decided to maximize its profits—and give itself a competitive edge over other copyshops—by declining to pay the royalties requested by the holders of the copyrights.[2]

The defendants' use of excerpts from the books at issue here was no less commercial in character than was *The Nation* magazine's use of copyrighted material in *Harper & Row*, where publication of a short article containing excerpts from the still unpublished manuscript of a book by

---

use constitutes fair use *ipso facto*. Judge Merritt's reading of the statute would be unassailable if Congress had said that "the use of a copyrighted work for purposes such as teaching (including multiple copies for classroom use) is not an infringement of copyright." But that is not what Congress said. It said, rather, that "the fair use of a copyrighted work, including such use [i.e., including 'fair use'] ... for purposes such as ... teaching (including multiple copies for classroom use) ... is not an infringement of copyright." When read in its entirety, as Judge Ryan's dissent correctly recognizes, the quoted sentence says that fair use of a copyrighted work for purposes such as teaching (including multiple copies for classroom use) is not an infringement. And the statutory factors set forth in the next sentence must be considered in determining whether the making of multiple copies for classroom use is a fair use in "any particular case," just as the statutory factors must be considered in determining whether any other use referred to in the first

sentence is a fair use in a particular case. To hold otherwise would be to subvert the intent manifested in the words of the statute and confirmed in the pertinent legislative history.

2. Two of the dissents suggest that a copyshop merely stands in the shoes of its customers and makes no "use" of copyrighted materials that differs materially from the use to which the copies are put by the ultimate consumer. But subject to the fair use exception, 17 U.S.C. § 106 gives the copyright owner the "exclusive" right "to reproduce the copyrighted work in copies...." And if the fairness of making copies depends on what the ultimate consumer does with the copies, it is hard to see how the manufacture of pirated editions of any copyrighted work of scholarship could ever be an unfair use. As discussed in Part IIIA, *infra*, the dissenters' suggestion—which proposes no limiting principle—runs counter to the legislative history of the Copyright Act and has properly been rejected by the courts.

President Ford was held to be an unfair use. Like the students who purchased unauthorized coursepacks, the purchasers of *The Nation* did not put the contents of the magazine to commercial use—but that did not stop the Supreme Court from characterizing the defendant's use of the excerpts as "a publication [that] was commercial as opposed to nonprofit...." *Harper & Row*, 471 U.S. at 562. And like the use that is being challenged in the case now before us, the use challenged in *Harper & Row* was "presumptively an unfair exploitation of the monopoly privilege that belongs to the owner of the copyright." *Id., quoting Sony*, 464 U.S. at 451.

The strength of the *Sony* presumption may vary according to the context in which it arises, and the presumption disappears entirely where the challenged use is one that transforms the original work into a new artistic creation. See *Campbell*, 510 U.S. at 587–89. Perhaps the presumption is weaker in the present case than it would be in other contexts. There is a presumption of unfairness here, nonetheless, and we are not persuaded that the defendants have rebutted it.

If we are wrong about the existence of the presumption—if the challenged use is not commercial, in other words, and if the plaintiff publishers have the burden of proving an adverse effect upon either the potential market for the copyrighted work or the potential value of the work—we believe that the publishers have carried the burden of proving a diminution in potential market value.

One test for determining market harm—a test endorsed by the Supreme Court in *Sony, Harper & Row*, and *Campbell*—is evocative of Kant's categorical imperative. "[T]o negate fair use," the Supreme Court has said, "one need only show that *if the challenged use 'should become widespread, it would adversely affect the potential market* for the copyrighted work.'" *Harper & Row*, 471 U.S. at 568, *quoting Sony*, 464 U.S. at 451 (emphasis supplied in part). Under this test, we believe, it is reasonably clear that the plaintiff publishers have succeeded in negating fair use.

As noted above, most of the copyshops that compete with MDS in the sale of coursepacks pay permission fees for the privilege of duplicating and selling excerpts from copyrighted works. The three plaintiffs together have been collecting permission fees at a rate approaching $500,000 a year. If copyshops across the nation were to start doing what the defendants have been doing here, this revenue stream would shrivel and the potential value of the copyrighted works of scholarship published by the plaintiffs would be diminished accordingly.

The defendants contend that it is circular to assume that a copyright holder is entitled to permission fees and then to measure market loss by reference to the lost fees. They argue that market harm can only be measured by lost sales of books, not permission fees. But the circularity argument proves too much. Imagine that the defendants set up a printing press and made exact reproductions—asserting that such reproductions constituted "fair use"—of a book to which they did not hold the copyright. Under the defendants' logic it would be circular for the copyright holder to argue market harm because of lost copyright revenues, since this would assume that the copyright holder had a right to such revenues.

A "circularity" argument indistinguishable from that made by the defendants here was rejected by the Second Circuit in *American Geophysical [Union v. Texaco Inc.]*, 60 F.3d at 929–31 (Jon O. Newman, C.J.), where the photocopying of scientific articles for use by Texaco researchers was held to be an unfair use. It is true, the Second Circuit acknowledged, that "a copyright holder can always assert some degree of adverse [e]ffect on its potential licensing revenues as a consequence of [the defendant's use] . . . simply because the copyright holder has not been paid a fee to permit that particular use." *Id.* at 929 n.17. But such an assertion will not carry much weight if the defendant has "filled a market niche that the [copyright owner] simply had no interest in occupying." *Id.* at 930 (quoting *Twin Peaks Prods., Inc. v. Publications Int'l, Ltd.*, 996 F.2d 1366, 1377 (2d Cir.1993)). Where, on the other hand, the copyright holder clearly does have an interest in exploiting a licensing market—and especially where the copyright holder has actually succeeded in doing so—"it is appropriate that potential licensing revenues for photocopying be considered in a fair use analysis." *American Geophysical*, 60 F.3d at 930. Only "traditional, reasonable, or likely to be developed markets" are to be considered in this connection, and even the availability of an existing system for collecting licensing fees will not be conclusive. *Id.* at 930–31. . . .

The approach followed by Judges Newman and Leval in the *American Geophysical* litigation is fully consistent with the Supreme Court case law. In *Harper & Row*, where there is no indication in the opinion that the challenged use caused any diminution in sales of President Ford's memoirs, the Court found harm to the market for the licensing of excerpts. The Court's reasoning—which was obviously premised on the assumption that the copyright holder was entitled to licensing fees for use of its copyrighted materials—is no more circular than that employed here. And in *Campbell*, where the Court was unwilling to conclude that the plaintiff had lost licensing revenues under the fourth statutory factor, the Court reasoned that a market for critical parody was not one "that creators of original works would in general develop or license others to develop." *Campbell*, 510 U.S. at 592.

The potential uses of the copyrighted works at issue in the case before us clearly include the selling of permission to reproduce portions of the works for inclusion in coursepacks—and the likelihood that publishers actually will license such reproduction is a demonstrated fact. A licensing market already exists here, as it did not in a case on which the plaintiffs [sic] rely, *Williams & Wilkins Co. v. United States*, 487 F.2d 1345 (1973), *aff'd by an equally divided Court*, 420 U.S. 376 (1975). Thus there is no circularity in saying, as we do say, that the potential for destruction of this market by widespread circumvention of the plaintiffs' permission fee system is enough, under the *Harper & Row* test, "to negate fair use."

Our final point with regard to the fourth statutory factor concerns the affidavits of the three professors who assigned one or more of the copyrighted works to be read by their students. The defendants make much of the proposition that these professors only assigned excerpts when they would not have required their students to purchase the entire work. But what seems significant to us is that none of these affidavits shows that the professor executing the affidavit would have refrained from assigning the copyrighted work if the position taken by the copyright holder had been sustained beforehand. . . .

III

In the context of nontransformative uses, at least, and except insofar as they touch on the fourth factor, the other statutory factors seem considerably less important. We shall deal with them relatively briefly.

A

As to "the purpose and character of the use, including whether such use is of a commercial nature or is for nonprofit educational purposes," 17 U.S.C. § 107(1), we have already explained our reasons for concluding that the challenged use is of a commercial nature.

The defendants argue that the copying at issue here would be considered "nonprofit educational" if done by the students or professors themselves. The defendants also note that they can profitably produce multiple copies for less than it would cost the professors or the students to make the same number of copies. Most of the copyshops with which the defendants compete have been paying permission fees, however, and we assume that these shops too can perform the copying on a more cost-effective basis than the professors or students can. This strikes us as a more significant datum than the ability of a black market copyshop to beat the do-it-yourself cost.

As to the proposition that it would be fair use for the students or professors to make their own copies, the issue is by no means free from doubt. We need not decide this question, however, for the fact is that the copying complained of here was performed on a profit-making basis by a commercial enterprise. And "[t]he courts have . . . properly rejected attempts by for-profit users to stand in the shoes of their customers making nonprofit or noncommercial uses." Patry, Fair Use in Copyright Law, at 420 n.34. As the House Judiciary Committee stated in its report on the 1976 legislation, "[I]t would not be possible for a non-profit institution, by means of contractual arrangements with a commercial copying enterprise, to authorize the enterprise to carry out copying and distribution functions that would be exempt if conducted by the non-profit institution itself." H.R. Rep. No. 1476, 94th Cong., 2d Sess. at 74 (1976), U.S. Code Cong. & Admin. News 5659, 5687–88.

It should be noted, finally, that the degree to which the challenged use has transformed the original copyrighted works—another element in the first statutory factor—is virtually indiscernible. If you make verbatim copies of 95 pages of a 316–page book, you have not transformed the 95 pages very much—even if you juxtapose them to excerpts from other works and package everything conveniently. This kind of mechanical "transformation" bears little resemblance to the creative metamorphosis accomplished by the parodists in the *Campbell* case.

B

The second statutory factor, "the nature of the copyrighted work," is not in dispute here. The defendants acknowledge that the excerpts copied for the coursepacks contained creative material, or "expression;" it was certainly not telephone book listings that the defendants were reproducing. This factor too cuts against a finding of fair use.

C

The third statutory factor requires us to assess "the amount and substantiality of the portion used in relation to the copyrighted work as a whole." Generally speaking, at least, "the larger the volume (or the greater the importance) of what is taken, the greater the affront to the interests of the copyright owner, and the less likely that a taking will qualify as a fair use." Pierre N. Leval, *Toward a Fair Use Standard*, 103 Harv. L. Rev. 1105, 1122 (1990).

The amounts used in the case at bar—8,000 words in the shortest excerpt—far exceed the 1,000–word safe harbor that we shall discuss in the next part of this opinion. See H.R. Rep. No. 1476, 94th Cong., 2d Sess. (1976), reprinted after 17 U.S.C.A. § 107. The defendants were using as much as 30 percent of one copyrighted work, and in no case did they use less than 5 percent of the copyrighted work as a whole. These percentages are not insubstantial. And to the extent that the third factor requires some type of assessment of the "value" of the excerpted material in relation to the entire work, the fact that the professors thought the excerpts sufficiently important to make them required reading strikes us as fairly convincing "evidence of the qualitative value of the copied material." *Harper & Row*, 471 U.S. at 565. We have no reason to suppose that in choosing the excerpts to be copied, the professors passed over material that was more representative of the major ideas of the work as a whole in preference to material that was less representative.

The third factor may have more significance for the 95–page excerpt from the black politics book than for the 17–page excerpt from the Vietnam book. In each instance, however, the defendants have failed to carry their burden of proof with respect to "amount and substantiality."

IV

We turn now to the pertinent legislative history. The general revision of the copyright law enacted in 1976 was developed through a somewhat unusual process. Congress and the Register of Copyrights initiated and supervised negotiations among interested groups—groups that included authors, publishers, and educators—over specific legislative language. Most of the language that emerged was enacted into law or was made a part of the committee reports. See Jessica Litman, *Copyright, Compromise, and Legislative History*, 72 Cornell L. Rev. 857 (1987). The statutory fair use provisions are a direct result of this process. *Id.* at 876–77. So too is the "Agreement on Guidelines for Classroom Copying in Not-for-Profit Educational Institutions With Respect to Books and Periodicals"—commonly called the "Classroom Guidelines"—set out in H.R. Rep. No. 1476 at 68–71, 94th Cong., 2d Sess. (1976). The House and Senate conferees explicitly accepted the Classroom Guidelines "as part of their understanding of fair use," H.R. Conf. Rep. No. 1733, 94th Cong. 2d Sess., at 70 (1976), and the Second Circuit has characterized the guidelines as "persuasive authority...." *American Geophysical*, 60 F.3d at 919 n.5, *citing Kinko's*, 758 F. Supp. at 1522–36.

There are strong reasons to consider this legislative history. The statutory factors are not models of clarity, and the fair use issue has long been a particularly troublesome one....

Although the Classroom Guidelines purport to "state the minimum and not the maximum standards of educational fair use," they do evoke a general idea, at least, of the type of educational copying Congress had in mind. The guidelines allow multiple copies for classroom use provided that (1) the copying meets the test of brevity (1,000 words, in the present context); (2) the copying meets the test of spontaneity, under which "[t]he inspiration and decision to use the work and the moment of its use for maximum teaching effectiveness [must be] so close in time that it would be unreasonable to expect a timely reply to a request for permission"; (3) no more than nine instances of multiple copying take place during a term, and only a limited number of copies are made from the works of any one author or from any one collective work; (4) each copy contains a notice of copyright; (5) the copying does not substitute for the purchase of "books, publishers' reprints or periodicals"; and (6) the student is not charged any more than the actual cost of copying. The Classroom Guidelines also make clear that unauthorized copying to create "anthologies, compilations or collective works" is prohibited. H.R. Rep. No. 1476, at 69.

In its systematic and premeditated character, its magnitude, its anthological content, and its commercial motivation, the copying done by MDS goes well beyond anything envisioned by the Congress that chose to incorporate the guidelines in the legislative history. Although the guidelines do not purport to be a complete and definitive statement of fair use law for educational copying, and although they do not have the force of law, they do provide us general guidance. The fact that the MDS copying is light years away from the safe harbor of the guidelines weighs against a finding of fair use.

. . .

V

We take as our text for the concluding part of this discussion of fair use Justice Stewart's well-known exposition of the correct approach to "ambiguities" (see *Sony*, 464 U.S. at 431–32) in the copyright law: "The immediate effect of our copyright law is to secure a fair return for an 'author's' creative labor. But the ultimate aim is, by this incentive, to stimulate artistic creativity for the general public good. 'The sole interest of the United States and the primary object in conferring the monopoly,' this Court has said, 'lie in the general benefits derived by the public from the labors of authors.' ... When technological change has rendered its literal terms ambiguous, the Copyright Act must be construed in light of this basic purpose." *Twentieth Century Music Corp. v. Aiken*, 422 U.S. 151, 156 (1975) (footnotes and citations omitted).

The defendants attach considerable weight to the assertions of numerous academic authors that they do not write primarily for money and that they want their published writings to be freely copyable. The defendants suggest that unlicensed copying will "stimulate artistic creativity for the general public good."

This suggestion would be more persuasive if the record did not demonstrate that licensing income is significant to the publishers. It is the publishers who hold the copyrights, of course—and the publishers obviously need economic incentives to publish scholarly works, even if the scholars do not need direct economic incentives to write such works.

The writings of most academic authors, it seems fair to say, lack the general appeal of works by a Walter Lippmann, for example. (Lippmann is the only non-academic author whose writings are involved in this case.) One suspects that the profitability of at least some of the other books at issue here is marginal. If publishers cannot look forward to receiving permission fees, why should they continue publishing marginally profitable books at all? And how will artistic creativity be stimulated if the diminution of economic incentives for publishers to publish academic works means that fewer academic works will be published?

The fact that a liberal photocopying policy may be favored by many academics who are not themselves in the publishing business has little relevance in this connection. As Judge Leval observed in *American Geophysical*, "[i]t is not surprising that authors favor liberal photocopying; generally such authors have a far greater interest in the wide dissemination of their work than in royalties—all the more so when they have assigned their royalties to the publisher. But the authors have not risked their capital to achieve dissemination. The publishers have. Once an author has assigned her copyright, her approval or disapproval of photocopying is of no further relevance." 802 F. Supp. at 27.

In the case at bar the district court was not persuaded that the creation of new works of scholarship would be stimulated by depriving publishers of the revenue stream derived from the sale of permissions. Neither are we. On the contrary, it seems to us, the destruction of this revenue stream can only have a deleterious effect upon the incentive to publish academic writings....

[In Part VI of its opinion, the court majority concluded, contrary to the district judge, that the defendants' belief that their copying constituted fair use was not so unreasonable as to bespeak willfulness, so that the issue of statutory damages was remanded. In Part VII, the court remanded the question of the scope of the injunction, which had barred "copying from any of plaintiffs' existing or future copyrighted works without first obtaining the necessary permission." Although the district judge clearly did not intend to bar copying of works that were not protected by copyright, there was uncertainty as to whether she had considered allowing copying that was clearly a fair use; the court was, however, prepared to affirm that part of the injunction barring the copying of future copyrighted works.]

■ Boyce F. Martin, Jr., Chief Judge, dissenting.

. . . The fair use doctrine, which requires unlimited public access to published works in educational settings, is one of the essential checks on the otherwise exclusive property rights given to copyright holders under the Copyright Act.

Ironically, the majority's rigid statutory construction of the Copyright Act grants publishers the kind of power that Article I, Section 8 of the Constitution is designed to guard against. The Copyright Clause grants Congress the power to create copyright interests that are limited in scope. Consequently, the Copyright Act adopted the fair use doctrine to protect society's vested interest in the sharing of ideas and information against pursuits of illegitimate or excessive private proprietary claims. While it may seem unjust that publishers must share, in certain situations, their work-product with others, free of charge, that is not some "unforeseen byproduct of a statutory scheme"; rather, it is the "essence of copyright" and a "constitutional requirement." *Feist Publications, Inc. v. Rural Tel. Serv. Co.*, 499 U.S. 340, 349 (1991).

Michigan Document Services provided a service to the University of Michigan that promoted scholarship and higher education. Michigan Document Services was paid for its services; however, that fact does not obviate a fair use claim under these facts. Requiring Michigan Document Services to pay permission fees in this instance is inconsistent with the primary mission of the Copyright Act. The individual rights granted by the Act are subservient to the Act's primary objective, which is the promotion of creativity generally. We must therefore consider the fair use provision of Section 107 of the Act in light of the sum total of public benefits intended by copyright law. In this instance, there is no adverse economic impact on Princeton University Press that can outweigh the benefits provided by Michigan Document Services. . . .

That the majority lends significance to the identity of the person operating the photocopier is a profound indication that its approach is misguided. Given the focus of the Copyright Act, the only practical difference between this case and that of a student making his or her own copies is that commercial photocopying is faster and more cost-effective. Censuring incidental private sector profit reflects little of the essence of copyright law. Would the majority require permission fees of the Professor's teaching assistant who at times must copy, at the Professor's behest, copyrighted materials for dissemination to a class, merely because such assistant is paid an hourly wage by the Professor for this work?

The majority's strict reading of the fair use doctrine promises to hinder scholastic progress nationwide. By charging permission fees on this kind of job, publishers will pass on expenses to colleges and universities that will, of course, pass such fees on to students. Students may also be harmed if added expenses and delays cause professors to opt against creating such specialized anthologies for their courses. Even if professors attempt to reproduce the benefits of such a customized education, the added textbook cost to students is likely to be prohibitive....

In limiting the right to copy published works in the Copyright Act, Congress created an exception for cases like the one before us. When I was in school, you bought your books and you went to the library for supplemental information. To record this supplemental information, in order to learn and benefit from it, you wrote it out long-hand or typed out what you needed—not easy, but effective. Today, with the help of free enterprise and technology, this fundamental means of obtaining information for study has been made easier. Students may now routinely acquire inexpensive copies of the information they need without all of the hassle. The trend of an instructor giving information to a copying service to make a single set of copies for each student for a small fee is just a modern approach to the classic process of education. To otherwise enforce this statute is nonsensical. I therefore dissent.

■ MERRITT, CIRCUIT JUDGE, dissenting.

The copying done in this case is permissible under the plain language of the copyright statute that allows "multiple copies for classroom use": "[T]he fair use of a copyrighted work ... for purposes such as ... teaching (including multiple copies for classroom use), ... is not an infringement of copyright." 17 U.S.C. § 107....

I

... For academic institutions, the practical consequences of the Court's decision in this case are highly unsatisfactory, to say the least. Anyone who makes multiple copies for classroom use for a fee is guilty of copyright infringement unless the portion copied is just a few paragraphs long. Chapters from a book or articles from a journal are verboten. No longer may Kinko's and other corner copyshops, or school bookstores, libraries and student-run booths and kiosks copy anything for a fee except a small passage. I do not see why we should so construe plain statutory language that on its face permits "multiple copies for classroom use." The custom of making copies for classroom use for a fee began during my college and law school days forty years ago and is now well-established. I see no justification for overturning this long-established practice.

I disagree with the Court's method of analyzing and explaining the statutory language of § 107 providing a fair use exception. Except for "teaching," the statute is cast in general, abstract language that allows fair use for "criticism," "comment," "news reporting" and "research." The scope or extent of copying allowed for these uses is left undefined. Not so for "teaching." This purpose, and this purpose alone, is immediately followed by a definition. The definition allows "multiple copies for classroom use" of copyrighted material. The four factors to be considered, e.g., market effect and the portion of the work used, are of limited assistance when the teaching use at issue fits squarely within the specific language of the statute, i.e., "multiple copies for classroom use." In the present case that is all we have—"multiple copies for classroom use."

There is nothing in the statute that distinguishes between copies made for students by a third person who charges a fee for their [sic] labor and copies made by students themselves who pay a fee only for use of the copy machine. Our political economy generally encourages the division and specialization of labor. There is no reason why in this instance the law should discourage high schools, colleges, students and professors from hiring the labor of others to make their copies any more than there is a reason to discourage lawyers from hiring paralegals to make copies for clients and courts. The Court's distinction in this case based on the division of labor—who does the copying—is short sighted and unsound economically.

Our Court cites no authority for the proposition that the intervention of the copyshop changes the outcome of the case. The Court errs by focusing on the "use" of the materials made by the copyshop in making the copies rather than upon the real user of the materials—the students. Neither the District Court nor our Court provides a rationale as to why the copyshops cannot "stand in the shoes" of their customers in making copies for noncommercial, educational purposes where the copying would be fair use if undertaken by the professor or the student personally.

Rights of copyright owners are tempered by the rights of the public. The copyright owner has never been accorded complete control over all possible uses of a work. . . . The public has the right to make fair use of a copyrighted work and to exercise that right without requesting permission from, or paying any fee to, the copyright holder. The essence of copyright is the promotion of learning—not the enrichment of publishers.

II

Even if the plain language of the statute allowing "multiple copies for classroom use" were less clear, the Court's analysis of the fair use factors is off base. There is nothing in the fair use analysis that casts doubt on the plain meaning of "multiple copies for classroom use."

Money changes hands and makes the transaction "commercial" because the copyshop has freed the student from undertaking the physical task of copying. The copyshop makes its money based on the number of pages copied, not the content of those pages. The students paid the copyshop solely for the time, effort and materials that each student would otherwise have expended in copying the material himself or herself. The money paid is not money that would otherwise go to the publishers. . . .

The statute also assesses the "amount and substantiality of the portion used in relation to the copyrighted work as a whole." The excerpts here were a small percentage of the total work. The District Court recognized that the excerpts were "truly 'excerpts' and do not purport to be replacements for the original works." *Princeton Univ. Press v. Michigan Doc. Servs., Inc.*, 855 F. Supp. 905, 910 (E.D.Mich.1994). This factor does not weigh against a finding of fair use, and our Court errs in reaching a contrary conclusion. . . .

Turning to the effect of the use upon the potential market for or value of the copyrighted work, plaintiffs here have failed to demonstrate that the photocopying done by defendant has caused even marginal economic harm to their publishing business. . . . The facts demonstrate that it is only wishful thinking on the part of the publishers that the professors who assigned the works in question would have directed their students to purchase the entire work if the excerpted portions were unavailable for copying. The excerpts copied were a small percentage of the total work, and, as the professors testified, it seems more likely that they would have omitted the work altogether instead of requiring the students to purchase the entire work.

The use complained of by plaintiffs here has been widespread for many years and the publishers have not been able to demonstrate any significant harm to the market for the original works during that time. . . .

It is also wrong to measure the amount of economic harm to the publishers by loss of a presumed license fee—a criterion that assumes that the publishers have the right to collect such fees in all cases where the user copies any portion of published works. . . .

The publishers have no right to such a license fee. Simply because the publishers have managed to make licensing fees a significant source of income from copyshops and other users of their works does not make the income from the licensing a factor on which we must rely in our analysis. If the publishers have no right to the fee in many of the instances in which they are collecting it, we should not validate that practice by now using the income derived from it to justify further imposition of fees. Our job is simply to determine whether the use here falls within the § 107 exception for "multiple copies for classroom use." If it does, the publisher cannot look to us to force the copyshop to pay a fee for the copying. . . .

■ RYAN, CIRCUIT JUDGE, dissenting.

It is clear from the application of the four fair use factors of 17 U.S.C. § 107 that MDS's copying of the publishers' copyrighted works in this case is fair use and, thus, no infringement of the publishers' rights. . . .

In my judgment, my colleagues have erred in 1. focusing on the loss of permission fees in evaluating "market effect" under section 107(4); 2. finding that the evidence supports the conclusion that permission fees provide an important incentive to authors to create new works or to publishers to publish new works; and 3. using legislative history, specifically the "Classroom Guidelines," to decide the issue of classroom use. . . .

... I agree with the majority that the production and use of the coursepacks must be examined under all four factors enumerated in section 107.

A

... [T]here is no occasion to address the transformative aspect because that inquiry is not conducted at all in the case of multiple copies for classroom use.... Thus, although the transformative value of the coursepacks is slight, it does not in any respect weigh against MDS's reproduction of excerpts for classroom use....

[In assessing whether the unauthorized use is commercial or nonprofit,] we must first decide whose use of the coursepacks must be evaluated. The majority accepts the publishers' position that the only relevant "use" under the first factor is MDS's sale of the coursepacks to students, not the use of the purchased coursepacks by the professors and students.... But [MDS] does not "use" the material independent of the university professors' and students' use; it is a participant in their use and its profits are derived only from photoreproduction services the students pay it to perform.

The business of producing and selling coursepacks is more properly viewed as the commercial exploitation of professional copying technologies and of the inability of academic parties to reproduce printed materials efficiently, not the exploitation of copyrighted, creative materials.... The for-profit nature of MDS's service does not weigh against a finding of fair use because MDS, the for-profit actor, does not represent an institutional threat to authors' and publishers' rightful profits....

... Society benefits from the additional circulation of ideas in the educational setting when those who direct the practice have no personal financial interests that would drive them to copy beyond the parameters of purely educational, and fair, use. The professors have no financial reason to copy mere excerpts when the entire works should be assigned, and their selections should not be presumed to harm the market for the original works and lessen the incentives for authors to write or publishers to publish new works. Rather, such harm must be demonstrated. Society benefits when professors provide diverse materials that are not central to the course but that may enrich or broaden the base of knowledge of the students.... [S]tudents are not benefited or authors/publishers justly compensated if students are required to purchase entire works in order to read the 5% or 30% of the work that is relevant to the course....

The coursepacks fit within the exception to the "transformative" quality requirement, and the predominant character of the use of excerpts in coursepacks is not commercial but "nonprofit educational." The first factor therefore favors a finding of fair use.

B

... [As to] the second fair use factor, "the nature of the copyrighted work," ... I agree with the majority that the materials copied in this case are much closer to the core of work protected by copyright than to the mere compilations of raw data in the phone books in *Feist*. . . .

C

The third factor considers "the amount and substantiality of the portion used in relation to the copyrighted work as a whole." 17 U.S.C. § 107(3). . . . [T]he fact that the professors required students to read the excerpts says nothing whatsoever about the "substantiality" of the excerpted material in relation to the entire work. To the extent that the professors' decision to excerpt the material has any meaning, it suggests that the excerpts stand separate from the entire work, not that they are central and substantial to the entire work. . . .

The lengthiest excerpt used in one of the coursepacks comprised 30% of Farewell to the Party of Lincoln: Black Politics in the Age of FDR, by Nancy J. Weiss, the original copyrighted work. Other excerpts ranged from 5% to 18% of the original works. There is no evidence to suggest that even the 30% selected from Weiss's book extracted the heart of the work rather than just those portions that the professor deemed instructive for his limited classroom purposes. The record is simply silent on the point. *Cf. Harper & Row*, 471 U.S. at 565–66. Given the uncontroverted declarations of the professors that they would not have assigned the original works even if copied excerpts were not available, there is no basis to conclude that the portions extracted from the copyrighted works were so substantial that the resulting coursepacks superseded the originals. . . . Thus, the third factor favors a finding of fair use.

D

The fourth fair use factor is "the effect of the use upon the potential market for or value of the copyrighted work." 17 U.S.C. § 107(4). . . . For plaintiffs to prevail, there must be at least a meaningful likelihood that future harm to a potential market for the copyrighted works will occur. . . . The original panel opinion, now vacated, stated: [E]vidence of lost permission fees does not bear on market effect. The right to permission fees is precisely what is at issue here. It is circular to argue that a use is unfair, and a fee therefore required, on the basis that the publisher is otherwise deprived of a fee. . . .

The majority's logic would always yield a conclusion that the market had been harmed because any fees that a copyright holder could extract from a user if the use were found to be unfair would be "lost" if the use were instead found to be "fair use." . . .

The majority cites *Harper & Row* and *Campbell* as support for its reasoning that the mere loss of licensing fees—to which the copyright holder may or may not be entitled—is proof of market harm. . . . [I]n *Harper & Row*, the value of the original work in a derivative market that was targeted by the copyright holder was harmed by the unauthorized use of the work. There is no similar evidence of injury to the value of a work in this case.

First, there is no evidence that the publishers, here, planned to create any products for a derivative market; no evidence, for instance, that the copyright holders sought to publish or license a competing compilation of excerpts to attract the interest, for instance, of the students in Professor Dawson's interdisciplinary course "Black Americans and the Political System." Second, even if there was evidence that the publishers had contemplated such a product, there is no evidence that the publishers' derivative compilation would be devalued by defendant's production of coursepacks; that is, there is no evidence that such a compilation would earn less because of the existence of coursepacks....

The fact is that the plaintiffs are not able to create a market for the product that MDS produces. To the extent that MDS serves a market at all, it is one created by the individual professors who have determined which excerpts from which writers they wish to comprise the required reading for a particular course.... The publishers do not identify potentially marketable specialty materials and license copyshops to produce the compilations as true derivative works; rather, the publishers reject any active role in identifying potential derivative markets or creating derivative works and seek to impose a tax/surcharge on the unique compilations that are designed by individual professors and assembled by MDS for use in a specific course. Thus, the facts do not suggest that the value of any conceived derivative work has been damaged by the defendant's production of coursepacks....

E

I disagree with the majority's conclusion that copyshop permission fees provide an important incentive to authors and publishers.... More than one hundred authors declared on the record that they write for professional and personal reasons such as making a contribution to a particular discipline, providing an opportunity for colleagues to evaluate and critique the authors' ideas and theories, enhancing the authors' professional reputations, and improving career opportunities. These declarants stated that the receipt of immediate monetary compensation such as a share of licensing fees is not their primary incentive to write....

The majority dismisses the motives of the authors—the actual creators—and concludes that what matters is the incentives to the publishers who hold the copyrights. The majority further concludes, without any evidence, that the licensing income from the permission-to-copy market is significant to publishers in individual cases, and that publishers need the economic incentive of licensing fees to publish academic works....

Despite the initial appeal of this reasoning, it is far from clear that the licensing income is significant to publishers in their decisions about whether to publish marginally profitable books. The fact that licensing income provides some welcome income in the aggregate does not mean that it provides an incentive to publishers to act in individual cases. There is, in fact, no indication that the paltry permission fees affect the publishers' decisions about whether to publish in individual cases....

F

Finally, a word about the majority's argument that the unenacted legislative history of the Copyright Act instructs us that MDS's copying function is not a fair use under the enacted provisions of sections 106 and 107.... I wish to emphasize in the strongest terms that it is entirely inappropriate to rely on the Copyright Act's legislative history at all.... The Classroom Guidelines do not become more authoritative by their adoption into a Committee Report. "[I]t is the statute, and not the Committee Report, which is the authoritative expression of the law." ...

In sum, even if the four statutory factors of section 107 are not "models of clarity" and their application to the facts of this case is "troublesome"—a challenge of the kind federal appellate judges are paid to face every day—the four factors are not ambiguous. Therefore, we may not properly resort to legislative history. I am satisfied to rely exclusively upon the evidence and lack of evidence on the record before us and the plain language of the Copyright Act and its construction in the case law; and they lead me to conclude that MDS's compilation into coursepacks of excerpts selected by professors is a "fair use" of the copyrighted materials....

QUESTIONS

1. As to the first fair use factor, which is the sounder view as to the "commercial" nature of MDS's activities? Is it properly to be regarded as a profitmaking entity, or as one that "stands in the shoes" of the teachers and students for whom it is making coursepack copies? Is the fact that "multiple copies for classroom use" is expressly mentioned in the first sentence of § 107 an all-but-dispositive indicator of congressional intent to allow the duplication of coursepacks by commercial copyshops?

2. As to the fourth fair use factor, which is the sounder view as to the "circularity" issue? That is, can a court properly take into account the permission fees that are not being collected from MDS, or does that not simply assume that the publishers are indeed entitled to such fees, which is the very issue for the court to decide? How relevant is it that other commercial copyshops, with which MDS is currently in competition, are already paying such fees to the publishers (often through the Copyright Clearance Center)?

Must the publishers, as MDS argues, prove that the unauthorized marketing of coursepacks is interfering with sales of books? If so, what is to be made of the professors' affidavits, and of the out of print status of some of the plaintiffs' books?

3. What are the implications of this decision for coursepack duplication and distribution by nonprofit bookstores that are formally part of a college or university, or by copy centers that are located in various schools and departments? If you were a professor, what steps would you take in reaction to the court's opinion? Would you, for example, refuse to deal any longer with a commercial copyshop, or would you do so only if the copyshop gave explicit assurances that it would secure the permission of the publishers? Would you give up such anthologizing altogether, change your syllabus, and require your students to buy the books? Would you give your students a reading list and either instruct them to read the books in the library (with a few copies of the books placed on reserve) or instruct them to do their own photocopying?

4. The court majority would presumably look at least as unfavorably upon the making of multiple copies of copyrighted materials for a commercial bar review course or for a program of continuing legal education for practicing lawyers and judges. How would the dissenting judges likely deal with those situations?

5. Do the materials copied for your law courses appear to satisfy the requirements of the Classroom Guidelines? If the "brevity" component of the Guidelines is satisfied, why should it be necessary to satisfy as well the "spontaneity" and cumulative-effect criteria? Is it wise or practicable to implement the latter criterion, especially in a university context? Was dissenting Judge Ryan correct in forbidding recourse to such legislative history in light of the clarity of the terms of § 107?

6. A public school district wishes to conduct a music-performance competition. A well-regarded panel of music educators has been selected to serve as judges. The school district wishes to know whether it is free to make photocopies of the complete piece of music to be performed by the students, so that each judge may have a copy of the piece to facilitate appraisal of the students' performances? Is such photocopying permissible? *See Kansas Attorney General's Opinion*, 1981 CCH Copyr. L. Dec. ¶ 25,331 (Aug. 25, 1981).

American Geophysical Union v. Texaco, Inc.

60 F.3d 913 (2d Cir.1994).

■ JON O. NEWMAN, CHIEF JUDGE:

This interlocutory appeal presents the issue of whether, under the particular circumstances of this case, the fair use defense to copyright infringement applies to the photocopying of articles in a scientific journal. . . .

Background

The District Court Proceedings. Plaintiffs American Geophysical Union and 82 other publishers of scientific and technical journals (the "publishers") brought a class action claiming that Texaco's unauthorized photocopying of articles from their journals constituted copyright infringement. Among other defenses, Texaco claimed that its copying was fair use under section 107 of the Copyright Act, 17 U.S.C. § 107 (1988). Since it appeared likely that the litigation could be resolved once the fair use defense was adjudicated, the parties agreed that an initial trial should be limited to whether Texaco's copying was fair use, and further agreed that this issue would be submitted for decision on a written record.

Although Texaco employs 400 to 500 research scientists, of whom all or most presumably photocopy scientific journal articles to support their Texaco research, the parties stipulated—in order to spare the enormous expense of exploring the photocopying practices of each of them—that one scientist would be chosen at random as the representative of the entire group. The scientist chosen was Dr. Donald H. Chickering, II, a scientist at Texaco's research center in Beacon, New York. For consideration at trial, the publishers selected from Chickering's files photocopies of eight particular articles from the *Journal of Catalysis*.

In a comprehensive opinion, reported at 802 F. Supp. 1, the District Court considered the statutory fair use factors identified in section 107, weighed other equitable considerations, and held that Texaco's photocopying of these eight articles for Chickering did not constitute fair use. The District Court certified its ruling for interlocutory appeal under 28 U.S.C. § 1292(b) (1988).

Essential Facts. Employing between 400 and 500 researchers nationwide, Texaco conducts considerable scientific research seeking to develop new products and technology primarily to improve its commercial performance in the petroleum industry. As part of its substantial expenditures in support of research activities at its Beacon facility, Texaco subscribes to many scientific and technical journals and maintains a sizable library with these materials. Among the periodicals that Texaco receives at its Beacon research facility is the *Journal of Catalysis* ("*Catalysis*"), a monthly publication produced by Academic Press, Inc., a major publisher of scholarly journals and one of the plaintiffs in this litigation. Texaco had initially purchased one subscription to *Catalysis* for its Beacon facility, and increased its total subscriptions to two in 1983. Since 1988, Texaco has main maintained three subscriptions to *Catalysis*.

Each issue of *Catalysis* contains articles, notes, and letters (collectively "articles"), ranging in length from two to twenty pages. All of the articles are received by the journal's editors through unsolicited submission by various authors. Authors are informed that they must transfer the copyright in their writings to Academic Press if one of their articles is accepted for publication, and no form of money payment is ever provided to authors whose works are published. Academic Press typically owns the copyright for each individual article published in *Catalysis,* and every issue of the journal includes a general statement that no part of the publication is to be reproduced without permission from the copyright owner. The average monthly issue of *Catalysis* runs approximately 200 pages and comprises 20 to 25 articles.

Chickering, a chemical engineer at the Beacon research facility, has worked for Texaco since 1981 conducting research in the field of catalysis, which concerns changes in the rates of chemical reactions. To keep abreast of developments in his field, Chickering must review works published in various scientific and technical journals related to his area of research. Texaco assists in this endeavor by having its library circulate current issues of relevant journals to Chickering when he places his name on the appropriate routing list.

The copies of the eight articles from *Catalysis* found in Chickering's files that the parties have made the exclusive focus of the fair use trial were photocopied in their entirety by Chickering or by other Texaco employees at Chickering's request. Chickering apparently believed that the material and data found within these articles would facilitate his current or future professional research. The evidence developed at trial indicated that Chickering did not generally use the *Catalysis* articles in his research immediately upon copying, but placed the photocopied articles in his files to have them available for later reference as needed. Chickering became aware of six of the photocopied articles when the original issues of *Catalysis* containing the articles were circulated to him. He learned of the other two articles upon seeing a reference to them in another published article. As it turned out, Chickering did not have occasion to make use of five of the articles that were copied.

Discussion

I.   *The Nature of the Dispute*

The parties and many of the *amici curiae* have approached this case as if it concerns the broad issue of whether photocopying of scientific articles is fair use, or at least the only slightly more limited issue of whether photocopying of such articles is fair use when undertaken by a research scientist engaged in his own research. Such broad issues are not before us. Rather, we consider whether Texaco's photocopying by 400 or 500 scientists, as represented by Chickering's example, is a fair use. This includes the question whether such institutional, systematic copying increases the number of copies available to scientists while avoiding the necessity of paying for license fees or for additional subscriptions. We do not deal with the question of copying by an individual, for personal use in research or otherwise (not for resale), recognizing that under the fair use doctrine or the *de minimis* doctrine, such a practice by an individual might well not constitute an infringement. In other words, our opinion does not decide the case that would arise if Chickering were a professor or an independent scientist engaged in copying and creating files for independent research, as opposed to being employed by an institution in the pursuit of his research on the institution's behalf. . . .

A.   *Fair Use and Photocopying*

We consider initially the doctrine of fair use and its application to photocopying of documents. . . .

. . . As a leading commentator astutely notes, the advent of modern photocopying technology creates a pressing need for the law "to strike an appropriate balance between the authors' interest in preserving the integrity of copyright, and the public's right to enjoy the benefits that photocopying technology offers." 3 Nimmer on Copyright § 13.05[E][1], at 13–226.

Indeed, if the issue were open, we would seriously question whether the fair use analysis that has developed with respect to works of authorship alleged to use portions of copyrighted material is precisely applicable to copies produced by mechanical means. The traditional fair use analysis, now codified in section 107, developed in an effort to adjust the competing interests of authors—the author of the original copyrighted work and the author of the secondary work that "copies" a portion of the original work in the course of producing what is claimed to be a new work. Mechanical "copying" of an entire document, made readily feasible and economical by the advent of xerography, see *SCM Corp. v. Xerox Corp.,* 463 F. Supp. 983, 991–94 (D.Conn.1978), *aff'd,* 645 F.2d 1195 (2d Cir.1981), *cert. denied,* 455 U.S. 1016 (1982), is obviously an activity entirely different from creating a work of authorship. Whatever social utility copying of this sort achieves, it is not concerned with creative authorship.

Though we have been instructed to defer to Congress "when major technological innovations alter the market for copyrighted materials," *Sony,* 464 U.S. at 431, Congress has thus far provided scant guidance for resolving fair use issues involving photocopying, legislating specifically only as to library copying, see 17 U.S.C. § 108, and providing indirect advice concerning classroom copying. See generally 3 Nimmer on Copyright § 13.05[E]. However, we learn from the Supreme Court's consideration of copying achieved by use of a videotape recorder that mechanical copying is to be assessed for fair use purposes under the traditional mode of analysis, including the four statutory factors of section 107. See *Sony,* 464 U.S. at 447–56. We therefore are obliged to apply that analysis to the photocopying that occurred in this case.

B. *The Precise Copyrights at Issue*

. . .

From the outset, this lawsuit concerned alleged infringement of the copyrights in individual journal articles, copyrights assigned by the authors to the publishers. More specifically, by virtue of the parties' stipulation, this case now concerns the copyrights in the eight articles from *Catalysis* found in Chickering's files, copyrights now owned by Academic Press. There are no allegations that raise questions concerning Academic Press's potential copyrights in whole issues or annual volumes of *Catalysis* as collective works.

C. *Burdens of Proof and Standard of Review*

Fair use serves as an affirmative defense to a claim of copyright infringement, and thus the party claiming that its secondary use of the original copyrighted work constitutes a fair use typically carries the burden of proof as to all issues in the dispute. See *Campbell,* 114 S. Ct. at 1177. Moreover, since fair use is a "mixed question of law and fact," *Harper & Row,* 471 U.S. at 560, we review the District Court's conclusions on this issue de novo, though we accept its subsidiary findings of fact unless clearly erroneous, see *Twin Peaks,* 996 F.2d at 1374.

II. *The Enumerated Fair Use Factors of Section 107*

Section 107 of the Copyright Act identifies four non-exclusive factors that a court is to consider when making its fair use assessment, see 17 U.S.C. § 107(1)-(4). The District Court concluded that three of the four statutory factors favor the publishers. As detailed below, our analysis of certain statutory factors differs somewhat from that of the District Court, though we are in agreement on the ultimate determination. Our differences stem primarily from the fact that, unlike the District Court, we have had the benefit of the Supreme Court's important decision in *Campbell,* decided after Judge Leval issued his opinion.

A. *First Factor: Purpose and Character of Use*

The first factor listed in section 107 is "the purpose and character of the use, including whether such use is of a commercial nature or is for nonprofit educational purposes." 17 U.S.C. § 107(1). Especially pertinent to an assessment of the first fair use factor are the precise circumstances under which copies of the eight *Catalysis* articles were made. After noticing six of these articles when the original copy of the journal issue containing each of them was circulated to him, Chickering had them photocopied, at least initially, for the same basic purpose that one would normally seek to obtain the original—to have it available on his shelf for ready reference if and when he needed to look at it. The library circulated one copy and invited all the researchers to make their own photocopies. It is a reasonable inference that the library staff wanted each journal issue moved around the building quickly and returned to the library so that it would be available for others to look at. Making copies enabled all researchers who might one day be interested in examining the contents of an article in the issue to have the issue readily available in their own offices. In Chickering's own words, the copies of the articles were made for "my personal convenience," since it is "far more convenient to have access in my office to a photocopy of an article than to have to go to the library each time I wanted to refer to it." Affidavit of Donald Chickering at 11 (submitted as direct trial testimony) [hereinafter Chickering testimony]. Significantly, Chickering did not even have occasion to use five of the photocopied articles at all, further revealing that the photocopies of the eight *Catalysis* articles were primarily made just for "future retrieval and reference." *Id.*

It is true that photocopying these articles also served other purposes. The most favorable for Texaco is the purpose of enabling Chickering, if the need should arise, to go into the lab with pieces of paper that (a) were not as bulky as the entire issue or a bound volume of a year's issues, and (b) presented no risk of damaging the original by exposure to chemicals. And these purposes might suffice to tilt the first fair use factor in favor of Texaco if these purposes were dominant. For example, if Chickering had asked the library to buy him a copy of the pertinent issue of *Catalysis* and had placed it on his shelf, and one day while reading it had noticed a chart, formula, or other material that he wanted to take right into the lab, it might be a fair use for him to make a photocopy, and use that copy in the lab (especially if he did not retain it and build up a mini-library of photocopied articles). This is the sort of "spontaneous" copying that is part of the test for permissible nonprofit classroom copying. *See Agreement on Guidelines for Classroom Copying in Not-for-Profit Educational Institutions, quoted in* Patry, The Fair Use Privilege, at 308.[5] But that is not what happened here as to the six items copied from the circulated issues.

As to the other two articles, the circumstances are not quite as clear, but they too appear more to serve the purpose of being additions to Chickering's office "library" than to be spontaneous copying of a critical page that he was reading on his way to the lab. One was copied apparently when he saw a reference to it in another article, which was in an issue circulated to him. The most likely inference is that he decided that he ought to have copies of both items—again for placement on his shelf for later use if the need arose. The last article was copied, according to his affidavit, when he saw a reference to it "elsewhere." Chickering testimony at 22. What is clear is that this item too was simply placed "on the shelf." As he testified, "I kept a copy to refer to in case I became more involved in support effects research." *Id.*

The photocopying of these eight *Catalysis* articles may be characterized as "archival"—i.e., done for the primary purpose of providing numerous Texaco scientists (for whom Chickering served as an example) each with his or her own personal copy of each article without Texaco's having to purchase another original journal. The photocopying "merely 'supersedes the objects' of the original creation," *Campbell*, 114 S. Ct. at 1171 (quoting *Folsom v. Marsh*, 9 F. Cas. 342, 348 (C.C.D.Mass.1841) (No. 4,901)), and tilts the first fair use factor against Texaco. We do not mean to suggest that no instance of archival copying would be fair use, but the first factor tilts against Texaco in this case because the making of copies to be placed on the shelf in Chickering's office is part of a systematic process of encouraging employee researchers to copy articles so as to multiply available copies while avoiding payment.

Texaco criticizes three aspects of the District Court's analysis of the first factor. Relying largely on the Supreme Court's discussion of fair use in *Sony*, the District Court suggested that a secondary user will "win" this first factor by showing a "transformative (or productive) nonsuperseding use of the original, or [a] noncommercial use, generally for a socially beneficial or widely accepted purpose." 802 F. Supp. at 12. The District Court then concluded that Texaco's copying is "neither transformative nor

---

5. These guidelines were included in the legislative history of the 1976 revision of the Copyright Act, see H.R. Rep. No. 1476, 94th Cong., 2d Sess. 68–71 (1976), and were endorsed by the House Judiciary Committee as "a reasonable interpretation of the minimum standards of fair use." *Id.* at 72. Though these guidelines are not considered necessarily binding on courts, see *Marcus v. Rowley*, 695 F.2d 1171, 1178 (9th Cir.1983), they exist as a persuasive authority marking out certain minimum standards for educational fair uses, see *Basic Books, Inc. v. Kinko's Graphics Corp.*, 758 F. Supp. 1522–36 (S.D.N.Y.1991). *See generally* 3 Nimmer on Copyright § 13.05[E][3][a], at 13–226.1 to 13–226.2 (discussing nature and impact of guidelines); Patry, The Fair Use Privilege, at 307–09, 404–07 (same).

noncommercial," *id.* at 13: not transformative because Texaco "simply makes mechanical photocopies of the entirety of relevant articles" and the "primary aspect" of Texaco's photocopying is to multiply copies, see *id.* at 13–15; and not noncommercial because, though it facilitates research, this research is conducted solely for commercial gain, see *id.* at 15–16.

Texaco asserts that the District Court mischaracterized the inquiry under the first factor and overlooked several relevant considerations. First, Texaco contends that the District Court inappropriately focussed on the character of the user rather than the nature of the use in labeling Texaco's copying as commercial. Texaco claims that its status as a for-profit corporation has no bearing on the fair use analysis, and that its use should be considered noncommercial since it photocopied articles in order to aid Chickering's research. Texaco emphasizes that "research" is explicitly listed in the preamble of section 107, a circumstance that Texaco contends should make its copying favored under the first factor and throughout the entire fair use analysis.[7]

Second, Texaco contends that the District Court put undue emphasis on whether its use was "transformative," especially since the Supreme Court appears to have rejected the view that a use must be transformative or productive to be a fair use. *See Sony,* 464 U.S. at 455 n.40 ("The distinction between 'productive' and 'unproductive' uses may be helpful in calibrating the balance [of interests], but it cannot be wholly determinative."). Texaco asserts that the "transformative use" concept is valuable only to the extent that it focuses attention upon whether a second work unfairly competes with the original. Texaco states that in this case, where the photocopies it made were not sold or distributed in competition with the original, the nontransformative nature of its copying should not prevent a finding of fair use. Texaco also suggests that its use should be considered transformative: photocopying the article separated it from a bulky journal, made it more amenable to markings, and provided a document that could be readily replaced if damaged in a laboratory, all of which "transformed" the original article into a form that better served Chickering's research needs.

Finally, Texaco claims that it should prevail on the first factor because, as the District Court acknowledged, the type of photocopying it conducted is widespread and has long been considered reasonable and customary. Texaco stresses that some courts and commentators regard custom and common usage as integral to the fair use analysis. *See, e.g., Williams & Wilkins Co. v. United States,* 487 F.2d 1345, 1353–56 (Ct.Cl.1973), *aff'd by equally divided Court,* 420 U.S. 376 (1975); Lloyd L. Weinreb, *Fair's Fair: A Comment on the Fair Use Doctrine,* 103 Harv. L. Rev. 1137, 1140 (1990)

---

7. Though Texaco claims that its copying is for "research" as that term is used in the preamble of section 107, this characterization might somewhat overstate the matter. Chickering has not used portions of articles from *Catalysis* in his own published piece of research, nor has he had to duplicate some portion of copyrighted material directly in the course of conducting an experiment or investigation. Rather, entire articles were copied as an intermediate step that might abet Chickering's research.

[hereinafter Weinreb, *Fair's Fair*]. We consider these three lines of attack separately.

1. *Commercial use.* We generally agree with Texaco's contention that the District Court placed undue emphasis on the fact that Texaco is a for-profit corporation conducting research primarily for commercial gain. Since many, if not most, secondary users seek at least some measure of commercial gain from their use, unduly emphasizing the commercial motivation of a copier will lead to an overly restrictive view of fair use. *See Campbell,* 114 S. Ct. at 1174; see also *Maxtone-Graham v. Burtchaell,* 803 F.2d 1253, 1262 (2d Cir.1986) (noting that if "commercial" nature of a secondary use is over-emphasized in the analysis, "fair use would be virtually obliterated"), *cert. denied,* 481 U.S. 1059 (1987). See generally 3 Nimmer on Copyright § 13.05[A][1][c], at 13–162 to 13–163 (categorical rule against commercial uses unwarranted since this "would cause the fair use analysis to collapse in all but the exceptional case of nonprofit exploitation"). Though the Supreme Court stated in *Sony* that every commercial use was "presumptively" unfair, see 464 U.S. at 451, that Court and lower courts have come to explain that the commercial nature of a secondary use simply " 'tends to weigh against a finding of fair use.' " *Campbell....*

"Indeed, *Campbell* warns against 'elevat[ing] ... to a *per se* rule' *Sony*'s language about a presumption against fair use arising from commercial use.... *Campbell* discards that language in favor of a more subtle, sophisticated approach, which recognizes that 'the more transformative the new work, the less will be the significance of other factors, like commercialism, that may weigh against a finding of fair use.' ... The Court states that 'the commercial or nonprofit educational purpose of a work is only one element of the first factor enquiry,' ... and points out that '[i]f, indeed, commerciality carried presumptive force against a finding of fairness, the presumption would swallow nearly all of the illustrative uses listed in the preamble paragraph of section 107.... *Id.*"

We do not mean to suggest that the District Court overlooked these principles; in fact, the Court discussed them insightfully, see 802 F. Supp. at 12–13. Rather, our concern here is that the Court let the for-profit nature of Texaco's activity weigh against Texaco without differentiating between a direct commercial use and the more indirect relation to commercial activity that occurred here. Texaco was not gaining direct or immediate commercial advantage from the photocopying at issue in this case—i.e., Texaco's profits, revenues, and overall commercial performance were not tied to its making copies of eight *Catalysis* articles for Chickering. *Cf. Basic Books, Inc. v. Kinko's Graphics Corp.,* 758 F. Supp. 1522 (S.D.N.Y.1991) (revenues of reprographic business stemmed directly from selling unauthorized photocopies of copyrighted books). Rather, Texaco's photocopying served, at most, to facilitate Chickering's research, which in turn might have led to the development of new products and technology that could have improved Texaco's commercial performance. Texaco's photocopying is more appropriately labeled an "intermediate use." *See Sega Enterprises,* 977 F.2d at 1522–23 (labeling secondary use "intermediate" and finding first factor in favor of for-profit company, even though ultimate purpose of copying was to develop competing commercial product, because immediate purpose of copying computer code was to study idea contained within computer program).

We do not consider Texaco's status as a for-profit company irrelevant to the fair use analysis. Though Texaco properly contends that a court's focus should be on the use of the copyrighted material and not simply on the user, it is overly simplistic to suggest that the "purpose and character of the use" can be fully discerned without considering the nature and objectives of the user.[8]

Ultimately, the somewhat cryptic suggestion in section 107(1) to consider whether the secondary use "is of a commercial nature or is for nonprofit educational purposes" connotes that a court should examine, among other factors, the value obtained by the secondary user from the use of the copyrighted material. *See Rogers,* 960 F.2d at 309 ("The first factor . . . asks whether the original was copied in good faith to benefit the public or primarily for the commercial interests of the infringer."); *MCA, Inc. v. Wilson,* 677 F.2d 180, 182 (2d Cir.1981) (court is to consider "whether the alleged infringing use was primarily for public benefit or for private commercial gain"). The commercial/nonprofit dichotomy concerns the unfairness that arises when a secondary user makes unauthorized use of copyrighted material to capture significant revenues as a direct consequence of copying the original work. *See Harper & Row,* 471 U.S. at 562 ("The crux of the profit/nonprofit distinction is . . . whether the user stands to profit from exploitation of the copyrighted material without paying the customary price.").

Consistent with these principles, courts will not sustain a claimed defense of fair use when the secondary use can fairly be characterized as a form of "commercial exploitation," i.e., when the copier directly and exclusively acquires conspicuous financial rewards from its use of the copyrighted material. . . . The greater the private economic rewards reaped by the secondary user (to the exclusion of broader public benefits), the more likely the first factor will favor the copyright holder and the less likely the use will be considered fair.

As noted before, in this particular case the link between Texaco's commercial gain and its copying is somewhat attenuated: the copying, at most, merely facilitated Chickering's research that might have led to the production of commercially valuable products. Thus, it would not be accurate to conclude that Texaco's copying of eight particular *Catalysis* articles amounted to "commercial exploitation," especially since the imme-

---

8. *See* Patry, The Fair Use Privilege, at 416–17 (noting that the nature of person or entity engaging in use affects the character of the use); Report of the Register of Copyrights—Library Reproduction of Copyrighted Works (17 U.S.C. 108) 85 (1983) (explaining that though a scientist in a for-profit firm and a university student may engage in the same photocopying of scholarly articles to facilitate their research, "the copyright consequences are different: [the scientist's] copying is of a clearly commercial nature, and less likely to be fair use") *quoted in* Patry, The Fair Use Privilege, at 417 n.307.

diate goal of Texaco's copying was to facilitate Chickering's research in the sciences, an objective that might well serve a broader public purpose. *See Twin Peaks,* 996 F.2d at 1375; *Sega Enterprises,* 977 F.2d at 1522. Still, we need not ignore the for-profit nature of Texaco's enterprise, especially since we can confidently conclude that Texaco reaps at least some indirect economic advantage from its photocopying. As the publishers emphasize, Texaco's photocopying for Chickering could be regarded simply as another "factor of production" utilized in Texaco's efforts to develop profitable products. Conceptualized in this way, it is not obvious why it is fair for Texaco to avoid having to pay at least some price to copyright holders for the right to photocopy the original articles.

2. *Transformative Use.* The District Court properly emphasized that Texaco's photocopying was not "transformative." After the District Court issued its opinion, the Supreme Court explicitly ruled that the concept of a "transformative use" is central to a proper analysis under the first factor, see *Campbell,* 114 S. Ct. at 1171–73. The Court explained that though a "transformative use is not absolutely necessary for a finding of fair use, . . . the more transformative the new work, the less will be the significance of other factors, like commercialism, that may weigh against a finding of fair use." *Id.* at 1171.

The "transformative use" concept is pertinent to a court's investigation under the first factor because it assesses the value generated by the secondary use and the means by which such value is generated. To the extent that the secondary use involves merely an untransformed duplication, the value generated by the secondary use is little or nothing more than the value that inheres in the original. Rather than making some contribution of new intellectual value and thereby fostering the advancement of the arts and sciences, an untransformed copy is likely to be used simply for the same intrinsic purpose as the original, thereby providing limited justification for a finding of fair use. *See Weissmann v. Freeman,* 868 F.2d 1313, 1324 (2d Cir.) (explaining that a use merely for the same "intrinsic purpose" as original "moves the balance of the calibration on the first factor against" secondary user and "seriously weakens a claimed fair use"), *cert. denied,* 493 U.S. 883 (1989).

In contrast, to the extent that the secondary use "adds something new, with a further purpose or different character," the value generated goes beyond the value that inheres in the original and "the goal of copyright, to promote science and the arts, is generally furthered." *Campbell,* 114 S. Ct. at 1171; *see also* Pierre N. Leval, *Toward a Fair Use Standard,* 103 Harv. L. Rev. 1105, 1111 (1990) [hereinafter Leval, *Toward a Fair Use Standard*]. It is therefore not surprising that the "preferred" uses illustrated in the preamble to section 107, such as criticism and comment, generally involve some transformative use of the original work. *See* 3 Nimmer on Copyright § 13.05[A][1][b], at 13–160.

Texaco suggests that its conversion of the individual *Catalysis* articles through photocopying into a form more easily used in a laboratory might constitute a transformative use. However, Texaco's photocopying merely transforms the material object embodying the intangible article that is the copyrighted original work. *See* 17 U.S.C. §§ 101, 102 (explaining that copyright protection in literary works subsists in the original work of authorship "regardless of the nature of the material objects . . . in which they are embodied"). Texaco's making of copies cannot properly be regarded as a transformative use of the copyrighted material. *See* Steven D. Smit, *"Make a Copy for the File . . .": Copyright Infringement by Attorneys*, 46 Baylor L. Rev. 1, 15 & n.58 (1994); *see also Basic Books*, 758 F. Supp. at 1530–31 (repackaging in anthology form of excerpts from copyrighted books not a transformative use).

Even though Texaco's photocopying is not technically a transformative use of the copyrighted material, we should not overlook the significant independent value that can stem from conversion of original journal articles into a format different from their normal appearance. *See generally Sony*, 464 U.S. at 454, 455 n.40 (acknowledging possible benefits from copying that might otherwise seem to serve "no productive purpose"); Weinreb, *Fair's Fair*, at 1143 & n.29 (discussing potential value from nontransformative copying). As previously explained, Texaco's photocopying converts the individual *Catalysis* articles into a useful format. Before modern photocopying, Chickering probably would have converted the original article into a more serviceable form by taking notes, whether cursory or extended;[10] today he can do so with a photocopying machine. Nevertheless, whatever independent value derives from the more usable format of the photocopy does not mean that every instance of photocopying wins on the first factor. In this case, the predominant archival purpose of the copying tips the first factor against the copier, despite the benefit of a more usable format.

3. *Reasonable and Customary Practice.* Texaco contends that Chickering's photocopying constitutes a use that has historically been considered "reasonable and customary." We agree with the District Court that whatever validity this argument might have had before the advent of the photocopying licensing arrangements discussed below in our consideration of the fourth fair use factor, the argument today is insubstantial. As the District Court observed, "To the extent the copying practice was 'reasonable' in 1973 [when *Williams & Wilkins* was decided], it has ceased to be 'reasonable' as the reasons that justified it before [photocopying licensing] have ceased to exist." 802 F. Supp. at 25.

· · ·

---

10. In stating that a handwritten copy would have been made, we do not mean to imply that such copying would necessarily have been a fair use. Despite the 1973 dictum in *Williams & Wilkins* asserting that "it is almost unanimously accepted that a scholar can make a handwritten copy of an entire copyrighted article for his own use . . .," 487 F.2d at 1350, the current edition of the Nimmer treatise reports that "there is no reported case on the question of whether a single handwritten copy of all or substantially all of a book or other protected work made for the copier's own private use is an infringement or fair use." 3 Nimmer on Copyright § 1305[E][4][a], at 13–229.

Moreover, the concept of a "transformative" use would be extended beyond recognition if it was applied to Chickering's copying simply because he acted in the course of doing research. The purposes illustrated by the categories listed in section 107 refer primarily to the work of authorship alleged to be a fair use, not to the activity in which the alleged infringer is engaged. Texaco cannot gain fair use insulation for Chickering's archival photocopying of articles (or books) simply because such copying is done by a company doing research. It would be equally extravagant for a newspaper to contend that because its business is "news reporting" it may line the shelves of its reporters with photocopies of books on journalism or that schools engaged in "teaching" may supply its faculty members with personal photocopies of books on educational techniques or substantive fields. Whatever benefit copying and reading such books might contribute to the process of "teaching" would not for that reason satisfy the test of a "teaching" purpose.

On balance, we agree with the District Court that the first factor favors the publishers, primarily because the dominant purpose of the use is a systematic institutional policy of multiplying the available number of copies of pertinent copyrighted articles by circulating the journals among employed scientists for them to make copies, thereby serving the same purpose for which additional subscriptions are normally sold, or, as will be discussed, for which photocopying licenses may be obtained.

B. Second Factor: Nature of Copyrighted Work

The second statutory fair use factor is "the nature of the copyrighted work." 17 U.S.C. § 107(2)....

. . .

Though a significant measure of creativity was undoubtedly used in the creation of the eight articles copied from *Catalysis,* even a glance at their content immediately reveals the predominantly factual nature of these works.[11] Moreover, though we have previously recognized the importance of strong copyright protection to provide sufficient incentives for the creation of scientific works, see *Weissmann,* 868 F.2d at 1325, nearly every category of copyrightable works could plausibly assert that broad copyright protection was essential to the continued vitality of that category of works.

Ultimately, then, the manifestly factual character of the eight articles precludes us from considering the articles as "within the core of the copyright's protective purposes," *Campbell,* 114 S. Ct. at 1175; see also *Harper & Row,* 471 U.S. at 563 ("The law generally recognizes a greater need to disseminate factual works than works of fiction or fantasy."). Thus,

---

11. Not only are the *Catalysis* articles essentially factual in nature, but the evidence suggests that Chickering was interested exclusively in the facts, ideas, concepts, or principles contained within the articles. Though scientists surely employ creativity and origi- nality to develop ideas and obtain facts and thereafter to convey the ideas and facts in scholarly articles, it is primarily the ideas and facts themselves that are of value to other scientists in their research.

in agreement with the District Court, we conclude that the second factor favors Texaco.

C. *Third Factor: Amount and Substantiality of Portion Used*

The third statutory fair use factor is "the amount and substantiality of the portion used in relation to the copyrighted work as a whole." 17 U.S.C. § 107(3). The District Court concluded that this factor clearly favors the publishers because Texaco copied the eight articles from *Catalysis* in their entirety. . . .

Texaco's suggestion that we consider that it copied only a small percentage of the total compendium of works encompassed within *Catalysis* is superficially intriguing, especially since *Catalysis* is traditionally market- ed only as a periodical by issue or volume. However, as the District Court recognized, each of the eight articles in *Catalysis* was separately authored and constitutes a discrete "original work[ ] of authorship," 17 U.S.C. § 102. As we emphasized at the outset, each article enjoys independent copyright protection, which the authors transferred to Academic Press, and what the publishers claim has been infringed is the copyright that subsists in each individual article—not the distinct copyright that may subsist in each journal issue or volume by virtue of the publishers' original compila- tion of these articles. The only other appellate court to consider the propriety of photocopying articles from journals also recognized that each article constituted an entire work in the fair use analysis. *See Williams & Wilkins,* 487 F.2d at 1353.

Despite Texaco's claims that we consider its amount of copying "mi- nuscule" in relation to the entirety of *Catalysis,* we conclude, as did the District Court, that Texaco has copied entire works. Though this conclusion does not preclude a finding of fair use, it militates against such a finding, see *Sony,* 464 U.S. at 449–50, and weights the third factor in favor of the publishers. . . .

D. *Fourth Factor: Effect Upon Potential Market or Value*

The fourth statutory fair use factor is "the effect of the use upon the potential market for or value of the copyrighted work." 17 U.S.C. § 107(4). Assessing this factor, the District Court detailed the range of procedures Texaco could use to obtain authorized copies of the articles that it photo- copied and found that "whatever combination of procedures Texaco used, the publishers' revenues would grow significantly." 802 F. Supp. at 19. The Court concluded that the publishers "powerfully demonstrated entitlement to prevail as to the fourth factor," since they had shown "a substantial harm to the value of their copyrights" as the consequence of Texaco's copying. See *id.* at 18–21.

Prior to *Campbell,* the Supreme Court had characterized the fourth factor as "the single most important element of fair use," *Harper & Row.* . . . However, *Campbell*'s discussion of the fourth factor conspicuously omits this phrasing. Apparently abandoning the idea that any factor enjoys primacy, *Campbell* instructs that "[a]ll [four factors] are to be explored, and the results weighed together, in light of the purposes of copyright." ___ U.S. at ___, 114 S. Ct. at 1171.

In analyzing this fourth factor, which the Supreme Court and commentators recognize as "the single most important element of fair use," *Harper & Row,* 471 U.S. at 566; accord 3 Nimmer on Copyright § 13.05[A][4], at 13–183, it is important (1) to bear in mind the precise copyrighted works, namely the eight journal articles, and (2) to recognize the distinctive nature and history of "the potential market for or value of" these particular works. Specifically, though there is a traditional market for, and hence a clearly defined value of, journal issues and volumes, in the form of per-issue purchases and journal subscriptions, there is neither a traditional market for, nor a clearly defined value of, individual journal articles. As a result, analysis of the fourth factor cannot proceed as simply as would have been the case if Texaco had copied a work that carries a stated or negotiated selling price in the market.

Like most authors, writers of journal articles do not directly seek to capture the potential financial rewards that stem from their copyrights by personally marketing copies of their writings. Rather, like other creators of literary works, the author of a journal article "commonly sells his rights to publishers who offer royalties in exchange for their services in producing and marketing the author's work." *Harper & Row,* 471 U.S. at 547. In the distinctive realm of academic and scientific articles, however, the only form of royalty paid by a publisher is often just the reward of being published, publication being a key to professional advancement and prestige for the author, see *Weissmann,* 868 F.2d at 1324 (noting that "in an academic setting, profit is ill-measured in dollars. Instead, what is valuable is recognition because it so often influences professional advancement and academic tenure."). The publishers in turn incur the costs and labor of producing and marketing authors' articles, driven by the prospect of capturing the economic value stemming from the copyrights in the original works, which the authors have transferred to them. Ultimately, the monopoly privileges conferred by copyright protection and the potential financial rewards therefrom are not directly serving to motivate authors to write individual articles; rather, they serve to motivate publishers to produce journals, which provide the conventional and often exclusive means for disseminating these individual articles. It is the prospect of such dissemination that contributes to the motivation of these authors.

Significantly, publishers have traditionally produced and marketed authors' individual articles only in a journal format, i.e., in periodical compilations of numerous articles. In other words, publishers have conventionally sought to capture the economic value from the "exclusive rights" to "reproduce" and "distribute copies" of the individual articles, see 17 U.S.C. § 106(1) & (3), solely by compiling many such articles together in a periodical journal and then charging a fee to subscribe. Publishers have not traditionally provided a simple or efficient means to obtain single copies of individual articles; reprints are usually available from publishers only in bulk quantities and with some delay.

This marketing pattern has various consequences for our analysis of the fourth factor. First, evidence concerning the effect that photocopying individual journal articles has on the traditional market for journal subscriptions is of somewhat less significance than if a market existed for the sale of individual copies of articles. Second, this distinctive arrangement raises novel questions concerning the significance of the publishers' establishment of an innovative licensing scheme for the photocopying of individual journal articles.

1. *Sales of Additional Journal Subscriptions, Back Issues, and Back Volumes.* Since we are concerned with the claim of fair use in copying the eight individual articles from *Catalysis,* the analysis under the fourth factor must focus on the effect of Texaco's photocopying upon the potential market for or value of these individual articles. Yet, in their respective discussions of the fourth statutory factor, the parties initially focus on the impact of Texaco's photocopying of individual journal articles upon the market for *Catalysis* journals through sales of *Catalysis* subscriptions, back issues, or back volumes.

. . .

These considerations persuade us that evidence concerning the effect of Texaco's photocopying of individual articles within *Catalysis* on the traditional market for *Catalysis* subscriptions is of somewhat limited significance in determining and evaluating the effect of Texaco's photocopying "upon the potential market for or value of" the individual articles. We do not mean to suggest that we believe the effect on the marketability of journal subscriptions is completely irrelevant to gauging the effect on the market for and value of individual articles. Were the publishers able to demonstrate that Texaco's type of photocopying, if widespread,[14] would impair the marketability of journals, then they might have a strong claim under the fourth factor. Likewise, were Texaco able to demonstrate that its type of photocopying, even if widespread, would have virtually no effect on the marketability of journals, then it might have a strong claim under this fourth factor.

On this record, however, the evidence is not resounding for either side. The District Court specifically found that, in the absence of photocopying, (1) "Texaco would not ordinarily fill the need now being supplied by photocopies through the purchase of back issues or back volumes . . . [or] by enormously enlarging the number of its subscriptions," but (2) Texaco still "would increase the number of subscriptions somewhat." 802 F. Supp. at 19.[15] This moderate conclusion concerning the actual effect on the

---

14. Properly applied, the fourth factor requires a court to consider "not only . . . particular actions of the alleged infringer, but also 'whether unrestricted and widespread conduct of the sort engaged in by the defendant . . . would result in a substantially adverse impact on the potential market' for the original." *Campbell,* 114 S. Ct. at 1177 (quot-

ing 3 Nimmer on Copyright § 13.05[A][4]). *Accord Harper & Row,* 471 U.S. at 568–69; *Rogers,* 960 F.2d at 312.

15. Texaco assails the conclusion that, without photocopying, it would increase subscriptions "somewhat" as an improper inference unsupported by the evidence. Though marketability of journals, combined with the uncertain relationship between the market for journals and the market for and value of individual articles, leads us to conclude that the evidence concerning sales of additional journal subscriptions, back issues, and back volumes does not strongly support either side with regard to the fourth factor. Cf. *Sony,* 464 U.S. at 451–55 (rejecting various predictions of harm to value of copyrighted work based on speculation about possible consequences of secondary use). At best, the loss of a few journal subscriptions tips the fourth factor only slightly toward the publishers because evidence of such loss is weak evidence that the copied articles themselves have lost any value.

2. *Licensing Revenues and Fees.* The District Court, however, went beyond discussing the sales of additional journal subscriptions in holding that Texaco's photocopying affected the value of the publishers' copyrights. Specifically, the Court pointed out that, if Texaco's unauthorized photocopying was not permitted as fair use, the publishers' revenues would increase significantly since Texaco would (1) obtain articles from document delivery services (which pay royalties to publishers for the right to photocopy articles), (2) negotiate photocopying licenses directly with individual publishers, and/or (3) acquire some form of photocopying license from the Copyright Clearance Center Inc. ("CCC").[16] *See* 802 F. Supp. at 19. Texaco claims that the District Court's reasoning is faulty because, in determining that the value of the publishers' copyrights was affected, the Court assumed that the publishers were entitled to demand and receive licensing royalties and fees for photocopying. Yet, continues Texaco, whether the publishers can demand a fee for permission to make photocopies is the very question that the fair use trial is supposed to answer.

we accept Texaco's assertion that additional subscriptions provide an imperfect substitute for the copies of individual articles that scientists need and prefer, we cannot conclude that the District Court's factual finding that "Texaco would add at least a modest number of subscriptions," 802 F. Supp. at 19, is clearly erroneous.

First, though Texaco claims that there is no reliable evidence suggesting that photocopying served to facilitate journal circulation, the evidence concerning Texaco's routing practices supports the District Court's inference that, without photocopying, Texaco will need a greater number of subscriptions to insure the prompt circulation of journals. Second, as discussed in connection with the first statutory factor, the dominant reason for, and value derived from, the copying of the eight particular *Catalysis* articles was to make them available on Chickering's shelf for ready reference when he needed to look at them. Thus, it is reasonable to conclude that

Texaco would purchase at least a few additional subscriptions to serve this purpose, i.e., to provide certain researchers with personal copies of particular articles in their own offices.

16. The CCC is a central clearing-house established in 1977 primarily by publishers to license photocopying. The CCC offers a variety of licensing schemes; fees can be paid on a per copy basis or through blanket license arrangements. Most publishers are registered with the CCC, but the participation of for-profit institutions that engage in photocopying has been limited, largely because of uncertainty concerning the legal questions at issue in this lawsuit. A more extended discussion of the formation, development, and effectiveness of the CCC and its licensing schemes is contained in Stanley M. Besen & Sheila N. Kirby, Compensating Creators of Intellectual Property: Collectives that Collect (1989); see also *American Geophysical Union v. Texaco Inc.,* 802 F. Supp. at 7–9.

It is indisputable that, as a general matter, a copyright holder is entitled to demand a royalty for licensing others to use its copyrighted work, see 17 U.S.C. § 106 (copyright owner has exclusive right "to authorize" certain uses), and that the impact on potential licensing revenues is a proper subject for consideration in assessing the fourth factor....

However, not every effect on potential licensing revenues enters the analysis under the fourth factor. Specifically, courts have recognized limits on the concept of "potential licensing revenues" by considering only traditional, reasonable, or likely to be developed markets when examining and assessing a secondary use's "effect upon the potential market for or value of the copyrighted work." *See Campbell*, 114 S. Ct. at 1178 ("The market for potential derivative uses includes only those that creators of original works would in general develop or license others to develop."); *Harper & Row*, 471 U.S. at 568 (fourth factor concerned with "use that supplants any part of the *normal* market for a copyrighted work") (emphasis added)....

For example, the Supreme Court recently explained that because of the "unlikelihood that creators of imaginative works will license critical reviews or lampoons" of their works, "the law recognizes no derivative market for critical works," *Campbell*, 114 S. Ct. at 1178. Similarly, other courts have found that the fourth factor will favor the secondary user when the only possible adverse effect occasioned by the secondary use would be to a potential market or value that the copyright holder has not typically sought to, or reasonably been able to, obtain or capture. *See Twin Peaks*, 996 F.2d at 1377 (noting that fourth factor will favor secondary user when use "filled a market niche that the [copyright owner] simply had no interest in occupying"); *Pacific and Southern Co. v. Duncan*, 744 F.2d 1490, 1496 (11th Cir.1984), *cert. denied*, 471 U.S. 1004 (1985) (noting that the fourth factor may not favor copyright owner when the secondary user "profits from an activity that the owner could not possibly take advantage of").

Thus, Texaco is correct, at least as a general matter, when it contends that it is not always appropriate for a court to be swayed on the fourth factor by the effects on potential licensing revenues. Only an impact on potential licensing revenues for traditional, reasonable, or likely to be developed markets should be legally cognizable when evaluating a secondary use's "effect upon the potential market for or value of the copyrighted work."

Though the publishers still have not established a conventional market for the direct sale and distribution of individual articles, they have created, primarily through the CCC, a workable market for institutional users to obtain licenses for the right to produce their own copies of individual articles via photocopying. The District Court found that many major corporations now subscribe to the CCC systems for photocopying licenses. 802 F. Supp. at 25. Indeed, it appears from the pleadings, especially Texaco's counterclaim, that Texaco itself has been paying royalties to the CCC. Since the Copyright Act explicitly provides that copyright holders have the "exclusive rights" to "reproduce" and "distribute copies" of their works, see 17 U.S.C. § 106(1) & (3), and since there currently exists a viable market for licensing these rights for individual journal articles, it is appropriate that potential licensing revenues for photocopying be considered in a fair use analysis.

Despite Texaco's claims to the contrary, it is not unsound to conclude that the right to seek payment for a particular use tends to become legally cognizable under the fourth fair use factor when the means for paying for such a use is made easier. This notion is not inherently troubling: it is sensible that a particular unauthorized use should be considered "more fair" when there is no ready market or means to pay for the use, while such an unauthorized use should be considered "less fair" when there is a ready market or means to pay for the use. The vice of circular reasoning arises only if the availability of payment is conclusive against fair use. Whatever the situation may have been previously, before the development of a market for institutional users to obtain licenses to photocopy articles, see *Williams & Wilkins*, 487 F.2d at 1357–59, it is now appropriate to consider the loss of licensing revenues in evaluating "the effect of the use upon the potential market for or value of" journal articles. It is especially appropriate to do so with respect to copying of articles from *Catalysis*, a publication as to which a photocopying license is now available. We do not decide how the fair use balance would be resolved if a photocopying license for *Catalysis* articles were not currently available.

In two ways, Congress has impliedly suggested that the law should recognize licensing fees for photocopying as part of the "potential market for or value of" journal articles. First, section 108 of the Copyright Act narrowly circumscribes the conditions under which libraries are permitted to make copies of copyrighted works. *See* 17 U.S.C. § 108. Though this section states that it does not in any way affect the right of fair use, see *id.* § 108(f)(4), the very fact that Congress restricted the rights of libraries to make copies implicitly suggests that Congress views journal publishers as possessing the right to restrict photocopying, or at least the right to demand a licensing royalty from nonpublic institutions that engage in photocopying. Second, Congress apparently prompted the development of CCC by suggesting that an efficient mechanism be established to license photocopying, see S. Rep. No. 983, 93d Cong., 2d Sess. 122 (1974); S. Rep. No. 473, 94th Cong., 1st Sess. 70–71 (1975); H.R. Rep. No. 83, 90th Cong., 1st Sess. 33 (1968). It is difficult to understand why Congress would recommend establishing such a mechanism if it did not believe that fees for photocopying should be legally recognized as part of the potential market for journal articles.

Primarily because of lost licensing revenue, and to a minor extent because of lost subscription revenue, we agree with the District Court that "the publishers have demonstrated a substantial harm to the value of their copyrights through [Texaco's] copying," 802 F. Supp. at 21, and thus conclude that the fourth statutory factor favors the publishers.

E. *Aggregate Assessment*

We conclude that three of the four statutory factors, including the important first and the critical fourth factor, favor the publishers. We recognize that the statutory factors provide a nonexclusive guide to analysis, see *Harper & Row,* 471 U.S. at 560, but to whatever extent more generalized equitable considerations are relevant, we are in agreement with the District Court's analysis of them. *See* 802 F. Supp. at 21–27. We therefore agree with the District Court's conclusion that Texaco's photocopying of eight particular articles from the *Journal of Catalysis* was not fair use.

Though we recognize the force of many observations made in Judge Jacobs's dissenting opinion, we are not dissuaded by his dire predictions that our ruling in this case "has ended fair-use photocopying with respect to a large population of journals," or, to the extent that the transactional licensing scheme is used, "would seem to require that an intellectual property lawyer be posted at each copy machine." Our ruling is confined to the archival photocopying revealed by the record—the precise copying that the parties stipulated should be the basis for the District Court's decision now on appeal and for which licenses are in fact available. And the claim that lawyers need to be stationed at copy machines is belied by the ease with which music royalties have been collected and distributed for performances at thousands of cabarets, without the attendance of intellectual property lawyers in any capacity other than as customers. If Texaco wants to continue the precise copying we hold not to be a fair use, it can either use the licensing schemes now existing or some variant of them, or, if all else fails, purchase one more subscription for each of its researchers who wish to keep issues of *Catalysis* on the office shelf.

Conclusion

The order of the District Court is affirmed.[19]

■ JACOBS, CIRCUIT JUDGE, dissenting:

The stipulated facts crisply present the fair use issues that govern the photocopying of entire journal articles for a scientist's own use, either in the laboratory or as part of a personal file assisting that scientist's particular inquiries. I agree with much in the majority's admirable review of the facts and the law. Specifically, I agree that, of the four nonexclusive considerations bearing on fair use enumerated in section 107, the second factor (the nature of the copyrighted work) tends to support a conclusion of fair use, and the third factor (the ratio of the copied portion to the whole copyrighted work) militates against it. I respectfully dissent, however, in respect of the first and fourth factors. As to the first factor: the purpose

---

19. Though neither the limited trial nor this appeal requires consideration of the publishers' remedy if infringement is ultimately found, we note that the context of this dispute appears to make ill-advised an injunction, which, in any event, has not been sought. If the dispute is not now settled, this appears to be an appropriate case for exploration of the possibility of a court-imposed compulsory license. *See Campbell,* 114 S. Ct. at 1171 n.10; 3 Nimmer on Copyright § 13.05[E][4][e], at 13–241 to 13–242.

and character of Dr. Chickering's use is integral to transformative and productive ends of scientific research. As to the fourth factor: the adverse effect of Dr. Chickering's use upon the potential market for the work, or upon its value, is illusory. For these reasons, and in light of certain equitable considerations and the overarching purpose of the copyright laws, I conclude that Dr. Chickering's photocopying of the *Catalysis* articles was fair use.

A. *Purpose and Character of the Use*

The critical facts adduced by the majority are that Dr. Chickering is a chemical engineer employed at a corporate research facility who keeps abreast of developments in his field by reviewing specialized scientific and technical journals, and who photocopies individual journal articles in the belief that doing so will facilitate his current or future professional research. I agree with the majority that the immediate goal of the photocopying was "to facilitate Chickering's research in the sciences, an objective that might well serve a broader public purpose." The photocopying was therefore integral to ongoing research by a scientist. In my view, all of the statutory factors organize themselves around this fact. The four factors listed in section 107 (and reviewed one by one in the majority opinion) are considerations that bear upon whether a particular use is fair; but those factors are informed by a preamble sentence in section 107 that recites in pertinent part that "the fair use of a copyrighted work, including such use by reproduction in copies . . . for purposes such as . . . scholarship, or research, is not an infringement of copyright." . . .

. . .

A use that is reasonable and customary is likely to be a fair one. *See Harper & Row Publishers, Inc. v. Nation Enterprises,* 471 U.S. 539, 550 (1985) ("The fair use doctrine was predicated on the author's implied consent to 'reasonable and customary' use"). The district court, the majority and I start from the same place in assessing whether Dr. Chickering's photocopying is a reasonable and customary use of the material: making single photocopies for research and scholarly purposes has been considered both reasonable and customary for as long as photocopying technology has been in existence. *See Williams & Wilkins Co. v. United States,* 487 F.2d 1345, 1355–56 (Ct.Cl.1973), *aff'd by an equally divided court,* 420 U.S. 376 (1975). The majority quotes the district court's short answer to this important insight: "To the extent the copying practice was 'reasonable' in 1973 [when *Williams v. Wilkins* was decided], it has ceased to be 'reasonable' as the reasons that justified it before [photocopying licensing] have ceased to exist." 802 F. Supp. at 25. I do not agree at all that a reasonable and customary use becomes unfair when the copyright holder develops a way to exact an additional price for the same product. Moreover, I view the advent of the CCC as an event that bears analytically upon the distinct question of whether Dr. Chickering's use supersedes the original (the fourth factor). I therefore reach an issue—reasonable and customary use—not explored by the district court or by the majority.

Consider what Dr. Chickering actually does with scientific journals. As a research scientist, he routinely sifts through the latest research done by his peers, much of which is printed in journals such as *Catalysis*. He determines which articles potentially assist his specific trains of thought and lines of inquiry, and he photocopies them. Relative to the volume of articles in each issue, his photocopying is insubstantial. He then files the articles for possible future use or study. As the majority observes, "before modern photocopying, Chickering probably would have converted the original article into a more serviceable form by taking notes, whether cursory or extended; today he can do so with a photocopying machine." The majority's footnote 10, appended to this passage, questions whether or not a scholar's handwritten copy of a full work is "necessarily" a fair use. As the majority adds, however, *Williams & Wilkins* says:

> It is almost unanimously accepted that a scholar can make a handwritten copy of an entire copyrighted article for his own use, and in the era before photoduplication it was not uncommon (and not seriously questioned) that he could have his secretary make a typed copy for his personal use and files. These customary facts of copyright-life are among our givens.

Williams & Wilkins, 487 F.2d at 1350. What Dr. Chickering does is simply a technologically assisted form of note-taking, such as has long been customary among researchers: the photocopy machine saves Dr. Chickering the toil and time of recording notes on index cards or in notebooks, and improves the accuracy and range of the data, charts, and formulas he can extract from the passing stream of information; but the note-taking purpose remains the same....

... Dr. Chickering's filing away of these photocopies does not subvert his claim of fair use. Like the majority, I am convinced that his deposit of the photocopied articles in his personal file, pending his personal use of them in the future, is an important fact bearing upon fair use; but the dominant significance of that fact, under the first factor of section 107, is that (whether he "uses" them or files them) the articles are not re-sold or retailed in any way. If the copies were sold by Dr. Chickering, that would be a telling—possibly determinative—fact. What Dr. Chickering has done reinforces the view that his photocopying was not commercial in purpose or character.

... Good notes, being as precise and copious as time allows, do not aspire to transform the original text, but are useful in research only to the extent that they faithfully record the original. Accordingly, I find the nature and purpose of the use to be fully transformative....

The nature and purpose of the use is not affected by Texaco's size or institutional nature, or by Texaco's circulation of its subscription journals to its scientists. I therefore find that this factor weighs clearly in favor of Texaco.

B. *Effect Upon Potential Market or Value*

In gauging the effect of Dr. Chickering's photocopying on the potential market or value of the copyrighted work, the majority properly considers two separate means of marketing: (1) journal subscriptions and sales, and (2) licensing revenues and fees.

. . .

(2) *Licensing Revenues and Fees*.... In this case the only harm to a market is to the supposed market in photocopy licenses. The CCC scheme is neither traditional nor reasonable; and its development into a real market is subject to substantial impediments. There is a circularity to the problem: the market will not crystallize unless courts reject the fair use argument that Texaco presents; but, under the statutory test, we cannot declare a use to be an infringement unless (assuming other factors also weigh in favor of the secondary user) there is a market to be harmed. At present, only a fraction of journal publishers have sought to exact these fees. I would hold that this fourth factor decisively weighs in favor of Texaco, because there is no normal market in photocopy licenses, and no real consensus among publishers that there ought to be one.

The majority holds that photocopying journal articles without a license is an infringement. Yet it is stipulated that (a) institutions such as Texaco subscribe to numerous journals, only 30 percent of which are covered by a CCC license; (b) not all publications of each CCC member are covered by the CCC licenses; and (c) not all the articles in publications covered by the CCC are copyrighted. It follows that no CCC license can assure a scientist that photocopying any given article is legal....

It is hard to escape the conclusion that the existence of the CCC—or the perception that the CCC and other schemes for collecting license fees are or may become "administratively tolerable"—is the chief support for the idea that photocopying scholarly articles is unfair in the first place. The majority finds it "sensible" that a use "should be considered 'less fair' when there is a ready market or means to pay for the use." That view is sensible only to a point. There is no technological or commercial impediment to imposing a fee for use of a work in a parody, or for the quotation of a paragraph in a review or biography. Many publishers could probably unite to fund a bureaucracy that would collect such fees. The majority is sensitive to this problem, but concludes that "the vice of circular reasoning arises only if the availability of payment is conclusive against fair use." That vice is not avoided here. The majority expressly declines to "decide how the fair use balance would be resolved if a photocopying license for *Catalysis* articles were not currently available." Moreover, the "critical" fourth factor tips in favor of the publishers (according to the majority) "primarily because of lost licensing revenue" and only "to a minor extent" on the basis of journal sales and subscriptions.

I do not agree with the majority that the publishers "have created, primarily through the CCC, a workable market for institutional users to obtain licenses for the right to produce their own copies of individual articles via photocopying." By the CCC's admission, in its correspondence with the Antitrust Division of the Justice Department, "the mechanism for the negotiation of a photocopy license fee is often not even in place.... Nor can it be said that CCC's current licensing programs have adequately met the market's needs." There is nothing workable, and there is no market.

Even if the CCC is or becomes workable, the holder of a CCC blanket license is not thereby privileged to photocopy journal articles published by non-members of the CCC, as to which articles there is no "ready market or means to pay for the fair use." ... This Court has ended fair-use photocopying with respect to a large population of journals, but the CCC mechanism allows fair-use photocopying only of some of them. The facts before us demonstrate that the holder of a blanket license must still deal separately with CCC-member Bell Labs as to certain hundreds of its publications. With respect to the journals for which the publishers do not market licenses, users will either (a) research which publications are in this category and copy them longhand, in typescript or in partial photocopy, or (b) ignore our fair-use doctrine as unworkable. Neither option serves scientific inquiry or respect for copyright. In any event, it seems to me that when a journal is used in a customary way—a way that the authors uniformly intend and wish—the user should not be subjected on a day to day basis to burdens that cannot be satisfied without a team of intellectual property lawyers and researchers.

The fourth factor tips decidedly in Texaco's favor because there is no appreciable impairment of the publishing revenue from journal subscriptions and sales; because the publisher captures additional revenue from institutional users by charging a double subscription price (and can presumably charge any price the users will pay); and because the market for licensing is cumbersome and unrealized....

QUESTIONS

1. With respect to the first factor in § 107, what is meant by "commercial nature"? Does it contemplate only competitive marketing of the plaintiff's work by the defendant? Or does it embrace as well an assessment of the overall profitmaking character of the defendant?

2. How would (and should) the court have analyzed the case had it involved a university science (or law) professor having his or her secretary making single photocopies of articles that bear upon the professor's field of research and teaching? *Compare Television Digest, Inc. v. United States Tel. Ass'n,* 841 F.Supp. 5 (D.D.C.1993) (nonprofit trade association made multiple copies from a single subscription to a communications-industry newsletter).

3. Still with respect to the first factor, both the majority and dissent in *Texaco* made much of the question whether the defendant's use was "transformative," drawing inspiration from the Supreme Court decision in the *Campbell (2 Live Crew)* case. What do you take the word "transformative" to mean? Does it embrace the exact photoduplication of the text of a journal article? What are Texaco's strongest arguments that it does?

4. How much weight should be given to Texaco's assertion that its photocopying practices were "reasonable and customary"? Is the analogy to hand note-taking a sound one? Should the emergence of the CCC be taken into account? Should it matter if the plaintiffs can show that they had, since approximately 1980, instituted targeted lawsuits against comparable photocopying practices and had secured favorable settlements?

5. With respect to the fourth factor, would the plaintiffs' case have been lost in *Texaco* had they not convinced the court that uncollected CCC licensing fees should be taken into account in assessing "the potential market for or value of the copyrighted work"? *Should* such uncollected fees be taken into account, or is it "circular" to do so, as the dissenting judge contends?

6. Texaco filed a petition for certiorari but before the filing of a responsive pleading, the lawsuit was settled, with Texaco agreeing to pay to the plaintiff publishers a seven-figure amount, to pay a retroactive one-year licensing fee to the CCC, and to subscribe to the CCC for a period of five years (and to urge other photocopiers to subscribe too). Is this a settlement that should satisfy both sides?

7. Aerial Images, Inc. (Aerial) entered into, and implemented, an agreement with Perini Construction Company, by which Aerial was to provide several hundred photographic images, taken from the air, of a large construction site on which Perini was providing construction services. This is often done as a safeguard in the event of future construction disputes and litigation. Perini selected 300 color images from Aerial's 50 fly-overs of the site to record the progress of the construction. When the developer of the site grew dissatisfied with Perini's work, and ordered Perini off the property, Perini invoked the arbitration provision of its construction agreement, and instituted arbitration proceedings against the developer. Perini, needing six copies of all of the images—to provide to the three arbitrators, the lawyers and witnesses—asked Aerial to make those copies; Aerial asked for $10 per copy (or $18,000) for color copies. Believing that to be exorbitant, Perini went to a photocopying service, which copied the 300 Aerial photographs for only $1 per black-and-white copy (or $1800). Aerial has sued Perini for copyright infringement, and Perini asserts the defense of fair use. Evaluate the likelihood of success. *See Images Audio Visual Prods, Inc. v. Perini Bldg. Co.*, 91 F. Supp. 2d 1075 (E.D.Mich.2000).

COPYING BY NONPROFIT LIBRARIES

Section 108 of the 1976 Act sets forth a special regime favoring certain acts of copying by (primarily) nonprofit libraries. Congress in the 1976 Act thus recognized the unique social and educational functions libraries perform.

Although at least some of the copying in which nonprofit libraries engage might well qualify for the fair use exemption, § 108 explicitly requires library copying to be considered separately (though not necessarily exclusively) from the § 107 fair use factors. Therefore, when assessing the ability of a library to copy a protected work, the relationship between §§ 107 and 108 should be properly understood. The statute seems to be clear in providing the § 108 exemption entirely apart from any fair use possibilities enjoyed by the library. Section 108(f)(4). This has led to the library position that § 108 "merely identifies certain copying situations which are conclusively presumed to be legal without affecting the right of fair use which continues as a general and flexible concept of law." Library Photocopying and the U.S. Copyright Law of 1976, p. vii (Special Libraries Association Pamphlet, Dec. 29, 1977). On the other hand, the author/publisher groups take the view that "[s]ection 108 authorizes certain kinds of library photocopying that could not qualify as 'fair use.'" Photocopying by Academic, Public and Nonprofit Research Libraries 5 (Association of American Publishers, Inc., and Authors League Pamphlet, May 1978). In any event, the library exemption in § 108 does not extend to the library patron, who therefore must still rely on the § 107 formulation of fair use. Section 108(f)(2).

The provisions of § 108 may be summarized as follows: (1) It defines the coverage of works negatively through partial exclusions set forth in § 108(h). The net result is that the section is most important with respect to books, periodicals, sound recordings, and television news programs (§ 108(f)(3)). (2) It sets forth general preconditions for library copying in § 108(a) and (g). (3) It specifies in § 108(b), (c), (d), and (e) the situations in which, under limitations and conditions over and above those in (a) and (g), works may be reproduced. (4) It covers miscellaneous matters in § 108(f) and provides in § 108(i) for a report from the Register in 1983 and at five-year intervals thereafter "setting forth the extent to which this section has achieved the intended statutory balancing of the rights of creators, and the needs of users."

To qualify, a library or archives need not be nonprofit or open to the public. It must, however, make the reproduction and distribution of material "without any purpose of direct or indirect commercial advantage" and, if not open to the public, be open at least to persons doing research in a specialized field who are not necessarily affiliated with the institution in question. The legislative interpretation of these requirements finally permitted libraries in a for-profit organization potentially to qualify, but subject to all the conditions and prohibitions of the section. H.R. Rep. No. 94–1733, *supra,* at 73–74. *But cf.* Brennan, *Legislative History and Chapter 1 of S.22,* 22 N.Y.L.S. L. Rev. 193, 202 (1976); S. Rep. No. 94–473, *supra,* at 67. Thus it is the reproduction and distribution that must be nonprofit, not the enterprise.

Additionally, the library copy must contain the notice of copyright that appears on the copied work. If no notice appears, the library must include a legend stating that the work may be protected by copyright. Section 108(a)(3). The privilege is to make "no more than one copy or phonorecord of a work" (§ 108(a)), except as permitted under subsections (b) and (c). This means no more than one *at a time,* as long as the reproduction is "isolated and unrelated" and not "the related or concerted reproduction or distribution of multiple copies or phonorecords of the same material. . . ." Section 108(g)(1). The additional limitation against "systematic reproduction or distribution," which applies to periodical articles, is discussed below.

The 1998 amendments to § 108 expanded the scope of additional copying permitted under subsections (b) and (c). Subsection (b) had allowed one facsimile (i.e. photocopied) reproduction of unpublished works for archival preservation; it now permits three copies or phonorecords. Moreover, the medium of the copy is no longer limited to facsimiles. Copies may be reproduced in digital format so long as the copy is not otherwise distributed in digital form and is not made available to the public outside of the library. Congress thus sought to avoid the rampant further reproduction that might follow were the library's digital copies to become generally available, for example over the Internet. (The subsection (b) privilege, as well as others provided in § 108, is subject to any contractual obligation undertaken by the library in connection with the deposit of a manuscript. Section 108(f)(4).)

Subsection (c) permits reproduction of three copies of a published work solely for the replacement of a copy or phonorecord "that is damaged, deteriorating, lost, or stolen, or if the existing format in which the work is stored has become obsolete," but only "if the library or archives has, after a reasonable effort, determined that an unused replacement cannot be obtained at a fair price." Any replacement copy made in digital format may not be made available to the public in digital format outside the premises of the library. The format has become obsolete "if the machine or device necessary to render perceptible a work stored in that format is no longer manufactured or is no longer reasonably available in the commercial marketplace." Section 108(c)(2).

Unavailability of copies at a fair price after reasonable investigation is also the standard for the slightly more controversial "out of print" provision in § 108(e). This permits the reproduction, under such circumstances, of an entire work for a user if the library has no notice that the material will be used for other than "private study, scholarship, or research" and it prominently posts a warning to be prescribed by regulation. Section 108(e). *See* 37 C.F.R. § 201.14 (1988).

This provision was introduced in 1969 (S. 543, 91st Cong.) as librarians responded to the commencement of the *Williams & Wilkins* case. See Williams & Wilkins Co. v. United States, 487 F.2d 1345 (Ct. of Claims 1973), *aff'd without opinion by an equally divided Court*, 420 U.S. 376 (1975)(reversing trial judge and finding extensive photocopying of medical journals by National Institute of Health and National Library of Medicine to be fair use). After the trial decision favorable to the publisher in 1972, efforts were redoubled to secure an exemption for journal articles even if not "out of print." The result was the special provision in § 108(d), subject to the limiting provisions in § 108(g)(2) and partially clarified by another set of guidelines. This complex structure dealing with a narrow question may be traced as follows:

A reproduction, directly or through interlibrary "loan," may be made of "no more than one article or other contribution to a copyrighted collection or periodical issue" or of a "small part of any other copyrighted work" under the same provisions as to good faith and posted warnings as in the "out of print" provision in section 108(e). But such reproduction, as indicated above, must be "isolated and unrelated" and specifically must not be "systematic." Section 108(g)(2). Examples of "systematic" copying are furnished in the Senate Report.

Senate Report

S. Rep. No. 94–473 at 70–71 (1975).

Multiple copies and systematic reproduction

Subsection (g) provides that the rights granted by this section extend only to the "isolated and unrelated reproduction of a single copy," but this section does not authorize the related or concerted reproduction of multiple copies of the same material whether made on one occasion or over a period of time, and whether intended for aggregate use by one individual or for separate use by the individual members of a group. For example, if a college professor instructs his class to read an article from a copyrighted journal, the school library would not be permitted, under subsection (g), to reproduce copies of the article for the members of the class.

Subsection (g) also provides that section 108 does not authorize the systematic reproduction or distribution of copies or phonorecords of articles or other contributions to copyrighted collections or periodicals or of small parts of other copyrighted works whether or not multiple copies are reproduced or distributed. Systematic reproduction or distribution occurs when a library makes copies of such materials available to other libraries or to groups of users under formal or informal arrangements whose purpose or effect is to have the reproducing library serve as their source of such material. Such systematic reproduction and distribution, as distinguished from isolated and unrelated reproduction or distribution, may substitute the copies reproduced by the source library for subscriptions or reprints or other copies which the receiving libraries or users might otherwise have purchased for themselves, from the publisher or the licensed reproducing agencies.

While it is not possible to formulate specific definitions of "systematic copying," the following examples serve to illustrate some of the copying prohibited by subsection (g).

(1) A library with a collection of journals in biology informs other libraries with similar collections that it will maintain and build its own collection and will make copies of articles from these journals available to them and their patrons on request. Accordingly, the other libraries discontinue or refrain from purchasing subscriptions to these journals and fulfill their patrons' requests for articles by obtaining photocopies from the source library.

(2) A research center employing a number of scientists and technicians subscribes to one or two copies of needed periodicals. By reproducing photocopies of articles the center is able to make the material in these periodicals available to its staff in the same manner which otherwise would have required multiple subscriptions.

(3) Several branches of a library system agree that one branch will subscribe to particular journals in lieu of each branch purchasing its own subscriptions, and the one subscribing branch will reproduce copies of articles from the publication for users of the other branches.

———

Because librarians contended that the "systematic" disqualification thus introduced in the Senate swallowed up the whole exemption, a proviso was inserted by the House committee in § 108(g)(2) as follows:

> That nothing in this clause prevents a library or archives from participating in interlibrary arrangements that do not have, as their purpose or effect, that the library or archives receiving such copies or phonorecords for distribution does so *in such aggregate quantities as to substitute for a subscription to or purchase of such work.* (Emphasis added.)

This proviso, which addresses itself only to the interlibrary situation and not reproduction by a library directly for its patrons, was accepted in the House-passed version of S. 22.

The question whether this proviso would be accepted by the Senate conferees was eased by the clarification of its scope. This was accomplished by the development of guidelines by the interested parties under the aegis of the National Commission on New Technological Uses of Copyrighted Works (CONTU), directed solely to the definition of "such aggregate quantities" in the proviso to § 108(g)(2). H.R. Rep. No. 94–1733, *supra,* at 72–73. For example, the basic formula deemed to warrant subscription to a given periodical is a group of requests "within any calendar year for a total of six or more copies of an article or articles published in such periodical within five years prior to the date of the request." *Id.*

The result of this particular development is as follows: A library whose requests exceed the number set forth in the guidelines is deemed to be substituting for subscription or purchase and is therefore engaging in "systematic reproduction" within the meaning of § 108(g)(2); it would therefore lose the exemption in § 108(d). Its only recourse, unless other parts of § 108 apply, is to argue that, despite the foregoing, it is still engaging in fair use within the meaning of § 107.

It is no wonder that some libraries, preferring to avoid the mine field described above, are removing themselves from photocopying activities. Some install coin-operated machines seeking to avail themselves of the provision in § 108(f)(1) that:

Nothing in this section—

(1) shall be construed to impose liability for copyright infringement upon a library or archives or its employees for the unsupervised use of reproducing equipment located on its premises: *Provided,* That such equipment displays a notice that the making of a copy may be subject to the copyright law. . . .

QUESTIONS

1.   To what extent, if any, do §§ 108 and 107 excuse the following acts:

(a) Seeking to fill in gaps in its collection of Ernest Hemingway novels, Columbus University library secures by interlibrary loan from the Penn University library copies of the missing volumes, photocopies these, and returns the originals to Penn.

(b) Same as above, except that Columbus scans the volumes into its database.

(c) Same as (a), except that the copied works are unpublished letters of Hemingway, none of them currently or previously in Columbus' collection.

(d) Same as (c), except that Columbus scans the letters.

(e) Same as (a), except that the library copies the volumes at the request of a member of the university faculty.

(f) Same as (e), except that the copies are requested by an editor employed by a for-profit textbook company.

2.   (a) The Columbus University law school library, seeking to alleviate overcrowding on its shelves, and to save subscription costs, discards its three extra sets of the West federal reporters (retaining one complete hardcopy set), and makes the cases available to users via on-line services, such as WESTLAW and LEXIS.

(b) Same as (a), except that the Columbus library scans the West reporters, and makes the database thus generated available to users.

3.   (a) Students at Columbus University scan newspaper articles from the Metropolis Bugle and post them on a student website, inviting others to comment on the articles. Cf. *L.A. Times v. Free Republic, infra* this chapter.

(b) Same as (a), except that the website is not affiliated with Columbus University, and it accepts advertising.

A & M Records, Inc., v. Napster, Inc.

239 F.3d 1004 (9th Cir.2001).

■ BEEZER, CIRCUIT JUDGE:

Plaintiffs are engaged in the commercial recording, distribution and sale of copyrighted musical compositions and sound recordings. The complaint alleges that Napster, Inc. ("Napster") is a contributory and vicarious copyright infringer. On July 26, 2000, the district court granted plaintiffs' motion for a preliminary injunction. The injunction was slightly modified by written opinion on August 10, 2000. *A & M Records, Inc. v. Napster, Inc.*, 114 F. Supp. 2d 896 (N.D.Cal.2000). The district court preliminarily enjoined Napster "from engaging in, or facilitating others in copying, downloading, uploading, transmitting, or distributing plaintiffs' copyrighted musical compositions and sound recordings, protected by either federal or state law, without express permission of the rights owner." *Id. at 927....*

We entered a temporary stay of the preliminary injunction pending resolution of this appeal. We have jurisdiction pursuant to 28 U.S.C. § 1292(a)(1). We affirm in part, reverse in part and remand.

I

We have examined the papers submitted in support of and in response to the injunction application and it appears that Napster has designed and operates a system which permits the transmission and retention of sound recordings employing digital technology.

In 1987, the Moving Picture Experts Group set a standard file format for the storage of audio recordings in a digital format called MPEG–3, abbreviated as "MP3." Digital MP3 files are created through a process colloquially called" ripping." Ripping software allows a computer owner to copy an audio compact disk ("audio CD") directly onto a computer's hard drive by compressing the audio information on the CD into the MP3 format. The MP3's compressed format allows for rapid transmission of digital audio files from one computer to another by electronic mail or any other file transfer protocol.

Napster facilitates the transmission of MP3 files between and among its users. Through a process commonly called "peer-to-peer" file sharing, Napster allows its users to: (1) make MP3 music files stored on individual computer hard drives available for copying by other Napster users; (2) search for MP3 music files stored on other users' computers; and (3) transfer exact copies of the contents of other users' MP3 files from one computer to another via the Internet. These functions are made possible by Napster's MusicShare software, available free of charge from Napster's Internet site, and Napster's network servers and server-side software. Napster provides technical support for the indexing and searching of MP3 files, as well as for its other functions, including a "chat room," where users can meet to discuss music, and a directory where participating artists can provide information about their music.

A.   Accessing the System

In order to copy MP3 files through the Napster system, a user must first access Napster's Internet site and download the MusicShare software to his individual computer. See http://www.Napster.com. Once the software is installed, the user can access the Napster system. A first-time user is required to register with the Napster system by creating a "user name" and password.

B.   Listing Available Files

If a registered user wants to list available files stored in his computer's hard drive on Napster for others to access, he must first create a "user library" directory on his computer's hard drive. The user then saves his MP3 files in the library directory, using self-designated file names. He next must log into the Napster system using his user name and password. His MusicShare software then searches his user library and verifies that the available files are properly formatted. If in the correct MP3 format, the names of the MP3 files will be uploaded from the user's computer to the Napster servers. The content of the MP3 files remains stored in the user's computer.

Once uploaded to the Napster servers, the user's MP3 file names are stored in a server-side "library" under the user's name and become part of a "collective directory"of files available for transfer during the time the user is logged onto the Napster system. The collective directory is fluid; it tracks users who are connected in real time, displaying only file names that are immediately accessible.

C.   Searching For Available Files

Napster allows a user to locate other users' MP3 files in two ways: through Napster's search function and through its "hotlist" function.

Software located on the Napster servers maintains a" search index" of Napster's collective directory. To search the files available from Napster users currently connected to the net-work servers, the individual user accesses a form in the MusicShare software stored in his computer and enters either the name of a song or an artist as the object of the search. The form is then transmitted to a Napster server and automatically compared to the MP3 file names listed in the server's search index. Napster's server compiles a list of all MP3 file names pulled from the search index which include the same search terms entered on the search form and transmits the list to the searching user. The Napster server does not search the contents of any MP3 file; rather, the search is limited to "a text search of the file names indexed in a particular cluster. Those file names may contain typographical errors or otherwise inaccurate descriptions of the content of the files since they are designated by other users." *Napster*, 114 F. Supp. 2d at 906.

To use the "hotlist" function, the Napster user creates a list of other users' names from whom he has obtained MP3 files in the past. When logged onto Napster's servers, the system alerts the user if any user on his list (a "hotlisted user") is also logged onto the system. If so, the user can access an index of all MP3 file names in a particular hotlisted user's library and request a file in the library by selecting the file name. The contents of the hotlisted user's MP3 file are not stored on the Napster system.

D.   Transferring Copies of an MP3 file

To transfer a copy of the contents of a requested MP3 file, the Napster server software obtains the Internet address of the requesting user and the Internet address of the" host user" (the user with the available files). The Napster servers then communicate the host user's Internet address to the requesting user. The requesting user's computer uses this information to establish a connection with the host user and downloads a copy of the contents of the MP3 file from one computer to the other over the Internet, "peer-to-peer." A downloaded MP3 file can be played directly from the user's hard drive using Napster's Music–Share program or other software. The file may also be transferred back onto an audio CD if the user has access to equipment designed for that purpose. In both cases, the quality of the original sound recording is slightly diminished by transfer to the MP3 format.

This architecture is described in some detail to promote an understanding of transmission mechanics as opposed to the content of the transmissions. The content is the subject of our copyright infringement analysis.

. . .

III

Plaintiffs claim Napster users are engaged in the wholesale reproduction and distribution of copyrighted works, all constituting direct infringement.[2] The district court agreed. We note that the district court's conclusion that plaintiffs have presented a prima facie case of direct infringement by Napster users is not presently appealed by Napster. We only need briefly address the threshold requirements.

A.   Infringement

Plaintiffs must ... demonstrate that the alleged infringers violate at least one exclusive right granted to copyright holders under 17 U.S.C. § 106.... The record supports the district court's determination that "as much as eighty-seven percent of the files available on Napster may be copyrighted and more than seventy percent may be owned or administered by plaintiffs." *Napster*, 114 F. Supp. 2d at 911.

The district court further determined that plaintiffs' exclusive rights under § 106 were violated:" here the evidence establishes that a majority of Napster users use the service to download and upload copyrighted music. ...And by doing that, it constitutes—the uses constitute direct infringement of plaintiffs' musical compositions, recordings." *A & M Records, Inc. v. Napster, Inc.*, Nos. 99–5183, 00–0074, 2000 WL 1009483, at *1 (N.D.Cal. July 26, 2000) (transcript of proceedings). The district court also noted that "it is pretty much acknowledged ... by Napster that this is infringement." *Id.* We agree that plaintiffs have shown that Napster users infringe at least two of the copyright holders' exclusive rights: the rights of reproduction, § 106(1); and distribution, § 106(3). Napster users who upload file names to the search index for others to copy violate plaintiffs' distribution rights.

---

2. Secondary liability for copyright infringement does not exist in the absence of direct infringement by a third party. *Religious Tech. Ctr. v. Netcom On–Line Communication Servs., Inc., 907 F. Supp. 1361, 1371 (N.D.Cal.1995)* ("There can be no contributo- ry infringement by a defendant without direct infringement by another."). It follows that Napster does not facilitate infringement of the copyright laws in the absence of direct infringement by its users.

Napster users who download files containing copyrighted music violate plaintiffs' reproduction rights.

Napster asserts an affirmative defense to the charge that its users directly infringe plaintiffs' copyrighted musical compositions and sound recordings.

B.   Fair Use

Napster contends that its users do not directly infringe plaintiffs' copyrights because the users are engaged in fair use of the material. *See* 17 U.S.C. § 107 ("The fair use of a copyrighted work ... is not an infringement of copyright."). Napster identifies three specific alleged fair uses: sampling, where users make temporary copies of a work before purchasing; space-shifting, where users access a sound recording through the Napster system that they already own in audio CD format; and permissive distribution of recordings by both new and established artists.

The district court considered factors listed in 17 U.S.C. § 107, which guide a court's fair use determination. These factors are: (1) the purpose and character of the use; (2) the nature of the copyrighted work; (3) the "amount and substantiality of the portion used" in relation to the work as a whole; and (4) the effect of the use upon the potential market for the work or the value of the work. See 17 U.S.C. § 107. The district court first conducted a general analysis of Napster system uses under § 107, and then applied its reasoning to the alleged fair uses identified by Napster. The district court concluded that Napster users are not fair users. We agree. We first address the court's overall fair use analysis.

1.   Purpose and Character of the Use

This factor focuses on whether the new work merely replaces the object of the original creation or instead adds a further purpose or different character. In other words, this factor asks "whether and to what extent the new work is 'transformative.'" See *Campbell v. Acuff–Rose Music, Inc.*, 510 U.S. 569, 579 (1994).

The district court first concluded that downloading MP3 files does not transform the copyrighted work. *Napster*, 114 F. Supp. 2d at 912. This conclusion is supportable. Courts have been reluctant to find fair use when an original work is merely retransmitted in a different medium. See, e.g., *Infinity Broadcast Corp. v. Kirkwood*, 150 F.3d 104, 108 (2d Cir.1998) (concluding that retransmission of radio broadcast over telephone lines is not transformative); *UMG Recordings, Inc. v. MP3.Com, Inc.*, 92 F. Supp. 2d 349, 351 (S.D.N.Y.) (finding that reproduction of audio CD into MP3 format does not "transform" the work), certification denied, 2000 U.S. Dist. LEXIS 7439, 2000 WL 710056 (S.D.N.Y. June 1, 2000) ("Defendant's copyright infringement was clear, and the mere fact that it was clothed in the exotic webbing of the Internet does not disguise its illegality.").

This "purpose and character" element also requires the district court to determine whether the allegedly infringing use is commercial or noncommercial. See *Campbell*, 510 U.S. at 584–85. A commercial use weighs against a finding of fair use but is not conclusive on the issue. Id. The district court determined that Napster users engage in commercial use of the copyrighted materials largely because (1) "a host user sending a file cannot be said to engage in a personal use when distributing that file to an anonymous requester" and (2) "Napster users get for free something they would ordinarily have to buy." *Napster*, 114 F. Supp. 2d at 912. The district court's findings are not clearly erroneous.

[handwritten margin note: Commercial: Getting something of value for free.]

Direct economic benefit is not required to demonstrate a commercial use. Rather, repeated and exploitative copying of copyrighted works, even if the copies are not offered for sale, may constitute a commercial use. See *Worldwide Church of God v. Philadelphia Church of God*, 227 F.3d 1110, 1118 (9th Cir.2000) (stating that church that copied religious text for its members "unquestionably profited" from the unauthorized "distribution and use of [the text] without having to account to the copyright holder"); *American Geophysical Union v. Texaco, Inc.*, 60 F.3d 913, 922 (2d Cir.1994) (finding that researchers at for-profit laboratory gained indirect economic advantage by photocopying copyrighted scholarly articles). In the record before us, commercial use is demonstrated by a showing that repeated and exploitative unauthorized copies of copyrighted works were made to save the expense of purchasing authorized copies. See *Worldwide Church*, 227 F.3d at 1117–18; *Sega Enters. Ltd. v. MAPHIA*, 857 F. Supp. 679, 687 (N.D.Cal.1994) (finding commercial use when individuals downloaded copies of video games "to avoid having to buy video game cartridges"); see also *American Geophysical*, 60 F.3d at 922. Plaintiffs made such a showing before the district court.

We also note that the definition of a financially motivated transaction for the purposes of criminal copyright actions includes trading infringing copies of a work for other items, "including the receipt of other copyrighted works." See No Electronic Theft Act ("NET Act"), Pub. L. No. 105–147, 18 U.S.C. § 101 (defining "Financial Gain").

2.   The Nature of the Copyrighted Work

Works that are creative in nature are "closer to the core of intended copyright protection" than are more fact-based works. See *Campbell*, 510 U.S. at 586. The district court determined that plaintiffs' "copyrighted musical compositions and sound recordings are creative in nature ... which cuts against a finding of fair use under the second factor." *Napster*, 114 F. Supp. 2d at 913. We find no error in the district court's conclusion.

3.   The Portion Used

"While 'wholesale copying does not preclude fair use per se,' copying an entire work 'militates against a finding of fair use.' " *Worldwide Church*, 227 F.3d at 1118 (quoting *Hustler Magazine, Inc. v. Moral Majority, Inc.*, 796 F.2d 1148, 1155 (9th Cir.1986)). The district court determined that Napster users engage in "wholesale copying" of copyrighted work because file transfer necessarily "involves copying the entirety of the copyrighted work." *Napster*, 114 F. Supp. 2d at 913. We agree. We note, however, that under certain circumstances, a court will conclude that a use is fair even when the protected work is copied in its entirety. See, e.g., *Sony Corp. v. Universal City Studios, Inc.*, 464 U.S. 417, 449–50 (1984) (acknowledging that fair use of time-shifting necessarily involved making a full copy of a protected work).

4. Effect of Use on Market

"Fair use, when properly applied, is limited to copying by others which does not materially impair the marketability of the work which is copied." *Harper & Row Publishers, Inc. v. Nation Enters.*, 471 U.S. 539, 566–67 (1985). "The importance of this [fourth] factor will vary, not only with the amount of harm, but also with the relative strength of the showing on the other factors." *Campbell*, 510 U.S. at 591 n.21. The proof required to demonstrate present or future market harm varies with the purpose and character of the use:

> A challenge to a noncommercial use of a copy-righted work requires proof either that the particular use is harmful, or that if it should become wide-spread, it would adversely affect the potential market for the copyrighted work. . . . *If the intended use is for commercial gain, that likelihood [of market harm] may be presumed. But if it is for a noncommercial purpose, the likelihood must be demonstrated.*

Sony, 464 U.S. at 451 (emphases added).

Addressing this factor, the district court concluded that Napster harms the market in "at least" two ways: it reduces audio CD sales among college students and it "raises barriers to plaintiffs' entry into the market for the digital downloading of music." *Napster*, 114 F. Supp. 2d at 913. The district court relied on evidence plaintiffs submitted to show that Napster use harms the market for their copyrighted musical compositions and sound recordings. In a separate memorandum and order regarding the parties' objections to the expert reports, the district court examined each report, finding some more appropriate and probative than others. *A & M Records, Inc. v. Napster*, Inc., 114 F. Supp. 2d 896, 2000 WL 1182467 (N.D. Cal. 2000). Notably, plaintiffs' expert, Dr. E. Deborah Jay, conducted a survey (the "Jay Report") using a random sample of college and university students to track their reasons for using Napster and the impact Napster had on their music purchases. *Id.* at *2. The court recognized that the Jay Report focused on just one segment of the Napster user population and found "evidence of lost sales attributable to college use to be probative of irreparable harm for purposes of the preliminary injunction motion." 114 F. Supp. 2d at 923, *Id.* at *3.

Plaintiffs also offered a study conducted by Michael Fine, Chief Executive Officer of Soundscan, (the "Fine Report") to determine the effect of online sharing of MP3 files in order to show irreparable harm. Fine found that online file sharing had resulted in a loss of "album" sales within college markets. After reviewing defendant's objections to the Fine Report and expressing some concerns regarding the methodology and findings, the district court refused to exclude the Fine Report insofar as plaintiffs offered it to show irreparable harm. *Id.* at *6.

Plaintiffs' expert Dr. David J. Teece studied several issues ("Teece Report"), including whether plaintiffs had suffered or were likely to suffer harm in their existing and planned businesses due to Napster use. *Id.* Napster objected that the report had not undergone peer review. The district court noted that such reports generally are not subject to such scrutiny and overruled defendant's objections. *Id.*

As for defendant's experts, plaintiffs objected to the report of Dr. Peter S. Fader, in which the expert concluded that Napster is beneficial to the music industry because MP3 music file-sharing stimulates more audio CD sales than it displaces. *Id.* at *7. The district court found problems in Dr. Fader's minimal role in overseeing the administration of the survey and the lack of objective data in his report. The court decided the generality of the report rendered it "of dubious reliability and value." The court did not exclude the report, however, but chose "not to rely on Fader's findings in determining the issues of fair use and irreparable harm." 114 F. Supp. 2d at 912, *Id.* at *8.

The district court cited both the Jay and Fine Reports in support of its finding that Napster use harms the market for plaintiffs' copyrighted musical compositions and sound recordings by reducing CD sales among college students. The district court cited the Teece Report to show the harm Napster use caused in raising barriers to plaintiffs' entry into the market for digital downloading of music. *Napster*, 114 F. Supp. 2d at 910. The district court's careful consideration of defendant's objections to these reports and decision to rely on the reports for specific issues demonstrates a proper exercise of discretion in addition to a correct application of the fair use doctrine. Defendant has failed to show any basis for disturbing the district court's findings.

We, therefore, conclude that the district court made sound findings related to Napster's deleterious effect on the present and future digital download market. Moreover, lack of harm to an established market cannot deprive the copyright holder of the right to develop alternative markets for the works. See *L.A. Times v. Free Republic*, 2000 U.S. Dist. LEXIS 5669, 54 U.S.P.Q.2D (BNA) 1453, 1469–71 (C.D.Cal.2000) (stating that online market for plaintiff newspapers' articles was harmed because plaintiffs demonstrated that "[defendants] are attempting to exploit the market for viewing their articles online"); see also *UMG Recordings*, 92 F. Supp. 2d at 352 (" Any allegedly positive impact of defendant's activities on plaintiffs' prior market in no way frees defendant to usurp a further market that directly derives from reproduction of the plaintiffs' copyrighted works."). Here, similar to L.A. Times and UMG Recordings, the record supports the district court's finding that the "record company plaintiffs have already expended considerable funds and effort to commence Internet sales and licensing for digital downloads." 114 F. Supp. 2d at 915. Having digital downloads available for free on the Napster system necessarily harms the copyright holders' attempts to charge for the same downloads.

Judge Patel did not abuse her discretion in reaching the above fair use conclusions, nor were the findings of fact with respect to fair use considerations clearly erroneous. We next address Napster's identified uses of sampling and space-shifting.

5.   Identified Uses

Napster maintains that its identified uses of sampling and space-shifting were wrongly excluded as fair uses by the district court.

a.   Sampling

Napster contends that its users download MP3 files to "sample" the music in order to decide whether to purchase the recording. Napster argues that the district court: (1) erred in concluding that sampling is a commercial use because it conflated a noncommercial use with a personal use; (2) erred in determining that sampling adversely affects the market for plaintiffs' copyrighted music, a requirement if the use is non-commercial; and (3) erroneously concluded that sampling is not a fair use because it determined that samplers may also engage in other infringing activity.

The district court determined that sampling remains a commercial use even if some users eventually purchase the music. We find no error in the district court's determination. Plaintiffs have established that they are likely to succeed in proving that even authorized temporary downloading of individual songs for sampling purposes is commercial in nature. *See Napster*, 114 F. Supp. 2d at 913. The record supports a finding that free promotional downloads are highly regulated by the record company plaintiffs and that the companies collect royalties for song samples available on retail Internet sites. Id. Evidence relied on by the district court demonstrates that the free downloads provided by the record companies consist of thirty-to-sixty second samples or are full songs programmed to "time out," that is, exist only for a short time on the downloader's computer. *Id.* at 913–14. In comparison, Napster users download a full, free and permanent copy of the recording. *Id.* at 914–15. The determination by the district court as to the commercial purpose and character of sampling is not clearly erroneous.

The district court further found that both the market for audio CDs and market for online distribution are adversely affected by Napster's service. As stated in our discussion of the district court's general fair use analysis: the court did not abuse its discretion when it found that, overall, Napster has an adverse impact on the audio CD and digital download markets. Contrary to Napster's assertion that the district court failed to specifically address the market impact of sampling, the district court determined that "even if the type of sampling supposedly done on Napster were a non-commercial use, plaintiffs have demonstrated a substantial likelihood that it would adversely affect the potential market for their copyrighted works if it became widespread." *Napster*, 114 F. Supp. 2d at 914. The record supports the district court's preliminary determinations that: (1) the more music that sampling users download, the less likely they are to eventually purchase the recordings on audio CD; and (2) even if the audio CD market is not harmed, Napster has adverse effects on the developing digital download market.

Napster further argues that the district court erred in rejecting its evidence that the users' downloading of "samples" increases or tends to increase audio CD sales. The district court, however, correctly noted that "any potential enhancement of plaintiffs' sales ... would not tip the fair use analysis conclusively in favor of defendant." *Id.* at 914. We agree that increased sales of copyrighted material attributable to unauthorized use should not deprive the copyright holder of the right to license the material. *See Campbell*, 510 U.S. at 591 n.21 ("Even favorable evidence, without more, is no guarantee of fairness. Judge Leval gives the example of the film producer's appropriation of a composer's previously unknown song that turns the song into a commercial success; the boon to the song does not make the film's simple copying fair."); *see also L.A. Times*, 54 U.S.P.Q.2D (BNA) at 1471–72. Nor does positive impact in one market, here the audio CD market, deprive the copyright holder of the right to develop identified alternative markets, here the digital download market. See *id.* at 1469–71.

We find no error in the district court's factual findings or abuse of discretion in the court's conclusion that plaintiffs will likely prevail in establishing that sampling does not constitute a fair use.

b. Space–Shifting

Napster also maintains that space-shifting is a fair use. Space-shifting occurs when a Napster user downloads MP3 music files in order to listen to music he already owns on audio CD. See id. at 915–16. Napster asserts that we have already held that space-shifting of musical compositions and sound recordings is a fair use. See *Recording Indus. Ass'n of Am. v. Diamond Multimedia Sys., Inc.*, 180 F.3d 1072, 1079 (9th Cir.1999) ("Rio [a portable MP3 player] merely makes copies in order to render portable, or 'space-shift, 'those files that already reside on a user's hard drive. ...Such copying is a paradigmatic noncommercial personal use."). *See also generally Sony*, 464 U.S. at 423 (holding that "time-shifting," where a video tape recorder owner records a television show for later viewing, is a fair use).

We conclude that the district court did not err when it refused to apply the "shifting" analyses of *Sony* and *Diamond*. Both *Diamond* and *Sony* are inapposite because the methods of shifting in these cases did not also simultaneously involve distribution of the copyrighted material to the general public; the time or space-shifting of copyrighted material exposed the material only to the original user. In *Diamond*, for example, the copyrighted music was transferred from the user's computer hard drive to the user's portable MP3 player. So too *Sony*, where "the majority of VCR purchasers ... did not distribute taped television broadcasts, but merely enjoyed them at home." *Napster*, 114 F. Supp. 2d at 913. Conversely, it is obvious that once a user lists a copy of music he already owns on the Napster system in order to access the music from another location, the song becomes "available to millions of other individuals," not just the original CD owner. See *UMG Recordings*, 92 F. Supp. 2d at 351–52 (finding spaceshifting of MP3 files not a fair use even when previous ownership is demonstrated before a download is allowed); cf. *Religious Tech. Ctr. v. Lerma*, 1996 U.S. Dist. LEXIS 15454, No. 95–1107 A, 1996 WL 633131, at

*6 (E.D.Va. Oct.4, 1996) (suggesting that storing copyrighted material on computer disk for later review is not a fair use).

c. Other Uses

Permissive reproduction by either independent or established artists is the final fair use claim made by Napster. The district court noted that plaintiffs did not seek to enjoin this and any other noninfringing use of the Napster system, including: chat rooms, message boards and Napster's New Artist Program. *Napster*, 114 F. Supp. 2d at 917. Plaintiffs do not challenge these uses on appeal.

We find no error in the district court's determination that plaintiffs will likely succeed in establishing that Napster users do not have a fair use defense.

. . .

[Editors' note: the court's discussion of Napster's liability for the infringements committed by its users is excerpted *infra*, Chapter 8.]

UMG Recordings, Inc. v. MP3.Com, Inc.

92 F. Supp. 2d 349 (S.D.N.Y.2000).

■ JED S. RAKOFF, DISTRICT JUDGE.

The complex marvels of cyberspatial communication may create difficult legal issues; but not in this case. Defendant's infringement of plaintiff's copyrights is clear. Accordingly, on April 28, 2000, the Court granted defendant's [sic] motion for partial summary judgment holding defendant liable for copyright infringement. This opinion will state the reasons why.

The pertinent facts, either undisputed or, where disputed, taken most favorably to defendant, are as follows:

The technology known as "MP3" permits rapid and efficient conversion of compact disc recordings ("CDs") to computer files easily accessed over the Internet. See generally *Recording Industry Ass'n of America v. Diamond Multimedia Systems Inc.*, 180 F.3d 1072, 1073–74 (9th Cir.1999). Utilizing this technology, defendant MP3.com, on or around January 12, 2000, launched its "My.MP3.com" service, which it advertised as permitting subscribers to store, customize, and listen to the recordings contained on their CDs from any place where they have an internet connection. To make good on this offer, defendant purchased tens of thousands of popular CDs in which plaintiffs held the copyrights, and, without authorization, copied their recordings onto its computer servers so as to be able to replay the recordings for its subscribers.

Specifically, in order to first access such a recording, a subscriber to MP3.com must either "prove" that he already owns the CD version of the recording by inserting his copy of the commercial CD into his computer CD–Rom drive for a few seconds (the "Beam-it Service") or must purchase the CD from one of defendant's cooperating online retailers (the "Instant Listening Service"). Thereafter, however, the subscriber can access via the

Internet from a computer anywhere in the world the copy of plaintiffs' recording made by defendant. Thus, although defendant seeks to portray its service as the "functional equivalent" of storing its subscribers' CDs, in actuality defendant is re-playing for the subscribers converted versions of the recordings it copied, without authorization, from plaintiffs' copyrighted CDs. On its face, this makes out a presumptive case of infringement under the Copyright Act of 1976.

Defendant argues, however, that such copying is protected by the affirmative defense of "fair use." . . .

Regarding the first [statutory fair use] factor—"the purpose and character of the use"—defendant does not dispute that its purpose is commercial, for while subscribers to My.MP3.com are not currently charged a fee, defendant seeks to attract a sufficiently large subscription base to draw advertising and otherwise make a profit. Consideration of the first factor, however, also involves inquiring into whether the new use essentially repeats the old or whether, instead, it "transforms" it by infusing it with new meaning, new understanding, or the like. Here, although defendant recites that My.MP3.com provides a transformative "space shift" by which subscribers can enjoy the sound recordings contained on their CDs without lugging around the physical discs themselves, this is simply another way of saying that the unauthorized copies are being retransmitted in another medium—an insufficient basis for any legitimate claim of transformation. . . .

Here, defendant adds no "new aesthetics, new insights and understandings" to the original music recordings it copies, *see Castle Rock*, 150 F.3d at 142 (internal quotation marks omitted), but simply repackages those recordings to facilitate their transmission through another medium. While such services may be innovative, they are not transformative.

Regarding the second factor—"the nature of the copyrighted work"—the creative recordings here being copied are "close[] to the core of intended copyright protection," and, conversely, far removed from the more factual or descriptive work more amenable to "fair use[.]" . . .

Regarding the third factor—"the amount and substantiality of the portion [of the copyrighted work] used [by the copier] in relation to the copyrighted work as a whole"—it is undisputed that defendant copies, and replays, the entirety of the copyrighted works here in issue, thus again negating any claim of fair use. . . .

Regarding the fourth factor—"the effect of the use upon the potential market for or value of the copyrighted work"—defendant's activities on their face invade plaintiffs' statutory right to license their copyrighted sound recordings to others for reproduction. Defendant, however, argues that, so far as the derivative market here involved is concerned, plaintiffs have not shown that such licensing is "traditional, reasonable, or likely to be developed." *American Geophysical*, 60 F.3d at 930 & n.17. Moreover, defendant argues, its activities can only enhance plaintiffs' sales, since subscribers cannot gain access to particular recordings made available by

MP3.com unless they have already "purchased" (actually or purportedly), or agreed to purchase, their own CD copies of those recordings.

Such arguments—though dressed in the garb of an expert's "opinion" (that, on inspection, consists almost entirely of speculative and conclusory statements)—are unpersuasive. Any allegedly positive impact of defendant's activities on plaintiffs' prior market in no way frees defendant to usurp a further market that directly derives from reproduction of the plaintiffs' copyrighted works. *See Infinity Broadcast*, 150 F.3d at 111. This would be so even if the copyrightholder had not yet entered the new market in issue, for a copyrightholder's "exclusive" rights, derived from the Constitution and the Copyright Act, include the right, within broad limits, to curb the development of such a derivative market by refusing to license a copyrighted work or by doing so only on terms the copyright owner finds acceptable. Here, moreover, plaintiffs have adduced substantial evidence that they have in fact taken steps to enter that market by entering into various licensing agreements....

Finally, regarding defendant's purported reliance on other factors, this essentially reduces to the claim that My.MP3.com provides a useful service to consumers that, in its absence, will be served by "pirates." Copyright, however, is not designed to afford consumer protection or convenience but, rather, to protect the copyrightholders' property interests. Moreover, as a practical matter, plaintiffs have indicated no objection in principle to licensing their recordings to companies like MP3.com; they simply want to make sure they get the remuneration the law reserves for them as holders of copyrights on creative works. Stripped to its essence, defendant's "consumer protection" argument amounts to nothing more than a bald claim that defendant should be able to misappropriate plaintiffs' property simply because there is a consumer demand for it. This hardly appeals to the conscience of equity.

In sum, on any view, defendant's "fair use" defense is indefensible and must be denied as a matter of law....

. . .

Accordingly, the Court, for the foregoing reasons, has determined that plaintiffs are entitled to partial summary judgment holding defendant to have infringed plaintiffs' copyrights.

[Editors' Note: At a subsequent stage of the proceedings, the district court determined that, in awarding statutory damages under section 504, all of the tracks on an unlawfully copied CD were to count as a single work, that the defendant's infringement was willful and that it should pay $25,000 per CD, and that—temporarily accepting the defendant's contention that the copyrights in no more than 4,700 CDs were owned by plaintiff UMG (the other record-company plaintiffs having settled)—statutory damages would amount to approximately $118 million. UMG Recordings, Inc. v. MP3.COM, Inc., 109 F. Supp. 2d 223 (S.D.N.Y.2000). Before the intended final hearing to determine damages, UMG and MP3 also settled, with MP3 agreeing to pay $53.4 million in exchange for a license to deliver the entire

UMG music catalog over the My.MP3.com service. On December 4, 2000, MP3 revived its My.MP3.com service offering both an annual subscription account and a free account (supported by advertising revenues) that features fewer services and recordings.

QUESTIONS

1. The advent of digital networks has vastly increased the power of users, be they commercial or individual, to copy and redisseminate copyrighted works. In many instances, new media open up new or distant markets that can enhance the value of the copyright. Should it make a difference whether the copyright owner's efforts led to the development of the new market? Should it make a difference whether the copyright owner currently intends to exploit the new market? Should it matter whether the "public benefit" claim of fair use addresses increased availability of the same (plaintiff's) work rather than the increased creativity stemming from (defendant's) transformative use?

2. What are the differences between the way My.MP3.com conducts its business and Napster? Do these differences counsel different results?

3. Suppose you emailed MP3 files from your music collection to your 5 best friends: fair use? To your 50 closest friends? Suppose you joined a chat group that "traded" MP3 files: Is your participation fair use? Who else's liability might be implicated in the chatroom example (see also *infra* Chapter 8)?

4. Suppose that instead of creating a database of 80,000 copied CDs, My.MP3.com created cyber-storage lockers for each of its subscribers, so that each subscriber uploaded her MP3 files to a location accessible only to her, from which the recordings would be streamed back to the user on request. Prima facie infringement? Fair use?

IS THE USE "TRANSFORMATIVE" OR MERELY REDISTRIBUTIVE?

Two recent decisions, immediately below, address the concept of "transformative" use in the context of copying material from one Internet site for placement on another. In neither case was the copied work incorporated into a new and independent work of criticism or commentary; rather, the defendants asserted "transformative use" because their websites allegedly served purposes different from those served by the websites from which the works were copied. In other words, these cases pose the question, *inter alia*, whether audience-shifting is fair use. The cases also present questions specific to fair use on the Internet: if a work is already on the Web, is it more or less subject to lawful unlicensed copying than are hard copy works? The arguments cut both ways. On the one hand, for the copyright owner to make works available in such easily copyable media could be taken as a tacit acknowledgment of their fair vulnerability to reproduction and redissemination; on the other, there is less need to copy when the Internet permits linking to the referenced documents.

Kelly v. Arriba Soft Corp.

77 F. Supp. 2d 1116 (C.D.Cal.1999), *appeal pending*.

■ GARY L. TAYLOR, DISTRICT JUDGE.

On apparent first impression, the Court holds the use by an Internet "visual search engine" of others' copyrighted images is a prima facia copyright violation, but it may be justified under the "fair use" doctrine. The Court finds that, under the particular circumstances of this case, the "fair use" doctrine applies. . . .

Defendant's Motion for Partial Summary Judgment on Plaintiff's First and Second Claims for Relief is GRANTED. Plaintiff's Motion for Partial Summary Judgment is DENIED.

I.   BACKGROUND

Defendant Ditto (formerly known as Arriba) operates a "visual search engine" on the Internet. Like other Internet search engines, it allows a user to obtain a list of related Web content in response to a search query entered by the user. Unlike other Internet search engines, Defendant's retrieves images instead of descriptive text. It produces a list of reduced, "thumbnail" pictures related to the user's query.

During the period when most of the relevant events in this case occurred, Defendant's visual search engine was known as the Arriba Vista Image Searcher. By "clicking" on the desired thumbnail, an Arriba Vista user could view the "image attributes" window displaying the full-size version of the image, a description of its dimensions, and an address for the Web site where it originated.[1] By clicking on the address, the user could link to the originating Web site for the image.[2]

Ditto's search engine (in both of its versions) works by maintaining an indexed database of approximately two million thumbnail images. These thumbnails are obtained through the operation of Ditto's "crawler," a computer program that travels the Web in search of images to be converted into thumbnails and added to the index.[3] Ditto's employees conduct a final

---

1. This full-size image was not technically located on Defendant's Web site. It was displayed by opening a link to its originating Web page. But only the image itself, and not any other part of the originating Web page, was displayed on the image attributes page. From the user's perspective, the source of the image matters less than the context in which it is displayed.

2. Defendant's current search engine, ditto.com, operates in a slightly different manner. When a ditto.com user clicks on a thumbnail, two windows open simultaneously. One window contains the full-size image; the other contains the originating Web page in full.

3. Images are briefly stored in full on Defendant's server until the thumbnail is made; they are then deleted. Joint Stip. P 32. There is no claim that Defendant provides any access to the full-sized images during this period.

screening to rank the most relevant thumbnails and eliminate inappropriate images.

Plaintiff Kelly is a photographer specializing in photographs of California gold rush country and related to the works of Laura Ingalls Wilder. He does not sell the photographs independently, but his photographs have appeared in several books. Plaintiff also maintains two Web sites, one of which (www.goldrush1849.com) provides a "virtual tour" of California's gold rush country and promotes Plaintiff's book on the subject, and the other (www.showmethegold.com) markets corporate retreats in California's gold rush country.

In January 1999, around thirty five of Plaintiff's images were indexed by the Ditto crawler and put in Defendant's image database. As a result, these images were made available in thumbnail form to users of Defendant's visual search engine.

After being notified of Plaintiff's objections, Ditto removed the images from its database, though due to various technical problems some of the images reappeared a few times. Meanwhile Plaintiff, having sent Defendant a notice of copyright infringement in January, filed this action in April. Plaintiff argues its copyrights in the images were infringed by Defendant's actions. . . .

II. DISCUSSION

These cross motions for summary adjudication present two questions of first impression. The first is whether the display of copyrighted images by a "visual search engine" on the Internet constitutes fair use under the Copyright Act. . . .

A. Fair Use . . .

1. Purpose and Character Of The Use

. . . There is no dispute Defendant operates its Web site for commercial purposes. Plaintiff's images, however, did not represent a significant element of that commerce, nor were they exploited in any special way.[5] They were reproduced as a result of Defendant's generally indiscriminate method of gathering images. Defendant has a commercial interest in developing a comprehensive thumbnail index so it can provide more complete results to users of its search engine. The Ditto crawler is designed to obtain large numbers of images from numerous sources without seeking authorization. Plaintiff's images were indexed as a result of these methods. While the use here was commercial, it was also of a somewhat more incidental and less exploitative nature than more traditional types of "commercial use."

5. The use in this case is commercial, but it is unusual and less serious than many other commercial uses. If, for example, Plaintiff's images were used without authorization in advertising for Defendant's Web site, a finding of fair use would be much less likely.The use in this case is commercial, but it is unusual and less serious than many other commercial uses. If, for example, Plaintiff's images were used without authorization in advertising for Defendant's Web site, a finding of fair use would be much less likely.

The most significant factor favoring Defendant is the transformative nature of its use of Plaintiff's images. Defendant's use is very different from the use for which the images were originally created. Plaintiff's photographs are artistic works used for illustrative purposes. Defendant's visual search engine is designed to catalog and improve access to images on the Internet. The character of the thumbnail index is not esthetic, but functional; its purpose is not to be artistic, but to be comprehensive.

To a lesser extent, the Arriba Vista image attributes page also served this purpose by allowing users to obtain more details about an image. The image attributes page, however, raises other concerns. It allowed users to view (and potentially download) full-size images without necessarily viewing the rest of the originating Web page. At the same time, it was less clearly connected to the search engine's purpose of finding and organizing Internet content for users. The presence of the image attributes page in the old version of the search engine somewhat detracts from the transformative effect of the search engine. But, when considering purpose and character of use in a new enterprise of this sort, it is more appropriate to consider the transformative purpose rather than the early imperfect means of achieving that purpose. The Court finds the purpose and character of Defendant's use was on the whole significantly transformative.

The Court finds the first factor weighs in favor of fair use.

2.   Nature of the Copyrighted Work

The second factor in § 107 is an acknowledgment "that some works are closer to the core of intended copyright protection than others, with the consequence that fair use is more difficult to establish when the former works are copied." *Campbell, supra*;, 510 U.S. at 586. Artistic works like Plaintiff's photographs are part of that core. The Court finds the second factor weighs against fair use.

3.   Amount and Substantiality of the Portion Used

The third fair use factor assesses whether the amount copied was "reasonable in relation to the purpose of the copying." *Id*. The analysis focuses on "the persuasiveness of a [copier's] justification for the particular copying done, and the enquiry will harken back to the first of the statutory factors, for . . . the extent of permissible copying varies with the purpose and character of the use." *Id*. at 586–87.

In the thumbnail index, Defendant used Plaintiff's images in their entirety, but reduced them in size. Defendant argues it is necessary for a visual search engine to copy images in their entirety so users can be sure of recognizing them, and the reduction in size and resolution mitigates damage that might otherwise result from copying. As Defendant has illustrated in its brief, thumbnails cannot be enlarged into useful images. Use of partial images or images further reduced in size would make images difficult for users to identify, and would eliminate the usefulness of Defendant's search engine as a means of categorizing and improving access to Internet resources.

As with the first factor, the Arriba Vista image attributes page presents a greater problem because it displayed a full-size image separated from the surrounding content on its originating Web page. Image attributes (e.g. dimensions and the address of the originating site) could have been displayed without reproducing the full-size image, and the display of the full image was not necessary to the main purposes of the search engine.[8]

If only the thumbnail index were at issue, Defendant's copying would likely be reasonable in light of its purposes. The image attributes page, however, was more remotely related to the purposes of the search engine. The Court finds the third factor weighs slightly against fair use.

4. Effect of the Use On The Potential Market or Value

. . .

The relevant market is Plaintiff's Web sites as a whole. The photographs are used to promote the products sold by Plaintiff's Web sites (including Plaintiff's books and corporate tour packages) and draw users to view the additional advertisements posted on those Web sites. The fourth factor addresses not just the potential market for a particular photo, but also its "value." The value of Plaintiff's photographs to Plaintiff could potentially be adversely affected if their promotional purposes are undermined.

Defendant argues there is no likely negative impact because its search engine does not compete with Plaintiff's Web sites and actually increases the number of users finding their way to those sites.

Plaintiff argues the market for his various products has been harmed. Defendant's conduct created a possibility that some users might improperly copy and use Plaintiff's images from Defendant's site. Defendant's search engine also enabled users to "deep link" directly to the pages containing retrieved images, and thereby bypass the "front page" of the originating Web site. As a result, these users would be less likely to view all of the advertisements on the Web sites or view the Web site's entire promotional message. However, Plaintiff has shown no evidence of any harm or adverse impact.

In the absence of any evidence about traffic to Plaintiff's Web sites or effects on Plaintiff's businesses, the Court cannot find any market harm to Plaintiff. The Defendant has met its burden of proof by offering evidence tending to show a lack of market harm, and Plaintiff has not refuted that evidence. The Court finds the fourth factor weighs in favor of fair use.

5. Conclusion—Fair Use

The Court finds two of the four factors weigh in favor of fair use, and two weigh against it. The first and fourth factors (character of use and lack of market harm) weigh in favor of a fair use finding because of the

---

8. The newer search engine, ditto.com, appears to lessen this problem by eliminating the image attributes page and simultaneously opening the originating Web page along with a full-size image.

established importance of search engines and the "transformative" nature of using reduced versions of images to organize and provide access to them. The second and third factors (creative nature of the work and amount or substantiality of copying) weigh against fair use.

The first factor of the fair use test is the most important in this case. Defendant never held Plaintiff's work out as its own, or even engaged in conduct specifically directed at Plaintiff's work. Plaintiff's images were swept up along with two million others available on the Internet, as part of Defendant's efforts to provide its users with a better way to find images on the Internet. Defendant's purposes were and are inherently transformative, even if its realization of those purposes was at times imperfect. Where, as here, a new use and new technology are evolving, the broad transformative purpose of the use weighs more heavily than the inevitable flaws in its early stages of development.

The Court has weighed all of the § 107 factors together. The Court finds Defendant's conduct constituted fair use of Plaintiff's images. There is no triable issue of material fact remaining to be resolved on the question of fair use, and summary adjudication is appropriate. Defendant's motion is GRANTED and Plaintiff's motion is DENIED as to the copyright infringement claims.

Los Angeles Times v. Free Republic

54 U.S.P.Q.2d 1453 (C.D.Cal., April 4, 2000).

■ MARGARET M. MORROW, DISTRICT JUDGE

Plaintiffs Los Angeles Times and The Washington Post Company publish newspapers in print and online versions. Defendant Free Republic is a "bulletin board" website whose members use the site to post news articles to which they add remarks or commentary. Other visitors to the site then read the articles and add their comments. For the most part, Free Republic members post the entire text of articles in which they are interested; among these are verbatim copies of articles from the Los Angeles Times and Washington Post websites. Plaintiffs' complaint alleges that the unauthorized copying and posting of the articles on the Free Republic site constitutes copyright infringement.

Defendants have now moved for summary judgment. They assert that the copying of news articles onto their website is protected by the fair use doctrine....

I.   FACTUAL BACKGROUND

A.   The Parties

Plaintiffs publish the Los Angeles Times and The Washington Post in print and online at "http://www.latimes.com" and "http://www.washington-post.com." Their respective websites contain the current edition of the newspaper, which can be viewed free of charge, and archived articles that users must pay to view.... [T]he websites also produce advertising and licensing revenue for the papers [which] depends on the volume of traffic the sites experience during a given period. The parties dispute the extent to which being able to access archived articles at a different site for free affects plaintiffs' ability to advertise, license, and sell the archived articles.

. . .

II. DISCUSSION

. . .

C. The Fair Use Defense . . .

1. The Purpose And Character Of The Use . . .

a. The Purpose Of Free Republic's Use And The Extent To Which Its Work Is Transformative

There is no dispute that at least some of the items posted on the Free Republic website are exact copies of [whole or substantial portions of] plaintiffs' articles. . . .

There is little transformative about copying the entirety or large portions of a work verbatim. [citations omitted]

Defendants proffer two reasons why their full text copying of plaintiffs' articles is nonetheless transformative. First, they assert that the copies of the articles found on the Free Republic site do not in reality substitute for the originals found on plaintiffs' web pages. Second, they contend they copy no more than necessary to fulfill their purpose of criticizing the manner in which the media covers current events and politics. Each of these contentions will be examined in turn.

Defendants' first argument . . . focuses on readers' ability to access and review specific articles in which they are interested. Defendants contend that using the Free Republic site to read current articles would be impractical since there is a delay between the time information is posted to the site and the time it is indexed by third-party search engines. Additionally, they assert that the imprecision of search language makes it difficult to locate archived articles at the site. These arguments overlook the fact that the Free Republic site has its own search engine that apparently has immediate search capability.

Even were this not true, the articles posted on the Free Republic site ultimately serve the same purpose as "that [for which] one would normally seek to obtain the original—to have it available . . . for ready reference if and when [website visitors adding comments] need[] to look at it." *American Geophysical Union v. Texaco, Inc.*, 60 F.3d 913, 918 (2d Cir.1994) (the court held that the first fair use factor weighed against a defendant that encouraged its employees to make unauthorized photocopies of articles in scientific and medical journals and keep them in their offices for ready reference).

Defendants' web page acknowledges this. It states, inter alia, that the Free Republic site is a place where visitors "can often find breaking news and up to the minute updates." Indeed, it is clear from the content of the representative pages submitted by defendants that visitors can read copies of plaintiffs' current and archived articles at the Free Republic site. For those who visit the site regularly, therefore, the articles posted there serve as substitutes for the originals found on plaintiffs' websites or in their newspapers.

Defendants next argue that their use of plaintiffs' works is transformative because registered Free Republic users add comments and criticism concerning the articles following a posting. Copying portions of a copyrighted work for the purpose of criticism or commentary is often considered fair use. The fact that criticism is involved, however, does not end the inquiry. Rather, it must be considered in combination with other circumstances to determine if the first factor favors defendants.

Since the first posting of an article to the Free Republic site often contains little or no commentary, it does not significantly transform plaintiffs' work. In *Netcom On–Line* defendant posted verbatim copies of works copyrighted by the Church of Scientology to an Internet website "with little or no added comment or criticism." The court found that the works were only "minimally transformative" because "unlike the typical critic, [defendant] added little new expression to the Church's works." The court specifically rejected defendant's argument that his copying was fair use because subsequent visitors added further comments. It concluded that while the copying of "works that were previously posted by their authors on the basis of an implied license or fair use argument" might be justified, such a defense would not be available "where the first posting made an unauthorized copy of a copyrighted work."

. . .

Additionally, even where copying serves the "criticism, comment and news reporting" purposes highlighted in § 107, its extent cannot exceed what is necessary to the purpose. Thus, an individualized assessment of the purpose for which defendants are copying the works and a comparison of that purpose to the amount copied is required.

Here, it seems clear that the primary purpose of the postings to the Free Republic site is to facilitate discussion, criticism and comment by registered visitors. Defendants contend that copying all or parts of articles verbatim is necessary to facilitate this purpose. They argue that full text posting is required because links expire after a week or two, and because unsophisticated Internet users will have difficulty accessing a linked site. Defendants' assertion that links expire after a period of time is presumably a reference to the fact that articles are available on plaintiffs' websites free of charge only for a certain number of days. Thereafter, there is a charge for viewing and/or printing them. That this is so does not make linking plaintiffs' websites to the Free Republic site "impractical." It merely requires that Free Republic visitors pay a fee for viewing plaintiffs' articles just as other members of the public do. Similarly, defendants' suggestion that articles are posted to the Free Republic site long after they are published is not supported by the representative postings they have submitted. These reflect that the vast majority of comments are posted the same day the articles appear or within one to three days afterwards. Finally, defendants' assertion that unsophisticated Internet users would be confused by links is unpersuasive. Linking is familiar to most Internet users, even those who are new to the web.

As evidence that verbatim copying is in fact not necessary to defendants' purpose, plaintiffs cite the fact that defendants provided a hypertext link to Jewish World Review's website at its request, and requested that registered Free Republic visitors no longer copy the publication's articles verbatim. That defendants accommodated Jewish World Review belies their current contention that only verbatim posting of articles will serve the criticism and comment purposes of the Free Republic site. Indeed, they acknowledge that honoring Jewish World Review's request "did not significantly detract from the purpose of the freerepublic.com website."

The fact that linking the text of an article as it appears on plaintiffs' websites to the Free Republic site, or summarizing the article's text, is not as easy or convenient for Free Republic users as full text posting does not render the practice a fair use. Rather, the focus of the inquiry must be whether verbatim copying is necessary to defendants' critical purpose.

Defendants have not met their burden of demonstrating that verbatim copying of all or a substantial portion of plaintiffs' articles is necessary to achieve their critical purpose. They argue that the purpose of full text posting is to enable Free Republic users to criticize the manner in which the media covers current events. The statement or purpose found on the website, however, is somewhat different. There, defendants state that visitors to the Free Republic site "are encouraged to comment on the news of the day . . . and . . . to contribute whatever information they may have to help others better understand a particular story." In fact, a review of the representative articles submitted by defendants reveals that visitors' commentary focuses much more on the news of the day than it does on the manner in which the media reports that news.This is significant, since the extent of copying that might be necessary to comment on the nature of the media's coverage of a news event is arguably greater than the amount needed to facilitate comment on the event itself. Commentary on news events requires only recitation of the underlying facts, not verbatim repetition of another's creative expression of those facts in a news article. So too, the fact that a particular media outlet published a given story, or approached that story from a particular angle can be communicated to a large degree without posting a full text copy of the report. For this reason, the court concludes that verbatim posting of plaintiffs' articles is "more than is necessary" to further defendants' critical purpose.

For all these reasons, the court concludes that defendants' use of plaintiffs' articles is minimally, if at all, transformative.

   b.   Commercial Nature Of The Free Republic Website

   . . . [T]he Second Circuit has described the proper analysis as "differentiating between a direct commercial use and [a] more indirect relation to

... commercial activity." *American Geophysical, supra*, 60 F.3d at 921. In *American Geophysical*, the court stated that the heart of "the commercial/nonprofit dichotomy concerns the unfairness that arises when a secondary user makes unauthorized use of copyrighted material to capture significant revenues as a direct consequence of copying the original work." Since, in the case before it, Texaco did not derive direct or immediate revenue or profits from photocopying articles in scientific and medical journals for members of its research staff, the court held that its use was "intermediate," and that the link between the copying and Texaco's commercial gain was "somewhat attenuated." Nonetheless, it concluded that Texaco "reaped at least some indirect benefit from its photocopying," and that this in turn had some impact on its ability to develop marketable products. Accordingly, the court stated, "it is not obvious why it is fair for Texaco to avoid having to pay at least some price to copyright holders for the right to photocopy the original articles."

Here, the analysis is much the same. Defendants do not generate revenue or profits from posting plaintiffs' articles on the Free Republic website. At most, they derive indirect economic benefit by enhancing the website's cachet, increasing registrations, and hence increasing donations and other forms of support. Coupled with the fact that Free Republic has many of the attributes of a non-profit organization, this indirect benefit argues against a finding that the use is strictly commercial. Rather, it is more appropriate to conclude that, while defendants do not necessarily "exploit" the articles for commercial gain, their posting to the Free Republic site allows defendants and other visitors to avoid paying the "customary price" charged for the works.

c.   Conclusion Regarding First Fair Use Factor

... Since the "central purpose" of the inquiry on the first fair use factor is to determine "whether the new work merely 'supersede[s] the objects' of the original creation, ... or instead adds something new", the court finds that the non-transformative character of the copying in this case tips the scale in plaintiffs' favor, and outweighs the non-profit/public benefit nature of the purpose for which the copying is performed. This is particularly true since the posting of plaintiffs' articles to the Free Republic site amounts to "systematic ... multiplying [of] the available number of copies" of the articles, "thereby serving the same purpose" for which licenses are sold or archive charges imposed. The first fair use factor thus favors plaintiffs.

2.   The Nature Of The Copyrighted Work

... While plaintiffs' news articles certainly contain expressive elements, they are predominantly factual. Consequently, defendants' fair use claim is stronger than it would be had the works been purely fictional. The court concludes that the second factor weighs in favor of a finding a fair use of the news articles by defendants in this case.

3.   The Amount And Substantiality Of The Portion Used In Relation To The Copyrighted Work As A Whole

Defendants concede that they have copied and posted entire articles published in plaintiffs' newspapers. . . . [V]erbatim copying of entire articles or substantial portions thereof is the norm. . . .

The fact that exact copies of plaintiffs' article are posted to the Free Republic site weighs strongly against a finding of fair use in this case.

. . . . Defendants also contend that copying all or a substantial portion of the articles is essential to the critical purpose of the Free Republic website. In assessing such an argument, *Campbell* [*v. Acuff–Rose Music, Inc.*, at p. 611 of casebook] instructs that the court focus on "the persuasiveness of a [copier's] justification for the particular copying done," and noted that "the enquiry will harken back to the first of the statutory factors, for . . . the extent of the permissible copying varies with the purpose and character of the use."

As detailed in the court's consideration of the first fair use factor, defendants have not offered a persuasive argument that full-text copying is essential to the critical purpose of the Free Republic site. Contrasted with the purpose and character of the use, the wholesale copying of plaintiffs' articles weighs against a finding of fair use.

4. The Effect Of The Use On The Potential Market For Or Value Of The Copyrighted Work

. . . . [T]he undisputed evidence shows that the Free Republic website has approximately 20,000 registered users, receives as many as 100,000 hits per day, and attracts between 25 and 50 million page views each month. . . . [F]or those individuals who visit the site, the articles posted to freerepublic.com do substitute for the original works. Given the number of registered visitors, hits and page views Free Republic attracts, the court cannot accept defendants' assertion that the site has only a de minimis effect on plaintiffs' ability to control the market for the copyrighted works. . . .

Plaintiffs assert they have lost and will lose revenue because visitors to the Free Republic site can read plaintiffs' archived news articles without paying the fee they would be charged for accessing the articles at plaintiffs' sites. Similarly, plaintiffs contend that defendants' use affects their ability to generate licensing revenue, since the fact that the articles are available for free viewing on Free Republic's web page diminishes their value to licensees. Finally, plaintiffs argue that defendants' copying reduces the number of people visiting their sites, and thus causes them to lose advertising revenue calculated on the number of hits they receive.

Defendants respond that plaintiffs have not adduced evidence of lost revenue resulting from operation of the Free Republic site. This, however, is not determinative. In [*Los Angeles News Serv. v. Reuters Television, Int'l*, 149 F.3d 987 (9th Cir.1998)], defendants copied plaintiffs' news footage without permission. Plaintiffs could not prove that they had lost sales of the footage or that they had suffered any actual adverse market effect. *Id.* The court noted that allowing a customer to buy the footage from defendants rather than plaintiffs lessened the market for plaintiffs' footage, and concluded that "such actions if permitted would result in a substantially adverse impact on the potential market for the original works." [citation omitted] Here, plaintiffs have shown that they are attempting to exploit the market for viewing their articles online, for selling copies of archived articles, and for licensing others to display or sell the articles. Defendants' use "substitutes" for the originals, and has the potential of lessening the frequency with which individuals visit plaintiffs' websites, of diminishing the market for the sale of archived articles, and decreasing the interest in licensing the articles.

Defendants counter that there is no evidence that people who view the articles on the Free Republic site would ever have visited plaintiffs' websites. It is not necessary, however, to show with certainty that future harm will result. That likelihood is present when articles that would otherwise be available only at sites controlled or licensed by plaintiffs are available at a different site as well. The likelihood only increases when one considers the impact on the market if defendants' practice of full text copying were to become widespread.

Defendants also contend that plaintiffs actually benefit from having their articles posted verbatim on the Free Republic site.... [Free Republic's expert] states that the Los Angeles Times' website receives approximately 20,000 hits per month from users who visit the Free Republic site before accessing the Times' site.... [H]owever, he does not address how many hits are diverted from plaintiffs' websites as a consequence of the posting of articles to the Free Republic site, and this is the pertinent inquiry in terms of potential market harm.

Defendants assert the evidence regarding referral hits demonstrates that Free Republic is creating a demand for plaintiffs' works. Even if this is the case, it does not mandate a conclusion that the fourth fair use factor favors defendants. Courts have routinely rejected the argument that a use is fair because it increases demand for the plaintiff's copyrighted work....

5.   Balancing The Fair Use Factors

In sum, three of the four fair use factors weigh in plaintiffs' favor. Moreover, the factor that favors defendants—the nature of the copyrighted work—does not provide strong support for a fair use finding, since defendants copied both the factual and the expressive elements of plaintiffs' news articles. Conversely, the amount and substantiality of the copying and the lack of any significant transformation of the articles weigh heavily in favor of plaintiffs on this issue. The court thus finds that defendants may not assert a fair use defense to plaintiffs' copyright infringement claim.

D.   First Amendment Defense

Defendants assert, as a separate defense, the fact that the First Amendment protects their posting of copies of plaintiffs' news articles to the Free Republic website. Defendants contend that visitors to the Free Republic site will be unable to express their views concerning the manner in which the media covers current events since the omissions and biases in the articles will be difficult to communicate to readers without the full text of the article available.

... Even assuming [the Supreme Court has entertained the possibility of a distinct First Amendment defense when the copyrighted work's expression is itself particularly newsworthy], defendants have failed to show that copying plaintiffs' news articles verbatim is essential to communication of the opinions and criticisms visitors to the website express. As discussed above in connection with analysis of defendants' fair use defense, visitors' comments more often concern the underlying news event than they do the manner in which that event was covered by the media. And, even where media coverage is the subject of the critique, the gist of the comments (which concern the fact that a particular media outlet published a story or approached the story from a particular angle) can generally be communicated without full text copying of the article. The availability of alternatives—such as linking and summarizing—further undercuts any claim that First Amendment rights are implicated. While defendants and other users of the Free Republic site may find these options less ideal than copying plaintiffs' articles verbatim, this does not demonstrate that a First Amendment violation will occur if full text posting is prohibited

QUESTIONS

1. In *Kelly v. Arriba*, what are the elements of the defendant's use of the plaintiff's photographic images that make it "transformative"? Shrinking their size? Moving them to the defendant's website (i.e., "audience-shifting")? Compiling them with other images? Indexing all of those images?

If a website took all of the songs written by, say, Irving Berlin, and duplicated only the melody lines (without any harmonies or musical arrangements)—and then made them available, along with the melodies written by many other prominent songwriters, and indexed them—would that be a transformative use of the Berlin melodies that would "significantly" cut in favor of fair use? Is there any difference between doing this in hardcopy form and doing it electronically on an internet website? Does it matter whether the Berlin tunes are already on the Internet, on other authorized websites?

2. The court in *Kelly v. Arriba* points out that the plaintiff photographer failed to show how the defendant's image index might have caused him adverse economic injury. If you were counsel for the plaintiff, how would you go about identifying and proving such injury?

3. Suppose the defendant in *Free Republic* had posted only those articles that were no longer accessible by linking? Or suppose it had limited its website to reader comments that addressed only the "bias" of the reporting disclosed in the copied excerpts. Would/should this have made a difference to the fair use analysis?

GENERAL REVIEW QUESTIONS

1.   Assume that a cartographer explores a hitherto uncharted geographic area and that she prepares, publishes, and copyrights a painstakingly detailed map of that area. Another individual refers to that map and makes an unauthorized chart that lists the distances between all points on the map, as well as altitudes and population (also shown on the map for the first time). Has the copyright on the map been infringed? Does the answer rest upon an analysis of copyrightability? Of infringement? Of fair use? Is there any difference in the determining factors under these analyses?

2.   Tom Tilden is a teacher of high school English, who regularly has his students read some of the plays of Shakespeare. Last month, the copyrighted motion picture of *Hamlet* was shown on television. Tilden used his videotape machine to make a tape of the film as it was being shown on television, and last week he ran the tape through a classroom television set so that the film could be viewed by his students during the school day. Has the Copyright Act been violated? If so, what are the remedies? *See Encyclopaedia Britannica Educ. Corp. v. Crooks,* 542 F.Supp. 1156 (W.D.N.Y.1982), and 558 F.Supp. 1247 (W.D.N.Y.1983).

CHAPTER 8

ENFORCEMENT OF COPYRIGHT

§ 501. Infringement of copyright

(a) Anyone who violates any of the exclusive rights of the copyright owner as provided by sections 106 through [121] or of the author as provided in section 106A, or who imports copies or phonorecords into the United States in violation of section 602, is an infringer of the copyright or right of the author, as the case may be. For purposes of this chapter (other than section 506), any reference to copyright shall be deemed to include the rights conferred by section 106A(a). As used in this subsection, the term "anyone" includes any State, any instrumentality of a State, and any officer or employee of a State or instrumentality of a State acting in his or her official capacity. Any State, and any such instrumentality, officer, or employee, shall be subject to the provisions of this title in the same manner and to the same extent as any nongovernmental entity.

(b) The legal or beneficial owner of an exclusive right under a copyright is entitled, subject to the requirements of section 411, to institute an action for any infringement of that particular right committed while he or she is the owner of it. The court may require such owner to serve written notice of the action with a copy of the complaint upon any person shown, by the records of the Copyright Office or otherwise, to have or claim an interest in the copyright, and shall require that such notice be served upon any person whose interest is likely to be affected by a decision in the case. The court may require the joinder, and shall permit the intervention, of any person having or claiming an interest in the copyright.

A.   INJUNCTIONS

Injunctive relief is grounded on long-established principles of equity. Section 502(a) of the 1976 Act provides that (except as against the Government) a court "may ... grant temporary and final injunctions on such terms as it may deem reasonable to prevent or restrain infringement of a copyright." The Act also provides, in § 502(b), for nationwide service of such injunctions and certain mechanics for out-of-district enforcement.

Whenever equity has jurisdiction to grant an injunction by final decree, it has the power to grant a preliminary injunction, generally for the purpose of maintaining the status quo. Preliminary injunctions have been very important in copyright cases, and it is generally acknowledged that courts issue them far more routinely in such cases than in other sorts of disputes. A long-held view has been that if the plaintiff establishes a prima facie case as to validity of copyright and its infringement, a temporary injunction will generally be issued. Recent appellate cases have concluded that irreparable injury may be presumed once the plaintiff satisfactorily proves that it will likely prevail on the merits. *See, e.g., Apple Computer, Inc. v. Formula International, Inc.,* 725 F.2d 521, 525 (9th Cir.1984).

It is also true that a permanent injunction routinely issues when copyright validity and infringement are ultimately found. Again, it is normally assumed that compensatory relief will not adequately redress the injury, often because it is difficult to assess, and that the infringement will likely continue in the future unless enjoined. An interesting and difficult issue arises when the defendant's work, rather than being merely an exact or close reiteration of the plaintiff's, incorporates the plaintiff's protectible expression only in part but adds a significant measure of independent creative elements.

In *Stewart v. Abend,* 495 U.S. 207 (1990), for example, the defendant's well-known motion picture, Rear Window, was based upon a copyrighted short story, but added creative contributions of the screen writers, the director Alfred Hitchcock, the actors Jimmy Stewart and Grace Kelly and others, the cinematographer and the composer of the musical score. Once it was determined that the continued distribution of the film was a copyright infringement, after the renewal term of the underlying short story had vested in the successors of the story writer, should the court enjoin future distribution, exhibition, and other marketing of the motion picture? (See the opinion below, *Abend v. MCA, Inc.,* 863 F.2d 1465 (9th Cir.1988).) Would an injunction in the latter case unduly penalize the film makers and deprive the public of their valuable creative contributions, and might the plaintiff's interests be adequately protected through a judicial decree allowing continued distribution and exhibition upon the payment of a reasonable royalty—equivalent to a judicially created compulsory license? Is this within the power of a court of equity?

The Supreme Court has hinted that this kind of compromise remedy may well be possible. In *Campbell v. Acuff–Rose Music, Inc., supra* Chapter 7.B, the Supreme Court in effect abandoned the time-tested maxim that injunctive relief should be routine when infringement is found—at least when the infringing work is "transformative" in its borrowing from the copyrighted work, e.g., parody. In such a situation, the public interest might well be served by permitting the defendant to make its new contributions publicly available upon payment of a reasonable royalty to the copyright owner. In *New York Times Co. v. Tasini, supra* Chapter 3B, the Court returned to its suggestion that injunctive relief may not always be the most appropriate way of resolving a copyright dispute. Responding to the *Times'* contention that a ruling for the authors would oblige the collective works copyright owner to remove all free-lance authors' contributions from licensed databases and CD ROM products, thereby gravely compromising "history," the Court rejoined:

Notwithstanding the dire predictions from some quarters, it hardly follows from today's decision that an injunction against the inclusion of these Articles in the Databases (much less all freelance articles in any databases) must issue. See 17 U.S.C. § 502(a) (court "may" enjoin infringement); *Campbell v. Acuff–Rose Music, Inc.*, 510 U.S. 569, 578, n. 10 (1994) (goals of copyright law are "not always best served by automatically granting injunctive relief"). The parties (Authors and Publishers) may enter into an agreement allowing continued electronic reproduction of the Authors' works; they, and if necessary the courts and Congress, may draw on numerous models for distributing copyrighted works and remunerating authors for their distribution.

Is this analysis an invitation to trial judges to create nonstatutory compulsory licenses in all cases involving "productive" or "transformative" or otherwise socially beneficial infringing defendants? Is that sound? Is it consistent with the remedial provisions of the Copyright Act? Is it consistent with the Supreme Court's decision in *Stewart v. Abend, supra* Chapter 4.B?

Compare the response of the Court of Appeals for the Ninth Circuit to Napster's contention that the public interest militated against entry of an injunction obliging Napster to block access to infringing copies of recorded music:

> Napster tells us that "where great public injury would be worked by an injunction, the courts might ... award damages or a continuing royalty instead of an injunction in such special circumstances." *Abend v. MCA, Inc.*, 863 F.2d 1465, 1479 (9th Cir.1988) (quoting 3 Melville B. Nimmer & David Nimmer, Nimmer On Copyright § 14.06[B](1988)), *aff'd*, 495 U.S. 207 (1990). We are at a total loss to find any "special circumstances" simply because this case requires us to apply well-established doctrines of copyright law to a new technology. Neither do we agree with Napster that an injunction would cause "great public injury." Further, we narrowly construe any suggestion that compulsory royalties are appropriate in this context because Congress has arguably limited the application of compulsory royalties to specific circumstances, none of which are present here. *See* 17 U.S.C. § 115.

> The Copyright Act provides for various sanctions for infringers. *See, e.g.,* 17 U.S.C. § § 502 (injunctions); 504 (damages); and 506 (criminal penalties); *see also* 18 U.S.C. § 2319A (criminal penalties for the unauthorized fixation of and trafficking in sound recordings and music videos of live musical performances). These statutory sanctions represent a more than adequate legislative solution to the problem created by copyright infringement.

> Imposing a compulsory royalty payment schedule would give Napster an "easy out" of this case. If such royalties were imposed, Napster would avoid penalties for any future violation of an injunction, statutory copyright damages and any possible criminal penalties for continuing infringement. The royalty structure would also grant Napster the luxury of either choosing to continue and pay royalties or shut down.

On the other hand, the wronged parties would be forced to do business with a company that profits from the wrongful use of intellectual properties. Plaintiffs would lose the power to control their intellectual property: they could not make a business decision not to license their property to Napster, and, in the event they planned to do business with Napster, compulsory royalties would take away the copyright holders' ability to negotiate the terms of any contractual arrangement.

(For other parts of the court's opinion, see Chapters 7.C *supra* and 8.F *infra*.) How would you reconcile the Ninth Circuit's amenability in *Abend* to substituting compensation for injunctive relief with its hostility to a similar result in *Napster*? How is *Napster* different in that regard from *Abend*, *Tasini* or *Campbell*?

A question sometimes arises whether an injunction against an infringing defendant should be limited to the precise work in issue in the case. Assume, for example, that a T-shirt distributor has been found liable for infringing the copyright on the Disney characters Mickey and Minnie Mouse, and the trial court has found that, absent an injunction, there is a likelihood of continued infringements. Disney asks the court to include in its injunctive order a direction to refrain from copying, as well, Donald Duck, Huey, Duey, Louie, Pluto, Goofy and Roger Rabbit—all characters in whom Disney owns the copyright. Should this broad injunction be issued? *See Walt Disney Co. v. Powell*, 897 F.2d 565 (D.C.Cir.1990).

Somewhat more difficult is the question whether an injunction should extend so as to bar copying of works that the plaintiff will create in the future, and that the court concludes the defendant is likely to infringe unless directed otherwise. Suppose, for example, a "videoclip" service is in the business of making what the court finds to be infringing videotapes of copyrighted news broadcasts, and markets the clips to the persons or institutions depicted in the various news segments. Is it proper for the trial court to enjoin taping of the plaintiff's future news programs for such an illicit purpose? Or does this, as the defendant argues, undermine the requirement in § 411(a) of the Copyright Act that copyright in a work be registered before an infringement action may be brought? Is the answer to be found in the text of § 502(a)? *See ibid.*; *Basic Books v. Kinko's Graphics Corp.*, 758 F.Supp. 1522, 1542 (S.D.N.Y.1991).

In addition to an injunction, other specific nonmonetary relief—such as impounding and destruction of the infringing articles—is available to a successful plaintiff under both the 1909 and 1976 statutes. For the mechanics to be utilized under the 1976 Act, see § 503 and the House Report at 160.

B. DAMAGES

§ 504. Remedies for infringement: Damages and profits

(a) *In General*—Except as otherwise provided by this title, an infringer of copyright is liable for either—

(1) the copyright owner's actual damages and any additional profits of the infringer, as provided by subsection (b); or

(2) statutory damages, as provided by subsection (c).

(b) *Actual Damages and Profits*—The copyright owner is entitled to recover the actual damages suffered by him or her as a result of the infringement, and any profits of the infringer that are attributable to the infringement and are not taken into account in computing the actual damages. In establishing the infringer's profits, the copyright owner is required to present proof only of the infringer's gross revenue, and the infringer is required to prove his or her deductible expenses and the elements of profit attributable to factors other than the copyrighted work.

. . .

House Report
H.R. Rep. No. 94–1476, 94th Cong., 2d Sess. 162 (1976).

In allowing the plaintiff to recover "the actual damages suffered by him or her as a result of the infringement," plus any of the infringer's profits "that are attributable to the infringement and are not taken into account in computing the actual damages," section 504(b) recognizes the different purposes served by awards of damages and profits. Damages are awarded to compensate the copyright owner for losses from the infringement, and profits are awarded to prevent the infringer from unfairly benefiting from a wrongful act. Where the defendant's profits are nothing more than a measure of the damages suffered by the copyright owner, it would be inappropriate to award damages and profits cumulatively, since in effect they amount to the same thing. However, in cases where the copyright owner has suffered damages not reflected in the infringer's profits, or where there have been profits attributable to the copyrighted work but not used as a measure of damages, subsection (b) authorizes the award of both.

The language of the subsection makes clear that only those profits "attributable to the infringement" are recoverable; where some of the defendant's profits result from the infringement and other profits are caused by different factors, it will be necessary for the court to make an apportionment. However, the burden of proof is on the defendant in these cases; in establishing profits the plaintiff need prove only "the infringer's gross revenue," and the defendant must prove not only "his or her deductible expenses" but also "the elements of profit attributable to factors other than the copyrighted work."

Davis v. The Gap, Inc.
246 F.3d 152 (2d Cir.2001).

[Plaintiff Davis designs jewelry worn over the eyes in the manner of eyeglasses, and describes it as "sculptured metallic ornamental wearable art." Defendant The Gap is a retailer of clothing and accessories with an international business and annual revenues of several billions of dollars. The Gap, without permission, used in an advertisement a photograph of an individual wearing Davis's copyrighted eyewear. Davis registered his copyright in the design and brought an action against The Gap for a declaratory judgment of infringement. He sought actual damages in the amount of $2.5 million (representing licensing fees that he claims he should have been paid for The Gap's unauthorized use), a percentage of The Gap's profits, $10 million in punitive damages, and attorney's fees. The district court granted summary judgment for The Gap, concluding among other things that the claims for actual damages and profits were speculative. The court of appeals reversed in part. Its discussion of remedies follows.]

■ LEVAL, CIRCUIT JUDGE:

. . .

B.   Compensatory Damages

17 U.S.C. § 504 imposes two categories of compensatory damages. Taking care to specify that double recovery is not permitted where the two categories overlap, the statute provides for the recovery of both the infringer's profits and the copyright owner's "actual damages." It is important that these two categories of compensation have different justifications and are based on different financial data. The award of the infringer's profits examines the facts only from the infringer's point of view. If the infringer has earned a profit, this award makes him disgorge the profit to insure that he not benefit from his wrongdoing. The award of the owner's actual damages looks at the facts from the point of view of the copyright owner; it undertakes to compensate the owner for any harm he suffered by reason of the infringer's illegal act. *See generally Fitzgerald Publ'g Co. v. Baylor Publ'g Co.*, 807 F.2d 1110, 1118 (2d Cir.1986); *Walker v. Forbes, Inc.*, 28 F.3d 409, 412 (4th Cir.1994).

. . . We agree with the district court as to the defendant's profits, but not as to Davis's claim for damages based on the Gap's failure to pay him a reasonable license fee.

1.   Infringer's profits

Davis submitted evidence that, during and shortly after the Gap's advertising campaign featuring the "fast" ad, the corporate parent of the Gap stores realized net sales of $1.668 billion, an increase of $146 million over the revenues earned in the same period of the preceding year. The district court considered this evidence inadequate to sustain a judgment in the plaintiff's favor because the overall revenues of the Gap, Inc. had no reasonable relationship to the act of alleged infringement. *See Davis I*, 1999 WL 199005, at *6. Because the ad infringed only with respect to Gap label stores and eyewear, we agree with the district court that it was incumbent on Davis to submit evidence at least limited to the gross revenues of the Gap label stores, and perhaps also limited to eyewear or accessories. Had he done so, the burden would then have shifted to the defendant under the terms of § 504(b) to prove its deductible expenses and elements of profits from those revenues attributable to factors other than the copyrighted work.

It is true that a highly literal interpretation of the statute would favor Davis. It says that "the copyright owner is required to present proof only of the infringer's gross revenue," 17 U.S.C. § 504(b), leaving it to the infringer to prove what portions of its revenue are not attributable to the infringement. Nonetheless we think the term "gross revenue" under the statute means gross revenue reasonably related to the infringement, not unrelated revenues.

Thus, if a publisher published an anthology of poetry which contained a poem covered by the plaintiff's copyright, we do not think the plaintiff's statutory burden would be discharged by submitting the publisher's gross revenue resulting from its publication of hundreds of titles, including trade books, textbooks, cookbooks, etc. In our view, the owner's burden would require evidence of the revenues realized from the sale of the anthology containing the infringing poem. The publisher would then bear the burden of proving its costs attributable to the anthology and the extent to which its profits from the sale of the anthology were attributable to factors other than the infringing poem, including particularly the other poems contained in the volume.... [T]he statutory term "infringer's gross revenue" should not be construed so broadly as to include revenue from lines of business that were unrelated to the act of infringement.

... Applying this reasoning to our case, we think the district court was correct in ruling that Davis failed to discharge his burden by submitting The Gap, Inc.'s gross revenue of $1.668 billion—revenue derived in part from sales under other labels within the Gap, Inc.'s corporate family that were in no way promoted by the advertisement, not to mention sales under the "Gap" label of jeans, khakis, shirts, underwear, cosmetics, children's clothing, and infantwear.

2. *The copyright owner's actual damages: Davis's failure to receive a reasonable licensing fee*

Among the elements Davis sought to prove as damages was the failure to receive a reasonable license fee from the Gap for its use of his copyrighted eyewear. The complaint asserted an entitlement to a $2.5 million licensing fee. The district court rejected the claim ... [T]he court found that Davis's claim was too speculative—that is, insufficiently supported by evidence....

a. *Was Davis's evidence too speculative?*

While there was no evidence to support Davis's wildly inflated claim of entitlement to $2.5 million, in our view his evidence did support a much more modest claim of a fair market value for a license to use his design in the ad. In addition to his evidence of numerous instances in which rock music stars wore Onoculii eyewear in photographs exhibited in music publications, Davis testified that on one occasion he was paid a royalty of

$50 for the publication by Vibe magazine of a photo of the deceased musician Sun Ra wearing Davis's eyewear.

On the basis of this evidence, a jury could reasonably find that Davis established a fair market value of at least $50 as a fee for the use of an image of his copyrighted design. This evidence was sufficiently concrete to support a finding of fair market value of $50 for the type of use made by Vibe. And if Davis could show at trial that the Gap used the image in a wider circulation than Vibe, that might justify a finding that the market value for the Gap's use of the eyewear was higher than $50. Therefore, to the extent the district court dismissed the case because Davis's evidence of the market value of a license fee was too speculative, we believe this was error.

. . .

c. Actual damages under § 504(a) and (b)

. . . [W]e proceed to consider whether [the use of a reasonable license fee theory] is permissible under the statute.

The question is as follows: Assume that the copyright owner proves that the defendant has infringed his work. He proves also that a license to make such use of the work has a fair market value, but does not show that the infringement caused him lost sales, lost opportunities to license, or diminution in the value of the copyright. The only proven loss lies in the owner's failure to receive payment by the infringer of the fair market value of the use illegally appropriated. Should the owner's claim for "actual damages" under § 504(b) be dismissed? Or should the court award damages corresponding to the fair market value of the use appropriated by the infringer?

Neither answer is entirely satisfactory. If the court dismisses the claim by reason of the owner's failure to prove that the act of infringement caused economic harm, the infringer will get his illegal taking for free, and the owner will be left uncompensated for the illegal taking of something of value. On the other hand, an award of damages might be seen as a windfall for an owner who received no less than he would have if the infringer had refrained from the illegal taking. In our view, the more reasonable approach is to allow such an award in appropriate circumstances.

Section 504(a) and (b) employ the broad term "actual damages." Courts and commentators agree it should be broadly construed to favor victims of infringement. *See* William F. Patry, Copyright Law and Practice 1167 (1994) ("Within reason, any ambiguities should be resolved in favor of the copyright owner."); 4 Nimmer § 14.02[A], at 14–12 ("[U]ncertainty will not preclude a recovery of actual damages if the uncertainty is as to amount, but not as to the fact that actual damages are attributable to the infringement."); *Fitzgerald Publ'g Co.*, 807 F.2d at 1118 ("[A]ctual damages are not . . . narrowly focused."); *Sygma Photo News, Inc. v. High Society Magazine*, 778 F.2d 89, 95 (2d Cir.1985) (stating that when courts are confronted with imprecision in calculating damages, they "should err on the side of guaranteeing the plaintiff a full recovery")....

A principal objective of the copyright law is to enable creators to earn a living either by selling or by licensing others to sell copies of the copyrighted work....

If a copier of protected work, instead of obtaining permission and paying the fee, proceeds without permission and without compensating the owner, it seems entirely reasonable to conclude that the owner has suffered damages to the extent of the infringer's taking without paying what the owner was legally entitled to exact a fee for. We can see no reason why, as an abstract matter, the statutory term "actual damages" should not cover the owner's failure to obtain the market value of the fee the owner was entitled to charge for such use....

It is important to note that under the terms of § 504(b), unless such a foregone payment can be considered "actual damages," in some circumstances victims of infringement will go uncompensated. If the infringer's venture turned out to be unprofitable, the owner can receive no recovery based on the statutory award of the "infringer's profits." And in some instances, there will be no harm to the market value of the copyrighted work. The owner may be incapable of showing a loss of either sales or licenses to third parties. To rule that the owner's loss of the fair market value of the license fees he might have exacted of the defendant do not constitute "actual damages," would mean that in such circumstances an infringer may steal with impunity. We see no reason why this should be so. Of course, if the terms of the statute compelled that result, our perception of inequity would make no difference; the statute would control. But in our view, the statutory term "actual damages" is broad enough to cover this form of deprivation suffered by infringed owners.

We recognize that awarding the copyright owner the lost license fee can risk abuse. Once the defendant has infringed, the owner may claim unreasonable amounts as the license fee—to wit Davis's demand for an award of $2.5 million. The law therefore exacts that the amount of damages may not be based on "undue speculation." *Abeshouse*, 754 F.2d at 470. The question is not what the owner would have charged, but rather what is the fair market value. In order to make out his claim that he has suffered actual damage because of the infringer's failure to pay the fee, the owner must show that the thing taken had a fair market value. But if the plaintiff owner has done so, and the defendant is thus protected against an unrealistically exaggerated claim, we can see little reason not to consider the market value of the uncollected license fee as an element of "actual damages" under § 504(b).[5]

---

5. Furthermore, the fair market value to be determined is not of the highest use for which plaintiff might license but the use the infringer made. Thus, assuming the defendant made infringing use of a Mickey Mouse image for a single performance of a school play before schoolchildren, teachers and parents with tickets at $3, the fair market value would not be the same as the fee customarily charged by the owner to license the use of this image in a commercial production.

We recognize also that finding the fair market value of a reasonable license fee may involve some uncertainty. But that is not sufficient reason to refuse to consider this as an eligible measure of actual damages. Many of the accepted methods of calculating copyright damages require the court to make uncertain estimates.... Many copyright owners are represented by agents who have established rates that are regularly paid by licensees. In such cases, establishing the fair market value of the license fee of which the owner was deprived is no more speculative than determining the damages in the case of a stolen cargo of lumber or potatoes. Given our long-held view that in assessing copyright damages "courts must necessarily engage in some degree of speculation," *id*. at 14, some difficulty in quantifying the damages attributable to infringement should not bar recovery. *See* 4 Nimmer § 14.02[A], at 14–12 ("[U]ncertainty will not preclude a recovery of actual damages if the uncertainty is as to amount, but not as to the fact that actual damages are attributable to the infringement."); II Paul Goldstein, Copyright § 12.1.1, at 12:6 (2d ed. 2000) ("Once the copyright owner shows a connection between infringement and damage, uncertainty about the amount of damages will not bar an award."); *Szekely*, 242 F.2d at 269 (where "legal injury is certain ... [w]e should not allow difficulty in ascertaining precisely the value of the right destroyed, which difficulty arises largely from the destruction, to enable the infringer to escape without compensating the owner of the right").

d. Governing Authority

The decisions of this and other courts support the view that the owner's actual damages may include in appropriate cases the reasonable license fee on which a willing buyer and a willing seller would have agreed for the use taken by the infringer.

. . .

e. Commentators

Commentators on copyright law are divided on the question whether actual damages may be calculated based on lost license or royalty fees. Professor Goldstein's treatise regards an award to the copyright owner representing the fair market value of the royalty payment that the defendant avoided by infringing as clearly included within the concept of the copyright owner's "actual damages." *See* II Goldstein § 12.1, at 12:4. Indeed this discussion is prominently featured in [the] opening discussion of "Damages and Profits." At the outset of his discussion of damages, Professor Goldstein offers the illustrative hypothetical in which Publisher B publishes an unauthorized French translation of Publisher A's novel. The treatise postulates:

> If, instead of infringing, ... B had negotiated with ... A for a license ..., the parties would probably have agreed upon a license fee giving ... A royalties roughly equal to the royalties that some other transla-

tor would have been willing to pay for the license and, at the same time, offering the prospect of profit to ... B. The negotiated license fee that Publishers A and B would have agreed upon represents the damage that Publisher A will suffer when Publisher B publishes its translation without obtaining a license.

Id. (emphasis added) (footnote omitted).

In exploring the subject in greater detail, Goldstein remarks:

If the infringer occupies the same market as the copyright owner, courts usually employ [the owner's] lost sales as the measure of damages on the assumption that every sale made by the defendant is one that the plaintiff otherwise could have made. If the infringer occupies a market that the copyright owner has not yet entered, courts usually employ a market value or reasonable royalty measure of damages on the assumption that the value of the copyrighted work in defendant's market corresponds to the sum that the copyright owner and the infringer would have agreed upon for licensing the work's use in that market.

II Goldstein § 12.1.1.1, at 12:7 (emphasis added) (footnote omitted).

... Goldstein thus justifies such an award by the fact that the infringer has illegally taken something of value and may properly be required to pay for its fair market value.... As the Goldstein treatise explains, whether the infringer might in fact have negotiated with the owner or purchased at the owner's price is irrelevant to the purpose of the test. See II Goldstein § 12.1.1.1, at 12:13.... The usefulness of the test does not depend on whether the copyright infringer was in fact himself willing to negotiate for a license. The honest purchaser is hypothesized solely as a tool for determining the fair market value of what was illegally taken....

We conclude that Section 504(b) permits a copyright owner to recover actual damages, in appropriate circumstances, for the fair market value of a license covering the defendant's infringing use. Davis adduced sufficiently concrete evidence of a modest fair market value of the use made by the Gap. The Gap's use of the infringed matter was substantial. If Davis were not compensated for the market value of the use taken, he would receive no compensation whatsoever.

C.   Punitive Damages

The district court correctly held that Davis is not entitled to punitive damages under the Copyright Act. See Davis I, 1999 WL 199005, at *8. As a general rule, punitive damages are not awarded in a statutory copyright infringement action. See 4 Nimmer § 14.02[B], at 14–23 to 24; Oboler v. Goldin, 714 F.2d 211, 213 (2d Cir.1983). The purpose of punitive damages—to punish and prevent malicious conduct—is generally achieved under the Copyright Act through the provisions of 17 U.S.C. § 504(c)(2), which allow increases to an award of statutory damages in cases of willful infringement. See 4 Nimmer § 14.02[B], at 14–23 to 24; Kamakazi Music

Corp. v. Robbins Music Corp., 534 F.Supp. 69, 78 (S.D.N.Y.1982). In any event, the question need not detain us long because Davis has failed to show willfulness on the Gap's part. [The court also concluded that statutory damages and attorney's fees could not be awarded to Davis because he had registered his copyright only after The Gap's infringement had commenced, § 412.] . . .

Frank Music Corp. v. Metro–Goldwyn–Mayer, Inc.
772 F.2d 505 (9th Cir.1985).

[The plaintiffs own the copyright in the 1953 Broadway musical *Kismet* and the songs from that show. Pursuant to a license from the plaintiffs, MGM produced and released in 1955 a motion picture version of *Kismet*. In April 1974, defendant MGM Grand Hotel staged a musical revue in its Ziegfeld Theatre; the revue, titled *Hallelujah Hollywood*, was staged, produced and directed by defendant Arden, and contained ten acts of singing, dancing and variety performances. One of the acts was billed as a tribute to the musical film *Kismet*. The act was comprised of four scenes, featured persons in the costumes of ancient Baghdad, and featured five songs from the plaintiffs' *Kismet*; of the eleven minutes consumed by this act in the hotel revue, approximately six minutes of music was taken from the plaintiffs' play. The total running time of *Hallelujah Hollywood* was approximately 100 minutes, except on Saturday evenings when it was shortened to 75 minutes (which included the full *Kismet* act) so that it could be performed three times rather than the usual two times per night. The revue continued to be performed with the *Kismet* act until July 1976 when, after protest from the plaintiffs, new music was substituted. In total, the *Kismet* sequence was used in approximately 1,700 performances of the hotel show.

[The defendants claimed that their performances of the *Kismet* songs were no infringement because they had been licensed by ASCAP on behalf of the plaintiffs. The court, however, construed the ASCAP license not to extend to the performances involved here because they were in the context of visual representations of the *Kismet* stage costumes and scenery. The court then turned to the question of remedies. Although the case was governed by the 1909 Act, all of the court's discussion would be pertinent to the application of the remedial provisions of the 1976 Act.]

1. *Actual Damages*

"Actual damages" are the extent to which the market value of a copyrighted work has been injured or destroyed by an infringement. 3 M. Nimmer, Nimmer on Copyright § 14.02, at 14–6 (1985). In this circuit, we have stated the test of market value as "what a willing buyer would have been reasonably required to pay to a willing seller for plaintiffs' work." *Krofft I* [*Sid & Marty Krofft T.V. Prods., Inc. v. McDonald's Corp.*, 562 F.2d 1157, 1174 (9th Cir.1977).]

The district court declined to award actual damages. The court stated that it was "unconvinced that the market value of plaintiffs' work was in any way diminished as a result of defendant's infringement." ... Plaintiffs contend the district court's finding is clearly erroneous in light of the evidence they presented concerning the royalties *Kismet* could have earned in a full Las Vegas production. Plaintiffs did offer evidence of the royalties *Kismet* had earned in productions around the country. They also introduced opinion testimony, elicited from plaintiff Lester and from *Kismet's* leasing agent, that a full production of *Kismet* could have been licensed in Las Vegas for $7,500 per week. And they introduced other opinion testimony to the effect that *Hallelujah Hollywood* had destroyed the Las Vegas market for a production of plaintiffs' *Kismet*.

In a copyright action, a trial court is entitled to reject a proffered measure of damages if it is too speculative. *See Peter Pan Fabrics, Inc. v. Jobela Fabrics, Inc.*, 329 F.2d 194, 196–97 (2d Cir.1964). Although uncertainty as to the amount of damages will not preclude recovery, uncertainty as to the fact of damages may. *Universal Pictures Co. v. Harold Lloyd Corp.*, 162 F.2d at 369; *see also* 3 M. Nimmer, *supra*, § 14.02, at 14–8 to –9. It was the *fact* of damages that concerned the district court. The court found that plaintiffs "failed to establish *any* damages attributable to the infringement." (Emphasis in original.) This finding is not clearly erroneous.

Plaintiffs offered no disinterested testimony showing that *Hallelujah Hollywood* precluded plaintiffs from presenting *Kismet* at some other hotel in Las Vegas. It is not implausible to conclude, as the court below apparently did, that a production presenting six minutes of music from *Kismet,* without telling any of the story of the play, would not significantly impair the prospects for presenting a full production of that play. Based on the record presented, the district court was not clearly erroneous in finding that plaintiffs' theory of damages was uncertain and speculative.

2. *Infringer's Profits*

[A] prevailing plaintiff in an infringement action is entitled to recover the infringer's profits to the extent they are attributable to the infringement. 17 U.S.C. § 101(b); *Krofft,* 562 F.2d at 1172. In establishing the infringer's profits, the plaintiff is required to prove only the defendant's sales; the burden then shifts to the defendant to prove the elements of costs to be deducted from sales in arriving at profit. 17 U.S.C. § 101(b). Any doubt as to the computation of costs or profits is to be resolved in favor of the plaintiff. *Shapiro, Bernstein & Co. v. Remington Records, Inc.*, 265 F.2d 263 (2d Cir.1959). If the infringing defendant does not meet its burden of proving costs, the gross figure stands as the defendant's profits. *Russell v. Price,* 612 F.2d 1123, 1130–31 (9th Cir.1979), *cert. denied,* 446 U.S. 952, 100 S. Ct. 2919, 64 L. Ed. 2d 809 (1980).

The district court, following this approach, found that the gross revenue MGM Grand earned from the presentation of *Hallelujah Hollywood* during the relevant time period was $24,191,690. From that figure, the court deducted direct costs of $18,060,084 and indirect costs (overhead) of $3,641,960, thus arriving at a net profit of $2,489,646.

Plaintiffs' challenge these computations on a number of grounds. . . .

. . .

We find ... merit in plaintiffs' ... challenge to the deduction of overhead costs. They argue that defendants failed to show that each item of claimed overhead assisted in the production of the infringement. The evidence defendants introduced at trial segregated overhead expenses into general categories, such as general and administrative costs, sales and advertising, and engineering and maintenance. Defendants then allocated a portion of these costs to the production of *Hallelujah Hollywood* based on a ratio of the revenues from that production as compared to MGM Grand's total revenues. The district court adopted this approach.

We do not disagree with the district court's acceptance of the defendants' method of allocation, based on gross revenues. Because a theoretically perfect allocation is impossible, we require only a "reasonably acceptable formula." *Sammons v. Colonial Press, Inc.,* 126 F.2d at 349; *see Kamar International, Inc. v. Russ Berrie & Co.,* 752 F.2d at 1333. We find, as did the district court, that defendants' method of allocation is reasonably acceptable.

We disagree with the district court, however, to the extent it concluded the defendants adequately showed that the claimed overhead expenses actually contributed to the production of *Hallelujah Hollywood*. Recently, in *Kamar International,* we stated that a deduction for overhead should be allowed "only when the infringer can demonstrate that [the overhead expense] was of actual assistance in the production, distribution or sale of the infringing product." 752 F.2d at 1332. . . .

We do not doubt that some of defendants' claimed overhead contributed to the production of *Hallelujah Hollywood*. The difficulty we have, however, is that defendants offered no evidence of what costs were included in general categories such as "general and administrative expenses," nor did they offer any evidence concerning how these costs contributed to the production of *Hallelujah Hollywood*. The defendants contend their burden was met when they introduced evidence of their total overhead costs allocated on a reasonable basis. The district court apparently agreed with this approach. That is not the law of this circuit. Under *Kamar International,* a defendant additionally must show that the categories of overhead actually contributed to sales of the infringing work. 752 F.2d at 1332. We can find no such showing in the record before us. Therefore, we conclude the district court's finding that "defendants have established that the items of general expense [the general categories of claimed overhead] contributed to the production of 'Hallelujah Hollywood' " was clearly erroneous.

Plaintiffs next challenge the district court's failure to consider MGM Grand's earnings on hotel and gaming operations in arriving at the amount of profits attributable to the infringement. The district court received evidence concerning MGM Grand's total net profit during the relevant time period, totaling approximately $395,000,000, but its memorandum decision does not mention these indirect profits and computes recovery based solely on the revenues and profits earned on the production of *Hallelujah Hollywood* (approximately $24,000,000 and $2,500,000 respectively). We surmise from this that the district court determined plaintiffs were not entitled to recover indirect profits, but we have no hint as to the district court's reasons.

Whether a copyright proprietor may recover "indirect profits" is one of first impression in this circuit. We conclude that under the 1909 Act indirect profits may be recovered.

The 1909 Act provided that a copyright proprietor is entitled to "all the profits which the infringer shall have made from such infringement.... " 17 U.S.C. § 101(b). The language of the statute is broad enough to permit recovery of indirect as well as direct profits....

The allowance of indirect profits was considered in *Sid & Marty Krofft Television Productions, Inc. v. McDonald's Corp.*, 1983 Copyright L. Rep. (CCH) ¶ 25,572 at 18,381 (C.D. Cal. 1983) (*Krofft II*), *on remand from* 562 F.2d 1157 (9th Cir.1977), a case involving facts analogous to those presented here. The plaintiffs, creators of the "H.R. Pufnstuf" children's television program, alleged that they were entitled to a portion of the profits McDonald's earned on its food sales as damages for the "McDonaldland" television commercials that infringed plaintiffs' copyright. The district court rejected as speculative the plaintiffs' formula for computing profits attributable to the infringement. However, the court's analysis and award of in lieu damages indicate that it considered indirect profits recoverable. The court stated, in awarding $1,044,000 in statutory damages, that "because a significant portion of defendants' profits made from the infringement are not ascertainable, a higher award of [statutory] in lieu damages is warranted." *Id.*, at 18,384; *see also Cream Records Inc. v. Jos. Schlitz Brewing Co.*, 754 F.2d 826, 828–29 (9th Cir.1985) (awarding profits from the sale of malt liquor for Schlitz's infringing use of plaintiff's song in television commercial).

Like the television commercials in *Krofft II*, *Hallelujah Hollywood* had promotional value. Defendants maintain that they endeavor to earn profits on all their operations and that *Hallelujah Hollywood* was a profit center. However, that fact does not detract from the promotional purposes of the show—to draw people to the hotel and the gaming tables. MGM's 1976 annual report states that "[t]he hotel and gaming operations of the MGM Grand–Las Vegas continued to be materially enhanced by the popularity of the hotel's entertainment[, including] 'Hallelujah Hollywood', the spectacularly successful production revue.... " Given the promotional nature of *Hallelujah Hollywood,* we conclude indirect profits from the hotel and gaming operations, as well as direct profits from the show itself, are recoverable if ascertainable.

3. *Apportionment of Profits*

How to apportion profits between the infringers and the plaintiffs is a complex issue in this case. Apportionment of direct profits from the production as well as indirect profits from the hotel and casino operations

[is] involved here, although the district court addressed only the former at the first trial.

When an infringer's profits are attributable to factors in addition to use of plaintiff's work, an apportionment of profits is proper.... The burden of proving apportionment, (i.e., the contribution to profits of elements other than the infringed property), is the defendant's.... We will not reverse a district court's findings regarding apportionment unless they are clearly erroneous....

After finding that the net profit earned by *Hallelujah Hollywood* was approximately $2,500,000, the district court offered the following explanation of apportionment:

> While no precise mathematical formula can be applied, the court concludes in light of the evidence presented at trial and the entire record in this case, a fair approximation of the profits of Act IV attributable to the infringement is $22,000.

The district court was correct that mathematical exactness is not required. However, a reasonable and just apportionment of profits is required. *Sheldon II,* 309 U.S. at 408, 60 S. Ct. at 688; *Universal Pictures Co. v. Harold Lloyd Corp.,* 162 F.2d at 377.

Arriving at a proper method of apportionment and determining a specific amount to award is largely a factual exercise. Defendants understandably argue that the facts support the district court's award. They claim that the infringing material, six minutes of music in Act IV, was an unimportant part of the whole show, that the unique features of the Ziegfeld Theater contributed more to the show's success than any other factor. This is proved, they argue, by the fact that when the music from *Kismet* was removed from *Hallelujah Hollywood* in 1976, the show suffered no decline in attendance and the hotel received no complaints.

Other evidence contradicts defendants' position. For instance, defendant Donn Arden testified that *Kismet* was "a very important part of the show" and "[he] hated to see it go." Moreover, while other acts were deleted from the shortened Saturday night versions of the show, Act IV "Kismet" never was.

We reject defendants' contention that the relative unimportance of the *Kismet* music was proved by its omission and the show's continued success thereafter. *Hallelujah Hollywood* was a revue, comprised of many different entertainment elements. Each element contributed significantly to the show's success, but no one element was the sole or overriding reason for that success. Just because one element could be omitted and the show goes on does not prove that the element was not important in the first instance and did not contribute to establishing the show's initial popularity.

The difficulty in this case is that the district court has not provided us with any reasoned explanation of or formula for its apportionment. We know only the district court's bottom line: that the plaintiffs are entitled to $22,000. Given the nature of the infringement, the character of the infringed property, the success of defendants' show, and the magnitude of the defendants' profits, the amount seems to be grossly inadequate. It amounts to less than one percent of MGM Grand's profits from the show, or roughly $13 for each of the 1700 infringing performances.[11]

On remand, the district court should reconsider its apportionment of profits, and should fully explain on the record its reasons and the resulting method of apportionment it uses. Apportionment of indirect profits may be a part of the calculus. If the court finds that a reasonable, nonspeculative formula cannot be derived, or that the amount of profits a reasonable formula yields is insufficient to serve the purposes underlying the statute, then the court should award statutory damages. . . .

4. *Liability of Joint Infringers*

The district court granted judgment of $22,000 "against defendants" in the plural. Yet if the district court intended that each of the defendants be jointly and severally liable for the $22,000 award, this was error.

When a copyright is infringed, all infringers are jointly and severally liable for plaintiffs' *actual damages,* but each defendant is severally liable for his or its own illegal *profit*; one defendant is not liable for the profit made by another. *MCA, Inc. v. Wilson,* 677 F.2d 180, 186 (2d Cir.1981); 3 M. Nimmer, *supra,* § 12.04[C][3], at 12–50; *see Cream Records, Inc. v. Jos. Schlitz Brewing Co.,* 754 F.2d at 829.

. . .

■ Reinhardt, Circuit Judge, concurring:

I concur fully in the majority opinion, except for Section B.1, I would hold that the district court clearly erred in finding that appellants "failed to establish *any* damage attributable to the infringement." It seems evident to me that the inclusion of "Kismet" as a part of 1,700 performances of *Hallelujah Hollywood* served to reduce the market value of appellant's property in the Las Vegas area. The testimony in the record amply supports this proposition. There is no evidence that would support the

---

11. The apportionment percentages in similar cases are markedly higher. *See, e.g., Universal Pictures Co. v. Harold Lloyd Corp.,* 162 F.2d at 377 (infringing use of one comedy sketch in motion picture; court affirmed award of 20% of the infringing movie's profits); *MCA, Inc. v. Wilson,* 677 F.2d 180, 181–82 (2d Cir.1981) (defendants copied substantial portion of plaintiff's song, "Boogie Woogie Bugle Boy," substituted "dirty" lyrics, and performed the song as a portion of an erotic nude show; court affirmed special master's award of approximately $244,000 representing 5% of defendants' total profits from the show); *Lottie Joplin Thomas Trust v. Crown Publishers, Inc.,* 592 F.2d at 657 (in-fringing songs filled one side of five-record set; court affirmed award of 50% of profits because inclusion of infringing songs made record set the only "complete" collection of Scott Joplin's works); *ABKCO Music, Inc. v. Harrisongs Music, Ltd.,* 508 F. Supp. 798, 800–801 (S.D.N.Y.1981) (infringing song reproduced on one side of single record, "flip side" contained noninfringing song, court awarded 70% of profits from sales of the single because infringing song was more popular than noninfringing song; similarly, court awarded 50% of profits for reproduction of same song on album containing twenty-one other songs).

opposite conclusion. Under these circumstances, I believe the district court clearly erred in disregarding the testimony offered by appellants.

———

Cream Records, Inc. v. Jos. Schlitz Brewing Co., 754 F.2d 826 (9th Cir.1985). Schlitz Brewing Co. used in one of its beer commercials some music from a copyrighted rhythm and blues composition, "The Theme From 'Shaft'." The trial court accepted the contention of the copyright owner, Cream, that the value of a license to use the entire song for a year was $80,000; and concluded that a reasonable license fee for the small part used by Schlitz would be some 15% of that amount, or $12,000. Because there was evidence that another manufacturer approached Cream for a license but withdrew when the Schlitz commercial was aired, and because there was no evidence that Cream was willing to grant a license for use of less than the entire copyrighted work, the court of appeals concluded that the full $80,000 was the proper measure of the extent to which Schlitz's "unauthorized use destroyed the value of the copyrighted work" for licensing purposes.

Cream also claimed a percentage of Schlitz's profits on the sale of malt liquor for the period during which the infringing commercial was broadcast; total profits were $4.876 million, and Cream sought 1.37% of that amount, or $66,800, as the portion attributable to the infringement. It argued that the expenditure for the infringing commercial constituted 13.7% of Schlitz's advertising budget for the year, and that the infringing music was responsible for 10% of the commercial's advertising power. The trial court concluded that the infringement was "minimal," consisting principally of a repeated ten-note accompaniment pattern; that the infringing material did not add substantially to the value of the commercial; that while the commercial was successful and "sold some beer" and that the "music had a portion of it," the portion was "minuscule." He concluded: "I have interpolated as best I can. They made a profit of $5 million. One-tenth of 1 percent is $5,000," and he awarded that. Cream contended that it was entitled to all of its claimed allocable profits, because Schlitz failed to introduce evidence of the portions of its profits not attributable to the infringement.

The court of appeals rejected this contention, and upheld the allocation made by the trial court. "[W]here it is clear, as it is in this case, that not all of the profits are attributable to the infringing material, the copyright owner is not entitled to recover all of those profits merely because the infringer fails to establish with certainty the portion attributable to the non-infringing elements. [In such cases, where] the evidence suggests some division which may rationally be used as a springboard it is the duty of the court to make some apportionment." The court quoted from a decision of Learned Hand: "[W]e are resolved to avoid the one certainly unjust course of giving the plaintiff everything, because the defendants cannot with certainty compute their own share. In cases where plaintiffs fail to prove their damages exactly, we often make the best estimate we can, even though it is really no more than a guess (*Pieczonka v. Pullman Co.,* 2 Cir., 102 F.2d 432, 434), and under the guise of resolving all doubts against the defendants we will not deny the one fact that stands undoubted." It then concluded—

> By claiming only 1.37% of Schlitz's malt liquor profits, Cream recognizes the impropriety of awarding Cream all of Schlitz's profits on a record that reflects beyond argument that most of these profits were attributable to elements other than the infringement. As to the amount of profits attributable to the infringing material, "what is required is . . . only a reasonable approximation," *Sheldon v. Metro-Goldwyn Pictures Corp.,* 309 U.S. at 408, 60 S. Ct. at 688; see also *Twentieth Century–Fox Film Corp. v. Stonesifer,* 140 F.2d 579, 583–84 (9th Cir.1944); *MCA, Inc. v. Wilson,* 677 F.2d 180, 186 (2d Cir.1981), and Cream's calculation is in the end no less speculative than that of the court. The disparity between the amount sought by Cream and the amount awarded by the court appears to rest not so much upon a difference in methods of calculation as upon a disagreement as to the extent to which the commercial infringed upon the copyright and the importance of the copyrighted material to the effectiveness of the commercial. These were determinations for the district court to make. . . .

QUESTIONS

1. On the issue of damages, more particularly the plaintiff's lost opportunity to license others after the infringing use of its music, is the decision in *Frank Music* reconcilable with the decisions in *Cream Records* and *The Gap*? How could you have reformulated the lost-license claim in *Frank Music,* so as to enhance the likelihood of a compensatory award?

2. On the issue of profits, was it proper for the Ninth Circuit to require Schlitz to disgorge some of its beer profits; and if so, how should it be shown (and by which party) what portion of those profits are properly allocable to the use of a repeating ten-note bass pattern in one of its beer commercials? Was it proper for that court to require the MGM Grand to disgorge some of the profits from its hotel rooms and casinos; and if so, how should it be shown (and by which party) what portion of those profits are properly allocable to the use of five of plaintiffs' songs in an eleven-minute act in a musical revue in the hotel theater?

3. A jury found that the popular song "Feelings," written by Morris Albert, infringed the plaintiff's song "Pour Toi," and brought in a verdict in the amount of $500,000. Albert consults you on the question whether the jury award can be reduced by the trial judge so as to apportion them between the infringing music and the noninfringing lyrics. What kind of evidence might you present on this issue? What is the likelihood of success? *See Gasté v. Kaiserman,* 863 F.2d 1061 (2d Cir.1988).

4. Recall the motion picture, "Letty Lynton" in *Sheldon v. Metro-Goldwyn Pictures Corp., supra* Chapter 6.A. Since not all of the defendants'

motion picture was taken from the plaintiff's play, and a substantial part of
its success was no doubt attributable to other elements (e.g., the public
domain story itself, the cinematic contributions of the MGM studio, Joan
Crawford as the star), what should the remedy be? Should MGM be
enjoined from further exhibition? Should plaintiff be awarded damages
measured by her lost opportunity to sell her play to Hollywood? If so, what
is to be made of the fact that her play was apparently unsalable under the
obscenity standards of the period? Should MGM disgorge its profits from
the exhibition of the infringing film? How are "profits" to be calculated
and, more obviously, should MGM be permitted to reduce the award by the
profits attributable to the non-infringing components mentioned above? *See
Sheldon v. Metro–Goldwyn Pictures Corp.*, 309 U.S. 390 (1940).

In defending against a claim for profits, can the defendant reduce its
gross revenues by proving its overhead expenses, such as rent, insurance,
entertainment, public relations, and depreciation? *See Hamil America, Inc.
v. GFI*, 193 F.3d 92 (2d Cir.1999). May it reduce its gross revenues by
proving the income taxes paid on those revenues? *See Three Boys Music
Corp. v. Bolton*, 212 F.3d 477 (9th Cir.2000). Should it matter whether the
infringement is willful or merely inadvertent or subconscious?

5.   Suppose the defendant infringes the plaintiff's copyright by embodying
the plaintiff's design for costume jewelry (selling for $8.00) into gold
jewelry (selling for $800). How should the defendant's profits be appor-
tioned so as to afford the plaintiff an appropriate recovery?

---

§ 504.   Remedies for infringement: Damages and profits

.   .   .

(c) *Statutory Damages—*

(1) Except as provided by clause (2) of this subsection, the copyright
owner may elect, at any time before final judgment is rendered, to recover,
instead of actual damages and profits, an award of statutory damages for
all infringements involved in the action, with respect to any one work, for
which any one infringer is liable individually, or for which any two or more
infringers are liable jointly and severally, in a sum of not less than [$750]
or more than [$30,000] as the court considers just. For the purposes of this
subsection, all the parts of a compilation or derivative work constitute one
work.

(2) In a case where the copyright owner sustains the burden of
proving, and the court finds, that infringement was committed willfully,
the court in its discretion may increase the award of statutory damages to a
sum of not more than [$150,000]. In a case where the infringer sustains the
burden of proving, and the court finds, that such infringer was not aware
and had no reason to believe that his or her acts constituted an infringement of copyright, the court in its discretion may reduce the award of
statutory damages to a sum of not less than $200. The court shall remit
statutory damages in any case where an infringer believed and had reasonable grounds for believing that his or her use of the copyrighted work was a

fair use under section 107, if the infringer was: (i) an employee or agent of a nonprofit educational institution, library, or archives acting within the scope of his or her employment who, or such institution, library, or archives itself, which infringed by reproducing the work in copies or phonorecords; or (ii) a public broadcasting entity which or a person who, as a regular part of the nonprofit activities of a public broadcasting entity (as defined in subsection (g) of section 118) infringed by performing a published nondramatic literary work or by reproducing a transmission program embodying a performance of such a work.

———

On December 9, 1999, President Clinton signed into law Public Law No. 106–610, that raised the dollar amounts set forth in § 504(c) by 50 percent. The legislation bore the title "Digital Theft Deterrence and Copyright Damages Improvement Act." For nonwillful infringements, statutory damages under § 504(c)(1) are to be no less than $750 or more than $30,000; statutory damages for willful infringements under § 504(c)(2) may be as high as $150,000.

House Report

H.R. Rep. No. 94–1476, 94th Cong., 2d Sess. 161–63 (1976).

. . . Recovery of actual damages and profits under section 504(b) or of statutory damages under section 504(c) is alternative and for the copyright owner to elect; as under the present law, the plaintiff in an infringement suit is not obliged to submit proof of damages and profits and may choose to rely on the provision for minimum statutory damages. However, there is nothing in section 504 to prevent a court from taking account of evidence concerning actual damages and profits in making an award of statutory damages within the range set out in subsection (c).

Statutory damages

Subsection (c) of section 504 makes clear that the plaintiff's election to recover statutory damages may take place at any time during the trial before the court has rendered its final judgment. The remainder of clause (1) of the subsection represents a statement of the general rates applicable to awards of statutory damages. Its principal provisions may be summarized as follows:

. . .

2. Although, as explained below, an award of minimum statutory damages may be multiplied if separate works and separately liable infringers are involved in the suit, a single award in the [$750 to $30,000] range is to be made "for all infringements involved in the action." A single infringer of a single work is liable for a single amount between [$750 and $30,000], no matter how many acts of infringement are involved in the action and

regardless of whether the acts were separate, isolated, or occurred in a related series.

3. Where the suit involves infringement of more than one separate and independent work, minimum statutory damages for each work must be awarded. For example, if one defendant has infringed three copyrighted works, the copyright owner is entitled to statutory damages of at least [$2250] and may be awarded up to [$90,000]. Subsection (c)(1) makes clear, however, that, although they are regarded as independent works for other purposes, "all the parts of a compilation or derivative work constitute one work" for this purpose. Moreover, although the minimum and maximum amounts are to be multiplied where multiple "works" are involved in the suit, the same is not true with respect to multiple copyrights, multiple owners, multiple exclusive rights, or multiple registrations. This point is especially important since, under a scheme of divisible copyright, it is possible to have the rights of a number of owners of separate "copyrights" in a single "work" infringed by one act of a defendant.

———

Engel v. Wild Oats, Inc., 644 F.Supp. 1089 (S.D.N.Y.1986). Plaintiff is the daughter and executrix of the late and renowned photographer Ruth Orkin Engel. Defendant Wild Oats manufactured T-shirts and sweatshirts bearing reproductions of one of Ms. Engel's still-life color photographs of Central Park, taken from a book of her photographs. These shirts were marketed by defendant New World Sales. Liability for infringement was conceded, and the only issue was damages. At the hearing, plaintiff Engel produced no evidence of either her damages or defendants' profits; she testified to her mother's reputation as a photographer, but stated that the damage to that reputation resulting from the copyright infringement was difficult to ascertain. Wild Oats, with 104 employees, produces 360,000 shirts per month; it produced some 2,500 shirts with the infringing design, on which its records showed net profits and sales commissions of $1,878.52. Plaintiff sought statutory damages ($50,000, then the statutory maximum for willful infringement), and defendants argued that such damages should be limited by defendants' profits.

The court invoked § 504(c) and stated that it was for the plaintiff to choose, at any time before final judgment, whether to elect actual damages and profits, or statutory damages; and that it was for the court, within a wide discretion, to determine a "just" award. Such flexibility accords with the goals of providing the copyright owner with "a potent arsenal of remedies against the infringer" and of discouraging further infringement. The court disagreed with the defendants' contention that their profits should "control" the determination of statutory damages; such profits are to be considered, but only along with other factors, including "the nature of the copyright, the difficulty of proving actual damages, the circumstances of the infringement, and in particular whether the infringement was willful."

The latter factor may warrant increasing the ceiling for statutory damages to $50,000. The court continued:

> The court finds that the infringement by Wild Oats was willful. The preponderance of the evidence indicates that the art director at Wild Oats copied the late Ms. Engel's photograph from the copyrighted book *More Pictures from My Window.* The art director knew or should have known that the unauthorized reprinting of a photograph from the book was a copyright violation. See *Fallaci v. New Gazette Literary Corp., supra,* 568 F. Supp. at 1173. Although the Court finds no direct proof of the art director's actual knowledge of the copyright infringement, the compelling circumstantial evidence of his reckless disregard for, if not actual knowledge of, plaintiff's rights in the photograph is sufficient to establish willfulness. *Wow & Flutter Music v. Len's Tom Jones Tavern, Inc.,* 606 F.Supp. 554, 556 (W.D.N.Y.1985); see *Lauratex Textile Corp. v. Allton Knitting Mills, Inc.,* 519 F.Supp. 730, 733 (S.D.N.Y.1981).

> The court also takes note of circumstances apart from Wild Oats' willfulness surrounding the infringement in this case. The nature of plaintiff's copyright—ownership of a rarefied, artistic subject matter— is unusually susceptible to damage when reproduced on the rather less rarefied medium of a T-shirt or sweat shirt. The scale of the infringement was not slight as defendants have distributed approximately 2,500 shirts in the open market. At the same time, the extent of plaintiff's actual damage is virtually impossible to ascertain. The harm of the infringement to the late Ms. Engel's artistic reputation, in the form of lost revenues from her works, may become evident only over the years to come.

> In light of all of these circumstances, the court has determined that $20,000 is the proper award of damages in this case. The award is adequate both to compensate plaintiff for her losses and to remind defendants and other would-be infringers of the seriousness of copyright violations.

> . . .

QUESTIONS

1. Under what circumstances should a plaintiff elect statutory damages? At what point in the proceeding? Can the court decide to award statutory damages under the 1976 Act or is the election solely the plaintiff's?

2. Suppose a Christmas line of six plush toys infringes copyright by depicting a comic strip character in different poses. A year later, the Christmas line of the same manufacturer includes four different versions of the character. If a successful copyright infringement suit for statutory damages is brought against all these items in the latter year, what is the maximum recovery? *See Walt Disney Co. v. Powell,* 897 F.2d 565 (D.C.Cir. 1990).

3. Author has written three one-act plays, one in 1999, one in 2000, and one in 2001. She publishes them under one cover in 2002. Zenith Drama Company, without authorization, performs the plays in a commercial playhouse in Chicago—the first play every night in April, the second play every night in May, and the third play every night in June. What is the maximum amount of statutory damages that Author can properly claim? *See Cormack v. Sunshine Food Stores, Inc.*, 675 F.Supp. 374 (E.D.Mich. 1987); *Robert Stigwood Group Ltd. v. O'Reilly*, 530 F.2d 1096 (2d Cir.), *cert. denied*, 429 U.S. 848 (1976).

What if the plays were instead separate installments of a television series? *See MCA T.V., Ltd. v. Feltner*, 89 F.3d 766 (11th Cir.1996), *cert. denied*, 520 U.S. 1117 (1997) (each episode of a TV series is a separate "work" for purposes of calculating statutory damages); *Columbia Pictures T.V. v. Krypton Broadcasting of Birmingham, Inc.*,106 F.3d 284 (9th Cir.1997), *rev'd on other grounds sub nom. Feltner v. Columbia Pictures T.V., Inc.*, 523 U.S. 340 (1998); *Lyons Partnership LP v. AAA Entertainment, Inc.*, 53 U.S.P.Q.2d 1397 (S.D.N.Y.1999) (Barney the Dinosaur costume was held to infringe character depicted on films, videocassettes, and plush toys, but not audio recordings or radio programs; counting separate television programs on the Barney series as separate infringed works, $500 in statutory damages was assessed for each of 97 infringements).

4. Horty Culture has published a book about the planting and care of flowers; the book contains 132 color photographs of seedlings. Seeds Incorporated markets flower seeds in small packets, and each packet is adorned by a color photograph of the pertinent seedling, reproduced directly from the photographs in Culture's copyrighted book. Culture sues Seeds, and claims statutory damages, 132–times over. Seeds, claiming that its infringement was not willful, concedes liability in the maximum amount of only $20,000. Who has the stronger case? *See Stokes Seeds, Ltd. v. Geo. W. Park Seed Co.*, 783 F.Supp. 104 (W.D.N.Y.1991).

5. In the *Krofft v. McDonald's* litigation discussed by the court in the *Frank Music* case, *supra,* there was a finding that the infringed Pufnstuf characters made their first appearance on a television cartoon show, and that they subsequently appeared in other such shows, in comic books, and in various merchandise items (such as masks, stickers and puzzles); and also that the McDonald's infringements were manifested in 114 different and frequently aired television commercials, 66 promotional items (such as McDonaldland cookies, puppets, glasses, posters), and 60 personal appearances by persons dressed as McDonaldland characters. Advise Krofft regarding the amount of statutory damages to which it would be entitled under § 504(c). How does your figure compare with that actually awarded by the *Krofft* court under the 1909 Act, after finding willful infringement—$1,044,000!

STATE IMMUNITY UNDER THE ELEVENTH AMENDMENT

As originally enacted, § 501(a) provided that "anyone who violates any of the exclusive rights of the copyright owner ... is an infringer." Several courts considered, and reached differing conclusions about, the question whether "anyone" included a state of the U.S., or an instrumentality of a state, such as a public school or university. The source of concern was the Eleventh Amendment to the U.S. Constitution, which provides: "The Judicial power of the United States shall not be construed to extend to any suit in law or equity, commenced or prosecuted against one of the United States by Citizens of another State, or by Citizens or Subjects of any Foreign State." Most courts concluded, relying on Supreme Court precedent, that a state could be sued for violating a federal statute enacted under the Commerce Clause or some comparable provision in Article I such as the Copyright Clause; it was assumed that by endorsing these constitutional provisions, states were to that extent waiving their sovereign immunity to federal enforcement actions. To resolve the matter clearly, Congress in 1990 added the third and fourth sentences now found in §§ 501(a) and 511 of the Copyright Act, making states and state instrumentalities fully liable for copyright infringement and remedies.

However, soon after, the key Court precedent on which the copyright decisions, and indeed Congress, had relied was overruled, and the Court held in *Seminole Tribe of Fla. v. Florida*, 517 U.S. 44 (1996), that the Commerce Clause is not a source of congressional authority to overturn states' sovereign immunity. Justice Stevens, writing in dissent for three other Justices as well, opined that the Court had effectively deprived Congress of the authority to hold states liable for violations of the bankruptcy, antitrust and copyright laws. Chief Justice Rehnquist, however, writing for the majority, noted that the Eleventh Amendment had long been interpreted not to bar injunction actions against state officials threatening to commit or to continue federal statutory violations—and he noted that only one decision in the lower courts had held that states could be sued for money damages for copyright infringement.

That case, then pending before the Court, was remanded to the court of appeals, which quickly conformed its decision so as to uphold sovereign immunity against copyright actions. In *Chavez v. Arte Publico Press*, 139 F.3d 504 (5th Cir.1998), the court interpreted *Seminole Tribe* to require voiding §§ 501(a) and 511 insofar as they subjected states to actions for money damages in the federal courts for copyright infringement. In this case, Ms. Chavez alleged that the University of Houston and its publishing arm had violated an agreement for the publication of her books, and she framed the action as one for copyright infringement (as distinguished from breach of contract, for which state-court relief was clearly available). The court held that Congress could not abrogate the sovereign immunity of the states by invoking its powers under Article I of the Constitution, including the Patent and Copyright Clause, and that the sole possible source of such congressional power is Section 5 of the Fourteenth Amendment; this empowers Congress to enforce by appropriate legislation the provisions of that Amendment, which include a prohibition against states depriving any person of "property" without due process of law. Chavez contended that her contract right (i.e., her publishing contract which regulated the copyright) and her copyright ownership constituted "property" the impairment of which by the state could be remedied under the Copyright Act. But the court of appeals rejected this argument, lest Congress be permitted to dilute state sovereign immunity simply by characterizing all sorts of federal rights as "property"—and so make an "end-run" around the limitation that *Seminole Tribe* imposes upon Congress's powers under Article I.

In decisions of major moment in the jurisprudence of constitutional federalism, a sharply divided Supreme Court held in June 1999 that the Fourteenth Amendment does not empower Congress to subject states to federal court actions for money damages for violations of the federal Patent Act and the federal Trademark Act (the Lanham Act). *College Savings Bank v. Florida Prepaid Postsecondary Educ. Expense Bd.*, 527 U.S. 666 (1999) (Lanham Act); *Florida Prepaid Postsecondary Educ. Expense Bd. v. College Savings Bank*, 527 U.S. 627 (1999) (Patent Act). Those two decisions grew out of a single incident of business competition, in which a New Jersey bank, College Savings Bank, created and sold certificates of deposit (for which it obtained a patent) designed to provide individuals with sufficient funds to cover future college expenses. Florida Prepaid Postsecondary Education Expenses Board, an entity created by the State of Florida, offered similar tuition prepayment contracts to state residents. College Savings Bank brought two separate actions in the New Jersey federal district court claiming violation of the Patent Act and § 43(a) of the Lanham Act (in view of certain alleged misrepresentations by Florida Prepaid in its brochures and reports). Congress had, in 1990, amended both of those statutes in precisely the same terms as are found in the contemporaneous amendments concerning §§ 501 and 511 of the Copyright Act, so as to make explicit and unequivocal the congressional intention to subject states and state instrumentalities to the terms of those statutes.

The Supreme Court majority (in 5-to-4 decisions) held that state sovereign immunity could not constitutionally be overturned by Congress in those cases—either through its Article I powers under the Commerce Clause (for the Lanham Act case) or the Patent and Copyright Clause (for the Patent Act case), or through its power to implement the Fourteenth Amendment. The former holding was concisely based on the earlier decision in *Seminole Tribe*. As to the latter, the Court held that the injury resulting from a business competitor's misrepresentations (whether or not those of a state or of a private corporation) cannot properly be characterized as a denial of "property"; and that even though a patent could indeed be characterized as "property," Congress had made no adequate showing that the states were "persistently" interfering with individuals' patent rights ("Congress identified no pattern of patent infringement by the States") such that sovereign immunity could constitutionally be overturned by application of the pertinent Supreme Court precedents. The Court also rejected the contention that a state "waives" its immunity when it enters upon a business that Congress has regulated, and it peremptorily rejected any concerns for national uniformity in the interpretation of federal statutes.

Although the two Court decisions did not expressly speak to sovereign immunity under the Copyright Act, the inferences to be drawn are strong indeed. Moreover, the limitations of the Court's holding—and thus the opportunities for congressional remediation—are apparently narrow. Chief Justice Rehnquist, in the *Florida Prepaid* decision, held for the majority that a state's infringement of a single patent cannot be viewed in itself as a violation of the Constitution, and that "[O]nly where the State provides no remedy, or only inadequate remedies, to injured patent owners for its infringement of their patent could a deprivation of property without due process result." The Court indeed suggested that Congress *could* constitutionally subject states to suits for patent infringement if those states offered only "questionable" remedies under state law or there was a "high incidence of [state] infringement." (In a footnote to his dissenting opinion, Justice Stevens opined that the Copyright Act provisions subjecting states to infringement actions might be distinguished and upheld, by virtue of the apparently greater incidence of state violations of copyrights, particularly in public universities.) Elsewhere, the majority indicated that the same was true for "willful" state infringements. Finally, the Court reiterated that injunctive actions remain available, as well as actions instituted by the federal government as distinguished from private individuals.

In the next stage of *Chavez v. Arte Publico Press*, 204 F.3d 601 (5th Cir.2000), the Patent Act *Florida Prepaid* decision was held dispositive in an action brought under the Copyright Act against a state agency. The court held, once again, that the 1990 amendments to the Copyright Act purporting to render states fully liable for copyright infringement exceeded Congress's power under the First and Fourteenth Amendments.

The implications of the state sovereign immunity decisions—if, like the court of appeals *Chavez* decisions suggest, they apply to the Copyright Act—are very substantial. Public libraries and state schools and universities (and university presses)—without regard to the wide range of other state instrumentalities—are in the business of copying and distributing vast amounts of copyrighted materials. The possibilities of infringement are great, and the competitive advantage in this respect afforded state schools over private nonprofit educational institutions is troubling. Some have suggested that the strictures of the Eleventh Amendment might be avoided through the highly extraordinary step of having Congress extend jurisdiction over such infringement actions to the state courts—in light of the bar in the amendment only against federal-court actions. In addition to the expectable concerns about state-court competence and disuniformities in the law, a third Supreme Court decision rendered on the same day in June 1999 raises serious doubts about congressional power to force a state—which may have its own laws according sovereign immunity—to defend a copyright infringement action in its own courts. *Alden v. Maine*, 527 U.S. 706 (1999) (Fair Labor Standards Act).

If you were a member of Congress, would you be concerned about the need to subject states to liability for money damages for copyright infringement? If so, what legislative amendments would you propose?

Senator Leahy has introduced legislation that would induce states to waive their Eleventh Amendment immunity against actions under the federal copyright, patent and trademark laws. The Intellectual Property Protection Restoration Act (IPPRA), S. 1835, 106th Cong. 1st Sess. (1999), would condition a state's receipt of future benefits under the federal intellectual property laws upon an unambiguous waiver of sovereign immunity; states that do not "opt in" to the federal systems by waiving their sovereign immunity would be denied the power to apply for federal IP rights and to sue for damages to enforce any such rights of their own. Among the findings set forth in support of the Leahy bill are that state violations of IP rights discourage technological innovation and artistic creation, and that some states by violating IP rights but refusing to waive their immunity have secured an unfair economic advantage over private entities.

Is the proposed *quid pro quo* waiving state sovereign immunity in return for federal intellectual property protection unconstitutionally coercive? Or might it instead be ineffective: might states have more to gain from intellectual property violations than from intellectual property protection? See generally, Mitchell N. Berman, R. Anthony Reese and Ernest A. Young, *State Accountability for Violations of Intellectual Property Rights: How to "Fix" Florida Prepaid (and How Not to)*, 79 Texas L. Rev. 1037 (2001).

RIGHT TO JURY TRIAL FOR STATUTORY DAMAGES CLAIMS

Feltner v. Columbia Pictures Television, Inc., 523 U.S. 340 (1998). The Supreme Court resolved an important issue that had long divided the federal courts of appeals: Whether, and to what extent, is a party entitled to a jury trial in cases in which the plaintiff seeks statutory damages under § 504(c) rather than actual damages and profits? The Court held that, although the Copyright Act does not grant a statutory right to jury trial, the Seventh Amendment to the Constitution affords such a right.

Columbia licensed several copyrighted television shows to three television stations owned by Feltner (and his company Krypton). Feltner continued to broadcast the programs after his license was terminated for failure to pay royalties. Columbia secured a summary judgment for willful infringement and requested statutory damages; the district court rejected Feltner's request for a jury trial on damages and awarded Columbia $8.8 million in statutory damages ($20,000 for each of 440 willful infringements, treating each separate TV episode as a separately infringed work and each of the three stations as committing separate violations) and $750,000 in attorneys' fees. The court of appeals held that there was no jury right in statutory-damages cases either under the Copyright Act or the Constitution.

Justice Thomas, writing for eight Justices, concluded that all of the references in § 504(c) to "the court" determining statutory damages, particularly in the context of other uses of that term elsewhere in the Act, make it clear that Congress intended that the trial judge is to assess statutory damages. The Court therefore proceeded to address the constitutional issue. The Seventh Amendment guarantees a jury trial in "suits at common law," which has been interpreted to embrace even actions to enforce statutory rights that are "analogous" to common law claims. Justice Thomas found that, before and contemporaneous with the adoption of the Seventh Amendment, in both England and the United States (including in the separate state copyright acts before the ratification of the Constitution), claims for damages were triable to a jury whether based on common law or statutory copyright. These were consistently treated as actions "at law" (pleaded "on the case" or "in an action of debt") and not "in equity." Moreover, the Court rejected Columbia's claim that statutory damages are "equitable in nature":

> We have recognized the "general rule" that monetary relief is legal, ... and that an award of statutory damages may serve purposes traditionally associated with legal relief, such as compensation and punishment.... Nor ... is a monetary remedy rendered equitable simply because it is "not fixed or readily calculable from a fixed formula." ... And there is historical evidence that cases involving discretionary monetary relief were tried before juries.... Accordingly, we must conclude that the Seventh Amendment provides a right to a jury trial where the copyright owner elects to recover statutory damages.

The jury is to decide all issues pertinent to the award of statutory damages, including the amount. Justice Scalia, in a separate concurring opinion, concluded that in order to avoid invalidating the provision in § 504(c) for a trial to the judge only, it was "fairly permissible" to construe the term "the court" to include both judge and jury.

The defendant ultimately fared quite poorly on remand in his trial before a jury. At the retrial in April 1999, the jury returned a damages award of nearly $32 million, about three and one-half times the amount originally awarded by the district judge. This is reportedly the largest award of statutory damages ever rendered for copyright infringement. The defendant then resourcefully argued that the Supreme Court had not simply declared the judge-jury allocation of § 504 unconstitutional but had declared the entire subsection on statutory damages to be unconstitutional, so that the jury award had to be altogether overturned as unsupported in the statute. Not surprisingly, the court of appeals ruled otherwise, and held that the Supreme Court finding of unconstitutionality was more narrowly based, and that the basic provision for statutory damages survives, to be implemented by juries. *Columbia Pictures Television, Inc. v. Krypton Broadcasting, Inc.*, 259 F.3d 1186 (9th Cir. 2001).

C.   Costs and Attorney's Fees

Fogerty v. Fantasy, Inc., 510 U.S. 517 (1994). The Supreme Court was confronted with a split among the circuits on the standard to be utilized in awarding attorneys' fees under § 505. The Ninth Circuit, for example, awarded such fees rather routinely to successful plaintiffs, but successful defendants had to show that the lawsuit was brought in bad faith or frivolously (the so-called "dual standard"). The Third Circuit, on the other hand, interpreted § 505 to allow the trial court to exercise its discretion in an evenhanded manner.

The Supreme Court reversed a decision of the Ninth Circuit Court of Appeals which had denied an award of counsel fees to defendant Fogerty simply because he could not prove that the infringement action was frivolous or in bad faith. The Court began by rejecting as controlling an earlier Court decision in a Title VII case, which had found in that civil rights statute a pro-plaintiff (often an impecunious "private attorney general") policy regarding the award of attorneys' fees.

The "dual approach" adopted by the Ninth Circuit relied heavily on the argument that routinely awarding attorneys' fees to prevailing plaintiffs encourages litigation of meritorious claims of copyright infringement, which promotes the public interest in creativity and the like. The Supreme Court rejected this argument.

> We think the argument is flawed because it expresses a one-sided view of the purposes of the Copyright Act. While it is true that *one* of the goals of the Copyright Act is to discourage infringement, it is by no means the *only* goal of that Act. In the first place, it is by no means always the case that the plaintiff in an infringement action is the only holder of a copyright; often times, defendants hold copyrights too. . . .

> More importantly, the policies served by the Copyright Act are more complex, more measured, than simply maximizing the number of meritorious suits for copyright infringement. . . . Because copyright law ultimately serves the purpose of enriching the general public through access to creative works, it is peculiarly important that the boundaries of copyright law be demarcated as clearly as possible. To that end, defendants who seek to advance a variety of meritorious copyright defenses should be encouraged to litigate them to the same extent that plaintiffs are encouraged to litigate meritorious claims of infringement. . . . [A] successful defense of a copyright infringement action may further the policies of the Copyright Act every bit as much as a successful prosecution of an infringement claim by the holder of a copyright.

The Court also, however, rejected the argument of the defendant Fogerty that § 505 was intended to adopt the "British Rule" of awarding attorneys' fees, as a matter of course, to whichever party prevails in the infringement action. "Prevailing plaintiffs and prevailing defendants are to be treated alike, but attorney's fees are to be awarded to prevailing parties only as a matter of the court's discretion"—as indicated by the use of the word "may" in § 505. The Court endorsed consideration by a trial judge of such factors as frivolousness, motivation, objective unreasonableness, and the need in certain cases to advance considerations of compensation and deterrence (so long as applied evenhandedly to prevailing plaintiffs and defendants).

In what is likely to be the final installment of *Fantasy, Inc. v. Fogerty*, the Court of Appeals for the Ninth Circuit, at 94 F.3d 553 (1996), affirmed an award to songwriter Fogerty of more than $1.35 million in attorneys' fees and court costs incurred by him from the initial jury trial, through the proceedings in the Ninth Circuit and the Supreme Court, and even including the lawyer's work in establishing a reasonable fee (a matter that was itself litigated). This appears to be the largest fee award ever entered in a copyright infringement case.

D. STATUTE OF LIMITATIONS

A significant limitation upon the rights of a copyright owner to sue for infringement is, of course, the statute of limitations. Under § 507, the period of limitations for both criminal and civil proceedings is three years. Statute of limitations questions are usually straightforward enough, but courts have had to grapple with some difficult issues of application.

First, is the running of the statute "tolled" until the plaintiff actually learns of the infringement, or does the statute begin to run as soon as acts of infringement occur? If the defendant "fraudulently conceals" the acts of infringement, the statute will be tolled. The prevailing rule is that even absent such concealment, the statute will be tolled during the period when a reasonable person in the plaintiff's shoes would not have discovered the infringement. *E.g., Taylor v. Meirick*, 712 F.2d 1112 (7th Cir.1983).

A more troubling question is whether repeated acts of infringement constitute a single "continuing" wrong, so that the plaintiff may sue for all infringing acts if the last one falls within the three-year statutory period. Suppose, for example, that a book club in 1985 advertises and sells almost all of its 10,000 copies of a book that contains infringing material; the only sales after that year are in 1988, when it "remainders" its copies by selling its inventory of 100 copies at sharply reduced prices to discount book stores. The copyright owner sues in 1990.

The defendant book club claims that damages must be limited to the 100 copies sold within the previous three years; it claims that, otherwise, substantial and possibly ruinous liability might be extended forever, so long as there is one infringing act within the three years prior to suit. The copyright owner contends, however, that the infringing sales are all part of a single continuing transaction, which is not ended for purposes of starting the running of the statutory period until the last infringing act is committed; otherwise, the copyright owner to protect its rights would have to bring successive piecemeal lawsuits. Which is the sounder view? The courts are sharply divided. *Compare Taylor v. Meirick, supra, with Gaste v. Kaiserman,* 669 F.Supp. 583 (S.D.N.Y.1987). *See Roley v. New World Pictures, Ltd.,* 19 F.3d 479 (9th Cir.1994) (rejecting a "rolling statute of limitations" and prohibiting plaintiffs to sue on *all* allegedly infringing acts whenever *any* infringement occurs within three years preceding the filing of the suit).

E.   CRIMINAL LIABILITY

Section 506 of the Copyright Act imposes federal criminal liability for various acts (not all of which would render the actor liable for civil remedies). Section 506(a) provides: "Any person who infringes a copyright willfully and for purposes of commercial advantage or private financial gain shall be punished as provided in section 2319 of title 18."

The named section of the criminal code was amended in significant respects in October 1992. Previously, the section declared to be a felony only the large-scale and willful reproduction and distribution of pirated or bootlegged motion pictures and musical records or tapes. As amended, the unauthorized reproduction or public distribution (but no other exclusive right of the copyright owner) of *any* kind of copyrighted work may be a felony, if the acts are willful (i.e., with knowledge that the conduct is prohibited by law), if they are for purposes of commercial advantage or private financial gain, and if at least ten copies with a retail value of more than $2,500 are reproduced or distributed within a 180–day period; this is punishable by up to five years' imprisonment. Up to ten years' imprisonment may be imposed for a second or subsequent offense. In all other cases, the defendant may be imprisoned for up to one year. Fines may be imposed up to $250,000 for individuals and $500,000 for organizations. When Congress amended the Copyright Act in 1990 so as to accord rights of integrity and attribution to visual artists (§ 106A(a)), it also provided, in § 506(f), that violations of those rights cannot give rise to criminal liability.

As the language of § 506(a) makes clear, although innocent intent is not a defense to civil copyright liability, in criminal prosecutions the government must prove that the accused intended to infringe (rather than merely to make or distribute copies). Section 506(b) requires that the court order the forfeiture and destruction of all copies or phonorecords, and manufacturing devices, in a criminal case—a remedy that is left to the court's discretion in civil cases.

Section 506(c) criminalizes the knowing placement of a false copyright notice or the knowing distribution or importation of any article bearing such notice; and § 506(d) penalizes the fraudulent removal of a copyright notice. The maximum fine under either of these two sections is $2,500. It should be noted that the acts condemned by these two subsections are not infringements of copyright for which civil remedies are available. *See Eden Toys, Inc. v. Florelee Undergarment Co.,* 697 F.2d 27, 37 n. 10 (2d Cir.1982); *Scarves by Vera, Inc. v. American Handbags, Inc.,* 188 F.Supp. 255 (S.D.N.Y.1960). This may help to explain why they have apparently never been successfully invoked as a basis for a criminal prosecution. Finally, § 506(e) imposes criminal liability for false representations of material fact in applying for copyright registration.

In *Dowling v. United States,* 473 U.S. 207 (1985) (6–to –3 decision), the Supreme Court addressed the issue whether liability for copyright offenses could arise under federal criminal statutes aside from the relevant sections of the Copyright Act. After reviewing the language and legislative history of the National Stolen Property Act (NSPA), 18 U.S.C. § 2314, which proscribes interstate and foreign transport of "goods" knowing the same to have been "stolen, converted, or taken by fraud," the Court determined that distributing "bootleg" phonorecords did not fall within the ambit of that Act. The rationale of *Dowling* is that given the very specific provisions of the amended Copyright Act of 1976, and in particular of 17 U.S.C. § 506(a), Congress did not intend broad criminal laws regarding stolen property—with punishments up to ten years in prison—to encompass copyright infringement. Justice Blackmun, writing for the Court, stated: "The copyright owner . . . holds no ordinary chattel. A copyright, like other intellectual property, comprises a series of carefully defined and carefully delimited interests to which the law affords correspondingly exact protections." Thus it seems clear that without explicit congressional authorization, courts will not impose criminal penalties for conduct within the ban of the Copyright Act.

The interpretation in *Dowling* was applied in *United States v. Brown,* 925 F.2d 1301 (10th Cir.1991). There, the defendant had been employed as a computer programmer and had made an unauthorized copy of a source code in which his employer held the copyright, although the hard computer disk onto which he copied the program did not belong to the employer. The court held that criminal convictions under the NSPA had always involved stolen physical goods, and it was not the intent of Congress that the NSPA was to function so as to criminalize copyright infringement. (The court observed that ambiguities in a criminal statute should be resolved in favor of the accused.)

With the exception of sound recordings made before 1972 (see § 301(c)) of the Copyright Act), persons accused of conduct which creates criminal or civil liability under the federal Copyright Act are exempt from state criminal prosecution. *See, e.g., Crow v. Wainwright,* 720 F.2d 1224 (11th Cir.1983), *cert. denied,* 469 U.S. 819 (1984) (preemption of state stolen-property crime, held equivalent to copyright infringement under the federal act). Even more clearly, actions that are lawful under the Copyright Act cannot be rendered criminal by state statutes.

On December 16, 1997, President Clinton signed into law an amendment to the Copyright Act (and U.S. criminal code) that toughens criminal penalties for willful copyright infringement. Pub. L. No. 105–147, 111 Stat. 2678 (1997). Focused largely on infringement through use of the Internet, the legislation was named the No Electronic Theft (NET) Act. Among other things, the Act increased the statute of limitations for criminal proceedings, in § 507(a), from three years to five years.

A principal purpose of the legislation was to address the problem created by the decision in *United States v. La Macchia,* 871 F.Supp. 535 (D.Mass.1994), in which a computer bulletin board operator who provided users with free unauthorized copies of copyrighted software was held not to have violated the federal wire fraud statute because his activities lacked the necessary element of commercial gain. The NET Act clarifies § 506(a) of the Copyright Act, which rests criminal liability for copyright infringement upon willful conduct "for purposes of commercial advantage or private financial gain," by adding to § 101 a definition of "financial gain": "receipt, or the expectation of receipt, of anything of value, including the receipt of other copyrighted works." A new subsection (a)(2) was also added to § 506, which declares criminal the willful infringement of a copyright "by the reproduction or distribution, including by electronic means, during any 180–day period, of 1 or more copies or phonorecords of 1 or more copyrighted works, which have a total retail value of more than $1,000." (This would clearly cover the conduct of Mr. La Macchia, even if he transmitted copyrighted software to others for free.) The NET Act also enlarged the extent of criminal penalties (fines and jail) for willful infringement, based on retail value, under 18 U.S.C. § 2319.

As will be seen below, Chapter 8.G, the Digital Millennium Copyright Act of 1998 imposed certain prohibitions upon the circumvention of anticopying devices and the removal of "copyright management information." (Sections 1201, 1202 of the Act.) Although violation is technically not a copyright infringement, these prohibitions are embraced within Title 17 of the U.S. Code. Section 1204 provides that violations that are willful and for purposes of "commercial advantage or private financial gain" can result in severe fines (up to $1 million) and substantial prison terms (up to ten years).

F. INDIVIDUAL, VICARIOUS, AND CONTRIBUTORY LIABILITY

It must always be remembered that copyright infringement is in the nature of a tort. Accordingly all persons participating therein are liable. In a typical case, this may include the publisher, printer, and vendor. *See American Code Co. v. Bensinger*, 282 F. 829 (2d Cir.1922). But the net of liability may extend much farther—to those having a less direct involvement in the infringement as well as to individuals perpetrating the infringing acts on behalf of a corporate employer. And although absence of knowledge or intention may affect the shaping of remedies, it is not a defense. *See* Latman & Tager, *Liability of Innocent Infringers of Copyrights,* 2 Studies on Copyright 1045 (Arthur Fisher mem. ed. 1963).

1. GENERAL PRINCIPLES

Sony Corp. of America v. Universal City Studios, Inc., 464 U.S. 417 (1984). Although the Copyright Act makes no specific reference to contributory infringement, the Supreme Court endorsed the possibility of imposing liability for copyright infringement on persons who have not themselves engaged in the infringing activities, because the concept "is merely a species of the broader problem of identifying the circumstances in which it is just to hold one individual accountable for the actions of another." The Court determined, however, that vicarious liability could not be imposed solely on the ground that defendants "have sold equipment with the constructive knowledge that their customers may use that equipment to make unauthorized copies of copyrighted material." Rather, analogizing from the patent law, which expressly recognizes contributory infringement, and which also affords an exemption for "staple article[s] or commodit[ies] of commerce suitable for substantial noninfringing uses," 35 U.S.C. § 271(a), (b), the Court held that the ability of a videocassette recorder to copy copyrighted motion pictures would not render the manufacturers of the machine liable for contributory infringement "if the product is widely used for legitimate, unobjectionable purposes. Indeed it need merely be capable of substantial noninfringing uses." The Court concluded—because many copyright owners of television programs do not object to home videotaping and because even unauthorized home videotaping, for time shifting purposes, is a fair use—that "the Betamax is, therefore, capable of substantial noninfringing uses. Sony's sale of such equipment to the general public does not constitute contributory infringement of respondent's copyrights."

[handwritten margin note: No liability if there are legitimate uses]

QUESTION

MAPHIA operates a computer bulletin board service which encourages its subscribers to upload and exchange copies of Sega videogames. These activities are carried out without Sega's authorization. Under the standard set out in *Sony*, is MAPHIA contributorily infringing Sega's copyrights in its videogames? *See Sega Enters. v. MAPHIA*, 857 F.Supp. 679 (N.D.Cal. 1994) (granting preliminary injunction); 948 F.Supp. 923 (N.D.Cal.1996) (holding MAPHIA liable).

Fonovisa, Inc. v. Cherry Auction, Inc.

76 F.3d 259 (9th Cir.1996).

■ SCHROEDER, J.

This is a copyright and trademark enforcement action against the operators of a swap meet, sometimes called a flea market, where third-party vendors routinely sell counterfeit recordings that infringe on the plaintiff's copyrights and trademarks. The district court dismissed on the pleadings, holding that the plaintiffs, as a matter of law, could not maintain any cause of action against the swap meet for sales by vendors who leased its premises. The district court's decision is published. *Fonovisa, Inc. v. Cherry Auction, Inc.*, 847 F. Supp. 1492 (E.D.Cal.1994). We reverse.

Background

The plaintiff and appellant is Fonovisa, Inc., a California corporation that owns copyrights and trademarks to Latin/Hispanic music recordings. Fonovisa filed this action in district court against defendant-appellee, Cherry Auction, Inc., and its individual operators (collectively "Cherry Auction"). For purposes of this appeal, it is undisputed that Cherry Auction operates a swap meet in Fresno, California, similar to many other swap meets in this country where customers come to purchase various merchandise from individual vendors. The vendors pay a daily rental fee to the swap meet operators in exchange for booth space. Cherry Auction supplies parking, conducts advertising and retains the right to exclude any vendor for any reason, at any time, and thus can exclude vendors for patent and trademark infringement. In addition, Cherry Auction receives an entrance fee from each customer who attends the swap meet.

There is also no dispute for purposes of this appeal that Cherry Auction and its operators were aware that vendors in their swap meet were selling counterfeit recordings in violation of Fonovisa's trademarks and copyrights. Indeed, it is alleged that in 1991, the Fresno County Sheriff's Department raided the Cherry Auction swap meet and seized more than 38,000 counterfeit recordings. The following year, after finding that vendors at the Cherry Auction swap meet were still selling counterfeit recordings, the Sheriff sent a letter notifying Cherry Auction of the on-going sales of infringing materials, and reminding Cherry Auction that they had agreed to provide the Sheriff with identifying information from each vendor. In addition, in 1993, Fonovisa itself sent an investigator to the Cherry Auction site and observed sales of counterfeit recordings.

Fonovisa filed its original complaint in the district court on February 25, 1993, and on March 22, 1994, the district court granted defendants' motion to dismiss pursuant to Federal Rule of Civil Procedure 12(b)(6). In this appeal, Fonovisa does not challenge the district court's dismissal of its claim for direct copyright infringement, but does appeal the dismissal of its claims for contributory copyright infringement, vicarious copyright infringement and contributory trademark infringement.

The copyright claims are brought pursuant to 17 U.S.C. §§ 101 et seq. Although the Copyright Act does not expressly impose liability on anyone other than direct infringers, courts have long recognized that in certain circumstances, vicarious or contributory liability will be imposed. See *Sony Corp. of America v. Universal City Studios, Inc.*, 464 U.S. 417 (1984) (explaining that "vicarious liability is imposed in virtually all areas of the law, and the concept of contributory infringement is merely a species of the broader problem of identifying circumstances in which it is just to hold one individually accountable for the actions of another").....

Vicarious Copyright Infringement

The concept of vicarious copyright liability was developed in the Second Circuit as an outgrowth of the agency principles of *respondeat superior*. The landmark case on vicarious liability for sales of counterfeit recordings is *Shapiro Bernstein and Co. v. H. L. Green Co.*, 316 F.2d 304 (2d Cir.1963). In *Shapiro*, the court was faced with a copyright infringement suit against the owner of a chain of department stores where a concessionaire was selling counterfeit recordings. Noting that the normal agency rule of *respondeat superior* imposes liability on an employer for copyright infringements by an employee, the court endeavored to fashion a principle for enforcing copyrights against a defendant whose economic interests were intertwined with the direct infringer's, but who did not actually employ the direct infringer.

Shapiro fashioned liability out of respondeat superior [handwritten marginalia]

The *Shapiro* court looked at the two lines of cases it perceived as most clearly relevant. In one line of cases, the landlord-tenant cases, the courts had held that a landlord who lacked knowledge of the infringing acts of its tenant and who exercised no control over the leased premises was not liable for infringing sales by its tenant. *See e.g. Deutsch v. Arnold*, 98 F.2d 686 (2d Cir.1938); *cf. Fromont v. Aeolian Co.*, 254 F. 592 (S.D.N.Y.1918). In the other line of cases, the so-called "dance hall cases," the operator of an entertainment venue was held liable for infringing performances when the operator (1) could control the premises and (2) obtained a direct financial benefit from the audience, who paid to enjoy the infringing performance. *See, e.g., Buck v. Jewell–LaSalle Realty Co.*, 283 U.S. 191, 198–199 (1931); *Dreamland Ball Room, Inc. v. Shapiro, Bernstein & Co.*, 36 F.2d 354 (7th Cir.1929).

From those two lines of cases, the *Shapiro* court determined that the relationship between the store owner and the concessionaire in the case before it was closer to the dance-hall model than to the landlord-tenant model. It imposed liability even though the defendant was unaware of the infringement. *Shapiro* deemed the imposition of vicarious liability neither unduly harsh nor unfair because the store proprietor had the power to cease the conduct of the concessionaire, and because the proprietor derived an obvious and direct financial benefit from the infringement. 316 F.2d at 307. The test was more clearly articulated in a later Second Circuit case as follows: "[E]ven in the absence of an employer-employee relationship one may be vicariously liable if he has the right and ability to supervise the infringing activity and also has a direct financial interest in such activities." *Gershwin Publishing Corp. v. Columbia Artists Management, Inc.*, 443 F.2d 1159, 1162 (2d Cir.1971)....

Liability even though defendant was unaware of the infringement [handwritten marginalia]

The district court in this case agreed with defendant Cherry Auction that Fonovisa did not, as a matter of law, meet either the control or the financial benefit prong of the vicarious copyright infringement test articulated in *Gershwin*, *supra*. Rather, the district court concluded that based on the pleadings, "Cherry Auction neither supervised nor profited from the vendors' sales." 847 F. Supp. at 1496. In the district court's view, with respect to both control and financial benefit, Cherry Auction was in the same position as an absentee landlord who has surrendered its exclusive right of occupancy in its leased property to its tenants.

This analogy to absentee landlords is not in accord with the facts as alleged in the district court and which we, for purposes of appeal, must accept. The allegations below were that vendors occupied small booths within premises that Cherry Auction controlled and patrolled. According to the complaint, Cherry Auction had the right to terminate vendors for any reason whatsoever and through that right had the ability to control the activities of vendors on the premises. In addition, Cherry Auction promoted the swap meet and controlled the access of customers to the swap meet area. In terms of control, the allegations before us are strikingly similar to those in *Shapiro* and *Gershwin*.

In *Shapiro*, for example, the court focused on the formal licensing agreement between defendant department store and the direct infringer-concessionaire. There, the concessionaire selling the bootleg recordings had a licensing agreement with the department store (H. L. Green Company) that required the concessionaire and its employees to "abide by, observe and obey all regulations promulgated from time to time by the H. L. Green Company," and H. L. Green Company had the "unreviewable discretion" to discharge the concessionaires' employees. 316 F.2d at 306. In practice, H. L. Green Company was not actively involved in the sale of records and the concessionaire controlled and supervised the individual employees. *Id.* Nevertheless, H. L. Green's ability to police its concessionaire—which parallels Cherry Auction's ability to police its vendors under Cherry Auction's similarly broad contract with its vendors—was sufficient to satisfy the control requirement. *Id.* at 308.

In *Gershwin*, the defendant lacked the formal, contractual ability to control the direct infringer. Nevertheless, because of defendant's "pervasive participation in the formation and direction" of the direct infringers, including promoting them (i.e. creating an audience for them), the court found that defendants were in a position to police the direct infringers and held that the control element was satisfied. 443 F.2d at 1163. As the promoter and organizer of the swap meet, Cherry Auction wields the same level of control over the direct infringers as did the *Gershwin* defendant. *See also Polygram*, 855 F. Supp. at 1329 (finding that the control requirement was satisfied because the defendant (1) could control the direct infringers through its rules and regulations; (2) policed its booths to make sure the regulations were followed; and (3) promoted the show in which direct infringers participated).

The district court's dismissal of the vicarious liability claim in this case was therefore not justified on the ground that the complaint failed to allege sufficient control.

. . .

... The facts alleged by Fonovisa ... reflect that the defendants reap substantial financial benefits from admission fees, concession stand sales and parking fees, all of which flow directly from customers who want to buy the counterfeit recordings at bargain basement prices. The plaintiff has sufficiently alleged direct financial benefit.

Our conclusion is fortified by the continuing line of cases, starting with the dance hall cases, imposing vicarious liability on the operator of a business where infringing performances enhance the attractiveness of the venue to potential customers.... In this case, the sale of pirated recordings at the Cherry Auction swap meet is a "draw" for customers, as was the performance of pirated music in the dance hall cases and their progeny.

Plaintiffs have stated a claim for vicarious copyright infringement.

Contributory Copyright Infringement

Contributory infringement originates in tort law and stems from the notion that one who directly contributes to another's infringement should be held accountable. *See Sony v. Universal City*, 464 U.S. at 417; 1 Neil Boorstyn, Boorstyn on Copyright § 10.06[2], at 10–21 (1994) ("In other words, the common law doctrine that one who knowingly participates in or furthers a tortious act is jointly and severally liable with the prime tortfeasor, is applicable under copyright law"). Contributory infringement has been described as an outgrowth of enterprise liability, *see* 3 Nimmer § 1204[a][2], at 1275; *Demetriades v. Kaufmann*, 690 F. Supp. 289, 292 (S.D.N.Y.1988), and imposes liability where one person knowingly contributes to the infringing conduct of another. The classic statement of the doctrine is in *Gershwin*, 443 F.2d 1159, 1162: "One who, with knowledge of the infringing activity, induces, causes or materially contributes to the infringing conduct of another, may be held liable as a 'contributory' infringer." [Citations omitted.]

There is no question that plaintiff adequately alleged the element of knowledge in this case. The disputed issue is whether plaintiff adequately alleged that Cherry Auction materially contributed to the infringing activity. We have little difficulty in holding that the allegations in this case are sufficient to show material contribution to the infringing activity. Indeed, it would be difficult for the infringing activity to take place in the massive quantities alleged without the support services provided by the swap meet. These services include, *inter alia*, the provision of space, utilities, parking, advertising, plumbing, and customers.

Here again Cherry Auction asks us to ignore all aspects of the enterprise described by the plaintiffs, to concentrate solely on the rental of space, and to hold that the swap meet provides nothing more. Yet Cherry Auction actively strives to provide the environment and the market for counterfeit recording sales to thrive. Its participation in the sales cannot be termed "passive," as Cherry Auction would prefer.

The district court apparently took the view that contribution to infringement should be limited to circumstances in which the defendant "expressly promoted or encouraged the sale of counterfeit products, or in some manner protected the identity of the infringers." 847 F. Supp. 1492, 1496. Given the allegations that the local sheriff lawfully requested that Cherry Auction gather and share basic, identifying information about its vendors, and that Cherry Auction failed to comply, the defendant appears to qualify within the last portion of the district court's own standard that posits liability for protecting infringers' identities. Moreover, we agree with the Third Circuit's analysis in *Columbia Pictures Industries, Inc. v. Aveco, Inc.*, 800 F.2d 59 (3d Cir.1986), that providing the site and facilities for known infringing activity is sufficient to establish contributory liability. *See* 2 William F. Patry, Copyright Law & Practice 1147 ("Merely providing the means for infringement may be sufficient" to incur contributory copyright liability) . . . .

QUESTION

On the one hand, how can one justify imputing vicarious liability in any circumstances going beyond the narrow employer-employee relationship? On the other hand, why should not even a landlord be required to pay for the infringements of its tenants?

A & M Records, Inc. v. Abdallah, 948 F.Supp. 1449 (C.D.Cal.1996). Defendant Abdallah sold hundreds of thousands of "time-loaded" audiocassettes to clients who used the cassettes to produce and market illegally counterfeited phonorecords. Time-loaded cassettes contain precisely enough tape to correspond to time requirements imposed by the customer, thus avoiding both risks presented by standard-duration blank cassettes: excess blank tape at the end or insufficient tape for the material to be recorded. Abdallah's customers requested blank tape corresponding to the duration of the sound recordings being duplicated; for some customers, Abdallah would time the targeted sound recordings in order to determine what length of tape the customer should order. A & M Records sued Abdallah for contributory infringement. The court found that Abdallah not only supplied the means for his customers to commit record piracy, but that Abdallah knew the purpose to which his time-loaded cassettes would be put. In rejecting Abdallah's defense that time-loaded cassettes were capable of substantially noninfringing use, the court distinguished *Sony v. Universal Studios*:

> In the present case, Mr. Abdallah argues that, just as VCR's have legitimate, noninfringing uses, the time-loaded cassettes that he sold also have legitimate, noninfringing uses[5]
>
> This Court rejects the defendant's argument for three reasons. First, the Supreme Court developed the *Sony* doctrine by borrowing a concept from patent law, which provides that the sale of a "staple article or commodity of commerce suitable for substantial noninfringing use cannot constitute contributory infringement." *See* 35 U.S.C. § 271(c) (1984); *Sony* at 439–40. Arguably, the *Sony* doctrine only applies to "staple articles or commodities of commerce," such as VCR's, photocopiers, and blank, standard-length cassette tapes. Its protection would not extend to products specifically manufactured for counterfeiting activity, even if such products have substantial noninfringing uses. Second, even if the *Sony* doctrine does apply to items specifically designed for counterfeit use, *Sony* requires that the product being sold have a "substantial" noninfringing use, and although time-loaded cassettes can be used for legitimate purposes, these purposes are insubstantial given the number of Mr. Abdallah's customers that were using them for counterfeiting purposes.

5. Mr. Abdallah testified that most of his customers used the time-loaded cassettes to record their own original works, such as church sermons, language classes, or advertisements. The plaintiffs did not dispute the fact that Mr. Abdallah had some legitimate customers for his time-loaded cassettes, although they claimed that the vast majority of his customers were counterfeiters.

Finally, even if *Sony* protected the defendant's sale of a product specifically designed for counterfeiters to a known counterfeiter, the evidence in this case indicated that Mr. Abdallah's actions went far beyond merely selling blank, time-loaded tapes. He acted as a contact between his customers and suppliers of other material necessary for counterfeiting, such as counterfeit insert cards; he sold duplicating machines to help his customers start up a counterfeiting operation or expand an existing one; he timed legitimate cassettes for his customers to assist them in ordering time-loaded cassettes; and he helped to finance some of his customers when they were starting out or needed assistance after a police raid. Therefore, even if *Sony* were to exonerate Mr. Abdallah for his selling of blank, time-loaded cassettes, this Court would conclude that Mr. Abdallah knowingly and materially contributed to the underlying counterfeiting activity.

[handwritten margin note: Other activities besides just selling cassettes]

QUESTIONS

1. The *Abdallah* court declined to extend *Sony* to providing goods that, albeit capable in the abstract of being put to noninfringing use, are not in fact so used. Its inquiry therefore differs from the Supreme Court's in that *Sony* appears to focus on the possible uses of the goods defendant provides, while *Abdallah* stresses the nature of defendant's activities. Are the two approaches consistent?

2. How should the court decide the following case? Songwriter *A* claims that his song "Blue of the Night" is infringed by the song "Gold of the Day," which was written and recorded by Rock Group *B* and published by *C* Corp. (which owns the copyright in the latter song). *A* brings an action against *B* and *C* for infringement. *A* also sues The Harry Fox Agency, Inc.; Fox, you will recall, licenses third persons to make recordings and collects royalties for the copyright holders. Fox has done so for "Gold of the Day" and collected royalties that it paid over to *C*. *A* can prove that Fox exercises some discretion in granting and monitoring recording licenses and that it receives commissions on the basis of the royalties it collects. Fox moves for summary judgment, claiming it is merely an agent for a fully disclosed principal, *C*. Should the case against Fox be dismissed? *See Dixon v. Atlantic Recording Corp.*, 227 U.S.P.Q. 559 (S.D.N.Y.1985).

A & M Records, Inc., v. Napster, Inc.

239 F.3d 1004 (9th Cir.2001).

[The Court of Appeals for the Ninth Circuit, having affirmed the District Court's holding that Napster users were not engaging in fair use, see *supra*, Chapter 7C, then turned to Napster's contributory and vicarious liability]

. . .

We first address plaintiffs' claim that Napster is liable for contributory copyright infringement. Traditionally, "one who, with knowledge of the infringing activity, induces, causes or materially contributes to the infringing conduct of another, may be held liable as a 'contributory' infringer.'' *Gershwin Publ'g Corp. v. Columbia Artists Mgmt., Inc.*, 443 F.2d 1159, 1162 (2d Cir.1971); *see also Fonovisa, Inc. v. Cherry Auction, Inc.*, 76 F.3d 259, 264 (9th Cir.1996). Put differently, liability exists if the defendant engages in "personal conduct that encourages or assists the infringement." *Matthew Bender & Co. v. West Publ'g Co.*, 158 F.3d 693, 706 (2d Cir.1998).

The district court determined that plaintiffs in all likelihood would establish Napster's liability as a contributory infringer. The district court did not err; Napster, by its conduct, knowingly encourages and assists the infringement of plaintiffs' copyrights.

A. Knowledge

Contributory liability requires that the secondary infringer "know or have reason to know" of direct infringement. *Cable/Home Communication Corp. v. Network Prods., Inc.*, 902 F.2d 829, 845 & 846 n. 29 (11th Cir.1990); *Religious Tech. Ctr. v. Netcom On–Line Communication Servs., Inc.*, 907 F. Supp. 1361, 1373–74 (N.D.Cal.1995) (framing issue as " 'whether Netcom knew or should have known of' the infringing activities). The district court found that Napster had both actual and constructive knowledge that its users exchanged copyrighted music. The district court also concluded that the law does not require knowledge of 'specific acts of infringement' and rejected Napster's contention that because the company cannot distinguish infringing from noninfringing files, it does not 'know' of the direct infringement." 114 F. Supp. 2d at 917.

It is apparent from the record that Napster has knowledge, both actual and constructive,[5] of direct infringement. Napster claims that it is nevertheless protected from contributory liability by the teaching of *Sony Corp. v. Universal City Studios, Inc.*, 464 U.S. 417 (1984). We disagree. We observe that Napster's actual, specific knowledge of direct infringement renders *Sony*'s holding of limited assistance to Napster. We are compelled to make a clear distinction between the architecture of the Napster system and Napster's conduct in relation to the operational capacity of the system.

The *Sony* Court refused to hold the manufacturer and retailers of video tape recorders liable for contributory infringement despite evidence that such machines could be and were used to infringe plaintiffs' copyrighted television shows. *Sony* stated that if liability "is to be imposed on petitioners in this case, it must rest on the fact that they have sold equipment with constructive knowledge of the fact that their customers may use that equipment to make unauthorized copies of copy-righted material." *Id.* at

---

5. The district court found actual knowledge because: (1) a document authored by Napster co-founder Sean Parker mentioned "the need to remain ignorant of users' real names and IP addresses' since they are exchanging 'pirated music' "; and (2) the Recording Industry Association of America ("RIAA") informed Napster of more than 12,000 infringing files, some of which are still available. 114 F. Supp. 2d at 918. The district court found constructive knowledge because: (a) Napster executives have recording industry experience; (b) they have enforced intellectual property rights in other instances; (c) Napster executives have downloaded copyrighted songs from the system; and (d) they have promoted the site with "screen shots listing infringing files." *Id.* at 919.

439 (emphasis added). The *Sony* Court declined to impute the requisite level of knowledge where the defendants made and sold equipment capable of both infringing and "substantial noninfringing uses." *Id.* at 442 (adopting a modified "staple article of commerce" doctrine from patent law). See also *Universal City Studios, Inc. v. Sony Corp.*, 480 F. Supp. 429, 459 (C.D.Cal.1979) ("This court agrees with defendants that their knowledge was insufficient to make them contributory infringers."), *rev'd*, 659 F.2d 963 (9th Cir.1981), *rev'd*, 464 U.S. 417 (1984); Alfred C. Yen, Internet Service Provider Liability for Subscriber Copyright Infringement, Enterprise Liability, and the First Amendment, 88 Geo. L.J. 1833, 1874 & 1893 n. 210 (2000) (suggesting that, after *Sony*, most Internet service providers lack "the requisite level of knowledge" for the imposition of contributory liability).

We are bound to follow *Sony*, and will not impute the requisite level of knowledge to Napster merely because peer-to-peer file sharing technology may be used to infringe plaintiffs' copyrights. See 464 U.S. at 436 (rejecting argument that merely supplying the " 'means' to accomplish an infringing activity" leads to imposition of liability). We depart from the reasoning of the district court that Napster failed to demonstrate that its system is capable of commercially significant noninfringing uses. See *Napster*, 114 F. Supp. 2d at 916, 917–18. The district court improperly confined the use analysis to current uses, ignoring the system's capabilities. See generally *Sony*, 464 U.S. at 442–43 (framing inquiry as whether the video tape recorder is "capable of commercially significant noninfringing uses") (emphasis added). Consequently, the district court placed undue weight on the proportion of current infringing use as compared to current and future noninfringing use. See generally *Vault Corp. v. Quaid Software Ltd.*, 847 F.2d 255, 264–67 (5th Cir.1988) (single noninfringing use implicated *Sony*). Nonetheless, whether we might arrive at a different result is not the issue here. See *Sports Form, Inc. v. United Press Int'l, Inc.*, 686 F.2d 750, 752 (9th Cir.1982). The instant appeal occurs at an early point in the proceedings and "the fully developed factual record may be materially different from that initially before the district court. ..." *Id.* at 753. Regardless of the number of Napster's infringing versus noninfringing uses, the evidentiary record here supported the district court's finding that plaintiffs would likely prevail in establishing that Napster knew or had reason to know of its users' infringement of plaintiffs' copyrights.

This analysis is similar to that of *Religious Technology Center v. Netcom On–Line Communication Services, Inc.*, which suggests that in an online context, evidence of actual knowledge of specific acts of infringement is required to hold a computer system operator liable for contributory copyright infringement. 907 F. Supp. at 1371....

. . .

We agree that if a computer system operator learns of specific infringing material available on his system and fails to purge such material from the system, the operator knows of and contributes to direct infringement. See *Netcom*, 907 F. Supp. at 1374. Conversely, absent any specific information which identifies infringing activity, a computer system operator cannot be liable for contributory infringement merely because the structure of the system allows for the exchange of copyrighted material. See *Sony*, 464 U.S. at 436, 442–43. To enjoin simply because a computer network allows for infringing use would, in our opinion, violate *Sony* and potentially restrict activity unrelated to infringing use.

We nevertheless conclude that sufficient knowledge exists to impose contributory liability when linked to demonstrated infringing use of the Napster system. The record supports the district court's finding that Napster has actual knowledge that specific infringing material is available using its system, that it could block access to the system by suppliers of the infringing material, and that it failed to remove the material. See *Napster*, 114 F. Supp. 2d at 918, 920–21.

B.   Material Contribution

Under the facts as found by the district court, Napster materially contributes to the infringing activity. Relying on *Fonovisa*, the district court concluded that "without the support services defendant provides, Napster users could not find and download the music they want with the ease of which defendant boasts." *Napster*, 114 F. Supp. 2d at 919–20 ("Napster is an integrated service designed to enable users to locate and download MP3 music files."). We agree that Napster provides "the site and facilities" for direct infringement. See *Fonovisa*, 76 F.3d at 264; *cf. Netcom*, 907 F. Supp. at 1372 ("Netcom will be liable for contributory infringement since its failure to cancel [a user's] infringing message and thereby stop an infringing copy from being distributed world-wide constitutes substantial participation."). The district court correctly applied the reasoning in *Fonovisa*, and properly found that Napster materially contributes to direct infringement.

We affirm the district court's conclusion that plaintiffs have demonstrated a likelihood of success on the merits of the contributory copyright infringement claim. . . .

V

We turn to the question whether Napster engages in vicarious copyright infringement. . . . In the context of copyright law, vicarious liability extends beyond an employer/employee relationship to cases in which a defendant "has the right and ability to supervise the infringing activity and also has a direct financial interest in such activities." . . .

Before moving into this discussion, we note that *Sony*'s "staple article of commerce" analysis has no application to Napster's potential liability for vicarious copyright infringement. . . .

A.   Financial Benefit

The district court determined that plaintiffs had demonstrated they would likely succeed in establishing that Napster has a direct financial interest in the infringing activity. *Napster*, 114 F. Supp. 2d at 921–22. We agree. Financial benefit exists where the availability of infringing material "acts as a 'draw' for customers." *Fonovisa*, 76 F.3d at 263–64 (stating that financial benefit may be shown "where infringing performances enhance the attractiveness of a venue"). Ample evidence supports the district court's finding that Napster's future revenue is directly dependent upon "increases in user-base." More users register with the Napster system as the "quality and quantity of available music increases." 114 F. Supp. 2d at 902. We conclude that the district court did not err in determining that Napster financially benefits from the availability of protected works on its system.

B. Supervision

The district court determined that Napster has the right and ability to supervise its users' conduct. *Napster*, 114 F. Supp. 2d at 920–21 (finding that Napster's representations to the court regarding "its improved methods of blocking users about whom rights holders complain . . . is tantamount to an admission that defendant can, and sometimes does, police its service"). We agree in part.

The ability to block infringers' access to a particular environment for any reason whatsoever is evidence of the right and ability to supervise. . . . Here, plaintiffs have demonstrated that Napster retains the right to control access to its system. Napster has an express reservation of rights policy, stating on its website that it expressly reserves the "right to refuse service and terminate accounts in [its] discretion, including, but not limited to, if Napster believes that user conduct violates applicable law . . . or for any reason in Napster's sole discretion, with or without cause."

To escape imposition of vicarious liability, the reserved right to police must be exercised to its fullest extent. Turning a blind eye to detectable acts of infringement for the sake of profit gives rise to liability. . . .

The district court correctly determined that Napster had the right and ability to police its system and failed to exercise that right to prevent the exchange of copyrighted material. The district court, however, failed to recognize that the boundaries of the premises that Napster "controls and patrols" are limited. . . . Put differently, Napster's reserved "right and ability" to police is cabined by the system's current architecture. As shown by the record, the Napster system does not "read" the content of indexed files, other than to check that they are in the proper MP3 format.

Napster, however, has the ability to locate infringing material listed on its search indices, and the right to terminate users' access to the system. The file name indices, therefore, are within the "premises" that Napster has the ability to police. We recognize that the files are user-named and may not match copyrighted material exactly (for example, the artist or song could be spelled wrong). For Napster to function effectively, however, file names must reasonably or roughly correspond to the material contained in the files, otherwise no user could ever locate any desired music. As a practical matter, Napster, its users and the record company plaintiffs have equal access to infringing material by employing Napster's "search function."

Our review of the record requires us to accept the district court's conclusion that plaintiffs have demonstrated a likelihood of success on the merits of the vicarious copyright infringement claim. Napster's failure to police the system's "premises," combined with a showing that Napster financially benefits from the continuing availability of infringing files on its system, leads to the imposition of vicarious liability.

VI

We next address whether Napster has asserted defenses which would preclude the entry of a preliminary injunction. Napster . . . asserts that its users engage in actions protected by § 1008 of the Audio Home Recording Act of 1992, 17 U.S.C. § 1008. . . .

A. Audio Home Recording Act

The statute states in part:

> No action may be brought under this title alleging infringement of copyright based on the manufacture, importation, or distribution of a digital audio recording device, a digital audio recording medium, an analog recording device, or an analog recording medium, or based on the noncommercial use by a consumer of such a device or medium for making digital musical recordings or analog musical recordings.

17 U.S.C. § 1008. Napster contends that MP3 file exchange is the type of "noncommercial use" protected from infringement actions by the statute. Napster asserts it cannot be secondarily liable for users' nonactionable exchange of copyrighted musical recordings.

The district court rejected Napster's argument, stating that the Audio Home Recording Act is "irrelevant" to the action because: (1) plaintiffs did not bring claims under the Audio Home Recording Act; and (2) the Audio Home Recording Act does not cover the downloading of MP3 files. *Napster,* 114 F. Supp. 2d at 916 n. 19.

We agree with the district court that the Audio Home Recording Act does not cover the downloading of MP3 files to computer hard drives. First, "under the plain meaning of the Act's definition of digital audio recording devices, computers (and their hard drives) are not digital audio recording devices because their 'primary purpose' is not to make digital audio copied recordings." *Recording Indus. Ass'n of Am. v. Diamond Multimedia Sys., Inc.,* 180 F.3d 1072, 1078 (9th Cir.1999). Second, notwithstanding Napster's claim that computers are "digital audio recording devices," computers do not make "digital music recordings" as defined by the Audio Home Recording Act. *Id.* at 1077 (citing S. Rep. 102–294) ("There are simply no grounds in either the plain language of the definition or in the legislative history for interpreting the term 'digital musical recording' to include songs fixed on computer hard drives.").

. . . .

[*Editors' Note*: On September 24, 2001, Napster announced that it had reached a settlement with the songwriter and music publisher plaintiffs (the settlement does not include the record producers and performers). Napster will pay $26 million for past infringements, and will pay an advance of $10 million against future licensing royalties. Following the division established in the Audio Home Recording Act, the licensing royalties will be divided 2/3 to sound recording copyright holders, and 1/3 to musical composition copyright holders.]

QUESTIONS

1. Suppose that teen hacker Roger Jolly devises and distributes a program he calls "Prankster." It works like Napster, but unlike Napster, it permits "sharing" not only of MP3 files, but of any kind of file, including text and images. While many MP3 files may well be suspect, as most music and sound recording copyright owners have not yet authorized distribution of their works in unprotected MP3 format, many text and image files are created to circulate freely. Although the "Prankster" program currently appeals most to music "sharers" (this would be especially true following issuance of an injunction against Napster), Roger anticipates an increased volume of authorized text and image-sharing as well. Under the Ninth Circuit's analysis, is Roger's knowledge that Prankster proves popular among music sharers sufficient to render him contributorily liable? What more would a copyright owner have to show? How likely is he or she to be able to show it?

2. After *Napster*, what should the analysis be if a system's "architecture" did not permit separation of infringing and non-infringing uses or users? Would it follow that there is no contributory infringement? Would that mean that one who deliberately builds an online system in a way that confounds the distinction between infringing and non-infringing uses should escape liability? The copyright owner may have the burden of discovering and notifying about infringement, but is the potential contributory infringer entitled to make that burden insuperable?

Intellectual Reserve, Inc. v. Utah Lighthouse Ministry, Inc.

75 F. Supp. 2d 1290 (D.Utah 1999).

■ TENA CAMPBELL, DISTRICT JUDGE.

This matter is before the court on plaintiff's motion for preliminary injunction. Plaintiff claims that unless a preliminary injunction issues, defendants will directly infringe and contribute to the infringement of its copyright in the Church Handbook of Instructions ("Handbook"). Defendants do not oppose a preliminary injunction, but argue that the scope of the injunction should be restricted to only prohibit direct infringement of plaintiff's copyright....

Discussion

... To determine the proper scope of the preliminary injunction, the court considers the likelihood that plaintiff will prevail on either or both of its claims.

A.   Direct Infringement

... Defendants initially conceded in a hearing, for purposes of the temporary restraining order and preliminary injunction, that plaintiff has a valid copyright in the Handbook, and that defendants directly infringed plaintiff's copyright by posting substantial portions of the copyrighted material....

B.   Contributory Infringement

According to plaintiff, after the defendants were ordered to remove the Handbook from their website, the defendants began infringing plaintiff's copyright by inducing, causing, or materially contributing to the infringing conduct of others. It is undisputed that defendants placed a notice on their website that the Handbook was online, and gave three website addresses of websites containing the material defendants were ordered to remove from their website. Defendants also posted e-mails on their website that encouraged browsing those websites, printing copies of the Handbook and sending the Handbook to others....

Liability for contributory infringement is imposed when "one who, with knowledge of the infringing activity, induces, causes or materially contributes to the infringing conduct of another." *Gershwin Publ'g Corp. v. Columbia Artists Mgt., Inc.*, 443 F.2d 1159, 1162 (2d Cir.1971). Thus, to prevail on its claim of contributory infringement, plaintiff must first be able to establish that the conduct defendants allegedly aided or encouraged could amount to infringement. Defendants argue that they have not contributed to copyright infringement by those who posted the Handbook on websites nor by those who browsed the websites on their computers.

1.   Can the Defendants Be Liable Under a Theory of Contributory Infringement for the Actions of Those Who Posted the Handbook on the Three Websites?

a.   Did those who posted the Handbook on the websites infringe plaintiff's copyright?

During a hearing on the motion to vacate the temporary restraining order, defendants accepted plaintiff's proffer that the three websites contain the material which plaintiff alleges is copyrighted. Therefore, plaintiff at trial is likely to establish that those who have posted the material on the three websites are directly infringing plaintiff's copyright.

b.   Did the defendants induce, cause or materially contribute to the infringement?

The evidence now before the court indicates that there is no direct relationship between the defendants and the people who operate the three websites. The defendants did not provide the website operators with the plaintiff's copyrighted material, nor are the defendants receiving any kind of compensation from them. The only connection between the defendants and those who operate the three websites appears to be the information defendants have posted on their website concerning the infringing sites. Based on this scant evidence, the court concludes that plaintiff has not shown that defendants contributed to the infringing action of those who operate the infringing websites.

2.   Can the Defendants Be Liable Under a Theory of Contributory Infringement for the Actions of Those Who Browse the Three Infringing Websites?

Defendants make two arguments in support of their position that the activities of those who browse the three websites do not make them liable under a theory of contributory infringement. First, defendants contend that those who browse the infringing websites are not themselves infringing plaintiff's copyright; and second, even if those who browse the websites are infringers, defendants have not materially contributed to the infringing conduct.

a.   Do those who browse the websites infringe plaintiff's copyright?

The first question, then, is whether those who browse any of the three infringing websites are infringing plaintiff's copyright. Central to this inquiry is whether the persons browsing are merely viewing the Handbook (which is not a copyright infringement), or whether they are making a copy of the Handbook (which is a copyright infringement).

"Copy" is defined in the Copyright Act as: "material objects . . . in which a work is fixed by any method now known or later developed, and from which the work can be perceived, reproduced, or otherwise communicated, either directly or with the aid of a machine or device." 17 U.S.C. § 101. "A work is fixed ' . . . when its . . . sufficiently permanent or stable to permit it to be perceived, reproduced, or otherwise communicated for a period of more than transitory duration.' " *Id.*

When a person browses a website, and by so doing displays the Handbook, a copy of the Handbook is made in the computer's random access memory (RAM), to permit viewing of the material. And in making a copy, even a temporary one, the person who browsed infringes the copyright. *See MAI Systems Corp. v. Peak Computer, Inc.*, 991 F.2d 511, 518 (9th Cir.1993) (holding that when material is transferred to a computer's RAM, copying has occurred; in the absence of ownership of the copyright or express permission by licence, such an act constitutes copyright infringement); *Marobie-Fl., Inc. v. National Ass'n of Fire Equip. Distrib.*, 983 F. Supp. 1167, 1179 (N.D.Ill.1997) (noting that liability for copyright infringement is with the persons who cause the display or distribution of the infringing material onto their computer); *see also* Nimmer on Copyright § 8.08(A)(1) (stating that the infringing act of copying may occur from "loading the copyrighted material . . . into the computer's random access memory (RAM)"). Additionally, a person making a printout or re-posting a copy of the Handbook on another website would infringe plaintiff's copyright.

b.   Did the defendants induce, cause or materially contribute to the infringement?

Actively encouraged

The court now considers whether the defendants' actions contributed to the infringement of plaintiff's copyright by those who browse the three websites.

The following evidence establishes that defendants have actively encouraged the infringement of plaintiff's copyright.[6] After being ordered to remove the Handbook from their website, defendants posted on their website: "Church Handbook of Instructions is back online!" and listed the three website addresses. Defendants also posted e-mail suggesting that the lawsuit against defendants would be affected by people logging onto one of the websites and downloading the complete handbook. One of the e-mails posted by the defendants mentioned sending a copy of the copyrighted material to the media. In response to an e-mail stating that the sender had unsuccessfully tried to browse a website that contained the Handbook, defendants gave further instruction on how to browse the material. At least one of the three websites encourages the copying and posting of copies of the allegedly infringing material on other websites. (*See* Ex. 4 ("Please mirror these files.... It will be a LOT quicker for you to download the compressed version ... Needless to say, we need a LOT of mirror sites, as absolutely soon as possible.").)

Based on the above, the court finds that the first element necessary for injunctive relief is satisfied....

QUESTION

Note the nature of the primary infringement announced in this case: reading the documents online. When users access the sites to read the postings, they make RAM copies, even if they do not make retention copies. For the District of Utah, the RAM copies constitute infringements, since the posting of the documents, and therefore their temporary copying, were unauthorized. As a matter of copyright doctrine, is this sound?

2.   SECONDARY LIABILITY OF INTERNET SERVICE PROVIDERS

Religious Technology Center v. Netcom On–Line Communication Services, Inc.

907 F.Supp. 1361 (N.D.Cal.1995).

[This case concerned the unauthorized dissemination of unpublished documents of the Church of Scientology. A disgruntled former Scientologist (Erlich) had posted the documents to an online bulletin board (Klemesrud);

---

6. Plaintiff at this point has been unable to specifically identify persons who have infringed its copyright because they were induced or assisted by defendants' conduct[;] however, there is a substantial likelihood that plaintiff will be able to do so after conducting discovery. There is evidence that at least one of the websites has seen a great increase in "hits" recently. Also, plaintiff does not have to establish that the defendants' actions are the sole cause of another's infringement; rather plaintiff may prevail by establishing that defendants' conduct induces or materially contributes to the infringing conduct of another.

the Church brought a copyright infringement claim against the bulletin board and against the online Internet access provider (Netcom). The court considered whether either of these actors could be contributorily or vicariously liable for infringing the Church's copyrights. With respect to contributory infringement, the court stated:]

a. *Knowledge of Infringing Activity*

Plaintiffs insist that Netcom knew that Erlich was infringing their copyrights at least after receiving notice from plaintiffs' counsel indicating that Erlich had posted copies of their works onto a.r.s. [Usenet newsgroup "alt.religion.scientology"] through Netcom's system. Despite this knowledge, Netcom continued to allow Erlich to post messages to a.r.s. and left the allegedly infringing messages on its system so that Netcom's subscribers and other Usenet servers could access them. Netcom argues that it did not possess the necessary type of knowledge because (1) it did not know of Erlich's planned infringing activities when it agreed to lease its facilities to Klemesrud, (2) it did not know that Erlich would infringe prior to any of his postings, (3) it is unable to screen out infringing postings before they are made, and (4) its knowledge of the infringing nature of Erlich's postings was too equivocal given the difficulty in assessing whether the registrations were valid and whether Erlich's use was fair. The court will address these arguments in turn.

Netcom cites cases holding that there is no contributory infringement by the lessors of premises that are later used for infringement unless the lessor had knowledge of the intended use at the time of the signing of the lease. *See, e.g., Deutsch v. Arnold*, 98 F.2d 686, 688 (2d Cir.1938). The contribution to the infringement by the defendant in Deutsch was merely to lease use of the premises to the infringer. Here, Netcom not only leases space but also serves as an access provider, which includes the storage and transmission of information necessary to facilitate Erlich's postings to a.r.s. Unlike a landlord, Netcom retains some control over the use of its system. Thus, the relevant time frame for knowledge is not when Netcom entered into an agreement with Klemesrud. It should be when Netcom provided its services to allow Erlich to infringe plaintiffs' copyrights. *Cf. Screen Gems–Columbia Music, Inc. v. Mark–Fi Records, Inc.*, 256 F. Supp. 399, 403 (S.D.N.Y.1966) (analyzing knowledge at time that defendant rendered its particular service). It is undisputed that Netcom did not know that Erlich was infringing before it received notice from plaintiffs. . . .

However, the evidence reveals a question of fact as to whether Netcom knew or should have known that Erlich had infringed plaintiffs' copyrights following receipt of plaintiffs' letter. Because Netcom was arguably participating in Erlich's public distribution of plaintiffs' works, there is a genuine issue as to whether Netcom knew of any infringement by Erlich before it was too late to do anything about it. If plaintiffs can prove the knowledge element, Netcom will be liable for contributory infringement since its failure to simply cancel Erlich's infringing message and thereby stop an infringing copy from being distributed worldwide constitutes substantial participation in Erlich's public distribution of the message. *Cf.* R.T. Nim-

[handwritten margin notes:] Lessors not liable unless they knew when lease was signed.

Access providers retain control over use. More than lessors.

Must show knowledge at any time before too late.

mer, The Law of Computer Technology ¶ 15.11B, at § 15–42 (2d ed. 1994) (opining that "where information service is less directly involved in the enterprise of creating unauthorized copies a finding of contributory infringement is not likely").

Netcom argues that its knowledge after receiving notice of Erlich's alleged infringing activities was too equivocal given the difficulty in assessing whether registrations are valid and whether use is fair. Although a mere unsupported allegation of infringement by a copyright owner may not automatically put a defendant on notice of infringing activity, Netcom's position that liability must be unequivocal is unsupportable. While perhaps the typical infringing activities of BBSs will involve copying software, where BBS operators are better equipped to judge infringement, the fact that this involves written works should not distinguish it. Where works contain copyright notices within them, as here, it is difficult to argue that a defendant did not know that the works were copyrighted. . . . Where a BBS operator cannot reasonably verify a claim of infringement, either because of a possible fair use defense, the lack of copyright notices on the copies, or the copyright holder's failure to provide the necessary documentation to show that there is a likely infringement, the operator's lack of knowledge will be found reasonable and there will be no liability for contributory infringement for allowing the continued distribution of the works on its system.

Since Netcom was given notice of an infringement claim before Erlich had completed his infringing activity, there may be a question of fact as to whether Netcom knew or should have known that such activities were infringing. Given the context of a dispute between a former minister and a church he is criticizing, Netcom may be able to show that its lack of knowledge that Erlich was infringing was reasonable. However, Netcom admits that it did not even look at the postings once given notice and that had it looked at the copyright notice and statements regarding authorship it would have triggered an investigation into whether there was infringement. These facts are sufficient to raise a question as to Netcom's knowledge once it received a letter from plaintiffs on December 29, 1994.

b.   *Substantial Participation*

Where a defendant has knowledge of the primary infringer's infringing activities, it will be liable if it "induces, causes or materially contributes to the infringing conduct of" the primary infringer. *Gershwin Publishing*, 443 F.2d at 1162. Such participation must be substantial. [Citations omitted.]

Providing a service that allows for the automatic distribution of all Usenet postings, infringing and noninfringing, goes well beyond renting a premises to an infringer. [The court cited the subsequently reversed district court opinion in *Fonovisa*.] It is more akin to the radio stations that were found liable for rebroadcasting an infringing broadcast. *See, e.g., Select Theatres Corp. v. Ronzoni Macaroni Co.*, 59 U.S.P.Q. 288, 291 (S.D.N.Y. 1943). Netcom allows Erlich's infringing messages to remain on its system and be further distributed to other Usenet servers worldwide. It does not completely relinquish control over how its system is used, unlike a landlord. Thus, it is fair, assuming Netcom is able to take simple measures to prevent further damage to plaintiffs' copyrighted works, to hold Netcom liable for contributory infringement where Netcom has knowledge of Erlich's infringing postings yet continues to aid in the accomplishment of Erlich's purpose of publicly distributing the postings. Accordingly, plaintiffs do raise a genuine issue of material fact as to their theory of contributory infringement as to the postings made after Netcom was on notice of plaintiffs' infringement claim.

3. *Vicarious Liability*

Even if plaintiffs cannot prove that Netcom is contributorily liable for its participation in the infringing activity, it may still seek to prove vicarious infringement based on Netcom's relationship to Erlich. A defendant is liable for vicarious liability for the actions of a primary infringer where the defendant (1) has the right and ability to control the infringer's acts and (2) receives a direct financial benefit from the infringement. Unlike contributory infringement, knowledge is not an element of vicarious liability. 3 Nimmer on Copyright § 12.04[A][1], at 12–70.

a. *Right and Ability to Control*

The first element of vicarious liability will be met if plaintiffs can show that Netcom has the right and ability to supervise the conduct of its subscribers. Netcom argues that it does not have the right to control its users' postings before they occur. Plaintiffs dispute this and argue that Netcom's terms and conditions, to which its subscribers[22] must agree, specify that Netcom reserves the right to take remedial action against subscribers. Plaintiffs argue that under "netiquette," the informal rules and customs that have developed on the Internet, violation of copyrights by a user is unacceptable and the access provider has a duty to take measures to prevent this; where the immediate service provider fails, the next service provider up the transmission stream must act. Further evidence of Netcom's right to restrict infringing activity is its prohibition of copyright infringement and its requirement that its subscribers indemnify it for any damage to third parties. Plaintiffs have thus raised a question of fact as to Netcom's right to control Erlich's use of its services.

Netcom argues that it could not possibly screen messages before they are posted given the speed and volume of the data that goes through its system. Netcom further argues that it has never exercised control over the content of its users' postings. Plaintiffs' expert opines otherwise, stating that with an easy software modification Netcom could identify postings that contain particular words or come from particular individuals. Plaintiffs further dispute Netcom's claim that it could not limit Erlich's access to Usenet without kicking off all 500 subscribers of Klemesrud's BBS. As

---

22. In this case, Netcom is even further removed from Erlich's activities. Erlich was in a contractual relationship only with Klemesrud. Netcom thus dealt directly only with Klemesrud. However, it is not crucial that Erlich does not obtain access directly through Netcom. The issue is Netcom's right and ability to control the use of its system, which it can do indirectly by controlling Klemesrud's use.

evidence that Netcom has in fact exercised its ability to police its users' conduct, plaintiffs cite evidence that Netcom has acted to suspend subscribers' accounts on over one thousand occasions. *See* Ex. J (listing suspensions of subscribers by Netcom for commercial advertising, posting obscene materials, and off-topic postings). Further evidence shows that Netcom can delete specific postings. Whether such sanctions occurred before or after the abusive conduct is not material to whether Netcom can exercise control. The court thus finds that plaintiffs have raised a genuine issue of fact as to whether Netcom has the right and ability to exercise control over the activities of its subscribers, and of Erlich in particular.

b.   *Direct Financial Benefit*

Plaintiffs must further prove that Netcom receives a direct financial benefit from the infringing activities of its users. For example, a landlord who has the right and ability to supervise the tenant's activities is vicariously liable for the infringements of the tenant where the rental amount is proportional to the proceeds of the tenant's sales. However, where a defendant rents space or services on a fixed rental fee that does not depend on the nature of the activity of the lessee, courts usually find no vicarious liability because there is no direct financial benefit from the infringement. [Citations omitted.]

... Plaintiffs cannot provide any evidence of a direct financial benefit received by Netcom from Erlich's infringing postings.... Netcom receives a fixed fee. There is no evidence that infringement by Erlich, or any other user of Netcom's services, in any way enhances the value of Netcom's services to subscribers or attracts new subscribers.... Because plaintiffs have failed to raise a question of fact on this vital element, their claim of vicarious liability fails....

SERVICE PROVIDER LIABILITY UNDER THE DMCA

Although the judicial trend favored the exoneration from direct liability of "mere conduit" service providers, the prospect of even indirect liability for contributory infringement appears to have spurred service providers to lobby Congress for exemptions or reductions in their liability to copyright owners. After extensive negotiations between service providers and copyright owners, Congress in 1998 passed the "Digital Millennium Copyright Act," adjusting the risks of copyright owners and service providers to place the burden on copyright owners to identify and notify "mere conduit" service providers of infringements carried by or residing on the providers' systems. By contrast, the law makes no special provision for service providers who originate or are otherwise actively implicated in the content residing on their servers or transiting through their systems.

A summary of the pertinent provisions of the Act follows. As you review them, consider whether the Act adequately balances the interests of copyright owners, service providers, and users. Pay particular attention to the "notice and take down and put back" provisions in §§ 512(c) and (g): how well do they reconcile the need of the copyright owner to prevent further dissemination of infringing communications with the interests of users in access to content?

New § 512 does not purport to define the conduct of an online service provider (OSP) that would render it liable for direct, contributory or vicarious infringement of copyright. Rather, it identifies several different OSP activities and specifies conditions—in the event the OSP is held to infringe by those activities—for immunizing the OSP against monetary relief and for limiting its exposure to injunctive relief. (The term "service provider" is elaborately defined in § 512(k), and can cover, for example, universities and schools as well as the more well-known commercial providers.)

Thus, § 512(a) applies to the case of an OSP that sends digital communications of others across digital networks, such as the Internet. It will be immunized against monetary liability if it plays the role of what might be called a "mere conduit" for the communications of others; i.e., the communication containing the infringing material must be initiated by a person other than the OSP, the OSP communicates the material through an automatic technical process without selecting the material, the OSP does not select the recipients of the material, the material is not maintained on the system for a period longer than necessary for transmission, routing, or connection, and the OSP does not modify the content of the material in the course of transmission. Comparable "conduit"-type conditions are set forth in § 512(b) for "system caching" by the OSP, i.e., when the OSP temporarily stores material so that network congestion, and delays to popular sites, will be reduced.

The very elaborate § 512(c) deals with the situation in which the OSP stores on a network allegedly infringing material for a longer time, at the direction of a user of that material. (The subsection does not limit liability when it is the OSP that stores the material through its own acts or decisions.) Examples of such storage covered by § 512(c) include providing server space for a user's website, for a chatroom, or for some other forum in which material may be posted at the direction of users. In such situations, the liability of the OSP will be limited if it satisfies three conditions.

One is that the OSP "does not have actual knowledge that the material or activity is infringing," or "in the absence of such actual knowledge, is not aware of facts or circumstances from which infringing activity is apparent," or "if upon obtaining such knowledge or awareness" (referred to in the legislative history as a "red flag") "the service provider acts expeditiously to remove or disable access to, the material." (The OSP need not monitor its service for, or affirmatively seek facts indicating, infringing activity.) A second, and cumulative, condition for limitation of liability is that the OSP "does not receive a financial benefit directly attributable to the infringing activity, where the service provider has the right and ability to control such activity." (This is very much like the standard test for vicarious copyright liability.) The third is that, if the OSP receives from the copyright owner (or its authorized agent) what has come to be known as a "take-down notice" identifying allegedly infringing material, the OSP "responds expeditiously to remove, or disable access to, the material that is claimed to be infringing or to be the subject of infringing activity." (Section 512 does not require that a copyright owner give a take-down notice as a condition for prevailing in a subsequent copyright infringement action; nor is it essential that the OSP, in order to assert valid defenses in such an action, have responded positively to the take-down notice.) Section 512(c) specifies the requirements for an effective take-down notification by the copyright owner; among other things, it must be in a signed writing, it must identify the copyrighted work, and it must identify the allegedly infringing material and its location (e.g., the URL address of the web page which is alleged to contain the infringing material).

———

In **ALS Scan, Inc. v. RemarQ Communities, Inc.**, 239 F.3d 619 (4th Cir.2001), the court addressed what kind of notification would substantially comply with the notice and take-down requirement. The district court had dismissed plaintiff's infringement claim alleging unauthorized posting of plaintiff's pornographic photos to news groups hosted by the defendant, on the ground that the plaintiff's notice requesting that the defendant service take down the photos lacked sufficient specificity under the statute. The plaintiff had not listed the photographs in the notification, but had contended that the sites clearly contained plaintiff's copyrighted works, and served no purpose other than to exchange plaintiff's photos, because the titles of the sites bore plaintiff's "ALS" name. The Fourth Circuit reversed the dismissal of plaintiff's complaint:

> In the spirit of achieving a balance between the responsibilities of the service provider and the copyright owner, the DMCA requires that a copyright owner put the service provider on notice in a detailed manner but allows notice by means that comport with the prescribed format only "substantially," rather than perfectly. The Act states: "To be effective under this subsection, a notification of claimed infringement must be a written communication provided to the designated agent of a service provider that includes *substantially* the following.... " 17 U.S.C. § 512(c)(3)(A) (emphasis added). In addition to substantial compliance, the notification requirements are relaxed to the extent that, with respect to multiple works, not all must be identified—only a "representative" list. See id. § 512(c)(3)(A)(ii). And with respect to location information, the copyright holder must provide information that is *"reasonably* sufficient" to permit the service provider to "locate" this material. Id. § 512(c)(3)(A)(iii) (emphasis added). This subsection specifying the requirements of a notification does not seek to burden copyright holders with the responsibility of identifying every infringing work—or even most of them—when multiple copyrights are involved. Instead, the requirements are written so as to reduce the burden of holders of multiple copyrights who face extensive infringement of their works. Thus, when a letter provides notice

equivalent to a list of representative works that can be easily identified by the service provider, the notice substantially complies with the notification requirements.

In this case, ALS Scan provided RemarQ with information that (1) identified two sites created for the sole purpose of publishing ALS Scan's copyrighted works, (2) asserted that virtually all the images at the two sites were its copyrighted material, and (3) referred RemarQ to two web addresses where RemarQ could find pictures of ALS Scan's models and obtain ALS Scan's copyright information. In addition, it noted that material at the site could be identified as ALS Scan's material because the material included ALS Scan's "name and/or copyright symbol next to it." We believe that with this information, ALS Scan substantially complied with the notification requirement of providing a representative list of infringing material as well as information reasonably sufficient to enable RemarQ to locate the infringing material. To the extent that ALS Scan's claims about infringing materials prove to be false, RemarQ has remedies for any injury it suffers as a result of removing or disabling noninfringing material. See 17 U.S.C. § 512(f), (g).

Section 512(d) deals with the situation in which the OSP "links" users to an online location containing infringing material or activity; it contemplates a subscriber using "information location tools" such as hyperlink directories and indexes, which refer to an infringing site. The section incorporates the "notification and take down" structure just described, both when so-called "red-flag" facts come to the attention of the OSP (e.g., when there is an obvious "pirate site" that uses "bootleg" or other slang terms in its URL to show the availability of pirated software, books, movies or music) and when a formal written notice is given by the copyright owner. The OSP will be afforded a "safe harbor" when it acts expeditiously to sever the link to the allegedly infringing online location.

Upon receiving the notification, the provider must "expeditiously" remove or block access to the alleged infringing material, or else face the full range of liability should the author prevail in an infringement suit. But the provider who removes or blocks the material must also so notify the subscriber; the subscriber may then send a "counter notification" (whose contents the law prescribes). See § 512(g)(3). In that event, the provider must send the counter notification to the person who notified the service of the alleged infringement, and must inform that person that the service will replace the material within 10 business days. The copyright owner must within that time "file[] an action seeking a court order to restrain the subscriber from engaging in infringing activity relating to the material on the service provider's system or network." See § 512(g)(2)(C). If the copyright owner does not initiate the action, and so inform the service provider's designated agent, then the service provider must put back the material "not less than 10, nor more than 14, business days following receipt of the counter notice . . . ." Id.

The purpose of the latter provision is to ensure that § 512 does not make it too easy for copyright owners to compel the removal of allegedly infringing material without judicial process. Section 512 encourages providers who have received notice to take down the material immediately, since the text insulates service providers who comply with the statutory requirements from suit by persons (including the subscriber) disgruntled at the removal of the material from the server. *See* § 512(g)(1). Moreover, any person who knowingly misrepresents that material or activity is infringing will be subject to damages incurred by any person injured as a result of the service provider's removal of the material. *See* § 512(f). From the point of view of authors and copyright owners, the strong incentives to remove material may offer an effective means of enforcement, since the author's first goal will often be to get the material taken down before it can be copied/disseminated further. On the other hand, there is the risk that timorous service providers will remove material whose posting was not infringing because, for example, the posting constituted fair use. Hence the opportunity for the posting subscriber to demand that the material be "put back," and a corresponding obligation for the copyright owner to initiate judicial proceedings if the copyright owner wishes to ensure that the "take down" of the material remains in effect.

QUESTIONS

1. Is the relief available to copyright owners against service providers under § 512 fully effective? Assess the following arguments offered on their behalf. The Act's inducements to remove allegedly infringing material can ensure a speedy response, but the preclusion of monetary relief may leave significant remedial gaps. In foreclosing monetary claims against service providers, Congress has also denied any practical prospect of recovery in damages when the primary infringer is underage or otherwise unable to satisfy a money judgment. Yet, this class of infringers is likely to be significant on the Internet, since one may anticipate that "Internet cowboys" will upload unauthorized copies, not for commercial gain, but to "liberate the content" of copyrighted works for all to enjoy. Even if not commercially motivated, this kind of conduct can have deleterious commercial consequences for copyright owners.

2. Recall *Napster*: users engaged in "peer to peer file sharing" through the Internet. After interrogating the Napster database to learn which users currently online had made the requested song available on their hard drives, the requesting user clicks on an entry and is sent directly to the other user's hard drive, from which she copies the song. No music resides on Napster's own servers. Napster seeks your advice as to whether § 512 would shield it in whole or in part for liability for contributory infringement. Which subsections of § 512 are at issue, and would they apply? See *A & M Records v. Napster*, 239 F.3d 1004 (9th Cir.2001).

G. TECHNOLOGICAL PROTECTION MEASURES

Works disseminated in digital form may be particularly susceptible to unauthorized copying, not only because these works can be easy to copy, but because the quality of the copy is as good as that of the original. Recall the discussion, *supra*, Chapter 6.A, of the impetus for the 1992 Audio Home Recording Act. That statute featured a novel development in U.S. copyright law—it mandated inclusion of "serial copy management system" (SCMS) copy-protection devices in all U.S.-manufactured or distributed digital audio tape recorders, and made it illegal to disable or tamper with the SCMS devices. In the absence of a legislative provision outlawing the disabling of or tampering with this anticopying device, it is likely that such conduct would not have violated Title 17, particularly in the wake of the Supreme Court's broad pronouncement in *Sony v. Universal Studios* that the supplier of copying equipment will not be liable for contributory copyright infringement so long as the device is "merely capable of substantial noninfringing uses."

Digital dissemination of copyrighted works poses other threats, and opportunities. The digital format may facilitate the copyright owner's licensing the work if the work is disseminated with information about authorship, ownership, and terms and conditions attached. In the future, click-on licenses obtained directly from the copyright owners through this kind of information may become the norm, but only if the information is reliable (and the work the licensing information accompanies is authentic). Here, again, promotion of digital dissemination and licensing depends on the security of the product and its licensing terms.

The need to accompany works disseminated in digital format with effective copy-protection and copyright management information measures, and the further need to insure those measures against alteration or defeat by unauthorized third parties, was recognized by the 160 nations that came together in Geneva in December 1996 to produce the World Intellectual Property Organization Copyright Treaty, CRNR/DC/89/eng (Dec. 20, 1996) (WCT). See Appendix G in the Statutory Appendix. That treaty, now open for ratification, contains two provisions concerning copyright owners' technological self-help measures. Under the Treaty, copyright owners have the option of disseminating their works together with anti-copying measures or copyright management information, but there is no obligation to do so. However, if the copyright owner chooses to resort to technological protections of the work and related licensing information, then treaty member countries must enforce that choice. The uncertainty, in light of *Sony v. Universal Studios*, whether U.S. law already afforded effective protection against the manufacture and sale of circumvention devices, or against tampering with copyright management information, led Congress to enact a new Chapter 12 of Title 17, as part of the 1998 "Digital Millennium Copyright Act" (DMCA).

1.   Protection Against Circumvention

With respect to technological protections, the DMCA distinguishes between measures used by the copyright owner to control initial access to the work and measures that prevent subsequent copying from a lawfully acquired copy. As you review the following provisions, consider the difference in impact between the treatment of technological measures protecting against "access" and technological measures that "effectively protect a right of a copyright owner."

§ 1201. Circumvention of copyright protection systems

(a) Violations Regarding Circumvention of Technological Protection Measures.—

(1)(A) No person shall circumvent a technological protection measure that effectively controls access to a work protected under this title. . . .

. . .

(2) No person shall manufacture, import, offer to the public, provide or otherwise traffic in any technology, product, service, device, component, or part thereof that—

(A) is primarily designed or produced for the purpose of circumventing a technological protection measure that effectively controls access to a work protected under this title;

(B) has only limited commercially significant purpose or use other than to circumvent a technological protection measure that effectively controls access to a work protected under this title; or

(C) is marketed by that person or another acting in concert with that person with that person's knowledge for use in circumventing a technological protection measure that effectively controls access to a work protected under this title.

(3) As used in this subsection—

(A) to "circumvent a technological protection measure" means to descramble a scrambled work, to decrypt an encrypted work, or otherwise to avoid, bypass, remove, deactivate, or impair a technological protection measure, without the authority of the copyright owner; and

(B) a technological protection measure "effectively controls access to a work" if the measure, in the ordinary course of its operation, requires the application of information, or a process or a treatment, with the authority of the copyright owner, to gain access to the work. . . .

[Section 1201(b) forbids manufacture or distribution of a product or service primarily designed to circumvent "protection afforded by" a technological protection measure that "effectively protects a right of a copyright owner" in a work—and otherwise parallels the terms of section 1201(a).]

(c) Other Rights, Etc., Not Affected.—

(1) Nothing in this section shall affect rights, remedies, limitations, or defenses to copyright infringement, including fair use, under this title.

(2) Nothing in this section shall enlarge or diminish vicarious or contributory liability for copyright infringement in connection with any technology, product, service, device, component or part thereof....

[Section 1201(d)–(j) sets forth exceptions to the prohibition on circumvention of technological protections of access. These include:

nonprofit libraries, archives and educational institutions: they may circumvent access controls in order to determine whether to purchase a protected work, if the work is not otherwise available for inspection. § 1201(d);

law enforcement activities and security testing: § 1201(e) entitles federal, state and local law enforcement officers to defeat access controls in order to conduct an authorized investigation. Similarly, § 1201(j) permits circumvention for purposes of "security testing," defined as "good faith testing, investigating or correcting a security flaw or vulnerability, with the authorization of the owner or operator of such computer, computer system, or computer network."

reverse engineering: circumvention of access controls is permitted if performed by a person who has "lawfully obtained the right to use a copy of a computer program ... for the sole purpose of identifying and analyzing those elements of the [access-protected] program that are necessary to achieve interoperability of an independently created computer program with other programs, and that have not previously been readily available to the person engaging in the circumvention, to the extent any such acts of identification and analysis do not constitute infringement under this title." § 1201(f);

encryption research: circumvention of access controls is permitted if necessary to conduct encryption research, performed by a person who has "lawfully obtained the encrypted copy," and who "made a good faith effort to obtain authorization before the circumvention." The statute includes a variety of factors designed to ensure the *bona fides* of the research and the researcher. § 1201(g);

exceptions regarding minors: permits the use of screening devices that include a "component or part" that circumvents access controls, but that is necessary to a device that "does not itself violate the provisions of this title" and has the "sole purpose to prevent the access of minors to material on the Internet." § 1201(h);

protection of personally identifying information: permits users to circumvent an access control in order to discover and disable an *undisclosed* information-gathering feature, but does not entitle the user to "gain access to any work." § 1201(i).]

WHAT IS "ACCESS"?

The DMCA distinguishes between access to the work and use of the work once accessed. In hardcopy terms, the distinction might be between acquiring a copy in the first place, and what one does with the copy thereafter. The fair use doctrine deals primarily with the second stage.

That is, it may be fair use to make non-profit research photocopies of pages from a lawfully acquired book, but it is not fair use to steal the book in order to make the photocopies. To that extent, the notion of "access" appears to resemble the traditional copyright concepts inherent in the § 106(3) exclusive distribution right. In *Harper & Row v. Nation Enterprises, supra* Chapter 7.B, the Supreme Court construed this right to give the author control over the determination to grant "access" to her work, that is, to disclose and offer it to the public for purchase if she chooses.

But it also seems that the "access" that § 1201(a) protects goes beyond traditional copyright prerogatives. Indeed, the text indicates that "access" is distinct from a "right of the copyright owner under this title." The difference becomes apparent if one compares the consequences of protecting a technological measure controlling " ... access to *a work* ... " with a measure controlling " ... access to *a copy of* a work ... " The latter corresponds to "access" in the copyright sense of the right to distribute copies of the work; the former is the new right introduced in the DMCA. The following example illustrates the difference between "access to a work" and "access to a copy of a work."

Suppose you purchase a CD–ROM containing a copyrighted work, such as a videogame. Suppose also that to view and play the game, you must register with the producer, using the modem in your computer. The producer in turn communicates a password to you. A technological measure included in the CD–ROM recognizes the password, and the computer. Thenceforth, each time you wish to play the game, you must enter your password, and play the game on the same computer. This means that you cannot use that copy of the game on another computer, nor may you lend your copy to a friend (to whom you would also disclose your password) to play on another computer.

In this scenario, by purchasing the CD–ROM, you have acquired lawful access to a *copy* of the work. Section 101 of the Copyright Act defines "copies" as "material objects" in which "a work" is fixed. The CD–ROM you purchased is a material object. But you do not access "the work" until you have entered the password (from the correct computer). Thus, you will be violating § 1201(a) if you try to bypass the access controls even to perform acts that are lawful under the Copyright Act, such as using your copy in another computer or lending it to a friend—acts permitted to the owner of the copy under the "first sale doctrine" codified in § 109(a), and under § 117, which allows the owner of a copy of a computer program to use it in a computer. By contrast, had the law barred circumvention of technological measures controlling access to "a copy" of a work, then once you had lawfully acquired your copy, you should have been able to use it in a computer, or to circulate that copy, without further prohibitions imposed or reinforced by the Copyright Act. (If you want to make or transmit *additional* copies, however, you would most likely infringe the reproduction or public performance/display rights, and might also run afoul of post-access technological protections attached to your copy.)

In granting copyright owners a right to prevent circumvention of technological controls on "access," Congress may in effect have extended copyright to cover "use" of works of authorship (subject to the exceptions permitting access-control circumvention). But in theory, copyright does not reach "use"; it prohibits unauthorized reproduction, adaptation, distribution, and public performance or display (communication to the public). Not all "uses" correspond to these acts. But because "access" is a prerequisite to "use," by controlling the former, the copyright owner may well end up preventing or conditioning the latter.

Does this result in overprotection, or is it a necessary adaptation to the digital world? That is, do traditional categories of rights under copyright fail to respond to the way works are (or will be) exploited in digital media, so that new rights are needed? "Access" probably will become the most important right pertaining to digitally expressed works, and its recognition, whether by the detour of prohibitions on circumvention of access controls, or by express addition to the list of exclusive rights under copyright, may be inevitable. But if "access" becomes a right (express or *de facto*), it is also necessary to consider whether that right should be subjected to limitations. Congress has indeed provided a variety of exceptions permitting users to circumvent access controls, and has instructed the Copyright Office to consider others, but it remains to be seen how the copyright balance will fare under the new "access" protection.

In October 2000, The Copyright Office concluded the first of its Congressionally-mandated ongoing triennial inquiries into the impact of access controls on non-infringing uses of copyrighted works. Congress had given the Librarian of Congress authority to declare classes of works for which access controls have compromised non-infringing uses, and to exempt those classes from application of the ban on circumvention. Although the Copyright Office study emphasized that, on the record of the first rulemaking, no significant showing of "digital lockup" had been made, the Office may well perceive a need to list more exempted classes should copyright owners prove overreaching in their implementation of access controls, and should non-protected formats become less publicly available. At the conclusion of its first Rulemaking, the Copyright Office listed two classes of works whose access controls would be subject to circumvention without liability:

1.   Compilations consisting of lists of websites blocked by filtering software applications; and

2.   Literary works, including computer programs and databases, protected by access control mechanisms that fail to permit access because of malfunction, damage or obsolescence.

See Rulemaking, 65 Fed. Reg. 64,556 (2000) (to be codified at 37 CFR Part 201) (also available at http://www.loc.gov/copyright/fedreg/65fr64555.html).

QUESTIONS

1. Victor Viewer purchases a videodisc containing a copy of the cult horror film, "It Came From the Titanic." The disc is played on Victor's home computer-entertainment center and is programmed to permit one viewing of the film; subsequent viewings require additional payment (by communicating the user's credit card number via modem to the rights holder). The computer-adept Victor disables the program that blocks subsequent unpaid viewings and watches the movie several more times on his home entertainment center. Has Victor violated "a right of a copyright owner"? Has Victor violated § 1201(a)?

2. Has the ease with which digital media permit copying and dissemination of copyrighted works forced Congress to alter fundamentally the nature of the copyright owner's rights? What reconceptualization of copyright law do these changes betoken? Is this a salutary development?

Two decisions so far have construed the § 1201(a)(2) provisions prohibiting the distribution of devices primarily designed to circumvent access controls. One controversy, *RealNetworks, Inc. v. Streambox, Inc.*, 2000 WL 127311 (W.D. Wash. 2000) concerned the commercial distribution of a product designed to convert streaming-only RealAudio music files into files that defendant's customers could download and retain. The other case, *Universal City Studios v. Reimerdes*, 82 F. Supp. 2d 211 (S.D.N.Y.2000), *appeal pending*, was initiated by members of the Motion Picture Association of America against the operators of websites that had posted the "hack" to defeat the encryption on DVDs. Both found violations of § 1201(a)(2), despite defendants' invocation of exceptions to the ban on circumvention.

Realnetworks, Inc. v. Streambox, Inc.

2000 WL 127311 (W.D. Wash. 2000).

■ Marsha J. Pechman, District Judge.

[RealNetworks develops and markets software products designed to enable owners of digitized audio and video content to send their content to computer users over the internet through a process known as "streaming." When a sound or video clip is "streamed" to a consumer, no trace of the clip is left on the consumer's computer, so that it cannot be accessed repeatedly at will or redistributed to others over the internet. Content owners use the RealNetworks software so that their copyrighted material—typically stored on the content owners' websites—can be transmitted securely and without fear of unauthorized reproduction by consumers. Content owners can encode (or encrypt) their material through a RealNetworks product; can send that content in RealMedia files to be stored on a RealServer; and can authorize the downloading of streamed material by a RealPlayer, a software program that resides on an end-user's computer.

[RealNetworks utilizes two security devices for the copyrighted material that it hosts: the so-called "Secret Handshake" and the so-called "Copy Switch." The "secret handshake" is an authentication mechanism that assures that files hosted on a RealServer will be sent only to a RealPlayer. After the RealServer recognizes the RealPlayer, it sends the Player the requested musical recording in streaming format.The "secret handshake" is thus an access control measure within the definition of § 1201(a)(3)(B) because it "requires the application of information, or a process or treatment, with the authority of the copyright owner, to gain access to the work," here, to tell the RealServer to communicate the work to the RealPlayer so that users may listen to the music.

[Copyright owners who make their works available through RealNetworks designate whether they wish the works to be delivered as streaming only, so that recipients cannot copy the work, or as a downloadable stream. The "Copy Switch" on the RealServer indicates whether the work may or may not be copied. Most copyright owners choose not to permit copying. The RealPlayer reads the information on the server; if the Copy Switch is turned off, the RealPlayer will deliver the work in streaming-only format.

[Streambox reverse engineered the RealPlayer software to ascertain the code that produces the "secret handshake," and then incorporated the code into its "VCR" product so that when a Streambox VCR contacts a RealNetworks server, the server will "think" it is communicating with a RealPlayer, and will give the VCR access to the works on the server. Unlike the RealPlayer, however, the StreamboxVCR will ignore the Copy Switch, and therefore will make copies whether or not the copyright owner has instructed the server to permit copying. Thus, by emulating the "secret handshake," the VCR circumvents an access protection in violation of § 1201(a)(2); and by avoiding the Copy Switch, the VCR circumvents an anticopying measure in violation of § 1201(b), the court held.]

CONCLUSIONS OF LAW

... Parts of the VCR Are Likely to Violate Sections 1201(a)(2) and 1201(b)

7.   Under the DMCA, the Secret Handshake that must take place between a RealServer and a RealPlayer before the RealServer will begin streaming content to an end-user appears to constitute a "technological measure" that "effectively controls access" to copyrighted works. See 17 U.S.C. § 1201(a)(3)(B) (measure "effectively controls access" if it "requires the application of information or a process or a treatment, with the authority of the copyright holder, to gain access to the work"). To gain access to a work protected by the Secret Handshake, a user must employ a RealPlayer, which will supply the requisite information to the RealServer in a proprietary authentication sequence.

8.   In conjunction with the Secret Handshake, the Copy Switch is a "technological measure" that effectively protects the right of a copyright owner to control the unauthorized copying of its work. See 17 U.S.C. § 1201(b)(2)(B) (measure "effectively protects" right of copyright holder if it "prevents, restricts or otherwise limits the exercise of a right of a copyright owner"); 17 U.S.C. § 106(a) (granting copyright holder exclusive right to make copies of its work). To access a RealMedia file distributed by

a RealServer, a user must use a RealPlayer. The RealPlayer reads the Copy Switch in the file. If the Copy Switch in the file is turned off, the RealPlayer will not permit the user to record a copy as the file is streamed. Thus, the Copy Switch may restrict others from exercising a copyright holder's exclusive right to copy its work.

9.   Under the DMCA, a product or part thereof "circumvents" protections afforded a technological measure by "avoiding, bypassing, removing, deactivating or otherwise impairing" the operation of that technological measure. 17 U.S.C. §§ 1201(b)(2)(A), 1201(a)(2)(A). Under that definition, at least a part of the Streambox VCR circumvents the technological measures RealNetworks affords to copyright owners. Where a RealMedia file is stored on a RealServer, the VCR "bypasses" the Secret Handshake to gain access to the file. The VCR then circumvents the Copy Switch, enabling a user to make a copy of a file that the copyright owner has sought to protect.

10.   Given the circumvention capabilities of the Streambox VCR, Streambox violates the DMCA if the product or a part thereof: (i) is primarily designed to serve this function; (ii) has only limited commercially significant purposes beyond the circumvention; or (iii) is marketed as a means of circumvention. 17 U.S.C. §§ 1201(a)(2)(A–C), 1201(b)(1)(A–C). These three tests are disjunctive. Id. A product that meets only one of the three independent bases for liability is still prohibited. Here, the VCR meets at least the first two.

11.   The Streambox VCR meets the first test for liability under the DMCA because at least a part of the Streambox VCR is primarily, if not exclusively, designed to circumvent the access control and copy protection measures that RealNetworks affords to copyright owners. 17 U.S.C. §§ 1201(a)(2)(A), 1201(b)(1)(A).

12.   The second basis for liability is met because [the] portion of the VCR that circumvents the Secret Handshake so as to avoid the Copy Switch has no significant commercial purpose other than to enable users to access and record protected content. 17 U.S.C. § 1201(a)(2)(B), 1201(b)(1)(B). There does not appear to be any other commercial value that this capability affords.

13.   Streambox's primary defense to Plaintiff's DMCA claims is that the VCR has legitimate uses. In particular, Streambox claims that the VCR allows consumers to make "fair use" copies of RealMedia files, notwithstanding the access control and copy protection measures that a copyright owner may have placed on that file.

14.   The portions of the VCR that circumvent the secret handshake and copy switch permit consumers to obtain and redistribute perfect digital copies of audio and video files that copyright owners have made clear they do not want copied. For this reason, Streambox's VCR is entitled to the same "fair use" protections the Supreme Court afforded to video cassette recorders used for "time-shifting" in *Sony Corp. v. Universal City Studios, Inc.*, 464 U.S. 417 (1984).

15.   The *Sony* decision turned in large part on a finding that substantial numbers of copyright holders who broadcast their works either had authorized or would not object to having their works time-shifted by private viewers. Here, by contrast, copyright owners have specifically chosen to prevent the copying enabled by the Streambox VCR putting their content on RealServers and leaving the Copy Switch off.

16.   Moreover, the *Sony* decision did not involve interpretation of the DMCA. Under the DMCA, product developers do not have the right to distribute products that circumvent technological measures that prevent consumers from gaining unauthorized access to or making unauthorized copies of works protected by the Copyright Act. Instead, Congress specifically prohibited the distribution of the tools by which such circumvention could be accomplished. The portion of the Streambox VCR that circumvents the technological measures that prevent unauthorized access to and duplication of audio and video content therefore runs afoul of the DMCA.

17.   This point is underscored by the leading treatise on copyright, which observes that the enactment of the DMCA means that "those who manufacture equipment and products generally can no longer gauge their conduct as permitted or forbidden by reference to the *Sony* doctrine. For a given piece of machinery might qualify as a stable [sic] item of commerce, with a substantial noninfringing use, and hence be immune from attack under *Sony*'s construction of the Copyright Act—but nonetheless still be subject to suppression under Section 1201." 1 Nimmer on Copyright (1999 Supp.), § 12A.18[B]. As such, "equipment manufacturers in the twenty-first century will need to vet their products for compliance with Section 1201 in order to avoid a circumvention claim, rather than under *Sony* to negate a copyright claim." *Id.*

18.   Streambox also argues that the VCR does not violate the DMCA because the Copy Switch that it avoids does not "effectively protect" against the unauthorized copying of copyrighted works as required by § 1201(a)(3)(B). Streambox claims this "effective" protection is lacking because an enterprising end-user could potentially use other means to record streaming audio content as it is played by the end-user's computer speakers. This argument fails because the Copy Switch, in the ordinary course of its operation when it is on, restricts and limits the ability of people to make perfect digital copies of a copyrighted work. The Copy Switch therefore constitutes a technological measure that effectively protects a copyright owner's rights under section 1201(a)(3)(B).

19.   In addition, the argument ignores the fact that before the Copy Switch is even implicated, the Streambox VCR has already circumvented the Secret Handshake to gain access to an unauthorized RealMedia file. That alone is sufficient for liability under the DMCA. See 17 U.S.C. § 1201(i)(e). . . .

20.   Streambox's last defense to liability for the VCR rests on Section 1201(c)(3) of the DMCA which it cites for the proposition that the VCR is not required to respond to the Copy Switch. Again, this argument fails to

address the VCR's circumvention of the Secret Handshake, which is enough, by itself, to create liability under Section 1201(a)(2).

21.   Moreover, Section 1201(c)(3) states that "nothing in this section shall require ... a response to any particular technological measure, so long as ... the product ... does not otherwise fall within the prohibitions of subsections (a) (2) or (b)(1)." As the remainder of the statute and the leading copyright commentator make clear, Section 1201(c)(3) does not provide immunity for products that circumvent technological measures in violation of Sections 1201(a)(2) or (b)(1). If the statute meant what Streambox suggests, any manufacturer of circumvention tools could avoid DMCA liability simply by claiming it chose not to respond to the particular protection that its tool circumvents.

22.   As set forth above, the Streambox VCR falls within the prohibitions of sections 1201(a)(2) and 1201(b)(1). Accordingly, Section 1201(c)(3) affords Streambox no defense....

26.   An injunction against the VCR also would serve the public interest because the VCR's ability to circumvent RealNetworks' security measures would likely reduce the willingness of copyright owners to make their audio and video works accessible to the public over the Internet.

Universal City Studios, Inc. v. Reimerdes

111 F. Supp. 2d 294 (S.D.N.Y. 2000), *aff'd sub nom.* Universal City Studios, Inc. v. Corley (2d Cir. Nov. 28, 2001).

■ LEWIS KAPLAN, DISTRICT JUDGE.

Plaintiffs, eight major United States motion picture studios, distribute many of their copyrighted motion pictures for home use on digital versatile disks ("DVDs"), which contain copies of the motion pictures in digital form. They protect those motion pictures from copying by using an encryption system called CSS. CSS-protected motion pictures on DVDs may be viewed only on players and computer drives equipped with licensed technology that permits the devices to decrypt and play—but not to copy—the films.

Late last year, computer hackers devised a computer program called DeCSS that circumvents the CSS protection system and allows CSS-protected motion pictures to be copied and played on devices that lack the licensed decryption technology. Defendants quickly posted DeCSS on their Internet web site, thus making it readily available to much of the world. Plaintiffs promptly brought this action under the Digital Millennium Copyright Act (the "DMCA") to enjoin defendants from posting DeCSS and to prevent them from electronically "linking" their site to others that post DeCSS. Defendants responded with what they termed "electronic civil disobedience"—increasing their efforts to link their web site to a large number of others that continue to make DeCSS available.

Defendants contend that their actions do not violate the DMCA and, in any case, that the DMCA, as applied to computer programs, or code, violates the First Amendment. This is the Court's decision after trial, and the decision may be summarized in a nutshell.

Defendants argue first that the DMCA should not be construed to reach their conduct, principally because the DMCA, so applied, could prevent those who wish to gain access to technologically protected copyrighted works in order to make fair—that is, non-infringing—use of them from doing so. They argue that those who would make fair use of technologically protected copyrighted works need means, such as DeCSS, of circumventing access control measures not for piracy, but to make lawful use of those works.

Technological access control measures have the capacity to prevent fair uses of copyrighted works as well as foul. Hence, there is a potential tension between the use of such access control measures and fair use. Defendants are not the first to recognize that possibility. As the DMCA made its way through the legislative process, Congress was preoccupied with precisely this issue. Proponents of strong restrictions on circumvention of access control measures argued that they were essential if copyright holders were to make their works available in digital form because digital works otherwise could be pirated too easily. Opponents contended that strong anticircumvention measures would extend the copyright monopoly inappropriately and prevent many fair uses of copyrighted material.

Congress struck a balance. The compromise it reached, depending upon future technological and commercial developments, may or may not prove ideal. But the solution it enacted is clear. The potential tension to which defendants point does not absolve them of liability under the statute. There is no serious question that defendants' posting of DeCSS violates the DMCA.

Defendants' constitutional argument ultimately rests on two propositions—that computer code, regardless of its function, is "speech" entitled to maximum constitutional protection and that computer code therefore essentially is exempt from regulation by government. But their argument is baseless.

Computer code is expressive. To that extent, it is a matter of First Amendment concern. But computer code is not purely expressive any more than the assassination of a political figure is purely a political statement. Code causes computers to perform desired functions. Its expressive element no more immunizes its functional aspects from regulation than the expressive motives of an assassin immunize the assassin's action. . . .

I.   The Genesis of the Controversy

As this case involves computers and technology with which many are unfamiliar, it is useful to begin by defining some of the vocabulary.

The Vocabulary of this Case

* * *

4. Portable Storage Media

Digital files may be stored on several different kinds of storage media, some of which are readily transportable. Perhaps the most familiar of these are so called floppy disks or "floppies," which now are 3 1/2 inch magnetic disks upon which digital files may be recorded. For present purposes, however, we are concerned principally with two more recent developments, CD–ROMs and digital versatile disks, or DVDs.

A CD–ROM is a five-inch wide optical disk capable of storing approximately 650 MB of data. To read the data on a CD–ROM, a computer must have a CD–ROM drive. DVDs are five-inch wide disks capable of storing more than 4.7 GB of data. In the application relevant here, they are used to hold full-length motion pictures in digital form. They are the latest technology for private home viewing of recorded motion pictures and result in drastically improved audio and visual clarity and quality of motion pictures shown on televisions or computer screens.

5. The Technology Here at Issue

CSS, or Content Scramble System, is an access control and copy prevention system for DVDs developed by the motion picture companies, including plaintiffs. It is an encryption-based system that requires the use of appropriately configured hardware such as a DVD player or a computer DVD drive to decrypt, unscramble and play back, but not copy, motion pictures on DVDs. The technology necessary to configure DVD players and drives to play CSS-protected DVDs has been licensed to hundreds of manufacturers in the United States and around the world.

DeCSS is a software utility, or computer program, that enables users to break the CSS copy protection system and hence to view DVDs on unlicensed players and make digital copies of DVD movies. The quality of motion pictures decrypted by DeCSS is virtually identical to that of encrypted movies on DVD.

DivX is a compression program available for download over the Internet. It compresses video files in order to minimize required storage space, often to facilitate transfer over the Internet or other networks.

B. Parties

Plaintiffs are eight major motion picture studios. Each is in the business of producing and distributing copyrighted material including motion pictures. Each distributes, either directly or through affiliates, copyrighted motion pictures on DVDs. Plaintiffs produce and distribute a large majority of the motion pictures on DVDs on the market today.

Defendant Eric Corley is viewed as a leader of the computer hacker community and goes by the name Emmanuel Goldstein, after the leader of the underground in George Orwell's classic, *1984*. He and his company, defendant 2600 Enterprises, Inc., together publish a magazine called *2600: The Hacker Quarterly*, which Corley founded in 1984, and which is something of a bible to the hacker community. The name "2600" was derived from the fact that hackers in the 1960's found that the transmission of a 2600 hertz tone over a long distance trunk connection gained access to "operator mode" and allowed the user to explore aspects of the telephone system that were not otherwise accessible. Mr. Corley chose the name because he regarded it as a "mystical thing," commemorating something that he evidently admired. Not surprisingly, *2600: The Hacker Quarterly* has included articles on such topics as how to steal an Internet domain name, access other people's e-mail, intercept cellular phone calls, and break into the computer systems at Costco stores and Federal Express. One issue contains a guide to the federal criminal justice system for readers charged with computer hacking. In addition, defendants operate a web site located at <http://www.2600.com> ("2600.com"), which is managed primarily by Mr. Corley and has been in existence since 1995.[47]

Prior to January 2000, when this action was commenced, defendants posted the source and object code for DeCSS on the 2600.com web site, from which they could be downloaded easily. At that time, 2600.com contained also a list of links to other web sites purporting to post DeCSS.

C. The Development of DVD and CSS

* * *

CSS involves encrypting, according to an encryption algorithm, the digital sound and graphics files on a DVD that together constitute a motion picture. A CSS-protected DVD can be decrypted by an appropriate decryption algorithm that employs a series of keys stored on the DVD and the DVD player. In consequence, only players and drives containing the appropriate keys are able to decrypt DVD files and thereby play movies stored on DVDs.

As the motion picture companies did not themselves develop CSS and, in any case, are not in the business of making DVD players and drives, the technology for making compliant devices, i.e., devices with CSS keys, had to be licensed to consumer electronics manufacturers.[60] In order to ensure that the decryption technology did not become generally available and that compliant devices could not be used to copy as well as merely to play CSS-protected movies, the technology is licensed subject to strict security requirements. Moreover, manufacturers may not, consistent with their licenses, make equipment that would supply digital output that could be used in copying protected DVDs....

With CSS in place, the studios introduced DVDs on the consumer market in early 1997. All or most of the motion pictures released on DVD were, and continue to be, encrypted with CSS technology. Over 4,000 motion pictures now have been released in DVD format in the United

---

47. Tr. (Corley) at 790; Ex. 52–54, 64, 79 (Corley Dec.) P20; 97.

Interestingly, defendants' copyright both their magazine and the material on their web site to prevent others from copying their works. Tr. (Corley) at 832; Ex. 96 (Corley Dep.) at 23–24.

60. The licensing function initially was performed by MEI and Toshiba. Subsequent-

ly, MEI and Toshiba granted a royalty free license to the DVD Copy Control Association ("DVD CCA"), which now handles the licensing function. Tr. (King) at 485–86, 510; Ex. XXY (Attaway Dep.) at 31. The motion picture companies themselves license CSS from the DVD CCA. Ex. XYY (Attaway Dep.) at 31–32.

States, and movies are being issued on DVD at the rate of over 40 new titles per month in addition to rereleases of classic films. Currently, more than five million households in the United States own DVD players, and players are projected to be in ten percent of United States homes by the end of 2000.

DVDs have proven not only popular, but lucrative for the studios. Revenue from their sale and rental currently accounts for a substantial percentage of the movie studios' revenue from the home video market. Revenue from the home market, in turn, makes up a large percentage of the studios' total distribution revenue.

D.   The Appearance of DeCSS

In late September 1999, Jon Johansen, a Norwegian subject then fifteen years of age, and two individuals he "met" under pseudonyms over the Internet, reverse engineered a licensed DVD player and discovered the CSS encryption algorithm and keys. They used this information to create DeCSS, a program capable of decrypting or "ripping" encrypted DVDs, thereby allowing playback on non-compliant computers as well as the copying of decrypted files to computer hard drives.[72] Mr. Johansen then posted the executable code on his personal Internet web site and informed members of an Internet mailing list that he had done so. Neither Mr. Johansen nor his collaborators obtained a license from the DVD CCA....

E.   The Distribution of DeCSS

In the months following its initial appearance on Mr. Johansen's web site, DeCSS has become widely available on the Internet, where hundreds of sites now purport to offer the software for download.... In November 1999, defendants' web site began to offer DeCSS for download. It established also a list of links to several web sites that purportedly "mirrored" or offered DeCSS for download....

F.   The Preliminary Injunction and Defendants' Response

* * * After a hearing at which defendants presented no affidavits or evidentiary material, the Court granted plaintiffs' motion for a preliminary injunction barring defendants from posting DeCSS. At the conclusion of the hearing, plaintiffs sought also to enjoin defendants from linking to other sites that posted DeCSS, but the Court declined to entertain the application at that time in view of plaintiffs' failure to raise the issue in their motion papers.

Following the issuance of the preliminary injunction, defendants removed DeCSS from the 2600.com web site. In what they termed an act of "electronic civil disobedience," however, they continued to support links to other web sites purporting to offer DeCSS for download, a list which had grown to nearly five hundred by July 2000. Indeed, they carried a banner saying "Stop the MPAA" and, in a reference to this lawsuit, proclaimed:

---

72. Mr. Johansen testified that the "De" in DeCSS stands for "decrypt." Tr. (Johansen) at 628.

"We have to face the possibility that we could be forced into submission. For that reason it's especially important that as many of you as possible, all throughout the world, take a stand and mirror these files."

Thus, defendants obviously hoped to frustrate plaintiffs' recourse to the judicial system by making effective relief difficult or impossible.

At least some of the links currently on defendants' mirror list lead the user to copies of DeCSS that, when downloaded and executed, successfully decrypt a motion picture on a CSS-encrypted DVD.

G. *Effects on Plaintiffs*

The effect on plaintiffs of defendants' posting of DeCSS depends upon the ease with which DeCSS decrypts plaintiffs' copyrighted motion pictures, the quality of the resulting product, and the convenience with which decrypted copies may be transferred or transmitted.

As noted, DeCSS was available for download from defendants' web site and remains available from web sites on defendants' mirror list. Downloading is simple and quick—plaintiffs' expert did it in seconds. The program in fact decrypts at least some DVDs. Although the process is computationally intensive, plaintiffs' expert decrypted a store-bought copy of *Sleepless in Seattle* in 20 to 45 minutes. The copy is stored on the hard drive of the computer. The quality of the decrypted film is virtually identical to that of encrypted films on DVD. The decrypted file can be copied like any other.

The decryption of a CSS-protected DVD is only the beginning of the tale, as the decrypted file is very large—approximately 4.3 to 6 GB or more depending on the length of the film—and thus extremely cumbersome to transfer or to store on portable storage media. One solution to this problem, however, is DivX, a compression utility available on the Internet that is promoted as a means of compressing decrypted motion picture files to manageable size.

DivX is capable of compressing decrypted files constituting a feature length motion picture to approximately 650 MB at a compression ratio that involves little loss of quality. While the compressed sound and graphic files then must be synchronized, a tedious process that took plaintiffs' expert between 10 and 20 hours, the task is entirely feasible. Indeed, having compared a store-bought DVD with portions of a copy compressed and synchronized with DivX (which often are referred to as "DivX'd" motion pictures), the Court finds that the loss of quality, at least in some cases, is imperceptible or so nearly imperceptible as to be of no importance to ordinary consumers.

The fact that DeCSS-decrypted DVDs can be compressed satisfactorily to 650 MB is very important. A writeable CD–ROM can hold 650 MB. Hence, it is entirely feasible to decrypt a DVD with DeCSS, compress and synchronize it with DivX, and then make as many copies as one wishes by burning the resulting files onto writeable CD–ROMs, which are sold blank for about one dollar apiece. Indeed, even if one wished to use a lower compression ratio to improve quality, a film easily could be compressed to about 1.3 GB and burned onto two CD–ROMs. But the creation of pirated copies of copyrighted movies on writeable CD–ROMs, although significant, is not the principal focus of plaintiffs' concern, which is transmission of pirated copies over the Internet or other networks.... [T]ransmission times ranging from three to twenty minutes to six hours or more for a feature length film are readily achievable, depending upon the users' precise circumstances.... While not everyone with Internet access now will find it convenient to send or receive DivX'd copies of pirated motion pictures over the Internet, the availability of high speed network connections in many businesses and institutions, and their growing availability in homes, make Internet and other network traffic in pirated copies a growing threat.

These circumstances have two major implications for plaintiffs. First, the availability of DeCSS on the Internet effectively has compromised plaintiffs' system of copyright protection for DVDs, requiring them either to tolerate increased piracy or to expend resources to develop and implement a replacement system unless the availability of DeCSS is terminated. It is analogous to the publication of a bank vault combination in a national newspaper. Even if no one uses the combination to open the vault, its mere publication has the effect of defeating the bank's security system, forcing the bank to reprogram the lock. Development and implementation of a new DVD copy protection system, however, is far more difficult and costly than reprogramming a combination lock and may carry with it the added problem of rendering the existing installed base of compliant DVD players obsolete.

Second, the application of DeCSS to copy and distribute motion pictures on DVD, both on CD–ROMs and via the Internet, threatens to reduce the studios' revenue from the sale and rental of DVDs. It threatens also to impede new, potentially lucrative initiatives for the distribution of motion pictures in digital form, such as video-on-demand via the Internet.

In consequence, plaintiffs already have been gravely injured. As the pressure for and competition to supply more and more users with faster and faster network connections grows, the injury will multiply.

II. The Digital Millennium Copyright Act

A. Background and Structure of the Statute

* * * The DMCA contains two principal anticircumvention provisions. The first, Section 1201(a)(1), governs "the act of circumventing a technological protection measure put in place by a copyright owner to control access to a copyrighted work," an act described by Congress as "the electronic equivalent of breaking into a locked room in order to obtain a copy of a book."[131] The second, Section 1201(a)(2), which is the focus of this case, "supplements the prohibition against the act of circumvention in paragraph (a)(1) with prohibitions on creating and making available certain

---

131. H.R. REP. No. 105–551(I), 105th Cong., 2d Sess. ("JUDICIARY COMM. REP."), at 17 (1998).

technologies ... developed or advertised to defeat technological protections against unauthorized access to a work." As defendants are accused here only of posting and linking to other sites posting DeCSS, and not of using it themselves to bypass plaintiffs' access controls, it is principally the second of the anticircumvention provisions that is at issue in this case.

B. Posting of DeCSS

1. Violation of Anti–Trafficking Provision

Section 1201(a)(2) of the Copyright Act, part of the DMCA, provides that:

"No person shall ... offer to the public, provide or otherwise traffic in any technology ... that—

"(A) is primarily designed or produced for the purpose of circumventing a technological measure that effectively controls access to a work protected under [the Copyright Act];

"(B) has only limited commercially significant purpose or use other than to circumvent a technological measure that effectively controls access to a work protected under [the Copyright Act]; or

"(C) is marketed by that person or another acting in concert with that person with that person's knowledge for use in circumventing a technological measure that effectively controls access to a work protected under [the Copyright Act]."

In this case, defendants concededly offered and provided and, absent a court order, would continue to offer and provide DeCSS to the public by making it available for download on the 2600.com web site. DeCSS, a computer program, unquestionably is "technology" within the meaning of the statute. "Circumvent a technological measure" is defined to mean descrambling a scrambled work, decrypting an encrypted work, or "otherwise to avoid, bypass, remove, deactivate, or impair a technological measure, without the authority of the copyright owner," so DeCSS clearly is a means of circumventing a technological access control measure. In consequence, if CSS otherwise falls within paragraphs (A), (B) or (C) of Section 1201(a)(2), and if none of the statutory exceptions applies to their actions, defendants have violated and, unless enjoined, will continue to violate the DMCA by posting DeCSS.

a. Section 1201(a)(2)(A)

(1) CSS Effectively Controls Access to Copyrighted Works

* * * [T]he statute expressly provides that "a technological measure 'effectively controls access to a work' if the measure, in the ordinary course of its operation, requires the application of information or a process or a treatment, with the authority of the copyright owner, to gain access to a work." One cannot gain access to a CSS-protected work on a DVD without application of the three keys that are required by the software. One cannot lawfully gain access to the keys except by entering into a license with the DVD CCA under authority granted by the copyright owners or by purchasing a DVD player or drive containing the keys pursuant to such a license.

In consequence, under the express terms of the statute, CSS "effectively controls access" to copyrighted DVD movies. It does so, within the meaning of the statute, whether or not it is a strong means of protection.

* * *

(2) DeCSS Was Designed Primarily to Circumvent CSS

As CSS effectively controls access to plaintiffs' copyrighted works, the only remaining question under Section 1201(a)(2)(A) is whether DeCSS was designed primarily to circumvent CSS. The answer is perfectly obvious. By the admission of both Jon Johansen, the programmer who principally wrote DeCSS, and defendant Corley, DeCSS was created solely for the purpose of decrypting CSS—that is all it does. Hence, absent satisfaction of a statutory exception, defendants clearly violated Section 1201(a)(2)(A) by posting DeCSS to their web site.

b.   Section 1201(a)(2)(B)

As the only purpose or use of DeCSS is to circumvent CSS, the foregoing is sufficient to establish a *prima facie* violation of Section 1201(a)(2)(B) as well.

c.   The Linux Argument

Perhaps the centerpiece of defendants' statutory position is the contention that DeCSS was not created for the purpose of pirating copyrighted motion pictures. Rather, they argue, it was written to further the development of a DVD player that would run under the Linux operating system, as there allegedly were no Linux compatible players on the market at the time....

2.   Statutory Exceptions

Earlier in the litigation, defendants contended that their activities came within several exceptions contained in the DMCA and the Copyright Act and constitute fair use under the Copyright Act. Their post-trial memorandum appears to confine their argument to the reverse engineering exception. In any case, all of their assertions are entirely without merit.

a.   Reverse engineering

Defendants claim to fall under Section 1201(f) of the statute, which provides in substance that one may circumvent, or develop and employ technological means to circumvent, access control measures in order to achieve interoperability with another computer program provided that doing so does not infringe another's copyright and, in addition, that one may make information acquired through such efforts "available to others, if the person [in question] ... provides such information solely for the purpose of enabling interoperability of an independently created computer program with other programs, and to the extent that doing so does not constitute infringement...." They contend that DeCSS is necessary to achieve interoperability between computers running the Linux operating system and DVDs and that this exception therefore is satisfied. This contention fails.

First, Section 1201(f)(3) permits information acquired through reverse engineering to be made available to others only by the person who acquired the information. But these defendants did not do any reverse engineering. They simply took DeCSS off someone else's web site and posted it on their own.

Defendants would be in no stronger position even if they had authored DeCSS. The right to make the information available extends only to dissemination "solely for the purpose" of achieving interoperability as defined in the statute. It does not apply to public dissemination of means of circumvention, as the legislative history confirms. These defendants, however, did not post DeCSS "solely" to achieve interoperability with Linux or anything else.

Finally, it is important to recognize that even the creators of DeCSS cannot credibly maintain that the "sole" purpose of DeCSS was to create a Linux DVD player. DeCSS concededly was developed on and runs under Windows—a far more widely used operating system. The developers of DeCSS therefore knew that DeCSS could be used to decrypt and play DVD movies on Windows as well as Linux machines. They knew also that the decrypted files could be copied like any other unprotected computer file. Moreover, the Court does not credit Mr. Johansen's testimony that he created DeCSS solely for the purpose of building a Linux player. Mr. Johansen is a very talented young man and a member of a well known hacker group who viewed "cracking" CSS as an end it itself and a means of demonstrating his talent and who fully expected that the use of DeCSS would not be confined to Linux machines. Hence, the Court finds that Mr. Johansen and the others who actually did develop DeCSS did not do so solely for the purpose of making a Linux DVD player if, indeed, developing a Linux-based DVD player was among their purposes.

Accordingly, the reverse engineering exception to the DMCA has no application here.

b.   Encryption research

* * *

In determining whether one is engaged in good faith encryption research [sheltered by Section 1201(g)(4)], the Court is instructed to consider factors including whether the results of the putative encryption research are disseminated in a manner designed to advance the state of knowledge of encryption technology versus facilitation of copyright infringement, whether the person in question is engaged in legitimate study of or work in encryption, and whether the results of the research are communicated in a timely fashion to the copyright owner.

Neither of the defendants remaining in this case was or is involved in good faith encryption research. They posted DeCSS for all the world to see. There is no evidence that they made any effort to provide the results of the DeCSS effort to the copyright owners. Surely there is no suggestion that either of them made a good faith effort to obtain authorization from the copyright owners. Accordingly, defendants are not protected by Section 1201(g).

* * *

d. Fair use

Finally, defendants rely on the doctrine of fair use.... Defendants have focused on a significant point. Access control measures such as CSS do involve some risk of preventing lawful as well as unlawful uses of copyrighted material. Congress, however, clearly faced up to and dealt with this question in enacting the DMCA.

The Court begins its statutory analysis, as it must, with the language of the statute. Section 107 of the Copyright Act provides in critical part that certain uses of copyrighted works that otherwise would be wrongful are "not ... infringement[s] of copyright." Defendants, however, are not here sued for copyright infringement. They are sued for offering and providing technology designed to circumvent technological measures that control access to copyrighted works and otherwise violating Section 1201(a)(2) of the Act. If Congress had meant the fair use defense to apply to such actions, it would have said so. Indeed, as the legislative history demonstrates, the decision not to make fair use a defense to a claim under Section 1201(a) was quite deliberate.

Congress was well aware during the consideration of the DMCA of the traditional role of the fair use defense in accommodating the exclusive rights of copyright owners with the legitimate interests of noninfringing users of portions of copyrighted works. It recognized the contention, voiced by a range of constituencies concerned with the legislation, that technological controls on access to copyrighted works might erode fair use by preventing access even for uses that would be deemed "fair" if only access might be gained. And it struck a balance among the competing interests.

The first element of the balance was the careful limitation of Section 1201(a)(1)'s prohibition of the act of circumvention to the act itself so as not to "apply to subsequent actions of a person once he or she has obtained authorized access to a copy of a [copyrighted] work. ..." By doing so, it left "the traditional defenses to copyright infringement, including fair use, ... fully applicable" provided "the access is authorized."

Second, Congress delayed the effective date of Section 1201(a)(1)'s prohibition of the act of circumvention for two years pending further investigation about how best to reconcile Section 1201(a)(1) with fair use concerns. Following that investigation, which is being carried out in the form of a rule-making by the Register of Copyright, the prohibition will not apply to users of particular classes of copyrighted works who demonstrate that their ability to make noninfringing uses of those classes of works would be affected adversely by Section 1201(a)(1).

Third, it created a series of exceptions to aspects of Section 1201(a) for certain uses that Congress thought "fair," including reverse engineering, security testing, good faith encryption research, and certain uses by non-profit libraries, archives and educational institutions.

* * *

The policy concerns raised by defendants were considered by Congress. Having considered them, Congress crafted a statute that, so far as the applicability of the fair use defense to Section 1201(a) claims is concerned, is crystal clear. In such circumstances, courts may not undo what Congress so plainly has done by "construing" the words of a statute to accomplish a result that Congress rejected....

C. *Linking to Sites Offering DeCSS*

Plaintiffs seek also to enjoin defendants from "linking" their 2600.com web site to other sites that make DeCSS available to users.... The dispositive question is whether linking to another web site containing DeCSS constitutes "offering [DeCSS] to the public" or "providing or otherwise trafficking" in it within the meaning of the DMCA Answering this question requires careful consideration of the nature and types of linking.

* * *

As noted earlier, the links that defendants established on their web site are of several types. Some transfer the user to a web page on an outside site that contains a good deal of information of various types, does not itself contain a link to DeCSS, but that links, either directly or via a series of other pages, to another page on the same site that posts the software. It then is up to the user to follow the link or series of links on the linked-to web site in order to arrive at the page with the DeCSS link and commence the download of the software. Others take the user to a page on an outside web site on which there appears a direct link to the DeCSS software and which may or may not contain text or links other than the DeCSS link. The user has only to click on the DeCSS link to commence the download. Still others may directly transfer the user to a file on the linked-to web site such that the download of DeCSS to the user's computer automatically commences without further user intervention.

The statute makes it unlawful to offer, provide or otherwise traffic in described technology. To "traffic" in something is to engage in dealings in it, conduct that necessarily involves awareness of the nature of the subject of the trafficking. To "provide" something, in the sense used in the statute, is to make it available or furnish it. To "offer" is to present or hold it out for consideration. The phrase "or otherwise traffic in" modifies and gives meaning to the words "offer" and "provide." In consequence, the anti-trafficking provision of the DMCA is implicated where one presents, holds out or makes a circumvention technology or device available, knowing its nature, for the purpose of allowing others to acquire it.

To the extent that defendants have linked to sites that automatically commence the process of downloading DeCSS upon a user being transferred by defendants' hyperlinks, there can be no serious question. Defendants are engaged in the functional equivalent of transferring the DeCSS code to the user themselves.

Substantially the same is true of defendants' hyperlinks to web pages that display nothing more than the DeCSS code or present the user only with the choice of commencing a download of DeCSS and no other content. The only distinction is that the entity extending to the user the option of downloading the program is the transferee site rather than defendants, a distinction without a difference.

Potentially more troublesome might be links to pages that offer a good deal of content other than DeCSS but that offer a hyperlink for download-ing, or transferring to a page for downloading, DeCSS. If one assumed, for the purposes of argument, that the *Los Angeles Times* web site somewhere contained the DeCSS code, it would be wrong to say that anyone who linked to the *Los Angeles Times* web site, regardless of purpose or the manner in which the link was described, thereby offered, provided or otherwise trafficked in DeCSS merely because DeCSS happened to be available on a site to which one linked. But that is not this case. Defen-dants urged others to post DeCSS in an effort to disseminate DeCSS and to inform defendants that they were doing so. Defendants then linked their site to those "mirror" sites, after first checking to ensure that the mirror sites in fact were posting DeCSS or something that looked like it, and proclaimed on their own site that DeCSS could be had by clicking on the hyperlinks on defendants' site. By doing so, they offered, provided or otherwise trafficked in DeCSS, and they continue to do so to this day.

III.   *The First Amendment*

Defendants argue that the DMCA, at least as applied to prevent the public dissemination of DeCSS, violates the First Amendment to the Constitution. They claim that it does so in two ways. First, they argue that computer code is protected speech and that the DMCA's prohibition of dissemination of DeCSS therefore violates defendants' First Amendment rights. Second, they contend that the DMCA is unconstitutionally over-broad, chiefly because its prohibition of the dissemination of decryption technology prevents third parties from making fair use of plaintiffs' en-crypted works, and vague. They argue also that a prohibition on their linking to sites that make DeCSS available is unconstitutional for much the same reasons.

* * *

The anti-trafficking provision of the DMCA furthers an important governmental interest—the protection of copyrighted works stored on digital media from the vastly expanded risk of piracy in this electronic age. The substantiality of that interest is evident both from the fact that the Constitution specifically empowers Congress to provide for copyright pro-tection and from the significance to our economy of trade in copyrighted materials. Indeed, the Supreme Court has made clear that copyright protection itself is "the engine of free expression." That substantial interest, moreover, is unrelated to the suppression of particular views expressed in means of gaining access to protected copyrighted works. Nor is the incidental restraint on protected expression—the prohibition of trafficking in means that would circumvent controls limiting access to unprotected materials or to copyrighted materials for noninfringing purposes—broader than is necessary to accomplish Congress' goals of preventing infringement and promoting the availability of content in digital form.

* * *

Accordingly, this Court holds that the anti-trafficking provision of the DMCA as applied to the posting of computer code that circumvents measures that control access to copyrighted works in digital form is a valid exercise of Congress' authority. It is a content neutral regulation in furtherance of important governmental interests that does not unduly restrict expressive activities. In any case, its particular functional characteristics are such that the Court would apply the same level of scrutiny even if it were viewed as content based. Yet it is important to emphasize that this is a very narrow holding. The restriction the Court here upholds, notwithstanding that computer code is within the area of First Amendment concern, is limited (1) to programs that circumvent access controls to copyrighted works in digital form in circumstances in which (2) there is no other practical means of preventing infringement through use of the programs, and (3) the regulation is motivated by a desire to prevent performance of the function for which the programs exist rather than any message they might convey. One readily might imagine other circumstances in which a governmental attempt to regulate the dissemination of computer code would not similarly be justified.

* * *

VI. *Conclusion*

In the final analysis, the dispute between these parties is simply put if not necessarily simply resolved.

Plaintiffs have invested huge sums over the years in producing motion pictures in reliance upon a legal framework that, through the law of copyright, has ensured that they will have the exclusive right to copy and distribute those motion pictures for economic gain. They contend that the advent of new technology should not alter this long established structure.

Defendants, on the other hand, are adherents of a movement that believes that information should be available without charge to anyone clever enough to break into the computer systems or data storage media in which it is located. Less radically, they have raised a legitimate concern about the possible impact on traditional fair use of access control measures in the digital era.

Each side is entitled to its views. In our society, however, clashes of competing interests like this are resolved by Congress. For now, at least, Congress has resolved this clash in the DMCA and in plaintiffs' favor.

Given the peculiar characteristics of computer programs for circumventing encryption and other access control measures, the DMCA as applied to posting and linking here does not contravene the First Amendment. Accordingly, plaintiffs are entitled to appropriate injunctive and declaratory relief.

SO ORDERED.

Editors' Note: The Second Circuit's decision affirming the district court's order primarily addressed the appellants' first amendment arguments. At the end of its lengthy opinion, however, the court turned to the Appellants' challenge to Judge Kaplan's determination that in enacting section 1201(a), Congress deliberately excluded a fair use defense to circumvention of access controls. Appellants had contended that fair use is constitutionally compelled, and that users therefore enjoyed a constitutionally-protected right to access and make digital copies of DVD movies in order to make fair uses of the works. Writing for a unanimous panel, Judge Newman observed that the Supreme Court had never held that fair use is "constitutionally required," and that, in any event, the DMCA did not "eliminate fair use," as Appellants had "extravagant[ly] claim[ed]." Moreover, the constitution does not mandate maximal convenience in the exercise of fair uses:

> [T]he Appellants have provided no support for their premise that fair use of DVD movies is constitutionally required to be made by copying the original work in its original format. Their examples of the fair uses that they believe others will be prevented from making all involve copying in a digital format those portions of a DVD movie amenable to fair use, a copying that would enable the fair user to manipulate the digitally copied portions. One example is that of a school child who wishes to copy images from a DVD movie to insert into the student's documentary film. We know of no authority for the proposition that fair use, as protected by the Copyright Act, much less the Constitution, guarantees copying by the optimum method or in the identical format of the original. Although the Appellants insisted at oral argument that they should not be relegated to a "horse and buggy" technique in making fair use of DVD movies, such as commenting on their content, quoting excerpts from their screenplays, and even recording portions of the video images and sounds on film or tape by pointing a camera, a camcorder, or a microphone at a monitor as it displays the DVD movie. The fact that the resulting copy will not be as perfect or as manipulable as a digital copy obtained by having direct access to the DVD movie in its digital form, provides no basis for a claim of unconstitutional limitation of fair use. A film critic making fair use of a movie by quoting selected lines of dialogue has no constitutionally valid claim that the review (in print or on television) would be technologically superior if the reviewer had not been prevented from using a movie camera in the theater, nor has an art student a valid constitutional claim to fair use of a painting by photographing it in a museum. Fair use has never been held to be a guarantee of access to copyrighted

material in order to copy it by the fair user's preferred technique or in the format of the original.

QUESTIONS

1. Suppose your copyright course has a website, which the professor updates to include discussion of current copyright issues. As part of that effort, your professor has placed on the website the text of the District Court decision in *Reimerdes*, as well as links to sites carrying De–CSS. Has your professor violated the DMCA? Would he or she have a stronger First Amendment defense than Corley?

2. The Recording Industry Association of America has invited hackers and other computer-adept members of the public to participate in a contest to "Hack SDMI." SDMI, the "secure digital music initiative," includes a technological measure that protects access to copyrighted sound recordings. Edward Felton, a professor of computer science at Princeton University, and several of his students and colleagues, succeed in breaking the access protection. They decline the reward for winning the contest—and the concomitant agreement to keep their results confidential—in favor of publishing an academic paper in which they discuss how they succeeded in circumventing the protection measure. In response to the RIAA's letter urging against publishing the paper, Felton has filed an action seeking a declaratory judgment that publication of his paper does not violate section 1201(a). Alternatively, were the court to find liability under section 1201(a), then Felton asks the court to hold that the DMCA violates the First Amendment. How should the court rule?

3. Suppose that Felton has not yet formally published his paper, but has made it available to several websites, and now it can be found on many more. What liability do the website operators face? What liability do the service providers that host the websites face?

2.   Copyright Management Information

The second WIPO norm that required U.S. implementation addressed "Obligations Concerning Rights Management Information." Under art. 12 of the WCT, contracting States must provide adequate and effective legal remedies against one who engages in the knowing removal or alteration of rights management information, "knowing or having reasonable grounds to know that it will induce, enable, facilitate or conceal an infringement of any right covered by this Treaty or the Berne Convention." Congress implemented this obligation in new § 1202.

Section 1202(c) defines copyright management information to include: the name of the author; the name of the copyright owner; and the "terms and conditions for use of the work." Section 1202(a) prohibits knowingly providing false copyright management information, with the intent to facilitate or conceal infringement. The provision also prohibits in § 1202(b) knowingly or intentionally altering or removing copyright management information, knowing (or having reasonable grounds to know) that the alteration or removal will facilitate or conceal infringement.

The provision is designed to promote the dissemination of copyrighted works by facilitating the grant or license of rights under copyright (particularly through electronic contracting). Because accurate and reliable information about the work is essential to its distribution (particularly online), the bill identifies that information and protects it against falsification, removal or alteration. These are important goals whose achievement will further the interests of the public and of authors in the digital communication of works of authorship.

A precursor to § 1202 was § 1002(d) and (e) of the 1992 Audio Home Recording Act (AHRA), concerning "encoding of information on digital musical recordings." As you review new § 1202, compare it with the AHRA provision (for § 1002, see the Statutory Appendix), and consider whether, and to what extent, new legislation was necessary.

§ 1202.   Integrity of copyright management information

(a) False Copyright Management Information—No person shall knowingly and with the intent to induce, enable, facilitate or conceal infringement—

> (1) provide copyright management information that is false, or

> (2) distribute or import for distribution copyright management information that is false.

(b) Removal or Alteration of Copyright Management Information—No person shall, without the authority of the copyright owner or the law—

> (1) intentionally remove or alter any copyright management information,

> (2) distribute or import for distribution copyright management information knowing that the copyright management information has been removed or altered without authority of the copyright owner or the law, or

> (3) distribute, import for distribution, or publicly perform works, copies of works, or phonorecords, knowing that copyright management information has been removed or altered without authority of the copyright owner or the law, knowing, or, with respect to civil remedies under section 1203, having reasonable grounds to know, that it will

induce, enable, facilitate or conceal an infringement of any right under this title.

(c) Definition—As used in this section, the term "copyright management information" means any of the following information conveyed in connection with copies or phonorecords of a work or performances or displays of a work, including in digital form, except that such term does not include any personally identifying information about a user of a work or of a copy, phonorecord, performance or display of a work:

(1) The title and other information identifying the work, including the information set forth on a notice of copyright.

(2) The name of, and other identifying information about, the author of a work.

(3) The name of, and other identifying information about, the copyright owner of the work, including the information set forth in a notice of copyright.

(4) With the exception of public performances of works by radio and television broadcast stations, the name of, and other identifying information about, a performer whose performance is fixed in a work other than an audiovisual work.

(5) With the exception of public performances of works by radio and television broadcast stations, in the case of an audiovisual work, the name of, and other identifying information about, a writer, performer, or director who is credited in the audiovisual work.

(6) Terms and conditions for use of the work.

(7) Identifying numbers or symbols referring to such information or links to such information.

(8) Such other information as the Register of Copyrights may prescribe by regulation, except that the Register of Copyrights may not require the provision of any information concerning the user of a copyrighted work.

. . .

———

How well does § 1202 achieve the desired reliability and accuracy of information relevant to proper identification of works and to electronic (or other) transactions in rights under copyright? Section 1202 may fall short in at least one respect. Linking the violation of the copyright management information provisions to copyright infringement does not effectively achieve the objective of ensuring the accuracy and reliability of a key component of copyright management information—proper identification of the author (as opposed to the copyright holder). Apart from the § 106A right of attribution with respect to works of visual art (see *supra* Chapter 6.B.2), there is no right *under copyright* to be credited as the author of a work. By contrast, there is a right under the Berne Convention to authorship credit. (*See* art. 6*bis*.) This means that willfully removing or altering the author's name is not in itself copyright infringement. This gap in § 1202's coverage disserves the general public interest in knowing who is the author of the work. Congress recognized the public benefit of authorship credit, since § 1202(c)'s definition of copyright management information includes "the name of, and other identifying information about, the author of a work." Section 1202 does not oblige the rights owner to attach copyright management information to distributions of the work, but if the rights holder does attach copyright management information, then that information should include the name of the author. Thus understood, § 1202 expresses a public policy favoring author identification as part of a reliable system of dissemination (especially electronic distribution) of copyrighted works.

QUESTIONS

1. Why, do you suppose, does § 1202(c) exempt radio and television broadcasters from liability for removing or altering copyright management information? What about webcasters?

2. When § 1202(c) states that copyright management information includes "the author of a work," does that mean the author as understood in the Copyright Act? If so, might there be instances of unfairness to individual creators? (*See* § 201(b).)

———

Kelly v. Arriba Soft Corp., 77 F. Supp. 2d 1116 (C.D.Cal.1999). In addition to presenting fair use issues, *see supra* chapter 7.C, *Kelly* was the first case to interpret the "copyright management information" provisions of the DMCA, § 1202. Defendant's index incorporated thumbnails of plaintiff's images; the thumbnails did not include the copyright management information that appeared in the text of plaintiff's web site because defendant's "crawler" retrieved only the plaintiff's images. Plaintiff therefore alleged a violation of § 1202(b), which prohibits the removal of copyright management information in certain circumstances. Defendant attempted to compensate for the non-inclusion of copyright management information by providing a separate "copyright" page for users to click open, on which defendant warned users about potential copyright restrictions.

The court held that plaintiff failed to establish a violation of § 1202(b)(1) because plaintiff had not embedded the copyright management information in the images themselves, but had included it elsewhere on his webpages. As a result, the court determined that defendant's copying of the images did not remove any copyright management information from plaintiff's works. (This holding is arguably inconsistent with the court's earlier determination that plaintiff's "works" were the webpages, not the separate photographs.) In addition, the court held that defendant did not intentionally omit copyright management information. The court further found that the defendant did not violate the § 1202(b)(3) prohibition on distribution of copies of works knowing that copyright management information has been removed. Although defendant displayed plaintiff's images out of the context of their web sites, in thumbnail (and, initially, in full-sized) versions, without their copyright management information, the court stressed defendant's provision of the name of the originating web site, a link for getting there, and a notice about potential copyright infringement. As a result, ruled the court, defendant did not have "reasonable grounds to know" that it could cause users to infringe the copyrights. Moreover, the court found that plaintiff's images are vulnerable to user infringement by virtue of their location on the web, and that defendant did not heighten plaintiff's vulnerability.

The court may have misconstrued § 1202 in holding that defendant did not remove copyright management information from plaintiff's works when the information was located on another part of plaintiff's webpage. § 1202 does not require that the information be embedded in the photographs; the definition of copyright management information covers information "conveyed in connection with copies or phonorecords of a work or performances or displays of a work, including in digital form. . . . " The appearance of the information on the webpage should have sufficed to meet the "in connection with" standard. But even if the court wrongly interpreted § 1202 as to this issue, the result nonetheless seems consonant with the statute. Under § 1202(b), the wrongful act is not simply removing the information, or distributing or publicly performing the work without the information. The statute also requires that those who distribute or perform the work have known that the information was removed without the copyright owner's authorization, *and* that those who remove the information, or who distribute or perform works whose information has been removed, do so "knowing, or . . . having reasonable grounds to know that it will induce, enable, facilitate, or conceal an infringement of any right under this title." Defendant may have intentionally removed the information, by deliberately separating the images from the information on plaintiff's webpage, and defendant therefore would have known that the images it communicated lacked the information. Nonetheless, it would be difficult to prove that defendant knew or had reasonable grounds to know that its acts would promote copyright infringement, particularly when the later version of defendant's index sent users from the thumbnails back to plaintiff's own webpage, on which the information did appear.

Kelly thus illustrates the relative weakness of § 1202's protection of copyright management information: even intentional removal is not unlawful if the copyright owner cannot show that the removal would encourage or facilitate copyright infringement. § 1202 therefore may require a rather high threshold of bad faith before a violation is established.

H.   OVERENFORCEMENT: COPYRIGHT MISUSE

In a number of recent copyright infringement cases, the defendant has attempted to introduce a relatively novel defense, i.e., that the plaintiff has used the monopoly power accorded by the copyright to extract incidental economic rewards to which it is not entitled and which are contrary to public policy. This defense, first significantly articulated in *Lasercomb America, Inc. v. Reynolds*, 911 F.2d 970 (4th Cir.1990), draws its inspiration from what has come to be known as the "patent misuse" defense recognized half a century before by the Supreme Court in *Morton Salt Co. v. G.S. Suppiger*, 314 U.S. 488 (1942). There, Morton Salt claimed that the defendant had infringed its patent on a salt-depositing machine. Although the salt tablets that the machine deposited were not patented, Morton's license required its licensees to use only salt tablets produced by Morton. The Court held that Morton had improperly used its patent to restrain competition in the sale of an item not within the scope of its patent. As already noted in Chapter 7 on Fair Use, a plaintiff's "unclean hands" are sometimes considered as a factor, beyond those set forth in § 107, in sustaining a fair use defense. Cases such as the one below, which endorse the extension of the "misuse" doctrine from patents to copyrights, in effect embrace the "unclean hands" principle altogether outside the sphere of the fair use doctrine. *See also Alcatel USA, Inc. v. DGI Techs., Inc.*, 166 F.3d 772 (5th Cir.1999).

Practice Management Information Corp. v. American Medical Ass'n, 121 F.3d 516 (9th Cir.1997). In this case, the court of appeals set forth the strongest statement of what had been developing as a doctrine of copyright misuse, in which an infringer may assert as a complete defense that the copyright owner is using its copyright in an unfairly anticompetitive manner.

For more than thirty years, the American Medical Association (AMA) has designed and published a detailed numerical code to enable physicians to identify particular medical procedures with precision; its book embodying the code is titled Physician's Current Procedural Technology (CPT). In 1977, Congress required a federal health agency, the Health Care Financing Administration (HCFA) to establish a uniform code for identifying medical procedures, to be used in connection with reimbursement claims under federal programs. HCFA entered into an agreement with the AMA, in which the AMA granted a non-exclusive, royalty free and irrevocable license to the CPT, and in exchange HCFA agreed not to use any other system of nomenclature for reporting physicians' services and to require use of the CPT in its programs; HCFA thereafter adopted regulations requiring applicants for Medicaid reimbursement to use the CPT.

Practice Management publishes and distributes medical books, including the CPT, which it has purchased from the AMA for resale. When the AMA denied its request for a volume discount, Practice Management decided to attack the AMA copyright by initiating an action for declaratory judgment. Its first major claim was that the copyright in the CPT was lost when its use was required by the HCFA in connection with Medicaid reimbursement applications. The court of appeals rejected the contention that the CPT had been in effect converted into a public document. The court, however, sustained Practice Management's claim that the contract in which the AMA secured a promise that HCFA would not use any competing coding system constituted a misuse of the AMA copyright, resulting in its invalidation. The court found it irrelevant that it was HCFA that initiated the idea of exclusivity, and that even apart from its contractual commitment the HCFA would have used the CPT exclusively because using another coding system in addition or instead would have been grossly inefficient.

> The controlling fact is that HCFA is prohibited from using any other coding system by virtue of the binding commitment it made to the AMA to use the AMA's copyrighted material exclusively. The absence of the agreement would not preclude HCFA from doing what AMA suggests would be proper—deciding on its own to use only the AMA's system. What offends the copyright misuse doctrine is not HCFA's decision to use the AMA's coding system exclusively, but the limitation imposed by the AMA licensing agreement on HCFA's rights to decide whether or not to use other forms as well. Conditioning the license on HCFA's promise not to use competitors' products constituted a misuse of the copyright by the AMA.

The court also concluded that it was not necessary, in order to invoke the copyright misuse doctrine, that there be proof that the copyright owner had technically committed a violation of the antitrust laws.

> [The student should consider the wisdom of the court creating such a "common law" defense that falls in between the two pertinent federal statutes: the Copyright Act which contemplates that the copyright owner will exercise monopoly power through its "exclusive rights," and the antitrust laws, which the court holds need not be violated in order to warrant striking down the copyright. What exactly are the contours of the copyright misuse doctrine?]

QUESTION

Suppose HCFA had not entered into a binding agreement with the AMA precluding HCFA from using any other coding system. Once HCFA had adopted the AMA codes as its standard for identifying medical procedures, wouldn't the same result have been achieved?

CHAPTER 9

FEDERAL PREEMPTION OF STATE LAW

A. STATE LAWS RESTRICTING COPYING

Although the law of copyright affords potentially broad protection for creative works, it by no means exhausts the theories providing support for claims of intellectual property. At the federal level, we have seen that the utility and design patent laws, and the Lanham Trademark Art, overlap with the Copyright Act in regulating competition in the marketing of goods, services and intangible creations of the mind. We have, for example, examined the tensions created between patent and copyright as reflected in the dichotomy between idea and expression and in the concept of "separability" of shape and function of useful articles. We have also examined the relationship between copyright and trademark in pictorial works, such as the Peter Rabbit drawings at issue in *Frederick Warne & Co. v. Book Sales, Inc.* (Chapter 1.E), that have arguably acquired "secondary meaning."

There are also bodies of state law that must be taken into account—by business planners and by litigators—in determining the respective rights of creators and competitors in the field of intellectual property. Since the founding of the Republic, state theories have been called into play to restrict the copying of works that are arguably, or actually, within the scope of the federal copyright law. What follows is a sketch of those theories, with illustrations of their possible pertinence to the field of intellectual property. (An excellent discussion of several of these theories may be found in *Restatement (Third) of Unfair Competition* (1995).) The bulk of this chapter will then be devoted to considering the extent to which these state laws remain viable within a federal system that is dominated by the comprehensive provisions of the U.S. Copyright Act.

1. ***Common Law Copyright.*** Until 1978, as the student is aware, the principal body of law regulating the right to copy, sell and perform unpublished works has been state law. Because typically it has been fashioned by state-court judges, this state law has been known as common law copyright. Common law copyright is rooted, in part, in concerns about individual privacy (most obviously, in the case of unauthorized publication of private letters or photographs) and, additionally, in a belief that creative authors and artists should have control over the timing and placement of the first publication of their works (a good illustration is President Ford's memoirs as litigated in *Harper & Row v. Nation Enterprises*, set forth in Chapter 7.B). Federal statutory copyright for published works (and also for

some unpublished works commonly exploited by performance rather than printing) and state copyright for unpublished works existed side-by-side for nearly two centuries. Once the owner of the state copyright, typically the author, exercised the "right of first publication," state rights were divested and protection against copying could be secured only by complying with the formalities of the federal Copyright Act, principally by placing a copyright notice on all publicly distributed copies.

Since January 1, 1978, § 301 of the Act has displaced common law copyright for works whose subject matter falls within § 102 or 103. Federal coverage attaches as soon as a work is "fixed" in a tangible medium of expression, so that the exclusive right to make and distribute copies for the first time, as well as subsequently, is governed exclusively by § 106. Such preemption is inapplicable to works not fixed in a tangible medium (§ 301(b)(1)), so that unauthorized reproduction—most typically through the making of phonorecords in the form of audiocassettes—of improvised and "unfixed" musical or comedy-dramatic performances can be forbidden by state courts under state law. Although Congress in 1994 amended the Copyright Act so as to give federal redress against the unauthorized taping or broadcasting of a "live musical performance" (§ 1101(a)), it expressly provided that state rights and remedies were not to be displaced (§ 1101(d)).

Although § 301 is understood principally to preempt state common law copyright, it is clear that a state cannot escape this preemptive mandate simply by giving the same relief under the same theory while simply using a different name for the tort. As will be seen below, courts have routinely struck down state claims as equivalent to copyright even though parading under a name such as "conversion" or "interference with contract." It is sometimes difficult, however, to determine where to draw the line between preempted and nonpreempted state laws. This will be explored at greater length below.

2. ***Unfair Competition: "Passing Off."*** A person or entity will commit the tort of unfair competition under state law when it so promotes its goods or services as to create a likelihood that consumers will believe them to be (or to be associated with) the goods or services of another. The purpose of the tort rule is to protect the reputation or goodwill of that other person and to protect the consuming public against confusion or deception. The application of the "passing off" theory to literary property cases is rather straightforward. We have seen, in the *Peter Rabbit* case (Chapter 1.E), a claim that certain drawings used in connection with the marketing of children's books, clothing and toys had acquired the "secondary meaning" of signifying a particular book publisher, so that the unauthorized use of the drawings by a competitor on similar products constituted a legal wrong. The claim was based upon the federal Lanham Act for the protection of trademarks and service marks, but such a claim can be founded upon state trademark or unfair competition law as well, and such state law—which well antedated the Lanham Act—is expressly preserved against federal preemption.

It has also been held, for example, that when a successful play entitled "the Gold Diggers" was made into a successful motion picture entitled "Gold Diggers of Broadway," it was unlawful for another to market a motion picture entitled "Gold Diggers of Paris" (at least without a conspicuous disclaimer that the picture was not based on the play or the earlier motion picture). *Warner Bros. Pictures, Inc. v. Majestic Pictures Corp.*, 70 F.2d 310 (2d Cir.1934). And it has also been held unlawful to draw popular comic-strip characters, using their names, in comic-strip settings unauthorized by the creator of the characters. The court concluded that "the figures and names have been so connected with the [artist] as their originator or author that the use by another of new cartoons exploiting the characters ... would be unfair to the public and to the plaintiff." *Fisher v. Star Co.*, 231 N.Y. 414, 132 N.E. 133 (1921) ("Mutt and Jeff"). The Gold Diggers motion picture and the Mutt and Jeff cartoons may ultimately lose their copyright protection (or the copyright may be transferred), but protection against "passing off" is available to the creator even thereafter, provided it can prove secondary meaning and customer confusion; the interests of third parties or of the public can be preserved by allowing copying but requiring conspicuous labeling so as to dispel the confusion as to source.

A variation on this theme, which has particular pertinence to works of art, is the possible claim for "trade-dress" infringement deriving from copying the "style" and pictorial themes of an earlier artist so as to lead the public to believe that the earlier artist has produced the late-comer's art. *See Romm Art Creations Ltd. v. Simcha Int'l, Inc.*, 786 F.Supp. 1126 (E.D.N.Y.1992) (see the photographs at pages 494 and 495, *supra*).

3. *Unfair Competition: Misappropriation.* The other major branch of state unfair competition law is known as "misappropriation." In effect, its tortious elements are the converse of those involved in passing off. In passing off, copyist C markets a work of its own while creating the impression it was in fact authored by A; in misappropriation, copyist C markets a work in fact authored by A while creating the impression that C is the author. In passing off, the confusion as to source can injure A, whose reputation and goodwill are place beyond its control; in misappropriation, the reverse confusion as to source allows C to get credit (and income) for a work actually generated by another who is not known to be the source. The following classic case exemplifies the tort of misappropriation.

International News Service v. Associated Press, 248 U.S. 215 (1918). Both AP (the plaintiff below) and INS are news-gathering organizations whose newspaper members pay a fee to receive news items gathered, written and communicated by the organization (which newspaper members also gather and report news to the organization in return). AP (a New York corporation) had annual operating costs of some $3.5 million, and it served about 950 newspapers; INS (a New Jersey corporation) had annual costs of more than $2 million, and it served about 400 newspapers. INS was accused of having taken news items from AP or AP-member newspapers and reported them to INS-member newspapers for publication there. The news items thus misappropriated were not copyrighted, because of the volume of AP dispatches and because of AP's concession that the substance of news is not eligible for copyright protection. INS argued that once AP published its news in newspapers or bulletin boards, INS and other members of the public were free to copy it.

The Court noted that the jurisdiction of the federal court below was based on diversity of citizenship; the law it applied was therefore (in those days before *Erie R.R. Co. v. Tompkins,* 304 U.S. 64 (1938)) federal tort law of unfair competition, fashioned by the federal judiciary. Justice Pitney, speaking for the Court majority, stated that the content of the news was not the creation of any writer and was therefore freely to be copied by the public: "It is not to be supposed that the framers of the Constitution ... intended to confer upon one who might happen to be the first to report a historic event the exclusive right for any period to spread the knowledge of it." What was at issue, however, was the "business of making it known to the world," in which AP and INS were competitors, each of whom thus had a "duty so to conduct its own business as not unnecessarily or unfairly to injure that of the other." Although neither of them, after publishing the news, had any rights against the public, they did have rights against one another, for the news was its "stock in trade, to be gathered at the cost of enterprise, organization, skill, labor, and money" from the sale of which they expected to make their profits. To that extent, as between them the news "must be regarded as *quasi* property."

In noting that INS had transmitted AP-gathered news to INS-member newspapers so as to allow publication at the same time as, and often before, publication in some AP-member newspapers (particularly on the West Coast), the Court concluded that INS "in appropriating it and selling it as its own is endeavoring to reap where it has not sown, and by disposing of it to newspapers that are competitors of [AP's] members is appropriating to itself the harvest of those who have sown"—"with special advantage to [INS] in the competition because of the fact that it is not burdened with any part of the expense of gathering the news." This was unquestionably "unfair competition in business."

The Court cautioned that it was not conferring upon AP an exclusive right to gather and disseminate news without complying with the copyright act, but only to "postpone" its competitor's activities in reproducing news that it had not gathered "and only to the extent necessary to prevent that competitor from reaping the fruits of complainant's efforts and expenditure." Relief against unfair competition was not to be limited to the common cases of "palming off" one's good as those made another: "instead of selling its own goods as those of complainant, [INS] substitutes misappropriation in the place of misrepresentation, and sells complainant's goods as its own." Although INS wrongly appropriates the credit actually due AP, the gist of the wrong goes deeper than this misrepresentation, and cannot be cured simply by a disclaimer. The Court, although noting its lack of specificity, upheld the preliminary injunction against INS's use of news issued by AP "until its commercial value as news to [AP] and all of its members has passed away."

In a separate opinion, Justice Holmes concluded that the gist of INS's wrong was the implied misrepresentation that it was the first to gather the news. He would have cured this with an injunction requiring that INS give an express credit for any news appropriated from AP. Justice Brandeis's dissenting opinion is almost as well known as the decision of the majority, and warrants reading in full. Basically, he asserted that the content of the news, being unprotected by any statutory exclusive right such as copyright, may be freely copied, absent breach of contract, trust or fiduciary obligation; the public interest so requires and is not overcome merely by characterizing the behavior as misappropriation. "He who follows the pioneer into a new market, or who engages in the manufacture of an article newly introduced by another, seeks profits due largely to the labor and expense of the first adventurer; but the law sanctions, indeed encourages, the pursuit." Although "the injustice of such action [by INS] is obvious," and although courts often fashion new rights by analogy or expansion to correct an injustice, this is best and wisely done when only private interests are at stake. When the public interest must be considered, the problem generally becomes too complex for courts, and the limitations and conditions upon the asserted private right—such as that of AP—and the machinery for its enforcement can properly be established only through legislation.

The common-law rule of misappropriation announced by the Supreme Court in *INS v. AP* has been imported into the jurisprudence of many states, as a form of unfair competition. In a closely analogous situation, for example, the Supreme Court of Pennsylvania, in *Pottstown Daily News Pub'g Co. v. Pottstown Broadcasting Co.*, 411 Pa. 383, 192 A.2d 657 (1963), enjoined a radio station which based (but did not substantially copy verbatim) its broadcast news programs on the content of news items carried in the local morning newspapers.

To the extent that one agrees with Justice Pitney in *INS v. AP* that the gist of the tort of misappropriation is not so much the taking of undeserved credit from the true author (which could be corrected by a disclaimer or by explicitly giving credit), but is rather the "reaping where one has not sown," it very much reduces itself to the tort of unauthorized copying—or more precisely, unauthorized copying from a competitor. This claim is thus essentially congruent with a claim of copyright infringement. For this reason, there is serious question whether the state tort of misappropriation can coexist with the comprehensive rules set forth in the Copyright Act. Section 301 of the Act means to displace state laws granting "all legal or equitable rights that are equivalent to any of the exclusive rights within the general scope of copyright." Certainly that was meant to preempt state common-law copyright, i.e., the right of first publication. It would also appear to preempt state law forbidding the unauthorized making of subsequent copies as well—which is what took place in *INS v. AP*. Is the case for preemption made weaker or stronger by the fact that what was copied by INS in that case was the content of the news, that is, "facts" which clearly cannot be protected by the Copyright Act, as we are reminded by § 102(b) of that Act? The continuing viability of the misappropriation tort is one of the more vexing issues that remain after the enactment of § 301. This issue will be explored at greater length below.

4. ***Breach of Contract, and Idea Protection.*** A more long-established and less controversial state theory that can be utilized to forbid unauthorized copying is breach of contract. If A turns over a manuscript to B, and in exchange for some form of consideration secures a promise from B that B will keep that manuscript secret, B's subsequent publication will constitute a breach of contract, for which A can secure compensatory damages and, in appropriate circumstances, an injunction against future publication—essentially the same relief that is available in an action for copyright infringement. Even if a party such as B has permission to publish, but only upon certain conditions—for example, only after October 1, 2000 or only in the City of Philadelphia—B's publication at an earlier date or in a different place will be a breach of contract. We have seen, in the *Monty Python* case (Chapter 6.B), that unauthorized editing of a television program, contrary to the limitations in the agreement between the scriptwriters and the producer, can give rise to an action not only for copyright infringement and trademark infringement under the Lanham Act but also for breach of contract (at least against the party with whom the author is in "privity").

Contract law is the principal basis upon which claims for "idea protection" rest. As we are reminded by § 102(b) of the Copyright Act, and also by various cases such as *Baker v. Selden*, "ideas" are not protected by the Act against unauthorized dissemination. If someone in a Hollywood restaurant overhears a conversation in the next booth in which the speaker discloses an idea for a game show or the general plot outline of a television series, appropriating that idea may be a bit shady, but it is not illegal. Many amateur creators seek to disclose their ideas to others who are in a better position to convert them into a copyrightable work or can produce or market them; the only way this disclosure can safely be done is through a return promise—best reduced to writing—not to use without compensation. (Even then there may be obstacles to protecting the idea, including the frequently implemented judicial requirement that the idea be "novel.") *See generally Blaustein v. Burton*, 9 Cal.App.3d 161, 88 Cal.Rptr. 319 (Dist. Ct. App. 1970).

5. ***Breach of Trust.*** In the idea-protection situation just described, the idea-originator will often be in such a position that he can add to his claim for breach of contract a related claim for breach of trust or of a confidential relationship. This will be the case when the person entrusted with the secret idea is the attorney, or the literary agent, of the originator, or someone else in a similar fiduciary relationship. This state-law theory of course can also apply when what is put into the possession of the agent is a fully completed and unpublished manuscript, protected by the Copyright Act against unauthorized reproduction and dissemination.

6. *Trade-Secret Protection.* Although typically closer to the law of patents than to the law of copyright, it should be noted that a long-established theory of state legal protection against copying is that of trade secret protection. A trade secret can be any information that is used in one's business and affords a competitive advantage against those who do not know it; an example would be a mechanical or chemical process (or the formula for the syrup used in Coca–Cola) or a specially compiled factual database (such as a customer list). To derive commercial benefit from the trade secret, it is of course necessary to disclose it to others, but its status as a secret is preserved so long as it has been confided under the express or implied restriction of nondisclosure to others. *See generally* Restatement (Third) of Unfair Competition §§ 39–45 (1995).

The law of trade secrets is often invoked when a former employee discloses to a new employer secrets learned while having been employed with a predecessor employer. State courts will frequently enjoin the employee and the second employer in such a situation. If the secret is reduced to writing and it falls within the subject matter of copyright—for example, a compilation derived from minimally creative selection or arrangement, such as a customer list—then unauthorized reproduction or public dissemination will also be a copyright infringement. The overlap between state trade secret law and federal copyright has become a particularly visible issue since the development of the computer program, which may embody processes the substance of which may be protected as a trade secret and the "expression" of which may be protected by copyright.

7. *Defamation.* If A writes a letter to B in which A says false and scurrilous things about C, publication of the letter by B (or by a third party) may constitute an actionable written defamation, or libel, for which redress can be sought by C in the state courts under state law. A can also presumably secure an injunction against publication by B or by another, on a theory of copyright infringement. (A is presumed to retain the copyright in the text of the letter despite mailing the piece of paper to B. *See* § 202 of the Copyright Act.) If A, instead, writes a textbook, and her publisher P makes revisions that are careless and inaccurate and then publishes the book without A's approval, A may well have an action against P for defamation by having attributed such a reputation-shattering work to A. *See, e.g., Clevenger v. Baker Voorhis & Co.*, 203 N.Y.S.2d 812, 168 N.E.2d 643 (1960). (There will very likely also be potential claims for copyright infringement for the unauthorized creation of a derivative work, a Lanham Act violation for false attribution as developed in the *Monty Python* case, and breach of contract.)

8. *Breach of Privacy and Publicity.* If A's letter to B discloses certain highly intimate matters about himself, and A can reasonably assume that B will keep them secret, B's publication of the letter can give rise to a state-law claim for breach of privacy as well as a copyright infringement claim. And if B is in possession of a photograph of A, given to him by A several months before, A will generally be afforded protection under state law against B incorporating A's image into the packaging of a

product manufactured by B or into advertising material promoting that product. These two theories of protection against copying were devised by state courts. The rights of privacy and of publicity have been the subject of an extensive scholarly literature. Two of the best known law review articles ever written addressed, and significantly shaped, these theories of legal protection: Warren & Brandeis, *The Right to Privacy*, 4 Harv. L. Rev. 193 (1890), reprinted in Hofstadter & Horowitz, The Right to Privacy 289 (1964); and Prosser, *Privacy*, 48 Calif. L. Rev. 383 (1960). Although the right of publicity historically evolved from the right of privacy, which has itself been variously divided into sub-rights, they are very different in their basic core. The privacy right is meant to protect the interest in being left alone, having sensitive life-facts kept undisclosed, and not being portrayed in a distorted light; while the publicity right is meant to assure being compensated for the unauthorized exploitation of one's name or image in connection with the commercial marketing of goods or services. These rights, particularly the right of publicity, have been increasingly embodied in legislation, which has dealt with such matters as whether the right descends to the individual's heirs upon his or her death. (For a comprehensive treatment, see J.T. McCarthy, *The Rights of Publicity and Privacy*; *see also* Restatement (Third) of Unfair Competition §§ 46–49 (1995).)

Several cases have involved a potential overlap of federal copyright protection and state-law protection of the rights of privacy and publicity. Examples are the unauthorized use of photographic images of Elvis Presley in posters, e.g., *Estate of Presley v. Russen*, 513 F.Supp. 1339 (D.N.J.1981); the unauthorized sculpting and sale of busts of the Reverend Martin Luther King, Jr., see *Martin Luther King. Jr., Center for Social Change, Inc. v. American Heritage Prods., Inc.*, 250 Ga. 135, 296 S.E.2d 697 (1982); the unauthorized use of photographs in sports cards or board games, e.g., *Haelan Labs., Inc. v. Topps Chewing Gum, Inc.*, 202 F.2d 866 (2d Cir.1953); the use of recordings (or imitations of recordings) of well-known performing artists singing copyrighted songs, *Motown Record Corp. v. Geo. A. Hormel & Co.*, 657 F.Supp. 1236 (C.D.Cal.1987); and the respective rights of professional sports teams and players (as alleged "performers"), in *Baltimore Orioles, Inc. v. Major League Baseball Players Ass'n*, 805 F.2d 663 (7th Cir.1986).

9. *Artists' Rights.* A dozen states have enacted statutes providing for "artists' rights" against mutilation and distortion of their works and to accurate attribution. These statutes have been noted above in Chapter 6.B. Some of these statutes define protected individuals and works quite broadly, including motion pictures, and some extend the rights of integrity and attribution to reproductions as well as to the original protected works themselves. The purpose is to protect the personality, reputation and artistic integrity of the artist, and to some extent to preserve the state's cultural heritage. These laws inspired the Visual Artists Rights Act enacted by Congress in 1990. The federal act—incorporated principally in § 106A of the Copyright Act—is relatively narrow in scope with respect to both the works of art that are protected and the kinds of "distortions" that are proscribed. There is also an overlap between the rights granted in state

artists' rights laws and the right granted in the Copyright Act to prepare derivative works.

———

There are yet other state-law theories that might be brought to bear in an action to forbid or restrict copying of creative works—including conversion, trespass and antitrust. These laws often create tensions and incompatibilities when laid alongside the comprehensive body of copyright legislation enacted by Congress. It is to this issue that we now turn.

B. SUPREME COURT PREEMPTION DECISIONS IN INTELLECTUAL PROPERTY CASES

An issue that has arisen with frequency throughout the life of the copyright and patent acts is whether a state court, invoking state law, may ban or restrict the copying of materials that are—or are not—protected under those federal statutes. There may be several reasons for resorting to state law: the work may fall outside the subject matter of the federal statute (e.g., unfixed dramatic or musical performances), or there may be doubt as to whether there is sufficiently creative authorship to warrant protection (e.g., factual compilations akin to telephone directories), or the term of statutory protection has expired (or has never properly been invoked because of the failure to comply with formalities such as copyright notice), or the statutory period of limitations (i.e., three years for civil copyright infringement actions, § 507(b)) has expired. Alternatively, even though federal statutory remedies may be fully available, it may be that the plaintiff's attorney simply feels more comfortable trying the case in the state courts.

Whether in such circumstances state-law claims remain viable is a question of constitutional dimension. The Supremacy Clause of the U.S. Constitution, Article VI, clause 2, provides:

> This Constitution, and the Laws of the United States which shall be made in Pursuance thereof; and all Treaties made, or which shall be made, under the Authority of the United States, shall be the supreme Law of the Land; and the Judges in every State shall be bound thereby, any Thing in the Constitution or Laws of any State to the contrary notwithstanding.

Two different theories of preemption of state law within the realm of copyright have been asserted. The broader finds state anti-copying laws to be preempted by virtue of the Patent and Copyright Clause of the Constitution itself, apart from any implementing legislation that Congress may enact. This theory views the constitutional clause as manifesting an intention on the part of the Framers to occupy the field of legal regulation of authors and writings, so as to exclude all state law within that field.

If this is meant to exclude state laws in the nature of copyright with respect to non-"writings," then obviously such a theory is flawed, because it has long been recognized that states may forbid the taping, and other forms of fixing, and subsequent dissemination or broadcast of a "live" performance. Even with respect to "writings," state common law copyright has been a recognized feature of the legal landscape throughout our history, until § 301 of the 1976 Copyright Act came into effect on January 1, 1978. As will be seen below, the Supreme Court in *Goldstein v. California*—a case challenging the power of the state of California to ban the "pirating" of recordings released before 1972—held that the framers contemplated a substantial role for state anti-copying laws to protect "writings" of "authors," at least when it can plausibly be argued that commerce in these works is a "local" matter. Thus, just as the Commerce Clause has not been interpreted as altogether excluding states from regulating some aspects of interstate commerce—but rather as contemplating some "concurrent" regulation by the states—the same is generally said to be the case under the Patent and Copyright Clause.

A narrower and more refined theory of preemption—what might be called the "conflict" theory rather than the "exclusion" theory—is that state anti-copying laws should be preempted only when they are expressly or impliedly inconsistent with a provision of the statute enacted by Congress in implementation of its constitutional powers. It is often stated that state law must not be enforced if it "stands as an obstacle to the accomplishment and execution of the full purposes and objectives of the Congress"—or if a provision of the Copyright Act would be "set at naught, or its benefits denied." This theory is of course anchored in the Supremacy Clause, which makes state law subservient to federal statutory law. An obvious example of a preemptive conflict would be a state copyright statute governing written works that provides for a term of protection ending 100 years after the death of the author or that purports to do away with the fair use privilege.

It is this approach to preemption analysis that has dominated the major Supreme Court decisions. Because neither the Patent Act nor the Copyright Act of 1909 expressly dealt with the issue of preemption of related state laws (except for § 2 of the 1909 Act, which saved state-law protection of unpublished writings), the Supreme Court had to address this issue by inferring from the statutory terms and policies what the preemptive intention of Congress was. That interpretive process, and the Court's important conclusions, are evidenced in the case summaries that follow. The decisions are arguably not altogether compatible; the broad preemptive premises of the *Sears, Roebuck* and *Compco* cases gave way to a more refined conflict analysis somewhat more hospitable to state anti-copying law in the *Goldstein* and *Kewanee* cases, and later to an attempt at synthesis (with something of a swing backward) in *Bonito Boats*.

Since Congress attempted to make the preemptive reach of the Copyright Act clear—and wide-ranging—in § 301, there is not quite the need that previously existed for courts to extrapolate the congressional intent from the substantive provisions of the Act. Even so, there is much in the analysis and illustrations found in the earlier cases that helps in the interpretation of § 301. Beyond that, as will be seen in greater detail below, state-law issues have arisen that do not fall precisely within the scope of § 301 and that still require the courts to assess the conflict between state and federal law. In these situations, the older Supreme Court cases still provide some helpful signposts.

Sears, Roebuck & Co. v. Stiffel Co., 376 U.S. 225 (1964). Stiffel designed and secured design and mechanical patents on the "pole lamp," which proved to be a commercial success. Sears then began to sell a substantially identical lamp, at a cheaper price. Stiffel brought a federal court action for infringement of its patents and for unfair competition under Illinois law (alleging confusion in the trade as to the source of the lamps resulting from the identical shapes). The District Court found the patents to be invalid for want of invention, but issued an injunction under state law against Sears' marketing lamps identical to or confusingly similar to Stiffel's; the Court of Appeals affirmed, holding (in the words of the Supreme Court) "Sears liable for doing no more than copying and marketing an unpatented article." The Supreme Court reversed.

The Court noted that the federal patent and copyright statutes since 1790 "are the supreme law of the land" and that "when state law touches upon the area of these federal statutes, it is 'familiar doctrine' that the federal policy 'may not be set at naught, or its benefits denied' by the state law." It then continued:

> Thus the patent system is one in which uniform federal standards are carefully used to promote invention while at the same time preserving free competition. Obviously a State could not, consistently with the Supremacy Clause of the Constitution, extend the life of a patent beyond its expiration date or give a patent on an article which lacked the level of invention required for federal patents. To do either would run counter to the policy of Congress of granting patents only to true inventions and then only for a limited time. Just as a State cannot encroach upon the federal patent laws directly, it cannot, under some other law, such as that forbidding unfair competition, give protection of a kind that clashes with the objectives of the federal patent laws.

> In the present case the "pole lamp" sold by Stiffel has been held not to be entitled to the protection of either a mechanical or a design patent. An unpatentable article, like an article on which the patent has expired, is in the public domain and may be made and sold by whoever chooses to do so. What Sears did was to copy Stiffel's design and to sell lamps almost identical to those sold by Stiffel. This it had every right to do under the federal patent laws. That Stiffel originated the pole lamp and made it popular is immaterial. "Sharing in the goodwill of an article unprotected by patent or trade-mark is the exercise of a right possessed by all—and in the free exercise of which the consuming public is deeply interested." *Kellogg Co. v. National Biscuit Co., supra,*

305 U.S., at 122. To allow a State by use of its law of unfair competition to prevent the copying of an article which represents too slight an advance to be patented would be to permit the State to block off from the public something which federal law has said belongs to the public. The result would be that while federal law grants only 14 or 17 years' protection to genuine inventions, see 35 U.S.C. §§ 154, 173, States could allow perpetual protection to articles too lacking in novelty to merit any patent at all under federal constitutional standards. This would be too great an encroachment on the federal patent system to be tolerated.

   . . . [M]ere inability of the public to tell two identical articles apart is not enough to support an injunction against copying or an award of damages for copying that which the federal patent laws permit to be copied. Doubtless a State may, in appropriate circumstances, require that goods, whether patented or unpatented, be labeled or that other precautionary steps be taken to prevent customers from being misled as to the source, just as it may protect businesses in the use of their trademarks, labels, or distinctive dress in the packaging of goods so as to prevent others, by imitating such markings, from misleading purchasers as to the source of the goods. But because of the federal patent laws a State may not, when the article is unpatented and uncopyrighted, prohibit the copying of the article itself or award damages for such copying. . . .

Compco Corp. v. Day–Brite Lighting, Inc., 376 U.S. 234 (1964). Plaintiff Day–Brite secured a design patent on a cross-ribbed reflector in its fluorescent lighting fixtures. Compco's predecessor copied it and marketed the copies, and Day–Brite brought this action for patent infringement and for unfair competition under Illinois law. Although the District Court held the design patent invalid and thus dismissed the patent infringement claim, it found that Compco had engaged in unfair competition by marketing a copied reflector having the same shape as Day–Brite's—a shape that identified Day–Brite in the trade—and thereby caused customer confusion. The Court of Appeals affirmed, and the Supreme Court granted certiorari. The Court, accepting the District Court's findings of fact regarding copying and confusion, nonetheless reversed.

   The Court broadly interpreted the *Sears* decision to stand for the proposition that "when an article is unprotected by a patent or a copyright, state law may not forbid others to copy that article. To forbid copying would interfere with the federal policy, found in Art. I, § 8, cl. 8, of the Constitution and in the implementing federal statutes, of allowing free access to copy whatever the federal patent and copyright laws leave in the public domain." Because Day–Brite's design and mechanical patents were invalid, its fixture was thus "in the public domain and can be copied in every detail by whoever pleases."

   Even though the ribbing pattern on the fixture identified Day–Brite to the trade and had thus acquired "secondary meaning," if the design "is not entitled to a design patent or other federal statutory protection, then it can be copied at will.... That an article copied from an unpatented article could be made in some other way, that the design is "nonfunctional" and not essential to the use of either article, that the configuration of the article copied may have a "secondary meaning" which identifies the maker to the trade, or that there may be "confusion" among purchasers as to which article is which or as to who is the maker, may be relevant evidence in applying a State's law requiring such precautions as labeling; however, and regardless of the copier's motives, neither these facts nor any others can furnish a basis for imposing liability for or prohibiting the actual acts of copying and selling." A state may, however, impose by law a requirement that those who make and sell copies must take precautions to label their products as their own.

Goldstein v. California, 412 U.S. 546 (1973). Petitioners made and marketed to the public through retail stores "pirated" tapes that copied the sounds of musical performances from commercially sold recordings, without the permission of or payment to the recording companies or performing artists. The pirated tapes were labeled with the name of the original recording and performers, but expressly disclaimed any relationship with those performers or with the original record company. The petitioners were convicted under § 653h of the California Penal Code, which declared such conduct a misdemeanor. (The petitioners activity had taken place in 1970 and 1971, before the U.S. Copyright Act was amended to accord for the first time copyright protection against record piracy; the federal statute expressly left to state law any rights with respect to sound recordings made before February 15, 1972.) The petitioners challenged the constitutionality of the California statute by virtue of the Supremacy Clause. They claimed, invoking the *Sears* and *Compco* cases, that Congress intended to allow individuals to copy any work which was not protected by a federal copyright. The Supreme Court disagreed, and affirmed the state convictions.

The Court turned first to the Copyright Clause of the Constitution to determine whether it reflected a relinquishing by the states of a copyright power that would otherwise be retained by them. The purpose of the constitutional provision authorizing Congress to enact copyright legislation was concededly to promote authorship through a single uniform system, without the need for multiple state registrations. But this "does not indicate that all writings are of national interest or that state legislation is, in all cases, unnecessary or precluded." Given the variety and diversity of the American population, and of its business and industry, "it is unlikely that all citizens in all parts of the country place the same importance on works relating to all subjects. Since the subject matter to which the Copyright Clause is addressed may thus be of purely local importance and not worthy of national attention or protection, we cannot discern such an unyielding national interest as to require an inference that state power to grant copyrights has been relinquished to *exclusive* federal control."

The Court determined that differences in copyright regulation among the states would not frustrate their respective interests, one against the other, and then turned to the question whether such state-law differences would frustrate national interests.

> ... [I]t is difficult to see how the concurrent exercise of the power to grant copyrights by Congress and the States will necessarily and inevitably lead to difficulty. At any time Congress determines that a particular category of "writing" is worthy of national protection and the incidental expenses of federal administration, federal copyright protection may be authorized. Where the need for free and unrestricted distribution of a writing is thought to be required by the national interest, the Copyright Clause and the Commerce Clause would allow Congress to eschew all protection. In such cases, a conflict would develop if a State attempted to protect that which Congress intended to be free from restraint or to free that which Congress had protected. However, where Congress determines that neither federal protection nor freedom from restraint is required by the national interest, it is at liberty to stay its hand entirely. Since state protection would not then conflict with federal action, total relinquishment of the State's power to grant copyright protection cannot be inferred.

> ... No reason exists why Congress must take affirmative action either to authorize protection of all categories of writings or to free them from all restraint. We therefore conclude that, under the Constitution, the States have not relinquished all power to grant to authors "the exclusive Right to their respective Writings."

The Court also rejected the petitioners' contention that the constitutional Copyright Clause, with its "limited times" provision, barred state copyright protection—such as California's against record piracy—that was indefinite in duration. The Court found the constitutional time limitation to speak only to congressional copyright legislation. Unlike an indefinite federal copyright, which would grant exclusive rights against all citizens and in all states, a state copyright, even unlimited in duration, "is confined to its borders.... [A]ny tendency to inhibit further progress in science or the arts is narrowly circumscribed. The challenged statute cannot be voided for lack of a durational limitation."

Even though California did not surrender its power to issue copyrights, its criminal statute could conceivably be invalidated under the Supremacy Clause, if it were to stand "as an obstacle to the accomplishment and execution of the full purposes and objectives of Congress" reflected in the Copyright Act. The Court found that sound recordings were among the "writings" that the Constitution empowered Congress to regulate, but that Congress has the discretion to decide what specific classes of writings it will protect. Petitioners claimed that, by virtue of the congressional exclusion of sound recordings from the coverage of the 1909 Copyright Act (as distinguished from the musical compositions recorded), the states cannot bar their copying.

> ... [*Sears, Roebuck & Co. v. Stiffel Co.*, 376 U.S. 225 (1964), and *Compco Corp. v. Day–Brite Lighting*, 376 U.S. 234 (1964)], on which petitioners rely, do not support their position. In those cases, the

question was whether a State could, under principles of a state unfair competition law, preclude the copying of mechanical configurations which did not possess the qualities required for the granting of a federal design or mechanical patent. . . .

In regard to mechanical configurations, Congress had balanced the need to encourage innovation and originality of invention against the need to insure competition in the sale of identical or substantially identical products. The standards established for granting federal patent protection to machines thus indicated not only which articles in this particular category Congress wished to protect, but which configurations it wished to remain free. The application of state law in these cases to prevent the copying of articles which did not meet the requirements for federal protection disturbed the careful balance which Congress had drawn and thereby necessarily gave way under the Supremacy Clause of the Constitution. No comparable conflict between state law and federal law arises in the case of recordings of musical performances. In regard to this category of "Writings," Congress has drawn no balance; rather, it has left the area unattended, and no reason exists why the State should not be free to act. . . . Congress has indicated neither that it wishes to protect, nor to free from protection, recordings of musical performances fixed prior to February 15, 1972. . . . Until and unless Congress takes further action with respect to recordings fixed prior to February 15, 1972, the California statute may be enforced against acts of piracy such as those which occurred in the present case.

There were two dissenting opinions filed, for a total of four Justices. Justice Douglas (for Justices Brennan and Blackmun as well) emphasized the concern expressed in the *Sears* and *Compco* decisions for national uniformity and competition in the areas of patent and copyright, and how inconsistent with those objectives were state copyright laws providing broad and unwarranted perpetual monopolies. Justice Marshall (also speaking for Justices Brennan and Blackmun) also supported preemption of the California statute. He concluded that Congress's listing of protected writings within the 1909 Act should be understood as mandating competition (i.e., the freedom to copy) with respect to other subject matter, such as pre–1972 sound recordings.

In view of the importance of not imposing unnecessary restraints on competition, the Court adopted in those cases [*Sears* and *Compco*] a rule of construction that, unless the failure to provide patent or copyright protection for some class of works could clearly be shown to reflect a judgment that state regulation was permitted, the silence of Congress would be taken to reflect a judgment that free competition should prevail. . . . [I cannot find] in the course of legislation sufficient evidence to convince me that Congress determined to permit state regulation of the reproduction of sound recordings. For, whenever technological advances made extension of copyright protection seem wise, Congress has acted promptly. . . .

... In light of the presumption of *Sears* and *Compco* that congressional silence betokens a determination that the benefits of competition outweigh the impediments placed on creativity by the lack of copyright protection, and in the absence of a congressional determination that the opposite is true, we should not let our distaste for "pirates" interfere with our interpretation of the copyright laws. I would therefore hold that, as to sound recordings fixed before February 15, 1972, the States may not enforce laws limiting reproduction.

Kewanee Oil Co. v. Bicron Corp., 416 U.S. 470 (1974). Plaintiff-petitioner brought a diversity-of-citizenship action for misappropriation of trade secrets against certain former employees who had formed or joined the defendant company, a competing manufacturer of synthetic crystals. Petitioner alleged that the former employees, who had signed nondisclosure agreements while employed by Kewanee, had disclosed certain secret production processes to Bicron. The trial court, relying on Ohio trade-secret law, enjoined the disclosure of the process; but the Court of Appeals for the Sixth Circuit reversed, finding that state law protection of the petitioner's trade secret, in commercial use for more than one year, was preempted by 35 U.S.C. § 101 of the federal patent law. Because four courts of appeals had held that state trade-secret law was not preempted, the Supreme Court granted certiorari; it reversed the judgment of the Sixth Circuit.

Ohio treats the petitioner's process as a protectible trade secret because, under the familiar definition in § 757 of the Restatement of Torts, it "is used in one's business, and ... gives him an opportunity to obtain an advantage over competitors who do not know or use it"; disclosure or unauthorized use "by those to whom the secret has been confided under the express or implied restriction of nondisclosure or nonuse" may be enjoined. Discovery of the trade secret is lawful, however, if achieved by independent invention, accidental disclosure, or by so-called reverse engineering. Novelty as required by the patent law is not required for trade secrets, although some novelty is required for otherwise the "secret" would be generally known.

The Supreme Court held, first, relying on *Goldstein*, that the Constitution does not oust the states from regulating discoveries that fall within the general subject matter of the patent and copyright clause. It then turned to whether there was a specific conflict with federally enacted patent law, inconsistent with the Supremacy Clause of the Constitution. The Court stated that a central purpose of the patent laws, to provide "an incentive for inventors to risk the often enormous costs in terms of time, research, and development," was achieved by providing 17 years (then the statutory term) of exclusive use, in exchange for which the inventor must disclose the invention by filing an application that fully and clearly describes the "manner and process of making and using" the invention, 35 U.S.C. § 112. The policies underlying trade-secret law are the maintenance of standards of commercial ethics and the encouragement of invention. The Court examined the interaction of these two systems of protection of intellectual property, to determine whether state law presents "too great an encroachment on the federal patent system to be tolerated."

With regard to subject matter that trade-secret law can protect (e.g., customer lists or methods of doing business) but that are not within the subject matter of the patent laws (i.e., processes, machines, manufactures, compositions of matter), abolition of trade-secret protection would not result in increased disclosure of discoveries to the public; by hypothesis, patent protection is unavailable and disclosure through patent applications cannot be induced. As to patentable subject matter, there is no general conflict when the incentive to invent provided by the patent system is reinforced by the incentive to invent provided by trade-secret protection.

"The more difficult objective of the patent law to reconcile with trade secret law is that of disclosure, the *quid pro quo* of the right to exclude." The Court then separately considered three different categories of trade secrets to determine whether inventors will refrain from applying for patents because of the existence of trade-secret protection: "(1) The trade secret believed by its owner to constitute a validly patentable invention; (2) the trade secret known to its owner not to be so patentable; and (3) the trade secret whose valid patent ability is considered dubious." The Court concluded that, with respect to all of these categories, the barring of state trade-secret protection would not advance the underlying policies of the patent laws, including disclosure; and that, indeed, the retention of trade-secret protection would in most situations reinforce patent policy.

The Court therefore concluded that state trade-secret law ought not be preempted by virtue of the Supremacy Clause.

Trade secret law encourages the development and exploitation of those items of lesser or different invention than might be accorded protection under the patent laws, but which items still have an important part to play in the technological and scientific advancement of the Nation. Trade secret law promotes the sharing of knowledge, and the efficient operation of industry; it permits the individual inventor to reap the rewards of his labor by contracting with a company large enough to develop and exploit it. Congress, by its silence over these many years, has seen the wisdom of allowing the States to enforce trade secret protection. Until Congress takes affirmative action to the contrary, States should be free to grant protection to trade secrets.

Justice Marshall concurred. Contrary to the majority, he believed there was a significant possibility that inventors—particularly those who intend to use or sell the invention themselves rather than license it to others—would find trade-secret protection, indefinite in duration, preferable to patent protection, thus depriving society of public disclosure. Nonetheless, he inferred from the long coexistence of trade secrets and patent protection that Congress has not intended to exert pressure on inventors to use the patent system exclusively by withdrawing all other forms of legal protection. Justice Douglas (joined by Justice Brennan) dissented. He interpreted the *Sears* and *Compco* cases to stand for the proposition that "when an article is unprotected by a patent, state law may not forbid others to copy it, because every article not covered by a valid patent is in the public domain" so that free competition may prevail. Because the synthetic crystals produced by the petitioner were within the subject matter of the patent laws, Justice Douglas concluded that they should be subject to the policy of disclosure adopted by Congress rather than secrecy, and the inventor should be allowed a limited 17–year (now 20–year) monopoly.

Bonito Boats, Inc. v. Thunder Craft Boats, Inc.

489 U.S. 141 (1989).

[Plaintiff, a boat manufacturer, sought to enjoin defendant's use of a "direct molding process" to duplicate plaintiff's unpatented boat hulls. Plaintiff invoked a Florida statute that made "[i]t ... unlawful for any person to use the direct molding process to duplicate for the purpose of sale any manufactured vessel hull or component part of a vessel made by another without the written permission of that other person." Fla. Stat. § 559.94(2) (1987). The statute also made it unlawful for a person to "knowingly sell a vessel duplicated in violation of subsection (2)." The Florida Supreme Court held the statute conflicted with the federal patent law and was therefore invalid under the Supremacy Clause of the federal Constitution. The United States Supreme Court affirmed.]

■ JUSTICE O'CONNOR delivered the opinion of the [unanimous] Court.

[The federal patent law requires a] backdrop of free competition in the exploitation of unpatented designs and innovations. The novelty and non-obviousness requirements of patentability embody a congressional understanding, implicit in the Patent Clause itself, that free exploitation of ideas will be the rule, to which the protection of a federal patent is the exception.... The ultimate goal of the patent system is to bring new designs and technology into the public domain through disclosure. State law protection for techniques and designs whose disclosure has already been induced by market rewards may conflict with the very purpose of the patent laws by decreasing the range of ideas available as the building blocks of further innovation. The offer of federal protection from competitive exploitation of intellectual property would be rendered meaningless in a world where substantially similar state law protections were readily available. To a limited extent the federal patent laws must determine not only what is protected but also what is free for all to use....

Thus ... state regulation of intellectual property must yield to the extent that it clashes with the balance struck by Congress in our patent laws. The tension between the desire to freely exploit the full potential of our inventive resources and the need to create an incentive to deploy those resources is constant. Where it is clear how the patent laws strike that balance in a particular circumstance, that is not a judgment the states may second guess....

. . .

We believe that the Florida statute at issue in this case so substantially impedes the public use of the otherwise unprotected design and utilitarian ideas embodied in unpatented boat hulls as to run afoul of the teaching of our decisions in *Sears* and *Compco*. It is readily apparent that the Florida statute does not operate to prohibit "unfair competition" in the usual sense that the term is understood. The law of unfair competition has its roots in the common-law tort of deceit: its general concern is with protecting consumers from confusion as to source. While that concern may result in the creation of "quasi-property rights" in communicative symbols, the focus is on the protection of consumers, not the protection of producers as an incentive to product innovation. . . .

With some notable exceptions, including the interpretation of the Illinois law of unfair competition at issue in *Sears* and *Compco,* the common-law tort of unfair competition has been limited to protection against copying of nonfunctional aspects of consumer products which have acquired secondary meaning such that they operate as a designation of source. . . . The "protection" granted a particular design under the law of unfair competition is thus limited to one context where consumer confusion is likely to result; the design "idea" itself may be freely exploited in all other contexts.

In contrast to the operation of unfair competition law, the Florida statute is aimed directly at preventing the exploitation of the design and utilitarian conceptions embodied in the product itself. . . . Like the patentee, the beneficiary of the Florida statute may prevent a competitor from "making" the product in what is evidently the most efficient manner available and from "selling" the product when it is produced in that fashion. The Florida scheme offers this protection for an unlimited number of years to all boat hulls and their component parts, without regard to their ornamental or technological merit. Protection is available for subject matter for which patent protection has been denied or has expired, as well as for designs which have been freely revealed to the consuming public by their creators. . . .

Our decisions since *Sears* and *Compco* have made it clear that the Patent and Copyright Clauses do not, by their own force or by negative implication, deprive the States of the power to adopt rules for the promotion of intellectual creation within their own jurisdictions. Thus, where "Congress determines that neither federal protection nor freedom from restraint is required by the national interest," *Goldstein* [*v. California*], [412 U.S. 546], 559 [(1973)], States remain free to promote originality and creativity in their own domains.

Nor does the fact that a particular item lies within the subject matter of the federal patent laws necessarily preclude the States from offering limited protection which does not impermissibly interfere with the federal patent scheme. As Sears itself makes clear, States may place limited regulations on the use of unpatented designs in order to prevent consumer confusion as to source. In *Kewanee,* we found that state protection of trade secrets, as applied to both patentable and unpatentable subject matter, did not conflict with the federal patent laws. In both situations, state protection was not aimed exclusively at the promotion of invention itself, and the state restrictions on the use of unpatented ideas were limited to those necessary to promote goals outside the contemplation of the federal patent scheme. Both the law of unfair competition and state trade secret law have coexisted harmoniously with federal patent protection for almost 200 years, and Congress has given no indication that their operation is inconsistent with the operation of the federal patent laws.

Indeed, there are affirmative indications from Congress that both the law of unfair competition and trade secret protection are consistent with the balance struck by the patent laws. [For support, the Court referred to the Lanham Act, through which Congress has recognized many of the concerns that underlie the state tort of unfair competition, and the very longstanding existence of state trade-secret laws, known to but never disapproved by Congress.] ... The same cannot be said of the Florida statute at issue here, which offers protection beyond that available under the law of unfair competition or trade secret, without any showing of consumer confusion, or breach of trust or secrecy.

The Florida statute is aimed directly at the promotion of intellectual creation by substantially restricting the public's ability to exploit ideas that the patent system mandates shall be free for all to use. Like the interpretation of Illinois unfair competition law in *Sears* and *Compco,* the Florida statute represents a break with the tradition of peaceful coexistence between state market regulation and federal patent policy. The Florida law substantially restricts the public's ability to exploit an unpatented design in general circulation, raising the specter of state-created monopolies in a host of useful shapes and processes for which patent protection has been denied or is otherwise unobtainable. It thus enters a field of regulation which the patent laws have reserved to Congress. The patent statute's careful balance between public right and private monopoly to promote certain creative activity is a "scheme of federal regulation ... so pervasive as to make reasonable the inference that Congress left no room for the States to supplement it." *Rice v. Santa Fe Elevator Corp.,* 331 U.S. 218, 230 (1947).

Congress has considered extending various forms of limited protection to industrial design either through the copyright laws or by relaxing the restrictions on the availability of design patents. See generally Brown, *Design Protection: An Overview,* 34 UCLA L. Rev. 1341 (1987). Congress explicitly refused to take this step in the copyright laws, see 17 U.S.C. § 101; H. R. Rep. No. 94–1476, p. 55 (1976), and despite sustained criticism for a number of years, it has declined to alter the patent protections presently available for industrial design. See Report of the President's Commission on the Patent System, S. Doc. No. 5, 90th Cong., 1st Sess., 20–21 (1967). It is for Congress to determine if the present system of design and utility patents is ineffectual in promoting the useful arts in the context of industrial design. By offering patent-like protection for ideas deemed unprotected under the present federal scheme, the Florida statute conflicts with the "strong federal policy favoring free competition in ideas which do not merit patent protection." *Lear, Inc.,* 395 U.S., at 656. We therefore agree with the majority of the Florida Supreme Court that the Florida statute is preempted by the Supremacy Clause, and the judgment of that court is hereby affirmed.

QUESTIONS

1. Do the same policies that apply to preemption analysis in the field of patents also apply in the field of copyrights? Is there, for example, a greater need for a single uniform body of law regulating the copying of inventions, as contrasted with the copying of works of literary, art and music—such that the exclusion by Congress of certain matter from the coverage of the Patent Act suggests more strongly that the states should be required to allow free and competitive copying?

2. On a related point, do you understand the treatment by the Supreme Court in the *Goldstein* case of various forms of creative works as lending themselves more readily to "local" as distinguished from "national" regulation? Is this consistent with the earlier analysis in the *Sears* and *Compco* decisions, and do you find any indication that the Supreme Court meant to apply the same analysis to patent and to copyright cases?

3. The Court in *Goldstein* distinguished between works which are not covered by the Copyright Act and which as a result must be available for free and uninhibited copying by the public, and other uncovered works which Congress meant to leave "unattended" and so subject to state anti-copying laws. How does a court decide which inference to draw from congressional noncoverage? Can you think of works that fall into the former category? Can you think of works, other than sound recordings, that fall into the latter category?

4. Review the Supreme Court decisions summarized above, and try to compile a list of the sorts of state-law legal theories, or causes of action, in the general areas of patent and copyright that the Court would view as *not* preempted by virtue of application of the Supremacy Clause.

C. COPYRIGHT PREEMPTION UNDER SECTION 301 OF THE 1976 ACT

If the core purpose of the Supremacy Clause is to restrict the lawmaking powers of the states so as not to conflict with the policies and provisions endorsed by the Congress, then Congress itself can eliminate the need for the kind of implication and inference undertaken in the above-summarized Supreme Court cases—simply by expressly declaring which state anti-copying laws are to be preempted and which are to be tolerated. Congress in fact attempted to do just that, in § 301 of the 1976 Act. In the words of the House Report, the preemption principles set forth in § 301 are "intended to be stated in the clearest and most unequivocal language possible, so as to foreclose any conceivable misinterpretation of its unqualified intention that Congress shall act preemptively, and to avoid the development of any vague borderline areas between State and Federal protection." In exploring the following materials, the student should consider whether this congressional objective has been achieved.

§ 301. Preemption with respect to other laws

(a) On and after January 1, 1978, all legal or equitable rights that are equivalent to any of the exclusive rights within the general scope of copyright as specified by section 106 in works of authorship that are fixed in a tangible medium of expression and come within the subject matter of copyright as specified by sections 102 and 103, whether created before or after that date and whether published or unpublished, are governed exclusively by this title. Thereafter, no person is entitled to any such right or equivalent right in any such work under the common law or statutes of any State.

(b) Nothing in this title annuls or limits any rights or remedies under the common law or statutes of any State with respect to—

(1) subject matter that does not come within the subject matter of copyright as specified by sections 102 and 103, including works of authorship not fixed in any tangible medium of expression; or

(2) any cause of action arising from undertakings commenced before January 1, 1978; or

(3) activities violating legal or equitable rights that are not equivalent to any of the exclusive rights within the general scope of copyright as specified by section 106; or

(4) State and local landmarks, historic preservation, zoning, or building codes, relating to architectural works protected under section 102(a)(8).

(c) With respect to sound recordings fixed before February 15, 1972, any rights or remedies under the common law or statutes of any State shall not be annulled or limited by this title until February 15, 2047....

(d) Nothing in this title annuls or limits any rights or remedies under any other Federal statute.

[Subsections (e) and (f), respectively, refer to the Berne Convention and provide for preemption of equivalent state laws regarding works of visual art that are covered by the Visual Artists Rights Act of 1990.]

————

There is hardly a more significant (and probably no more troublesome) question underlying the Act than the preemptive effect of this provision. Basically, this question is: How much of the common law (or state statutory law), particularly that of unfair competition, is left standing or is permitted to develop by the Copyright Act?

In the analysis of this complex question, several things at least are clear:

(1) The statute covers, as it must, only works "fixed in a tangible medium of expression." This is clearly intended to be most comprehensive and to cover not only things such as sound recordings, computer-readable material, and other known forms of fixation but also works fixed by any method "later developed." Moreover, it has already been seen that the limitation of preemption to "subject matter of copyright as specified by sections 102 and 103" still covers a very broad area of material. Nevertheless oral works (such as improvised speeches), live jazz performances, and live demonstrations or displays by cathode rays are frequently never fixed in a tangible medium of expression. (As already noted, live broadcasts simultaneously taped are considered "fixed" under § 101.) Accordingly, copying and other copyright-type uses of such material are not treated as infringements, and state regulation thereof is not preempted. (Under § 1101, however, incorporated in Title 17 in 1994, "bootleg" recordings and broadcasts of live musical performances are now outlawed; technically, they are not copyright infringements regulated under the Copyright Clause of the Constitution, but are subject to copyright-like remedies. Section 1101(d) expressly provides that state law is not preempted.)

(2) Rights or remedies under other *federal* statutes are expressly saved from preemption by § 301(d). The patent statute, Title 35, U.S.C., is an example of such other (non-preempted) federal statute; and so too is the Federal Communications Act, 47 U.S.C. § 151 et seq. *See, e.g.,* § 111 of the Copyright Act. Perhaps the most intriguing statutory exception is offered by the Lanham Act, 15 U.S.C. § 1051 et seq., not only in its provision for trademark registration of shapes which might otherwise be copyrightable, see, e.g., *In re Morton–Norwich Prods., Inc.,* 671 F.2d 1332 (C.C.P.A. 1982); *In re Mogen David Wine Corp.,* 328 F.2d 925 (C.C.P.A. 1964), 372 F.2d 539 (C.C.P.A. 1967), but also in its more open-ended "false representation" provision, § 43(a), 15 U.S.C. § 1125(a). *See, e.g., Scholastic, Inc. v. Stouffer,* 124 F. Supp. 2d 836 (S.D.N.Y.2000) (preserving federal § 43(a) and state unfair competition claims regarding false attribution of authorship of "Muggles" characters in "Harry Potter" novels). *Contra,* Lacour v. Time Warner, Inc., 2000 WL 688946 (N.D.Ill.2000) (Copyright Act displaces "reverse passing off" claim under both Lanham Act and state law). *Cf. Gilliam v. American Broadcasting Co.,* 538 F.2d 14 (2d Cir.1976), *supra* Chapter 6.B.2.

(3) Section 301 expressly obliterates "publication" as the dividing line between federal protection under the statute and common law protection (the new dividing line being "creation," i.e., "fixation"). Works are protected under the statute "whether published or unpublished" and indeed whether created before or after January 1, 1978. This means, at the very least, the abolition of common law literary property, often called "common law copyright," covering the copying of manuscripts, letters, diaries, private presentations, and other unpublished material fixed in a tangible medium of expression.

We turn now to aspects of § 301 that are not so clear. The statute sets forth two requirements for preemption under that section: a "subject matter" test and an "equivalent rights" test. These will be explored in detail below. Focusing on the latter test for the moment, just what Congress meant by state rights "that are not equivalent to any of the exclusive rights within the general scope of copyright as specified by Section 106" is not at all apparent—and was not even apparent to the enacting Congress. Although Congress expressed a generally resounding preemptive intent, it vacillated on the question of what state rights are nonequivalent.

An earlier version of § 301(b)(3) included the following list of putatively nonequivalent state claims:

> [R]ights against misappropriation not equivalent to any of such exclusive rights, breaches of contract, breaches of trust, trespass, conversion, invasion of privacy, defamation, and deceptive trade practices such as passing off and false representation.

As you read the House Report accompanying this version of § 301, note the discussion of these state claims and ask yourself whether preservation of such claims does not undermine the creation of a uniform federal copyright system.

House Report

H.R. Rep. No. 94–1476, 94th Cong., 2d Sess. 129–33 (1976).

Single Federal System

Section 301, one of the bedrock provisions of the bill, would accomplish a fundamental and significant change in the present law. Instead of a dual system of "common law copyright" for unpublished works and statutory copyright for published works, which has been the system in effect in the United States since the first copyright statute in 1790, the bill adopts a single system of Federal statutory copyright from creation. Under section 301 a work would obtain statutory protection as soon as it is "created" or, as that term is defined in section 101, when it is "fixed in a copy or phonorecord for the first time." Common law copyright protection for works coming within the scope of the statute would be abrogated, and the concept of publication would lose its all-embracing importance as a dividing line between common law and statutory protection and between both of these forms of legal protection and the public domain.

By substituting a single Federal system for the present anachronistic, uncertain, impractical, and highly complicated dual system, the bill would greatly improve the operation of the copyright law and would be much more effective in carrying out the basic constitutional aims of uniformity and the promotion of writing and scholarship. The main arguments in favor of a single Federal system can be summarized as follows:

1. One of the fundamental purposes behind the copyright clause of the Constitution, as shown in Madison's comments in The Federalist, was to promote national uniformity and to avoid the practical difficulties of determining and enforcing an author's rights under the differing laws and in the separate courts of the various States. Today, when the methods for

dissemination of an author's work are incomparably broader and faster than they were in 1789, national uniformity in copyright protection is even more essential than it was then to carry out the constitutional intent.

2.   "Publication," perhaps the most important single concept under the present law, also represents its most serious defect. Although at one time, when works were disseminated almost exclusively through printed copies, "publication" could serve as a practical dividing line between common law and statutory protection, this is no longer true. With the development of the 20th-century communications revolution, the concept of publication has become increasingly artificial and obscure. To cope with the legal consequences of an established concept that has lost much of its meaning and justification, the courts have given "publication" a number of diverse interpretations, some of them radically different. Not unexpectedly, the results in individual cases have become unpredictable and often unfair. A single Federal system would help to clear up this chaotic situation.

3.   Enactment of section 301 would also implement the "limited times" provision of the Constitution, which has become distorted under the traditional concept of "publication." Common law protection in "unpublished" works is now perpetual, no matter how widely they may be disseminated by means other than "publication"; the bill would place a time limit on the duration of exclusive rights in them. The provision would also aid scholarship and the dissemination of historical materials by making unpublished, undisseminated manuscripts available for publication after a reasonable period.

4.   Adoption of a uniform national copyright system would greatly improve international dealings in copyrighted material. No other country has anything like our present dual system. In an era when copyrighted works can be disseminated instantaneously to every country on the globe, the need for effective international copyright relations, and the concomitant need for national uniformity, assume ever greater importance.

Under section 301, the statute would apply to all works created after its effective date, whether or not they are ever published or disseminated. With respect to works created before the effective date of the statute and still under common law protection, section 303 of the statute would provide protection from that date on, and would guarantee a minimum period of statutory copyright.

Preemption of State Law

The intention of section 301 is to preempt and abolish any rights under the common law or statutes of a State that are equivalent to copyright and that extend to works coming within the scope of the Federal copyright law. The declaration of this principle in section 301 is intended to be stated in the clearest and most unequivocal language possible, so as to foreclose any conceivable misinterpretation of its unqualified intention that Congress shall act preemptively, and to avoid the development of any vague borderline areas between State and Federal protection.

Under section 301(a) all "legal or equitable rights that are equivalent to any of the exclusive rights within the general scope of copyright as specified by section 106 ... are governed exclusively by" the Federal copyright statute if the works involved are "works of authorship that are fixed in a tangible medium of expression and come within the subject matter of copyright as specified by sections 102 and 103." All corresponding State laws, whether common law or statutory, are preempted and abrogated. Regardless of when the work was created and whether it is published or unpublished, disseminated or undisseminated, in the public domain or copyrighted under the Federal statute, the States cannot offer it protection equivalent to copyright. Section 1338 of title 28, United States Code, also makes clear that any action involving rights under the Federal copyright law would come within the exclusive jurisdiction of the Federal courts. The preemptive effect of section 301 is limited to State laws: as stated expressly in subsection (d) of section 301, there is no intention to deal with the question of whether Congress can or should offer the equivalent of copyright protection under some constitutional provision other than the patent-copyright clause of article 1, section 8.

As long as a work fits within one of the general subject matter categories of sections 102 and 103, the bill prevents the States from protecting it even if it fails to achieve Federal statutory copyright because it is too minimal or lacking in originality to qualify, or because it has fallen into the public domain. On the other hand, section 301(b) explicitly preserves common law copyright protection for one important class of works: works that have not been "fixed in any tangible medium of expression." Examples would include choreography that has never been filmed or notated, an extemporaneous speech, "original works of authorship" communicated solely through conversations or live broadcasts, and a dramatic sketch or musical composition improvised or developed from memory and without being recorded or written down. As mentioned above in connection with section 102, unfixed works are not included in the specified "subject matter of copyright." They are therefore not affected by the preemption of section 301, and would continue to be subject to protection under State statute or common law until fixed in tangible form.

The preemption of rights under State law is complete with respect to any work coming within the scope of the bill, even though the scope of exclusive rights given the work under the bill is narrower than the scope of common law rights in the work might have been.

. . .

In a general way subsection (b) of section 301 represents the obverse of subsection (a).... The numbered clauses of subsection (b) list three general areas left unaffected by the preemption: (1) subject matter that does not come within the subject matter of copyright; (2) causes of action arising under State law before the effective date of the statute; and (3) violations of rights that are not equivalent to any of the exclusive rights under copyright.

The examples in clause (3), while not exhaustive, are intended to illustrate rights and remedies that are different in nature from the rights comprised in a copyright and that may continue to be protected under State common law or statute. The evolving common law rights of "privacy," "publicity," and trade secrets, and the general laws of defamation and fraud, would remain unaffected as long as the causes of action contain elements, such as an invasion of personal rights or a breach of trust or confidentiality, that are different in kind from copyright infringement. Nothing in the bill derogates from the rights of parties to contract with each other and to sue for breaches of contract; however, to the extent that the unfair competition concept known as "interference with contract relations" is merely the equivalent of copyright protection, it would be preempted.

The last example listed in clause (3)—"deceptive trade practices such as passing off and false representation"—represents an effort to distinguish between those causes of action known as "unfair competition" that the copyright statute is not intended to preempt and those that it is. Section 301 is not intended to preempt common law protection in cases involving activities such as false labeling, fraudulent representation, and passing off even where the subject matter involved comes within the scope of the copyright statute.

"Misappropriation" is not necessarily synonymous with copyright infringement, and thus a cause of action labeled as "misappropriation" is not preempted if it is in fact based neither on a right within the general scope of copyright as specified by section 106 nor on a right equivalent thereto. For example, state law should have the flexibility to afford a remedy (under traditional principles of equity) against a consistent pattern of unauthorized appropriation by a competitor of the facts (i.e., not the literary expression) constituting "hot" news, whether in the traditional mold of *International News Service v. Associated Press*, 248 U.S. 215 (1918), or in the newer form of data updates from scientific, business, or financial data bases. Likewise, a person having no trust or other relationship with the proprietor of a computerized data base should not be immunized from sanctions against electronically or cryptographically breaching the proprietor's security arrangements and accessing the proprietor's data. The unauthorized data access which should be remediable might also be achieved by the intentional interception of data transmissions by wire, microwave or laser transmissions, or by the common unintentional means of "crossed" telephone lines occasioned by errors in switching. . . .

. . .

Nothing contained in section 301 precludes the owner of a material embodiment of a copy or a phonorecord from enforcing a claim of conversion against one who takes possession of the copy or phonorecord without consent.

When the bill discussed above came up for debate on the floor of the House of Representatives on September 22, 1976, an amendment was proposed to delete from the bill the list of nonequivalent state claims. The list was indeed deleted, after a brief and confusing dialogue that left the significance of the deletion altogether unfathomable. The Department of Justice had protested the language saving the state laws, particularly the claim of misappropriation; this position was endorsed by the Congressman making the motion, who feared that incorporating a list of allowable state claims would "render the preemption section meaningless." The proponents of the bill, including the Chairman of the Judiciary subcommittee that drafted it, acquiesced in the deletion, stating their understanding that it would nonetheless leave the various state laws unchanged *and* be consistent with the position of the Justice Department. The Senate conferees acquiesced in the deletion of the list, and the Conference Report contains no comment on the intended effect of the deletion. For more detailed accounts of the tortuous legislative history of § 301, see, e.g., Brown, *Unification: A Cheerful Requiem for Common Law Copyright*, 24 UCLA L. Rev. 1070, 1089–1102 (1977); Diamond, *Preemption of State Law*, 25 Bull. Copyr. Soc'y 204, 209–12 (1978). *See generally* P. Goldstein, Copyright, ch. 15; M. & D. Nimmer, Nimmer on Copyright § 1.01[B]. For the judicial reaction, see, e.g., *Architectronics, Inc. v. Control Sys., Inc.*, 935 F.Supp. 425 (S.D.N.Y.1996) (breach of contract).

1. WORKS COMING WITHIN THE SUBJECT MATTER OF COPYRIGHT

Baltimore Orioles, Inc. v. Major League Baseball Players Ass'n, 805 F.2d 663 (7th Cir.1986), *cert. denied*, 480 U.S. 941 (1987). In the midst of a dispute between major league baseball clubs and their players about the allocation of revenues from television broadcasts of games, the players wrote letters to the clubs and to television and cable companies asserting that game telecasts were unlawful. The players claimed that their consent to such telecasts had not been secured, and that the telecasts misappropriated their property rights in their athletic performances. Lawsuits were brought by the clubs and the players to secure a declaration regarding their respective rights in the game telecasts.

The court of appeals affirmed the judgment of the district court against the players. It held that telecasts of baseball games are copyrightable works, involving authorship regarding such matters as "camera angles, types of shots, the use of instant replays and split screens, and shot selection"; and that the clubs own the copyright, while the athletic performances of the players are contributed as employees to the televised "works made for hire." Despite this holding on the copyright issue, the players contended that broadcast of the games without their express consent "violates their rights to publicity in their performances." The clubs argued that any such publicity claim is preempted under § 301 of the Copyright Act, both because the players' athletic performances are within the subject matter of copyright and because the right of publicity is equivalent to a copyright claim.

On the former issue, the principal dispute concerned whether the players' performances are "fixed" so as to be covered by the Copyright Act. Although the game telecasts are recorded simultaneously with their transmission, and are therefore "fixed" within the definition in § 101 of the Act, the players contended that they were claiming rights in their performances, which are separate from the telecast and are not fixed. The court disagreed. Whatever might have been the case had the ballgames been played in a stadium without being broadcast or recorded,

> the Players' performances are embodied in a copy, *viz,* the videotape of the telecast, from which the performances can be perceived, reproduced, and otherwise communicated indefinitely. Hence, their performances are fixed in tangible form, and any property rights in the performances that are equivalent to any of the rights encompassed in a copyright are preempted.

The players also argued that their performances, "because they lack sufficient creativity," are not works of authorship within the subject matter of copyright under § 102. The court rejected this contention as well. It concluded that so long as a work falls within the listed categories in § 102, preemption of state claims equivalent to copyright will follow "even if [the work] fails to achieve Federal copyright because it is too minimal or lacking in originality to qualify." The court found, in any event, that the players' performances are brought within the scope of § 301 preemption by virtue of their incorporation in the recorded game telecasts, which *are* sufficiently creative.

The court then turned to the question whether the state-law right asserted by the players, the right of publicity, was equivalent to any of the rights included in § 106 of the Copyright Act. Because the players' right of publicity was allegedly violated merely by the telecasting of baseball games in which they played, the court found this alleged right to be equivalent to the right under § 106(4) publicly to perform an audiovisual work. Accordingly, § 301 compelled preemption of the state claim.

QUESTION

Bluesy Recording Company has lawfully rereleased older recordings by well-known blues artists. Bluesy, without asking permission, placed the names and photographs of those artists on the CD and cassette covers. Several of the performers have sued Bluesy for violating their right of publicity under state law, i.e., the exclusive right to use their name and likeness for commercial purposes. Bluesy relies upon the *Baltimore Orioles* case in support of its motion to dismiss; the plaintiffs contend, among other things, that their name and likeness are not the "writings" of "authors" and that in any event the cited case is clearly distinguishable on its facts. How should the court decide? *See Brown v. Ames,* 201 F.3d 654 (5th Cir.2000).

———

EQUIVALENT SUBJECT MATTER

In preserving state law rights (including copyright-equivalent rights) regarding "Subject matter that does not come within the subject matter of copyright as specified by Sections 102 and 103, including works of authorship not fixed in any tangible medium of expression," what did Congress have in mind? The language of § 301(b)(1) suggests a congressional intent not to preempt state claims concerning a class of works or subject matter that extends beyond the class of unfixed works. What further uncopyrightable subject matter did Congress allow the states to regulate?

For example, assume that a literary work sets forth certain ideas or concepts, and that a state seeks to forbid the copying of those ideas or concepts. Is this preempted because the literary work is subject matter embraced by the Copyright Act, or is the state law viable because the incorporated ideas and concepts fall outside the protection of the Act?

There is some authority for the latter view. In *Bromhall v. Rorvik,* 478 F.Supp. 361 (E.D.Pa.1979), the court rejected a preemption challenge to plaintiff's claim that defendant, who had read plaintiff's eight-page thesis abstract on the cloning of rabbits, had misappropriated plaintiff's rabbit cloning ideas in writing a book about the cloning of humans. Observing that under § 102(b) "copyright protection extends only to the *expression* of an idea, not the idea itself" (emphasis added), the court determined that claims relating to the idea itself were preserved under § 301(b)(1). See also *Past Pluto Prods. Corp. v. Dana,* 627 F.Supp. 1435 (S.D.N.Y.1986)(dictum that idea of making simple replica of Statue of Liberty crown could be protected by state law despite lack of sufficient originality for copyright); United States Golf Ass'n v. Arroyo Software Corp., 81 Cal.Rptr.2d 708, 49 U.S.P.Q.2d 1979 (Cal. App. 1st Dist. 1999)(allowing state misappropriation claim regarding golf handicapping formulas, despite contention that they were "systems" and "processes" rendered unprotectible by the Copyright Act). *Accord* Goldstein, *Preempted State Doctrines, Involuntary Transfers and Compulsory Licenses: Testing the Limits of Copyright,* 24 UCLA L. Rev. 1107, 1119 (1977).

The prevailing view, however, holds that once the work at issue is a copyrightable "work of authorship," all claims concerning copying, whether of protected or unprotected material, are governed exclusively by federal law. Thus, in *Harper & Row v. Nation Enters.,* 723 F.2d 195 (2d Cir.1983), *rev'd on other grounds,* 471 U.S. 539 (1985), the Second Circuit stated that state claims regarding the unauthorized advance publication of portions of the memoirs of Former President Gerald R. Ford concerned a "work of authorship" exclusively governed by federal law.

> The fact that portions of the Ford memoirs may consist of uncopyrightable material ... does not take the work as a whole outside the subject matter protected by the Act. Were this not so, states would be free to expand the perimeters of copyright protection to their own liking, on the theory that preemption would be no bar to state protection of material not meeting federal standards. That interpretation would run directly afoul of one of the Act's central purposes, to "avoid the

development of any vague borderline areas between State and Federal protection."

Accord Gorman, *Fact or Fancy: The Implications for Copyright,* 29 J. Copyright Soc'y 560, 604 (1982):

When Congress declares in section 102(b) that copyright in ... a literary work does not "extend to any idea" described, explained or embodied therein, it is not declaring such an idea outside of the subject matter of copyright so much as it is affirmatively declaring—as clearly as it can, and for the clearest of reasons—that ideas are free to be copied, adapted and disseminated, and that no court is to construe the federal copyright monopoly as inhibiting that freedom. The implication for state law is equally clear: neither can the states. This is a compelling illustration of the kind of congressional declaration that the *Goldstein* Court had in mind when it said:

Where the need for free and unrestricted distribution of a writing is thought to be required by the national interest, the Copyright Clause and the Commerce Clause would allow Congress to eschew all protection. In such cases, a conflict would develop if a State attempted to protect that which Congress intended to be free from restraint....

... The same can be said concerning the facts, principles, discoveries, and systems embodied in maps, directories, printed forms, and works of history or biography. All of these tangible works are either literary or graphic, and thus within the subject matter of copyright under section 102(a), such that the preemptive mandate of section 301 applies. A state may therefore not make it a tort to exercise rights equivalent to those in section 106, such as reproducing those works in copies, preparing adaptations or translations, making the first sale of copies to the public, or displaying them publicly. Nor may a state forbid the dissemination of the principles, discoveries, and systems embodied therein.

A federal court of appeals has recently endorsed this view. In *United States ex rel. Berge v. Board of Trustees of Univ. of Ala.,* 104 F.3d 1453 (4th Cir.1997), a former graduate student sought relief under Alabama law for conversion of intellectual property resulting from plagiarism of the ideas and methods developed in her Ph.D. dissertation; she claimed that these subjects fell outside the subject matter of the Copyright Act, so that state-law relief was not preempted. The court disagreed. It held that the Copyright Act's "scope" (i.e., subject matter) and its "protection" are not synonymous. "[T]he shadow actually cast by the Act's preemption is notably broader than the wing of its protection." *See also Nobel v. Bangor Hydro–Elec. Co.,* 584 A.2d 57 (Me.1990) (phrase "energy light" used in advertising jingle is within subject matter of copyright for purposes of preemption analysis).

QUESTIONS

Which, if any, of the following state statutes address subject matter reserved under § 301(b)(1)?

(1) A proposed state statute protecting artistically designed buildings, furniture, refrigerators, food processors, automobiles, and other useful articles. *See Vermont Castings, Inc. v. Evans Prods. Co.,* 215 U.S.P.Q. 758 (D.Vt.1981); *H₂O Swimwear Ltd. v. Lomas,* 164 A.D.2d 804, 560 N.Y.S.2d 19 (1st Dep't 1990).

(2) A proposed state statute protecting book design and typeface. *See Leonard Storch Enters. v. Mergenthaler Linotype,* 202 U.S.P.Q. 623 (E.D.N.Y.1979).

(3) A proposed state statute protecting characters. *See Universal City Studios, Inc. v. T–Shirt Gallery, Ltd.,* 634 F.Supp. 1468 (S.D.N.Y.1986).

(4) A proposed state statute protecting against the extraction of information from databases.

(5) A proposed state statute protecting works whose federal copyrights have expired.

(6) A proposed state statute protecting derivative works created without the authorization of the owner of copyright in the underlying work.

2. Rights Equivalent to Copyright

a. MISAPPROPRIATION

National Basketball Ass'n v. Motorola, Inc.

105 F.3d 841 (2d Cir.1997).

■ Winter, Circuit Judge:

Motorola, Inc. and Sports Team Analysis and Tracking Systems ("STATS") appeal from a permanent injunction entered by Judge Preska. The injunction concerns a handheld pager sold by Motorola and marketed under the name "SportsTrax," which displays updated information of professional basketball games in progress. The injunction prohibits appellants, absent authorization from the National Basketball Association and NBA Properties, Inc. (collectively the "NBA"), from transmitting scores or other data about NBA games in progress via the pagers, STATS's site on America On–Line's computer dial-up service, or "any equivalent means."

The crux of the dispute concerns the extent to which a state law "hot-news" misappropriation claim based on *International News Service v. Associated Press,* 248 U.S. 215, 63 L. Ed. 211, 39 S. Ct. 68 (1918) ("*INS*"), survives preemption by the federal Copyright Act and whether the NBA's claim fits within the surviving *INS*-type claims. We hold that a narrow "hot-news" exception does survive preemption. However, we also hold that appellants' transmission of "real-time" NBA game scores and information tabulated from television and radio broadcasts of games in progress does not constitute a misappropriation of "hot news" that is the property of the NBA.

.   .   .

I. BACKGROUND

The facts are largely undisputed. Motorola manufactures and markets the SportsTrax paging device while STATS supplies the game information that is transmitted to the pagers. The product became available to the public in January 1996, at a retail price of about $200. SportsTrax's pager has an inch-and-a-half by inch-and-a-half screen and operates in four basic modes: "current," "statistics," "final scores" and "demonstration." It is the "current" mode that gives rise to the present dispute. In that mode, SportsTrax displays the following information on NBA games in progress: (i) the teams playing; (ii) score changes; (iii) the team in possession of the ball; (iv) whether the team is in the free-throw bonus; (v) the quarter of the game; and (vi) time remaining in the quarter. The information is updated every two to three minutes, with more frequent updates near the end of the first half and the end of the game. There is a lag of approximately two or three minutes between events in the game itself and when the information appears on the pager screen.

SportsTrax's operation relies on a "data feed" supplied by STATS reporters who watch the games on television or listen to them on the radio. The reporters key into a personal computer changes in the score and other information such as successful and missed shots, fouls, and clock updates. The information is relayed by modem to STATS's host computer, which compiles, analyzes, and formats the data for retransmission. The information is then sent to a common carrier, which then sends it via satellite to various local FM radio networks that in turn emit the signal received by the individual SportsTrax pagers.

Although the NBA's complaint concerned only the SportsTrax device, the NBA offered evidence at trial concerning STATS's America On–Line ("AOL") site. Starting in January, 1996, users who accessed STATS's AOL site, typically via a modem attached to a home computer, were provided with slightly more comprehensive and detailed real-time game information than is displayed on a SportsTrax pager. On the AOL site, game scores are updated every 15 seconds to a minute, and the player and team statistics are updated each minute.... [W]e regard the legal issues as identical with respect to both products, and our holding applies equally to SportsTrax and STATS's AOL site.

The NBA's complaint asserted six claims for relief....

The district court dismissed all of the NBA's claims except the first—misappropriation under New York law.... Finding Motorola and STATS liable for misappropriation, Judge Preska entered the permanent injunction, reserved the calculation of damages for subsequent proceedings, and stayed execution of the injunction pending appeal. Motorola and STATS appeal from the injunction....

II. THE STATE LAW MISAPPROPRIATION CLAIM

A. *Summary of Ruling*

... The issues before us are ones that have arisen in various forms over the course of this century as technology has steadily increased the speed and quantity of information transmission. Today, individuals at home, at work, or elsewhere, can use a computer, pager, or other device to obtain highly selective kinds of information virtually at will. *International News Service v. Associated Press*, 248 U.S. 215 (1918) ("*INS*"), was one of the first cases to address the issues raised by these technological advances, although the technology involved in that case was primitive by contemporary standards. *INS* involved two wire services, the Associated Press ("AP") and International News Service ("INS"), that transmitted news stories by wire to member newspapers. *Id.* INS would lift factual stories from AP bulletins and send them by wire to INS papers. *Id.* at 231. INS would also take factual stories from east coast AP papers and wire them to INS papers on the west coast that had yet to publish because of time differentials. *Id.* at 238. The Supreme Court held that INS's conduct was a common-law misappropriation of AP's property. *Id.* at 242.

With the advance of technology, radio stations began "live" broadcasts of events such as baseball games and operas, and various entrepreneurs began to use the transmissions of others in one way or another for their own profit. In response, New York courts created a body of misappropriation law, loosely based on *INS*, that sought to apply ethical standards to the use by one party of another's transmissions of events. . . .

The 1976 amendments ... contained provisions preempting state law claims that enforced rights "equivalent" to exclusive copyright protections when the work to which the state claim was being applied fell within the area of copyright protection. See 17 U.S.C. 301. Based on legislative history of the 1976 amendments, it is generally agreed that a "hot-news" *INS*-like claim survives preemption. H.R. No. 94–1476 at 132 (1976), reprinted in 1976 U.S.C.C.A.N. 5659, 5748. However, much of New York misappropriation law after *INS* goes well beyond "hot-news" claims and is preempted.

We hold that the surviving "hot-news" *INS*-like claim is limited to cases where: (i) a plaintiff generates or gathers information at a cost; (ii) the information is time-sensitive; (iii) a defendant's use of the information constitutes free-riding on the plaintiff's efforts; (iv) the defendant is in direct competition with a product or service offered by the plaintiffs; and (v) the ability of other parties to free-ride on the efforts of the plaintiff or others would so reduce the incentive to produce the product or service that its existence or quality would be substantially threatened. We conclude that SportsTrax does not meet that test.

B. *Copyrights in Events or Broadcasts of Events*

The NBA asserted copyright infringement claims with regard both to the underlying games and to their broadcasts. The district court dismissed these claims, and the NBA does not appeal from their dismissal. Nevertheless, discussion of the infringement claims is necessary to provide the framework for analyzing the viability of the NBA's state law misappropriation claim in light of the Copyright Act's preemptive effect.

1. *Infringement of a Copyright in the Underlying Games*

In our view, the underlying basketball games do not fall within the subject matter of federal copyright protection because they do not constitute "original works of authorship" under 17 U.S.C. 102(a). Section 102(a) lists eight categories of "works of authorship" covered by the act, including such categories as "literary works," "musical works," and "dramatic works." The list does not include athletic events, and, although the list is concededly non-exclusive, such events are neither similar nor analogous to any of the listed categories.

Sports events are not "authored" in any common sense of the word. There is, of course, at least at the professional level, considerable preparation for a game. However, the preparation is as much an expression of hope or faith as a determination of what will actually happen. Unlike movies, plays, television programs, or operas, athletic events are competitive and have no underlying script. Preparation may even cause mistakes to succeed, like the broken play in football that gains yardage because the opposition could not expect it. Athletic events may also result in wholly unanticipated occurrences, the most notable recent event being in a championship baseball game in which interference with a fly ball caused an umpire to signal erroneously a home run.

What "authorship" there is in a sports event, moreover, must be open to copying by competitors if fans are to be attracted. If the inventor of the T-formation in football had been able to copyright it, the sport might have come to an end instead of prospering. Even where athletic preparation most resembles authorship—figure skating, gymnastics, and, some would uncharitably say, professional wrestling—a performer who conceives and executes a particularly graceful and difficult—or, in the case of wrestling, seemingly painful—acrobatic feat cannot copyright it without impairing the underlying competition in the future. A claim of being the only athlete to perform a feat doesn't mean much if no one else is allowed to try.

For many of these reasons, Nimmer on Copyright concludes that the "far more reasonable" position is that athletic events are not copyrightable. 1 M. Nimmer & D. Nimmer, Nimmer on Copyright 2.09[F] at 2–170.1 (1996). Nimmer notes that, among other problems, the number of joint copyright owners would arguably include the league, the teams, the athletes, umpires, stadium workers and even fans, who all contribute to the "work."

. . .

... We believe that the lack of caselaw is attributable to a general understanding that athletic events were, and are, uncopyrightable. Indeed, prior to 1976, there was even doubt that broadcasts describing or depicting such events, which have a far stronger case for copyrightability than the events themselves, were entitled to copyright protection. Indeed, as described in the next subsection of this opinion, Congress found it necessary to extend such protection to recorded broadcasts of live events. The fact that Congress did not extend such protection to the events themselves confirms our view that the district court correctly held that appellants were not infringing a copyright in the NBA games.

2. *Infringement of a Copyright in the Broadcasts of NBA Games*

As noted, recorded broadcasts of NBA games—as opposed to the games themselves—are now entitled to copyright protection. The Copyright Act was amended in 1976 specifically to insure that simultaneously-recorded transmissions of live performances and sporting events would meet the Act's requirement that the original work of authorship be "fixed in any tangible medium of expression." 17 U.S.C. 102(a). Accordingly, Section 101 of the Act, containing definitions, was amended to read:

> A work consisting of sounds, images, or both, that are being transmitted, is "fixed" for purposes of this title if a fixation of the work is being made simultaneously with its transmission.

... In explaining how game broadcasts meet the Act's requirement that the subject matter be an "original work[] of authorship," 17 U.S.C. 102(a), the House Report stated:

> When a football game is being covered by four television cameras, with a director guiding the activities of the four cameramen and choosing which of their electronic images are sent out to the public and in what order, there is little doubt that what the cameramen and the director are doing constitutes "authorship."

H.R. No. 94–1476 at 52, reprinted in 1976 U.S.C.C.A.N. at 5665.

Although the broadcasts are protected under copyright law, the district court correctly held that Motorola and STATS did not infringe NBA's copyright because they reproduced only facts from the broadcasts, not the expression or description of the game that constitutes the broadcast. The "fact/expression dichotomy" is a bedrock principle of copyright law that "limits severely the scope of protection in fact-based works." *Feist Publications, Inc. v. Rural Tel. Service Co.*, 499 U.S. 340, 350 (1991). " 'No author may copyright facts or ideas. The copyright is limited to those aspects of the work—termed 'expression'—that display the stamp of the author's originality.' " *Id.* (quoting *Harper & Row, Inc. v. Nation Enters.*, 471 U.S. 539, 547–48, 85 L. Ed. 2d 588, 105 S. Ct. 2218 (1985)).

We agree with the district court that the "defendants provide purely factual information which any patron of an NBA game could acquire from the arena without any involvement from the director, cameramen, or others who contribute to the originality of a broadcast." 939 F. Supp. at 1094. Because the SportsTrax device and AOL site reproduce only factual information culled from the broadcasts and none of the copyrightable expression of the games, appellants did not infringe the copyright of the broadcasts.

C.   The State–Law Misappropriation Claim

The district court's injunction was based on its conclusion that, under New York law, defendants had unlawfully misappropriated the NBA's property rights in its games. The district court reached this conclusion by holding: (i) that the NBA's misappropriation claim relating to the underlying games was not preempted by Section 301 of the Copyright Act; and (ii) that, under New York common law, defendants had engaged in unlawful misappropriation. *Id.* at 1094–1107. We disagree.

1. *Preemption Under the Copyright Act*

   a) *Summary*

   . . .

The district court concluded that the NBA's misappropriation claim was not preempted because, with respect to the underlying games, as opposed to the broadcasts, the subject matter requirement was not met. 939 F. Supp. at 1097. The court dubbed as "partial preemption" its separate analysis of misappropriation claims relating to the underlying games and misappropriation claims relating to broadcasts of those games. . . .

   b) *"Partial Preemption" and the Subject Matter Requirement*

The subject matter requirement is met when the work of authorship being copied or misappropriated "falls within the ambit of copyright protection." *Harper & Row, Inc. v. Nation Enters.,* 723 F.2d 195, 200 (1983), *rev'd on other grounds,* 471 U.S. 539 (1985). We believe that the subject matter requirement is met in the instant matter and that the concept of "partial preemption" is not consistent with Section 301 of the Copyright Act. . . .

Copyrightable material often contains uncopyrightable elements within it, but Section 301 preemption bars state law misappropriation claims with respect to uncopyrightable as well as copyrightable elements. . . .

Adoption of a partial preemption doctrine—preemption of claims based on misappropriation of broadcasts but no preemption of claims based on misappropriation of underlying facts—would expand significantly the reach of state law claims and render the preemption intended by Congress unworkable. It is often difficult or impossible to separate the fixed copyrightable work from the underlying uncopyrightable events or facts. Moreover, Congress, in extending copyright protection only to the broadcasts and not to the underlying events, intended that the latter be in the public domain. Partial preemption turns that intent on its head by allowing state law to vest exclusive rights in material that Congress intended to be in the public domain and to make unlawful conduct that Congress intended to allow. . . .

   c) *The General Scope Requirement*

Under the general scope requirement, Section 301 "preempts only those state law rights that 'may be abridged by an act which, in and of itself, would infringe one of the exclusive rights' provided by federal copyright law." *Computer Assocs. Int'l, Inc. v. Altai, Inc.*, 982 F.2d 693, 716 (2d Cir.1992) (quoting *Harper & Row*, 723 F.2d at 200). However, certain forms of commercial misappropriation otherwise within the general scope requirement will survive preemption if an "extra-element" test is met. As stated in *Altai*:

> But if an "extra element" is "required instead of or in addition to the acts of reproduction, performance, distribution or display, in order to constitute a state-created cause of action, then the right does not lie 'within the general scope of copyright,' and there is no preemption."

Id. (quoting 1 Nimmer on Copyright 1.01[B] at 1–15). . . .

We turn, therefore, to the question of the extent to which a "hot-news" misappropriation claim based on *INS* involves extra elements and is not the equivalent of exclusive rights under a copyright. Courts are generally agreed that some form of such a claim survives preemption. *Financial Information, Inc. v. Moody's Investors Service, Inc.*, 808 F.2d 204, 208 (2d Cir.1986), *cert. denied*, 484 U.S. 820, 98 L. Ed. 2d 42, 108 S. Ct. 79 (1987) (*"FII"*). This conclusion is based in part on the legislative history of the 1976 amendments. The House Report stated:

> "Misappropriation" is not necessarily synonymous with copyright infringement, and thus a cause of action labeled as "misappropriation" is not preempted if it is in fact based neither on a right within the general scope of copyright as specified by section 106 nor on a right equivalent thereto. For example, state law should have the flexibility to afford a remedy (under traditional principles of equity) against a consistent pattern of unauthorized appropriation by a competitor of the facts (i.e., not the literary expression) constituting "hot" news, whether in the traditional mold of *International News Service v. Associated Press*, 248 U.S. 215 (1918), or in the newer form of data updates from scientific, business, or financial data bases.

. . .

The theory of the New York misappropriation cases relied upon by the district court is considerably broader than that of *INS*. For example, the district court quoted at length from *Metropolitan Opera Ass'n v. Wagner–Nichols Recorder Corp.*, 199 Misc. 786, 101 N.Y.S.2d 483 (N.Y.Sup.Ct.1950), *aff'd*, 279 A.D. 632, 107 N.Y.S.2d 795 (1st Dep't 1951). *Metropolitan Opera* described New York misappropriation law as standing for the "broader principle that property rights of commercial value are to be and will be protected from any form of commercial immorality"; that misappropriation law developed "to deal with business malpractices offensive to the ethics of [ ] society"; and that the doctrine is "broad and flexible." 939 F. Supp. at 1098–1110 (quoting *Metropolitan Opera*, 101 N.Y.S.2d at 492, 488–89).

However, we believe that *Metropolitan Opera*'s broad misappropriation doctrine based on amorphous concepts such as "commercial immorality" or society's "ethics" is preempted. Such concepts are virtually synonymous for wrongful copying and are in no meaningful fashion distinguishable from infringement of a copyright. The broad misappropriation doctrine relied upon by the district court is, therefore, the equivalent of exclusive rights in copyright law.

Indeed, we said as much in *FII*. That decision involved the copying of financial information by a rival financial reporting service and specifically repudiated the broad misappropriation doctrine of *Metropolitan Opera*. We explained:

> We are not persuaded by FII's argument that misappropriation is not "equivalent" to the exclusive rights provided by the Copyright Act.... Nor do we believe that a possible exception to the general rule of preemption in the misappropriation area—for claims involving "any form of commercial immorality," ... quoting *Metropolitan Opera Ass'n v. Wagner–Nichols Recorder Corp.*, 199 Misc. 786, 101 N.Y.S.2d 483, ... —should be applied here. We believe that no such exception exists and reject its use here. Whether or not reproduction of another's work is "immoral" depends on whether such use of the work is wrongful. If, for example, the work is in the public domain, then its use would not be wrongful. Likewise, if, as here, the work is unprotected by federal law because of lack of originality, then its use is neither unfair nor unjustified.

FII, 808 F.2d at 208. In fact, *FII* only begrudgingly concedes that even narrow "hot news" *INS*-type claims survive preemption. *Id.* at 209.

Moreover, *Computer Associates Int'l, Inc. v. Altai, Inc.* indicated that the "extra element" test should not be applied so as to allow state claims to survive preemption easily. 982 F.2d at 717. "An action will not be saved from preemption by elements such as awareness or intent, which alter 'the action's scope but not its nature'.... Following this 'extra element' test, we have held that unfair competition and misappropriation claims grounded solely in the copying of a plaintiff's protected expression are preempted by section 301." *Id.* (citation omitted)....

Our conclusion, therefore, is that only a narrow "hot-news" misappropriation claim survives preemption for actions concerning material within the realm of copyright.[6] ...[7]

---

6. State law claims involving breach of fiduciary duties or trade-secret claims are not involved in this matter and are not addressed by this discussion. These claims are generally not preempted because they pass the "extra elements" test. See *Altai*, 982 F.2d at 717.

7. Quite apart from Copyright Act preemption, *INS* has long been regarded with skepticism by many courts and scholars and often confined strictly to its facts. In particular, Judge Learned Hand was notably hostile to a broad reading of the case. He wrote:

> We think that no more was covered than situations substantially similar to those then at bar. The difficulties of understanding it otherwise are insuperable. We are to suppose that the court meant to create a sort of common-law patent or copyright for reasons of justice. Either would flagrantly conflict with the scheme which Congress has for more than a century devised to cover the subject-matter.

Cheney Bros. v. Doris Silk Corp., 35 F.2d 279, 280 (2d Cir.1929), *cert. denied*, 281 U.S. 728, 74 L. Ed. 1145, 50 S. Ct. 245 (1930). See also Restatement (Third) of Unfair Competition 38 cmt. c (1995):

In our view, the elements central to an *INS* claim are: (i) the plaintiff generates or collects information at some cost or expense, see *FII*, 808 F.2d at 206; *INS*, 248 U.S. at 240; (ii) the value of the information is highly time-sensitive, see *FII*, 808 F.2d at 209; *INS*, 248 U.S. at 231; Restatement (Third) Unfair Competition, 38 cmt. c.; (iii) the defendant's use of the information constitutes free-riding on the plaintiff's costly efforts to generate or collect it, see *FII*, 808 F.2d at 207; *INS*, 248 U.S. at 239–40; Restatement 38 at cmt. c.; McCarthy, 10:73 at 10–139; (iv) the defendant's use of the information is in direct competition with a product or service offered by the plaintiff, *FII*, 808 F.2d at 209; *INS*, 248 U.S. at 240; (v) the ability of other parties to free-ride on the efforts of the plaintiff would so reduce the incentive to produce the product or service that its existence or quality would be substantially threatened, *FII*, 808 F.2d at 209; Restatement, 38 at cmt. c.; *INS*, 248 U.S. at 241 ("[INS's conduct] would render [AP's] publication profitless, or so little profitable as in effect to cut off the service by rendering the cost prohibitive in comparison with the return.").[8]

INS is not about ethics; it is about the protection of property rights in time-sensitive information so that the information will be made available to the public by profit-seeking entrepreneurs. If services like AP were not assured of property rights in the news they pay to collect, they would cease to collect it. The ability of their competitors to appropriate their product at only nominal cost and thereby to disseminate a competing product at a lower price would destroy the incentive to collect news in the first place. The newspaper-reading public would suffer because no one would have an incentive to collect "hot news."

The facts of the *INS* decision are unusual and may serve, in part, to limit its rationale.... The limited extent to which the *INS* rationale has been incorporated into the common law of the states indicates that the decision is properly viewed as a response to unusual circumstances rather than as a statement of generally applicable principles of common law. Many subsequent decisions have expressly limited the *INS* case to its facts.

8. Some authorities have labeled this element as requiring direct competition between the defendant and the plaintiff in a primary market. "In most of the small number of cases in which the misappropriation doctrine has been determinative, the defendant's appropriation, like that in *INS*, resulted in direct competition in the plaintiffs' primary market.... Appeals to the misappropriation doctrine are almost always rejected when the appropriation does not intrude upon the plaintiff's primary market,"

Restatement (Third) of Unfair Competition, 38 cmt. c, at 412–13; see also *National Football League v. Delaware*, 435 F. Supp. 1372 (D.Del.1977). In that case, the NFL sued Delaware over the state's lottery game which was based on NFL games. In dismissing the wrongful misappropriation claims, the court stated:

While courts have recognized that one has a right to one's own harvest, this proposition has not been construed to preclude others from profiting from demands for collateral services generated by the success of one's business venture.

Id. at 1378. The court also noted, "It is true that Delaware is thus making profits it would not make but for the existence of the NFL, but I find this difficult to distinguish from the multitude of charter bus companies who generate profit from servicing those of plaintiffs' fans who want to go to the stadium or, indeed, the sidewalk popcorn salesman who services the crowd as it surges towards the gate." *Id.*

We therefore find the extra elements—those in addition to the elements of copyright infringement—that allow a "hot-news" claim to survive preemption are: (i) the time-sensitive value of factual information, (ii) the free-riding by a defendant, and (iii) the threat to the very existence of the product or service provided by the plaintiff.

2. *The Legality of SportsTrax*

We conclude that Motorola and STATS have not engaged in unlawful misappropriation under the "hot-news" test set out above. To be sure, some of the elements of a "hot-news" *INS*-claim are met. The information transmitted to SportsTrax is not precisely contemporaneous, but it is nevertheless time sensitive. Also, the NBA does provide, or will shortly do so, information like that available through SportsTrax. It now offers a service called "Gamestats" that provides official play-by-play game sheets and half-time and final box scores within each arena. It also provides such information to the media in each arena. In the future, the NBA plans to enhance Gamestats so that it will be networked between the various arenas and will support a pager product analogous to SportsTrax. SportsTrax will of course directly compete with an enhanced Gamestats.

However, there are critical elements missing in the NBA's attempt to assert a "hot-news" *INS*-type claim. As framed by the NBA, their claim compresses and confuses three different informational products. The first product is generating the information by playing the games; the second product is transmitting live, full descriptions of those games; and the third product is collecting and retransmitting strictly factual information about the games. The first and second products are the NBA's primary business: producing basketball games for live attendance and licensing copyrighted broadcasts of those games. The collection and retransmission of strictly factual material about the games is a different product: e.g., box-scores in newspapers, summaries of statistics on television sports news, and real-time facts to be transmitted to pagers. In our view, the NBA has failed to show any competitive effect whatsoever from SportsTrax on the first and second products and a lack of any free-riding by SportsTrax on the third.

With regard to the NBA's primary products—producing basketball games with live attendance and licensing copyrighted broadcasts of those games—there is no evidence that anyone regards SportsTrax or the AOL site as a substitute for attending NBA games or watching them on television. In fact, Motorola markets SportsTrax as being designed "for those times when you cannot be at the arena, watch the game on TV, or listen to the radio. . . . "

The NBA argues that the pager market is also relevant to a "hot-news" INS-type claim and that SportsTrax's future competition with Gamestats satisfies any missing element. We agree that there is a separate market for the real-time transmission of factual information to pagers or similar devices, such as STATS's AOL site. However, we disagree that SportsTrax is in any sense free-riding off Gamestats.

An indispensable element of an *INS* "hot-news" claim is free-riding by a defendant on a plaintiff's product, enabling the defendant to produce a directly competitive product for less money because it has lower costs. SportsTrax is not such a product. The use of pagers to transmit real-time information about NBA games requires: (i) the collecting of facts about the games; (ii) the transmission of these facts on a network; (iii) the assembling of them by the particular service; and (iv) the transmission of them to pagers or an on-line computer site. Appellants are in no way free-riding on Gamestats. Motorola and STATS expend their own resources to collect purely factual information generated in NBA games to transmit to SportsTrax pagers. They have their own network and assemble and transmit data themselves.

To be sure, if appellants in the future were to collect facts from an enhanced Gamestats pager to retransmit them to SportsTrax pagers, that would constitute free-riding and might well cause Gamestats to be unprofitable because it had to bear costs to collect facts that SportsTrax did not. If the appropriation of facts from one pager to another pager service were allowed, transmission of current information on NBA games to pagers or similar devices would be substantially deterred because any potential transmitter would know that the first entrant would quickly encounter a lower cost competitor free-riding on the originator's transmissions.[9]

. . . For the foregoing reasons, the NBA has not shown any damage to any of its products based on free-riding by Motorola and STATS, and the NBA's misappropriation claim based on New York law is preempted.[10]

. . .

QUESTIONS

1. Is *NBA*'s identification of "extra elements" persuasive? The second element, "free-riding" may be a pejorative description of copying, but is it not still copying? Indeed, by distinguishing STATS' gathering of the information from a hypothetical diversion of information from "Gamestats," the *NBA* court made it clear that "free-riding" means copying. Similarly, does not the last "extra element"—whether the copying threatens to put the claimant out of business—have more to do with the extent of the damage wrought by defendant's copying than with the nature of the rights?

This leaves the "time sensitive" nature of "hot news" as the sole distinguishing "extra element." The compilation has value because its information is especially current; that is, the value is not so much in the

---

9. It may well be that the NBA's product, when enhanced, will actually have a competitive edge because its Gamestats system will apparently be used for a number of in-stadium services as well as the pager market, resulting in a certain amount of cost-sharing. Gamestats might also have a temporal advantage in collecting and transmitting official statistics. Whether this is so does not affect our disposition of this matter, although it does demonstrate the gulf between this case and *INS*, where the free-riding created the danger of no wire service being viable.

10. In view of our disposition of this matter, we need not address appellants' First Amendment and laches defenses.

content as in the timing of its delivery. Stock quote information that is valuable one hour may be worthless the next. The qualitatively different right, then, would be the right to protect the timing of the information's public disclosure. But how different is that right from copyright's distribution right, which includes the right of first publication (recall *Harper & Row v. Nation, supra*)?

2. If claims regarding "time sensitive" information resist preemption, it becomes important to define "time sensitivity." In *NBA*, the information changed by the second. But other dynamic compilations may change more slowly. For example, a database of traffic conditions might be updated every ten minutes. A database of weather reports might be updated hourly. A database of airline schedules might change daily or weekly. Time is of the essence to these databases to the extent that the information must be accurate at the moment it is consulted. But are these compilations "time sensitive" in the "hot news" sense?

b.   CONTRACT

ProCD, Inc. v. Zeidenberg

86 F.3d 1447 (7th Cir.1996).

■ EASTERBROOK, CIRCUIT JUDGE.

Must buyers of computer software obey the terms of shrinkwrap licenses? The district court held not, for two reasons: first, they are not contracts because the licenses are inside the box rather than printed on the outside; second, federal law forbids enforcement even if the licenses are contracts. 908 F. Supp. 640 (W.D.Wis.1996). The parties and numerous amici curiae have briefed many other issues, but these are the only two that matter—and we disagree with the district judge's conclusion on each. Shrinkwrap licenses are enforceable unless their terms are objectionable on grounds applicable to contracts in general (for example, if they violate a rule of positive law, or if they are unconscionable). Because no one argues that the terms of the license at issue here are troublesome, we remand with instructions to enter judgment for the plaintiff.

I

ProCD, the plaintiff, has compiled information from more than 3,000 telephone directories into a computer database. We may assume that this database cannot be copyrighted, although it is more complex, contains more information (nine-digit zip codes and census industrial codes), is organized differently, and therefore is more original than the single alphabetical directory at issue in *Feist Publications, Inc. v. Rural Telephone Service Co.,* 499 U.S. 340, 111 S. Ct. 1282, 113 L. Ed. 2d 358 (1991). See Paul J. Heald, *The Vices of Originality*, 1991 Sup. Ct. Rev. 143, 160–68. ProCD sells a version of the database, called SelectPhone (trademark), on CD–ROM discs. (CD–ROM means "compact disc—read only memory." The "shrinkwrap license" gets its name from the fact that retail software packages are covered in plastic or cellophane "shrinkwrap," and some vendors, though not ProCD, have written licenses that become effective as soon as the customer tears the wrapping from the package. Vendors prefer "end user license," but we use the more common term.) A proprietary method of compressing the data serves as effective encryption too. Customers decrypt and use the data with the aid of an application program that ProCD has written. This program, which is copyrighted, searches the database in response to users' criteria (such as "find all people named Tatum in Tennessee, plus all firms with 'Door Systems' in the corporate name"). The resulting lists (or, as ProCD prefers, "listings") can be read and manipulated by other software, such as word processing programs.

The database in SelectPhone (trademark) cost more than $10 million to compile and is expensive to keep current. It is much more valuable to some users than to others. The combination of names, addresses, and sic codes enables manufacturers to compile lists of potential customers. Manufacturers and retailers pay high prices to specialized information intermediaries for such mailing lists; ProCD offers a potentially cheaper alternative. People with nothing to sell could use the database as a substitute for calling long distance information, or as a way to look up old friends who have moved to unknown towns, or just as an electronic substitute for the local phone book. ProCD decided to engage in price discrimination, selling its database to the general public for personal use at a low price (approximately $150 for the set of five discs) while selling information to the trade for a higher price....

If ProCD had to recover all of its costs and make a profit by charging a single price—that is, if it could not charge more to commercial users than to the general public—it would have to raise the price substantially over $150.... To make price discrimination work, however, the seller must be able to control arbitrage.... [A] consumer could buy the software and resell to a commercial user. That arbitrage would break down the price discrimination and drive up the minimum price at which ProCD would sell to anyone.

Instead of tinkering with the product and letting users sort themselves—for example, furnishing current data at a high price that would be attractive only to commercial customers, and two-year-old data at a low price—ProCD turned to the institution of contract. Every box containing its consumer product declares that the software comes with restrictions stated in an enclosed license. This license, which is encoded on the CD–ROM disks as well as printed in the manual, and which appears on a user's screen every time the software runs, limits use of the application program and listings to non-commercial purposes.

Matthew Zeidenberg bought a consumer package of SelectPhone (trademark) in 1994 from a retail outlet in Madison, Wisconsin, but decided to ignore the license. He formed Silken Mountain Web Services, Inc., to resell the information in the SelectPhone (trademark) database. The corporation makes the database available on the Internet to anyone willing to pay its price—which, needless to say, is less than ProCD charges its commercial customers. Zeidenberg has purchased two additional Select-

Phone (trademark) packages, each with an updated version of the database, and made the latest information available over the World Wide Web, for a price, through his corporation. ProCD filed this suit seeking an injunction against further dissemination that exceeds the rights specified in the licenses (identical in each of the three packages Zeidenberg purchased). The district court held the licenses ineffectual because their terms do not appear on the outside of the packages. The court added that the second and third licenses stand no different from the first, even though they are identical, because they might have been different, and a purchaser does not agree to—and cannot be bound by—terms that were secret at the time of purchase. 908 F. Supp. at 654.

II

Following the district court, we treat the licenses as ordinary contracts accompanying the sale of products, and therefore as governed by the common law of contracts and the Uniform Commercial Code.... Zeidenberg [argues], and the district court held, that placing the package of software on the shelf is an "offer," which the customer "accepts" by paying the asking price and leaving the store with the goods.... So far, so good—but one of the terms to which Zeidenberg agreed by purchasing the software is that the transaction was subject to a license. Zeidenberg's position therefore must be that the printed terms on the outside of a box are the parties' contract—except for printed terms that refer to or incorporate other terms. But why would Wisconsin fetter the parties' choice in this way? Vendors can put the entire terms of a contract on the outside of a box only by using microscopic type, removing other information that buyers might find more useful (such as what the software does, and on which computers it works), or both. The "Read Me" file included with most software, describing system requirements and potential incompatibilities, may be equivalent to ten pages of type; warranties and license restrictions take still more space. Notice on the outside, terms on the inside, and a right to return the software for a refund if the terms are unacceptable (a right that the license expressly extends), may be a means of doing business valuable to buyers and sellers alike....

Transactions in which the exchange of money precedes the communication of detailed terms are common. Consider the purchase of insurance. [Judge Easterbrook then mentioned the purchase of insurance, the purchase of an airline ticket, the purchase of a concert ticket by telephone or electronic data service, and the purchase of a radio or of pharmaceuticals (which come with warranties and warnings in the box).]

Next consider the software industry itself. Only a minority of sales take place over the counter, where there are boxes to peruse. A customer may place an order by phone in response to a line item in a catalog or a review in a magazine. Much software is ordered over the Internet by purchasers who have never seen a box. Increasingly software arrives by wire. There is no box; there is only a stream of electrons, a collection of information that includes data, an application program, instructions, many limitations ("MegaPixel 3.14159 cannot be used with BytePusher 2.718"), and the terms of sale. The user purchases a serial number, which activates the software's features. On Zeidenberg's arguments, these unboxed sales are unfettered by terms—so the seller has made a broad warranty and must pay consequential damages for any shortfalls in performance, two "promises" that if taken seriously would drive prices through the ceiling or return transactions to the horse-and-buggy age.

According to the district court, the UCC does not countenance the sequence of money now, terms later. (Wisconsin's version of the UCC does not differ from the Official Version in any material respect, so we use the regular numbering system. Wis. Stat. § 402.201 corresponds to UCC § 2–201, and other citations are easy to derive.) . . . .

What then does the current version of the UCC have to say? We think that the place to start is § 2–204(1): "A contract for sale of goods may be made in any manner sufficient to show agreement, including conduct by both parties which recognizes the existence of such a contract." A vendor, as master of the offer, may invite acceptance by conduct, and may propose limitations on the kind of conduct that constitutes acceptance. A buyer may accept by performing the acts the vendor proposes to treat as acceptance. And that is what happened. ProCD proposed a contract that a buyer would accept by using the software after having an opportunity to read the license at leisure. This Zeidenberg did. He had no choice, because the software splashed the license on the screen and would not let him proceed without indicating acceptance. So although the district judge was right to say that a contract can be, and often is, formed simply by paying the price and walking out of the store, the UCC permits contracts to be formed in other ways. ProCD proposed such a different way, and without protest Zeidenberg agreed. Ours is not a case in which a consumer opens a package to find an insert saying "you owe us an extra $10,000" and the seller files suit to collect. Any buyer finding such a demand can prevent formation of the contract by returning the package, as can any consumer who concludes that the terms of the license make the software worth less than the purchase price. Nothing in the UCC requires a seller to maximize the buyer's net gains.

. . . Zeidenberg has not located any Wisconsin case—for that matter, any case in any state—holding that under the UCC the ordinary terms found in shrinkwrap licenses require any special prominence, or otherwise are to be undercut rather than enforced. In the end, the terms of the license are conceptually identical to the contents of the package. Just as no court would dream of saying that SelectPhone (trademark) must contain 3,100 phone books rather than 3,000, or must have data no more than 30 days old, or must sell for $100 rather than $150—although any of these changes would be welcomed by the customer, if all other things were held constant—so, we believe, Wisconsin would not let the buyer pick and choose among terms. Terms of use are no less a part of "the product" than are the size of the database and the speed with which the software compiles listings. Competition among vendors, not judicial revision of a package's contents, is how consumers are protected in a market economy. *Digital Equipment Corp. v. Uniq Digital Technologies, Inc.*, 73 F.3d 756 (7th Cir.1996). ProCD has rivals, which may elect to compete by offering superior software, monthly updates, improved terms of use, lower price, or a better compromise among these elements. As we stressed above, adjusting terms in buyers' favor might help Matthew Zeidenberg today (he already has the software) but would lead to a response, such as a higher price, that might make consumers as a whole worse off.

III

The district court held that, even if Wisconsin treats shrinkwrap licenses as contracts, § 301(a) of the Copyright Act, 17 U.S.C. § 301(a), prevents their enforcement. 908 F. Supp. at 656–59. The relevant part of § 301(a) preempts any "legal or equitable rights [under state law] that are equivalent to any of the exclusive rights within the general scope of copyright as specified by section 106 in works of authorship that are fixed in a tangible medium of expression and come within the subject matter of copyright as specified by sections 102 and 103." ProCD's software and data are "fixed in a tangible medium of expression," and the district judge held that they are "within the subject matter of copyright." The latter conclusion is plainly right for the copyrighted application program, and the judge thought that the data likewise are "within the subject matter of copyright" even if, after *Feist*, they are not sufficiently original to be copyrighted.... One function of § 301(a) is to prevent states from giving special protection to works of authorship that Congress has decided should be in the public domain, which it can accomplish only if "subject matter of copyright" includes all works of a type covered by sections 102 and 103, even if federal law does not afford protection to them. Cf. *Bonito Boats, Inc. v. Thunder Craft Boats, Inc.*, 489 U.S. 141, 109 S. Ct. 971, 103 L. Ed. 2d 118 (1989) (same principle under patent laws).

But are rights created by contract "equivalent to any of the exclusive rights within the general scope of copyright"? Three courts of appeals have answered "no." *National Car Rental System, Inc. v. Computer Associates International, Inc.*, 991 F.2d 426, 433 (8th Cir.1993); *Taquino v. Teledyne Monarch Rubber*, 893 F.2d 1488, 1501 (5th Cir.1990); *Acorn Structures, Inc. v. Swantz*, 846 F.2d 923, 926 (4th Cir.1988). The district court disagreed with these decisions, 908 F. Supp. at 658, but we think them sound. Rights "equivalent to any of the exclusive rights within the general scope of copyright" are rights established by law—rights that restrict the options of persons who are strangers to the author. Copyright law forbids duplication, public performance, and so on, unless the person wishing to copy or perform the work gets permission; silence means a ban on copying. A copyright is a right against the world. Contracts, by contrast, generally affect only their parties; strangers may do as they please, so contracts do not create "exclusive rights." Someone who found a copy of SelectPhone (trademark) on the street would not be affected by the shrinkwrap license—though the federal copyright laws of their own force would limit the finder's ability to copy or transmit the application program.

Think for a moment about trade secrets. One common trade secret is a customer list. After *Feist*, a simple alphabetical list of a firm's customers, with address and telephone numbers, could not be protected by copyright. Yet *Kewanee Oil Co. v. Bicron Corp.*, 416 U.S. 470, 94 S. Ct. 1879, 40 L. Ed. 2d 315 (1974), holds that contracts about trade secrets may be enforced—precisely because they do not affect strangers' ability to discover and use the information independently. If the amendment of § 301(a) in 1976 overruled *Kewanee* and abolished consensual protection of those trade secrets that cannot be copyrighted, no one has noticed—though abolition is a logical consequence of the district court's approach. Think, too, about everyday transactions in intellectual property. A customer visits a video store and rents a copy of *Night of the Lepus*. The customer's contract with the store limits use of the tape to home viewing and requires its return in two days. May the customer keep the tape, on the ground that § 301(a) makes the promise unenforceable?

A law student uses the LEXIS database, containing public domain documents, under a contract limiting the results to educational endeavors; may the student resell his access to this database to a law firm from which LEXIS seeks to collect a much higher hourly rate? Suppose ProCD hires a firm to scour the nation for telephone directories, promising to pay $100 for each that ProCD does not already have. The firm locates 100 new directories, which it sends to ProCD with an invoice for $10,000. ProCD incorporates the directories into its database; does it have to pay the bill? Surely yes; *Aronson v. Quick Point Pencil Co.*, 440 U.S. 257, 99 S. Ct. 1096, 59 L. Ed. 2d 296 (1979), holds that promises to pay for intellectual property may be enforced even though federal law (in *Aronson*, the patent law) offers no protection against third-party uses of that property. See also *Kennedy v. Wright*, 851 F.2d 963 (7th Cir.1988). But these illustrations are what our case is about. ProCD offers software and data for two prices: one for personal use, a higher price for commercial use. Zeidenberg wants to use the data without paying the seller's price; if the law student and Quick Point Pencil Co. could not do that, neither can Zeidenberg.

Although Congress possesses power to preempt even the enforcement of contracts about intellectual property—or railroads, on which see *Norfolk & Western Ry. v. American Train Dispatchers*, 499 U.S. 117, 111 S. Ct. 1156, 113 L. Ed. 2d 95 (1991)—courts usually read preemption clauses to leave private contracts unaffected. *American Airlines, Inc. v. Wolens*, 513 U.S. 219, 115 S. Ct. 817, 130 L. Ed. 2d 715 (1995), provides a nice illustration. A federal statute preempts any state "law, rule, regulation, standard, or other provision . . . relating to rates, routes, or services of any air carrier." 49 U.S.C. App. § 1305(a)(1). Does such a law preempt the law of contracts—so that, for example, an air carrier need not honor a quoted price (or a contract to reduce the price by the value of frequent flyer miles)? The Court allowed that it is possible to read the statute that broadly but thought such an interpretation would make little sense. Terms and conditions offered by contract reflect private ordering, essential to the efficient functioning of markets. ___ U.S. at ___-___, 115 S. Ct. at 824–25.... Section 301(a) plays a role similar to § 1301(a)(1): it prevents states from substituting their own regulatory systems for those of the national government. Just as § 301(a) does not itself interfere with private transactions in intellectual property, so it does not prevent states from respecting those transactions. Like the Supreme Court in *Wolens*, we think it prudent to refrain from adopting a rule that anything with the label "contract" is necessarily outside the preemption clause: the variations and possibilities are too numerous to foresee. *National Car Rental* likewise recognizes the possibility that some applications of the law of contract could interfere with the attainment of national objectives and therefore come within the domain of § 301(a). But general enforcement of shrinkwrap licenses of the kind before us does not create such interference.

Aronson emphasized that enforcement of the contract between Aronson and Quick Point Pencil Company would not withdraw any information from the public domain. That is equally true of the contract between ProCD and Zeidenberg. Everyone remains free to copy and disseminate all 3,000 telephone books that have been incorporated into ProCD's database. Anyone can add sic codes and zip codes. ProCD's rivals have done so. Enforcement of the shrinkwrap license may even make information more readily available, by reducing the price ProCD charges to consumer buyers. . . . Licenses may have other benefits for consumers: many licenses permit users to make extra copies, to use the software on multiple computers, even to incorporate the software into the user's products. But whether a particular license is generous or restrictive, a simple two-party contract is not "equivalent to any of the exclusive rights within the general scope of copyright" and therefore may be enforced.

Reversed and remanded.

QUESTIONS

1. In the *ProCD* case, the court invoked several commercial contexts in which state courts enforce against consumer purchasers contract terms that become known only after money changes hands. But did the court unfairly neglect to mention that certain of those transactions—for example, insurance, transportation, and pharmaceuticals—are subjected to extremely comprehensive governmental regulation in the interest of consumer protection?

2. The *ProCD* court concluded that enforcement of individual contractual limits on the dissemination of the uncopyrightable telephone database will not significantly interfere with the copyright policy of allowing the public more generally to have access to such a database. It states, for example, that a person finding the CD–ROM on the street, unaccompanied by the shrinkwrap license, is not bound by its terms and may lawfully disseminate the CD–ROM contents widely (presumably even on the Internet). How often will such a curbside discovery take place? Does there not come a point at which contractually enforceable restrictions in shrinkwrap licenses become so pervasive that they would indeed conflict with the strong public domain policy of the copyright laws as articulated in the *Feist* case? Is *ProCD* an example of such a situation? (Indeed, would not a contract be formed when the CD–ROM-finder loaded the disk, encountered the license terms "splashed on the screen," and clicked her assent?)

3. Presumably the key "extra" element in a state contract-enforcement action is that of the bargained-for exchange between negotiating parties, which gives rise to reasonable expectations. Is that model of contract enforcement at all pertinent to the shrink-wrap license, which is very much like a unilateral declaration by the licensor, meant to be binding "on the world" without any negotiation or bargained-for exchange? If not, should contractual relief be preempted as equivalent to an infringement action? Would a legend behind the title page of a book, to the effect that "any and all reproduction of any portion of this book is forbidden," properly provide the basis for a nonpreempted contract-enforcement action against someone copying a short passage?

For a decision at odds with *ProCD* with respect to the breach of a contract or license where there has been no bargaining, *see Information Handling Services Inc. v. LRP Pubs., Inc.*, 54 U.S.P.Q.2d 1571 (E.D.Pa. 2000) (compilation of legal materials relating to employment law). *See also Softman Prods. Co. v. Adobe Sys., Inc.*, 2001 WL 1343955 (C.D.Cal.2001) (court interprets shrinkwrap transaction as sale rather than license, and applies first-sale doctrine).

4. In *Vault Corp. v. Quaid Software, Ltd.*, 847 F.2d 255 (5th Cir.1988), the court held that a state claim to enforce a shrink-wrap license forbidding copying or adapting the software program was preempted on the ground that it conflicted with § 117 of the Copyright Act, which permits owners of copies of programs to copy and adapt them in conjunction with the running of the computer, and to make backup copies. The court in *ProCD* did not refer to, let alone attempt to distinguish, the *Vault* decision. Are the conclusions compatible? If not, which do you regard as more convincing?

Wrench LLC v. Taco Bell Corp.

256 F.3d 446 (6th Cir.2001).

[The plaintiffs are creators of the "Psycho Chihuahua" cartoon character—a clever, feisty dog "with an attitude"—which they promote, market and license. Representatives of the defendant food company became engaged in a course of communications with the plaintiffs and their licensing representatives during 1996 and 1997, for the purpose of using the dog in Taco Bell advertising. In these discussions and meetings, the idea of using the animated dog evolved into one using a real dog manipulated by computer graphics imaging, and some specific advertising themes were discussed. There was also a discussion of the costs to the defendant of using the plaintiffs' ideas, but no specific amounts were mentioned. In mid–1997, a recently retained advertising agency for Taco Bell presented an idea—allegedly originated altogether independently—of an advertising campaign based on a feisty chihuahua, and nationwide commercials focusing on the dog began airing on television in December 1997. Plaintiffs brought suit in January 1998, alleging breach of an implied-in-fact contract as well as various tort and statutory claims under state law. The district court granted summary judgment for defendant, finding that the claims were preempted because equivalent to the exclusive rights under copyright. The court of appeals reversed and remanded. At the outset, it determined that, even though the plaintiffs were objecting to the copying of their ideas and concepts, these were "within the subject matter of copyright as specified by sections 102 and 103" for purposes of preemption analysis under section 301. It then turned to the second element of preemption analysis.]

■ GRAHAM, DISTRICT JUDGE (sitting by designation):

The second prong of the preemption analysis—the so-called "equivalency" or "general scope" requirement—augments the subject matter inquiry by asking whether the state common law or statutory action at issue asserts rights that are the same as those protected under § 106 of the Copyright Act. Under § 301(a), even if appellants' state law claims concern works within the subject matter of copyright, such claims will only be preempted if they assert rights that are "equivalent to any of the exclusive rights within the general scope of copyright as specified by section 106[.]" 17 U.S.C. § 301(a).

Equivalency exists if the right defined by state law may be abridged by an act which in and of itself would infringe one of the exclusive rights. See *Harper & Row*, 723 F.2d at 200. Conversely, if an extra element is required instead of or in addition to the acts of reproduction, performance, distribution or display in order to constitute a state-created cause of action, there is no preemption, provided that the extra element changes the nature of the action so that it is qualitatively different from a copyright infringement claim. . . . We find that appellants' state law implied-in-fact contract claim survives preemption under these rules.

Under Michigan law, "[a]n implied contract, like other contracts, requires mutual assent and consideration." *Spruytte v. Dep't of Corr.*, 82 Mich.App. 145, 266 N.W.2d 482, 483 (1978). Michigan draws a clear distinction between contracts implied in fact and contracts implied in law:

> The first does not exist, unless the minds of the parties meet, by reason of words or conduct. The second is quasi or constructive, and does not require a meeting of minds, but is imposed by fiction of law[.]

Cascaden v. Magryta, 247 Mich. 267, 225 N.W. 511, 512 (1929).

The gist of appellants' state law implied-in-fact contract claim is breach of an actual promise to pay for appellants' creative work. It is not the use of the work alone but the failure to pay for it that violates the contract and gives rise to the right to recover damages. Thus, the state law right is not abridged by an act which in and of itself would infringe one of the exclusive rights granted by § 106, since the right to be paid for the use of the work is not one of those rights.

An extra element is required instead of or in addition to the acts of reproduction, performance, distribution or display, in order to constitute the state-created cause of action. The extra element is the promise to pay. This extra element does change the nature of the action so that it is qualitatively different from a copyright infringement claim. The qualitative difference includes the requirement of proof of an enforceable promise and a breach thereof which requires, inter alia, proof of mutual assent and consideration, as well as proof of the value of the work and appellee's use thereof.

This qualitative difference is further reflected by the difference in the remedy afforded by the state law claim. Under Michigan law, a plaintiff's remedy for breach of an implied-in-fact contract includes recovery of the reasonable value of the services rendered, considering factors such as the general practice of the industry. . . .

Under the Copyright Act, remedies for infringement are limited to injunctions; impounding and destruction of infringing articles; recovery of the copyright owner's actual damages and any additional profits of the infringer or statutory damages; and costs and attorneys fees. See 17 U.S.C. §§ 502, 503, 504 and 505. The remedies available under copyright law do not include damages for the reasonable value of the defendants' use of the work. See *Business Trends Analysts, Inc. v. Freedonia Group, Inc.*, 887 F.2d 399, 406–07 (2nd Cir.1989).

. . . [Here] there is another crucial act that stands as a condition to the appellee's liability, to wit: its promise to pay for the use of the work. Thus, this is a case in which the breach of contract cause of action alleges more than reproduction, adaptation, etc., simplicter.

In finding that appellants' state law contract claim is not preempted, we do not embrace the proposition that all state law contract claims survive preemption simply because they involve the additional element of promise. See, e.g., *[ProCD, Inc. v.] Zeidenberg*, 86 F.3d at 1454;[6] *Taquino v. Teledyne Monarch Rubber*, 893 F.2d 1488, 1501 (5th Cir.1990) (appendix). Under that rationale, a contract which consisted only of a promise not to reproduce the copyrighted work would survive preemption even though it was limited to one of the exclusive rights enumerated in 17 U.S.C. § 106. If the promise amounts only to a promise to refrain from reproducing, performing, distributing or displaying the work, then the contract claim is preempted. The contrary result would clearly violate the rule that state law rights are preempted when they would be abridged by an act which in and of itself would infringe one of the exclusive rights of § 106. As the authors note in 1 Nimmer on Copyright § 1.01[B][1][a] at 1–22: "Although the vast majority of contract claims will presumably survive scrutiny . . . nonetheless preemption should continue to strike down claims that, though denominated 'contract,' nonetheless complain directly about the reproduction of expressive materials."

. . . [In finding that the plaintiff's implied contract claim was preempted, the district court relied principally upon a case that in turn cited] *Nimmer on Copyright* § 1.01[B][1][a] at 1–19, [g] at 1–34 (1997), for the proposition that "implied contracts as a species of *quasi*-contract 'should be

---

6. The Seventh Circuit in *Zeidenberg* did qualify somewhat its broad holding that because contracts, unlike the Copyright Act, do not create exclusive rights but generally affect only their parties, they are not preempted, stating, "[W]e think it prudent to refrain from adopting a rule that anything with the label 'contract' is necessarily outside the preemption clause: the variations and possibilities are too numerous to foresee." 86 F.3d at 1455.

regarded as an "equivalent right" and pre-empted [.]' "Id. In the instant case, however, appellants' claim is not based on *quasi*-contract; instead, it is based upon an implied-in-fact contract which, under Michigan law, does not exist unless the minds of the parties meet by reason of words or conduct.

The authors of *Nimmer on Copyright* warn against confusing contracts implied in law (*quasi*-contract) and contracts implied in fact:

> Unfortunately, many courts in dealing with idea cases fail to distinguish between a contract implied in law and a contract implied in fact. An action in quasi contract is not a true contract since " 'quasi contracts, unlike true contracts, are not based upon the apparent intention of the parties to undertake the performances in question, nor are they promises. They are obligations created by law for reasons of justice.' ... Quasi contractual recovery is based upon benefit accepted or derived from which the law implies an obligation to pay." An implied in fact contract on the other hand is a consensual agreement presenting the same elements as are found in an express contract except that in an implied in fact contract the promise is not expressed in words but is rather implied from the promisor's conduct.

4 Nimmer on Copyright § 16.03 at 10–10 to 16–11 (quoting *Weitzenkorn v. Lesser*, 40 Cal.2d 778, 794, 256 P.2d 947, 959 (1953)) (footnotes omitted).

For the purpose of the preemption analysis, there is a crucial difference between a claim based on *quasi*-contract, *i.e.*, a contract implied in law, and a claim based upon a contract implied in fact. In the former, the action depends on nothing more than the unauthorized use of the work. Thus, an action based on a contract implied in law requires no extra element in addition to an act of reproduction, performance, distribution or display, whereas an action based on a contract implied in fact requires the extra element of a promise to pay for the use of the work which is implied from the conduct of the parties....

Here, appellants' implied-in-fact contract claim contains the essential element of expectation of compensation which is an element not envisioned by § 106. See *Cascaden* [*v. Magryta*, 247 Mich. 267], 225 N.W. at 511–12 ("Plaintiffs cannot recover on the theory of a contract implied in fact, for the work was not done ... under circumstances authorizing plaintiffs to entertain an expectation of pay from defendants.").

We conclude that the district court erred with respect to the equivalency prong of the preemption analysis and find that appellants' state law implied-in-fact contract claim is not preempted by the Copyright Act.

[The court concluded that genuine issues of material fact were presented by the defendant's claim that it had originated the Chihuahua idea without copying from the plaintiffs. It also held that under Michigan law it was not necessary that the plaintiffs prove that their ideas were "novel" in order to prevail. Accordingly, the summary judgment for the defendant was reversed and the case was remanded to the district court.]

QUESTIONS

1. If awarding judgment to a plaintiff on a contract claim will render only the defendant liable for copying, and not all potential copiers, why should not *all* contract claims—both express and implied—be allowed and non-preempted under the Copyright Act? (Isn't that supported by the congressional language deleted at the last minute in the discussion of section 301 on the floor of the House?)

2. Some courts have held that if a defendant has simply promised not to copy an author's copyrighted material, and nothing more, then breach of that promise—simply by copying—is equivalent to a copyright infringement and a state-law action framed as breach of contract should be preempted. Do you agree?

3. Assume that Publisher agrees to publish Author's book and to pay a $2.00 royalty for each copy of the book sold. After its first week of distributing the book to retail stores, Publisher repudiates the publishing contract and refuses to pay. Advise Author as to what tenable claims she has against Publisher, what court(s) she may sue in, and what remedies she can get.

c. CONVERSION OF CHATTELS; TRADE SECRET

Ehat v. Tanner

780 F.2d 876 (10th Cir.1985), *cert. denied,* 479 U.S. 820 (1986).

■ SEYMOUR, CIRCUIT JUDGE.

Andrew Ehat brought this action against Gerald and Sandra Tanner, dba Modern Microfilm Company (the Tanners), alleging injury from the Tanners' unauthorized reproduction and sale of literary material in which Ehat claimed a proprietary interest. Judgment was entered against the Tanners, and they appeal. We reverse.

Ehat was a scholar engaged in post-graduate research on the history of the Church of Jesus Christ of Latter–Day Saints (the LDS Church). The Tanners publish and distribute documents and works relevant to the LDS Church. In the course of his research, Ehat examined and took notes from a 350–page transcript of the William Clayton Journals at the LDS Church Archives.[1] Ehat gave to his colleague, Lyndon Cook, material consisting of quotations he and another researcher had taken from the Journals as well as his own notes and comments. This material was surreptitiously taken from Cook's office, copied, and replaced. One of these unauthorized copies found its way to the Tanners, who had no part in the original removal from Cook's office. They blacked out the material added by Ehat, printed the original extracts, and sold them to the public.

---

1. William Clayton lived during the 1800's and was for a time the private secretary to Joseph Smith, the first president of the LDS Church. The Journals at issue were kept by Clayton from 1842 to 1846 while he and Joseph Smith lived in Nauvoo, Illinois.

Ehat's complaint asserted claims under the federal copyright statutes, on which the judge granted summary judgment for the Tanners. In addition, the complaint alleged state common law claims for unfair competition and unjust enrichment. Following a bench trial on these claims, the Court entered judgment for Ehat. On appeal, the Tanners assert that the district court erred in awarding damages on Ehat's common law claims because those claims are preempted by the federal copyright statutes. We agree.

Federal copyright law was amended by the Copyright Act of 1976 to preempt state law ... Congress expressly stated that section 301 is intended to prevent "the States from protecting ... [a work] even if it fails to achieve Federal statutory copyright because it is too minimal or lacking in originality to qualify, or because it has fallen into the public domain." H.R. Rep. No. 1476, 94th Cong., 2d Sess. 131, *reprinted in* 1976 U.S. Code Cong. & Ad. News 5659, 5747. State law forbidding others to copy an article "unprotected by a patent or a copyright ... would interfere with the federal policy, found in Art. I, § 8, cl. 8, of the Constitution and in the implementing federal statutes, of allowing free access to copy whatever the federal patent and copyright laws leave in the public domain." *Compco Corp. v. Day–Brite Lighting, Inc.,* 376 U.S. 234, 237, 84 S. Ct. 779, 782, 11 L. Ed. 2d 669 (1964); *see also Suid v. Newsweek Magazine,* 503 F. Supp. 146, 148 (D.D.C.1980).

Under section 301, a state common law or statutory claim is preempted if: (1) the work is within the scope of the "subject matter of copyright" as specified in 17 U.S.C. §§ 102, 103; and (2) the rights granted under state law are equivalent to any exclusive rights within the scope of federal copyright as set out in 17 U.S.C. § 106....

Literary works, including compilations and derivative works, are within the subject matter of copyright if they are original works of authorship fixed in any tangible medium of expression. *See* 17 U.S.C. §§ 102, 103. This is so notwithstanding the material could not be copyrighted. *See Harper & Row,* 723 F.2d at 200. The material at issue here clearly falls within the subject matter of copyright. The district court did not address this issue, and Ehat does not argue otherwise on appeal.

We now turn to whether the rights Ehat seeks to assert under state common law are equivalent to those exclusive rights within the scope of copyright. Under federal law, the owner of copyright has the exclusive right "to reproduce the copyrighted work" and "to distribute copies" to the public by sale. *See* 17 U.S.C. §§ 106(1), (3).

> When a right defined by state law may be abridged by an act which, in and of itself, would infringe one of the exclusive rights, the state law in question must be deemed preempted.... Conversely, when a state law violation is predicated upon an act incorporating elements beyond mere reproduction or the like, the rights involved are not equivalent and preemption will not occur.

Harper & Row, 723 F.2d at 200 (citations omitted).

In an effort to distinguish this case from a preempted claim, the district court granted Ehat relief based on its finding that, by printing and selling Ehat's notes, the Tanners "bodily appropriated the work product of plaintiff" and derived a profit from their misappropriation. Rec., vol. V, at 13–14. We need not decide whether this misappropriation of material states a claim for relief under Utah law. Assuming that it does, *see generally International News Service v. Associated Press,* 248 U.S. 215, 39 S. Ct. 68, 63 L. Ed. 211 (1918); Prosser & Keeton on Torts § 130 at 1020–22 (5th ed. 1984), we see no distinction between such a state right and those exclusive rights encompassed by the federal copyright laws. *See Warner Bros., Inc. v. American Broadcasting Cos.,* 720 F.2d 231, 247 (2d Cir.1983) ("state law claims that rely on the misappropriation branch of unfair competition are preempted"); *Schuchart & Associates,* 540 F. Supp. at 943–44 (same). *See generally* 1 Nimmer § 1.01[B], at 1–16 to 1–22. We cannot agree with the district court that Ehat's state claim was not within the scope of copyright because it was based on his right in the notes "as a physical matter and property." Rec., vol. V, at 9. Ehat did not allege a state law claim of conversion to recover for the physical deprivation of his notes. Instead, he sought to recover for damage flowing from their reproduction and distribution. *See Harper & Row,* 723 F.2d at 200–01. Such reproduction interferes with an intangible literary or artistic property right equivalent to copyright. *See* 1 Nimmer § 1.01[B], at 1–14.4 n.51.

Our view of the nature of Ehat's claim is confirmed by the district court's award of damages. The court awarded $960, representing the Tanners' profits from the printing and sale of their publication, which is clearly an award for the reproduction of Ehat's work. The court also awarded $3,000 which it found Ehat suffered as a reduction in the market value of his master's thesis due to the misappropriation. This damage also flows from the reproduction of the material rather than from its physical taking. *See Harper & Row,* 723 F.2d at 201. Finally, the court awarded Ehat $12,000 for general damage to his reputation as a scholar resulting from "defendant's unlawful and improper publication." Rec., vol. V, at 15. Because the reputation injury arose out of the copying of Ehat's work, that claim is preempted as well. *See* 1 Nimmer § 1.10[B], at 1.14.2 n.49.

. . .

Ehat "cannot achieve by an unfair competition claim what [he] failed to achieve under [his] copyright claim." *See Durham Industries, Inc. v. Tomy Corp.,* 630 F.2d 905, 918 (2d Cir.1980).

. . .

Accordingly, Ehat's state law claim is preempted. The case is reversed and remanded for further proceedings consistent with this opinion.

———

Harper & Row Publishers, Inc. v. Nation Enterprises, 723 F.2d 195 (2d Cir.1983), *rev'd on other grounds,* 471 U.S. 539 (1985). The facts of the case are set forth *supra* Chapter 7.B. The manuscript of the Ford memoirs was improperly taken and turned over to The Nation magazine which, shortly before the publication of the Ford book, published an article borrowing substantial quotations from the manuscript. Time magazine, which had contracted to publish excerpts in conjunction with the publication of the Harper & Row book, decided not to do so and to withhold $12,500 payable to Harper & Row. Harper & Row and Reader's Digest brought an action for copyright infringement and for certain state law violations, including conversion and tortious interference with contractual relations. The district court found copyright infringement and no fair use, but dismissed the state-law claims as preempted. The court of appeals reversed on the copyright claim, finding fair use (this was reversed in turn by the Supreme Court), and it affirmed the dismissal of the state claims.

The court of appeals stated that a state-law claim is preempted if it can be established simply by proving acts, such as reproduction and the preparation of a derivative work, that violate § 106 of the Copyright Act. It found the plaintiffs' state claims to be of this kind.

The conversion claim was viewed by the court as ambiguous. To the extent it rested upon unauthorized publication of the Ford manuscript, it is "coextensive with an exclusive right already safeguarded by the Act— namely, control over reproduction and derivative use of copyrighted material," and is preempted. To the extent the plaintiffs complain about unauthorized possession of the papers themselves, such a theory would not be preempted: "Conversion, as thus described, is a tort involving acts— possession and control of chattels—which are qualitatively different from those proscribed by copyright law." However, a conversion claim was not adequately supported; "merely removing one of a number of copies of a manuscript (with or without permission) for a short time, copying parts of it, and returning it undamaged, constitutes far too insubstantial an interference with property rights to demonstrate conversion." (The lesser tort of trespass to chattels also would fail, for lack of actual damage to the property interfered with.)

The plaintiffs also asserted that The Nation had tortiously interfered with their contractual relations, "by destroying the exclusive right of an author and his licensed publishers to exercise and enjoy the benefit of the pre-book publication serialization rights." The court of appeals also found this claim to be preempted.

> If there is a qualitative difference between the asserted right and the exclusive right under the Act of preparing derivative works based on the copyrighted work, we are unable to discern it. In both cases, it is the act of unauthorized publication which causes the violation. The enjoyment of benefits from derivative use is so intimately bound up with the right itself that it could not possibly be deemed a separate element. *See* 1 Nimmer on Copyright § 1.01[B], at n. 46 (1983). As the trial court noted, the fact that cross-appellants pleaded additional elements of awareness and intentional interference, not part of a copyright infringement claim, goes merely to the scope of the right; it

does not establish qualitatively different conduct on the part of the infringing party, nor a fundamental nonequivalence between the state and federal rights implicated.

Computer Associates International, Inc. v. Altai, Inc., 982 F.2d 693 (2d Cir.1992) (For a fuller statement of the facts of this case, see Chapter 6.A.1). Defendant Altai created its OSCAR 3.5 program by a "clean room" examination of plaintiff CA's ADAPTER program, after learning that the OSCAR 3.4 program had been copied from ADAPTER by an Altai programmer who formerly worked for CA. The district court, affirmed by the Second Circuit, held that OSCAR 3.5 did not infringe the copyright in ADAPTER. Plaintiff also alleged that defendant's examination and reconstitution of the ideas of the ADAPTER program violated plaintiff's trade secret rights in the program. The court of appeals reversed the district court's finding of preemption, and held that trade secret claims have an "extra element" that changes the "nature of the action so that it is qualitatively different from a copyright infringement claim." The court explained its conclusion as follows:

> [M]any state law rights that can arise in connection with instances of copyright infringement satisfy the extra element test, and thus are not preempted by section 301. These include unfair competition claims based upon breaches of confidential relationships, breaches of fiduciary duties and trade secrets.... Trade secret protection, the branch of unfair competition law at issue in this case, remains a "uniquely valuable" weapon in the defensive arsenal of computer programmers. *See* 1 Milgrim on Trade Secrets § 2.06A[5][c], at 2–172.4. Precisely because trade secret doctrine protects the discovery of ideas, processes, and systems which are explicitly precluded from coverage under copyright law, courts and commentators alike consider it a necessary and integral part of the intellectual property protection extended to computer programs....
>
> The legislative history of section 301 states that "[t]he evolving common law rights of ... trade secrets ... would remain unaffected as long as the causes of action contain elements, such as ... a breach of trust or confidentiality, that are different in kind from copyright infringement." House Report, at 5748.... Trade secret claims often are grounded upon a defendant's breach of a duty of trust or confidence to the plaintiff through improper disclosure of confidential material.... The defendant's breach of duty is the gravamen of such trade secret claims, and supplies the "extra element" that qualitatively distinguishes such trade secret causes of action from claims for copyright infringement that are based solely upon copying.

The district court had read the plaintiff's trade secret claims to be based on no more than Altai's *use* of CA's program (which would in substance be merely a claim of illicit copying). But the court of appeals read those claims to include more pertinently an assertion that Altai had unlawfully *acquired* the program through its hiring of Arney, a former CA employee, who had violated his duty of loyalty and confidentiality. Proving CA's trade secret claims would turn upon whether Altai had actual or constructive notice of the fact that Arney was incorporating CA's trade secrets into the 3.4 and 3.5 programs that Altai developed. Because these latter issues had not been explored by the district court, the court remanded for further proceedings.

QUESTIONS

1. In *Ehat,* should the court have given greater weight to defendants' usurpation of plaintiff's interest in publishing the (apparently) public domain documents *first*? (Should the court of appeals in the *Harper & Row* case have done so as well?) Are copyright or other public policies advanced by precluding all remedies against the unauthorized first publication of public domain materials laboriously gathered by another?

2. The *Ehat* court appears to hold that even a defamation claim is preempted if the reputation injury flows simply from the act of unauthorized publication. Do you agree? Is this conclusion consistent with the legislative history of § 301 of the Copyright Act? Must not closer attention be paid to the precise nature of the reputational injury? For example, is the preemption conclusion affected by whether the injury to a plaintiff's reputation stems from: (a) the appearance, as in *Ehat,* that a plaintiff-scholar was not the first to discover and publish, but was actually the "copycat"; (b) the poor grammar, spelling and organization in the plaintiff-scholar's draft, which would have assuredly been corrected in the editing process; or (c) the scurrilous comments made about a third person in the document published without authorization, when that third person sues?

3. Do you understand the difference, emphasized in *Altai,* between "wrongful acquisition" and "misappropriation by copying"? Why is the latter preempted, but not the former?

4. eBay is an Internet trading site that offers sellers the ability to list all manner of items for sale and prospective buyers the ability to search those listings and bid on items. A potential purchaser can access the eBay site and perform a key word search for relevant auctions; eBay has over 7 million registered users, adds 400,000 new items to the site every day, and handles 100 million searches per day on its database. Bidder's Edge (BE) is an internet company that uses "robots" to access websites such as eBay, to gather the auction information compiled thereon, and to create its own composite listings of auction items (with eBay's by far the largest source). A software robot is a computer program which operates across the internet to perform searching, copying and retrieving functions on the websites of others; its activities consume the processing and storage resources of another's system, making that portion of it unavailable to other users and also slowing the processing of information there. eBay has attempted to block access by BE to the eBay website, but has been unsuccessful in doing so; the same is true of eBay's insistence that BE cease using its robots on the eBay site.

eBay has brought an action against BE for copyright infringement and a variety of state torts including trespass. (Will the infringement action be successful? What other information would you need to know?) As to the latter, eBay asserts its servers (upon which the auction data are stored) are private property, and that the electronic signals sent by BE to retrieve information from eBay's servers are "sufficiently tangible" to interfere with eBay's possessory interest in its computer system and thus to support a trespass cause of action. eBay claims that, under this element of its complaint, it is seeking relief not against BE's use (e.g., copying) of the auction data it accesses but rather against the access itself, which eBay asserts is the equivalent of an unauthorized interference with physical personal property: BE deprives eBay and others of the use of the eBay bandwidth and system capacity.

Is the trespass action preempted by § 301 of the Copyright Act? *See eBay, Inc. v. Bidder's Edge, Inc.*, 100 F. Supp. 2d 1058 (N.D.Cal.2000).

3.   A Suggested Preemption Analysis

Some tentative steps might be taken here toward the formulation of a more constructive analysis for the implementation of § 301. State anti-copying claims might usefully be divided into three categories. The first category is of the kind about which Congress might say the following:

> "These state causes of action do contain elements which are not necessary in order to state a claim for copyright infringement. But those elements—loss of a contract with a third party, unjust enrichment, willful competitive injury—*can* be considered in the copyright action, and fitting remedies can be fashioned for redress."

If that is so, then copyright and its attendant rights and remedies should be treated as "occupying the field," and this category of state claim should be preempted.

As to a second category of state claim, Congress might say the following:

> "Here too, the state cause of action embraces elements which are not necessary in order to state a claim for copyright infringement. But here, these elements are of incidental concern or of no concern at all in determining appropriate remedies in the copyright action. Conversely, the fact that there has been copying is only incidental to the state claim, which is really designed to protect other and independent interests."

State causes of action for breach of contract, breach of a fiduciary or confidential relationship, trespass and conversion regarding tangible property, and privacy and defamation claims are of this kind. Because the Copyright Act focuses upon the economic injury resulting basically from copying itself, and is rather inattentive to the enforcement of promises, the protection of special relationships and physical property, and the personal hurt resulting from exposure or ridicule, preemption should not operate, and the state claims can survive.

The third category of state claim forces us to grapple with the fact that Congress' failure in the Copyright Act to embrace a particular interest within the statutory rights and remedies (as in the second category) may signal not hospitability toward state protection of that interest but rather congressional opposition. In this third category, there is once again an element in the state claim which is not of the kind which a federal court is invited to consider in a copyright action; but unlike the second category, the economic injury resulting from copying as such is not incidental to the state claim but is the essence of it. An example would be a state law barring phonorecord manufacturers from imitating the sounds on another's recording (as distinguished from "pirating" the actual sounds on that person's recording, which *is* a copyright infringement under §§ 106(1) and 114(b)). There would be no recovery for such imitation in a copyright action. When a state treats that particular form of copying, exempted from the copyright owner's monopoly, as at the core of its cause of action, it is likely to be affronting Congress' infringement (and exemption) policies and should thus be preempted.

QUESTIONS

1. Do you agree with the above analysis of nonequivalent state claims?

2. Which, if any, of the following state statutes or claims seek to protect rights equivalent to rights within the general scope of copyright?

(a) A New York statute which provides:

Whenever a work of fine art is sold or otherwise transferred by or on behalf of the artist who created it, or his heirs or personal representatives, the right of reproduction thereof is reserved to the grantor until it passes into the public domain by act or operation of law unless such right is sooner expressly transferred by an instrument, note or memorandum in writing signed by the owner of the rights conveyed or his duly authorized agent. Nothing herein contained, however, shall be construed to prohibit the fair use of such work of art.

See Ronald Litoff, Ltd. v. American Express Co., 621 F.Supp. 981 (S.D.N.Y. 1985).

(b) A provision of the penal law which makes it a misdemeanor to distribute commercially a phonograph record, disc, tape or other article embodying an illegally recorded performance without the consent of the owner of such recorded performance. *See Crow v. Wainwright,* 720 F.2d 1224 (11th Cir.1983).

(c) A state law "droit moral" statute, forbidding mutilation or distortion of works of art, literature, or music. What if the statute is limited to forbidding owners of works of the fine arts from mutilating or destroying them?

(d) A state statute forbidding forgery of works of art.

(e) A state statute granting a performance right to recording artists in their sound recordings.

(f) A state statute banning rentals of records, audiotapes, and video-cassettes.

(g) A state statute mandating a resale royalty (i.e., a continuing royalty on subsequent sales) to creators of works of the fine arts. *See Morseburg v. Balyon,* 621 F.2d 972 (9th Cir.), *cert. denied,* 449 U.S. 983 (1980).

3. The song "Baby Love" was performed by the female singing trio "The Supremes" in the 1960s; their formal gowns and bouffant hairstyle were as familiar as their singing style. Recently, a television advertisement for "Dinty Moore" brand beef stew depicted, in part, three young black women, with bouffant hair, in sequined formal gowns singing "Dinty Moore, My Dinty Moore," to the tune of "Baby Love." The owner of copyright in the song, along with Motown Records (which owns the federally registered trademark "The Supremes"), and the singers who have comprised the trio through the years have brought an action against Dinty Moore in a state court. They assert a number of state-law claims. One claim is for unfair competition; the advertisement is said to convey the false impression that the copyright owner, Motown, and the singers have given their permission for the use of the song and the images of The Supremes. Another claim is for intentional and negligent interference with prospective business advantage; it is said that the advertisement impairs the copyright owner's ability to exploit the composition, and impairs the rights of The Supremes to exploit their recordings and other materials. A third claim is that the use of Supreme look-alikes and the performance of the song violate a state statute barring the "knowing use of another's name, voice or likeness for purposes of advertising or selling products without such person's prior consent." A fourth claim is that defendant's imitation of plaintiffs' vocal style and physical appearance for commercial purposes constitutes common-law misappropriation. Fifth, plaintiffs assert that defendant's conduct should be deemed to create a constructive trust for the payment of its profits to the plaintiffs. Finally, plaintiffs claim that they have a protected right in the likeness, style and image (the "persona") of The Supremes that is protectible under § 43(a) of the Lanham Act. How should the court rule on the defendant's motion for summary judgment? *See Motown Record Corp. v. Geo. A. Hormel & Co.,* 657 F.Supp. 1236 (C.D.Cal.1987); *Universal City Studios, Inc. v. T–Shirt Gallery, Ltd.,* 634 F.Supp. 1468 (S.D.N.Y.1986).

4. Will application of the following state laws survive a defendant's challenge based on preemption by the Copyright Act?

(a) An Ohio criminal statute provides that "no person shall knowingly use or operate the property of another without the consent of the owner or person authorized to give consent." The criminal defendant operated an electronic bulletin board on which he placed software by Microsoft Corp. without its consent. *See State of Ohio v. Perry,* 83 Ohio St.3d 41, 697 N.E.2d 624 (1998).

(b) The California Civil Code provides for a right of publicity, making it unlawful to "knowingly use another's name, voice, signature, photograph, or likeness, in any manner, or on any products . . ., or for purposes of advertising or selling . . . without such person's prior consent." Alan Actor performed in a motion picture but was not paid by the producer; CBS secured distribution rights from the producer and released the film on videotape, with a picture of Actor on the videotape box. Pending his being paid for his services, Actor has sued CBS and has sought to enjoin continued distribution, claiming a violation of his right of publicity. *See Fleet v. CBS, Inc.*, 58 Cal.Rptr.2d 645 (Cal.App.1996).

(c) South Carolina recognizes at common law the torts of outrage (based on a particularly willful and egregious infliction of emotional distress) and the loss of consortium. A cookbook author and her husband have, respectively, asserted these claims against a publisher that published a substantial number of her recipes in a competing book, without her consent and without crediting her. *See Griggs v. South Carolina Elec. & Gas Co.*, 463 S.E.2d 608 (S.C.1995).

5. Paramount Pictures, which owns the copyright to the celebrated television program *Cheers*, authorized the Host Company to operate bars in certain airports to be designed along the lines of the bar in the program, and to place on bar stools two "animatronic robot figures" resembling the characters portrayed by the television actors George Wendt and John Ratzenberger. Wendt and Ratzenberger have sued Host Company for violation of their right of publicity by virtue of the copying of their likenesses. (See Question 5(b), supra.) Host has argued that the robots are authorized derivative works based on the characters incorporated in the copyrighted Paramount television program, so that the plaintiffs' publicity claims are preempted. How should the court rule? *See Wendt v. Host International, Inc.*, 197 F.3d 1284 (9th Cir.1999) (Kozinski, J., dissenting from denial of petition for rehearing).

BROADER DISPLACEMENT OF STATE LAW BY "CONFLICT" ANALYSIS

In its precise terms, § 301 deals only with preemption of state laws that grant rights that are equivalent to reproduction, the preparation of derivative works, public distribution, and public performance and display. Technically, that section does not oust state law on matters such as copyright ownership. It is clear, however, that—for example—a state would be barred, by application of the Supremacy Clause, from fixing copyright ownership rights in an employee who had prepared a literary work within the scope of his employment. The allocation of rights between employer and employee is carefully treated in the Copyright Act, and the application of state law would be an obstacle to the policies reflected in the federal statute. The same would be true if a state, whether calling it a matter of contract or of property, were to purport to make the transfer of ownership in a physical object (a literary manuscript or an oil painting on canvas) conclusive evidence of the transfer of copyright ownership as well, in flat contradiction of § 202 of the Copyright Act. It has also been held that state doctrines of agency law—such as an agent's "apparent authority" to make binding, albeit unauthorized, commitments on behalf of a property owner— must be subordinated to copyright doctrine such as that which makes innocence no defense to an infringement action. *See Pinkham v. Sara Lee Corp.*, 983 F.2d 824 (8th Cir.1992).

In such instances, in which the terms and structure of § 301 appear not to apply, it becomes necessary to invoke more longstanding and generic approaches to preemption analysis, asking such questions as whether the federal policies reflected in one or another provision of the Copyright Act would be "set at naught, or its benefits denied" by the application of state law. This form of preemption is sometimes referred to as "conflict preemption," in contrast to the "express preemption" derived from § 301. In such a generic approach, the pre–1978 Supreme Court cases dealing with preemption under the patent and copyright laws—including *Sears* and *Compco*—continue to provide useful sources for analysis.

In a recent decision of the Court of Appeals for the Eleventh Circuit, the court summarized and applied the Supreme Court's general jurisprudence dealing with federal preemption—developed outside of Copyright law—in a case involving the respective rights of primary and secondary infringers. In **Foley v. Luster**, 249 F.3d 1281 (11th Cir.2001), Luster was a videographer who made videotapes intended to promote the services of a group of "high level" distributors of Amway products. Those videotapes included recordings of copyrighted music, for which Luster had secured no licenses. Several recording companies sued Luster and the distributors for copyright infringement, and the distributors—after reaching a settlement— filed a cross-claim against Luster to have him indemnify them. A jury ruled for certain of the distributors, but Luster claimed on appeal that the indemnification claim, based on Florida law, was preempted by the Copyright Act. The Court of Appeals ruled against his preemption contention.

First, the court concluded that the so-called "extra element" test— requiring, to avoid preemption under section 301(a), that the state-law claim have an extra element instead of or in addition to the exclusive rights set forth in section 106—was inapplicable, because the issue was not the rights of the copyright owner but rather the respective liabilities of the several infringers among themselves. That test was therefore not a bar to the cross-claim for indemnification. The court explained why, and it then proceeded to determine whether that state law cross-claim was barred by virtue of three other types of preemption analysis:

> It is important to understand why this extra element test is not applicable to the case before us. The extra element test was developed to protect the "exclusive rights" of copyright holders. See Altai, 982 F.2d at 716. The Act establishes a comprehensive set of rights and remedies to protect copyrights, and preempts most state actions so that the rights and remedies will be consistent for all copyright holders. The indemnity case before us, however, does not concern the rights of a

copyright holder. Rather, it concerns the allocation of responsibility between copyright infringers. Whether or not Luster indemnifies the distributors for their share of the settlement fund and attorneys' fees is "not equivalent to any of the exclusive rights within the general scope of copyright as specified by section 106." 17 U.S.C. § 301(a). Because the question before us does not fall within this provision of the Act, the exception found in § 301(b)(3) is irrelevant, and, therefore, the extra element test does not apply. Instead, we apply general preemption law to determine whether an indemnity case brought pursuant to Florida common law is preempted by the Act.

Under Article VI of the U.S. Constitution, federal law is the "supreme Law of the Land," and any state law that is in conflict with a federal law is preempted. See Maryland v. Louisiana, 451 U.S. 725, 746, 101 S.Ct. 2114, 2128–29, 68 L.Ed.2d 576 (1981). In an effort to explain preemption, the Supreme Court has clarified that

> Congress' intent may be explicitly stated in the statute's language or implicitly contained in its structure and purpose. In the absence of an express congressional command, state law is pre-empted if that law actually conflicts with federal law, or if federal law so thoroughly occupies a legislative field as to make reasonable inference that Congress left no room for the States to supplement it.

Cipollone v. Liggett Group, Inc., 505 U.S. 504, 516, 112 S.Ct. 2608, 2617, 120 L.Ed.2d 407 (1992) (quotations and citations omitted). These bases for preemption are commonly referred to as explicit preemption, conflict preemption, and field preemption. When determining whether a state law is preempted under one of these bases, we look to the intent of Congress in passing the federal law. Malone v. White Motor Corp., 435 U.S. 497, 504, 98 S.Ct. 1185, 1190, 55 L.Ed.2d 443 (1978) (" 'The purpose of Congress is the ultimate touchstone' " of preemption.) (quoting Retail Clerks v. Schermerhorn, 375 U.S. 96, 103, 84 S.Ct. 219, 223, 11 L.Ed.2d 179 (1963)). By applying each basis for preemption to Luster's argument, we find that an indemnity claim under the common law of Florida is not preempted by the Act.

1. Explicit Preemption

Explicit preemption is evident when "Congress' command is explicitly stated in the statute's language or implicitly contained in its structure and purpose." Jones v. Rath Packing Co., 430 U.S. 519, 525, 97 S.Ct. 1305, 1309, 51 L.Ed.2d 604 (1977). Section 301 explicitly preempts all claims that are covered under § 106 of the Act, if they come within the subject matter of §§ 102 and 103. . . . It is evident that the congressional intent in § 106 was to protect the rights of copyright holders, not to govern cases between infringers. Nothing in the language of § 301 explicitly prohibits indemnity suits, nor is there a message in the structure of §§ 301 and 106 read together that implies a preemption of indemnity suits. Therefore, such suits are not explicitly preempted by the Act.

2. Conflict Preemption

Conflict preemption "arises when compliance with both federal and state regulations is a physical impossibility, or where state law stands as an obstacle to the accomplishment and execution of the full purposes and objectives of Congress." Pacific Gas and Elec. Co. v. State Energy Res. Conservation and Dev. Comm'n, 461 U.S. 190, 204, 103 S.Ct. 1713, 1722, 75 L.Ed.2d 752 (1983) (quotations and citations omitted). Again, a suit for indemnity between defendants in a copyright infringement case is not an obstacle to congressional intent, which was to protect copyright holders in a comprehensive and uniform way that was consistent with Article I, Section 8, clause 8 of the U.S. Constitution. Further, it is certainly permissible for a plaintiff to sustain a copyright infringement suit while the defendants litigate an indemnity suit as a cross-claim. Therefore, a state indemnity suit is not barred by the principles of conflict preemption.

3. Field Preemption

Finally, preemption is evident where "[t]he scheme of federal regulation [is] so pervasive as to make reasonable the inference that Congress left no room for the States to supplement it." Rice v. Santa Fe Elevator Corp., 331 U.S. 218, 230, 67 S.Ct. 1146, 1152, 91 L.Ed. 1447 (1947). In this situation, "the federal interest is so dominant that the federal system will be assumed to preclude enforcement of state laws on the same subject." Id. If the distributors had brought any type of copyright claim against Luster, this area of preemption may have precluded the suit. However, the Act does not touch on the field of common law indemnity, and indemnity does not intrude upon the field of rights guaranteed by the Act. Accordingly, the indemnity claim is not preempted by any of the bases for federal preemption, and the district court properly denied the motion for judgment as a matter of law on these grounds.

Turning to Florida indemnification law—which would shield Luster from a duty to indemnify in the event that the distributors were culpable for the videotape infringement to any degree, however slight—the court determined that the jury had been properly instructed, and it therefore denied Luster's motion for judgment as a matter of law.

A number of other courts have had to address the question whether a "state law stands as an obstacle to the accomplishment and execution of the full purposes and objectives of Congress" as reflected in the Copyright Act—that is, whether there is "conflict preemption." Courts can frequently disagree, depending upon how broadly (or narrowly) they construe the commands and policies of the federal statute and how broadly (or narrowly) they construe the commands and policies of the pertinent state law. Some courts are more willing than others to effect an "accommodation" of the federal and state laws, and thus to deny that the state law is preempted. Two examples will suffice. One deals with whether the copyright ownership of an author-spouse must be shared with his or her mate in community-property states; and the other deals with the power of a transferor of a copyright interest to terminate in less than the 35 years mentioned in section 203(a) of the Copyright Act when this would be permitted under state law.

A California appellate court, in the case of **In re Marriage of Susan M. & Frederick L. Worth**, 241 Cal.Rptr. 135, 195 Cal.App.3d 768 (1st Dist. 1987), held that copyrights in works written during the marriage are community property; that § 201(d)(1) accommodates transfer of the copyright "by operation of law" from the author-husband, in whom the copyright had initially vested, to the community; and that the federal Copyright Act does not preempt the application of state community property laws. The court left unclear whether the wife in that case was not only entitled to half of the royalties generated by the work of the divorced author-husband but was also entitled—as a true joint owner—to license or assign rights in the work without first securing the author's consent.

The potential breadth of the rights of the nonauthor spouse, in a community property regime, induced the lower court in a later case, arising in Louisiana, to conclude that there was "conflict preemption": the state law had to give way, lest transactions in copyrights be unduly muddled by the various potentially applicable state rules regarding property ownership between spouses, particularly divorced spouses. Yet, the court of appeals reversed, finding that the federal provisions awarding copyright ownership to the author-spouse and the federal policy favoring efficient copyright transactions could be readily accommodated to the Louisiana community property (and civil law) rules. In **Rodrigue v. Rodrigue**, 218 F.3d 432 (5th Cir.2000), the husband during and after his 26–year marriage created numerous paintings that included recurring images of the "Blue Dog." In the state proceedings on the division of marital property, the wife claimed to be co-owner of all copyrights generated during the community, as well as of derivative works created after the divorce that were based on such earlier created works. The husband filed suit in federal court seeking a declaratory judgment that Louisiana's community property laws were preempted by the Copyright Act. The court of appeals concluded that there was no conflict preemption, by accommodating the federal and state rules, rather than giving one or the other full sway.

As to the Copyright Act, the court held that although an author is given initial ownership of the copyright by section 201(a), that is comprised of the listed exclusive rights (in section 106), but not necessarily the enjoyment of economic benefits that derive therefrom. ("Notably, none of these rights either expressly or implicitly include the exclusive right to enjoy income or any of the other economic benefits produced by or derived from copyrights.... Moreover, by its very title, § 201(a) addresses only initial—not permanent—vesting of the copyright in the author. And, even though the author's copyright arises at the moment of creation of the work, the Act explicitly allows for subsequent vesting in non-authors, either jointly with the author or subsequent to him by virtue of transfer of all or lesser portions of the copyright.")

As to state law, the court first referred to Article 2338 of the Louisiana Civil Code: "[P]roperty acquired during the existence of [marriage] through the effort, skill, or industry of either spouse" is community property. The court then noted that property ownership under Louisiana law is comprised of three elements: *usus* (the right to use or possess), *abusus* (the right to encumber or alienate), and *fructus* (the right to enjoy the revenues derived from the property). These component rights can be parceled out to different individuals, e.g., the owner of a legal "usufruct" has the right to use and enjoy revenues generated by the property but does not have the right to alienate the property. The court concluded that the policies of both federal and state law can be fostered and accommodated by allowing the non-author spouse, upon the divorce, to continue to share in the revenues from the copyrighted work prepared by her husband during the marriage; but giving the author spouse the exclusive right to transfer the copyrights, and to license rights thereunder, to third persons. The court reasoned:

> . . . . Numerous examples of exclusive management of community property and shared enjoyment of those assets exist: A paycheck issued by the employer in the name of the employee-spouse alone can be cashed, deposited, or otherwise negotiated only by that spouse; yet, the proceeds of the paycheck, representing earnings of one spouse in community, belong to the community. . . .

> In concluding that copyrights should be treated the same as paychecks, cars, and partnership interests, we rely initially on Louisiana Civil Code article 2351 which proclaims that "[a] spouse has the exclusive right to manage, alienate, encumber, or lease movables issued or registered in his name as provided by law." This right of exclusive management of those kinds of movables is not coterminous with the community but continues as long as the copyright is vested in the author-spouse, even after partition of the property formerly belonging to the community is complete. Under Louisiana law a copyright is a "movable," and under federal law a copyright is issued or registered in the name of the author-spouse. In compatible combination, these two systems of law provide for the author-spouse's *exclusive management* of copyrights created during the existence of the community and thereafter until completion of the partition of the property of the former community, while at the same time ensuring that the non author-spouse is not deprived of his or her right to one-half of the economic benefits of the copyright.

> The *economic benefits* that flow from particular types of one-spouse assets, including but not limited to cars, paychecks, partnership interests—and copyrights—can inure to the benefit of the community without doing violence to the legal results intended by the Louisiana Legislature or Congress in providing for vesting of title in one spouse only, results designed with third parties in mind, not spouses or other co-owners. In the context of these clearly established concepts and

principles, we conclude that federal copyright law does not conflict with, and therefore does not preempt, Louisiana community property law to the extent of denying the entitlement of the non-author spouse (Veronica) to an undivided one-half interest in the economic benefits of the copyrighted works created by the author (George) during the existence of the community, and of the derivatives of such works following its termination.

. . . . [As to George's claim of "express preemption" by virtue of section 301(a),] [n]otably absent from the Copyright Act's exclusive sub-bundle of five rights is the right to enjoy the earnings and profits of the copyright. Nothing in the copyright law purports to prevent non-preempted rights from being enjoyed by the community during its existence or thereafter by the former spouses in community as co-owners of equal, undivided interests. . . .

George nevertheless insists in the alternative that, even if § 301 preemption does not apply, "conflict preemption" does because designating copyrights as community property would do substantial damage to important federal interests.] In this argument, George fails (or refuses) to recognize the jurisprudential corollary that "[s]tate family and family-property law must do 'major damage' to 'clear and substantial' federal interests before the Supremacy Clause will demand that state law be overridden." . . . George argues that (1) copyrights will not be amenable to efficient or predictable exchange if spouses have equal rights to impair or dispose of such rights, possibly in conflicting manners, (2) predictability and uniformity will not be served if varying state laws are applied to copyright management issues, and (3) authors will have less incentive to create if they must share the fruits of their creative works. His reliance on these three arguments is misplaced.

George's first contention is negated by our ready recognition today that the author-spouse has the exclusive right to manage and control the copyright. . . . As equal management does not apply to copyrights, federal interests in predictability and efficiency are not impaired by it. A potential purchaser or licensee will still be able to obtain good "title" from the author-spouse alone free of interference from the other spouse.

George's second contention does not persuade us that allowing differing state laws—in particular, community property laws that differ from state to state among the eight that presently have some version of such marital property regimes [Arizona, California, Idaho, Louisiana, Nevada, New Mexico, Texas, Washington]—to apply just to the economic benefit derived from copyrights will somehow damage the federal interests in predictability and uniformity. Indeed, the Act itself subjects copyrights to varying state laws for other purposes. . . . The litigation and management issues arising from [the application of state law to] contractual conveyance and post-mortem devolution of copyrights has not resulted in obstruction of federal interests leading to preemption of state law, and we discern no reason why the community property result we decree today should fare differently.

As for George's third contention—that community entitlement to the "fruits" of copyrights would lessen the author's incentive to create or exploit his works, thereby conflicting with the federal interest in encouraging authorship—we decline to assume globally that the commercial and economic interests of spouses during marriage are so at odds that one spouse would be disinclined to create copyrightable works merely because the economic benefits of his endeavors would inure to the benefit of their community rather than to his separate estate. As for a former spouse's lack of incentive following divorce, ... we are convinced that the duty imposed by Louisiana [to "manage prudently" former community property] is consistent with—not contrary to—the federal interest in encouraging authorship and exploitation of copyrights, just as we are convinced that most if not all authors will continue to exploit their copyrights after termination of the community rather than cutting off their noses to spite their faces by letting copyrighted works languish.

The court of appeals concluded that, although the district court on remand was "to enter judgment recognizing Veronica's entitlement to an undivided one-half interest in the net economic benefits generated by or resulting from copyrighted works created by George during the existence of the community and from any derivatives thereof," it is for the *state* court "that has jurisdiction over judicial partition and settlement of the Rodrigue community to determine both the proper method for establishing the value of Veronica's share of these net economic benefits and the proper procedure for delivery of that share to her, whether that be, for example, by (1) an accounting based on the present value of the appraised fair market value of the fully exploited copyrights and derivatives during their expected lifetimes, (2) periodic accountings and payments to Veronica as the copyrights and derivatives are exploited and proceeds are derived from them, or (3) some other altogether different procedure."

"Conflict preemption" analysis has also been invoked—with inconsistent results—by three courts of appeals dealing with the question of the relationship between section 203 of the Copyright Act, allowing for termination of a copyright grant after 35 years, and state law allowing for immediate termination when the parties have been silent about the matter.

Rano v. Sipa Press, Inc., 987 F.2d 580 (9th Cir.1993). Rano, a professional photographer, in 1978 entered into an oral license agreement of unspecified duration with Sipa Press, a photograph distribution syndicate; he gave Sipa a nonexclusive license to distribute his photographs, and Sipa agreed to pay him 50 percent of the net royalties. The relationship went smoothly for some eight years, but in 1986, Rano informed Sipa that he was changing agencies (claiming that Sipa, among other alleged delinquencies, had been failing to pay timely royalties); and in 1987 Rano wrote Sipa that he "did not authorize Sipa to sell any more of [his] photographs."

Sipa, nonetheless, continued to do so, and Rano sued for copyright infringement and also made a number of state-law claims. The principal question for decision was whether Rano had effectively terminated the 1978 license agreement, thus making later distributions of his photographs by Sipa a copyright infringement.

Rano's first contention was that he was entitled to terminate the license agreement at any time by virtue of California contract law, which allows either party to an agreement of nonspecified duration to terminate it at will. The Court of Appeals for the Ninth Circuit, however, rejected that contention and held that the California law on this issue was preempted.

> [A]pplication of this principle of California contract law here would directly conflict with federal copyright law. Under Section 203 of the Copyright Act, licensing agreements are not terminable at will from the moment of creation; instead, they are terminable at the will of the author only during a five year period beginning at the end of thirty-five years from the date of execution of the license unless they explicitly specify an earlier termination date. 17 U.S.C. § 203(a). Since California law and federal law are in direct conflict, federal law must control.... Section 203 applies to non-exclusive, as well as exclusive, licenses executed by the author on or after January 1, 1978....

The court further held that Rano, as copyright owner, could properly claim infringement in the event that Sipa committed a material breach of contract, but the court found any alleged breach by Sipa to be only minor; it remanded for a ruling upon Rano's state-law claim for breach of contract.

Walthal v. Rusk, 172 F.3d 481 (7th Cir.1999). The plaintiffs, members of a musical group, had by a 1984 oral agreement (without any specified time limit) given the defendant a license to manufacture and sell their recordings; the parties agreed to divide the net profits 50–50. In 1995, the group wanted to increase their share of profits to 80 percent and wanted the agreement to end in three years. The defendant refused to change the terms and the plaintiffs sent a letter terminating the still oral agreement. Under the governing Illinois law, as with the California law in the *Rano* case, a contract of unspecified length is terminable at will. When the defendant continued making and selling their recordings, the plaintiffs sued for copyright infringement. The defendant claimed that termination was prohibited by the 35–year termination provision in § 203(a).

The court strongly disagreed with the defendant, and with the *Rano* decision in the Court of Appeals for the Ninth Circuit which, it observed, had been so thoroughly criticized in the scholarly literature that "if [it] were a Broadway show, bad reviews would have forced it to close after opening night." The court found, particularly in the legislative history, an intention to make 35 years the maximum term of a license rather than the minimum term, in light of the author-protective purpose of the provision, and an intention to allow parties to negotiate for an earlier termination date. The court saw no sense in finding that a contract for a shorter specified term of years does not conflict with § 203, while a contract terminable at will by operation of law does so conflict. The Illinois law in effect impliedly incorporates into the oral license agreement a power to terminate at any time, even short of 35 years. The court stated: "We conclude that allowing terminations under Illinois law does not conflict with § 203, but rather is, in fact, in keeping with the intent of § 203. Therefore, there is no issue of preemption. Under Illinois law, this contract can be terminated, and it is undisputed that the [plaintiffs'] letter of December 8, 1995 did just that. That letter rendered the license agreement *kaput,*" so that the recording company lost its defense to the plaintiffs' action for copyright infringement.

The same year, the Court of Appeals for the Eleventh Circuit addressed the same question—and embraced the analysis and conclusion of the Seventh Circuit—in **Korman v. HBC Florida, Inc.**, 182 F.3d 1291 (11th Cir.1999). The court ended its opinion as follows: "We join the Seventh Circuit in rejecting *Rano*'s conversion of 'casual oral permission into a thirty-five year straitjacket.' 3 Nimmer on Copyright § 11.01[B], at 11–9 (1994). We hold that if state law provides that licenses of indefinite duration may be terminated in less than 35 years, it is state law and not section 203 that governs the question of termination before 35 years."

QUESTIONS

1. In the *Rodrigue* "blue dog" case, do you believe that the court effectively accommodated the federal and state laws so as to avoid any conflict and thus preemption of the latter? For example, do you agree that the Copyright Act, in giving the author spouse the initial ownership of the copyright, gives to him or her only the listed exclusive rights in section 106 but not the exclusive enjoyment of the pertinent revenues? Is that consistent with the "incentive/reward" rationale for copyright? Is it consistent with the policies underlying the § 203(b) termination right?

2. In the *Rodrigue* case, the court stated: "We leave for another day the question whether the author-spouse, in exercising his exclusive rights to exploit and alienate the copyright both during the existence of the community and after its dissolution, has some agency or fiduciary-like duty to the non-author spouse, such as the duty to act in good faith and not in a manner contrary to her interests.... For reasons that are not apparent to us, neither party has invited us to consider Civil Code article 2369.3, which imposes an affirmative duty on a spouse 'to preserve and to manage prudently former community property under his control' and makes him 'answerable for any damage caused by his fault, default, or neglect.' " Would such an obligation—to exploit the copyright so as to enrich the nonauthor spouse—conflict with the right given by the Copyright Act simply to hoard the copyright and bar its use by all others? (Is there such a federal right?)

3. In *Rodrigue*, would you have extended the equal division of royalties between the former spouses so as to embrace all derivative art works created by the husband after the divorce? Would that include red-dog drawings as well as the blue? Animated cartoons (with dialogue provided by the artist) as well as two-dimensional drawings? Red-cat drawings in the same style?

4. On the question presented in the *Rano, Walthal* and *Korman* cases— i.e., the displacement of state rules for terminating a license agreement by the 35–year period in the Copyright Act—which do you regard as the correct result?

5. The Medical College Achievement Test (MCAT) is a copyrighted examination widely used by medical schools in their admissions process; the copyright covers the test forms, test questions and answer sheets. The Association of American Medical Colleges (AAMC) is the copyright owner of these materials, which it attempts to keep secret, and the Copyright Office has "secure test" regulations that permit registration while preserving secrecy. The State of New York has enacted a Truth in Testing Act that declares materials such as the MCAT to be "public records" that are subject to involuntary disclosure. The principal purpose of the statute is to permit citizens to confirm or challenge the validity and objectivity of the test questions and answers.

AAMC has brought an action in a federal court against the Governor and other officials of the State of New York. The Association claims that by forcing AAMC to disclose tests, answers and forms, the state is undermining AAMC's exclusive rights under the Copyright Act to reproduce and distribute these materials, and is facilitating infringement of those rights by others. AAMC claims that the New York statute must therefore be preempted and its enforcement enjoined.

The State of New York contends that, under the Supremacy Clause of the U.S. Constitution, the New York statute should be preempted only if its implementation "stands as an obstacle to the accomplishment and execution of the full purposes and objectives of Congress in proscribing copyright infringement"—which is not the situation here. It also contends that its disclosure requirement should be understood to be a fair use of the copyrighted MCAT materials, such that the policies of the Copyright Act will not be frustrated by the New York statute.

Under either § 301 or the broader Supremacy Clause analysis proffered by the defendant, should an injunction issue against the enforcement of the New York statute? *See Association of Am. Med. Colleges v. Cuomo,* 928 F.2d 519 (2d Cir.), *cert. denied,* 502 U.S. 862, 112 S.Ct. 184, 116 L.Ed.2d 146 (1991).

6. A Pennsylvania statute requires that a motion picture distributor (usually a studio or its authorized distributor) may grant exclusive exhibition rights to a particular movie theater for no more than 42 days, after which it must license a different theater in the same geographic area for the second-run showing of the film. The purpose is to curtail monopolistic and anti-competitive practices. A film distributor and its first-run movie house in Philadelphia have challenged the Pennsylvania statute as inconsistent with the exclusive public-distribution and public-performance rights given to the copyright owner (here, the studio) by the Copyright Act. Must the Pennsylvania act be invalidated? *See Orson, Inc. v. Miramax Film Corp.*, 189 F.3d 377 (3d Cir. *en banc* 1999).

7. ASCAP and BMI, which enforce public-performance rights on behalf of music copyright owners, often utilize undercover investigators who go to establishments—sometimes through repeated visits over a period of time, to detect a pattern of infringement—and monitor and take notes concerning copyrighted music being performed there. In 1995, New York enacted a statute requiring groups such as ASCAP and BMI to provide proprietors with written notice of an investigation within 72 hours after the first undercover visit. The statute empowers the alleged infringer to bring an action against organizations that fail to comply with the notice requirement, and to secure relief such as an injunction, actual damages and attorneys' fees (and to file a state counterclaim therefore in the event a copyright infringement action is brought in a federal court). ASCAP and BMI seek an injunction against implementation of the state statute, as impliedly preempted by the Copyright Act. Should the injunction issue? If so, can the state achieve its objectives through less objectionable measures? *See ASCAP v. Pataki*, 930 F.Supp. 873 (S.D.N.Y.1996); *see also* 1997 Copyr. L. Dec. ¶ 27,649 (S.D.N.Y. 1997).

CHAPTER 10

INTERNATIONAL DIMENSIONS OF COPYRIGHT

A. INTRODUCTION

Protection of exclusive rights in works of authorship has existed in some form since at least the dissemination of printing technology in the late fifteenth century. This protection, however, whether by way of royal privilege or of copyright, was exclusively territorial. Citizens of one nation or city-state might prevent unauthorized reproductions on their own soil, but rarely could they obtain recognition and enforcement of their rights abroad.

International protection of authors' rights developed during the nineteenth century. By the middle of that century, a few European nations had entered into bilateral treaties, or had passed legislation protecting foreign works on the basis of reciprocity.[1] Nonetheless, until the late 1800s, most authors had little recourse beyond endeavoring to secure protection outside their home countries through complex and cumbersome attempts to attribute multiple nationality status to their works. They sought to achieve this by publishing the work simultaneously in the countries whose protection they wished to obtain; under conflicts of law principles still recognized today, a work of authorship assumes the nationality (and hence, entitlement to local protection) of the country where it was first published.[2] *See, e.g., Routledge v. Low*, 3 H.L. 100 (1868) (works first published in Great Britain protected regardless of author's citizenship or domicile); S. Ricketson, *The Berne Convention for the Protection of Literary and Artistic Works 1886–1986*, at 22–23 (1987), listing countries protecting works on the basis of publication within the local territory.

By the mid-nineteenth century, authors' groups were calling for international agreements promoting formality-free protection for works of literature and art. These demands culminated in the adoption, in 1886, of the Berne Union for the Protection of Literary and Artistic Works (discussed

---

1. *See* Abelman & Berkowitz, International Copyright Law, 22 N.Y.L.S. L. Rev. 619, 621–22 (1977). In 1852, however, France took the unusual step of according protection to all works of authorship, regardless of country of origin, and without reference to reciprocity. *See* S. Ricketson, The Berne Convention for the Protection of Literary and Artistic Works 1886–1986, 20–21 (1987).

2. This procedure, however, did not always succeed; failure to achieve simultaneity of first publication, or inadequate compliance with local formalities, such as deposit and registration of the work, often frustrated authors' efforts.

infra Subchapter C.1 of this chapter). Original signatories included most of the Western European nations, as well as one African country, and some Caribbean and Latin–American nations. The United States was not a party to the original Berne Convention, and did not join the Treaty until 1989. This treaty, revised at several instances from 1908 to 1971, is one of two major international copyright agreements currently in force.

In this century, the international dimension of copyright law has assumed increasing importance, particularly to U.S. authors, copyright holders and policy makers. There is now a worldwide market for U.S. copyrighted works, particularly computer software, audiovisual works (including video games), and popular music. There is also worldwide piracy of U.S. copyright works, both in traditional formats, and online. As a result, there has been an increasing linkage of copyright and trade as a part of U.S. policy. This phenomenon began in the late 1980s and accelerated in the 1990s. The economic significance of the core copyright industries to the United States economy in part explains this linkage: $457.2 billion—or 4.9% of the U.S. gross domestic product (GDP)—representing the largest export industry sector in the U.S.[3] The world-wide piracy losses reported by the copyright industries and the U.S. government also account for the trade policy emphasis on copyright protection. The U.S. copyright industries estimate at least $20–22 billion in losses annually due to piracy outside the United States, according to survey results published by the International Intellectual Property Alliance in 2000.[4]

From the isolationist position that characterized U.S. international copyright relations until the middle of this century, the U.S. has become one of the leading proponents of adequate and effective transnational copyright protection. United States efforts in the last half-century to promote and secure international trade in copyrighted works have included sponsorship and membership in the other leading international copyright treaty, the Universal Copyright Convention. In 1988 the U.S. adopted the legislative changes necessary to join the Berne Convention, and treaty accession became effective on March 1, 1989. The U.S. has also entered into many bilateral agreements. These take two forms—either copyright bilateral agreements establishing a point of attachment and substantive rights for works of the United States and another country, or trade-related bilateral agreements. The latter usually impose obligations on foreign governments to increase levels of protection and enforcement for copyrighted works (and

---

3. Stephen E. Siwek & Gale Mosteller, *Copyright Industries in the U.S. Economy* (1998), Report prepared for the International Intellectual Property Alliance.

4. *See* 2001 Special 301 Recommendations of the International Intellectual Property Alliance (IIPA), filing of February 16, 2001 cover letter of Eric H. Smith, President IIPA to Joseph Papovich, Assistant USTR

for Services, Investment and Intellectual Property; Office of the United States Trade Representative. The IIPA filed its annual report on piracy detailing copyright law and enforcement deficiencies in 58 countries (total estimated losses of $7.9 billion in 2000) in response to a January 16, 2001 Federal Register Request for Written Submissions. The entire report, including the cover letter, is available at http://www.iipa.com.

sound recordings) in exchange for the U.S. granting preferable trade benefits (or, for failure to meet perceived international standards, imposing trade-based sanctions on such countries). The trade-based approach led the U.S. to promote the TRIPs (Trade Related Aspects of Intellectual Property) accord, as part of the multilateral trade negotiations that produced the World Trade Organization agreement of 1994. This multilateral approach increased the international standards of protection of copyrighted material, and especially copyright enforcement, in WTO member countries, supplementing the Berne Convention's minimum levels of protection. Most recently, in 1998, the U.S. ratified the 1996 WIPO Copyright Treaty (WCT) and the 1996 WIPO Performers and Phonograms Treaty (WPPT) to add new obligations for copyright and neighboring rights for the use of material in "digital" formats.

B. EARLY HISTORY OF U.S. INTERNATIONAL COPYRIGHT RELATIONS

Sandison, The Berne Convention and the Universal Copyright Convention: The American Experience, 11 Colum.-V.L.A. J.L. & Arts 89, 90–95 (1986)

[Former Register of Copyrights Barbara Ringer has stated: "Until the Second World War the United States had little reason to take pride in its international copyright relations; in fact, it had a great deal to be ashamed of. With few exceptions its role in international copyright was marked by short-sightedness, political isolationism, and narrow economic self-interest."[5]

The grounds for this American self-criticism are twofold: in the first place, up to 1891, the United States denied copyright protection altogether to published works by nonresident foreigners; secondly, up to 1955 [when the United States joined the Universal Copyright Convention], the United States refused to enter into multilateral copyright relations outside the Western Hemisphere. Thus, for almost 200 years, it is fair to describe the American approach to international copyright relations as essentially isolationist.

The roots of American isolationism are clearly evident in the U.S. Copyright Act of 1790, which afforded protection to published works only if their authors were citizens or residents of the United States. In this respect, the first federal copyright statute merely mirrored antecedent state copyright statutes enacted by all but one of the 13 newly independent states between 1783 and 1786, which limited their protection to the works of U.S. residents. Of course, the United States was not alone in denying copyright protection to nonresident foreigners at that time: it was not until

---

5. Ringer, *The Role of the United States in International Copyright—Past, Present,* *and Future,* 56 Geo. L.J. 1050, 1051 (1968).

the first half of the 19th century that such protection was allowed, first by Denmark in 1828 and then by the other major nations of Europe. However, subsequent revisions of the U.S. copyright statute in 1802, 1831, 1856, 1865 and 1870, while greatly expanding the subject matter of protection, still left published works by nonresident foreigners unprotected.

In the absence of copyright protection under U.S. law, literary piracy of foreign—and particularly British—works grew dramatically in the 19th century. Not surprisingly, this produced great resentment among British authors, and none was more vociferous in his condemnation of U.S. law than Charles Dickens. Reporting on a visit to North America in 1842, Dickens wrote to his future biographer:

> I spoke, as you know, of international copyright, at Boston; and I spoke of it again at Hartford. My friends were paralysed with wonder at such audacious daring. The notion that I, a man alone by himself, in America, should venture to suggest to the Americans that there was one point on which they were neither just to their own countrymen nor to us, actually struck the boldest dumb! Washington Irving, Prescott, Hoffman, Bryant, Halleck, Dana, Washington Allston—every man who writes in this country is devoted to the question, and not one of them *dares* to raise his voice and complain of the atrocious state of the law. It is nothing that of all men living I am the greatest loser by it. It is nothing that I have a claim to speak and be heard. The wonder is that a breathing man can be found with temerity enough to suggest to the Americans the possibility of their having done wrong. I wish you could have seen the faces that I saw, down both sides of the table at Hartford, when I began to talk about Scott. I wish you could have heard how I gave it out. My blood so boiled as I thought of the monstrous injustice that I felt as if I were twelve feet high when I thrust it down their throats.

Unsuccessful attempts to establish copyright treaty relations with Great Britain were made in 1837, in 1853, and again in 1880–81, foundering each time on the opposition of American publishers who believed that their financial success depended upon being able to sell cheap reprints of British books. . . .

Notwithstanding the opposition of the "book-selling leviathans" [as Anthony Trollope branded American publishers] and their friends in Congress, the movement for international copyright protection continued to gain ground in the United States in the second half of the 19th century, supported by a majority of American authors as well as a growing number of publishers. Most American authors favored copyright protection for foreign works, not only as a matter of principle, but also on economic grounds: without international copyright protection, they faced unfair competition from unauthorized reprints of British books which were cheaper because their British authors received no royalties. As Max Kampelman has noted, "American readers were less inclined to read the novels of Cooper or Hawthorne for a dollar when they could buy a novel of Scott or Dickens for a quarter." American authors were also hurt by the lack of reciprocal protection abroad. Longfellow, for example, complained that, although he had twenty-two publishers in England and Scotland, "only four of them took the slightest notice of my existence, even so far as to send me a copy of the book." American publishers, too, increasingly felt that action was needed to combat widespread literary piracy of foreign works, although they qualified their position by insisting that a foreign work should not be protected unless it was domestically manufactured.

Agitation for international copyright protection in the United States finally achieved success in the International Copyright Act of 1891. This legislation made copyright protection available to published works by nonresident foreigners on the basis of a proclamation by the President to the effect that their nation either afforded U.S. citizens copyright protection "on substantially the same basis as its own citizens" or was a party to an international agreement, to which the United States was also a party, providing for "reciprocity in the granting of copyright."[29] At the same time, however, the 1891 Act introduced a new requirement of domestic manufacture as a condition of copyright protection for every "book, photograph, chromo or lithograph."[30]

As Barbara Ringer has noted, this so-called "Manufacturing Clause" was the "compromise that made the Act of 1891 possible," since it effectively neutralized the opposition of American publishers. On the other hand, she points out that the requirements of the Manufacturing Clause "were so rigid that they made the extension of copyright protection to foreigners illusory." . . .

Under the authority of the 1891 Act, Presidential proclamations were issued in that year extending U.S. protection to the nationals of Great Britain and three other European nations. From 1891 to 1955, these and subsequent Presidential proclamations were in fact the principal source of international copyright relations between the United States and the rest of the world. The United States stayed out of Berne, and although it entered into two multilateral copyright treaties prior to 1955—the Mexico City Convention of 1902 and the Buenos Aires Convention of 1910—these so-called "Pan American" Conventions were of limited application: their membership was confined to nations of the Western Hemisphere and they did not relieve the nationals of one member nation of the obligation of complying with the domestic formalities of another member nation.

. . .

29. Act of March 3, 1891, ch. 565, § 13, 26 Stat. 1110 (1891). The Copyright Act of 1909 added a third basis for a presidential proclamation, namely, the granting by a foreign nation to American citizens of "copyright protection substantially equal to the protection secured" such foreign nation's nationals by American law or treaty. Copyright Act of 1909, § 8, 35 Stat. 1075 (1909).

30. Acts of March 3, 1891, ch. 565, § 3, 26 Stat. 1106 (1891). The other formalities of domestic copyright protection—including registration and deposit of copies—were also made applicable to foreign works under the 1891 Act. See Ringer, *supra* note 5, at 1056–57.

[Editors' Note: The United States finally joined a worldwide multilateral copyright treaty in 1955, when it ratified the Universal Copyright Convention [UCC]. As part of UCC adherence, the U.S. abandoned the requirement that foreign English-language works be printed in the U.S. The Manufacturing Clause, however, continued to apply to U.S. authors. As a result, a provision once intended to deprive foreigners of meaningful U.S. copyright protection now burdened U.S. authors, for it prevented U.S. parties from reducing production costs by importing authorized copies made more cheaply abroad. Nonetheless, the Manufacturing Clause remained in the 1976 act, despite increasing opposition from authors' groups. The 1976 compromise called for the clause's expiration in 1984. That year, however, Congress again voted, over the President's veto, to extend the clause until 1986. The Manufacturing Clause survived a first amendment challenge in *Authors League of Am. v. Oman,* 790 F.2d 220 (2d Cir.1986), but finally expired at the end of 1986.]

C. INTERNATIONAL CONVENTIONS AND AGREEMENTS

The U.S. is now party to the two leading international copyright agreements, the Berne Convention and the Universal Copyright Convention. As of October 2001, the former convention had 148 members, and as of May 1999, the latter had 96. The memberships are not completely overlapping, however. As of 2001, dozens of countries belonged only to the Berne Convention, but very few (e.g. Saudi Arabia) adhered to the UCC but not to Berne. Adherents to the Berne Convention, but not the UCC, are especially common in the Middle East, Africa, and the former republics of the Soviet Union.* In many instances, the U.S. had no copyright relations with these countries before becoming a party to Berne.

In order to understand the U.S.'s treaty obligations and benefits, the student should first apprehend the general framework of these, and certain other copyright-related, treaties. Finally, it is also important to sketch U.S. bilateral copyright arrangements, not only because these afford our only copyright relationships with certain nations, but because bilaterals may be assuming increasing importance in the U.S.'s strategy for international copyright protection, and in the protection of older works that are not otherwise protected by Berne or the UCC, and for certain materials such as sound recordings, the "neighboring rights" treaties, such as the Geneva Phonograms Convention.

1. THE STRUCTURE OF THE LEADING MULTILATERAL COPYRIGHT TREATIES

The Berne Convention, the WTO/TRIPs accord, the WCT and the Universal Copyright Convention all combine imposition of supranational substantive rules with the principle of national treatment. The supranational substantive rules address both the subject matter protected and the rights afforded. The more recent multilateral instruments, the TRIPs and

* See U.S. Copyright Office Circular 38a, available at www.loc.gov/copyright.

the WCT, heighten the threshold of minimum protection, notably with regard to digital uses of works created in traditional and electronic form.

The criteria for a work's inclusion in the treaties' ambit are essentially the same in both the Berne and Universal Copyright Conventions. A work will qualify for protection under the treaties if its country of origin is a signatory. The notion of country of origin is generous: the Conventions set forth many points of contact so as to increase the possibility of a work's inclusion. In general, country of origin is determined according to the author's citizenship or residence, or according to the country of first publication. A work will come within the treaties' reach if, whether the work is published or unpublished, its author is a national or resident of a member country. It will also be protected if it is first published in a member country. Under both Conventions, moreover, "first" publication encompasses publication in a member country within 30 days of actual initial publication, if that act occurs in a nonsignatory country. (*See* Berne, art. 3; UCC, art. II. See also 17 U.S.C. § 104(b).)

With regard to the legal regime of protection, in most instances the treaties operate on the principle of National Treatment: they provide that a qualifying foreign work shall receive, at a minimum, the same protection as would a local work. As a result, under these treaties, the law applicable to determine the scope of protection is the law of the country where protection is sought—generally, the law of the forum.

Designation of the forum's law to resolve most questions of infringement advances the principle of nondiscrimination against foreign authors. It also presents a practical advantage: local courts need not master a foreign copyright law. On the other hand, some anomalies result from the national treatment rule. If local laws substantively differ, a work may receive different degrees of protection depending on which side of an international border an infringement occurs. Indeed, the work may be protected in member countries even though it never qualified for protection in its country of origin. (*See* Berne, art. 5.2). The national treatment rule therefore does not necessarily enhance predictability of outcome in the international trade in copyrighted works. Two features of the treaties, however, temper the disruption that disparity of local laws might otherwise provoke. First, the treaties provide for certain substantive minima of protection, thus preventing a member country from refusing to accord effective protection to core classes of copyrighted works. Second, the treaties provide either explicitly, or implicitly, for some exceptions to applicability of the forum's law.

With respect to substantive minima, both the Berne Convention and the Universal Copyright Convention prescribe categories of works to be protected, minimum periods of protection, limitations on imposition of formalities, and forms of exploitation in which exclusive rights, or in some instances, at least equitable remuneration, must be assured. The categories of works encompass a broad range of literary and artistic works, including musical compositions and audiovisual works. The TRIPs accord and the WCT have added computer programs and databases to the list (TRIPs, art.

10; WCT, arts. 4 & 5). Sound recordings, however, do not come within the ambit of these categories. *See* Berne, art. 2; UCC, art. I; *but see* WPPT, discussed *infra* subsection 2. Regarding duration of copyright, the Berne Convention generally specifies a minimum period of life plus 50 years (or, for cinematographic, anonymous and pseudonymous works—when the author's identity is in fact unknown, 50 years) (art. 7), while the Universal Copyright Convention generally requires protection for no less than the life of the author plus 25 years or no less than 25 years from publication.

The Conventions diverge somewhat over the question of formalities. The Berne Convention categorically states: "The enjoyment and exercise of these rights [under copyright] shall not be subject to any formality" (art. 5.2). That treaty therefore prohibits not only formalities prerequisite to securing copyright protection (such as, under the U.S. 1909 Act, the notice requirement), but those necessary to its effective exercise and pursuit (such as, under the U.S. 1976 Act, the requirement of registration before initiation of a copyright infringement suit). The UCC allows member countries to require compliance with formalities, but somewhat simplifies their array. Under UCC art. III, all of a member country's conditions on the initial existence of copyright shall be deemed satisfied if the foreign work was first and continuously published with an accompanying notice described in the Treaty. (UCC, art. III notice is essentially the same as the notice required by the U.S. 1976 Act before the 1988 amendments.) As a result of U.S. adherence for the Berne Convention, affixation of notice is no longer necessary for domestic protection, nor to protection in other Berne countries. It is required, however, for coverage in those few countries which are UCC, but not Berne, adherents, and which impose formalities.

The UCC also permits member countries to demand compliance with "procedural" formalities, such as registration and deposit prior to initiation of suit. (Art. III.3). Most interpretations of the Berne Convention, by contrast, deem such pre-suit conditions to be just as much proscribed as are formalities going to the initial existence of copyright. Although the 1988 amendments to the U.S. copyright act eliminated the pre-suit registration prerequisite for foreign works from Berne countries, the requirement is retained for U.S. and other foreign works.

The primary forms of exploitation guaranteed by the Conventions are the rights of reproduction and public performance (including broadcasting). (Berne, arts. 9.1, 11^{bis}1, 11ter; *UCC, art. 4^{bis}1*). The WCT has generalized the public performance right into a "right of communication to the public" (art. 8), including by digital means. (The WPPT art. 15, adds a right to remuneration for broadcasting and communication to the public for performers and producers of sound recordings, discussed *infra*.). The right of translation is another form of exploitation both treaties explicitly grant (subject to certain limitations, some of which are available to all states, and others of which specifically favor third-world nations). (Berne, arts. 8, 11.2, appendix; UCC, arts. V.1, V$^{bis,\ ter,\ quater}$). *The Berne Convention further specifies the protection of moral rights. (Art. 6bis).* The TRIPs accord, however, which incorporates most of the Berne Convention, explicitly excludes moral rights from the treaty requirements (art. 9.1).

Concerning limitations on exclusive rights, the Berne Convention imposes no exceptions but permits member countries to institute certain compulsory licenses, particularly in the domains of mechanical reproduction and broadcast-cable. (Arts. 13, 11^{bis}2). That treaty also authorizes a limited exemption from the reproduction right for purposes of teaching, criticism, and commentary (art. 10). Moreover, member countries may provide for other exceptions to the reproduction right, (1) in certain special cases, so long as these (2) do not conflict with a normal exploitation of the work, and (3) do not unreasonably prejudice the legitimate interests of the author (art. 9.2). The WCT (and WPPT) generalized this "three-step test" to apply to exceptions and limitations to all the exclusive rights under copyright (art. 10). *See also* TRIPs, art. 13. The Universal Copyright Convention tolerates any exception that does "not conflict with the spirit and provisions of" that treaty, so long as member countries "nevertheless accord a reasonable degree of effective protection to each of the rights to which exception has been made." (UCC, art. IV^{bis}2).

The treaties further reduce the likelihood of highly disparate results in transnational protection by providing for certain exceptions to the rule of National Treatment. Most significantly, both documents state that where the duration of protection is shorter in the country of origin than in the forum country, the shorter period prevails. (Berne, art. 7.8; UCC, art. IV.4).[6] Curiously, neither treaty clearly designates which law, that of the country of origin or of the forum, generally governs the ownership and transfer of rights under copyright,[7] but these issues, at least in some instances, may also fall outside the national treatment rule. We will return to the topic of copyright ownership later.

2.   OTHER MAJOR MULTILATERAL TREATIES RELATED TO COPYRIGHT

As mentioned earlier, neither the Berne Convention nor the Universal Copyright Convention covers sound recordings.[8] This is primarily because many countries other than the U.S. do not believe that the making of a sound recording comprehends sufficient originality of authorship, as op-

---

6. The UCC provision, however, is not self-executing. Thus, an adherent must enact specific legislation to limit other member countries' works to their national copyright terms, otherwise the work will automatically receive the forum's term. The U.S. Congress has determined that the Berne Convention is not self-executing, Berne Convention Implementation Act of 1988, § 2, Pub. L. No. 100–568, 102 Stat. 2853 (1988), hence, absent specific legislation, the U.S. would not apply the Berne shorter term rule either.

7. An exception is Berne, art. 14*bis*, making the law of the "country where protection is claimed" the governing legislation regarding certain questions of ownership and transfer of rights in cinematographic works.

8. However, they nevertheless can be covered by these conventions. For example, since the U.S. does protect "sound recordings" under copyright law, see § 102(a)(7), foreign sound recordings in the U.S. are afforded Berne subject matter protection unilaterally.

posed to technical expertise, to qualify for copyright protection. A separate treaty, the Geneva Phonograms Convention, protects rights of reproduction, public distribution, and importation of sound recordings. This treaty also operates on the principle of national treatment, leaving it to member countries to protect sound recordings either by means of copyright, of a specific right, of unfair competition, or by criminal sanctions. Another "neighboring rights" treaty is the Rome Convention, but the U.S. is not a party to it.

The 1996 WIPO Performers and Phonograms Treaty updates the Geneva Phonograms Convention, notably by clarifying the application of the phonogram producer's exclusive reproduction right "in any manner or form" including digital media (art. 7 and Agreed Statement), and a distribution right (art. 8). With respect to performers' rights, the treaty elaborates on the rights set forth in the TRIPs agreement (art. 14.1) to prevent the fixation, reproduction and broadcasting and communication to the public of their live performances. The WPPT also provides for a performers' and producers' right of remuneration for broadcasting and communication to the public, but permits member States to limit or decline to apply this provision (art. 15).

3. BILATERAL COPYRIGHT ARRANGEMENTS

Before the U.S. joined the Universal Copyright Convention in 1955, bilateral copyright agreements provided the predominant basis of overseas protection of U.S. works, and, correspondingly, of U.S. protection of foreign works (essentially from 1891 until 1955). The 1909 Act authorized protection for alien authors if the foreign nation granted nondiscriminatory or reciprocal protection to U.S. authors; the President was to determine by proclamation that the foreign state was according such protection (a similar provision persists in the 1976 Act, 17 U.S.C. § 104, discussed *infra*).

Following U.S. adherence to the UCC, bilateral arrangements receded from the U.S. international copyright scene. There were almost no states with which the U.S. had had bilateral arrangements who were not also UCC members. Now that the U.S. is a Berne and WTO/TRIPS member, even fewer bilateral agreements remain important as the sole point of attachment (though they may protect older works not covered by the UCC, and, in a very few cases, Berne). In fact, only one country, Vietnam, is known to rely on a bilateral agreement as a point of attachment.

Beginning in the late 1980s however, the U.S. signed many bilateral trade agreements containing intellectual property rights (IPR) provisions. These agreements required signatories to amend their domestic copyright and neighboring rights laws (and civil and criminal codes) to raise the minimum levels of protection and enforcement. In particular, as Eastern Europe and the former Soviet Union moved to democratic governments and market economies, bilateral agreements were signed by the U.S. with virtually every country in that region in exchange for preferential trade benefits (Most Favored Nation (MFN) status, now known as Normal Trade Relations (NTR)).[9]

9. *See* Eric Schwartz, *Recent Developments in the Copyright Regimes of the Soviet* Union and Eastern Europe, 38 J. Copyright Soc'y, 123 (1991) (although this article was

The bilateral route offers some attractions. First, as noted, it ensures protection for U.S. works prior to the foreign state's adherence to a multilateral treaty. Second, it may in fact secure a *greater* degree of protection than available under a multilateral treaty, especially in the case of trade agreements that raised the UCC or Berne minima to 1980 or 1990 levels of protection and enforcement. As of 2001, the U.S. had entered into bilateral copyright and trade arrangements with IPR obligations with at least 30 nations.

D.   U.S.–BASED COPYRIGHT ACTIONS WITH AN INTERNATIONAL DIMENSION

1.   PROTECTION OF ALIEN AUTHORS

The Register's Report on Revision of the U.S. Copyright Law recommended in 1961 that all foreign and domestic works be protected on the same basis, without regard to the nationality of the author (subject to restriction by presidential proclamation). *Report of the Register of Copyrights on the General Revision of the U.S. Copyright Law, Report to House Committee on the Judiciary,* 87th Cong., 1st Sess. 119 (1961). But this proposal never saw the light of legislative day; at least as to published works, the 1976 Act carries forward, though in liberalized form, the policy laid down in the Act of 1891, 26 Stat. 1106, and followed in the 1909 Act. Under this policy, the United States demands a quid pro quo for the extension of the copyright privilege to the nationals of any foreign state or nation who are not domiciled here.[10]

Absent treaty obligations, most foreign countries likewise condition copyright for non-domiciliary aliens on the existence of protection for their own nationals in the alien's country. Even France, which had long pursued a policy of protecting foreign authors regardless of the absence of reciprocal protection of French works in the author's country of origin, see generally H. Desbois, Le Droit D'Auteur en France 916–22 (3d ed. 1978), finally reserved the right to deny protection to works from countries that do not protect French works. Decree of July 8, 1964.

Once a foreign work qualifies for protection, the basic rule of treatment, both in the United States and abroad, is "national" rather than strictly "reciprocal" treatment: protection is granted on the same terms as

written before the dissolution of the Soviet Union, it discusses, and includes copies of, bilateral agreements still in force with many Eastern European countries).

10. But, when the United States joined the WTO/TRIPs Agreement, effective January 1, 1996, the U.S. provided full retroactive protection for pre-existing works, including sound recordings, for all Berne, UCC and WTO member countries without regard to any reciprocal treatment of American works in each such country. *See* 17 U.S.C. § 104A.

apply to a U.S. citizen and not on the terms of protection available in the alien's country.

In its coverage of all unpublished material (much of which had been protected by the common law), the 1976 Act adopts the common law rule of protection for unpublished works irrespective of the nationality or domicile of the author. *See* § 104(a). With respect to published works, however, protection is available under § 104(b), as amended in 1998, only if at least one of the following four conditions is satisfied:

(1) one or more of the authors is, at the time of first publication, a national or domiciliary of:

(a) the United States, or

(b) a country with which we have a copyright or similar treaty, including the Berne Convention and the Universal Copyright Convention (or the author is the sovereign authority of such a country), the WTO Agreement, or the WCT or WPPT (the latter for sound recordings only), or

(c) no country, i.e., a stateless person. *Cf. Houghton Mifflin Co. v. Stackpole Sons, Inc.,* 104 F.2d 306 (2d Cir.), *cert. denied,* 308 U.S. 597 (1939) (stateless persons protected under general grant of § 9 of 1909 law, since only citizens of foreign states must meet the specified nationality requirements);

(2) the work is first published in the United States or in a Berne or Universal Copyright Convention or WTO or WCT or WPPT (for sound recordings), country;

(3) the work is first published by the United Nations (or any of its specialized agencies) or the Organization of American States; or

(4) the work comes within the scope of a presidential proclamation finding that the author's country accords nondiscriminatory or national treatment to works of United States authorship or first publication. (Preexisting proclamations remain in force until further presidential action. Trans. & Suppl. § 104 (90 Stat. 2599).)

Domicile within the meaning of this section is no different from the ordinary usage of this legal term. To acquire domicile in the U.S., there must be residence with intention to remain in the United States, which may be inferred from various circumstances such as declarations, marriage to an American, payment of taxes, establishment of a home, etc. *See G. Ricordi & Co. v. Columbia Graphophone Co.,* 258 F. 72 (S.D.N.Y.1919).

Of course, aside from these specific provisions, another basis of protection is any treaty supplementing Title 17 of the United States Code as the copyright "law of the land."

QUESTIONS

1. France is a member of the Berne Convention. Vietnam has recently entered into a bilateral agreement with the United States that includes mutual obligations with respect to copyright. Iraq is one of the countries with which the United States has no copyright relations.

Which, if any, of the following works would be protected in the United States?:

(a) A work by a Vietnamese author, first published in Iraq.

(b) A work by an Iraqi author, first published in Vietnam.

(c) A work by an Iraqi author, first published in France.

(d) A work by an Iraqi author living in France.

(e) A work by an Iraqi author employed by a French company.

2. A foreign nation is neither a member of a multilateral copyright treaty nor party to a bilateral treaty with the United States. Indeed, that country has no domestic copyright law. You are counsel to an American company interested in becoming the United States distributor for dolls created and initially distributed in the foreign country by local creators. What problems do you see? What advice would you give your client?

3. Under § 104, first publication in the U.S. affords foreigners one means of protecting their works in the U.S. Whether the first publication occurred in the U.S., however, may not always be evident. Section 101 defines publication as public distribution of copies, or as the "offering to distribute copies or phonorecords to a group of persons for purposes of further distribution, public performance, or public display." Suppose a national of a country with whom the U.S. has no copyright relations seeks a U.S. distributor for the work. Assume further that the work has yet to be publicly distributed anywhere. Does an exchange of correspondence and/or telephone calls to and from the U.S. and the foreign state regarding the proposed distribution constitute an offering in the U.S. for purposes of § 101? If the offeree-distributor is a single "person," natural or juridical, does the offering fail to meet § 101 criteria? Does § 101's reference to "further" distribution, public performance, or public display imply initial acts in the U.S.?

4. If a work is first publicly disclosed over the Internet, what is its country of first publication?

2. JURISDICTION OF U.S. COURTS TO ADJUDICATE COPYRIGHT CLAIMS PRESENTING AN EXTRATERRITORIAL ELEMENT

It is important here to keep in mind the distinction between jurisdiction to adjudicate, and choice of law. The U.S. federal courts may have subject matter jurisdiction over an international copyright claim by virtue of the grant of federal jurisdiction over copyright claims set forth in 28 U.S.C. § 1338(a), to which the foreign copyright claims are "supplemental," see 28 U.S.C. § 1367. Or, the federal court may exercise subject matter jurisdiction by virtue of diversity of the parties' citizenship (and an amount in controversy of $75,000 or more) under 28 U.S.C. § 1332(a)(2). In the latter instance, a U.S. federal court has jurisdiction to adjudicate a claim of violation of a foreign copyright law, if the suit is between "citizens of a State and citizens or subjects of a foreign state." The following decisions discuss the circumstances under which a U.S. court might retain jurisdiction over a copyright infringement action, even though U.S. law does not apply to the claim.

London Film Productions, Ltd. v. Intercontinental Communications, Inc.

580 F.Supp. 47 (S.D.N.Y.1984).

■ ROBERT L. CARTER, DISTRICT JUDGE.

This case presents a novel question of law. Plaintiff, London Film Productions, Ltd. ("London"), a British corporation, has sued Intercontinental Communications, Inc. ("ICI"), a New York corporation based in New York City, for infringements of plaintiff's British copyright. The alleged infringements occurred in Chile and other South American countries. In bringing the case before this Court, plaintiff has invoked the Court's diversity jurisdiction. 28 U.S.C. § 1332(a)(2). Defendant has moved to dismiss plaintiff's complaint, arguing that the Court should abstain from exercising jurisdiction over this action.

Background

London produces feature motion pictures in Great Britain, which it then distributes throughout the world. ICI specializes in the licensing of motion pictures, produced by others, that it believes are in the public domain. London's copyright infringement claim is based mainly on license agreements between ICI and Dilatsa S.A., a buying agent for Chilean television stations. The agreements apparently granted the latter the right to distribute and exhibit certain of plaintiff's motion pictures on television in Chile. London also alleges that ICI has marketed several of its motion pictures in Venezuela, Peru, Equador, Costa Rica and Panama, as well as in Chile.

Plaintiff alleges that the films that are the subjects of the arrangements between Dilatsa S.A. and defendant are protected by copyright in Great Britain as well as in Chile and most other countries (but not in the United States) by virtue of the terms and provisions of the Berne Convention.* The license agreements, it maintains, have unjustly enriched defendants and deprived plaintiff of the opportunity to market its motion pictures for television use.

Defendant questions this Court's jurisdiction because plaintiff has not alleged any acts of wrongdoing on defendant's part that constitute violations of United States law,[3] and, therefore, defendant claims that this Court lacks a vital interest in the suit. In addition, assuming jurisdiction, defendant argues that because the Court would have to construe "alien treaty rights," with which it has no familiarity, the suit would violate, in

---

* [Editors' Note: At the time of this decision the U.S. was not party to the Berne Convention.]

3. The films named, although formerly subject to United States copyrights, are no longer so subject.

principle, the doctrine of *forum non conveniens*. In further support of this contention, defendant maintains that the law would not only be foreign, but complex, since plaintiff's claims would have to be determined with reference to each of the South American states in which the alleged copyright infringements occurred.

Determination

There seems to be no dispute that plaintiff has stated a valid cause of action under the copyright laws of a foreign country. Also clear is the fact that this Court has personal jurisdiction over defendant; in fact, there is no showing that defendant may be subject to personal jurisdiction in another forum. Under these circumstances, one authority on copyright law has presented an argument pursuant to which this Court has jurisdiction to hear the matter before it. M. Nimmer, 3 Nimmer on Copyright (1982). It is based on the theory that copyright infringement constitutes a transitory cause of action,[4] and hence may be adjudicated in the courts of a sovereign other than the one in which the cause of action arose. *Id.* at § 1703. That theory appears sound in the absence of convincing objections by defendant to the contrary.

Although plaintiff has not alleged the violation of any laws of this country by defendant, this Court is not bereft of interest in this case. The Court has an obvious interest in securing compliance with this nation's laws by citizens of foreign nations who have dealings within this jurisdiction. A concern with the conduct of American citizens in foreign countries is merely the reciprocal of that interest. An unwillingness by this Court to hear a complaint against its own citizens with regard to a violation of foreign law will engender, it would seem, a similar unwillingness on the part of a foreign jurisdiction when the question arises concerning a violation of our laws by one of its citizens who has since left our jurisdiction. This Court's interest in adjudicating the controversy in this case may be indirect, but its importance is not thereby diminished.

Of course, not every violation of foreign law by a citizen of this country must be afforded a local tribunal, and defendants cite several cases in which, basically under general principles of comity, it would be inappropriate for this Court to exercise its jurisdiction. *Cf. Kalmich v. Bruno,* 404 F. Supp. 57, 61 (N.D.Ill.1975), *rev'd on other grounds,* 553 F.2d 549 (7th Cir.1977), *cert. denied,* 434 U.S. 940 (1977). This is not one of those. The line of cases on which defendants rely can be distinguished on significant points. The Court in *Vanity Fair Mills, Inc. v. T. Eaton, Ltd.,* 234 F.2d 633 (2d Cir.), *cert. denied,* 352 U.S. 871 (1956), the principal case of those cited, found that the district court had not abused its discretion in declining to assume jurisdiction over a claim for acts of alleged trademark infringement and unfair competition arising in Canada under Canadian law. As defendant here has acknowledged, the complaint raised a "crucial issue" as to

---

4. *See* 3 Nimmer, *supra* at § 12.01[C] (copyright is intangible incorporeal right; it has no situs apart from domicile of proprietor).

the validity of Canadian trademark law. This factor weighed heavily in the Court's decision.

> We do not think it the province of United States district courts to determine the validity of trademarks which officials of foreign countries have seen fit to grant. To do so would be to welcome conflicts with the administrative and judicial officers of the Dominion of Canada.

Id. at 647. But as Nimmer has noted, "[i]n adjudicating an infringement action under a foreign copyright law there is . . . no need to pass upon the validity of acts of foreign government officials," 3 Nimmer, *supra,* at § 1703, since foreign copyright laws, by and large, do not incorporate administrative formalities which must be satisfied to create or perfect a copyright. *Id.*

The facts in this case confirm the logic of Nimmer's observation. The British films at issue here received copyright protection in Great Britain simply by virtue of publication there. Copinger, Law of Copyright (9th ed. 1958), 21 et seq. Chile's adherence to the Berne Convention in 1970 automatically conferred copyright protection on these films in Chile. Therefore, no "act of state" is called into question here. Moreover, there is no danger that foreign courts will be forced to accept the inexpert determination of this Court, nor that this Court will create "an unseemly conflict with the judgment of another country." *See Packard Instrument Co. v. Beckman Instruments, Inc.,* 346 F. Supp. 408, 410 (N.D.Ill.1972). The litigation will determine only whether an American corporation has acted in violation of a foreign copyright, not whether such copyright exists, nor whether such copyright is valid.

With respect to defendant's *forum non conveniens* arguments, it is true that this case will likely involve the construction of at least one, if not several foreign laws.[6] However, the need to apply foreign law is not in itself reason to dismiss or transfer the case. *Manu Int'l S.A. v. Avon Products, Inc.,* 641 F.2d 62, 67–68 (2d Cir.1981). Moreover, there is no foreign forum in which defendant is the subject of personal jurisdiction, and an available forum is necessary to validate dismissal of an action on the ground of *forum non conveniens,* for if there is no alternative forum "the plaintiff might find himself with a valid claim but nowhere to assert it." *Farmanfarmaian v. Gulf Oil Corp.,* 437 F. Supp. 910, 915 (S.D.N.Y.1977) (Carter, J.), *aff'd,* 588 F.2d 880 (2d Cir.1978).

While this Court might dismiss this action subject to conditions that would assure the plaintiff of a fair hearing, *Mizokami Bros. of Ariz. v. Mobay Chemical Corp.,* 660 F.2d 712, 719 (8th Cir.1981), neither plaintiff nor defendant has demonstrated the relative advantage in convenience that

---

6. Plaintiff has alleged infringements in Chile, Venezuela, Peru, Ecuador, Costa Rica and Panama. Since, under the Berne Convention, the applicable law is the copyright law of the state in which the infringement oc- curred, [sic] defendant seems correct in its assumption that the laws of several countries will be involved in the case. 3 Nimmer, *supra* at § 17.05.

another forum, compared to this one, would provide. *Overseas Programming Companies v. Cinematographische Commerz–Anstalt*, 684 F.2d 232, 235 (2d Cir.1982). The selection of a South American country as an alternative forum, although it would afford greater expertise in applying relevant legal principles, would seem to involve considerable hardship and inconvenience for both parties. A British forum might similarly provide some advantages in the construction of relevant law, however, it would impose additional hardships upon defendant, and would raise questions, as would the South American forum, regarding enforceability of a resulting judgment. *See American Rice, Inc. v. Arkansas Rice Growers Co-op. Ass'n,* 701 F.2d 408, 417 (5th Cir.1983). Where the balance does not tip strongly in favor of an alternative forum it is well-established that the plaintiff's choice of forum should not be disturbed.

For all of the above reasons, the Court finds it has jurisdiction over the instant case and defendant's motion to dismiss is denied, as is its motion to have the Court abstain from exercising its jurisdiction here. . . .

———

Armstrong v. Virgin Records, 91 F. Supp. 2d 628 (S.D.N.Y.2000). The plaintiff, a U.S. resident performing artist, brought a copyright infringement action against British performers and record producers, alleging that defendants' work unlawfully "sampled" his recorded performances. Defendants' recordings had been distributed in the U.K. and the U.S., but were made in the U.K. The defendants moved to dismiss for lack of subject matter jurisdiction, on the ground that U.S. copyright law did not apply to the making of the recordings in the U.K., and that the U.S. court lacked jurisdiction to apply English copyright law to the acts committed in the U.K. The court agreed that, absent a "predicate act" in the U.S. (see *infra* part 3.b), U.S. copyright law did not reach U.K. acts. Nonetheless, the court ruled that it was competent to hear plaintiff's claim regarding alleged copyright infringements in England:

> The question presented is whether, if any of the defendants committed acts of infringement abroad actionable under the laws of foreign nations, this Court may exercise subject matter jurisdiction over such claims—not whether it is advisable, convenient, or wise to hear such claims. . . .
>
> > While certain courts have, at times, demonstrated their reluctance to "enter the bramble bush of ascertaining and applying foreign law without an urgent reason to do so," [citation omitted] there is no principled reason to bar, in absolute fashion, copyright claims brought under foreign law for lack of subject matter jurisdiction. Not only is this Court called upon to enter bramble bushes, briar patches, and other thorny legal thickets on a routine basis, but a number of persuasive authorities and commentators have also indicated that the exercise of subject matter jurisdiction

is appropriate in cases of transnational copyright infringement. [citations omitted] As Professor Nimmer has explained:

> Even if the United State Copyright Act is clearly inoperative with respect to acts occurring outside of its jurisdiction, it does not necessarily follow that American courts are without [subject matter] jurisdiction in such a case. If the plaintiff has a valid cause of action under the copyright laws of a foreign country, and if personal jurisdiction of the defendant can be obtained in an American court, it is arguable that an action may be brought in such court for infringement of a foreign copyright law. This would be on a theory that copyright infringement constitutes a transitory cause of action, and hence, may be adjudicated in the courts of a sovereign other than the one in which the cause of action arose.

3 Nimmer § 17.03; see 3 Goldstein § 16.2 ("Causes of action for copyright infringement are transitory and may be brought in any court that has jurisdiction over the defendant. Subject to jurisdictional requirements, a copyright owner may sue an infringer in United States courts even though the only alleged infringement occurred in another country. Under the territoriality principle, the copyright law of the other country, and not United States copyright law, will govern the action in the United States.").

In the present case, this Court would unquestionably have subject matter jurisdiction over any claims properly arising under United States copyright law, potentially allowing the Court to exercise pendent jurisdiction over claims arising under foreign law. Moreover, there would appear to be complete diversity as among the parties to this action.

Accord, *Carell v. Shubert Org.,* 104 F. Supp. 2d 236 (S.D.N.Y.2000) (make-up designer for musical *Cats* alleged infringement of her designs by producers of the musical in U.S., Australia, Canada, Japan and U.K.; court sustains its subject matter jurisdiction over foreign claims).

For a striking example of adjudication of multiple territory copyright claims, see *Monroig v. RMM Records & Video Corp,* 196 F.R.D. 214, 220 (D.P.R. 2000), in which plaintiff's song was modified and reproduced without authorization in phonorecords and on the sound track of a film distributed in Puerto Rico, Venezuela, Chile, Panama, Nicaragua, Costa Rica, Guatemala, Ecuador, Peru, Mexico, Spain, Portugal, Japan, Uruguay and Colombia. Plaintiff did not receive authorship credit as the composer. The court found violations not only of the songwriter's reproduction rights under the U.S. Copyright Act, but also of his moral rights in each of the countries of distribution. The court awarded $5,000,000 for the combined foreign moral rights violations.

———

The *London Film* court retained jurisdiction, despite the application of foreign copyright law, at least in part because the defendant was American and because it was not clear that a superior foreign forum was available. These factors were also emphasized, and the criteria for *forum non conveniens* developed further, in the following case.

Boosey & Hawkes Music Publishers, Ltd. v. Walt Disney & Co., 145 F.3d 481 (2d Cir.1998). This case involved a dispute over ownership of worldwide videocassette rights to Stravinsky's *Rite of Spring* as recorded on the soundtrack to Disney's motion picture *Fantasia* pursuant to a 1939 contract made in New York. The trial court granted Disney's motion to dismiss the claims for copyright infringement in at least 18 foreign nations in which the videocassettes had been distributed, holding that the substantive copyright issues would best be tried in the countries whose domestic copyright laws would be called into play. The court of appeals reversed, concluding that the application of possibly 18 different foreign laws should not be a dispositive obstacle to litigation in a federal court in New York. The pertinent parts of its decision follow:

> District courts enjoy broad discretion to decide whether to dismiss an action under the doctrine of forum non conveniens. *See Scottish Air Int'l Inc. v. British Caledonian Group, PLC*, 81 F.3d 1224, 1232 (2d Cir.1996). Nevertheless, this discretion is subject to "meaningful appellate review." *R. Maganlal & Co. v. M.G. Chem. Co., Inc.*, 942 F.2d 164, 167 (2d Cir.1991). A dismissal for forum non conveniens will be upset on appeal where a defendant has failed to demonstrate that "an adequate alternative forum exists" and that "the balance of convenience tilts strongly in favor of trial in the foreign forum." *Id.*; *see also Manu Int'l S.A. v. Avon Products Inc.*, 641 F.2d 62, 65 (2d Cir.1981) (emphasizing appellate obligation to enforce principle that "unless the balance is strongly in favor of the defendant, the plaintiff's choice of forum should rarely be disturbed") (quoting *Gulf Oil Corp. v. Gilbert*, 330 U.S. 501, 508).

> We recently explained that a motion to dismiss under forum non conveniens is decided in two steps. *See Peregrine Myanmar Ltd. v. Segal*, 89 F.3d 41, 46 (2d Cir.1996). The district court first must determine whether there exists an alternative forum with jurisdiction to hear the case. *Id.* If so, the court then weighs the factors set out in *Gilbert*, 330 U.S. at 508–09 ("the *Gilbert* factors"), to decide which "forum ... will be most convenient and will best serve the ends of justice." *Peregrine Myanmar*, 89 F.3d at 46. [The *Gilbert* factors are: (1) the "relative ease of access to sources of proof"; (2) "the cost of obtaining attendance of willing [ ] witnesses,"; (3), the enforceability of judgments; (4) the "availability of compulsory process for attendance of unwilling" witnesses; and (5) "practical problems that make trial of a case easy, expeditious and inexpensive." *Gilbert*, 330 U.S. at 508.]

> The district court failed to consider whether there were alternative fora capable of adjudicating Boosey's copyright claims.... It made no

determination whether Disney was subject to jurisdiction in the various countries where the court anticipated that trial would occur and did not condition dismissal on Disney's consent to jurisdiction in those nations.

Furthermore, consideration of the *Gilbert* factors makes plain that forum non conveniens is inappropriate here. The district court must carefully weigh the private and public interests set forth in *Gilbert* and may grant the forum non conveniens motion only if these considerations strongly support dismissal.... Relevant private interests of the litigants include access to proof, availability of witnesses and "all other practical problems that make trial of a case easy, expeditious and inexpensive." *Gilbert*, 330 U.S. at 508.

The private interests of the litigants favor conducting the litigation in New York where the plaintiff brought suit. Disney does not allege that a New York forum is inconvenient. The necessary evidence and witnesses are available and ready for presentation. A trial here promises to begin and end sooner than elsewhere, and would allow the parties to sort out their rights and obligations in a single proceeding. This is not a circumstance where the plaintiff's choice of forum is motivated by harassment.... Indeed, it seems rather more likely that Disney's motion seeks to split the suit into 18 parts in 18 nations, complicate the suit, delay it, and render it more expensive.

In dismissing the cases, the court relied on the "public interests" identified in *Gilbert*. It reasoned that the trial would require extensive application of foreign copyright and antitrust jurisprudence, bodies of law involving strong national interests best litigated "in their respective countries." *Boosey & Hawkes*, 934 F. Supp. at 124. The court concluded as well that these necessary inquiries into foreign law would place "an undue burden on our judicial system." *Id.*

While reluctance to apply foreign law is a valid factor favoring dismissal under *Gilbert*, standing alone it does not justify dismissal.... District courts must weigh this factor along with the other relevant considerations.... Numerous countervailing considerations suggest that New York venue is proper: defendant is a U.S. corporation, the 1939 agreement was substantially negotiated and signed in New York, and the agreement is governed by New York law. The plaintiff has chosen New York and the trial is ready to proceed here. Everything before us suggests that trial would be more "easy, expeditious and inexpensive" in the district court than dispersed to 18 foreign nations.... We therefore vacate the dismissal of the foreign copyright claims and remand for trial.

By contrast, in *Murray v. British Broadcasting Corp.*, 81 F.3d 287 (2d Cir.1996), the Second Circuit ruled that a dispute about ownership between two British citizens, governed by British contract law, with events having taken place in the U.K., should be tried there. Although Murray was contesting the BBC's right to authorize U.S. television exhibition of his "Mr. Blobby" character, the Second Circuit held that the BBC's rights in the U.S. market depended on the scope of rights the BBC had received from Murray under the English contract. *Cf. Gilliam v. ABC*, 538 F.2d 14 (2d Cir.1976) (defendant ABC could not claim to have received rights to edit "Monty Python" programs from the BBC, because the BBC had not received those rights from the authors). As a result, the highly attenuated U.S. interest in the case, and the close nexus of the English forum with the parties and the claim, justified the *forum non conveniens* dismissal.

3.   WHEN U.S. COURTS EXERCISE JURISDICTION OVER CLAIMS PRESENTING EXTRATERRITORIAL ELEMENTS, WHAT LAW APPLIES—

Suppose a foreign plaintiff asserts that the defendant has unlawfully copied or publicly performed her work in the U.S. and abroad. Defendant counters by challenging the validity of the copyright, as well as the plaintiff's title to it. Defendant also asserts that, with respect to alleged acts of infringement that occur outside the United States, U.S. copyright law cannot apply. As between U.S. law and that of the source country of the work or, for that matter, some other country's law, what law determines whether the work is protectible in the U.S.? What law determines who owns rights in the work? What national law determines the lawfulness of acts committed across multiple territories?

a.   —TO DETERMINE COPYRIGHT OWNERSHIP OF A FOREIGN WORK

Itar–Tass Russian News Agency v. Russian Kurier, Inc.

153 F.3d 82 (2d Cir.1998).

■ JON O. NEWMAN, CIRCUIT JUDGE:

This appeal primarily presents issues concerning the choice of law in international copyright cases and the substantive meaning of Russian copyright law as to the respective rights of newspaper reporters and newspaper publishers. The conflicts issue is which country's law applies to issues of copyright ownership and to issues of infringement. The primary substantive issue under Russian copyright law is whether a newspaper publishing company has an interest sufficient to give it standing to sue for copying the text of individual articles appearing in its newspapers, or whether complaint about such copying may be made only by the reporters who authored the articles. Defendants-appellants Russian Kurier, Inc. ("Kurier") and Oleg Pogrebnoy (collectively "the Kurier defendants") appeal from the March 25, 1997, judgment of the District Court for the Southern District of New York (John G. Koeltl, Judge) enjoining them from copying articles that have appeared or will appear in publications of the plaintiffs-appellees, mainly Russian newspapers and a Russian news agency, and awarding the appellees substantial damages for copyright infringement.

On the conflicts issue, we conclude that, with respect to the Russian plaintiffs, Russian law determines the ownership and essential nature of the copyrights alleged to have been infringed and that United States law determines whether those copyrights have been infringed in the United States and, if so, what remedies are available. . . .

Background

The lawsuit concerns Kurier, a Russian language weekly newspaper with a circulation in the New York area of about 20,000. It is published in New York City by defendant Kurier. Defendant Pogrebnoy is president and sole shareholder of Kurier and editor-in-chief of Kurier. The plaintiffs include corporations that publish, daily or weekly, major Russian language newspapers in Russia and Russian language magazines in Russia or Israel; Itar–Tass Russian News Agency ("Itar–Tass"), formerly known as the Telegraph Agency of the Soviet Union (TASS), a wire service and news gathering company centered in Moscow, functioning similarly to the Associated Press; and the Union of Journalists of Russia ("UJR"), the professional writers union of accredited print and broadcast journalists of the Russian Federation.

The Kurier defendants do not dispute that Kurier has copied about 500 articles that first appeared in the plaintiffs' publications or were distributed by Itar–Tass. The copied material, though extensive, was a small percentage of the total number of articles published in Kurier. The Kurier defendants also do not dispute how the copying occurred: articles from the plaintiffs' publications, sometimes containing headlines, pictures, bylines, and graphics, in addition to text, were cut out, pasted on layout sheets, and sent to Kurier's printer for photographic reproduction and printing in the pages of Kurier.

Most significantly, the Kurier defendants also do not dispute that, with one exception, they had not obtained permission from any of the plaintiffs to copy the articles that appeared in Kurier. . . .

Discussion

I. *Choice of Law*

The threshold issue concerns the choice of law for resolution of this dispute. That issue was not initially considered by the parties, all of whom turned directly to Russian law for resolution of the case. . . .

Choice of law issues in international copyright cases have been largely ignored in the reported decisions and dealt with rather cursorily by most commentators. Examples pertinent to the pending appeal are those decisions involving a work created by the employee of a foreign corporation. Several courts have applied the United States work-for-hire doctrine, see 17 U.S.C. § 201(b), without explicit consideration of the conflicts issue. *See, e.g., Aldon Accessories Ltd. v. Spiegel, Inc.,* 738 F.2d 548, 551–53 (2d Cir.1984) (U.S. law applied to determine if statuettes crafted abroad were works for hire);[4] *Dae Han Video Productions, Inc. v. Kuk Dong Oriental*

---

4. Though *Aldon*'s use of the "actual supervision and control" test for applying the work-for-hire doctrine has since been rejected, see *Community for Creative Non–Violence*

Food, Inc., 19 U.S.P.Q.2d (BNA) 1294 (D.Md.1990) (U.S. law applied to determine if scripts written abroad were works for hire);[5] *P & D International v. Halsey Publishing Co.,* 672 F. Supp. 1429, 1435–36 (S.D.Fla.1987) (U.S. work for hire law assumed to apply). Other courts have applied foreign law. *See Frink America, Inc. v. Champion Road Machinery Ltd.,* 961 F. Supp. 398 (N.D.N.Y.1997) (Canadian copyright law applied on issue of ownership); *Greenwich Film Productions v. DRG Records Inc.,* 1992 U.S. Dist. LEXIS 14770, 1992 WL 279357 (S.D.N.Y. 1992) (French law applied to determine ownership of right to musical work commissioned in France for French film); *Dae Han Video Production Inc. v. Dong San Chun,* 17 U.S.P.Q.2d (BNA) 1306, 1310 n. 6 (E.D.Va.1990) (foreign law relied on to determine that alleged licensor lacks rights). . . . The conflicts issue was identified but ruled not necessary to be resolved in *Greenwich Film Productions S.A. v. D.R.G. Records, Inc.,* 25 U.S.P.Q.2d (BNA) 1435, 1437–38 (S.D.N.Y.1992).

The Nimmer treatise briefly (and perhaps optimistically) suggests that conflicts issues "have rarely proved troublesome in the law of copyright." *See* Nimmer on Copyright § 17.05 (1998) ("Nimmer") (footnote omitted). Relying on the "national treatment" principle of the Berne Convention and the Universal Copyright Convention ("U.C.C."), Nimmer asserts, correctly in our view, that "an author who is a national of one of the member states of either Berne or the U.C.C., or one who first publishes his work in any such member state, is entitled to the same copyright protection in each other member state as such other state accords to its own nationals." *Id.* (footnotes omitted). Nimmer then somewhat overstates the national treatment principle: "The applicable law is the copyright law of the state in which the infringement occurred, not that of the state of which the author is a national, or in which the work is first published." *Id.* (footnote omitted). The difficulty with this broad statement is that it subsumes under the phrase "applicable law" the law concerning two distinct issues—ownership and substantive rights, i.e., scope of protection.[8] Another com-

---

v. Reid, 490 U.S. 730 (1989), its use of U.S. law as the source of the work-for-hire doctrine remains unimpaired, though the precedential force of the implicit conflicts ruling is weakened by the absence of any discussion of the issue. Under principles we discuss below, United States law was properly applied to the ownership issue since the country of origin of the work was the United States, the work having been first published in the United States and "authored" by a U.S. citizen.

5. To the extent that this decision applied the U.S. work-for-hire doctrine simply because copyright certificates had been issued by the United States Copyright Office, it relied on an unpersuasive ground. Issuance of the certificate is not a determination concerning applicability of the work-for-hire doctrine

or a resolution of any issue concerning ownership. *See* Jane C. Ginsburg, *Ownership of Electronic Rights and the Private International Law of Copyright,* 22 Colum.-VLA J.L. & Arts 165, 171 n.22 (1998).

8. Prof. Patry's brief, as Amicus Curiae, helpfully points out that the principle of national treatment is really not a conflicts rule at all; it does not direct application of the law of any country. It simply requires that the country in which protection is claimed must treat foreign and domestic authors alike. Whether U.S. copyright law directs U.S. courts to look to foreign or domestic law as to certain issues is irrelevant to national treatment, so long as the scope of protection would be extended equally to foreign and domestic authors.

mentator has also broadly stated the principle of national treatment, but described its application in a way that does not necessarily cover issues of ownership. "The principle of national treatment also means that both the question of whether the right exists and the question of the scope of the right are to be answered in accordance with the law of the country where the protection is claimed." S.M. Stewart, International Copyright and Neighboring Rights § 3.17 (2d ed. 1989). We agree with the view of the Amicus that the Convention's principle of national treatment simply assures that if the law of the country of infringement applies to the scope of substantive copyright protection, that law will be applied uniformly to foreign and domestic authors. *See Murray v. British Broadcasting Corp.*, 906 F. Supp. 858 (S.D.N.Y.1995), *aff'd*, 81 F.3d 287 (1996).

Source of conflicts rules. Our analysis of the conflicts issue begins with consideration of the source of law for selecting a conflicts rule. Though Nimmer turns directly to the Berne Convention and the U.C.C., we think that step moves too quickly past the Berne Convention Implementation Act of 1988, Pub L. 100–568, 102 Stat. 2853, 17 U.S.C.A. § 101 note. Section 4(a)(3) of the Act amends Title 17 to provide: "No right or interest in a work eligible for protection under this title may be claimed by virtue of ... the provisions of the Berne Convention.... Any rights in a work eligible for protection under this title that derive from this title ... shall not be expanded or reduced by virtue of ... the provisions of the Berne Convention." 17 U.S.C. § 104(c).

We start our analysis with the Copyrights Act itself, which contains no provision relevant to the pending case concerning conflicts issues. We therefore fill the interstices of the Act by developing federal common law on the conflicts issue. *See D'Oench, Duhme & Co. v. FDIC*, 315 U.S. 447 (1942); *id.* at 472 (Jackson, J., concurring) ("The law which we apply to this case consists of principles of established credit in jurisprudence, selected by us because they are appropriate to effectuate the policy of the governing Act."). In doing so, we are entitled to consider and apply principles of private international law, which are " 'part of our law.' " *Maxwell Communication Corp. v. Société Générale*, 93 F.3d 1036, 1047 (2d Cir.1996) (*quoting Hilton v. Guyot*, 159 U.S. 113, 143 (1895)).

The choice of law applicable to the pending case is not necessarily the same for all issues. *See* Restatement (Second) of Conflict of Laws § 222 ("The courts have long recognized that they are not bound to decide all issues under the local law of a single state."). We consider first the law applicable to the issue of copyright ownership.

Conflicts rule for issues of ownership. Copyright is a form of property, and the usual rule is that the interests of the parties in property are determined by the law of the state with "the most significant relationship" to the property and the parties. *See id.* The Restatement recognizes the applicability of this principle to intangibles such as "a literary idea." *Id.* Since the works at issue were created by Russian nationals and first published in Russia, Russian law is the appropriate source of law to determine issues of ownership of rights. That is the well-reasoned conclusion of the Amicus Curiae, Prof. Patry, and the parties in their supplemental briefs are in agreement on this point. In terms of the United States Copyrights Act and its reference to the Berne Convention, Russia is the "country of origin" of these works, see 17 U.S.C. § 101 (definition of "country of origin" of Berne Convention work); Berne Convention, Art. 5(4), although "country of origin" might not always be the appropriate country for purposes of choice of law concerning ownership.[10]

To whatever extent we look to the Berne Convention itself as guidance in the development of federal common law on the conflicts issue, we find nothing to alter our conclusion. The Convention does not purport to settle issues of ownership, with one exception not relevant to this case.[11] *See* Jane C. Ginsburg, *Ownership of Electronic Rights and the Private International Law of Copyright*, 22 Colum.-VLA J. L. & Arts 165, 167–68 (1998) (The Berne Convention "provides that the law of the country where protection is claimed defines what rights are protected, the scope of the protection, and the available remedies; the treaty does not supply a choice of law rule for determining ownership.") (footnote concerning Art. 14*bis*(2)(a) omitted). Selection of Russian law to determine copyright ownership is, however, subject to one procedural qualification. Under United States law, an owner (including one determined according to foreign law) may sue for infringement in a United States court only if it meets the standing test of 17 U.S.C. § 501(b), which accords standing only to the legal or beneficial owner of an "exclusive right."

Conflicts rule for infringement issues. On infringement issues, the governing conflicts principle is usually *lex loci delicti*, the doctrine generally applicable to torts. *See Lauritzen v. Larsen,* 345 U.S. 571, 583 (1953). We have implicitly adopted that approach to infringement claims, applying United States copyright law to a work that was unprotected in its country of origin. *See Hasbro Bradley, Inc. v. Sparkle Toys, Inc.,* 780 F.2d 189, 192–93 (2d Cir.1985). In the pending case, the place of the tort is plainly the United States. To whatever extent *lex loci delicti* is to be considered only one part of a broader "interest" approach, see *Carbotrade S.p.A. v. Bureau Veritas,* 99 F.3d 86, 89–90 (2d Cir.1996), United States law would still apply to infringement issues, since not only is this country the place of the tort, but also the defendant is a United States corporation.

---

10. In deciding that the law of the country of origin determines the ownership of copyright, we consider only initial ownership, and have no occasion to consider choice of law issues concerning assignments of rights.

11. The Berne Convention expressly provides that "ownership of copyright in a cinematographic work shall be a matter for legislation in the country where protection is claimed." Berne Convention, Art. 14*bis*(2)(a). With respect to other works, this provision could be understood to have any of three meanings. First, it could carry a negative implication that for other works, ownership is not to be determined by legislation in the country where protection is claimed. Second, it could be thought of as an explicit assertion for films of a general principle already applicable to other works. Third, it could be a specific provision for films that was adopted without an intention to imply anything about other works. In the absence of any indication that either the first or second meanings were intended, we prefer the third understanding.

The division of issues, for conflicts purposes, between ownership and infringement issues will not always be as easily made as the above discussion implies. If the issue is the relatively straightforward one of which of two contending parties owns a copyright, the issue is unquestionably an ownership issue, and the law of the country with the closest relationship to the work will apply to settle the ownership dispute. But in some cases, including the pending one, the issue is not simply who owns the copyright but also what is the nature of the ownership interest. Yet as a court considers the nature of an ownership interest, there is some risk that it will too readily shift the inquiry over to the issue of whether an alleged copy has infringed the asserted copyright. Whether a copy infringes depends in part on the scope of the interest of the copyright owner. Nevertheless, though the issues are related, the nature of a copyright interest is an issue distinct from the issue of whether the copyright has been infringed, see, e.g., *Kregos v. Associated Press,* 937 F.2d 700, 709–10 (2d Cir.1991) (pointing out that although work survives summary judgment on issue of copyrightability of compilation, scope of protection against claim of infringement might be limited). The pending case is one that requires consideration not simply of who owns an interest, but, as to the newspapers, the nature of the interest that is owned.

. . .

QUESTIONS

1. How far does one extend the principle that the law of the country with the "most significant relationship" to the work (generally, the source country) determines ownership status? For example, disparities between U.S. copyright law and foreign laws exist not only with respect to the status of employers as owners of copyright, but also regarding joint authorship. Under U.S. law, given the prerequisite intent, the joint authors' contributions may comprise either an inseparable or an interdependent but separable whole. In certain other countries, however, only inseparable contributions form a joint work. Suppose that a foreign work is a dramatico-musical composition, comprising the efforts of a composer and a lyricist. Under most countries' rules of duration of copyright, a joint work's copyright endures until a determined number of years (70 in the European Union and the U.S.; generally 50 elsewhere) from the death of the last surviving author. Assume a musical comedy was created in 1979 in an EU country which requires inseparable contributions (and considers dramatico-musical works to be separable). The composer died in 1980; the lyricist in 1990. Under the law of the source country, the copyright in the music will expire in 2050; the copyright in the lyrics in 2060. Under U.S. law, the copyright in the work as a whole will expire in 2060. When will the music fall into the public domain in the U.S.? The answer will depend on whether the U.S. definition or the source country definition of a joint work applies.

2. Is the law of the country of exploitation relevant to determining the scope of a grant of rights in a foreign work, when the contract of transfer is governed by a foreign law? Normally, the law chosen by the parties controls the scope of the grant. Nonetheless, to some extent the answer may depend on whether the issue is considered one of contract law or of substantive copyright law. Recall *Corcovado Music v. Hollis Music*, 981 F.2d 679 (2d Cir.1993), *supra* Chapter 4. Although the contract of transfer between the Brazilian composer and his Brazilian publisher was subject to Brazilian law, the Second Circuit held that U.S. copyright law governed the validity of the transfer of the U.S. renewal term.

A similar result may apply when a U.S. work is exploited abroad. For example, some foreign copyright laws, such as that of Germany, state that the rights to new forms of exploitation, unknown at the time of contracting, accrue to the author, not to the grantee, even if the contract purported to transfer all the author's interest. Others, for example France, permit transfers of unknown new technology rights, but demand that the transfer be explicit. Suppose that in 1970, an author granted "publication rights," and that under New York law (chosen by the parties to govern the contract), the burden falls on the author to reserve future technology rights. Suppose further that the publisher-grantee seeks now to digitize the work and to exploit it over internationally-accessible digital networks. May the U.S. author prevent the publisher's digital exploitation of the work in Germany and/or France? Would the choice of forum matter?

3. Because the Berne Convention imposes no choice of law rule regarding copyright ownership (outside the context of cinematographic works, see art. 14^{bis}2), it is possible that other countries would follow the *Itar–Tass* approach of applying the law of the source country to determine initial copyright ownership. But the outcome may be different when authorship status, rather than ownership of economic rights, is at issue. Authorship status determines entitlement to "moral rights" in most foreign jurisdictions. These are independent of economic rights, and are personal to the actual creator of the work. As a result, the creator continues to enjoy certain prerogatives of "authorship" with respect to a work in which another person, perhaps the author's employer, owns the copyright. The question therefore may arise whether a U.S. employee-for-hire may claim authorship status in these countries, and thus avail herself of local moral rights protections. For an affirmative answer, rendered by the French courts in a claim brought by the heirs of director John Huston against the French broadcaster of a colorized version of *The Asphalt Jungle*, see *Huston v. La Cinq*, Cour de cassation 1991, English translation at 15 Colum.-VLA J. L. & Arts 159 (1991), *discussed in* Jane C. Ginsburg & Pierre Sirinelli, *Authors and Exploitations in International Private Law: The French Supreme Court and the Huston Film Colorization Controversy*, 15 Colum.-VLA J. L. & Arts 135 (1991).

b.   —TO INFRINGEMENTS OCCURRING, AT LEAST IN PART, BEYOND U.S. BORDERS

Subafilms, Ltd. v. MGM–Pathé Communications Co.

24 F.3d 1088 (9th Cir.) (en banc), *cert. denied,* 513 U.S. 1001 (1994).

■ D.W. NELSON, CIRCUIT JUDGE:

In this case, we consider the "vexing question" of whether a claim for infringement can be brought under the Copyright Act, 17 U.S.C. § 101 et seq. (1988), when the assertedly infringing conduct consists solely of the authorization within the territorial boundaries of the United States of acts that occur entirely abroad. We hold that such allegations do not state a claim for relief under the copyright laws of the United States.

Factual and Procedural Background

In 1966, the musical group The Beatles, through Subafilms, Ltd., entered into a joint venture with the Hearst Corporation to produce the animated motion picture entitled "Yellow Submarine" (the "Picture"). Over the next year, Hearst, acting on behalf of the joint venture (the "Producer"), negotiated an agreement with United Artists Corporation ("UA") to distribute and finance the film. Separate distribution and financing agreements were entered into in May, 1967. Pursuant to these agreements, UA distributed the Picture in theaters beginning in 1968 and later on television.

In the early 1980s, with the advent of the home video market, UA entered into several licensing agreements to distribute a number of its films on videocassette. Although one company expressed interest in the Picture, UA refused to license "Yellow Submarine" because of uncertainty over whether home video rights had been granted by the 1967 agreements. Subsequently, in 1987, UA's successor company, MGM/UA Communications Co. ("MGM/UA"), over the Producer's objections, authorized its subsidiary MGM/UA Home Video, Inc. to distribute the Picture for the domestic home video market, and, pursuant to an earlier licensing agreement, notified Warner Bros., Inc. ("Warner") that the Picture had been cleared for international videocassette distribution. Warner, through its wholly owned subsidiary, Warner Home Video, Inc., in turn entered into agreements with third parties for distribution of the Picture on videocassette around the world.

In 1988, Subafilms and Hearst ("Appellees") brought suit against MGM/UA, Warner, and their respective subsidiaries (collectively the "Distributors" or "Appellants"), contending that the videocassette distribution of the Picture, both foreign and domestic, constituted copyright infringement and a breach of the 1967 agreements. The case was tried before a retired California Superior Court Judge acting as a special master. The special master found for Appellees on both claims.... [T]he district court adopted all of the special master's factual findings and legal conclusions. Appellees were awarded $2,228,000.00 in compensatory damages, split evenly between the foreign and domestic home video distributions. In addition, Appellees received attorneys' fees and a permanent injunction that prohibited the Distributors from engaging in, or authorizing, any home video use of the Picture.

A panel of this circuit, in an unpublished disposition, affirmed the district court's judgment on the ground that both the domestic and foreign distribution of the Picture constituted infringement under the Copyright

Act. . . . With respect to the foreign distribution of the Picture, the panel concluded that it was bound by this court's prior decision in *Peter Starr Prod. Co. v. Twin Continental Films, Inc.*, 783 F.2d 1440 (9th Cir.1986), which it held to stand for the proposition that, although "infringing actions that take place entirely outside the United States are not actionable' [under the Copyright Act, an] 'act of infringement within the United States' [properly is] alleged where the illegal authorization of international exhibitions t[akes] place in the United States," *Subafilms*, slip op. at 4917–18 (quoting *Peter Starr*, 783 F.2d at 1442, 1443 (emphasis in original) (alterations added)). Because the Distributors had admitted that the initial authorization to distribute the Picture internationally occurred within the United States, the panel affirmed the district court's holding with respect to liability for extraterritorial home video distribution of the Picture.[3]

We granted Appellants' petition for rehearing en banc to consider whether the panel's interpretation of *Peter Starr* conflicted with our subsequent decision in *Lewis Galoob Toys, Inc. v. Nintendo of Am., Inc.*, 964 F.2d 965 (9th Cir.1992), *cert. denied*, 113 S. Ct. 1582 (1993), which held that there could be no liability for authorizing a party to engage in an infringing act when the authorized "party's use of the work would not violate the Copyright Act," *id.* at 970. . . . Because we conclude that there can be no liability under the United States copyright laws for authorizing an act that itself could not constitute infringement of rights secured by those laws, and that wholly extraterritorial acts of infringement are not cognizable under the Copyright Act, we overrule *Peter Starr* insofar as it held that allegations of an authorization within the United States of infringing acts that take place entirely abroad state a claim for infringement under the Act. Accordingly, we vacate the panel's decision in part and return the case to the panel for further proceedings.

Discussion

I.   *The Mere Authorization of Extraterritorial Acts of Infringement Does Not State a Claim Under the Copyright Act*

As the panel in this case correctly concluded, *Peter Starr* held that the authorization within the United States of entirely extraterritorial acts stated a cause of action under the "plain language" of the Copyright Act. *Peter Starr*, 783 F.2d at 1442–43. Observing that the Copyright Act grants a copyright owner "the *exclusive rights* to do and *to authorize*" any of the activities listed in 17 U.S.C. § 106(1)–(5), *id.* at 1442 (emphasis in original), and that a violation of the "authorization" right constitutes infringement

---

3. At oral argument before this court Appellants' counsel conceded that the relevant authorization occurred within the United States. Counsel for Appellees, accepting this concession, additionally insisted that the authorization necessarily included the making of a copy of the negative of the Picture within the United States. Appellants' counsel responded that this contention was made before neither the special master nor the panel, and was not supported by the record. For the purposes of this decision, we assume, as apparently the panel did, that each of the defendants made a relevant "authorization" within the United States, and that the acts of authorization consisted solely of entering into licensing agreements.

under section 501 of the Act, the *Peter Starr* court reasoned that allegations of an authorization within the United States of extraterritorial conduct that corresponded to the activities listed in section 106 "allege[d] an act of infringement within the United States," *id.* at 1442–43. Accordingly, the court determined that the district court erred "in concluding that 'Plaintiff allege[d] only infringing acts which took place outside of the United States,'" and reversed the district court's dismissal for lack of subject matter jurisdiction. *Id.* at 1443.

The *Peter Starr* court accepted, as does this court, that the acts authorized from within the United States themselves could not have constituted infringement under the Copyright Act because "[i]n general, United States copyright laws do not have extraterritorial effect," and therefore, "infringing actions that take place entirely outside the United States are not actionable." *Peter Starr*, 783 F.2d at 1442 (citing *Robert Stigwood Group, Ltd. v. O'Reilly*, 530 F.2d 1096, 1101 (2d Cir.), *cert. denied*, 429 U.S. 848 (1976)). The central premise of the *Peter Starr* court, then, was that a party could be held liable as an "infringer" under section 501 of the Act merely for authorizing a third party to engage in acts that, had they been committed within the United States, would have violated the exclusive rights granted to a copyright holder by section 106.

Since *Peter Starr*, however, we have recognized that, when a party authorizes an activity not proscribed by one of the five section 106 clauses, the authorizing party cannot be held liable as an infringer. In *Lewis Galoob*, we rejected the argument that "a party can unlawfully authorize another party to use a copyrighted work even if that party's use of the work would not violate the Copyright Act," *Lewis Galoob*, 964 F.2d at 970, and approved of Professor Nimmer's statement that " 'to the extent that an activity does not violate one of th[e] five enumerated rights [found in 17 U.S.C. § 106], authorizing such activity does not constitute copyright infringement,'" *id.* (quoting 3 David Nimmer & Melville B. Nimmer, Nimmer on Copyright § 12.04[A][3][a], at 12–80 n.82 (1991)). Similarly, in *Columbia Pictures*, we held that no liability attached under the Copyright Act for providing videodisc players to hotel guests when the use of that equipment did not constitute a "public" performance within the meaning of section 106 of the Act, see *Columbia Pictures*, 866 F.2d at 279–81.

The apparent premise of *Lewis Galoob* was that the addition of the words "to authorize" in the Copyright Act was not meant to create a new form of liability for "authorization" that was divorced completely from the legal consequences of authorized conduct, but was intended to invoke the preexisting doctrine of contributory infringement. *See Lewis Galoob*, 964 F.2d at 970 ("Although infringement by authorization is a form of direct infringement [under the Act], this does not change the proper focus of our inquiry; a party cannot authorize another party to infringe a copyright unless the authorized conduct would itself be unlawful."). We agree.

. . .

Although the *Peter Starr* court recognized that the addition of the authorization right in the 1976 Act "was intended to remove the confusion surrounding contributory . . . infringement," *Peter Starr,* 783 F.2d at 1443, it did not consider the applicability of an essential attribute of the doctrine: that contributory infringement, even when triggered solely by an "authorization," is a form of third party liability that requires the authorized acts to constitute infringing ones. We believe that the *Peter Starr* court erred in not applying this principle to the authorization of acts that cannot themselves be infringing because they take place entirely abroad. As Professor Nimmer has observed:

> Accepting the proposition that a direct infringement is a prerequisite to third party liability, the further question arises whether the direct infringement on which liability is premised must take place within the United States. Given the undisputed axiom that United States copyright law has no extraterritorial application, it would seem to follow necessarily that a primary activity outside the boundaries of the United States, not constituting an infringement cognizable under the Copyright Act, cannot serve as the basis for holding liable under the Copyright Act one who is merely related to that activity within the United States.

3 Nimmer, *supra,* § 12.04[A][3][b], at 12–86 (footnotes omitted).

Appellees resist the force of this logic, and argue that liability in this case is appropriate because, unlike in *Lewis Galoob* and *Columbia Pictures,* in which the alleged primary infringement consisted of acts that were entirely outside the purview of 17 U.S.C. § 106(1)–(5) (and presumably lawful), the conduct authorized in this case was precisely that prohibited by section 106, and is only uncognizable because it occurred outside the United States. Moreover, they contend that the conduct authorized in this case would have been prohibited under the copyright laws of virtually every nation. *See also* 1 Goldstein, *supra,* § 6.1, at 706 n.4 (suggesting that "*Peter Starr*'s interpretation of section 106's authorization right would appear to be at least literally correct since the statute nowhere requires that the direct infringement occur within the United States").

. . .

Even assuming *arguendo* that the acts authorized in this case would have been illegal abroad, we do not believe the distinction offered by Appellees is a relevant one. Because the copyright laws do not apply extraterritorially, each of the rights conferred under the five section 106 categories must be read as extending "no farther than the [United States'] borders." 2 Goldstein, *supra,* § 16.0, at 675. *See, e.g., Robert Stigwood,* 530 F.2d at 1101 (holding that no damages could be obtained under the Copyright Act for public performances in Canada when preliminary steps were taken within the United States and stating that "[t]he Canadian performances, while they may have been torts in Canada, were not torts here"); *see also Filmvideo Releasing Corp. v. Hastings,* 668 F.2d 91, 93 (2d Cir.1981) (reversing an order of the district court that required the defendant to surrender prints of a film because the prints could be used to further conduct abroad that was not proscribed by United States copyright laws). In light of our above conclusion that the "authorization" right refers to the doctrine of contributory infringement, which requires that the authorized act itself could violate one of the exclusive rights listed in section 106(1)–(5), we believe that "[i]t is simply not possible to draw a principled distinction" between an act that does not violate a copyright because it is not the type of conduct proscribed by section 106, and one that does not violate section 106 because the illicit act occurs overseas. In both cases, the authorized conduct could not violate the exclusive rights guaranteed by section 106. In both cases, therefore, there can be no liability for "authorizing" such conduct. *See also* 3 Nimmer, *supra*, § 12.04[A][3][b], at 12–87 to 12–88.

To hold otherwise would produce the untenable anomaly, inconsistent with the general principles of third party liability, that a party could be held liable as an infringer for violating the "authorization" right when the party that it authorized could not be considered an infringer under the Copyright Act. Put otherwise, we do not think Congress intended to hold a party liable for merely "authorizing" conduct that, had the authorizing party chosen to engage in itself, would have resulted in no liability under the Act. *Cf. Robert Stigwood,* 530 F.2d at 1101.

Appellees rely heavily on the Second Circuit's doctrine that extraterritorial application of the copyright laws is permissible "when the type of infringement permits further reproduction abroad." *Update Art, Inc. v. Modiin Publishing, Ltd.,* 843 F.2d 67, 73 (2d Cir.1988). Whatever the merits of the Second Circuit's rule, and we express no opinion on its validity in this circuit, it is premised on the theory that the copyright holder may recover damages that stem from a direct infringement of its exclusive rights that occurs within the United States. *See Robert Stigwood,* 530 F.2d at 1101; *Sheldon v. Metro–Goldwyn Pictures Corp.,* 106 F.2d 45, 52 (2d Cir.1939) (L. Hand, J.) ("The negatives were 'records' from which the work could be 'reproduced,' and it was a tort to make them in this country. The plaintiffs acquired an equitable interest in them as soon as they were made, which attached to any profits from their exploitation...."), *aff'd,* 309 U.S. 390 (1940)....[9] In these cases, liability is not based on contributory infringement, but on the theory that the infringing use would have been actionable even if the subsequent foreign distribution that stemmed from that use never took place. *See, e.g., Famous Music,* 201 F. Supp. at 569 ("[T]hat a copyright has no extraterritorial effect[ ] does not solve th[e] problem of [whether liability should attach for preparing within the United States tapes that were part of a] manufacture [completed abroad] since plaintiffs seek to hold defendant for what it did *here* rather

---

9. Professor Nimmer formulates the doctrine in the following terms: "[I]f and to the extent a part of an 'act' of infringement occurs within the United States, then, although such act is completed in a foreign jurisdiction, those parties who contributed to the act within the United States may be rendered liable under American copyright law." 3 Nimmer, *supra,* 17.02, at 17–19 (footnotes omitted).

than what it did abroad." (emphasis in original)). These cases, therefore, simply are inapplicable to a theory of liability based merely on the authorization of noninfringing acts.

Accordingly, accepting that wholly extraterritorial acts of infringement cannot support a claim under the Copyright Act, we believe that the *Peter Starr* court, and thus the panel in this case, erred in concluding that the mere authorization of such acts supports a claim for infringement under the Act.

II. *The Extraterritoriality of the Copyright Act*

Appellees additionally contend that, if liability for "authorizing" acts of infringement depends on finding that the authorized acts themselves are cognizable under the Copyright Act, this court should find that the United States copyright laws do extend to extraterritorial acts of infringement when such acts "result in adverse effects within the United States." Appellees buttress this argument with the contention that failure to apply the copyright laws extraterritorially in this case will have a disastrous effect on the American film industry, and that other remedies, such as suits in foreign jurisdictions or the application of foreign copyright laws by American courts, are not realistic alternatives.

We are not persuaded by Appellees' parade of horribles.[10] More fundamentally, however, we are unwilling to overturn over eighty years of consistent jurisprudence on the extraterritorial reach of the copyright laws without further guidance from Congress.

The Supreme Court recently reminded us that "[i]t is a long-standing principle of American law 'that legislation of Congress, unless a contrary intent appears, is meant to apply only within the territorial jurisdiction of the United States.' " *EEOC v. Arabian American Oil Co. (Aramco)*, 111 S. Ct. 1227, 1230 (1991) (quoting *Foley Bros., Inc. v. Filardo*, 336 U.S. 281, 285 (1949)). Because courts must "assume that Congress legislates against the backdrop of the presumption against extraterritoriality," unless "there is 'the affirmative intention of the Congress clearly expressed' " congressional enactments must be presumed to be " 'primarily concerned with domestic conditions.' " *Id.* at 1230 (quoting *Foley Bros.*, 336 U.S. at 285 and *Benz v. Compania Naviera Hidalgo, S.A.*, 353 U.S. 138, 147 (1957)).

---

10. As Appellants note, breach of contract remedies (such as those pursued in this case) remain available. Moreover, at least one court has recognized that actions under the copyright laws of other nations may be brought in United States courts. *See London Film Prods., Ltd. v. Intercontinental Communications, Inc.*, 580 F. Supp. 47, 48–50 (S.D.N.Y.1984). *See generally* 2 Goldstein, *supra*, 16.3, at 683 ("Subject to jurisdictional requirements, a copyright owner may sue an infringer in United States courts even though the only alleged infringement occurred in another country.") *But see ITSI*, 785 F. Supp. at 866 (discerning, despite *London Film*, "no clear authority for exercising such jurisdiction" (citing David R. Toraya, Note, *Federal Jurisdiction Over Foreign Copyright Actions: An Unsolicited Reply to Professor Nimmer*, 70 Cornell L. Rev. 1165 (1985)), and stating that "American courts should be reluctant to enter the bramble bush of ascertaining and applying foreign law without an urgent reason to do so"). . . .

The "undisputed axiom," 3 Nimmer, *supra,* § 12.04[A][3][b], at 12–86, that the United States' copyright laws have no application to extraterritorial infringement predates the 1909 Act, see, e.g., *United Dictionary Co. v. G. & C. Merriam Co.,* 208 U.S. 260, 264–66 (1908) (Holmes, J.), and, as discussed above, the principle of territoriality consistently has been reaffirmed, see, e.g., *Capitol Records, Inc. v. Mercury Records Corp.,* 221 F.2d 657, 662 (2d Cir.1955) (citing *American Code Co. v. Bensinger,* 282 F. 829, 833 (2d Cir.1922)) ("The copyright laws of one country have no extraterritorial operation, unless otherwise provided." (citing *Ferris v. Frohman,* 223 U.S. 424 (1912)); sources cited *supra* pp. 4917–20. There is no clear expression of congressional intent in either the 1976 Act or other relevant enactments to alter the preexisting extraterritoriality doctrine....

Furthermore, we note that Congress chose in 1976 to expand one specific "extraterritorial" application of the Act by declaring that the unauthorized importation of copyrighted works constitutes infringement even when the copies lawfully were made abroad. *See* 17 U.S.C.A. § 602(a) (West Supp. 1992). Had Congress been inclined to overturn the preexisting doctrine that infringing acts that take place wholly outside the United States are not actionable under the Copyright Act, it knew how to do so. *See Argentine Republic v. Amerada Hess Shipping Corp.,* 488 U.S. 428, 440 (1989) ("When it desires to do so, Congress knows how to place the high seas within the jurisdictional reach of a statute." (quoted in *Aramco,* 111 S. Ct. at 1235)). Accordingly, the presumption against extraterritoriality, "far from being overcome here, is doubly fortified by the language of [the] statute," *Smith v. United States,* 113 S. Ct. 1178, 1183 (1993) (quoting *United States v. Spelar,* 338 U.S. 217, 222 (1949)), as set against its consistent historical interpretation.

... Extraterritorial application of American law would be contrary to the spirit of the Berne Convention, and might offend other member nations by effectively displacing their law in circumstances in which previously it was assumed to govern. Consequently, an extension of extraterritoriality might undermine Congress's objective of achieving " 'effective and harmonious' copyright laws among all nations." House Report, *supra,* at 20. Indeed, it might well send the signal that the United States does not believe that the protection accorded by the laws of other member nations is adequate, which would undermine two other objectives of Congress in joining the convention: "strengthen[ing] the credibility of the U.S. position in trade negotiations with countries where piracy is not uncommon" and "rais[ing] the like[li]hood that other nations will enter the Convention." S. Rep. 352, 100th Cong., 2d Sess. 4–5, *reprinted in* 1988 U.S.C.C.A.N., 3706, 3709–10.

... Accordingly, because an extension of the extraterritorial reach of the Copyright Act by the courts would in all likelihood disrupt the international regime for protecting intellectual property that Congress so recently described as essential to furthering the goal of protecting the works of American authors abroad, ... we reaffirm that the United States copyright laws do not reach acts of infringement that take place entirely abroad. It is for Congress, and not the courts, to take the initiative in this field....

Conclusion

We hold that the mere authorization of acts of infringement that are not cognizable under the United States copyright laws because they occur entirely outside of the United States does not state a claim for infringement under the Copyright Act. *Peter Starr* is overruled insofar as it held to the contrary....

Vacated in Part and Remanded.

Update Art, Inc. v. Modiin Publishing, 843 F.2d 67 (2d Cir.1988). This action concerned an Israeli newspaper's unauthorized publication of a photograph of plaintiff U.S.-citizen's "Ronbo" poster, depicting Ronald Reagan's head atop a gun-toting torso resembling Sylvester Stallone's in the film *Rambo.*

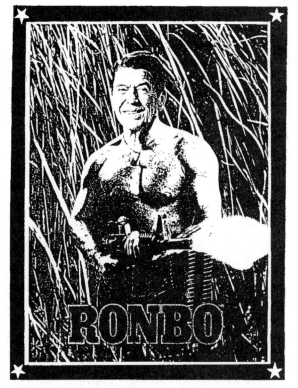

Reproduced with permission of Update Art, Inc.

The court stated:

It is well established that copyright laws generally do not have extraterritorial application. There is an exception when the type of infringement permits further reproduction abroad—such as the unauthorized manufacture of copyrighted material in the United States. [citations omitted.]

> Appellants [defendants] concede the magistrate's jurisdiction over the newspapers distributed in the United States. As the applicability of American copyright laws over the Israeli newspapers [distributed in Israel] depends on the occurrence of a predicate act in the United States, the geographic location of the illegal reproduction is crucial. If the illegal reproduction of the poster occurred in the United States and then was exported to Israel, the magistrate properly could include damages accruing from the Israeli newspapers. Since a large portion of the damage award accrued from the Israeli newspapers, our determination on this issue affects substantially the final judgment.

The court then held that in light of plaintiff's assertion that defendant made an initial copy of the Ronbo poster in the U.S., and of defendant's failure to produce contrary evidence (and its repeated failure to respond to discovery orders), "[d]amages accruing from the illegal infringement in the Israeli newspapers properly were awarded to Update [plaintiff]."

———

Curb v. MCA, 898 F.Supp. 586 (M.D.Tenn.1995). In a case involving the alleged unlicensed "authorization" from the U.S. to make and distribute country music phonorecords outside the U.S., the court criticized the Ninth Circuit's *Subafilms* decision:

> Curb argues that it did nothing more than sign contracts with entities abroad to distribute copies of sound recordings in which Curb held a license to reproduce. Curb's argument at law is this: Even assuming that such an action violated U.S. copyright law, such illegality is beyond the reach of this Court. There is recent precedent outside the Sixth Circuit that bears examination. [The court described *Subafilms*.]

> Even if the Court accepted *Subafilms'* interpretation lashing the § 106 authorization right solely to claims of contributory infringement, however, a critical question remains: Is there any primary infringement? ...

> This threshold question may be called "localizing infringement." Paul E. Geller & Melville B. Nimmer, eds., 1 International Copyright Law and Practice, Intr. § 3[b][i] (6th ed. 1994) ("Geller & Nimmer"). "More generally, in dealing with transborder conduct, it is advisable to analyze it down into discrete component acts country by country, before asking which law or laws should apply to which acts." Simply put, the Court must determine whether an act of copyright infringement occurred within the boundaries of the United States. For if it did, even *Subafilms* concedes that further extraterritorial acts will not thwart a U.S. court's jurisdiction....

> In this case, MCA indisputably held copyrights in the sound recordings at issue. By the Licensing Agreement, MCA authorized

Curb to reproduce and distribute copies of the recordings in the United States, Canada, and the United Kingdom.

MCA argues that when Curb expanded the market for these recordings to other countries, it infringed upon at least three of MCA's exclusive rights: reproduction, distribution, and authorization. . . .

MCA has produced copies of Curb's sublicensing agreements with entities in Hong Kong, Japan, and Australia. Each agreement required Curb to deliver duplicate master recordings to facilitate their reproduction. Curb's unauthorized creation of duplicate master tapes for release into these countries would appear to amount to an infringement of MCA's reproduction right.

Curb responds that the Licensing Agreement permitted Curb to reproduce the recordings anyway. However, the Licensing Agreement clearly restricts Curb's rights to the United States, Canada, and the United Kingdom. If Curb's argument were valid, it could make as many copies of MCA's recordings as it wished, so long as the copies were not used for infringing purposes. While this argument sounds fine at first blush, it is undercut by its own faulty premise: Why would any copyright holder authorize reproduction for the domestic market when such a transfer could lead to unsanctionable reproduction for wholesale distribution in foreign markets?

Curb's reproduction of the masters, if it occurred (and it did unless Curb shipped its only copy in a circuit from foreign distributor to distributor), for distribution into unauthorized territory, therefore amounts to a primary infringement of MCA's exclusive rights. . . .

The Ninth Circuit rejected the argument that the 1978 addition of the words "to authorize" in § 106 created an independent right, just as the words "to do" do. Instead, *Subafilms* holds that "to authorize" merely codifies the doctrine of contributory infringement. *Subafilms*, thus, reads the authorization right out of the Act in cases of foreign infringement.

But piracy has changed since the Barbary days. Today, the raider need not grab the bounty with his own hands; he need only transmit his go-ahead by wire or telefax to start the presses in a distant land. *Subafilms* ignores this economic reality, and the economic incentives underpinning the Copyright Clause designed to encourage creation of new works, and transforms infringement of the authorization right into a requirement of domestic presence by a primary infringer. Under this view, a phone call to Nebraska results in liability; the same phone call to France results in riches. In a global marketplace, it is literally a distinction without a difference.

A better view, one supported by the text, the precedents, and, ironically enough, the legislative history to which the *Subafilms* court cited, would be to hold that domestic violation of the authorization right is an infringement, sanctionable under the Copyright Act, whenever the authorizee has committed an act that would violate the copyright owner's § 106 rights....

In this case, even taking Curb's argument that it lawfully acquired and reproduced copies of MCA's sound recordings as true, the act of authorizing the distribution of the recordings for sale to a worldwide public seems equally sanctionable under sections 106 and 501. That Curb authorized these sales does not appear to be in dispute....

The Court is sensitive to the sovereignty and rule of law in other countries.... However, a careful exercise of domestic jurisdiction is consistent with the approach of the leading treatise in the field of international copyright law:

> A U.S. court, for example, could grant injunctive remedies under U.S. law for acts that commence a course of infringing conduct in the United States, for example, acts of authorizing or copying, without regard for whether eventual exploitation is to take place at home or abroad. Such an injunction would be justifiable if it forestalled piracy, whether at home or abroad, but did not risk interfering with such relief as might be granted under foreign laws for exploitation abroad

Geller & Nimmer, *supra*, § 3[b][ii], at INT–51–52.

QUESTIONS

1. In rejecting liability under U.S. copyright law for mere acts of "authorization" of copying to be done abroad, the *Subafilms* court specified that it was not reaching the question of the application of U.S. law to extraterritorial acts when at least one act of copying did occur in the United States (compare *Update Art, supra*). The root copy approach seems well-entrenched elsewhere, however, see, e.g., *Gasté v. Kaiserman,* 863 F.2d 1061 (2d Cir.1988) (public performances abroad made from sound recording unlawfully made in the U.S.); *Monroig v. RMM Records & Video Corp,* 196 F.R.D. 214 (D.P.R. 2000) (master copies of sound recordings made in U.S. and shipped to 14 foreign countries for further reproduction and distribution). What practical difference might it make were foreign laws rather than U.S. law to apply to the foreign-made copies from the U.S. masters?

2. In a decision subsequent to *Subafilms, Los Angeles News Serv. v. Reuters T.V. Int'l, Ltd.,* 149 F.3d 987 (9th Cir.1998), the Ninth Circuit upheld liability under the U.S. Copyright Act for an unauthorized transmission of videotaped scenes of riots in Los Angeles, because an initial infringing copy of the videotape was made in New York before the contents were transmitted from the U.S. to Europe and Africa. By contrast, in *Allarcom Pay T.V., Ltd. v. General Instrument Corp.,* 69 F.3d 381 (9th Cir.1995), the Ninth Circuit rejected application of U.S. law to unauthorized transmissions commenced in the U.S. but culminating abroad. The court stated:

> [D]efendants either initiated a potential infringement in the United States by broadcasting the Showtime signal, which contained copy-

righted material, or defendants authorized people in Canada to engage in infringement. In either case, the potential infringement was only completed in Canada once the signal was received and viewed. Accordingly, U.S. copyright law did not apply. . . .

Compare *NFL v. Primetime 24, infra.* Is this distinction between initial copies and initial transmissions persuasive as a matter of statutory interpretation? As a matter of policy? As a matter of fact? (Recall that digital technology blurs the distinction between reproduction and public performance.) Does the *Curb v. MCA* court offer a more satisfying approach? *Cf. Expediters Int'l of Washington, Inc. v. Direct Line Cargo Mgt. Servs., Inc.,* 995 F.Supp. 468 (D.N.J.1998) (following *Curb*).

3. In *Subafilms,* the disputed ''authorizations'' for international distribution of videocassettes of *Yellow Submarine* were at least made under color of right, since the licensor had financed and initially distributed the film, pursuant to an agreement with the Beatles. Should it make a difference to the applicability of U.S. law to extraterritorial exploitation if, as in *Curb v. MCA,* the ''authorizing'' party had exceeded the scope of its license from the copyright owner? What if the ''authorizing'' party had *no* prior relationship with the initial copyright owner? For example, what if defendant, a stranger to the Beatles, had from its U.S. offices directed the counterfeiting and sale in Southeast Asia of videocassettes of *Yellow Submarine? Cf. Ocean Garden, Inc. v. Marktrade Co.,* 953 F.2d 500 (9th Cir.1991) (applying Lanham Trademarks Act to a U.S. defendant who allegedly, from its California headquarters, directed the affixation on cans of tuna, fished and packaged in Mexico and sold in the Far East, of labels confusingly similar to plaintiff's labels for canned tuna).

4. In *Subafilms,* the Ninth Circuit characterized § 602(a)'s prohibition on unauthorized importation of copies lawfully made abroad as an ''extraterritorial'' application of U.S. law. Would it not be more accurate to describe this provision as one that declines to give effect, in the United States, to a foreign country's copyright law? In other words, rather than exemplifying an extraterritorial application of U.S. law, does not § 602(a) reinforce the *territoriality* of U.S. copyright law?

5. Defendant U.S. company authorizes (without the U.S. copyright owner's consent) the production of copies of the work abroad for reshipment to the U.S. by defendant's foreign partner. Does this act of authorization violate the U.S. copyright law? Or must the U.S. copyright owner wait until the copies arrive in the U.S.? *See Metzke v. May Department Stores Co.,* 878 F.Supp. 756 (W.D.Pa.1995); *BG Marketing USA, Inc. v. Gerolsteiner Brunnen GmbH & Co.,* 782 F.Supp. 763 (W.D.N.Y.1991).

———

Twentieth Century Fox Film Corp. v. iCraveTV, No 00–121 (W.D. Pa. Jan. 20, 2000). iCrave TV, a Toronto-based website, converted into videostreaming format the broadcast signals from Canadian programs, and from U.S. television programming received across the border, and made the programming available via its website. iCrave TV claimed that its capture, conversion, and redistribution of the U.S. programming was lawful under Canadian law concerning secondary transmissions of broadcast performances.

The producers brought suit in the Western District of Pennsylvania, where iCrave TV's President and its International Sales Manager resided. With respect to the Canadian business entities, the court found general personal jurisdiction over the non-resident defendants on the basis of their continuous and systematic contacts with Pennsylvania. Among the contacts the court identified were: sales of advertising out of a Pittsburgh office, employment of an agent in Pittsburgh to work in that office, and domain name registration for iCraveTV.com in the U.S., with technical and billing contacts listed in Pennsylvania. The court further found that defendants' activities in Pennsylvania were "integrally a part of the activities giving rise to the cause of action asserted." Finally, the court noted that defendants had streamed plaintiffs' programming to U.S. citizens throughout the U.S. overall, and had attempted to sell advertising throughout the U.S. through agents in New York and Pennsylvania.

On choice of law, the court found sufficient points of attachment with the U.S. to apply the U.S. Copyright Act to defendants' activities. The court found that the alleged infringement occurred in the United States when U.S. citizens "received and viewed defendants' streaming of the copyrighted materials," without plaintiffs' authorization, even though the streaming began in Canada. The receipt of the transmissions in the U.S. constituted public performances under U.S. copyright law. Moreover, the transmissions to the U.S. accounted for a substantial portion of iCrave TV's total business. For example, on January 17, 2000, an iCraveTV employee reported that log books monitoring traffic showed that approximately 45% of iCrave TV's traffic was from U.S.-based users; a January 25, 2000 report from a "private ad serving system" counted 1.6 million impressions from U.S. visitors (second only to Canadian visitors); "Real Video" logs of Internet addresses showed "substantial numbers of persons in the U.S. received the streaming of programming." The court ordered iCrave TV to cease retransmitting U.S. television programming. Following initiation of a suit in Canada alleging that iCrave TV's retransmissions were not permitted under Canadian law either, iCrave TV and the producers settled, and iCrave has ceased retrans-mitting U.S. television programming.

National Football League v. PrimeTime 24, 211 F.3d 10 (2d Cir.2000). This case presented the reverse of the *iCrave TV* coin. There, the retransmission originated from Canada, but was receivable in the U.S. Here, defendant captured plaintiff's U.S. broadcast signals in the U.S., but sent the retransmitted signals to Canadian households. Primetime 24 asserted that its service of Canadian households fell outside the scope of the U.S. copyright act, because the signals were received in Canada; no "public performance" occurred in the U.S. The Second Circuit disagreed:

The issue in this case is whether PrimeTime publicly performed or displayed NFL's copyrighted material. PrimeTime argues that capturing or uplinking copyrighted material and transmitting it to a satellite does not constitute a public display or performance of that material. PrimeTime argues that any public performance or display occurs during the downlink from the satellite to the home subscriber in Canada, which is in a foreign country where the Copyright Act does not apply.

In *WGN Continental Broad. Co. v. United Video, Inc.*, 693 F.2d 622, 624–25 (7th Cir.1982), the Seventh Circuit considered whether an intermediate carrier had publicly performed copyrighted television signals by capturing broadcast signals, altering them and transmitting them to cable television systems. The court determined that "the Copyright Act defines 'perform or display ... publicly' broadly enough to encompass indirect transmission to the ultimate public." Consequently, the *WGN* court concluded that an intermediate carrier is not immune from copyright liability simply because it does not retransmit a copyrighted signal to the public directly but instead routes the signal to cable systems, which then retransmit to the public.

Judge Posner, writing for the court in *WGN*, noted that a contrary result would render the passive carrier exemption in the Act superfluous. The passive carrier exemption provides that a secondary transmission is not copyright infringement if the transmitter has no control over the content or selection of the original signal or over the recipients of the secondary transmission and provides only the wires, cables, or communication channels for the use of others. *See* 17 U.S.C. § 111(a)(3). In other words, if a copyrighted signal is publicly performed or displayed only when received by viewers, there would be no need for a passive carrier exemption because these passive intermediate carriers "do not transmit directly to the public." ...

District courts in this Circuit have agreed that a transmission need not be made directly to the public in order for there to be a public performance or display. For example, in *David v. Showtime/The Movie Channel, Inc.*, 697 F.Supp. 752, 759 (S.D.N.Y.1988), Judge Tenney concluded that "Congress intended the definitions of 'public' and 'performance' to encompass each step in the process by which a protected work wends its way to its audience." Judge Tenney further stated that the definition of transmit "is broad enough to include all conceivable forms and combinations of wired or wireless communications media." ...

The Court of Appeals for the Ninth Circuit has suggested a different result. When considering whether the Copyright Act preempted state law, that Court stated that copyright infringement does not occur until the signal is received by the viewing public. See *Allarcom Pay Television, Ltd. v. General Instrument Corp.*, 69 F.3d 381, 387 (9th Cir.1995). This opinion has been subject to some non-judicial criticism, which we need not repeat. See Jane C. Ginsburg, *Extraterritoriality and Multiterritoriality in Copyright Infringement*, 37 Va. J. Int'l L. 587, 598 (1997); Andreas P. Reindl, *Choosing Law in Cyberspace: Copyright Conflicts on Global Networks*, 19 Mich. J. Int'l L. 799, 823 n.84 (1998). We accord the decision little weight largely because it contains no analysis of the Copyright Act.

We believe the most logical interpretation of the Copyright Act is to hold that a public performance or display includes "each step in the process by which a protected work wends its way to its audience." Under that analysis, it is clear that PrimeTime's uplink transmission of signals captured in the United States is a step in the process by which NFL's protected work wends its way to a public audience. In short, PrimeTime publicly displayed or performed material in which the NFL owns the copyright. Because PrimeTime did not have authorization to make such a public performance, PrimeTime infringed the NFL's copyright. . . .

QUESTION

Can a U.S. copyright plaintiff have it both ways: assert violation of U.S. law when a transmission originating abroad is received in the U.S., but also claim application of U.S. law when a U.S.-originated transmission is received abroad?

*

GENERAL REVIEW PROBLEMS

The following Problems cover a variety of issues in copyright law. They may afford the student a helpful means of review.

PROBLEM 1

The Museum of Moderately Modern Art (hereafter MOMMA) is planning a major show of twentieth-century American and European artists. Some of the works on display are part of MOMMA's permanent collection, some are on loan from other museums. Most of the works are well known to the public through their display in museums and their inclusion in scholarly and coffee table art books. But the highlights of the show will be several works by Picasso never previously exhibited, specially loaned by Picasso family members, as well as two new works by contemporary feminist political artist Barbara Kruger.

MOMMA anticipates many visitors to the show and hopes to recover its costs, and perhaps to defray general museum expenses, not only through ticket sales but through sales of postcards, catalogs, posters, and a variety of related merchandise, including calendars, note cards, shopping bags, scarves, placemats, decorative plates, board games, bed sheets, shower curtains, lunch boxes, kitchen canisters, and dish towels, all bearing full or partial productions of works in the show.

MOMMA has traditionally taken the position that it has the right to make and sell postcards, etc., of any work that it owns or exhibits. Recently, however, several artists have expressed disagreement with the museum's assertions and have threatened to initiate court action. Although MOMMA publicly adheres to its position, Curt Curator, the show's organizer, is concerned about what right the museum does in fact have to make and sell postcards and other merchandizing properties of the works to be included in the show. He further inquires whether, to the extent MOMMA may not have pertinent rights, they may be secured, and if so, how? You are counsel to MOMMA. Advise Mr. Curator.

PROBLEM 2

Your client has sent you the following draft advertisement detailing her plans for a new magazine:

Attention Wine Lovers!

Do you want to know the best wines and best values in America today?

Do you want the most recent reviews and vintage reports on the wines of Bordeaux, Burgundy, Germany, Italy, California and other important wine districts? Would you like to know the opinions of the world's leading wine writers, the ratings made by the top wine journals—all this in one convenient publication?

Announcing BACCH/ANNALS, America's first wine-review newspaper.

It reports on the published wine reviews and opinions of every important wine columnist and wine writer printed in America today, plus the top wine authorities of England and France. It does so without their approval or involvement so it can objectively evaluate their reviews without bias or personal obligation.

BACCH/ANNALS is published mid-monthly so you can receive the latest wine news and reviews shortly after they appear in their original publications. BACCH/ANNALS is conveniently organized in a country-by-country, district-by-district, and wine-type by wine type format that is a breeze to use. Each review is in a consistent style regardless of the newspaper or magazine it appeared in.

Retailers, Importers, Wine Producers and other
members of the wine trade, read this!

You get *all* the ratings from *all* the foremost wine writers from *all* the best wine reviews; you will save hundreds of dollars each year when you subscribe to BACCH/ANNALS. Best of all, BACCH/ANNALS is published on paper that is easy to reproduce in ads or catalogs or enlarge for in-store displays.

Based on the description set forth in the advertisement, advise your client concerning:

A.   The risk of copyright liability she may incur if she publishes the magazine as it is described in the advertisement;

B.   How she might modify the content of the magazine to diminish the risk of liability for copyright infringement.

PROBLEM 3

Seeking a publisher for his projected first detective novel, an aspiring young writer, Artiste Manqué, sends the following submission to Scrivener & Sons, Publishers:

"A strange case of poisoning pervaded Paris. Someone had unleashed a flock of infected bees in the Jardin de Luxembourg, with the design, successfully realized, of allowing the bees to mingle among the chestnut blossoms, poisoning the pollen, and asphyxiating all who might breather the air through which the pollen wafted. The Sureté's crack detective, Commissaire Maldefoie, was dispatched to root out the evil-doer.

"Commissaire Maldefoie was the sort of robust *bon bourgeois* to be found at many a sidewalk café, but with a difference: he ate only the finest escargots, washed down with Sauternes—a combination to curdle the stomachs of his countrymen, but one which he maintained aided his famous mental acuity. When on a case, Maldefoie would often make notes while standing on his head in a yoga position and simultaneously barking orders to his hapless assistant, Inspecteur Vautrien.

"In unraveling the mystery of the poisoned pollen, Maldefoie meets up with a seductive part-time beekeeper who, during a break in a show at the Folies Bergeres (where she also works in the chorus line), discloses the names of the members of an international insect-raising gang, which may or may not be involved in the crime. From a disgruntled street sweeper, Maldefoie learns of CIA infiltration into the public gardeners' union. At a rendezvous with an informer in the Louvre, Maldefoie begins to suspect that Vautrien has been playing a double-game. These suspicions are confirmed when Maldefoie discovers his assistant hanged from the headless neck of the Winged Victory above the museum's monumental staircase.

"As the exciting denouement of a complicated plot, Maldefoie gathers all the suspects, including the beekeeper, the informant, the international insect raisers, and several CIA operatives, at the top of the Eiffel Tower, to reveal the name of the poisoner.

"If you want to know who did it and how Maldefoie found out, send me a publishing contract and a $100,000 advance."

Joyce Eliot, an enterprising editor in Scrivener's unsolicited manuscripts department, reads Manqué's submission and is enthusiastic about its possibilities. At first inclined to recommend a contract for Manqué, she then determines to send Manqué a rejection letter, and to work from his submission to write the novel herself. Eliot's finished novel incorporates and builds on the plot and characters as disclosed in Manqué's submission. It proves an enormous popular and financial success, and is optioned for a television series detailing the further adventures of Maldefoie.

Upon reading Eliot's novel, Manqué is enraged and commences an action alleging:

1. Co-ownership of copyright in the novel as a joint author;
2. Infringement of the copyright in the material submitted through Eliot's use of his plot and characters;
3. Misappropriation;
4. Misrepresentation.

Ms. Eliot has hired you to advise her about defending the suit. Set forth the factual and legal (including jurisdictional) bases of each claim; identify and elaborate on defenses you would raise with respect to each claim; and give your evaluation of the likelihood of success of these defenses. You may assume that all events transpired after January 1, 1978.

PROBLEM 4

Harold Hacker, a fifteen-year-old computer enthusiast, has developed an educational service for his high school classmates who have experienced difficulty in the Algebra course. Having correctly guessed the password to gaining access to the math department computer at Major University, Hacker has discovered that the computer includes in its data base the text of the Algebra textbook used in his high school, as well as the text of the

Teacher's Manual with all of the solutions to the problems in the textbook. Hacker has stored the Teacher's Manual solutions on one of his computer disks. Hacker does not know much about copyright, but he suspects that printing out and distributing copies of the Manual from his disk may not be a good idea. Instead, therefore, Hacker invites his classmates, for a fee, to come over to his house to read the computer screen display of the Manual generated by Hacker's disk. As word spreads among high school students concerning Hacker's service, students from other schools contact Hacker about coming over to see the Manual. Unable to accommodate all the requests, Hacker agrees, for a fee, to go to a designated vacant lot to deliver a lecture disclosing the solutions contained in the Manual to students from other high schools.

You know more about copyright than Hacker does. Which of the following acts constitute infringement of what rights under copyright and why or why not?

1. Gaining access to Major University's computer.

2. Inputting the Teacher's Manual on a disk.

3. Inviting classmates over to read the screen display generated by the disk.

4. The lecture.

PROBLEM 5

Your client is Color Technology, Inc. (CTI), which has perfected a technique for adding realistic colors to black-and-white motion picture films. The process works as follows. A single film frame from each scene is selected by a CTI "colorist" who, with the use of a computer, codes the frame with a variety of colors chosen by the technician. In part, the colors chosen are intended to reproduce the actual colors of a person's hair, skin etc., and of the scenic background, such as a flag or building; in part, the colors chosen are freely selected with a view toward an overall appealing color pattern. The computer is able to take account of movement from frame-to-frame within the scene, and can thus carry the selected colors onto any number of frames on the film.

CTI has recently acquired copies of several motion picture films that are in good enough condition to use for "colorizing." These films, upon their initial release, had all been commercially distributed and exhibited in the customary manner, i.e., the authorized distributor rented the film for a limited time to a motion picture theater for exhibition, and the theatre promised to return the film to the distributor at the end of that period and not to give possession to anyone else or to make any copies. The oldest of the four films is from 1910; it bears a copyright notice with that date, and your research shows that its copyright was renewed in 1938. Another film in CTI's possession was released in 1970, and a third in 1980; neither, however, bears a copyright notice. A fourth film was just released in September 1989; it also has no copyright notice.

(a) CTI asks you whether it must secure anyone's permission before "colorizing" the four black-and-white films and then marketing the colorized versions for television broadcasting and videocassette sales and rentals. Give your advise, with reasons.

(b) CTI also asks you whether CTI will be able to stop others who would wish to make copies of the colorized CTI films, and whether any steps should be taken by CTI in order to protect its right. Give your advice, with reasons.

PROBLEM 6

Don's Supermarket decided to place an advertisement in one of the local newspapers at the time of the Thanksgiving holiday. Don went to the Daily Planet, and spoke to the head of the advertising staff, Paula Penn. Don gave Paula his business card, which contained a drawing of his supermarket and of some fruits and vegetables, and also the address and telephone number and business hours of the store. Don asked Paula to use the business card as the basis for the advertisement and to have the Daily Planet's advertising staff add some of the usual brief complimentary phrases about the freshness, quality and price of the products sold at Don's Supermarket.

Although Don did not see the finished advertisement prior to publication, he was pleased with it when it was printed prior to the Thanksgiving holiday, and he sent a check to the Daily Planet, to the attention of Paula Penn, in the amount of $300 as had been agreed upon. The check contained the legend on the back: "In full payment for the advertisement prepared by the Daily Planet as a work made for hire, and for the transfer of all other rights." Paula endorsed the check and the Daily Planet deposited it in the newspaper's bank account.

A few days ago, Don informed you of his intention to have the advertisement published in the other four local newspapers during the Christmas shopping season. Is he free to do so? Give your advice, with reasons.

PROBLEM 7

Paramount Pictures, Inc., produces and distributes motion pictures made for theatre and television exhibition. It owns the copyright in most of those films. You are its general counsel, and your specialty is intellectual property. Paramount's executives have formulated several questions, recounted below, on which they would like your advice in the form of a reasoned memorandum. Prepare that memorandum.

(a) Paramount has learned that airlines are considering making available to passengers flying in First Class a hand-held videotape player and a choice of videocassettes of motion picture films for personal viewing on long-distance flights. (This would be particularly attractive to the traveler who, for example, has already seen the film that is being shown to all of the passengers on the plane.) Paramount wants to know whether the airlines must secure its consent before making Paramount-owned films available in this fashion; if so, Paramount would consider requiring the payment of a reasonable royalty.

(b) Several members of the House and Senate have introduced identical bills to

amend the Copyright Act so that the commercial rental of a videotaped films would be an infringement. These bills are modeled on the Record Rental Amendment of 1984 and the Computer Software Rental Amendment of 1990. Paramount supports such legislation, which would afford it an opportunity to enter into negotiated royalty agreements with video store owners. Paramount wishes to know what the strongest arguments are that will likely be made against these bills as well as whether there are any changes that Paramount might consider in order to improve them or to reduce legislative opposition.

(c) A few of Paramount's copyrighted films are musicals. Songs written under contract for use in those films are electronically fixed on the soundtrack so as to synchronize with the dramatic action on the film frames. Paramount has learned that a popular singer has just made a recording that includes several songs from one of Paramount's musical films and that this recording is selling very well in record stores across the country. Because Paramount believes that the singer's recorded performances are of very poor quality, it wishes to know whether it may prevent the continued sale of the records.

PROBLEM 8

An action has been brought for infringement of a statue. The statue, familiarly known as the Three Servicemen Statue, is part of the Vietnam Veterans Memorial in Washington. It as commissioned, and was selected after a juried competition. The defendant is manufacturing and selling small three-dimensional replicas of the statue. Neither the plaintiff's originality nor the defendant's copying is denied.

The defendant, however, has interposed several defenses. First, he claims that the artistic elements of the statue are not separable from its utilitarian function of honoring Vietnam veterans. Second, he claims that the statue, although sculpted by a civilian, was commissioned by the federal government and is therefore beyond the protection of copyright. Third, he claims that in any event the statue is a work made for hire, and the plaintiff has no standing to sue. Fourth, he claims that because the statue is open to view in a public place, the 1990 amendments to the Copyright Act permit the making of unauthorized reproductions.

How should the court dispose of these issues?

PROBLEM 9

Mellifluous Editions Inc., a commercial (albeit not very profitable) publisher specializing in works about music, wishes to compile and publish a catalogue of U.S. and European doctoral dissertations on modern music written during the last twenty years. No such listings are currently available from a single source. Mellifluous would acquire information for its listings from the following sources:

1. *Universal Dissertations Abstracts.* This CD ROM product lists all completed U.S. and Canadian doctoral dissertations in all academic fields. The listings are organized chronologically. Each academic discipline in which a thesis is written has a code number. The user can enter the code onto the CD ROM reader and thereby call up listings only for the dissertations in the field corresponding to the code. There is a code for Music and Music History, but no subcodes breaking the field down by period. The CD ROM contains two levels of information about each dissertation. At the first level, the CD ROM displays the title of the dissertation, the author's name, the school awarding the degree, and the year in which the doctoral degree was conferred. At the second level, the CD ROM offers abstracts of each listed dissertation. The abstracts are written by the dissertation authors, and present a one-paragraph outline and summary of the dissertation.

2. *MusiqueChronique.* The June issue of this French academic journal lists dissertations completed in Europe since publication of the prior year's listings. The listings are organized by field within Music History, for example, Renaissance, Baroque, Romantic, Modern. Within each field, the listings include the university conferring the degree, the title of the dissertation, and name of the author.

While *MusiqueChronique* is in conventional hard-copy format, *Universal Dissertation Abstracts* is available only on CD ROM. The CD ROM is made available to libraries subject to a "site license," through which the library agrees to permit patrons to access the information on the CD ROM only if they agree to the following terms and conditions:

Any printing or downloading or information from *Universal Dissertation Abstracts* is permitted for personal use only and may not be used for other purposes.

Mellifuous is concerned that its project may pose copyright problems. In addition to identifying the problems, suggest how Mellifluous might go about working with the above sources in order to create listings, yet avoid liability to any of the publishers of the sources.

PROBLEM 10

I–Gulf, an online auction house, offers buyers and sellers a forum for sales of goods to the highest online bidder. Sellers post notices on the I–Gulf websites, identifying the goods, the starting price, and the duration of the bidding period; buyers respond within the allotted period; I–Gulf takes a commission from the sellers on each sale conducted through the site. Once the sale is concluded, the buyer sends a check directly to the seller, and the seller mails the goods to the buyer. It has recently come to the attention of Tinychip, a leading software producer, that many sellers on the I–Gulf site are selling copies of Tinychip Office for $28.00 or less. The product normally retails for $400. Most of the low-priced copies of Office are offered in large lots.

After making several online purchases from large lot sellers through I–Gulf, Tinychip learns that the suspiciously low-priced copies of Office fall into four categories. Some are counterfeit. Others, as the British English spelling conventions employed in the user's manuals reveals, are copies of Office that have been imported from foreign markets where Tinychip's foreign licensees sell them at a lower price than Tinychip charges in the U.S. Still others are used copies, resold in violation of the shrinkwrap license that accompanies each retail package of Office. Finally, some of the copies have been resold after removal or disabling of the anti-copying codes that Tinychip had incorporated in its software.

You are counsel to Tinychip. Citing pertinent provisions of Title 17 where relevant, as well as applicable judicial interpretation, identify and analyze the claims Tinychip may have against the large lot sellers and against I–Gulf, and the defenses you should anticipate.

PROBLEM 11

You are in-house counsel to Graphic Ubiquitous Solutions Technology (GUST), a major computer software producer. GUST contacted Tippy Temps, an agency supplying temporary office workers, to request the services of a computer programmer to assist on the Help Line GUST makes available to customers who phone in with questions or problems concerning GUST software. Tippy Temps sent Orville Wilbur, one of its experienced programmers. While answering customer questions for GUST about the software, Orville came to believe that the GUST Help Line's call receiving system was inefficient and could be improved. He set about to improve it by writing a new program for the Help Line. Orville discussed the project with his supervisor, Katherine Deeds, who allowed him to use GUST equipment to write the program. When not answering the phone, Orville worked on the program at GUST's offices. He also worked on it at home on his own computer.

When the program was half completed, Orville left Tippy Temps. He continued to work on the GUST helpline program, at home and at GUST. Shortly before completing the program, Orville informed Katherine that he would not make the program available to GUST unless GUST acquired a license from him for the use of the program. Katherine temporized, saying she would have to obtain the approval of her superiors. Hoping that GUST would ultimately take a license, Orville completed the program, installed it on GUST's LAN, and trained GUST's Help Line staff in the program's operation.

GUST, however, did not agree to take a license from Orville. After Orville threatened to take action against GUST, and fearing that Orville would remove or destroy all GUST's copies of the program, GUST obtained a court order prohibiting Orville from entering GUST's premises. Orville had anticipated GUST's lockout. As a precaution, he had programmed the new Help Line software to recognize his login; if he did not log in for four consecutive days, the software would self-destruct. And it did.

Undaunted, GUST assigned an in-house programmer to write a new Help Line program implementing Orville's ideas for improvement of the prior system. The programmer did not consult Orville's program when writing the new program, but the programmer was very familiar with Orville's program, having frequently worked with it from the time of its installation until its self-destruction.

Orville has commenced an action for an injunction and damages, alleging (1) copyright infringement of the Help Line program he wrote, and (2) common-law conversion of the value of his services in writing the program. Orville has also sought to license his program to other software producers for their Help Lines. How should GUST respond to Orville's claims and acts?

PROBLEM 12

Professor Donna Prima, of the Columbus University School of Law, teaches a course in Popular Culture and the Law. Her "reading list" includes popular music, articles from periodicals, excerpts from books, judicial decisions and statutes that Professor Prima has uploaded to her website. Because Professor Donna Prima believes fervently in academic freedom and open communication, she has not restricted access to her course webpage to students enrolled in the course, or even to those enrolled at Columbus Law School. Because Professor Prima is web-adept (or has hired student teaching assistants who are web-adept), her course webpage has very high production values. It includes the cartoon of the week, scanned from sources such as the New Yorker, and the Sunday comics; the webpage's soundtrack features the song of the week, downloaded from a variety of MP3 sites. This week's song is the appallingly post-feminist hit by Normandie Swords: "Beat Me Baby, Yet Again." The webpage also has a chatroom that allows students and others to comment on the classes and on the "readings." Sometimes, participants post excerpts from other works as part of the online discussions. Not surprisingly, Professor Prima's webpage has developed quite a following within and without Columbus Law School; the webpage's counter shows thousands of "hits" to the site. Columbus Dean Willard Worried has become concerned that Professor Prima's site may pose copyright problems. He wonders what, short of shutting the site down (which would spark tremendous resentment), he can do to minimize risks of liability to Columbus.

Professor Prima's instruction is not merely virtual. She is a dynamic lecturer and her classes are very popular. So popular in fact, that a student enrolled in the class, Roger Jolly, has responded to a business opportunity offered to him by LegalEd.com, to post his class notes on their website. Jolly's notes, while purporting to convey the content of Professor Prima's lectures, are sometimes inaccurate, not to mention frequently misspelled. When Professor Prima learns what Roger Jolly has been doing (and how ineptly he has been doing it), she is outraged, and demands that LegalEd.com take down the posting. Dean Worried sends LegalEd.com a cease and desist letter on Professor Prima's and the school's behalf. LegalEd.com replies that the notes are the student's intellectual property that he has transferred to LegalEd.com, and that they therefore are entitled to post the notes on their for-profit website.

You are General Counsel to Columbus University. Advise your client concerning its exposure to liability for copyright infringement resulting from Professor Prima's website, and as to its rights against LegalEd.com.

PROBLEM 13

Assume that you were enrolled last year in a law school seminar, in which there was a requirement that you write an extended research paper. Pursuant to the instructor's course requirements, you discussed the paper topic with him; you thereafter submitted a detailed outline, upon which he made extended comments and returned it to you; you thereafter submitted a first draft of your paper, and again received extended written comments from the professor (most of which you addressed in your subsequent revision); and you then prepared and presented your final draft. At the end of the seminar, you were given a fine grade based upon the quality of your final paper.

During the course of last summer, while you were working for a law firm, you learned to your surprise that the law school, without your permission, had placed 10 pages of excerpts from the 50–page text of your final paper on the law school's website on the internet. The accompanying statement on the website noted that your paper, and five others heavily quoted there, were examples of the cutting-edge work done by students in their courses and seminars. The law school website can, of course, be accessed by all persons who own a computer and who contract with an internet service provider.

Your initial pleasure at learning of this development turned to embarrassment and anger, when you were informed that the position you espoused in your paper was flatly contrary to one that your summer law firm was taking at the time in an ongoing dispute; your firm subtly conveyed its displeasure to you.

(1) You have brought an action for copyright infringement against your law school. Explain briefly which exclusive rights you claim have been violated. Might you name other defendants? Might you have any claims other than copyright infringement?

(2) The law school defends against your copyright infringement claim by asserting several defenses: (a) The paper was a work for hire and its copyright is owned by the school; (b) the paper was a joint work the copyright to which was partly owned by the professor (who gave his permission to its posting on the website); (c) the law school's copying was insubstantial; and (d) the copying was in any event fair use. What is the likely outcome of the lawsuit? Explain.

BIBLIOGRAPHY

The following is a selective list of secondary materials, organized according to the chapters herein, that the casebook authors believe to be particularly useful background reading, beyond those already cited in the text.

For general reference regarding domestic U.S. copyright law, the Copyright Office Webpage, www.loc.gov/copyright, is a very useful starting point. The Copyright Office page includes recent legislative developments, Copyright Office documents, and links to a multitude of public and private sources concerning copyright law. Leading treatises include Melville Nimmer & David Nimmer, *Nimmer on Copyright,* and Paul Goldstein, *Copyright: Principles, Law and Practice* (2d ed. 1996, with updates). *See also* William Patry, *Copyright Law and Practice* (1994, 2000 supp.). Marshall Leaffer, *Understanding Copyright* (3d ed. 1999), is a useful one-volume treatment. Two of the leading journals in the field are the *Journal of the Copyright Society of the USA* and the *Columbia-VLA Journal of Law & the Arts.*

The authors also recommend a number of readable and provocative books that explore many of the general issues of copyright and its history: Benjamin Kaplan, *An Unhurried View of Copyright* (1967); Paul Goldstein, *Copyright's Highway: From Gutenberg to the Celestial Jukebox* (1995); Edward Samuels, *The Illustrated Story of Copyright* (2000); Jessica Litman, *Digital Copyright* (2001).

For general reference regarding international and comparative copyright law, the World Intellectual Property Organization's website, www.wipo.org, offers a helpful introduction. The leading treatises are: Sam Ricketson, *The Berne Convention for the Protection of Literary and Artistic Works 1886–1986* (1987); Stephen M. Stewart, *International Copyright and Neighboring Rights* (2d ed. 1989); and Paul Edward Geller & Melville B. Nimmer, *International Copyright Law and Practice* (2000) (with updates). Leading international and comparative copyright journals publishing articles in English include: *RIDA,* (Revue Internationale du Droit d'Auteur) (France); *IIC* (International Intellectual Property and Copyright) (Germany); and *EIPR,* (European Intellectual Property Reporter) (UK).

CHAPTER 1. THE CONCEPT OF COPYRIGHT

Howard B. Abrams, *The Historic Foundation of American Copyright: Exploding the Myth of Common Law Copyright,* 29 Wayne L. Rev. 1119 (1983)

Stanley M. Besen & Leo Raskind, *An Introduction to the Law and Economics of Intellectual Property,* 5 J. Econ. Perspectives 3 (1991)

Zachariah Chafee, Jr., *Reflections on the Law of Copyright,* 45 Colum. L. Rev. 503, 719 (1945)

Francine Crawford, *Pre-Constitutional Copyright Statutes,* 23 Bull. Copyright Soc'y 11 (1975)

Robert C. Denicola, *Mostly Dead?: Copyright Law in the New Millennium*, 47 J. Copyright Soc'y 193 (2000)

Paul Edward Geller, *Copyright History and the Future: What's Culture Got to Do with It?*, 47 J. Copyright Soc'y 209 (2000)

Jane C. Ginsburg, *Authors and Users in Copyright*, 45 J. Copyright Soc'y 1 (1997)

Jane C. Ginsburg, *Can Copyright Be Made User–Friendly? Essay Review of Jessica Litman's* Digital Copyright, 25 Colum.-VLA J.L. & Arts (2001).

Paul Goldstein, *Copyright*, 38 J. Copyright Soc'y 109 (1991)

Wendy J. Gordon, *An Inquiry into the Merits of Copyright: The Challenges of Consistency, Consent, and "Encouragement" Theory*, 41 Stan. L. Rev. 1343 (1989)

Marci A. Hamilton, *Copyright at the Supreme Court: A Jurisprudence of Deference*, 47 J. Copyright Soc'y 317 (2000)

I. Trotter Hardy, *Property (and Copyright) in Cyberspace*, 1996 U. Chi. L. F. 217 (1996)

Paul J. Heald & Suzanna Sherry, *Implied Limits on the Legislative Power: The Intellectual Property Clause as an Absolute Constraint on Congress*, 2000 U. Ill. L. Rev. 1119

Robert Patrick Merges & Glenn Harlan Reynolds, *The Proper Scope of the Copyright and Patent Power*, 37 Harv. J. on Legis. 45 (2000)

Neil Weinstock Netanel, *Copyright and a Democratic Society*, 106 Yale L.J. 283 (1996)

Thomas P. Olson, *The Iron Law of Consensus: Congressional Responses to Proposed Copyright Reforms Since the 1909 Act*, 36 J. Copyright Soc'y 109 (1989)

L. Ray Patterson, Copyright in Historical Perspective (1968)

L. Ray Patterson, *Copyright in the New Millennium: Resolving the Conflict between Property Rights and Political Rights*, 62 Ohio St. L.J. 703 (2001)

L. Ray Patterson, *Understanding the Copyright Clause*, 47 J. Copyright Soc'y 365 (2000)

Shira Perlmutter, *Convergence and the Future of Copyright*, 24 Colum.-VLA J.L. & Arts 163 (2001)

Edward Samuels, *The Public Domain in Copyright Law*, 41 J. Copyright Soc'y 137 (1993)

Pamela Samuelson, *Economic and Constitutional Influences on Copyright Law in the United States*, 23 Eur. Intell. Prop. Rep. 409 (2001)

Jeremy Waldron, *From Authors to Copiers: Individual Rights and Social Values in Intellectual Property*, 68 Chi.-Kent L. Rev. 841 (1993)

Alfred C. Yen, *Copyright Opinions and Aesthetic Theory*, 71 S. Cal. L. Rev. 247 (1998)

CHAPTER 2. COPYRIGHTABLE SUBJECT MATTER

A. IN GENERAL

Ralph S. Brown, *Eligibility for Copyright Protection: A Search for Principled Standards,* 70 Minn. L. Rev. 579 (1985)

Gregory S. Donat, Note, *Fixing Fixation: A Copyright with Teeth for Improvisational Performers,* 97 Colum. L. Rev. 1363 (1997)

David Nimmer, *Copyright in the Dead Sea Scrolls: Authorship and Originality,* 38 Hous. L. Rev. 1 (2001)

Pamela Samuelson, *Some New Kinds of Authorship Made Possible by Computers and Some Intellectual Property Questions They Raise,* 53 U. Pitt. L. Rev. 865 (1992)

Lloyd L. Weinreb, *Copyright for Functional Expression,* 111 Harv. L. Rev. 1149 (1998)

B. THE "IDEA/EXPRESSION DICHOTOMY"

Scott Abrahamson, Comment, *Seen One, Seen Them All? Making Sense of the Copyright Merger Doctrine,* 45 UCLA L. Rev. 1125 (1998)

Amy B. Cohen, *Copyright Law and the Myth of Objectivity: The Idea–Expression Dichotomy and the Inevitability of Artistic Value Judgments,* 66 Ind. L. Rev. 175 (1990)

Edward Samuels, *The Idea–Expression Dichotomy in Copyright Law,* 56 Tenn. L. Rev. 321 (1989)

Richard H. Stern, *Scope-of-Protection Problems With Patents and Copyrights on Methods of Doing Business,* 10 Fordham Intell. Prop. Media & Ent. L.J. 105 (1999)

C. FACTS AND COMPILATIONS

Jonathan Band & Makoto Kono, *The Database Protection Debate in the 106th Congress,* 62 Ohio St. L.J. 869 (2001)

Paula Baron, *Back to the Future: Learning from the Past in the Database Debate,* 62 Ohio St. L.J. 879 (2001)

Robert C. Denicola, *Copyright in Collections of Facts: A Theory for the Protection of Nonfiction Literary Works,* 81 Colum. L. Rev. 516 (1981)

Jane C. Ginsburg, *Copyright, Common Law, and Sui Generis Protection of Databases in the United States and Abroad,* 66 U. Cin. L. Rev. 151 (1997)

Jane C. Ginsburg, *Creation and Commercial Value: Copyright Protection for Works of Information,* 90 Colum. L. Rev. 1865 (1990)

Robert A. Gorman, *Fact or Fancy? The Implications for Copyright,* 29 J. Copyright Soc'y 590 (1982)

Robert A. Gorman, *Copyright Protection for the Collection and Representation of Facts,* 76 Harv. L. Rev. 1569 (1963)

Paul J. Heald, *The Extraction/Duplication Dichotomy: Constitutional Line–Drawing in the Database Debate*, 62 Ohio St. L.J. 933 (2001)

Dennis S. Karjala, *Copyright in Electronic Maps*, 35 Jurimetrics J. 295 (1995)

Malla Pollack, *The Right to Know?: Delimiting Database Protection at the Juncture of the Commerce Clause, The Intellectual Property Clause, and the First Amendment*, 17 Cardozo Arts & Ent. L.J. 47 (1999)

J.H. Reichman & Pamela Samuelson, *Intellectual Property Rights in Data?*, 50 Vand. L. Rev. 51 (1997)

D.   DERIVATIVE WORKS

Steven S. Boyd, *Deriving Originality in Derivative Works: Considering the Quantum of Originality Needed to Attain Copyright Protection in a Derivative Work*, 40 Santa Clara L. Rev. 325 (2000)

Paul Goldstein, *Derivative Rights and Derivative Works in Copyright*, 30 J. Copyright Soc'y 209 (1982)

Robert A. Gorman, *Copyright Courts and Aesthetic Judgments: Abuse or Necessity?*, 25 Colum.-VLA J.L. & Arts 1 (2001)

E.   COMPUTER PROGRAMS

Kenneth W. Dam, *Some Economic Considerations in the Intellectual Property Protection of Software*, 24 J. Legal Studies 321 (1995)

Marci A. Hamilton & Ted Sabety, *Computer Science Concepts in Copyright Cases: The Path to a Coherent Law*, 10 Harv. J.L. & Tech. 239 (1997)

Dennis S. Karjala, *A Coherent Theory for the Copyright Protection of Computer Software and Recent Judicial Interpretations*, 66 U. Cin. L. Rev. 53 (1997)

Peter S. Menell, *Tailoring Legal Protection for Computer Software*, 39 Stan. L. Rev. 1329 (1987)

Arthur R. Miller, *Copyright Protection for Computer Programs, Databases, and Computer–Generated Works: Is Anything New Since CONTU?*, 106 Harv. L. Rev. 977 (1993)

Symposium, *Toward a Third Intellectual Property Paradigm*, 94 Colum. L. Rev. 2307 (1994)

F.   PICTORIAL, GRAPHIC AND SCULPTURAL WORKS

Ralph S. Brown, *Design Protection: An Overview*, 34 UCLA L. Rev. 1341 (1987)

Robert C. Denicola, *Applied Art and Industrial Design: A Suggested Approach to Copyright in Useful Articles*, 67 Minn. L. Rev. 707 (1983)

Daniel Goldenberg, *The Long and Winding Road, A History of the Fight over Industrial Design Protection in the United States*, 45 J. Copyright Soc'y 21 (1997)

Shira Perlmutter, *Conceptual Separability and Copyright in the Designs of Useful Articles,* 37 J. Copyright Soc'y 339 (1990)

J.H. Reichman, *Design Protection After the Copyright Act of 1976: A Comparative View of the Emerging Interim Models,* 31 J. Copyright Soc'y 267 (1984)

J.H. Reichman, *Design Protection and the Legislative Agenda,* 55 Law & Contemp. Probs. 281 (1992)

J.H. Reichman, *Design Protection in Domestic and Foreign Copyright Law: From the Berne Revision of 1948 to the Copyright Act of 1976,* 1983 Duke L.J. 1143

G.   ARCHITECTURAL WORKS

Christopher C. Dremann, *Copyright Protection for Architectural Works,* 23 AIPLA Q.J. 325 (1995)

Jane C. Ginsburg, *Copyright in the 101st Congress: Commentary on the Visual Artists' Rights Act and the Architectural Works Copyright Protection Act of 1990,* 14 Colum.-VLA J.L. & Arts 477 (1990)

Melissa M. Mathis, *Note: Function, Nonfunction, and Monumental Works of Architecture: An Interpretive Lens in Copyright Law,* 22 Cardozo L. Rev. 595 (2001)

Raleigh W. Newsam, *Architecture and Copyright—Separating the Poetic from the Prosaic,* 71 Tul. L. Rev. 1073 (1997)

H.   CHARACTERS

Mark Bartholomew, *Protecting the Performers: Setting a New Standard for Character Copyrightability,* 41 Santa Clara L. Rev. 341 (2001)

Michael Todd Helfand, Note, *When Mickey Mouse Is as Strong as Superman: The Convergence of Intellectual Property Laws to Protect Fictional Literary and Pictorial Characters,* 44 Stan. L. Rev. 623 (1992)

Leslie A. Kurtz, *The Independent Legal Lives of Fictional Characters,* 1986 Wis. L. Rev. 429

Francis M. Nevins, *Copyright + Character = Catastrophe,* 39 J. Copyright Soc'y 303 (1992)

Dean D. Niro, *Protecting Characters Through Copyright Law: Paving a New Road Upon Which Literary, Graphic and Motion Picture Characters Can All Travel,* 41 DePaul L. Rev. 359 (1992)

Keith Poliakoff, *License to Copyright: The Ongoing Dispute Over the Ownership of James Bond,* 18 Cardozo Arts & Ent. L.J. 387 (2000)

Richard Wincor, The Art of Character Licensing (1996)

I.   GOVERNMENT WORKS AND OTHER PUBLIC POLICY ISSUES

Marvin J. Nadiff, *Copyrightability of Works of the Federal and State Governments Under the 1976 Act,* 29 St. Louis U. L.J. 91 (1984)

Malla Pollack, *Intellectual Property Protection for the Creative Chef, or How to Copyright a Cake: A Modest Proposal*, 12 Cardozo L. Rev. 1477 (1991)

CHAPTER 3. OWNERSHIP

Stacey M. Byrnes, *Copyright Licenses, New Technology and Default Rules: Converging Media, Diverging Courts?*, 20 Loy. L.A. Ent. L. Rev. 243 (2000)

Dane S. Ciolino, *Why Copyrights Are Not Community Property*, 60 La. L. Rev. 127 (1999)

Rochelle Cooper Dreyfuss, *The Creative Employee and the Copyright Act of 1976*, 54 U. Chi. L. Rev. 590 (1987)

Robert A. Gorman, *Copyright Conflicts on the University Campus*, 47 J. Copyright Soc'y 291 (2000)

Alice Haemmerli, *Insecurity Interests: Where Intellectual Property and Commercial Law Collide*, 96 Colum. L. Rev. 1645 (1996)

Jonathan Hudis, *Software "Made for Hire": Make Sure Its Really Yours*, 40 J. Copyright Soc'y 8 (1996)

John M. Kernochan, *Ownership and Control of Intellectual Property Rights in Audiovisual Works: Contracts and Practice*, 20 Colum.-VLA J.L. & Arts 359 (1996)

Robert A. Kreiss, *The "In Writing" Requirement for Copyright and Patent Transfers: Are the Circuits in Conflict?*, 26 Dayton L. Rev. 43 (2000)

Mary LaFrance, *Authorship, Dominance, and the Captive Collaborator: Preserving the Rights of Joint Authors*, 50 Emory L.J. 193 (2001)

Scott Miller, Jr., *Photography and the Work-for-Hire Doctrine*, 1 Tex. Wesleyan L. Rev. 81 (1994)

Pamela Samuelson, *Allocating Ownership Rights in Computer–Generated Works*, 47 U. Pitt. L. Rev. 1185 (1986)

Nancy P. Spyke, *The Joint Works Dilemma: The Separately Copyrightable Contribution Requirement and Co–Ownership Principles*, 40 J. Copyright Soc'y 463 (1993)

Amanda Trefethen, *Copyright as Community Property*, 11 J. Contemp. Legal Issues 256 (2000)

Russ VerSteeg, *Defining "Author" for the Purposes of Copyright*, 45 Am. U. L. Rev. 1323 (1996)

Russ VerSteeg, *Copyright and the Educational Process: The Right of Teacher Inception*, 75 Iowa L. Rev. 381 (1990)

CHAPTER 4. DURATION AND RENEWAL AND TERMINATION OF TRANSFERS

Suzanne D. Anderson, Note, *Bleak House Revisited: An Appraisal of the Termination Provisions of the 1976 Copyright Act—Sections 203 and 304(c)*, 65 Or. L. Rev. 829 (1986)

Robert L. Bard & Lewis Kurlantzick, *Copyright Duration at the Millenium*, 47 J. Copyright Soc'y 13 (2000)

Michael H. Davis, *Extending Copyright and the Constitution: "Have I Stayed Too Long?"*, 52 Fla. L. Rev. 989 (2000)

Jane C. Ginsburg, Wendy J. Gordon, Arthur R. Miller, William F. Patry, *The Constitutionality of Copyright Term Extension: How Long is Too Long?*, 18 Cardozo Arts & Ent. L.J. 651 (2000)

Lawrence Lessig, *Copyright's First Amendment*, 48 UCLA L. Rev. 1057 (2001)

CHAPTER 5. FORMALITIES

Thomas P. Arden, *The Questionable Utility of Copyright Notice: Statutory and Non–Legal Incentives in the Post–Berne Era,* 24 Loy. U. Chi. L.J. 259 (1993)

E. Fulton Brylawski, *Publication: Its Role in Copyright Matters, Both Past and Present*, 31 J. Copyright Soc'y 507 (1984)

Irwin Karp, John B. Koegel, Arthur Levine, Charles Ossola, Shira Permutter, Bernard R. Sorkin, The Herbert Tenzer Memorial Conference, *Copyright in the Twenty–First Century, Formalities and the Future: The Fate of Sections 411 and 412*, 13 Cardozo Art. & Ent. L.J. 521 (1995)

CHAPTER 6. EXCLUSIVE RIGHTS UNDER COPYRIGHT

A. THE RIGHT TO REPRODUCE THE WORK IN COPIES AND PHONORECORDS UNDER § 106(1)

Karen Bevill, *Note, Copyright Infringement and Access: Has the Access Requirement Lost Its Probative Value?*, 52 Rutgers L. Rev. 311 (1999)

Amy B. Cohen, *Masking Copyright Decisionmaking: The Meaninglessness of Substantial Similarity*, 20 U.C. Davis L. Rev. 719 (1987)

Jane C. Ginsburg, *Copyright and Control Over New Technologies of Dissemination*, 101 Colum. L. Rev. 1613 (2001)

Alice J. Kim, Note, *Expert Testimony and Substantial Similarity: Facing the Music in (Music) Copyright Infringement Cases,* 19 Colum.-VLA J.L. & Arts. 109 (1995)

Alan Latman, *"Probative Similarity" as Proof of Copyright: Toward Dispelling Some Myths in Copyright Infringement*, 90 Colum. L. Rev. 1187 (1990)

Joseph P. Liu, *Owning Digital Copies: Copyright Law and the Incidents of Copy Ownership*, 42 Wm. and Mary L. Rev. 1245 (2001)

B. THE RIGHT TO PREPARE DERIVATIVE WORKS UNDER § 106(2) AND MORAL RIGHTS

Christopher D. Abramson, *Note: Digital Sampling and the Recording Musician: A Proposal for Legislative Protection*, 74 N.Y.U. L. Rev. 1660 (1999)

Ralph S. Brown, *The Widening Gyre: Are Derivative Works Getting Out of Hand?*, 3 Cardozo Arts & Ent. L.J. 1865 (1990)

Thomas F. Cotter, *Pragmatism, Economics, and the Droit Moral,* 76 N.C. L. Rev. 1 (1997)

Edward J. Damich, *State "Moral Rights" Statutes: An Analysis and Critique,* 13 Colum.-VLA J.L. & Arts 291 (1989)

Jane C. Ginsburg, *Copyright in the 101*st *Congress: Commentary on the Visual Artists' Rights Act and the Architectural Works Copyright Protection Act of 1990,* 14 Colum.-VLA J.L. & Arts 477 (1990)

Jane C. Ginsburg, *Have Moral Rights Come of (Digital) Age in the U.S.?,* 19 Cardozo Arts & Ent. L.J. 9 (2001)

Paul Goldstein, *Derivative Rights and Derivative Works in Copyright,* 30 J. Copyright Soc'y 209 (1982)

Robert A. Gorman, *Federal Moral Rights Legislation: The Need for Caution,* 14 Nova L. Rev. 421 (1990)

Roberta Rosenthal Kwall, *How Fine Art Fares Post VARA,* 1 Marq. Intel. Prop. L. Rev. 1 (1997)

William M. Landes, *Copyright, Borrowed Images, and Appropriation Art: An Economic Approach*, 9 Geo. Mason L. Rev. 1 (2000)

Mark A. Lemley, *Rights of Attribution and Integrity in Online Communications*, 1995 J. Online L. art. 2

Mark A. Lemley, *The Economics of Improvement in Intellectual Property Law,* 75 Tex. L. Rev. 989 (1997)

Randolph S. Sergent, *Building Reputational Capital: The Right of Attribution Under Section 43 of the Lanham Act,* 19 Colum.-VLA J.L. & Arts 45 (1995)

Russ VerSteeg, *Federal Moral Rights for Visual Artists: Contract Theory and Analysis*, 67 Wash. L. Rev. 827 (1992)

Naomi A. Voegtli, *Rethinking Derivative Rights,* 63 Brook. L. Rev. 1213 (1997)

C. THE RIGHT TO DISTRIBUTE UNDER § 106(3)

Nancy A. Bloom, *Protecting Copyright Owners of Digital Music—No More Free Access to Cyber Tunes,* 45 J. Copyright Soc'y 179 (1997)

Steve Lauff, Note, *Decompilation of Collective Works: When the First Sale Doctrine Is a Mirage,* 76 Tex. L. Rev. 869 (1997)

Lee D. Neumann, *The Berne Convention and Droit de Suite Legislation in the United States: Domestic and International Consequences of Federal Incorporation of State Law for Treaty Implementation,* 16 Colum.-VLA J.L. & Arts 157 (1992)

Shira Perlmutter, *Resale Royalties for Artists: An Analysis of the Register of Copyrights' Report,* 16 Colum.-VLA J.L. & Arts 395 (1992)

Jennifer M. Schneck, Note, *Closing the Book on the Public Lending Right,* 63 N.Y.U. L. Rev. 878 (1989)

U.S. Copyright Office, *Droit de Suite: The Artist's Resale Royalty* (1992 Report), summarized at 16 Colum.-VLA J. L. & Arts 381 (1992)

D. Rights of Public Performance and Display Under § 106(4), (5), (6)

Laura N. Gasaway, Impasse*: Distance Learning and Copyright,* 62 Ohio St. L.J. 783 (2001)

Thomas M. Goetzl & Stuart A. Sutton, *Copyright and the Visual Artist's Display Right: A New Doctrinal Analysis,* 9 Art & L. 15 (1984)

Robert A. Gorman, *The Recording Musician and Union Power: A Case Study of the American Federation of Musicians,* 37 Sw. L.J. 697 (1983)

Laurence R. Helfer, *World Music on a U.S. Stage: A Berne/TRIPS and Economic Analysis of the Fairness in Music Licensing Act,* 80 B.U. L. Rev. 93 (2000)

Herman Cohen Jehoram, *The Future of Copyright Collecting Societies,* 23 Eur. Intell. Prop. Rep. 134 (2001)

John M. Kernochan, *Music Performing Rights Organizations in the United States of America: Special Characteristics, Restraints, and Public Attitudes,* 10 Colum.-VLA J.L. & Arts 333 (1986)

Mark A. Lemley, *Privileges on the Internet: Dealing with Overlapping Copyrights on the Internet,* 22 Dayton L. Rev. 547 (1997)

David Nimmer, *Ignoring the Public, Part I: On the Absurd Complexity of the Digital Audio Transmission Right,* 7 UCLA Ent. L. Rev. 189 (2000)

R. Anthony Reese, *Copyright and Internet Music Transmissions: Existing Law, Major Controversies, Possible Solutions,* 55 U. Miami L. Rev. 237 (2001)

R. Anthony Reese, *The Public Display Right: The Copyright Act's Neglected Solution to the Controversy over RAM "Copies",* 2001 U. Ill. L. Rev. 83

CHAPTER 7. FAIR USE

Tom W. Bell, *Fair Use vs. Fared Use?: The Impact of Automated Rights Management on Copyright's Fair Use Doctrine,* 76 N.C. L. Rev. 557 (1998)

Kenneth D. Crews, *The Law of Fair Use and the Illusion of Fair–Use Guidelines,* 62 Ohio St. L.J. 599 (2001)

William A. Fisher, *Reconstructing the Fair Use Doctrine,* 101 Harv. L. Rev. 1659 (1988)

Stephen Fraser, *The Conflict Between the First Amendment and Copyright Law and Its Impact on the Internet,* 16 Cardozo Arts & Ent. L.J. 1 (1998)

Laura N. Gasaway, *Values Conflict in the Digital Environment: Librarians Versus Copyright Holders,* 24 Colum.-VLA J.L. & Arts 115 (2000)

Paul Goldstein, *Copyright and the First Amendment,* 70 Colum. L. Rev. 983 (1970)

Wendy J. Gordon, *Fair Use as Market Failure: A Structural and Economic Analysis of the Betamax Case and its Predecessors,* 82 Colum. L. Rev. (1982)

Marshall Leaffer, *The Uncertain Future of Fair Use in a Global Information Marketplace,* 62 Ohio St. L.J. 849 (2001)

Pierre N. Leval, *Toward a Fair Use Standard,* 103 Harv. L. Rev. 1105 (1990)

Pierre N. Level, *Nimmer Lecture: Fair Use Rescued,* 44 UCLA L. Rev. 1449 (1997)

Robert P. Merges, *Are You Making Fun of Me? Notes on Market Failure and the Parody Defense in Copyright,* 21 AIPLA Q.J. 305 (1993)

Melville B. Nimmer, *Does Copyright Abridge the First Amendment Guarantees of Free Speech and Press?,* 17 UCLA L. Rev. 1180 (1970)

Kate O'Neill, *Against Dicta: A Legal Method for Rescuing Fair Use from the Right of First Publication,* 89 Cal. L. Rev. 369 (2001)

L. Ray Patterson, *Free Speech, Copyright, and Fair Use,* 40 Vand. L. Rev. 1 (1987)

Richard A. Posner, *When Is Parody Fair Use?,* 21 J. Legal Stud. 67 (1992)

Leo J. Raskind, *A Functional Interpretation of Fair Use,* 31 J. Copyright Soc'y 601 (1984)

Lloyd L. Weinreb, *Fair Use and How it Got That Way,* 45 J. Copyright Soc'y 634 (1998)

Lloyd L. Weinreb, *Fair's Fair: A Comment on the Fair Use Doctrine,* 103 Harv. L. Rev. 1337 (1990)

Alfred C. Yen, *When Authors Won't Sell: Parody, Fair Use and Efficiency in Copyright Law,* 62 U. Colo. L. Rev. 79 (1991)

Geri J. Yonover, *The Precarious Balance: Moral Rights, Parody, and Fair Use,* 14 Cardozo Arts & Ent. L.J. 79 (1996)

Diane Leenheer Zimmerman, *The More Things Change, the Less They Seem "Transformed": Some Reflections on Fair Use,* 46 J. Copyright Soc'y 251 (1999)

CHAPTER 8. ENFORCEMENT OF COPYRIGHT

A. INJUNCTION

Mark Lemley and Eugene Volokh, *Freedom of Speech and Injunctions in Intellectual Property Cases,* 48 Duke L.J. 147 (1998)

B. DAMAGES

Mitchell N. Berman, R. Anthony Reese & Ernest A. Young, *State Accountability for Violations of Intellectual Property Rights: How to "Fix" Florida Prepaid (and How Not to),* 79 Tex. L. Rev. 1039 (2001)

Roger D. Blair & Thomas F. Cotter, *An Economic Analysis of Damages Rules in Intellectual Property Law*, 39 Wm. & Mary L. Rev. 1585 (1998)

Ralph S. Brown, *Civil Remedies for Intellectual Property Invasions: Themes and Variations*, 55 Law & Contemp. Probs. 45 (1992)

Dane S. Ciolino, *Reconsidering Restitution in Copyright*, 8 Emory L.J. 1 (1999)

Wendy J. Gordon, *Of Harms and Benefits: Torts, Restitution and Intellectual Property*, 21 J. Legal Stud. 449 (1992)

Paul J. Heald & Michael L. Wells, *Remedies for the Misappropriation of Intellectual Property by State and Municipal Governments Before and After Seminole Tribe: The Eleventh Amendment and Other Immunity Doctrines*, 55 Wash. & Lee L. Rev. 849 (1998)

C.   COSTS AND ATTORNEY'S FEES

Jeffrey Edward Barnes, *Comment: Attorney's Fee Awards in Federal Copyright Litigation After Fogerty v. Fantasy: Defendants Are Winning Fees More Often, but the New Standard Still Favors Prevailing Plaintiffs*, 47 UCLA L. Rev. 1381 (2000)

D.   CRIMINAL LIABILITY

Note, *The Criminalization of Copyright Infringement in the Digital Era*, 112 Harv. L. Rev. 1705 (1999)

Lydia Pallas Loren, *Digitization, Commodification, Criminalization: The Evolution of Criminal Copyright Infringement and the Importance of the Willfulness Requirement*, 77 Wash. U. L.Q. 835 (1999)

E.   INDIVIDUAL, VICARIOUS, CONTRIBUTORY LIABILITY

David Nimmer, *An Odyssey Through Copyright's Vicarious Defenses*, 73 N.Y.U. L. Rev. 162 (1998)

F.   TECHNOLOGICAL PROTECTION MEASURES

Julie E. Cohen, *Lochner in Cyberspace: The New Economic Orthodoxy of Rights Management*, 97 Mich. L. Rev. 462 (1998)

Jane C. Ginsburg, *Copyright Use and Excuse on the Internet*, 24 Colum.-VLA J.L. & Arts 1 (2000)

Jane C. Ginsburg, *Copyright Legislation for the "Digital Millennium"*, 23 Colum.-VLA J.L. & Arts 137 (1999)

Glynn S. Lunney, Jr., *The Death of Copyright: Digital Technology, Private Copying, and the Digital Millennium Copyright Act*, 87 Va. L. Rev. 813 (2001)

Dean S. Marks & Bruce H. Turnbull, *Technical Protection Measures: The Intersection of Technology, Law and Commercial Licenses*, 22 Eur. Intell. Prop. Rep. 198 (2000)

Pamela Samuelson, *Intellectual Property and the Digital Economy: Why the Anti–Circumvention Regulations Need to Be Revised*, 14 Berkeley Tech. L.J. 519 (1999)

G.   Copyright Misuse

Leo J. Raskind, *Licensing Under Antitrust Law*, 20 Brook. J. Int'l L. 49 (1993)

CHAPTER 9.   FEDERAL PREEMPTION OF STATE LAW

Douglas G. Baird, *Common Law Intellectual Property and the Legacy of International News Service v. Associated Press*, 50 U. Chi. L. Rev. 411 (1983)

Samuel M. Bayard, *Note: Chihuahuas, Seventh Circuit Judges, and Movie Scripts, Oh My!: Copyright Preemption of Contracts to Protect Ideas*, 86 Cornell L. Rev. 603 (2001)

Ralph S. Brown, *Copyright and Its Upstart Cousins: Privacy, Publicity, Unfair Competition*, 33 J. Copyright Soc'y 301 (1986)

Ralph D. Clifford, *Simultaneous Copyright and Trade Secret Claims: Can the Copyright Misuse Defense Prevent Constitutional Doublethink?* 104 Dick. L. Rev. 247 (2000)

Paul Goldstein, *Copyright and Its Substitutes*, 1997 Wis. L. Rev. 865

Dennis S. Karjala, *Copyright and Misappropriation*, 17 U. Dayton L. Rev. 885 (1992)

Mark A. Lemley, *Beyond Preemption: The Law and Policy of Intellectual Property Licensing*, 87 Cal. L. Rev. 111 (1999)

Maureen O'Rourke, *Copyright Preemption After the ProCD Case: A Market–Based Approach*, 12 Berkeley Tech. L.J. 53 (1997)

Pamela Samuelson & Kurt Opsahl, *Licensing Information in the Global Information Market: Freedom of Contract Meets Public Policy*, 21 Eur. Intell. Prop. Rep. 386 (1999)

CHAPTER 10.   INTERNATIONAL DIMENSIONS OF COPYRIGHT

Graeme W. Austin, *Domestic Laws and Foreign Rights: Choice of Law in Transnational Copyright Infringement Litigation*, 23 Colum.-VLA J.L. & Arts 1 (1999)

Irene Segal Ayers, *The Future of Global Copyright Protection: Has Copyright Law Gone Too Far?*, 62 U. Pitt. L. Rev. 49 (2000)

Graeme B. Dinwoodie, *The Development and Incorporation of International Norms in the Formation of Copyright Law*, 62 Ohio St. L.J. 733 (2001)

Graeme B. Dinwoodie, *A New Copyright Order: Why National Courts Should Create Global Norms*, 149 U. Pa. L. Rev. 469 (2000)

Paul E. Geller, *Conflicts of Laws in Cyberspace: Rethinking International Copyright in a Digitally Networked World*, 20 Colum.-VLA J.L. & Arts 571 (1996)

Jane C. Ginsburg, *Copyright Without Borders? Choice of Forum and Choice of Law for Copyright Infringement in Cyberspace*, 15 Cardozo Arts. & Ent. L.J. 153 (1997)

Jane C. Ginsburg, *The Cyberian Captivity of Copyright: Territoriality and Authors' Rights in a Networked World*, 15 Computer & High Tech. L.J. 347 (1999)

Jane C. Ginsburg, *Extraterritoriality and Multiterritoriality in Copyright Infringement*, 37 Va. J. Int'l L. 587 (1997)

Jane C. Ginsburg, *International Copyright: From a "Bundle" of National Copyright Laws to a Supranational Code?*, 47 J. Copyright Soc'y 265 (2000)

Jane C. Ginsburg & John M. Kernochan, *One Hundred and Two Years Later: The United States Adheres to the Berne Convention*, 13 Colum.-VLA J.L. & Arts 1 (1988)

Laurence R. Helfer, *A European Human Rights Analogy for Adjudicating Copyright Claims Under TRIPS*, 21 Eur. Intell. Prop. Rep. 8 (1999)

Michel A. Jaccard, *Securing Copyright in Transnational Cyberspace: The Case for Contracting with Potential Infringers*, 35 Colum. J. Transnat'l L. 619 (1997)

Beryl R. Jones, *An Introduction to the European Economic Community and Intellectual Property*, 18 Brooklyn J. Int'l L. 665 (1992)

Marshall A. Leaffer, *Protecting U.S. Intellectual Property Abroad: Toward a New Multilateralism*, 76 Iowa L. Rev. 273 (1991)

Rebecca F. Martin, *The WIPO Performances and Phonograms Treaty: Will the U.S. Whistle a New Tune?*, 44 J. Copyright Soc'y 157 (1997)

Neil W. Netanel, *The Next Round: The Impact of the WIPO Copyright Treaty on TRIPS Dispute Settlement*, 37 Va. J. Int'l L. 441 (1997)

David W. Nimmer, *The Death of Copyright*, 48 Vand. L. Rev. 1385 (1996)

Ruth Okediji, *Toward an International Fair Use Doctrine*, 39 Colum. J. Transnat'l L. 75 (2000)

Pamela Samuelson, *Challenges for the World Intellectual Property Organisation and the Trade-Related Aspects of Intellectual Property Rights Council in Regulating Intellectual Property Rights in the Information Age*, 21 Eur. Intell. Prop. Rep. 578 (1999)

Pamela Samuelson, *The U.S. Digital Agenda at WIPO*, 37 Va. J. Int'l L. 369 (1997)

*

INDEX

References are to Pages

†

1–58778–375–4

9 781587 783753